Literature
and the Language Arts

Experiencing Literature

THE EMC MASTERPIECE SERIES

SECOND EDITION

EMCParadigm Publishing Saint Paul, Minnesota

Staff Credits

Editorial

Laurie Skiba
Editor

Brenda Owens
Associate Editor

Lori Ann Coleman
Associate Editor

Diana Moen
Associate Editor

Jennifer Joline Anderson
Assistant Editor

Gia Marie Garbinsky
Assistant Editor

Janice Johnson
Curriculum Specialist

Paul Spencer
Art and Photo Researcher

Chris Bohen
Editorial Assistant

Katherine S. Link
Editorial Assistant

Design

Shelley Clubb
Production Manager

C. Vern Johnson
Senior Designer

Michelle Lewis
Senior Design Specialist

Jennifer Wreisner
Senior Designer

Julie L. Hansen
Design Specialist

Bill Connell
Design Specialist

Leslie Anderson
Design Specialist

Cover Credits

Cover Designer: C. Vern Johnson

Gas [Detail], 1940. Edward Hopper.
The Starry Night [Detail], 1889. Vincent van Gogh.
Last of the Buffalo [Detail], 1889. Albert Bierstadt.
His Hammer in His Hand [Detail], from the *John Henry Series,* 1944–47. Palmer Hayden.

ISBN 0-8219-2106-1 (Student Edition)
©2003, 2001 by EMC Corporation

Published by EMC/Paradigm Publishing
875 Montreal Way
St. Paul, Minnesota 55102
800-328-1452
www.emcp.com
E-mail: educate@emcp.com

Printed in the United States of America.
10 9 8 7 6 5   XXX   06 05 04 03

Literature
and the Language Arts
SECOND EDITION

REDWOOD LEVEL
DISCOVERING LITERATURE

WILLOW LEVEL
UNDERSTANDING LITERATURE

CEDAR LEVEL
EXPLORING LITERATURE

PINE LEVEL
THE AMERICAN TRADITION

OAK LEVEL
RESPONDING TO LITERATURE

MAPLE LEVEL
THE BRITISH TRADITION

BIRCH LEVEL
EXPERIENCING LITERATURE

CYPRESS LEVEL
WORLD LITERATURE

Consultants and Writers

Senior Consultant
Dr. Edmund J. Farrell
Emeritus Professor of English
    Education
University of Texas at Austin
Austin, Texas

Gwendolyn Alexander
Educational Consultant
Washington, DC

Amy Bergstrom
Instructor
English Education Department
University of Minnesota
Duluth, Minnesota

Diana Blythe
Senior Content Manager
Humanities Software,
    a division of Advantage
    Learning Systems, Inc.
Hood River, Oregon

Cherie Boen
National Board Certified
    Teacher
Educational Consultant
Minneapolis, Minnesota

Gloria Canson
English Instructor
Roosevelt High School
Portland, Oregon

Linda Christopherson
Educational Writer
Charlotte, North Carolina

Arlene Clark
English Teacher/Debate Coach
West Ottawa High School
Holland, Michigan

Bob Crepeau
Educational Writer
San Diego, California

Mary Curfman
Language Arts Supervisor
Department of Curriculum
    and Professional Development
Clark County Schools
Las Vegas, Nevada

Deanna and Roger Hebbert
Educational Writers
Longmont, Colorado

Sara Hyry
Freelance Education Writer
Easthampton, Massachusetts

Christina Kolb
Educational Writer
Newton, Massachusetts

Sharon Kremer
English Department Chair
A. O. Calhoun Middle School
Denton, Texas

Jon Madian
Senior Instructional Designer
Humanities Software,
    a division of Advantage
    Learning Systems, Inc.
Hood River, Oregon

Beverly Martin
Managing Editor
Humanities Software,
    a division of Advantage
    Learning Systems, Inc.
Hood River, Oregon

Michael McDonald
Educational Writer
Portland, Oregon

Laura Mezner Nelson
Educational Writer
Minnetonka, Minnesota

Margaret Palmer
English Department Chair
Samuel Clemens High School
Shertz, Texas

Geoff Penrose
Educational Writer
Wasilla, Alaska

David Rathbun
English Instructor
South High School
Minneapolis, Minnesota

Carol Satz
Clinician
Center for Reading and Writing
Rider University
Lawrenceville, New Jersey

Eric Schneider
English Instructor
Patrick Henry High School
Minneapolis, Minnesota

Elnora Shields
Educational Consultant
Durham, North Carolina

Dr. Jane S. Shoaf
Educational Consultant
Edenton, North Carolina

Kendra Sisserson
Research Associate
University of Chicago
Chicago, Illinois

James W. Swanson
Educational Consultant
Minneapolis, Minnesota

Anita Usmiani
Language Arts Supervisor
Hamilton Township School
    District
Hamilton, New Jersey

Hope Vasholz
Teacher of English
Hammond High School
Columbia, Maryland

Dr. Gary Wiener
Language Arts Chair
Brighton High School
Rochester, New York

TABLE OF CONTENTS

Landscape with the Fall of Icarus, c.1558. Pieter Bruegel.

The House of Mystery, 1926. Sydney Lee.

Orange Boats, 1998. Ann Phong.

The Acrobat, c.1900s. Marc Chagall.

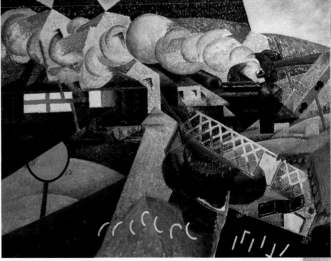

Red Cross Train Passing a Village, 1915. Gino Severini.

Man at the Crossroads, 1934. Diego Rivera.

Fox Hunt, 1893. Winslow Homer.

To the Student

Features of Your Textbook

A Guide for Reading

When you open your *EMC Masterpiece Series* textbook, you will find great literature, both classic and contemporary, by a wide variety of authors. You will also find useful step-by-step study strategies for each selection, helpful background information, and activities that allow you to relate the literature to your own experiences and share your point of view.

The **Guided Reading** program in this *EMC Masterpiece Series* book gives you tips before, during, and after you read each selection. Read on for a description of the features you will find in your textbook.

- **Reader's Resource** gives you background and other information you'll need for the reading.

- **Literary Tools** features point out and explain literary techniques that are used in the selection.

- A **Graphic Organizer** is provided to help you sort out the important points on paper.

- **Guided Reading Questions** within the selection help you check your understanding of the reading.

- **Words for Everyday Use** includes the definition and pronunciation for new vocabulary. A sample sentence demonstrates the use of the word in context.

- **Footnotes** explain unfamiliar terms or unusual words.

- **Art Note** features provide information about the history, culture, or artistic technique of the fine art throughout the textbook and foster critical viewing of the art.

- **Respond to the Selection** allows you to relate the literature to your own experiences.

- **Investigate, Inquire, and Imagine** contains questions you need to perfect your understanding of the reading, from basic recalling and interpreting to questions that ask you to analyze, synthesize, evaluate, and extend your ideas. Some questions also ask you to look at a specific point of view, or examine a different perspective.

- **Understanding Literature** follows up on the literary techniques introduced in Reader's Toolbox and asks you questions to further your understanding.

- **Writer's Journal** gives you three quick-writing options to help you build writing skills.

- **Integrating the Language Arts** contain creative activities that tie literature to other language arts areas such as grammar, vocabulary development, public speaking, study and research, collaborative learning, media literacy, and applied English.

A Guide for Writing

At the end of each unit of your textbook you will find a **Guided Writing** activity that takes you through the steps of the writing process. The lesson includes models from professional writers and students. Also included are graphic organizers, questions to get you thinking, and an integrated **Language, Grammar, and Style** lesson to help you brush up on grammar points.

A Guide for Language Arts Skills

The **Language Arts Survey** in the back of your textbook is your resource for information about how to use the English language effectively. It includes tips on what you need to know to write, speak, and read effectively. There are six sections in the Language Arts Survey: the **Reading Resource**, the **Writing Resource**, the **Language, Grammar, and Style Resource**, the **Speaking and Listening Resource**, the **Study and Research Resource**, and the **Applied English Resource**. Do you need to correct a passive sentence? include an Internet site in a research paper? interview someone in the community? write a letter? It's all here for you.

Genres in Literature
PART ONE

Hoosick River, Summer, 1952. Grandma Moses. Private Collection.

The FOLK Tradition

" If a nation loses its storytellers,
it loses its childhood. "

—Peter Handle

ELEMENTS of THE FOLK TRADITION

Are there favorite stories that people in your family like to tell? When you were a child, did people tell you bedtime stories? Did you learn rhymes and jingles and songs from your friends? Have you ever sat around a campfire and told ghost stories? Have you ever heard a minister, priest, rabbi, or teacher tell a story to make a point? If so, then you have experienced the oral tradition.

One good definition of human beings is that we are storytelling creatures. Long before people invented writing, they were telling stories about their gods and heroes and experiences. The best of these stories were passed by word of mouth from generation to generation to form the basis of the literature that we know today. Some early stories were told in the form of poems. Some were in the form of songs. Others were in the form of what we would now call prose tales.

The passing of stories, poems, and songs by word of mouth from person to person is called oral transmission. The body of work created in this way in a particular culture is called that culture's oral tradition.

Types of Oral Literature

MYTHS. Myths are stories that explain objects or events in the natural world as resulting from the action of some supernatural force or entity, most often a god. Every early culture around the globe has produced its own myths. Two Greek myths appear in this unit: "Echo and Narcissus," retold by Walker Brents, and "The Story of Dædalus and Icarus," translated by Rolfe Humphries.

LEGENDS. Legends are stories coming down from the past, often based on real events or characters from older times. Unlike myths, legends are popularly regarded as historical; however, they may contain elements that are fantastic or unverifiable. An example of a legend is the story of George Washington chopping down the cherry tree. An example in this unit is "The Silver Pool," which tells a story of the legendary Irish, or Celtic, hero Fionn MacCumhail.

FOLK TALES. Folk tales are brief stories passed by word of mouth from generation to generation. "Goha and the Pot," found in this unit, is a North African folk tale.

TALL TALES. Tall tales are also folk tales. Tall tales are often lighthearted or humorous, and contain highly exaggerated, unrealistic elements. The stories of Paul Bunyan and Pecos Bill are tall tales.

FAIRY TALES. Fairy tales are stories that deal with mischievous spirits and other supernatural occurrences, often in medieval settings. The name is generally applied to stories of the kinds collected by Charles Perrault in France and the Brothers Grimm in Germany or told by Hans Christian Andersen of Denmark. "Cinderella" and "The Little Mermaid" are famous examples. "The White Snake," found in this unit, is another famous fairy tale from the European oral tradition.

PARABLES. Parables are very brief stories told to teach a moral lesson. The most famous parables are those told by Jesus in the Bible. "The Prodigal Son," found in this unit, is one such parable.

FABLES. Fables are brief stories, often with animal characters, told to express a moral. Famous fables include those of Æsop and Jean de La Fontaine. In this unit you will find the fable "The Fox and the Crow," by Æsop.

FOLK SONGS. Folk songs are traditional or composed songs typically made up of stanzas, a refrain, and a simple melody. A form of folk literature, folk songs are expressions of commonly shared ideas or feelings and may be narrative or lyric in style. Traditional folk songs are anonymous songs that have been transmitted orally. Examples include the ballad "John Henry," found in this unit.

Shah-nameh: First Meeting Between Rostam and His Lord Sam, c.1500s. Persian artist.
Musée Conde, Chantilly, France.

SPIRITUALS. Spirituals are religious songs from the African-American folk tradition. Two spirituals are included in this unit: "Steal Away" and "Go Down, Moses."

EPICS. An **epic** is a long story, often told in verse, involving heroes and gods. Epics have often been passed on orally and may have anonymous authors. Grand in length and scope, an epic provides a portrait of an entire culture, of the legends, beliefs, values, laws, arts, and ways of life of a people. Homer's *Odyssey,* Unit 2, is an example of an epic poem.

PROVERBS. A **proverb,** or *adage*, is a traditional saying, such as "You can lead a horse to water, but you can't make it drink" or the title of Shakespeare's play *All's Well That Ends Well.*

Literary TOOLS

SUSPENSION OF DISBELIEF. Suspension of disbelief is the act by which the reader willingly sets aside his or her skepticism to participate imaginatively in the work being read. As you read, think about which elements of the story require you to suspend your disbelief.

MYTH. A **myth** is a story that explains objects or events in the natural world as resulting from the action of some supernatural force or entity, most often a god.

Organizer

As you read, make a chart. On the left, list examples of natural phenomena that are explained in this myth. On the right, describe how the phenomena are explained.

Natural Phenomena	Explanation

Reader's JOURNAL

What qualities do you find attractive in another person? Is physical appearance as important as other aspects such as personality or intellectual qualities? Why, or why not?

"Echo and Narcissus"

retold by Walker Brents

Reader's resource

HISTORY CONNECTION. The world of the ancient Greeks and Romans was populated with gods and goddesses. These supernatural beings were more powerful than humans, but they experienced human emotions such as jealousy and passion. The Greeks and the Romans worshipped many of the same gods and goddesses but had different names for them. In **"Echo and Narcissus,"** the gods and goddesses are referred to by their Greek names; in **"The Story of Dædalus and Icarus,"** the story that follows on page 11, they are referred to by their Roman names. Two of the gods named in these selections are Zeus, or Jove, the supreme god; and Hera, or Juno, his wife. Also important in "Echo and Narcissus" are nymphs, or lesser goddesses. Naiads were water nymphs who dwelled in rivers, lakes, and springs; dryads were tree nymphs.

Narcissus is a genus of plant belonging to the amaryllis (*Amaryllidaceae*) family of lilylike flowers. *Narcissi* have showy yellow or white blooms with cuplike centers. Jonquils and daffodils are types of *Narcissus*.

PSYCHOLOGY CONNECTION. Famous pyschoanalyst Sigmund Freud first used the term **narcissism**, derived from this myth, to mean extreme self-absorption or egoism.

About the AUTHOR

Walker Brents (1959–) is a poet and storyteller who has studied myths since he discovered at the age of five the myths of Hercules and the Greek gods. After majoring in English and philosophy at Drury College in Springfield, Missouri, Brents worked with the Jesuit Volunteer Corps in the early 1980s. It was while working at a refugee center in southern California that he was able to listen to the many stories of Vietnamese, Romanian, Laotian, and Cambodian refugees. Brents now tells Hindu, Japanese, and Chinese myths and folk tales at the Asian Art Museum in San Francisco and teaches at Berkwood Hedge School in Berkeley. He has published poetry in a number of literary magazines, including the *Berkeley Review of Books*, *Moksha Journal*, and *Galley Sail Review*. He has also been a featured performer at various cafes, as well as at the Marsh, a theater in San Francisco.

Echo & Narcissus

retold by Walker Brents

Liriope the river nymph gave birth to a beautiful child. She brought him to the blind seer Tiresias to ask his destiny. Tiresias predicted that the boy would live a long life, but only if he never "came to know himself."

The child was named Narcissus. As he grew, his beauty increased. His dazzling looks had a strange effect upon the woodland spirits, the naiads and the dryads,[1] around whom he spent his days. They all fell in love with him, but he was <u>oblivious</u>, interested only in hunting in the hills with his companions. His pride in his beauty grew so great that he had nothing but scorn for the feelings of others.

There was one nymph, Echo by name, who saw Narcissus chasing deer into nets in the hills. Echo was instantly seized by love and could not overcome it. Secretly, she followed him through the wilderness, waiting for her chance to make herself known to him—but one thing held her back: she could not initiate speech on her own. She could only repeat what was said to her. This was her condition, and it

How do others react to Narcissus? How does he treat them?

---

1. **the naiads and the dryads.** Nymphs of the water and of trees

words for everyday use	o • bliv • i • ous (ə bliv´ē əs) *adj.*, unaware; lacking attention. *Pete cranked up the volume of the television, <u>oblivious</u> to the fact that he was disturbing everyone's sleep.*

had come about because one day the goddess Hera was questioning the nymphs about her husband Zeus. She asked them where Zeus was, suspecting that the unfaithful god had been chasing the lovely nymphs and dwelling among them. Indeed he had, and while he was making his escape Echo distracted Hera with a flow of entertaining conversation. When Hera learned she had been fooled, she cursed Echo, saying, "From now on your words will not be your own. You will only be able to repeat what is said to you. That way your powers to beguile and distract will be curtailed."

Who has punished Echo? What is the punishment?

Thereafter Echo could only repeat the words she heard. She could not announce herself to Narcissus. She trailed him silently, hoping for the right circumstance to meet him and declare her love. One day Narcissus had wandered away from his companions, and was in the forest looking for them. Echo was nearby, but Narcissus did not see her. "Is anyone here?" he cried. "Here," she answered. "Come to me," he called out. "Come to me," she replied. "Do not avoid me," he pleaded. She said the same to him. "Let us meet," he announced. This was her chance. She stepped out of hiding and stood before him smiling, saying, "Let us meet." He fell back from her scornfully. "You are not the one I seek. I would die before I would be near you." Echo advanced toward him, pleading, "I would be near you." But he ran from her.

Haunted by his rejection and crushed by shame, Echo hid herself in caves and covered herself with leaves. She began to waste away and disappear. In the end only her bones were left, and these became rocks. But her

What happens to Echo?

voice remained. Travelers and wanderers heard it sometimes, answering them with their own words. Still Echo did not forget Narcissus.

Meanwhile, Narcissus too fell victim to a curse. Another nymph had fallen in love with him, but was also spurned. This one cried to the heavens for vengeance: "May Narcissus fall into a love that is not returned!" The goddess of righteous anger, Nemesis, heard these words. And so it happened that on a sunny and hot day Narcissus found himself at a pond to which no shepherd's flocks had been, from which no goats had drunk. It was a wild place. A green meadow surrounded it, and tall trees shaded it from the sun and sheltered it from winds. Putting his face to the waters in order to quench his thirst, Narcissus caught sight for the first time of his own reflection. He was astonished by the beautiful face that met his eye.

"What star-like eyes are these; what smooth skin! That forehead, that jaw, that gorgeous flowing hair! Who are you? Draw near to me!" He reached his hands to the water, but the reflected image disintegrated. He waited for it to reappear. "Only the surface of these waters parts us. No fortress gates nor city walls; no long rocky highway, no impenetrable forest nor unclimbable mountain stands between us. Yet I cannot reach you! How can this be?" He cried to the endless skies, "How is it that when I find my love his very nearness keeps us far apart?" But there was no answer.

What happens to Narcissus as he bends over the pool for a drink?

Narcissus could not leave this place. Entranced by his own reflection, he began to waste away from hunger and thirst. His strength and his life ebbed away and did not return. Echo

---

words for everyday use

be • guile (bi gīal´) vt., lead by deception; distract. *When my little brother screamed for a toy he wanted, I beguiled him with the promise of an ice cream cone.*

cur • tail (kər tāl´) vt., make less as if by cutting away a part. *The dictator's power was curtailed when his army was defeated.*

dis • in • te • grate (di sin´ tə grāt´) vt., break apart. *The note disintegrated into tiny pieces after it had accidentally gone through the wash.*

ebb (eb´) vi., decline; fall to a lower or worse state. *My determination ebbed, and I became depressed as I realized how difficult it would be to reach my goal.*

---

hovered around him, invisible and unforgetting. Her disembodied voice repeated his final word, which was "Alas." He died, and his spirit left his body. Even on the boat of souls, crossing the river between this world and the other one, Narcissus leaned over the edge, looking into those waters, trying to catch a glimpse of the image that so captivated him.

The nymphs heard of his death and went to the pond to retrieve his body for the funeral ceremony. But when they got there, they found no corpse, only a new blossom with snowy petals and a yellow corona.[2] The flower came to be called "Narcissus," in honor of one who, in the <u>enigmatic</u> words of Tiresias, "came to know himself," and fell in love. ■

How is Narcissus transformed?

---

2. **corona.** Trumpet-shaped cup of flowers such as the daffodil

Narcissus, 1600. Michelangelo Merisi da Caravaggio.
Galleria Nazionale d'Arte Antica, Rome.

art note

Narcissus, 1600. Michelangelo Merisi da Caravaggio.

The brief and violent life of Caravaggio (1573–1610) was as dramatic as his paintings. Although this painting is more subdued than most of Caravaggio's works, it has the same *chiaroscuro*, or severe contrast between light and shadow. What films or television shows can you think of that use this method of lighting?

words for everyday use

en • ig • ma • tic (e´ nig ma´ tik) *adj.*, mysterious; hard to decipher. *Julia is so <u>enigmatic</u>; I can never seem to understand where she is coming from.*

Respond *to the* SELECTION

Do you feel sympathy toward Narcissus, or do you think he deserves his fate?

Investigate, Inquire, and Imagine

Recall: GATHERING FACTS → Interpret: FINDING MEANING

1a. What is unusual about Echo's speech? What caused this peculiarity?

1b. How does Echo manage to express herself despite her speech limitation? How well does she succeed?

2a. How is Narcissus described? What effect does he have on other creatures? How does Narcissus respond to Echo?

2b. How would you describe Narcissus's character?

3a. With whom does Narcissus fall in love? Who caused this to happen?

3b. Why does Nemesis punish Narcissus?

Analyze: TAKING THINGS APART → Synthesize: BRINGING THINGS TOGETHER

4a. What metamorphoses, or transformations, occur in "Echo and Narcissus"?

4b. This story explains two phenomena in nature. What are these phenomena, and how are they explained?

Perspective: LOOKING AT OTHER VIEWS → Empathy: SEEING FROM INSIDE

5a. From the nymphs' perspective, what is Narcissus's crime? Explain whether you think Narcissus's punishment is appropriate to the crime.

5b. Imagine you were Narcissus and everyone was instantly captivated by your exceptional good looks. Would you find this annoying? How would you react?

Understanding Literature

SUSPENSION OF DISBELIEF. Review the definition for **suspension of disbelief** in the Handbook of Literary Terms. The willingness to suspend disbelief, to participate imaginatively in a story being read, is the most important attribute, beyond literacy, that a person can bring to the act of reading literature. Which elements of the story require you to suspend your disbelief? Why?

MYTH. Review the definition for **myth** in the Handbook of Literary Terms. Features of myth are shared by other kinds of literature. *Fairy tales* deal with extraordinary beings and events but lack the authority of myth. *Sagas* and *epics* claim authority and truth but reflect specific historical settings. Discuss how the selection shows the characteristics of myths.

"The Story of Dædalus and Icarus"

from the *Metamorphoses*

by Ovid, translated by Rolfe Humphries

Reader's resource

HISTORY CONNECTION. The works of Ovid present Roman myths, many of which were borrowed from the ancient Greeks. Such myths were part of the culture of the ancient world and were carried about by traveling singers and bards before they were written down by poets such as Ovid.

SCIENCE CONNECTION. Astronomers have tracked and cataloged more than 2,000 asteroids, also known as planetoids and minor planets, orbiting the sun. Scientists speculate that thousands more exist that have yet to be charted. Unlike the major planets, which are sphere-shaped, asteroids have an irregular shape. Many of them have been given Roman names. Ceres, for example, is the largest-known asteroid, with a diameter of approximately 470 miles. The three next largest are Pallas, Vesta, and Juno. Astronomers have named an asteroid after the mythical figure Icarus as well. Its orbit is considered the most eccentric, or unpredictable, of all known asteroids.

BACKGROUND. "The Story of Dædalus and Icarus" is about the brilliant mythical inventor Dædalus and his son who escape from captivity in Crete, an island ruled by King Minos.

About the AUTHOR

Ovid is the pen name of Publius Ovidius Naso (43 BC–AD 18), one of the greatest of the Latin poets. Ovid lived at the time of the emperor Augustus) when the Roman Empire was in its golden age. Popular in his time, he was best known for his love poetry, including *Ars amatoria (The Art of Love)*. Ovid's masterpiece is now considered to be the *Metamorphoses*, an epic poem in fifteen books that covers the history of the world and focuses on changes, often on the transformation of beings into different forms. In the *Metamorphoses*, Ovid retold many myths of the ancient world.

Literary TOOLS

MORAL. A **moral** is a practical or moral lesson, usually relating to the principles of right and wrong, to be drawn from a story or other work of literature. As you read, find the moral of the story.

FORESHADOWING. **Foreshadowing** is the act of presenting materials that hint at events to occur later in a story.

Organizer

Make a cluster chart to list the examples of foreshadowing in "The Story of Dædalus and Icarus."

Foreshadowing

Dædalus kisses Icarus goodbye

Reader's Journal

Humans fantasized about flying long before airplanes were invented. In your journal, write about an improbable adventure you would like to experience.

Landscape with the Fall of Icarus, c.1558. Pieter Bruegel. Musées Royaux des Beaux-Arts, Brussels.

The Story of Dædalus and Icarus

FROM THE Metamorphoses

Ovid, translated by Rolfe Humphries

Homesick for homeland, Dædalus hated Crete
And his long exile there, but the sea held him.
"Though Minos blocks escape by land or water,"
Dædalus said, "surely the sky is open,
5   And that's the way we'll go. Minos' <u>dominion</u>
Does not include the air." He turned his thinking
Toward unknown arts, changing the laws of nature.
He laid out feathers in order, first the smallest,
A little larger next it, and so continued,

> What is Dædalus's plan for leaving Crete? What does he create?

words for everyday use

do • min • ion (də min′yən) *n.*, governed territory. *Until 1973 the Bahama Islands in the Caribbean were within the <u>dominion</u> of Great Britain.*

10 The way that pan-pipes[1] rise in gradual sequence.
He fastened them with twine and wax, at middle,
At bottom, so, and bent them, gently curving,
So that they looked like wings of birds, most surely.
And Icarus, his son, stood by and watched him,
15 Not knowing he was dealing with his downfall,
Stood by and watched, and raised his shiny face
To let a feather, light as down, fall on it,
Or stuck his thumb into the yellow wax,
Fooling around, the way a boy will, always,
20 Whenever a father tries to get some work done.
Still, it was done at last, and the father hovered,
Poised, in the moving air, and taught his son:
"I warn you, Icarus, fly a middle course:
Don't go too low, or water will weigh the wings down;
25 Don't go too high, or the sun's fire will burn them.
Keep to the middle way. And one more thing,
No fancy steering by star or constellation,
Follow my lead!" That was the flying lesson,
And now to fit the wings to the boy's shoulders.
30 Between the work and warning the father found
His cheeks were wet with tears, and his hands trembled.
He kissed his son (*Good-bye*, if he had known it),
Rose on his wings, flew on ahead, as fearful
As any bird launching the little nestlings[2]
35 Out of high nest into thin air. *Keep on,*
Keep on, he signals, *follow me!* He guides him
In flight—O fatal art!—and the wings move
And the father looks back to see the son's wings moving.
Far off, far down, some fisherman is watching
40 As the rod dips and trembles over the water,
Some shepherd rests his weight upon his crook,
Some ploughman on the handles of the ploughshare,
And all look up, in absolute amazement,
At those air-borne above. They must be gods!
45 They were over Samos, Juno's sacred island,
Delos and Paros toward the left, Lebinthus
Visible to the right, and another island,
Calymne, rich in honey. And the boy
Thought *This is wonderful!* and left his father,
50 Soared higher, higher, drawn to the vast heaven,
Nearer the sun, and the wax that held the wings
Melted in that fierce heat, and the bare arms

According to Dædalus, what should Icarus avoid?

Who looks up in amazement as Icarus flies?

---

1. **pan-pipes.** Instruments made of reeds of various lengths
2. **nestlings.** Young birds that have not left the nest yet

Beat up and down in air, and lacking oarage[3]
Took hold of nothing. *Father!* he cried, and *Father!*
55 Until the blue sea hushed him, the dark water
Men call the Icarian now. And Dædalus,
Father no more, called "Icarus, where are you!
Where are you, Icarus? Tell me where to find you!"
And saw the wings on the waves, and cursed his talents,
60 Buried the body in a tomb, and the land
Was named for Icarus.
                              During the burial
A noisy partridge, from a muddy ditch,
Looked out, drummed with her wings in loud approval.
No other bird, those days, was like the partridge,
65 Newcomer to the ranks of birds; the story
Reflects no credit on Dædalus. His sister,
Ignorant of the fates, had sent her son
To Dædalus as apprentice, only a youngster,
Hardly much more than twelve years old, but clever,
70 With an inventive turn of mind. For instance,
Studying a fish's backbone for a model,
He had notched a row of teeth in a strip of iron,
Thus making the first saw, and he had bound
Two arms of iron together with a joint
75 To keep them both together and apart,
One standing still, the other <u>traversing</u>
In a circle, so men came to have the compass.
And Dædalus, in envy, hurled the boy
Headlong from the high temple of Minerva,
80 And lied about it, saying he had fallen
Through accident, but Minerva, kind protectress
Of all inventive wits, stayed him in air,
Clothed him with <u>plumage</u>; he still retained his aptness
In feet and wings, and kept his old name, Perdix,
85 But in the new bird-form, Perdix, the partridge,
Never flies high, nor nests in trees, but flutters
Close to the ground, and the eggs are laid in hedgerows.
The bird, it seems, remembers, and is fearful
Of all high places.   ■

---

3. **oarage.** Ability to propel

What ends the flight of Icarus? Where does Icarus fall?

Why had Dædalus's sister sent her son to Dædalus? What sort of mind did the boy have?

What did Dædalus do to his nephew? Why?

What becomes of the young boy?

words for everyday use

tra • verse (trə vurs´) *vi.,* turn; swivel. *The point guard snatched the ball and quickly <u>traversed</u> to the other side of the court.*

plum • age (ploom´ij) *n.,* bird's feathers. *The parrot catches the eye because of its bright blue <u>plumage</u>.*

The Story of "Dædalus and Icarus" is one of the most familiar stories in Western literature. Why do you think it has remained so popular over the centuries?

Investigate, *Inquire,* and Imagine

Recall: GATHERING FACTS

1a. What is the problem Dædalus has at the beginning of the story? How does he try to solve it?

2a. What advice does Dædalus give Icarus before they try to fly? What happens to Icarus?

3a. What inventions does Dædalus's nephew make? What is the fate of Dædalus's nephew?

Interpret: FINDING MEANING

1b. What special gift does Dædalus have?

2b. Why does Icarus not follow Dædalus's advice about how to fly? What is the reason for Icarus's death? Should the boy's death be blamed on Dædalus, who defied the laws of nature, or does the blame lie with Icarus? What do you think the ancients thought? What do you think?

3b. What does the episode of Dædalus's nephew reveal about Dædalus?

Analyze: TAKING THINGS APART

4a. How does the role of the supernatural differ in the stories of Echo and Narcissus and Dædalus and Icarus?

Synthesize: BRINGING THINGS TOGETHER

4b. What do you think is the moral of each of the two selections?

Evaluate: MAKING JUDGMENTS

5a. Dædalus was considered the greatest inventor in ancient times. What did you learn about Dædalus from Ovid's story? Do you think he was justly punished? Explain.

Extend: CONNECTING IDEAS

5b. What did the people of the ancient world believe about their gods?

Understanding *Literature*

MORAL. Review the definition for **moral** in the Handbook of Literary Terms. What advice does Dædalus give Icarus that can be taken as the moral of the story?

FORESHADOWING. Review the definition for **foreshadowing** in Literary Tools and the graphic organizer you made. The episode in which Icarus plays with the wax can be said to foreshadow or at least explain his later actions. Explain why.

Writer's Journal

1. Icarus became so caught up in the thrill of flying that he forgot about the danger of flying too close to the sun. Think about a time you did something thrilling, such as going on a roller coaster, rock climbing, or rollerblading. Write a **description** about how you felt during the experience and afterward.

2. Narcissus has a human failing, his egoism, that results in his downfall. Write a **character sketch** about a person with a tragic human failing.

3. Write a **myth** to tell the origin of something in the world around you. You could tell about the origin of something in nature, like a flower or bird, or a technological innovation such as television or computers. You might want to include supernatural elements such as the intervention of the gods found in the two selections.

Integrating the Language Arts

Language, Grammar, and Style

FUNCTIONS OF THE SENTENCE. Sentences are the basic unit of expression in the English language. Four different kinds of sentences express four different kinds of thoughts and feelings, and each has characteristic end punctuation: **declarative, interrogative, imperative,** and **exclamatory**. For more information refer to the Language Arts Survey 3.17, "Functions of Sentences."

Identify the function of each sentence below by writing *dec* (declarative), *int* (interrogative), *imp* (imperative), or *exc* (exclamatory). Add appropriate end punctuation.

1. Tell me how Dædalus made the wings.

2. Stay away from the sun, Icarus.

3. Have you ever dreamed of flying.

4. Icarus didn't listen to his father.

5. Come down now.

Media Literacy

MEDIA REFERENCES TO GREEK AND ROMAN MYTHOLOGY. Many references to mythological characters or occurrences can be found in magazine articles, television shows and movies, and in product names and advertising. With a partner, find three references to Greek or Roman mythology in the media. If possible, photocopy or clip any articles and advertisements. What references to Greek and Roman mythology do you find in each example?

Collaborative Learning

RETELLING MYTHS. Working in a small group, select gods and goddesses from Greek or Roman mythology. Make a poster that includes the names, descriptions, and, if possible, pictures of traditional representations of the gods and goddesses. Find myths or tales in which each god or goddess has an important role. You should each select a myth for a different god or goddess and be prepared to retell it to the class as your group displays its poster.

"The White Snake"

by Jacob and Wilhelm Grimm, translated by Lucy Crane

Reader's resource

Many of the fairy tales you may be familiar with began as folk songs and stories from the European oral tradition and were later transcribed on paper. The Grimm brothers, Jacob and Wilhelm, collected oral stories such as "Rapunzel" in their native Germany. In France, Charles Perrault (1628–1703) wrote down other folk stories, including "Cinderella" and "Sleeping Beauty." In Denmark, Hans Christian Andersen (1805–1874) retold such tales as "The Princess and the Pea," "The Ugly Duckling," and "The Emperor's New Clothes."

CULTURE CONNECTION. Similar tales are told in many different countries and cultures. For example, versions of the Cinderella tale have been told for centuries by the Chinese and Native Americans.

About the AUTHORS

Jacob Grimm (1785–1863) and his brother **Wilhelm** (1786–1859) were German scholars. Among young people around the globe, the Grimm brothers are famous for collecting folk songs and folk tales from the European oral tradition. The brothers transcribed these traditional tales as people related them and are credited with giving folk tales a readable form without changing their essential character. The Grimms' collection became a classic of world literature. The two hundred stories they collected convey the spirit and imagination of generations of people. Jacob was also a highly esteemed scholar of the history of European languages. He demonstrated that sounds change in regular ways and showed how certain languages in Europe and western Asia evolved from other languages.

Literary TOOLS

FAIRY TALE. A **fairy tale** is a story that deals with mischievous spirits and other supernatural occurrences, often in medieval settings. As you read, identify elements of this story that you find typical of fairy tales.

CHARACTER. A **character** is a person (or sometimes an animal) who figures in the action of a literary work. A *one-dimensional character, flat character,* or *caricature* is one who exhibits a single dominant quality, or character trait. A *three-dimensional, full,* or *rounded character* is one who exhibits the complexity of traits associated with actual human beings. As you read, list the details you learn about the servant in this fairy tale.

MOTIF. A **motif** is any element that recurs in a literary work. Read the entry on *motif* in the Handbook of Literary Terms. As you read "The White Snake," note the fairy tale motif of items occurring in sets of three.

Graphic Organizer

Create a cluster chart like the one below to record the motif of items occurring in sets of three.

Items in Sets of Three

Three Tasks

Reader's Journal

In this story, the king grants the hero one favor. If a powerful person promised you one favor, what would you choose? Explain.

THE WHITE

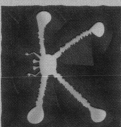

SNAKE

Jacob and
Wilhelm Grimm,

translated by
Lucy Crane

The Keepsake, 1901. Kate Elizabeth Bunce.
Birmingham Museums and Art Gallery, Birmingham, England.

A long time ago there lived a King whose wisdom was noised <u>abroad</u> in all the country. Nothing remained long unknown to him, and it was as if the knowledge of hidden things was brought to him in the air. However, he had one curious custom. Every day at dinner, after the table had been cleared and every one gone away, a trusty servant had to bring in one other dish. But it was covered up, and the servant himself did not know what was in it, and no one else knew, for the King waited until he was quite alone before he uncovered it. This had gone on a long time, but at last there came a day when the servant could restrain his curiosity no longer, but as he was carrying the dish away he took it into his own room. As soon as he had fastened the door securely, he lifted the cover, and there he saw a white snake lying on the dish. After seeing it he could not resist the desire to taste it, and so he cut off a small piece and put it in his mouth. As soon as it touched his tongue he heard outside his window a strange chorus of delicate voices. He went and listened, and found that it was the sparrows talking together, and telling each other all they had seen in the fields and woods. The virtue of the snake had given him power to understand the speech of animals.

> How does the servant learn the King's secret? What is the secret?

> What ability does the servant acquire? What gives him this ability?

Now it happened one day that the Queen lost her most splendid ring, and suspicion fell upon the trusty servant, who had the general <u>superintendence</u>, and he was accused of stealing it. The King summoned him to his presence, and after many reproaches told him that if by the next day he was not able to name the thief he should be considered guilty, and punished. It was in vain that he protested his innocence; he could get no better sentence. In his uneasiness and <u>anxiety</u> he went out into the courtyard, and began to consider what he could do in so great a necessity. There sat the ducks by the running water and rested themselves, and <u>plumed</u> themselves with their flat bills, and held a comfortable chat. The servant stayed where he was and listened to them. They told how they had waddled about all yesterday morning and found good food; and then one of them said pitifully, "Something lies very heavy in my craw,[1]—it is the ring that was lying under the Queen's window; I swallowed it down in too great a hurry."

> In what way does the servant's new ability help him?

art note

Kate Elizabeth Bunce (1856–1927) was an English artist who painted in the style of the Pre-Raphaelites, a group that went against convention by looking for inspiration in art that predated the Renaissance. Their subject matter was often very romanticized visions of women. But the movement attracted women artists at a time when women were discouraged from pursuing art as a profession and Bunce won awards and commissions in competition with male painters. Does this picture remind you of a certain part of the story?

---

1. **craw.** Stomach of an animal

---

words for everyday use

a • broad (ə brôd´) *adv.*, far and wide. *News of President Lincoln's assasination quickly spread <u>abroad</u> in the land.*

su • per • in • ten • dence (sōō´pər in tend´ens) *n.*, supervision; management. *City officials have given <u>superintendence</u> of the arts festival to Ms. Irene Pizzuti.*

anx • i • e • ty (aŋ zī´ə tē) *n.*, worry; apprehension. *Feeling a certain amount of <u>anxiety</u> before giving a speech is perfectly normal.*

plume (plōōm) *vt.*, preen, or clean and arrange one's feathers. *After splashing in the birdbath, the cardinal sat on the edge and <u>plumed</u> itself.*

Then the servant seized her by the neck, took her into the kitchen, and said to the cook,

"Kill this one, she is quite ready for cooking."

"Yes," said the cook, weighing it in her hand; "there will be no trouble of fattening this one—it has been ready ever so long."

She then slit up its neck, and when it was opened the Queen's ring was found in its craw. The servant could now clearly prove his innocence, and in order to make up for the injustice he had suffered the King permitted him to ask some favour for himself, and also promised him the place of greatest honour in the royal household.

But the servant refused it, and only asked for a horse and money for travelling, for he had a fancy to see the world, and look about him a little. So his request was granted, and he set out on his way; and one day he came to a pool of water, by which he saw three fishes who had got entangled in the rushes, and were panting for water. Although fishes are usually considered dumb creatures, he understood very well their lament that they were to perish so miserably; and as he had a compassionate heart he dismounted from his horse, and put the three fishes back again into the water. They quivered all over with joy, stretched out their heads, and called out to him,

"We will remember and reward thee, because thou hast delivered us." He rode on, and after a while he heard a small voice come up from the sand underneath his horse's feet. He listened, and understood how an ant-king was complaining,

> What does the young man do for the three fishes? for the ants? What do both the fishes and the ants say to him?

"If only these men would keep off, with their great awkward beasts! Here comes this stupid horse treading down my people with his hard hoofs!"

The man then turned his horse to the side-path, and the ant-king called out to him,

"We will remember and reward thee!"

The path led him through a wood, and there he saw a father-raven and mother-raven standing by their nest and throwing their young ones out.

"Off with you! young gallows-birds!"[2] cried they; "we cannot stuff you any more; you are big enough to fend for yourselves!" The poor young ravens lay on the ground, fluttering, and beating the air with their pinions, and crying,

"We are poor helpless things, we cannot fend for ourselves, we cannot even fly! we can only die of hunger!"

Then the kind young man dismounted, killed his horse with his dagger, and

> What other animals does the young man help?

left it to the young ravens for food. They came hopping up, feasted away at it, and cried,

"We will remember and reward thee!"

So now he had to use his own legs, and when he had gone a long way he came to a great town. There was much noise and thronging in the streets, and there came a man on a horse, who proclaimed,

"That the King's daughter seeks a husband, but he who wishes to marry her must perform a difficult task, and if he cannot carry it through successfully, he must lose his life."

Many had already tried, but had lost their lives, in vain. The young man, when he saw the King's daughter, was so dazzled by her great beauty, that he forgot all danger, went to the King and offered himself as a wooer.

> What is the reward for completing the difficult task? What danger lies in attempting this task? Why does the young man decide to undertake the task?

Then he was led to the sea-side, and a gold ring was thrown into the water before his eyes. Then the King told him that he must fetch the ring up again from the bottom of the sea, saying,

"If you come back without it, you shall be put under the waves again and again until you are drowned."

---

2. **gallows-birds.** Creatures who deserve to be hanged

Every one pitied the handsome young man, but they went, and left him alone by the sea. As he was standing on the shore and thinking of what he should do, there came three fishes swimming by, none other than those he had set free. The middle one had a mussel in his mouth, and he laid it on the strand at the young man's feet; and when he took it up and opened it there was the gold ring inside! Full of joy he carried it to the King, and expected the promised reward; but the King's daughter, proud of her high birth,[3] despised him, and set him another task to perform. She went out into the garden, and strewed about over the grass ten sacks full of millet seed.[4]

"By the time the sun rises in the morning you must have picked up all these," she said, "and not a grain must be wanting."

The young man sat down in the garden and considered how it was possible to do this task, but he could <u>contrive</u> nothing, and stayed there, feeling very sorrowful, and expecting to be led to death at break of day. But when the first beams of the sun fell on the garden he saw that the ten sacks were all filled, standing one by the other, and not even a grain was missing. The ant-king had arrived in the night with his thousands of ants, and the grateful creatures had picked up all the millet seed, and filled the sacks with great industry. The King's daughter came herself into the garden and saw with astonishment that the young man had performed all that had

What enables the young man to complete the second task?

been given him to do. But she could not let her proud heart melt, but said,

"Although he has completed the two tasks, he shall not be my bridegroom unless he brings me an apple from the tree of life."

The young man did not know where the tree of life was to be found, but he set out and went on and on, as long as his legs could carry him, but he had no hope of finding it. When he had gone through three kingdoms he came one evening to a wood, and seated himself under a tree to go to sleep; but he heard a rustling in the boughs, and a golden apple fell into his hand. Immediately three ravens flew towards him, perched on his knee, and said,

How was the young man able to find the apple from the tree of life?

"We are the three young ravens that you delivered from starving; when we grew big, and heard that you were seeking the golden apple, we flew over the sea to the end of the earth, where the tree of life stands, and we fetched the apple."

Full of joy the young man set off on his way home, and brought the golden apple to the King's beautiful daughter, who was without any further excuse.

So they divided the apple of life, and ate it together; and their hearts were filled with love, and they lived in undisturbed happiness to a great age. ■

What happens at the end of the story?

---

3. **high birth.** Being born into a noble family
4. **millet seed.** Seed of a grain grown for food

---

words for everyday use

con • trive (kən trīv´) *vt.,* devise, plan; bring about by strategy or difficulty. *After several days, Kaila finally <u>contrived</u> a way to finish the science experiment.*

Respond *to the* SELECTION

Which fairy tales were your favorites when you were younger, and why?

Investigate, Inquire, and Imagine

Recall: GATHERING FACTS

1a. What does the servant do out of curiosity at the beginning of the story? How does his curiosity help him with the problem he has concerning the ring?

2a. What does the servant choose when the king grants him a favor? What three groups of animals does the servant meet? How does he help them?

3a. Why does the servant choose to perform the tasks set for him? How do the animals he previously met help him?

Interpret: FINDING MEANING

1b. What elements in the first two paragraphs make it clear that this is a fairy tale?

2b. Why do you think the servant chose the favor he did? What do the servant's encounters with the animals show about his character?

3b. What is the nature of the tasks that the servant has to perform to win the princess's hand? Why does the servant need supernatural helpers to perform these tasks?

Analyze: TAKING THINGS APART

4a. How is this fairy tale similar to the first two myths in this unit? How is it different?

Synthesize: BRINGING THINGS TOGETHER

4b. How is this tale similar to other fairy tales you know? List the similar elements. For example, this tale, like many others, has a happy ending. Why might this sort of ending be common in fairy tales?

Evaluate: MAKING JUDGMENTS

5a. Do you think the tasks are fair? Why does the princess continue to ask more tasks of the young man? What motivates the young man to continue despite the tremendous odds? Do you think he is foolish, or should he be admired for his determination?

Extend: CONNECTING IDEAS

5b. What qualities were admired in young men at the time this fairy tale was first being told? What qualities were admired in young women? What idea of love is presented in this tale?

Understanding Literature

FAIRY TALE. Review the definition for **fairy tale** in the Handbook of Literary Terms and the list you made in Literary Tools on page 17. What elements occur frequently in fairy tales that you know? List these elements. Here are some ideas to prompt your thinking: tests, curses, good versus evil. Why do you think that fairy tales are traditionally told or read to children?

CHARACTER. Review the definition for **character** in the Handbook of Literary Terms and the list you made in Literary Tools. List the details you know about the servant in this fairy tale. Is the servant a one- or three-dimensional character? How important is strong character development in fairy tales?

MOTIF. Review the definition for **motif** in the Handbook of Literary Terms and the cluster chart you completed on page 17. One common fairy tale motif found in "The White Snake" is items or events occurring in sets of three. Discuss the examples of the motif of threes that you found in the story.

Writer's Journal

1. Compose a **poem** for a wedding card that the animals in the story might have given to the servant and princess.
2. In this fairy tale, animals speak. What would happen if your pet or another animal you encountered suddenly talked? What would it say? Would it be shy, helpful, hip, or haughty? Write a **summary** of a short story about a talking animal.
3. Write a **retelling** of a section of "The White Snake," changing its setting to the present. For example, you can change the challenges the hero faces and how he or she meets them. You can also include modern machinery to help the hero, but make sure to retain some supernatural elements to make your story fit the fairy tale genre.

Integrating the Language Arts

Language, Grammar, and Style

COMPLETE SUBJECTS AND PREDICATES IN SENTENCES. English sentences have two major parts, the *subject* and the *predicate*. In the most common English sentence (a declarative sentence), first the sentence tells us what it is talking about. This is the **complete subject**. Second, it gives us information about the subject; this second part of the sentence is called the **complete predicate**. Every word in a sentence is part of the complete subject or the complete predicate. For more information, refer to the Language Arts Survey 3.19, "Finding the Complete Subject and Complete Predicate in a Sentence."

In each of the sentences below, underline the complete subject once and the complete predicate twice.

1. The curious servant discovered a white snake on the plate.
2. The three fish were put back in the water.
3. The young man fell in love with the king's daughter
4. The lucky young man had completed two tasks.
5. Three ravens helped him get an apple from the tree of life.

Study and Research

THE MEDIEVAL PERIOD IN EUROPE. Many fairy tales are set in the medieval era, or the Middle Ages. Select a fairy tale from a country in Europe (such as Denmark, Germany, Ireland, England, or France) and research what that country was like during medieval times. How did the common person live? How was the country ruled? Finally, explain which elements of your fairy tale reflect the way of life as it was during the medieval period.

Collaborative Learning

FAIRY TALES ACROSS CULTURES, TIMES, AND MEDIA. Working with other students in a small group, choose a popular fairy tale to research. Gather several versions of the tale from various sources and analyze them to discover differences in their settings, plots, characters, and themes. Present the results of your comparisons to the rest of the class.

Literary TOOLS

PARABLE. A **parable** is a very brief story told to teach a moral lesson. As you read, write down the verses that serve as an introduction to the parable of the prodigal son.

SYMBOL. A **symbol** is a thing that stands for or represents itself and something else. In this parable, there are many symbols.

Graphic Organizer

Make a chart. On the left, identify the symbol. On the right, write what it represents. One example has been done for you.

Symbol	What It Represents
shepherd	God

Reader's Journal

If you suddenly had a lot of money to spend, how would you spend it, and why?

"THE PRODIGAL SON"
from the King James Bible

Reader's resource

"The Prodigal Son" is one of several parables found in the New Testament of the Bible told by Jesus to answer questions posed to him and to serve as a guide to moral behavior.

CULTURE CONNECTION. The Bible has had a profound effect on Western culture. Whatever your own religious beliefs might be, becoming familiar with the Bible will help you to understand the culture and literature of Western civilization. For two thousand years, the stories in the Bible have influenced the literature, art, music, and ways of life of people in the Middle East, Europe, and Latin America. In addition, for much of the history of the United States, the one book found in most homes was a copy of the Bible. If you have knowledge of the most familiar stories from the Bible, many aspects of culture will be open to you. These titles of great novels in the English language, taken from lines in the Bible, point to the influence of the Bible on literature.

The Golden Bowl, by Henry James
The Sun Also Rises, by Ernest Hemingway
The Violent Bear It Away, by Flannery O'Connor
East of Eden and *The Grapes of Wrath*, by John Steinbeck
The Power and the Glory, by Graham Greene
Stranger in a Strange Land, by Robert Heinlein

Knowing biblical stories will help you to recognize such references, or allusions, in the literature that you will read throughout your life.

About the AUTHOR

The **King James Bible** was published in England in 1611 during the reign of King James I. This work was a translation into English done by forty-seven scholars who used both previous translations and texts in the original ancient languages in which the Bible was written. The poetic King James translation of the Bible had a profound effect on the English language. Words and quotations from the King James Bible, familiar from Sunday services and from Bible reading, became interwoven in the speech of everyday life.

THE PRODIGAL[1] SON

from the King James Bible

Then drew near unto him all the publicans[2] and sinners for to hear him.

2   And the Pharisees[3] and scribes murmured, saying, This man receiveth sinners, and eateth with them.

3   And he spake this parable unto them, saying,

4   What man of you, having an hundred sheep, if he lose one of them, doth not leave the ninety and nine in the wilderness, and go after that which is lost, until he find it?

5   And when he hath found it, he layeth it on his shoulders, rejoicing.

6   And when he cometh home, he calleth together his friends and neighbors, saying unto them, Rejoice with me; for I have found my sheep which was lost.

What would a person do if a sheep or a piece of silver were lost? What would happen when the sheep or the silver was found? What would cause a similar reaction in heaven?

7   I say unto you, that likewise joy shall be in heaven over one sinner that repenteth,[4] more than over ninety and nine just persons, which need no repentance.

8   Either what woman having ten pieces of silver, if she lose one piece, doth not light a candle and sweep the house, and seek <u>diligently</u> till she find it?

---

1. **Prodigal.** Extravagant; characterized by wasteful expenditure
2. **publicans.** Collectors of revenue in ancient Judea
3. **Pharisees.** Members of an ancient Jewish party or fellowship
4. **repenteth.** Repents, feels sorry for sins

The Return of the Prodigal Son, 1662. Rembrandt van Rijn.
Hermitage Museum, St. Petersburg, Russia.

art note

The Return of the Prodigal Son, 1662.
Rembrandt van Rijn.
In his use of light, the Dutch master Rembrandt (1606–1669) was influenced by Caravaggio (page 9). Why are some faces brightly lit and others in shadow? What does it mean to be "enlightened"? How does that relate to the way the characters in the story react to the prodigal son's return?

words for everyday use
dil • i • gent • ly (dil´ə jənt lē) *adv.,* carefully and steadily. *Because Mrs. Chang <u>diligently</u> weeds and waters her vegetable garden, it produces abundantly.*

9   And when she hath found it, she calleth her friends and her neighbors together, saying, Rejoice with me for I have found the piece which I had lost.

10   Likewise, I say unto you, there is joy in the presence of the angels of God over one sinner that repenteth.

11   And he said, A certain man had two sons:

12   And the younger of them said to his father, Father, give me the portion of goods that falleth to me. And he divided unto them his living.

13   And not many days after the younger son gathered all together, and took his journey into a far country, and there wasted his substance with <u>riotous</u> living.

> What does the younger son do with his money?

14   And when he had spent all, there arose a mighty <u>famine</u> in that land; and he began to be in want.

15   And he went and joined himself to a citizen of that country; and he sent him into his fields to feed swine.

16   And he would fain[5] have filled his belly with the husks that the swine did eat: and no man gave unto him.

17   And when he came to himself, he said, How many hired servants of my father's have bread enough and to spare, and I perish with hunger!

18   I will arise and go to my father, and will say unto him, Father, I have sinned against heaven, and before thee,

19   And am no more worthy to be called thy son: make me as one of the hired servants.

20   And he arose, and came to his father. But when he was yet a great way off, his father saw him, and had <u>compassion</u> and ran, and fell on his neck and kissed him.

21   And the son said unto him Father, I have sinned against heaven, and in thy sight and am no more worthy to be called thy son.

22   But the father said to his servants, Bring forth the best robe, and put it on him; and put a ring on his hand, and shoes on his feet:

23   And bring hither the fatted calf, and kill it, and let us eat, and be merry:

24   For this my son was dead, and is alive again; he was lost, and is found. And they began to be merry.

25   Now his elder son was in the field: and as he came and drew nigh to the house, he heard music and dancing.

26   And he called one of the servants, and asked what these things meant.

27   And he said unto him, Thy brother is come; and thy father hath killed the fatted calf, because he hath received him safe and sound.

28   And he was angry, and would not go in: therefore came his father out, and <u>entreated</u> him.

> How does the older son react?

29   And he answering said to his father, Lo, these many years do I serve thee, neither <u>transgressed</u> I at any time thy commandment: and yet thou never gavest me a kid, that I might make merry with my friends:

30   But as soon as this thy son was come, which hath devoured thy living with harlots, thou hast killed for him the fatted calf.

31   And he said unto him, Son, thou art ever with me, and all that I have is thine.

> What explanation does the father give for his actions?

32   It was meet[6] that we should make merry, and be glad: for this thy brother was dead, and is alive again; and was lost, and is found. ■

---

5. **fain.** Gladly
6. **meet.** Fitting

Write about a time in which you forgave someone for a wrong that he or she committed. How did forgiving the person make you feel?

Investigate, *Inquire,* and Imagine

Recall: GATHERING FACTS

1a. What does the younger son request at the beginning of the story?

2a. How does the younger son spend his money? Why does he decide to return home?

3a. How is the younger son greeted when he returns home? What is his father's reaction? What is his brother's reaction?

Interpret: FINDING MEANING

1b. Do you consider what the younger son does at the beginning of the parable to be usual or unusual for a young person? Give reasons to support your opinion.

2b. Why is "The Prodigal Son" an appropriate name for the parable? Do you think it takes courage for the younger son to return home? Explain.

3b. Why does the father greet his son as he does? Why does the older brother react as he does?

Analyze: TAKING THINGS APART

4a. Identify the characteristics of the prodigal son, the father, and the elder son, and identify the relationship of the father to each of his sons. What role does the elder son play in the parable?

Synthesize: BRINGING THINGS TOGETHER

4b. What lesson does the parable teach? How do the characters and their roles make this an effective vehicle for this lesson?

Evaluate: MAKING JUDGMENTS

5a. Describe, then evaluate, the father's relationship to each of his sons. Do you think he treats them fairly? Explain.

Extend: CONNECTING IDEAS

5b. Put yourself in the younger son's place. How will you live your life now that you have returned home and have been forgiven by your father?

Understanding *Literature*

PARABLE. Review the definition for **parable** in the Handbook of Literary terms and the notes you took in Literary Tools on page 24. Which verses serve as an introduction to the parable of the prodigal son? Which verses tell the parable of the prodigal son?

SYMBOL. Review the definition for **symbol** in the Handbook of Literary Terms and the chart you made for Literary Tools. What do the lost sheep, the lost silver coin, and the prodigal son symbolize? Why does the writer of this parable provide so many examples?

Writer's Journal

1. Imagine you are the older brother of the prodigal son. Do you think your brother has truly reformed, or will he go back to his old ways if he gets a chance? Form an opinion, then write a **journal entry** supporting your opinion.

2. Write a brief **comparison-contrast essay** comparing this parable to another work you have read in this unit. How is it different from the myths and the fairy tale, for example, and how is it similar?

3. Do you believe that parents should be forgiving and accepting of their children, or do you believe that strict discipline is important for building character? Write a **parable**, or lesson story, of your own demonstrating your point of view. For example, you could write a parable about a father who disciplines his son too harshly and gets negative consequences.

Integrating the Language Arts

Language, Grammar, and Style

IDENTIFYING AND CORRECTING SENTENCES. A **fragment** is a piece of a sentence—it might be just a subject or a part of a predicate. It is not a sentence because it does not express a complete thought—just part of a thought. Refer to the Language Arts Survey 3.33, "Correcting Sentence Fragments," for examples.

If the group of words is a complete sentence, underline the complete subject once and the complete predicate twice. If it is a fragment, add material to make the group of words into a complete sentence.

1. It was appropriate for everyone to celebrate the returned son.
2. Who has wasted your money on foolish living.
3. I will go to the house of my father.
4. Begged to be a servant in his father's house.
5. Went off to live a wild life among strangers.

Speaking and Listening

DEBATE. Hold a class debate about whether the prodigal son has truly reformed or whether he will continue in his prodigal ways. You may also debate whether his father's treatment of him is wise or overly indulgent. Those students who wrote about this topic for Writer's Journal should share their ideas. Be sure to listen to others in your class and to give everyone a chance to share his or her opinion. For more information, see the Language Arts Survey 4.21, "Participating in a Debate."

Collaborative Learning

WRITING AN ADAPTATION. Working in groups of three, write an adaptation of the parable of the prodigal son in which the story takes place in a contemporary setting, perhaps in your city or town. Brainstorm together for ideas before writing. Use your imagination, but be sure to keep the message of the parable intact. When you have finished, share your modern parables with the rest of the class.

"GOHA AND THE POT"

North African Folk Tale, retold by Mahmoud Ibrahim Mostafa

Reader's resource

Trickster tales are traditional stories that are passed on by word of mouth. The tales usually involve deceit, or a trick of some kind. The trickster figure, usually a clever underdog, typically outwits a slower-witted character. Trickster tales have been told around the world, especially in native North and South American cultures and in Africa. In Africa, common trickster animals include the hare, the spider, and the tortoise. Many African tales also feature human tricksters. "**Goha and the Pot**" is a trickster tale.

GEOGRAPHY CONNECTION. "Goha and the Pot" is a folk tale from North Africa. North Africa includes the countries of Morocco, Algeria, Tunisia, Libya, and Egypt. The area is bounded to the north and west by the Mediterranean Sea and the Atlantic Ocean, and to the east by the Red Sea. Most people in North Africa live along the coast; the southern area of the region is a vast desert called the Sahara. The Atlas Mountains separate the coastal areas from the Sahara Desert.

HISTORY CONNECTION. The population of North Africa is mainly Berber and Arab. Berbers are a native African tribe. Arab peoples invaded North Africa in AD 643 and brought the Islamic religion with them. As a result, most people in North Africa are Muslim. In the 1800s, North Africa was colonized by Europeans—the French in Algeria and Tunisia, the Italians in Libya, and the French and the Spanish in Morocco. Since 1962, when Algeria achieved its independence, all the countries of North Africa have been independent. In some North African regions, French, Spanish, and Italian are still written and spoken.

About the AUTHOR

Mahmoud Ibrahim Mostafa (1943–) was born in Shubra, Cairo, Egypt. A physician, he has practiced in Columbia, South Carolina, for many years.

Literary TOOLS

FOLK TALE AND AIM. A **folk tale** is a story passed by word of mouth from generation to generation. A writer's **aim** is his or her purpose, or goal. For a more complete definition of *aim,* see the Handbook of Literary Terms. As you read, decide what you think is the principal aim of this folk tale.

PERSONIFICATION. Personification is a figure of speech in which something not human is described as if it were human. As you read, identify what is personified in this story.

Reader's Journal

When have you seen or heard of people behaving foolishly because of greed?

GOHA AND THE POT

North African Folk Tale, retold by Mahmoud Ibrahim Mostafa

One day, many, many years ago, Goha wanted to fix a meal for his family. He found that he needed a big pot, so he went to his next door neighbor to ask if he might borrow a big brass pot. The neighbor was reluctant to lend him the pot, but Goha promised that he would return it to his neighbor the following day.

To the surprise of his neighbor, Goha returned the next day with the big brass pot that he had borrowed and another one, smaller than the first. The neighbor felt that Goha must have made a mistake since he had lent Goha one pot, but Goha said that there was no mistake at all. He explained that overnight the pot he had borrowed went into labor and gave birth to this nice, shiny, little pot, and Goha insisted that the small pot also belonged to his neighbor!

A few days later, Goha returned to the same neighbor and asked if he could borrow another pot. This time the neighbor did not have any trouble giving him two big pots, thinking that Goha would return with more pots anyway. And indeed, when Goha returned the two big pots, he also brought two smaller, shining pots, much to the delight of his neighbor.

> Why is the neighbor not reluctant to lend Goha a pot the second time?

The next time Goha knocked on his neighbor's door, before he could even say a word, the neighbor gave him a basket full of big pots. In fact he gave Goha all the pots he had in his possession. His neighbor did not stop there, however; he even helped to carry the pots to Goha's house.

Days passed, then weeks, and the neighbor began to worry, but he did not mention his concern to Goha, hoping that Goha would come by some day soon with a whole room full of pots. After three whole months had gone by, the neighbor decided to go to Goha to inquire about his pots. Upon his inquiry, Goha with a very sad face said to his neighbor, "My dear neighbor, I'm saddened to tell you that your pots are all dead!"

The neighbor was furious, and he shouted, "Are you a madman? Pots don't die!"

Then Goha quietly said, "My dear neighbor, you were very willing to accept the fact that pots can have babies, weren't you? Why for goodness' sake don't you accept that they can also die?" ∎

> What did Goha tell his neighbor about the pots?

Mosaic [Detail]. African artist. Bordol Museum, Tunisia.

Respond *to the* SELECTION

If you were Goha's neighbor, how would you feel about being tricked? Would the trick cause you to reevaluate your own behavior? Explain.

Investigate, *Inquire,* and Imagine

Recall: GATHERING FACTS

1a. In "Goha and the Pot," what does Goha ask to borrow from his neighbor, and what is his neighbor's reaction to the request? What "surprise" does Goha give his neighbor when he returns the next day? What explanation does Goha provide for this surprise?

2a. What happens when Goha asks to borrow a pot the second time? the third time?

3a. How long does the neighbor wait before asking Goha about his pots? What does Goha say has happened to the neighbor's pots? What does Goha say when the neighbor becomes angry?

Interpret: FINDING MEANING

1b. What does the neighbor's reaction reveal about his character? Do you think the neighbor really believes Goha's explanation? Why is the neighbor willing to accept this explanation?

2b. Why does the neighbor give Goha so many pots? Why do you think Goha returns with more pots the first two times he borrows a pot?

3b. Why does the neighbor wait so long before asking Goha about his pots? Do you think Goha is really "saddened" to tell the neighbor what has happened to the pots? What do you think has really happened to the pots?

Analyze: TAKING THINGS APART

4a. Analyze the character of the neighbor based on his actions throughout the story. What kind of a person is he? Why do you think Goha tricks his neighbor?

Synthesize: BRINGING THINGS TOGETHER

4b. What do you think is the moral, or lesson, of "Goha and the Pot"?

Evaluate: MAKING JUDGMENTS

5a. What do you think of Goha's behavior toward his neighbor? Is he clever or cruel? Does his neighbor deserve to be tricked? Why, or why not?

Extend: CONNECTING IDEAS

5b. What would happen today in your community if someone like Goha performed a trick on his neighbor like the one in "Goha and the Pot"?

Understanding *Literature*

FOLK TALE AND AIM. Review the definitions for **folk tale** and **aim** in the Handbook of Literary Terms. Why do you think this story was passed on among the people of North Africa? What was the aim in creating this tale?

PERSONIFICATION. Review the definition for **personification** in the Handbook of Literary Terms. What is personified in this story? What human qualities are given to this object or objects? What events does personification explain in this story? What does the story's outcome suggest about personification?

Writer's Journal

1. Imagine that you were helping Goha carry out his plan in "Goha and the Pot." Write a **birth announcement** for the "baby" pot, to be sent to Goha's neighbor.

2. Imagine that you are an advice columnist in Goha's village and that Goha's neighbor writes you to ask for advice in getting his pots back. Write an **advice column** that includes his letter and your response.

3. Imagine that you are the neighbor at the end of the story. Write a **journal entry** describing the incident with Goha. Explain how you feel about being tricked, and what you plan to do next.

Integrating the Language Arts

Language, Grammar, and Style

FINDING THE VERB (SIMPLE PREDICATE) OF A SENTENCE. The **verb**, or **simple predicate**, is the *complete predicate* without any complements or modifiers. The verb provides the action of the sentence. For additional help in finding the verb in a sentence refer to the Language Arts Survey 3.21, "How to Find the Simple Subject and Verb."

Underline the verb in each of the following sentences:

1. Goha <u>borrowed</u> a pot from the neighbor.
2. He was <u>cooking</u> a meal for his family.
3. The next day two pots had been <u>returned.</u>
4. At night the pot had <u>birthed</u> a little pot.
5. Goha <u>gave</u> the neighbor both pots.

Media Literacy

TELEVISION ADVERTISING. Advertisers sometimes create commercials and "infomercials" to advertise products that are "revolutionary," "the answer to everyone's problems," and "too good to be true." For example, they might advertise a way for people to lose weight without exercising or dieting. Or they might claim to have a way for people to earn millions without doing any work. How are such advertising techniques similar to the "trickster" technique Goha used? Why are people willing to try such products, even if the claims made by the advertisers are so difficult to believe?

Create a fictional television commercial advertising a product that is "too good to be true." Refer to the Language Arts Survey 5.3, "Avoiding False Arguments and Propaganda," for help in persuading your audience to buy this product. If you wish, use props to show your viewers how your product works. You might want to use charts or graphs or actual "samples" of your product. Then act out your commercial in front of the class. If possible, videotape the commercial.

"The Fox and the Crow"
by Æsop

Reader's resource

CULTURE CONNECTION. "The Fox and the Crow" features a fox as one of its main characters. The fox is a popular character in fairy tales and fables around the world. Many fables from ancient times involved foxes, as well as crows, mice, and lions. The clever fox Renart, or Reynard (from the French *renard* for fox), was the hero of epics written in the European Middle Ages. Chinese folklore and superstition portrays the fox as a magical being, able to change itself into a human form to tempt and trick unlucky humans. Korean and Japanese folklore, highly influenced by the Chinese, tells of fox-maidens that lure young men to their doom. Shape-shifting foxes are also found in South American tales, and similar legends featuring the fox's relative, the coyote, can be found in Native American tradition. Undoubtedly the craftiness of the fox inspired so many cultures to feature it as a trickster animal and assign it magical traits.

About the AUTHOR

Æsop may or may not have been a real person. His name has traditionally been associated with a collection of Greek fables, but since no reliable historical record of Æsop exists, it might be that the fables simply originated in the oral tradition of Greece. According to some ancient writers, however, Æsop was a real person born around 620 BC in Samos, Greece. Some say he was a slave who was later freed for his storytelling abilities, while others say he was an advisor to a king. According to one legend, Æsop met his death in Delphi while working as an ambassador for King Croesus of Lydia. The story goes that Æsop was supposed to distribute a tribute of gold to the Delphians, but, disgusted with the people's greed, he refused to do so. The people were so angry they had Æsop condemned for heresy and forced him off a cliff.

Reader's Journal

In your opinion, is there a difference between flattery and praise? Explain.

Literary TOOLS

FABLE. A **fable** is a brief story, often with animal characters, told to express a moral. As you read, try to determine the moral in "The Fox and the Crow."

CHARACTER. A **character** is a person (or sometimes an animal) who figures in the action of a literary work. A *one-dimensional character* is one who exhibits a single dominant quality, or character trait. A *three-dimensional character* is one who exhibits the complexity of traits associated with actual human beings. A *stock character* is one who is found again and again in different literary works. As you read, decide which type or types of characters are found in this fable.

Organizer

The characters in the selection you are about to read are similar in some ways to those in the African folk tale "Goha and the Pot." On your own paper, make a Venn diagram like the one below to fill in as you read. The differences between the characters of each story should go in each individual oval, while the similarities should go in the space where the ovals overlap.

Characters in "Goha and the Pot"   Characters in "The Fox and the Crow"

Fox Hunt, 1893. Winslow Homer. The Pennsylvania Academy of Fine Arts, Philadelphia.

The Fox and the Crow

Æsop

A Fox once saw a Crow fly off with a piece of cheese in its beak and settle on a branch of a tree. "That's for me, as I am a Fox," said Master Reynard,[1] and he walked up to the foot of the tree.

"Good day, Mistress Crow," he cried. "How well you are looking today: how glossy your feathers; how bright your eye. I feel sure your voice must surpass that of other birds, just as your figure does; let me hear but one song from you that I may greet you as the Queen of Birds."

The Crow lifted up her head and began to caw her best, but the moment she opened her mouth the piece of cheese fell to the ground, only to be snapped up by Master Fox. "That will do," said he. "That was all I wanted. In exchange for your cheese I will give you a piece of advice for the future—

"Do not trust flatterers." ■

> What does the Fox say to the Crow? What does he ask her to do? Why does he make this request?

---

1. **Master Reynard.** Fox in the medieval beast epic *Reynard the Fox*

---

words for everyday use

sur • pass (sər pas´) vt., go beyond. *Because Matt grew like a weed, he soon surpassed the other boys in height.*

SELECTION

Explain why a person might offer insincere praise to someone else.

Investigate, *Inquire,* and *Imagine*

Recall: GATHERING FACTS

1a. What is the Fox's decision at the start of the story?

2a. How does the Fox convince the Crow to open her mouth?

3a. Why does the Crow lose the cheese?

Interpret: FINDING MEANING

1b. What does the Fox's decision at the start of the story tell about his character?

2b. What is humorous about the Fox's flattery of the Crow?

3b. Why doesn't the Crow realize that she is going to lose the cheese?

Analyze: TAKING THINGS APART

4a. What character traits does the Crow have that make her accept the Fox's flattery so readily?

Synthesize: BRINGING THINGS TOGETHER

4b. How would you state the moral, or lesson, of the fable?

Evaluate: MAKING JUDGMENTS

5a. How do you think the Crow feels about the Fox's flattery? How might she feel after realizing she has been tricked? Do you think the Crow deserved to be tricked in this way? Do you feel sympathy for her?

Extend: CONNECTING IDEAS

5b. With respect to characterization, literary technique, and aim, how is this story similar to the African folk tale "Goha and the Pot"? Explain, using examples from the selection.

Understanding *Literature*

FABLE. Review the definition for **fable** in the Handbook of Literary Terms. What characteristics make this tale a fable? How is a fable similar to and different from folk tales and parables?

CHARACTER. Review the definitions for **character**, **one-dimensional character**, and **three-dimensional character** in the Handbook of Literary Tools. What kind of character is the Fox? the Crow? What traits does each exhibit?

Writer's Journal

1. The crow is always being tricked by the fox, so she (or he) writes a letter to an advice columnist, asking how to outfox the fox. Imagine you are an advice columnist. Write the crow's letter to you and your **advice column** letter giving the crow options for his predicament.

2. Many fables like those of Æsop are told to children to teach them moral lessons. Rewrite a traditional **fable** in comic-book form to make it appealing to children.

3. Find a traditional fable and retell it in a **summary** either by using modern characters or by adding a twist to it. You could, for example, rewrite the fable of the fox and the crow so that the crow keeps the cheese, outsmarting the fox and teaching him a lesson. Or, you could change the character of the fox into a crafty thief and the crow's character into a wary victim.

Integrating the Language Arts

Language, Grammar, and Style

FINDING THE SIMPLE SUBJECT. The **simple subject** is the *complete subject* without any of its modifiers. For additional help in finding the simple subject of a sentence refer to the Language Arts Survey 3.21, "How to Find the Simple Subject and Verb."

In the following sentences, underline the simple subject once and the verb twice. Be sure to find the verb before you begin to find the simple subject.

1. Many stories are told about the clever fox.
2. The clever fox flattered the crow.
3. The crow was carrying cheese in its beak.
4. The fox asked about the crow's voice.
5. The crow dropped the cheese.

Collaborative Learning

FABLE CONTEST. Find a book of fables. Choose one that appeals to you and make a copy of it. Write out the moral of the fable on a separate sheet of paper, deciding what you think it is meant to teach. You and your classmates should put the copies of the fables you found on a bulletin board, labeled with numbers, and put the morals scattered underneath, labeled with letters. Then have a contest in which the fables are to be matched to the morals.

Critical Thinking

COMPARING AND CONTRASTING FABLES. Locate a copy of James Thurber's retelling of "The Fox and the Crow" in the library. Note places where the speaker in Thurber's tale seems to be deliberately parodying (making fun of) or reworking elements of Æsop's tale. List both places in which the speaker establishes himself as part of the folklore tradition and in which the speaker attempts to differentiate himself from this tradition. What are the differences in the morals of the two versions of the fable?

"The Silver Pool"

from *The Tangle-Coated Horse and Other Tales: Episodes from the Fionn Saga*

by Ella Young

Reader's resource

Fionn MacCumhail, or "Finn McCool" as English speakers call him, is one of the greatest legendary heroes of Ireland. In the minds of many Irish, Fionn is "giant-big" and capable of nearly impossible feats. According to legend, Fionn followed in his father's footsteps to become chief of the King of Ireland's army, a band of warriors called the **Fianna**. Like all Fianna, Fionn could jump as high as his head height and duck as low as his knee height, pull thorns from his feet while running, and escape through woods without breaking a branch. Some say that Fionn is still alive today, asleep in a cave, and will awaken someday when the people of Ireland call for his aid. Others say that Fionn grew old and buried himself beside the Liffy River in Northern Ireland—and that his giant head lies under a hill looming on the riverbank.

HISTORY CONNECTION. Irish legends were passed on orally from ancient times and were recorded by Christian monks in the twelfth century. Today these legends serve as semihistorical records of ancient Ireland. The stories of Fionn MacCumhail, collectively known as the Fionn Saga, reflect a period prior to the eighth century when Ireland was organized into clans, all of which paid homage to the high king of Ireland at Tara. Despite the constant warring among the clans, literature and art flourished. Each clan chief or king kept an official poet, or Druid, who preserved the oral traditions of the people. In "The Silver Pool," Fionn seeks out the Druid Finnegas to learn the ancient poetry and tales of his land.

About the AUTHOR

Ella Young (1867–1956) was born in the small village of Feenagh in County Antrim, Ireland. "From childhood I heard tales of ghosts, banshees, haunted castles, mischievous and friendly sprites, snatches of ballads, and political arguments," she explained. After she grew older and moved to Dublin, Ella met some Irish literature scholars. Then, she said, "I read every translation I could get, learned Irish, and betook myself to Gaelic Ireland where, by turf fires, I could hear the poems of the Fianna recited by folk who had heard the faery music and danced in faery circles." In her story collection *The Tangle-Coated Horse*, Ella retold many of these old tales of Fionn and the Fianna.

Literary TOOLS

LEGEND. A **legend** is a story coming down from the past, often based on real events or characters from older times. Unlike myths, legends are popularly regarded as historical; however, they may contain elements that are fantastic or unverifiable. What elements make "The Silver Pool" a legend?

IRONY AND IRONY OF SITUATION. Irony is a difference between appearance and reality. **Irony of situation** is when an event occurs that violates the expectations of the characters, the reader, or the audience. As you read, look for examples of irony or irony of situation in this story.

Organizer

Make a chart like the one below. As you read, record instances of irony, situations in which appearance, or expectations, differ from reality or what really happens. One example has been done for you.

APPEARANCE (what is expected)	REALITY (what really happens)
Fionn appears to be a common churl.	He is the son of a great chief of the Fianna.

Reader's Journal

Do you believe in destiny—in the idea that the future is already determined for you—or do you think that people create their own future? Explain.

Still Life of a Salmon on a Riverbank in a Mountainous Landscape, c.1700s. John Russell. Bonhams, London.

The Silver Pool

Ella Young

Fionn walked sturdily forward. Birds were singing in leafy branches. The river Boyne showed a gleam of silver between tree-trunks; it made a soft plashing sound among its reeds. Fionn whistled a little tune as he walked. He had no plan in his mind, save to meet what happened: and day by day to grow tall and strong so that some day he might wrest the Treasure-Wallet from Lia of Luachra; avenge his father's wrong; and win to the headship of the Fianna. Many moons had withered in the sky since he had said farewell to Bovemall and Liath[1] and the kindly oak forest. Many a <u>buffet</u> fate had dealt him since then: many a sharp and evil chance he had known; many a good happening. He had set eyes on many a hill, many a valley since then: he had seen many a proud chieftain's lime-washed dune.[2] Sun had tanned him. His bright hair was cropped like the hair of a <u>churl</u>, chariot-dust of the roadway had grimed his deerskin tunic: save for the pride

What are Fionn's plans?

---

1. **Bovemall and Liath.** Two old women who raised Fionn in the forest
2. **Dune.** Hill or ridge of sand piled up by the wind

---

words for everyday use

buf • fet (buʹ fət) *n.,* blow, esp. by the hand. *Ann swung her hand and accidentally delivered a sharp <u>buffet</u> to her friend's face.*

churl (chʉrl) *n.,* rude, vulgar, or unsophisticated person. *The man who cut ahead in line is obviously a <u>churl</u>.*

of his walk there was little to betray the chief's son in him.

The morning was hot, and the plashy sound of the Boyne drew Fionn to the river side. Picking his way between alder and willow and flowering rush he came to where the water swirled in silvery singing reaches in the pool that is called the Pool of the Star-Dance. By the pool was a man in the garb of the fisher-folk drawing to land a small casting-net. There were silver-gleaming trout spotted with crimson in the net, but the man took them one by one and threw them into the pool again.

"Greeting to you," said Fionn, as he drew near, "and luck on your fishing."

"I have no luck on my fishing," said the man.

"It is a strange thing, indeed," said Fionn, "that you make naught of the red-spotted trout of the Boyne. There's few but yourself would grumble at so good a catch."

"One fish alone I am eager to snare," said the man, "and that is the purple-finned crimson-banded Salmon of Knowledge that has gold of the sun and silver of the moon in every scale of him."

What is the fisherman trying to catch?

"A wise woman taught me," said Fionn, "that the Salmon of Knowledge swims in the Heaven-World in the pool of the Sacred Hazels."

"She might have taught you, to boot," said the man, "that whatever happens in the Heaven-World makes a shadow of itself here. It is in this pool, they say, that the shadow-self of the Salmon of Knowledge swims. I would snare it."

"I have heard that men of learning and poets can snare the Salmon in a net made of their dreams," said Fionn, "and have thereafter one shining scale of him. You that are the Flower of Poets and the Jewel of Learning should have more than one scale."

"Why do you use this manner of speech to me, that am naught but a plain fisherman?"

"I know you for the King's Poet," said Fionn. "In the year of the Great Assembly I saw you riding on a white stallion with the mane and tail dyed purple; you were wearing the singing robe and the head-dress of a royal poet, and you had fifty princes in your train. I was crouching in the thickness of an oak-bough when you rode past the Wood of the Golden Hawks, and I thought that if I had choice of speech with any one man that went by me there in a flashing chariot, or on a proud-stepping horse, I would choose to have speech with you."

Who is the fisherman?

"What help is there in words?" said the man. "You could not teach me how to snare the Salmon: I could not teach you more wood-craft than you know already."

"You could teach me poetry," said Fionn; "and I could serve you: cut rushes for your bed; bring you eggs of the wild duck; and deer from the mountain, with swift hares of the valley."

"What learning and what arts and what weapon-knowledge have you come by?" asked the man.

"Sword-craft I had from a robber that forced me to consort with him. I herded cows for a herb-leech and learned the virtues of herbs. The ways of horses I learned among horse-boys. The forest taught me wood-craft; but he who is ignorant of poetry is but a churl!"

What does Fionn say about poetry?

"You shall serve me," said the man, "what name have you? I am, as is known to you, Finnegas the Poet."

"Demna is my name," said Fionn, and in this he spake truth, for the name Fionn, which means Beautiful One, was a nickname.

---

words for everyday use

garb (gärb) *n.*, style of clothing. *Santa Claus is typically represented as wearing red garb.*

naught (nôt) *n.*, nothing. *All of the dance committee's efforts came to naught when a huge snowstorm forced the cancellation of the Snowball Dance.*

con • sort (kən sôrt') *vi.*, unite, associate. *Jaime decided never to consort with the gang members in his neighborhood.*

So it came to pass that Fionn abode with the King's Poet. He plaited mats of rushes, he snared wild fowl, he culled water-cress and sweet and bitter herbs of the field such as go with savory meats, he pounded acorns and made bread as he had seen Bovemall do in the forest. And the King's Poet talked with him of heroes and kings and of the art of verse and the ceremonial of palaces. Fionn stored these conversations in his mind: and always he practised with his sling at casting stones, and with a sword of wood at thrusting and parrying, and with a pole cut from an ash tree he practised the hurling of spears. He ran, and jumped, and wrestled with tough boughs and saplings, so that he might grow in strength and hardihood. He put words together in praise of forest things and in praise of the small blossoms of the field

What does Fionn learn from Finnegas?

and the songs of the blackbird and thrush: the King's Poet taught him how to shape them till he could make good well-hammered verse.

On a day of the days it chanced that Fionn had been praised for a poem, and in lightness of heart he set off to search for eggs of the plover[3] that are delicate to the taste, for he had in mind to make festival for the King's Poet: that had naught himself in mind but the swirling of the Boyne and the Salmon that might lurk in the shallows, or in deep melodious reaches of the waters.

Fionn got the eggs and turned homeward. As he went, his foot struck on something hard, and stooping he saw a piece of strangely shaped greenish metal that had thrust from the marsh-soil. There was something familiar in the curve of it, and his hands dug eagerly into the grass-roots; more and more eagerly as the treasure unbared itself. At last he

What treasure does Fionn find?

drew it forth—a bronze sword, double-edged and perfect! A sword that Gobniu the Smith might have fashioned: a sword that Lugh might have reddened in the battle of Moytirra. Fionn rubbed it with a bunch of grass till it shone greenly, he fingered the finely tapered edges, he gripped the hilt: and all the while the tears ran down his face.

"My Treasure," he cried, "If Uail could see you; or Bovemall that had no sword to give me! If Crimmall[4] knew I had you, his heart would be glad. I will show you to the sunlight. I will take you where you can hear loud battle-shouts— loud as those you heard before the man that had you flung you from him lest his slayers should boast of you! Flame of Battle be glad of me—be glad of me!"

"I have snared him! I have snared him," the King's Poet was shouting, "I have snared the Salmon of Knowledge!"

Fionn leaped to his feet, flung the sword into the air, caught it midway and whirled it about his head. Then he gathered up his plover eggs and set off at a run.

As he neared the pool where the King's Poet fished, day in and day out, he saw that something must have happened. The King's Poet was coming hastily to him gesticulating and shouting. Fionn hurried a little more and caught the words.

"I have snared him! I have snared him," the King's Poet was shouting, "I have snared the Salmon of Knowledge!"

---

3. **plover.** Shore-inhabiting bird similar to the sandpiper
4. **Crimmall.** Fionn's uncle, the brother of his father Uail

---

words for everyday use

plait (plāt) vt., braid or weave. *Sherie plaited her hair into two long braids.*
cull (kul) vt., select from a group; choose. *The selective coach culled the best players for the starting lineup.*
par • ry (par′ ē) vt., ward off a weapon or a blow. *The boxer parried the powerful jabs of his opponent.*

And sure enough a small salmon, all silver-scaled and blue and <u>carmine</u> spotted, lay glinting on the bank.

"By what token do you know it for the Salmon of Knowledge?" asked Fionn.

"Never have I snared the like of it," said the King's Poet, "and there is a <u>prophecy</u> that the Salmon of Knowledge will be snared in this pool, and eaten by a poet named Finnegas or Fionn. Now I am Finnegas and I will eat this Salmon."

What is prophesied about the Salmon of Knowledge?

"Indeed you shall eat it with heartiness and enjoyment," said Fionn, "and I will broil it for you as Bovemall taught me to broil the salmon of the Shannon[5] that are kings' food. I have plover eggs too, and sharptasting herbs: sweet and bitter."

"I will touch naught but the Salmon, that I may have wisdom through it," said Finnegas.

Fionn made ready an oven and broiled the Salmon: but sitting by it, his mind wandered to the sword, and a flame licked the salmon-scales. Fionn turned the fish hastily and as he did so, a little bit of scale stuck to his thumb and burned him. He thrust his thumb into his mouth without thinking and so tasted the Salmon. He watched his work carefully after that, and when the fish was cooked through and through he brought it to Finnegas. Finnegas prepared to eat it as one should eat a sacred fish.

Fionn sat by the river bank and his thoughts were on his sword. Suddenly he was aware that the King's Poet stood beside him.

"A strange thing has happened, Demna," said the Poet, "the savor and virtue of the Salmon have gone. It is as any other fish. Can it be that you have tricked me and have eaten of it?"

What happens when Fionn accidentally tastes the Salmon?

"Nay," said Fionn, "I have not tasted of it, save for a scale that clung, burning, to my thumb."

"That scale has taken the <u>virtue</u> of the fish," said the Poet, "and yet it is strange that a prophecy could be so easily broken. The Salmon was for a poet called Fionn, or Finnegas—and you are Demna!"

"Demna is my name, but I am called Fionn: it is a nickname that stuck to me."

What is Fionn's given name? What is his "true" name?

"Fionn, henceforth, will be your true name: for now I see that the Salmon was meant for you. It is not to one who is weary of mart and court and battleground that the Salmon of Knowledge will give himself, but to one who is eager for the sword-hilt and <u>amorous</u> of life."

"I have a sword," cried Fionn, "a sword for a king it is! a luck-bringer, a battle-queller, a singer of war-songs!"

He held up the sword, his eyes caressing it. Finnegas took it in his hands.

"May luck be with it," he said, "it is indeed a royal sword. How came you by it?"

Fionn told the story of its finding.

"Some Lord of the Shining Folk[6] has blessed this day for you," said Finnegas. "Salmon and Sword! What have you in mind to do with your fortune?"

"I have in mind to avenge my father that was treacherously slain."

"What man was your father?" asked Finnegas, "I know well you are no churl's son."

"I would name my father," said Fionn, "only to one that had loved him, or to the High King of Ireland on that day when I win

What happened to Fionn's father? What does Fionn say about him?

---

5. **Shannon.** The Shannon River, which flows in western Ireland
6. **Shining Folk.** Gods

words for everyday use

car • mine (kär′ mīn) adj., vivid red. *The stagehand opened the <u>carmine</u> velvet curtains.*
pro • phe • cy (prä′ fə sē) n., prediction of something to come. *Many people believed the <u>prophecy</u> that the world would come to an end at the close of the century.*
vir • tue (vʉr′ chü) n., beneficial quality or power of a thing. *Herbalists say that one <u>virtue</u> of Echinacea root is its ability to prevent the common cold.*
am • o • rous (a′ mə rəs) adj., being in love, enamored (usually used with of). *Romeo was famously <u>amorous</u> of Juliet.*

back my heritage. I am no churl's son, Finnegas, and if I live I will set poetry as a craft for warriors. I will come, too—if I win out—to seek you in whatever place you may be!"

"I know not in what place I may be," said Finnegas, "mayhap[7] at Tara with the High King; mayhap in some mountain wilderness; mayhap in this hut by the river, if I be not under the sod—but tell me what way of life do you plan for yourself: for I know you will not <u>tarry</u> with me longer."

"I purpose to join with myself other lads, as I find them," said Fionn, "and

What will Fionn do next?

practise feats and <u>stratagems</u> till we can make ourselves felt in some <u>foray</u> and come by weapons: then we will seek a warrior that is kin to me—outlawed now and in hiding—and do as his wisdom counsels."

"I dare predict that you will win your heritage," said the King's Poet. "Eat now the Salmon, and we will spend the hours that remain to us in the telling of tales and the recital of poems and in sound sleep: that tomorrow may be fortunate for your setting forth."

So Fionn ate the Salmon, and wondered if its wisdom would help him to find lads like himself, eager to venture; comrades of the Sword

and the Treasure-Wallet. And the King's Poet ate the plover eggs with the sweet and bitter herbs; and wondered whether it would be wise to go back again to the bright-colored loud-sounding life of palaces; or wiser to stay in the little hut by the Boyne, watching cloud-shadows: and herons brooding on reedy pools. ∎

What does Fionn wonder? What does Finnegas wonder?

---

7. **mayhap.** Perhaps

Finn McCool, 1928. Vera Bock.

words for everyday use

tar • ry (tar′ē) *vi.*, delay or be tardy; stay in or at a place. *Red Riding Hood <u>tarried</u> in the woods picking flowers.*
stra • ta • gem (strā′tə jem) *n.*, trick or scheme used to gain an end. *The bank robber's <u>stratagem</u> for gaining access to the vault was a very clever scheme, but it failed.*
for • ay (fôr′ā) *n.*, sudden invasion or attack: raid. *Smelling the cookies cooling on the counter, I made a sneaky <u>foray</u> into the kitchen.*

Respond *to the* SELECTION

How would you feel at the end of the story if you were Finnegas?

Investigate, *Inquire,* and Imagine

Recall: GATHERING FACTS

1a. In the beginning, what are Fionn's goals? Whom is he seeking?

2a. Who is the fisherman Fionn encounters at the Pool of the Star-Dance? What fish is he trying to catch, and what has been prophesied about this fish?

3a. What does Fionn find buried? What happens to the fish?

Interpret: FINDING MEANING

1b. Why does Fionn seek this person? How will this person help him reach his goals?

2b. What is special about the fish? Why does the fisherman feel confident that he will eventually catch it?

3b. What do these events mean for Fionn?

Analyze: TAKING THINGS APART

4a. What clues can you find in this story that Fionn is the person meant by the prophecy? How does Finnegas know that the prophecy was fulfilled correctly?

Synthesize: BRINGING THINGS TOGETHER

4b. What role does destiny play in this story?

Evaluate: MAKING JUDGMENTS

5a. The legendary Fianna of Ireland were noble and skilled warriors. To join the Fianna, one had to pass strict tests and abide by codes of honor. Yet the Fianna also had to be cultured, and more specifically they had to be poets. Why do you think the Celts valued poetry enough to make it a requirement for their warriors? Fionn says that "men of learning and poets can snare the Salmon in a net made of their dreams." Why do you think only educated people and poets are able to snare the Salmon? What does this tell you about Celtic belief?

Extend: CONNECTING IDEAS

5b. What role does Fionn think poetry should play in a person's life, especially a warrior's life? What does he think about people who are ignorant of poetry? Do you think that poetry, or art in general, is as crucial to a person's life as is more practical or technical knowledge? Why, or why not? Do you think being cultured and well mannered makes someone a better person? Explain.

Understanding *Literature*

LEGEND. Review the definition for **legend** in the Handbook of Literary Terms. Why is "The Silver Pool" considered a legend rather than a fairy tale or myth? Which elements of the story are based on fact? Which are fantastic?

IRONY AND IRONY OF SITUATION. Review the definition of **irony** in the Handbook of Literary Terms. What example or examples of **irony of situation** did you find in "The Silver Pool"? Were your expectations violated by the irony of situation in the story? Why, or why not?

Writer's Journal

1. Write a **prophecy** about what will happen next to Fionn.

2. Imagine you are Finnegas at the end of the story. Write a brief **poem** about how you feel now and what you will do next with your life. The poem does not have to rhyme.

3. A field guide is a book used by naturalists and botanists to identify animals and plants found in nature. It includes descriptions and often drawings or photographs of different species. Write a **field guide entry** for the Salmon of Knowledge. How would you describe the magical fish so that visitors to the area would be able to recognize it? If you'd like, you may also draw the fish.

Integrating
the Language Arts

Language, Grammar, and Style

USING THE PARTS OF SPEECH IN WRITING. Many words in English can be used as more than one part of speech. Identify the part of speech of each italicized word below. Then, write a new sentence using each word as the part of speech given in parentheses. Read the Language Arts Survey 3.49, "Namers—Nouns and Pronouns," 3.59, "Expressers—Verbs," 3.65, "Modifiers—Adjectives and Adverbs," and 3.69, "Prepositions," for more information.

EXAMPLE: The *drama* class will perform some well-known folk tales. (Use as a noun.)
ANSWER: Adjective. Used as a *noun:* The audience found the *drama* very entertaining.

1. The operator isn't able to make the telephone call go *through*. (Use as a preposition.)
2. "*Well*, I guess I'll sing the folk song," Tony volunteered reluctantly. (Use as an adverb.)
3. Benjamin Franklin originated the aphorism "*Time* is money." (Use as a verb.)
4. As Fionn walked homeward, his foot struck something *hard* that was buried in the soil. (Use as an adverb.)
5. Admission to the *storytelling* festival is free. (Use as a noun.)

Media Literacy

CREATING A NEWS SEGMENT. Imagine that you are a television reporter in Fionn MacCumhail's day. The news has reached you that the Salmon of Knowledge has been caught, and you would like to do a feature story on Fionn MacCumhail. Form groups of four students. One of you should play the anchorperson; another, the on-site reporter; another, Fionn; and another, Finnegas. The anchorperson should introduce the breaking story, telling some background information, while the on-site reporter should get brief comments from Fionn and Finnegas, as well as tell viewers about the site and circumstances in which the Salmon was found. If possible, film the story with a videocamera. If you have access to film editing equipment, edit the story so that the sound bites and clips are smooth.

Critical Thinking

COMPARING LEGENDS AND FAIRY TALES. The legend "The Silver Pool" and the fairy tale "The White Snake" have certain motifs and elements in common. With a partner, read the entries for *motif, fairy tale,* and *legend* in the Handbook of Literary Terms. What are the motifs in each story? Which motifs do the stories have in common? Why do you think one is considered a legend, while the other is considered a fairy tale? Could the labels be interchanged? Why, or why not?

"John Henry"

from *Mules and Men*
retold by Zora Neale Hurston

Reader's resource

"**John Henry**," an African-American folk song, tells the story of a steel driver, a railroad worker whose job it was to drill holes in rock for explosives used to blast railroad tunnels. Steel drivers had a grueling job. They would pound a steel bit into solid rock with a sledge hammer. According to the legend, John Henry was working on the Big Bend Tunnel in West Virginia when he bet his foreman he could drive steel faster than a new steam drill. The effort killed mighty John Henry, but he is remembered as a symbol of the unconquerable spirit of the American worker. This selection, recorded by Zora Neale Hurston, is just one of 100 or more versions of the famous folk song, which originated in the oral tradition and has no single known author.

HISTORY CONNECTION. John Stephens of Hoboken, New Jersey, built the first steam locomotive in 1825. Over the next fifty years, railroads were built stretching from the east coast to the west, bringing thousands of settlers to the western United States. According to some sources, John Henry was hired by the C&O Railroad, a company that was extending its line from Virginia to Ohio, sometime the 1870s. Working alongside many other blacks who had just been freed from slavery by the Civil War, John Henry put his sweat and blood into building America's railroads.

About the AUTHOR

Zora Neale Hurston (1891–1960) was an African-American writer and novelist. Her best-known novel, *Their Eyes Were Watching God* (1937), tells the story of an African-American woman's journey of self-discovery. Hurston was born in Eatonville, Florida, a town founded by African Americans. She graduated in 1928 from Barnard College, where she studied anthropology. Ever fascinated with folklore, Hurston collected African-American folk tales, folk remedies, curses, and spells in *Mules and Men* (1935), the book from which this selection is taken.

Literary TOOLS

FOLK SONG. A **folk song** is a traditional or composed song typically made up of stanzas, a refrain, and a simple melody. A form of folk literature, folk songs are expressions of commonly shared ideas or feelings and may be narrative or lyric in style. Traditional folk songs are anonymous songs that have been transmitted orally. As you read "John Henry," look for characteristics that make it a folk song.

DIALECT. A **dialect** is a version of a language spoken by the people of a particular place, time, or social group. Some of the language of "John Henry" is from a dialect spoken in the past in the rural South.

Organizer

As you read, make a chart. On the left, list examples of dialect in the song. On the right, list their equivalents in standard English. One example has been done for you.

Dialect	Standard English
'fore	before

Reader's Journal

In what kinds of contests have you participated? Which have been the most difficult?

John Henry

from *Mules and Men*
retold by Zora Neale Hurston

John Henry driving[1] on the right hand side,
Steam drill driving on the left,
Says, 'fore I'll let your steam drill beat me down
I'll hammer my fool self to death,
5   Hammer my fool self to death.

John Henry told his Captain,
When you go to town
Please bring me back a nine pound hammer
And I'll drive your steel on down,
10   And I'll drive your steel on down.

John Henry told his Captain,
Man ain't nothing but a man,
And 'fore I'll let that steam drill beat me down
I'll die with this hammer in my hand,
15   Die with this hammer in my hand.

Captain ast John Henry,
What is that storm I hear?
He says Cap'n that ain't no storm,
'Tain't nothing but my hammer in the air,
20   Nothing but my hammer in the air.

John Henry told his Captain,
Bury me under the sills of the floor,
So when they get to playing good old Georgy skin,[2]
Bet 'em fifty to a dollar more,
25   Fifty to a dollar more.

John Henry had a little woman,
The dress she wore was red,
Says I'm going down the track,
And she never looked back.
30   I'm going where John Henry fell dead,
Going where John Henry fell dead.

What does John Henry decide about the steam drill?

What did John Henry ask his captain to bring? What will John Henry do?

Who is the woman in the folk song?

---

1. **driving.** Using a hammer to drive metal stakes into railroad ties
2. **Georgy skin.** Gambling game played by railroad workers

Who's going to shoe your pretty lil feet?
And who's going to glove your hand?
Who's going to kiss your dimpled cheek?
35   And who's going to be your man?
Who's going to be your man?

My father's going to shoe my pretty lil feet;
My brother's going to glove my hand;
My sister's going to kiss my dimpled cheek;
40   John Henry's going to be my man,
John Henry's going to be my man.

Where did you get your pretty lil dress?
The shoes you wear so fine?
I got my shoes from a railroad man,
45   My dress from a man in the mine,
My dress from a man in the mine.   ∎

His Hammer in His Hand, from the *John Henry Series,* 1944–1947. Palmer Hayden.
Museum of African American Art, Los Angeles.

art n o t e

Palmer Hayden (1890–1973) had heard the ballad of John Henry many times as a child and became interested in painting it when he discovered that it was based on a true story. Hayden wanted to depict the heroic John Henry as a real person. He traveled to the Big Bend Tunnel in West Virginia to get accurate scenery and illustrated twelve lines from the song as real events.

Hayden worked at hard, physical jobs throughout his life to support himself as an artist. What do you think he might be saying with his portrait of John Henry?

December 8, 1998

'White House' mystery may be solved

■ **Site mentioned in 'John Henry' song a prison morgue?**

LINDA WHEELER WASHINGTON POST

A century-old riddle in the ballad of John Henry, the legendary black railroad man who was so strong he could work faster than a machine, may have been solved by a College of William and Mary history professor who stumbled upon a clue on the Internet.

A reference in the song to the "White House" had puzzled historians and folklorists for years because they thought it meant the presidential White House. An early version ends with this verse:

"They took John Henry to the White House,
And buried him in the san',
And every locomotive come roarin' by,
Says there lays that steel drivin' man,
Says there lays that steel drivin' man."

Scott Nelson, an assistant professor of history at William and Mary, said he often hummed the ballad while researching Civil War-era railroad companies, which used forced labor. The steel-driving men, who drove rods into rock to create dynamite pockets, were an integral part of the process.

Nelson knew that prisoners from the Virginia state penitentiary had been used to blast tunnels through the Appalachian mountains, and he searched the Internet for a picture of the Richmond prison, which was built before the Civil War. In early November, he found a hand-colored postcard of the prison that showed a white machine shop or barracks nearby.

"The lyrics were going off in my head, and then, there in the middle of my screen, is a big white house," he said. "It all clicked together. It wasn't my plan to talk about John Henry as a convict, but it came together. It all made sense."

"Local knowledge among prisoners was not the White House in Washington, but the white house at the penitentiary," he said. "When they said someone was going to the white house, they meant someone was going to get buried."

In 1990, the state closed the penitentiary and sold the property. Three years later, construction workers digging a drainage field found skulls and bones at the rear of the property near what had been a railroad bed.

Katharine Beidleman, the archaeologist on the project, was amazed. Her research had not indicated any burial grounds on the penitentiary property. But excavation over a three-month period turned up the remains of about 300 men, women and children.

Records were found that listed women, as well as children as young as 10, as prisoners, she said. Among the bones were pieces of jewelry similar to those made by Civil War prisoners, who melted hard rubber buttons and combs to create rings and brooches.

The remains were sent to the Smithsonian Institution. Doug Owsley, head of the forensic anthropology division in the National Museum of Natural History, said that while staff shortages have delayed a final report, preliminary findings indicate that black and white men were buried in the unmarked graves, along with a few women, infants and children. Among them were "very robust individuals," Owsley said, but without a physical description or a picture, it's unlikely anyone will ever know if John Henry was in the mass grave.

Nelson, the professor, said he believes John Henry was one of the hundreds of black prisoners rented to the Chesapeake and Ohio Railroad in 1871 to build the Big Bend Tunnel at Talcott, in southern West Virginia. Talcott has long claimed the title of the birthplace of the John Henry legend, and atop Big Bend Mountain is a hulking statue of the steel-driving man, a hammer in his hand.

There are many versions of the ballad. Nelson used what is believed to be the earliest published version, which says John Henry died when he accidentally struck himself with his hammer after he had bested a steam drill in a contest to see whether man or machine was faster.

If so, Nelson said, John Henry was among the 10 percent who were horribly injured or killed on the Big Bend job that year. The dead were sent, along with the injured, back to prison for burial. Newspapers at the time reported a scandal: burying prisoners at the jail instead of in a "decent" burial ground. The city council moved to end the practice, forcing penal authorities to buy land for a cemetery outside the city in 1877.

Nelson presented his findings Nov. 21 to the Social Science History Association at a Chicago meeting.

West Virginia historian Ed Cabbell has spent years studying John Henry, whom he calls "a great black American hero." He is convinced John Henry was a former slave, probably from Richmond, who worked on the Big Bend Tunnel and who did win a contest with the steam drill that made him famous among railroad workers. And while he doesn't agree that John Henry was a prisoner, Cabbell said, he hasn't discounted the theory.

"With the lack of records on blacks in general, and particularly during that time period, anything you can get, even with the slightest possible development of a truth, is worth listening to and checking out," he said. "When dealing with African-Americans, our history is oral, and you have to track down every possible source and give it serious consideration."

'John Henry' lyrics

Historians have searched the lyrics of the ballad "John Henry" for clues about the black "steel drivin' " railroad man. Following are selected stanzas of the song from the book *John Henry: Tracking Down a Negro Legend* by Guy B. Johnson (1929, University of North Carolina Press):

> Some say he's from Georgia,
> Some say he's from Alabama,
> But it's wrote on the rock at the
> Big Ben Tunnel,
> That he's an East Virginia man,
> That he's an East Virginia man.
>   John Henry was a steel drivin' man,
> He died with a hammah in his han'
> Oh, come along boys and line the track,
> For John Henry ain't never comin' back
> For John Henry ain't ever comin' back.
>   John Henry, he could hammah.
> He could whistle, he could sing,
> He went to the mountain early in the mornin'
> To hear the hammah ring,
> To hear the hammah ring.
>   John Henry went to the section boss,
> Says the section boss what kin you do?
> Says I can line a track, I kin histe a jack,
> I kin pick and shovel too,
> I kin pick and shovel too.
>   John Henry told the cap'n,
> When you go to town
> Buy me a nine pound hammah
> An' I'll drive the steel drill down,
> An' I'll drive the steel drill down.

> Cap'n said to John Henry,
> You've got a willin' mind.
> But you just well lay yoh hammah down
> You'll nevah beat this drill of mine,
> You'll nevah beat this drill of mine.
>   John Henry went to the tunnel
> And they put him in lead to drive,
> The rock was so tall and John Henry so small
> That he laid down his hammah and he cried,
> That he laid down his hammah and he cried.
>   The steam drill was on the right han' side,
> John Henry was on the left,
> Says before I let this steam drill bear me down,
> I'll hammah myself to death.
> I'll hammah myself to death.
>   Then John Henry he did hammah,
> He did make his hammah soun',
> Says now one more lick fore quittin' time,
> An' I'll beat this steam drill down,
> An' I'll beat this steam drill down.
>   The hammah that John Henry swung,
> It weighed over nine poun',
> He broke a rib in his left han' side,
> And his intrels fell on the groun',
> And his intrels fell on the groun'.
>   All the women in the West
> That heard of John Henry's death,
> Stood in the rain, flagged the east bound train,
> Goin' where John Henry dropped dead,
> Goin' where John Henry dropped dead.
>   They took John Henry to the White House,
> And buried him in the san',
> And every locomotive come roarin' by,
> Says there lays that steel drivin' man,
> Says there lays that steel drivin' man. ■

ABOUT THE RELATED READING

This Related Reading offers some clues historians have uncovered about the identity of legendary railroad man John Henry. The two articles in the Related Reading were first published in *The Washington Post* on December 8, 1998.

What can machines do better than you, and what can you do better than machines?

Investigate, *Inquire*, and *Imagine*

Recall: GATHERING FACTS

1a. What does John Henry decide in verse 1 of the song?

2a. What is John Henry doing in verse 4?

3a. What does John Henry's woman decide in verse 6 of the song?

Interpret: FINDING MEANING

1b. What tone and mood are set in verse 1? What elements of the verse help to establish this tone and mood?

2b. What example of exaggeration is there in verse 4?

3b. What do verses 7–9 tell about the role of women in the society in which "John Henry" was written?

Analyze: TAKING THINGS APART

4a. Identify John Henry's characteristics, as revealed in his dialogue with the Captain.

Synthesize: BRINGING THINGS TOGETHER

4b. What makes John Henry a hero?

Evaluate: MAKING JUDGMENTS

5a. Why do you think John Henry put himself against the power and speed of the steam drill? What did it mean to him? What did he value more than technological innovation?

Extend: CONNECTING IDEAS

5b. Make a list of modern situations in which people oppose technology. Can people who are against "progress" win? Why, or why not?

Understanding *Literature*

FOLK SONG. Review the definition for **folk song** in the Handbook of Literary Terms. What elements make "John Henry" a folk song? Could John Henry also be considered a legend, similar to Fionn MacCumhail in "The Silver Pool"? Explain.

DIALECT. Review the definition for **dialect** in the Handbook of Literary Terms and the chart you made for Literary Tools. Some of the language of "John Henry" is from a dialect spoken in the past in the rural South. How does keeping this dialect in modern versions of the song add to the song's effect?

Writer's Journal

1. Imagine a time in the future when all work is done by machines. Write a **diary entry** that might be written by a person living in such a time. Start by making a chart in which you write in the left-hand column what work a person might actually do in a typical day in our time, and in the right-hand column how various tasks might change if machines did them.

2. An **elegy** is a song or a poem written for someone who is dead. In your journal, compose a short elegy for John Henry. Your elegy should praise John Henry and say how he will be remembered by those he left behind.

3. Write **song lyrics** for a story in this unit or another story that you know.

Integrating the Language Arts

Language, Grammar, and Style

VARIETIES OF ENGLISH. As you have learned, the song "John Henry" was written using the dialect appropriate to its setting. How would the song be different if this dialect were not included? Read the Language Arts Survey 3.5, "Dialects of English." Then, rewrite the song in standard English. Your opinion? Which version of the song is better? Explain.

Collaborative Learning

COMPARING TWO VERSIONS OF "JOHN HENRY." Read the Related Reading, "'John Henry' Lyrics." Then, in groups of three or four, examine the similarities and differences between the two versions of John Henry's story. What elements are most important to the legend? What information is given in the related reading that was not revealed in Hurston's version of the story? Is there any information in the Related Reading that contradicts Hurston's version of the song?

Study and Research

RESEARCHING AMERICAN RAILROADS. The building of railroads changed the face of America by allowing goods to be transported more quickly throughout the land. Many towns were built up near railroad tracks, and a transcontinental railroad allowed Americans to travel from the East Coast all the way to California. Using library resources, research the development of railroads of the United States. When were the main railroads built? Who engineered and built them? Why are they no longer as prominent as they once were in this country? When you have finished your research, prepare a report to be handed in to your teacher.

Literary
T O O L S

REPETITION. Repetition is the writer's conscious reuse of a sound, word, phrase, sentence, or other element. Spirituals often contain repeated lines or phrases. Note how repetition is used in the two selections.

ALLUSION. An **allusion** is a figure of speech in which reference is made to a person, event, object, or work from history or literature.

Organizer

Read the following passages from the Bible: Matthew 24:29–31 and 25:30–46 and Exodus 9–11. Then make a chart for the two songs. On the left, note the biblical allusions that can be found in the songs. On the right, explain the biblical allusions. One example has been done for you.

Allusions	Explanations
the trumpet sounds within my soul	the trumpet announces Judgment Day

Reader's
Journal

Write about songs you know that have a particularly powerful effect on you because they express your strongest feelings.

"Steal Away"
"Go Down, Moses"

Anonymous

Reader's
resource

"Steal Away" and **"Go Down, Moses"** are examples of a kind of music called the **spiritual**, part of the African-American folk tradition. As the name suggests, spirituals deal with religious subjects. "Steal Away" tells of Judgment Day and stealing away from earthly life to an afterlife in heaven. "Go Down, Moses" tells a story from the Bible. According to the Book of Exodus in the Bible, Moses was the Hebrew prophet who led his people, the Israelites, out of captivity in Egypt, which was ruled by a king, or Pharaoh.

Most spirituals were composed by anonymous singers during the era of slavery in the United States, and many have a secondary meaning related to escape from slavery into a better life here on earth (or the afterlife). For example, both "Steal Away" and "Go Down, Moses" can be interpreted as expressions of the desire of an enslaved people to gain freedom. Thus the Israelites can be seen as African Americans under slavery, Egypt as a slave state, Pharaoh as a typical slave master or plantation owner, and Moses as a potential liberator.

MUSIC CONNECTION. Although spirituals had long been part of the African-American tradition, it was only in the 1870s that the country at large began to become aware of this rich tradition, when the Fisk Jubilee Singers from Fisk University in Nashville, Tennessee, began to tour the country, singing programs of these songs. Since that time, spirituals have had an important influence on the development of several American musical styles, including gospel, blues, jazz, country, and rock.

Steal Away

Anonymous

1

My Lord calls me, He calls me by the thunder;
The trumpet sounds within my soul, I don't have long to stay here.

Chorus

Steal away, steal away, steal away to Jesus.
Steal away, steal away home, I don't have long to stay here.

2

Green trees are bending, poor sinners, they stand trembling,
The trumpet sounds within my soul, I don't have long to stay here.

(Repeat Chorus)

3

My Lord he calls me, He calls me by the lightning,
The trumpet sounds within my soul, I don't have long to stay here.

(Repeat Chorus)

A Ride for Liberty [Detail],
c.1862. Eastman Johnson.

Verse

My Lord____ calls me, He calls me by the thun - der; the

trum-pet sounds with-in___ my soul, I don't have long to stay here.

Chorus

Steal a - way, steal a - way, steal a - way to Je - sus.

Steal a - way, steal a - way, home, I don't have long to stay here.

A Ride for Liberty, c.1862. Eastman Johnson. Brooklyn Museum of Art.

Why might an anonymous African American living under slavery have been motivated to create this song?

Investigate, *Inquire,* and Imagine

Recall: GATHERING FACTS

1a. Who is calling the speaker in this song?

2a. To what are green trees compared?

3a. What does the speaker say is sounding in his or her soul?

Interpret: FINDING MEANING

1b. What message is the speaker receiving? To what is the voice calling the speaker compared?

2b. What similarity might exist between green trees and sinners?

3b. What does the sound of the trumpet in this song represent? Read this passage from Matthew 24:31.

> And he shall send his angels with a great sound of a trumpet, and they shall gather together his elect from the four winds, from one end of heaven to the other.

Analyze: TAKING THINGS APART

4a. Why might this song be interpreted as an expression of slaves' desire for freedom? What elements of this song support that interpretation?

Synthesize: BRINGING THINGS TOGETHER

4b. How might singing songs like "Steal Away" make slaves' spirits strong during the difficult times of slavery?

art note

Eastman Johnson (1824–1906) witnessed the scene on the facing page during the Civil War: a family of slaves making a dash for freedom through the middle of a battlefield. Just as spirituals used biblical metaphors for slavery, some critics have seen a parallel between this painting and the story of the flight of Mary, Joseph, and Jesus into Egypt. What effect might this painting have had on people who saw it during the Civil War?

Underground Railroad, c.1945. William H. Johnson.
National Museum of American Art, Washington, DC.

Go Down, Moses

Anonymous

1
When Israel was in Egypt's land,
Let my people go!
Oppressed so hard they could not stand,
Let my people go!

Chorus
"Go down, Moses,
'Way down in Egypt's land,
Tell old Pharaoh
To let my people go!"

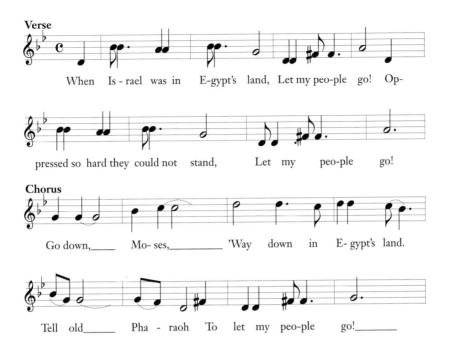

Verse

When Is - rael was in E-gypt's land, Let my peo-ple go! Op-

pressed so hard they could not stand, Let my peo-ple go!

Chorus

Go down,____ Mo- ses,_____ 'Way down in E- gypt's land.

Tell old____ Pha - raoh To let my peo-ple go!_____

2

"Thus spoke the Lord," bold Moses said,
"Let my people go!
If not, I'll smite[1] your firstborn dead,
Let my people go!"

(Repeat Chorus)

3

"No more shall they in bondage toil,
Let my people go!
Let them come out with Egypt's spoil,[2]
Let my people go!"

(Repeat Chorus) ■

---

1. **smite.** Kill
2. **spoil.** Riches

Which types of music do people seem to find most uplifting? In what way might this song have helped to raise the spirits of slaves?

Investigate, *Inquire,* and Imagine

Recall: GATHERING FACTS

1a. According to the song, who is "in Egypt's land"?

2a. In whose name does Moses speak in stanza 2?

Interpret: FINDING MEANING

1b. According to stanza 1, what was life like for the Israelites in Egypt?

2b. What message does Moses deliver to Pharaoh?

Analyze: TAKING THINGS APART

3a. What elements of this song communicate the resolve and power of Moses?

Synthesize: BRINGING THINGS TOGETHER

3b. Why might someone living in slavery have found the story of the delivery of the Israelites from slavery so appealing? Why might Moses have been a hero to such a person?

Evaluate: MAKING JUDGMENTS

4a. When slaves arrived from Africa, they were not Christian: they were converted by slave owners to Christianity. Why do you think the slave owners wanted their slaves to become Christian? What did Christianity contribute to the lives of the slaves? Cite evidence from "Go Down, Moses."

Extend: CONNECTING IDEAS

4b. Why do you think the slaves made Christianity, a religion imposed by their masters, into an expression of their own experience?

Understanding *Literature*

REPETITION. Review the definition of **repetition** in the Handbook of Literary Terms. Spirituals often contain repeated lines or phrases. How is repetition used in the two selections?

ALLUSION. Review the definition of **allusion** and the chart you made for Literary Tools. What allusions to materials from the Bible are made in "Steal Away" and "Go Down, Moses"?

Writer's Journal

1. Spirituals offered consolation and a source of hope to the African Americans who composed and sang them. What role does music play in your life? Write a **personal essay** about music and what it means to you.
2. Write **interview questions** to ask a slave about the spirituals he or she sings.
3. Write **lyrics** for a spiritual based on a biblical allusion. Allude to something from the Bible other than the Judgment Day or Moses.

Integrating the Language Arts

Language, Grammar, and Style

COMPOUND SIMPLE SUBJECTS AND COMPOUND VERBS. Sometimes a sentence has more than one simple subject, more than one verb, or both. Find the simple subject(s) and verb(s) of the following sentences using the steps found in the Language Arts Survey 3.21, "How to Find the Simple Subject and Verb." Underline the subject(s) once and the verb(s) twice.

1. Moses was a Hebrew prophet and led his people out of captivity.
2. "Steal Away" tells of Judgment Day and stealing away from earthly life.
3. Spirituals and folk songs have influenced gospel, blues, and jazz.
4. Pharaoh was a typical slave master and plantation owner.
5. Both spirituals express the desire of enslaved people to gain freedom.

Study and Research

RESEARCHING HARRIET TUBMAN AND MOSES. Harriet Tubman, who led many African Americans to freedom in the North during the mid-nineteenth century, is often called "the Moses of Her People." Research the life and work of Harriet Tubman. Then read Exodus chapters 2–16 in the Bible, which tells about the life of Moses and his deliverance of the Israelites from bondage in Egypt. Write a brief essay comparing the two leaders. How and why did they begin their work of leading people to freedom? What special qualities or opportunities did they have that made them successful, and what beliefs and ideas did they have regarding the work they did?

Collaborative Learning

AFRICAN-AMERICAN MUSIC FESTIVAL. African Americans have played central roles in creating and developing many of the most interesting and important American musical forms, including spirituals, gospel, blues, jazz, ragtime, bluegrass, rock, and rap. As a class, organize a festival to honor African-American contributions to American music. Divide into groups and assign each group a particular type of music to research. Prepare presentations on various artists, styles, and famous pieces, and find recordings to play. Give each group the responsibility of preparing a presentation on one type of music, including introductory speeches and selections from recorded music.

Language Arts *in Action*

National Storytelling Youth Olympics

The National Storytelling Youth Olympics is an event where thousands of kids from grades 6 to 12 compete against each other by telling stories. It is sponsored by the Master's Degree Program in Reading and Storytelling at East Tennessee State University. The sole purpose of this event is to promote and encourage both the arts and science of storytelling among middle school and high school students. Although this event is competitive, its underlying intent and goal is to provide students across the nation with a reason to practice numerous noncompetitive skills. Those skills include sportsmanship, responsible behavior, and an attitude of respect for others and the storytelling genre. The eventual goal of the National Storytelling Youth Olympics is to encourage every classroom in America to discover (or rediscover) the beauty of storytelling and story performance.

Joe Bowman and his teacher Diane Judy, displaying the trophy Joe won at the National Storytelling Youth Olympics in 1999.

The National Storytelling Youth Olympics takes place usually around the first weekend in March. Students from all over the country arrive by bus, plane, or automobile in Johnson City, Tennessee. They usually arrive on Thursday or Friday. Those that arrive on Thursday take advantage of their early arrival by telling stories at local schools. On Friday, an evening meal is prepared for all contestants, coaches, and parents. Games are played, stories are told, and lifetime friendships begin. Saturday is the day of the big event. A luncheon is held in the afternoon so contestants can familiarize themselves with the surroundings and do a sound check.

The event is divided into three categories separated by grades. Contestants are judged not only by their storytelling performance, but also by the attitude and behavior they display during the entire weekend. A winner is picked from each of the three categories; however, there is an overall winner who is granted the name of Grand Torch Bearer. This person is selected not only by the judges, but also by the contestants. After the winners have been announced, the contestants retreat back to their hotel where a celebratory ice cream party is held; and believe it or not, they tell more stories! This is what the National Storytelling Youth Olympics is all about: developing a love for the art of storytelling.

Joe Bowman did just that. He has been developing his love for storytelling since the sixth grade. His efforts and hard work were rewarded when he received the title Grand Torch Bearer in 1999 with the story titled, "The Pirate." This story was actually a song that he rewrote to tell as a story. It is the story of a young pirate who wants to become a Broadway singer. "The Pirate" reflects Joe's favorite type of story to tell—humorous. He also likes to tell folk tales and stories with lessons, especially lessons that teach character in people. As a tenth grader at Daniel Boone High School in Gray, Tennessee, he keeps busy by telling these types of stories at libraries, homes for the elderly, local coffee houses, elementary schools, churches, and competitions. Joe is also involved in the school choir and drill team. He will be competing in the National Storytelling Convention to be held in Kingsport, Tennessee, in the summer of 2000.

Joe Bowman storytelling at his local elementary school in Gray, Tennessee.

> "The written word is the only record we will have of this our present, or our past, to leave behind for future generations."
>
> —Langston Hughes

RECORDING AN ORAL HISTORY

1492: Columbus sails to New World. 1776: Colonists declare their independence from Great Britain. 1804: Sacajawea helps guide Lewis and Clark through Louisiana Territory. 1863: Lincoln signs Emancipation Proclamation. 1969: Armstrong walks on moon. Great stories—told and retold—have etched these events into the minds of many people.

Yet hundreds of other stories wait to be told. 1878: Great-Great-Grandpa Edwin migrates from Canada to Dakota Territory; 1902: Great-Grandma Sophia disembarks at Ellis Island; 1961: Tîo Carlos arrives in Miami from Havana. For each of these events, an important story for generations of families and their communities awaits uncovering. Why did Edwin leave Canada for the unknown Dakota prairie? What did Sophia carry in her trunk from the Old Country? How did Carlos find work in Miami? The stories that answer these questions reveal much about who we are, where we've been, what we've learned, and what we value.

WRITING ASSIGNMENT. Interview a person you know to uncover a true story and then record it. The story may be about an event, a memory, or an object that holds special meaning for that person. The person may be a grandparent, great-grandparent, or another acquaintance two or more generations older than you.

Professional Model

Excerpt from "Echo and Narcissus"
Retold by Walker Brents
page 7

Liriope the river nymph gave birth to a beautiful child . . . The child was named Narcissus. As he grew, his beauty increased. His dazzling looks had a strange effect upon the woodland spirits . . . around whom he spent his days. They all fell in love with him, but he was oblivious, interested only in hunting in the hills with his companions. His pride in his beauty grew so great that he had nothing but scorn for the feelings of others.

. . . Another nymph had fallen in love with him, but was also spurned. This one cried to the heavens for vengeance: "May Narcissus fall into a love that is not returned!" The goddess of righteous anger, Nemesis, heard these words. And so it happened that on a sunny and hot day Narcissus found himself at a pond. . . . Putting his face to the waters in order to quench his thirst, Narcissus caught sight for the first time of his own reflection. He was astonished by the beautiful face that met his eye.

"What star-like eyes are these; what smooth skin! That forehead, that jaw, that gorgeous flowing hair! Who are you? Draw near to me!" He reached his hands to the water, but the reflected image disintegrated. He waited for it to reappear. "Only the surface of these waters parts us. . . . Yet I cannot reach you! How can this be?". . . . But there was no answer.

Narcissus could not leave this place. Entranced by his own reflection, he began to waste away from hunger and thirst. . . . He died, and his spirit left his body. . . .

The nymphs heard of his death and went to the pond to retrieve his body for the funeral ceremony. But when they got there, they found no corpse, only a new blossom with snowy petals and a yellow corona. The flower came to be called "Narcissus."

EXAMINING THE MODEL. This ancient story of gods and goddesses with human flaws would have been carried about by traveling singers and poets before it was written down. What is it about this story that would make it worth repeating? Tell the beginning, middle, and end of the story. How is Narcissus described? What does it suggest to you when you read, "he was oblivious, interested only in hunting in the hills with his companions"? Find the lines where the author shows that Narcissus has a character flaw. What one word names the weakness? Look at the actual words of Narcissus. What do they show about his character? What sensory details has Brents used? Pay special attention to the conclusion. What impact does it have on you as the reader?

Prewriting

FINDING YOUR VOICE. Even though the narrative you write will be told to you by another person, it is your voice that will convey the story. Your voice uniquely expresses that story through your word choice, sentence structure, and tone. Carefully choosing the subject of your interview, conveying interest in the interview itself, and committing yourself to the writing that follows will help you develop a voice that is honest, effective, and engaging.

IDENTIFYING YOUR AUDIENCE. Certainly the person that you interview will want to read the oral history that you record. That person's family members may be interested in reading it, too. Whom else might you consider as an audience? Members of local historical societies, your classmates, and even future readers such as a grandchild or great-grandchild may be interested in your writing.

What considerations do you need to make for your audience? You will want to convey ideas and details that engage the reader and make the narrative come alive. You might also need to include some necessary background information to establish the place and time for the event.

As you prepare for this assignment, see the Language Arts Survey 4.14, "Conducting an Interview." Also see the Language Arts Survey 2.14, "Questioning: Using the 5 *W*s and an *H*," for more help in preparing questions to ask in your interview.

WRITING WITH A PLAN. Your first task is to select a person to interview. Before you select whom to interview for your narrative, consider a pre-interview with several people to determine the types of experiences each person has had. Decide whose experiences and background are of the greatest interest to you and then make your selection. Arrange with that person a specific time and place for the interview to take place. When you make the contact, be sure to explain your mission—to record oral history. Also explore with your interview subject what event, memory, or object he or she would like to tell about. You may not know exactly what your focus will be until you begin the interview, but this is a good time to start focusing your material.

Before the interview, prepare a list of questions to elicit from the person everything he or she can possibly recall about the event, memory, or object you plan to discuss. A good selection of who, what, where, when, why, and how questions will help you to gather pertinent details and explanations. Be open to the possibility that the focus of your interview may change. For example, you may plan to interview your grandfather about the medals you've seen in his house, but instead he may want to tell you about the first time he traveled by plane. Be open to the unexpected. After the interview, you can narrow what you actually write about.

- Begin the interview by double-checking that you have the person's permission to take notes or tape-record and to print or otherwise share what is said.
- Be certain you have the person's name spelled correctly.
- Ask about newspaper clippings, photographs, scrapbooks, clothing, jewelry, or other mementos that will spark more details about the event or time period.
- If possible, record the interview. Also, write down main ideas, key words, your observations, and direct quotations on paper or with a laptop computer.
- Keep your questions handy.
- Observe the subject's facial expressions and mannerisms for possible inclusion in the narrative. You can use your observations as you write to develop your subject's character.
- Be careful not to become so preoccupied with the business of interviewing that you miss the opportunity to converse and get to know this person better.
- Of course, as the interview concludes, thank your subject, give a date when you expect to have the writing completed, and offer to share the finished project.
- If time allows before completion of the assignment, perhaps you can take and develop a photograph.

Neil, who planned to interview his Grandpa Johnson, used the following graphic organizer to prepare for his interview. After reviewing Neil's information, copy the graphic organizer on your paper. Add the specific information about your interview and your questions. Then complete the organizer as you conduct your interview.

> "One line of dialogue that rings true reveals character in a way that pages of description can't."
>
> —Anne Lamott

Student Model—Graphic Organizer

Oral History Interview Organizer

Interview with: *my grandfather, Dennis Neil August Johnson*
Date: *September 28*
Time: *2 PM*
Place: *Grandpa's home at 186 S. Oak St. See if we can meet in his study, where he keeps all those old photos and souvenirs*

Permission to take notes, tape-record, and print: *Yes*

My goal for the interview: *learn about his cross-country trip in 1922 Buick*

The event, memory, or object: *cross-country trip in 1924 with his parents and five siblings*

Questions for the interview:

Who?
1. Who went on the trip?
2. Whom did you meet or see on the trip?

What?
1. What did you do on the trip?
2. What did your parents and siblings do?
3. What did you see that you would never forget?

Where?
1. Where did you start?
2. Where did the trip end?
3. Where was your favorite place on the trip? Where was your least favorite?

When?
1. When, or what time of year, did you go on the trip?
2. When during the day did you travel?

Why?
1. Why did you go on the trip?
2. Why especially do you remember the trip?
3. Why was it such an important trip for your family to take?

How?
1. How did the trip affect you at the time?
2. How did the trip change the way you saw things?
3. How did the trip affect the people in your family?

continued on page 66

continued

Mementos: *(newspaper clippings, photographs, scrapbooks, clothing, jewelry)*

Direct quotations:

Main ideas, key words, and observations:

Gestures and expressions worth noting:

Drafting

Review your notes and, if you used a tape recorder, listen to the taped interview several times until the story is clear and complete in your mind. You may also want to transcribe—type out—the interview or parts of it. If necessary, mark your notes to identify the correct time order for the events. Put a question mark in your notes beside anything that is unclear to you and, if possible, check back with the person you interviewed and clarify those questions. Work to include sensory details that will make your writing memorable.

If you haven't already done so, determine the focus. If you're stuck, invite a friend or parent to hear the interview, read your notes, and suggest a focus. Once you have the main idea for your narrative, begin telling the events of the story in chronological order. Telling the story in time order will help your reader understand and experience just what your subject has shared with you.

The first paragraph should introduce and identify the subject, specify the time period, and indicate the focus of the story. Notice how the following paragraph accomplishes this.

> When my father's Great Aunt Tillie was born, the *Titanic* had just sunk and New Mexico was soon to celebrate statehood. Since then, Matilda Mae (Tillie) Aldrich has lived her entire life on a ranch and knows the hardships as well as the satisfaction ranch life has to offer. She fondly recalls spring roundup and branding, in particular in 1932 when she met the wrangler who was to become her husband.

Continue to tell the story in several more paragraphs, drawing from your notes and the recorded interview. Use your observations to develop your subject's character. Include direct quotations and interesting details, such as the stained hat Tillie remembers her husband-to-be wearing that day or the standard fare served during branding. This is also the time to incorporate what you observed of your subject when you interviewed her: "Great Aunt Tillie dabbed the corners of her eyes with a lacy white hankie whenever she mentioned Great Uncle Benny."

After the story is told, wrap it up with a short conclusion. You might wish to summarize the years that followed in the life of the subject or explain the situation at the present time. The

---

> "Whatever we conceive well we express clearly."
>
> —Boileau

Reflecting

Before you begin to write your narrative, think about the stories that you have heard told and retold. Which stories are the most interesting to you? What experiences and memories did the writer capture? How did the writer convey those experiences and memories? How did you benefit from hearing the stories? Considering answers to these questions can help you write a narrative that your readers will want to read again and again.

conclusion is the place for you to editorialize a bit, too. How did you benefit from talking with this person? What has been captured for the benefit or enjoyment of others?

Student Model—Draft

My grandfather, Dennis Neil August Johnson, was born in 1910. Recently, he recalled his trip to the West Coast in the summer of 1924. At that time he was thirteen, almost fourteen, and had five siblings, soon to be six.

Grandpa Dennis's father, Sam Johnson, had been *"Incorrect to use both; & "and"* suffering from ulcers; and) it was difficult for him to farm his land just north of Sioux Falls, South Dakota. So Sam and his wife Ovida decided to take a trip. They rented out the farm and then the family *sold stock & machinery* of eight packed up the 1922 Buick open touring car with wooden wheels. They started their journey to the West *this is abrupt* Coast. *Grandpa said it was an adventure from the moment they left.*

combine these two sentences to avoid repeating "roads" The family traveled due west toward Wyoming on graveled <u>roads</u>. Even in the mountains, the <u>roads</u> didn't have guardrails. The small town of Presho, South Dakota, 213 miles west of Sioux Falls, was the first campsite on the. *good detail* journey. They camped out in their car for the whole trip. When it rained they put up curtains to keep the rain out

Language, Grammar, and Style

Sentence Variety
IDENTIFYING DIFFERENT TYPES OF SENTENCES. Even the most exciting story might sound dull if the writer does not use a variety of sentence structures. There are four types of sentences that you can use to keep your writing interesting: simple, compound, complex, and compound-complex.

Simple Sentence
A **simple sentence** is made up of one independent clause. As you have learned in Unit 1, a simple sentence has a complete subject and predicate. Look at the example below.

The sky turned grayish green.

Compound Sentence
Combining two or more simple sentences makes a **compound sentence**. The independent clauses are usually combined with a **coordinating conjunction** such as *and, but, for, nor, or,* or *yet*. A comma is usually placed before the connecting word in a compound sentence. Read the example below.

continued on page 68

The sky turned grayish green, and then the tornado hit.

Look at the two independent clauses in the example below. Combine them into a compound sentence using one of the following coordinating conjunctions: *and, but, for, nor, or,* or *yet.*

The tornado was over in minutes. The cleanup took weeks!

Instead of using a coordinating conjunction to combine independent clauses, you can use a semicolon between the clauses. Look at the example below.

Trees were split in two; a foot of water filled the street.

Combine the two independent clauses below using a semicolon.

Bricks from the neighbor's chimney had fallen into our sunroom. My mother's prized sewing machine was nicked and dented.

Look at the Professional Model and identify any compound sentences. Do the sentences use a comma and a coordinating conjunction or a semicolon between the independent clauses?

continued on page 69

why did they get wet? ————

and the family dry and comfortable. Three of Dennis's sisters slept together in the back seat, his brother Astor on the front seat, Dennis and his sister Doris each on a cot, and the parents on a double cot. They mostly ate fried foods, siphoning gas from the Buick for their stove. *good image & detail*

Since Sam was ill and Ovida did not know how to drive, my grandpa drove the whole trip. The family stopped in *Incredible! Good for him* Yellowstone National Park to visit the *Include some dialog?* forest and geysers. Ovida was afraid that one of the children would fall into *How could that happen g. not fenced off* a geyser. The family got quite a scare, when a shaggy-headed bear stuck its head into an open window of the Buick. The *Good detail* children were so scared that they threw that day's lunch out of the car so the bear would leave them alone. They left Yellowstone and traveled on into Idaho and then Washington. Driving through *spell out* Washington, the (6) children were amazed to see (24) horses pulling a combine with one man filling wheat sacks. The family took a trip down to the harbor in Portland to see the logging industry.

Self- and Peer Evaluation

After you finish your first draft, complete a self-evaluation of your writing. If time allows, you may want to get one or two peer evaluations. For more information, see the Language Arts Survey 2.37, "Self- and Peer Evaluation."

As you evaluate your narrative or that of a classmate, answer the following questions:

- What is your overall impression of the narrative? Is it inviting to read, interesting, and purposeful? What areas excel in this? What areas could use improvement?
- Does the narrative present a complete story with a beginning, middle, and end?
- What information is presented to create a sense of time and place for the narrative? What information is still needed?
- What techniques does the narrative use to give the reader a sense of the subject's character?
- What details could be added to help the reader get to know the subject better?
- How well do the sensory details create a vivid picture of the story's events and characters? How could the sensory details be improved?
- Does the narrative contain extraneous information that could be eliminated? What could be eliminated?
- How do word choice and tone contribute to an honest, effective, and engaging voice?
- What variety of sentence structures does the narrative use? Where would the narrative benefit from a greater variety of sentence structures?
- How significant is the story to the storyteller? the author? the reader? What might make the story more significant to the reader?

Revising and Proofreading

If possible, let your draft and evaluation comments rest a day before you begin editing. Reading it aloud is an excellent technique you can use to hear as well as see where you need to make changes or corrections. Think about the strengths and weaknesses identified in the evaluation comment. Using these comments, decide how to revise your draft so that the final narrative is interesting, lively, and significant.

Proofread for mechanical and grammatical errors. For more information, see the Language Arts Survey 2.45, "A Proofreading Checklist."

Student Model—Revised

```
On the Road with Grandpa
by Neil Hebbert

    My grandfather, Dennis Neil August
Johnson, was born in 1910. Recently, he
recalled his trip to the West Coast in
the summer of 1924. At that time he was
thirteen, almost fourteen, and had five
siblings, soon to be six.
    Grandpa Dennis's  father, Sam
Johnson, had been suffering from
```

Complex Sentence

Combining an independent clause with at least one dependent clause makes a **complex sentence**. Look at the example below.

> When the sky turned grayish green, we ran to the basement.

Words that are used to begin dependent clauses are called subordinating conjunctions. These conjunctions include *after, although, as, as if, because, before, even if, even though, if, if only, rather than, since, that, though, unless, until, when, where, whereas, wherever, whether, which,* and *while*.

Combine each independent clause with the dependent clause in the examples below. The dependent clause may either begin or end a complex sentence, but when it begins the sentence, a comma must follow it.

> Although the tornado didn't last long. It did a significant amount of damage.

> You should know what to do. When there is a tornado warning.

Look at the Professional Model and identify each complex sentence. Is the dependent clause at the beginning or at the end of the sentence?

continued on page 70

Compound-Complex

You can create a **compound-complex** sentence by combining a dependent clause with two or more independent clauses. Look at the example below.

> As the wind began to blow, the lawn chairs flew off the front porch, and we ran to the basement.

Combine the dependent clause and the two independent clauses below into a compound-complex sentence. Use a coordinating conjunction between the two independent clauses.

> After the tornado was over. The street was flooded. Tree limbs floated down the street.

FIXING INCORRECT COMPOUND AND COMPLEX SENTENCES.

Identify and correct the error in each compound sentence below.

> Grandpa Dennis's father, Sam Johnson, had been suffering from ulcers; and it was difficult for him to farm his land just north of Sioux Falls, South Dakota.

> They rented out the farm and then the family of eight packed up the 1922 Buick open touring car with wooden wheels.

Identify and correct the error in each complex sentence below.

continued on page 71

ulcers, making it difficult to farm his land just north of Sioux Falls, South Dakota. So Sam and his wife Ovida decided to take a trip. They sold much of their stock and machinery, but kept their car, a 1922 Buick open touring car with wooden wheels. The family of eight packed up the Buick and started on their journey to the West Coast. "It was an adventure from the moment we left the farm," Grandpa said.

The family traveled due west toward Wyoming on graveled roads in South Dakota that didn't even have guardrails. The small town of Presho, South Dakota, 213 miles west of Sioux Falls, was the first campsite on the journey. They camped out in their car for the whole trip. When it rained, they put up curtains to keep rain out and the family dry and comfortable. Three of Dennis's sisters slept together in the back seat, his brother Astor on the front seat, Dennis and his sister Doris each on a cot, and the parents on a double cot. "We mostly ate fried foods, siphoning gas from the Buick for our stove," Grandpa said. "It wasn't the smartest idea in the world because it wasn't very safe, but we didn't think about that at the time."

Since Sam was ill and Ovida did not know how to drive, my grandpa drove the whole trip. "Not a bad adventure for a young 'un," Grandpa told me, tipping his head back with a laugh. The family stopped in Yellowstone National Park to visit the forest and geysers. "My mother—your Great-Grandmother Ovida— was afraid that one of the children would fall into a geyser," Grandpa remembered, explaining that, at that time, the geysers were not fenced off. The family got quite a scare when a shaggy-headed bear stuck its head into an open window of the Buick. The children were so frightened that they threw that day's lunch out of the car so the bear would leave them alone. They left Yellowstone and traveled on into Idaho and then Washington. Driving through the countryside of Washington, the six children were amazed to see twenty-four horses pulling a combine with one man filling wheat sacks.

The family took a trip down to the harbor in Portland to see the logging industry. After Portland, they headed back home to the farm. Grandpa Dennis was still driving. He remembers celebrating his fourteenth birthday in Idaho. One week after their return at the end of August, Calvin Johnson, the seventh, youngest, and final child of the family was born. "Your Great-Grandma Ovida always said that it was easier camping out for over two months with a husband and six children than preparing three meals and two lunches a day for a crew of farmhands," Grandpa said. "I suppose she was right."

My grandpa eventually inherited the farm and has worked it all his life. Recently when we were discussing where I was going to attend college, he exclaimed, "That will really be an experience for you. But I went to college behind four cows in a field at the farm!" I laughed and thought about all the things that he has experienced in his lifetime. Life has been his school—and what a scholar he is.

When it rained they put up curtains to keep the rain out and the family dry and comfortable.

The family got quite a scare, when a shaggy-headed bear stuck its head into an open window of the Buick.

USING A VARIETY OF SENTENCES. Examine the kinds of sentences that you have used in your writing. You will want to vary the length and type of your sentences.

Try to combine two simple sentences into a compound sentence. Next, combine other sentences to create a complex sentence. Try putting the dependent clause at the beginning of the complex sentence. Then create another complex sentence with the dependent clause at the end of the sentence.

Reading out loud is a good way to check the rhythm and flow of your writing. Continue to experiment with sentence structure until you have the effect you want to achieve.

For more information, see the Language Arts Survey 3.36, "Combining and Expanding Sentences."

Publishing and Presenting

Your narrative could become a piece of your family's or your community's history. How can you best present and preserve it? You might create a booklet that includes your story, a short biographical entry about the person whose story you have told, photographs, and photocopies of any newspaper clippings or mementos associated with the story. You might work with several classmates or your entire class to create a book that includes all of your class's narratives. Be sure to make your narrative available to the person that you interviewed.

UNIT 1 review
The Folk Tradition

Words for Everyday Use

Check your knowledge of the following vocabulary words from the selections in this unit. Write short sentences using each of these words in context to make the meaning clear. To review the definition or usage of a word, refer back to the page number(s) listed or the Glossary of Words for Everyday Use.

abroad, 19	contrive, 21	famine, 26	prophecy, 41
amorous, 41	cull, 40	foray, 42	riotous, 26
anxiety, 19	curtail, 8	garb, 39	stratagem, 42
beguile, 8	diligently, 25	naught, 39	surpass, 34
buffet, 38	disintegrate, 8	oblivious, 7	superintendence, 19
carmine, 41	dominion, 12	parry, 40	tarry, 42
churl, 38	ebb, 8	plait, 40	transgress, 26
compassion, 26	enigmatic, 9	plumage, 14	traverse, 14
consort, 39	entreat, 26	plume, 19	virtue, 41

Literary Tools

Define each of the following terms, giving concrete examples of how they are used in the selections in this unit. To review a term, refer to the page number(s) indicated or to the Handbook of Literary Terms.

aim, 29	folk tale, 29	myth, 6
allusion, 52	foreshadowing, 11	parable, 24
character, 17, 33	irony, 37	personification, 29
dialect, 45	irony of situation, 37	repetition, 52
fable, 33	legend, 37	suspension of disbelief, 6
fairy tale, 17	moral, 11	symbol, 24
folk song, 45	motif, 17	

Reflecting on your reading

Genre Studies

1. What are the primary differences between myths and legends? between fables and fairy tales? Explain, using examples from the selections in this unit.

2. Compare and contrast the role of the supernatural in these three stories: "Echo and Narcissus," "The Story of Dædalus and Icarus," and "The White Snake."

3. What characteristics do parables and fables have in common? Explain, using examples from "The Prodigal Son" and "The Fox and the Crow."

4. The stories, poems, and songs of the folk tradition serve many purposes other than simple entertainment. What are some of the purposes served by myths, parables, fables, folk songs, and spirituals? Explain, using specific examples from the selections in this unit.

Thematic Studies

5. **HEROISM.** Fionn MacCumhail was a legendary Irish hero, and John Henry was a legendary African-American hero. What qualities made each man a hero? What aspects of the two men's stories are based on fact?

6. **DESTINY.** Discuss the theme of destiny in "Echo and Narcissus" and the Celtic legend "The Silver Pool."

7. **PUNISHMENT AND FORGIVENESS.** Punishment is a theme in the following selections: "Echo and Narcissus," "The Story of Dædalus and Icarus," "Goha and the Pot," and "The Fox and the Crow." Who is punished in these stories, and why? What does each story reveal about the values of the people who first told it? Next consider the parable "The Prodigal Son." In this story, someone is spared punishment. Why? What values was this parable intended to convey?

8. **RELIGION AND FREEDOM.** Discuss the dual themes of religion and freedom in the African-American spirituals "Steal Away" and "Go Down, Moses." How were both of these themes present in the songs? Explain.

for your READING LIST

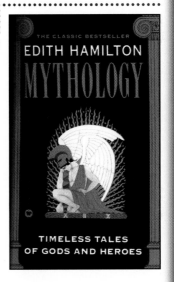

Mythology: Timeless Tales of Gods and Heroes by Edith Hamilton. Edith Hamilton's *Mythology* is an anthology of classical mythology that gives the reader a knowledge of the classic myths, as well as an idea of what the writers who told them were like—who have, in Hamilton's words, "been proved, by two thousand years and more, to be immortal."

Independent Reading Activity

COMPARING AND CONTRASTING. Read Ovid's telling of the story of Narcissus found in Edith Hamilton's *Mythology*. Compare this telling with the one found in this unit by Walker Brents on page 7. How are the retellings similar or different? How are the characters of Narcissus and Echo portrayed in each telling?

Selections for Additional Reading

Bird Girl and the Man Who Followed the Sun: An Athabaskan Indian Legend from Alaska by Velma Wallace. Rooted in the legends of Alaska's Athabaskan Indians, this novel about two young rebels teaches that the search for individualism often comes at a high price but can be the foundation for finding true wisdom.

The Power of Myth by Joseph Campbell with Bill Moyers. This interview with Joseph Campbell, a preeminent scholar, writer, and teacher, conducted by Bill Moyers, one of America's most prominent journalists, provides a guide to recognizing and understanding the meaning of the symbols of mythology and legend.

How the Spider Became Bald: Folktales and Legends from West Africa by Peter Eric Adotey Addo. *How the Spider Became Bald* collects twenty-five traditional folk tales, retold by a native of Ghana in the lively, spontaneous style of the classic storytelling tradition.

The Starry Night, 1889. Vincent van Gogh. The Museum of Modern Art, New York.

Poetry

UNIT TWO

ELEMENTS *of* POETRY

The word "poem" comes from the Greek root *poíema,* which means "work," and is derived from *poieín,* to make. Finding a good definition for poetry is difficult, especially because poems can take so many forms. Poetry does not have to be written down; it can be chanted or sung, spontaneous or memorized. Some poems rhyme and have regular, rhythmical patterns, but others do not. Many poems depend on special devices of sound such as onomatopoeia and alliteration, and many use special techniques of meaning such as metaphor and symbolism. Some are simply designs or word pictures, like this concrete poem:

```
              O   O
     B A L L       N
```

Poetry differs from prose in that it compresses more meaning into fewer words, and often uses meter, rhyme, rhythm, and techniques such as metaphor and simile. Poetry is often arranged in lines and stanzas as opposed to sentences and paragraphs, and it can be more free in the ordering of words and the use of punctuation. One thing that all poems have in common is that they use imaginative language carefully chosen and arranged to communicate experiences, thoughts, or emotions. Here are some interesting definitions of poetry put forward by important literary figures from the past:

Poetry is . . .

"the spontaneous overflow of powerful feelings."
—William Wordsworth

"the best words in the best order."
—Samuel Taylor Coleridge

"the record of the best and happiest moments of the happiest and best minds."
—Percy Bysshe Shelley

"[language that] strike[s] the reader as a wording of his own highest thoughts, and appear[s] almost a remembrance."
—John Keats

"musical thought."
—Thomas Carlyle

"conceived and composed in the soul."
—Matthew Arnold

"a mixture of common sense, which not all have, with an uncommon sense, which very few have."
—John Masefield

"the supreme fiction."
—Wallace Stevens

"what gets lost in translation."
—Robert Frost

"not an assertion of truth, but the making of that truth more fully real to us."
—T. S. Eliot

TYPES OF POETRY

NARRATIVE POETRY. A **narrative poem** is a verse that tells a story. Narrative poems in this unit are Gabriela Mistral's "Song" and James Weldon Johnson's "The Creation." Another example of a narrative poem is Margaret Atwood's "Death of a Young Son by Drowning" (Unit 10).

DRAMATIC POETRY. A **dramatic poem** is a verse that relies heavily on dramatic elements such as **monologue** (speech by a single character) or **dialogue** (conversation involving two or more characters). Often dramatic poems are narratives as well. In other words, they often tell stories. A **dramatic monologue** is a poem that presents the speech of a single character in a dramatic situation. Audre Lorde's "Hanging Fire" (Unit 7) could be considered a dramatic poem.

LYRIC POETRY. A **lyric poem** is a highly musical verse that expresses the emotions of a speaker. There are many types of lyric poems. Among the most common types are the following:

Sonnet. A **sonnet** is a fourteen-line poem that follows one of a number of different rhyme schemes. Many sonnets deal with the subject of love.

The Calumet, 1961. Robert Indiana. Rose Art Museum, Brandeis University, Waltham, Massachusetts.

art
n o t e

Robert Indiana (1928–   ) is considered a Pop artist, but his work differs from those who use commercial products as subject matter, such as Andy Warhol with his soup cans. Inspired by road signs and advertisements, Indiana paints textual references to American popular culture. With *The Calumet* he used a line from Longfellow's classic poem "Song of Hiawatha" in the outer ring and the names of Native American tribes in the inner rings. How does Indiana's choice of lettering and his arrangement of the words affect the way you think of the text? What other ways is poetry incorporated into contemporary life and art?

Ode. An **ode** is a lofty lyric poem on a serious theme. It may employ alternating stanza patterns, developed from the choral ode of Greek dramatic poetry. These stanza patterns are called the strophe, the antistrophe, and the epode. However, not all odes follow this pattern.

Free Verse. **Free verse** is poetry that avoids use of regular rhyme, rhythm, meter, or division into stanzas. Examples of free-verse poems include N. Scott Momaday's "A Simile" (Unit 2) and Nikki Giovanni's "Nikki-Rosa" (Unit 7).

Elegaic Lyric. An **elegaic lyric** expresses a speaker's feelings of loss, often because of the death of a loved one or friend.

Imagist Poem. An **imagist poem** is a lyric that presents a single vivid picture in words.

TECHNIQUES OF POETRY: METER AND STANZA FORM

Metrical verse follows a set rhythmical pattern. **Free verse**, or *vers libre*, does not. Instead, it follows the rhythms of ordinary speech.

METER. The **meter** of a poem is its rhythmical pattern. English verse usually is described as being made up of rhythmical units called **feet**. A **foot** consists of some combination of **weakly stressed** (˘) and **strongly stressed** (/) syllables, as follows:

TYPE OF FOOT	PATTERN	EXAMPLE
iamb, or iambic foot	˘ /	afraid
trochee, or trochaic foot	/ ˘	freedom
anapest, or anapestic foot	˘ ˘ /	in a flash
dactyl, or dactylic foot	/ ˘ ˘	feverish
spondee, or spondaic foot	/ /	baseball

Some writers on meter also use the term **pyrrhee**, or **pyrrhic foot**, to describe a foot with two weak stresses, as follows:

anapest   pyrrhee

˘ ˘ / | ˘ ˘

un re li | a ble

The following terms are used to describe the number of feet in a line of poetry:

TERM	# OF FEET	EXAMPLE
monometer	one foot	˘ / Today ˘ / We play
dimeter	two feet	/ ˘ ˘ / ˘ Following | closely / ˘ ˘ / ˘ Through the | forest
trimeter	three feet	˘ / ˘ / ˘ / God shed | His light | on thee
tetrameter	four feet	/ ˘ / ˘ / ˘ / ˘ In the | greenest | of our | valleys
pentameter	five feet	˘ / ˘ / ˘ / A vast | re pub | lic famed| ˘ / ˘ / through ev | ry clime
hexameter or Alexandrine	six feet	˘ / ˘ / ˘ / In o | ther's eyes | we see | ˘ / ˘ / ˘ / ourselves | the truth | to tell

A complete description of the meter of a line includes both the term for the type of foot that predominates in the line and the term for the number of feet in the line. The most common meters in English are **iambic tetrameter** and **iambic pentameter**.

STANZA FORM. A **stanza** is a group of lines in a poem. The following are some common types of stanza:

COUPLET *(two lines)*

We dance round in a ring and suppose,
But the Secret sits in the middle and knows.

—Robert Frost, "The Secret Sits"

TRIPLET OR TERCET *(three lines)*

Children picking up our bones
Will never know that these were once
As quick as foxes on the hill;

—Wallace Stevens, "A Postcard from the Volcano"

QUATRAIN (four lines)

By the rude bridge that arched the flood,
  Their flag to April's breeze unfurl'd,
Here once the embattled farmers stood,
  And fired the shot heard round the world.

> —Ralph Waldo Emerson, "Hymn Sung
> at the Completion of the Concord
> Monument, April 19, 1836"

QUINTAIN (five lines)

Gaunt the shadow on your green,
  Shenandoah!
The cut is on the crown
  (Lo, John Brown),
And the stabs shall heal no more.

> —Herman Melville, "The Portent"

SESTET (six lines)

Over these writings I bent my head.
Now you are considering them. If you
turn away I will look up: a bridge
that was there will be gone.
For the rest of your life I will stand here,
reaching across.

> —William Stafford, "Sending These Messages"

HEPTASTICH (seven lines)

In Heaven a spirit doth dwell
  "Whose heart-strings are a lute;"
None sing so wildly well
As the angel Israfel,
And the giddy stars (so legends tell)
Ceasing their hymns, attend the spell
  Of his voice, all mute.

> —Edgar Allan Poe, "Israfel"

OCTAVE (eight lines)

The God who made New Hampshire
Taunted the lofty land
With little men;—
Small bat and wren
House in the oak:—
If earth-fire cleave
The upheaved land, and bury the folk,
The southern crocodile would grieve.

> —Ralph Waldo Emerson,
> "Ode, Inscribed to
> W. H. Channing"

TECHNIQUES OF POETRY: SOUND*

RHYTHM. The **rhythm** is the pattern of beats or stresses in a line of verse or prose. A regular rhythmic pattern is called a meter.

RHYME. Rhyme is the repetition of sounds at the ends of words. The following are some types of rhyme:

End Rhyme. End rhyme is rhyme that occurs at the ends of lines.

INTERNAL RHYME. Internal rhyme is the use of rhyming words within lines.

Slant Rhyme. A **slant rhyme**, half rhyme, near rhyme, or off rhyme is the substitution of assonance or consonance for true rhyme. The pairs *world/boiled* and *bear/bore* are examples.

ALLITERATION. Alliteration is the repetition of initial consonant sounds. Some writers also use the term to describe repeated initial vowel sounds. Edgar Allan Poe's "The Bells" in this unit contains the following example of alliteration: "**W**hat a **w**orld of **m**erriment their **m**elody foretells!"

ASSONANCE. Assonance is the repetition of vowel sounds in stressed syllables that end with different consonant sounds, as in "From the m**o**lten-g**o**lden n**o**tes," also in "The Bells."

CONSONANCE. Consonance is a kind of slant rhyme in which the ending consonant sounds of two words match, but the preceding vowel sound does not, as in the words *wind* and *sound*.

ONOMATOPOEIA. Onomatopoeia is the use of words or phrases that sound like the things to which they refer. Examples of onomatopoeia include words such as *pow, caw, clink,* and *murmur.*

*Note: These techniques are used commonly, but not exclusively, in poetry.

Literary T O O L S

REPETITION. Repetition is the writer's conscious reuse of a sound, word, phrase, sentence, or other element. As you read, pay attention to the words and phrases that are repeated in the poem.

ONOMATOPOEIA. Onomatopoeia (ä nə mä tə pē ə) is the use of words or phrases that sound like the things to which they refer.

Organizer

As you read, make a chart. On the left, list onomatopoeic words from the poem. On the right, list the kind of bells with which these sounds are associated. One example has been done for you.

Onomatopoeia	Bells
jingling	sleigh bells

Reader's JOURNAL

What types of bells have you heard in your life? With what events or life stages were the bells associated?

"The Bells" by Edgar Allan Poe

Reader's resource

A friend of Poe, Marie Louise Shew, suggested the idea for "**The Bells.**" Poe was in poor mental and physical health, and the ringing of the many church bells near Shew's house disturbed him greatly. When he expressed the need to write a poem for immediate publication, she suggested the topic of the bells. Poe wrote a brief poem that was later expanded into the poem that exists today. Through techniques such as *assonance, alliteration,* and *repetition,* the poem creates an *onomatopoeic* rendering of the sounds of four types of bells and the resulting emotional responses.

About *the* A U T H O R

Edgar Allan Poe (1809–1849) led a short, troubled life but managed in his forty years to make major contributions to literary form and criticism. Considered to be one of the two creators of the modern short story (the other being Nathanial Hawthorne), Poe also invented detective fiction, wrote lyric poetry, and pioneered the psychological horror story. Few writers have had such enduring popularity and influence as Poe.

Poe's tragic life was plagued with insecurity. His father deserted the family when Edgar was a year old. His mother died at the age of twenty-four, and Poe, two years old, was taken in by John Allan, a prosperous Richmond, Virginia, merchant. Poe briefly attended the University of Virginia and did well in his studies. He joined the army after publishing *Tamerlane and Other Poems* in 1827, and was appointed to West Point, but poor class attendance led to his expulsion from the academy.

Poe later held various editorial jobs, reviewed literary works, and wrote one novel, *The Narrative of Arthur Gordon Pym*, in addition to producing numerous short stories and poems. Briefly famous and successful after the publication of his poem "The Raven," Poe nonetheless spent most of his adult life in poverty, losing one job after another due to drinking and quarrelsomeness. Several of his works, including "The Bells," were published after his death.

Other well-known work by Poe includes the poem "Annabel Lee" and the stories "The Fall of the House of Usher," "The Masque of the Red Death," "The Black Cat," "The Cask of Amontillado," "The Purloined Letter," and "The Tell-Tale Heart."

art note

Charles Burchfield (1893–1967) tried to represent the invisible forces of sound and motion in his painting. Of course, sound cannot be seen, but Burchfield uses "force lines" to represent the sound emanating from the bells. Where else have you seen techniques like this used in pictures?

The Bells

Edgar Allan Poe

Church Bells Ringing, Rainy Winter Night, 1917. Charles Burchfield. The Cleveland Museum of Art.

I

       *H*ear the sledges[1] with the bells—
          Silver bells!
What a world of merriment their melody foretells!
       How they tinkle, tinkle, tinkle,
5   In the icy air of night!
      While the stars that oversprinkle
      All the heavens seem to twinkle
         With a crystalline delight;
         Keeping time, time, time,
10   In a sort of Runic rhyme,[2]
To the tintinnabulation[3] that so musically wells
      From the bells, bells, bells, bells,
           Bells, bells, bells—
From the jingling and the tinkling of the bells.

What kind of bells are described here? What do these bells foretell? What sound do they make?

---

1. **sledges.** Sleds or sleighs
2. **Runic rhyme.** Ancient verse written in an alphabet known as Runic
3. **tintinnabulation.** Ringing sound

II

15 Hear the mellow wedding bells,
            Golden bells!
    What a world of happiness their harmony foretells!
            Through the <u>balmy</u> air of night
            How they ring out their delight!
20   From the molten-golden notes,
                And all in tune,
            What a liquid ditty floats
    To the turtle-dove that listens, while she gloats
                On the moon!
25   Oh, from out the sounding cells
    What a gush of euphony[4] <u>voluminously</u> wells!
                How it swells!
                How it dwells
            On the Future! how it tells
30   Of the rapture that impels
        To the swinging and the ringing
            Of the bells, bells, bells,
    Of the bells, bells, bells, bells,
            Bells, bells, bells—
35 To the rhyming and the chiming of the bells!

What sounds do the wedding bells make? What do they tell?

III

    Hear the loud alarum bells[5]—
            Brazen bells!
    What a tale of terror, now, their turbulency[6] tells!
            In the startled ear of night
40   How they scream out their affright![7]
            Too much horrified to speak,
            They can only shriek, shriek,
                Out of tune,
    In a clamorous appealing to the mercy of the fire,
45 In a mad expostulation[8] with the deaf and frantic fire,
            Leaping higher, higher, higher,
            With a desperate desire,

What message do the alarm bells have? What noise do they use to convey this message?

---

4. **euphony.** Pleasing sound
5. **alarum bells.** Alarm bells (archaic)
6. **turbulency.** Violent agitation
7. **affright.** Great fright or terror (archaic)
8. **expostulation.** Objection, disagreement

words for everyday use

balm • y (bäm´ē) *adj.,* soothing; mild; pleasant. *A <u>balmy</u> breeze wafted over us as we lay on the hammock.*

vo • lu • mi • nous • ly (və lōō´ mə nəs lē) *adv.,* largely; fully. *Numerous petticoats <u>voluminously</u> filled the actor's wide skirt.*

And a resolute endeavor
Now—now to sit, or never,
50   By the side of the pale-faced moon.
Oh, the bells, bells, bells!
What a tale their terror tells
Of despair!
How they clang, and clash, and roar!
55   What a horror they outpour
On the bosom of the <u>palpitating</u> air!
Yet the ear it fully knows,
By the twanging,
And the clanging,
60   How the danger ebbs and flows;
Yet the ear distinctly tells,
In the jangling,
And the wrangling,
How the danger sinks and swells,
65   By the sinking or the swelling in the anger of the bells—
Of the bells—
Of the bells, bells, bells, bells,
Bells, bells, bells—
In the <u>clamor</u> and the clangor of the bells!

IV

70   *H*ear the tolling of the bells
Iron bells!
What a world of solemn thought their melody compels!
In the silence of the night,
How we shiver with affright
75   At the <u>melancholy</u> menace of their tone!
For every sound that floats
From the rust within their throats
Is a groan.
And the people—ah, the people—
80   They that dwell up in the steeple,
All alone,
And who tolling, tolling, tolling,
In that muffled monotone,
Feel a glory in so rolling
85   On the human heart a stone—

What does the ear know of danger?

What effect do the iron bells have on us?

words for everyday use

pal • pi • tat • ing (pal´pə tāt´ing) *part.*, beating rapidly; fluttering. *After running a mile, Shawna could feel her heart palpitating.*

clam • or (kla´mər) *n.*, loud continuous noice. *The clamor of children playing at recess got on Mrs. Green's nerves.*

mel • an • chol • y (mel´ən käl´ē) *adj.*, sad; gloomy; depressed. *The doctor insisted that Michael's melancholy mood could be treated with medication.*

They are neither man nor woman—
They are neither brute nor human—
They are Ghouls:[9]
And their king it is who tolls;
90   And he rolls, rolls, rolls,
Rolls
A pæan[10] from the bells!
And his merry bosom swells
With the pæan of the bells!
95   And he dances, and he yells;
Keeping time, time, time,
In a sort of Runic rhyme,
To the pæan of the bells—
Of the bells:
100   Keeping time, time, time,
In a sort of Runic rhyme,
To the throbbing of the bells—
Of the bells, bells, bells—
To the sobbing of the bells;
105   Keeping time, time, time,
As he knells, knells, knells,
In a happy Runic rhyme,
To the rolling of the bells—
Of the bells, bells, bells—
110   To the tolling of the bells,
Of the bells, bells, bells, bells—
Bells, bells, bells—
To the moaning and the groaning of the bells. ■

> What does the king of the Ghouls do?

> How does this contrast with the bells in the opening stanza?

---

9. **Ghouls.** Evil spirits
10. **pæan.** Song of joy, triumph, or praise

words for everyday use

knell (nel) *vi.*, sound ominously or mournfully. *After the boat sank in the stormy sea, the buoy bell knelled for the lives that were lost.*

Respond to the SELECTION

Which bell would be the most pleasing to hear? Which would be the most unpleasant?

Investigate, Inquire, and Imagine

Recall: GATHERING FACTS

1a. What do the bells in the first two stanzas foretell?

2a. What bells are introduced in stanza 3? What story do these bells tell? What kind of sound do they produce?

3a. What bells does the speaker describe in stanza 4? What do these bells make people do?

Interpret: FINDING MEANING

1b. In what way are the bells in the first two stanzas similar?

2b. How does the effect of the sound produced by the bells in stanza 3 differ from the effect of the sounds made by the bells in stanzas 1 and 2?

3b. The bells in both stanza 1 and stanza 4 are described as "keeping time, time, time in a sort of Runic rhyme." Does the meaning of this line differ for the two types of bells?

Analyze: TAKING THINGS APART

4a. Identify the different meanings bells have for the speaker.

Synthesize: BRINGING THINGS TOGETHER

4b. Why are the sounds so significant to the speaker? What do they represent?

Evaluate: MAKING JUDGMENTS

5a. Decide whether or not there is a pattern to sentence and stanza length in the poem.

Extend: CONNECTING IDEAS

5b. Using Poe's style, write a stanza for a funeral bell.

Understanding Literature

REPETITION. Review the definition for **repetition** in the Handbook of Literary Terms. The word *bells* is repeated many times within each stanza. What other words are repeated? What two-line phrase is repeated twice exactly and a third time, slightly altered, in stanza 4? Where else in the poem is the line repeated?

ONOMATOPOEIA. Review the definition for **onomatopoeia** in the Handbook of Literary Terms. Then refer to the chart that you created for Literary Tools on page 80. Which words sound like small, light bells? Which words sound like large, heavy bells? What repeated phrases in the poem have the rhythmic quality of ringing bells?

Writer's Journal

1. Write a **letter** to Poe telling him which description of bells is the most effective and why, or recommending to him other bells you believe should have been included and giving reasons why.

2. Write **performance notes** telling a chorus how to read a selection from "The Bells." Mark the stanzas for rate of delivery, pitch, and volume, depending on which bells are highlighted in that part of the poem.

3. Consider the way Poe uses the sounds of words to create the sounds and moods of different bells. Think about another sound that can have different meanings. For example, a dog might make a welcoming bark, a pained yelp, or a menacing growl. Choose a sound and write a **poem** about it to read to the class or to share with a classmate. Try to use the techniques of onomatopoeia and repetition. You may find it useful to consult a thesaurus to find synonyms with appropriate sounds.

Integrating the Language Arts

Language, Grammar, and Style

UNDERSTOOD SUBJECT: *You.* **Understood subjects** are sometimes used in sentences that make requests or give commands. Poe's poem "The Bells" uses an understood subject throughout. This is the one place in English when a subject is not stated. We understand that the writer is talking to us, the reader. If we were to state the subject it would be *you.* Understood subjects are indicated by putting the pronoun *you* in parentheses: (you).

EXAMPLE: (You) hear the sledges with the bells—.

Review the Language Arts Survey 3.32, "Avoiding Problems Caused by Understood Subjects and Nouns of Direct Address." Then find the subject and verb for each of the following sentences:

1. The bells are keeping time.
2. Hear the alarm bells.
3. Hear the tolling of the bells.
4. You can see and hear the bells of the poem.
5. Use appropriate sound in your poetry!

Study and Research & Applied English

RESEARCHING POE ON THE INTERNET. Imagine that you want to apply for a grant to research places associated with Edgar Allan Poe. Use the Internet to find locations that you would want to visit. One site you may find useful is http://www.comnet.ca/~forrest/haunts.html. Then write a grant proposal stating what places you need to visit, and why.

Speaking and Listening

CHORAL READING. In a group of three prepare a choral reading of one section of "The Bells." Consider single voices for some lines. Decide the pitch, speed, and articulation of the words of each line to create the sound and dramatic effect of the bells. Then give your oral interpretation to the class.

"The Song of Wandering Aengus" by W. B. Yeats

Reader's resource

"The Song of Wandering Aengus" was published in *The Wind Among the Reeds* (1899). William Butler Yeats drew much inspiration for his poetry from Celtic myths. Aengus was the Celtic god of love who spent much of his life wandering. He became enamored of a fairy woman and spent his life fruitlessly trying to find her again.

About *the* AUTHOR

William Butler (W. B.) Yeats (1865–1939) is remembered as an important Irish cultural leader, as a major playwright, and as one of the greatest poets of the twentieth century. Born in Dublin, Yeats grew up in London and County Sligo, Ireland. He studied art before leaving school to pursue his writing. As a young man, he fell deeply in love with a beautiful actress and Irish revolutionary named Maude Gonne, who inspired many of his poems about love. For her, Yeats took up the cause of the Irish nationalist movement for independence.

In 1889 Yeats published his first major poem, *The Wanderings of Oisin,* based on Irish folklore. It grew out of his involvement with the Celtic Revival, a movement against the cultural influences of English rule in Ireland during the Victorian period. The movement sought to promote the spirit of Ireland's native heritage.

Along with Lady Augusta Gregory, Yeats founded the Irish National Theatre, now known as the Abbey Theatre, and Yeats became its director. For the theater he wrote plays based on Irish themes, some of which used innovative costuming and movement derived from Japanese Nō drama. In 1917, Yeats married Georgie Hyde-Lees and moved into a restored Norman tower called Thoor Ballylee. Yeats had always had a keen interest in spiritualism. As a young man living in London he became interested in mysticism and joined the Theosophical Society. In 1922, Yeats became a member of the Irish senate in the Irish Free State (Eire). The following year he won the Nobel Prize for literature. When he died at the age of 73, he left behind a varied, fascinating body of work.

Literary TOOLS

ALLEGORY. An **allegory** is a work in which each element symbolizes, or represents, something else. This poem is traditionally read as an allegory for a person's aging. As you read, try to figure out how this poem could be read as an allegory for the creative process.

RHYME. Rhyme is the repetition of sounds at the ends of words. *End rhyme* is the use of rhyming words at the ends of lines.

Graphic Organizer

As you read, figure out the rhyme scheme of each stanza in the poem. The first stanza has been done for you.

	RHYME SCHEME
Stanza 1	*abcbdefe*
Stanza 2	
Stanza 3	

Reader's Journal

Did you ever meet someone who vanished from your life whom you would like to see again? Describe that person and what interested you about him or her.

The Song of Wandering Aengus

W. B. Yeats

I went out to the hazel wood,[1]
Because a fire was in my head,
And cut and peeled a hazel wand,
And hooked a berry to a thread;
5   And when white moths were on the wing,
And moth-like stars were flickering out,
I dropped the berry in a stream
And caught a little silver trout.

When I had laid it on the floor
10 I went to blow the fire aflame,
But something rustled on the floor,
And some one called me by my name:
It had become a glimmering girl
With apple blossom in her hair
15 Who called me by my name and ran
And faded through the brightening air.

Though I am old with wandering
Through hollow lands and hilly lands,
I will find out where she has gone,
20 And kiss her lips and take her hands;
And walk among long <u>dappled</u> grass,
And pluck till time and times are done
The silver apples of the moon,
The golden apples of the sun. ∎

---

1. **hazel wood.** Woods made up of hazel trees from the birch family

Why did the speaker
go to the hazel wood?

What did the speaker
catch?

What happened to
the trout?

What will the speaker
do "till time and
times are done"?

**words
for
everyday
use**   dap • pled (dap´əld) adj., spotted. The <u>dappled</u> pony with all her spots was my favorite.

Imagine that you are Aengus as an old man. Are you imagining the girl as she once was or how she would be today? Explain.

Investigate, *Inquire,* and Imagine

Recall: GATHERING FACTS → ### Interpret: FINDING MEANING

1a. What reason does the speaker give for going to the hazel wood?

1b. What does this reason suggest about the speaker's age and character?

2a. Into what does the trout change?

2b. What effect does the trout's transformation have on the speaker's life?

3a. What does the speaker want to do with the girl once he finds her again?

3b. What is the speaker's attitude toward his search? toward aging?

Analyze: TAKING THINGS APART → ### Synthesize: BRINGING THINGS TOGETHER

4a. Identify the verb tenses of the three stanzas and explain why the tenses change.

4b. What will finding the girl enable the speaker to do?

Evaluate: MAKING JUDGMENTS → ### Extend: CONNECTING IDEAS

5a. To what degree has the speaker changed by the end of the poem?

5b. How are youth, adulthood, and old age portrayed in popular culture? How do these portrayals contrast to those in the poem?

Understanding *Literature*

ALLEGORY. Review the definition for **allegory** in the Handbook of Literary Terms. How can this poem be read as an allegory for the creative process? What might the fire in the speaker's head symbolize in this interpretation? What might the transformation of the fish symbolize? What might the quest of the aged speaker symbolize?

RHYME. Review the definition for **rhyme** in the Handbook of Literary Terms. Then look at the chart you made in Literary Tools on page 87. Which two stanzas share the same rhyme scheme? What effect does Yeats's repetition accomplish by this rhyme scheme?

Writer's Journal

1. Imagine you are the speaker. Write a **love letter** to the person you are seeking, explaining what he or she means to you.

2. Imagine that you are the speaker as an old man. Write a **journal entry** describing the most inspirational event in your life. What happened? How did the event transform your life? How does it continue to affect your life?

3. In the poem, Aengus, as an old man, says that he will pluck the "silver apples of the moon" and the "golden apples of the sun." Write a **paragraph** explaining what this means.

Integrating the Language Arts

Language, Grammar, and Style

SENTENCE COMPLETERS FOR ACTION VERBS #1. Review the Language Arts Survey 3.22, "Sentence Completers for Action Verbs." In the sentence "The Irish love Yeats's poetry," the verb is *love* and the subject is *Irish*. After subject and verb are found, two more steps will identify a completer. Ask "*Irish love* what?" The answer is *Yeats's poetry*. Now, eliminate any extra words. *Yeats* can be eliminated, so the direct object is *poetry*. Remember that some verbs do not need completers!

In the following sentences, underline the subject once, the verb twice, and circle the direct object.

1. Yeats had been collecting ancient stories.
2. These tales capture Irish history and dreams.
3. The poet's plays, poems, and stories retell these myths.
4. Poetry captures the Irish spirit.
5. Cab drivers, servers, street cleaners have memorized and can recite Yeats's poems.

Speaking and Listening

EXTENDING THE DIALOGUE. Imagine that Aengus meets the girl again. With a partner, play the roles of Aengus and the girl. Ask each other questions that are based on underlying ideas in the poem. For example, Aengus might ask, "Why did you call out my name?" The girl might ask, "Why was I turned into a girl?"

Study and Research

YEATS IN MUSIC. Songwriter and singer Van Morrison, a fellow Irishman, makes references to Yeats's poetry in his songs. Listen to one of the songs below and read the Yeats poem that it references. Study the poem and the song. Then write a paragraph describing the meaning that Van Morrison ascribes to the references and indicate if he changes the original meaning of the poem's lyrics. Here is a partial list of Yeats's poems and Van Morrison's songs that reference them:

Yeats Poems	Van Morrison Songs
"A Vision"	"Rave On, John Donne"
"Crazy Jane on God"	"Crazy Jane on God"
"Under Ben Bulben"	"Here Comes the Knight"

Literary
T O O L S

SPEAKER AND EFFECT. The **speaker** is the character who speaks in, or narrates, a poem—the voice assumed by the writer. The **effect** of a literary work is the general impression or emotional impact that it achieves. As you read, determine with what kind of eye the speaker creates the descriptions in the poem and what effect the poem creates upon the reader.

IMAGE. An **image** is language that creates a concrete representation of an object or an experience.

Graphic Organizer

As you read, fill in the sensory detail chart below.

SIGHT	
SOUND	gravel-voiced
TOUCH	
TASTE	
SMELL	

Reader's Journal

What is unique about the place where you live?

"Local Sensibilities"
by Wing Tek Lum

Reader's resource

"**Local Sensibilities**" was originally published in Wing Tek Lum's volume of verse *Expounding the Doubtful Points* (1987). Lum, in a series of vignettes, or descriptive scenes, paints a living portrait of his native Hawaii. He gives us a look at the industry, characters, animal life, vocabulary, and history that create this "unique universe" that he calls home.

GEOGRAPHY CONNECTION. In 1959 Hawaii became the fiftieth state. It consists of eight major islands and numerous islets in the Pacific Ocean. The Hawaiian islands—Hawaii, Oahu, Kahoolawe, Kauai, Lanai, Maui, Molokai, and Niihau—are of volcanic origin and are edged with coral reefs. Tourists flock to Hawaii to enjoy its abundant sunshine, green plants, gaily colored flowers, coral beaches with rolling white surf, and palm trees. Sugarcane and pineapples, grown chiefly on large company-owned plantations, are the major agricultural products and the basis of the islands' principal industry, food processing. More ethnic and cultural groups are represented in Hawaii than in any other state. These include Chinese, Filipinos, Koreans, Portuguese, Germans, Japanese, and Puerto Ricans. Due to intermarriage, pureblooded Hawaiians make up only a very small percentage of the population. Japanese now represent roughly a third of the population. During World War II, many Japanese and Japanese Americans were sent to relocation centers because the U.S. government feared they would assist the Japanese if Japan invaded the United States. The evacuees suffered property losses estimated at $400 million, and the government was severely criticized for depriving citizens of their civil liberties.

About *the* AUTHOR

Wing Tek Lum lives in Hawaii. When asked to provide biographical information about himself, he declined, saying that readers should "let the poem speak for itself."

Local Sensibilities

Wing Tek Lum

Monument to Duke Kahanamoku, the father of modern surfing, in Waikiki, Hawaii.

When I see a pineapple,
I do not think of an <u>exotic</u> fruit sliced in rings
    to be served with ham,
more the summer jobs at the cannery
5   driving a forklift or packing wedges on the line.

When I hear the name "Duke,"[1]
I envision someone other than that movie cowboy,

What does the speaker think of when he sees a pineapple?

---

1. **"Duke."** American movie actor John Wayne, who starred in *True Grit* and many other Westerns and war films

words for everyday use

ex • ot • ic (ig zä´tik) *adj.*, not native to the place where found; foreign; exciting or mysterious. *Our vacation destination was the <u>exotic</u> island of Tahiti.*

gravel-voiced, a true grit idol of the late night set;
instead I see a white-haired surfer by his long board,
10   palms so large, flashing smiles along the beach.

When I think of a man-of-war,
it is not the name of a Triple Crown horse
          pacing a stud farm that comes to mind first;
rather I picture the Portuguese kind
15   whose stings must be salved by rubbing sand.

How can you remedy a sting by a man-of-war?

When I use the word "packages,"
it is usually not a reference to the parcels
          waiting for me at the post office,
rather the paper sacks I get
20   from the supermarket to lug my groceries home.

When I read the term "Jap,"
the image of a kamikaze[2] pilot now turned to Sony exports
          is not what I see;
mainly it is the Sand Island roundup[3] and those old men
25   who still wince long after the 442nd has marched back.

What happened to Japanese-American men during World War II?

When I think of Hawaii,
I do not fancy myself lolling under palm trees,
          a backdrop of <u>verdant</u> cliffs, caressed by a balmy breeze;
instead I give thanks for classmates and our family graves,
30   this unique universe that we have called our home. ∎

Where does the speaker live? For what does he give thanks?

---

2. **kamikaze.** Member of a Japanese air attack corps in
World War II assigned to make a suicidal crash on a target
3. **Sand Island roundup.** Roundup of Japanese
Americans who were sent to detention in relocation centers during World War II

words for everyday use

ver • dant (ver´dənt) adj., green. In Gauguin's landscapes of Tahiti, <u>verdant</u> hills and purple mountains abound.

Respond to the SELECTION

Imagine you are the speaker. How do you see Hawaii differently than the tourists do?

Investigate, Inquire, and Imagine

Recall: GATHERING FACTS

1a. Where do many local people work in the summer?

2a. What special characters, animal life, vocabulary, and history does the speaker associate with Hawaii?

3a. What does the speaker think of when he thinks of Hawaii?

Interpret: FINDING MEANING

1b. What do most people think of when they see a pineapple?

2b. What point of view does the speaker use in giving his descriptions?

3b. How do tourists view Hawaii? What do they do when they go there?

Analyze: TAKING THINGS APART

4a. Identify how the speaker creates a sense of place in the poem.

Synthesize: BRINGING THINGS TOGETHER

4b. Why is the poem titled "Local Sensibilities"?

Evaluate: MAKING JUDGMENTS

5a. Evaluate how effectively the poet portrays Hawaii as a separate, special place that goes beyond the stereotypes a tourist might have. How does he do it?

Extend: CONNECTING IDEAS

5b. Write one or more stanzas for a free-verse poem that describes where you live, using Lum's poem as a model.

Understanding Literature

SPEAKER AND EFFECT. Review the definitions for **speaker** and **effect** in the Handbook of Literary Terms. With what kind of eye does the speaker create the descriptions in the poem? What effect, or general impression, does the poem create upon the reader?

IMAGE. Review the definition for **image** in the Handbook of Literary Terms. An image is also the vivid mental picture created in the reader's mind by that language. The images in a literary work are referred to, collectively, as the work's *imagery*. Refer to the sensory detail chart you made as a graphic organizer on page 92. How does the imagery used in poem appeal to your senses of sight, sound, touch, taste, and smell? What setting does the poem's imagery evoke?

Writer's Journal

1. Imagine you are a tourist in Hawaii. Write a **postcard** to a friend describing what you notice about the island.

2. Imagine you are the speaker. Write an **editorial** for the local newspaper describing what troubles you when you see the older Japanese-American men and think about the Sand Island roundup.

3. Write a **tour guide** for visitors who want to see Hawaii in a way that most tourists never would.

Integrating the Language Arts

Language, Grammar, and Style

SENTENCE COMPLETERS FOR ACTION VERBS #2. Sometimes the direct object is received by someone or something. This receiver is called the **indirect object**.

EXAMPLE: Mike gave me a red pencil.

Follow the steps in the Language Arts Survey 3.22 to find the direct object listed in the sentence above: verb = *gave*; subject = *Mike*, direct object (pencil). In this sentence someone received the pencil. To find this receiver (called the **indirect object**), add an additional step: Ask who received the pencil (direct object). The answer is *me*. A sentence without a direct object cannot have an indirect object.

In each of the following sentences, identify the subject, the verb, the direct object, and the indirect object if one is present.

1. Wing Tek Lum shows us native Hawaiian attitudes.
2. Scholars have given everyone several explanations.
3. Few purebred native people still exist.
4. Intermarriage and easy travel can explain many reasons.
5. Everyone can go everywhere and marry anyone.

Study and Research

RELOCATION CENTERS. Research the use of relocation centers for Japanese Americans in World War II. Why were Japanese Americans interned? How many evacuees were there? Where were the relocation centers located? What did those in the camps do? What were the conditions of the relocation camps? In what way, if any, was restitution eventually made to these Japanese Americans? Write an outline and a composition to demonstrate what you have learned. You may want to read the Language Arts Survey 2.30, "Formal Outlines," and 2.24–2.28, "Organizing Ideas."

Speaking and Listening

ORAL INTERPRETATION. With two or three classmates, locate another poem that celebrates a specific location. Write an introduction for the poem, and then rehearse the poems in your small group using expression, gesture, and body movements. You might also want to include music, visual images such as a slide show, and authentic food from the area. Finally, present your poem to the class. Before you begin, you may want to read the Language Arts Survey 4.19, "Oral Interpretation."

"A Simile"
by N. Scott Momaday

and

"Metaphor"
by Eve Merriam

 Literary T O O L S

THEME. A **theme** is a central idea in a literary work. As you read each poem, think about what its theme or themes might be.

FIGURATIVE LANGUAGE. **Figurative language** is writing or speech meant to be understood imaginatively instead of literally. Many writers, especially poets, use figurative language to help readers to see things in new ways. Simile and metaphor are two examples of figurative language. A *simile* is a comparison using *like* or *as*. For example, if you say, "Jennifer dances like a willow," you would be using a simile. A *metaphor* is a figure of speech in which one thing is spoken or written about as if it were another. For example, if you say "Jennifer is a dancing willow," you would be using a metaphor. Similes and metaphors encourage you to make comparisons between two things. The two "things" involved are the writer's actual subject, the *tenor* of the figure of speech, and another thing to which the subject is likened, the *vehicle* of the figure of speech. In the example sentences, *Jennifer* is the tenor and *willow* is the vehicle.

Graphic Organizer

As you read the two poems, make a chart for each one. On the left, give the tenor of the figure of speech. On the right, list the vehicle.

"A Simile"

Tenor	Vehicle

"Metaphor"

Tenor	Vehicle

Reader's resource

"**A Simile**," by N. Scott Momaday, uses a simile to explore what can happen to body language when people become tense because they aren't getting along well. "A Simile" has been published in a number of Native American anthologies, including *Carriers of the Dream* (1975).

In "**Metaphor**," Eve Merriam uses a metaphor to explore how to get the most out of each new day. "Metaphor" was published in *A Sky Full of Poems* (1986).

 Reader's Journal

What figurative language would you use to describe your attitude toward a tense relationship with someone and your attitude toward a new day?

A Simile

N. Scott Momaday

What did we say to each other
that now we are as the deer
who walk in single file
with heads high
5   with ears forward
with eyes watchful
with hooves always placed on firm
ground in whose limbs there is latent
flight   ■

How do the deer walk?

Respond*to the*
SELECTION

What words do you think were exchanged between the speaker of "A Simile" and the other
person referred to in the poem?

Metaphor

Eve Merriam

Morning is
a new sheet of paper
for you to write on.

According to the speaker, what is morning?

Whatever you want to say,
5   all day,
until night
folds it up
and files it away.

What happens at night?

The bright words and the
dark words are gone
until dawn
and a new day
to write on. ■

What does dawn bring?

Respond *to the* SELECTION

What do you want to write on your sheet of paper today?

About *the* AUTHORS

N. Scott Momaday (1934–), poet, novelist, playwright, and nonfiction writer, has spent his life teaching and writing about Native American folklore, history, and mythology. Proud of his Native American heritage, the author grew up on Kiowa, Navajo, Apache, and Pueblo Indian reservations. After graduating from the University of New Mexico, Momaday earned a doctorate in English literature at Stanford University. He currently teaches English at the University of Arizona. In 1969, Momaday won the Pulitzer Prize for his novel *House Made of Dawn,* which tells the story of a young Native American torn between his ancestral roots and twentieth-century mainstream society. In his best-known work, *The Way to Rainy Mountain* (1969), the author combines history, personal anecdotes, and myths imagistically. His collections of poetry include *Angle of Geese and Other Poems* (1974) and *The Gourd Dancer* (1976). Also an artist, Momaday has illustrated some of his books.

Eve Merriam (1916–1992), an award-winning poet and playwright, wrote more than thirty books. Born in Philadelphia, Pennsylvania, she attended Cornell University, the University of Pennsylvania, the University of Wisconsin, and Columbia University. She taught and lectured at many colleges. Her first book of poetry, *Family Circle* (1946), was selected for the Yale Series of Younger Poets by the renowned poet Archibald MacLeish. Other poetry collections include *The Trouble with Love* and *It Doesn't Have to Rhyme* (1964). Her books *After Nora Slammed the Door* (1964) and *Growing Up Female in America: Ten Lives* (1971) are about women's rights. Merriam also wrote television scripts, advertising copy, song lyrics, fiction, and children's books. In 1981, she was named the winner of the National Council for Teachers of English Award for Excellence in Poetry for Children. Merriam was a resident of New York City for many years.

Investigate, *Inquire,* and Imagine

Recall: GATHERING FACTS

1a. In "A Simile," what does the speaker wonder about?

2a. In "A Simile," how do the two people walk?

3a. In "Metaphor," what is morning?

4a. In "Metaphor," what does night do?

Interpret: FINDING MEANING

1b. In "A Simile," what kind of words do you think were spoken between the two people?

2b. In "A Simile," what does the deerlike stance of the two people reveal?

3b. In "Metaphor," what does the new day mean if viewed as it is in this poem?

4b. In "Metaphor," what happens to everything that one does during the day?

Analyze: TAKING THINGS APART

5a. Tone is the emotional attitude toward the reader or toward the subject implied by a literary work. Identify the tone of the two poems. How did you arrive at your assessment?

Synthesize: BRINGING THINGS TOGETHER

5b. What might the speaker suggest to resolve the conflict in "A Simile"? What do you think the speaker of "Metaphor" might suggest if you make mistakes on your paper?

Understanding *Literature*

THEME. Review the definition for **theme** in the Handbook of Literary Terms. What do you think is the major theme of "A Simile"? What is the principal theme of "Metaphor"?

FIGURATIVE LANGUAGE. Review the definition for **figurative language** in the Handbook of Literary Terms and the graphic organizer you made. What simile is used in "A Simile"? What metaphor is used in "Metaphor"?

Writer's Journal

1. Write three **similes** comparing yourself to animals or objects that you believe help reflect who you are.
2. Write an **extended metaphor** about a friendship or other relationship you have with someone. An extended metaphor is a point-by-point presentation of one thing as though it were another. Eve Merriam's poem is an extended metaphor.
3. Write a **paragraph** in which you explore the theme for a poem you want to write.

Integrating the Language Arts

Language, Grammar, and Style

CONTRACTIONS IN SENTENCES. **Contractions** can cause students problems because they may combine two different sentence parts in one word. Before finding the parts of the sentence, always write out the words that the contraction combines: doesn't = does not, It's = it is, I'll = I will. Review the Language Arts Survey 3.29, "Working with Negatives and Contractions."

In each of the following sentences, write out all contractions. Then identify the simple subject and verb.

1. N. Scott Momaday's poems don't present Hollywood stereotypes.
2. Many of the best poets won't use tired images.
3. Old images can't arouse vivid mental pictures.
4. Readers shouldn't expect tired stuff in poems.
5. Wonderful ancient adventures haven't bored people.

Speaking and Listening & Collaborative Learning

ORAL INTERPRETATION. Form small groups of four or five students. Each student should select a poem with a simile or metaphor. You may want to review the Language Arts Survey 4.19, "Oral Interpretation" before you begin. Then sit in a circle and take turns presenting your poems. As you listen to the speaker before you, take notes on his or her poem. Then write a transition to present a logical connection to your selection. The first presenter can write an introduction to all the poems. Finally, make a presentation to the class, including transitional statements and the introduction. You might find it useful to look for appropriate poems in poetry anthologies. If you are interested in a certain poet, try finding examples of his or her work on the Internet.

Applied English

RÉSUMÉ. Imagine that you have had ten years experiencing each day as a new piece of paper. Think about what you will have accomplished in those years. Write a résumé listing what you would most like your résumé to reflect about you. You should include a career objective, work experience, education, hobbies, and references. Before you begin, you might find it useful to examine the sample résumé in the Language Arts Survey 6.8, "Writing a Résumé."

"Boast Not, Proud English" by Roger Williams

Reader's resource

HISTORY CONNECTION. Roger Williams, a minister living in colonial America, recognized that Native Americans were not the uncivilized savages that many of the colonists believed them to be. He criticized people who called them heathens, maintaining that no Christian is completely good and free of sin. Williams expresses these beliefs in his poem **"Boast Not, Proud English."**

About the AUTHOR

Roger Williams (c.1603–1683), colonist, minister, and reformer, developed an interest in church reform while serving as a chaplain to Sir William Masham at Otis in Essex County. He became a Puritan and left England for the American colonies. He soon dissociated himself from the Puritans, however, and moved first to the Separatist Plymouth Colony and then to Salem, where he served as a pastor and practiced his democratic views of church government. The Massachusetts General Court sentenced him to exile for his firm opposition to authoritarianism. He fled, seeking refuge in Rhode Island. There he founded the city of Providence and became state governor for several years. Williams believed deeply in personal and religious freedom and made Providence Plantations open to all religions. While Williams contributed greatly to establishing religious freedom, he did oppose some groups himself.

Williams's religious ideas were not popular, nor were his relatively liberal ideas about Native Americans. He developed a good relationship with the Native American people of Rhode Island, but in his last years as governor, difficulties developed between the colonists and the indigenous people. One of Williams's most impressive writings is *A Key into the Language of America*. This book became a useful tool for people who wanted to convert Native Americans to Christianity.

Literary TOOLS

COUPLET. A **couplet** is two lines of verse that usually rhyme. As you read, decide which two couplets do not rhyme conventionally.

AIM. A writer's **aim** is his or her purpose or goal. People may write with one or more aims in mind. Among possible aims are the following: to inform (expository/informational writing); to entertain, enrich, enlighten, and/or use an artistic medium, such as fiction or poetry, to share a perspective (imaginative writing); to share a story about an event (narrative writing); to reflect (personal/expressive writing); to persuade readers or listeners to respond in some way, such as to agree with a position, change a view on an issue, reach an agreement, or perform an action (persuasive/argumentative writing).

Organizer

As you read, make a chart. On the left, list important points that Williams makes in the poem. On the right, list the aim Williams intended for each point. One example has been done for you.

Points	Aim
English settlers should not boast about being superior to Native Americans.	persuade

Reader's Journal

When have you stood up for your beliefs? What happened as a result?

Boast Not, Proud English

Roger Williams

Corn Planter, 1786. Bartoli. Private Collection.

Boast not, proud English, of thy birth and blood:
　Thy brother Indian is by birth as good.
Of one blood God made him, and thee, and all.
　As wise, as fair, as strong, as personal.[1]
By nature, wrath's his portion, thine, no more
　Till Grace his soul and thine in Christ restore.[2]
Make sure thy second birth,[3] or thou shalt see
　Heaven ope[4] to Indians wild, but shut to thee. ∎

1. **as personal.** As much a person (as you)
2. **wrath's his portion, . . . restore.** The Puritans believed that every person deserved God's wrath because of Adam's original sin and that only through God's grace could people be saved, or "restored." Williams is saying that in this respect, as in others, the Native American and the English settler are alike.
3. **second birth.** Religious or spiritual awakening
4. **ope.** Open

Whom does the speaker address in this poem?

In what way, according to the speaker, are the Native Americans and the English connected?

What does the speaker warn that boastful English people might see?

What did many of the English settlers believe about Native Americans?

Investigate, *Inquire,* and Imagine

Recall: GATHERING FACTS

1a. What does the speaker tell the English settlers not to do?

2a. What might the English settlers find if they do not make sure of their "second birth"?

Interpret: FINDING MEANING

1b. What reasons does the speaker give for the warning he issues to the settlers?

2b. How do you think the settlers would have reacted to the last two lines? Why?

Analyze: TAKING THINGS APART

3a. Identify the beliefs about religion that are expressed in the poem.

Synthesize: BRINGING THINGS TOGETHER

3b. Today Williams is considered one of the visionaries who helped to formulate the ideas of pluralism, democracy, freedom of speech and religion, and equality under the law enshrined in the United States Constitution. Why do you think this might be so?

Evaluate: MAKING JUDGMENTS

4a. How effective would Williams's arguments be today?

Extend: CONNECTING IDEAS

4b. Some people find it difficult to accept and understand cultures different from their own. Name some cultures in the United States that are frequently misunderstood and explain why this might be the case.

Understanding *Literature*

COUPLET. Review the definition for **couplet** in the Handbook of Literary Terms. Which two couplets do not rhyme in modern English?

AIM. Review the definition for **aim** in the Handbook of Literary Terms. Then review the chart you made as a graphic organizer on page 103. What were Williams's aims in writing "Boast Not, Proud English"? What points does Williams provide to achieve these aims?

Writer's Journal

1. Write a **paragraph** for your social studies teacher explaining what many English settlers believed in the seventeenth century about the Native Americans.

2. Imagine that you are a seventeenth-century English settler. Write a **newspaper editorial** expressing your reaction to Williams's poem.

3. Using contemporary language, write a **lyric poem** encouraging Americans to accept minorities. You may or may not want to use couplets.

Integrating
the Language Arts

Language, Grammar, and Style

PERSONAL AND INDEFINITE PRONOUNS IN SENTENCES. Pronouns are words that take the place of nouns. You are already familiar with **personal pronouns**, which substitute for the names of specific persons or things. The personal pronouns include *I, me, you, he, him, she, her, it, we, us, they,* and *them.*

   Indefinite pronouns refer to unspecified or unknown persons or things. These pronouns include *somebody, several, few, anyone, everyone,* and *all.* More are listed in the table in the Language Arts Survey 3.54, "Types of Pronouns."

   Identify the personal pronouns and indefinite pronouns in each of the following sentences.

1. Roger Williams's poem teaches everyone lessons.
2. Many have different cultures.
3. Roger Williams wrote a poem for one of these.
4. They should not be disrespected, according to Williams.
5. Roger Williams showed them respect; he thought everybody deserved polite treatment.

Media Literacy & Applied English

BOOK JACKET. Design a book jacket for the writings of Roger Williams about Native Americans. On the front draw a picture suggestive of Williams's views. On the inside cover, write a summary highlighting the contents of the book and promotional copy that will prompt readers to buy the book. You will need to do some research about Williams's other writings about Native Americans.

Study and Research & Media Literacy

TELEVISION INTERVIEW. With a partner, research the life and beliefs of Roger Williams. Then conduct a television interview. One student should play the role of a television interviewer, while the other should play the role of Williams.

"BIRCHES"

by Robert Frost

Reader's resource

The *setting* is the time and place of a literary work. Robert Frost's **"Birches"** recalls a winter setting in rural New England. Sometimes, in that part of the country, winter rain falls on trees and becomes frozen, so that the branches and twigs appear to be made of crystal. Young birches, carrying that heavy load of ice, are often bent to the ground.

A few months after returning to the United States from England in 1915, Frost was asked by Tufts University to read three of his as yet unpublished poems: "Birches," "The Road Not Taken," and "The Sound of Trees." The next day, at a meeting, *The Atlantic Monthly* asked Frost if he had any new poems that the magazine could publish. The editor said he was willing to publish them sight unseen. Frost pulled out of his pocket the three poems that he had written only the night before. And so, in the August 1915 issue of *The Atlantic Monthly,* "A Group of Poems by Robert Frost" appeared, marking the first time any of Frost's poems were published in the United States since his volume *North of Boston.*

About the AUTHOR

Robert Frost (1874–1963) was born in San Francisco and raised in New Hampshire and Massachusetts. In 1892, he graduated from high school in Lawrence, Massachusetts, as co-valedictorian with Elinor White, whom he married three years later. After spending less than a semester at Dartmouth College in 1892, Frost returned to Lawrence, where he worked in a textile mill and taught school. Five years later, Frost entered Harvard. There he studied Latin, which he felt helped him to develop word sense. He studied at Harvard for three years before leaving for an experiment in poultry farming. In 1900, Frost moved to a farm in Derry, New Hampshire. When he was thirty-eight, he sold his farm and sailed with his wife and four children from Boston to Glasgow, determined to make his reputation as a poet in England. While there he published his first book of poetry, *A Boy's Will,* in 1913, and his second, *North of Boston,* a year later. Frost returned home in 1915 with the reputation he had been seeking.

In his lifetime, Frost received many awards and honors, including Pulitzer Prizes for several of his books and over forty honorary degrees from colleges and universities. In 1960 he was invited to read at the inauguration of President John F. Kennedy.

BIRCHES

Robert Frost

When I see birches bend to left and right
Across the lines of straighter darker trees,
I like to think some boy's been swinging them.
But swinging doesn't bend them down to stay

5   As ice storms do. Often you must have seen them
        Loaded with ice a sunny winter morning
        After a rain. They click upon themselves
        As the breeze rises, and turn many-colored
        As the stir cracks and crazes their enamel.[1]

10   Soon the sun's warmth makes them shed crystal shells
        Shattering and avalanching on the snow crust—
        Such heaps of broken glass to sweep away
        You'd think the inner dome of heaven had fallen.
        They are dragged to the withered <u>bracken</u> by the load,

15   And they seem not to break; though once they are bowed
        So low for long, they never right themselves:
        You may see their trunks arching in the woods
        Years afterwards, trailing their leaves on the ground
        Like girls on hands and knees that throw their hair

20   Before them over their heads to dry in the sun.
        But I was going to say when Truth broke in
        With all her matter of fact about the ice storm,
        I should prefer to have some boy bend them
        As he went out and in to fetch the cows—

25   Some boy too far from town to learn baseball,
        Whose only play was what he found himself,
        Summer or winter, and could play alone.
        One by one he <u>subdued</u> his father's trees
        By riding them down over and over again

What does the speaker like to think bends the birches? What actually bends the birches?

To what does the speaker compare the broken ice?

To what does the speaker compare the bent birches?

What kind of boy does the speaker imagine bending the birches?

---

1. **crazes their enamel.** Scratches the shiny white surface of the birch trunks

words for everyday use

brack • en (brak´ən) n., large, coarse, weedy ferns occurring in meadows and woods. *The deer heard the hunter step on the <u>bracken</u> and vanished.*

sub • due (sub dōō´) vt., overcome; control; reduce. *With their powerful longbows, the English soldiers quickly <u>subdued</u> the Scottish rebels.*

30   Until he took the stiffness out of them,
      And not one but hung limp, not one was left
      For him to conquer. He learned all there was
      To learn about not launching out too soon
      And so not carrying the tree away

35   Clear to the ground. He always kept his poise
      To the top branches, climbing carefully
      With the same pains you use to fill a cup
      Up to the brim, and even above the brim.
      Then he flung outward, feet first, with a swish,

40   Kicking his way down through the air to the ground.
      So was I once myself a swinger of birches.
      And so I dream of going back to be.
      It's when I'm weary of considerations,
      And life is too much like a pathless wood

45   Where your face burns and tickles with the cobwebs[2]
      Broken across it, and one eye is weeping
      From a twig's having <u>lashed</u> across it open.
      I'd like to get away from earth awhile
      And then come back to it and begin over.

50   May no fate willfully misunderstand me
      And half grant what I wish and snatch me away
      Not to return. Earth's the right place for love:
      I don't know where it's likely to go better.
      I'd like to go by climbing a birch tree,

55   And climb black branches up a snow-white trunk
      Toward heaven, till the tree could bear no more,
      But dipped its top and set me down again.
      That would be good both going and coming back.
      One could do worse than be a swinger of birches. ■

What kind of endeavor is bending a birch? To what activity is swinging a birch compared?

When does the speaker dream of becoming a swinger of birches? Why does the speaker wish for this?

Does the speaker wish to leave the earth forever? Why, or why not?

---

2. **cobwebs.** The speaker refers to the weblike pattern of lines across the face, perhaps brought on by his grief as well as his age.

words for everyday use   lash (lash) *vt.,* strike hard with great force. *The driver <u>lashed</u> the horse so it would gallop.*

Which explanation for the bent birches do you prefer, that they were bent by ice or by a boy? Why?

Investigate, *Inquire,* and Imagine

Recall: GATHERING FACTS

1a. What does the speaker like to think is the cause when he or she sees bent birches? What really caused them to bend?

2a. How does the narrator describe the birch trees when they lose their ice? What makes the narrator talk about the reality of ice storms and their effect on birches?

3a. What does the speaker say the boy learned about trees? What happened when he got to the top? What does the speaker know about swinging from trees?

Interpret: FINDING MEANING

1b. Why does the speaker prefer to think this has caused the trees to bend?

2b. What does it say about human frailty and the power of nature if an ice storm and not some boy bent the trees?

3b. How does the speaker's imagination show in this story of the boy?

Analyze: TAKING THINGS APART

4a. In the last line, the narrator says, "One could do worse than be a swinger of birches." What does it mean to be a swinger of birches?

Synthesize: BRINGING THINGS TOGETHER

4b. Why does the speaker want to be a swinger of birches?

Perspective: LOOKING AT OTHER VIEWS

5a. Why is the speaker content to merely "dream" about swinging from birches?

Empathy: SEEING FROM INSIDE

5b. Imagine yourself in the speaker's place. How could you make the experience come alive again?

Understanding *Literature*

SYMBOL. Review the definition for **symbol** in the Handbook of Literary Terms. What does swinging on a birch tree toward heaven symbolize?

METAPHOR AND SIMILE. Review the definitions for **metaphor** and **simile** in the Handbook of Literary Terms. Then refer to the chart you made as a graphic organizer. Is the comparison of ice-coated branches and crystal shells a metaphor or a simile? Is the comparison of life to a pathless wood a metaphor or a simile? What characteristic of life is represented by a pathless wood?

Writer's Journal

1. Imagine you are a young person swinging from birches. Write step-by-step **directions** for a friend, telling how to swing from birches.

2. Imagine that you are the speaker of the poem. Write a **journal entry** describing problems in your life that prompt you to want to swing from birches again.

3. Write an **explanation** of a natural event you have seen, such as a sunset, a covering of frost on a cold morning, or a violent thunderstorm. You may wish to explain some of the actual reasons for such an occurrence, but you should focus on an imaginative reason of your own. Use similes and metaphors to enrich your writing.

Integrating the Language Arts

Language, Grammar, and Style

MODIFIERS: ADJECTIVES AND ADVERBS. Adjectives and **adverbs**, two kinds of **modifiers**, add meaning to other words. Read the Language Arts Survey 3.66, "Adjectives," and 3.67, "Adverbs."

Each of the sentences below has one or more underlined words. Label each underlined word as an adjective or adverb.

1. Robert Frost <u>always</u> wrote beautiful <u>nature</u> poetry.
2. <u>Frost's</u> boy took all <u>the</u> stiffness out of the trees.
3. <u>Bent</u> birches <u>often</u> trail <u>their</u> leaves on the ground.
4. Frost doesn't use <u>very</u> <u>much</u> onomatopoeia.
5. Birches may represent <u>people's</u> challenges in <u>this</u> poem.

Media Literacy & Speaking and Listening

AUDIO FILES. Access the American Academy of Poets at http://www.poets.org and click on "Listening Booth" to hear Robert Frost read his poem "The Road Not Taken." Then select a poem by Frost to tape-record in the style and manner of Frost reading his own poems. You might find it useful to make a photo copy of your selected poem and mark it for pitch, emphasis, and volume.

Study and Research

RESEARCHING ON THE INTERNET. Using the Internet, locate other poems by Robert Frost and read them. Then make a booklet, either a booklet of other nature poems or a booklet of your favorite poems by Frost. One site you will find useful is the Poet's Corner at http://www.geocities.com/spanoudi/poems/poem-ef.html.

"Song"
by Gabriela Mistral, translated by Langston Hughes

Reader's resource

A **prose poem** is a work of prose, usually a short work, that makes such extensive use of poetic language, such as figures of speech and words that echo their sense, that the line between prose and poetry becomes blurred. In the prose poem **"Song,"** the poet uses personification to express how nature reacts to a woman's mournful, beautiful singing.

CULTURE CONNECTION. The government of Chile supports cultural endeavors with technical assistance, special lines of financial credit, and competitions such as those organized by the National Fund for the Development of the Arts and Culture (Fondart) to sponsor and promote the development of cultural industries and to save and protect Chile's national heritage. Various private foundations have also taken on the task of sustaining and promoting the work of talented artists, and of financing halls, museums, and exhibitions. Chile is the only Latin American nation to be home to two Nobel laureates in Literature, Gabriela Mistral in 1945, and Pablo Neruda in 1971.

About the AUTHOR

Gabriela Mistral (1889–1957) was born Lucila Godoy y Alcayaga in Vicuña, Chile. She renamed herself after the archangel Gabriel and the mistral wind—a dry, cold wind that blows in France. Largely self-educated, she began teaching when she was fifteen years old. At eighteen she fell in love with a young railway worker who took his own life two years later; she expressed the depth of her grief at her loss by writing a series of prize-winning sonnets. By 1922, she had become the most popular poet in the Spanish-speaking countries of Latin America.

Mistral collaborated with the Mexican minister of education to create an education reform program for rural areas and served in the diplomatic corps in Latin America, Europe, and the United States. In 1945, Mistral was the first Latin American woman to receive the Nobel Prize for literature.

Mistral also became the first woman to adorn a peso note in her native Chile. In 1981 the South American country introduced a new 5,000-peso note featuring a portrait of the poet, who died in 1957 in Hempstead, New York.

Literary TOOLS

NARRATIVE POEM. A **narrative poem** is a verse that tells a story. As you read, decide what story "Song" tells.

PERSONIFICATION. Personification is a figure of speech in which an idea, animal, or thing is described as if it were a person.

Organizer

As you read, make a chart. On the left, write examples of personification from the poem. On the right, write what human characteristics the objects have. One example has been done for you.

Personification	Human Characteristics
Night grows maternal.	motherly

Reader's Journal

When have you felt really sad? What did you do to express your emotions?

Woman in Cordilleran Night, 1966. María Eugenia Terrazas.
Private Collection.

Song

Gabriela Mistral

A woman is singing in the valley. The shadows falling blot her out, but her song spreads over the fields.

Her heart is broken, like the jar she dropped this afternoon among the pebbles in the brook. As she sings, the hidden wound sharpens on the thread of her song, and becomes thin and hard. Her voice in <u>modulation</u> dampens with blood.

In the fields the other voices die with the dying day, and a moment ago the song of the last slow-poke bird stopped. But her deathless heart, alive with grief, gathers all the silent voices into her voice, sharp now, yet very sweet.

Does she sing for a husband who looks at her silently in the dusk, or for a child whom her song caresses? Or does she sing for her own heart, more helpless than a babe at nightfall.

Night grows maternal before this song that goes to meet it; the stars, with a sweetness that is human, are beginning to come out; the sky full of stars becomes human and understands the sorrows of this world.

Her song, as pure as water filled with light, cleanses the plain and rinses the mean air of day in which men hate. From the throat of the woman who keeps on singing, day rises nobly evaporating toward the stars. ■

> How can you tell the woman is in the darkened valley?

> What does the woman gather into her voice?

> Why might she be singing?

> What impact does the woman's singing have?

words for everyday use

mod • u • la • tion (mod ōō lā´shən) *n.*, inflection of tone or pitch of the voice. *The singer's* <u>modulation</u> *changed so that her inflection expressed the joyfulness of the song.*

If you were the woman, what would make you stop singing? Why?

Investigate, *Inquire,* and *Imagine*

Recall: GATHERING FACTS

1a. Where is the woman? What is she doing?

2a. What happens to the voices in the fields?

3a. Why might the woman be singing her mournful song?

Interpret: FINDING MEANING

1b. Why does the woman's voice dampen with blood?

2b. Why is the woman's lamentation "sharp" yet "sweet"?

3b. Why doesn't the speaker tell us what caused the woman's grief?

Analyze: TAKING THINGS APART

4a. Identify how nature responds to the woman's singing at night.

Synthesize: BRINGING THINGS TOGETHER

4b. How does the woman's song affect nature?

Evaluate: MAKING JUDGMENTS

5a. How believably does the poem reflect the woman's grief?

Extend: CONNECTING IDEAS

5b. What strategies have you seen people use to express their grief?

Understanding *Literature*

NARRATIVE POEM. Review the definition for **narrative poem** in the Handbook of Literary Terms. What story does "Song" tell?

PERSONIFICATION. Review the definition for **personification** in Literary Tools on page 113. Then look at the chart you made in Literary Tools. What objects are personified in this poem? What human characteristics do these objects have?

Writer's Journal

1. Imagine you are the woman who sings in the poem. Write **song lyrics** that describe what happened to fill you with such grief.

2. Imagine that this poem is being adapted as a short film. Write a **screenplay** describing the scene in the valley. Tell what the viewers hear and see.

3. When the woman sings, she "gathers all the silent voices into her voice." Write a **paragraph** describing what characteristics the silent voices add to her song.

Integrating the Language Arts

Language, Grammar, and Style

WORKING WITH NEGATIVES/AVOIDING DOUBLE NEGATIVES. Negatives such as *not* and *never* affect verbs, but they are not verbs, themselves. They tell the reader that the action is the opposite of what the verb says. Many languages use double negatives; however, standard English does not. Review the Language Arts Survey 3.29, "Working with Negatives and Contractions."

In the following sentences, underline the negatives. If you find a double negative, make sure to change it so that there is only one negative to a sentence. If the sentence is without errors, write *Correct*.

1. Gabriela Mistral didn't never write in the English language.
2. You might not have read her poems in Spanish class either.
3. U.S. language students don't hardly ever read poems in foreign languages.
4. A Spanish-speaking woman hadn't never been awarded a Nobel Prize for literature before.
5. I have never written any poetry neither.

Speaking and Listening

ORAL INTERPRETATION. Select a favorite poem that tells a story. If it is long, select an appropriate cutting. Write an introduction to the piece. Then decide how you will use volume, pitch, stress, tone, gestures, facial expression, and body language to present the work effectively. You may want to write notes on your script to help you as you practice. Finally, perform your selection for the class. During your performance, have your audience focus on finding the answers to several questions that you have prepared in advance. Before you begin, you may find it useful to read the Language Arts Survey 4.19, "Oral Interpretation."

Collaborative Learning

WRITING A PROSE POEM. With a partner, select a poem in verse that you like. Perhaps there is one in this unit that you would like to choose. Then rewrite the poem in prose and share it with the class.

"The Creation"

by James Weldon Johnson

Reader's resource

"The Creation" is included in Johnson's book *God's Trombones,* a collection of seven sermons and a prayer. The creation of the world and the beginning of life is a common theme in religions around the world. Johnson's poem, with its vivid imagery and rhetoric reminiscent of Southern preaching, is widely considered one of the most memorable of all retellings of this familiar story.

About *the* AUTHOR

James Weldon Johnson (1871–1938) was born in Jacksonville, Florida, and educated at Atlanta University and Columbia University. Johnson's talents ran the gamut from writing poetry and prose to writing songs for Broadway productions, teaching, and practicing law and politics. In a rich and varied career, Johnson worked as a high school principal, a vaudeville comedian, a national secretary to the National Association for the Advancement of Colored People (NAACP), a United States consul to Venezuela and Nicaragua, and a professor of creative literature at Fisk University in Nashville, Tennessee. He edited several collections of poetry and wrote poems of his own.

Collections of Johnson's poetry include *God's Trombones* (1927) and *Selected Poems* (1935). The anonymously published novel *Autobiography of an Ex-Colored Man* (1912) garnered new attention when Johnson was revealed as its author after its reissue in 1927. Another influential prose work by Johnson was his autobiography, *Along This Way* (1933).

Literary TOOLS

SIMILE. A **simile** is a comparison using *like* or *as.* As you read, look for the simile that is used to describe the creation of people.

NARRATIVE POEM. A **narrative poem** is a verse that tells a story.

Organizer

As you read, make a chart like the one below to show events in the poem. On the left, cite events that occur in the poem. On the right, paraphrase the event. One example has been done for you.

Citations	Paraphrasings
"God smiled"	God smiled to create light

Reader's Journal

What have you created that took great time and effort? What thoughts did you experience while creating this thing?

The Creation

James Weldon Johnson

And God stepped out on space,
And he looked around and said:
I'm lonely—
I'll make me a world.

5   And far as the eye of God could see
Darkness covered everything,
Blacker than a hundred midnights
Down in a cypress swamp.[1]

Then God smiled,
10   And the light broke,
And the darkness rolled up on one side,
And the light stood shining on the other,
And God said: That's good!

Then God reached out and took the light in His hands,
15   And God rolled the light around in His hands
Until He made the sun;
And He set that sun a-blazing in the heavens.
And the light that was left from making the sun
God gathered it up in a shining ball
20   And flung it against the darkness,
Spangling the night with the moon and stars.
Then down between
The darkness and the light
He hurled the world;

What exists before creation?

How does God create light? What does God say when it is created? What does this passage reveal about God?

To what is the creation of celestial elements (moon, stars, and the world) compared?

---

1. **cypress swamp.** Swamp of evergreen, cone-bearing trees native to North America, Europe, and Asia

25   And God said: That's good!

Then God himself stepped down—
And the sun was on His right hand,
And the moon was on His left;
The stars were clustered about His head,
30   And the earth was under His feet.
And God walked, and where He trod
His footsteps hollowed the valleys out
And bulged the mountains up.

Then He stopped and looked and saw
35   That the earth was hot and <u>barren</u>.
So God stepped over to the edge of the world
And He spat out the seven seas—
He batted His eyes, and the lightnings flashed—
He clapped His hands, and the thunders rolled—
40   And the waters above the earth came down,
The cooling waters came down.

Then the green grass sprouted,
And the little red flowers blossomed,
The pine tree pointed his finger to the sky,
45   And the oak spread out his arms,
The lakes cuddled down in the hollows of the ground,
And the rivers ran down to the sea;
And God smiled again,
And the rainbow appeared,
50   And curled itself around His shoulder.

Then God raised His arm and He waved His hand
Over the sea and over the land,
And He said: Bring forth! Bring forth!
And quicker than God could drop His hand,

The Creation, 1935. Aaron Douglas.
The Howard University Gallery of Art,
Washington, DC.

art note

Aaron Douglas was the foremost
artist of the Harlem Renaissance, a
movement of great artistic output by African-
American writers and artists in the 1920s and
1930s. He drew the illustrations for Johnson's
book *God's Trombones* and later made paintings based on them, such as this one. Douglas
based his distinctive style on a wide range of
sources, including the tribal art of Africa, the art
of ancient Egypt and Greece, and Modern
European painting. Can you identify one of
those influences in this painting?

**words
for
everyday
use**

bar • ren (ba´rən) *adj.,* empty; not producing crops. *Nothing moved in the flat, treeless landscape; it
looked as <u>barren</u> as the moon.*

55   Fishes and fowls
And beasts and birds
Swam the rivers and the seas,
Roamed the forests and the woods,
And split the air with their wings.
60   And God said: That's good!

Then God walked around,
And God looked around
On all that He had made.
He looked at His sun,
65   And He looked at His moon,
And He looked at His little stars;
He looked on His world
With all its living things,
And God said: I'm lonely still.

70   Then God sat down—
On the side of a hill where He could think;
By a deep, wide river He sat down;
With His head in His hands,
God thought and thought,
75   Till He thought: I'll make me a man!

Up from the bed of the river
God scooped the clay;
And by the bank of the river
He kneeled Him down;
80   And there the great God Almighty
Who lit the sun and fixed it in the sky,
Who flung the stars to the most far corner of the night,
Who rounded the earth in the middle of His hand;
This Great God,
85   Like a mammy[2] bending over her baby,
Kneeled down in the dust
Toiling over a lump of clay
Till He shaped it in His own image;

Then into it He blew the breath of life,
90   And man became a living soul.
Amen. Amen.

> To what is God compared?

---

2. **mammy.** Southern term for "Mama"

What part of the creation story is reflected in the painting by Aaron Douglas?

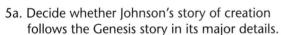
and Imagine

Recall: GATHERING FACTS

1a. What does God see when He looks around? What does God decide to do?

2a. How does God create light? How does He make the sun, stars, and moon?

3a. What happens when God walks on the land? How does He create the seas, thunder, lightning, and rain? How does He create the animals?

→ **Interpret:** FINDING MEANING

1b. How does God feel at the beginning of the poem? How is this emotion related to the creation of the world?

2b. Why is light the first thing that God makes? How does He feel when He has created the sun, stars, and moon?

3b. How does God feel about His creation?

Analyze: TAKING THINGS APART

4a. Identify how God creates humans differently from His other creations.

→ **Synthesize:** BRINGING THINGS TOGETHER

4b. Why does God create humans?

Evaluate: MAKING JUDGMENTS

5a. Decide whether Johnson's story of creation follows the Genesis story in its major details.

→ **Extend:** CONNECTING IDEAS

5b. Compare and contrast Johnson's creation story with one from another culture.

Understanding *Literature*

SIMILE. Review the definition for **simile** in the Handbook of Literary Terms. What simile is used to describe God creating a person? To what is God compared? How are these two things similar? Johnson says that God "kneeled down in the dust toiling over a lump of clay," so he could have compared God to a sculptor. What kind of relationship would that have established between God and humans? How would that differ from the relationship developed through the simile Johnson does use?

NARRATIVE POEM. Review the definition for **narrative poem** in the Handbook of Literary Terms. Then refer to the chart you made in Literary Tools on page 117. What story does "The Creation" tell? Why do you think the story was written in verse? The poem was written as a sermon. How might that have affected the tone or style of the poem?

Writer's Journal

1. Imagine that you are God in the poem. Write a **letter** to humankind explaining why you created the world and what expectations you have.

2. Imagine you are the first person that God created. Write a **journal entry** describing your awe at what you see in the world around you.

3. Write a **video script** giving directions for a film shot depicting one of God's actions in "The Creation."

Integrating the Language Arts

Language, Grammar, and Style

PRONOUNS AS SUBJECTS AND OBJECTS. Review the Language Arts Survey 3.54–3.56, "Types of Pronouns," "Personal Pronouns," and "Indefinite Pronouns." The following examples have personal or indefinite pronouns as subjects, or direct or indirect objects:

1. <u>We</u> gave <u>several</u> a ride. (Personal pronoun = subject; indefinite pronoun = indirect object)

2. <u>Two</u> fit in the back seat. (Indefinite pronoun = subject)

3. Timmy got <u>everyone</u> into his car. (Indefinite pronoun = direct object)

In the sentences below, 1) identify the pronouns; 2) tell if the pronouns are personal or indefinite; 3) identify the subject, the verb, and the direct object.

1. I'll make me a world.
2. Then God reached out, took the light, and held it.
3. Few knew or read James Weldon Johnson's poems.
4. The Civil Rights movement changed that.
5. Work by African Americans and others were included in poetry texts for students.

Study and Research

RESEARCHING CREATION STORIES. Research creation stories from other cultures. Find two that are similar and compare and contrast them in an essay. You may want to review comparison and contrast order in the Language Arts Survey 2.27, "Choosing a Method of Organization."

Speaking and Listening

ORAL INTERPRETATION. Select a cutting from "The Creation" and write an introduction for it. Rehearse your cutting, and then present it to the class or a small group. Use vocal expression, gesture, and body movement in your presentation. Before you begin, you may want to read the Language Arts Survey 4.19, "Oral Interpretation."

THE *ODYSSEY*

from **BOOK NINE** and **BOOK TWELVE**
by Homer, translated by Robert Fitzgerald

Reader's *resource*

Background: Genre. Read the definitions of **epic** and **heroic epic** in Literary Tools. One of the oldest and greatest of all epic poems is the *Odyssey.* This poem, attributed to Homer, tells the story of the hero Odysseus, king of the Greek city of Ithaca, whose name in ancient Greek means "wanderer" or "voyager." In the *Odyssey,* a Greek people named the Achaeans go to war against the city of Troy to rescue Helen, the wife of the Achaean king Menelaus. For ten long years, the Achaeans attempt unsuccessfully to conquer the walled city. Finally, they are able to do so by means of a famous trick thought up by the crafty Odysseus. They build a large wooden horse and secretly put soldiers inside it. Then they pretend to leave. The Trojans, believing the wooden horse to be a gift left by the defeated Achaeans, wheel the horse into their city. Then, at night, the Greeks steal out of the horse and open the city gates, allowing their soldiers to enter. After the defeat of the Trojans, Odysseus sets sail for Ithaca, which lies across the Mediterranean Sea.

Much of the *Odyssey* tells of Odysseus's ten-year voyage home, during which time his son Telemachus and his wife Penelope wait in Ithaca, attempting to maintain their authority in Odysseus's absence. On his journey, Odysseus has many adventures. In the land of the Lotus-Eaters, his shipmates become lazy and unwilling to leave because they have eaten the lotus plant, and only with difficulty does Odysseus rescue them. In the land of the Cyclopes, the giant, one-eyed sons of the sea god Poseidon, Odysseus and his men are captured and escape only by means of another of Odysseus's tricks. Of Odysseus's twelve ships, eleven are destroyed by a cannibal named Laistrygones. Odysseus then travels to the land of a sorceress, Circe, who turns many of his men into pigs. Odysseus has numerous other adventures, including visiting the land of the dead and navigating in a narrow stretch of water between two monsters, Scylla and Charybdis. He is lured into staying for years on the island of the nymph Calypso, but eventually he returns home. Back in Ithaca, he is recognized at first only by his dog and by his now elderly nurse. With Telemachus, he fights against the many suitors who have come in his absence to win Penelope's hand and to become king of Ithaca.

Literary TOOLS

EPIC AND HEROIC EPIC. An **epic** is a long story, often told in verse, involving heroes and gods. Grand in length and scope, an epic provides a portrait of an entire culture, of the legends, beliefs, values, laws, arts, and ways of life of a people. A **heroic epic** is an epic that has a main purpose of telling the life story of a great hero. As you read, determine what powers the gods have in the *Odyssey* and what makes Odysseus a hero.

PERSONIFICATION. Personification is a figure of speech in which an idea, animal, or thing is described as if it were a person. Dawn is personified in both the story of the Cyclops and the story of the Sirens.

Organizer

As you read, make a cluster chart, listing how Homer personifies Dawn.

- personification of Dawn
- "Dawn spread out her finger tips of rose."

Reader's Journal

What qualities do you think make a person a hero?

The following pages present two selections from Robert Fitzgerald's translation of the *Odyssey*. In the first, Odysseus and his sailors meet the mighty Cyclops Polyphemos. In the second, they encounter the Sirens, whose singing is so enchanting that sailors are tempted to follow the sound and so steer their ships into death-dealing rocks.

About *the* AUTHOR

In ancient Greece, before the development of writing, poets created long poems that told stories of heroic adventures. These poems, partly memorized and partly improvised, were written down long after their creation. According to tradition, the greatest of the oral poets, or bards, of ancient Greece was **Homer**. Nothing is known of the historical Homer. However, according to legend, he was blind and came from Ionia, in Asia Minor (site of modern-day Turkey). To Homer is attributed the composition of the two greatest poems of ancient Greece, the *Iliad* and the *Odyssey*, both of which probably date from the seventh century BC.

from THE ODYSSEY

Homer

Ulysses and the Sirens, 1891. John Waterhouse. National Gallery of Victoria, Melbourne, Australia.

from BOOK NINE

. . . In the next land we found were Cyclopes,[1]
giants, louts, without a law to bless them.
In ignorance leaving the fruitage of the earth in mystery
to the immortal gods, they neither plow

How do the Cyclopes' lives differ from those of civilized people?

---

1. **Cyclopes.** One-eyed giants

5   nor sow by hand, nor till the ground, though grain—
     wild wheat and barley—grows untended, and
     wine-grapes, in clusters, ripen in heaven's rain.
     Cyclopes have no muster and no meeting,
     no consultation or old tribal ways,
10   but each one dwells in his own mountain cave
     dealing out rough justice to wife and child,
     indifferent to what the others do.

                              Well, then:
     across the wide bay from the mainland
     there lies a desert island, not far out
15   but still not close inshore. Wild goats in hundreds
     breed there; and no human being comes
     upon the isle to startle them—no hunter
     of all who ever tracked with hounds through forests
     or had rough going over mountain trails.
20   The isle, unplanted and untilled, a wilderness,
     pastures goats alone. And this is why:
     good ships like ours with cheekpaint at the bows
     are far beyond the Cyclopes. No shipwright
     toils among them, shaping and building up
25   symmetrical trim hulls to cross the sea
     and visit all the seaboard towns, as men do
     who go and come in commerce over water.
     This isle—seagoing folk would have annexed it
     and built their homesteads on it: all good land,
30   fertile for every crop in season: lush
     well-watered meads[2] along the shore, vines in profusion,
     prairie, clear for the plow, where grain would grow
     chin high by harvest time, and rich sub-soil.
     The island cove is landlocked, so you need
35   no hawsers[3] out astern, bow-stones or mooring:
     run in and ride there till the day your crews
     chafe to be under sail, and a fair wind blows.
     You'll find good water flowing from a cavern
     through dusky poplars into the upper bay.
40   Here we made harbor. Some god guided us
     that night, for we could barely see our bows

Pronunciation Guide

Achaen (ə kē′ on)
Agamemnon (a gə mem′ non)
Apollo (ə po′ lō)
Athena (ə thē nə)
Atreus (a′ trē əs)
Cicones (si kō′ nes)
Circe (sər′ sē)
Cyclopes (sī′ klops)
Euanthês (yü an′ thēs)
Eur'ylokhos (you ri′ lō kəs)
Eurymos (yü′ ryē mos)
Helios (hē′ le os)
Ismanos (is mā′ nəs)
Ithaca (i′ tha kə)
Kronos (krō′ nōs)
Laërtês (lā er′ tēs)
Maron (me′ ron)
Odysseus (ō di′ sē əs)
Perimêdês (pe ri me′ des)
Polyphemos (po lē fē′ məs)
Poseidon (pō sī′ dən)
Siren (sī′ ren)
Télemos (te′ le məs)
Zeus (zoos)

What force helps the Greeks reach a safe harbor?

---

2. **meads.** Meadows
3. **hawsers.** Large ropes for mooring or towing a ship

---

words for everyday use

an • nex (ə neks′) *vt.*, add on or attach. *Hitler annexed Poland in 1939, adding it to the countries he claimed for Germany.*

chafe (chāf) *vi.*, be impatient or vexed. *Sitting in bumper-to-bumper traffic, Bernice chafed at the delay.*

in the dense fog around us, and no moonlight
filtered through the overcast. No look-out,
nobody saw the island dead ahead,
45   nor even the great landward rolling billow
that took us in: we found ourselves in shallows,
keels grazing shore: so furled our sails
and disembarked where the low ripples broke.
There on the beach we lay, and slept till morning.

Where do the Greeks spend the night?

50   When Dawn[4] spread out her finger tips of rose
we turned out marvelling, to tour the isle,
while Zeus's shy nymph daughters flushed wild goats
down from the heights—a breakfast for my men.
We ran to fetch our hunting bows and long-shanked
55   lances from the ships, and in three companies
we took our shots. Heaven gave us game a-plenty:
for every one of twelve ships in my squadron
nine goats fell to be shared; my lot was ten.
So there all day, until the sun went down,
60   we made our feast on meat galore, and wine—
wine from the ship, for our supply held out,
so many jars were filled at Ismaros
from stores of the Cicones[5] that we <u>plundered</u>.
We gazed, too, at Cyclopes Land, so near;
65   we saw their smoke, heard bleating from their flocks.
But after sundown, in the gathering dusk,
we slept again above the wash of ripples.

What does Dawn do?

When the young Dawn with finger tips of rose
came in the east, I called my men together
and made a speech to them:

70   "Old shipmates, friends,
the rest of you stand by; I'll make the crossing
in my own ship, with my own company,
and find out what the mainland natives are—

Notice that the description in line 68 is similar to the one in line 50. Why might a poet who composed his work orally use stock phrases, or formulas, again and again?

---

4. **Dawn.** The Greek goddess of dawn is called Eos; in Roman mythology her name is Aurora.

5. **Cicones.** Allies of the Trojans and Odysseus's enemies. Odysseus and his men had attacked the Cicones and taken jars of supplies from them.

words for everyday use

plun • der (plun´dər) vt., steal or take by trickery or by force. *In 1204 European crusaders burned and <u>plundered</u> Constantinople, the jewel of the Byzantine Empire.*

for they may be wild savages, and lawless,
75   or hospitable and god fearing men."

At this I went aboard, and gave the word
to cast off by the stern. My oarsmen followed,
filing in to their benches by the rowlocks,
and all in line dipped oars in the grey sea.

80   As we rowed on, and nearer to the mainland,
at one end of the bay, we saw a cavern
yawning above the water, screened with laurel,
and many rams and goats about the place
inside a sheepfold—made from slabs of stone
85   earthfast between tall trunks of pine and rugged
towering oak trees.

A <u>prodigious</u> man
slept in this cave alone, and took his flocks
to graze afield—remote from all companions,
knowing none but savage ways, a brute
90   so huge, he seemed no man at all of those
who eat good wheaten bread; but he seemed rather
a shaggy mountain reared in solitude.
We beached there, and I told the crew
to stand by and keep watch over the ship;
95   as for myself I took my twelve best fighters
and went ahead. I had a goatskin full
of that sweet liquor that Euanthês' son,
Maron, had given me. He kept Apollo's
holy grove at Ismaros; for kindness
100   we showed him there, and showed his wife and child,
he gave me seven shining golden talents[6]
perfectly formed, a solid silver winebowl,
and then this liquor—twelve two-handled jars
of brandy, pure and fiery. Not a slave
105   in Maron's household knew this drink; only
he, his wife and the storeroom mistress knew;
and they would put one cupful—ruby-colored,
honey-smooth—in twenty more of water,
but still the sweet scent hovered like a <u>fume</u>

> To what is the
> Cyclops compared?

---

6. **talents.** Coins

words for everyday use

pro • di • gious (prō dij´əs) *adj.*, exceptional; of great size or power. *The young violinist had <u>prodigious</u> talent and tremendous energy.*

fume (fyōōm) *n.*, smoke, gas, or vapor. *As Vaughn filled the tank, he turned his head away to avoid breathing the gasoline <u>fumes</u>.*

110 over the winebowl. No man turned away
when cups of this came round.

A wineskin full
I brought along, and victuals[7] in a bag,
for in my bones I knew some towering brute
would be upon us soon—all outward power,
115 a wild man, ignorant of civility.

We climbed, then, briskly to the cave. But Cyclops
had gone afield, to pasture his fat sheep,
so we looked round at everything inside:
a drying rack that sagged with cheeses, pens
120 crowded with lambs and kids, each in its class:
firstlings apart from middlings, and the "dewdrops,"
or newborn lambkins, penned apart from both.
And vessels full of whey[8] were brimming there—
bowls of earthenware and pails for milking.
My men came pressing round me, pleading:

125 "Why not
take these cheeses, get them stowed, come back,
throw open all the pens, and make a run for it?
We'll drive the kids and lambs aboard. We say
put out[9] again on good salt water!"

Ah,
130 how sound that was! Yet I refused. I wished
to see the caveman, what he had to offer—
no pretty sight, it turned out, for my friends.

We lit a fire, burnt an offering,
and took some cheese to eat; then sat in silence
135 around the embers, waiting. When he came
he had a load of dry boughs on his shoulder
to stoke his fire at suppertime. He dumped it
with a great crash into that hollow cave,
and we all scattered fast to the far wall.
140 Then over the broad cavern floor he ushered
the ewes he meant to milk. He left his rams

What does Odysseus bring along to offer to the Cyclops?

What mistake does Odysseus make? What is foreshadowed, or hinted at, in these lines?

---

7. **victuals.** Food
8. **whey.** Milky liquid left over from the making of cheese
9. **put out.** Set sail

words for everyday use

civ • il • i • ty (sə vil´ə tē) n., manners; civilized ways. *The pet store owner always treats us with civility, even when we make a complaint.*

stow (stō) vt., put away, especially aboard a ship. *The flight attendant stowed my heavy bag in the overhead compartment.*

and he-goats in the yard outside, and swung
high overhead a slab of solid rock
to close the cave. Two dozen four-wheeled wagons,
145   with heaving wagon teams, could not have stirred
the tonnage of that rock from where he wedged it
over the doorsill. Next he took his seat
and milked his bleating ewes. A practiced job
he made of it, giving each ewe her suckling;
150   thickened his milk, then, into curds and whey,
sieved out the curds to drip in withy[10] baskets,
and poured the whey to stand in bowls
cooling until he drank it for his supper.
When all these chores were done, he poked the fire,
155   heaping on brushwood. In the glare he saw us.

"Strangers," he said, "who are you? And where from?
What brings you here by sea ways—a fair traffic?[11]
Or are you wandering rogues, who cast your lives
like dice, and ravage other folk by sea?"
160   We felt a pressure on our hearts, in dread
of that deep rumble and that mighty man.
But all the same I spoke up in reply:

"We are from Troy, Achaeans, blown off course
by shifting gales on the Great South Sea;
165   homeward bound, but taking routes and ways
uncommon; so the will of Zeus would have it.
We served under Agamemnon, son of Atreus—
the whole world knows what city
he laid waste, what armies he destroyed.
170   It was our luck to come here; here we stand,
beholden for your help, or any gifts
you give—as custom is to honor strangers.[12]
We would entreat you, great Sir, have a care
for the gods' courtesy; Zeus will avenge
the unoffending guest."

How strong is the Cyclops? How do you know?

---

10. **withy.** Made of willow twigs
11. **fair traffic.** Honest trade
12. **as custom . . . strangers.** Among the ancient Greeks, treating visitors well was considered a sacred obligation.

words for everyday use

rogue (rōg) *n.*, wicked or rascally person. *"Stop, rogue," cried the cavalier, brandishing his sword.*

a • venge (ə venjʹ) *vt.*, get revenge for a wrongdoing. *War broke out between the two countries when one side sought to avenge an attack on a small village.*

175   He answered this
from his brute chest, unmoved:

                          "You are a ninny,
or else you come from the other end of nowhere,
telling me, mind the gods! We Cyclopes
care not a whistle for your thundering Zeus

180   or all the gods in bliss; we have more force by far.
I would not let you go for fear of Zeus—
you or your friends—unless I had a whim to.
Tell me, where was it, now, you left your ship—
around the point, or down the shore, I wonder?"

185   He thought he'd find out, but I saw through this,
and answered with a ready lie:

                          "My ship?
Poseidon Lord,[13] who sets the earth a-tremble,
broke it up on the rocks at your land's end.
A wind from seaward served him, drove us there.

190   We are survivors, these good men and I."

Neither reply nor pity came from him,
but in one stride he clutched at my companions
and caught two in his hands like squirming puppies
to beat their brains out, spattering the floor.

195   Then he dismembered them and made his meal,
gaping and crunching like a mountain lion—
everything: innards, flesh, and marrow bones.
We cried aloud, lifting our hands to Zeus,
powerless, looking on at this, appalled;

200   but Cyclops went on filling up his belly
with manflesh and great gulps of whey,
then lay down like a mast among his sheep.
My heart beat high now at the chance of action,
and drawing the sharp sword from my hip I went

205   along his flank to stab him where the midriff
holds the liver. I had touched the spot
when sudden fear stayed me: if I killed him
we perished there as well, for we could never

---

13. **Poseidon Lord.** Greek god of the sea

> Why doesn't Odysseus tell the Cyclops the truth?

> How large would you estimate the Cyclops to be?

> To what is the Cyclops compared?

> Why can't Odysseus kill the Cyclops?

move his <u>ponderous</u> doorway slab aside.
210 So we were left to groan and wait for morning.

When the young Dawn with finger tips of rose
lit up the world, the Cyclops built a fire
and milked his handsome ewes, all in due order,
putting the sucklings to the mothers. Then,
215 his chores being all dispatched, he caught
another brace of men to make his breakfast,
and whisked away his great door slab
to let his sheep go through—but he, behind,
reset the stone as one would cap a quiver.[14]
220 There was a <u>din</u> of whistling as the Cyclops
rounded his flock to higher ground, then stillness.
And now I pondered how to hurt him worst
if but Athena[15] granted what I prayed for.
Here are the means I thought would serve my turn:

225 a club, or staff, lay there along the fold—
an olive tree, felled green and left to season
for Cyclops' hand. And it was like a mast
a lugger of twenty oars, broad in the beam—
a deep-sea-going craft—might carry:
230 so long, so big around, it seemed. Now I
chopped out a six-foot section of this pole
and set it down before my men, who scraped it;
and when they had it smooth, I hewed again
to make a stake with pointed end. I held this
235 in the fire's heart and turned it, toughening it,
then hid it, well back in the cavern, under
one of the dung piles in profusion there.
Now came the time to toss for it: who ventured
along with me? whose hand could bear to thrust
240 and grind that spike in Cyclops' eye, when mild
sleep had mastered him? As luck would have it,
the men I would have chosen won the toss—

How big is the Cyclops's club or staff? What does Odysseus do with it?

What does Odysseus plan to do with the stake?

----

14. **cap a quiver.** Put the top on a container for arrows
15. **Athena.** Greek goddess of wisdom to whom Odysseus, known for his intelligence, often turns for guidance

words for everyday use

pon • der • ous (pän′dər əs) *adj.*, heavy; bulky; massive. *The old haywagon creaked and swayed under its <u>ponderous</u> load.*

din (din) *n.*, noise. *The <u>din</u> of the cafeteria made it impossible for them to talk quietly.*

four strong men, and I made five as captain.

245 At evening came the shepherd with his flock,
his woolly flock. The rams as well, this time,
entered the cave: by some sheep-herding whim—
or a god's bidding—none were left outside.
He hefted[16] his great boulder into place
250 and sat him down to milk the bleating ewes
in proper order, put the lambs to suck,
and swiftly ran through all his evening chores.
Then he caught two more men and feasted on them.
My moment was at hand, and I went forward
holding an ivy bowl of my dark drink,
looking up, saying:

255   "Cyclops, try some wine.
Here's liquor to wash down your scraps of men.
Taste it, and see the kind of drink we carried
under our planks. I meant it for an offering
if you would help us home. But you are mad,
260 unbearable, a bloody monster! After this,
will any other traveler come to see you?"

He seized and drained the bowl, and it went down
so fiery and smooth he called for more:

"Give me another, thank you kindly. Tell me,
265 how are you called? I'll make a gift will please you.
Even Cyclopes know the wine-grapes grow
out of grassland and loam in heaven's rain,
but here's a bit of nectar and ambrosia!"[17]

Three bowls I brought him, and he poured them down.
270 I saw the fuddle and flush come over him,
then I sang out in cordial tones:

                          "Cyclops,
you ask my honorable name? Remember

---

16. **hefted.** Lifted
17. **ambrosia.** Food of the gods

words for everyday use

cor • dial (kôr´jəl) adj., friendly. *The Red Cross nurses were cordial, greeting Brent warmly when he went to give blood.*

the gift you promised me, and I shall tell you.
My name is Nohbdy: mother, father, and friends,
everyone calls me Nohbdy."

275   And he said:

"Nohbdy's my meat, then, after I eat his friends.
Others come first. There's a noble gift, now."
Even as he spoke, he reeled and tumbled backward,
his great head lolling to one side; and sleep
280   took him like any creature. Drunk, hiccuping,
he dribbled streams of liquor and bits of men.

Now, by the gods, I drove my big hand spike
deep in the embers, charring it again,
and cheered my men along with battle talk
285   to keep their courage up: no quitting now.
The pike of olive, green though it had been,
reddened and glowed as if about to catch.
I drew it from the coals and my four fellows
gave me a hand, lugging it near the Cyclops
290   as more than natural force nerved them; straight
forward they sprinted, lifted it, and rammed it
deep in his crater eye, and I leaned on it
turning it as a shipwright turns a drill
in planking, having men below to swing
295   the two-handled strap that spins it in the groove.
So with our brand we bored that great eye socket
while blood ran out around the red hot bar.
Eyelid and lash were seared; the pierced ball
hissed broiling, and the roots popped.

In a smithy
300   one sees a white-hot axehead or an adze[18]
plunged and wrung in a cold tub, screeching steam—
the way they make soft iron hale and hard—:
just so that eyeball hissed around the spike.
The Cyclops bellowed and the rock roared round him,

305   and we fell back in fear. Clawing his face
he tugged the bloody spike out of his eye,

What "gift" does the Cyclops offer to Odysseus in exchange for the drink?

What parts of the description of the Cyclops show him to be monstrous and revolting?

What do Odysseus and his companions do to the Cyclops?

---

18. **adze.** Axe-like tool with a curved blade

threw it away, and his wild hands went groping;
then he set up a howl for Cyclopes
who lived in caves on windy peaks nearby.
310 Some heard him; and they came by divers[19] ways
to clump around outside and call:

"What ails you,
Polyphemos? Why do you cry so sore
in the starry night? You will not let us sleep.
Sure no man's driving off your flock? No man
has tricked you, ruined you?"

315 Out of the cave
the mammoth Polyphemos roared in answer:

"Nohbdy, Nohbdy's tricked me, Nohbdy's ruined me!"

To this rough shout they made a <u>sage</u> reply:

"Ah well, if nobody has played you foul
320 there in your lonely bed, we are no use in pain
given by great Zeus. Let it be your father,
Poseidon Lord, to whom you pray."

So saying
they trailed away. And I was filled with laughter
to see how like a charm the name deceived them.
325 Now Cyclops, wheezing as the pain came on him,
fumbled to wrench away the great doorstone
and squatted in the breach with arms thrown wide
for any silly beast or man who bolted—
hoping somehow I might be such a fool.
330 But I kept thinking how to win the game:
death sat there huge; how could we slip away?
I drew on all my wits, and ran through tactics,
reasoning as a man will for dear life,
until a trick came—and it pleased me well.
335 The Cyclops' rams were handsome, fat, with heavy
fleeces, a dark violet.

> Why do you think Odysseus tells the Cyclops that his name is Nohbdy? What mistake is made by the other Cyclopes when they hear this name?

---

19. **divers.** Various; several

words for everyday use

sage (sāj) *adj.*, wise. *Shakespeare offers <u>sage</u> advice, as in* Hamlet *when he says, "To thine own self be true."*

Three abreast

I tied them silently together, twining
cords of willow from the ogre's bed;
then slung a man under each middle one
340   to ride there safely, shielded left and right.
So three sheep could convey each man. I took
the woolliest ram, the choicest of the flock,
and hung myself under his kinky belly,
pulled up tight, with fingers twisted deep
345   in sheepskin ringlets for an iron grip.
So, breathing hard, we waited until morning.

When Dawn spread out her finger tips of rose
the rams began to stir, moving for pasture,
and peals of bleating echoed round the pens
350   where dams[20] with udders full called for a milking.
Blinded, and sick with pain from his head wound,
the master stroked each ram, then let it pass,
but my men riding on the <u>pectoral</u> fleece
the giant's blind hands blundering never found.
355   Last of them all my ram, the leader, came,
weighted by wool and me with my meditations.
The Cyclops patted him, and then he said:

"Sweet cousin ram, why lag behind the rest
in the night cave? You never linger so
360   but graze before them all, and go afar
to crop sweet grass, and take your stately way
leading along the streams, until at evening
you run to be the first one in the fold.
Why, now, so far behind? Can you be grieving
365   over your Master's eye? That <u>carrion</u> rogue
and his accurst companions burnt it out
when he had conquered all my wits with wine.
Nohbdy will not get out alive, I swear.
Oh, had you brain and voice to tell
370   where he may be now, dodging all my fury!

---

20. **dams.** Female sheep

words for everyday use

pec • tor • al (pek´tə rəl) *adj.,* located in or on the chest. *Bench-pressing heavy weights develops the <u>pectoral</u> muscles.*

car • ri • on (kar´ē ən) *adj.,* literally, like a piece of dead meat; figuratively, something disgusting or repulsive. *The vultures gathered for a <u>carrion</u> feast in the middle of the road.*

Bashed by this hand and bashed on this rock wall
his brains would strew the floor, and I should have
rest from the outrage Nohbdy worked upon me."

He sent us into the open, then. Close by,
375   I dropped and rolled clear of the ram's belly,
going this way and that to untie the men.
With many glances back, we rounded up
his fat, stiff-legged sheep to take aboard,
and drove them down to where the good ship lay.
380   We saw, as we came near, our fellows' faces
shining; then we saw them turn to grief
tallying those who had not fled from death.
I hushed them, jerking head and eyebrows up,
and in a low voice told them: "Load this herd;
385   move fast, and put the ship's head toward the breakers."
They all pitched in at loading, then embarked
and struck their oars into the sea. Far out,
as far off shore as shouted words would carry,
I sent a few back to the adversary:

390   "O Cyclops! Would you feast on my companions?
Puny, am I, in a Caveman's hands?
How do you like the beating that we gave you,
you damned cannibal? Eater of guests
under your roof! Zeus and the gods have paid you!"

395   The blind thing in his doubled fury broke
a hilltop in his hands and heaved it after us.
Ahead of our black prow it struck and sank
whelmed in a spuming geyser, a giant wave
that washed the ship stern foremost back to shore.
400   I got the longest boathook out and stood
fending us off, with furious nods to all
to put their backs into a racing stroke—
row, row, or perish. So the long oars bent
kicking the foam sternward,[21] making head
405   until we drew away, and twice as far.
Now when I cupped my hands I heard the crew
in low voices protesting:
                        "Godsake, Captain!
Why bait the beast again? Let him alone."

"That tidal wave he made on the first throw
all but beached us."

What do the Greeks do with the Cyclops's sheep?

How has the Cyclops paid for not honoring his guests?

What happens as a result of Odysseus's taunts?

---

21. **sternward.** Toward the rear of a ship or boat

Polyphemus Attacking Odysseus's Ship, 1855. Alexandre Gabriel DeCamps. Musée des Beaux-Arts, Rouen, France.

410   "All but stove us in!"
 "Give him our bearing with your trumpeting,
 he'll get the range and lob a boulder."

         "Aye.
 He'll smash our timbers and our heads together!"

 I would not heed them in my glorying spirit,
 but let my anger flare and yelled:

415   "Cyclops,
 if ever mortal man inquire
 how you were put to shame and blinded, tell him
 Odysseus, raider of cities, took your eye:
 Laërtês' son, whose home's on Ithaca!"

420 At this he gave a mighty sob and rumbled:

 "Now comes the weird²² upon me, spoken of old.
 A wizard, grand and wondrous, lived here—Télemos,

---

22. **weird.** Fate or destiny

a son of Eurymos; great length of days
he had in wizardry among the Cyclopes,
425   and these things he foretold for time to come:
my great eye lost, and at Odysseus's hands.
Always I had in mind some giant, armed
in giant force, would come against me here.
But this, but you—small, pitiful and twiggy—
430   you put me down with wine, you blinded me.
Come back, Odysseus, and I'll treat you well,
praying the god of earthquake[23] to befriend you—
his son I am, for he by his avowal
fathered me, and, if he will, he may
435   heal me of this black wound—he and no other
of all the happy gods or mortal men."

Few words I shouted in reply to him:

"If I could take your life I would and take
your time away, and hurl you down to hell!
440   The god of earthquake could not heal you there!"

At this he stretched his hands out in his darkness
toward the sky of stars, and prayed Poseidon:

"O hear me, lord, blue girdler of the islands,
if I am thine indeed, and thou art father:
445   grant that Odysseus, raider of cities, never
see his home: Laërtês' son, I mean,
who kept his hall on Ithaca. Should destiny
intend that he shall see his roof again
among his family in his father land,
450   far be that day, and dark the years between.
Let him lose all companions, and return
under strange sail to bitter days at home."

In these words he prayed, and the god heard him.
Now he laid hands upon a bigger stone
455   and wheeled around, <u>titanic</u> for the cast,
to let it fly in the black-prowed vessel's track.

> Who is Polyphemos's father?

> As it turns out, it takes Odysseus ten years to get back home. Why might this be so?

---

23. **the god of earthquake.** Poseidon, god of the seas, who could cause earthquakes and tidal waves with his three-pronged spear, or trident

words for everyday use

ti • tan • ic (tī tan′ik) adj., of great size, strength, or power. *The <u>titanic</u> blue whale is larger than many of the largest dinosaurs.*

But it fell short, just aft the steering oar,
and whelming seas rose giant above the stone
to bear us onward toward the island.
                                                    There
460   as we ran in we saw the squadron waiting,
the trim ships drawn up side by side, and all
our troubled friends who waited, looking seaward.
We beached her, grinding keel[24] in the soft sand,
and waded in, ourselves, on the sandy beach.
465   Then we unloaded all the Cyclops' flock
to make division, share and share alike,
only my fighters voted that my ram,
the prize of all, should go to me. I slew him
by the sea side and burnt his long thighbones
470   to Zeus beyond the stormcloud, Kronos' son,[25]
who rules the world. But Zeus disdained my offering;
destruction for my ships he had in store
and death for those who sailed them, my companions.
Now all day long until the sun went down
475   we made our feast on mutton and sweet wine,
till after sunset in the gathering dark
we went to sleep above the wash of ripples.

When the young Dawn with finger tips of rose
touched the world, I roused the men, gave orders
480   to man the ships, cast off the mooring lines;
and filing in to sit beside the rowlocks
oarsmen in line dipped oars in the gray sea.
So we moved out, sad in the vast offing,[26]
having our precious lives, but not our friends.

What offering does Odysseus make to Zeus? Is his offering successful?

Why are Odysseus and his companions sad despite the fact that they have escaped with their lives?

from BOOK TWELVE

. . . As Circe[27] spoke, Dawn mounted her golden throne,
and on the first rays Circe left me, taking
her way like a great goddess up the island.
I made straight for the ship, roused up the men
5   to get aboard and cast off at the stern;
They scrambled to their places by the rowlocks
and all in line dipped oars in the gray sea.

---

24. **keel.** Bottom ridge of a ship
25. **Kronos' son.** Kronos, or Chronos, the god of time, was the father of Zeus, the chief of the Greek gods.
26. **offing.** Leaving
27. **Circe.** Sorceress who, by means of drugs and incantations, was able to change humans into animals. She was the daughter of Helios and the ocean nymph Perse.

Odysseus and the Sirens, c.470 BC. Greek artist. British Museum, London.

But soon an off-shore breeze blew to our liking—
a canvas-bellying breeze, a lusty shipmate
10 sent by the singing nymph with sunbright hair.
So we made fast the braces,²⁸ and we rested,
letting the wind and steersman work the ship.
The crew being now silent before me, I
addressed them, sore at heart:

                                        "Dear friends,
15 more than one man, or two, should know those things
Circe foresaw for us and shared with me,
so let me tell her forecast: then we die
with our eyes open, if we are going to die,
or know what death we baffle if we can. Sirens
20 weaving a haunting song over the sea
we are to shun, she, and their green shore
all sweet with clover; yet she urged that I
alone should listen to their song. Therefore
you are to tie me up, tight as a splint,
25 erect along the mast, lashed to the mast,
and if I shout and beg to be untied,
take more turns of the rope to muffle me."

---

28. **made fast the braces.** Tied down the ropes that
control the movement of the sails

art note

Compare this ancient Greek vase to the painting on page 125. The vase was created about 100 years after Homer's time and the painting about 2,400 years after that. Do you think that the English painter John Waterhouse (1849–1917) may have seen the vase? What similarities and differences do you see between the two works?

Of what has Circe warned Odysseus?

What does Odysseus ask his men to do? Why doesn't he want to be free to move when he hears the Sirens' song?

I rather dwelt on this part of the forecast,
while our good ship made time, bound outward down
the wind for the strange island of Sirens.
Then all at once the wind fell, and a calm
came over all the sea, as though some power
lulled the swell.

The crew were on their feet
briskly, to furl the sail, and stow it; then,
each in place, they poised the smooth oar blades
and sent the white foam scudding by. I carved
a massive cake of beeswax into bits
and rolled them in my hands until they softened—
no long task, for a burning heat came down
from Helios,[29] lord of high noon. Going forward
I carried wax along the line, and laid it
thick on their ears. They tied me up, then, plumb
amidships, back to the mast, lashed to the mast,
and took themselves again to rowing. Soon,
as we came smartly within hailing distance,
the two Sirens, noting our fast ship
off their point, made ready, and they sang:

Why does Odysseus stop the ears of the sailors with wax?

This way, oh turn your bows,
Achaea's glory,
As all the world allows—
Moor and be merry.

Sweet coupled airs we sing.
No lonely seafarer
Holds clear of entering
Our green mirror.

Pleased by each purling[30] *note*
Like honey twining
From her throat and my throat,
Who lies a-pining?

Sea rovers here take joy
Voyaging onward,
As from our song of Troy
Graybeard and rower-boy

29. **Helios.** Sun god
30. ***purling.*** Swirling; rippling

Goeth more learnèd.[31]

65   *All feats on that great field*
          In the long warfare,
        Dark days the bright gods willed,
          Wounds you bore there,

        Argos'[32] *old soldiery*
70   *On Troy beach teeming,*
        Charmed out of time we see.
        No life on earth can be
          Hid from our dreaming.

      The lovely voices in <u>ardor</u> appealing over the water
75   made me crave to listen, and I tried to say,
      "Untie me!" to the crew, jerking my brows;
      but they bent steady to the oars. Then Perimêdês
      got to his feet, he and Eur'ylokhos,
      and passed more line about, to hold me still.
80   So all rowed on, until the Sirens
      dropped under the sea rim, and their singing
      dwindled away.
                            My faithful company
      rested on their oars now, peeling off
      the wax that I had laid thick on their ears;
85   then set me free. . . .   ■

How does Odysseus try to communicate with his crew? Why do they ignore him?

---

31. *learnèd.* The accent over the *e* shows that it is to be pronounced as a separate syllable.
32. *Argos.* Ancient Greek city-state

words for everyday use

ar • dor (är´dər) *n.,* eagerness; passion; enthusiasm. *Daniel Webster spoke with such* <u>ardor</u> *that even his opponents listened with awe.*

Respond *to the* SELECTION

Which qualitites do you admire in Odysseus? Why?

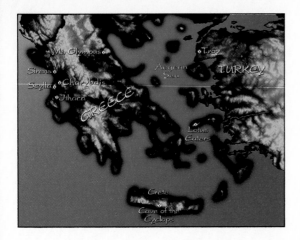

Exploring the Greece of Odysseus

by Laurel Miranda

Odysseus is alive and well. He may be impossible to verify historically, however. Was he legend? Was he fact? Archeologists, including Heinrich Schliemann, the man who discovered Troy and Mycenae, have tried to find Odysseus's palace, but have failed. But still, people who know the amazing story of the *Odyssey* pursue its hero with the hope of finding some aspect of him in the rocks, the water, the islands, the light of Greece.

It would be hard to find a more arresting character from Greek mythology, especially as Homer has characterized him. As Ellen Switzer says in *Gods, Heroes and Monsters,* Odysseus is known only for his cleverness in Homer's *Iliad.* It is not until the *Odyssey* that "Odysseus is intelligent and imaginative, but also loyal, brave, and, on occasion, kind. His physical strength is not what is most admirable about him; his moral and intellectual strength is what the reader is supposed to admire" (Switzer 191).

We were on a mission to find him. My husband and I had lived in Greece a few years earlier. Now our six-year-old son, Forest, would be seeing Greece for the first time. Even before we planned our trip, Forest was reading about Odysseus's adventures from the Wishbone Classics version of Homer's *Odyssey.* This retelling, complete with humor that only a dog as narrator can provide ("Seven years! I'd hate to be on a leash for that long") had Forest's

complete attention. He filled his notebooks with drawings: Odysseus strapped to the mast of his ship as the creepily beautiful Sirens sang, Odysseus battling the one-eyed Cyclops, Odysseus and his ship's crew trying to escape the watery clutches of Scylla and Charybdis. For Forest, going to Greece would mean swimming every day and eating his favorite souvlaki[1] and seeing the friends we had told him about for so long. But we had to add one task to our travel plans: Find Odysseus.

Americans, living as we do in a relatively new country, have a hard time realizing how possible it is for the ancient past and its heroes and gods to overlap the present. When you are in Greece, things that happened in the Dark Ages or the Classical Era seem physically real, not just the stuff of textbooks. The Akropolis rises above sprawling, chaotic Athens in such a way that you begin to believe you might walk up the Parthenon steps and hear Socrates discoursing about philosophy. Children and streets are named after gods and heroes: Athena, Hermes, Aristotle. Greeks call automobiles with one headlight missing "Cyclopes." They call jellyfish "Medusas." Finding Odysseus, or at least retracing the paths he once roamed, was not an unreasonable request for a six-year-old to make.

Ellen Switzer writes, "In many places in Greece, Odysseus is thought of as a real person, rather than a fictitious character. Since his travels presumably took him to almost every island and coastal harbor on the Aegean Sea, in

---

1. **souvlaki.** Greek shish-kebob

most villages there is someone who insists that he or she knows a special place where Odysseus hid or camped out while on his journey back home. The cave of Odysseus is almost like the bed in which Washington slept. It's anywhere someone thinks it is" (Switzer 191).

Library research before our trip confirmed this. We learned of seven archeological digs in Ithaka in search of Odysseus's palace between 1805 and 1938. The latest and ongoing expedition, initiated in 1984 on the island at Aetos, has had several excavation seasons. Its director, Professor Sarantis Symeonoglou, maintains that this location "corresponds best to the setting described in Homer's great epic, the *Odyssey*" (Symeonoglou, "Odyssey Project" Web Site).

The presence of Odysseus and the events that Homer chronicled are not limited to archeological sites. People on the island of Corfu claim that the shipwrecked Odysseus was washed up and discovered by Nausicaa at the beaches at Palocastritsa (Gage 200). Others have asserted that the temple of Apollo in Sicyon housed Odysseus's cloak and breastplate, and a sample of his wife Penelope's weaving (MacKendrick 407). And at Tiryns, people still like to say that the Cyclops built the huge walls that are 30 feet high and 27 feet thick in some places (Time-Life Books 134). As Ellen Switzer says, "Greek mythology is unique in that it is so totally earthbound. In today's Greece, any tourist who asks the right questions will be shown the cave (though some may say it was a hut) where Odysseus hid before entering Ithaca" (Switzer vii).

We didn't find that exact cave on the island of Ithaka, but we found plenty of other little caves and crevices on the nearby islands of Zakynthos and Kephalonia that served as well. No matter where we went in Greece, Forest scanned the horizon for castles in the rocky hillsides, caverns where the Cyclops might live, the beach where Odysseus had washed up on shore. It was all so real to him that he didn't require documentation. At one point, things got a little too real: I made the mistake of telling him that Scylla and Charybdis, the sea monsters that had capsized Odysseus's ship and killed his men, were just ahead of our boat as we crossed the water to the next island. He was terrified. We managed to calm him enough to get through the ferry ride, but that night we had a sleepless night battling the Scylla and Charybdis of nightmares.

But if Odysseus could make it past such treacherous monsters, so could he. The next morning Forest was up and swimming through caverns along the beach as if nothing had happened the night before. A stick became a sword, he did the battles he needed to do with Cyclops, and he managed to sail his inflatable raft between a three-headed craggy rock and his father, who provided added drama as the whirlpool. Later I learned of Professor Spyridon Marinatos, an archeologist who discovered Santorini as the lost island of Atlantis. "Whenever he set sail, he liked to imagine himself accompanied by Odysseus, the hero of Homer's *Odyssey*, and about to encounter similar adventures" (Time-Life Books 56). Forest, it seemed, was in good company.

Works Cited

Gage, Nicholas. *Hellas: A Portrait of Greece.* New York: Villard Books, 1987.

MacKendrick, Paul. *The Greek Stones Speak: The Story of Archaeology in Greek Lands.* Second Edition. New York, Norton, 1981.

Switzer, Ellen, and Costas. *Greek Myths: Gods, Heroes and Monster.* New York. Atheneum, 1988.

Symeonoglou, Sarantis. "Odyssey Project Homepage." <http://www.artsci.wustl.edu/~ssymeono/summary.html> Site maintained by Department of Art History & Archaeology, Washington University, St. Louis, MO.

Time-Life Books. *Wondrous Realms of the Aegean.* Alexandra, Virginia. Time-Life Books. 1993.

Wishbone Classics. Homer. The *Odyssey.* Retold by Joanne Mattern. New York: HarperCollins, 1996.

Investigate, *Inquire,* and Imagine

Recall: GATHERING FACTS

1a. What do Odysseus's men suggest when they arrive at the land of the Cyclopes? Why do they not follow this plan?

2a. What does Odysseus tell the Cyclops his name is? How do Odysseus and his men escape from the Cyclops? What does Odysseus do when he and his sailors have left the island of the Cyclopes?

3a. What warning does Odysseus share with his men? What preparations do they make?

Interpret: FINDING MEANING

1b. What does Odysseus's desire to wait for the inhabitant of the cave tell you about his personality? What happens as a result of Odysseus's decision?

2b. Why does Odysseus identify himself with a false name? What aspects of Odysseus's personality are revealed by the plan he concocts to free himself and his remaining men from the Cyclops? Why does Odysseus shout to the Cyclops when he and his men are away from the island?

3b. What characterizes the words of the Sirens' song?

Analyze: TAKING THINGS APART

4a. Identify the mythological characters that help or hinder Odysseus on his journey.

Synthesize: BRINGING THINGS TOGETHER

4b. Explain how Odysseus's beliefs in these mythological characters affect his behavior.

Evaluate: MAKING JUDGMENTS

5a. On a scale of one to ten, rate the effectiveness of Odysseus as a leader. Explain your answer.

Extend: CONNECTING IDEAS

5b. Compare Odysseus to other legendary heroes and discuss how they are similar and different.

Understanding *Literature*

EPIC AND HEROIC EPIC. Review the definition for **epic** and **heroic epic** in the Handbook of Literary Terms. What powers do the gods possess? How do they use their powers? What makes Odysseus a hero?

PERSONIFICATION. Review the definition for **personification** in the Handbook of Literary Terms and the cluster chart you made in Literary Tools on page 123. Why is it logical for Homer to personify Dawn?

Writer's Journal

1. Imagine that, as Odysseus, you decided to heed the warning of your men and did not shout out to Polyphemos. Write the Cyclops a **letter** instead, explaining why you blinded him.

2. Imagine that you are Odysseus. Write a **ship's log entry** explaining how you lost several men and describing the effect of your loss.

3. Imagine that you are one of Odysseus's men and you have entered the twenty-first century by means of a time capsule. Write a set of **beliefs** that you lived by to share with people of this century. Explain why each belief was important to you.

Integrating the Language Arts

Language, Grammar, and Style

AGREEMENT OF PRONOUNS AND ANTECEDENTS. Check the pronouns in the sentences below to be sure they agree in number and gender with their antecedents (the words to which they refer). Begin by underlining the pronouns and circling their antecedents. Next, identify whether the agreement problem is incorrect because of number or gender. Then rewrite the sentences to achieve pronoun-antecedent agreement. An example has been done for you. For more information, see the Language Arts Survey 3.45, "Getting Pronouns and Antecedents to Agree."

EXAMPLE:
Telemachus waited for <u>her</u> father to return. (incorrect gender)
Revised: Telemachus waited for his father to return.

1. Odysseus wanted to meet the Cyclops in their cave.
2. Dawn spread out his finger tips of rose.
3. Each of Odysseus's sailors struck their oars into the sea.
4. Did Odysseus or did the Cyclops lose their courage?
5. The crew on the ship is hoping they can escape the Sirens.

Study and Research & Collaborative Learning

ALLUSIONS. With a partner, read poems from the eighteenth and nineteenth centuries that make allusions to characters found in the *Odyssey*. Then make a quotations booklet listing relevant lines under topics such as the Cyclopes, the Sirens, Zeus, Circe, Dawn (Eos), and Poseidon. Finally, find paintings and statues from the eighteenth and nineteenth centuries that portray these mythological characters.

Speaking and Listening & Study and Research

ART EXHIBIT. Find a copy of a painting that illustrates an episode from the *Odyssey* in the library and make a photocopy. Then describe to the class what is happening in the painting. Finally, you might want to post your painting in the classroom, along with those of your classmates, to create an art exhibit on the *Odyssey*.

Language Arts in Action

COWBOY POETRY GATHERINGS HELP PRESERVE WESTERN TRADITIONS

Cowboy poetry rides as high as the great western landscape at the original Cowboy Poetry Gathering, which meets each January in Elko, Nevada. Started in 1985 by the Western Folklife Center, a nonprofit organization dedicated to preserving the folk arts of the American West, the Gathering continues to grow in popularity with each passing year. It celebrates the tradition of cowboy poetry, an art form that traces its roots to Anglo-Saxon and Celtic balladry, but is distinctly American.

Most of the first cowboys emigrated from the British Isles in the mid-nineteenth century and moved west to find work herding and driving cattle on ranches. Bringing with them their native storytelling tradition, these immigrants fused their past with the broad horizons of their new identity in the American West. Into that mixture also went the traditions of Moorish and Spanish horsemanship, European cavalry, African improvisation, and Native American experience.

The poetry and songs of the cowboys celebrated the "cowboy lifestyle," that of a rugged individual able to exist in the vast and often harsh territory of the West. When the trail drives became obsolete in the late 1800s due to the growth and convenience of railroad shipping, the cowboy way of life threatened to become extinct as well. However, the spirit of that life survives today in cowboy poetry.

The highlight of every gathering is the chance to see and hear cowboy poets perform their work. Cowboy poetry is at its best when read or sung aloud. As Eddie Nickens writes in his article "Bards of the Bunkhouse,"[1] "In its written form some might call this poetry simplistic, unpolished. Like a horse in need of a rider, however, these words need a human voice to guide them, and when that voice is deft—or gifted—the result is poetry of emotional clarity and unabashed honesty that speaks eloquently to those far removed from the cowboy experience." Some poems can be sad and wistful, hearkening back to the lost days of the open range. Others are uproariously funny tall tales about rodeo mishaps and the vengeful sweethearts of roamin' cowpokes. They all retain the flavor of the West.

The Cowboy Poetry Gathering in Elko, Nevada, was the first effort to formally pay homage to the cowboy poetry tradition. Since then, other gatherings throughout the West have helped renew a burgeoning interest in all things western. Along with the poetry and music, these yearly Gatherings offer a variety of educational programs to help preserve the cowboy heritage, including workshops on blacksmithing, horsehair hitching, ranch-style cooking, and fancy knot tying.

With all their diverse offerings, the Gatherings are very popular with young people. Many organizers have tailored their programs to attract young adults to the ways of the cowboy lifestyle, hoping that future generations will carry forward the best of the West. Many of the Gatherings offer youth poetry contests with prizes and scholarships awarded at each year's events. The following poem by ninth-grader Austin Huckabee won an award at the National Cowboy Symposium in Lubbock, Texas.

---

1. Eddie Nickens, "Bards of the Bunkhouse," Historic Preservation,
May 1 June 1994. Excerpted at http://www.westfolk.org/w.b.histpres.html.

continued on page 150

THE WESTERN FOLKLIFE CENTER
PRESENTS

THE 15TH COWBOY POETRY
GATHERING
JANUARY 23-30 · 1999 · ELKO · NEVADA

WILD HORSES OF NEVADA, 1927, BY MAYNARD DIXON · COLLECTION OF THE WILLIAM A. KARGES FAMILY TRUST

From "THE RHYME OF THE RESTLESS ONES" By Robert Service

Oh, they shook us off and shipped us o'er the foam,
To the larger lands that lure a man to roam;
And we took the chance they gave
Of a far and foreign grave,
and we bade good-by for evermore to home.

. . . And you'll find us herding cattle in the South.
We like strong drink and fun, and, when the race is run,
We often die with curses in our mouth.
We are wild as colts unbroke, but never mean,
Of our sins we've shoulders broad to bear the blame;
But we'll never stay in town and we'll never settle down,
And we'll never have an object or an aim.

MAJOR SUPPORT FOR THE COWBOY POETRY GATHERING AND THE WESTERN FOLKLIFE CENTER IS PROVIDED BY: NEVADA COMMISSION FOR CULTURAL AFFAIRS · LILA WALLACE-READER'S DIGEST FUND · NATIONAL ENDOWMENT FOR THE ARTS · R. HAROLD BURTON FOUNDATION · WILLIAM & FLORA HEWLETT FOUNDATION · JOHN BEN SHON MEMORIAL TRUST · GEORGE GUND III · CITY OF ELKO · THE WILLIAM RANDOLPH HEARST FOUNDATIONS · NEVADA ARTS COUNCIL · ANNE PATTEE · RUTH MOTT FUND · LILA WALLACE-READER'S DIGEST COMMUNITY FOLKLIFE PROGRAM · FULL HOUSE, INC. · UTAH TRAVEL COUNCIL · MEL AND SUE DIXON · BARRICK GOLDSTRIKE · ELKO COUNTY RECREATION BOARD · PHILIP MORRIS COMPANIES · THE BRETZLAFF FOUNDATION · WILLIAM AND SALLY SEARLE · NEVADA COMMISSION ON TOURISM · NEVADA HUMANITIES COMMITTEE AND MANY OTHER BUSINESSES AND INDIVIDUALS. SPECIAL THANKS TO THE ELKO CONVENTION AND VISITORS AUTHORITY · GREAT BASIN COLLEGE · NORTHEASTERN NEVADA MUSEUM AND THE ELKO CHAMBER OF COMMERCE

The Last Cowboys

by Austin Huckabee, Veribest Junior High, 9th Grade

In this big world of computers and digital phones
There ain't no room for the last cowboys to roam.

They're supposed to go on drives and fix broken fences
Not be forced to leave for "economical businesses."

Nowhere to go, so they're forced to settle down
Take roots & stay, or go live in town.

They need room to stray, need wide open spaces
All these cities and suburbs bring sadness to their faces.

Where will they go? Where will they stay?
There's nowhere to sleep at the end of the day.

This world is too crowded, there's nowhere to roam
There's not any place for the last cowboys to call home.

Ninth-grade poet Austin Huckabee
of Veribest, Texas.

Since the first Gathering at Elko, Nevada in 1985, many others have followed. To find out how you and your classmates can get involved, investigate one of the following poetry gatherings or resources:

- **Cowboy Poetry Gathering,** Elko, Nevada.
  This is the original gathering. For more information, visit http://www.westernfolklife.org; send a letter to 501 Railroad St., Elko, NV 89801; or call 775-738-7508.
- **Cochise Cowboy Poetry & Music Gathering,** Sierra Vista, Arizona.
  For information, visit http://www.cowboypoets.com; write to P.O. Box 3201, Sierra Vista, AZ 85636-3201; or call 520-459-3868.
- **Lincoln County Symposium,** Ruidoso Downs, New Mexico.
  Visit http://www.zianet.com/lccs/.
- **National Cowboy Symposium and Celebration,** Lubbock, Texas.
  For general information, visit http://www.cowboy.org or write to 4124 62nd Drive, Lubbock, Texas 79413. For information specifically about the youth poetry contest, visit http://www.cowboy.org/ypoets.htm.
- **Texas Cowboy Poetry Gathering,** Sul Ross State University, Alpine, Texas.
  Visit http://www.sulross.edu/~poetry/.
- **Omar West's Cowboy Poetry at the Bar-D Ranch**
  This site, located at http://www.cowboypoetry.com/, offers a poetry contest. Winners have a chance at becoming the "Lariat Laureate." It also contains a number of cowboy poetry links and a collection of Omar West's poems.

Guided Writing

COMPOSING A PERSONAL ESSAY

Look at your heroes. Surely, some of them are probably legends from the past: George Washington, Abraham Lincoln, or Martin Luther King. Others may be considered more modern, legends in our own time: Mother Teresa, Christopher Reeve, or Michael Jordan. Each culture and age adds its own heroes to the mix.

Sometimes poets celebrate heroes and their heroic acts in epic poems. That can keep the legend alive for all time. But what is it that makes a hero? Some heroes, like Odysseus, conquer brutish foes and outwit clever enemies. Some achieve outstanding goals against all odds. Some help others, sacrificing their lives for the good of all people. The specific details of their courageous acts provide the basis for the poem, story, or legend sung, written, or spun about heroes' lives.

What legend or legend-in-the-making do you admire? You might consider someone who has spent a long time away from family and friends—perhaps someone captured during a war— and recognize a modern Odysseus.

WRITING ASSIGNMENT. Write a personal essay with documentation about a person that you consider a hero. By researching the life of someone you admire, you can learn more about what traits make that person the way he or she is and why you call him or her a hero.

Professional Model

from "Exploring the Greece of Odysseus"
by Laurel Miranda
page 144

Odysseus is alive and well....people who know the amazing story of the *Odyssey* pursue its hero with the hope of finding some aspect of him in the rocks, the water, the islands, the light of Greece....

We were on a mission to find him. My husband and I had lived in Greece a few years earlier. Now our six-year-old son, Forest, would be seeing Greece for the first time....[and that] would mean swimming every day and

EXAMINING THE MODEL. "Exploring the Greece of Odysseus" investigates some of the historical remnants of an ancient, larger-than-life hero. Does this descriptive piece help bring Odysseus to life for you the way it does for Forest and the author? What details does the author include that make Odysseus seem like a real person? What did you learn about Odysseus that you didn't already know? Which piece of new information did you find most interesting? Why? What is the central point of this essay? Which details do you think the author needed to research? How does this essay help you better define the essence of a hero?

The American Heritage Dictionary defines **hero** as someone in mythology or legend who "who is endowed with great courage and strength," or someone "noted for great feats of courage or nobility of purpose."

eating his favorite souvlaki and seeing the friends we had told him about for so long. But we had to add one task to our travel plans: Find Odysseus....

Ellen Switzer writes, "In many places in Greece, Odysseus is thought of as a real person, rather than a fictitious character....The cave of Odysseus is almost like the bed in which Washington slept. It's anywhere someone thinks it is" (Switzer 191)....

We didn't find that exact cave on the island of Ithaka, but we found plenty of other little caves and crevices on the nearby islands of Zakynthos and Kephalonia that served as well. No matter where we went in Greece, Forest scanned the horizon for castles in the rocky hillsides, caverns where the Cyclops might live, the beach where Odysseus had washed up on shore....

....A stick became a sword, he did the battles he needed to do with Cyclops, and he managed to sail his inflatable raft between a three-headed craggy rock and his father, who provided added drama as the whirlpool. Later I learned of Professor Spyridon Marinatos, an archeologist who discovered Santorini as the lost island of Atlantis. "Whenever he set sail, he liked to imagine himself accompanied by Odysseus, the hero of Homer's *Odyssey*, and about to encounter similar adventures" (Time-Life Books 56). Forest, it seemed, was in good company.

Partial Bibliography

Gage, Nicholas. *Hellas: A Portrait of Greece.* New York: Villard Books, 1987.

MacKendrick, Paul. *The Greek Stones Speak: The Story of Archaeology in Greek Lands.* Second Edition. New York, Norton, 1981.

Switzer, Ellen, and Costas. *Greek Myths: Gods, Heroes and Monster.* New York. Atheneum, 1988.

Prewriting

WRITING WITH A PLAN. Look at the poems you read in this section that identify heroes—the *Odyssey* and "Local Sensibilities" are examples. What makes the characters heroic? Are there any striking similarities (or differences) between these fictional heroes and your hero? Brainstorm with classmates what characteristics a figure must possess to be called a hero. After you have a list of everyone's responses, discuss in a small group the traits you want in your final definition of *hero*. Consider, as a start, the dictionary definition at left. You will probably want to add other characteristics as your group develops the definition you consider most complete. Circle the traits as your group reaches consensus.

Pick one of your heroes and research his or her life. There are a number of places to look for information: books, newspapers, magazines, video, and the Internet. From your research, list some of the more memorable things that have happened to this person or that he or she has accomplished. Discover what there is about this person that qualifies him or her as a hero. When you research a topic, even one with which you are very familiar, you usually discover something you didn't know before. What new facts about your hero did you learn? Did they change the way you look at this person? How? Do you have enough information to write about this event in detail? If not, go back to your notes and research sources with this more specific question and look for more details.

Niko used the graphic organizer below to decide what information to include in his paper.

In your group work, remember to:
- Ask questions of one another about which traits to include.
- Listen to others' responses.
- Give reasons for your ideas.

Student Model—Graphic Organizer

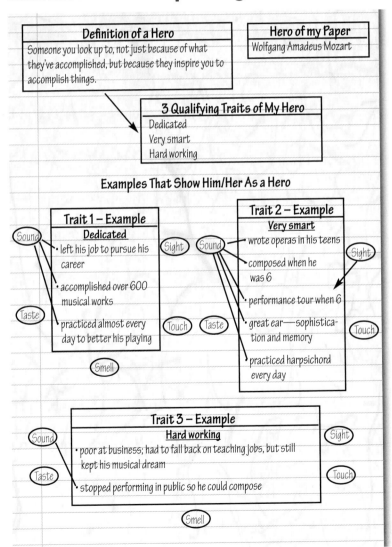

Definition of a Hero
Someone you look up to, not just because of what they've accomplished, but because they inspire you to accomplish things.

Hero of my Paper
Wolfgang Amadeus Mozart

3 Qualifying Traits of My Hero
Dedicated
Very smart
Hard working

Examples That Show Him/Her As a Hero

Trait 1 – Example
Dedicated
- left his job to pursue his career
- accomplished over 600 musical works
- practiced almost every day to better his playing

(Sound) (Taste) (Sight) (Touch) (Smell)

Trait 2 – Example
Very smart
- wrote operas in his teens
- composed when he was 6
- performance tour when 6
- great ear—sophistication and memory
- practiced harpsichord every day

(Sound) (Taste) (Sight) (Touch)

Trait 3 – Example
Hard working
- poor at business; had to fall back on teaching jobs, but still kept his musical dream
- stopped performing in public so he could compose

(Sound) (Taste) (Sight) (Touch) (Smell)

> "I find that a great part of the information I have was acquired by looking up something and finding something else on the way."
> —Franklin P. Adams

Copy the graphic organizer and complete it for your own hero. Use at least two senses in each of your examples. Draw an arrow to the sense from the detail that uses it. Then circle the heroic traits you want to describe and the examples and incidents you will use to illustrate those choices. Be sure to include the sensory details—images of sight, sound, touch, taste, or smell—to capture your readers' attention when you describe the hero in action. These details will help bring your hero to life. Remember, an effective introduction will catch the reader's interest and map out the journey your reader is about to take, while a satisfactory conclusion will wrap up the sequence of ideas as a complete package.

FINDING YOUR VOICE. Your voice will reveal your attitude toward your subject. Think for a moment: What is it about this person that you most admire? How can you make your reader feel this admiration? What is there about your topic that makes it irresistible? Look at how Forest idolized Odysseus. What do you think made this ancient and imaginary character so real to this young boy? What is there about your hero that will stir your readers' hearts and minds? Write one sentence or phrase that captures this spirit. Now rewrite the phrase several times, each time experimenting with the language you use. Work toward writing the phrase in such a way that it personally touches you and whoever else might read your paper.

Notice the difference in voice in this:

Forest always looked for the places where Odysseus might have been.

and this:

No matter where we went in Greece, Forest scanned the horizon for castles in the rocky hillsides, caverns where the Cyclops might live, the beach where Odysseus had washed up on shore.

How do word choice, sentence structure, and tone contribute to voice?

IDENTIFYING YOUR AUDIENCE. Who will be interested in reading what you have found out about your hero? What lessons and examples from your research best describe what your hero has to offer your audience? What examples clearly define why this person is a hero? Why? What special background knowledge do they need to understand the message? Will your audience include readers likely to be familiar with the topic? If so, are there certain assumptions you can make about your readers' familiarity with your material? How much detail is too much and how much is not enough?

DOCUMENTATION. You need to give credit to the authors for the information you use in your research. For more information about documenting sources, see the Language Arts Survey 5.36, "Documenting Sources."

Drafting

After your research is complete, and your details are at hand and organized cohesively in your graphic organizer, you are ready to begin. Base your report on these details. Work in the details you researched to support your statements. Be sure that you give credit to your sources.

At this point, don't focus on spelling, grammar, usage, and mechanics. Instead, concentrate on two things: 1) creating a picture of your hero with words, and 2) describing the experience or experiences that have made him or her someone to be admired. Just put your ideas down on paper and write a rough draft.

Student Model—Draft

> Mozart was a very smart person. He was born in Salzburg, Austria in 1756. Before he was even four years old he already showed his talents for memory and ear-sophistication. When his father realized that Mozart had a talent for music he signed him up for harpsichord lessons. A harpsichord is an old instrument, like a piano. —— *Add sensory detail*
>
> Mozzart started to write opera in his teens and his first opera, Mitridate ~*Italics* was performed when he was only fouteen! Even at such a young age, critics compared him to Handel ⁁another famous composer). When he was fifteen he was made the concertmaster in the orchestra of the Archbishop of Salzburg. Things didn't go very well at this job because Mozart didn't get along very well with the Archbishop, ~~and~~ ⁁left for Vienna/ against his father's wishes. *He* *Documentation?*

Language, Grammar, and Style

Pronoun and Antecedent Agreement

IDENTIFYING PRONOUN AND ANTECEDENT ERRORS. A **pronoun** is a word that takes the place of a noun or stands in for an unknown noun. The noun that the pronoun replaces is called its **antecedent.** A pronoun must agree with or match its antecedent because it is a substitute for the noun. Look at the example below from the professional model:

> …in most villages there is someone who insists that he or she knows a special place where Odysseus hid or camped out while on his journey back home.

Who, he, she, and *someone* are four pronouns that broadly refer to a specific person who believes he or she has special knowledge of Odysseus. *Where* is a pronoun whose antecedent is "a place." Finally, *his* connects "journey" with Odysseus.

Read the example below from the professional model:

> …people who know the amazing story of the *Odyssey* pursue its hero with the hope of finding some aspect of him in the rocks, the water, the islands, the light of Greece….

continued on page 156

Reorganize so that you put facts and examples about the same trait in one paragraph. Put all the things about his being smart in one paragraph. Put all the things about being dedicated (producing even under hardship) together. A third paragraph could be about how hard he worked. Give examples and facts with sensory detail for each trait.

Give detail about what this is all about.

Identify the pronouns and their antecedents. Explain why they are in agreement.

Go to the professional model and identify all the pronouns. What are their antecedents? To what do they refer? Explain.

FIXING PRONOUN AND ANTECEDENT ERRORS. Look at the following line from Niko's rough draft and identify an error in pronoun-antecedent agreement. Rewrite the sentence to correct the error(s) in agreement.

A hero is someone you look up to, not just because of what they've accomplished, but because they inspire you to accomplish things.

continued on page 157

Now that Mozart was a grown man his thrived in Vienna. Even so, he was poor at business and sometimes had to fall back on teaching jobs. He stopped performing in public in 1788 and decided to compose more instead. At thirty‸five years old he died.

Though Mozart had a short life he completed many amazing works. Mozart *back this up with some facts* was a child prodigy and genous as his life continued. Mozart was a dedicated musician ~~and~~ *at* such a young age. He gave everything he had into what he did. When he didn't like what he was doing when he was being the concertmaster he left for refuge in Vienna for a musical career. That definately shows how didicated Mozart was to his passion.

Self- and Peer Evaluation

After you finish your first draft, complete a self-evaluation of your writing. If time allows, you may want to get one or two peer evaluations. See the Language Arts Survey 2.37 for more details about self- and peer evaluation. As you evaluate your research paper or that of a classmate, answer the following questions:

- On what qualities of a hero does this paper focus? How does this paper convey the theme of what made the hero a hero?
- What specific, vivid details help the experience of the hero become real, alive, and important for the reader?
- How does reading about the hero affect you? What are your reactions to the heroic deeds presented here? Are you impressed? stirred? awed?

- How does the voice invite you along to share the experience? Does it seem that the author is talking to you?
- Where can word choices be improved? What words could be added or changed to make the details more concrete, specific, and descriptive?
- Where does the writer employ metaphor and simile, comparisons, to create more specific images that convey the uniqueness of the subject to the audience?
- Where, if anywhere, are there problems with pronoun-antecedent agreement?

Revising and Proofreading

If possible, wait a day before you revise your personal essay. Review your self- and peer evaluations. Revise your writing according to decisions you make about these comments. Consider the focus and content, as well as the agreement of all your pronouns and their antecedents. Concentrate on the realism of the examples you use and how clearly it comes across.

Publishing and Presenting

Finally, write or print a final copy of your essay and give it to a relative or friend to read, especially someone for whom the message might have special significance. You and your classmates may also want to share your reports. You might want to use the topic and details of your essay as a basis for a different type of writing. For instance, how would your incident translate into an epic or even humorous or satiric poem, news article, or short story. Consider illustrating your work.

Reflecting

Consider the value of taking the time to reflect on events and experiences in your own life that are similar to or have some connection with those of your hero and write these reflections down. How have you gained from this experience? How might you continue to gain from this experience if you reread your report when you are twenty? when you are thirty?

What was the reaction of the person or persons who read your essay? Compare your reflective essay with one or more of the reports in your class. Are there any similarities between the themes, incidents, thoughts, or feelings? Are the same topics still valid or do they seem dated? Why, or why not? What has changed and what hasn't?

See the Student Model—Revised on pages 158–159.

For more help on fixing pronoun-antecedent agreement errors, see the Language Arts Survey 3.45. For help on identifying a subject and a verb, see the Language Arts Survey 3.21.

USING PRONOUN AND ANTECEDENT AGREEMENT. Circle the pronoun and underline the antecedent in each sentence of your personal essay. Check the pronoun-antecedent agreement for case, number, and ambiguity. Singular antecedents need singular pronouns. Plural antecedents need plural pronouns. Subject case antecedents require subject case pronouns. Object case antecedents require object case pronouns. The relationship between antecedents and pronouns must be obvious, explicit, and clear.

If a number of words separate the pronoun from the antecedent, temporarily removing the words in between can help you isolate the antecedent and pronoun and determine whether they agree.

Mozart...My Hero
by Niko Tsubota

A hero is someone that you look up to, not just because of what he or she has accomplished, but because he inspires you to accomplish things. Because of this definition of a hero, I chose to write about one of my heroes, Wolfgang Amadeus Mozart. Mozart is a hero to me because whenever I listen to one of his many piano pieces or symphonies it inspires me to do my best in practicing and performing.

Mozart was a very smart person, a child prodigy and genius. He was born in Salzburg, Austria, in 1756. Before he was even four years old he already showed his talents for memory and ear-sophistication. When his father realized that Mozart had a talent for music he signed him up for harpsichord lessons. A harpsichord is an old instrument, like a piano, but it has a raspy sound and fewer keys. Mozart quickly mastered it. Mozart started to compose music when he was six years old and toured Vienna at this age with his piano pieces. Mozart started to write operas in his teens. His first opera, *Mitridate*, was performed when he was only fourteen! Critics compared him to Handel, another famous composer of those days, even at such a young age (Scime). Though Mozart had a short life he completed many amazing works. He composed over 600 different musical works; 21 stage and operas, over 50 symphonies, 25 piano concertos, 12 violin concertos, 17 piano sonatas, 26 string quartets, and many others (Chew).

Mozart was a dedicated musician starting at a young age. He put everything he had into working with music. When he had to perform in front of royalty it must have been very nerve-racking for him. He had to wear very fancy clothes that people wore in the 1700s. I imagine he even had to wear one of the white flour wigs they wore back then; that would make me sneeze! Despite all of this he always got through the performances well. It must have been a sight for the people he played in front of: a little boy sitting behind a giant piano playing everything so perfectly. When he was fifteen he was hired as the concertmaster of the Archbishop of Salzburg's orchestra. Things didn't go very well at this job because Mozart didn't get along well with the archbishop. Mozart left for Vienna against his father's wishes. This shows how dedicated he was to his music. He left behind something certain, a job he could hold, and left for the unknown just because he wanted to compose and play his music (LeCargo).

Mozart was also a hard worker. While he was traveling through Vienna when he was about six years old the conditions from show to show were terrible! On many occasions the family had to travel in a carriage that was unheated and on a worn suspension system. That didn't help at all when they hit all of the rocks and such on the roadway. Somehow he got through all the awful conditions on the trips. When Mozart was on his own he thrived in Vienna. Even so, he was poor at business and sometimes had to fall back on teaching jobs to support himself, but music was always in his heart and soul. When he did have enough money to keep following his dream, he did. He never stopped learning and working for what he wanted. He stopped performing in public in 1788 so that he could concentrate on composing music. He died when he was only thirty-five (Boerner).

When I learned about everything that Mozart had accomplished in his short life, it made me want to strive even more to be a better piano player and try my best at everything I do. Not just in the musical area, but even when I'm doing schoolwork I can think about how dedicated Mozart was. It makes me think about how much I could be doing if I tried my hardest. A hero to many people is just someone to admire, but to me a hero is something more. A hero makes you think about what you've done, or are doing, with your life and makes you strive to be a better person.

Bibliography

Boerner, Steve. "The Mozart Project." 1999.
   <http://www.mozartproject.org/>.
Chew, Robin. "Wolfgang Amadeus Mozart." 1996.
   <http://www2.lucidcafe.com/lucidcafe/library/96jan/mozart.html.>
Scime, Toniann. "W.A. Mozart." 1999.
   <http://members.tripod.com/wamozart/bio.html>.
LeCargo. "A Tribute to Wolfgang Amadeus Mozart."
   <http://208.4.223.8/lecagot/mozart.asp>.

UNIT 2 review
Poetry

Words for Everyday Use

Check your knowledge of the following vocabulary words from the selections in this unit. Write a short sentence using each of these words in context to make the meaning clear. To review the definition or usage of a word, refer back to the page number(s) listed or the Glossary of Words for Everyday Use.

annex, 126	civility, 129	lash, 110	rogue, 130
ardor, 143	clamor, 83	melancholy, 83	sage, 135
avenge, 130	cordial, 133	modulation, 114	stow, 129
balmy, 82	dappled, 89	palpitating, 83	subdue, 109
barren, 119	din, 132	pectoral, 136	titanic, 139
bracken, 109	exotic, 93	plunder, 127	verdant, 94
carrion, 136	fume, 128	ponderous, 132	voluminously, 82
chafe, 126	knell, 84	prodigious, 128	

Literary Tools

Define each of the following terms, giving concrete examples of how they are used in the selections in this unit. To review a term, refer to the page number(s) indicated or the Handbook of Literary Terms.

aim, 103	heroic epic, 123	repetition, 80
allegory, 87	image, 92	rhyme, 87
couplet, 103	metaphor, 97, 107	simile, 97, 107, 117
effect, 92	narrative poem, 113, 117	speaker, 92
epic, 123	onomatopoeia, 80	symbol, 107
figurative language, 97	personification, 113, 123	theme, 97

Reflecting
on your reading

Genre Studies

1. Select a lyric poem and a narrative poem from the unit and explain how they differ. Use specific examples from the poems to define what a lyric poem and a narrative poem are.

2. What examples can you find in the unit of each of the following techniques of sound: onomatopoeia, repetition, and rhyme? How do these techniques enrich the meaning of the poems?

3. Find examples of figurative language in the selections from this unit, specifically, personification, simile, and metaphor. What idea is expressed by each example?

4. What is a heroic epic? How does the poem the *Odyssey* meet that definition? What makes the poem an epic? How does the character Odysseus meet the Greek ideal of the hero?

Thematic Studies

5. **LOCATION.** How does the location of "Local Sensibilities" inform the meaning of the poem? How would the poem be different if it had a different location?

6. **GOALS.** How does having a goal affect the speakers of "The Song of Wandering Aengus" and "Birches"? What is each speaker's goal? How does each speaker plan to attain his goal?

7. **CREATION.** Explore the theme of creation in "The Creation" and "Song." What is being created in each poem? What was the impetus to create? How does the creator feel about his or her creation?

8. **ADVICE.** Both "Metaphor" and "Boast Not, Proud English" give advice to the reader on how to live. What is that advice? What will the reader gain if he or she heeds that advice?

for your READING LIST

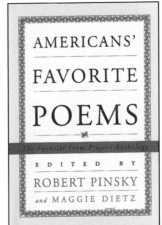

Americans' Favorite Poems: The Favorite Poem Project Anthology edited by Robert Pinsky and Maggie Dietz. Yes, ordinary Americans do read poetry. Poet laureate Robert Pinsky set out to show that not only do Americans of all ages, backgrounds, and walks of life read poetry, but also that poetry plays a significant role in their lives. He invited Americans to submit their favorite poem along with a brief description of the reasons for their choice. The overwhelming response led to this anthology, which includes everything from Shakespearean sonnets to Lewis Carroll's "Jabberwocky." What sets this anthology apart from any other, though, is the words of the very diverse group of people who chose the poems. The thoughts of teenagers and grandparents, prisoners and artists, housewives and executives who chose the poems help to make this book not just a collection of poetry, but a portrait of America as well.

Independent Reading Activity

COMPILE YOUR OWN ANTHOLOGY. Working with your book circle or club, compile an anthology of your favorite poems. You may want to solicit choices from a wider group, perhaps the entire class, the entire school, or your families. Invite each person to include a brief statement of why he or she chose a particular poem and what special meaning the poem holds for him or her.

Selections for Additional Reading

I Am Wings: Poems about Love by Ralph Fletcher. These thirty-three poems capture the experiences of falling in and out of love with titles such as "Phone Call," "Crush Blush," and "Changing Channels."

Poetry for Young People: Edgar Allan Poe edited by Brod Bagert. This book of the suspenseful poetry and prose of Edgar Allan Poe is modernized with colorful and spooky illustration.

Poems for Youth, Emily Dickinson edited by Alfred Leete Hampson. This collection of seventy-eight poems written by Emily Dickinson includes poems on the themes of friendship, nature, and the cycles of time, and is enhanced with black-and-white drawings by Thomas B. Allen.

Fiction

> " Fiction is truth's
> elder sister. "
>
> —*Rudyard Kipling*

ELEMENTS *of* FICTION

The term *fiction* comes from the Latin *fictio*, meaning "something invented." Thus fiction is any prose writing that tells an invented or imaginary story. Some fiction, the historical novel, for example, is based on fact, while other forms, such as the fantasy tale, are highly unrealistic. Fictional works also vary in structure and length, from the newly recognized **short short** (a very brief short story) to the book-length **novel**. Other forms include the traditional **short story** and the **novella**, a fictional work of intermediate length.

The Development of Fiction

The oldest fictions are the prose stories told in the oral tradition, which include myths, legends, and fables. Early written prose fictions include Petronius's *Satyricon* and Apuleius's *The Golden Ass*, written by Romans in the first and second centuries. The first novel, *The Tale of Genji*, was written by a Japanese woman, Lady Murasaki Shikibu, in the eleventh century. Early fictions from Europe include Boccaccio's *Decameron*, a collection of short prose tales written in the mid-fourteenth century, and Cervantes's *Don Quixote*, a satire of medieval romance tales written in the early seventeenth century.

The Novel

The novel developed from various kinds of non-fictional writing, including autobiographies, biographies, travel sketches, journals, and letters. Arguably, the first full-fledged novel in English was Aphra Behn's *Oroonoko*, published in 1688. Other early novels in English include Daniel Defoe's *Robinson Crusoe* (1719) and *Moll Flanders* (1722), and Samuel Richardson's *Pamela* (1740) and *Clarissa* (1747–1748). By the mid-1800s, the novel had become a popular form in the United States. Important American novelists include Nathaniel Hawthorne (1804–1864), Herman Melville

(1819–1891), Mark Twain (1835–1910), Henry James (1843–1916), Kate Chopin (1850–1904), Edith Wharton (1862–1937), Stephen Crane (1871–1945), Willa Cather (1873–1947), Zora Neale Hurston (1891–1960), F. Scott Fitzgerald (1896–1940), William Faulkner (1897–1962), Ernest Hemingway (1899–1961), Richard Wright (1908–1960), John Steinbeck (1902–1968), Eudora Welty (1909–   ), Saul Bellow (1915–   ), James Baldwin (1924–1987), Toni Morrison (1931–   ), John Updike (1932–   ), and Alice Walker (1944–   ).

Important novelists from around the world include Honoré de Balzac (1799–1850), Victor Hugo (1802–1885), and Marcel Proust (1871–1922) from France; Jane Austen (1775–1817), Emily Brontë (1818–1848), and James Joyce (1882–1941) from Great Britain; Fyodor Dostoyevsky (1821–1881) and Leo Tolstoy (1828–1910) from Russia; Yasunari Kawabata (1899–1972) from Japan; Kamala Markandaya (1923–   ) from India; Gabriel García Márquez (1928–   ) from Colombia; Chinua Achebe (1930–   ) from Nigeria; Carlos Fuentes (1928–   ) and Laura Esquivel (1950–   ) from Mexico; Isabel Allende (1942–   ) from Chile; Julia Alvarez (1950–   ) from the Dominican Republic; and Mark Mathabane (1960–   ) from South Africa.

The Short Story

The short story genre, or type, originated in the United States. Important American figures in the development of the short story include Washington Irving (1783–1859), Nathaniel Hawthorne (1804–1864), and Edgar Allan Poe (1809–1849). Poe was instrumental in defining the genre, which he described as a short work that creates a single dominant impression on the reader. According to Poe, every detail in a short story should contribute to creating that overall impression or effect.

Night in Bologna, 1958. Paul Cadmus. National Museum of American Art, Washington DC.

There are many short stories in this textbook. In this unit, you will find among others "The Monkey's Paw" by W. W. Jacobs, "The Handsomest Drowned Man in the World" by Gabriel García Márquez, "Everyday Use" by Alice Walker, and "The Gift of the Magi" by famed short story master O. Henry. Elsewhere in the book you will find "Catch the Moon" by Judith Ortiz Cofer (Unit 9), "The Interlopers" by Saki (Unit 9), "The Leap" by Louise Erdrich (Unit 10), and "The Feeling of Power" by Isaac Asimov (Unit 12).

ELEMENTS OF FICTION

CHARACTER. A **character** is a person (or sometimes an animal) who figures in the action of a story. The following are some useful terms for describing characters:

A **protagonist,** or *main character,* is the central figure in a story.

An **antagonist** is a character who is pitted against a protagonist.

A **major character** is one with a significant role in the action of a story. A **minor character** is one who plays a lesser role. Because of limitations of length and focus, most short stories have, at most, one or two major characters.

A **one-dimensional character**, or *flat character,* or *caricature* is one who exhibits a single dominant quality, or **character trait.**

A **three-dimensional character**, or *full,* or *rounded character* is one who exhibits the complexity of traits associated with actual human beings.

A **static character** is one who does not change during the course of the story.

A **dynamic character** is one who does change during the course of the story.

A **stock character** is one found again and again in different literary works. Examples of stock characters include the mad scientist and the absent-minded professor.

Motivation is a force that moves a character to think, feel, or behave in a certain way. For example, a character may be **motivated** by greed, love, or friendship. The particular reasons or causes behind a character's actions are his or her **motives.**

CHARACTERIZATION. **Characterization** is the use of literary techniques to create a character. Writers use three major techniques to create characters: *direct description, portrayal of characters' behavior,* and *representations of characters' internal states.* When using direct description, the writer, through a speaker, a narrator, or another character, simply comments on the character, telling the reader about such matters as the character's appearance, habits, dress, background, personality, motivations, and so on. Skillful writers are able to create characterizations through a few well-chosen, significant details. In portrayal of a character's behavior, the writer presents the actions and speech of the character, allowing the reader to draw his or her own conclusions from what the character says or does. When using representations of internal states, the writer reveals directly the character's private thoughts and emotions, often by means of what is known as the **internal monologue.**

SETTING AND MOOD. The **setting** is the time and place in which a story occurs, together with all the details used to create a sense of a particular time and place. The **mood** is the emotion created in the reader by part or all of a literary work. A writer creates mood through judicious use of concrete details. These details might include descriptions of the setting, of characters, and of events. In fiction, setting is most often revealed by means of description of such elements as landscape, scenery, buildings, furniture, clothing, weather, and the season. It also can be revealed by how characters talk and behave. In its widest sense, setting includes the general social, political, moral, and psychological conditions in which characters find themselves. Many American novels and short stories deal with particular regions of the country (New York City, the western frontier, small towns in the South or Midwest, and so on). Writing in which particular settings play an important role is called **regional fiction.** The details used to create a particular regional setting are called **local color.**

CONFLICT. A **conflict** is a struggle between two forces in a literary work. A plot involves the introduction, development, and eventual resolution of a conflict. One side of the central conflict in a work of fiction usually is taken by the main character. That character may struggle against another character, against the forces of nature, against society or social norms, against fate, or against some element within himself or herself. A struggle that takes place between a character and some outside force is called an **external conflict.** A struggle that takes place within a character is called an **internal conflict.**

PLOT. A **plot** is a series of events related to a central conflict, or struggle. Often the events of a plot are causally connected. The English novelist E. M. Forster explained, famously, that if the king dies and then the queen dies, that is a story, but if the king dies and then the queen dies of grief, that is a plot. A typical plot involves the following elements:

The **exposition,** or *introduction,* sets the tone and mood, introduces the characters and the setting, and provides necessary background information.

The **inciting incident** is the event that introduces the central conflict.

The **rising action,** or *complication,* develops the conflict to a high point of intensity.

The **climax** is the high point of interest or suspense.

The **crisis,** or *turning point,* often the same event as the climax, is the point in the plot where something decisive happens to determine the future course of events and the eventual working out of the conflict.

The **falling action** is all the events that follow the climax.

The **resolution** is the point at which the central conflict is ended, or resolved.

The **dénouement** is any material that follows the resolution and that ties up loose ends.

Plots are often illustrated using the diagram shown below, known as a plot pyramid. However, many plots do not include all of these elements, and in short stories, the climax often occurs very late in the plot.

THEME. A **theme** is a central idea in a literary work. A long work such as a novel may deal with several interrelated themes.

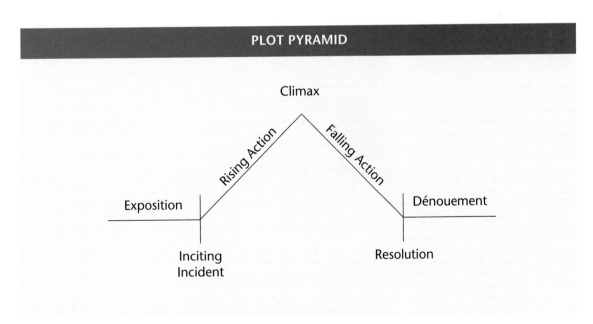

PLOT PYRAMID

Climax

Rising Action

Falling Action

Exposition

Dénouement

Inciting Incident

Resolution

Literary
T O O L S

FORESHADOWING. Foreshadowing is the act of presenting materials that hint at events to occur later in a story. As you read the selection, look for two examples of foreshadowing.

SETTING. The **setting** of a literary work is the time and place in which it occurs, together with all the details used to create a sense of a particular time and place.

Graphic Organizer

As you read, fill in the cluster chart below to describe the setting. One example has been done for you.

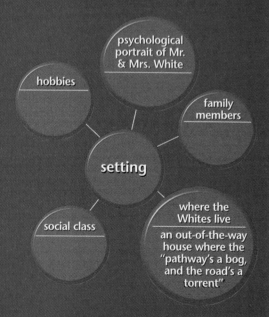

- psychological portrait of Mr. & Mrs. White
- hobbies
- family members
- **setting**
- social class
- where the Whites live
- an out-of-the-way house where the "pathway's a bog, and the road's a torrent"

"The Monkey's Paw"
by W. W. Jacobs

Reader's
r e s o u r c e

"The Monkey's Paw" was published in 1902. One year later, Louis Napoleon Parker, British playwright and composer, dramatized the story as a one-act play, which was produced in 1903 at the London Haymarket. A classic horror story, "The Monkey's Paw" creates in the reader a sense of foreboding dread. Jacobs achieves this suspenseful effect by introducing into the ordinary, everyday life of the White family the odd artifact of the monkey's paw. As you read the story, note the details that help to create its suspenseful mood.

HISTORY CONNECTION. Sergeant-Major Morris in the story has returned from a tour of duty in India, which was controlled by Britain for three and a half centuries. India did not gain its independence from Britain until 1947.

About *the*
A U T H O R

W. W. Jacobs (1863–1943), born in London, England, grew up in a house along the Thames River wharf. He later drew upon his childhood memories to write comic tales about the misadventures of sailors. *Many Cargoes,* Jacobs's first collection of stories, was immediately successful. Although his work is collected in more than twenty volumes, it is for the horror story "The Monkey's Paw" that Jacobs is best known.

Reader's
Journal

If you were granted three wishes, what would they be?

The Monkey's Paw

W. W. Jacobs

Without, the night was cold and wet, but in the small parlor of Laburnum Villa the blinds were drawn, and the fire burned brightly.

Father and son were at chess, the former, who possessed ideas about the game involving radical changes, putting his king into such sharp and unnecessary perils that it even <u>provoked</u> comment from the white-haired old lady knitting placidly by the fire.

"Hark at the wind," said Mr. White, who, having seen a fatal mistake after it was too late, was <u>amiably</u> desirous of preventing his son from seeing it.

"I'm listening," said the latter, grimly surveying the board as he stretched out his hand. "Check."

"I should hardly think that he'd come tonight," said his father, with his hand <u>poised</u> over the board.

"Mate,"[1] replied the son.

"That's the worst living so far out," bawled Mr. White, with sudden and unlooked-for violence. "Of all the beastly slushy, out-of-the-way places to live in, this is the worst. Pathway's a bog, and the road's a <u>torrent</u>. I don't know what people are thinking about. I suppose because only two houses in the road are let; they think it doesn't matter."

"Never mind, dear," said his wife soothingly. "Perhaps you'll win the next one."

Mr. White looked up sharply, just in time to <u>intercept</u> a knowing glance between mother and son. The words died away on his lips, and he hid a guilty grin in his thin gray beard.

"There he is," said Herbert White, as the gate banged loudly and heavy footsteps came toward the door.

The old man rose with hospitable haste, and opening the door, was heard <u>condoling</u> with the new arrival. The new arrival also condoled with himself, so that Mrs. White said, "Tut, tut!" and coughed gently as her husband entered the room, followed by a tall, <u>burly</u> man, beady of eye and rubicund of visage.[2]

"Sergeant-Major Morris," he said, introducing him.

The sergeant-major shook hands, and taking the <u>proffered</u> seat by the fire, watched contentedly while his host got out whisky and tumblers and stood a small copper kettle on the fire.

At the third glass, his eyes got brighter, and he began to talk; the little family circle regarding with eager interest this visitor from distant parts, as he squared his broad shoulders in the chair and spoke of wild scenes and doughty[3] deeds; of wars and plagues and strange peoples.

"Twenty-one years of it," said Mr. White, nodding at his wife and son. "When he went away he was a slip of a youth in the warehouse. Now look at him."

"He don't look to have taken much harm," said Mrs. White politely.

"I'd like to go to India myself," said the old man, "just to look round a bit, you know."

"Better where you are," said the sergeant-major, shaking his head. He put down the empty glass, and sighing softly, shook it again.

"I should like to see those old temples and fakirs[4] and jugglers," said the old man. "What was that you started telling me the other day about a monkey's paw or something, Morris?"

> What words and phrases in this passage create a suspenseful, ominous mood?

---

1. **Mate.** The winning move in chess, capturing your opponent's king, is announced with "Checkmate."
2. **rubicund of visage.** Pink-faced
3. **doughty.** Brave
4. **fakirs.** Person who, for religious purposes, lives a thoughtful life of poverty and self-denial

words for everyday use

pro • voke (prō vōk´) vt., stir up action or feeling. *Mary's teasing <u>provoked</u> a sharp response from Jeff.*
a • mi • a • bly (ā´mē ə blē) adv., pleasantly. *Mr. Stuart greeted me <u>amiably</u> and shook my hand.*
poised (poizd) part., suspended. *The kitten sat motionless, <u>poised</u> to pounce on the mouse.*
tor • rent (tôr´ənt) n., swift, violent stream. *The gentle stream becomes a raging <u>torrent</u> when the snow melts.*
in • ter • cept (in´tər sept´) vt., seize or stop on the way. *In class Reggie <u>intercepted</u> the note Sandy was sending to Brian.*
con • dole (kən dōl´) vi., sympathize. *I <u>condoled</u> with Yolanda about her failing grade.*
bur • ly (bur´lē) adj., big and strong. *Although not <u>burly</u> like many football players, John has speed and agility that make him a good running back.*
prof • fered (präf´ərd) part., offered courteously. *The cookie <u>proffered</u> to me by the hostess was dry and tasteless.*

"Nothing," said the soldier hastily. "Leastways, nothing worth hearing."

"Monkey's paw?" said Mrs. White curiously.

"Well, it's just a bit of what you might call magic, perhaps," said the sergeant-major offhandedly.

His three listeners leaned forward eagerly. The visitor absentmindedly put his empty glass to his lips and then set it down again. His host filled it for him.

"To look at," said the sergeant-major, fumbling in his pocket, "it's just an ordinary little paw, dried to a mummy."

He took something out of his pocket and proffered it. Mrs. White drew back with a grimace, but her son, taking it, examined it curiously.

"And what is there special about it?" inquired Mr. White as he took it from his son, and having examined it, placed it upon the table.

"It had a spell put on it by an old fakir," said the sergeant-major, "a very holy man. He wanted to show that fate ruled people's lives, and that those who interfered with it did so to their sorrow. He put a spell on it so that three separate men could each have three wishes from it."

Do you find the sergeant-major's story believable? Why, or why not?

His manner was so impressive that his hearers were conscious that their light laughter jarred somewhat.

"Well, why don't you have three, sir?" said Herbert White cleverly.

The soldier regarded him in the way that middle age is wont to regard presumptuous youth. "I have," he said quietly, and his blotchy face whitened.

"And did you really have the three wishes granted?" asked Mrs. White.

"I did," said the sergeant-major, and his glass tapped against his strong teeth.

"And has anybody else wished?" persisted the old lady.

"The first man had his three wishes. Yes," was the reply. "I don't know what the first two were, but the third was for death. That's how I got the paw."

His tones were so grave that a hush fell upon the group.

"If you've had your three wishes, it's no good to you now, then, Morris," said the old man at last. "What do you keep it for?"

The soldier shook his head.

"Fancy, I suppose," he said slowly. "I did have some idea of selling it, but I don't think I will. It has caused enough mischief already. Besides, people won't buy. They think it's a fairy tale; some of them, and those who do think anything of it, want to try it first and pay me afterward."

"If you could have another three wishes," said the old man, eyeing him keenly, "would you have them?"

"I don't know," said the other. "I don't know."

He took the paw, and dangling it between his forefinger and thumb, suddenly threw it upon the fire. White, with a slight cry, stooped down and snatched it off.

"Better let it burn," said the soldier solemnly.

"If you don't want it, Morris," said the other, "give it to me."

"I won't," said his friend doggedly. "I threw it on the fire. If you keep it, don't blame me for what happens. Pitch it on the fire again like a sensible man."

"Well, it's just a bit of what you might call magic, perhaps."

---

words for everyday use

pre • sump • tu • ous (prē zump´chōŏ əs) *adj.*, arrogant. *Allan was presumptuous to tell everyone he was the new class president before the votes were counted.*

per • sist (pər sist´) *vi.*, continue insistently. *Alicia persisted in talking to a classmate, even after the teacher asked for silence.*

keen • ly (kēn´lē) *adv.*, sharply. *Jerome listened keenly to Jim's play-by-play account because he didn't want to miss a detail about the game he hadn't been able to attend.*

The other shook his head and examined his new possession closely. "How do you do it?" he inquired.

"Hold it up in your right hand and wish aloud," said the sergeant-major, "but I warn you of the consequences."

"Sounds like the *Arabian Nights*," said Mrs. White, as she rose and began to set the supper. "Don't you think you might wish for four pairs of hands for me?"

Her husband drew the talisman[5] from his pocket, and then all three burst into laughter as the sergeant-major, with a look of alarm on his face, caught him by the arm.

Why is the sergeant-major alarmed?

"If you must wish," he said gruffly, "wish for something sensible."

Mr. White dropped it back into his pocket, and placing chairs, motioned his friend to the table. In the business of supper, the talisman was partly forgotten, and afterward the three sat listening in an <u>enthralled</u> fashion to a second installment of the soldier's adventures in India.

"If the tale about the monkey's paw is not more truthful than those he has been telling us," said Herbert, as the door closed behind their guest, just in time for him to catch the last train, "we shan't make much out of it."

"Did you give him anything for it, Father?" inquired Mrs. White, regarding her husband closely.

"A trifle," said he, coloring slightly. "He didn't want it, but I made him take it. And he pressed me again to throw it away."

"Likely," said Herbert, with pretended horror. "Why, we're going to be rich, and famous and happy. Wish to be an emperor, Father, to begin with; then you can't be henpecked."

He darted round the table, pursued by the <u>maligned</u> Mrs. White armed with an antimacassar.[6]

Mr. White took the paw from his pocket and eyed it <u>dubiously</u>. "I don't know what to wish for, and that's a fact," he said slowly. "It seems to me I've got all I want."

Why doesn't Mr. White know what to wish for?

"If you only cleared the house, you'd be quite happy, wouldn't you?" said Herbert, with his hand on his shoulder. "Well, wish for two hundred pounds, then; that'll just do it."

His father, smiling shamefacedly at his own <u>credulity</u>, held up the talisman, as his son, with a solemn face, somewhat marred by a wink at his mother, sat down at the piano and struck a few impressive chords.

"I wish for two hundred pounds," said the old man distinctly.

A fine crash from the piano greeted the words, interrupted by a shuddering cry from the old man. His wife and son ran toward him.

"It moved," he cried, with a glance of disgust at the object as it lay on the floor. "As I wished, it twisted in my hand like a snake."

What happens when Mr. White makes his wish?

"Well, I don't see the money," said his son as he picked it up and placed it on the table, "and I bet I never shall."

"It must have been your fancy, Father," said his wife, regarding him anxiously.

He shook his head. "Never mind, though; there's no harm done, but it gave me a shock all the same."

---

5. **talisman.** Magic charm
6. **antimacassar.** Cover on a chair or sofa, which prevents soiling

---

words for everyday use	en • thralled (en thrôld´) *adj.,* captivated. *Enthralled by the puppet show, the kindergarten class fell silent.* ma • ligned (mə līnd´) *adj.,* slandered. *The maligned plaintiff was seeking punitive damages.* du • bi • ous • ly (dōō´ bē əs lē) *adv.,* skeptically, doubtfully. *The teacher listened dubiously to Charlene's excuse for being late to class.* cre • du • li • ty (krə dōō´ lə tē) *n.,* tendency to believe too readily. *Brian took advantage of his little sister's credulity and told her eating more than three pieces of Halloween candy would make her sick.*

They sat down by the fire again while the two men finished their pipes. Outside, the wind was higher than ever, and the old man started nervously at the sound of a door banging upstairs. A silence unusual and depressing settled upon all three, which lasted until the old couple rose to retire for the night.

"I expect you'll find the cash tied up in a big bag in the middle of your bed," said Herbert, as he bade them good night, "and something horrible squatting up on top of the wardrobe watching you as you pocket your ill-gotten gains."

He sat alone in the darkness, gazing at the dying fire, and seeing faces in it. The last face was so horrible and so <u>simian</u> that he gazed at it in amazement. It got so vivid that, with a little uneasy laugh, he felt on the table for a glass containing a little water to throw over it. His hand grasped the monkey's paw, and with a little shiver, he wiped his hand on his coat and went up to bed.

In the brightness of the wintry sun next morning as it streamed over the breakfast table, he laughed at his fears. There was an air of <u>prosaic</u> wholesomeness about the room that it had lacked on the previous night, and the dirty, shrivelled little paw was pitched on the sideboard with a carelessness which betokened[7] no great belief in its virtues.

"I suppose all old soldiers are the same," said Mrs. White. "The idea of our listening to such nonsense! How could wishes be granted in these days? And if they could, how could two hundred pounds hurt you, Father?"

"Might drop on his head from the sky," said the <u>frivolous</u> Herbert.

"Morris said the things happened so naturally," said his father, "that you might if you so wished <u>attribute</u> it to coincidence."

"Well, don't break into the money before I come back," said Herbert as he rose from the table. "I'm afraid it'll turn you into a mean, <u>avaricious</u> man, and we shall have to disown you."

His mother laughed, and following him to the door, watched him down the road; and returning to the breakfast table, was very happy at the expense of her husband's credulity. All of which did not prevent her from scurrying to the door at the postman's knock, nor prevent her from referring somewhat shortly to retired sergeant-majors of bibulous[8] habits when she found that the post brought a tailor's bill.

What are the family's feelings about the wish in the morning?

"Herbert will have some more of his funny remarks, I expect, when he comes home," she said, as they sat at dinner.

"I dare say," said Mr. White, pouring himself out some beer. "But for all that, the thing moved in my hand; that I'll swear to."

"You thought it did," said the old lady soothingly.

"I say it did," replied the other. "There was no thought about it; I had just—What's the matter?"

His wife made no reply. She was watching the mysterious movements of a man outside, who, peering in an undecided fashion at the house, appeared to be trying to make up his mind to enter. In mental connection with the two hundred pounds, she noticed that the stranger was well dressed, and wore a silk hat of glossy newness. Three times he paused at the gate, and then walked on again. The fourth time he stood with his hands upon it, and then with sudden resolution flung it open and walked up the

---

7. **betokened.** Indicated
8. **bibulous.** Tending to drink too much

<table>
<tr><td rowspan="5">words
for
everyday
use</td><td>sim • i • an (sim´ē ən) adj., like an ape or a monkey. Jake's <u>simian</u> antics made his friends laugh.</td></tr>
<tr><td>pro • sa • ic (prō zā´ik) adj., commonplace; dull. <u>Prosaic</u> objects, such as vases and bowls, are the focus of many still-life paintings.</td></tr>
<tr><td>friv • o • lous (friv´ə ləs) adj., not properly serious. "If you don't change this <u>frivolous</u> attitude toward practicing," warned Mr. Linnehan, "you'll never become a good flute player."</td></tr>
<tr><td>at • trib • ute (ə trib´yoot) vt., think of as resulting from. Chandra <u>attributes</u> her sculpting ability to natural talent and hard work.</td></tr>
<tr><td>av • a • ri • cious (av´ə rish´əs) adj., greedy. Scrooge's <u>avaricious</u> habits left him without friends.</td></tr>
</table>

path. Mrs. White at the same moment placed her hands behind her, and hurriedly unfastening the strings of her apron, put that useful article of apparel beneath the cushion of her chair.

She brought the stranger, who seemed ill at ease, into the room. He gazed at her <u>furtively</u>, and listened in a preoccupied fashion as the old lady apologized for the appearance of the room, and her husband's coat, a garment that he usually reserved for the garden. She then waited, as patiently as her sex would permit, for him to broach his business; but he was at first strangely silent.

"I—was asked to call," he said at last, and stooped and picked a piece of cotton from his trousers. "I come from Maw and Meggins."

The old lady started. "Is anything the matter?" she asked breathlessly. "Has anything happened to Herbert? What is it? What is it?"

Her husband interposed. "There, there, Mother," he said hastily. "Sit down, and don't jump to conclusions. You've not brought bad news, I'm sure, sir," and he eyed the other wistfully.

"I'm sorry—" began the visitor.

"Is he hurt?" demanded the mother wildly.

The visitor bowed in assent. "Badly hurt," he said quietly, "but he is not in any pain."

"Oh, thank God!" said the old woman, clasping her hands. "Thank God for that! Thank—"

She broke off suddenly as the sinister meaning of the assurance dawned upon her, and she saw the awful confirmation of her fears in the other's <u>averted</u> face. She caught her breath, and turning to her slower-witted husband, laid her trembling old hand upon his. There was a long silence.

"He was caught in the machinery," said the visitor at length in a low voice.

"Caught in the machinery," repeated Mr. White, in a dazed fashion, "yes."

He sat staring blankly out at the window, and taking his wife's hand between his own, pressed it as he had been wont to do in their old courting days nearly forty years before.

"He was the only one left to us," he said, turning gently to the visitor. "It is hard."

The other coughed, and rising, walked slowly to the window. "The firm wished me to convey their sincere sympathy with you in your great loss," he said, without looking round. "I beg that you will understand I am only their servant and merely obeying orders."

There was no reply. The old woman's face was white, her eyes staring, and her breath <u>inaudible</u>. On the husband's face was a look such as his friend the sergeant-major might have carried into his first action.

"I was to say that Maw and Meggins disclaim all responsibility," continued the other. "They admit no <u>liability</u> at all, but in consideration of your son's services, they wish to present you with a certain sum as <u>compensation</u>."

Mr. White dropped his wife's hand, and rising to his feet, gazed with a look of horror at his visitor. His dry lips shaped the words, "How much?"

"Two hundred pounds," was the answer.

How does the first wish come true?

Unconscious of his wife's shriek, the old man smiled faintly, put out his hands like a sightless man, and dropped, a senseless heap, to the floor.

In the huge new cemetery, some two miles distant, the old people buried their dead, and came back to a house steeped in shadow and silence. It was all over so quickly that at first they could hardly realize it, and remained in a state of expectation as though of something else

---

words for everyday use

fur • tive • ly (fur´tiv lē) *adv.*, stealthily; not openly. *Kim looked around <u>furtively</u> before dropping her suggestion in the suggestion box.*

a • vert • ed (ə vurt´ id) *adj.*, turned away. *The <u>averted</u> drought saved hundreds of farmers from bankruptcy.*

in • au • di • ble (in ôd´ə bəl) *adj.*, that cannot be heard. *Although the whistle on the car is <u>inaudible</u> to humans, it signals deer and other animals that danger is approaching.*

li • a • bil • i • ty (lī´ə bil´ə tē) *n.*, state of legal obligation. *I don't see how the company can escape <u>liability</u> for selling dangerous toys.*

com • pen • sa • tion (käm´ pən sā´shən) *n.*, payment in amends for something. *Sherry expected generous <u>compensation</u> for baby-sitting the Blacks' three unruly children.*

to happen—something else that was to lighten this load, too heavy for old hearts to bear.

But the days passed, and expectation gave place to resignation—the hopeless resignation of the old, sometimes miscalled <u>apathy</u>. Sometimes they hardly exchanged a word, for now they had nothing to talk about, and their days were long to weariness.

It was about a week after, that the old man, waking suddenly in the night, stretched out his hand and found himself alone. The room was in darkness, and the sound of <u>subdued</u> weeping came from the window. He raised himself in bed and listened.

"Come back," he said tenderly. "You will be cold."

"It is colder for my son," said the old woman, and wept afresh.

The sound of her sobs died away on his ears. The bed was warm, and his eyes heavy with sleep. He dozed fitfully, and then slept, until a sudden wild cry from his wife awoke him with a start.

"The paw!" she cried wildly. "The monkey's paw!"

He started up in alarm. "Where? Where is it? What's the matter?"

She came stumbling across the room toward him. "I want it," she said quietly. "You've not destroyed it?"

"It's in the parlor, on the bracket," he replied, marvelling. "Why?"

She cried and laughed together, and bending over, kissed his cheek.

"I only just thought of it," she said hysterically. "Why didn't I think of it before? Why didn't *you* think of it?"

"Think of what?" he questioned.

"The other two wishes," she replied rapidly. "We've only had one."

"Was not that enough?" he demanded fiercely.

"No," she cried triumphantly. "We'll have one more. Go down and get it quickly, and wish our boy alive again."

The man sat up in bed and flung the bed-clothes from his quaking limbs. "Good God, you are mad!" he cried, aghast.

"Get it," she panted. "Get it quickly, and wish—Oh, my boy, my boy!"

Her husband struck a match and lit the candle. "Get back to bed," he said unsteadily. "You don't know what you are saying."

"We had the first wish granted," said the old woman feverishly. "Why not the second?"

"A coincidence," stammered the old man.

"Go and get it and wish," cried his wife, quivering with excitement.

The old man turned and regarded her, and his voice shook. "He has been dead ten days, and besides he—I would not tell you else, but—I could only recognize him by his clothing. If he was too terrible for you to see then, how now?"

"Bring him back," cried the old woman, and dragged him toward the door. "Do you think I fear the child I have nursed?"

He went down in the darkness, and felt his way to the parlor, and then to the mantelpiece. The talisman was in its place, and a horrible fear that the unspoken wish might bring his mutilated son before him ere

Why does Mrs. White want the monkey's paw?

"We had the first wish granted," said the old woman feverishly. "Why not the second?"

What fear does Mr. White have?

---

words for everyday use

ap • a • thy (ap´ə thē) *n.*, indifference; lack of emotion. *The media blamed low voter turnout on citizens' <u>apathy</u> over the mayoral candidates.*

sub • dued (səb dōō´d) *part.*, diminished; lessened in intensity. *The art exhibit balanced the intense colors of Monica's oil paintings with the more <u>subdued</u> tones of Vanessa's watercolors.*

he could escape from the room seized upon him, and he caught his breath as he found that he had lost the direction of the door. His brow cold with sweat, he felt his way round the table, and groped along the wall until he found himself in the small passage with the unwholesome thing in his hand.

Even his wife's face seemed changed as he entered the room. It was white and expectant, and to his fears, seemed to have an unnatural look upon it. He was afraid of her.

"*Wish!*" she cried, in a strong voice.

"It is foolish and wicked," he faltered.

"*Wish!*" repeated his wife.

He raised his hand. "I wish my son alive again."

The talisman fell to the floor, and he regarded it fearfully. Then he sank trembling into a chair as the old woman, with burning eyes, walked to the window and raised the blind.

He sat until he was chilled with the cold, glancing occasionally at the figure of the old woman peering through the window. The candle-end, which had burned below the rim of the china candlestick, was throwing pulsating shadows on the ceiling and walls, until, with a flicker larger than the rest, it expired. The old man, with an unspeakable sense of relief at the failure of the talisman, crept back to his bed, and a minute or two afterward the old woman came silently and apathetically beside him.

Neither spoke, but lay silently listening to the ticking of the clock. A stair creaked, and a squeaky mouse scurried noisily through the wall. The darkness was <u>oppressive</u>, and after

> Why does the man hesitate before making the wish?

"For God's sake, don't let it in," cried the old man, trembling.

lying for some time screwing up his courage, he took the box of matches, and striking one, went downstairs for a candle.

At the foot of the stairs the match went out, and he paused to strike another; and at the same moment a knock, so quiet and stealthy as to be scarcely audible, sounded on the front door.

The matches fell from his hand and spilled in the passage. He stood motionless, his breath suspended until the knock was repeated. Then he turned and fled swiftly back to his room, and closed the door behind him. A third knock sounded through the house.

"*What's that?*" cried the old woman, starting up.

"A rat," said the old man in shaking tones—"a rat. It passed me on the stairs."

His wife sat up in bed listening. A loud knock resounded through the house.

"It's Herbert!" she screamed. "It's Herbert!"

She ran to the door, but her husband was before her, and catching her by the arm, held her tightly.

"What are you going to do?" he whispered hoarsely.

"It's my boy; it's Herbert!" she cried, struggling mechanically. "I forgot it was two miles away. What are you holding me for? Let go. I must open the door."

> Why is the man afraid?

"For God's sake, don't let it in," cried the old man, trembling.

"You're afraid of your own son," she cried, struggling. "Let me go. I'm coming, Herbert; I'm coming."

There was another knock, and another. The old woman, with a sudden wrench, broke free

---

words for everyday use

op • pres • sive (ə pres´iv) *adj.*, hard to put up with. *The heavy silence of libraries is <u>oppressive</u> to me; I prefer to study at home with music in the background.*

The House of Mystery, 1926. Sydney Lee.
Harris Museum and Art Gallery, Preston, UK.

and ran from the room. Her husband followed to the landing, and called after her appealingly as she hurried downstairs. He heard the chain rattle back and the bottom bolt drawn slowly and stiffly from the socket. Then the old woman's voice, strained and panting.

"The bolt," she cried loudly. "Come down. I can't reach it."

But her husband was on his hands and knees, groping wildly on the floor in search of the paw. If he could only find it before the thing outside got in. A perfect fusillade[9] of knocks <u>reverberated</u> through the house, and he heard the scraping of a chair as his wife put it down in the passage against the door. He heard the creaking of the bolt as it came slowly back, and at the same moment he found the monkey's paw, and frantically breathed his third and last wish.

> What was the man's third wish?

The knocking ceased suddenly, although the echoes of it were still in the house. He heard the chair drawn back, and the door opened. A cold wind rushed up the staircase, and a long, loud wail of disappointment and misery from his wife gave him courage to run down to her side, and then to the gate beyond. The street lamp flickering opposite shone on a quiet and deserted road. ∎

---

9. **fusillade.** Simultaneous discharge of many firearms

| words for everyday use | **re • ver • ber • ate** (ri vʉr´bə rāt´) *vi.,* resound; echo. *Must you play your music so loudly that it <u>reverberates</u> throughout the whole house?* |

Imagine that you are Mr. White. Reflect on the night of Sergeant-Major Morris's visit, when he brought the monkey's paw to your home. Explain how your view of the monkey's paw changed after that.

Investigate, *Inquire,* and Imagine

Recall: GATHERING FACTS ➔

1a. What spell was put on the monkey's paw by a fakir? Why did the fakir put the spell on the paw?

2a. What is Mr. White's first wish?

3a. Why does Mr. White make a second wish? What is it?

Interpret: FINDING MEANING

1b. What is probably troubling the Sergeant-Major about the White family's lightheartedness toward the paw?

2b. What event reveals the power of the monkey's paw?

3b. What relationship between human life and fate is described in this story? How are the fakir's ideas about fate proved true?

Analyze: TAKING THINGS APART ➔

4a. What human weaknesses are revealed by members of the White family in this story?

Synthesize: BRINGING THINGS TOGETHER

4b. Why does Mr. White make a third wish?

Evaluate: MAKING JUDGMENTS ➔

5a. Who believes most strongly in the power of the monkey's paw—Sergeant-Major Morris, Mr. White, or Mrs. White? Explain your answer.

Extend: CONNECTING IDEAS

5b. Do you believe fate, coincidence, or human will determines your future? Explain your answer.

Understanding *Literature*

FORESHADOWING. Review the definition for **foreshadowing** in Literary Tools on page 168. What two statements by Sergeant-Major Morris and Herbert foreshadow events in the story? What events do they foreshadow? How does the use of foreshadowing increase the suspense in the story?

SETTING. Review the definition for **setting** in the Handbook of Literary Terms. Use the graphic organizer you made for Literary Tools on page 168 to answer the following questions. How does the location of the Whites' house contribute to the development of the plot? Which psychological characteristic of the Whites allows them to believe in the monkey's paw?

Writer's Journal

1. Write an **epitaph** for Herbert, explaining how he died. An *epitaph* is an inscription on a tomb or grave.

2. Imagine that you are Mr. White at the end of the story. Write a **letter** to Sergeant-Major Morris, explaining what three wishes you wish you had made and instead of those you did.

3. Imagine that you are Sergeant-Major Morris. Write a **journal entry**, explaining what you believe about fate after your experience with the monkey's paw. Tell what you wish you had done with the monkey's paw, and why.

Integrating the Language Arts

1001

Language, Grammar, and Style

ACTION VERB OR LINKING VERB. Linking verbs are those verbs that do not express actions. They either express a condition (sometimes called *a state of being*), they join two concepts that mean the same thing, or they describe the subject. When *to be* verbs are part of an action verb, they are helpers; but when they are used without an action verb, they are *state of being verbs*. Using your own paper, underline the verbs in the sentences below. If there is no action present, go directly to your helping verb chart in the Language Arts Survey 3.8. Remember that helping verbs without actions may be linking verbs. Label each verb you find as an action or a linking verb.

1. The monkey's paw guaranteed three wishes.

2. The wishes may have dark sides.

3. The monkey's paw was a magic charm.

4. It had been a source for bad luck.

5. The Whites wanted the monkey's paw.

Collaborative Learning

DRAMATIC SKIT. With one, two, or three other students, write a dramatization of one of the scenes in "The Monkey's Paw." Choose a scene that you feel is particularly effective in creating suspense or dread. Write parts for each student in your group. You may want to use music to add to the suspenseful effect of your scene. Rehearse your skit and present it to the class.

Speaking and Listening

TELLING A HORROR STORY. In a small group, take turns telling a horror story that you make up as you go along. Each student talks for thirty seconds, adding details to the story that the first storyteller starts. You may want to put a limit on the number of times each speaker speaks. Be sure to pay attention to setting and psychological development as you tell your story.

"To Build a Fire"

by Jack London

Literary TOOLS

SETTING. The **setting** of a literary work is the time and place in which it occurs, together with all the details used to create a sense of a particular time and place. As you read the selection, decide which details are effective in creating the wintry Yukon setting.

PLOT AND CONFLICT. A **plot** is a series of events related to a central conflict, or struggle. A **conflict** is a struggle between two forces in a literary work. The protagonist may struggle against another character, against the forces of nature, against society or social norms, against fate, or against some element within himself or herself.

Graphic Organizer

As you read, make a sequence chart of the main events in the story and circle those that indicate a struggle. One example has been done for you.

| Protagonist tries to walk to camp. | → | Climbs the high earth-bank leading to the trail. | → |

Reader's Journal

How do you know when to listen to someone's advice and when to follow your own ideas instead?

Reader's resource

Published in 1908, **"To Build a Fire"** is one of the twenty-eight stories included in London's *Northland Saga*. In addition, the *Northland Saga* comprises four novels, one play, and six nonfiction pieces.

"To Build a Fire" is an example of Naturalism. Naturalism was a literary movement of the late nineteenth and early twentieth centuries that saw actions and events as resulting inevitably from biological or environmental forces. Often these forces were beyond the comprehension or control of the characters subjected to them. Taken to its extreme, Naturalism views all events as mechanically determined by external forces, including decisions made by people. Much of modern fiction, with its emphasis on social conditions leading to particular consequences, is Naturalistic in this sense. Jack London was one of many authors influenced by the philosophy of Naturalism.

HISTORY CONNECTION. One of hundreds of thousands of people who joined the Klondike Gold Rush, Jack London had firsthand experience surviving a winter in the Yukon, a region in northwestern Canada and the setting of "To Build a Fire." Read the Related Reading excerpt on page 193, "A Short Life Intensely Lived: The Adventures of Jack London," for more information on London's experiences in the Yukon, an area acquired by the Canadian government from the Hudson's Bay Company in 1870 and made into a territory in 1898.

About the AUTHOR

Jack London (1876–1916), born in San Francisco, supported himself and helped support his family from the time he was fourteen. By age eighteen, he had worked in a cannery, as an oyster pirate, seaman, jute-mill worker, and coal shoveler. While still a teenager, he tramped halfway across the continent with the "army of the unemployed" in its "March on Washington," then struck out on his own for the Northeast. After spending thirty days in jail for vagrancy, London decided it was time to improve his life. He returned to California, entered the state university, and took English classes. He soon left, disenchanted with his fellow students, his professors, and the formal educational system, and was on his way to the gold rush in the Klondike.

By the time London returned to Oakland from his adventures in the Klondike, he was determined to make a living as a writer. He won a local writing contest, which was followed by numerous rejections and then a string of small sales. His break came when the *Atlantic Monthly* paid $120 for his story "The Odyssey of the North." Although London often said he disliked his profession and wrote to make money, he nevertheless was a master storyteller who published prodigiously during his career. His two most famous novels, *The Call of the Wild* (1903) and *The Sea-Wolf* (1904), were written before he was thirty. Among his other works are *The People of the Abyss* (1903), *War of the Classes* (1905), *White Fang* (1906), *The Iron Heel* (1908), and *Martin Eden* (autobiographical novel, 1909).

To Build a Fire

Jack London

Day had broken
cold and gray, exceedingly cold
and gray, when the man turned aside
from the main Yukon¹ trail and climbed the
high earth-bank, where a dim and little-traveled
trail led eastward through the fat spruce timberland.

1. **Yukon.** Territory and river in northwestern Canada

It was a steep bank, and he paused for breath at the top, excusing the act to himself by looking at his watch. It was nine o'clock. There was no sun nor hint of sun, though there was not a cloud in the sky. It was a clear day, and yet there seemed an intangible <u>pall</u> over the face of things, a subtle gloom that made the day dark, and that was due to the absence of sun. This fact did not worry the man. He was used to the lack of sun. It had been days since he had seen the sun, and he knew that a few more days must pass before that cheerful orb, due south, would just peep above the skyline and dip immediately from view.

What is the day like? Why does it have this atmosphere?

The man flung a look back along the way he had come. The Yukon lay a mile wide and hidden under three feet of ice. On top of this ice were as many feet of snow. It was all pure white, rolling in gentle <u>undulations</u> where the ice jams of the freeze-up had formed. North and south, as far as his eye could see, it was unbroken white, save for a dark hairline that curved and twisted from around the spruce-covered island to the south, and that curved and twisted away into the north, where it disappeared behind another spruce-covered island. This dark hairline was the trail—the main trail—that led south five hundred miles to the Chilcoot Pass, Dyea,[2] and salt water; and that led north seventy miles to Dawson, and still on to the north a thousand miles to Nulato,[3] and finally to St. Michael on Bering Sea, a thousand miles and half a thousand more.

But all this—the mysterious, far-reaching hairline trail, the absence of sun from the sky, the tremendous cold, and the strangeness and weirdness of it all—made no impression on the man. It was not because he was long used to it. He was a newcomer in the land, a *chechaquo*,[4]

and this was his first winter. The trouble with him was that he was without imagination. He was quick and alert in the things of life, but only in the things, and not in the significances. Fifty degrees below zero meant eighty-odd degrees of frost. Such fact impressed him as being cold and uncomfortable, and that was all. It did not lead him to meditate upon his frailty as a creature of temperature, and upon man's frailty in general, able only to live within certain narrow limits of heat and cold; and from there on it did not lead him to the <u>conjectural</u> field of immortality and man's place in the universe. Fifty degrees below zero stood for a bite of frost that hurt and that must be guarded against by the use of mittens, earflaps, warm moccasins, and thick socks. Fifty degrees below zero was to him just precisely fifty degrees below zero. That there should be anything more to it than that was a thought that never entered his head.

What is the man's limitation?

As he turned to go on, he spat speculatively. There was a sharp, explosive crackle that startled him. He spat again. And again, in the air, before it could fall to the snow, the spittle crackled. He knew that at fifty below spittle crackled on the snow, but this spittle had crackled in the air. Undoubtedly it was colder than fifty below—how much colder he did not know. But the temperature did not matter. He was bound for the old claim on the left fork of Henderson Creek, where the boys were already. They had come over across the divide from the Indian Creek country, while he had

What is the man's errand?

2. **Chilcoot Pass, Dyea.** *Chilcoot Pass*—mountain pass leading to the Klondike; *Dyea*—once a town in Alaska that marked the beginning of the Yukon trail
3. **Dawson . . . Nulato.** Gold-mining towns in the Yukon
4. *chechaquo.* Newcomer

---

words for everyday use

pall (pôl) *n.,* covering that obscures or cloaks gloomily. *A heavy <u>pall</u> of disappointment hung over the crowd after the announcement was made that the band would not play.*

un • du • la • tion (un′dyo͞o lā′shən) *n.,* wave; curve. *The <u>undulations</u> of the water reached our dangling feet.*

con • jec • tur • al (kən jek′chər əl) *adj.,* based on guesses. *The study of the universe is highly <u>conjectural</u>, based as it is on theories.*

come the roundabout way to take a look at the possibilities of getting out logs in the spring from the islands in the Yukon. He would be in to camp by six o'clock: a bit after dark, it was true, but the boys would be there, a fire would be going, and a hot supper would be ready. As for lunch, he pressed his hand against the protruding bundle under his jacket. It was also under his shirt, wrapped up in a handkerchief and lying against the naked skin. It was the only way to keep the biscuits from freezing. He smiled agreeably to himself as he thought of those biscuits, each cut open and sopped in bacon grease, and each enclosing a generous slice of fried bacon.

He plunged in among the big spruce trees. The trail was faint. A foot of snow had fallen since the last sled had passed over, and he was glad he was without a sled, traveling light. In fact, he carried nothing but the lunch wrapped in the handkerchief. He was surprised, however, at the cold. It certainly was cold, he concluded, as he rubbed his numb nose and cheekbones with his mittened hand. He was a warm-whiskered man, but the hair on his face did not protect the high cheekbones and the eager nose that thrust itself aggressively into the frosty air.

At the man's heels trotted a dog, a big native husky, the proper wolf dog, gray-coated and without any visible or temperamental difference from its brother, the wild wolf. The animal was depressed by the tremendous cold. It knew that it was no time for traveling. Its instinct told it a truer tale than was told to the man by the man's judgment. In reality, it was not merely colder than fifty below zero: it was colder than sixty below, than seventy below. It was seventy-five below zero. Since the freezing point is thirty-two above

In what way is the dog more advanced than the man?

zero, it meant that one hundred and seven degrees of frost obtained. The dog did not know anything about thermometers. Possibly in its brain there was no sharp consciousness of a condition of very cold such as was in the man's brain. But the brute had its instinct. It experienced a vague but menacing <u>apprehension</u> that subdued it and made it slink along at the man's heels, and that made it question eagerly every unwonted movement of the man as if expecting him to go into camp or to seek shelter somewhere and build a fire. The dog had learned fire, and it wanted fire, or else to burrow under the snow and cuddle its warmth away from the air.

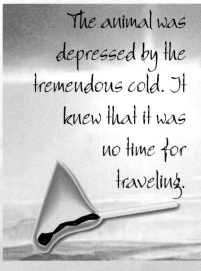

The animal was depressed by the tremendous cold. It knew that it was no time for traveling.

The frozen moisture of its breathing had settled on its fur in a fine powder of frost, and especially were its jowls, muzzle, and eyelashes whitened by its crystalled breath. The man's red beard and mustache were likewise frosted, but more solidly, the deposit taking the form of ice and increasing with every warm, moist breath he exhaled. Also, the man was chewing tobacco, and the muzzle of ice held his lips so rigidly that he was unable to clear his chin when he expelled the juice. The result was that a crystal beard of the color and solidity of amber was increasing its length on his chin. If he fell down it would shatter itself, like glass, into brittle fragments. But he did not mind the appendage. It was the penalty all tobacco chewers paid in that country, and he had been out before in two cold snaps. They had not been so cold as this, he knew, but by the spirit thermometer[5] at Sixty Mile he knew they had been registered at fifty below and at fifty-five.

He held on through the level stretch of woods for several miles, crossed a wide flat, and dropped down a bank to the frozen bed of a small stream. This was Henderson Creek, and he knew he was ten miles from the forks. He looked at his watch. It was ten o'clock. He was making four miles an hour, and he calculated that he would arrive at the forks at half past twelve. He decided to celebrate that event by eating his lunch there.

The dog dropped in again at his heels, with a tail drooping discouragement, as the man swung along the creek bed. The furrow of the old sled trail was plainly visible, but a dozen inches of snow covered the marks of the last runners. In a month no man had come up or down that silent creek. The man held steadily on. He was not much given to thinking, and just then particularly he had nothing to think about save that he would eat lunch at the forks and that at six o'clock he would be in camp with the boys. There was nobody to talk to; and, had there been, speech would have been impossible because of the ice-muzzle on his mouth. So he continued monotonously to chew tobacco and to increase the length of his amber beard.

Once in a while the thought <u>reiterated</u> itself that it was very cold and that he had never experienced such cold. As he walked along he rubbed his cheekbones and nose with the back of his mittened hand. He did this automatically, now and again changing hands. But rub as he would, the instant he stopped his cheekbones went numb, and the following instant the end of his nose went numb. He was sure to frost his cheeks; he knew that, and experienced a pang of regret that he had not devised a nose strap of the sort Bud wore in cold snaps. Such a strap passed across the cheeks, as well, and saved them. But it didn't matter much, after all. What were frosted cheeks? A bit painful, that was all: they were never serious.

Empty as the man's mind was of thoughts, he was keenly observant, and he noticed the changes in the creek, the curves and bends and timber jams, and always he sharply noted where he placed his feet. Once, coming around a bend, he shied abruptly, like a startled horse, curved away from the place where he had been walking, and retreated several paces back along the trail. The creek he knew was frozen clear to the bottom— no creek could contain water in that arctic winter—but he knew also that there were springs that bubbled out from the hillsides and ran along under the snow and on top the ice of the creek. He knew that the coldest snaps never froze these springs, and he knew likewise their danger. They were traps. They hid pools of water under the snow that might be three inches deep, or three feet. Sometimes a skin of ice half an inch thick covered them, and in turn was covered by the snow. Sometimes there were alternate layers of water and ice skin, so that when one broke through he kept on breaking through for a while, sometimes wetting himself to the waist.

What danger does the man know?

That was why he had shied in such panic. He had felt the give under his feet and heard the crackle of a snow-hidden ice skin. And to get his feet wet in such a temperature meant trouble and danger. At the very least it meant delay, for he would be forced to stop and build a fire, and under its protection to bare his feet while he dried his socks and moccasins. He stood and studied the creek bed and its banks, and decided

5. **spirit thermometer.** Thermometer that uses alcohol instead of mercury because of the lower freezing point of alcohol

words for everyday use	re • it • er • ate (rē it´ ə rāt´) *vt.*, repeat. *The teachers <u>reiterated</u> to the principal their argument for smaller class sizes.*

that the flow of water came from the right. He reflected awhile, rubbing his nose and cheeks, then skirted to the left, stepping gingerly and testing the footing for each step. Once clear of the danger, he took a fresh chew of tobacco and swung along at his four-mile gait.

In the course of the next two hours he came upon several similar traps. Usually the snow above the hidden pools had a sunken, candied appearance that advertised the danger. Once again, however, he had a close call; and once, suspecting danger, he compelled the dog to go on in front. The dog did not want to go. It hung back until the man shoved it forward, and then it went quickly across the white, unbroken surface. Suddenly it broke through, floundered to one side, and got away to firmer footing. It had wet its forefeet and legs, and almost immediately the water that clung to it turned to ice. It made quick efforts to lick the ice off its legs, then dropped down in the snow and began to bite out the ice that had formed between the toes. This was a matter of instinct. To permit the ice to remain would mean sore feet. It did not know this. It merely obeyed the mysterious prompting that arose from the deep crypts of its being. But the man knew, having achieved a judgment on the subject, and he removed the mitten from his right hand and helped tear out the ice particles. He did not expose his fingers more than a minute, and was astonished at the swift numbness that smote them. It certainly was cold. He pulled on the mitten hastily, and beat the hand savagely across his chest.

At twelve o'clock the day was at its brightest. Yet the sun was too far south on its winter journey to clear the horizon. The bulge of the earth intervened between it and Henderson Creek, where the man walked under a clear sky at noon and cast no shadow. At half-past twelve, to the minute, he arrived at the forks of the creek. He was pleased at the speed he had made. If he kept it up, he would certainly be with the boys by six. He unbuttoned his jacket and shirt and drew forth his lunch. The action consumed no more than a quarter of a minute, yet in that brief moment the numbness laid hold of the exposed fingers. He did not put the mitten on, but, instead, struck the fingers a dozen sharp smashes against his leg. Then he sat down on a snow-covered log to eat. The sting that followed upon the striking of his fingers against his leg ceased so quickly that he was startled. He had had no chance to take a bite of biscuit. He struck the fingers repeatedly and returned them to the mitten, baring the other hand for the purpose of eating. He tried to take a mouthful. but the ice muzzle prevented. He had forgotten to build a fire and thaw out. He chuckled at his foolishness, and as he chuckled he noted the numbness creeping into the exposed fingers. Also, he noted that the stinging which had first come to his toes when he sat down was already passing away. He wondered whether the toes were warm or numb. He moved them inside the moccasins and decided that they were numb.

He pulled the mitten on hurriedly and stood up. He was a bit frightened. He stamped up and down until the stinging returned into the feet. It certainly was cold, was his thought. That man from Sulphur Creek had spoken the truth when telling how cold it sometimes got in the country. And he had laughed at him at the time! That showed one must not be too sure of things. There was no mistake about it, it was cold. He strode up and down, stamping his feet and threshing his arms, until reassured by the returning warmth. Then he got out matches and proceeded to make a

What is the man starting to feel? Whom had he met? What had he been told?

---

words for everyday use

thresh (thresh) *vt.*, thrash; beat or strike; move or stir about violently. *Before vacuum cleaners, women threshed rugs with brooms and sticks.*

fire. From the undergrowth, where high water of the previous spring had lodged a supply of seasoned twigs, he got his firewood. Working carefully from a small beginning, he soon had a roaring fire, over which he thawed the ice from his face and in the protection of which he ate his biscuits. For the moment the cold of space was outwitted. The dog took satisfaction in the fire, stretching out close enough for warmth and far enough away to escape being singed.

When the man had finished, he filled his pipe and took his comfortable time over a smoke. Then he pulled on his mittens, settled the earflaps of his cap firmly about his ears, and took the creek trail up the left fork. The dog was disappointed and yearned back toward the fire. This man did not know cold. Possibly all the generations of his ancestry had been ignorant of cold, of real cold, of cold one hundred and seven degrees below freezing point. But the dog knew; all its ancestry knew, and it had inherited the knowledge. And it knew that it was not good to walk abroad in such fearful cold. It was the time to lie snug in a hole in the snow and wait for a curtain of cloud to be drawn across the face of outer space whence this cold came. On the other hand, there was no keen intimacy between the dog and the man. The one was the toil slave of the other, and the only caresses it had ever received were the caresses of the whiplash and of harsh and menacing throat sounds that threatened the whiplash. So the dog made no effort to communicate its apprehension to the man. It was not concerned in the welfare of the man; it was for its own sake that it yearned back toward the fire. But the man whistled, and spoke to it with the sound of whiplashes, and the dog swung in at the man's heels and followed after.

> What does the dog think should happen?

The man took a chew of tobacco and proceeded to start a new amber beard. Also, his moist breath quickly powdered with white his mustache, eyebrows, and lashes. There did not seem to be so many springs on the left fork of the Henderson, and for half an hour the man saw no signs of any. And then it happened. At a place where there were no signs, where the soft, unbroken snow seemed to advertise solidity beneath, the man broke through. It was not deep. He wet himself halfway to the knees before he floundered out to the firm crust.

> What happens unexpectedly?

He was angry, and cursed his luck aloud. He had hoped to get into camp with the boys at six o'clock, and this would delay him an hour, for he would have to build a fire and dry out his footgear. This was imperative at that low temperature— he knew that much; and he turned aside to the bank, which he climbed. On top, tangled in the underbrush about the trunks of several small spruce trees, was a high-water deposit of dry firewood—sticks and twigs, principally, but also larger portions of seasoned branches and fine, dry, last year's grasses. He threw down several large pieces on top of the snow. This served for a foundation and prevented the young flame from drowning itself in the snow it otherwise would melt. The flame he got by touching a match to a small shred of birch bark that he took from his pocket. This burned even more readily than paper. Placing it on the foundation, he fed the young flame with wisps of dry grass and with the tiniest dry twigs.

> What does the man see as the negative consequences of his accident?

He worked slowly and carefully, keenly aware of his danger. Gradually, as the flame grew stronger, he increased the size of the twigs with which he fed it. He squatted in the snow,

---

words for everyday use   im • per • a • tive (im per´ə tiv) *adj.*, absolutely necessary. *"It is <u>imperative</u> that you be at work when the shift starts,"* the supervisor explained.

pulling the twigs out from their entanglement in the brush and feeding directly to the flame. He knew there must be no failure. When it is seventy-five below zero, a man must not fail in his first attempt to build a fire—that is, if his feet are wet. If his feet are dry, and he fails, he can run along the trail for half a mile and restore his circulation. But the circulation of wet and freezing feet cannot be restored by running when it is seventy-five below. No matter how fast one runs, the wet feet will freeze the harder.

All this the man knew. The old-timer on Sulphur Creek had told him about it the previous fall, and now he was appreciating the advice. Already all sensation had gone out of his feet. To build the fire he had been forced to remove his mittens, and the fingers had quickly gone numb. His pace of four miles an hour had kept his heart pumping blood to the surface of his body and to all the extremities. But the instant he stopped, the action of the pump eased down. The cold of space smote the unprotected tip of the planet, and he, being on that unprotected tip, received the full force of the blow. The blood of his body recoiled before it. The blood was alive, like the dog, and like the dog it wanted to hide away and cover itself up from the fearful cold. So long as he walked four miles an hour, he pumped that blood, willy-nilly, to the surface; but now it ebbed away and sank down into the recesses of his body. The extremities were the first to feel its absence. His wet feet froze the faster, and his exposed fingers numbed the faster, though they had not yet begun to freeze. Nose and cheeks were already freezing, while the skin of all his body chilled as it lost its blood.

But he was safe. Toes and nose and cheeks would be only touched by the frost, for the fire

> To what is the man's blood compared? In what way are they similar?

was beginning to burn with strength. He was feeding it with twigs the size of his finger. In another minute he would be able to feed it with branches the size of his wrist, and then he could remove his wet foot-gear, and, while it dried, he could keep his naked feet warm by the fire, rubbing them at first, of course, with snow. The fire was a success. He was safe. He remembered the advice of the old-timer on Sulphur Creek, and smiled. The old-timer had been very serious in laying down the law that no man must travel alone in the Klondike after fifty below. Well, here he was; he had had the accident; he was alone; and he had saved himself. Those old-timers were rather womanish, some of them, he thought. All a man had to do was to keep his head, and he was all right. Any man who was a man could travel alone. But it was surprising, the rapidity with which his cheeks and nose were freezing. And he had not thought his fingers could go lifeless in so short a time. Lifeless they were, for he could scarcely make them move together to grip a twig, and they seemed remote from his body and from him. When he touched a twig, he had to look and see whether or not he had hold of it. The wires were pretty well down between him and his finger ends.

All of which counted for little. There was the fire, snapping and crackling and

When it is seventy-five below zero, a man must not fail in his first attempt to build a fire—that is, if his feet are wet.

> What does the fire symbolize in such cold?

promising life with every dancing flame. He started to untie his moccasins. They were coated with ice; the thick German socks were like sheaths of iron halfway to the knees; and the moccasin strings were like rods of steel all twisted and knotted as by some conflagration. For a moment he tugged with his numb fingers, then, realizing the folly of it, he drew his sheath-knife.

But before he could cut the strings, it happened. It was his own fault or, rather, his mistake. He should not have built the fire under the spruce tree. He should have built it in the open. But it had been easier to pull the twigs from the brush and drop them directly on the fire. Now the tree under which he had done this carried a weight of snow on its boughs. No wind had blown for weeks, and each bough was fully freighted. Each time he had pulled a twig he had communicated a slight agitation to the tree—an imperceptible agitation, so far as he was concerned, but an agitation sufficient to bring about the disaster. High up in the tree one bough capsized its load of snow. This fell on the boughs beneath, capsizing them. This process continued, spreading out and involving the whole tree. It grew like an avalanche, and it descended without warning upon the man and the fire, and the fire was blotted out! Where it had burned was a mantle of fresh and disordered snow.

The man was shocked. It was as though he had just heard his own sentence of death.

What terrible mistake does the man make?

The man was shocked. It was as though he had just heard his own sentence of death. For a moment he sat and stared at the spot where the fire had been. Then he grew very calm. Perhaps the old-timer on Sulphur Creek was right. If he had only had a trail mate he would have been in no danger now. The trail mate could have built the fire. Well, it was up to him to build the fire over again, and this second time there must be no failure. Even if he succeeded, he would most likely lose some toes. His feet must be badly frozen by now, and there would be some time before the second fire was ready.

Such were his thoughts, but he did not sit and think them. He was busy all the time they were passing through his mind. He made a new foundation for a fire, this time in the open, where no treacherous tree could blot it out. Next, he gathered dry grasses and tiny twigs from the high-water flotsam.[6] He could not bring his fingers together to pull them out, but he was able to gather them by the handful. In this way he got many rotten twigs and bits of green moss that were undesirable, but it was the best he could do. He worked methodically, even collecting an armful of the larger branches to be used later when the fire gathered strength. And all the while the dog sat and watched him, a certain yearning wistfulness in its eyes, for it looked upon him as the fire provider, and the fire was slow in coming.

When all was ready, the man reached in his pocket for a second piece of birch bark. He knew the bark was there, and, though he could not feel it with his fingers, he could hear its crisp rustling as he fumbled for it. Try as he would, he could not clutch hold of it. And all the time, in his consciousness, was the knowledge that each

_____

6. **flotsam.** Odds and ends washed up by the water

---

words for everyday use

con • fla • gra • tion (kän´flə grā´shən) *n.*, destructive fire. *Fire stations from ten towns were called out to fight the conflagration in Ashton.*

ag • i • ta • tion (aj´ə tā´shən) *n.*, appreciable motion or disturbance. *The agitation of the washing machine made the box of detergent fall on the floor.*

instant his feet were freezing. This thought tended to put him in a panic, but he fought against it and kept calm. He pulled on his mittens with his teeth, and threshed his arms back and forth, beating his hands with all his might against his sides. He did this sitting down, and he stood up to do it; and all the while the dog sat in the snow, its wolf brush of a tail curled around warmly over its forefeet, its sharp wolf ears pricked forward intently as it watched the man. And the man, as he beat and threshed with his arms and hands, felt a great surge of envy as he regarded the creature that was warm and secure in its natural covering.

What does the man feel is happening? What is his reaction?

After a time he was aware of the first faraway signals of sensation in his beaten fingers. The faint tingling grew stronger till it evolved into a stinging ache that was excruciating, but which the man hailed with satisfaction. He stripped the mitten from his right hand and fetched forth the birch bark. The exposed fingers were quickly going numb again. Next he brought out his bunch of sulphur matches. But the tremendous cold had already driven the life out of his fingers. In his effort to separate one match from the others, the whole bunch fell in the snow. He tried to pick it out of the snow, but failed. The dead fingers could neither touch nor clutch. He was very careful. He drove the thought of his freezing feet, and nose, and cheeks, out of his mind, devoting his whole soul to the matches. He watched, using the sense of vision in place of that of touch, and when he saw his fingers on each side the bunch, he closed them—that is, he willed to close them, for the wires were down, and the fingers did not obey. He pulled the mitten on the right hand, and beat it fiercely against his knee. Then, with both mittened hands, he scooped the bunch of matches, along with much snow, into his lap. Yet he was no better off.

After some manipulation he managed to get the bunch between the heels of his mittened hands. In this fashion he carried it to his mouth. The ice crackled and snapped when by a violent effort he opened his mouth. He drew the lower jaw in, curled the upper lip out of the way, and scraped the bunch with his upper teeth in order to separate a match. He succeeded in getting one, which he dropped on his lap. He was no better off. He could not pick it up. Then he devised a way. He picked it up in his teeth and scratched it on his leg. Twenty times he scratched before he succeeded in lighting it. As it flamed he held it with his teeth to the birch bark. But the burning brimstone went up his nostrils and into his lungs, causing him to cough spasmodically. The match fell into the snow and went out.

The old-timer on Sulphur Creek was right, he thought in the moment of controlled despair that ensued: after fifty below, a man should travel with a partner. He beat his hands, but failed in exciting any sensation. Suddenly he bared both hands, removing the mittens with his teeth. He caught the whole bunch between the heels of his hands. His arm muscles not being frozen enabled him to press the hand heels tightly against the matches. Then he scratched the bunch along his leg. It flared into flame, seventy sulphur matches at once! There was no wind to blow them out. He kept his head to one side to escape the strangling fumes, and held the blazing bunch to the birch bark. As he so held it, he became aware of sensation in his hand. His flesh was burning. He could smell it. Deep down below the surface he could feel it. The sensation developed into pain that grew acute. And still he endured it, holding the flame of the matches clumsily to the bark that would not light readily because his own burning hands were in the way, absorbing most of the flame.

What advice did the man fail to heed?

At last, when he could endure no more, he jerked his hands apart. The blazing matches fell sizzling into the snow, but the birch bark was alight. He began laying dry grasses and the tiniest twigs on the flame. He could not pick and choose, for he had to lift the fuel between the heels of his hands. Small pieces of rotten wood and green moss clung to the twigs, and he bit them off as well as he could with his teeth. He cherished the flame carefully and awkwardly. It meant life, and it must not perish. The withdrawal of blood from the surface of his body now made him begin to shiver, and he grew more awkward. A large piece of green moss fell squarely on the little fire. He tried to poke it out with his fingers, but his shivering frame made him poke too far, and he disrupted the <u>nucleus</u> of the little fire, the burning grasses and tiny twigs separating and scattering. He tried to poke them together again, but in spite of the tenseness of the effort, his shivering got away with him, and the twigs were hopelessly scattered. Each twig gushed a puff of smoke and went out. The fire provider had failed. As he looked <u>apathetically</u> about him, his eyes chanced on the dog, sitting across the ruins of the fire from him, in the snow, making restless, hunching movements, slightly lifting one forefoot and then the other, shifting its weight back and forth on them with wistful eagerness.

The sight of the dog put a wild idea into his head.

The sight of the dog put a wild idea into his head. He remembered the tale of the man, caught in a blizzard, who killed a steer and crawled inside the carcass, and so was saved. He would kill the dog and bury his hands in the warm body until the numbness went out of them. Then he could build another

What plan does the man devise?

fire. He spoke to the dog, calling it to him; but in his voice was a strange note of fear that frightened the animal, who had never known the man to speak in such way before. Something was the matter, and its suspicious nature sensed danger—it knew not what danger, but somewhere, somehow, in its brain arose an apprehension of the man. It flattened its ears down at the sound of the man's voice, and its restless, hunching movements and the liftings and shiftings of its forefeet became more pronounced; but it would not come to the man. He got on his hand and knees and crawled toward the dog. This unusual posture again excited suspicion, and the animal sidled mincingly away.

The man sat up in the snow for a moment and struggled for calmness. Then he pulled on his mittens, by means of his teeth, and got upon his feet. He glanced down at first in order to assure himself that he was really standing up, for the absence of sensation in his feet left him unrelated to the earth. His erect position in itself started to drive the webs of suspicion from the dog's mind; and when he spoke <u>peremptorily</u>, with the sound of whiplashes in his voice, the dog rendered its customary allegiance and came to him. As it came within reaching distance, the man lost his control. His arms flashed out to the dog, and he experienced genuine surprise when he discovered that his hands could not clutch, that there was neither bend nor feeling in the fingers. He had forgotten for the moment that they were frozen and that they were freezing more and more. All this happened quickly, and before the animal could get away, he encircled its body with his arms. He sat down in the snow, and in this fashion held the dog, while it snarled and whined and struggled.

But it was all he could do, hold its body encircled in his arms and sit there. He realized that he could not kill the dog.

How does the plan proceed?

There was no way to do it. With his helpless hands he could neither draw nor hold his sheath-knife nor throttle the animal. He released it, and it plunged wildly away, with tail between its legs, and still snarling. It halted forty feet away and surveyed him curiously, with ears sharply pricked forward. The man looked down at his hands in order to locate them, and found them hanging on the ends of his arms. It struck him as curious that one should have to use his eyes in order to find out where his hands were. He began threshing his arms back and forth, beating the mittened hands against his sides. He did this for five minutes, violently, and his heart pumped enough blood up to the surface to put a stop to his shivering. But no sensation was aroused in the hands. He had an impression that they hung like weights on the ends of his arms, but when he tried to run the impression down, he could not find it.

A certain fear of death, dull and oppressive, came to him. This fear quickly became <u>poignant</u> as he realized that it was no longer a mere matter of freezing his fingers and toes, or of losing his hands and feet, but that it was a matter of life and death with the chances against him. This threw him into a panic, and he turned and ran up the creekbed along the old, dim trail. The dog joined in behind and kept up with him. He ran blindly, without intention, in fear such as he had never known in his life. Slowly, as he plowed and floundered through the snow, he began to see things again—the banks of the creek, the old timber

What does the man begin to realize?

jams, the leafless aspens, and the sky. The running made him feel better. He did not shiver. Maybe, if he ran on, his feet would thaw out: and, anyway, if he ran far enough, he would reach camp and the boys. Without doubt he would lose some fingers and toes and some of his face; but the boys would take care of him, and save the rest of him when he got there. And at the same time there was another thought in his mind that said he would never get to the camp and the boys;

What thoughts fight in his mind?

that it was too many miles away, that the freezing had too great a start on him, and that he would soon be stiff and dead. This thought he kept in the background and refused to consider. Sometimes it pushed itself forward and demanded to be heard, but he thrust it back and strove to think of other things.

It struck him as curious that he could run at all on feet so frozen that he could not feel them when they struck the earth and took the weight of his body. He seemed to himself to skim along above the surface, and to have no connection with the earth. Somewhere he had once seen a winged Mercury,[7] and he wondered if Mercury felt as he felt when skimming over the earth.

His theory of running until he reached camp and the boys had one flaw in it: he lacked the endurance. Several times he stumbled, and finally he tottered, crumpled up, and fell. When he tried to rise, he failed. He must sit and rest, he decided, and next time he would merely walk and keep on going. As he sat and regained his breath, he noted that he was feeling quite warm and comfortable. He was not shivering, and it even seemed that a warm glow had come to his chest and trunk. And yet, when he touched his

---

7. **Mercury.** In Roman mythology, Mercury, the messenger of the gods, is depicted with winged feet.

words for everyday use poign • ant (poin´yənt) *adj.*, sharp; painful. <u>Poignant</u> memories of his months in a refugee camp washed over Li.

nose or cheeks, there was no sensation. Running would not thaw them out. Nor would it thaw out his hands and feet. Then the thought came to him that the frozen portions of his body must be extending. He tried to keep this thought down, to forget it, to think of something else; he was aware of the panicky feeling that it caused, and he was afraid of the panic. But the thought asserted itself, and persisted, until it produced a vision of his body totally frozen. This was too much, and he made another wild run along the trail. Once he slowed down to a walk, but the thought of the freezing extending itself made him run again.

And all the time the dog ran with him, at his heels. When he fell down a second time, it curled its tail over its forefeet and sat in front of him, facing him, curiously eager and intent. The warmth and security of the animal angered him, and he cursed it till it flattened down its ears appeasingly. This time the shivering came more quickly upon the man. He was losing in his battle with the frost. It was creeping into his body from all sides. The thought of it drove him on, but he ran no more than a hundred feet, when he staggered and pitched headlong. It was his last panic. When he had recovered his breath and control, he sat up and entertained in his mind the conception of meeting death with dignity. However, the conception did not come to him in such terms. His idea of it was that he had been making a fool of himself, running around like a chicken with its head cut off—such was the simile that occurred to him. Well, he was bound to freeze anyway, and he might as well take it decently. With this new-found peace of mind came the first glimmerings of drowsiness. A good idea, he thought, to sleep off to death. It was like taking an anaesthetic. Freezing was not so bad as people thought. There were lots worse ways to die.

He pictured the boys finding his body next day. Suddenly he found himself with them, coming along the trail and looking for himself. And, still with them, he came around a turn in the trail and found himself lying in the snow. He did not belong with himself any more, for even then he was out of himself; standing with the boys and looking at himself in the snow. It certainly was cold, was his thought. When he got back to the States he could tell the folks what real cold was. He drifted on from this to a vision of the old-timer on Sulphur Creek. He could see him quite clearly, warm and comfortable, and smoking a pipe.

What are the man's final thoughts?

"You were right, old hoss; you were right," the man mumbled to the old-timer of Sulphur Creek.

Then the man drowsed off into what seemed to him the most comfortable and satisfying sleep he had ever known. The dog sat facing him and waiting. The brief day drew to a close in a long, slow twilight. There were no signs of a fire to be made, and, besides, never in the dog's experience had it known a man to sit like that in the snow and make no fire. As the twilight drew on, its eager yearning for the fire mastered it, and with a great lifting and shifting of forefeet, it whined softly, then flattened its ears down in anticipation of being chidden[8] by the man. But the man remained silent. Later, the dog whined loudly. And still later it crept close to the man and caught the scent of death. This made the animal bristle and back away. A little longer it delayed, howling under the stars that leaped and danced and shone brightly in the cold sky. Then it turned and trotted up the trail in the direction of the camp it knew, where were the other food providers and fire providers.

---

8. **chidden.** Scolded

from A Short Life Intensely Lived:
The Adventures of Jack London

MELISSA BURDICK HARMON

In 1897, a handsome 21-year-old named Jack London joined thousands of other courageous and foolhardy men who stormed north to Alaska, carried unbearable loads over steep and snow-covered trails to Canada's Yukon, built boats and tried not to drown in life-snatching rapids, and survived frigid temperatures and scurvy, all because they intended to become rich. The event was the great Klondike Gold Rush, and to the lawyers and stockbrokers and ministers and thieves who left everything behind to head north, the big bonanza, the great fortune in gold, was certain to be on the mining claim that they staked.

London stayed in the Yukon for just one year. He staked a mining claim but never worked it. He returned home the following summer, not with his fortune in gold, but with something just as valuable—a head crammed with the stories and settings that would make his career. In fact, not a single Klondike prospector did as well from that Gold Rush as Jack London did. For the Klondike made him famous, made him rich, and continued to inspire him as a writer until the end of his life.

Even today, 83 years after London's death, it is almost impossible to imagine the Far North without thinking of *The Call of the Wild*, *White Fang*, or the classic short story "To Build a Fire." Jack London, in fact, invented Alaska and the Yukon for millions of readers around the world. It was actually his plan all along: Before he had even arrived there, he told a fellow traveler that he was not going north to mine, but to gather material for books. And that is exactly what he did.

• • •

He left for the Klondike Gold Rush in July 1897, the youngest prospector aboard a ship called the *Umatilla*. He was financed by the adoring Eliza [Jack's half-sister] and was accompanied by her lawyer husband, who'd also heard the call, although a bit more faintly. Upon arrival in Skagway, Alaska, Eliza's husband took one look at the virtually vertical Chilkoot Trail over the mountains to the Yukon and decided to turn back. Jack went on, carrying 100 pounds on his back at a time, relaying his requisite 1,000 pounds of food and supplies (needed to gain admittance to Canada) up the trail, and reached the top before the professional Indian packers he had started with. Jack may have been the only stampeder whose gear included Darwin's *Origin of the Species*, Spencer's *Philosophy of Style* (with its arguments for socialism), *Das Kapital*, and *Paradise Lost*.

When Jack and three friends he'd made on the *Umatilla* moved on to Lake Linderman, no boats were available, so Jack and his crew built two. When the foursome arrived at the Yukon River, they found nearly 1,000 boats backed up there. The reason: Every party attempting to make it over the Whitehorse Rapids, the next phase of the journey, had drowned. But "Sailor Jack" shot the rapids with ease, as thousands of stampeders cheered from the shoreline. He arrived in the Klondike with the winter.

Jack London in his "office," 1905.

London packed his gear up the snowcovered Chilkhoot Pass near Skagway, Alaska, en route to the gold fields in the Yukon and Alaska.

Jack applied for placer-mining claim 54 on the left fork of Henderson Creek but didn't work it. (Much later, that area was dredged and found to be full of gold.) Instead, he spent his Klondike winter reading in his bunk and gossiping and playing cards and eating beans and bacon and biscuits. "He never done a tap of work," reported one miner who knew him. He did, however, make an extended visit to Dawson, then a tent city of 50,000, packed with prospectors and bars with dreamy names like El Dorado. There, of course, Jack did his real prospecting—picking up enough characters and color to last a lifetime.

After a winter without fruits and vegetables, London was suffering from scurvy—his handsome face now covered with sores, his few remaining real teeth about to fall out, his right leg crippled. He headed for home, earning his way down the Yukon by stoking the ship's furnace. When he arrived back in San Francisco, he found that John London [Jack's stepfather] was dead and that his mother—who had never been anything but an indifferent parent to Jack—had adopted one of John's grandchildren. He was expected to support both of them.

Jack did odd jobs, waited to hear about a position he'd applied for at the post office, pawned his possessions, courted the patient Mabel [Jack's girlfriend] once a week, copied out Kipling by hand to learn about style, and wrote and wrote and wrote, limiting himself to five hours sleep a night. Rejections poured in. Then, surprisingly, he received an unprecedented two acceptances, one right after the other. A literary magazine called *Overland Monthly* bought one of his Alaska stories, "To the Man on Trail," for $5, and *The Black Cat* bought an old story of his, complaining that it was "more lengthy than strengthy" but offering $40 anyway if he'd let them cut it. He was on his way.

• • •

Throughout his life, Jack London never stopped pushing himself in new and dangerous directions. He lived anonymously among the poor of London's East End and produced a powerful sociological treatise about it. He covered the Russo-Japanese War for Hearst, sailing a junk across the Yellow Sea, then riding a horse across Korea to get to the action before anyone else. He twice ran for mayor of Oakland on the Socialist Party ticket. He went to Mexico to cover the revolution in 1914. He invested a quarter of a million dollars to create a model farm, staffed largely by paroled convicts from Folsom and San Quentin, and never turned a penny's profit.

• • •

As a young man, Jack London had said that he wanted to be where the winds of adventure blew. He was there on his life-changing journey into the Yukon, and in fact, he was there for almost every one of the 40 years of his life. That constant eagerness to accept adventure may just have been Jack London's greatest accomplishment of all.

ABOUT THE RELATED READING

"A Short Life Intensely Lived: The Adventures of Jack London," appeared in the travel section of the July 1999 issue of *Biography* magazine. Melissa Burdick Harmon covers travel for the magazine. Biography.com's website at http://www.biography.com/ contains over 25,000 biographies of famous personalities.

Evaluating Author Websites

When researching an author, keep in mind that it takes time to find a quality, informative site among the clutter and gigantic mass of the Internet. Web browsers are a great place to start; most of the sites you will find there will be well organized and in-depth. The best sites are often those that the authors put together themselves. When a writer creates a home page, you can often find personal messages and anecdotes that allow you to get a real sense of who he or she is. Good secondary sites include those authorized by the author or his or her agent, literary societies, publishers, and fans of the author. Literary societies and publishers often have author websites that are easy to use and fun to view. However, you may find that publisher sites often provide only a short author biography and a list of the author's published works. Fan sites, while of greatly varying quality and depth, can be rich sources of offbeat information and quirky stories. The main drawback to using a fan-sponsored site as a resource is that the accuracy of the information may be unreliable.

Two sites, one fan-created and one maintained by the literary society of the University of California, Berkeley, serve as excellent examples of quality author websites. They both feature writer Jack London, best known for his novels *The Call of the Wild*, *White Fang*, and *The Sea-Wolf*. The Berkeley Digital Library SunSITE "The Jack London Collection," at http://sunsite.berkeley.edu/London/, is more scholarly, meant for use as a study tool. The fan site, "Jack London's Ranch Album,"

at http://www.geocities.com/~jacklondons/, is a "get-to-know" site, with many interesting anecdotes about London's life but with fewer specific details and research aids.

The Berkeley site is comprehensive and well organized. If you wanted to write a paper on Jack London, this would be the place to go for sheer volume of information. It provides several links to other quality sites, as well as links to photos of Jack, his family, his travels, and a growing collection of his writings. Many of London's books and other works are reproduced in full on the site, ready for printing or downloading. The site also lists fan and scholarly organizations devoted to London and his work.

The fan site provides a deeper look at Jack London's personality and gives a sense of the drama of his life. The focus of the site is London's California ranch and the museum it houses today, but it also

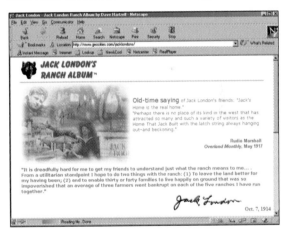

contains other information, such as tales of his travels in his sailing ship, the *Snark*. At first glance, the site has a warmer, friendlier look than the Berkeley site, but seems slightly less organized. This site is best suited for someone who has the time to go through and read, page by page, Jack London's exploits and life history. Links go back and forth from the main drive of the biography to comments, anecdotal stories, and London's own quotes.

Whether you are looking for factual biographical information or personal details about an author's private life, the Internet is a good place to begin your search.

Imagine that you are one of the men waiting at camp for the return of the solitary traveler. Why do you think he is late in returning to camp? What concerns do you have for his safety?

Investigate, *Inquire,* and Imagine

Recall: GATHERING FACTS

1a. What signals warn the man that it is much colder than he estimated?

2a. Why does the man call the dog to him?

3a. Against what does the man lose his battle?

Interpret: FINDING MEANING

1b. What responses does the man have toward the cold? What does he think about to motivate himself to continue?

2b. How is the dog wiser than the man?

3b. How will the boys at camp learn of the man's death?

Analyze: TAKING THINGS APART

4a. Identify the mistakes the man makes.

Synthesize: BRINGING THINGS TOGETHER

4b. Why does the author state that the man's limitation is that he is without imagination?

Evaluate: MAKING JUDGMENTS

5a. Evaluate the advice of the old-timer of Sulphur Creek.

Extend: CONNECTING IDEAS

5b. After reading the Related Reading about Jack London's real-life adventures, what personal experiences of the author do you think might have influenced him to write this story?

Understanding Literature

SETTING. Review the definition for **setting** in the Handbook of Literary Terms. Which details are effective in creating the wintry Yukon setting? In what ways does London's setting reflect his interest in Naturalism? (For more information on Naturalism, see the Reader's Resource on page 180.)

PLOT AND CONFLICT. Review the definitions for **plot** and **conflict** in the Handbook of Literary Terms. Looking at the sequence chart you completed for Literary Tools on page 180, what is the external conflict, or outside force, against which the main character struggles? What events cause the main character's downfall? Is his death inevitable? Why, or why not?

Writer's Journal

1. Write a **letter** to the man's family explaining how he died.
2. Imagine that you are the old-timer at Sulphur Creek. Write a brief **survival guide** specifying what is needed for travel in the Yukon.
3. Write **directions** for how to build a fire in the snow.

Integrating the Language Arts

Vocabulary

BASE WORDS AND SUFFIXES. Read the Language Arts Survey 1.19, "Learning Base Words, Prefixes, and Suffixes." Then underline the base word once and the suffix twice in each of the following words from "To Build a Fire." Next look up each suffix in a dictionary and write two additional words that end with the same suffix.

1. uncomfortable
2. solidity
3. eastward
4. numbness
5. sensation

Applied English

TECHNICAL WRITING. In the selection, London describes all the steps in the process of building a fire in the wilderness. Think of a procedure, such as programming a VCR, with which you are familiar, and write a set of guidelines documenting the procedure. (You may wish to refer to the Language Arts Survey 6.4, "Writing a Step-by-Step Procedure.") To get started, you may want to think through each step of the procedure. Then, break the task into a series of short, simple, chronological steps. Use simple and precise language, written in the second-person imperative.

Collaborative Learning

SKIT. With two or three partners, write a skit to dramatize what happens in the camp when the dog returns without the man. Write dialogue, assigning a role to each group member. The skit should describe the men's discovery of the dog, their hypotheses about what happened to the man, and their plans for finding him. Then perform your skit for the class.

Study and Research

JACK LONDON'S LETTERS. Access the Internet site http://sunsite.berkeley.edu/London/Documents. Read original letters by Jack London and take notes on the biographical data you collect. When you are done reading the letters, write a paragraph about what you learned about Jack London from using this primary source. You may also want to visit other websites. See Insights, "Evaluating Author Websites" on page 195.

Literary TOOLS

IRONY. Irony is a difference between appearance and reality. *Verbal irony* occurs when a statement is made that implies its opposite. *Irony of situation* occurs when an event violates the expectations of the characters. Look for an example of verbal irony and irony of situation as you read "The Most Dangerous Game."

PLOT AND CONFLICT. A **plot** is a series of events related to a central **conflict**, or struggle. A typical plot involves the introduction of a conflict, its development, and its eventual resolution. Types of conflict include person versus person, person versus nature, person versus society, person versus self, person versus machine, and person versus the supernatural.

Organizer

As you read the selection, make a sequence chart of the main events in the story, circling the events that point out a struggle, or conflict.

Rainsford falls off the yacht. → Rainsford enters the château and meets General Zaroff. →

Reader's Journal

Describe what you think it would be like to be shipwrecked. If you landed on a desert island, how would you find shelter and food?

"The Most DANGEROUS Game"
by Richard Connell

Reader's resource

In **"The Most Dangerous Game,"** published in 1924, techniques of characterization are used to create the characters of Rainsford and Zaroff. Highly skilled and experienced hunters, the famous Rainsford and cultured Zaroff share an enthusiasm for the sport of big-game hunting. Through various techniques of characterization, such as dialogue and direct description, the different physical traits, actions, and beliefs of each character are created.

CULTURE CONNECTION. In recent years big-game hunting has been banned in many countries because of dwindling populations of animals such as lions and tigers.

About the AUTHOR

Richard Connell (1893–1949) was born in Poughkeepsie, New York. At the age of ten, he took on his first writing assignment, covering baseball games for the local newspaper. After attending Georgetown University for one year, he entered and graduated from Harvard University. During World War I, Connell served with the American Expeditionary Force. After the war, he moved to New York City and became a freelance writer. The author of screenplays and hundreds of short stories, Connell also wrote numerous novels, including *Apes and Angels* (1924) and *The Mad Lover* (1927).

The Most DANGEROUS Game

Richard Connell

"Off there to the right—somewhere—is a large island," said Whitney. "It's rather a mystery—"

"What island is it?" Rainsford asked.

"The old charts call it 'Ship-Trap Island,' " Whitney replied. "A suggestive name, isn't it? Sailors have a curious dread of the place. I don't know why. Some superstition—"

> What is ominous about the name of the island?

"Can't see it," remarked Rainsford, trying to peer through the <u>dank</u> tropical night that was <u>palpable</u> as it pressed its thick warm blackness in upon the yacht.

"You've good eyes," said Whitney, with a laugh, "and I've seen you pick off a moose moving in the brown fall bush at four hundred yards, but even you can't see four miles or so through a moonless Caribbean night."

"Nor four yards," admitted Rainsford. "Ugh! It's like moist black velvet."

"It will be light enough in Rio,[1] promised Whitney. "We should make it in a few days. I hope the jaguar guns have come from Purdey's.

We should have some good hunting up the Amazon. Great sport, hunting."

"The best sport in the world," agreed Rainsford.

"For the hunter," amended Whitney. "Not for the jaguar."

"Don't talk rot, Whitney," said Rainsford. "You're a big-game hunter, not a philosopher. Who cares how a jaguar feels?"

"Perhaps the jaguar does," observed Whitney.

"Bah! They've no understanding."

"Even so, I rather think they understand one thing—fear. The fear of pain and the fear of death."

> What doesn't Rainsford understand?

"Nonsense," laughed Rainsford. "This hot weather is making you soft, Whitney. Be a <u>realist</u>. The world is made up of two classes—the hunters and the hunted. Luckily, you and I are

---

1. **Rio.** Rio de Janeiro, then the capital of Brazil

the hunters. Do you think we've passed that island yet?"

"I can't tell in the dark. I hope so."

"Why?" asked Rainsford.

"The place has a reputation—a bad one."

"Cannibals?" suggested Rainsford.

"Hardly. Even cannibals wouldn't live in such a God-forsaken place. But it's gotten into sailor lore, somehow. Didn't you notice that the crew's nerves seemed a bit jumpy today?"

"They were a bit strange, now you mention it. Even Captain Nielsen—"

"Yes, even that tough-minded old Swede, who'd go up to the devil himself and ask him for a light. Those fishy blue eyes held a look I never saw there before. All I could get out of him was: 'This place has an evil name among sea-faring men, sir.' Then he said to me, very gravely: 'Don't you feel anything?'—as if the air about us was actually poisonous. Now, you mustn't laugh when I tell you this—I did feel something like a sudden chill.

"There was no breeze. The sea was as flat as a plate-glass window. We were drawing near the island then. What I felt was a—a mental chill; a sort of sudden dread."

"Pure imagination," said Rainsford. "One superstitious sailor can <u>taint</u> the whole ship's company with his fear."

"Maybe. But sometimes I think sailors have an extra sense that tells them when they are in danger. Sometimes I think evil is a <u>tangible</u> thing— with wave lengths, just as sound and light have. An evil place can, so to speak, broadcast vibrations of evil. Anyhow, I'm glad we're getting out of this zone. Well, I think I'll turn in now, Rainsford."

"I'm not sleepy," said Rainsford. "I'm going to smoke another pipe on the afterdeck."[2]

"Good night, then, Rainsford. See you at breakfast."

"Right. Good night, Whitney."

There was no sound in the night as Rainsford sat there, but the muffled throb of the engine that drove the yacht swiftly through the darkness, and the swish and ripple of the wash of the propeller.

Rainsford, reclining in a steamer chair, <u>indolently</u> puffed on his favorite brier. The sensuous drowsiness of the night was on him. "It's so dark," he thought, "that I could sleep without closing my eyes; the night would be my eyelids—"

An abrupt sound startled him. Off to the right he heard it, and his ears, expert in such matters, could not be mistaken. Again he heard the sound, and again. Somewhere, off in the blackness, someone had fired a gun three times.

Rainsford sprang up and moved quickly to the rail, mystified. He strained his eyes in the direction from which the reports had come, but it was like trying to see through a blanket. He leaped upon the rail and balanced himself there, to get greater elevation; his pipe, striking a rope, was knocked from his mouth. He lunged for it; a short, hoarse cry came from his lips as he realized he had reached too far and had lost his balance. The cry was pinched off short as the blood-warm waters of the Caribbean Sea[3] closed over his head.

He struggled up to the surface and tried to cry out, but the wash from the speeding yacht slapped him in the face and the salt water in his open mouth made him gag and strangle. Desperately he struck out with strong strokes after the <u>receding</u> lights of the yacht, but he stopped before he had swum fifty feet. A cer-

---

2. **afterdeck.** Part of a ship's deck between the middle and the rear

3. **Caribbean Sea.** Tropical and subtropical body of water near the eastern coast of the Americas in the western Atlantic

words for everyday use

taint (tānt) vt., infect. *Many old houses have been <u>tainted</u> by lead in paint.*

tan • gi • ble (tan´jə bəl) adj., having actual form. *Although I had no <u>tangible</u> evidence, I felt certain that someone had gone through my locker.*

in • do • lent • ly (in´də lənt lē) adv., idly; lazily. *The cat lay <u>indolently</u> in her favorite sunny spot on the couch.*

re • ced • ing (ri sēd´iŋ) part., moving away from; becoming more distant. *We kidded Dad about his <u>receding</u> hairline.*

tain coolheadedness had come to him; it was not the first time he had been in a tight place. There was a chance that his cries could be heard by some one aboard the yacht, but that chance was slender, and grew more slender as the yacht raced on. He wrestled himself out of his clothes, and shouted with all his power. The lights of the yacht became faint and ever-vanishing fireflies; then they were blotted out entirely by the night.

Rainsford remembered the shots. They had come from the right, and doggedly he swam in that direction, swimming with slow, deliberate strokes, conserving his strength. For a seemingly endless time he fought the sea. He began to count his strokes; he could do possibly a hundred more and then—

Rainsford heard a sound. It came out of the darkness, a high screaming sound, the sound of an animal in an <u>extremity</u> of anguish and terror.

He did not recognize the animal that made the sound; he did not try to; with fresh vitality he swam toward the sound. He heard it again; then it was cut short by another noise, crisp, staccato.

"Pistol shot," muttered Rainsford, swimming on.

Ten minutes of determined effort brought another sound to his ears—the most welcome he had ever heard—the muttering and growling of the sea breaking on a rocky shore. He was almost on the rocks before he saw them; on a night less calm he would have been shattered against them. With his remaining strength he dragged himself from the swirling waters. Jagged crags appeared to jut into the opaqueness, he forced himself upward, hand over hand. Gasping, his hands raw, he reached a flat

Why does Rainsford swim in the direction of the shots?

What is unusual about the sound that Rainsford hears?

place at the top. Dense jungle came down to the very edge of the cliffs. What perils that tangle of trees and underbrush might hold for him did not concern Rainsford just then. All he knew was that he was safe from his enemy, the sea, and that utter weariness was on him. He flung himself down at the jungle edge and tumbled headlong into the deepest sleep of his life.

When he opened his eyes he knew from the position of the sun that it was late in the afternoon. Sleep had given him new vigor; a sharp hunger was picking at him. He looked about him, almost cheerfully.

"Where there are pistol shots, there are men. Where there are men, there is food," he thought. But what kind of men, he wondered, in so forbidding a place? An unbroken front of snarled and jagged jungle fringed the shore.

He saw no sign of a trail through the closely knit web of weeds and trees; it was easier to go along the shore, and Rainsford floundered along by the water. Not far from where he had landed, he stopped.

Some wounded thing, by the evidence a large animal, had thrashed about in the underbrush; the jungle weeds were crushed down and the moss was <u>lacerated</u>; one patch of weeds was stained crimson. A small, glittering object not far away caught Rainsford's eye and he picked it up. It was an empty cartridge.

"A twenty-two," he remarked. "That's odd. It must have been a fairly large animal too. The hunter had his nerve with him to tackle it with a light gun. It's clear that the brute put up a

It came out of the darkness, a high screaming sound, the sound of an animal in an extremity of anguish and terror.

words for everyday use

ex • trem • i • ty (ek strem´ə tē) n., greatest degree. *The marathon runner reached the <u>extremity</u> of her endurance at the twenty-sixth mile.*

lac • er • at • ed (las´ər āt´əd) part., torn; mangled. *Someone's feet could be <u>lacerated</u> by this broken glass on the sidewalk.*

fight. I suppose the first three shots I heard was when the hunter flushed his quarry[4] and wounded it. The last shot was when he trailed it here and finished it."

He examined the ground closely and found what he had hoped to find—the print of hunting boots. They pointed along the cliff in the direction he had been going. Eagerly he hurried along, now slipping on a rotten log or a loose stone, but making headway; night was beginning to settle down on the island.

What sign does Rainsford find? Why is he glad to see this sign?

Bleak darkness was blacking out the sea and jungle when Rainsford sighted the lights. He came upon them as he turned a crook in the coast line and his first thought was that he had come upon a village, for there were many lights. But as he forged along he saw to his great astonishment that all the lights were in one enormous building—a lofty structure with pointed towers plunging upward into the gloom. His eyes made out the shadowy outlines of a palatial château; it was set on a high bluff, and on three sides of it cliffs dived down to where the sea licked greedy lips in the shadows.

In his hand the man held a long-barreled revolver, and he was pointing it straight at Rainsford's heart.

"Mirage," thought Rainsford. But it was no mirage, he found, when he opened the tall spiked iron gate. The stone steps were real enough; the massive door with a leering gargoyle[5] for a knocker was real enough; yet about it all hung an air of unreality.

He lifted the knocker, and it creaked up stiffly, as if it had never before been used. He let it fall,

and it startled him with its booming loudness. He thought he heard steps within; the door remained closed. Again Rainsford lifted the heavy knocker, and let it fall. The door opened then, opened as suddenly as if it were on a spring, and Rainsford stood blinking in the river of glaring gold light that poured out. The first thing Rainsford's eyes discerned was the largest man Rainsford had ever seen—a gigantic creature, solidly made and black-bearded to the waist. In his hand the man held a long-barreled revolver, and he was pointing it straight at Rainsford's heart.

Out of the snarl of beard two small eyes regarded Rainsford.

"Don't be alarmed," said Rainsford, with a smile which he hoped was disarming. "I'm no robber. I fell off a yacht. My name is Sanger Rainsford of New York City."

The menacing look in the eyes did not change. The revolver pointed as rigidly as if the giant were a statue. He gave no sign that he understood Rainsford's words, or that he had even heard them. He was dressed in uniform, a black uniform trimmed with gray astrakhan.[6]

"I'm Sanger Rainsford of New York," Rainsford began again. "I fell off a yacht. I am hungry."

The man's only answer was to raise with his thumb the hammer of his revolver. Then Rainsford saw the man's free hand go to his forehead in a military salute, and he saw him click his heels together and stand at attention. Another man was coming down the broad marble steps, an erect, slender man in evening clothes. He advanced to Rainsford and held out his hand.

In a cultivated voice marked by a slight accent that gave it added precision and deliberateness, he said: "It is a very great pleasure and honor to

---

4. **flushed his quarry.** Forced the animal out of its hiding place
5. **gargoyle.** Grotesquely carved figure
6. **astrakhan.** Fur made from the pelt of young lambs

welcome Mr. Sanger Rainsford, the celebrated hunter, to my home."

Automatically Rainsford shook the man's hand.

For what is Rainsford known?

"I've read your book about hunting snow leopards in Tibet, you see," explained the man. "I am General Zaroff."

Rainsford's first impression was that the man was singularly handsome; his second was that there was an original, almost bizarre quality about the general's face. He was a tall man past middle age, for his hair was a vivid white; but his thick eyebrows and pointed military mustache were as black as the night from which Rainsford had come. His eyes, too, were black and very bright. He had high cheek bones, a sharp-cut nose, a spare, dark face, the face of a man used to giving orders, the face of an aristocrat. Turning to the giant in uniform, the general made a sign. The giant put away his pistol, saluted, withdrew.

"Ivan is an incredibly strong fellow," remarked the general, "but he has the misfortune to be deaf and dumb. A simple fellow, but I'm afraid, like all his race, a bit of a savage."

"Is he Russian?"

"He is a Cossack,"[7] said the general, and his smile showed red lips and pointed teeth. "So am I."

"Come," he said, "we shouldn't be chatting here. We can talk later. Now you want clothes, food, rest. You shall have them. This is a most restful spot."

Ivan had reappeared, and the general spoke to him with lips that moved but gave forth no sound.

"Follow Ivan, if you please, Mr. Rainsford," said the general. "I was about to have my dinner when you came. I'll wait for you. You'll find that my clothes will fit you, I think."

It was to a huge, beam-ceilinged bedroom with a canopied bed big enough for six men that Rainsford followed the silent giant. Ivan laid out an evening suit, and Rainsford, as he put it on, noticed that it came from a London tailor who ordinarily cut and sewed for none below the rank of duke.

The dining room to which Ivan conducted him was in many ways remarkable. There was a medieval magnificence about it; it suggested a baronial hall of feudal times[8] with its oaken panels, its high ceiling, its vast refectory table[9] where twoscore[10] men could sit down to eat. About the hall were the mounted heads of many animals—lions, tigers, elephants, moose, bears; larger or more perfect specimens Rainsford had never seen. At the great table the general was sitting, alone.

"You'll have a cocktail, Mr. Rainsford," he suggested. The cocktail was surpassingly good; and, Rainsford noted, the table appointments were of the finest—the linen, the crystal, the silver, the china.

They were eating borsch,[11] the rich, red soup with whipped cream so dear to Russian palates. Half apologetically General Zaroff said: "We do our best to preserve the amenities of civilization here. Please forgive any lapses. We are well off the beaten track, you know. Do you think the champagne has suffered from its long ocean trip?"

"Not in the least," declared Rainsford. He was finding the general a most thoughtful and affable host, a true cosmopolite.[12] But there was one small trait of the general's that made Rainsford uncomfortable. Whenever

What about General Zaroff makes Rainsford uncomfortable?

---

7. **Cossack.** Member of a group of people from southern Russia known for equestrian skill and fighting ability

8. **baronial hall of feudal times.** Dining room in a medieval mansion

9. **refectory table.** Large table in the dining room

10. **twoscore.** Forty

11. *borsch.* Russian soup made of beets

12. **cosmopolite.** Person having a worldwide rather than a provincial scope

---

words for everyday use

con • duct (kən dukt´) vt., lead. *The hostess conducted us to a quiet table by the window.*

me • di • e • val (mə dē´vəl) adj., suggestive of the Middle Ages. *Medieval European castles were built as fortresses.*

a • men • i • ty (ə men´ə tē) n., desirable feature. *What amenities does the Carlton Hotel offer?*

> "No thrill left in tigers, no real danger. I live for danger, Mr. Rainsford."

he looked up from his plate he found the general studying him, <u>appraising</u> him narrowly.

"Perhaps," said General Zaroff, "you were surprised that I recognized your name. You see, I read all books on hunting published in English, French, and Russian. I have but one passion in my life, Mr. Rainsford, and it is the hunt."

"You have some wonderful heads here," said Rainsford as he ate a particularly well cooked filet mignon. "That Cape buffalo is the largest I ever saw."

"Oh, that fellow. Yes, he was a monster."

"Did he charge you?"

"Hurled me against a tree," said the general. "Fractured my skull. But I got the brute."

"I've always thought," said Rainsford, "that the Cape buffalo is the most dangerous of all big game."

For a moment the general did not reply; he was smiling his curious redlipped smile. Then he said slowly: "No. You are wrong, sir. The Cape buffalo is not the most dangerous big game." He sipped his wine. "Here in my <u>preserve</u> on this island," he said in the same slow tone, "I hunt more dangerous game."

Rainsford expressed his surprise. "Is there big game on this island?"

The general nodded. "The biggest."

"Really?"

"Oh, it isn't here naturally, of course. I have to stock the island."

"What have you imported, General?" Rainsford asked. "Tigers?"

The general smiled. "No," he said. "Hunting tigers ceased to interest me some years ago. I exhausted their possibilities, you see. No thrill left in tigers, no real danger. I live for danger, Mr. Rainsford."

The general took from his pocket a gold cigarette case and offered his guest a long black cigarette with a silver tip; it was perfumed and gave off a smell like incense.

"We will have some capital hunting, you and I," said the general. "I shall be most glad to have your society."

"But what game—" began Rainsford.

"I'll tell you," said the general. "You will be amused, I know. I think I may say, in all modesty, that I have done a rare thing. I have invented a new sensation. May I pour you another glass of port, Mr. Rainsford?"

"Thank you, General."

The general filled both glasses and said: "God makes some men poets. Some He makes kings, some beggars. Me He made a hunter. My hand was made for the trigger, my father said. He was a very rich man with a quarter of a million acres in the Crimea,[13] and he was an ardent sportsman. When I was only five years old he gave me a little gun, specially made in Moscow for me, to shoot sparrows with. When I shot some of his prize turkeys with it, he did not punish me; he complimented me on my marksmanship. I killed my first bear in the Caucasus when I was ten. My whole life has been one prolonged hunt. I went into the army—it was expected of noblemen's sons—and for a time commanded a division of Cossack cavalry, but my real interest was always the hunt. I have hunted every kind of game in every land. It would be impossible for me to tell you how many animals I have killed."

13. **Crimea.** Peninsula on the Black Sea in southwestern Russia

---

words for everyday use

ap • praise (ə prāz´) vt., judge the worth of. *The jeweler <u>appraised</u> the diamond ring.*

pre • serve (prē zurv´) n., place maintained for regulated hunting. *The animals on the big-game <u>preserve</u> became endangered species.*

The general puffed at his cigarette.

"After the debacle in Russia[14] I left the country, for it was imprudent for an officer of the Czar to stay there. Many noble Russians lost everything. I, luckily, had invested heavily in American securities, so I shall never have to open a tea room in Monte Carlo or drive a taxi in Paris. Naturally, I continued to hunt—grizzlies in your Rockies, crocodiles in the Ganges,[15] rhinoceroses in East Africa. It was in Africa that the Cape buffalo hit me and laid me up for six months. As soon as I recovered I started for the Amazon to hunt jaguars, for I had heard they were unusually <u>cunning</u>. They weren't." The Cossack sighed. "They were no match at all for a hunter with his wits about him and a high-powered rifle. I was bitterly disappointed. I was lying in my tent with a splitting headache one night when a terrible thought pushed its way into my mind. Hunting was beginning to bore me! And hunting, remember, had been my life. I have heard that in America business men often go to pieces when they give up the business that has been their life."

"Yes, that's so," said Rainsford.

The general smiled. "I had no wish to go to pieces," he said. "I must do something. Now, mine is an <u>analytical</u> mind, Mr. Rainsford. Doubtless that is why I enjoy the problems of the chase."

"No doubt, General Zaroff."

"So," continued the general, "I asked myself why the hunt no longer fascinated me. You are much younger than I am, Mr. Rainsford, and have not hunted as much, but you perhaps can guess the answer."

"What was it?"

"Simply this: hunting had ceased to be what you call 'a sporting proposition.' It had become too easy. I always got my quarry. Always. There is no greater bore than perfection."

The general lit a fresh cigarette.

"No animal had a chance with me any more. That is no boast; it is a mathematical certainty. The animal had nothing but his legs and his instinct. Instinct is no match for reason. When I thought of this it was a tragic moment for me, I can tell you."

Rainsford leaned across the table, absorbed in what his host was saying.

"It came to me as an inspiration what I must do," the general went on.

"And that was?"

The general smiled the quiet smile of one who has faced an obstacle and surmounted it with success. "I had to invent a new animal to hunt," he said.

"A new animal? You're joking."

"Not at all," said the general. "I never joke about hunting. I needed a new animal. I found one. So I bought this island, built this house, and here I do my hunting. The island is perfect for my purposes—there are jungles with a maze of trails in them, hills, swamps—"

"But the animal, General Zaroff?"

"Oh," said the general, "it supplies me with the most exciting hunting in the world. No other hunting compares with it for an instant. Every day I hunt, and I never grow bored now, for I have a quarry with which I can match my wits."

Rainsford's bewilderment showed in his face.

"I wanted the ideal animal to hunt," explained the general. "So I said: 'What are the attributes of an ideal quarry?' And the answer was, of course: 'It must have courage, cunning, and, above all, it must be able to reason.'"

"But no animal can reason," objected Rainsford.

---

14. **debacle in Russia.** Russian Revolution of 1917 during which the czar was overthrown and wealthy landowners lost their property
15. **Ganges.** River in India, viewed by the Hindus as sacred

"My dear fellow," said the general, "there is one that can."

"But you can't mean—" gasped Rainsford.

"And why not?"

"I can't believe you are serious, General Zaroff. This is a grisly joke."

"Why should I not be serious? I am speaking of hunting."

"Hunting? General Zaroff, what you speak of is murder."

What animal does Zaroff hunt?

The general laughed with entire good nature. He regarded Rainsford quizzically. "I refuse to believe that so modern and civilized a young man as you seem to be harbors romantic ideas about the value of human life. Surely your experiences in the war—"

"Did not make me condone coldblooded murder," finished Rainsford stiffly.

Laughter shook the general. "How extraordinarily droll you are!" he said. "One does not expect nowadays to find a young man of the educated class, even in America, with such a naive, and, if I may say so, mid-Victorian point of view.[16] It's like finding a snuff-box in a limousine. Ah, well, doubtless you had Puritan ancestors. So many Americans appear to have had. I'll wager you'll forget your notions when you go hunting with me. You've a genuine new thrill in store for you, Mr. Rainsford."

"Thank you, I'm a hunter, not a murderer."

"Dear me," said the general, quite unruffled, "again that unpleasant word. But I think I can show you that your scruples are quite ill founded."

"Yes?"

"Life is for the strong, to be lived by the strong, and, if need be, taken by the strong. The weak of the world were put here to give the strong pleasure. I am strong.

What justification does General Zaroff give for his hobby?

Why should I not use my gift? If I wish to hunt, why should I not? I hunt the scum of the earth—a thoroughbred horse or hound is worth more than a score of them."

"But they are men," said Rainsford hotly.

"Precisely," said the general. "That is why I use them. It gives me pleasure. They can reason, after a fashion. So they are dangerous."

"But where do you get them?"

The general's left eyelid fluttered down in a wink. "This island is called Ship-Trap," he answered. "Sometimes an angry god of the high seas sends them to me. Sometimes, when Providence is not so kind, I help Providence a bit. Come to the window with me."

Rainsford went to the window and looked out toward the sea.

"Watch! Out there!" exclaimed the general, pointing into the night. Rainsford's eyes saw only blackness, and then, as the general pressed a button, far out to sea Rainsford saw the flash of lights.

The general chuckled. "They indicate a channel," he said, "where there's none; giant rocks with razor edges crouch like a sea monster with wide-open jaws. They can crush a ship as easily as I crush this nut." He dropped a walnut on the hardwood floor and brought his heel grinding down on it. "Oh, yes," he said casually, as if in answer to a question, "I have electricity. We try to be civilized here."

What indication does General Zaroff give of being civilized?

"Civilized? And you shoot down men?"

A trace of anger was in the general's black eyes; but it was there for but a second, and he said, in his most pleasant manner: "Dear me, what a

---

16. **mid-Victorian point of view.** During the reign of Queen Victoria, in the late nineteenth century, the English had a very strict code of moral behavior.

---

words for everyday use

gris • ly (griz´lē) *adj.*, terrifying; horrifying. *The jurors had to examine grisly photographs of the murder scene.*

con • done (kən dōn´) *vt.*, forgive or overlook an offense. *"Let it be known that I never condone cheating," exclaimed the teacher.*

scru • ple (skrōō´pəl) *n.*, qualm; uneasiness about something one thinks is wrong. *Breanna's scruples prevented her from keeping the fifty-dollar bill she found.*

righteous young man you are! I assure you I do not do the thing you suggest. That would be <u>barbarous</u>. I treat these visitors with every consideration. They get plenty of good food and exercise. They get into splendid physical condition. You shall see for yourself tomorrow."

"What do you mean?"

"We'll visit my training school," smiled the general. "It's in the cellar. I have about a dozen pupils down there now. They're from the Spanish bark San Lucar that had the bad luck to go on the rocks out there. A very inferior lot, I regret to say. Poor specimens and more accustomed to the deck than to the jungle."

He raised his hand, and Ivan, who served as waiter, brought thick Turkish coffee. Rainsford, with an effort, held his tongue in check.

"It's a game, you see," pursued the general blandly. "I suggest to one of them that we go hunting. I give him a supply of food and an excellent hunting knife. I give him three hours' start. I am to follow, armed only with a pistol of the smallest caliber and range. If my quarry eludes me for three whole days, he wins the game. If I find him"—the general smiled—"he loses."

"Suppose he refuses to be hunted?"

"Oh," said the general, "I give him his option, of course. He need not play the game if he doesn't wish to. If he does not wish to hunt, I turn him over to Ivan. Ivan once had the honor of serving as official knouter to the Great White Czar,[17] and he has his own ideas of sport. Invariably, Mr. Rainsford, invariably they choose the hunt."

"And if they win?"

The smile on the general's face widened. "To date I have not lost," he said.

Then he added, hastily: "I don't wish you to think me a braggart, Mr. Rainsford. Many of them afford only the most elementary sort of

Relaxing After the Safari, 1922. Guy Arnoux. Stapleton Collection, London.

problem. Occasionally I strike a tartar.[18] One almost did win. I eventually had to use the dogs."

"The dogs?"

"This way, please. I'll show you."

The general steered Rainsford to a window. The lights from the windows sent a flickering illumination that made grotesque patterns on the courtyard below, and Rainsford could see moving about there a dozen or so huge black shapes; as they turned toward him, their eyes glittered greenly.

"A rather good lot, I think," observed the general. "They are let out at seven every night.

---

17. **Ivan . . . Czar.** During the reign of Alexander III (1881–1894) of Russia, Ivan was the official flogger, who whipped prisoners severely.

18. **strike a tartar.** Meet one who is difficult to control

words for everyday use

bar • ba • rous (bär´bə rəs) *adj.*, cruel; brutal; uncultured. *The practice of applying leeches to purify the blood seems* <u>barbarous</u> *to us now.*

If anyone should try to get into my house—or out of it—something extremely regrettable would occur to him." He hummed a snatch of song from the Folies Bergère.

"And now," said the general, "I want to show you my new collection of heads. Will you come with me to the library?"

"I hope," said Rainsford, "that you will excuse me tonight, General Zaroff. I'm really not feeling at all well."

"Ah, indeed?" the general inquired solicitously. "Well, I suppose that's only natural, after your long swim. You need a good, restful night's sleep. Tomorrow you'll feel like a new man, I'll wager. Then we'll hunt, eh? I've one rather promising prospect—"

What is the real reason why Rainsford feels ill?

Rainsford was hurrying from the room.

"Sorry you can't go with me tonight," called the general. "I expect rather fair sport—a big, strong sailor. He looks resourceful—Well, good night, Mr. Rainsford; I hope you have a good night's rest."

The bed was good and the pajamas of the softest silk, and he was tired in every fiber of his being, but nevertheless Rainsford could not quiet his brain with the opiate of sleep. He lay, eyes wide open. Once he thought he heard stealthy steps in the corridor outside his room. He sought to throw open the door; it would not open. He went to the window and looked out. His room was high up in one of the towers. The lights of the château were out now, and it was dark and silent; but there was a fragment of sallow moon, and by its wan light he could see, dimly, the courtyard; there, weaving in and out in the pattern of shadow, were black, noiseless forms; the hounds heard him at the window and looked

Why can't Rainsford sleep?

up, expectantly, with their green eyes. Rainsford went back to the bed and lay down. By many methods he tried to put himself to sleep. He had achieved a doze when, just as morning began to come, he heard, far off in the jungle, the faint report of a pistol.

General Zaroff did not appear until luncheon. He was dressed faultlessly in the tweeds of a country squire. He was solicitous about the state of Rainsford's health.

"As for me," sighed the general, "I do not feel so well. I am worried, Mr. Rainsford. Last night I detected traces of my old complaint."

To Rainsford's questioning glance the general said: "Ennui. Boredom."

Then, taking a second helping of crêpes suzette,[19] the general explained: "The hunting was not good last night. The fellow lost his head. He made a straight trail that offered no problems at all. That's the trouble with these sailors. They have dull brains to begin with, and they do not know how to get about in the woods. They do excessively stupid and obvious things. It's becoming most annoying. Will you have another glass of Chablis, Mr. Rainsford?"

"General," said Rainsford firmly, "I wish to leave this island at once."

The general raised his thickets of eyebrows; he seemed hurt. "But, my dear fellow," the general protested, "you've only just come. You've had no hunting—"

"I wish to go today," said Rainsford. He saw the dead black eyes of the general on him, studying him. General Zaroff's face suddenly brightened.

He filled Rainsford's glass with venerable Chablis from a dusty bottle.

---

19. **crêpes suzette.** Thin pancakes eaten as a dessert

words for everyday use

so • lic • i • tous • ly (sə lisʹə təs lē) *adv.,* showing concern. *The nurse solicitously asked questions about the patient's injuries.*

pros • pect (präʹspekt ʹ) *n.,* likely candidate. *With her experience in middle-school government, Angela is an excellent prospect for class office in high school.*

wan (wän) *adj.,* pale; faint. *The wan glow of the flashlight indicated it needed new batteries.*

"Tonight," said the general, "we will hunt—you and I."

Rainsford shook his head. "No, General," he said, "I will not hunt."

The general shrugged his shoulders and delicately ate a hothouse grape. "As you wish, my friend," he said. "The choice rests entirely with you. But may I not venture to suggest that you will find my idea of sport more <u>diverting</u> than Ivan's?"

He nodded toward the corner to where the giant stood, scowling, his thick arms crossed on his huge chest.

"You don't mean—" cried Rainsford.

"My dear fellow," said the general, "have I not told you I always mean what I say about hunting? This is really an inspiration. I drink to a foe worthy of me at last."

The general raised his glass, but Rainsford sat staring at him.

"You'll find this game worth playing," the general said enthusiastically. "Your brain against mine. Your woodcraft against mine. Your strength and stamina against mine. Outdoor chess! And the stake is not without value, eh?"

"And if I should win—" began Rainsford huskily.

"I'll cheerfully <u>acknowledge</u> myself defeated if I do not find you by midnight of the third day," said General Zaroff. "My sloop will place you on the mainland near a town."

The general read what Rainsford was thinking.

"Oh, you can trust me," said the Cossack. "I will give you my word as a gentleman and a sportsman. Of course you, in turn, must agree to say nothing of your visit here."

"I'll agree to nothing of the kind," said Rainsford.

Whom does Zaroff propose to hunt?

"Tonight," said the general, "we will hunt—you and I."

"Oh," said the general, "in that case—But why discuss that now? Three days hence we can discuss it over a bottle of Veuve Cliquot, unless—"

The general sipped his wine.

Then a businesslike air <u>animated</u> him. "Ivan," he said to Rainsford, "will supply you with hunting clothes, food, a knife. I suggest you wear moccasins; they leave a poorer trail. I suggest too that you avoid the big swamp in the southeast corner of the island. We call it Death Swamp. There's quicksand there. One foolish fellow tried it. The <u>deplorable</u> part of it was that Lazarus followed him. You can imagine my feelings, Mr. Rainsford. I loved Lazarus; he was the finest hound in my pack. Well, I must beg you to excuse me now. I always take a siesta after lunch. You'll hardly have time for a nap, I fear. You'll want to start, no doubt. I shall not follow till dusk. Hunting at night is so much more exciting than by day, don't you think? *Au revoir;*[20] Mr. Rainsford, *au revoir.*"

General Zaroff, with a deep, courtly bow, strolled from the room.

From another door came Ivan. Under one arm he carried khaki hunting clothes, a haversack of food, a leather sheath containing a long-bladed hunting knife; his right hand rested on a cocked revolver thrust in the crimson sash about his waist. . . .

Rainsford had fought his way through the bush for two hours. "I must keep my nerve. I must keep my nerve," he said through tight teeth.

---

20. *Au revoir.* Until we meet again (French)

He had not been entirely clearheaded when the château gates snapped shut behind him. His whole idea at first was to put distance between himself and General Zaroff, and, to this end, he had plunged along, spurred on by the sharp rowels of something very like panic. Now he had got a grip on himself, had stopped, and was taking stock of himself and the situation.

He saw that straight flight was <u>futile</u>; inevitably it would bring him face to face with the sea. He was in a picture with a frame of water, and his operations, clearly, must take place within that frame.

"I'll give him a trail to follow," muttered

> What is Rainsford's plan?

Rainsford, and he struck off from the rude paths he had been following into the trackless wilderness. He executed a series of <u>intricate</u> loops; he doubled on his trail again and again, recalling all the lore of the fox hunt, and all the dodges of the fox. Night found him leg-weary, with hands and face lashed by the branches, on a thickly wooded ridge. He knew it would be insane to blunder on through the dark, even if he had the strength. His need for rest was imperative and he thought: "I have played the fox, now I must play the cat of the fable."[21] A big tree with a thick trunk and outspread branches was nearby,

> How does Rainsford plan to outwit General Zaroff?

and, taking care to leave not the slightest mark, he climbed up into the crotch, and stretching out on one of the broad limbs, after a fashion, rested. Rest brought him new confidence and almost a feeling of security. Even so zealous a hunter as General Zaroff could not trace him there, he told himself; only the devil himself could follow that complicated trail through the jungle after dark. But, perhaps, the general was a devil—

An apprehensive night crawled slowly by like a wounded snake, and sleep did not visit Rainsford, although the silence of a dead world was on the jungle. Toward morning when a dingy gray was varnishing the sky, the cry of some startled bird focused Rainsford's attention in that direction. Something was coming through the bush, coming slowly, carefully, coming by the same winding way Rainsford had come. He flattened himself down on the limb, and through a screen of leaves almost as thick as tapestry, he watched. The thing that was approaching was a man.

It was General Zaroff. He made his way along with his eyes fixed in utmost concentration on the ground before him. He paused, almost beneath the tree, dropped to his knees and studied the ground. Rainsford's impulse was to hurl himself down like a panther, but he saw the general's right hand held something metallic—a small automatic pistol.

The hunter shook his head several times, as if he were puzzled. Then he straightened up and took from his case one of his black cigarettes; its pungent incense-like smoke floated up to Rainsford's nostrils.

Rainsford held his breath. The general's eyes had left the ground and were traveling inch by inch up the tree. Rainsford froze there, every muscle tensed for a spring. But the sharp eyes of the hunter stopped before they reached the limb where Rainsford lay; a smile spread over his brown face. Very deliberately he blew a smoke ring into the air; then he turned his back on the tree and walked carelessly away, back along the trail

> Why does Zaroff blow the smoke ring? What does he want to communicate?

21. **"I have played . . . fable."** He has used the trickery of the fox to escape his pursuer; now he must use the cunning of a cat to further escape.

---

words for everyday use

fu • tile (fyo͞ot´'l) *adj.*, hopeless. *Nancy realized that her headache made it <u>futile</u> to keep studying.*

in • tri • cate (in´tri kit) *adj.*, complex. *The <u>intricate</u> design on the turquoise earrings reminded Melanie of a Navajo painting she had seen.*

he had come. The swish of the underbrush against his hunting boots grew fainter and fainter.

The pent-up air burst hotly from Rainsford's lungs. His first thought made him feel sick and numb. The general could follow a trail through the woods at night; he could follow an extremely difficult trail; he must have uncanny powers; only by the merest chance had the Cossack failed to see his quarry.

Rainsford's second thought was even more terrible. It sent a shudder of cold horror through his whole being. Why had the general smiled? Why had he turned back?

Rainsford did not want to believe what his reason told him was true, but the truth was as evident as the sun that had by now pushed through the morning mists. The general was playing with him! The general was saving him for another day's sport! The Cossack was the cat; he was the mouse. Then it was that Rainsford knew the full meaning of terror.

"I will not lose my nerve. I will not."

He slid down from the tree, and struck off again into the woods. His face was set and he forced the machinery of his mind to function. Three hundred yards from his hiding place he stopped where a huge dead tree leaned precariously on a smaller, living one. Throwing off his sack of food, Rainsford took his knife from its sheath and began to work with all his energy.

The job was finished at last, and he threw himself down behind a fallen log a hundred feet away. He did not have to wait long. The cat was coming again to play with the mouse.

Following the trail with the sureness of a bloodhound, came General Zaroff. Nothing escaped those searching black eyes, no crushed blade of grass, no bent twig, no mark, no matter how faint, in the moss. So intent was the Cossack on his stalking that he was upon the thing Rainsford had made before he saw it. His foot touched the protruding bough that was the trigger. Even as he touched it, the general sensed his danger and leaped back with the agility of an ape. But he was not quite quick enough; the dead tree, delicately adjusted to rest on the cut living one, crashed down and struck the general a glancing blow on the shoulder as it fell; but for his alertness, he must have been smashed beneath it. He staggered, but he did not fall; nor did he drop his revolver. He stood there, rubbing his injured shoulder, and Rainsford, with fear again gripping his heart, heard the general's mocking laugh ring through the jungle.

"Rainsford," called the general, "if you are within the sound of my voice, as I suppose you are, let me congratulate you. Not many men know how to make a Malay man-catcher. Luckily, for me, I too have hunted in Malacca.[22] You are proving interesting, Mr. Rainsford. I am going now to have my wound dressed; it's only a slight one. But I shall be back. I shall be back."

When the general, nursing his bruised shoulder, had gone, Rainsford took up his flight again. It was flight now, a desperate, hopeless flight, that carried him on for some hours. Dusk came, then darkness, and still he pressed on. The ground grew softer under his moccasins; the vegetation grew ranker, denser; insects bit him savagely. Then, as he stepped forward, his foot sank into the ooze. He tried

Rainsford's second thought was even more terrible. It sent a shudder of cold horror through his whole being.

_____
22. **Malacca.** Region in the southwestern Malay Peninsula in Asia

words for everyday use	un • can • ny (un kan´ē) adj., beyond normal. Joe has an uncanny sense of direction and never seems to get lost.
	pre • car • i • ous • ly (prē ker´ē əs lē) adv., insecurely. The bus in the film rested precariously at the edge of a cliff.
	pro • trud • ing (prō trōōd´iŋ) adj., jutting out. The babysitter knew where Ryan was hiding when she saw a small protruding foot.

to wrench it back, but the muck sucked viciously at his foot as if it were a giant leech. With a violent effort, he tore his foot loose. He knew where he was now. Death Swamp and its quicksand.

His hands were tight closed as if his nerve were something tangible that some one in the darkness was trying to tear from his grip. The softness of the earth had given him an idea. He stepped back from the quicksand a dozen feet or so, and, like some huge prehistoric beaver, he began to dig.

Rainsford had dug himself in in France, when a second's delay meant death. That had been a placid pastime compared to his digging now. The pit grew deeper; when it was above his shoulders, he climbed out and from some hard saplings cut stakes and sharpened them to a fine point. These stakes he planted in the bottom of the pit with the points sticking up. With flying fingers he wove a rough carpet of weeds and branches and with it he covered the mouth of the pit. Then, wet with sweat and aching with tiredness, he crouched behind the stump of a lightning-charred tree.

He knew his pursuer was coming; he heard the padding sound of feet on the soft earth, and the night breeze brought him the perfume of the general's cigarette. It seemed to Rainsford that the general was coming with unusual swiftness; he was not feeling his way along, foot by foot. Rainsford, crouching there, could not see the general, nor could he see the pit. He lived a year in a minute. Then he felt an impulse to cry aloud with joy, for he heard the sharp crackle of the breaking branches as the cover of the pit gave way; he heard the sharp scream of pain as the pointed stakes found their mark. He leaped up from his place of concealment. Then he cowered back. Three feet from the pit a man was standing, with an electric torch[23] in his hand.

"You've done well, Rainsford," the voice of the general called. "Your Burmese tiger pit[24] has claimed one of my best dogs. Again you score. I think, Mr. Rainsford, I'll see what you can do against my whole pack. I'm going home for a rest now. Thank you for a most amusing evening."

At daybreak Rainsford, lying near the swamp, was awakened by a sound that made him know that he had new things to learn about fear. It was a distant sound, faint and wavering, but he knew it. It was the baying of a pack of hounds.

Rainsford knew he could do one of two things. He could stay where he was and wait. That was suicide. He could flee. That was postponing the inevitable. For a moment he stood there, thinking. An idea that held a wild chance came to him, and, tightening his belt, he headed away from the swamp.

The baying of the hounds drew nearer, then still nearer, nearer, ever nearer. On a ridge Rainsford climbed a tree. Down a watercourse, not a quarter of a mile away, he could see the bush moving. Straining his eyes, he saw the lean figure of General Zaroff; just ahead of him Rainsford made out another figure whose wide shoulders surged through the tall jungle weeds; it was the giant Ivan, and he seemed pulled forward by some unseen force; Rainsford knew that Ivan must be holding the pack in leash.

They would be on him any minute now. His mind worked frantically. He thought of a native trick he had learned in Uganda. He slid down the tree. He caught hold of a springy young sapling and to it he fastened his hunting knife, with the blade pointing down the trail; with a bit of wild grapevine he tied back the sapling.

---

23. **torch.** Flashlight (British)
24. **Burmese tiger pit.** Deep pit used to trap tigers in Burma, a country located in Southeast Asia that is today known as Myanmar

Then he ran for his life. The hounds raised their voices as they hit the fresh scent. Rainsford knew now how an animal at bay feels.

He had to stop to get his breath. The baying of the hounds stopped abruptly, and Rainsford's heart stopped too. They must have reached the knife.

He shinned excitedly up a tree and looked back. His pursuers had stopped. But the hope that was in Rainsford's brain when he climbed died; for he saw in the shallow valley that General Zaroff was still on his feet. But Ivan was not. The knife, driven by the <u>recoil</u> of the springing tree, had not wholly failed.

> What happens to Ivan? How?

Rainsford had hardly tumbled to the ground when the pack took up the cry again.

"Nerve, nerve, nerve!" he panted, as he dashed along. A blue gap showed between the trees dead ahead. Ever nearer drew the hounds. Rainsford forced himself on toward that gap. He reached it. It was the shore of the sea. Across a cove he could see the gloomy gray stone of the château. Twenty feet below him the sea rumbled and hissed. Rainsford hesitated. He heard the hounds. Then he leaped far out into the sea. . . .

When the general and his pack reached the place by the sea, the Cossack stopped. For some minutes he stood regarding the blue-green expanse of water. He shrugged his shoulders. Then he sat down, took a drink of brandy from a silver flask, lit a perfumed cigarette, and hummed a bit from *Madame Butterfly*.[25]

General Zaroff had an exceedingly good dinner in his great paneled dining hall that evening. With it he had a bottle of Pol Roger and half a bottle of Chambertin. Two slight annoyances kept him from perfect enjoyment. One was the thought that it

> What two things bother General Zaroff?

would be difficult to replace Ivan; the other was that his quarry had escaped him; of course the American hadn't played the game—so thought the general as he tasted his after-dinner liqueur. In his library he read, to soothe himself, from the works of Marcus Aurelius.[26] At ten he went up to his bedroom. He was deliciously tired, he said to himself, as he locked himself in. There was a little moonlight, so, before turning on his light, he went to the window and looked down at the courtyard. He could see the great hounds, and he called: "Better luck another time," to them. Then he switched on the light.

A man, who had been hiding in the curtains of the bed, was standing there.

"Rainsford!" screamed the general. "How in God's name did you get here?"

"Swam," said Rainsford. "I found it quicker than walking through the jungle."

The general sucked in his breath and smiled. "I congratulate you," he said. "You have won the game."

Rainsford did not smile. "I am still a beast at bay," he said, in a low, hoarse voice. "Get ready, General Zaroff."

The general made one of his deepest bows. "I see," he said. "Splendid! One of us is to furnish a repast for the hounds. The other will sleep in this very excellent bed. En garde, Rainsford. . . ."

He had never slept in a better bed, Rainsford decided. ∎

25. *Madame Butterfly.* Opera by Puccini
26. **Marcus Aurelius.** Roman emperor and philosopher who ruled from AD 160 to 180

> Rainsford knew now how an animal at bay feels.

words for everyday use

re • coil (rē´koil´) *n.*, state of flying back when released. *Hiroshi smacked himself in the face with the <u>recoil</u> of the rubber band he meant to shoot at Tom.*

Imagine that you are the famous hunter Rainsford in this story. Think about an early comment you made to Whitney, "Who cares how a jaguar feels?" Explain how you feel differently after your experience with General Zaroff.

Investigate, *Inquire,* and Imagine

Recall: GATHERING FACTS →

1a. What sport does Rainsford consider to be the best in the world?

2a. What reason does General Zaroff give why the hunt no longer fascinates him?

3a. Why does Rainsford agree to become "the hunted" in General Zaroff's game?

Interpret: FINDING MEANING

1b. What statements support Rainsford's allegiance to the hunter, not the hunted, at the beginning of the story?

2b. What actions has General Zaroff taken to regain his interest in hunting?

3b. What actions on the part of Rainsford show his extraordinary skill as a hunter?

Analyze: TAKING THINGS APART →

4a. What different meanings does the word *game* have in the story?

Synthesize: BRINGING THINGS TOGETHER

4b. How do you think Rainsford will change after having been "the hunted"?

Perspective: LOOKING AT OTHER VIEWS→

5a. If you were Rainsford, would you consider Zaroff's rules of the game fair? Why, or why not?

Empathy: SEEING FROM INSIDE

5b. If you were Rainsford at the end of the story, how would you regard the captive men in the cellar? What would you do for them?

Understanding *Literature*

IRONY. Review the definitions for **irony**, **verbal irony**, and **irony of situation** in the Handbook of Literary Terms. What examples of verbal irony and irony of situation did you find in the selection?

PLOT AND CONFLICT. Review the definitions for **plot** and **conflict** in the Handbook of Literary Terms. Using the sequence chart you made in Literary Tools on page 198, identify the type of conflict established in the story. How does the opening dialogue between Whitney and Rainsford establish the conflict?

Writer's Journal

1. Imagine that you are a captive man who survived the hunt with General Zaroff. Write a **newspaper article** describing your experience to warn other sailors.
2. Imagine that you are General Zaroff after Rainsford has just arrived at the château. Write a **journal entry** on why you find him suitable prey.
3. Imagine that you are Rainsford before the hunt. Write a **goodbye note** to General Zaroff in case he wins.

Integrating the Language Arts

Language, Grammar, and Style

COMPLETERS FOR LINKING VERBS: PREDICATE ADJECTIVES. Sometimes these verbs link the subject of a sentence with an adjective that describes it. Frequently this description follows a linking verb that is not a form of the verb *to be*. To find the complement of a linking verb, ask the same questions you asked to find a direct object (see the Language Arts Survey 3.22). In each of the following sentences, identify the subject(s), the verb(s), and the predicate adjective.

1. Rainsford was confident.
2. He always had been skilled and alert.
3. A pleasant dinner became threatening.
4. The contest might be challenging.
5. The strange island appeared eerie.

Media Literacy

STORYBOARD. A storyboard, often used in advertising and film-making, is a large board on which the events of a story are sketched in sequence. These sketches often appear with captions and dialogue. As a class, identify the following plot elements in the story: **introduction, inciting incident, rising action, climax, turning point, falling action,** and **resolution.** Then form seven small groups, assigning one plot element to each group. Within each group, create the appropriate portion of a storyboard illustrating the key event for that plot element. When each group has finished, display all seven portions of the storyboard in the class to determine whether all key elements of the plot have been included.

Collaborative Learning

HUNTING DEBATE. Using library resources, research arguments for and against hunting. Then form teams to debate the issue. You may choose to limit your debate to hunting one type of animal popular in your area, such as deer. Another topic is to debate hunting animals, such as the wolf, that have been taken off the endangered species list. For more information, see the Language Arts Survey 4.21, "Participating in a Debate."

Literary
T O O L S

POINT OF VIEW. Point of view is the vantage point from which a story is told. Stories are typically written from a *first-person point of view,* in which the narrator uses words such as *I* and *we,* or from a *third-person point of view,* in which the narrator uses words such as *he, she, it* and *they.* What point of view is used in the story?

HYPERBOLE. A hyperbole is an exaggeration made for rhetorical effect. For example, in the selection the narrator relates that "Not only was he the tallest, strongest, most virile, and best built man they had ever seen, but even though they were looking at him, there was no room for him in their imagination." The hyperbole creates the impression that the stranger is godlike because he is not only larger than life, but even larger than the women's imagination. As you read, find another example of hyperbole.

MYTH. A myth is a story that explains objects or events in the natural world as resulting from the action of some supernatural force or entity, most often a god.

Organizer

As you read, complete the chart below. On the left write what is different about the village after Esteban's arrival. On the right explain why the changes occurred. One example has been done for you.

Changes in the Village	Why the Changes Occurred
wide doors	Esteban was wide

Reader's
JOURNAL

What would you do if you found a drowned man washed up on the beach?

"The Handsomest Drowned Man in the World" by Gabriel García Márquez
translated by Gregory Rabassa

Reader's
r e s o u r c e

Every culture on the globe has its legends. In the United States, legendary characters include Pocahontas, Annie Oakley, Davy Crockett, Daniel Boone, and Johnny Appleseed. All of these characters were actual historical figures. However, over time, many fantastic tales were told about them. The folk imagination transformed them from extraordinary actual people into mythical personages. **"The Handsomest Drowned Man in the World"** shows how such transformations of the ordinary into the mythical take place. In short, it is a story about how myths are born.

García Márquez is recognized as the master of Magical Realism. Magical Realism is a kind of fiction that is for the most part realistic but that contains elements of fantasy. In García Márquez's novels and short stories, characters emerge from mirrors and ascend to heaven without dying, and infants are born with curly tails as a form of divine punishment. In this story, watch how an extraordinary event affects ordinary people.

About *the*
A U T H O R

Gabriel García Márquez (1928–) was born in Aracataca, Colombia, a town that made its living from banana production. One of sixteen children born to the town telegrapher, he put himself through high school on a scholarship, quit law school after a year out of boredom, and became a newspaper reporter. "I have been told by the family that I started telling about things, stories and so on, almost ever since I was born," said the author. "I guess that's what got me into journalism and fiction writing, and the two went together all my life." For most of his life, Márquez has lived in self-imposed exile in Barcelona, Paris, Rome, New York, and Mexico City.

In *Leaf Storm* (1972), his first book, García Márquez introduced the fictional town of Macondo, a symbol of all underdeveloped Latin countries and the setting for many of his later works. His epic masterpiece, *One Hundred Years of Solitude* (1967), took twenty years to complete and has sold more copies around the world than any other work by a contemporary Spanish-speaking author. Other notable works by García Márquez include *Love in the Time of Cholera* (1985), *The General in His Labyrinth* (1989), and *Strange Pilgrims* (1992). In 1982 Márquez was awarded the Nobel Prize in literature "for his novels and short stories in which the fantastic and the realistic are combined in a richly composed world of imagination, reflecting a continent's life and conflicts."

The Handsomest DROWNED Man in the World

Gabriel García Márquez,
translated by Gregory Rabassa

The first children who saw the dark and slinky bulge approaching through the sea let themselves think it was an enemy ship. Then they saw it had no flags or masts and they thought it was a whale. But when it washed up on the beach, they removed the clumps of seaweed, the jellyfish tentacles, and the remains of fish and <u>flotsam</u>, and only then did they see that it was a drowned man.

They had been playing with him all afternoon, burying him in the sand and digging him up again, when someone chanced to see them and spread the alarm in the village. The men who carried him to the nearest house noticed that he weighed more than any dead man they had ever known, almost as much as a horse, and they said to each other that maybe he'd been floating too long and the water had got into his bones. When they laid him on the floor they said he'd been taller than all other men because there was barely enough room for him in the house, but they thought that maybe the ability to keep on growing after death was part of the nature of certain drowned men. He had the smell of the sea about him and only his shape gave one to suppose that it was the corpse of a human being, because the skin was covered with a crust of mud and scales.

They did not even have to clean off his face to know that the dead man was a stranger. The village was made up of only twenty-odd wooden houses that had stone courtyards with no flowers and which were spread about on the end of a desertlike <u>cape</u>. There was so little land that mothers always went about with the fear that the wind would carry off their children and the few dead that the years had caused among them had to be thrown off the cliffs. But the sea was calm and <u>bountiful</u> and all the men fit into seven boats. So when they found the drowned man they simply had to look at one another

> What do the men notice about the drowned man?

> Why do the people know right away that the man is a stranger? What is their village like?

words for everyday use

flot • sam (flät´səm) *n.*, debris floating on the sea. *Pieces of <u>flotsam</u> such as discarded plastic bags can be dangerous to whales if swallowed.*

cape (kāp) *n.*, piece of land projecting into a body of water. *Many lighthouses are located on <u>capes</u>.*

boun • ti • ful (boun´tə fəl) *adj.*, plentiful; abundant. *The <u>bountiful</u> harvest was celebrated with a festival in the village.*

Not only was he the tallest, strongest, most virile, and best built man they had ever seen, but even though they were looking at him there was no room for him in their imagination.

to see that they were all there. That night they did not go out to work at sea. While the men went to find out if anyone was missing in neighboring villages, the women stayed behind to care for the drowned man. They took the mud off with grass swabs, they removed the underwater stones entangled in his hair, and they scraped the crust off with tools used for scaling fish. As they were doing that they noticed that the vegetation on him came from faraway oceans and deep water and that his clothes were in tatters, as if he had sailed through <u>labyrinths</u> of coral. They noticed too that he bore his death with pride, for he did not have the lonely look of

What did the women notice as they cleaned the man?

other drowned men who came out of the sea or that haggard, needy look of men who drowned in rivers. But only when they finished cleaning him off did they become aware of the kind of man he was and it left them breathless. Not only was he the tallest, strongest, most virile, and best built man they had ever seen, but even though they were looking at him there was no room for him in their imagination.

They could not find a bed in the village large enough to lay him on nor was there a table solid enough to use for his wake. The tallest men's holiday pants would not fit him, nor the fattest ones' Sunday shirts, nor the shoes of the one with the biggest feet. Fascinated by his huge size and his beauty, the women then decided to make him

some pants from a large piece of sail and a shirt from some bridal brabant linen[1] so that he could continue through his death with dignity. As they sewed, sitting in a circle and gazing at the corpse between stitches, it seemed to them that the wind had never been so steady nor the sea so restless as on that night and they supposed that the change had something to do with the dead man. They thought that if that magnificent man had lived in the village, his house would have had the widest doors, the highest ceiling, and the strongest floor, his bedstead would have been made from a midship frame held together by iron bolts, and his wife would have been the happiest woman. They thought that he would have had so much authority that he could have drawn fish out of the sea simply by calling their names and that he would have put so much

What did they imagine the drowned man would do if he were a villager?

work into his land that springs would have burst forth from among the rocks so that he would have been able to plant flowers on the cliffs. They secretly compared him to their own men, thinking that for all their lives theirs were incapable of doing what he could do in one night, and they ended up dismissing them deep in their hearts as the weakest, meanest, and most useless creatures on earth. They were wandering through that maze of fantasy when the oldest woman, who as the oldest had looked upon the drowned man with more compassion than passion, sighed:

"He has the face of someone called Esteban."[2]

It was true. Most of them had only to take another look at him to see that he could not have any other name. The more stubborn among them, who were the youngest, still lived for a few hours with the <u>illusion</u> that when they put his

---

1. **brabant linen.** Linen from Brabant, a province on the border between Belgium and the Netherlands
2. **Esteban.** Spanish name for Stephen

---

words for everyday use

lab • y • rinth (lab´ ər inth´) n., complicated maze. *The garden was a <u>labyrinth</u> in shrubbery.*

il • lu • sion (i lōō´zhən) n., false perception. *Greg had an <u>illusion</u> that if he could only get to Hollywood he would find fame and fortune.*

After the Hurricane, Texas, 1899. Winslow Homer. The Art Institute of Chicago.

clothes on and he lay among the flowers in patent leather shoes his name might be Lautaro. But it was a vain illusion. There had not been enough canvas, the poorly cut and worse sewn pants were too tight, and the hidden strength of his heart popped the buttons on his shirt. After midnight the whistling of the wind died down and the sea fell into its Wednesday drowsiness. The silence put an end to any last doubts: he was Esteban. The women who had dressed him, who had combed his hair, had cut his nails and shaved him were unable to hold back a shudder of pity when they had to resign themselves to his being dragged along the ground. It was then that they understood how unhappy he must have been with that huge body since it bothered him even after death. They could see him in life, condemned to going through doors sideways, cracking his head on crossbeams, remaining on his feet during visits, not knowing what to do with his soft, pink, sea lion hands while the lady of the house looked for her most resistant chair and begged him, frightened to death, sit here, Esteban, please, and he, leaning against the wall, smiling, don't bother, ma'am, I'm fine where I am, his heels raw and his back roasted from having done the same thing so many times whenever he paid a visit, don't bother, ma'am, I'm fine where I am, just to avoid the embarrassment of breaking up the chair, and never knowing perhaps that the ones who said don't go, Esteban, at least wait till the coffee's ready, were the ones who later on would whisper the big boob finally left, how nice, the handsome fool has gone. That was what the women were thinking beside the body a little before dawn. Later, when they covered his face with a handkerchief so that the light would not bother him, he looked so forever dead, so defenseless, so much like their men that the first furrows of tears opened in their hearts. It was one of the younger ones who began the weeping. The others, coming to, went from sighs to wails, and the more they sobbed the more they felt like weeping, because the drowned man was becoming all the more Esteban for them, and so they wept so much, for he was the most destitute, most peaceful, and most obliging man on earth, poor Esteban. So when the men returned with the news that the drowned man was not from the neighboring villages either, the women felt an opening of jubilation in the midst of their tears.

"Praise the Lord," they sighed, "he's ours!"

The men thought the fuss was only womanish frivolity. Fatigued because of the difficult night-time inquiries, all they wanted was to get rid of the bother of the newcomer once and for all before the sun grew strong on that arid, windless day. They improvised a litter[3] with the remains of foremasts and gaffs, tying it together with rigging so that it would bear the weight of the body until they reached the cliffs. They wanted to tie the anchor from a cargo ship to him so that he would sink easily into the deepest waves, where fish are blind and divers die of nostalgia, and bad currents would not bring him back to shore, as had happened with other bodies. But the more they hurried, the more the women thought of ways to waste time. They walked about like startled hens, pecking with the

"Praise the Lord," they sighed, "he's ours!"

sea charms on their breasts, some interfering on one side to put a scapular of the good wind[4] on the drowned man, some on the other side to put a wrist compass[5] on him, and after a great deal of *get away from there, woman, stay out of the way, look, you almost made me fall on top of the dead man,* the men began to feel mistrust in their livers and started grumbling about why so many main-altar decorations for a stranger, because no matter how many nails and holy-water jars he had on him, the sharks would chew him all the same, but the women kept piling on their junk relics, running back and forth, stumbling, while they released in sighs what they did not in tears, so that the men finally exploded with *since when has there ever been such a fuss over a drifting corpse, a drowned nobody, a piece of cold Wednesday meat.* One of the women, mortified by so much lack of care, then removed the handkerchief from the dead man's face and the men were left breathless too.

He was Esteban. It was not necessary to repeat it for them to recognize him. If they had been told Sir Walter Raleigh, even they might have been impressed with his gringo accent, the macaw on his shoulder, his cannibal-killing blunderbuss,[6] but there could be only one Esteban in the world and there he was, stretched out like a sperm whale, shoeless, wearing the pants of an undersized child, and with those stony nails that had to be cut with

How do the men of the village feel about Esteban? What do they want to do with him? How do the women respond to this?

---

3. **litter.** Transportable cot used for moving injured or ill people
4. **scapular of the good wind.** Garment with religious significance
5. **wrist compass.** Compass placed on the wrist for the purpose of directing the soul to God
6. **Sir Walter Raleigh . . . blunderbuss.** English navigator and diplomat (1552–1618). He is portrayed here as having an English accent, a tropical bird on his shoulder, and a blunderbuss, an obsolete gun with a large muzzle, accurate only at short range.

words for everyday use

fur • row (fur'ō) *n.*, narrow groove. *Before machinery, wooden ploughs pulled by oxen made the furrows for planting.*
des • ti • tute (des'tə tōōt) *adj.*, abandoned; forsaken. *The homeless shelter offers food and lodging to destitute people.*
fri • vol • i • ty (fri väl'ə tē) *n.*, lack of seriousness. *After a semester of serious work, the students enjoyed the frivolity of a costume party.*
im • pro • vise (im'prə vīz') *vt.*, bring about with tools and materials. *Shelley improvised the recipe by adding yogurt instead of an egg, which she did not have.*
mor • ti • fied (môrt'ə fīd') *adj.*, shamed, humiliated. *Juan was mortified that Sarah found out that the love note, meant to be anonymous, came from him.*

a knife. They only had to take the handkerchief off his face to see that he was ashamed, that it was not his fault that he was so big or so heavy or so handsome, and if he had known that this was going to happen, he would have looked for a more <u>discreet</u> place to drown in, seriously, I even would have tied the anchor off a galleon around my neck and staggered off a cliff like someone who doesn't like things in order not to be upsetting people now with this Wednesday dead body, as you people say, in order not to be bothering anyone with this filthy piece of cold meat that doesn't have anything to do with me. There was so much truth in his manner that even the most mistrustful men, the ones who felt the bitterness of endless nights at sea fearing that their women would tire of dreaming about them and begin to dream of drowned men, even they and others who were harder still shuddered in the marrow of their bones at Esteban's sincerity.

What makes some of the men shudder?

That was how they came to hold the most splendid funeral they could conceive of for an abandoned drowned man. Some women who had gone to get flowers in the neighboring villages returned with other women who could not believe what they had been told, and those women went back for more flowers when they saw the dead man, and they brought more and more until there were so many flowers and so many people that it was hard to walk about. At the final moment it pained them to return him to the waters as an orphan and they chose a father and mother from among the best people, and aunts and uncles and cousins, so that through him all the inhabitants of the village became <u>kinsmen</u>. Some sailors who heard the weeping from a distance went off course and people heard of one who had himself

What do the people do before they return the man to the waters?

tied to the mainmast, remembering ancient fables about sirens.[7] While they fought for the privilege of carrying him on their shoulders along the steep <u>escarpment</u> by the cliffs, men and women became aware for the first time of the desolation of their streets, the dryness of their courtyards, the narrowness of their dreams as they faced the splendor and beauty of their drowned man. They let him go without an anchor so that he could come back if he wished and whenever he wished, and they all held their breath for the fraction of centuries the body took to fall into the abyss. They did not need to look at one another to realize that they were no longer all present, that they would never be. But they also knew that everything would be different from then on, that their houses would have wider doors, higher ceilings, and stronger floors so that Esteban's memory could go everywhere without bumping into beams and so that no one in the future would dare whisper the big boob finally died, too bad, the handsome fool has finally died, because they were going to paint their house fronts gay colors to make Esteban's memory <u>eternal</u> and they were going to break their backs digging for springs among the stones and planting flowers on the cliffs so that in future years at dawn the passengers on great liners would awaken, suffocated by the smell of gardens on the high seas, and the captain would have to come down from the bridge in his dress uniform, with his astrolabe,[8] his pole star, and his row of war medals and, pointing to the promontory of roses on the horizon, he would say in fourteen languages, look there, where the wind is so peaceful now that it's gone to sleep beneath the beds, over there, where the sun's so bright that the sunflowers don't know which way to turn, yes, over there, that's Esteban's village. ■

7. **sirens.** Sea nymphs who lured sailors to their deaths
8. **astrolabe.** Ancient marine navigational instrument

words for everyday use

dis • creet (di skrēt´) *adj.*, proper or prudent. *Claire promised Amy to be <u>discreet</u> when asking Jed if he was going to the dance.*

kins • man (kinz´mən) *n.*, relative. *Is your Uncle Billy really a <u>kinsman</u> or just a close family friend?*

es • carp • ment (e skärp´mənt) *n.*, steep slope. *Many mountain bikers love the thrill of speeding down a steep <u>escarpment</u>.*

e • ter • nal (ē tur´nəl) *adj.*, timeless; everlasting. *Nancy thought her love for David would be <u>eternal</u> until she met Eduardo.*

Was Esteban's arrival a positive or negative event for the village? Explain.

Investigate, *Inquire, and* Imagine

Recall: GATHERING FACTS

1a. Who takes care of the drowned man?

2a. What makes the men believe in Esteban?

3a. Why do the men make a litter for Esteban?

Interpret: FINDING MEANING

1b. What is the first thing the women do to immortalize the drowned man?

2b. How do the women and men view Esteban differently?

3b. What is probably the reason that the villagers "became aware for the first time of the desolation of their streets"?

Analyze: TAKING THINGS APART

4a. What actions on the part of the villagers ensure that the memory of Esteban will be kept alive?

Synthesize: BRINGING THINGS TOGETHER

4b. Why do the villagers have a mythic response to Esteban?

Evaluate: MAKING JUDGMENTS

5a. Evaluate whether the villagers are justified in making such a fuss over Esteban. What do their actions reveal about them?

Extend: CONNECTING IDEAS

5b. Imagine that you are a member of a primitive tribe who is visiting a modern city for the first time. Write a myth to explain one of the modern technological inventions that fascinates you.

Understanding *Literature*

POINT OF VIEW. Review the definition for **point of view** in the Handbook of Literary Terms. What point of view is used in the story? Why might the author have chosen to use that point of view?

HYPERBOLE. Review the definition for **hyperbole** in the Handbook of Literary Terms. Besides Esteban's size, what other example of hyperbole did you find? What effect is created by the hyperbole?

MYTH. Review the definition for **myth** in the Handbook of Literary Terms. Then refer to the chart you made for Literary Tools on page 216. Why are the doors in the village so wide, the ceilings so tall, and the floors so strong? Why does the village have brightly painted houses and flowers along the cliff?

Writer's Journal

1. Imagine that you were with Esteban when he drowned. Write a **journal entry** explaining what happened and why you could not save him.

2. Imagine you are a visitor to the village that adopted Esteban. Write a **letter** to your family describing the interesting characteristics of the village and their causes.

3. Imagine that you are a villager in Esteban's adoptive village. Write a **newspaper article** for a neighboring village describing the man that drowned and your village's reaction to him.

Integrating the Language Arts

Language, Grammar, and Style

COMPLETERS FOR LINKING VERBS: PREDICATE NOUNS AND PRONOUNS. Linking verbs can also take predicate nouns and pronouns. To find a predicate noun or pronoun, ask the same question as you did to find the direct object: the sentence structures are the same; the kinds of verbs are different. Predicate nouns and pronouns rename the subject. Refer to the Language Arts Survey 3.22–3.23. In each of the following sentences, identify the subject(s), the verb(s), and the predicate noun(s) and/or pronouns.

1. Many villagers were fishermen.
2. The drowned man was a gift from the sea.
3. Villagers might have seemed weak men.
4. The drowned man became a star.
5. The entire village became another town.

Collaborative Learning & Study and Research

RESEARCHING MYTHS. With two or three classmates, research Greek, Roman, Incan, Mayan, Native American, African, or Asian myths. Research myths that explain how elements in the natural world came to be. Then present the results of your research to the class, describing the culture or civilization you chose and retelling one or two myths. Read the Language Arts Survey 4.20, "Telling a Story."

Study and Research

INTERVIEW WITH THE AUTHOR. With a partner, research the influence of García Márquez's grandmother on the author's use of Magical Realism in his fiction. Consult a biography of García Márquez or articles in which the author has been interviewed. Then conduct a mock interview. One student should play the role of the interviewer, and the other should play the role of García Márquez.

Literary TOOLS

PLOT. A **plot** is a series of events related to a central conflict, or struggle. A typical plot involves the introduction of a *conflict,* its development, and its eventual resolution. The *crisis,* or *turning point,* is the point in the plot where something decisive happens to determine the future course of events and the eventual working out of the conflict. As you read, decide what the central conflict and crisis are.

CHARACTER AND CHARACTERIZATION. A **character** is a person who figures in the action of a literary work. A *protagonist,* or *main character,* is the central figure in a literary work. A *static character* is one who does not change during the course of the action. A *dynamic character* is one who does change. **Characterization** is the use of literary techniques to create a character. Writers use three major techniques to create characters: direct description, portrayal of characters' behavior, and representations of characters' internal states.

Graphic Organizer

As you read, make a chart. On the left, list descriptions of old Mrs. Pan's character traits and behavior before she decides to find a husband for Lili. On the right, list descriptions of old Mrs. Pan's character traits and behavior after she decides to find a husband for Lili. One example has been done for you.

Before	After
Did not look out the window.	Looks frequently out the window.

"THE GOOD DEED"
by Pearl S. Buck

Reader's resource

"**The Good Deed,**" originally published in *Woman's Home Companion* in 1953 under the title "A Husband for Lili," appeared in Pearl S. Buck's collection of short stories called *The Good Deed and Other Stories of Asia Past and Present* (1953). While the story's title may refer to one particular good deed that is at the heart of the story, the theme of good deeds ripples through the lives of all of the characters.

HISTORY CONNECTION. Immigration from China to the United States began in the middle of the nineteenth century. Chinese immigrant laborers contributed to the building of the railroads in the West. The first immigration restrictions against any particular group were made in 1882 by the Chinese Exclusion Act, which denied entrance to Chinese laborers. The Chinese Exclusion Act was repealed by Congress in 1943, and Chinese immigrants again sought residence in the United States.

About the AUTHOR

Pearl S. Buck (1892–1973) was born in West Virginia to Presbyterian missionary parents. When Buck was five months old, her parents moved to China, where she spent her youth and received her early education. She returned to the United States for her college education, graduating in 1914. Upon returning to China, Buck taught in Nanking from 1921 to 1931. Her novel *The Good Earth* (1931), about the struggles of a Chinese peasant, was widely translated. Other of her novels include the trilogy *The House of Earth* (1935), *Dragon Seed* (1942), and *Imperial Woman* (1956). Among her short story collections are *The First Wife and Other Stories* (1933), *Far and Near* (1947), and *The Good Deed* (1953). Buck was awarded a Pulitzer Prize in 1932 and the Nobel Prize for literature in 1938.

Reader's Journal

What good deed have you performed for someone?

THE GOOD DEED

Pearl S. Buck

丰功偉績

Mr. Pan was worried about his mother. He had been worried about her when she was in China, and now he was worried about her in New York, although he had thought that once he got her out of his ancestral village in the province of Szechuen and safely away from the local bullies, who took over when the distant government fell, his anxieties would be ended. To this end he had risked his own life and paid out large sums of sound American money, and he felt that day when he saw her on the wharf, a tiny, dazed little old woman, in a lavender silk coat and black skirt, that now they would live happily together, he and his wife, their four small children and his beloved mother, in the huge safety of the American city.

It soon became clear, however, that safety was not enough for old Mrs. Pan. She did not even appreciate the fact, which he repeated again and again, that had she remained in the village, she would now have been dead, because she was the widow of the large land-owner who had been his father and therefore deserved death in the eyes of the rowdies in power.

Old Mrs. Pan listened to this without reply, but her eyes, looking very large in her small withered face, were haunted with homesickness.

How does old Mrs. Pan feel about being in an American city?

"There are many things worse than death, especially at my age," she replied at last, when again her son reminded her of her good fortune in being where she was.

"How is it," she once asked her son, "that the children do not know how to obey?"

He became impassioned when she said this. He struck his breast with his clenched fists and he shouted, "Could I have forgiven myself if I had allowed you to die? Would the ghost of my father have given me rest?"

"I doubt his ghost would have traveled over such a wide sea," she replied. "That man was always afraid of the water."

Yet there was nothing that Mr. Pan and his wife did not try to do for his mother in order to make her happy. They prepared the food that she had once enjoyed, but she was now beyond the age of pleasure in food, and she had no appetite. She touched one dish and another with the ends of her ivory chopsticks,[1] which she had brought with her from her home, and she thanked them prettily. "It is all good," she said, "but the water is not the same as our village water; it tastes of metal and not of earth, and so the flavor is not the same. Please allow the children to eat it."

> Why won't old Mrs. Pan eat?

She was afraid of the children. They went to an American school and they spoke English very well and Chinese very badly, and since she could speak no English, it distressed her to hear her own language maltreated by their careless tongues. For a time she tried to coax them to a few lessons, or she told them stories, to which they were too busy to listen. Instead they preferred to look at the moving pictures in the box that stood on a table in the living room. She gave them up finally and merely watched them contemplatively when they were in the same room with her and was glad when they were gone. She liked her son's wife. She did not understand how there could be a Chinese woman who had never been in China, but such her son's wife was. When her son was away, she could not say to her daughter-in-law, "Do you remember how the willows grew over the gate?" For her son's wife had no such memories. She had grown up here in the city and she did not even hear its noise. At the same time, though she was so foreign, she was very kind to the old lady, and she spoke to her always in a gentle voice, however she might shout at the children, who were often disobedient.

> What things disturb Mrs. Pan about her grandchildren?

The disobedience of the children was another grief to old Mrs. Pan. She did not understand how it was that four children could all be disobedient, for this meant that they had never been taught to obey their parents and revere their elders, which are the first lessons a child should learn.

"How is it," she once asked her son, "that the children do not know how to obey?"

Mr. Pan had laughed, though uncomfortably. "Here in America the children are not taught as we were in China," he explained.

"But my grandchildren are Chinese nevertheless," old Mrs. Pan said in some astonishment.

"They are always with Americans," Mr. Pan explained. "It is very difficult to teach them."

Old Mrs. Pan did not understand, for Chinese and Americans are different beings, one on the

---

1. **ivory chopsticks.** Thin pair of sticks used as eating utensils, made from elephant's tusks

---

words for everyday use	**im • pas • sioned** (im pash´ənd) *adj.,* having a strong feeling. *Jim is impassioned about social justice.* **mal • treat** (mal trēt´) *vt.,* handle in an abusive manner. *Jen thought the puppy was being maltreated and called the animal shelter.* **con • tem • pla • tive • ly** (kən tem´plə tiv´lē) *adv.,* in a thoughtful or studious way. *Newton never rushes to begin an assignment; first, he sits and considers the assignment contemplatively.* **re • vere** (ri vir´) *vt.,* regard with deep respect and love. *That the children revere their grandmother is apparent in the way they obey her requests.*

west side of the sea and one on the east, and the sea is always between. Therefore, why should they not continue to live apart even in the same city? She felt in her heart that the children should be kept at home and taught those things which must be learned, but she said nothing. She felt lonely and there was no one who understood the things she felt and she was quite useless. That was the most difficult thing: She was of no use here. She could not even remember which spout the hot water came from and which brought the cold. Sometimes she turned on one and then the other, until her son's wife came in briskly and said, "Let me, Mother."

So she gave up and sat uselessly all day, not by the window, because the machines and the many people frightened her. She sat where she could not see out; she looked at a few books, and day by day she grew thinner and thinner until Mr. Pan was concerned beyond endurance.

One day he said to his wife, "Sophia, we must do something for my mother. There is no use in saving her from death in our village if she dies here in the city. Do you see how thin her hands are?"

Why is Mr. Pan concerned about his mother?

"I have seen," his good young wife said. "But what can we do?"

"Is there no woman you know who can speak Chinese with her?" Mr. Pan asked. "She needs to have someone to whom she can talk about the village and all the things she knows. She cannot talk to you because you can only speak English, and I am too busy making our living to sit and listen to her."

Young Mrs. Pan considered. "I have a friend," she said at last, "a schoolmate whose family <u>compelled</u> her to speak Chinese. Now she is a social worker here in the city. She visits families in Chinatown and this is her work. I will call her

up and ask her to spend some time here so that our old mother can be happy enough to eat again."

"Do so," Mr. Pan said.

That very morning, when Mr. Pan was gone, young Mrs. Pan made the call and found her friend, Lili Yang, and she explained everything to her.

"We are really in very much trouble," she said finally. "His mother is thinner every day, and she is so afraid she will die here. She has made us promise that we will not bury her in foreign soil but will send her coffin back to the ancestral village. We have promised, but can we keep this promise, Lili? Yet I am so afraid, because I think she will die, and Billy will think he must keep his promise and he will try to take the coffin back and then he will be killed. Please help us, Lili."

Where does old Mrs. Pan wish to be buried?

Lili Yang promised and within a few days she came to the apartment and young Mrs. Pan led her into the inner room, which was old Mrs. Pan's room and where she always sat, wrapped in her satin coat and holding a magazine at whose pictures she did not care to look. She took up that magazine when her daughter-in-law came in, because she did not want to hurt her feelings, but the pictures frightened her. The women looked bold and evil, their bosoms bare, and sometimes they wore only a little silk stuff over their legs and this shocked her. She wondered that her son's wife would put such a magazine into her hands, but she did not ask questions. There would have been no end to them had she once begun, and the ways of foreigners did not interest her. Most of the time she sat silent and still, her head sunk on her breast, dreaming of the village, the big house there where she and her husband had lived

---

words for everyday use

com • pel (kəm pel´) *vt.,* force to do something. *My parents <u>compel</u> me to feed the dog and take out the trash.*

together with his parents and where their children were born. She knew that the village had fallen into the hands of their enemies and that strangers lived in the house, but she hoped even so that the land was tilled.[2] All that she remembered was the way it had been when she was a young woman and before the evil had come to pass.

She heard now her daughter-in-law's voice, "Mother, this is a friend. She is Miss Lili Yang. She has come to see you."

Old Mrs. Pan remembered her manners. She tried to rise but Lili took her hands and begged her to keep seated.

"You must not rise to one so much younger," she exclaimed.

Old Mrs. Pan lifted her head. "You speak such good Chinese!"

"I was taught by my parents," Lili said. She sat down on a chair near the old lady.

Mrs. Pan leaned forward and put her hand on Lili's knee. "Have you been in our own country?" she asked eagerly.

Lili shook her head. "That is my sorrow. I have not and I want to know about it. I have come here to listen to you tell me."

"Excuse me," young Mrs. Pan said, "I must prepare the dinner for the family."

She slipped away so that the two could be alone and old Mrs. Pan looked after her sadly. "She never wishes to hear; she is always busy."

"You must remember in this country we have no servants," Lili reminded her gently.

"Yes," old Mrs. Pan said, "and why not? I have told my son it is not fitting to have my daughter-in-law cooking and washing in the kitchen. We should have at least three servants: one for me, one for the children and one to clean and cook. At home we had many more but here we have only a few rooms."

Why doesn't old Mrs. Pan understand that the younger Mrs. Pan must do housework?

Lili did not try to explain. "Everything is different here and let us not talk about it," she said. "Let us talk about your home and the village. I want to know how it looks and what goes on there."

Old Mrs. Pan was delighted. She smoothed the gray satin of her coat as it lay on her knees and she began.

"You must know that our village lies in a wide valley from which the mountains rise as sharply as tiger's teeth."

"Is it so?" Lili said, making a voice of wonder.

"It is, and the village is not a small one. On the contrary, the walls encircle more than one thousand souls, all of whom are relatives of our family."

What is Mrs. Pan's conception of a large village? How does the size of the village compare to that of the city?

"A large family," Lili said.

"It is," old Mrs. Pan said, "and my son's father was the head of it. We lived in a house with seventy rooms. It was in the midst of the village. We had gardens in the courtyards. My own garden contained also a pool wherein are aged goldfish, very fat. I fed them millet[3] and they knew me."

"How amusing." Lili saw with pleasure that the old lady's cheeks were faintly pink and that her large beautiful eyes were beginning to shine and glow. "And how many years did you live there, Ancient One?"

"I went there as a bride. I was seventeen." She looked at Lili, questioning, "How old are you?"

Lili smiled, somewhat ashamed, "I am twenty-seven."

Mrs. Pan was shocked. "Twenty-seven? But my son's wife called you Miss."

"I am not married," Lili confessed.

Mrs. Pan was instantly concerned. "How is this?" she asked. "Are your parents dead?"

"They are dead," Lili said, "but it is not their fault that I am not married."

Old Mrs. Pan would not agree to this. She shook her head with decision. "It is the duty of

"It is the duty of the parents to arrange the marriage of the children."

---

2. **tilled.** Plowed and fertilized to be ready for planting
3. **millet.** Cereal grass whose grain is used for food

the parents to arrange the marriage of the children. When death approached, they should have attended to this for you. Now who is left to perform the task? Have you brothers?"

"No," Lili said, "I am an only child. But please don't worry yourself, Madame Pan. I am earning my own living and there are many young women like me in this country."

Old Mrs. Pan was dignified about this. "I cannot be responsible for what other persons do, but I must be responsible for my own kind," she declared. "Allow me to know the names of the suitable persons who can arrange your marriage. I will stand in the place of your mother. We are all in a foreign country now and we must keep together and the old must help the young in these important matters."

Lili was kind and she knew that Mrs. Pan meant kindness. "Dear Madame Pan," she said. "Marriage in America is very different from marriage in China. Here the young people choose their own mates."

"Why do you not choose, then?" Mrs. Pan said with some spirit.

Lili Yang looked <u>abashed</u>. "Perhaps it would be better for me to say that only the young men choose. It is they who must ask the young women."

"What do the young women do?" Mrs. Pan inquired.

"They wait," Lili confessed.

"And if they are not asked?"

"They continue to wait," Lili said gently.

"How long?" Mrs. Pan demanded.

"As long as they live."

Old Mrs. Pan was <u>profoundly</u> shocked. "Do you tell me that there is no person who arranges such matters when it is necessary?"

> What does Mrs. Pan find shocking about American marriage traditions?

"Such an arrangement is not thought of here," Lili told her.

"And they allow their women to remain unmarried?" Mrs. Pan exclaimed. "Are there also sons who do not marry?"

"Here men do not marry unless they wish to do so."

Mrs. Pan was even more shocked. "How can this be?" she asked. "Of course, men will not marry unless they are compelled to do so to provide grandchildren for the family. It is necessary to make laws and create customs so that a man who will not marry is <u>denounced</u> as an unfilial[4] son and one who does not fulfill his duty to his ancestors."

> What solution does Mrs. Pan suggest to the problem of unmarried men?

"Here the ancestors are forgotten and parents are not important," Lili said unwillingly.

"What a country is this," Mrs. Pan exclaimed. "How can such a country endure?"

Lili did not reply. Old Mrs. Pan had unknowingly touched upon a wound in her heart. No man had ever asked her to marry him. Yet above all else she would like to be married and to have children. She was a good social worker, and the head of the Children's Bureau sometimes told her that he would not know what to do without her and she must never leave them, for then there would be no one to serve the people in Chinatown. She did not wish to leave except to be married, but how could she find a husband? She looked down at her hands, clasped in her lap, and thought that if she had been in her own country, if her father had not come here as a young man and married here, she would have been in China and by now the mother of many children.

> Does Lili have mixed feelings about living in America? Why, or why not?

---

4. **unfilial.** Not showing respect to one's parents

Instead what would become of her? She would grow older and older, and twenty-seven was already old, and at last hope must die. She knew several American girls quite well; they liked her, and she knew that they faced the same fate. They, too, were waiting. They tried very hard; they went in summer to hotels and in winter to ski lodges, where men gathered and were at leisure enough to think about them, and in confidence they told one another of their efforts. They compared their experiences and they asked anxious questions. "Do you think men like talkative women or quiet ones?" "Do you think men like lipstick or none?" Such questions they asked of one another and who could answer them? If a girl succeeded in winning a proposal from a man, then all the other girls envied her and asked her special questions and immediately she became someone above them all, a successful woman. The job which had

once been so valuable then became worthless and it was given away easily and gladly. But how could she explain this to old Mrs. Pan?

Meanwhile Mrs. Pan had been studying Lili's face carefully and with thought. This was not a pretty girl. Her face was too flat, and her mouth was large. She looked like a girl from Canton and not from Hangchow or Soochow. But she had nice skin, and her eyes, though small, were kind. She was the sort of girl, Mrs. Pan could see, who would make an excellent wife and a good mother, but certainly she was one for whom a marriage must be arranged. She was a decent, plain, good girl and, left to herself, Mrs. Pan could predict, nothing at all would happen. She would wither away like a dying flower.

Old Mrs. Pan forgot herself for the first time since she had been hurried away from the village without even being allowed to stop and see that the salted cabbage, drying on ropes across the big courtyard, was brought in for the winter. She had been compelled to leave it there and she had often thought of it with regret. She could have brought some with her had she known it was not to be had here. But there it was, and it was only one thing among others that she had left undone. Many people depended upon her and she had left them, because her son compelled her, and she was not used to this idleness that was killing her day by day.

Now as she looked at Lili's kind, ugly face it occurred to her that here there was something she could do. She could find a husband for this good girl, and it would be counted for merit when she went to heaven. A good deed is a good deed, whether one is in

Why does Mrs. Pan want to help Lili?

> A good deed is a good deed, whether one is in China or in America, for the same heaven stretches above all.

China or in America, for the same heaven stretches above all.

She patted Lili's clasped hands. "Do not grieve anymore," she said tenderly. "I will arrange everything."

"I am not grieving," Lili said.

"Of course, you are," Mrs. Pan retorted. "I see you are a true woman, and women grieve when they are not wed so that they can have children. You are grieving for your children."

Lili could not deny it. She would have been ashamed to confess to any other person except this old Chinese lady who might have been her grandmother. She bent her head and bit her lip; she let a tear or two fall upon her hands. Then she nodded. Yes, she grieved in the secret places of her heart, in the darkness of the lonely

nights, when she thought of the empty future of her life.

"Do not grieve," old Mrs. Pan was saying, "I will arrange it; I will do it."

It was so comforting a murmur that Lili could not bear it. She said, "I came to comfort you, but it is you who comfort me." Then she got up and went out of the room

What surprises Lili about the visit?

quickly because she did not want to sob aloud. She was unseen, for young Mrs. Pan had gone to market and the children were at school, and Lili went away telling herself that it was all absurd, that an old woman from the middle of China who could not speak a word of English would not be able to change this American world, even for her.

Old Mrs. Pan could scarcely wait for her son to come home at noon. She declined to join the family at the table, saying that she must speak to her son first.

When he came in, he saw at once that she was changed. She held up her head and she spoke to him sharply when he came into the room, as though it was her house and not his in which they now were.

"Let the children eat first," she commanded, "I shall need time to talk with you and I am not hungry."

He repressed his inclination to tell her that he was hungry and that he must get back to the office. Something in her look made it impossible for him to be disobedient to her. He went away and gave the children direction and then returned.

"Yes, my mother," he said, seating himself on a small and uncomfortable chair.

Then she related to him with much detail and repetition what had happened that morning; she

words for everyday use

ab • surd (ab surd´) adj., clearly ridiculous. *In Columbus's day most people thought it absurd that some believed the earth orbited around the sun.*

re • press (ri pres´) vt., hold back or restrain. *I could no longer repress my sadness, so I let the tears flow.*

declared with indignation that she had never before heard of a country where no marriages were arranged for the young, leaving to them the most important event of their lives and that at a time when their judgment was still unripe, and a mistake could bring disaster upon the whole family.

"Your own marriage," she reminded him, "was arranged by your father with great care, our two families knowing each other well. Even though you and my daughter-in-law were distant in this country, yet we met her parents through a suitable go-between, and her uncle here stood in her father's place, and your father's friend in place of your father, and so it was all done according to custom though so far away."

How does Mrs. Pan believe that her son came to be married?

Mr. Pan did not have the heart to tell his mother that he and his wife Sophia had fallen in love first, and then, out of kindness to their elders, had allowed the marriage to be arranged for them as though they were not in love, and as though, indeed, they did not know each other. They were both young people of heart, and although it would have been much easier to be married in the American fashion, they considered their elders.

How did Mr. Pan really come to be marrried?

"What has all this to do with us now, my mother?" he asked.

"This is what is to do," she replied with spirit. "A nice, ugly girl of our own people came here today to see me. She is twenty-seven years old and she is not married. What will become of her?"

"Do you mean Lili Yang?" her son asked.

"I do," she replied. "When I heard that she has no way of being married because, according to the custom of this country, she must wait for a man to ask her—"

Old Mrs. Pan broke off and gazed at her son with horrified eyes.

"What now," he asked.

"Suppose the only man who asks is one who is not at all suitable?"

"It is quite possible that it often happens thus," her son said, trying not to laugh.

"Then she has no choice," old Mrs. Pan said <u>indignantly</u>. "She can only remain unmarried or accept one who is unsuitable."

"Here she has no choice," Mr. Pan agreed, "unless she is very pretty, my mother, when several men may ask and then she has choice." It was on the tip of his tongue to tell how at least six young men had proposed to his Sophia, thereby distressing him continually until he was finally chosen, but he thought better of it. Would it not be very hard to explain so much to his old mother, and could she understand? He doubted it. Nevertheless, he felt it necessary at least to make one point.

"Something must be said for the man also, my mother. Sometimes he asks a girl who will not have him, because she chooses another, and then his sufferings are intense. Unless he wishes to remain unmarried he must ask a second girl, who is not the first one. Here also is some injustice."

Old Mrs. Pan listened to this attentively and then declared, "It is all barbarous.[5] Certainly it is very embarrassing to be compelled to speak of these matters, man and woman, face to face. They should be spared; others should speak for them."

Why does Mrs. Pan consider American marriage customs "barbarous"?

---

5. **barbarous.** Uncivilized

---

words for everyday use

in • dig • nant • ly (in dig´nənt lē) *adv.*, feeling anger as a reaction to ungratefulness. *"I'm hurt that you assumed I did it," Marie said <u>indignantly</u>.*

She considered for a few seconds and then she said with fresh indignation, "And what woman can change the appearance her ancestors have given her? Because she is not pretty is she less a woman? Are not her feelings like any woman's; is it not her right to have husband and home and children? It is well-known that men have no wisdom in such matters; they believe that a woman's face is all she has, forgetting that everything else is the same. They gather about the pretty woman, who is surfeited with them,[6] and leave alone the good woman. And I do not know why heaven has created ugly women always good but so it is, whether here or in our own country, but what man is wise enough to know that? Therefore his wife should be chosen for him, so that the family is not burdened with his follies."

What does Mrs. Pan say about women who are not beautiful?

Mr. Pan allowed all this to be said and then he inquired, "What is on your mind, my mother?"

Old Mrs. Pan leaned toward him and lifted her forefinger. "This is what I command you to do for me, my son. I myself will find a husband for this good girl of our people. She is helpless and alone. But I know no one; I am a stranger and I must depend upon you. In your business there must be young men. Inquire of them and see who stands for them, so that we can arrange a meeting between them and me; I will stand for the girl's mother. I promised it."

Now Mr. Pan laughed heartily. "Oh, my mother!" he cried. "You are too kind but it cannot be done. They would laugh at me, and do you believe that Lili Yang herself would like such an arrangement? I think she would not. She has been in America too long."

"And what woman can change the appearance her ancestors have given her? Because she is not pretty is she less a woman?"

Old Mrs. Pan would not yield, however, and in the end he was compelled to promise that he would see what he could do. Upon this promise she consented to eat her meal, and he led her out, her right hand resting upon his left wrist. The children were gone and they had a quiet meal together, and after it she said she felt that she would sleep. This was good news, for she had not slept well since she came, and young Mrs. Pan led her into the bedroom and helped her to lie down and placed a thin quilt over her.

When young Mrs. Pan went back to the small dining room where her husband waited to tell her what his mother had said, she listened thoughtfully.

"It is absurd," her husband said, "but what shall we do to satisfy my mother? She sees it as a good deed if she can find a husband for Lili Yang."

Here his wife surprised him. "I can see some good in it myself," she declared. "I have often felt for Lili. It is a problem, and our mother is right to see it as such. It is not only Lili—it is a problem here for all young women, especially if they are not pretty." She looked <u>quizzically</u> at her husband for a moment and then said, "I too used to worry when I was very young, lest I should not find a husband for myself. It is a great burden for a young woman. It would be nice to have someone else arrange the matter."

"Remember," he told her, "how often in the old country the wrong men are arranged for and how often the young men leave home because they do not like the wives their parents choose for them."

What does Mr. Pan dislike about arranged marriages?

---

6. **is surfeited with them.** Has had enough of them

words for everyday use

quiz • zi • cal • ly (kwiz´i kə lē) *adv.*, in a perplexed manner. *When our teacher dressed up for Halloween, we looked at him <u>quizzically</u>.*

"Well, so do they here," she said pertly. "Divorce, divorce, divorce!"

"Come, come," he told her. "It is not so bad."

"It is very bad for women," she insisted. "When there is divorce here, then she is thrown out of the family. The ties are broken. But in the old country, it is the man who leaves home and the woman stays on, for she is still the daughter-in-law and her children will belong to the family, and however far away the man wants to go, she has her place and she is safe."

Mr. Pan looked at his watch. "It is late and I must go to the office."

"Oh, your office," young Mrs. Pan said in an uppish[7] voice, "what would you do without it?"

They did not know it but their voices roused old Mrs. Pan in the bedroom, and she opened her eyes. She could not understand what they said for they spoke in English, but she understood that there was an argument. She sat up on the bed to listen, then she heard the door slam and she knew her son was gone. She was about to lie down again when it occurred to her that it would be interesting to look out of the window to the street and see what young men there were coming to and fro. One did not choose men from the street, of course, but still she could see what their looks were.

> Why does Mrs. Pan finally look out the window?

She got up and tidied her hair and tottered on her small feet over to the window and opening the curtains a little she gazed into the street really for the first time since she came. She was pleased to see many Chinese men, some of them young. It was still not late, and they loitered in the sunshine before going back to work, talking and laughing and looking happy. It was interesting to her to watch them, keeping in mind Lili Yang and thinking to herself that it might be this one or that one, although still one did not choose men from the street. She stood so long that at last she became tired and she pulled a small chair to the window and kept looking through the parted curtain.

Here her daughter-in-law saw her a little later, when she opened the door to see if her mother-in-law was awake, but she did not speak. She looked at the little satin-clad figure, and went away again, wondering why it was that the old lady found it pleasant today to look out of the window when every other day she had refused the same pleasure.

It became a pastime for old Mrs. Pan to look out of the window every day from then on. Gradually she came to know some of the young men, not by name but by their faces and by the way they walked by her window, never, of course looking up at her, until one day a certain young man did look up and smile. It was a warm day, and she had asked that the window be opened, which until now she had not allowed, for fear she might be assailed by the foreign winds and made ill. Today, however, was near to summer, she felt the room airless and she longed for freshness.

After this the young man habitually smiled when he passed or nodded his head. She was too old to have it mean anything but courtesy and so bit by bit she allowed herself to make a gesture of her hand in return. It was evident that he belonged in a china shop across the narrow street. She watched him go in and come out; she watched him stand at the door in his shirt sleeves on a fine day and talk and laugh, showing, as she observed, strong white teeth set off by two gold

> Why does Mrs. Pan feel free to gesture to the man?

---

7. **uppish.** Haughty or arrogant

words for everyday use

as • sail (ə sāl´) *vt.,* attack physically. *Once we were in the marsh we were <u>assailed</u> by mosquitoes.*

ones. Evidently he made money. She did not believe he was married, for she saw an old man who must be his father, who smoked a water pipe, and now and then an elderly woman, perhaps his mother, and a younger brother, but there was no young woman.

She began after some weeks of watching to fix upon this young man as a husband for Lili. But who could be the go-between except her own son?

She confided her plans one night to him, and, as always, he listened to her with courtesy and concealed amusement. "But the young man, my mother, is the son of Mr. Lim, who is the richest man on our street."

"That is nothing against him," she declared.

"No, but he will not submit to an arrangement, my mother. He is a college graduate. He is only spending the summer at home in the shop to help his father."

"Lili Yang has also been to school."

"I know, my mother, but, you see, the young man will want to choose his own wife, and it will not be someone who looks like Lili Yang. It will be someone who—"

He broke off and made a gesture which suggested curled hair, a fine figure and an air. Mrs. Pan watched him with disgust.

Why does Mrs. Pan become angry with her son?

"You are like all these other men, though you are my son," she said and dismissed him sternly.

Nevertheless, she thought over what he had said when she went back to the window. The young man was standing on the street picking his fine teeth and laughing at friends who passed, the sun shining on his glistening black hair. It was true he did not look at all obedient; it was perhaps true that he was no more wise

> "But the young man, my mother, is the son of Mr. Lim, who is the richest man on our street."

than other men and so saw only what a girl's face was. She wished that she could speak to him, but that, of course, was impossible. Unless—

She drew in a long breath. Unless she went downstairs and out into that street and crossed it and entered the shop, pretending that she came to buy something! If she did this, she could speak to him. But what would she say, and who would help her cross the street? She did not want to tell her son or her son's wife, for they would suspect her and laugh. They teased her often even now about her purpose, and Lili was so embarrassed by their laughter that she did not want to come anymore.

Old Mrs. Pan reflected on the difficulty of her position as a lady in a barbarous and strange country. Then she thought of her eldest grandson, Johnnie. On Saturday, when her son was at his office and her son's wife was at the market, she would coax Johnnie to lead her across the street to the china shop; she would pay him some money, and in the shop she would say she was looking for two bowls to match some that had been broken. It would be an <u>expedition</u>, but she might speak to the young man and tell him—what should she tell him? That must first be planned.

This was only Thursday and she had only two days to prepare. She was very restless during those two days, and she could not eat. Mr. Pan spoke of a doctor whom she indignantly refused to see, because he was a man and also because she was not ill. But Saturday came at last and everything came about as she planned. Her son went away, and then her son's wife, and she crept downstairs with much effort to the side-

---

words for everyday use

ex • pe • di • tion (eks´pə dish´ən) n., journey or voyage for a definite purpose. *The purpose of Lewis and Clark's expedition was to explore the West.*

walk where her grandson was playing marbles and beckoned him to her. The child was terrified to see her there and came at once, and she pressed a coin into his palm and pointed across the street with her cane.

"Lead me there," she commanded and, shutting her eyes tightly, she put her hand on his shoulder and allowed him to lead her to the shop. Then to her dismay he left her and ran back to play and she stood <u>wavering</u> on the threshold, feeling dizzy, and the young man saw her and came hurrying toward her. To her joy he spoke good Chinese, and the words fell sweetly upon her old ears.

> How does the man treat Mrs. Pan?

"Ancient One, Ancient One," he chided[8] her kindly. "Come in and sit down. It is too much for you."

He led her inside the cool, dark shop and she sat down on a bamboo chair.

"I came to look for two bowls," she said faintly.

"Tell me the pattern and I will get them for you," he said. "Are they blue willow pattern or the thousand flowers?"

"Thousand flowers," she said in the same faint voice, "but I do not wish to disturb you."

"I am here to be disturbed," he replied with the utmost courtesy.

He brought out some bowls and set them on a small table before her and she fell to talking with him. He was very pleasant; his rather large face was shining with kindness and he laughed easily. Now that she saw him close, she was glad to notice that he was not too handsome; his nose and mouth were big, and he had big hands and feet.

"You look like a countryman," she said. "Where is your ancestral home?"

"It is in the province of Shantung," he replied, "and there are not many of us here."

"That explains why you are so tall," she said. "These people from Canton are small. We of Szechuen are also big and our language is yours. I cannot understand the people of Canton."

From this they fell to talking of their own country, which he had never seen, and she told him about the village and how her son's father had left it many years ago to do business here in this foreign country and how he had sent for their son and then how she had been compelled to flee because the country was in fragments and torn between many leaders. When she had told this much, she found herself telling him how difficult it was to live here and how strange the city was to her and how she would never have looked out of the window had it not been for the sake of Lili Yang.

"Who is Lili Yang?" he asked.

Old Mrs. Pan did not answer him directly. That would not have been suitable. One does not speak of a reputable young woman to any man, not even one as good as this one. Instead she began a long speech about the virtues of young women who were not pretty, and how beauty in a woman made virtue unlikely, and how a woman not beautiful was always grateful to her husband and did not consider that she had done him a favor by the marriage, but rather that it was he who <u>conferred</u> the favor, so that she served him far better than she could have done were she beautiful.

To all this the young man listened, his small eyes twinkling with laughter.

"I take it that this Lili Yang is not beautiful," he said.

---

8. **chide.** Gently reprimand or scold

---

words for everyday use

wa • ver • ing (wā´ver iŋ) *part.*, swinging or swaying back and forth. *In the intense heat the air seemed to be* <u>wavering</u> *above the blistering pavement.*

con • fer (kən fur´) *vt.*, grant or bestow. *The queen* <u>conferred</u> *knighthood upon the actor.*

Old Mrs. Pan looked astonished. "I did not say so," she replied with spirit. "I will not say she is beautiful and I will not say she is ugly. What is beautiful to one is not so to another. Suppose you see her sometime for yourself, and then we will discuss it."

What method does Mrs. Pan use to encourage the young man to meet Lili?

"Discuss what?" he demanded.

"Whether she is beautiful."

Suddenly she felt that she had come to a point and that she had better go home. It was enough for the first visit. She chose two bowls and paid for them and while he wrapped them up she waited in silence, for to say too much is worse than to say too little.

When the bowls were wrapped, the young man said courteously, "Let me lead you across the street, Ancient One."

So, putting her right hand on his left wrist, she let him lead her across and this time she did not shut her eyes, and she came home again feeling that she had been a long way and had accomplished much. When her daughter-in-law came home she said quite easily, "I went across the street and bought these two bowls."

Young Mrs. Pan opened her eyes wide. "My mother, how could you go alone?"

"I did not go alone," old Mrs. Pan said tranquilly. "My grandson led me across and young Mr. Lim brought me back."

Each had spoken in her own language with helpful gestures.

How do Mrs. Pan and her daughter-in-law communicate?

Young Mrs. Pan was astonished and she said no more until her husband came home, when she told him. He laughed a great deal and said, "Do not interfere with our old one. She is enjoying herself. It is good for her."

But all the time he knew what his mother was doing and he joined in it without her knowledge. That is to say, he telephoned the same afternoon from his office to Miss Lili Yang, and when she answered, he said, "Please come and see my old mother again. She asks after you every day. Your visit did her much good."

Lili Yang promised, not for today but for a week hence, and when Mr. Pan went home he told his mother carelessly, as though it were nothing, that Lili Yang had called him up to say she was coming again next week.

Old Mrs. Pan heard this with secret excitement. She had not gone out again, but every day young Mr. Lim nodded to her and smiled, and once he sent her a small gift of fresh ginger root. She made up her mind slowly but she made it up well. When Lili Yang came again, she would ask her to take her to the china shop, pretending that she wanted to buy something, and she would introduce the two to each other; that much she would do. It was too much, but, after all, these were modern times, and this was a barbarous country, where it did not matter greatly whether the old customs were kept or not. The important thing was to find a husband for Lili, who was already twenty-seven years old.

Does Mrs. Pan mind deviating a little from her old ways?

So it all came about, and when Lili walked into her room the next week, while the fine weather still held, old Mrs. Pan greeted her with smiles. She seized Lili's small hand and noticed that the hand was very soft and pretty, as the hands of most plain-faced girls are, the gods being kind to such women and giving them pretty bodies when they see that ancestors have not bestowed pretty faces.

"Do not take off your foreign hat," she told Lili. "I wish to go across the street to that shop and buy some dishes as a gift for my son's wife. She is very kind to me."

Lili Yang was pleased to see the old lady so changed and cheerful and in all innocence she agreed and they went across the street and into

"What is beautiful to one is not so to another."

the shop. Today there were customers, and old Mr. Lim was there too, as well as his son. He was a tall, withered man, and he wore a small beard under his chin. When he saw old Mrs. Pan he stopped what he was doing and brought her a chair to sit upon while she waited. As soon as his customer was gone, he introduced himself, saying that he knew her son.

"My son has told me of your honored visit last week," he said. "Please come inside and have some tea. I will have my son bring the dishes, and you can look at them in quiet. It is too noisy here."

She accepted his courtesy, and in a few minutes young Mr. Lim came back to the inner room with the dishes while a servant brought tea.

Old Mrs. Pan did not introduce Lili Yang, for it was not well to embarrass a woman, but young Mr. Lim boldly introduced himself, in English.

"Are you Miss Lili Yang?" he asked. "I am James Lim."

"How did you know my name?" Lili asked, astonished.

"I have met you before, not face to face, but through Mrs. Pan," he said, his small eyes twinkling. "She has told me more about you than she knows."

Lili blushed. "Mrs. Pan is so old-fashioned," she murmured. "You must not believe her."

"I shall only believe what I see for myself," he said gallantly. He looked at her frankly and Lili kept blushing. Old Mrs. Pan had not done her justice, he thought. The young woman had a nice, round face, the sort of face he liked. She was shy, and he liked that also. It was something new.

> How does Mr. Lim feel about Lili's appearance?

Meanwhile old Mrs. Pan watched all this with amazement. So this was the way it was: The young man began speaking immediately, and the young woman blushed. She wished that she knew what they were saying but perhaps it was better that she did not know.

She turned to old Mr. Lim, who was sitting across the square table sipping tea. At least here she could do her duty. "I hear your son is not married," she said in a tentative way.

"Not yet," Mr. Lim said. "He wants first to finish learning how to be a Western doctor."

"How old is he?" Mrs. Pan inquired.

"He is twenty-eight. It is very old but he did not make up his mind for some years, and the learning is long."

"Miss Lili Yang is twenty-seven," Mrs. Pan said in the same <u>tentative</u> voice.

The young people were still talking in English and not listening to them. Lili was telling James Lim about her work and about old Mrs. Pan. She was not blushing anymore; she had forgotten, it seemed, that he was a young man and she a young woman. Suddenly she stopped and blushed again. A woman was supposed to let a man talk about himself, not about her.

"Tell me about your work," she said. "I wanted to be a doctor, too, but it cost too much."

"I can't tell you here," he said. "There are customers waiting in the shop and it will take a long time. Let me come to see you, may I? I could come on Sunday when the shop is closed. Or we could take a ride on one of the riverboats. Will you? The weather is so fine."

"I have never been on a riverboat," she said. "It would be delightful."

She forgot her work and remembered that he was a young man and that she was a young woman. She liked his big face and the way his

words for everyday use

ten • ta • tive (ten´tə tiv) adj., hesitant. *Jan wore a <u>tentative</u> smile when asked if her first day at work went well.*

black hair fell back from his forehead and she knew that a day on the river could be a day in heaven.

The customers were getting impatient. They began to call out and he got up. "Next Sunday," he said in a low voice. "Let's start early. I'll be at the wharf at nine o'clock."

"We do not know each other," she said, <u>reluctant</u> and yet eager. Would he think she was too eager?

He laughed. "You see my respectable father, and I know old Mrs. Pan very well. Let them guarantee us."

Why is the meeting between Lili and Mr. Lim respectable?

He hurried away, and old Mrs. Pan said immediately to Lili, "I have chosen these four dishes. Please take them and have them wrapped. Then we will go home."

Lili obeyed, and when she was gone, old Mrs. Pan leaned toward old Mr. Lim.

> *"All days are good, when one performs a good deed, and what is better than to arrange a marriage?"*

"I wanted to get her out of the way," she said in a low and important voice. "Now, while she is gone, what do you say? Shall we arrange a match? We do not need a go-between. I stand as her mother, let us say, and you are his father. We must have their horoscopes[9] read, of course, but just between us, it looks as though it is suitable, does it not?"

Mr. Lim wagged his head. "If you recommend her, Honorable Old Lady, why not?"

Why not, indeed? After all, things were not so different here, after all.

"What day is convenient for you?" she asked.

"Shall we say Sunday?" old Mr. Lim suggested.

"Why not?" she replied. "All days are good, when one performs a good deed, and what is better than to arrange a marriage?"

"Nothing is better," old Mr. Lim agreed. "Of all good deeds under heaven, it is the best."

They fell silent, both pleased with themselves, while they waited. ∎

---

9. **horoscopes.** Explanations about the effect on individuals of the positions of stars and planets at a particular point in time. In Chinese astrology, the most important time is conception—in this case, the time when Lili's (or James's) mother first began her pregnancy.

words for everyday use

re • luc • tant (ri luk´tənt) *adj.,* unwilling or disinclined. *Even though I knew the answer, I was <u>reluctant</u> to raise my hand.*

Respond *to the* SELECTION

Imagine that you are old Mrs. Pan. Why do you think that finding a husband for Lili has changed your behavior?

Investigate, *Inquire,* and Imagine

Recall: GATHERING FACTS

1a. What risks has Mr. Pan taken to bring his mother to New York?

2a. What kinds of things frighten old Mrs. Pan in New York?

3a. What does Lili want to talk about during her first visit with old Mrs. Pan? What promise does the elderly woman make to Lili?

Interpret: FINDING MEANING

1b. What is probably the reason that old Mrs. Pan does not "appreciate the fact" of her safety?

2b. What actions on the part of old Mrs. Pan show that she is very lonely? What actions on her part show that being of use renews her spirit?

3b. What actions on the part of Lili Yang and James Lim show that they do not object to old Mrs. Pan's arrangement?

Analyze: TAKING THINGS APART

4a. What differences between American and traditional Chinese customs of marriage are described in the story?

Synthesize: BRINGING THINGS TOGETHER

4b. How is the courtship between Lili and James a blending of Chinese and American customs?

Evaluate: MAKING JUDGMENTS

5a. Many good deeds are performed in the story. For example, Mr. Pan brings his mother to America, Lili comes to talk Chinese to old Mrs. Pan, old Mrs. Pan tries to find a husband for Lili, and James is courteous to old Mrs. Pan when she visits his store. Which deed do you consider the most generous? Why?

Extend: CONNECTING IDEAS

5b. Imagine that you are in your late twenties and want a spouse but haven't found one yet. What resources could you use to try to find a spouse in contemporary society?

Understanding *Literature*

PLOT. Review the definition for **plot** in the Handbook of Literary Terms. What are the central conflict and the crisis in the story? How is the crisis emphasized by the characterization of old Mrs. Pan?

CHARACTER AND CHARACTERIZATION. Review the definitions for **character** and **characterization** in the Handbook of Literary Terms and the chart you made for Literary Tools on page 224. Who is the protagonist of the story? Is the protagonist a static or a dynamic character? Analyze how the portrayal of old Mrs. Pan's behavior is effective in showing how she changes in the story.

Writer's Journal

1. Imagine you are Lili. Write a **thank-you note** to old Mrs. Pan for finding a husband for you. Explain how you regard the old Chinese marriage customs and courtship in America.
2. For the local newspaper's classified ads section, write a **personal ad** that seeks a husband for Lili.
3. Imagine you are Mrs. Pan. Write a **postcard** to a friend in your village in China describing how you find America and telling how you spend your days. Tell how you felt about meeting Lili and what decision has changed your life.

Integrating the Language Arts

Language, Grammar, and Style

SENTENCE COMPLETER REVIEW: DIRECT AND INDIRECT OBJECTS, PREDICATE NOUNS, PRONOUNS AND ADJECTIVES. For each of the sentences below, identify the simple subject(s), verb(s), and the complement(s) (if any are present). Then identify the kind of complement. Write down DO if the complement is a direct object, IO if it is an indirect object, PA if it is a predicate adjective, PN if it is a predicate noun, or PP if it is a predicate pronoun. For a review, refer to the Language Arts Survey 3.22–3.23.

1. Mrs. Pan's daughter-in-law has prepared and served a good dinner.
2. I will be your mother.
3. Pretty women do not need arranged marriages or go-betweens.
4. Mr. Lim and Mrs. Pan came from China.
5. James and Lili respected the old ways.

Speaking and Listening

INTERVIEW. With a partner, play the roles of old Mrs. Pan and an interviewer. If you play the interviewer, ask Mrs. Pan about her old life in China and her new life in America.

Applied English

BUSINESS LETTER. Imagine that you are Pearl S. Buck and that you have just written a short story called "The Good Deed." Write a letter to a magazine editor to try to get your story published. Tell the editor why you are writing, describe the plot and theme of your story, and inform the editor that you are including a self-addressed stamped envelope for his or her response. Before you begin writing, you might want to read the Language Arts Survey 6.5, "Writing a Business Letter."

Study and Research & Media Literacy

RESEARCHING ON THE INTERNET. Use the Internet to locate news items about Pearl S. Buck. One site you will find useful is The University of Pennsylvania's English Department website about Pearl S. Buck at http://dept.english.upenn.edu/Projects/Buck/. Then lay out pages of a newsletter dedicated to Buck, including articles about the author and her work.

Literary TOOLS

POINT OF VIEW. Point of view is the vantage point from which a story is told. Stories are typically written from a *first-person point of view*, in which the narrator uses words such as *I* and *we*, or from a *third-person point of view*, in which the narrator uses words such as *he, she, it,* and *they*. As you read, determine the point of view used in this story.

PLOT. A plot is a series of events related to a central conflict, or struggle. The *inciting incident* is the event that introduces the central conflict. The *climax* is the high point of interest or suspense in the plot. The *crisis*, or *turning point*, often the same event as the climax, is the point in the plot where something decisive happens to determine the future course of events and the eventual working out of the conflict. The *resolution* is the point at which the central conflict is ended, or resolved.

Graphic Organizer

As you read, make a sequence chart listing the main events of the story. One example has been done for you.

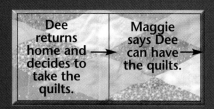

| Dee returns home and decides to take the quilts. | → | Maggie says Dee can have the quilts. | → |

Reader's Journal

What family heirloom is important to you?

"Everyday Use"
by Alice Walker

Reader's resource

"Everyday Use" was published in *In Love and Trouble* (1973). Like many of Alice Walker's writings, the story explores the idea of African-American heritage. In a conflict between a woman and her sister and mother, two different interpretations of heritage are presented.

"Everyday Use" is enriched by Walker's development of symbols. In particular, the contested quilts become the central metaphor of the story's theme; they represent the past of the women in the family. The central theme of the story concerns the importance of heritage and culture to an individual's understanding of his or her present life and identity. The debate over how the quilts should be treated—used or hung on the wall—represents the black woman's dilemma about how to face the future.

About the AUTHOR

Alice Walker (1944–   ) was raised in a sharecropping family in Eatonton, Georgia, and educated at Atlanta's Spelman College and then at Sarah Lawrence. In 1964, Walker visited Africa and then in 1966 took part in the voter registration drive in Mississippi. She tapped these experiences for her first book of poetry, *Once* (1968), which explores her roots and the African-American struggle for civil rights. Her first novel, *Meridian* (1976), also deals with civil rights and has been hailed as a sensitive portrayal of the movement. Her works reached a wider audience when her 1983 novel *The Color Purple* won the Pulitzer Prize for fiction and was made into a successful movie. A central theme in Walker's writing is her belief that "not enough credit has been given to the black woman who has been oppressed beyond recognition."

Everyday Use

for your grandmama

Alice Walker

I will wait for her in the yard that Maggie and I made so clean and wavy yesterday afternoon. A yard like this is more comfortable than most people know. It is not just a yard. It is like an extended living room. When the hard clay is swept clean as a floor and the fine sand around the edges lined with tiny, irregular grooves, anyone can come and sit and look up into the elm tree and wait for the breezes that never come inside the house.

Maggie will be nervous until after her sister goes: she will stand hopelessly in corners, <u>homely</u> and ashamed of the burn scars down her arms and legs, eying her sister with a mixture of envy and awe. She thinks her sister has held life always in the palm of one hand, that "no" is a word the world never learned to say to her.

How does Maggie feel toward her sister?

You've no doubt seen those TV shows where the child who has "made it" is confronted, as a surprise, by her own mother and father, tottering in weakly from backstage.[1] (A pleasant surprise, of course: What would they do if parent and child came on the show only to curse out and insult each other?) On TV mother and child embrace and smile into each other's faces. Sometimes the mother and father weep, the child wraps them in her arms and leans across the table to tell how she would not have made it without their help. I have seen these programs.

Sometimes I dream a dream in which Dee and I are suddenly brought together on a TV program of this sort. Out of a dark and soft-seated limousine I am <u>ushered</u> into a bright room filled with many people. There I meet a smiling, gray, sporty man like Johnny Carson[2] who shakes my hand and tells me what a fine girl I have. Then we are on the stage and Dee is embracing me with tears in her eyes. She pins on my dress a large orchid, even though she has told me once that she thinks orchids are tacky flowers.

In real life I am a large, big-boned woman with rough, man-working hands. In the winter I wear flannel nightgowns to bed and overalls during the day. I can kill and clean a hog as mercilessly as a man. My fat keeps me hot in zero weather. I can work outside

How does the speaker describe herself as being in real life? How does she visualize herself appearing on TV?

---

1. **TV shows . . . backstage.** Refers to *This Is Your Life*, a television show in which celebrities were surprised by a group of family and friends
2. **Johnny Carson.** Former host of *The Tonight Show*

all day, breaking ice to get water for washing; I can eat pork liver cooked over the open fire minutes after it comes steaming from the hog. One winter I knocked a bull calf straight in the brain between the eyes with a sledge hammer and had the meat hung up to chill before nightfall. But of course all this does not show on television. I am the way my daughter would want me to be: a hundred pounds lighter, my skin like an uncooked barley pancake. My hair glistens in the hot bright lights. Johnny Carson has much to do to keep up with my quick and witty tongue.

But that is a mistake. I know even before I wake up. Who ever knew a Johnson with a quick tongue? Who can even imagine me looking a strange white man in the eye? It seems to me I have talked to them always with one foot raised in flight, with my head turned in whichever way is farthest from them. Dee, though. She would always look anyone in the eye. Hesitation was no part of her nature.

"How do I look, Mama?" Maggie says, showing just enough of her thin body enveloped in pink skirt and red blouse for me to know she's there, almost hidden by the door.

"Come out into the yard," I say.

Have you ever seen a lame animal, perhaps a dog run over by some careless person rich enough to own a car, sidle up to someone who is ignorant enough to be kind to him? That is the way my Maggie walks. She has been like this, chin on chest, eyes on ground, feet in shuffle, ever since the fire that burned the other house to the ground.

Dee is lighter than Maggie, with nicer hair and a fuller figure. She's a woman now, though sometimes I forget. How long ago was it that the other house burned? Ten, twelve years? Sometimes I can still hear the flames and feel Maggie's arms sticking to me, her hair smoking and her dress falling off her in little black papery flakes. Her eyes seemed stretched open, blazed open by the flames reflected in them. And Dee. I see her

To what does the speaker compare Maggie?

standing off under the sweet gum tree she used to dig gum out of; a look of concentration on her face as she watched the last dingy gray board of the house fall in toward the red-hot brick chimney. Why don't you do a dance around the ashes? I'd wanted to ask her. She had hated the house that much.

What happened to the other house? What happened to Maggie? How did Dee appear to feel about the house?

I used to think she hated Maggie, too. But that was before we raised the money, the church and me, to send her to Augusta[3] to school. She used to read to us without pity; forcing words, lies, other folks' habits, whole lives upon us two, sitting trapped and ignorant underneath her voice. She washed us in a river of make-believe, burned us with a lot of knowledge we didn't necessarily need to know. Pressed us to her with the serious way she read, to shove us away at just the moment, like dimwits, we seemed about to understand.

Dee wanted nice things. A yellow organdy[4] dress to wear to her graduation from high school; black pumps to match a green suit she'd made from an old suit somebody gave me. She was determined to stare down any disaster in her efforts. Her eyelids would not flicker for minutes at a time. Often I fought off the temptation to shake her. At sixteen she had a style of her own: and knew what style was.

I never had an education myself. After second grade the school was closed down. Don't ask me why: in 1927 colored asked fewer questions than they do now. Sometimes Maggie reads to me. She stumbles along good-naturedly but can't see well. She knows she is not bright. Like good looks and money, quickness passed her by. She will marry John Thomas (who has mossy teeth in an earnest face) and then I'll be free to sit here and I guess just sing church songs to myself.

---

3. **Augusta.** City in Georgia where Paine College is located
4. **organdy.** Sheer cotton fabric

Although I never was a good singer. Never could carry a tune. I was always better at a man's job. I used to love to milk till I was hooked in the side[5] in '49. Cows are soothing and slow and don't bother you, unless you try to milk them the wrong way.

I have deliberately turned my back on the house. It is three rooms, just like the one that burned, except the roof is tin; they don't make shingle roofs any more. There are no real windows, just some holes cut in the sides, like the portholes in a ship, but not round and not square, with rawhide holding the shutters up on the outside. This house is in a pasture, too, like the other one. No doubt when Dee sees it she will want to tear it down. She wrote me once that no matter where we "choose" to live, she will manage to come see us. But she will never bring her friends. Maggie and I thought about this and Maggie asked me, "Mama, when did Dee ever *have* any friends?"

She had a few. Furtive boys in pink shirts hanging about on washday after school. Nervous girls who never laughed. Impressed with her they worshiped the well-turned phrase, the cute shape, the scalding humor that erupted like bubbles in lye.[6] She read to them.

In what way does the speaker characterize Dee's humor?

When she was courting Jimmy T she didn't have much time to pay to us, but turned all her faultfinding power on him. He *flew* to marry a cheap city girl from a family of ignorant flashy people. She hardly had time to recompose herself.

When she comes I will meet—but there they are!

Maggie attempts to make a dash for the house, in her shuffling way, but I stay her with my hand. "Come back here," I say. And she stops and tries to dig a well in the sand with her toe.

It is hard to see them clearly through the strong sun. But even the first glimpse of leg out of the car tells me it is Dee. Her feet were always neat-looking, as if God himself had shaped them with a certain style. From the other side of the car comes a short, stocky man. Hair is all over his head a foot long and hanging from his chin like a kinky mule tail. I hear Maggie suck in her breath. "Uhnnnh," is what it sounds like. Like when you see the wriggling end of a snake just in front of your foot on the road. "Uhnnnh."

Dee next. A dress down to the ground, in this hot weather. A dress so loud it hurts my eyes. There are yellows and oranges enough to throw back the light of the sun. I feel my whole face warming from the heat waves it throws out. Earrings gold, too, and hanging down to her shoulders. Bracelets dangling and making noises when she moves her arm up to shake the folds of the dress out of her armpits. The dress is loose and flows, and as she walks closer, I like it. I hear Maggie go "Uhnnnh" again. It is her sister's hair. It stands straight up like the wool on a sheep. It is black as night and around the edges are two long pigtails that rope about like small lizards disappearing behind her ears.

"Wa-su-zo-Tean-o!"[7] she says, coming on in that gliding way the dress makes her move. The

Cows are soothing and slow and don't bother you, unless you try to milk them the wrong way.

---

5. **hooked in the side.** Kicked by a cow
6. **lye.** Alkaline substance used to make soap
7. **Wa-su-zo-Tean-o!** African dialect greeting

---

words for everyday use

fur • tive (fur′tiv) *adj.,* sneaky; stealthy. *After furtive whispering, the girls selected members for their team.*

scald • ing (skôld′iŋ) *part.,* burning; injuring. *Scalding hot water turned the shellfish from brown to pink.*

re • com • pose (rē′kəm pōz′) *vt.,* restore calmness of mind. *Andrea recomposed herself after the heated tennis match.*

short stocky fellow with the hair to his navel is all grinning and he follows up with "Asalamalakim,[8] my mother and sister!" He moves to hug Maggie but she falls back, right up against the back of my chair. I feel her trembling there and when I look up I see the perspiration falling off her chin.

"Don't get up," says Dee. Since I am stout it takes something of a push. You can see me trying to move a second or two before I make it. She turns, showing white heels through her sandals, and goes back to the car. Out she peeks next with a Polaroid. She stoops down quickly and lines up picture after picture of me sitting there in front of the house with Maggie cowering behind me. She never takes a shot without making sure the house is included. When a cow comes nibbling around the edge of the yard she snaps it and me and Maggie *and* the house. Then she puts the Polaroid in the back seat of the car, and comes up and kisses me on the forehead.

Meanwhile Asalamalakim is going through motions with Maggie's hand. Maggie's hand is as limp as a fish, and probably as cold, despite the sweat, and she keeps trying to pull it back. It looks like Asalamalakim wants to shake hands but wants to do it fancy. Or maybe he don't know how people shake hands. Anyhow, he soon gives up on Maggie.

"Well," I say. "Dee."

"No, Mama," she says. "Not 'Dee,' Wangero Leewanika Kemanjo!"

"What happened to 'Dee'?" I wanted to know.

"She's dead," Wangero said. "I couldn't bear it any

Why might Dee want to include the house in all the photographs?

What reason does Dee cite for changing her name to Wangero?

longer, being named after the people who oppress me."

"You know as well as me you was named after your aunt Dicie," I said. Dicie is my sister. She named Dee. We called her "Big Dee" after Dee was born.

"But who was she named after?" asked Wangero.

"I guess after Grandma Dee," I said.

"And who was *she* named after?" asked Wangero.

"Her mother," I said, and saw Wangero was getting tired. "That's about as far back as I can trace it," I said. Though, in fact, I probably could have carried it back beyond the Civil War through the branches.

"Well," said Asalamalakim, "there you are."

"Uhnnnh," I heard Maggie say.

"There I was not," I said, "before 'Dicie' cropped up in our family, so why should I try to trace it that far back?"

He just stood there grinning, looking down on me like somebody inspecting a Model A car.[9] Every once in a while he and Wangero sent eye signals over my head.

"How do you pronounce this name?" I asked.

"You don't have to call me by it if you don't want to," said Wangero.

"Why shouldn't I?" I asked. "If that's what you want us to call you, we'll call you."

"I know it might sound awkward at first," said Wangero.

"I'll get used to it," I said. "Ream it out again."

Well, soon we got the name out of the way. Asalamalakim had a name twice as long and three times as hard. After I tripped over it two or three times he told me to just call him Hakim-a-barber. I wanted to ask him was he a barber, but I didn't really think he was so I didn't ask.

"You must belong to those beef-cattle peoples down the road," I said. They said

---

8. **Asalamalakim.** Muslim greeting
9. **Model A car.** One of the first American cars

"Asalamalakim" when they met you, too, but they didn't shake hands. Always too busy: feeding the cattle, fixing the fences, putting up salt-lick shelters,[10] throwing down hay. When the white folks poisoned some of the herd the men stayed up all night with rifles in their hands. I walked a mile and a half just to see the sight.

Hakim-a-barber said, "I accept some of their <u>doctrines</u>, but farming and raising cattle is not my style." (They didn't tell me, and I didn't ask, whether Wangero (Dee) had really gone and married him.)

We sat down to eat and right away he said he didn't eat collards[11] and pork was unclean. Wangero, though, went on through the chitlins and corn bread, the greens and everything else. She talked a blue streak over the sweet potatoes. Everything delighted her. Even the fact that we still used the benches her daddy made for the table when we couldn't afford to buy chairs.

"Oh, Mama!" she cried. Then turned to Hakim-a-barber. "I never knew how lovely these benches are. You can feel the rump prints," she said, running her hands underneath her and along the bench. Then she gave a sigh and her hand closed over Grandma Dee's butter dish. "That's it!" she said. "I knew there was something I wanted to ask you if I could have." She jumped up from the table and went over in the corner where the churn stood, the milk in it clabber[12] by now. She looked at the churn and looked at it.

"This churn top is what I need," she said. "Didn't Uncle Buddy whittle it out of a tree you all used to have?"

"Yes," I said.

"Uh huh," she said happily. "And I want the dasher, too."

Lone Star Quilt, 1930. American artist. Private Collection.

"Uncle Buddy whittle that, too?" asked the barber.

Dee (Wangero) looked up at me.

"Aunt Dee's first husband whittled the dash," said Maggie so low you almost couldn't hear her. "His name was Henry, but they called him Stash."

"Maggie's brain is like an elephant's," Wangero said, laughing. "I can use the churn top as a centerpiece for the <u>alcove</u> table," she said, sliding a plate over the churn, "and I'll think of something artistic to do with the dasher."

> For what is Dee going to use the churn top? the dasher? For what were the speaker and Maggie using them?

---

10. **salt-lick shelters.** Places where cows are kept out of the heat by being given salt to lick
11. **collards.** Leafy cabbage-like vegetable
12. **clabber.** Sour milk

When she finished wrapping the dasher the handle stuck out. I took it for a moment in my hands. You didn't even have to look close to see where hands pushing the dasher up and down to make butter had left a kind of sink in the wood. In fact, there were a lot of small sinks; you could see where thumbs and fingers had sunk into the wood. It was beautiful light yellow wood, from a tree that grew in the yard where Big Dee and Stash had lived.

After dinner Dee (Wangero) went to the trunk at the foot of my bed and started <u>rifling</u> through it. Maggie hung back in the kitchen over the dishpan. Out came Wangero with two quilts. They had been pieced by Grandma Dee and then Big Dee and me had hung them on the quilt frames on the front porch and quilted them. One was in the Lone Star pattern. The other was Walk Around the Mountain. In both of them were scraps of dresses Grandma Dee had worn fifty and more years ago. Bits and pieces of Grandpa Jarrell's Paisley shirts. And one teeny faded blue piece, about the size of a penny matchbox, that was from Great Grandpa Ezra's uniform that he wore in the Civil War.

"Mama," Wangero said sweet as a bird. "Can I have these old quilts?"

I heard something fall in the kitchen, and a minute later the kitchen door slammed.

"Why don't you take one or two of the others?" I asked. "These old things was just done by me and Big Dee from some tops your grandma pieced before she died."

"No," said Wangero. "I don't want those. They are stitched around the borders by machine."

"That'll make them last better," I said.

"That's not the point," said Wangero. "These are all pieces of dresses Grandma used to wear. She did all this stitching by hand. Imagine!" She held the quilts securely in her arms, stroking them.

"Some of the pieces, like those lavender ones, come from old clothes her mother handed down to her," I said, moving up to touch the quilts. Dee (Wangero) moved back just enough so that I couldn't reach the quilts. They already belonged to her.

"Maggie would put them on the bed and in five years they'd be in rags. Less than that!"

"Imagine!" she breathed again, clutching them closely to her bosom.

"The truth is," I said, "I promised to give them quilts to Maggie, for when she marries John Thomas."

She gasped like a bee had stung her.

"Maggie can't appreciate these quilts!" she said. "She'd probably be backward enough to put them to everyday use."

"I reckon she would," I said. "God knows I been saving 'em for long enough with nobody using 'em. I hope she will!" I didn't want to bring up how I had offered Dee (Wangero) a quilt when she went away to college. Then she had told me they were old-fashioned, out of style.

"But they're *priceless!*" she was saying now, furiously; for she has a temper. "Maggie would put them on the bed and in five years they'd be in rags. Less than that!"

"She can always make some more," I said. "Maggie knows how to quilt."

Dee (Wangero) looked at me with hatred. "You just will not understand. The point is these quilts, *these* quilts!"

"Well," I said, stumped. "What would *you* do with them?"

"Hang them," she said. As if that was the only thing you *could* do with quilts.

Maggie by now was standing in the door. I could almost hear the sound her feet made as they scraped over each other.

"She can have them, Mama," she said, like somebody used to never winning anything, or having anything reserved for her. "I can 'member Grandma Dee without the quilts."

I looked at her hard. She had filled her bottom lip with checkerberry snuff and it gave her face a kind of dopey, <u>hangdog</u> look. It was Grandma Dee and Big Dee who taught her how to quilt herself. She stood there with her scarred hands hidden in the folds of her skirt. She looked at her sister with something like fear but she wasn't mad at her. This was Maggie's portion. This was the way she knew God to work.

When I looked at her like that something hit me in the top of my head and ran down to the soles of my feet. Just like when I'm in church and the spirit of God touches me and I get happy and shout. I did something I never had done before: hugged Maggie to me, then dragged her on into the room, snatched the quilts out of Miss Wangero's hands and dumped them into Maggie's lap. Maggie just sat there on my bed with her mouth open.

What does the speaker do? To whom does she give the quilts?

"Take one or two of the others," I said to Dee.

But she turned without a word and went out to Hakim-a-barber.

"You just don't understand," she said, as Maggie and I came out to the car.

"What don't I understand?" I wanted to know.

"Your <u>heritage</u>," she said. And then she turned to Maggie, kissed her, and said, "You ought to try to make something of yourself, too, Maggie. It's really a new day for us. But from the way you and Mama still live you'd never know it."

She put on some sunglasses that hid everything above the tip of her nose and her chin.

Maggie smiled; maybe at the sunglasses. But a real smile, not scared. After we watched the car dust settle I asked Maggie to bring me a dip of snuff. And then the two of us sat there just enjoying, until it was time to go in the house and go to bed. ∎

---

words for everyday use

hang • dog (haŋ´dôg´) *adj.,* ashamed and cringing. *The little boy's <u>hangdog</u> expression indicated he was sorry for taking the cookie.*

her • it • age (her´i tij´) *n.,* cultural traditions handed down by ancestors. *Eating lefse was a part of Julia's Norwegian <u>heritage</u> that she enjoyed.*

Should family heirlooms be put to "everyday use"? Why, or why not?

Investigate, *Inquire,* and *Imagine*

Recall: GATHERING FACTS

1a. What does the speaker dream?

2a. To what does the mother compare Maggie?

3a. What is Dee wearing? What greeting does she give? To what has she changed her name?

Interpret: FINDING MEANING

1b. What does the speaker's dream reveal about what she would like her life to be like? What does it reveal about the reality of her life?

2b. In what ways are Maggie and Dee different in both personality and appearance?

3b. What did Dee think of life with her mother and Maggie? For what reasons did she make changes in her life?

Analyze: TAKING THINGS APART

4a. What does "heritage" mean to Dee, Maggie, and the mother? Who has the deepest understanding of their heritage?

Synthesize: BRINGING THINGS TOGETHER

4b. How do you think Maggie will lead her life? Will she follow Dee's advice to make something of herself by leaving the family home? Provide evidence for your response.

Evaluate: MAKING JUDGMENTS

5a. Who values the quilts more, Dee or Maggie? Why?

Extend: CONNECTING IDEAS

5b. If a quilt were made of your life so far, what scenes and symbols would it depict?

Understanding *Literature*

POINT OF VIEW. Review the definition for **point of view** in the Handbook of Literary Terms. What point of view is used in the story? What information do we learn from the narrator? What information is she unable to tell us? What might we know about Dee if the story were told by an omniscient narrator?

PLOT. Review the definition for **plot** in the Handbook of Literary Terms. What are the inciting incident, climax, crisis, and resolution of the plot?

Writer's Journal

1. Imagine you are Dee. Write a name change **greeting card** to your family telling them about your new identity. In your greeting card, use an African expression from the story or another one you know.
2. Imagine you are Maggie. Write a **wish list** for your life, explaining why each wish is important to you.
3. Imagine you are the mother. Write a **letter** to Maggie explaining why you gave the quilts to her rather than to Dee.

Integrating the Language Arts

Language, Grammar, and Style

NOUNS OF DIRECT ADDRESS. Sometimes, as you speak to a person or a group, you say the name of the person or group as you speak. This construction, called a **noun of direct address,** is *not* an essential part of the sentence. Review the Language Arts Survey 3.32, "Avoiding Problems Caused by Understood Subjects and Nouns of Direct Address."

For each of the sentences below, identify the simple subject, verb, and the complement(s). Also identify any noun of direct address, if there is one.

1. These are Maggie's quilts, Dee.
2. Maggie, we know Dee's motives.
3. I can use the antique quilts, Mother.
4. The quilting class is starting, everyone.
5. Lose some weight and become a television personality, Mother.

Speaking and Listening & Collaborative Learning

FAMILY HISTORY. Maggie knows many family stories and the histories of many items created by her family. With several students, take turns telling a story from your family. You might know a story about how your ancestors came to the United States, what life was like on the farm your great-grandparents owned, or how an object came to be important to your family. The story might also be an event that happened during your lifetime that you would like to be passed on to future generations. When everyone in the group has told his or her story, write from memory the story of one of your group members to share with the class. Use the first-person point of view.

Media Literacy & Speaking and Listening

TALK SHOW. The mother in the story dreams about appearing on a television talk show. Imagine that Dee, Maggie, and the mother go on a talk show to resolve the problem of who should get the quilts. One student plays the role of the talk show host who moderates the discussion, and the others play the roles of Dee, Maggie, and the mother. By the end of your show, it should be clear what the position is of each family member, whether or not the problem is actually resolved.

"The Devil and Daniel Webster"

by Stephen Vincent Benét

Literary TOOLS

SUSPENSION OF DISBELIEF. The **suspension of disbelief** is the act by which the reader willingly sets aside his or her skepticism to participate imaginatively in the work being read. As you read, decide what ideas you must set aside to participate imaginatively in "The Devil and Daniel Webster."

CHARACTER, TALL TALE, AND HYPERBOLE. A **character** is a person who figures in the action of a literary work. A **tall tale** is a story, often lighthearted or humorous, that contains highly exaggerated, unrealistic elements. These highly exaggerated elements, used for rhetorical effect, are **hyperbole**.

Organizer

As you read, make a cluster chart in which you list the character traits of Daniel Webster that are exaggerated. One example has been done for you.

Exaggerations of Daniel Webster

trout jump into his pockets

Reader's JOURNAL

When have you made a choice that commanded a very high price from you at a later time?

Reader's resource

This story about a man who makes a bargain with the devil features real figures from American history, such as Daniel Webster, along with fictional characters. Stephen Vincent Benét first published this story in 1936 in *The Saturday Evening Post*. Like Daniel Webster, Benét was a fiercely patriotic man who believed that, though our nation and form of government were not perfect, they were the best that had been developed.

HISTORY CONNECTION. Daniel Webster (1782–1852), one of the greatest orators in the history of American politics, argued many cases before the Supreme Court and served as a member of Congress, senator, and United States secretary of state. In his youth, Webster took strong stands on states' rights but later became a staunch supporter of the Union, ending one speech with the often-quoted line, "Liberty *and* Union, now and forever, one and inseparable!" Many of Webster's pro-Union supporters, however, turned against him for supporting Henry Clay's Missouri Compromise and the Fugitive Slave Act.

About the AUTHOR

Stephen Vincent Benét (1898–1943), poet and novelist, was born in Bethlehem, Pennsylvania. His travels and an interest in history greatly affected his writing. Benét began writing at age fifteen and two years later published his first book of poetry. He continued to write poetry while a student at Yale. Later Benét received a Guggenheim Fellowship and went to Paris, where he finished a book-length narrative poem about the Civil War, *John Brown's Body* (1928), for which he won his first Pulitzer Prize. The poem tells the story of the early days of the Civil War. Benét's story "Sobbin Women" (1926) was made into the musical *Seven Brides for Seven Brothers*, and his story "The Devil and Daniel Webster" (1937) was made into an opera and a movie. In 1944, Benét was awarded a second Pulitzer Prize posthumously for his epic poem on the westward migration, *Western Star.*

Benét frequently mixed material from American history with fictional characters and stories from American folklore. He once said, "We have our own folk gods and giants and figures of earth in this country. It's always seemed to me . . . that legends and yarns and folktales are as much a part of the real history of a country as proclamations and provisos and constitutional amendments. . . ." "The Devil and Daniel Webster" was one of Benét's attempts at writing such a tall tale.

Eagle Cliff, Franconia Notch, New Hampshire, 1858. Jasper Cropsey. North Carolina Museum of Art, Raleigh.

Stephen Vincent Benét

The DEVIL & Daniel Webster

It's a story they tell in the border country, where Massachusetts joins Vermont and New Hampshire.

Yes, Dan'l Webster's dead—or, at least, they buried him. But every time there's a thunderstorm around Marshfield, they say you can hear his rolling voice in the hollows of the sky. And they say that if you go to his grave and speak loud and clear, "Dan'l Webster—Dan'l Webster!" the ground'll begin to shiver and the trees begin to shake. And after a while you'll hear a deep voice saying, "Neighbor, how stands the Union?" Then you better answer the Union stands as she stood, rock-bottomed and copper-sheathed, one and indivisible, or he's liable to rear right out of the ground. At least, that's what I was told when I was a youngster.

You see, for a while, he was the biggest man in the country. He never got to be President, but he was the biggest man.

Who was the biggest man in the country?

There were thousands that trusted in him right next to God Almighty, and they told stories about him and all the things that belonged to him that were the stories of patriarchs and such. They said, when he stood up to speak, stars and stripes came right out of the sky, and once he spoke against a river and made it sink into the ground. They said, when he walked the woods with his fishing rod, Killall, the trout would jump out of the streams right into his pockets, for they knew it was no use putting up a fight against him; and, when he argued a case, he could turn on the harps of the blessed and the shaking of the earth underground. That was the kind of man he was, and his big farm up at Marshfield was suitable to him. The chickens he raised were all white meat down through the drumsticks, the cows were tended like children, and the big ram he called Goliath had horns with a curl like a morning-glory vine and could butt through an iron door. But Dan'l wasn't one of your gentlemen farmers; he knew all the ways of the land, and he'd be up by candlelight to see that the chores got done. A man with a mouth like a mastiff, a brow like a mountain and eyes like burning anthracite[1]— that was Dan'l Webster in his prime. And the biggest case he argued never got written down in the books, for he argued it against the devil, nip and tuck and no holds barred. And this is the way I used to hear it told.

Against whom did Daniel Webster argue his biggest case?

There was a man named Jabez Stone, lived at Cross Corners, New Hampshire. He wasn't a bad man to start with, but he was an unlucky man. If he planted corn, he got borers; if he planted potatoes, he got blight. He had good-enough land, but it didn't prosper him; he

What kind of luck did Jabez Stone have? What sorts of things happened to him?

had a decent wife and children, but the more children he had, the less there was to feed them. If stones cropped up in his neighbor's field, boulders boiled up in his; if he had a horse with the spavins[2], he'd trade it for one with the staggers and give something extra. There's some folks bound to be like that, apparently. But one day Jabez Stone got sick of the whole business.

He'd been plowing that morning and he'd just broke the plowshare on a rock that he could have sworn hadn't been there yesterday. And, as he stood looking at the plowshare, the off horse began to cough—that ropy kind of cough that means sickness and horse doctors. There were two children down with the measles, his wife was ailing, and he had a whitlow[3] on his thumb. It

---

1. **anthracite.** Hard natural coal that burns cleanly
2. **spavins.** Disease that affects the hock joint of horses, making them swollen or stiff
3. **whitlow.** Painful abscess

was about the last straw for Jabez Stone. "I vow," he said, and he looked around him kind of desperate, "I vow it's enough to make a man want to sell his soul to the devil! And I would, too, for two cents!"

What vow does Jabez Stone make? How does he feel about his vow later?

Then he felt a kind of queerness come over him at having said what he'd said; though, naturally, being a New Hampshireman, he wouldn't take it back. But, all the same, when it got to be evening and, as far as he could see, no notice had been taken, he felt relieved in his mind, for he was a religious man. But notice is always taken, sooner or later, just like the Good Book says. And, sure enough, next day, about suppertime, a soft-spoken, dark-dressed stranger drove up in a handsome buggy and asked for Jabez Stone.

> "I vow it's enough to make a man want to sell his soul to the devil! And I would, too, for two cents!"

Well, Jabez told his family it was a lawyer, come to see him about a legacy. But he knew who it was. He didn't like the looks of the stranger, nor the way he smiled with his teeth. They were white teeth, and plentiful—some say they were filed to a point, but I wouldn't vouch for that. And he didn't like it when the dog took one look at the stranger and ran away howling, with his tail between his legs. But having passed the word, more or less, he stuck to it, and they went

With whom does Jabez Stone strike a bargain? What does he ask for?

out behind the barn and made their bargain. Jabez Stone had to prick his finger to sign, and the stranger lent him a silver pin. The wound healed clean, but it left a little white scar.

After that, all of a sudden, things began to pick up and prosper for Jabez Stone. His cows got fat and his horses sleek, his crops were the envy of the neighborhood, and lightning might strike all over the valley, but it wouldn't strike his barn. Pretty soon he was one of the prosperous people of the county; they asked him to stand for selectman, and he stood for it; there began to be talk of running him for state senate. All in all, you might say the Stone family was as happy and contented as cats in a dairy. And so they were, except for Jabez Stone.

He'd been contented enough the first few years. It's a great thing when bad luck turns; it drives most other things out of your head. True, every now and then, especially in rainy weather, the little white scar on his finger would give him a twinge. And once a year, punctual as clockwork, the stranger with the handsome buggy would come driving by. But the sixth year the stranger lighted, and, after that, his peace was over for Jabez Stone.

The stranger came up through the lower field, switching his boots with a cane—they were handsome black boots, but Jabez Stone never liked the look of them, particularly the toes. And, after he'd passed the time of day, he said, "Well, Mr. Stone, you're a hummer! It's a very pretty property you've got here, Mr. Stone."

"Well, some might favor it and others might not," said Jabez Stone, for he was a New Hampshireman.

"Oh, no need to decry your industry!" said the stranger, very easy, showing his teeth in a smile. "After all, we know what's been done, and it's been according to contract and specifications. So

words for everyday use

le • ga • cy (le´ge sē) n., gift by will, especially of money or other personal property. *Cheryl's legacy was a cabin her aunt had willed to her on Lake Calhoun.*

se • lect • man (si lek[t]´man) n., elected town official in New England. *The new selectman garnered 57 percent of the vote.*

de • cry (dī krī´) vt., express strong disapproval. *Mr. Ayscue decried his son's laziness and couldn't understand his behavior.*

Daniel Webster, c.1840.
James Reid Lamdin.
Library of Congress.

when—ahem—the mortgage falls due next year, you shouldn't have any regrets."

"Speaking of that mortgage, mister," said Jabez Stone, and he looked around for help to the earth and the sky, "I'm beginning to have one or two doubts about it."

"Doubts?" said the stranger not quite so pleasantly.

"Why, yes," said Jabez Stone. "This being the U.S.A. and me always having been a religious man." He cleared his throat and got bolder. "Yes, sir," he said, "I'm beginning to have considerable doubts as to that mortgage holding in court."

"There's courts and courts," said the stranger, clicking his teeth. "Still, we might as well have a look at the original document." And he hauled out a big black pocketbook, full of papers. "Sherwin, Slater, Stevens, Stone," he muttered. "'I, Jabez Stone, for a term of seven years—' Oh, it's quite in order, I think."

But Jabez Stone wasn't listening, for he saw something else flutter out of the black pocketbook. It was something that looked like a moth, but it wasn't a moth. And as Jabez Stone stared at it, it seemed to speak to him in a small sort of piping voice, terrible small and thin, but terrible human. "Neighbor Stone!" It squeaked. "Neighbor Stone! Help me! For God's sake, help me!"

But before Jabez Stone could stir hand or foot, the stranger whipped out a big bandanna handkerchief, caught the creature in it, just like a butterfly, and started tying up the ends of the bandanna.

"Sorry for the interruption," he said. "As I was saying—"

But Jabez Stone was shaking all over like a scared horse.

"That's Miser Stevens' voice!" he said in a croak. "And you've got him in your handkerchief!"

The stranger looked a little embarrassed.

> Whose voice does Jabez Stone hear when the stranger comes to visit?

"Yes, I really should have transferred him to the collecting box," he said with a simper, "but there were some rather unusual specimens there and I don't want them crowded. Well, well, these little contretemps[4] will occur."

"I don't know what you mean by contertan," said Jabez Stone, "but that was Miser Stevens' voice! And he ain't dead! You can't tell me he is! He was just as <u>spry</u> and mean as a woodchuck Tuesday!"

"In the midst of life . . ." said the stranger, kind of pious. "Listen!" Then a bell began to toll in the valley and Jabez Stone listened, with the sweat running down his face. For he knew it was tolled for Miser Stevens and that he was dead.

"These long-standing accounts," said the stranger with a sigh; "one really hates to close them. But business is business."

He still had the bandanna in his hand, and Jabez Stone felt sick as he saw the cloth struggle and flutter.

"Are they all as small as that?" he asked hoarsely.

"Small?" said the stranger. "Oh, I see what you mean. Why, they vary." He measured Jabez Stone with his eyes, and his teeth showed. "Don't worry, Mr. Stone," he said. "You'll go with a very good grade. I wouldn't trust you outside the collecting box. Now, a man like Dan'l

---

4. **contretemps** (kän′ trə tän). Awkward occurrences

Webster, of course—well, we'd have to build a special box for him, and even at that, I imagine the wing spread would astonish you. He'd certainly be a prize. I wish we could see our way clear to him. But, in your case, as I was saying—"

"Put that handkerchief away!" said Jabez Stone, and he began to beg and to pray. But the best he could get at the end was a three years' extension, with conditions.

But till you make a bargain like that, you've got no idea of how fast four years can run. By the last months of those years Jabez Stone's known all over the state and there's talk of running him for governor—and it's dust and ashes in his mouth. For every day, when he gets up, he thinks, "There's one more night gone," and every night, when he lies down, he thinks of the black pocketbook and the soul of Miser Stevens, and it makes him sick at heart. Till, finally, he can't bear it any longer, and, in the last days of the last year, he hitches up his horse and drives off to seek Dan'l Webster. For Dan'l was born in New Hampshire, only a few miles from Cross Corners, and it's well known that he has a particular soft spot for old neighbors.

It was early in the morning when he got to Marshfield, but Dan'l was up already, talking Latin to the farm hands and wrestling with the ram, Goliath, and trying out a new trotter and working up speeches to make against John C. Calhoun.[5] But when he heard a New Hampshireman had come to see him, he dropped everything else he was doing, for that was Dan'l's way. He gave Jabez Stone a breakfast that five men couldn't eat, went into the living history of every man and woman in Cross Corners, and finally asked him how he could serve him.

Jabez Stone allowed that it was a kind of mortgage case.

"Well, I haven't <u>pleaded</u> a mortgage case in a long time, and I don't generally plead now, except before the Supreme Court," said Dan'l, "but if I can, I'll help you."

"Then I've got hope for the first time in ten years," said Jabez Stone and told him the details.

Dan'l walked up and down as he listened, hands behind his back, now and then asking a question, now and then plunging his eyes at the floor, as if they'd bore through it like gimlets.[6] When Jabez Stone had finished, Dan'l puffed out his cheeks and blew. Then he turned to Jabez Stone and a smile broke over his face like the sunrise over Monadnock.[7]

"You've certainly given yourself the devil's own row to hoe, Neighbor Stone," he said, "but I'll take your case."

> What does Daniel Webster agree to do?

"You'll take it?" said Jabez Stone, hardly daring to believe.

"Yes," said Dan'l Webster. "I've got about seventy-five other things to do and the Missouri Compromise[8] to straighten out, but I'll take your case. For if two New Hampshiremen aren't a match for the devil, we might as well give the country back to the Indians."

Then he shook Jabez Stone by the hand and said, "Did you come down here in a hurry?"

"Well, I admit I made time," said Jabez Stone.

"You'll go back faster," said Dan'l Webster, and he told 'em to hitch up Constitution and Constellation to the carriage. They were

---

5. **John C. Calhoun.** Senator whose historic debate with Daniel Webster defined the opposing positions on the issues of states' rights and slavery
6. **gimlet.** Small hand tool for boring holes
7. **Monadnock.** Mountain in New Hampshire
8. **Missouri Compromise.** Bill passed in 1820 that allowed slavery in Missouri but not anywhere else west of the Mississippi

---

words for everyday use   plead (plēd) *vi.*, argue a case in a court of law. *The plaintiff announced to the media that Mr. Nelson would <u>plead</u> her case.*

matched grays with one white forefoot, and they stepped like greased lightning.

Well, I won't describe how excited and pleased the whole Stone family was to have the great Dan'l Webster for a guest, when they finally got there. Jabez Stone had lost his hat on the way, blown off when they overtook a wind, but he didn't take much account of that. But after supper he sent the family off to bed, for he had most particular business with Mr. Webster. Mrs. Stone wanted him to sit in the front parlor, but Dan'l Webster knew front parlors and said he preferred the kitchen. So it was there they sat, waiting for the stranger, with a jug on the table between them and a bright fire on the hearth— the stranger being scheduled to show up on the stroke of midnight, according to specification.

Well, most men wouldn't have asked for better company than Dan'l Webster and a jug. But with every tick of the clock Jabez Stone got sadder and sadder. His eyes roved round, and though he sampled the jug you could see he couldn't taste it. Finally, on the stroke of 11:30 he reached over and grabbed Dan'l Webster by the arm.

"Mr. Webster, Mr. Webster!" he said, and his voice was shaking with fear and a desperate courage. "For God's sake, Mr. Webster, harness your horses and get away from this place while you can!"

"You've brought me a long way, neighbor, to tell me you don't like my company," said Dan'l Webster, quite peaceable, pulling at the jug.

"Miserable wretch that I am!" groaned Jabez Stone. "I've brought you a devilish way, and now I see my folly. Let him take me if he wills. I don't hanker after it, I must say, but I can stand it. But you're the Union's stay and New Hampshire's pride! He mustn't get you, Mr. Webster! He mustn't get you!"

Dan'l Webster looked at the distracted man, all gray and shaking in the firelight, and laid a hand on his shoulder.

"I'm obliged to you, Neighbor Stone," he said gently. "It's kindly thought of. But there's a jug on the table and a case in hand. And I never left a jug or a case half finished in my life."

And just at that moment there was a sharp rap on the door.

"Ah," said Dan'l Webster very coolly, "I thought your clock was a trifle slow, Neighbor Stone." He stepped to the door and opened it. "Come in!" he said.

The stranger came in—very dark and tall he looked in the firelight. He was carrying a box under his arm—a black japanned[9] box with little air holes in the lid. At the sight of the box Jabez Stone gave a low cry and shrank into a corner of the room.

"Mr. Webster, I presume," said the stranger, very polite, but with his eyes glowing like a fox's deep in the woods.

"Attorney of record for Jabez Stone," said Dan'l Webster, but his eyes were glowing too. "Might I ask your name?"

"I've gone by a good many," said the stranger carelessly. "Perhaps Scratch will do for the evening. I'm often called that in these regions."

Then he sat down at the table and poured himself a drink from the jug. The liquor was cold in the jug, but it came steaming into the glass.

"And now," said the stranger, smiling and showing his teeth, "I shall call upon you, as a law-abiding citizen, to assist me in taking possession of my property."

Well, with that the argument began—and it went hot and heavy. At first Jabez Stone had a flicker of hope, but when he saw Dan'l Webster being forced back at point after point, he just sat scrunched in his corner, with his eyes on that japanned box. For there wasn't any doubt as to the deed or the signature—that was the worst of it. Dan'l Webster twisted and turned and thumped his fist on the table, but he couldn't get away from that. He offered to compromise the case; the stranger wouldn't hear of it.

Who is losing the argument at this point?

---

9. **japanned.** Covered with a black, glossy enamel

He pointed out the property had increased in value, and state senators ought to be worth more; the stranger stuck to the letter of the law. He was a great lawyer, Dan'l Webster, but we know who's the King of Lawyers, as the Good Book tells us, and it seemed as if, for the first time, Dan'l Webster had met his match.

Finally, the stranger yawned a little. "Your spirited efforts on behalf of your client do you credit, Mr. Webster," he said, "but if you have no more arguments to adduce,[10] I'm rather pressed for time . . ." and Jabez Stone shuddered.

Dan'l Webster's brow looked dark as a thundercloud.

"Pressed or not, you shall not have this man!" he thundered. "Mr. Stone is an American citizen, and no American citizen may be forced into the service of a foreign prince. We fought England for that in '12 and we'll fight all hell for it again!"

"Foreign?" said the stranger. "And who calls me a foreigner?"

"Well, I never yet heard of the dev— of your claiming American citizenship," said Dan'l Webster with surprise.

"And who with better right?" said the stranger with one of his terrible smiles. "When the first wrong was done to the first Indian, I was there. When the first slaver put out for the Congo, I stood on her deck. Am I not in your books and stories and beliefs, from the first settlements on? Am I not spoken of still in every church in New England? 'Tis true the North claims me for a Southerner and the South for a Northerner, but I am neither. I am merely an honest American like yourself—and of the best descent—for, to tell the truth, Mr. Webster, though I don't like to boast of it, my name is older in this country than yours."

"Aha!" said Dan'l Webster with the veins standing out in his forehead. "Then I stand on the Constitution! I demand a trial for my client!"

"The case is hardly one for an ordinary court," said the stranger, his eyes flickering. "And, indeed, the lateness of the hour—"

"Let it be any court you choose, so it is an American judge and an American jury!" said Dan'l Webster in his pride. "Let it be the quick[11] or the dead; I'll abide the issue!"

> What does Daniel Webster demand for his client?

"You have said it," said the stranger, and pointed his finger at the door. And with that, and all of a sudden, there was a rushing of wind outside and a noise of footsteps. They came, clear and distinct, through the night. And yet they were not like the footsteps of living men.

"In God's name, who comes by so late?" cried Jabez Stone in an ague[12] of fear.

"The jury Mr. Webster demands," said the stranger, sipping at his boiling glass. "You must pardon the rough appearance of one or two; they will have come a long way."

And with that the fire burned blue and the door blew open and twelve men entered, one by one.

If Jabez Stone had been sick with terror before, he was blind with terror now. For there was Walter Butler, the loyalist, who spread fire and horror through the Mohawk Valley in the times of the Revolution; and there was Simon Girty, the renegade, who saw white men burned

> **A**nd yet they were not like the footsteps of living men.

---

10. **adduce.** To cite as an example, proving a point in an argument
11. **quick.** Living
12. **ague.** Fever

at the stake and whooped with the Indians to see them burn. His eyes were green, like a catamount's,[13] and the stains on his hunting shirt did not come from the blood of the deer. King Philip was there, wild and proud as he had been in life, with the great gash in his head that gave him his death wound, and cruel Governor Dale, who broke men on the wheel. There was Morton of Merry Mount, who so <u>vexed</u> the Plymouth Colony, with his flushed, loose, handsome face and his hate of the godly. There was Teach,[14] the bloody pirate, with his black beard curling on his breast. The Reverend John Smeet, with his strangler's hands and his Geneva gown, walked as daintily as he had to the gallows. The red print of the rope was still around his neck, but he carried a perfumed handkerchief in one hand. One and all, they came into the room with the fires of hell still upon them, and the stranger named their names and their deeds as they came, till the tale of twelve was told. Yet the stranger had told the truth—they had all played a part in America.

When the jury enters the room, what is still upon them?

"Are you satisfied with the jury, Mr. Webster?" said the stranger mockingly, when they had taken their places.

The sweat stood upon Dan'l Webster's brow, but his voice was clear.

"Quite satisfied," he said. "Though I miss General Arnold[15] from the company."

"Benedict Arnold is engaged upon other business," said the stranger with a glower. "Ah, you asked for a justice, I believe."

He pointed his finger once more, and a tall man, soberly clad in Puritan garb, with the burning gaze of the fanatic, stalked into the room and took his judge's place.

"Justice Hathorne is a jurist of experience," said the stranger. "He presided at certain witch trials once held in Salem. There were others who repented of the business later, but not he."

"Repent of such notable wonders and undertakings?" said the stern old justice. "Nay, hang them—hang them all!" And he muttered to himself in a way that struck ice into the soul of Jabez Stone.

Then the trial began, and, as you might expect, it didn't look anyways good for the defense. And Jabez Stone didn't make much of a witness in his own behalf. He took one look at Simon Girty and screeched, and they had to put him back in his corner in a kind of swoon.

It didn't halt the trial though; the trial went on, as trials do. Dan'l Webster had faced some hard juries and hanging judges in his time, but this was the hardest he'd ever faced, and he knew it. They sat there with a kind of glitter in their eyes, and the stranger's smooth voice went on and on. Every time he'd raise an objection, it'd be "Objection sustained," but whenever Dan'l objected, it'd be "Objection denied." Well, you couldn't expect fair play from a fellow like this Mr. Scratch.

What happens to each of Daniel Webster's objections?

It got to Dan'l in the end, and he began to heat, like iron in the forge. When he got up to speak he was going to flay[16] that stranger with every trick known to the law, and the judge and jury too. He didn't care if it was contempt of court or what would happen to him for it. He didn't care any more what happened to Jabez

---

13. **catamount.** Large, wild cat
14. **Teach.** Edward Teach, also known as Blackbeard, a notorious pirate of the Atlantic Seabord
15. **General Arnold.** Benedict Arnold, notorious American traitor during the Revolutionary War
16. **flay.** To lash, as with a whip

words for everyday use

vex (veks) *vt.*, bring trouble, distress, or agitation. *The protesters outside the grocery store <u>vexed</u> the customers.*

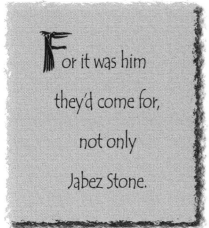

For it was him they'd come for, not only Jabez Stone.

Stone. He just got madder and madder, thinking of what he'd say. And yet, curiously enough, the more he thought about it, the less he was able to arrange his speech in his mind.

Till, finally, it was time for him to get up on his feet, and he did so, all ready to bust out with lightnings and denunciations. But before he started he looked over the judge and jury for a moment, such being his custom. And he noticed the glitter in their eyes was twice as strong as before, and they all leaned forward. Like hounds just before they get the fox, they looked, and the blue mist of evil in the room thickened as he watched them. Then he saw what he'd been about to do, and he wiped his forehead, as a man might who's just escaped falling into a pit in the dark.

For it was him they'd come for, not only Jabez Stone. He read it in the glitter of their eyes and in the way the stranger hid his mouth with one hand. And if he fought them with their own weapons, he'd fall into their power; he knew that, though he couldn't have told you how. It was his own anger and horror that burned in their eyes; and he'd have to wipe that out or the case was lost. He stood there for a moment, his black eyes burning like anthracite. And then he began to speak.

He started off in a low voice, though you could hear every word. They say he could call on the harps of the blessed when he chose. And this was just as simple and easy as a man could talk. But he didn't start out by condemning or <u>reviling</u>. He was talking about the things that make a country a country and a man a man.

What does Daniel Webster talk about?

And he began with the simple things that everybody's known and felt— the freshness of a fine morning when you're young, and the taste of food when you're hungry, and the new day that's every day when you're a child. He took them up and he turned them in his hands. They were good things for any man. But without freedom they sickened. And when he talked of those enslaved, and the sorrows of slavery, his voice got like a big bell. He talked of the early days of America and the men who had made those days. It wasn't a spread-eagle speech, but he made you see it. He admitted all the wrong that had ever been done. But he showed how, out of the wrong and the right, the suffering and the starvations, something new had come. And everybody had played a part in it, even the traitors.

Then he turned to Jabez Stone and showed him as he was—an ordinary man who'd had hard luck and wanted to change it. And, because he'd wanted to change it, now he was going to be punished for all eternity. And yet there was good in Jabez Stone, and he showed that good. He was hard and mean, in some ways, but he was a man. There was sadness in being a man, but it was a proud thing too. And he showed what the pride of it was till you couldn't help feeling it. Yes, even in hell, if a man was a man, you'd know it. And he wasn't pleading for any one person any more, though his voice rang like an organ. He was telling the story and the failures and the endless journey of mankind. They got tricked and trapped and bamboozled, but it was a great journey. And no demon that was ever foaled could know the inwardness of it—it took a man to do that.

words for everyday use

re • vile (ri vīl´) vt., subject to verbal abuse. *The deacon <u>reviled</u> the boy responsible for stealing from the collection box.*

The fire began to die on the hearth and the wind before morning to blow. The light was getting gray in the room when Dan'l Webster finished. And his words came back at the end to New Hampshire ground, and the one spot of land that each man loves and clings to. He painted a picture of that, and to each one of that jury he spoke of things long forgotten. For his voice could search the heart, and that was his gift and his strength. And to one his voice was like the forest and its secrecy, and to another like the sea and the storms of the sea; and one heard the cry of his lost nation in it, and another saw a little harmless scene he hadn't remembered for years. But each saw something. And when Dan'l Webster finished he didn't know whether or not he'd saved Jabez Stone. But he knew he'd done a miracle. For the glitter was gone from the eyes of judge and jury, and, for the moment, they were men again, and knew they were men.

How does Daniel Webster know he's had an impact on the judge and jury?

"The defense rests," said Dan'l Webster and stood there like a mountain. His ears were still ringing with his speech, and he didn't hear anything else till he heard Judge Hathorne say, "The jury will retire to consider its verdict."

Walter Butler rose in his place and his face had a dark, gay pride on it.

"The jury has considered its verdict," he said and looked the stranger full in the eye. "We find for the defendant, Jabez Stone."

Who wins the case?

With that, the smile left the stranger's face, but Walter Butler did not flinch.

"Perhaps 'tis not strictly in accordance with the evidence," he said, "but even the damned may salute the eloquence of Mr. Webster."

With that, the long crow of a rooster split the gray morning sky, and judge and jury were gone from the room like a puff of smoke and as if they had never been there. The stranger returned to Dan'l Webster, smiling <u>wryly</u>.

"Major Butler was always a bold man," he said. "I had not thought him quite so bold. Nevertheless, my congratulations, as between two gentlemen."

"I'll have that paper first, if you please," said Dan'l Webster, and he took it and tore it into four pieces. It was queerly warm to the touch. "And now," he said, "I'll have you!" and his hand came down like a bear trap on the stranger's arm. For he knew that once you bested anybody like Mr. Scratch in fair fight, his power on you was gone. And he could see that Mr. Scratch knew it too.

The stranger twisted and wriggled, but he couldn't get out of that grip. "Come, come, Mr. Webster," he said, smiling palely. "This sort of thing is ridic—ouch!—is ridiculous. If you're worried about the costs of the case, naturally, I'd be glad to pay—"

"And so you shall!" said Dan'l Webster, shaking him till his teeth rattled. "For you'll sit right down at that table and draw up a document, promising never to bother Jabez Stone nor his heirs or assigns[17] nor any other New Hampshireman till doomsday! For any hades[18] we want to raise in this state, we can raise ourselves, without assistance from strangers."

What does Daniel Webster demand from the devil?

"Ouch!" said the stranger. "Ouch! Well, they never did run very big to the barrel, but—ouch!—I agree!"

So he sat down and drew up the document. But Dan'l Webster kept his hand on his coat collar all the time.

"And now may I go?" said the stranger, quite humble, when Dan'l'd seen the document's in

---

17. **assign.** Person to whom property is transferred
18. **hades.** Underground in Greek mythology

words for everyday use

wry • ly (rī ́ lē) *adv.,* bitterly or disdainfully ironic. *Asked if he could parachute, James Bond smiled <u>wryly</u>.*

proper and legal form.

"Go?" said Dan'l, giving him another shake. "I'm still trying to figure out what I'll do with you. For you've settled the costs of the case, but you haven't settled with me. I think I'll take you back to Marshfield," he said, kind of reflective. "I've got a ram there named Goliath that can butt through an iron door. I'd kind of like to turn you loose in his field and see what he'd do."

Well, with that the stranger began to beg and to plead. And he begged and he pled so humble that finally Dan'l, who was naturally kindhearted, agreed to let him go. The stranger seemed terrible grateful for that and said, just to show they were friends, he'd tell Dan'l's fortune before leaving. So Dan'l agreed to that, though he didn't take much stock in fortunetellers ordinarily. But, naturally, the stranger was a little different.

Well, he pried and he peered at the lines in Dan'l's hands. And he told him one thing and another that was quite remarkable. But they were all in the past.

"Yes, all that's true, and it happened," said Dan'l Webster. "But what's to come in the future?"

The stranger grinned, kind of happily, and shook his head.

"The future's not as you think it," he said. "It's dark. You have a great ambition, Mr. Webster."

"I have," said Dan'l firmly, for everybody knew he wanted to be President.

"It seems almost within your grasp," said the stranger, "but you will not attain it. Lesser men will be made President and you will be passed over."

"And, if I am, I'll still be Daniel Webster," said Dan'l. "Say on."

"You have two strong sons," said the stranger, shaking his head. "You look to found a line. But each will die in war and neither reach greatness."

"Live or die, they are still my sons," said Dan'l Webster. "Say on."

"You have made great speeches," said the stranger. "You will make more."

"The future's not as you think it," he said. "It's dark."

"Ah," said Dan'l Webster.

"But the last great speech you make will turn many of your own against you," said the stranger. "They will call you Ichabod; they will call you by other names. Even in New England some will say you have turned your coat and sold your country, and their voices will be loud against you till you die."

"So it is an honest speech, it does not matter what men say," said Dan'l Webster. Then he looked at the stranger and their glances locked.

"One question," he said. "I have fought for the Union all my life. Will I see that fight won against those who would tear it apart?"

"Not while you live," said the stranger grimly, "but it will be won. And after you are dead, there are thousands who will fight for your cause, because of words that you spoke."

"Why, then, you long-barreled, slab-sided, lantern-jawed, fortune-telling note shaver," said Dan'l Webster with a great roar of laughter, "be off with you to your own place before I put my mark on you! For, by the thirteen original colonies, I'd go to the Pit itself to save the Union!"

And with that he drew back his foot for a kick that would have stunned a horse. It was only the tip of his shoe that caught the stranger, but he went flying out of the door with his collecting box under his arm.

"And now," said Dan'l Webster, seeing Jabez Stone beginning to rouse from his swoon, "let's see what's left in the jug, for it's dry work talking all night. I hope there's pie for breakfast, Neighbor Stone."

But they say that whenever the devil comes near Marshfield, even now, he gives it a wide berth. And he hasn't been seen in the state of New Hampshire from that day to this.

I'm not talking about Massachusetts or Vermont. ∎

> *What does the devil predict for Daniel Webster when he reads his fortune?*

If you were Jabez Stone, how would you live your life after the trial?

Investigate, Inquire, and Imagine

Recall: GATHERING FACTS

1a. What do the people in the tri-state area say about Daniel Webster after he died?

2a. Which clues indicate the real identity of the stranger? Who is he?

3a. What does Daniel Webster want to know most about the future?

Interpret: FINDING MEANING

1b. Why does the narrator describe the influence Daniel Webster had after death?

2b. How does Daniel Webster win his case against Scratch?

3b. What does the manner in which Daniel Webster accepts bad news about his future reveal about his character?

Analyze: TAKING THINGS APART

4a. How does Daniel Webster organize his speech to save Jabez Stone?

Synthesize: BRINGING THINGS TOGETHER

4b. Why does Daniel Webster win the case?

Evaluate: MAKING JUDGMENTS

5a. If you were a member of the jury, would you find for or against Jabez Stone? Why?

Extend: CONNECTING IDEAS

5b. Do you believe that people in contemporary society sometimes sell their souls? If so, what are they choosing over moral, religious, or patriotic values?

Understanding Literature

SUSPENSION OF DISBELIEF. Review the definition of **suspension of disbelief** in the Handbook of Literary Terms. What beliefs does the author ask you to suspend in order to appreciate and understand his story? What unrealistic events in the story were you able to believe?

CHARACTER, TALL TALE, AND HYPERBOLE. Review the definitions for **character**, **tall tale**, and **hyperbole** in the Handbook of Literary Tools. Then review the cluster chart you made for Literary Tools on page 252. What exaggerations about Daniel Webster's character does the narrator make? What purpose does this exaggeration serve? What comment does Stephen Vincent Benét make about the United States with his depiction of Daniel Webster? Looking at your graphic organizer, which example of hyperbole at the beginning of the story prepares the reader for Daniel Webster's winning his case against the devil?

Writer's Journal

1. Imagine that you are Jabez Stone the morning after the trial. Write a **thank-you note** to Daniel Webster for his help in saving your soul.

2. Scratch selected the jury, and the narrator described seven of these men. Imagine that Daniel Webster had been able to choose whom he wanted for jurors. Write a **paragraph** naming four jurors that Webster would have chosen. Be sure to explain why Webster would have chosen these people.

3. Imagine that you are Scratch. Write the **contract** between you and Jabez Stone, spelling out the things each of you agree to do in exchange for the other's commitment.

Integrating the Language Arts

Language, Grammar, and Style

CLAUSES AND COMPOUND SENTENCES. A clause is a group of words that has a subject and a verb; it may have completers as well. A sentence with only one clause is called a **simple sentence.** A **compound sentence** is formed by two or more clauses 1) connected by a semicolon, *or* 2) a coordinating conjunction + a comma. For a list of coordinating conjunctions see the Language Arts Survey 3.70, "Coordinating Conjunctions." For each of the sentences below, underline the simple subject(s) once, and the verb(s) twice.

1. Daniel Webster was a great orator; he outargued the devil.
2. Jabez Stone wanted better things, so he made a devilish bargain.
3. The devil came for him; Stone was afraid.
4. Stone contacted Daniel Webster; Webster would always help a neighbor.
5. Webster knew the right arguments, and he appealed to men, not devils.

Study and Research

COMPARISON-CONTRAST COMPOSITION. The theme of selling one's soul to the devil is common in Western civilization. Perhaps the most famous is the Faust legend in English and German literature, written by Christopher Marlowe in 1590, by Johann von Goethe in 1808, and by Thomas Mann in 1947. The American writer Washington Irving wrote "The Devil and Tom Walker" in 1800. More modern treatments of this theme include the film *Damn Yankees* and the Charlie Daniels band's song "The Devil Went Down to Georgia." Research one of these versions of the "pact with the devil" theme. Then write a comparison-contrast composition, discussing similarities and differences with "The Devil and Daniel Webster." Before you begin writing, you might want to review the order of comparison and contrast in the Language Arts Survey 2.27, "Choosing a Method of Organization."

Applied English & Study and Research

RÉSUMÉ. Research the life of Daniel Webster in order to write his résumé in the year he sought the presidency. Before you begin writing, you might want to review the résumé in the Language Arts Survey 6.8, "Writing a Résumé."

Literary T O O L S

METAPHOR. A **metaphor** is a figure of speech in which one thing is spoken or written about as if it were another. As you read, find the metaphor comparing hands on page 268 and decide what characteristic hands and the other subject of the comparison have in common.

THEME. A **theme** is a central idea in a literary work.

Organizer

As you read the selection, fill in the cluster chart below with the emotions Gwilan feels throughout the story. One example has been done for you.

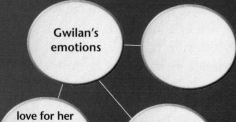

Gwilan's emotions

love for her harp was greater than love for herself

Reader's Journal

What activity are you involved in that is important to your identity?

"Gwilan's Harp"
by Ursula K. Le Guin

Reader's r e s o u r c e

"**Gwilan's Harp**" is a short story, but it contains many elements of **fables**, **fairy tales**, and **folk tales**. Like a fable, which is often told to express a moral, this story teaches a lesson. The setting of the story suggests the medieval setting of a fairy tale. Like a folk tale, a story passed from one generation to another in the oral tradition, this story tells of characters in a preliterate culture, one that transmits tales and legends through oral poets and singers rather than the written word.

MUSIC CONNECTION. The harp is a stringed musical instrument of ancient origin. The existence of the harp is recorded in paintings that date from the thirteenth century BC. In different forms it was played by peoples of nearly all lands throughout the ages.

About *the* A U T H O R

Ursula K. Le Guin (1929–) was born in Berkeley, California, and grew up in a stimulating home filled with books and visits from scientists and writers. Her father was an anthropologist and her mother a writer. "My father studied real cultures and I make them up—in a way, it's the same thing," says Le Guin. After receiving her bachelor's degree from Radcliffe College and her master's degree from Columbia University, she went to Paris on a Fulbright scholarship. Returning to the United States to live in Oregon, Le Guin began her prolific writing career, producing such diverse work as fantasy, science fiction, and realistic or mainstream fiction. Speaking of the importance of her types of fiction, Le Guin has said, "We are trained not to use our imaginations. And that's where I think science fiction, or speculative fiction, is really an important branch of literature. It shows us to think through dreadful results. It also, much more important to me, allows us to think of alternatives."

Le Guin is best known for her four novels, beginning with *A Wizard of Earthsea* (1968) and ending with *Tehanu* (1990), that are set in the imaginary land of Earthsea. Her futuristic novel *Always Coming Home* (1985) includes both poetry and prose, and is accompanied with a tape of music. Among her awards, the author has received five Hugo awards, five Nebulas, a Pushcart Prize, a National Book Award, and a Newbery Silver Medal.

Gwilan's Harp

Ursula K. Le Guin

The harp had come to Gwilan from her mother, and so had her mastery of it, people said. "Ah, they said when Gwilan played, "you can tell, that's Diera's touch," just as their parents had said when Diera played, "Ah, that's the true Penlin touch!" Gwilan's mother had had the harp from Penlin, a musician's dying gift to the worthiest of pupils. From a musician's hands Penlin too had received it: never had it been sold or <u>bartered</u> for, nor any value put upon it that can be said in numbers. A princely and most incredible instrument it was for a poor harper to own. The shape of it was perfection, and every part was strong and fine: the wood as hard and smooth as bronze, the fittings of ivory and silver. The grand curves of the frame bore silver mountings chased with long <u>intertwining</u> lines that became waves and the waves became leaves, and the eyes of gods and stags looked out from among the leaves that became waves and the waves became lines again. It was the work of great craftsmen, you could see that at a glance, and the longer you looked the clearer you saw it. But all this

How does Gwilan acquire the harp and her talent for playing it?

beauty was practical, obedient, shaped to the service of sound. The sound of Gwilan's harp was water running and rain and sunlight on the water, waves breaking and the foam on the brown sands, forests, the leaves and branches of the forest and the shining eyes of gods and stags among the leaves when the wind blows in the valleys. It was all that and none of that. When Gwilan played, the harp made music; and what is music but a little wrinkling of the air?

Play she did, wherever they wanted her. Her singing voice was true but had no sweetness, so when it was songs and ballads she accompanied the singers. Weak voices were borne up by her playing, fine voices gained a glory from it; the loudest, proudest singers might keep still a verse to hear her play alone. She played with flute and reed-flute and tambour,[1] and the music made for the harp to play alone, and the music that

---

1. **tambour.** Small drum

---

sprang up of itself when her fingers touched the strings. At weddings and festivals it was, "Gwilan will be here to play," and at music-day competitions, "When will Gwilan play?"

She was young; her hands were iron and her touch was silk; she could play all night and the next day too. She travelled from valley to valley, from town to town, stopping here and staying there and moving on again with other musicians on their wanderings. They walked, or a wagon was sent for them, or they got a lift on a farmer's cart. However they went, Gwilan carried her harp in its silk and leather case at her back or in her hands. When she rode she rode with the harp and when she walked she walked with the harp, and when she slept, no, she didn't sleep with the harp, but it was there where she could reach out and touch it. She was not jealous of it, and would change instruments with another harper gladly; it was a great pleasure to her when at last they gave her back her own, saying with <u>sober</u> envy, "I never played so fine an instrument." She kept it clean, the mountings[2] polished, and strung it with the harpstrings made by old Uliad, which cost as much apiece as a whole set of common harpstrings. In the heat of summer she carried it in the shade of her body, in the bitter winter it shared her cloak. In a firelit hall she did not sit with it very near the fire, nor yet too far away, for changes of heat and cold would change the voice of it, and perhaps harm the frame. She did not look after herself with half the care. Indeed she saw no need to. She knew there were other harpers, and

Harp Player, c.1109–1400. Spanish artist. San Vincente, Avila, Spain.

would be other harpers; most not as good, some better. But the harp was the best. There had not been and there would not be a better. Delight and service were due and fitting to it. She was

---

2. **mountings.** Knobs that hold the harp's strings

words for everyday use

so • ber (sō´bər) *adj.*, serious, solemn. *With a <u>sober</u> look, Jorge told me he was worried about his grandmother's health.*

not its owner but its player. It was her music, her joy, her life, the noble instrument.

What does the harp mean to Gwilan?

She was young; she travelled from town to town; she played *A Fine Long Life* at weddings, and *The Green Leaves* at festivals. There were funerals, with the burial feast, the singing of elegies,[3] and Gwilan to play *The Lament of Orioth*, the music that crashes and cries out like the sea and the seabirds, bringing relief and a burst of tears to the grief-dried heart. There were music-days, with a rivalry of harpers and a shrilling of fiddlers and a mighty outshouting of tenors. She went from town to town in sun and rain, the harp on her back or in her hands. So she was going one day to the yearly musicday at Comin, and the landowner of Torm Vale was giving her a lift, a man who so loved music that he had traded a good cow for a bad horse, since the cow would not take him where he could hear music played. It was he and Gwilan in a rickety cart, and the lean-necked roan stepping out down the steep, sunlit road from Torm.

A bear in the forest by the road, or a bear's ghost, or the shadow of a hawk: the horse shied half across the road. Torm had been discussing music deeply with Gwilan, waving his hands to conduct a choir of voices, and the reins went flipping out of those startled hands. The horse jumped like a cat, and ran. At the sharp curve of the road the cart swung round and smashed against the rocky cutting. A wheel leapt free and rolled, rocking like a top, for a few yards. The roan went plunging and sliding down the road with half the wrecked cart dragging behind, and was gone, and the road lay silent in the sunlight between the forest trees.

What happens to Torm and Gwilan as they travel?

Torm had been thrown from the cart, and lay stunned for a minute or two.

Gwilan had clutched the harp to her when the horse shied, but had lost hold of it in the smash. The cart had tipped over and dragged on it. It was in its case of leather and embroidered silk, but when, one-handed, she got the case out from under the wheel and opened it, she did not take out a harp, but a piece of wood, and another piece, and a tangle of strings, and a sliver of ivory, and a twisted shell of silver chased with lines and leaves and eyes, held by a silver nail to a fragment of the frame.

What happened to Gwilan's harp?

It was six months without playing after that, since her arm had broken at the wrist. The wrist healed well enough, but there was no mending the harp; and by then the landowner of Torm had asked her if she would marry him, and she had said yes. Sometimes she wondered why she had said yes, having never thought much of marriage before, but if she looked steadily into her own mind she saw the reason why.

She saw Torm on the road in the sunlight kneeling by the broken harp, his face all blood and dust, and he was weeping. When she looked at that she saw that the time for rambling and roving was over and gone. One day is the day for moving on, and overnight, the next day, there is no more good in moving on, because you have come where you were going to.

> *It was her music, her joy, her life, the noble instrument.*

---

3. **elegy.** Song expressing sorrow for the dead

words for everyday use

la • ment (lə ment´) *n.*, song of mourning. *The sorrowful lament followed the hearse through the Spanish streets.*
ri • val • ry (rī´vəl rē) *n.*, competition. *Angela hoped the rivalry over becoming captain of the soccer team would not ruin her friendship with Jane.*
ten • or (ten´ər) *n.*, singer with voice range one octave above and one octave below middle C. *Mark is a baritone, while Luigi is a tenor.*
roan (rōn) *n.*, solid-colored horse with a sprinkling of white hair. *Although the Arabian was beautiful, Marla's favorite horse in the stable was the roan.*
plunge (plunj) *vi.*, move rapidly downward. *Don't you wonder where paragliders find the courage to plunge over cliffs?*

Gwilan brought to the marriage a gold piece, which had been the prize last year at Four Valleys music-day; she had sewn it to her bodice as a brooch, because where on earth could you spend a gold piece. She also had two silver pieces, five coppers, and a good winter cloak. Torm contributed house and household, fields and forests, four tenant farmers even poorer than himself, twenty hens, five cows, and forty sheep.

What do Gwilan and Torm each contribute to the marriage?

They married in the old way, by themselves, over the spring where the stream began, and came back and told the household. Torm had never suggested a wedding, with singing and harp-playing, never a word of all that. He was a man you could trust, Torm was.

What began in pain, in tears, was never free from the fear of pain. The two of them were gentle to each other. Not that they lived together thirty years without some quarreling. Two rocks sitting side by side would get sick of each other in thirty years, and who knows what they say now and then when nobody is listening. But if people trust each other they can grumble, and a good bit of grumbling takes the fuel from <u>wrath</u>. Their quarrels went up and burnt out like bits of paper, leaving nothing but a feather of ash, a laugh in bed in the dark. Torm's land never gave more than enough, and there was no money saved. But it was a good house, and the sunlight was sweet on those high stony fields. There were two sons, who grew up into cheerful sensible men. One had a taste for roving, and the other was a farmer born; but neither had any gift of music.

Gwilan never spoke of wanting another harp. But about the time her wrist was healed, old Uliad had a traveling musician bring her one on loan; when he had an offer to buy it at its worth he sent for it back

What made it possible for Gwilan to start playing the harp again?

again. At that time Torm would have it that there was money from selling three good heifers[4] to the landowner of Comin High Farm, and the money should buy a harp, which it did. A year or two later an old friend, a flute player still on his travels and rambles, brought her a harp from the south as a present. The three-heifers harp was a common instrument, plain and heavy; the Southern harp was delicately carved and gilt, but cranky to tune and thin of voice. Gwilan could draw sweetness from the one and strength from the other. When she picked up a harp, or spoke to a child, it obeyed her.

She played at all festivities and funerals in the neighborhood, and with the musician's fees she bought good strings; not Uliad's strings, though, for Uliad was in his grave before her second child was born. If there was a music-day nearby she went to it with Torm. She would not play in the competitions, not for fear of losing but because she was not a harper now, and if they did not know it, she did. So they had her judge the competitions, which she did well and mercilessly. Often in the early years musicians would stop by on their travels, and stay two or three nights at Torm; with them she would play the Hunts of Orioth, the Dances of Cail, the difficult and learned music of the North, and learn from them the new songs. Even in winter evenings there was music in the house of Torm: she played the harp—usually the three-heifers one, sometimes the fretful Southerner—and Torm's good tenor voice, and the boys singing, first a sweet treble, later on in husky unreliable baritone;[5] and one of the farm's men was a lively fiddler; and the shepherd Keth, when he was there, played on the pipes, though he never could tune them to anyone

---

4. **heifers.** Young cows
5. **baritone.** Male singing voice lower than a tenor but higher than a bass

---

words for everyday use   **wrath** (rath) *n.,* anger. *Oona's failure to return before curfew inspired the <u>wrath</u> of her parents.*

else's note. "It's our own music-day tonight," Gwilan would say. "Put another log on the fire, Torm, and sing *The Green Leaves* with me, and the boys will take the descant."[6]

Her wrist that had been broken grew a little stiff as the years went on; then the arthritis came into her hands. The work she did in house and farm was not easy work. But then who, looking at a hand, would say it was made to do easy work? You can see from the look of it that it is meant to do difficult things, that it is the noble, willing servant of the heart and mind. But the best servants get clumsy as the years go on. Gwilan could still play the harp, but not as well as she had played, and she did not much like half-measures. So the two harps hung on the wall, though she kept them tuned. About that time the younger son went wandering off to see what things looked like in the north, and the elder married and brought his bride to Torm. Old Keth was found dead up on the mountain in the spring rain, his dog crouched silent by him and the sheep nearby. And the drouth[7] came, and the good year, and the poor year, and there was food to eat and to be cooked and clothes to wear and to be washed, poor year or good year. In the depth of a winter Torm took ill. He went from a cough to a high fever to quietness, and died while Gwilan sat beside him.

Thirty years, how can you say how long that is, and yet no longer than the saying of it: thirty years. How can you say how heavy the weight of thirty years is, and yet you can hold all of them together in your hand lighter than a bit of ash, briefer than a laugh in the dark. The thirty years began in pain; they passed in peace, contentment. But they did not end there. They ended where they began.

> *Why does Gwilan have to stop playing again?*

> "I thought my harp was myself. But it was not. It was destroyed, I was not."

Gwilan got up from her chair and went into the hearthroom. The rest of the household were asleep. In the light of her candle she saw the two harps hung against the wall, the three-heifers harp and the gilded Southern harp, the dull music and the false music. She thought, "I'll take them down at last and smash them on the hearthstone, crush them till they're only bits of wood and tangles of wire, like my harp." But she did not. She could not play them at all any more, her hands were far too stiff. It is silly to smash an instrument you cannot even play.

"There is no instrument left that I can play," Gwilan thought, and the thought hung in her mind for a while like a long chord, until she knew the notes that made it. "I thought my harp was myself. But it was not. It was destroyed, I was not. I thought Torm's wife was myself, but she was not. He is dead, I am not. I have nothing left at all now but myself. The wind blows from the valley, and there's a voice on the wind, a bit of a tune. Then the wind falls, or changes. The work has to be done, and we did the work. It's their turn now for that, the children. There's nothing left for me to do but sing. I never could sing. But you play the instrument you have." So she stood by the cold hearth and sang the melody of Orioth's Lament. The people of the household wakened in their beds and heard her singing, all but Torm; but he knew that tune already. The untuned strings of the harps hung on the wall wakened and answered softly, voice to voice, like eyes that shine among the leaves when the wind is blowing. ■

> *What instrument does Gwilan decide to use? What prompts her to use this instrument?*

---

6. **descant.** Musical line sung above the main melody to create harmony

7. **drouth.** Archaic spelling of *drought*, a prolonged period of time with no rain

Imagine that you are the young Gwilan and have just been given your mother's harp. Explain the meaning that the harp holds for you.

Investigate, *Inquire,* and Imagine

Recall: GATHERING FACTS

1a. What do people say about Gwilan's mastery of the harp?

2a. What happens to the harp during Gwilan's journey to Comin?

3a. Why does Gwilan hang the two harps on the wall but not play them?

Interpret: FINDING MEANING

1b. What gift is passed on with the harp?

2b. Why does Gwilan marry Torm?

3b. What events at the end of the story show the passage of time?

Analyze: TAKING THINGS APART

4a. Why does Gwilan start singing after she can no longer play the harp? Why does she sing Orioth's Lament?

Synthesize: BRINGING THINGS TOGETHER

4b. What lessons does the selection teach?

Evaluate: MAKING JUDGMENTS

5a. Decide whether or not Gwilan is defined by her roles as harpist and wife of Torm at the end of the story.

Extend: CONNECTING IDEAS

5b. Describe a story, novel, or movie in which a character rises above suffering and obstacles to take charge of his or her life. If you prefer, tell a real-life story with which you are familiar.

Understanding *Literature*

METAPHOR. Review the definition for **metaphor** in the Handbook of Literary Terms. To what does the narrator of "Gwilan's Harp" compare hands? What characteristics do hands and the other subject of the comparison have in common? What is the sound of Gwilan's harp compared to? What is the purpose of this metaphor?

THEME. Review the definition for **theme** in the Handbook of Literary Terms. Then, referring to the cluster chart you made in Literary Tools on page 266, decide which emotions of Gwilan point to a theme in the story. What do you think is the main theme of the selection?

Writer's Journal

1. Write **song lyrics** about the aged Gwilan telling her why you admire her.
2. Imagine that you are Torm and that it is Valentine's Day. Write a **free-verse poem** or **letter** to Gwilan telling her why you fell in love with her.
3. Imagine that you are Gwilan at the end of the story. Write a **journal entry** explaining how music has intertwined throughout all the stages and events of your life.

Integrating
the Language Arts

Language, Grammar, and Style

WORKING WITH INVERTED SENTENCES. Review the Language Arts Survey 3.19, "Finding the Complete Subject and Complete Predicate in a Sentence." A sentence is **inverted** when all or part of the **complete predicate** comes before the **subject**. Questions can be tricky because part of the verb may be in front of the subject. For each of the sentences below, identify the simple subject(s), verb(s), and the complement(s) if any are present. Then identify the kind of complement: DO, IO, PA, PN, or PP. Refer to the Language Arts Survey 3.26, "Working with Inverted Sentences."

1. Did Gwilan's mother give her music lessons?
2. Have you seen an Irish harp?
3. Are Irish musicians still respected?
4. Can the fairies have taught the musicians?
5. Can't ordinary people play extraordinary music?

Study and Research

RESEARCHING LE GUIN. In articles and books, read about the worlds Le Guin creates in her fantasy, science fiction, and mainstream novels and short stories. Then make a presentation to a classmate on an interesting aspect of Le Guin's imaginary world. Your aim is persuasive, that is, you want to get your classmate interested in learning more about Le Guin's works or in reading a specific work. Remember that in persuasion the purpose is to move the listener to adopt your point of view, which needs to be clearly stated.

Applied English & Study and Research

WRITING A WORK ORDER. Imagine that you are a harp maker and Gwilan has come to you for help because she wants you to replace her broken harp. Write a work order describing the size of the harp, its decorations, the quality of its sound, and the type of strings. You may want to do some research on harps before creating a work order form to fill in.

Literary TOOLS

IRONY AND IRONY OF SITUATION. Irony is a difference between appearance and reality. The ending of the story uses a particular type of irony—the irony of situation. **Irony of situation** occurs when an event in the story violates the expectations of the characters, the reader, or the audience. As you read, decide which expectations of Stella and Jim are violated.

PLOT AND THEME. A **plot** is a series of events related to a central conflict, or struggle. A **theme** is a central idea in a literary work. In "The Gift of the Magi," the plot focuses on a married couple who make personal sacrifices to buy Christmas gifts for each other. As you read, notice how the plot helps to develop the theme of the story.

Graphic Organizer

As you read this selection, complete a sequence chart like the one below. Map out each event as it happens. Try to determine what the plot reveals about the theme.

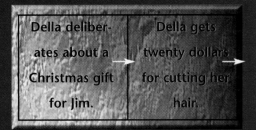

| Della deliber- ates about a Christmas gift for Jim. | → | Della gets twenty dollars for cutting her hair. | → |

Reader's Journal

What have you done to give a special gift to someone?

"The Gift of the Magi"
by O. Henry

Reader's resource

O. Henry's stories are famous for their distinctive surprise endings in which an ironic event occurs that violates expectations of the characters or the reader. "**The Gift of the Magi**" contains, perhaps, the most famous surprise ending of all.

First published in 1906, "The Gift of the Magi" appeared in the short story collection *The Four Million.* The twenty-five stories in the collection are set in the author's favorite locale, New York City, and peopled with his favorite characters—lower-middle-class workers, the unemployed, the homeless, and the forgotten. O. Henry selected the title of the collection, which refers to the population of New York City in 1906, in direct rebuttal to an infamous, elitist remark that "there are only about four hundred people in New York society."

About the AUTHOR

O. Henry (1862–1910) was the pseudonym of William Sydney Porter. Born in Greensboro, North Carolina, Henry moved to Texas, where he edited and published a humorous magazine, *The Rolling Stone,* and wrote for a newspaper. The magazine failed, and two years later Henry faced charges for embezzling funds from a bank. He escaped to Central America but later returned and served over three years in an Ohio federal prison. While imprisoned, Henry began to write short stories. After his release, he moved to New York City, the setting with which most of his work is identified, and published a story a week in *World.* Among the collections of O. Henry stories are *The Four Million, Heart of the West, The Voice of the City, Options,* and *Strictly Business.*

The Gift of the Magi

O. Henry

Only a Lock of Hair. Sir John Everett Millais. Manchester City Art Galleries, England.

One dollar and eighty-seven cents. That was all. And sixty cents of it was in pennies. Pennies saved one and two at a time by bulldozing the grocer and the vegetable man and the butcher until one's cheeks burned with the silent <u>imputation</u> of <u>parsimony</u> that such close dealing implied. Three times Della counted it. One dollar and eighty-seven cents. And the next day would be Christmas.

> How much money does Della have? How did she manage to save it?

words for everyday use

im • pu • ta • tion (im pyōō tā´shən) *n.*, charge; claim. *The defense attorney's <u>imputation</u> was that the plaintiff was not telling the whole truth.*

par • si • mo • ny (pär´sə mō´nē) *n.*, stinginess. *Bronwen's <u>parsimony</u> extended to leaving inadequate tips.*

Rapidly she pulled down her hair and let it fall to its full length.

There was clearly nothing to do but flop down on the shabby little couch and howl. So Della did it. Which instigates the moral reflection that life is made up of sobs, sniffles, and smiles, with sniffles <u>predominating</u>.

While the mistress of the home is gradually <u>subsiding</u> from the first stage to the second, take a look at the home. A furnished flat at $8 per week. It did not exactly beggar description, but it certainly had that word on the lookout for the mendicancy[1] squad.

In the vestibule below was a letter box into which no letter would go, and an electric button from which no mortal finger could coax a ring. Also <u>appertaining</u> thereunto was a card bearing the name "Mr. James Dillingham Young."

The "Dillingham" had been flung to the breeze during a former period of prosperity when its possessor was being paid $30 per week. Now, when the income was shrunk to $20, the letters of "Dillingham" looked blurred, as though they were thinking seriously of contracting to a modest and unassuming D. But whenever Mr. James Dillingham Young came home and reached his flat above he was called "Jim" and greatly hugged by Mrs. James Dillingham Young, already introduced to you as Della. Which is all very good.

Della finished her cry and attended to her cheeks with the powder rag. She stood by the window and looked out dully at a gray cat walking a gray fence in a gray backyard. Tomorrow would be Christmas Day, and she had only $1.87 with which to buy Jim a present. She had been saving every penny she could for months, with this result. Twenty dollars a week doesn't go far. Expenses had been greater than she had calculated. They always are. Only $1.87 to buy a present for Jim. Her Jim. Many a happy hour she had spent planning for something nice for him. Something fine and rare and sterling—something just a little bit near to being worthy of the honor of being owned by Jim.

Why does Della need money?

There was a pier glass[2] between the windows of the room. Perhaps you have seen a pier glass in an $8 flat. A very thin and very <u>agile</u> person may, by observing his reflection in a rapid sequence of longitudinal strips, obtain a fairly accurate conception of his looks. Della, being slender, had mastered the art.

Suddenly she whirled from the window and stood before the glass. Her eyes were shining brilliantly, but her face had lost its color within twenty seconds. Rapidly she pulled down her hair and let it fall to its full length.

Now, there were two possessions of the James Dillingham Youngs in which they both took a mighty pride. One was Jim's gold watch that had been his father's and his grandfather's. The other was Della's hair. Had the Queen of Sheba[3] lived in the flat across the air shaft, Della would have let her hair hang out the window some day to dry just to <u>depreciate</u> Her Majesty's jewels and gifts. Had King Solomon[3] been the janitor, with all his treasures piled up in the basement, Jim would have

Of what two possessions are the James Dillingham Youngs most proud?

---

1. **mendicancy.** Begging
2. **pier glass.** Narrow mirror set between two windows
3. **Queen of Sheba.** Biblical queen
4. **King Solomon.** Biblical king

---

words for everyday use

pre • dom • i • nate (prē däm´ ə nāt´) *vi.,* prevail. *Of the many types of birds that come to our backyard, finches seem to <u>predominate</u>.*

sub • side (səb sīd´) *vi.,* settle; lessen in intensity. *After his father's anger <u>subsided</u>, Luis asked to borrow the car.*

ap • per • tain (ap´ər tān´) *vi.,* be a part of. *I could not see how Margaret's anecdote <u>appertained</u> to the rest of our conversation.*

ag • ile (aj´əl) *adj.,* able to move quickly and easily. *The most <u>agile</u> recruit completed the obstacle course in eight minutes.*

de • pre • ci • ate (di prē´shē āt) *vt.,* lower in value. *Although the stock <u>depreciated</u>, Mr. Talbot hung onto it in the hope that its value would rise again.*

pulled out his watch every time he passed, just to see him pluck at his beard from envy.

So now Della's beautiful hair fell about her rippling and shining like a cascade of brown waters. It reached below her knee and made itself almost a garment for her. And then she did it up again nervously and quickly. Once she <u>faltered</u> for a minute and stood still while a tear or two splashed on the worn red carpet.

On went her old brown jacket; on went her old brown hat. With a whirl of skirts and with the brilliant sparkle still in her eyes, she fluttered out the door and down the stairs to the street.

Where she stopped the sign read: "Mme. Sofronie. Hair Goods of All Kinds." One flight up Della ran, and collected herself, panting. Madame, large, too white, chilly, hardly looked the "Sofronie."

"Will you buy my hair?" asked Della.

"I buy hair," said Madame. "Take yer hat off and let's have a sight at the looks of it."

Down rippled the brown cascade.

"Twenty dollars," said Madame, lifting the mass with a practiced hand.

> What does Della sell? How much money does she get?

"Give it to me quick," said Della.

Oh, and the next two hours tripped by on rosy wings. Forget the hashed metaphor. She was ransacking the stores for Jim's present.

She found it at last. It surely had been made for Jim and no one else. There was no other like it in any of the stores, and she had turned all of them inside out. It was a platinum fob chain[5] simple and chaste in design, properly proclaiming its value by substance alone and not by <u>meretricious</u> ornamentation—as all

> What does Della buy for Jim?

good things should do. It was even worthy of The Watch. As soon as she saw it she knew that it must be Jim's. It was like him. Quietness and value—the description applied to both. Twenty-one dollars they took from her for it, and she hurried home with the eighty-seven cents. With that chain on his watch Jim might be properly anxious about the time in any company. Grand as the watch was, he sometimes looked at it on the sly on account of the old leather strap that he used in place of a chain.

When Della reached home her intoxication gave way a little to <u>prudence</u> and reason. She got out her curling irons and lighted the gas and went to work repairing the ravages made by generosity added to love. Which is always a tremendous task, dear friends—a mammoth task.

> What does Della do when she gets home?

Within forty minutes her head was covered with tiny, close-lying curls that made her look wonderfully like a truant schoolboy. She looked at her reflection in the mirror long, carefully, and critically.

"If Jim doesn't kill me," she said to herself, "before he takes a second look at me, he'll say I look like a Coney Island[6] chorus girl. But what could I do—oh! what could I do with a dollar and eighty-seven cents?"

At seven o'clock the coffee was made and the frying pan was on the back of the stove hot and ready to cook the chops.

Jim was never late. Della doubled the fob chain in her hand and sat on the corner of the table near the door that he always entered. Then she heard his step on the stair away down on the first flight, and she turned white for just

---

5. **fob chain.** Chain for a pocket watch
6. **Coney Island.** Section of Brooklyn, New York, known for its amusement park

<table>
<tr><td>words
for
everyday
use</td><td>fal • ter (fôl´tər) vi., hesitate. I expected Kate to stumble over her words when giving the speech, but she never <u>faltered</u>.

mer • e • tri • cious (mer´ə trish´əs) adj., alluring in a false, showy way. Sonia cast aside the <u>meretricious</u> scarves and selected a modest one.

pru • dence (prood´ns) n., sound judgment. Jack showed <u>prudence</u> when he started a money market account with the money he received for Christmas.</td></tr>
</table>

a moment. She had a habit of saying little silent prayers about the simplest everyday things, and now she whispered: "Please God, make him think I am still pretty."

The door opened and Jim stepped in and closed it. He looked thin and very serious. Poor fellow, he was only twenty-two—and to be burdened with a family! He needed a new overcoat and he was without gloves.

Jim stopped inside the door, as immovable as a setter at the scent of quail. His eyes were fixed upon Della, and there was an expression in them that she could not read, and it terrified her. It was not anger, nor surprise, nor disapproval, nor horror, nor any of the sentiments that she had been prepared for. He simply stared at her fixedly with that peculiar expression on his face.

> How does Jim react to Della's appearance at first?

Della wriggled off the table and went for him.

"Jim, darling," she cried, "don't look at me that way. I had my hair cut off and sold it because I couldn't have lived through Christmas without giving you a present. It'll grow out again—you won't mind, will you? I just had to do it. My hair grows awfully fast. Say 'Merry Christmas,' Jim, and let's be happy. You don't know what a nice—what a beautiful, nice gift I've got for you."

"You've cut off your hair?" asked Jim, <u>laboriously</u>, as if he had not arrived at that patent fact yet even after the hardest mental labor.

"Cut it off and sold it," said Della. "Don't you like me just as well, anyhow? I'm me without my hair, ain't I?"

Jim looked about the room curiously.

"You say your hair is gone?" he said, with an air almost of idiocy.

"You needn't look for it," said Della. "It's sold, I tell you—sold and gone, too. It's Christmas Eve, boy. Be good to me, for it went for you. Maybe the hairs of my head were numbered," she went on with a sudden serious sweetness, "but nobody could ever count my love for you. Shall I put the chops on, Jim?"

Out of his trance Jim seemed quickly to wake. He enfolded his Della. For ten seconds let us regard with discreet <u>scrutiny</u> some <u>inconsequential</u> object in the other direction. Eight dollars a week or a million a year—what is the difference? A mathematician or a wit would give you the wrong answer. The magi[7] brought valuable gifts, but that was not among them. This dark assertion will be illuminated later on.

Jim drew a package from his overcoat pocket and threw it upon the table.

"Don't make any mistake, Dell," he said, "about me. I don't think there's anything in the way of a haircut or a shave or a shampoo that could make me like my girl any less. But if you'll unwrap that package you may see why you had me going awhile at first."

> Is Jim really upset about the haircut? What has he purchased for Della?

White fingers and <u>nimble</u> tore at the string and paper. And then an ecstatic scream of joy; and then, alas! a quick feminine change to hysterical tears and wails, necessitating the immediate employment of all the comforting powers of the lord of the flat.

For there lay The Combs—the set of combs, side and back, that Della had worshiped for long in a Broadway window. Beautiful combs, pure tortoise shell, with jeweled rims just the shade to wear in the beautiful vanished hair. They were expensive combs, she knew, and her heart had simply craved and yearned over them without the least hope of possession. And now, they were hers, but the tresses that should have

---

7. **magi.** Wise men from the East who brought gifts to the infant Jesus

adorned the coveted <u>adornments</u> were gone.

But she hugged them to her bosom, and at length she was able to look up with dim eyes and a smile and say: "My hair grows so fast, Jim!"

And then Della leaped up like a little singed cat and cried, "Oh, oh!"

Jim had not yet seen his beautiful present. She held it out to him eagerly upon her open palm. The dull precious metal seemed to flash with a reflection of her bright and ardent spirit.

"Isn't it a dandy, Jim? I hunted all over town to find it. You'll have to look at the time a hundred times a day now. Give me your watch. I want to see how it looks on it."

Instead of obeying, Jim tumbled down on the couch and put his hands under the back of his head and smiled.

Of all who give and receive gifts, such as they are wisest.

"Dell," said he, "let's put our Christmas presents away and keep 'em awhile. They're too nice to use just at present. I sold the watch to get the money to buy your combs. And now suppose you put the chops on."

The magi, as you know, were wise men—wonderfully wise men—who brought gifts to the Babe in the manger. They invented the art of giving Christmas presents. Being wise, their gifts were no doubt wise ones, possibly bearing the privilege of exchange in case of <u>duplication</u>. And here I have lamely related to you the uneventful chronicle of two foolish children in a flat who most unwisely sacrificed for each other the greatest treasures of their house. But in a last word to the wise of these days let it be said that of all who give gifts these two were the wisest. Of all who give and receive gifts, such as they are wisest. Everywhere they are wisest. They are the magi. ∎

What similarity exists between the magi and the characters in this story? Why does the narrator call Della and Jim not foolish but wise?

---

words for everyday use

a • dorn • ment (ə dôrn´mənt) *n.*, ornament, decoration. *The <u>adornment</u> of the Christmas tree was a family tradition.*

du • pli • ca • tion (doo´ pli kā´shən) *n.*, copy, double. *This letter is a <u>duplication</u> of the one I sent you last week that was lost in the mail.*

Respond *to the* SELECTION

Imagine that you are either Della or Jim in this story. Discuss why you wanted to give your spouse an expensive gift that you could not really afford.

Investigate, Inquire, and Imagine

Recall: GATHERING FACTS

1a. What amount of money has Della saved for Jim's Christmas present?

2a. What possession does Della sell for money to buy Jim's gift? How much money does she get for it?

3a. What possession does Jim sell for money to buy Della's gift?

Interpret: FINDING MEANING

1b. What troubles Della at the beginning of the story?

2b. What reaction does Della fear that Jim may have upon seeing her bobbed hair?

3b. How does Jim reassure Della?

Analyze: TAKING THINGS APART

4a. How does the narrator interact with the reader in this story? Provide several examples that illustrate this interaction. Then discuss (analyze) whether or not you find the narrator's commentary helpful or intrusive.

Synthesize: BRINGING THINGS TOGETHER

4b. Why does the narrator say about Della and Jim, "Of all who give and receive gifts these two were the wisest"? How does this passage relate to the title of the story?

Perspective: LOOKING AT OTHER VIEWS

5a. What in Della or Jim's character causes them to give the gifts they do? What do you think leads to such a capacity?

Empathy: SEEING FROM INSIDE

5b. Taking the perspective of Della or Jim, write a paragraph telling whether or not it was a mistake to buy the gift you did. For example, if you were Jim, would you take the combs back and try to buy back your watch? Why, or why not?

Understanding Literature

IRONY AND IRONY OF SITUATION. Review the definition for **irony** and **irony of situation** in the Handbook of Literary Terms. Then look at the sequence chart you made for Literary Tools on page 274. Which of Della's expectations are violated in the story? Circle the events in the sequence chart in which Della's expectations are violated. Then do the same for events in which Jim's expectations are violated. Which of the reader's expectations are violated?

PLOT AND THEME. Review the definitions for **plot** and **theme** in the Handbook of Literary Terms. What is the plot of the story? What do you consider to be its main theme?

Writer's Journal

1. Imagine that you are Jim. Write a **wish list** with at least ten items telling Della what you would give her if you had five hundred dollars. Explain why you would buy her each gift.
2. Imagine that you are Della or Jim. Write a **journal entry** describing the experience of seeing your spouse go without something important to him or her for your sake.
3. Imagine that Jim or Della has written a letter to the newspaper asking what they should do with the gifts they cannot use. Write an **advice column** giving the couple advice and sharing your thoughts about what their gift-giving experience means.

Integrating the Language Arts

Language, Grammar, and Style

SENTENCE REVIEW. For each of the sentences below, identify the simple subject(s), verb(s), and the complement(s), if any are present. Then identify the kind of complement: direct object (DO), indirect object (IO), predicate adjective (PA), predicate noun (PN), or predicate pronoun (PP). For review refer to the Language Arts Survey 3.19–3.25.

1. O. Henry was a skilled writer; he embezzled money and was punished.
2. The prisoner wrote short stories; today all Americans know his work.
3. The surprise ending was his specialty, and "The Gift of the Magi" has one.
4. Why didn't O. Henry use his own real name?
5. Frequently young people make bad decisions; Jim and Della made especially bad ones.

Speaking and Listening & Collaborative Learning

DRAMATIC SKIT. With a partner, write a dramatization of the scene from "The Gift of the Magi" where Jim and Della exchange gifts. Write a part for Jim and a part for Della. Include stage directions. (Stage directions are notes included in a play for the purpose of describing how something should be performed on stage. Stage directions describe setting, lighting, music, sound effects, entrances and exits, properties, and the movements of characters.) You may want to add music from the period to enhance the atmosphere of your scene. Rehearse your skit and present it to the class.

Study and Research & Media Literacy

COMMUNITY RESEARCH. As a community service project, visit a nursing home or retirement center and interview a resident about gift-giving in his or her youth. (Check with the nursing home staff first to make an appointment and to make sure your questions are appropriate.) You may want to include questions for people who lived through the Great Depression, when money was scarce. After your interview, share your story with a small group of classmates. Then write a newspaper article about what you learned in your group and from your nursing home visit. Generalize about gift-giving practices, give examples, and use quotations in your article.

Language Arts in *Action*

Mentor CONNECTION

In every high school there are inevitably students who feel restricted, who want more than the standard education. They are often "gifted" in some way or other, uniquely motivated toward some area of interest. Few opportunities exist for these students to flex their intellectual muscle outside the boundaries of traditional education. In 1984, a program was begun, funded by Northeast Metro Intermediate School District 916 in St. Paul, Minnesota, to give students the opportunity to go beyond high school into the "real world." That program is called Mentor Connection.

The author, Chris Nelson, displaying his completed project at the Mentor Connection's final presentation fair.

Mentor Connection is geared toward uniting a student with a person who is already engaged in the student's preferred study area. Mentors chosen are always experienced career adults. None are paid; all are volunteers who give of their time to educate these highly motivated students. One of the main goals of the program is to allow students access to places, people, and experiences that they would otherwise not reach until perhaps a college-level internship. Each student uses this access to create a project based on his or her topic of study. This active participation enhances the learning experience and is a vital part of the mentorship. Projects, like areas of interest, are always varied. The only restrictions to a project are safety, feasibility, and the limits of imagination.

Preparation for the mentorship begins even before classes start. Accepted students are asked to thoroughly research their topic at the University of Minnesota libraries the summer before they join the program. Since students will already have extensive book knowledge of their topic, mentors can concentrate on teaching the aspects of their field that are hard, or impossible, to learn from books.

In 1998, during his senior year, Chris Nelson was lucky enough to be chosen as one of the few to engage in this unique and challenging program. Chris said of this experience, "My dream, my passion, was writing. More specifically, writing science fiction. Learning to be a writer, however, was slightly different from learning to be a doctor, or a scientist, or an engineer. There weren't many books, or technical manuals, or step-by-step instructions for me to follow. The how-to books that I could find were some help, but for the most part the best preparation I could give myself was simply to start writing. Until my Mentor Connection experience, I only wrote when some sudden inspiration tackled me. This happened fairly often, but I would get so caught up in inspiration that I missed some of the most important aspects of writing. One of the few books I read on writing stated that a good writer depends on inspiration only 1 percent of the time. The other 99 percent of his or her work is dedication, hours of writing every day. Writing is like a sport: you have to practice it and stay 'in shape' to be good at what you do."

Chris had his inspiration—an idea for a story that came to him one day while letting his imagination run free. It started with an idea about a boy who, on certain moonless nights, would become a panther. "One of the great things about writing, especially science fiction writing, is that the possibilities are truly endless. My mentor, writer Bruce Bethke, helped open my mind to those endless possibilities and suggested new ways for my story to grow. We created a background for the boy's race. He gave me advice on how to develop my characters, and, most of all, encouraged me not to give up on my dream of being a writer," Chris said.

At the end of the school year Chris was proud to hand his mentor the first draft of his completed story. It was 145 pages in total—not very long for a science fiction novel, but by far his most ambitious work to date. He continues to work with the story in hopes that he can someday submit it for publication.

Excerpt from a work in progress, tentatively titled *Foreign Bodies*
by Christopher D. Nelson

"Do you know why you play that same melody over and over?" the man said, not looking at the boy but shifting their fire with a branch.

"It's my song. I don't know why I play it. It was the first song I ever wrote. I guess you could say it's the one thing I have to hold on to, that's really mine alone."

The man kept his eyes on the fire. "Well, that's not exactly true. You see, that song is thousands of years old. Even the oldest of your people don't know where it came from. It is something that you have in you from birth, a kind of universal mark. In the hands of an experienced musician, it has the power to influence others' emotions, even their thoughts. It is a powerful gift, indeed. It's how I knew where you were." The man looked up at the boy, intently.

The boy stared back, his eyes glistening hard in the flame. "That's . . . impossible. That song took me a year to perfect . . . and . . . what do you mean, my people?"

The man looked away, back at the fire. "Your . . . people. I guess that isn't exactly accurate." He paused a moment. "Ever wonder who your real parents are?"

"No. Phil is my real father, even though he's a jerk. My mom left him because of it. Why, was she some kind of Asian, or Indian, or something? My music definitely isn't native or Asian."

"You're right, it isn't. But she wasn't your biological mother. Tell me about your dream."

"What?"

"The dream you have. Describe it to me."

". . . which one?"

"Don't dodge the subject."

The boy gazed down at the ground. "The panther."

"Right."

Guided Writing

> "It's not only the scenery you miss by going too fast—you also miss the sense of where you are going and why."
>
> —Eddie Cantor

WRITING A COMPARISON AND CONTRAST ESSAY

Ever want to listen to some new music? To know where to buy used skis? Or to plan a perfect vacation? With a few clicks of your finger, the answers roll across your computer screen: graphics, photographs, information and options, sometimes accompanied by sounds. Welcome to the world of Internet websites. This evolving forum for communication combines text and media in a lively format that offers you unlimited choices and the chance to interact.

But right now it's time to "slow down" that computer search engine so you don't "miss the sense of where you are going and why."

The Internet holds millions of sites posted by individuals and organizations. Many sites contain useful information, but some do not. How can you evaluate whether a website is worth your time? One way to decide is by comparison and contrast. By observing ways that sites are alike and different, you can learn more about your topic and, at the same time, learn to critique the sites according to your own set of standards.

WRITING ASSIGNMENT. Write an essay comparing and contrasting two websites related to an author of your choice. You design a set of standards that will serve as the basis for making and supporting an informed opinion about the websites.

Professional Model

"Evaluating Author Websites"
page 195

When researching an author…Web browsers are a great place to start; most of the sites you will find there will be well organized and in-depth. The best sites are often those that the authors put together themselves….Good secondary sites include those authorized by the author or his or her agent, literary societies, publishers, and fans of the author….

The Berkeley site is comprehensive and well organized. If you wanted to write a paper on Jack London, this would be the place to go for sheer volume of information. It provides several links to other quality sites, as well as links to photos of Jack, his family, and his travels, and a growing collection of his writings. Many of London's books and other works are reproduced in full on the site....The site also lists fan and scholarly organizations devoted to London and his work.

The fan site provides a deeper look at Jack London's personality and gives a sense of the drama of his life. The focus of the site is London's California ranch, and the museum it houses today, but it also contains other information, such as tales of his travels in his sailing ship, the *Snark*. At first glance, the site has a warmer, friendlier look than the Berkeley site, but seems slightly less organized. This site is best suited for someone who has the time to go through and read, page by page, Jack London's exploits and life history.

"There are a bunch of hacker kids out there who can string a sentence together better than their blue-blooded peers simply because they log on all the time and write, write, write."

—Brock Meeks

EXAMINING THE MODEL. In the opening of this essay the writer introduces the general idea that the Internet is a good source of information and then narrows the topic to researching authors. The thesis classifies kinds of author websites and the information found in each.

In the body of the piece, you are given examples of two kinds of websites for the author Jack London. The writer compares and contrasts the two sites, one by the literary society of the University of California at Berkeley and the other by a fan.

Find the paragraph where the writer lumps together specific points about the Berkeley site. Now find the paragraph containing specific points about the fan site.

Grouping all your points together like this is called **block organization.** With block organization, you tell all about the first item and then you tell all about the second item. Block organization is easier to follow when you keep the order of presentation the same. That is, if you start your discussion of the first website with a point about its layout, begin your discussion of the second website with a point about its layout.

Think of block organization as big boxes containing information about one item:

IDENTIFYING YOUR AUDIENCE.
Your class could create a
collection of critiques to post
in the classroom, the
computer writing lab, or
school library as a research
resource. Or you might want
to offer your critique to the
school newspaper. In these
cases, the audience is other
students and perhaps teachers.

FINDING YOUR VOICE. Use your
natural voice, one that
expresses a commitment to
what you have learned about
the websites you have
analyzed. Since you want your
opinion to be heard, your
voice should be reasonable
and appropriate to your
audience.

For example, using slang
to describe websites, or
dismissing websites with
emotional language neither
convinces your reader nor
instills confidence in your
analytical abilities. This does
not mean you should adopt
an overly formal voice. Do
include original and fresh
descriptions, humor, or
other language that shows
honesty and conviction.

> "Rather than the
> sham of objectivity, I
> think you should put
> your perspective up
> front. That's only fair
> to the reader."
> —*Ralph Wiley*

Berkeley Website

Fan Website

Another way to organize a comparison and contrast essay is
to argue point-by-point. With **point-by-point organization**,
you jump back and forth from one item you are comparing
to the other. First you might argue a point about the layout
in website number 1 and then compare or contrast it to the
layout in website number 2. Next, you might argue a point
about the quality of the biography in website number 1 and
then discuss the biography in website number 2. Think of
point-by-point organization as small boxes containing
individual points.

Example of point-by-point argument:

The Berkeley site provides several links to other quality sites as well as links to photos of Jack, his family, and his travels.

The fan site has links that go back and forth from the main drive of the biography, inserting comments, stories, and quotes. Unfortunately, there is no search function....

Look at this statement about the Berkeley site. Read over the
essay and find a parallel statement from the fan site.

Berkeley Site:
If you wanted to write a paper on Jack London, this would be the place to go for sheer volume of information.

Fan Site:

Prewriting

WRITING WITH A PLAN. Choose an author you enjoy reading
who is respected and well known. This could be one of the
authors studied in class or some other author of literary
significance.

One way to find websites about your author is simply to
enter the author's name into a search engine and scan the list
that results. You may also want to try combinations of words
such as "author biographies" or "arts and literature." Consider

using several search engines—Lycos, AltaVista, Yahoo!—because each one offers a slightly different result.

Look over the websites that refer to your author and pick two. Note the Internet address and title at the top of the page.

First note the categories of information available. Then look at the physical layout of the sites. But don't stop there. See if you can find who wrote them and why. Often there is a brief explanation about the people posting the website or a link to another website that explains the origins of the material.

Individuals and organizations have many reasons for publishing information on the Internet. Is someone trying to sell books? There is nothing wrong with this. Just keep the motive in mind when you evaluate.

Now that you have carefully observed your two author websites, you are ready to begin analyzing your information.

Minna, a ninth grade student, used this graphic organizer to list the features of her two author sites. Create a chart on your paper like the one below. Fill in each square with information about the websites you found. A few categories are listed below from Minna's research, but you will want to add others from your sites. Be sure to also include categories about the physical layout, the way the website looks, and any of your observations about ease of use.

Student Model—Graphic Organizer

Website Comparison-Contrast Table

Website #1	Website #2
To Kill a Mockingbird and Harper Lee	Harper Lee
http://www.chebucto.ns.ca/culture/harperlee/index.html	http://www.kirjasto.sci.fi/harperle.html
Biographical Information	**Biographical Information**
1½ pages	½ page
well written with quotes	brief description
Links	**Links**
many links to other sites about the book and discussion groups	no links to other sites

Language, Grammar, and Style

Subject-Verb Agreement
IDENTIFYING SUBJECT-VERB AGREEMENT. Making subjects and verbs agree is easy in sentences in which the subject and verb are close together. But when sentences have phrases or clauses that separate the subject and verb, writers sometimes get confused. Still, even in complex sentences, matching subjects and verbs is easy if you remember a few common-sense rules.

1. **Look for the subject.** Always look for the subject—whom or what the sentence is about—and let that subject determine the form of your verb.

EXAMPLE:
That bag of green apples she brought back from the San Juan Islands seem fresh.

If you find the subject—and never mind the plural words *apples* and *Islands*—you will see that the verb should be singular: That <u>bag</u> <u>seems</u> fresh.

2. **Using compound subjects.** A **compound subject** is formed with two or more nouns or pronouns that are joined and have the same verb. A compound subject with *and* takes a plural verb, unless the compound subject refers to one person or thing.

continued on page 288

EXAMPLES:

The <u>dog</u> and the <u>cat</u> <u>are</u> sleeping.

My best <u>friend</u> and <u>hero</u> <u>is</u> my brother.

<u>Peanut butter</u> and <u>jelly</u> <u>is</u> my favorite.

A compound subject made up of two singular subjects joined with *or* or *nor* takes a singular verb. A compound subject made up of a singular and a plural subject takes the verb that agrees in number with the subject nearer the verb.

EXAMPLES:

Either <u>pen</u> or <u>pencil</u> <u>is</u> fine to use for filling out the form.

Neither <u>Odysseus</u> nor his <u>men</u> <u>were</u> able to resist the temptation of the sirens.

3. **Using pronoun subjects.** Sometimes your subject will be a pronoun. **Indefinite pronouns** such as *everybody, nobody, neither, both, few, most,* and *all* can cause confusion.

The following pronouns are singular and require a singular verb: **each, either, one, neither, everyone, no one, anybody, everybody, nobody, anything, everything, nothing.**

EXAMPLES:

<u>Neither</u> of us <u>is</u> happy.

<u>Everyone</u> <u>helps</u> after dinner.

The following pronouns are plural and require a plural verb: **few, many, both, several.**

continued on page 289

With your chart filled in, you are ready to evaluate the facts. Which website do you like better, and why? What standards are you using for your evaluation: easy to understand, easy to use, attractive and inviting graphics, excerpts that allowed you to get a flavor of the books your author wrote, lots of articles on your author?

Now write a thesis statement that describes which website you think is more effective, and why. This statement may change as you go along, so consider this a beginning. For additional help, refer to the Language Arts Survey 2.25, "Writing a Thesis Statement."

Drafting

Using your thesis as a starting point, write a draft that argues for one website over another. Your completed chart from the graphic organizer provides facts, evidence, and reasons for your opinion. Put these in the body of your piece.

You will need to decide whether to use point-by-point organization or block organization for your paper. If your websites are easy to match up, use point-by-point organization. If they are less comparable, you may find that block organization will work better.

Don't worry about creating a perfect draft at this point. Just try to get your most important points in writing.

Self- and Peer Evaluation

Use the questions below to guide you in making revisions on your first draft. If time allows, have another student evaluate your paper.

- Does the paper have a thesis that clearly states an opinion? What is the thesis statement?
- What specific standards or criteria did the writer use to form this opinion?
- What reasons, facts, or evidence does the paper use to support the thesis statement?
- Which arguments are the strongest, and why?
- Which arguments are least effective, and why?
- Which form of organization—block or point-by-point—does the paper follow? Identify any places where the organization could be clearer.
- Look for transitions between arguments. Are there places where the paper could use a transition to guide the reader from one idea to the next?
- Where, if anywhere, are there parts of the paper where the language does not sound convincing or real?
- Where, if anywhere, do you find errors in subject-verb agreement?

Revising and Proofreading

Based on the responses to your self- and peer evaluations, make changes in your essay that will help your reader better understand your point of view. Don't hesitate to play with your thesis until it reflects exactly what you want to say. A thesis with a strong and clear opinion is the glue that holds your paper together and the body of your essay will fall into place once you have it.

Think about adding more evidence to weak arguments and getting rid of repetitious points. Insert transitions where necessary.

When you are finished revising, proofread your paper for errors in capitalization, spelling, punctuation, and grammar usage such as subject-verb agreement.

Here is the final draft of Minna's paper comparing and contrasting author websites:

Student Model—Revised

by Minna Brown

One author whose work I really like is Harper Lee. Like so many others who read the book, I thought *To Kill a Mockingbird* was a real page-turner. Naturally, I would like to know more about her and other things she may have written.

I did a website search and found two that seemed reliable: "*To Kill a Mockingbird* and Harper Lee" at http://www.chebucto.ns.ca/culture/harperlee/index.html and "Harper Lee" at http://www.kirjasto.sci.fi/harperle.htm. It didn't take me long to realize I favored the first one over the second.

The first site, "*To Kill a Mockingbird* and Harper Lee," had an interesting, clean line layout. Three colors were used in all and there were no extravagant graphics, just a simple picture of Scout from the movie made from the novel. The first page clearly listed the categories that were included in the site and that was all. I clicked on the categories and saw more of the same layout with a few pictures and the same colors used sparingly. I liked that the whole site appeared uncluttered and was really easy to follow.

As for the content of the site, it didn't quite live up to my expectations. There was a lot of information, but with categories like a "Mockingbird FAQ,"

EXAMPLES:
Both of us are happy.

Many sing along.

These pronouns can be either singular or plural: **all, some, most, none, any.** You need to determine whether the pronoun is referring to one thing or more than one. Then you'll know which verb form to use. The pronoun *none* will almost always take a singular verb, because it means "not one." Only use a plural verb with *none* when it sounds wrong to use a singular one.

EXAMPLES:
Most of the food is bad.

Most of the people are leaving.

None of the links matches my interest.

None are as successful as those who try their best.

FIXING ERRORS IN SUBJECT-VERB AGREEMENT. In Minna's rough draft, she found these sentences with errors in subject-verb agreement. Identify and correct the errors in each sentence.

Her biography, along with shorter biographies of her family, were less than one page.

Neither site are good for finding out about the author's personal life.

None of the links matches my interest.

continued on page 290

Using Subject-Verb Agreement.

Search through your own essay for subjects and verbs that do not agree. Read your sentences aloud and check to see that singular subjects have singular verbs and plural subjects have plural verbs. Make the necessary changes to improve the readability of your paper.

Publishing and Presenting

Print a final copy of your essay and combine it with your classmates' essays into a website resource book. Your class could add graphics and a table of contents to create an attractive and readable handbook. Consider placing this resource in the school library or computer lab for other students to use.

Another option for publishing is to post your essay on the Internet. Does your school have a website? Perhaps there is a place for your critique there. Some websites and online magazines are looking for manuscripts about the Internet and may welcome your essay. You might even find that the authors of the websites you analyzed are eager to read your opinion of their site.

Reflecting

Your ability to evaluate websites by comparing and contrasting can serve you well. How might you benefit from this skill in the future? What do you think accounts for the differences in the two sites you examined? How might you get in the habit of judging the masses of information you see every day?

"Mockingbird quiz," and "*To Kill a Mockingbird*—the book," it was mostly covering the book and not Ms. Lee. There was also an address where you can e-mail the site creator to talk about the book. The biography in this site wasn't very thorough at around one and a half pages long. Also, there were somewhat shorter biographies of others in Harper Lee's family. This site might work better if you wanted a lot of information on her book and not as much on Harper Lee. It gave you some good details, but not too much information.

The second site, "Harper Lee," was much different. It was on a plain background with no color or graphics whatsoever. There were two pages of information but they seemed too crowded. I think the whole site could have been improved if the font size had been increased two points and if everything had been double-spaced. Graphics, colors, and photos would have added some eye-appeal to this lifeless site.

I noticed that, like the first site, there was probably more information on the book than on Harper Lee. In this site there were no links to any other sites or anything that would have helped you find more information. The biography was short. It was definitely not as long as the other site's biographical information, but it did give you a brief description of her life. In my opinion, this site was not very helpful because it gave so little information.

The first site was much better than the second on all three counts. It used a well-designed layout to draw both surfers and students into the page. The first one was crisp and clear, but the second one looked like it had taken barely any effort to create. I liked the content of the first site, and I found it to be more thorough. Links were there for me to expand my search. Although I was a little disappointed that more information on the author herself was not available on either site, the first had more than the second. A look at both shows a difference in quality and quantity. Both matter to me.

UNIT 3 review
Fiction

Words for Everyday Use

Check your knowledge of the following vocabulary words from the selections in this unit. Write short sentences using each of these words in context to make the meaning clear. To review the definition or usage of a word, refer back to the page number(s) listed or the Glossary of Words for Everyday Use.

abashed, 229
absurd, 231
acknowledge, 209
adornment, 279
agile, 276
agitation, 188
alcove, 247
amenity, 203
amiably, 170
analytical, 205
animate, 209
apathetically, 190
apathy, 175
appertain, 276
appraise, 204
apprehension, 183
assail, 234
attribute, 173
avaricious, 173
averted, 174
barbarous, 207
barter, 267
bountiful, 217
burly, 170
cape, 217
compel, 227
compensation, 174
condole, 170
condone, 206
conduct, 203
confer, 236
conflagration, 188
conjectural, 182
contemplatively, 226
cower, 212
credulity, 172
cunning, 205
dank, 199
decry, 255
denounce, 229

deplorable, 209
depreciate, 276
destitute, 220
disarming, 202
discreet, 221
diverting, 209
doctrine, 247
dubiously, 172
duplication, 279
ebb, 187
enthralled, 172
escarpment, 221
eternal, 221
expedition, 235
extremity, 201
falter, 277
flotsam, 217
forge, 202
frivolity, 220
frivolous, 173
furrow, 220
furtive, 245
furtively, 174
futile, 210
glaring, 202
grisly, 206
hangdog, 249
heritage, 249
homely, 243
illusion, 218
impassioned, 226
imperative, 186
improvise, 220
imputation, 275
inaudible, 174
inconsequential, 278
indignantly, 232
indolently, 200
inevitable, 212
intercept, 170

intertwining, 267
intricate, 210
keenly, 171
kinsman, 221
laboriously, 278
labyrinth, 218
lacerated, 201
lament, 269
legacy, 255
liability, 174
maligned, 172
maltreat, 226
mastiff, 254
medieval, 203
meretricious, 277
mortified, 220
nimble, 278
nucleus, 190
oppressive, 176
pall, 182
palpable, 199
parsimony, 275
patriarch, 254
peremptorily, 190
persist, 171
plead, 257
plunge, 269
poignant, 191
poised, 170
precariously, 211
predominate, 276
preserve, 204
presumptuous, 171
proffered, 170
profoundly, 229
prosaic, 173
prospect, 208
protruding, 211
provoke, 170
prudence, 277

quizzically, 233
realist, 199
receding, 200
recoil, 213
recompose, 245
reiterate, 184
reluctant, 239
renegade, 259
repress, 231
reverberate, 177
revere, 226
revile, 261
rifle, 248
rivalry, 269
roan, 269
scalding, 245
scruple, 206
scrutiny, 278
selectman, 255
sheathed, 254
simian, 173
sober, 268
solicitously, 208
spry, 256
subdued, 175
subside, 276
taint, 200
tangible, 200
tenor, 269
tentative, 238
thresh, 185
torrent, 170
uncanny, 211
undulation, 182
usher, 243
vex, 260
wan, 208
wavering, 236
wrath, 270
wryly, 262

Literary Tools

Define each of the following terms, giving concrete examples of how they are used in the selections in this unit. To review a term, refer to the page number(s) indicated or the Handbook of Literary Terms.

character, 224, 252
characterization, 224
conflict, 180, 198
foreshadowing, 168
hyperbole, 216, 252

irony, 198, 274
irony of situation, 198, 274
metaphor, 266
myth, 216
plot, 180, 198, 224, 242, 274

point of view, 216, 242
setting, 168, 180
suspension of disbelief, 252
tall tale, 252
theme, 266, 274

Reflecting on your reading

Genre Studies

1. Identify the elements of plot—exposition, inciting incident, rising action, climax, falling action, resolution, and dénouement—for "The Monkey's Paw" by W. W. Jacobs.

2. Review the definition for *point of view* in the Handbook of Literary Terms. Examine the point of view used in the short stories in this unit. Which stories use the same point of view? Discuss first-person point of view versus third-person point of view and limited versus omniscient point of view.

3. Discuss which techniques of characterization are used to draw the portraits of the man in "To Build a Fire" by Jack London and Dee in "Everyday Use" by Alice Walker. For each technique of characterization used, give an example from the story. Before you begin, review the definition for *characterization* in the Handbook of Literary Terms.

4. Review the definition for *setting* in the Handbook of Literary Terms. Describe the setting of "The Handsomest Drowned Man in the World" by Gabriel García Márquez. Be sure to describe the scenery, buildings, and weather.

Thematic Studies

5. THEME. Review the definition for *theme* in the Handbook of Literary Terms. Then identify the theme of "The Good Deed" by Pearl S. Buck.

6. GOOD DEEDS. What good deed is accomplished in "The Good Deed" by Pearl S. Buck and in "The Devil and Daniel Webster" by Stephen Vincent Benét? What motivates old Mrs. Pan and Daniel Webster to perform these good deeds? How do these good deeds change the lives of the characters they help?

7. POSSESSIONS. What possessions are valued in "Gwilan's Harp" by Ursula K. Le Guin and "Everyday Use" by Alice Walker? How do these possessions affect the lives of Gwilan and the narrator of "Everyday Use"?

8. ADVERSARIES. What adversarial relationships are developed in Jack London's "To Build a Fire" and Richard Connell's "The Most Dangerous Game"? What skills does each protagonist have to fight his adversary? In view of their respective skills, is the outcome of the stories predictable?

for your READING LIST

I Am the Cheese by Robert Cormier. Fourteen year-old Adam Farmer's whole life has unraveled. Nothing is what it seemed—his parents, his home, even his name. Who is he? Whom can he trust? In this psychological suspense novel, Robert Cormier tells the story of a boy who begins to suspect that his parents are hiding a secret, and ultimately that they are in danger. The novel is told in a series of flashbacks and conversations with an interviewer, in which Adam slowly remembers what really happened and who he really is. As each piece of the puzzle falls into place, a terrifying yet very plausible explanation for the deception takes shape. You won't be able to put this book down until you know what it is.

Independent Reading Activity

WRITE A BOOK REVIEW. Imagine that you are a book critic for your local newspaper, reviewing books for young adults. Write a review of *I Am the Cheese* by Robert Cormier. The readers of your review are likely to include both teenagers looking for good books to read, as well as their parents. Before you begin to write your review, think about both audiences. What questions would they have about the book? What information would they want if they were considering whether or not to read this book? You may also find it helpful to read some book reviews in your local newspaper or in the *New York Times Review of Books,* available at your local library. Notice the kinds of things usually included in a book review. The following questions and suggestions may be helpful:

- Include a brief summary of the plot of the book—but not enough detail to spoil the suspense.
- How well written is the book?
- Did you enjoy it? On a scale of one to ten, how would you rate it, and why?
- Was the story believable? Why, or why not?
- To what kind of reader would you recommend this book?

You may even want to submit your review to your local newspaper or to one of the many websites that accept reader reviews. Ask your school librarian or media specialist for help in locating these sites.

Selections for Additional Reading

Tunes for Bears to Dance To by Robert Cormier. Henry is faced with a terrible choice when his boss offers help to Henry's family in exchange for Henry agreeing to betray a friend.

The Best Short Stories of O. Henry edited by Bennett Cerf and Van Cartmell. This is an anthology of the thirty-six most popular stories by O. Henry.

An Architectural Fantasy, 1634. Dirck van Delen. National Gallery, London.

Drama

❝ Drama is life with
the dull bits cut out. ❞

—*Alfred Hitchcock*

UNIT FOUR

ELEMENTS of DRAMA

Drama is literature enacted in front of an audience by people who play the parts of the characters. No one knows for certain how drama originated, but we do know that ritual performances have been held by people around the globe since long before the beginning of recorded history.

The first literary dramas were created long ago in ancient Greece and may have developed from reenactments of ritual sacrifices. In fact, the ancient Greek word *tragōidia*, from which our word *tragedy* derives, meant "song of the goats." According to one theory, people in ancient Greece would come together to sacrifice an animal to win a god's favor. Eventually, that sacrifice developed into an elaborate show involving an actor, a priest, and a chorus with whom the priest interacted. In the fifth century BC, the Greek playwright Aeschylus added a second actor, and drama as we know it was born.

Types of Stages

In classical times, dramas were performed in open-air amphitheaters, or **arena stages**. In the Middle Ages, plays were often produced on the backs of wagons in the courtyards of inns. From these developed the **thrust stage** used in Elizabethan England, a platform that jutted into an area open to the sky. In the nineteenth and twentieth centuries, the **proscenium stage**, or **picture stage**, became common. Such a stage is a box-like area with three walls (or curtains) and a removed "fourth wall" through which the audience views the action.

Types of Drama

Most dramas can be classified as either comedies or tragedies. A **comedy**, in its original sense, was any work with a happy ending. The term is widely used today to refer to any humorous work, especially one prepared for the stage or the screen. A **tragedy** initially was a drama that told the story of the fall of a person of high status, though in recent years the word has been used to describe any play about the downfall of a central character, or protagonist, who wins the audience's sympathies in some way.

ELEMENTS OF DRAMA

PLAYWRIGHT. The author of a play is the **playwright**. The relationship between a playwright and the play is more tenuous than that of an ordinary author to his or her text. A novelist or poet has enormous control over the form in which his or her work will be presented to its audience, the reader. A playwright, in contrast, must depend upon the interpretations given his or her work by producers, directors, set designers, actors, and other persons involved in producing the work for the stage. The playwright's art involves the collaboration of many people.

SCRIPT. A **script** is the written form of the play. It contains stage directions and dialogue and may be divided into acts and scenes. Scripts for television screenplays, such as Rod Serling's "The Monsters Are Due on Maple Street" (Unit 12), include instructions for how the play should be filmed.

DIALOGUE. Dialogue is the term used to describe the speech of actors in a play. The dialogue usually consists of the characters' names and the words or other utterances to be spoken by the actors. The dialogue of a play may contain many **monologues**, or long speeches given by actors. A speech given by a lone character on stage is called a **soliloquy**. A statement intended to be heard by the audience or by a single other character but not by other characters on the stage is called an **aside**.

ACTS AND SCENES. An **act** is a major division of a drama. The plays of ancient Rome and of Elizabethan England were typically divided into **five acts**. Shakespeare's *Romeo and Juliet*, in this unit, consists of five acts. In the Modern Era, **three-act** and **one-act** plays are quite common. The acts may be divided into scenes. Typically, a **scene** begins with the entrance of one or more characters. The time and place of acts or scenes may change from one to the next.

STAGE DIRECTIONS. Stage directions are notes provided by the playwright to describe how something should be presented or performed on the stage. Stage directions often describe elements of the **spectacle**, such as lighting, music, sound effects, costumes, properties (props) or set design. They also may describe entrances and exits, the movements of characters, facial expressions, gestures, body language, tone of voice, or other elements related to the acting of the play. Sometimes, stage directions provide historical or background information. Stage directions usually are printed in italics and enclosed in brackets or parentheses. In stage directions, the parts of the stage are often described using the terms *up, down, right, left,* and *center,* which describe stage areas from the point of view of the actors.

STAGE AREAS.

THE PARTS OF A STAGE

Up Right	Up Center	Up Left
Right Center	Center	Left Center
Down Right	Down Center	Down Left

THE SPECTACLE

SPECTACLE. The **spectacle** is all the elements of the drama presented to the senses of the audience—the lights, sets, curtains, costumes, makeup, music, sound effects, properties, and movements of the actors, including any special movement such as pantomime or dance. Spectacle is one major feature that differentiates dramatic from nondramatic works. The following chart describes common parts of the spectacle.

ELEMENT OF SPECTACLE	DESCRIPTION
Stage	This is the area in which the action is performed. An **arena stage,** or **theater in the round,** is one in which the audience stands or sits around a circular or semicircular open space. A **thrust stage** is one that extends into the audience, which is situated on three sides of the playing area. A **proscenium,** or **picture stage,** is one that has an arch around an opening that acts as a removed "fourth wall."
Set	The set is everything placed upon the stage to give the impression of a particular setting, or time and place. Sets often include walls, furnishings, and painted backdrops.
Properties	Properties are items that can be carried on and off the stage by actors or manipulated by actors during scenes. Examples of properties include books, fans, gavels, and walking sticks.
Sound effects	These are sounds introduced to create mood or to indicate the presence of something. Common sound effects include thunder, ringing telephones, and police sirens.
Blocking	This is the act of determining how actors will move on a stage. Blocking is almost always done by the director of the play.

Literary T O O L S

PLOT, CENTRAL CONFLICT, AND INCITING INCIDENT. A **plot** is the series of events related to a **central conflict** or *struggle.* The event introducing the central conflict is called the **inciting incident.** As you read act 1, look for signs of the central conflict of the play.

MOTIF. A **motif** is any element that recurs in one or more works of literature or art. The star motif occurs in the prologue and in act 1, scene 4. As you read, chart the references to stars.

References to Stars	Speaker	Scene and Line
1. star-cross'd lovers	Chorus	Prologue, line 6

OXYMORON. An **oxymoron** is a statement that contradicts itself. Words like *bittersweet, tragicomic,* and *pianoforte* (literally "soft-loud") are oxymorons that develop a complex meaning from two seemingly contradictory elements. As you read act 1, scene 1, list any oxymorons you encounter.

SONNET. A **sonnet** is a fourteen-line poem that follows one of a number of different rhyme schemes. The English, Elizabethan, or Shakespearean sonnet is divided into four parts: three quatrains and a final couplet. The rhyme scheme is *abab cdcd efef gg.* Both the prologue to act 1 and act 1, scene 5, lines 91–104 are Elizabethan sonnets. As you read these lines, notice the rhyme scheme.

Reader's Journal

What causes people to fall in love?

THE TRAGEDY OF ROMEO AND JULIET

by William Shakespeare

Reader's resource

The Tragedy of Romeo and Juliet is a form of drama known as **tragedy.** Traditionally a tragedy presents a sad tale of the fall of a noble character or characters. In this play, there are two characters who suffer a downfall—the two young people whose names appear in the title. In most tragedies, the downfall of the central character is brought about by a personal failing called a **tragic flaw.** As you read *Romeo and Juliet,* think about what actions of the central characters lead them into trouble. Doing so will help you to identify their tragic flaws.

When Romeo, a Montague, and Juliet, a Capulet, fall in love, they know that their union will not be blessed by their warring families. This creates a **conflict,** or *struggle,* for the two young people that can lead only to disaster.

This play, like others written during the time of Queen Elizabeth I, is divided into five **acts.** An act is a major section of a play. Each act is divided into several **scenes,** short parts that begin and end with characters entering or exiting the stage.

Act 1 begins with a **prologue** spoken by the "Chorus." The Chorus is usually played by a group of actors who chant the lines together, but one actor can also play the part. A prologue is an introduction. It provides information about the work to come. The prologue in this play takes the form of a **sonnet.** Try reading the prologue aloud in class. Read the first four lines. Then stop to paraphrase them, or repeat what they are saying in your own words. Then do the same with the next four lines, with the four lines after that, and with the two lines that end the sonnet.

BACKGROUND. *Romeo and Juliet* is set in "fair Verona," a city in northern Italy. The time is the Renaissance. The central characters in the play are a young man and woman from two noble families, the Montagues and the Capulets, who are feuding with one another. A feud is a fight carried out over a long time between rival groups. In the first scene of the play, servants from these two families are seen dueling with swords. Their duel is typical of the "civil strife," or public quarrelings, that result from the Montague and Capulet feud. The reason for the long-running feud between the Montagues and the Capulets is never explained in the play; in fact, the characters may not know or remember the cause themselves. Therefore, the reader has no basis for judging whether or not the feud is justified or whose side may be the correct one. Shakespeare focuses only on the tragic outcome.

About *the* AUTHOR

William Shakespeare (1564–1616) is often called the greatest playwright who ever lived and is considered one of the greatest authors of any genre to write in the English language. Even now, nearly four hundred years after his death, audiences flock to see his plays. Despite the often-difficult Elizabethan English his characters speak, modern audiences enjoy his work because of his extraordinary skill in depicting human nature and the emotions and universal struggles all people face. Another reason for the enormous popularity of Shakespeare's plays is that they provide something for everyone. In his time, theater audiences included all segments of society with all levels of education, from the nobility to the poorest laborers. His plays include lyrical poetry expressing ideas about love; philosophical discourse on topics such as justice and fate; coarse, slapstick comedy; and swashbuckling sword fights.

Shakespeare was born to Mary Arden and John Shakespeare in Stratford-upon-Avon, a small English village on the banks of the river Avon. His father was a glove maker and local political figure. His mother was from a prosperous family who owned large amounts of land. William Shakespeare attended grammar school in Stratford, where he studied Latin, as was common for schoolchildren of his day. Little is known of his early life.

Stratford-upon-Avon was a rural town, and the plays that Shakespeare would grow up to write have many references to plants and animals of the woods and fields. As a young man, Shakespeare may have been a schoolteacher. He married Anne Hathaway, also of Stratford-upon-Avon, and had three children, Susanna, Hamnet, and Judith. By 1592, he was living and working in London, the largest city in England. There he became a successful actor, playwright, and theater owner. He also wrote magnificent poetry. His theater company, the Lord Chamberlain's Men (so called because the group's sponsor, or patron, was Lord Chamberlain, an official of the royal court), became the most popular troupe of actors in London. They performed at the Globe Theater and in a smaller indoor theater called Blackfriars. Shakespeare's company performed two plays before Queen Elizabeth I in 1594, and then, in 1603, the troupe became servants of King James I and changed their name to the King's Men. Shakespeare bought a large house in Stratford in 1597 called New Place, and it is believed that he divided his time thereafter between Stratford-upon-Avon and London. Increasingly, he devoted himself to writing rather than to acting. Altogether, he wrote at least thirty-six plays, including *Hamlet*, *Macbeth*, *Julius Cæsar*, *King Lear*, *Othello*, *A Midsummer Night's Dream*, *The Tempest*, and *Romeo and Juliet*. During a performance of *Henry VIII* in 1613, a cannon fired as a sound effect accidentally burned down the Globe Theater. Following that incident, Shakespeare retired to Stratford-upon-Avon. He died at the age of fifty-two, but his plays have lived on to delight audiences through the ages and around the world.

THE TRAGEDY OF ROMEO AND JULIET

WILLIAM SHAKESPEARE

CHARACTERS IN THE PLAY

CHORUS

ESCALUS, *Prince of Verona*
PARIS, *a young nobleman, kinsman to the Prince*
MONTAGUE ⎤ *heads of two houses at*
CAPULET ⎦ *variance with each other*
An OLD MAN, *of the Capulet family*
ROMEO, *son to Montague*
MERCUTIO, *kinsman to the Prince, and friend to Romeo*
BENVOLIO, *nephew to Montague, and friend to Romeo*
TYBALT, *nephew to Lady Capulet*
PETRUCHIO, *a (mute) follower of Tybalt*
FRIAR LAWRENCE ⎤ *Franciscans*
FRIAR JOHN ⎦
BALTHASAR, *servant to Romeo*
ABRAM, *servant to Montague*

SAMPSON ⎤
GREGORY ⎥ *servants to Capulet*
CLOWN ⎦
PETER, *servant to Juliet's nurse*
PAGE *to Paris*
APOTHECARY
Three MUSICIANS

LADY MONTAGUE, *wife to Montague*
LADY CAPULET, *wife to Capulet*
JULIET, *daughter to Capulet*
NURSE *to Juliet*
CITIZENS *of Verona; several* GENTLEMEN *and*
GENTLEWOMEN *of both houses;* MASKERS, TORCH-
BEARERS, PAGES, GUARDS, WATCHMEN, SERVANTS,
and ATTENDANTS

THE PROLOGUE

Enter CHORUS.

Two households, both alike in dignity,[1]
In fair Verona, where we lay our scene,
From ancient grudge break to new <u>mutiny</u>,
Where civil blood makes civil hands unclean.[2]
5　From forth the fatal loins of these two foes
A pair of star-cross'd[3] lovers take their life;
Whose misadventur'd piteous overthrows
Doth with their death bury their parents' strife.
The fearful passage of their death-mark'd love,
10　And the continuance of their parents' rage,
Which, but their children's end, nought could remove,
Is now the two hours' traffic[4] of our stage;
The which if you with patient ears attend,
What here shall miss, our toil shall strive to mend.[5]

What ends the long feud between the two families?

Exit.

ACT 1

SCENE 1: A PUBLIC PLACE IN VERONA

Enter SAMPSON *and* GREGORY, *with swords and bucklers, of the house of Capulet.*

SAMPSON.　Gregory, on my word, we'll not carry coals.[6]

GREGORY.　No, for then we should be colliers.[7]

SAMPSON.　I mean, and we be in choler,[8] we'll draw.

GREGORY.　Ay, while you live, draw your neck out of collar.[9]

5　**SAMPSON.**　I strike quickly, being mov'd.

GREGORY.　But thou art not quickly mov'd to strike.

SAMPSON.　A dog of the house of Montague moves me.

GREGORY.　To move is to stir, and to be valiant is to stand; therefore, if thou art mov'd, thou run'st away.

PROLOGUE / ACT 1, SCENE 1
　1. **alike in dignity.** Of the same rank (both noble)
　2. **civil blood . . . civil hands unclean.** Citizens are guilty of shedding one another's blood
　3. **star-cross'd.** Opposed by the stars, which were believed to control fate
　4. **traffic.** Business; action
　5. **What here . . . to mend.** What we do not do well in tonight's performance, we shall correct in the future, based on your reactions.

　6. **carry coals.** Perform menial work; figuratively, put up with insults
　7. **colliers.** Coal miners
　8. **be in choler.** Be angry
　9. **draw your neck . . . collar.** Keep from being hanged; note the play on words in "colliers," "choler," and "collar"

words for everyday use

mu • ti • ny (myo͞ot´'n ē) *n.*, revolt against constituted authority. *The crew's <u>mutiny</u> against Captain Bligh is recounted in* Mutiny on the Bounty.

10   SAMPSON.   A dog of that house shall move me to stand! I will take the wall[10] of any man or maid of Montague's.

GREGORY.   That shows thee a weak slave, for the weakest goes to the wall.[11]

SAMPSON.   'Tis true, and therefore women, being the weaker vessels, are ever thrust to the wall; therefore I will push Montague's men from the wall,

15   and thrust his maids to the wall.

GREGORY.   The quarrel is between our masters, and us their men.

SAMPSON.   'Tis all one; I will show myself a tyrant: when I have fought with the men, I will be civil with the maids; I will cut off their heads.

GREGORY.   The heads of the maids?

20   SAMPSON.   Ay, the heads of the maids, or their maidenheads, take it in what sense thou wilt.

GREGORY.   They must take it in sense that feel it.

SAMPSON.   Me they shall feel while I am able to stand, and 'tis known I am a pretty piece of flesh.

25   GREGORY.   'Tis well thou art not fish; if thou hadst, thou hadst been poor-John.[12] Draw thy tool, here comes two of the house of Montagues.

Enter two other servingmen ABRAM *and* BALTHASAR.

SAMPSON.   My naked weapon is out. Quarrel, I will back thee.[13]

GREGORY.   How, turn thy back and run?

SAMPSON.   Fear me not.

30   GREGORY.   No, marry, I fear thee!

SAMPSON.   Let us take the law of our sides,[14] let them begin.

GREGORY.   I will frown as I pass by, and let them take it as they list.[15]

SAMPSON.   Nay, as they dare. I will bite my thumb[16] at them, which is disgrace to them if they bear it.

35   ABRAM.   Do you bite your thumb at us, sir?

SAMPSON.   I do bite my thumb, sir.

ABRAM.   Do you bite your thumb at us, sir?

SAMPSON.   [*Aside to* GREGORY.] Is the law of our side if I say ay?

GREGORY.   [*Aside to* SAMPSON.] No.

40   SAMPSON.   No, sir, I do not bite my thumb at you, sir, but I bite my thumb, sir.

GREGORY.   Do you quarrel, sir?

ABRAM.   Quarrel, sir? No, sir.

> What is the cause of the fight predicted by Gregory and Sampson? Where does the real quarrel lie?

---

10. **take the wall.** Inner part of a sidewalk, near the wall, was cleaner, so people allowed their superiors to walk there as a matter of courtesy.
11. **weakest . . . wall.** The weakest gives way.
12. **poor-John.** Inexpensive fish

13. **back thee.** Assist you
14. **take the law of our sides.** Have the law on our side
15. **list.** Wish
16. **bite my thumb.** Gesture of contempt or insult

SAMPSON. But if you do, sir, I am for you. I serve as good a man as you.

45 **ABRAM.** No better?

SAMPSON. Well, sir.

Enter BENVOLIO.

GREGORY. Say "better," here comes one of my master's kinsmen.

SAMPSON. Yes, better, sir.

ABRAM. You lie.

50 **SAMPSON.** Draw, if you be men. Gregory, remember thy washing[17] blow.

They fight.

BENVOLIO. Part, fools!
Put up your swords, you know not what you do.   *Beats down their swords.*

Enter TYBALT.

TYBALT. What, art thou drawn among these heartless hinds?[18]
Turn thee, Benvolio, look upon thy death.

55 **BENVOLIO.** I do but keep the peace. Put up thy sword,
Or manage it to part these men with me.

Who tries to stop the fighting?

TYBALT. What, drawn and talk of peace? I hate the word
As I hate hell, all Montagues, and thee.
Have at thee, coward!   *They fight.*

What does Tybalt feel about peace?

Enter three or four CITIZENS *with clubs or partisans.*[19]

60 **CITIZENS.** Clubs, bills,[20] and partisans! Strike! Beat them down!
Down with the Capulets! Down with the Montagues!

Enter old CAPULET *in his gown, and his wife* LADY CAPULET.

CAPULET. What noise is this? Give me my long sword ho!

LADY CAPULET. A crutch, a crutch! why call you for a sword?

CAPULET. My sword, I say! Old Montague is come,
65 And <u>flourishes</u> his blade in spite of me.

Enter old MONTAGUE *and his wife* LADY MONTAGUE.

MONTAGUE. Thou villain Capulet!—Hold me not, let me go.

LADY MONTAGUE. Thou shalt not stir one foot to seek a foe.

---

17. **washing.** Slashing
18. **heartless hinds.** Cowardly creatures
19. *partisans.* Broad-bladed spears
20. **bills.** Hooked blades attached to long shafts

words for everyday use

flour • ish (flŭr´ish) vt., wave in the air. *The veteran <u>flourished</u> the American flag during the Memorial Day parade.*

Enter PRINCE ESCALUS *with his* TRAIN.

PRINCE.　　Rebellious subjects, enemies to peace,
Profaners of this neighbor-stained steel[21]—

70　　Will they not hear?—What ho, you men, you beasts!
That quench the fire of your <u>pernicious</u> rage
With purple fountains issuing from your veins—
On pain of torture, from those bloody hands
Throw your mistempered[22] weapons to the ground,

75　　And hear the sentence of your moved prince.
Three civil brawls, bred of an airy word,
By thee, old Capulet, and Montague,
Have thrice[23] disturb'd the quiet of our streets,
And made Verona's ancient citizens

80　　Cast by their grave beseeming ornaments[24]
To wield old partisans, in hands as old,
Cank'red[25] with peace, to part your cank'red hate;
If ever you disturb our streets again
Your lives shall pay the <u>forfeit</u> of the peace.

85　　For this time all the rest depart away.
You, Capulet, shall go along with me,
And, Montague, come you this afternoon,
To know our farther pleasure in this case,
To old Free-town, our common judgment-place.

90　　Once more, on pain of death, all men depart.

Exeunt all but MONTAGUE, LADY MONTAGUE, *and* BENVOLIO.

MONTAGUE.　　Who set this ancient quarrel new abroach?[26]
Speak, nephew, were you by when it began?

BENVOLIO.　　Here were the servants of your <u>adversary</u>,
And yours, close fighting ere[27] I did approach.

95　　I drew to part them. In the instant came
The fiery Tybalt, with his sword prepar'd,
Which, as he breath'd defiance to my ears,
He swung about his head and cut the winds,

> What are "purple fountains"? What fires do they put out?

> Why does the fighting between Capulets and Montagues disturb Prince Escalus? What punishment will they face if they do not stop fighting?

---

21. **Profaners . . . steel.** People who profane, or make contemptible, their weapons by staining them with their neighbors' blood
22. **mistempered.** Hardened for an improper use
23. **thrice.** Three times

24. **Cast . . . ornaments.** Throw aside those objects, like canes, appropriate for old age
25. **Cank'red.** Malignant
26. **abroach.** Open and flowing freely
27. **ere.** Before

---

words for everyday use

per • ni • cious (pər nish´əs) *adj.*, fatal; deadly. *The <u>pernicious</u> bullet, lodged in Dylan's lung, caused his death.*

for • feit (fôr´fit) *n.*, penalty or fine one pays because of a crime or infraction. *Because we did not have enough players on our team, we had to accept a <u>forfeit</u> and go home without playing.*

ad • ver • sar • y (ad´vər ser´ē) *n.*, opponent; enemy. *In court the defendant's <u>adversary</u> is the prosecuting attorney.*

Who, nothing hurt withal,[28] hiss'd him in scorn.

100 While we were interchanging thrusts and blows,
Came more and more, and fought on part and part,
Till the Prince came, who parted either part.

LADY MONTAGUE. O, where is Romeo? Saw you him today?
Right glad I am he was not at this <u>fray</u>.

105 **BENVOLIO.** Madam, an hour before the worshipp'd sun
Peer'd forth the golden window of the east,
A troubled mind drive[29] me to walk abroad,
Where, underneath the grove of sycamore
That westward rooteth from this city side,

110 So early walking did I see your son.
Towards him I made, but he was ware[30] of me,
And stole into the covert[31] of the wood.
I, measuring his affections by my own,
Which then most sought where most might not be found,

115 Being one too many by my weary self,
Pursued my humor not pursuing his,[32]
And gladly shunn'd who gladly fled from me.

MONTAGUE. Many a morning hath he there been seen,
With tears <u>augmenting</u> the fresh morning's dew,

120 Adding to clouds more clouds with his deep sighs,
But all so soon as the all-cheering sun
Should in the farthest east begin to draw
The shady curtains from Aurora's[33] bed,
Away from light steals home my heavy son,

125 And private in his chamber pens himself,
Shuts up his windows, locks fair daylight out,
And makes himself an artificial night.
Black and portendous[34] must this humor[35] prove,
Unless good counsel may the cause remove.

130 **BENVOLIO.** My noble uncle, do you know the cause?

MONTAGUE. I neither know it, nor can learn of him.

BENVOLIO. Have you importun'd[36] him by any means?

What happened when Benvolio saw Romeo?

According to his father, how does Romeo spend his nights and days?

---

28. **nothing hurt withal.** Not harmed as a result
29. **drive.** Drove
30. **ware.** Wary
31. **covert.** Cover; hiding place
32. **Pursued . . . his.** Followed my own mood by not following him

33. **Aurora's.** Of the Roman goddess of dawn
34. **portendous.** Ominous; portentous
35. **humor.** Moody behavior
36. **importun'd.** Questioned

words for everyday use

fray (frā) *n.*, noisy quarrel or fight. *The <u>fray</u> at the Martins' apartment woke the neighbors.*

aug • ment (ôg ment´) *vt.*, make greater in size, strength, or quantity. *Julian wanted his boss to <u>augment</u> his salary so he could earn more money.*

MONTAGUE.   Both by myself and many other friends,
But he, his own affections' counsellor,

135   Is to himself (I will not say how true)
But to himself so secret and so close,
So far from sounding[37] and discovery,
As is the bud bit with an envious[38] worm,
Ere he can spread his sweet leaves to the air

140   Or dedicate his beauty to the sun.
Could we but learn from whence[39] his sorrows grow,
We would as willingly give cure as know.

Enter ROMEO.

BENVOLIO.   See where he comes. So please you step aside,
I'll know his <u>grievance</u>, or be much denied.

What does Benvolio hope to learn?

145   **MONTAGUE.**   I would thou wert[40] so happy by thy stay
To hear true shrift.[41] Come, madam, let's away.

Exeunt MONTAGUE *and* LADY.

BENVOLIO.   Good morrow, cousin.

ROMEO.   Is the day so young?

BENVOLIO.   But new strook[42] nine.

ROMEO.   Ay me, sad hours seem long.
Was that my father that went hence[43] so fast?

150   **BENVOLIO.**   It was. What sadness lengthens Romeo's hours?

ROMEO.   Not having that which, having, makes them short.

BENVOLIO.   In love?

ROMEO.   Out—

BENVOLIO.   Of love?

What is the cause of Romeo's despair?

155   **ROMEO.**   Out of her favor where I am in love.

BENVOLIO.   Alas that love, so gentle in his view,
Should be so tyrannous and rough in proof!

ROMEO.   Alas that love, whose view is muffled still,[44]
Should, without eyes, see pathways to his will!

160   Where shall we dine? O me! what fray was here?

---

37. **sounding.** Being understood
38. **envious.** Vicious
39. **whence.** What place
40. **wert.** Were
41. **shrift.** Confession

42. **strook.** Struck
43. **hence.** From here
44. **whose view . . . still.** Love is conventionally pictured as blind.

words for everyday use   griev • ance (grēv´əns) n., complaint or resentment. *The teacher's <u>grievance</u> over reassignment to social studies classes was heard by a mediator.*

Yet tell me not, for I have heard it all:
Here's much to do with hate, but more with love.
Why then, O brawling love! O loving hate!
O any thing, of nothing first create![45]
165 O heavy lightness, serious vanity,
Misshapen chaos of well-seeming forms,
Feather of lead, bright smoke, cold fire, sick health,
Still-waking sleep, that is not what it is!
This love feel I, that feel no love in this.[46]
Dost thou not laugh?

What makes Benvolio sad? How does this affect Romeo?

170 **BENVOLIO.**   No, coz,[47] I rather weep.

ROMEO. Good heart, at what?

BENVOLIO.   At thy good heart's oppression.

ROMEO. Why, such is love's <u>transgression</u>.
Griefs of mine own lie heavy in my breast,
Which thou wilt <u>propagate</u> to have it press'd
175 With more of thine.[48] This love that thou hast shown
Doth add more grief to too much of mine own.
Love is a smoke made with the fume of sighs,
Being <u>purg'd</u>, a fire sparkling in lovers' eyes,
Being <u>vex'd</u>, a sea nourish'd with loving tears.
180 What is it else? a madness most discreet,
A choking gall, and a preserving sweet.
Farewell, my coz.

BENVOLIO.   Soft,[49] I will go along;
And if you leave me so, you do me wrong.

ROMEO. Tut, I have lost myself, I am not here:
185 This is not Romeo, he's some other where.

BENVOLIO. Tell me in sadness,[50] who is that you love?

ROMEO. What, shall I groan and tell thee?

BENVOLIO.   Groan? why, no;
But sadly tell me, who?

ROMEO. Bid a sick man in sadness make his will—

---

45. **O any thing . . . create!** All things created (by God) out of nothing
46. **O brawling love . . . no love in this.** Romeo's string of contradictions shows the confused state he is in. He feels good because he is in love and also feels bad because his love is not returned. His language suggests that he is in love with love.

47. **coz.** Cousin (said of any relative)
48. **Griefs of mine own . . . of thine.** The grief in my heart will multiply if it feels the further weight of your grief.
49. **Soft.** One moment; used as an interjection
50. **in sadness.** With gravity or seriousness

words for everyday use

trans • gres • sion (trans gresh´ən) *n.*, offense. *Jolene felt sorry for her <u>transgression</u> and put the money back in Kim's jacket.*
prop • a • gate (präp´ə gāt) *vt.*, reproduce; multiply. *Because the minks had <u>propagated</u>, the farmer had to build an additional pen.*
purge (pʉrj) *vt.*, cleanse of impurities. *Stalin wanted to <u>purge</u> the Soviet Union of dissenters.*
vex (veks) *vt.*, disturb; annoy; irritate. *Jim <u>vexed</u> his sister with repeated demands to borrow ten dollars.*

190   A word ill urg'd to one that is so ill!
In sadness, cousin, I do love a woman.

BENVOLIO.   I aim'd so near when I suppos'd you lov'd.

ROMEO.   A right good mark-man![51] And she's fair I love.

BENVOLIO.   A right fair mark,[52] fair coz, is soonest hit.

195   **ROMEO.**   Well, in that hit you miss: she'll not be hit
With Cupid's arrow, she hath Dian's wit;[53]
And in strong proof[54] of chastity well arm'd,
From Love's weak childish bow she lives uncharm'd.[55]
She will not stay[56] the siege of loving terms,
200   Nor bide th' encounter of assailing eyes,
Nor ope her lap to saint-seducing gold.[57]
O, she is rich in beauty, only poor
That, when she dies, with beauty dies her store.[58]

BENVOLIO.   Then she hath sworn that she will still[59] live chaste?

205   **ROMEO.**   She hath, and in that sparing[60] makes huge waste;
For beauty starv'd with her severity
Cuts beauty off from all posterity.
She is too fair, too wise, wisely too fair,
To merit bliss by making me despair.
210   She hath forsworn to love, and in that vow
Do I live dead that live to tell it now.

BENVOLIO.   Be rul'd by me, forget to think of her.

ROMEO.   O, teach me how I should forget to think.

BENVOLIO.   By giving liberty unto thine eyes:
215   Examine other beauties.

ROMEO.   'Tis the way
To call hers, exquisite, in question more.[61]
These happy masks that kiss fair ladies' brows,
Being black, puts us in mind they hide the fair.
He that is strooken[62] blind cannot forget

Why will Romeo's love, Rosaline, "not be hit with Cupid's arrow"?

What advice does Benvolio give to Romeo, who loves someone who does not love him?

---

51. **mark-man.** Marksman, one who shoots well
52. **mark.** Target
53. **Dian's wit.** Ideas or beliefs of Diana, the Roman goddess of chastity and of the hunt
54. **proof.** Armor
55. **uncharm'd.** Not under the spell of
56. **stay.** Abide
57. **Nor ope . . . gold.** The reference is to Danaë, in Roman mythology, whom Jupiter visited in the form of a shower of gold.
58. **dies her store.** Her beauty will die with her, for she left no children.
59. **still.** Always
60. **sparing.** Thriftiness
61. **'Tis the way . . . more.** That's the way to make her great beauty even more evident.
62. **strooken.** Struck

words for everyday use

siege (sēj) *n.*, persistent attempt to gain control. *During the siege of the castle, the baron's men spilled tar on the invaders.*

pos • ter • i • ty (päs ter´ə tē) *n.*, all succeeding generations. *The founding fathers wanted the Bill of Rights to be enjoyed by posterity.*

220　　The precious treasure of his eyesight lost.
　　　　Show me a mistress that is passing[63] fair,
　　　　What doth her beauty serve but as a note
　　　　Where I may read who pass'd that passing fair?
　　　　Farewell, thou canst not teach me to forget.

225　**BENVOLIO.**　I'll pay that doctrine, or else die in debt.[64]

　　　　　　　　　　　　　　　　　　　　　Exeunt.

SCENE 2: A STREET IN VERONA

Enter CAPULET, COUNTY PARIS, *and the Clown, Capulet's* SERVANT.

CAPULET.　But Montague is bound as well as I,
In penalty alike, and 'tis not hard, I think,
For men so old as we to keep the peace.

PARIS.　Of honorable reckoning[1] are you both,
5　And pity 'tis you liv'd at odds so long.
But now, my lord, what say you to my suit?[2]

CAPULET.　But saying o'er what I have said before:
My child is yet a stranger in the world,
She hath not seen the change of fourteen years;
10　Let two more summers wither in their pride,
Ere we may think her ripe to be a bride.

PARIS.　Younger than she are happy mothers made.

CAPULET.　And too soon marr'd are those so early made.
Earth hath swallowed all my hopes but she;
15　She's the hopeful lady of my earth.[3]
But woo her, gentle Paris, get her heart,
My will to her consent is but a part;
And she agreed, within her scope of choice
Lies my consent and fair according voice.
20　This night I hold an old accustom'd feast,
Whereto I have invited many a guest,
Such as I love, and you, among the store
One more, most welcome, makes my number more.
At my poor house look to behold this night
25　Earth-treading stars that make dark heaven light.
Such comfort as do lusty young men feel
When well-apparell'd April on the heel

How old is Juliet? What age does her father think appropriate for her marriage?

Who wishes to marry Juliet?

---

63. **passing.** Extremely; surpassing others
64. **pay that . . . debt.** Teach you that lesson or die still under obligation to you

ACT 1, SCENE 2
1. **Of honorable reckoning.** With a favorable reputation
2. **suit.** Pleading
3. **hopeful . . . earth.** The one who will inherit my land, and the one who makes my world seem hopeful

Of limping winter treads, even such delight
Among fresh fennel[4] buds shall you this night
30 Inherit[5] at my house; hear all, all see;
And like her most whose merit most shall be;
Which on more view of many, mine, being one,
May stand in number, though in reck'ning none.[6]
Come go with me. [*To* SERVANT.] Go, sirrah,[7] trudge about
35 Through fair Verona, find those persons out
Whose names are written there, and to them say,
My house and welcome on their pleasure stay.[8]   *Exit with* PARIS.

SERVANT.   Find them out whose names are written here! It is written that
the shoemaker should meddle with his yard and the tailor with his last, the
40 fisher with his pencil and the painter with his nets; but I am sent to find
those persons whose names are here writ, and can never find what names the
writing person hath here writ. I must to the learned. In good time!

Enter BENVOLIO *and* ROMEO.

BENVOLIO.   Tut, man, one fire burns out another's burning,
One pain is less'ned by another's anguish;
45 Turn giddy, and be holp[9] by backward turning;
One desperate grief cures with another's languish:[10]
Take thou some new infection to thy eye,
And the rank poison of the old will die.

ROMEO.   Your plantan leaf[11] is excellent for that.

50 BENVOLIO.   For what, I pray thee?

ROMEO.   For your broken shin.

BENVOLIO.   Why, Romeo, art thou mad?

ROMEO.   Not mad, but bound more than a madman is;
Shut up in prison, kept without my food,
Whipt and tormented and—God-den,[12] good fellow.

55 SERVANT.   God gi' god-den. I pray, sir, can you read?

ROMEO.   Ay, mine own fortune in my misery.

SERVANT.   Perhaps you have learn'd it without book.

---

4. **fennel.** Plant with yellow flowers and a sweet aroma
5. **Inherit.** Experience
6. **May stand . . . none.** She may be one of a number of women, but when you reckon, or make calculations, about which is the best, you will find that none compares to her.
7. **sirrah.** Form of address used by a person of higher rank when speaking to a person of a lesser social rank

8. **on their pleasure stay.** Wait to see what will be their pleasure
9. **holp.** Helped; cured
10. **languish.** State of depression
11. **plantan leaf.** Leaf of the plantain, applied to soothe minor wounds
12. **God-den.** Good evening

What advice does Capulet give Paris? Who gave similar advice to Romeo?

What is the servant's problem?

But I pray, can you read any thing you see?

ROMEO. Ay, if I know the letters and the language.

60 **SERVANT.** Ye say honestly, rest you merry!

ROMEO. Stay, fellow, I can read.
(*He reads the letter.*) "Signior Martino and his wife and daughters; County
Anselme and his beauteous sisters; the lady widow of Vitruvio; Signior Placentio
and his lovely nieces; Mercutio and his brother Valentine; mine uncle Capulet,
65 his wife, and daughters; my fair niece Rosaline, and Livia; Signior Valentio and
his cousin Tybalt; Lucio and the lively Helena." A fair assembly. Whither should
they come?

SERVANT. Up.

ROMEO. Whither? to supper?

70 **SERVANT.** To our house.

ROMEO. Whose house?

SERVANT. My master's.

ROMEO. Indeed I should have ask'd thee that before.

SERVANT. Now I'll tell you without asking. My master is the great rich
75 Capulet, and if you be not of the house of Montagues, I pray come and crush[13]
a cup of wine. Rest you merry! *Exit.*

BENVOLIO. At this same ancient feast of Capulet's
Sups the fair Rosaline whom thou so loves,
With all the admired beauties of Verona.
80 Go thither,[14] and with unattainted[15] eye
Compare her face with some that I shall show,
And I will make thee think thy swan a crow.

ROMEO. When the <u>devout</u> religion of mine eye
Maintains such falsehood, then turn tears to fires;
85 And these,[16] who, often drown'd, could never die,
Transparent heretics, be burnt for liars!
One fairer than my love! The all-seeing sun
Ne'er saw her match since first the world begun.

BENVOLIO. Tut, you saw her fair, none else being by,
90 Herself pois'd with herself in either eye;
But in that crystal scales let there be weigh'd
Your lady's love against some other maid

Whom does Romeo
love? What advice does
Benvolio give to Romeo?

---

13. **crush.** Drink
14. **thither.** There
15. **unattainted.** Untainted; not with preconceived ideas
16. **these.** These eyes

words for everyday use
de • vout (di vout´) *adj.,* religious; pious. *A <u>devout</u> woman, Mrs. Bacholl went to Mass every weekend.*

That I will show you shining at this feast,
And she shall scant show well that now seems best.

95   **ROMEO.**   I'll go along no such sight to be shown,
But to rejoice in splendor of mine own.   *Exeunt.*

What does Romeo decide to do?

SCENE 3: CAPULET'S HOUSE

Enter CAPULET'S WIFE, *and* NURSE.

LADY CAPULET.   Nurse, where's my daughter? Call her forth to me.

NURSE.   Now by my maidenhead at twelve year old,
I bade her come. What, lamb! What, ladybird!
God forbid! Where's this girl? What, Juliet!

Enter JULIET.

JULIET.   How now, who calls?

NURSE.   Your mother.

5   **JULIET.**   Madam, I am here,
What is your will?

LADY CAPULET.   This is the matter. Nurse, give leave[1] a while,
We must talk in secret. Nurse, come back again,
I have rememb'red me, thou s'[2] hear our counsel.

10   Thou knowest my daughter's of a pretty age.

NURSE.   Faith, I can tell her age unto an hour.

LADY CAPULET.   She's not fourteen.

NURSE.   I'll lay fourteen of my teeth—
And yet, to my teen[3] be it spoken, I have but four—
She's not fourteen. How long is it now
To Lammas-tide?[4]

15   **LADY CAPULET.**   A fortnight[5] and odd days.

NURSE.   Even or odd, of all days in the year,
Come Lammas-eve at night shall she be fourteen,
Susan and she—God rest all Christian souls!—
Were of an age. Well, Susan is with God,
20   She was too good for me. But as I said,
On Lammas-eve at night shall she be fourteen,
That shall she, marry, I remember it well.
'Tis since the earthquake now aleven[6] years,
And[7] she was wean'd—I never shall forget it—

ACT 1, SCENE 3
  1. **give leave.** Leave us
  2. **thou s'.** You shall or you should
  3. **teen.** Sorrow

  4. **Lammas-tide.** First of August
  5. **fortnight.** Fourteen nights
  6. **aleven.** Eleven
  7. **And.** Since

25 Of all the days of the year, upon that day;
For I had then laid wormwood to my dug,[8]
Sitting in the sun under the dove-house wall.
My lord and you were then at Mantua—
Nay, I do bear a brain—but as I said,
30 When it did taste the wormwood on the nipple
Of my dug and felt it bitter, pretty fool,
To see it teachy[9] and fall out wi' th' dug!
Shake, quoth the dove-house;[10] 'twas no need, I trow,[11]
To bid me trudge.
35 And since that time it is aleven years,
For then she could stand high-lone;[12] nay, by th' rood,[13]
She could have run and waddled all about;
For even the day before, she broke her <u>brow</u>,
And then my husband—God be with his soul!
40 'A[14] was a merry man—took up the child.
"Yea," quoth he, "dost thou fall upon thy face?
Thou wilt fall backward when thou hast more wit,
Wilt thou not, Jule?" and by my holidam,[15]
The pretty wretch left crying and said, "Ay."[16]
45 To see now how a jest shall come about![17]
I warrant,[18] and I should live a thousand years,
I never should forget it: "Wilt thou not, Jule?" quoth he;
And, pretty fool, it stinted[19] and said, "Ay."

LADY CAPULET.   Enough of this, I pray thee hold thy peace.

50 **NURSE.**   Yes, madam, yet I cannot choose but laugh
To think it should leave crying and say, "Ay."
And yet I warrant it had upon it[20] brow
A bump as big as a young cock'rel's stone[21]—
A perilous knock—and it cried bitterly.
55 "Yea," quoth my husband, "fall'st upon thy face?
Thou wilt fall backward when thou comest to age,

---

8. **laid wormwood to my dug.** Applied the bitter herb called wormwood to her breast to wean the child
9. **teachy.** Touchy
10. **Shake . . . dove-house.** The dove house shook because of the earthquake.
11. **trow.** Believe
12. **stand high-lone.** Stand upright
13. **rood.** Cross
14. **'A.** He

15. **holidam.** Holiness, sometimes referring to the Virgin Mary
16. **Ay.** Aye, or yes
17. **To see . . . about!** The nurse is expressing pleasure at seeing her husband's joke come true.
18. **warrant.** Swear or guarantee
19. **stinted.** Stopped (crying)
20. **it.** Its
21. **cock'rel's stone.** Part of a young male chicken

words for everyday use

brow (brou) *n.*, forehead. *Jed wiped the sweat from his <u>brow</u>.*

Wilt thou not, Jule?" It stinted and said, "Ay."

JULIET.   And stint thou too, I pray thee, nurse, say I.

NURSE.   Peace, I have done. God mark thee to his grace!²²
60   Thou wast the prettiest babe that e'er I nurs'd.
And I might live to see thee married once,
I have my wish.

LADY CAPULET.   Marry, that "marry" is the very theme
I came to talk of. Tell me, daughter Juliet,
65   How stands your dispositions to be married?

JULIET.   It is an honor that I dream not of.

NURSE.   An honor! were not I thine only nurse,
I would say thou hadst suck'd wisdom from thy teat.

LADY CAPULET.   Well, think of marriage now; younger than you,
70   Here in Verona, ladies of esteem,
Are made already mothers. By my count,
I was your mother much upon these years
That you are now a maid. Thus then in brief:
The valiant Paris seeks you for his love.

75   **NURSE.**   A man, young lady! Lady, such a man
As all the world—why, he's a man of wax.²³

LADY CAPULET.   Verona's summer hath not such a flower.

NURSE.   Nay, he's a flower, in faith, a very flower.

LADY CAPULET.   What say you? can you love the gentleman?
80   This night you shall behold him at our feast;
Read o'er the volume of young Paris' face,
And find delight writ there with beauty's pen;
Examine every married²⁴ <u>lineament</u>,
And see how one another lends content;
85   And what obscur'd in this fair volume lies
Find written in the margent²⁵ of his eyes.
This precious book of love, this unbound²⁶ lover,
To beautify him, only lacks a cover.
The fish lives in the sea, and 'tis much pride

What does Juliet say she feels about getting married?

What do Lady Capulet and the Nurse think of Paris and his wish to marry Juliet?

---

22. **God mark . . . grace!** God grant grace to you!
23. **he's a man of wax.** He is as handsome as a wax figure of a man. The nurse means this as a compliment, but a wax figure is less than a real person, so the compliment is unintentionally an insult.

24. **married.** Well matched or put together; also a pun on the usual sense of the word
25. **margent.** Margin, as in a book
26. **unbound.** Like a book unbound, he is unbound by marriage.

words for everyday use   lin • e • a • ment (lin´ē ə mənt) *n.*, definite shape, contour, or line, especially of the face. *Her fine <u>lineaments</u> made her the very image of her mother.*

90 For fair without the fair within to hide.[27]
    That book in many's eyes doth share the glory,
    That in gold clasps locks in the golden story;
    So shall you share all that he doth possess,
    By having him, making yourself no less.

95 **NURSE.**   No less! nay, bigger: women grow by men.

    LADY CAPULET.   Speak briefly, can you like of Paris' love?[28]

    JULIET.   I'll look to like, if looking liking move;
    But no more deep will I endart[29] mine eye
    Than your consent gives strength to make it fly.

    Enter SERVINGMAN.

> What does Juliet say is important about her choice of a husband?

100 **SERVINGMAN.**   Madam, the guests are come, supper serv'd up, you call'd, my young
    lady ask'd for, the nurse curs'd in the pantry,[30] and every thing in extremity. I must
    hence to wait; I beseech you follow straight.   *Exit.*

    LADY CAPULET.   We follow thee. Juliet, the County stays.[31]

    NURSE.   Go, girl, seek happy nights to happy days.   *Exeunt.*

SCENE 4: IN FRONT OF CAPULET'S HOUSE

Enter ROMEO, MERCUTIO, BENVOLIO, *with five or six other* MASKERS;[1] TORCH-BEARERS.

    ROMEO.   What, shall this speech be spoke for our excuse?
    Or shall we on without apology?

    BENVOLIO.   The date is out of such prolixity:[2]
    We'll have no Cupid hoodwink'd with a scarf,[3]
5   Bearing a Tartar's painted bow of lath,[4]
    Scaring the ladies like a crow-keeper,[5]
    Nor no without-book prologue,[6] faintly spoke
    After the prompter,[7] for our entrance;
    But let them measure us by what they will,
10 We'll measure them a measure[8] and be gone.

    ROMEO.   Give me a torch, I am not for this ambling;[9]
    Being but heavy, I will bear the light.

---

27. **The fish . . . hide.** It is as appropriate for a good man to be handsome as it is for a fish to live in the sea.
28. **like of Paris' love.** Love someone like Paris
29. **endart.** Shoot like a dart
30. **the nurse . . . pantry.** The kitchen help are cursing because the nurse is not there to help.
31. **the County stays.** The Count (Paris) waits.

ACT 1, SCENE 4

1. **Maskers.** People wearing masks, dressed in costumes for the party
2. **The date . . . prolixity.** Such a speech, given by maskers arriving at a party, is out of fashion.
3. **Cupid hoodwink'd with a scarf.** Cupid was the Roman god of love, said to pierce lovers with his arrows.

To be hoodwinked meant, literally, to be blindfolded with a scarf tied around the head.
4. **Bearing . . . lath.** Carrying, like Cupid or like a Tartar, a small bow of painted strips of wood
5. **crow-keeper.** Scarecrow
6. **without-book prologue.** Memorized introduction
7. **After the prompter.** Repeating lines given by a prompter, a person whose job it is to help an actor who has forgotten the lines
8. **measure them a measure.** Give them a dance
9. **Give me . . . ambling.** Romeo wishes to carry a torch because he wants to avoid ambling, or dancing, being too heavy-hearted for such frivolity.

MERCUTIO.   Nay, gentle Romeo, we must have you dance.

ROMEO.   Not I, believe me. You have dancing shoes
15   With nimble soles, I have a soul of lead
So stakes me to the ground I cannot move.

MERCUTIO.   You are a lover, borrow Cupid's wings,
And soar with them above a common bound.[10]

ROMEO.   I am too sore enpierced with his shaft
20   To soar with his light feathers, and so bound
I cannot bound a pitch above dull woe;
Under love's heavy burthen[11] do I sink.

MERCUTIO.   And, to sink in it, should you burthen love—
Too great oppression for a tender thing.

25   **ROMEO.**   Is love a tender thing? It is too rough,
Too rude, too boist'rous, and it pricks like thorn.

MERCUTIO.   If love be rough with you, be rough with love;
Prick love for pricking, and you beat love down.
Give me a case to put my <u>visage</u> in, [*Puts on a mask.*]
30   A visor for a visor![12] what care I
What curious eye doth cote[13] deformities?
Here are the beetle brows[14] shall blush for me.

BENVOLIO.   Come knock and enter, and no sooner in,
But every man betake him to his legs.[15]

35   **ROMEO.**   A torch for me. Let wantons light of heart
Tickle the senseless rushes[16] with their heels.
For I am proverb'd with a grandsire phrase,[17]
I'll be a candle-holder and look on:[18]
The game was ne'er so fair, and I am done.

40   **MERCUTIO.**   Tut, dun's the mouse, the constable's own word.[19]
If thou art Dun, we'll draw thee from the mire
Of this sir-reverence love, wherein thou stickest
Up to the ears. Come, we burn daylight,[20] ho!

> *What is Mercutio's attitude about Romeo's heavy heart?*

---

10. **a common bound.** Ordinary leap as might be made by an ordinary, untalented dancer
11. **burthen.** Burden
12. **visor for a visor!** A visor is a mask. Mercutio is suggesting that his face is also a mask because he is a jester, one who hides his feelings behind his wit.
13. **cote.** See; notice
14. **beetle brows.** Bushy eyebrows
15. **betake him to his legs.** Begin dancing
16. **rushes.** Plants used as a floor covering

17. **grandsire phrase.** Proverb, or phrase known to our grandfathers
18. **I'll be . . . look on.** Romeo recalls the proverb, "A good candle-holder or spectator makes a good gamester."
19. **dun's . . . word.** A mouse is dun—a dull, grayish brown. Romeo has just suggested that he will be an onlooker, which makes Mercutio think of a hidden, quiet mouse. A constable, or police officer, might describe a stealthy criminal in that way.
20. **burn daylight.** Waste time

---

words for everyday use   vis • age (viz´ij) *n.*, face. *Emily could tell from John's <u>visage</u> that he did not love her anymore.*

ROMEO. Nay, that's not so.

MERCUTIO.   I mean, sir, in delay
45   We waste our lights in vain, like lights by day!
Take our good meaning, for our judgment sits
Five times in that ere once in our five wits.

ROMEO. And we mean well in going to this mask,
But 'tis no wit to go.

MERCUTIO. Why, may one ask?

ROMEO. I dreamt a dream tonight.

50   **MERCUTIO.**   And so did I.

ROMEO. Well, what was yours?

MERCUTIO.   That dreamers often lie.[21]

ROMEO. In bed asleep, while they do dream things true.

MERCUTIO. O then I see Queen Mab[22] hath been with you.
She is the fairies' midwife, and she comes

Who is Queen Mab?

55   In shape no bigger than an agot-stone[23]
On the forefinger of an alderman,
Drawn with a team of little atomi[24]
Over men's noses as they lie asleep.
Her chariot is an empty hazel-nut,
60   Made by the joiner squirrel or old grub,
Time out a' mind the fairies' coachmakers.
Her waggon-spokes made of long spinners' legs,
The cover of the wings of grasshoppers,
Her traces of the smallest spider web,
65   Her collars of the moonshine's wat'ry beams,
Her whip of cricket's bone, the lash of film,
Her waggoner a small grey-coated gnat,
Not half so big as a round little worm
Prick'd from the lazy finger of a maid.[25]
70   And in this state she gallops night by night
Through lovers' brains, and then they dream of love;
O'er <u>courtiers</u>' knees, that dream on cur'sies[26] straight;
O'er lawyers' fingers, who straight dream on fees;

---

21. **lie.** Mercutio puns on the word *lie*, implying both
"rest" and "tell falsehoods."
22. **Queen Mab.** Fairy creature
23. **agot-stone.** Agate used as a stone in a ring

24. **atomi.** Tiny beings
25. **Not half . . . maid.** According to a folk belief,
worms grew in the fingers of lazy girls.
26. **on cur'sies.** Of curtsies, or bows

**words
for
everyday
use**   cour • ti • er (kôrt´ē ər) *n.*, attendant at a royal court. *The <u>courtier</u> lived at court and attended the king's entertainments.*

O'er ladies' lips, who straight on kisses dream,
75 Which oft the angry Mab with blisters plagues,
Because their breath with sweetmeats tainted are.
Sometime she gallops o'er a courtier's nose,
And then dreams he of smelling out a suit;[27]
And sometime comes she with a tithe-pig's[28] tail
80 Tickling a parson's nose as 'a lies asleep,
Then he dreams of another benefice.[29]
Sometime she driveth o'er a soldier's neck,
And then dreams he of cutting foreign throats,
Of breaches, ambuscadoes,[30] Spanish blades,
85 Of healths five fadom deep;[31] and then anon[32]
Drums in his ear, at which he starts and wakes,
And being thus frighted, swears a prayer or two,
And sleeps again. This is that very Mab
That plats the manes of horses in the night,
90 And bakes the elf-locks in foul sluttish hairs,
Which, once untangled, much misfortune bodes.[33]
This is the hag, when maids lie on their backs,
That presses them and learns them first to bear,
Making them women of good carriage.[34]
This is she—

95 **ROMEO.**   Peace, peace, Mercutio, peace!
Thou talk'st of nothing.

MERCUTIO.   True, I talk of dreams,
Which are the children of an idle brain,
Begot of nothing but vain fantasy,
Which is as thin of substance as the air,
100 And more inconstant than the wind, who woos
Even now the frozen bosom of the north,
And, being anger'd, puffs away from thence,
Turning his side to the dew-dropping south.

BENVOLIO.   This wind you talk of blows us from ourselves:
105 Supper is done, and we shall come too late.

ROMEO.   I fear, too early, for my mind misgives
Some consequence yet hanging in the stars
Shall bitterly begin his fearful date

> What does Queen Mab do by night?

27. **smelling out a suit.** Thinking of something to request for oneself of a high-born or noble person
28. **tithe-pig.** Pig given as payment of tithes, dues owed to a parish
29. **benefice.** Church office that provides a living for its holder
30. **breaches, ambuscadoes.** Breaching, or breaking through fortifications; ambushes

31. **healths five fadom deep.** Drinks five fathoms deep. A fathom is a unit of measure of water equal to six feet in depth.
32. **anon.** At once
33. **bakes . . . bodes.** A folk belief was that elves matted the hair of lazy or slovenly people and that to unmat this hair was to bring bad luck.
34. **good carriage.** Pun, one sense of which is "women who are carrying (babies)"

With this night's revels, and expire the term
110 Of a despised life clos'd in my breast
By some vile forfeit of untimely death.
But He that hath the steerage of my course
Direct my sail! On, lusty gentlemen!

BENVOLIO. Strike, drum.

They march about the stage and stand to one side.

What does Romeo fear?

SCENE 5: A HALL IN CAPULET'S HOUSE

And SERVINGMEN *come forth with napkins.*

1. SERVINGMAN. Where's Potpan, that he helps not to take away? He shift a trencher?[1] he scrape a trencher?

2. SERVINGMAN. When good manners shall lie all in one or two men's hands, and they unwash'd too, 'tis a foul thing.

5 **1. SERVINGMAN.** Away with the join-stools,[2] remove the court-cupboard, look to the plate. Good thou, save me a piece of marchpane,[3] and, as thou loves me, let the porter let in Susan Grindstone and Nell. [*Exit Second Servant.*] Anthony and Potpan!

Enter ANTHONY *and* POTPAN.

ANTHONY. Ay, boy, ready.

10 **1. SERVINGMAN.** You are look'd for and call'd for, ask'd for and sought for, in the great chamber.

POTPAN. We cannot be here and there too. Cheerly, boys, be brisk a while, and the longer liver take all.

Exeunt.

Enter CAPULET, LADY CAPULET, JULIET, TYBALT, NURSE, SERVINGMEN, *and all the* GUESTS *and* GENTLEWOMEN *to the Maskers.*

CAPULET. Welcome, gentlemen! Ladies that have their toes
15 Unplagu'd with corns will walk a bout with you.
Ah, my mistresses, which of you all
Will now deny to dance? She that makes dainty,[4]
She I'll swear hath corns. Am I come near ye now?
Welcome, gentlemen! I have seen the day
20 That I have worn a visor and could tell
A whispering tale in a fair lady's ear,

How does Capulet try to get the ladies to dance?

ACT 1, SCENE 5
  1. **trencher.** Platter
  2. **join-stools.** Wooden stools, made by carpenters called joiners

3. **marchpane.** Marzipan, a type of candy
4. **makes dainty.** Behaves shyly by refusing to dance

Such as would please; 'tis gone, 'tis gone, 'tis gone.
You are welcome, gentlemen! Come, musicians, play.

Music plays, and they dance.

A hall, a hall! give room! and foot it, girls.
25 More light, you knaves, and turn the tables up;
And quench the fire, the room is grown too hot.
Ah, sirrah, this unlook'd-for sport comes well.
Nay, sit, nay, sit, good cousin Capulet,
For you and I are past our dancing days.
30 How long is't now since last yourself and I
Were in a mask?

2. CAPULET.   By'r lady, thirty years.

CAPULET.   What, man? 'tis not so much, 'tis not so much:
'Tis since the <u>nuptial</u> of Lucentio,
Come Pentecost[5] as quickly as it will,
35 Some five and twenty years, and then we mask'd.

2. CAPULET.   'Tis more, 'tis more. His son is elder,[6] sir;
His son is thirty.

CAPULET.   Will you tell me that?
His son was but a ward two years ago.

ROMEO.   [*To a Servingman.*] What lady's that which doth enrich the hand
40 Of yonder knight?

SERVINGMAN.   I know not, sir.

ROMEO.   O, she doth teach the torches to burn bright!
It seems she hangs upon the cheek of night
As a rich jewel in an Ethiop's[7] ear—
45 Beauty too rich for use, for earth too dear!
So shows a snowy dove trooping with crows,
As yonder lady o'er her fellows shows.
The measure done, I'll watch her place of stand,
And touching hers, make blessed my rude hand.
50 Did my heart love till now? Forswear it, sight!
For I ne'er saw true beauty till this night.

Is Romeo speaking of Rosaline?

---

5. **Pentecost.** Christian festival occurring on the seventh Sunday after Easter, marking the descent of the Holy Spirit on the disciples after the resurrection of Jesus

6. **elder.** Older

7. **Ethiop's.** Of a person from Ethiopia, a country in Africa

words for everyday use   nup • tial (nup´shəl) *n.*, wedding; marriage (usu. used in plural). *The couple's <u>nuptials</u> were to be held in the bride's hometown.*

TYBALT. This, by his voice, should be a Montague.
Fetch me my rapier, boy. What dares the slave
Come hither, cover'd with an antic face,
55 To fleer[8] and scorn at our solemnity?
Now, by the stock and honor of my kin,
To strike him dead I hold it not a sin.

CAPULET. Why, how now, kinsman, wherefore storm you so?

TYBALT. Uncle, this is a Montague, our foe;
60 A villain that is hither come in spite
To scorn at our solemnity this night.

CAPULET. Young Romeo is it?

TYBALT. 'Tis he, that villain Romeo.

CAPULET. Content thee, gentle coz, let him alone,
'A bears him like a portly gentleman;[9]
65 And to say truth, Verona brags of him
To be a virtuous and well-govern'd youth.
I would not for the wealth of all this town
Here in my house do him disparagement;
Therefore be patient, take no note of him;
70 It is my will, the which if thou respect,
Show a fair presence and put off these frowns,
An ill-beseeming semblance for a feast.

TYBALT. It fits when such a villain is a guest.
I'll not endure him.

CAPULET. He shall be endured.
75 What, goodman boy?[10] I say he shall, go to!
Am I the master here, or you? go to!
You'll not endure him! God shall mend my soul,
You'll make a mutiny among my guests!
You will set cock-a-hoop![11] you'll be the man!

80 **TYBALT.** Why, uncle, 'tis a shame.

CAPULET. Go to, go to,
You are a saucy boy. Is't so indeed?
This trick may chance to scath you,[12] I know what.
You must contrary me![13] Marry, 'tis time.—
Well said, my hearts!—You are a princox,[14] go,
85 Be quiet, or—More light, more light!—For shame,
I'll make you quiet, what!—Cheerly, my hearts!

> How does Capulet feel about Romeo's presence at the feast?

---

8. **fleer.** Mock
9. **portly gentleman.** Well-mannered nobleman
10. **goodman boy.** The term *goodman* was used to address non-nobles. *Goodman boy* is an insult because Tybalt is being called both common and a boy.
11. **set cock-a-hoop.** Act wildly
12. **trick . . . you.** Behavior will hurt you
13. **contrary me.** Go contrary to me, or contradict me
14. **princox.** Sassy boy

TYBALT. Patience perforce with willful choler meeting
Makes my flesh tremble in their different greeting.
I will withdraw, but this intrusion shall,
90 Now seeming sweet, convert to bitt'rest gall.[15]

What does Tybalt plan?

Exit.

ROMEO. [*To Juliet.*] If I profane with my unworthiest hand
This holy shrine, the gentle sin[16] is this,
My lips, two blushing pilgrims, ready stand
To smooth that rough touch with a tender kiss.

95 **JULIET.** Good pilgrim, you do wrong your hand too much,
Which mannerly devotion shows in this:
For saints have hands that pilgrims' hands do touch,
And palm to palm is holy palmers'[17] kiss.

ROMEO. Have not saints lips, and holy palmers too?

100 **JULIET.** Ay, pilgrim, lips that they must use in pray'r.

ROMEO. O then, dear saint, let lips do what hands do,
They pray—grant thou, lest faith turn to despair.

JULIET. Saints do not move, though grant for prayers' sake.

ROMEO. Then move not while my prayer's effect I take.
105 Thus from my lips, by thine, my sin is purg'd.

Kissing her.

JULIET. Then have my lips the sin that they have took.

ROMEO. Sin from my lips? O trespass sweetly urg'd!
Give me my sin again.

Kissing her again.

JULIET.   You kiss by th' book.

NURSE. Madam, your mother craves a word with you.

ROMEO. What is her mother?

110 **NURSE.**   Marry, bachelor,
Her mother is the lady of the house,
And a good lady, and a wise and virtuous.
I nurs'd her daughter that you talk'd withal;[18]
I tell you, he that can lay hold of her
Shall have the chinks.[19]

115 **ROMEO.**   Is she a Capulet?
O dear account! my life is my foe's debt.[20]

BENVOLIO. Away, be gone, the sport is at the best.[21]

ROMEO. Ay, so I fear, the more is my unrest.

What does Romeo think when he learns Juliet's identity?

---

15. **gall.** Something bitter to endure
16. **sin.** Fine or penalty
17. **palmers'.** Of pilgrims
18. **withal.** With
19. **chinks.** Money

20. **my foe's debt.** Owed to my enemy; in that enemy's power
21. **sport . . . best.** Benvolio cautions Romeo to quit while he is ahead.

CAPULET.   Nay, gentlemen, prepare not to be gone,
120   We have a trifling foolish banquet towards.[22]   *They whisper in his ear.*
       Is it e'en so? Why then I thank you all.
       I thank you, honest gentlemen, good night.
       More torches here! Come on, then let's to bed.
       [*To Second Capulet.*] Ah, sirrah, by my fay,[23] it waxes late,
125   I'll to my rest.   *Exeunt all but* JULIET *and* NURSE.

       JULIET.   Come hither, nurse. What is yond gentleman?

       NURSE.   The son and heir of old Tiberio.

       JULIET.   What's he that now is going out of door?

       NURSE.   Marry, that, I think, be young Petruchio.

130   **JULIET.**   What's he that follows here, that would not dance?

       NURSE.   I know not.

       JULIET.   Go ask his name.—If he be married,
       My grave is like to be my wedding-bed.

       NURSE.   His name is Romeo, and a Montague,
135   The only son of your great enemy.

       JULIET.   My only love sprung from my only hate!
       Too early seen unknown, and known too late!
       Prodigious[24] birth of love it is to me
       That I must love a loathed enemy.

       NURSE.   What's tis? what's tis!

140   **JULIET.**   A rhyme I learnt even now
       Of one I danc'd withal.   *One calls within,* "Juliet!"

       NURSE.   Anon, anon!
       Come let's away, the strangers all are gone.   *Exeunt.*

       ---

22. **towards.** Coming
23. **fay.** Faith
24. **Prodigious.** Ominous

to *the*
SELECTION

What do you predict will happen between the feuding Capulets and Montagues? between Romeo and Juliet?

How does Juliet learn Romeo's identity without letting the Nurse know of her interest?

Investigate, *Inquire*, and Imagine

Recall: GATHERING FACTS

1a. When Escalus, the prince of Verona, arrives on the scene at the beginning of the play, what does he break up? What does the prince say will happen if the peace of his city is again disturbed in this way?

2a. With whom is Romeo in love at the beginning of the play? Why does he go to the Capulet feast?

3a. Whom do Capulet and Lady Capulet want Juliet to marry?

Interpret: FINDING MEANING

1b. What "ancient grudge" is referred to in line 3 of the prologue? Who has a grudge against whom? What have been the consequences of this grudge, or feud, for the city of Verona? Why is the prince so upset in scene 1?

2b. What happens to Romeo at the Capulet feast? What becomes of the love that he felt at the beginning of the play? What does this tell you about Romeo?

3b. How does Juliet react when her mother first speaks of a possible marriage? What does Juliet's reaction reveal about her? Is she a dutiful daughter? In what way was marriage different in the time of this play than it usually is today?

Analyze: TAKING THINGS APART

4a. What are Romeo's words and impressions on seeing Juliet for the first time? What is Juliet's first reaction to seeing Romeo? What mixed feelings do they have about each other at the end of act 1?

Synthesize: BRINGING THINGS TOGETHER

4b. What do the emotions Romeo and Juliet experience tell you about the two main characters? What struggle or conflict do you foresee for the two?

Evaluate: MAKING JUDGMENTS

5a. Evaluate the effectiveness of Lady Capulet at convincing Juliet to love Paris. What factors are most important to Juliet in considering Paris as a husband?

Extend: CONNECTING IDEAS

5b. What do you think of the idea of arranged marriages? Would Mrs. Pan in "The Good Deed" agree with the Capulets? Why do you think this practice was used among noble families? What would you do if your parents told you whom to date or marry?

Understanding *Literature*

PLOT, CENTRAL CONFLICT, AND INCITING INCIDENT. Review the definitions for **plot**, **central conflict**, and **inciting incident** in the Handbook of Literary Terms. What conflict is introduced at the end of act 1? What is the inciting incident in this play?

MOTIF. Review the definition for **motif** in the Handbook of Literary Terms. What is the significance of the motif of stars in the prologue and in scene 4? What is the playwright suggesting about the role of fate in people's lives? Do you agree that fate plays an important role in life? It is often said that "character is destiny." In other words, people's fates result from the sort of people they are. What sort of people are Romeo and Juliet? In what way do they act impulsively? What fate might result from their impulsiveness?

OXYMORON. Review the definition for **oxymoron** in the Handbook of Literary Terms. What oxymorons did you find in act 1, and who spoke them? What do these oxymorons indicate about the speaker's state of mind and his or her opinion of love?

SONNET. Review the definition for **sonnet** in the Handbook of Literary Terms and, on a sheet of paper, mark the rhyme scheme of the sonnet found in act 1, scene 5, lines 91–104. You may wish to read the sonnet aloud in order to hear the rhyme scheme. Notice that the lines of the sonnet form a conversation between Romeo and Juliet. Which two lines form the couplet? Why do you think Shakespeare used the form of a sonnet for the first words Romeo and Juliet speak to one another?

Writer's Journal

1. Imagine that you are Lady Capulet. Write a **party invitation** for the feast held in your home in act 1. Describe the food, the dancing, and the other activities in such a way as to make your invited guests look forward to the party.

2. Assume that you are Romeo or Juliet at the end of act 1 of this play. Write a **personal letter** to the other person you have met at the feast. Be sure to express your feelings about the other person as well as your hopes and fears for the future.

3. Play the role of an advice columnist to whom Romeo has written for help with his troubles in love. He has described his initial love for Rosaline, who felt no love for him, as well as his new love for Juliet, who returns his love but is the daughter of his father's enemy. He asks, "What should I do?" What advice would you have for Romeo? Write an **advice column** including Romeo's letter and your response.

Integrating the Language Arts

Language, Grammar, and Style

DETERMINING WHO VS. WHOM. Review the Language Arts Survey 3.44, "Using *Who* and *Whom*." Select the appropriate pronoun for each of the following sentences:

1. (Who/Whom) is going with me to Lady Capulet's party?
2. (Who/Whom) did you see on the street, a Capulet or a Montague?
3. The fair woman (who/whom) I love has expressed her indifference to me.
4. The playwright (who/whom) wrote so many comedies also wrote tragedies and romances.
5. She is the nurse of (who/whom) I was thinking.

Speaking and Listening

REWRITING SHAKESPEARE INTO INFORMAL ENGLISH. Refer to the Language Arts Survey 3.2, "Formal and Informal English." In small groups, read aloud the prologue to *Romeo and Juliet*. Discuss the meaning of the words. Then rewrite the prologue in modern, informal English, being careful not to change the meaning. Your rewrite should be understandable to modern listeners, though not in slang. Compare these two versions of the prologue and read each aloud again. Which version do you like better? Which is more meaningful? more beautiful in the way it sounds?

Study and Research & Speaking and Listening

RESEARCHING AND PRESENTING MYTHOLOGICAL REFERENCES. Shakespeare refers to several mythological characters in act 1. Choose one of these and research the legend behind it: Queen Mab, a fairy queen of English and Welsh legend; Diana, the Roman goddess of chastity and the hunt; or Cupid, the Roman god of love. Prepare a brief oral presentation and share what you have learned with your class. You may want to include visuals that depict your character.

Literary T O O L S

PLOT AND COMPLICATION. A **plot** is the series of events related to a central conflict or struggle. The **complication** is the part of the plot in which the conflict is developed or built to its high point of intensity. In this play, the central conflict is between Romeo and Juliet's love for one another and their families' opposition to this love. As you read act 2, take notes on the events that increase the conflict.

CHARACTER AND MOTIVATION. A **character** is a person who figures in the action of a literary work. **Motivation** is a force that moves a character to think, feel, or behave in a certain way. As you read about the actions of the characters in act 2, think about their motivation for these actions. For either Romeo or Juliet, draw on your own paper the following chart. Complete it as you read, noting the positive and negative aspects of the character you have chosen.

Organizer

Positive	Negative

Reader's Journal

How much would you risk for true love?

ACT 2

Enter CHORUS.

Now old desire doth in his death-bed lie,
And young affection gapes[1] to be his heir;
That fair[2] for which love groan'd for and would die,
With tender Juliet match'd[3] is now not fair.
5 Now Romeo is belov'd and loves again,[4]
Alike[5] bewitched by the charm of looks;
But to his foe suppos'd he must complain,[6]
And she steal love's sweet bait from fearful[7] hooks.
Being held a foe, he may not have access
10 To breathe such vows as lovers use to[8] swear,
And she as much in love, her means much less
To meet her new-beloved any where.
But passion lends them power, time means, to meet, Temp'ring[9] extremities[10] with extreme sweet.

Exit.

> What will give the lovers the power to meet? What will give them the means?

SCENE 1: CAPULET'S ORCHARD

Enter ROMEO *alone.*

ROMEO.   Can I go forward when my heart is here?
Turn back, dull earth,[11] and find thy center[12] out.

Enter BENVOLIO *with* MERCUTIO. ROMEO *withdraws.*

BENVOLIO.   Romeo! my cousin Romeo! Romeo!

MERCUTIO.   He is wise,
And, on my life, hath stol'n him home to bed.

5 **BENVOLIO.**   He ran this way and leapt this orchard[13] wall.
Call, good Mercutio.

MERCUTIO.   Nay, I'll conjure[14] too.
Romeo! humors! madman! passion! lover!
Appear thou in the likeness of a sigh!
Speak but one rhyme, and I am satisfied;

PROLOGUE / ACT 2, SCENE 1
  1. **gapes.** Desires
  2. **fair.** Beauty
  3. **match'd.** Compared
  4. **loves again.** Loves back
  5. **Alike.** Both
  6. **complain.** Speak (of his love)
  7. **fearful.** Dangerous
  8. **use to.** Usually
  9. **Temp'ring.** Lessening or making bearable
  10. **extremities.** Difficulties
  11. **dull earth.** The body, made of earth
  12. **center.** Romeo is saying that Juliet is the center of his life. He turns back to her as things on Earth fall toward its center.
  13. **orchard.** Garden
  14. **conjure.** Cause a spirit to appear

10   Cry but "Ay me!", pronounce but "love" and "dove,"
       Speak to my gossip[15] Venus one fair word,
       One nickname for her purblind[16] son and heir,
       Young Abraham[17] Cupid he that shot so trim,[18]
       When King Cophetua lov'd the beggar-maid![19]

15   He heareth not, he stirreth not, he moveth not,
       The ape is dead, and I must conjure him.
       I conjure thee by Rosaline's bright eyes,
       By her high forehead and her scarlet lip,
       By her fine foot, straight leg, and quivering thigh,

20   And the demesnes[20] that there <u>adjacent</u> lie,
       That in thy likeness thou appear to us!

       BENVOLIO.   And if[21] he hear thee, thou wilt anger him.

       MERCUTIO.   This cannot anger him; 'twould anger him
       To raise a spirit in his mistress' circle,[22]

25   Of some strange nature, letting it there stand
       Till she had laid it and conjur'd it down.
       That were some spite.[23] My <u>invocation</u>
       Is fair and honest; in his mistress' name
       I conjure only but to raise up him.

30   **BENVOLIO.**   Come, he hath hid himself among these trees
       To be consorted with the humorous[24] night.
       Blind is his love and best befits the dark.

       MERCUTIO.   If love be blind, love cannot hit the mark.
       Now will he sit under a medlar[25] tree,

35   And wish his mistress were that kind of fruit
       As maids call medlars, when they laugh alone.
       O, Romeo, that she were, O that she were
       An open-arse,[26] thou a pop'rin pear![27]
       Romeo, good night, I'll to my truckle-bed,[28]

40   This field-bed is too cold for me to sleep.
       Come, shall we go?

       BENVOLIO.   Go then, for 'tis in vain
       To seek him here that means not to be found.   *Exit with* MERCUTIO.

---

15. **gossip.** Busybody or crone
16. **purblind.** Weak-sighted
17. **Abraham.** Beggar
18. **trim.** Precisely; accurately
19. **King . . . maid.** Love story from a popular ballad
20. **demesnes.** Regions
21. **And if.** If
22. **To raise . . . circle.** To call up a spirit as in a seance

23. **spite.** Vexation
24. **consorted . . . humorous.** In harmony with the wet or mood-provoking
25. **medlar.** Fruit
26. **open-arse.** Another name for the medlar fruit
27. **pop'rin pear.** Kind of fruit
28. **truckle-bed.** Small bed that fits under a larger bed

words for everyday use

ad • ja • cent (ə jā´sənt) *adj.,* near or close to something. *The administrative office is <u>adjacent</u> to the guidance office.*

in • vo • ca • tion (in´və kā´shən) *n.,* act of calling on a god for blessing or inspiration. *After the <u>invocation</u>, the valedictorian gave her speech.*

SCENE 2: CAPULET'S ORCHARD

ROMEO *advances.*

ROMEO.   He jests at scars that never felt a wound.

Enter JULIET *above at her window.*

ROMEO.   But soft, what light through yonder window breaks?
It is the east, and Juliet is the sun.
Arise, fair sun, and kill the envious moon,
5   Who is already sick and pale with grief
That thou, her maid, art far more fair than she.
Be not her maid,[1] since she is envious;
Her vestal livery[2] is but sick and green,
And none but fools do wear it; cast it off.
10   It is my lady, O, it is my love!
O that she knew she were!
She speaks, yet she says nothing; what of that?
Her eye <u>discourses</u>, I will answer it.
I am too bold, 'tis not to me she speaks.
15   Two of the fairest stars in all the heaven,
Having some business, do entreat her eyes
To twinkle in their spheres[3] till they return.
What if her eyes were there, they in her head?
The brightness of her cheek would shame those stars,
20   As daylight doth a lamp; her eyes in heaven
Would through the airy region stream[4] so bright
That birds would sing and think it were not night.
See how she leans her cheek upon her hand!
O that I were a glove upon that hand,
That I might touch that cheek!

JULIET.   Ay me!

25   **ROMEO.**   She speaks!
O, speak again, bright angel, for thou art
As glorious to this night, being o'er my head,
As is a winged messenger of heaven
Unto the white-upturned[5] wond'ring eyes
30   Of mortals that fall back to gaze on him,

> What does Romeo wish that Juliet knew?

> What do two stars ask of Juliet's eyes?

ACT 2, SCENE 2
 1. **maid.** Servant
 2. **vestal livery.** Uniform belonging to a servant of
Vestia, the virgin Roman goddess

 3. **spheres.** Places in the heavens
 4. **stream.** Shine
 5. **white-upturned.** When the eyes look up, more of
the whites of them show.

words for everyday use   dis • course (dis kôrs´) *vi.*, express oneself. *The speaker <u>discoursed</u> on the problems of managed health care.*

When he bestrides the lazy puffing clouds,
And sails upon the bosom of the air.

JULIET.   O Romeo, Romeo, wherefore art thou Romeo?
Deny thy father and refuse thy name;
35   Or, if thou wilt not, be but sworn my love,
And I'll no longer be a Capulet.

What does "wherefore" mean? What is Juliet's dilemma? Does she know she is not alone?

ROMEO.   [*Aside*.] Shall I hear more, or shall I speak at this?

JULIET.   'Tis but thy name that is my enemy;
Thou art thyself, though not a Montague.[6]
40   What's Montague? It is nor hand nor foot,
Nor arm nor face, nor any other part
Belonging to a man. O, be some other name!
What's in a name? That which we call a rose
By any other word would smell as sweet;
45   So Romeo would, were he not Romeo call'd,
Retain that dear perfection which he owes[7]
Without that title. Romeo, doff thy name,
And for[8] thy name, which is no part of thee,
Take all myself.

ROMEO.   I take thee at thy word.
50   Call me but love, and I'll be new baptiz'd;
Henceforth I never will be Romeo.

For what reward would Romeo reject his name?

JULIET.   What man art thou that thus bescreen'd in night
So stumblest on my counsel?[9]

ROMEO.   By a name
I know not how to tell thee who I am.
55   My name, dear saint, is hateful to myself,
Because it is an enemy to thee;
Had I it written, I would tear the word.

JULIET.   My ears have yet not drunk a hundred words
Of thy tongue's uttering, yet I know the sound.
60   Art thou not Romeo, and a Montague?

ROMEO.   Neither, fair maid, if either thee dislike.

JULIET.   How camest thou hither, tell me, and wherefore?
The orchard walls are high and hard to climb,
And the place death, considering who thou art,
65   If any of my kinsmen find thee here.

ROMEO.   With love's light wings did I o'erperch[10] these walls,
For stony limits cannot hold love out,

---

6. **Thou . . . Montague.** If you were to change your name, it would not change who you are.
7. **owes.** Owns; has

8. **for.** In payment for
9. **counsel.** Meditations; private musings
10. **o'erperch.** Fly over

And what love can do, that dares love attempt;
Therefore thy kinsmen are no stop to me.

70   **JULIET.**   If they do see thee, they will murther[11] thee.

  ROMEO.   Alack, there lies more peril in thine eye
Than twenty of their swords! Look thou but sweet,
And I am proof[12] against their <u>enmity</u>.

  JULIET.   I would not for the world they saw thee here.

75   **ROMEO.**   I have night's cloak to hide me from their eyes,
And but thou love me,[13] let them find me here;
My life were better ended by their hate,
Than death prorogued,[14] wanting of[15] thy love.

  JULIET.   By whose direction foundst thou out this place?[16]

80   **ROMEO.**   By love, that first did prompt me to inquire;
He lent me counsel, and I lent him eyes.
I am no pilot, yet, wert thou as far
As that vast shore wash'd with the farthest sea,
I should adventure for such merchandise.[17]

85   **JULIET.**   Thou knowest the mask of night is on my face,
Else would a maiden blush bepaint my cheek
For that which thou hast heard me speak tonight.
Fain[18] would I dwell on form,[19] fain deny
What I have spoke, but farewell compliment![20]

90   Dost thou love me? I know thou wilt say, "Ay,"
And I will take thy word; yet, if thou swear'st,
Thou mayest prove false: at lovers' perjuries
They say Jove laughs. O gentle Romeo,
If thou dost love, pronounce it faithfully,

95   Or if thou thinkest I am too quickly won,
I'll frown and be perverse, and say thee nay,
So thou wilt[21] woo, but else not for the world.
In truth, fair Montague, I am too fond,[22]
And therefore thou mayest think my behavior light,

What holds more peril for Romeo than the hatred of Juliet's kinsmen?

What makes Juliet worry?

---

11. **murther.** Murder
12. **proof.** Protected
13. **And but thou love me.** If you do not love me
14. **prorogued.** Postponed
15. **wanting of.** Lacking
16. **By whose . . . place?** Who gave you directions to this place?
17. **I am . . . merchandise.** Romeo compares his willingness to work for her love to the willingness of sailors to risk dangerous voyages.
18. **Fain.** Gladly
19. **dwell on form.** Act formally
20. **compliment.** Etiquette, social graces
21. **So thou wilt.** So that you will
22. **fond.** Silly

words for everyday use

en • mi • ty (en′mə tē) *n.,* hostility; antagonism. *The <u>enmity</u> between the Hatfields and McCoys resulted in endless feuds.*

100 But trust me, gentleman, I'll prove more true
Than those that have more coying[23] to be strange.[24]
I should have been more strange, I must confess,
But that thou overheardst, ere I was ware,
My true-love passion; therefore pardon me,
105 And not <u>impute</u> this yielding to light love,
Which the dark night hath so discovered.[25]

ROMEO. Lady, by yonder blessed moon I vow,
That tips with silver all these fruit-tree tops—

JULIET. O, swear not by the moon, th' <u>inconstant</u> moon,
110 That monthly changes in her circled orb,[26]
Lest that thy love prove likewise variable.[27]

ROMEO. What shall I swear by?

JULIET.   Do not swear at all;
Or if thou wilt, swear by thy gracious self,
Which is the god of my <u>idolatry</u>,
And I'll believe thee.

115 **ROMEO.**   If my heart's dear love—

JULIET. Well, do not swear. Although I joy in thee,
I have no joy of this contract tonight,
It is too rash, too unadvis'd, too sudden,
Too like the lightning, which doth cease to be
120 Ere one can say it lightens. Sweet, good night!
This bud of love, by summer's ripening breath,
May prove a beauteous flow'r when next we meet.
Good night, good night! as sweet <u>repose</u> and rest
Come to thy heart as that within my breast!

125 **ROMEO.** O, wilt thou leave me so unsatisfied?

JULIET. What satisfaction canst thou have tonight?

ROMEO. Th' exchange of thy love's faithful vow for mine.

JULIET. I gave thee mine before thou didst request it;
And yet I would it were to give again.

130 **ROMEO.** Wouldst thou withdraw it? for what purpose, love?

How does Juliet feel about their newly confessed love?

---

23. **coying.** Coyness; skill at coquetry
24. **strange.** Distant; standoffish
25. **discovered.** Shown
26. **circled orb.** Orbit

27. **Lest . . . variable.** Because of its changes, the moon is a traditional symbol of inconsistency, or fickleness.

words for everyday use

im • pute (im pyōōt´) *vt.,* attribute. *I <u>impute</u> the pains in my hands to the damp weather.*

in • con • stant (in kän´stənt) *adj.,* not remaining firm in mind or purpose. *Due to Emily's <u>inconstant</u> demands, Jeremiah did not know how to make her happy.*

i • dol • a • try (ī däl´ə trē) *n.,* excessive devotion or reverence. *Jen's CD and poster collections demonstrate her <u>idolatry</u> of the rock star.*

re • pose (ri pōz´) *n.,* rest; sleep. *Jeff's <u>repose</u> was interrupted by the doorbell, and he woke up.*

JULIET.   But to be frank[28] and give it thee again,
And yet I wish but for the thing I have.
My <u>bounty</u> is as boundless as the sea,
My love as deep; the more I give to thee,
135 The more I have, for both are infinite.   NURSE *calls within.*
I hear some noise within; dear love, adieu!
Anon,[29] good nurse! Sweet Montague, be true.
Stay but a little, I will come again.   *Exit above.*

ROMEO.   O blessed, blessed night! I am afeard,
140 Being in night, all this is but a dream,
Too flattering-sweet to be <u>substantial</u>.

Enter JULIET *above.*

JULIET.   Three words, dear Romeo, and good night indeed.
If that thy bent of love[30] be honorable,
Thy purpose marriage, send me word tomorrow,
145 By one that I'll <u>procure</u> to come to thee,
Where and what time thou wilt perform the rite,
And all my fortunes at thy foot I'll lay,
And follow thee my lord throughout the world.

NURSE.   [*Within.*] Madam!

150 **JULIET.**   I come, anon.—But if thou meanest not well,
I do beseech thee—

NURSE.   [*Within.*] Madam!

JULIET.   By and by,[31] I come—
To cease thy strife,[32] and leave me to my grief.
Tomorrow will I send.

ROMEO.   So thrive my soul—

JULIET.   A thousand times good night!   *Exit above.*

155 **ROMEO.**   A thousand times the worse, to want thy light.
Love goes toward love as schoolboys from their books,
But love from love, toward school with heavy looks.   *Retiring.*

Enter JULIET *again above.*

JULIET.   Hist,[33] Romeo, hist! O, for a falc'ner's voice,

> What message does Juliet want Romeo to send her?

---

28. **frank.** Generous
29. **Anon.** Now, at once
30. **thy . . . love.** The purpose or inclination of your love

31. **By and by.** Now, at this moment
32. **strife.** Striving; endeavor. Other texts use the word "suit" here.
33. **Hist.** Falconer's call

---

words for everyday use

boun • ty (boun´tē) *n.,* something given freely; generous gift. *The Indians' <u>bounty</u> helped the Puritans to survive their first winter in America.*

sub • stan • tial (səb stan´shəl) *adj.,* real; actual; true. *The investigator found <u>substantial</u> verification of his client's claims.*

pro • cure (prō kyoor´) *vt.,* get or bring about by some effort. *Janet <u>procured</u> a backstage pass for the Rolling Stones concert.*

To lure this tassel-gentle[34] back again!
160 Bondage is hoarse, and may not speak aloud,
Else would I tear the cave where Echo lies,
And make her airy tongue more hoarse than mine,
With repetition of my Romeo's name. Romeo!

ROMEO.   It is my soul that calls upon my name.
165 How silver-sweet sound lovers' tongues by night,
Like softest music to attending ears!

JULIET.   Romeo!

ROMEO.   My niesse?[35]

JULIET.   What a' clock tomorrow
Shall I send to thee?

ROMEO.   By the hour of nine.

JULIET.   I will not fail, 'tis twenty year till then.
170 I have forgot why I did call thee back.

ROMEO.   Let me stand here till thou remember it.

JULIET.   I shall forget, to have thee still[36] stand there,
Rememb'ring how I love thy company.

ROMEO.   And I'll still stay, to have thee still forget,
175 Forgetting any other home but this.

JULIET.   'Tis almost morning, I would have thee gone—
And yet no farther than a wanton's bird,
That lets it hop a little from his hand,
Like a poor prisoner in his twisted gyves,[37]
180 And with a silken thread plucks it back again,
So loving-jealous of his liberty.

ROMEO.   I would I were thy bird.

JULIET.   Sweet, so would I,
Yet I should kill thee with much cherishing.
Good night, good night! Parting is such sweet sorrow
185 That I shall say good night till it be morrow.   *Exit above.*

ROMEO.   Sleep dwell upon thine eyes, peace in thy breast!
Would I were sleep and peace, so sweet to rest!
Hence will I to my ghostly sire's close cell,[38]
His help to crave, and my dear hap[39] to tell.   *Exit.*

---

34. **tassel-gentle.** Male falcon of a type
reserved to princes
35. **niesse.** Nestling hawk
36. **still.** Always

37. **gyves.** Chains around ankles
38. **ghostly sire's close cell.** Priest's (or confessor's)
secluded room
39. **hap.** Fortune

Enter FRIAR LAWRENCE *alone, with a basket.*

FRIAR LAWRENCE.   The grey-ey'd morn smiles on the frowning night,
Check'ring the eastern clouds with streaks of light,
And fleckled[1] darkness like a drunkard reels
From forth day's path and Titan's fiery wheels.[2]

5   Now ere the sun advance his burning eye,
The day to cheer and night's dank dew to dry,
I must up-fill this osier cage[3] of ours
With <u>baleful</u> weeds and precious-juiced flowers.
The earth that's nature's mother is her tomb;

10   What is her burying grave, that is her womb;
And from her womb children of divers kind
We sucking on her natural bosom find:
Many for many virtues excellent,
None but for some,[4] and yet all different.

15   O, mickle[5] is the powerful grace that lies
In plants, herbs, stones, and their true qualities;
For nought so vile that on the earth doth live
But to the earth some special good doth give;
Nor aught so good but, strain'd from that fair use,

20   Revolts from true birth,[6] stumbling on abuse.
Virtue itself turns[7] vice, being misapplied
And vice sometime by action dignified.[8]

Enter ROMEO.

Within the infant rind of this weak flower
Poison hath <u>residence</u> and medicine power;

25   For this, being smelt, with that part cheers each part,
Being tasted, stays all senses with the heart.[9]
Two such opposed kings encamp them still
In man as well as herbs, grace and rude will;
And where the worser is <u>predominant</u>,

30   Full soon the canker[10] death eats up that plant.

> What does Friar Lawrence say about good and evil?

ACT 2, SCENE 3
  1. **fleckled.** Flecked, spotted with color
  2. **Titan's fiery wheels.** Wheels of the chariot belonging to the sun god, Helios, one of the Titans
  3. **osier cage.** Willow basket
  4. **None . . . some.** None without some valuable property
  5. **mickle.** Great

  6. **true birth.** Its nature
  7. **turns.** Becomes
  8. **vice . . . dignified.** Vice may sometimes be made worthy by particular circumstances.
  9. **For this . . . heart.** Being smelled, it improves health; being tasted, it kills.
  10. **canker.** Worm in the bud of a plant

words for everyday use

bale • ful (bāl´fəl) *adj.,* sinister. *The robber's <u>baleful</u> countenance frightened the bank teller.*

res • i • dence (rez´i dəns) *n.,* place in which a person or thing resides or lives. *Many French people have a secondary <u>residence</u> in the country.*

pre • dom • i • nant (prē däm´ə nənt) *adj.,* having dominating influence over others; superior. *The <u>predominant</u> characteristic of the painting is geometrical forms.*

ROMEO.   Good morrow, father.

FRIAR LAWRENCE.   *Benedicite!*[11]
What early tongue so sweet saluteth me?
Young son, it argues a distempered[12] head
So soon to bid good morrow to thy bed.
35   Care keeps his watch in every old man's eye,
And where care lodges, sleep will never lie;
But where unbruised youth with unstuff'd brain
Doth couch his limbs, there golden sleep doth reign.
Therefore thy earliness doth me assure
40   Thou art up-rous'd with some distemp'rature;
Or if not so, then here I hit it right—
Our Romeo hath not been in bed tonight.

What assumptions does Friar Lawrence make about why Romeo is making such an early visit?

ROMEO.   That last is true—the sweeter rest was mine.

FRIAR LAWRENCE.   God pardon sin! Wast thou with Rosaline?

45   **ROMEO.**   With Rosaline? my ghostly father, no;
I have forgot that name, and that name's woe.

FRIAR LAWRENCE.   That's my good son, but where hast thou been then?

ROMEO.   I'll tell thee ere thou ask it me again.
I have been feasting with mine enemy,
50   Where on a sudden one hath wounded me
That's by me wounded; both our remedies
Within thy help and holy physic[13] lies.
I bear no hatred, blessed man, for lo
My intercession[14] likewise steads[15] my foe.

55   **FRIAR LAWRENCE.**   Be plain, good son, and homely in thy drift,[16]
Riddling <u>confession</u> finds but riddling shrift.[17]

ROMEO.   Then plainly know my heart's dear love is set
On the fair daughter of rich Capulet.
As mine on hers, so hers is set on mine,
60   And all combin'd, save what thou must combine
By holy marriage. When and where and how
We met, we woo'd, and made exchange of vow,
I'll tell thee as we pass, but this I pray,
That thou consent to marry us today.

What does Romeo want Friar Lawrence to do?

---

11. *Benedicite!* Bless you!
12. **distempered.** Disordered, disturbed
13. **physic.** Healing power
14. **intercession.** Petition, request
15. **steads.** Helps
16. **homely . . . drift.** Plain in your speech
17. **shrift.** Forgiveness, absolution of sin

words for everyday use

con • fes • sion (kən fesh´ən) *n.*, admission of guilt. *The burglar gave himself up to the police and made a <u>confession</u>.*

65   **FRIAR LAWRENCE.**   Holy Saint Francis, what a change is here!
Is Rosaline, that thou didst love so dear,
So soon forsaken? Young men's love then lies
Not truly in their hearts, but in their eyes.
Jesu Maria, what a deal of brine[18]
70   Hath wash'd thy sallow[19] cheeks for Rosaline!
How much salt water thrown away in waste,
To season love, that of it doth not taste!
The sun not yet thy sighs from heaven clears,
Thy old groans yet ringing in mine ancient ears;
75   Lo here upon thy cheek the stain doth sit
Of an old tear that is not wash'd off yet.
If e'er thou wast[20] thyself and these woes thine,
Thou and these woes were all for Rosaline.
And art thou chang'd? Pronounce this sentence then:
80   Women may fall, when there's no strength in men.

For what does Friar Lawrence scold Romeo?

ROMEO.   Thou <u>chidst</u> me oft for loving Rosaline.

FRIAR LAWRENCE.   For <u>doting</u>, not for loving, pupil mine.

ROMEO.   And badst me[21] bury love.

FRIAR LAWRENCE.   Not in a grave,
To lay one in, another out to have.

85   **ROMEO.**   I pray thee chide me not. Her I love now
Doth grace for grace and love for love allow;
The other did not so.

FRIAR LAWRENCE.   O, she knew well
Thy love did read by rote that could not spell.[22]
But come, young waverer, come go with me,
90   In one respect I'll thy assistant be;
For this alliance may so happy prove
To turn your households' <u>rancor</u> to pure love.

What is the hope Friar Lawrence finds in the love between a Montague and a Capulet?

ROMEO.   O, let us hence, I stand on[23] sudden haste.

FRIAR LAWRENCE.   Wisely and slow, they stumble that run fast.

Exeunt.

---

18. **brine.** Salt water; tears
19. **sallow.** Of a sickly, pale yellow color
20. **wast.** Was
21. **badst me.** Bade me, told me to

22. **Thy love . . . spell.** Your love was recited from memory, not really understood or felt.
23. **stand on.** Require

words for everyday use

chide (chīd) *vt.*, scold. *The nanny <u>chided</u> the child for breaking the figurine.*

dote (dōt) *vi.*, be foolishly or excessively fond. *"Grandma Ansell <u>dotes</u> on you," said Mrs. Capecchi to her son when her mother bought him another toy.*

ran • cor (raŋ´kər) *n.*, bitter hate or ill will. *<u>Rancor</u> between the parents prolonged the custody dispute.*

Enter BENVOLIO *and* MERCUTIO.

MERCUTIO.   Where the dev'l should this Romeo be?
Came he not home tonight?

BENVOLIO.   Not to his father's, I spoke with his man.

MERCUTIO.   Why, that same pale hard-hearted wench, that Rosaline,
5   Torments him so, that he will sure run mad.

BENVOLIO.   Tybalt, the kinsman to old Capulet,
Hath sent a letter to his father's house.

MERCUTIO.   A challenge, on my life.

What does Tybalt send to the Montague house? What does Benvolio think Romeo will do?

BENVOLIO.   Romeo will answer it.

10   **MERCUTIO.**   Any man that can write may answer a letter.

BENVOLIO.   Nay, he will answer the letter's master, how he dares,
being dar'd.

MERCUTIO.   Alas, poor Romeo, he is already dead, stabb'd with a white
wench's black eye, run through the ear with a love-song, the very pin[1] of
15   his heart cleft with the blind bow-boy's butt-shaft;[2] is he a man to
encounter Tybalt?

BENVOLIO.   Why, what is Tybalt?

MERCUTIO.   More than Prince of Cats.[3] O, he's the courageous captain
of compliments.[4] He fights as you sing prick-song,[5] keeps time, distance,
20   and proportion; he rests his minim[6] rests, one, two, and the third in your
bosom: the very butcher of a silk button,[7] a duellist, a duellist; a gentleman of the very first house, of the first and second cause. Ah, the immortal
passado, the *punto reverso*, the *hay!*[8]

Mercutio describes what skill of Tybalt's?

BENVOLIO.   The what?

25   **MERCUTIO.**   The pox of such antic, lisping, affecting phantasimes,
these new tuners of accent![9] "By Jesu, a very good blade! a very tall[10] man!
a very good whore!" Why, is not this a lamentable thing, grandsire, that
we should be thus afflicted with these strange flies, these fashion-
mongers, these pardon-me's,[11] who stand so much on the new form,[12]
30   that they cannot sit at ease on the old bench? O, their bones, their bones!

ACT 2, SCENE 4

1. **pin.** Bull's eye
2. **butt-shaft.** Blunt, nonbarbed arrow used for practice by the love god Cupid
3. **Prince of Cats.** Tybalt is the name of the Prince of Cats in a series of medieval tales about Reynard the Fox.
4. **captain of compliments.** Dueling master
5. **prick-song.** Printed music
6. **minim.** Short note in music

7. **butcher . . . button.** Swordsman good enough to pierce a particular button on an opponent's clothing
8. **a gentleman . . . hay.** Superb swordsman, knowledgeable about the rules and techniques of swordplay
9. **The pox . . . accent.** The sickness of smart, young people with their modern speech
10. **tall.** Large; intimidating
11. **pardon-me's.** Overly polite, affected people
12. **form.** Contemporary fashions or fads

Enter ROMEO.

BENVOLIO.   Here comes Romeo, here comes Romeo.

MERCUTIO.   Without his roe,[13] like a dried herring: O flesh flesh, how art thou fishified! Now is he for the numbers[14] that Petrarch flow'd in. Laura to his lady was a kitchen wench (marry, she had a better love to berhyme her), Dido a dowdy, Cleopatra a gipsy, Helen and Hero hildings[15] and harlots, Thisby[16] a gray eye or so, but not to the purpose. Signior Romeo, *bon jour!* there's a French salutation to your French slop.[17] You gave us the counterfeit fairly last night.

ROMEO.   Good morrow to you both. What counterfeit did I give you?

MERCUTIO.   The slip,[18] sir, the slip, can you not conceive?[19]

ROMEO.   Pardon, good Mercutio, my business was great, and in such a case as mine a man may strain courtesy.

MERCUTIO.   That's as much as to say, such a case as yours constrains a man to bow in the hams.

ROMEO.   Meaning to cur'sy.

MERCUTIO.   Thou hast most kindly hit it.

ROMEO.   A most courteous exposition.

MERCUTIO.   Nay, I am the very pink[20] of courtesy.

ROMEO.   Pink for flower.

MERCUTIO.   Right.

ROMEO.   Why then is my pump[21] well flower'd.[22]

MERCUTIO.   Sure wit! Follow me this jest now, till thou hast worn out thy pump, that when the single[23] sole of it is worn, the jest may remain, after the wearing, soly singular.

ROMEO.   O single-sol'd jest, soly <u>singular</u> for the singleness![24]

MERCUTIO.   Come between us, good Benvolio, my wits faints.

ROMEO.   Swits and spurs,[25] swits and spurs, or I'll cry a match.[26]

MERCUTIO.   Nay, if our wits run the wild-goose chase, I am done; for thou

---

13. **Without his roe.** Thin from not eating
14. **numbers.** Verses of poetry
15. **hildings.** Good-for-nothings
16. **Laura . . . Thisby.** Famous women in love stories
17. **French slop.** Pants
18. **The slip.** Counterfeit coins were called *slips.*
19. **conceive.** Understand
20. **pink.** Flower

21. **pump.** Shoe
22. **flower'd.** Decorated by pinking, or punching with holes
23. **single.** Thin
24. **O single-sol'd . . . singleness.** Feeble jest, unequaled in its silliness
25. **Swits and spurs.** Switches and spurs
26. **cry a match.** Claim victory

words for everyday use   sin • gu • lar (siŋ´ gyə lər) *adj.,* being the only one of its kind. *Elijah admired the <u>singular</u> beauty of the sculpture.*

60 hast more of the wild goose in one of thy wits than, I am sure, I have in my whole five. Was I with you there for the goose?

ROMEO. Thou wast never with me for any thing when thou wast not there for the goose.

MERCUTIO. I will bite thee by the ear for that jest.

ROMEO. Nay, good goose, bite not.

65 **MERCUTIO.** Thy wit is a very bitter sweeting,[27] it is a most sharp sauce.

ROMEO. And is it not then well serv'd in to a sweet goose?

MERCUTIO. O, here's a wit of cheverel,[28] that stretches from an inch narrow to an ell[29] broad!

ROMEO. I stretch it out for that word "broad," which, added to the goose,
70 proves thee far and wide a broad[30] goose.

MERCUTIO. Why, is not this better now than groaning for love? Now art thou sociable, now art thou Romeo; now art thou what thou art, by art as well as by nature, for this <u>drivelling</u> love is like a great natural[31] that runs lolling up and down to hide his bable[32] in a hole.

75 **BENVOLIO.** Stop there, stop there.

MERCUTIO. Thou desirest me to stop in my tale against the hair.[33]

BENVOLIO. Thou wouldst else have made thy tale large.

MERCUTIO. O, thou art deceiv'd; I would have made it short, for I was come to the whole depth of my tale, and meant indeed to occupy the
80 argument no longer.

ROMEO. Here's goodly gear!

Enter NURSE *and her man* PETER.

A sail, a sail!

MERCUTIO. Two, two: a shirt and a smock.[34]

NURSE. Peter!

85 **PETER.** Anon!

NURSE. My fan, Peter.

MERCUTIO. Good Peter, to hide her face, for her fan's the fairer face.

NURSE. God ye good morrow, gentlemen.

> What does Mercutio say is better for Romeo than being heartsick?

---

27. **sweeting.** Kind of apple
28. **cheverel.** Easily stretched kind of leather
29. **ell.** Measure equal to forty-five inches
30. **broad.** Large or obvious
31. **natural.** Fool, jester
32. **bable.** Bauble, stick carried by a court jester
33. **against the hair.** Against my wish
34. **shirt . . . smock.** Man and a woman

words for everyday use

driv • el • ling (driv´əl iŋ) *part.*, childish. *"Your <u>drivelling</u> arguments won't make me change my mind,"* Mrs. Tremblay told her husband.

MERCUTIO. God ye good den,[35] fair gentlewoman.

90 **NURSE.** Is it good den?

MERCUTIO. 'Tis no less, I tell ye, for the bawdy hand of the dial is now upon the prick[36] of noon.

NURSE. Out upon you, what a man[37] are you?

ROMEO. One, gentlewoman, that God hath made, himself to mar.

95 **NURSE.** By my troth,[38] it is well said; "for himself to mar," quoth 'a![39] Gentlemen, can any of you tell me where I may find the young Romeo?

ROMEO. I can tell you, but young Romeo will be older when you have found him than he was when you sought him. I am the youngest of that name, for fault of a worse.

100 **NURSE.** You say well.

MERCUTIO. Yea, is the worst well? Very well took, i' faith, wisely, wisely.

NURSE. If you be he, sir, I desire some confidence with you.

BENVOLIO. She will indite[40] him to some supper.

MERCUTIO. A bawd, a bawd, a bawd! So ho![41]

105 **ROMEO.** What hast thou found?

MERCUTIO. No hare,[42] sir, unless a hare, sir, in a lenten pie,[43] that is something stale and hoar[44] ere it be spent.[45]

He walks by them and sings.

An old hare hoar,
And an old hare hoar,
110 Is very good meat in Lent;
But a hare that is hoar
Is too much for a score,[46]
When it hoars ere it be spent.

Romeo, will you come to your father's? We'll to dinner thither.

115 **ROMEO.** I will follow you.

MERCUTIO. Farewell, ancient lady, farewell, *singing* "lady, lady, lady."

Exeunt MERCUTIO *and* BENVOLIO.

NURSE. I pray you, sir, what saucy merchant[47] was this, that was so full of his ropery?[48]

ROMEO. A gentleman, nurse, that loves to hear himself talk, and
120 will speak more in a minute than he will stand to in a month.

Why does the Nurse seek Romeo?

---

35. **good den.** Good afternoon
36. **prick.** Mark on a sundial or clock
37. **what a man.** What sort of person
38. **troth.** Faith
39. **quoth 'a.** Says he
40. **indite.** Invite
41. **So ho.** Hunter's cry
42. **hare.** Rabbit. There is a double meaning here, as well. *Hare* was a term used to refer to a woman of loose

character. Mercutio is referring to the nurse.
43. **lenten pie.** Meatless pie prepared during Lent, into which, Mercutio suggests, one might place an old rabbit left over from before the Lenten season
44. **hoar.** Moldy
45. **spent.** Eaten
46. **Is . . . score.** Costs too much
47. **saucy merchant.** Jesting, vulgar man
48. **ropery.** Vulgar jokes

NURSE. And 'a speak any thing against me, I'll take him down, and 'a were lustier than he is, and twenty such Jacks; and if I cannot, I'll find those that shall. Scurvy knave, I am none of his flirt-gills,[49] I am none of his skains-mates.[50] [*She turns to* PETER, *her man.*] And thou must stand by too and suffer every knave to use me at his pleasure!

What has made the Nurse angry?

125

PETER. I saw no man use you at his pleasure; if I had, my weapon should quickly have been out. I warrant you, I dare draw as soon as another man, if I see occasion in a good quarrel, and the law on my side.

NURSE. Now, afore God, I am so vex'd that every part about me quivers.

130 Scurvy knave! Pray you, sir, a word: and as I told you, my young lady bid me inquire you out; what she bid me say, I will keep to myself. But first let me tell ye, if ye should lead her in a fool's paradise, as they say, it were a very gross kind of behavior, as they say; for the gentlewoman is young; and therefore, if you should deal double[51] with her, truly it were an ill

135 thing to be off'red to any gentlewoman, and very weak[52] dealing.

What concerns the Nurse about Romeo's feelings for Juliet?

ROMEO. Nurse, commend me to thy lady and mistress. I protest unto thee—

NURSE. Good heart, and, i' faith, I will tell her as much.[53] Lord, Lord, she will be a joyful woman.

140 **ROMEO.** What wilt thou tell her, nurse? Thou dost not mark[54] me.

NURSE. I will tell her, sir, that you do protest, which, as I take it, is a gentle-man-like offer.

ROMEO. Bid her devise
Some means to come to shrift[55] this afternoon,

145 And there she shall at Friar Lawrence' cell
Be shriv'd and married. Here is for thy pains.

What plan does Romeo want the Nurse to disclose to Juliet?

NURSE. No, truly, sir, not a penny.

ROMEO. Go to, I say you shall.

NURSE. This afternoon, sir? Well, she shall be there.

150 **ROMEO.** And stay, good nurse—behind the abbey wall
Within this hour my man shall be with thee,
And bring thee cords made like a tackled stair,[56]
Which to the high top-gallant[57] of my joy
Must be my convoy[58] in the secret night.

155 Farewell, be trusty, and I'll quit[59] thy pains.
Farewell, commend me to thy mistress.

---

49. **flirt-gills.** Flirtatious, loose women
50. **skains-mates.** Outlaw women
51. **deal double.** Speak untruly or equivocatingly
52. **weak.** Poor; mean
53. **I will . . . much.** The nurse has not allowed Romeo to say anything.
54. **mark.** Listen to
55. **shrift.** Confession
56. **tackled stair.** Rope ladder
57. **top-gallant.** Highest mast of a ship
58. **convoy.** Means of passage
59. **quit.** Reward

NURSE.   Now God in heaven bless thee! Hark you, sir.

ROMEO.   What say'st thou, my dear nurse?

NURSE.   Is your man secret?[60] Did you ne'er hear say,
160   "Two may keep counsel,[61] putting one away"?[62]

ROMEO.   'Warrant thee, my man's as true as steel.

NURSE.   Well, sir, my mistress is the sweetest lady—Lord, Lord! when
'twas a little prating thing—O, there is a nobleman in town, one Paris,
that would fain lay knife aboard;[63] but she, good soul, had as lieve[64] see a
165   toad, a very toad, as see him. I anger her sometimes and tell her that Paris
is the properer[65] man, but I'll warrant you, when I say so, she looks as pale
as any clout[66] in the versal[67] world. Doth not rosemary and Romeo begin
both with a letter?[68]

ROMEO.   Ay, nurse, what of that? Both with an *R*.

170   **NURSE.**   Ah, mocker, that's the dog's name.[69] *R* is for the—no, I know it
begins with some other letter—and she hath the prettiest sententious[70] of
it, of you and rosemary, that it would do you good to hear it.

ROMEO.   Commend me to thy lady.

NURSE.   Ay, a thousand times. [*Exit* ROMEO.] Peter!

175   **PETER.**   Anon!

NURSE.   [*Handing him her fan.*] Before, and apace.

Exit after PETER.

SCENE 5: CAPULET'S ORCHARD

Enter JULIET.

JULIET.   The clock strook nine when I did send the nurse;
In half an hour she promised to return.
Perchance she cannot meet him—that's not so.
O, she is lame! Love's heralds should be thoughts,
5   Which ten times faster glides than the sun's beams,
Driving back shadows over low'ring hills;
Therefore do nimble-pinion'd doves draw Love,[1]
And therefore hath the wind-swift Cupid wings.
Now is the sun upon the highmost hill
10   Of this day's journey, and from nine till twelve

---

60. **secret.** Discreet
61. **keep counsel.** Keep a secret
62. **putting one away.** If one of them is away
63. **lay knife aboard.** Lay seige, or claim
64. **lieve.** Willingly
65. **properer.** Handsomer
66. **clout.** Cloth

67. **versal.** Universal; whole
68. **a letter.** The same letter
69. **the dog's name.** Because an *r* sounds like the growl of a dog
70. **sententious.** Sayings (The nurse is misusing a big word.)

ACT 2, SCENE 5
1. **draw Love.** Pull the chariot of Venus

Is three long hours, yet she is not come.
Had she affections and warm youthful blood,
She would be as swift in motion as a ball;
My words would bandy[2] her to my sweet love,
15   And his to me.
But old folks—many feign as they were dead,
Unwieldy, slow, heavy, and pale as lead.

Enter NURSE *and* PETER.

O God, she comes! O honey nurse, what news?
Hast thou met with him? Send thy man away.

20   **NURSE.**   Peter, stay at the gate.   *Exit* PETER.

JULIET.   Now, good sweet nurse—O Lord, why lookest thou sad?
Though news be sad, yet tell them merrily;
If good, thou shamest the music of sweet news
By playing it to me with so sour a face.

25   **NURSE.**   I am a-weary, give me leave a while.
Fie, how my bones ache! What a jaunce[3] have I!

JULIET.   I would thou hadst my bones, and I thy news.
Nay, come, I pray thee speak, good, good nurse, speak.

NURSE.   Jesu, what haste! Can you not stay[4] a while?
30   Do you not see that I am out of breath?

JULIET.   How art thou out of breath, when thou hast breath
To say to me that thou art out of breath?
The excuse that thou dost make in this delay
Is longer than the tale thou dost excuse.
35   Is thy news good or bad? Answer to that.
Say either, and I'll stay the circumstance.[5]
Let me be satisfied, is't good or bad?

NURSE.   Well, you have made a simple[6] choice, you know not how to choose a man.
Romeo! no, not he. Though his face be better than any
40   man's, yet his leg excels all men's, and for a hand and a foot and a body,
though they be not to be talk'd on,[7] yet they are past compare. He is not the flower
of courtesy, but I'll warrant him, as gentle as a lamb. Go thy ways, wench, serve God.
What, have you din'd at home?

JULIET.   No, no! But all this did I know before.
45   What says he of our marriage? what of that?

NURSE.   Lord, how my head aches! What a head have I!
It beats as it would fall in twenty pieces.
My back a' t'[8] other side—ah, my back, my back!

How long did it take the Nurse to complete her journey to see Romeo? In how much time had the Nurse promised to return?

---

2. **bandy.** Toss
3. **jaunce.** Bounce; difficult journey
4. **stay.** Wait
5. **stay the circumstance.** Wait for details
6. **simple.** Foolish
7. **be not . . . on.** Aren't worth talking about
8. **a' t'.** On the

Beshrew your heart[9] for sending me about
50 To catch my death with jauncing up and down!

JULIET. I' faith, I am sorry that thou art not well.
Sweet, sweet, sweet nurse, tell me, what says my love?

NURSE. Your love says, like an honest gentleman,
An' a courteous, and a kind, and a handsome,
55 And, I warrant, a virtuous—Where is your mother?

JULIET. Where is my mother! why, she is within,
Where should she be? How oddly thou repliest!
"Your love says, like an honest gentleman,
'Where is your mother?'"

NURSE.   O God's lady dear!
60 Are you so hot?[10] Marry,[11] come up,[12] I trow;
Is this the poultice for my aching bones?
Henceforward do your messages yourself.

JULIET. Here's such a coil![13] Come, what says Romeo?

NURSE. Have you got leave to go to shrift to-day?

65 **JULIET.** I have.

NURSE. Then hie[14] you hence to Friar Lawrence' cell,
There stays a husband to make you a wife.
Now comes the wanton[15] blood up in your cheeks,
They'll be in scarlet straight at any news.[16]
70 Hie you to church, I must another way,
To fetch a ladder, by the which your love
Must climb a bird's nest soon when it is dark.
I am the drudge, and toil in your delight;
But you shall bear the burthen soon at night.
75 Go, I'll to dinner, hie you to the cell.

JULIET. Hie to high fortune! Honest nurse, farewell.   *Exeunt.*

What message does
Juliet await from
Romeo? What must she
do to hear it from the
Nurse?

SCENE 6: FRIAR LAWRENCE'S CELL

Enter FRIAR LAWRENCE *and* ROMEO.

FRIAR LAWRENCE. So smile the heavens upon this holy act,
That after-hours with sorrow chide us not!

ROMEO. Amen, amen! but come what sorrow can,
It cannot countervail[1] the exchange of joy
5 That one short minute gives me in her sight.

---

9. **Beshrew your heart.** (Mild oath)
10. **hot.** Impatient
11. **Marry.** (Interjection)
12. **come up.** Stop now
13. **coil.** Fuss

14. **hie.** Hurry
15. **wanton.** Unrestrained
16. **They'll . . . news.** Any little thing makes you blush.
ACT 2, SCENE 6
  1. **countervail.** Match, equal

Do thou but close our hands with holy words,
Then love-devouring death do what he dare,
It is enough I may but call her mine.

FRIAR LAWRENCE.   These violent delights have violent ends,
10   And in their triumph die, like fire and powder,
Which as they kiss consume. The sweetest honey
Is loathsome in his own deliciousness,
And in the taste confounds[2] the appetite.
Therefore love moderately: long love doth so;
15   Too swift arrives as tardy as too slow.

Enter JULIET.

Here comes the lady. O, so light a foot
Will ne'er wear out the everlasting flint;
A lover may bestride the gossamers[3]
That idles in the wanton[4] summer air,
20   And yet not fall; so light is vanity.[5]

JULIET.   Good even to my ghostly confessor.

FRIAR LAWRENCE.   Romeo shall thank thee, daughter, for us both.

JULIET.   As much[6] to him, else is his thanks too much.

ROMEO.   Ah, Juliet, if the measure of thy joy
25   Be heap'd like mine, and that[7] thy skill be more
To blazon[8] it, then sweeten with thy breath
This neighbor air, and let rich music's tongue
Unfold the imagin'd happiness[9] that both
Receive in either by this dear encounter.

30   **JULIET.**   Conceit,[10] more rich in matter than in words,
Brags of[11] his substance, not of ornament;
They are but beggars that can count their worth,
But my true love is grown to such excess
I cannot sum up sum[12] of half my wealth.

35   **FRIAR LAWRENCE.**   Come, come with me, and we will make short work,
For by your leaves, you shall not stay alone
Till Holy Church incorporate two in one.   *Exeunt.*

To what does Friar Lawrence compare "fire and powder, / Which as they kiss, consume"?

---

2. **confounds.** Destroys
3. **gossamers.** Delicate threads like those spun by spiders
4. **wanton.** Sportive
5. **vanity.** Temporary joy of life
6. **As much.** A return of Romeo's greeting and kiss
7. **that.** If

8. **blazon.** Proclaim
9. **imagin'd happiness.** Unexpressed emotion
10. **Conceit.** Understanding
11. **Brags of.** Prides himself on
12. **sum up sum.** Determine the total

Respond *to the* SELECTION

Do you think it is more important to respond to true love or to follow your parents' wishes? Why?

Investigate, *Inquire,* and Imagine

Recall: GATHERING FACTS

1a. To what does Romeo compare Juliet's eyes in the opening of scene 2? What does Romeo swear by in line 107 of this scene? What is Juliet's response?

2a. What does Juliet say about the name *Montague* in the balcony scene? How does Romeo respond?

3a. Why does Romeo go to see Friar Lawrence? What does Romeo hope to do? For what purpose do Romeo and Juliet meet with Friar Lawrence at the end of act 2?

Interpret: FINDING MEANING

1b. How do Romeo and Juliet feel about one another, as revealed in the balcony scene? For what does each one hope? What does each one fear?

2b. What problem lies in the path of the two lovers? What is Romeo ready to renounce in exchange for Juliet's love?

3b. Why does Friar Lawrence want to marry the two young people to one another? What does he hope to accomplish by doing this?

Analyze: TAKING THINGS APART

4a. Analyze Juliet's statements about marriage and love, starting from act 1, scene 3, in which Lady Capulet asks her how she feels about marriage, through act 2, scene 2, in which Juliet speaks to Romeo from her balcony about their love and about marriage. How do Juliet's feelings change? Who first mentions the subject of marriage, Romeo or Juliet?

Synthesize: BRINGING THINGS TOGETHER

4b. What conclusions about Juliet's character do you draw from her response?

Evaluate: MAKING JUDGMENTS

5a. In what time of year and of day does the balcony scene take place? What do the two lovers both know at the end of the scene? How does what happens between the two young people differ from thinking something over carefully in the cold light of day?

Extend: CONNECTING IDEAS

5b. It is sometimes said that "The end justifies the means." This means that questionable methods may be used to accomplish a goal that is important or worthy. In the case of Romeo and Juliet, Friar Lawrence goes against the wishes of the Capulets and Montagues in marrying Romeo and Juliet, and helps deceive the families as well, in order to accomplish what he believes is a worthy goal. What examples can you recall in modern history in which this argument that "the end justifies the means" has been made? Do you agree that noble ends justify any means? Explain.

Understanding *Literature*

PLOT AND COMPLICATION. Review the definitions for **plot** and **complication** in the Handbook of Literary Terms. In this play, the central conflict is between Romeo and Juliet's love for one another and their families' opposition to this love. The central conflict is introduced in act 1. What happens in act 2 to develop this conflict even further?

CHARACTER AND MOTIVATION. Review the definitions for **character** and **motivation** in the Handbook of Literary Terms. Why does Romeo's presence in the garden make Juliet afraid? What does this part of scene 2 reveal about the character of Romeo? What motivates him? How strong is this motivation?

Writer's Journal

1. Imagine that you are Juliet. Write the **journal entry** she might write after the balcony scene in act 2, scene 2.
2. Play the role of Friar Lawrence, about to perform a wedding ceremony for Romeo and Juliet. Write the **marriage vows** for the couple.
3. Begin by writing notes, in prose, about how you think Rosaline might regard Romeo. Include in your notes a sentence or two comparing Romeo to the moon, which is sometimes full, sometimes partially full, and sometimes completely dark. Then study your notes and make a list of rhymes that you might use in your **poem**, such as *moon* and *soon, Romeo* and *below*.

Integrating the **Language Arts**

Vocabulary

USING VOCABULARY IN CONTEXT. Review the definition of each of these vocabulary words from act 2. Write sentences using each word correctly. Underline the vocabulary word. An example has been done for you.

Example: **inconstant**, not remaining firm in mind or purpose. *My sister and her boyfriend are so* <u>inconstant</u> *in their feelings for each other that they repeatedly make up and break up.*

adjacent	repose
substantial	enmity
procure	dote
singular	chide
predominant	bounty

Language, Grammar, and Style

AGREEMENT OF PRONOUNS AND ANTECEDENTS. Review the Language Arts Survey 3.45, "Getting Pronouns and Antecedents to Agree." Then correct the agreement errors in the following sentences:

1. Any woman who wants Romeo's affections will have to wait their turn.
2. Mercutio spends her time making jokes.
3. Friar Lawrence tells Romeo he can return to one's cell to marry Juliet in the morning.
4. Tybalt is known for her swordsmanship.
5. The Montagues and the Capulets would continue its feud if Romeo and Juliet did not marry.

Collaborative Learning & Study and Research

STAGECRAFT. Imagine that you are going to stage the balcony scene from act 2 in a contemporary theater. Working with other students, make plans for the costumes and set design for the scene. What will Romeo wear? What will Juliet wear? Do some research in the library to find out about Elizabethan dress and costumes. Based on this research, create written descriptions and drawings of the costumes. Then turn your attention to the set. Create a written description of the stage set telling what structures should appear there, what painted backdrops might be used, what objects might be placed on the stage, and what lighting effects the scene requires. Do a drawing of the stage that shows the parts of your set design.

THE PARTS OF A STAGE

Up Right	Up Center	Up Left
Right Center	Center	Left Center
Down Right	Down Center	Down Left

Study and Research & Collaborative Learning

RESEARCHING MEDICINAL HERBS AND FLOWERS. Friar Lawrence gathers herbs and flowers that are medicinal in small doses but poisonous in large quantities. With a partner, research herbs and flowers that have medicinal uses but are also poisonous. Prepare a presentation on your findings, including pictures of the plants and information about their uses.

Speaking and Listening

CHORAL READING. In act 2, scene 1, read the lines 1–14 out loud together as a class. After reading the lines, discuss the meaning of the lines and how this sets the stage for the scene to follow.

DRAMATIZATION. Working in pairs read aloud the famous balcony scene between Romeo and Juliet in act 2, scene 2, lines 2–60. This is one of the most famous dialogues in any of Shakespeare's plays. Rewrite the dialogue in modern language, as you would use to speak with a peer, and practice reading it aloud. Which version is more dramatic?

ACT 3
SCENE 1: A PUBLIC PLACE IN VERONA

Enter MERCUTIO, BENVOLIO, PAGE, *and* MEN.

BENVOLIO.   I pray thee, good Mercutio, let's retire.
The day is hot, the Capels are abroad,
And if we meet we shall not scape a brawl,
For now, these hot days, is the mad blood stirring.

5   **MERCUTIO.**   Thou art like one of these fellows that,
when he enters the confines of a tavern, claps me[1] his
sword upon the table, and says, "God send me no need of
thee!" and by the operation of the second cup draws him
on the drawer,[2] when indeed there is no need.

10   **BENVOLIO.**   Am I like such a fellow?

MERCUTIO.   Come, come, thou art as hot a Jack in thy
mood as any in Italy, and as soon mov'd to be moody, and
as soon moody[3] to be mov'd.

BENVOLIO.   And what to?

15   **MERCUTIO.**   Nay, and there were two[4] such, we should
have none shortly, for one would kill the other. Thou?
why, thou wilt quarrel with a man that hath a hair more
or a hair less in his beard than thou hast. Thou wilt
quarrel with a man for cracking nuts, having no other
20   reason but because thou hast hazel eyes. What eye but
such an eye would spy out such a quarrel? Thy head is as
full of quarrels as an egg is full of meat,[5] and yet thy head
hath been beaten as addle[6] as an egg for quarrelling. Thou
hast quarrell'd with a man for coughing in the street,
25   because he hath waken'd thy dog that hath lain asleep in
the sun. Didst thou not fall out with a tailor for wearing
his new doublet[7] before Easter? with another for tying his
new shoes with old riband?[8] and yet thou wilt tutor me
from[9] quarrelling!

30   **BENVOLIO.**   And I were so apt to quarrel as thou art,
any man should buy the fee-simple[10] of my life for an
hour and a quarter.

ACT 3, SCENE 1
1. **claps me.** Throws down
2. **draws . . . drawer.** Prepares to sword fight with the bartender
3. **moody.** Irritable
4. **two.** Retort to Benvolio's *to*
5. **meat.** Matter that can be eaten
6. **addle.** Confused, rotten (with reference to eggs)
7. **doublet.** Close-fitting jacket, with or without sleeves
8. **riband.** Shoelace
9. **tutor me from.** Instruct me not to be
10. **fee-simple.** Complete ownership

Literary
TOOLS

PLOT AND CRISIS. A **plot** is a series of events related to a central conflict or struggle. The **crisis** is the point in the plot where something decisive happens to determine the future course of events and the eventual working out of the conflict. In a tragedy, the main character's fortunes improve until the crisis. After the crisis, the main character's fortunes decline, or get worse. As you read, look for the crisis.

IRONY AND DRAMATIC IRONY. **Irony** is a difference between appearance and reality. In **dramatic irony**, something is known by the reader or audience but is unknown to the characters. There are several instances of dramatic irony in act 3. As you read, note the situations in which the audience knows something that the character does not know.

DRAMATIC IRONY	
Act, Scene, Line	act 1, scene 5, lines 59–80
Character who is unaware	Romeo
What audience knows	Capulet tells Tybalt to leave Romeo alone. Capulet finds Romeo an honorable man to whom he wishes no harm.
What would character do differently if he/she knew?	Romeo and Juliet might have been honest with Juliet's father and not married in secret.

Reader's
Journal

In what ways is society threatened if people settle their differences by fighting or dueling?

MERCUTIO. The fee-simple! O simple!

Enter TYBALT, PETRUCHIO, *and others.*

BENVOLIO. By my head, here comes the Capulets.

35 **MERCUTIO.** By my heel, I care not.

TYBALT. Follow me close, for I will speak to them.
Gentlemen, good den, a word with one of you.

MERCUTIO. And but one word with one of us?
Couple it with something, make it a word and a blow.

40 **TYBALT.** You shall find me apt enough to that, sir, and you will give me occasion.

MERCUTIO. Could you not take some occasion without giving?

TYBALT. Mercutio, thou consortest with Romeo—

MERCUTIO. Consort![11] what, dost thou make us <u>minstrels</u>? And thou make minstrels of us, look to hear nothing but discords. Here's my fiddlestick,[12] here's that
45 shall make you dance. 'Zounds,[13] consort!

BENVOLIO. We talk here in the public haunt of men.
Either withdraw unto some private place;
Or reason coldly of[14] your grievances,
Or else depart;[15] here all eyes gaze on us.

50 **MERCUTIO.** Men's eyes were made to look, and let them gaze;
I will not budge for no man's pleasure, I.

Enter ROMEO.

TYBALT. Well, peace be with you, sir, here comes my man.

MERCUTIO. But I'll be hang'd, sir, if he wear your livery.[16]
Marry, go before to field,[17] he'll be your follower;
55 Your worship in that sense may call him man.[18]

TYBALT. Romeo, the love I bear thee can afford
No better term than this: thou art a villain.

> How does Tybalt try to insult Romeo?

---

11. **Consort.** Mercutio means to "play music with." *Consort* refers to a group of musicians.
12. **fiddlestick.** Rapier, a type of sword
13. **'Zounds.** By God's (Christ's) wounds
14. **reason coldly of.** Speak about dispassionately
15. **depart.** Separate
16. **livery.** Mercutio responds as if Tybalt used *my man* to mean "my servant."
17. **field.** Setting for a duel
18. **man.** One deserving to be described as a man

words for everyday use   min • strel (min´strəl) *n.*, medieval entertainer who traveled from place to place. *The <u>minstrel</u> traveled from Paris to Aix, singing songs of love on his stops.*

Romeo. Tybalt, the reason that I have to love thee
Doth much excuse the appertaining rage[19]
60 To such a greeting. Villain am I none;
Therefore farewell, I see thou knowest me not.

Tybalt. Boy, this shall not excuse the injuries
That thou hast done me, therefore turn and draw.

Romeo. I do protest[20] I never injuried[21] thee,
65 But love thee better than thou canst devise,[22]
Till thou shalt know the reason of my love,

What does Romeo know that Tybalt does not?

19. **excuse . . . rage.** Lessen the appropriate anger
20. **protest.** Assert
21. **injuried.** Harmed
22. **devise.** Imagine

And so, good Capulet—which name I tender[23]
As dearly as mine own—be satisfied.

70 **MERCUTIO.**   O calm, dishonorable, vile <u>submission</u>!
Alla stoccato[24] carries it away.   *Draws.*
Tybalt, you rat-catcher,[25] will you walk?[26]

TYBALT.   What wouldst thou have with me?

MERCUTIO.   Good King of Cats, nothing but one of your nine lives; that I mean to
make bold withal, and as you shall use me hereafter,[27] dry-beat[28] the rest of the eight.
75 Will you pluck your sword out of his pilcher[29] by the ears?[30] Make haste, lest mine
be about your ears ere it be out.

TYBALT.   I am for you.   *Drawing.*

ROMEO.   Gentle Mercutio, put thy rapier up.

MERCUTIO.   Come, sir, your *passado*.[31]   *They fight.*

80 **ROMEO.**   Draw, Benvolio, beat down their weapons.
Gentlemen, for shame, forbear this outrage!
Tybalt, Mercutio, the Prince expressly hath
Forbid this bandying[32] in Verona streets.

> What do Tybalt and
> Mercutio do? How does
> Romeo respond?

ROMEO *steps between them.*

Hold, Tybalt! Good Mercutio!

TYBALT *under* ROMEO'S *arm thrusts* MERCUTIO *in.*
Away TYBALT *with his followers.*

MERCUTIO.   I am hurt.
85 A plague a' both houses! I am sped.[33]
Is he gone and hath nothing?

BENVOLIO.   What, art thou hurt?

MERCUTIO.   Ay, ay, a scratch,[34] a scratch, marry, 'tis enough.
Where is my page? Go, villain,[35] fetch a surgeon.   *Exit* PAGE.

ROMEO.   Courage, man, the hurt cannot be much.

---

23. **tender.** Cherish
24. *Alla stoccato.* Literally, "at the thrust" (fencing term). Mercutio suggests that Tybalt's attack has unarmed Romeo.
25. **rat-catcher.** Reference to his name
26. **walk.** Leave the premises
27. **as . . . hereafter.** Depending on how you treat me in the future
28. **dry-beat.** Beat up (without drawing blood)

29. **his pilcher.** Its sheath
30. **by the ears.** Implying that the sword resists being unsheathed
31. *passado.* Thrust
32. **bandying.** Fighting
33. **sped.** Spent, finished
34. **a scratch.** Another reference to Tybalt's name
35. **villain.** Person of lower class; boy

words for everyday use   sub • mis • sion (sub mish´ən) *n.,* yielding or surrendering. *The husband's <u>submission</u> was evident after he lost the argument with his wife.*

90   **MERCUTIO.**   No, 'tis not so deep as a well, nor so wide as a church-door,
but 'tis enough, 'twill serve. Ask for me tomorrow, and you shall find me
a grave man.[36] I am pepper'd, I warrant, for this world. A <u>plague</u> a' both
your houses! 'Zounds, a dog, a rat, a mouse, a cat, to scratch a man to death!
a braggart, a rogue, a villain, that fights by the book of arithmetic! Why the
95   dev'l came you between us? I was hurt under your arm.

     ROMEO.   I thought all for the best.

     MERCUTIO.   Help me into some house, Benvolio,
Or I shall faint. A plague a' both your houses!
They have made worms' meat of me. I have it,
100   And soundly too. Your houses!

Exeunt MERCUTIO *and* BENVOLIO.

     ROMEO.   This gentleman, the Prince's near ally,[37]
My very[38] friend, hath got this mortal hurt
In my behalf; my reputation stain'd
With Tybalt's slander—Tybalt, that an hour
105   Hath been my cousin! O sweet Juliet,
Thy beauty hath made me effeminate,
And in my temper[39] soft'ned <u>valor's</u> steel!

Enter BENVOLIO.

     BENVOLIO.   O Romeo, Romeo, brave Mercutio is dead!
That gallant spirit hath aspir'd[40] the clouds,
110   Which too untimely here did scorn the earth.

> What news does Benvolio bring of Mercutio?

     ROMEO.   This day's black fate on moe days doth depend,[41]
This but begins the woe others must end.

Enter TYBALT.

     BENVOLIO.   Here comes the furious Tybalt back again.

     ROMEO.   He gone in triumph, and Mercutio slain!
115   Away to heaven, respective[42] lenity,
And fire-ey'd fury be my conduct[43] now!
Now, Tybalt, take the "villain" back again
That late thou gavest me, for Mercutio's soul
Is but a little way above our heads,

> Why does Romeo challenge Tybalt?

---

36. **grave man.** Pun stating that he may be found in a
grave tomorrow
37. **ally.** Relative
38. **very.** Absolute
39. **temper.** Nature

40. **aspir'd.** Ascended to
41. **on . . . depend.** Affects days in the future
42. **respective.** Thoughtful
43. **conduct.** Guide

words for everyday use

plague (plāg) *n.*, anything that afflicts or troubles. *Alistair was troubled by a <u>plague</u> of money worries.*

val • or (val´ər) *n.*, marked courage or bravery. *The knight demonstrated his <u>valor</u> when he stormed the castle to free the princess.*

120 Staying for thine to keep him company.
Either thou or I, or both, must go with him.

TYBALT. Thou wretched boy, that didst consort him here,
Shalt with him hence.

ROMEO. This shall determine that.

They fight; TYBALT falls.

BENVOLIO. Romeo, away, be gone!
125 The citizens are up,[44] and Tybalt slain.
Stand not amazed,[45] the Prince will doom thee death
If thou art taken. Hence be gone, away!

ROMEO. O, I am fortune's fool!

BENVOLIO. Why dost thou stay? *Exit ROMEO.*

Enter CITIZENS.

1. CITIZEN. Which way ran he that kill'd Mercutio?
130 Tybalt, that murtherer, which way ran he?

BENVOLIO. There lies that Tybalt.

1. CITIZEN. Up, sir, go with me;
I charge thee in the Prince's name, obey.

Enter PRINCE, old MONTAGUE, CAPULET, their WIVES, and all.

PRINCE. Where are the vile beginners of this fray?

BENVOLIO. O noble Prince, I can discover[46] all
135 The unlucky manage[47] of this fatal brawl:
There lies the man, slain by young Romeo,
That slew thy kinsman brave Mercutio.

LADY CAPULET. Tybalt, my cousin! O my brother's child!
O Prince! O husband! O, the blood is spill'd
140 Of my dear kinsman! Prince, as thou art true,
For blood of ours, shed blood of Montague.
O cousin, cousin!

PRINCE. Benvolio, who began this bloody fray?

BENVOLIO. Tybalt, here slain, whom Romeo's hand did slay!
145 Romeo that spoke him fair, bid him bethink
How nice[48] the quarrel was, and urg'd withal
Your high displeasure; all this, uttered
With gentle breath, calm look, knees humbly bowed,
Could not take truce with the unruly spleen
150 Of Tybalt deaf to peace, but that he tilts

> Why must Romeo escape?

> What does Lady Capulet demand?

44. **up.** Have taken arms
45. **amazed.** Bewildered, astounded
46. **discover.** Uncover, divulge
47. **manage.** Process
48. **nice.** Slight

With piercing steel at bold Mercutio's breast,
Who, all as hot, turns deadly point to point,
And, with a martial scorn, with one hand beats
Cold death aside, and with the other sends

155 It back to Tybalt, whose <u>dexterity</u>
Retorts it. Romeo he cries aloud,
"Hold, friends! friends, part!" and swifter than his tongue,
His <u>agile</u> arm beats down their fatal points,
And 'twixt them rushes; underneath whose arm

160 An envious[49] thrust from Tybalt hit the life
Of stout[50] Mercutio, and then Tybalt fled;
But by and by comes back to Romeo,
Who had but newly entertain'd[51] revenge,
And to't they go like lightning, for, ere I

165 Could draw to part them, was stout Tybalt slain;
And as he fell, did Romeo turn and fly.
This is the truth, or let Benvolio die.

LADY CAPULET.   He is a kinsman to the Montague,
Affection makes him false, he speaks not true.

170 Some twenty of them fought in this black strife,
And all those twenty could but kill one life.
I beg for justice, which thou, Prince, must give:
Romeo slew Tybalt, Romeo must not live.

PRINCE.   Romeo slew him, he slew Mercutio;

175 Who now the price of his dear blood doth owe?

MONTAGUE.   Not Romeo, Prince, he was Mercutio's friend;
His fault concludes but what the law should end,
The life of Tybalt.

PRINCE.   And for that offense
Immediately we do exile him hence.

180 I have an interest[52] in your heart's proceeding;
My blood[53] for your rude brawls doth lie a-bleeding;
But I'll amerce[54] you with so strong a fine
That you shall all repent the loss of mine.
I will be deaf to pleading and excuses,

185 Nor tears nor prayers shall purchase out[55] abuses;

> Of what does Lady Capulet accuse Benvolio?

> What is Romeo's punishment? What could it have been?

> What further punishment does the Prince levy on both families?

---

49. **envious.** Spiteful
50. **stout.** Brave
51. **entertain'd.** Considered
52. **interest.** Concern

53. **My blood.** Mercutio and the prince are related
54. **amerce.** Inflict a fine
55. **purchase out.** Make amends for

words for everyday use

dex • ter • i • ty (deks ter´ə tē) *n.*, skill in using one's hands or body. *Mark's <u>dexterity</u> in making a beautiful shelf impressed his shop teacher.*

ag • ile (aj´əl) *adj.*, quick and easy of movement. *The <u>agile</u> movements of the aerobics teacher were hard for Christabel to imitate.*

Therefore use none. Let Romeo hence in haste,
Else, when he is found, that hour is his last.
Bear hence this body and attend our will;[56]
Mercy but murders,[57] pardoning those that kill.   *Exeunt.*

SCENE 2: CAPULET'S HOUSE

Enter JULIET *alone.*

JULIET.   Gallop apace, you fiery-footed steeds,[1]
Towards Phoebus' lodging;[2] such a waggoner
As Phaëton[3] would whip you to the west,
And bring in cloudy night immediately.
5   Spread thy close[4] curtain, love-performing night,
That th' runaway's[5] eyes may wink,[6] and Romeo
Leap to these arms untalk'd of and unseen!
Lovers can see to do their <u>amorous</u> rites
By their own beauties, or, if love be blind,
10   It best agrees with night. Come, civil[7] night,
Thou sober-suited <u>matron</u> all in black,
And learn me how to lose a winning match,
Play'd for a pair of stainless maidenhoods.
Hood[8] my unmann'd blood, bating[9] in my cheeks,
15   With thy black mantle; till strange[10] love grow[11] bold,
Think true love acted simple modesty.[12]
Come, night, come, Romeo, come, thou day in night,
For thou wilt lie upon the wings of night,
Whiter than new snow upon a raven's back.
20   Come, gentle night, come, loving, black-brow'd night,
Give me my Romeo, and, when I shall die,
Take him and cut him out in little stars,
And he will make the face of heaven so fine
That all the world will be in love with night,
25   And pay no worship to the garish sun.

---

56. **attend our will.** Listen to my judgment
57. **murders.** Encourages future murders

ACT 3, SCENE 2
  1. **steeds.** Horses that pull the chariot of the sun-god
  2. **Phoebus' lodging.** Beyond the western horizon
  3. **Phaëton.** Phaëthon, son of the sun-god, who lost control of the sun-chariot and was killed by Zeus
  4. **close.** Protective

  5. **runaway's.** Meaning is unclear; word possibly changed
  6. **wink.** Close and so not see
  7. **civil.** Solemn
  8. **Hood.** Hide
  9. **bating.** Beating
 10. **strange.** Restrained
 11. **grow.** Becomes
 12. **modesty.** Virtuousness

words for everyday use

am • o • rous (am´ə res) *adj.,* relating to love. *Durrell's <u>amorous</u> words did not soften Shamika's heart.*

ma • tron (mā´trən) *n.,* married woman or widow. *The funeral director gave the <u>matron</u> the book that mourners had signed at her husband's funeral.*

O, I have bought the mansion of a love,
But not possess'd it, and though I am sold,
Not yet enjoy'd. So tedious is this day
As is the night before some festival
30 To an impatient child that hath new robes
And may not wear them. O, here comes my nurse,

Enter NURSE *wringing her hands, with the ladder of cords in her lap.*

And she brings news; and every tongue that speaks
But Romeo's name speaks heavenly <u>eloquence</u>.
Now, nurse, what news? What hast thou there? the cords
That Romeo bid thee fetch?

35 **NURSE.**   Ay, ay, the cords.   *Throws them down.*

JULIET.   Ay me, what news? Why dost thou wring thy hands?

NURSE.   Ah, weraday,[13] he's dead, he's dead, he's dead!
We are undone, lady, we are undone!
Alack the day, he's gone, he's kill'd, he's dead!

JULIET.   Can heaven be so envious?[14]

40 **NURSE.**   Romeo can,
Though heaven cannot. O Romeo, Romeo!
Who ever would have thought it? Romeo!

JULIET.   What devil art thou that dost torment me thus?
This torture should be roar'd in dismal hell.
45 Hath Romeo slain himself? Say thou but ay,
And that bare vowel *I* shall poison more
Than the death-darting eye of cockatrice.[15]
I am not I, if there be such an ay,
Or those eyes shut,[16] that makes thee answer ay.
50 If he be slain, say ay, or if not, no.
Brief sounds determine my weal or woe.[17]

NURSE.   I saw the wound, I saw it with mine eyes—
God save the mark![18]—here on his manly breast.
A <u>piteous</u> corse,[19] a bloody piteous corse,
55 Pale, pale as ashes, all bedaub'd in blood,
All in gore blood; I sounded[20] at the sight.

> **What misunderstanding occurs with the Nurse's words?**

---

13. **weraday.** Pity
14. **envious.** Spiteful
15. **cockatrice.** Basilisk, mythical serpent that could kill with a glance
16. **Or . . . shut.** If Romeo dies

17. **determine . . . woe.** Decide whether I am happy or sad
18. **God . . . mark.** Expression used to ward off bad omens
19. **corse.** Dead body
20. **sounded.** Fainted

words for everyday use

el • o • quence (el´ə kwəns) *n.*, speech or writing that is vivid, forceful, and persuasive. *The president's <u>eloquence</u> convinced Congress to pass the bill.*

pit • e • ous (pit´ē əs) *adj.*, arousing or deserving pity or compassion. *The <u>piteous</u> cries of the mourners were heard in the streets the day the civil rights leader was slain.*

JULIET.   O, break, my heart, poor bankrout,[21] break at once!
To prison, eyes, ne'er look on liberty!
Vile earth,[22] to earth resign,[23] end motion here,
60 And thou and Romeo press one heavy <u>bier</u>!

NURSE.   O Tybalt, Tybalt, the best friend I had!
O courteous Tybalt, honest gentleman,
That ever I should live to see thee dead!

JULIET.   What storm is this that blows so contrary?
65 Is Romeo slaught'red? and is Tybalt dead?
My dearest cousin, and my dearer lord?
Then, dreadful trumpet,[24] sound the general doom,
For who is living, if those two are gone?

NURSE.   Tybalt is gone, and Romeo banished,
70 Romeo that kill'd him, he is banished.

JULIET.   O God, did Romeo's hand shed Tybalt's blood?

NURSE.   It did, it did, alas the day, it did!

JULIET.   O serpent heart, hid with a flow'ring[25] face!
Did ever dragon keep[26] so fair a cave?
75 Beautiful tyrant! fiend angelical!
Dove-feather'd raven! wolvish ravening lamb!
Despised substance[27] of divinest show![28]
Just opposite to what thou justly seem'st,[29]
A damned saint, an honorable villain!
80 O nature, what hadst thou to do in hell
When thou didst bower[30] the spirit of a fiend
In mortal paradise of such sweet flesh?
Was ever book containing such vile matter
So fairly bound? O that deceit should dwell
In such a gorgeous palace!

85 **NURSE.**   There's no trust,
No faith, no honesty in men, all perjur'd,
All forsworn, all naught,[31] all <u>dissemblers</u>.
Ah, where's my man? Give me some aqua-vitae;[32]

> To whom does Juliet refer when she says "Beautiful tyrant!"? What other oxymorons does she use to express her conflicting feelings?

---

21. **bankrout.** Emptiness
22. **Vile earth.** Body
23. **resign.** Relinquish yourself
24. **trumpet.** Signal of Judgment Day
25. **flow'ring.** Young, attractive
26. **keep.** Reside in
27. **substance.** Contemptible being

28. **show.** Appearance
29. **Just . . . seem'st.** Exactly the opposite of what you appear to be
30. **bower.** Enclose
31. **naught.** Evil
32. **aqua-vitae.** Strong liquor

words for everyday use

bier (bir) *n.*, coffin and its supporting platform. *The <u>bier</u> was lowered into the ground at the family's cemetery plot.*

dis • sem • bler (di sem´blir) *n.*, pretender. *Alex accused Jerry of being a <u>dissembler</u> when he pretended to support the Coyotes.*

These griefs, these woes, these sorrows make me old.
Shame come to Romeo!

90 **JULIET.**   Blister'd be thy tongue
For such a wish! he was not born to shame:
Upon his brow shame is asham'd to sit;
For 'tis a throne where honor may be crown'd
Sole <u>monarch</u> of the universal earth.

95 O, what a beast was I to chide at him!

NURSE. Will you speak well of him that kill'd your cousin?

JULIET. Shall I speak ill of him that is my husband?
Ah, poor my lord, what tongue shall smooth thy name,
When I, thy three-hours wife, have mangled it?

100 But wherefore, villain, didst thou kill my cousin?
That villain cousin would have kill'd my husband.
Back, foolish tears, back to your native spring,
Your tributary drops belong to woe,[33]
Which you, mistaking, offer up to joy.[34]

105 My husband lives that Tybalt would have slain,
And Tybalt's dead that would have slain my husband.
All this is comfort, wherefore weep I then?
Some word there was, worser than Tybalt's death,
That murd'red me; I would forget it fain,

110 But O, it presses to my memory
Like damned guilty deeds to sinners' minds:
"Tybalt is dead, and Romeo banished."
That "banished," that one word "banished,"
Hath slain ten thousand Tybalts. Tybalt's death

115 Was woe enough if it had ended there;
Or if sour woe delights in fellowship,
And needly[35] will be rank'd[36] with other griefs,
Why followed not, when she said, "Tybalt's dead,"
Thy father or thy mother, nay, or both,

120 Which modern[37] <u>lamentation</u> might have moved?
But with a rearward[38] following Tybalt's death,
"Romeo is banished," to speak that word,
Is father, mother, Tybalt, Romeo, Juliet,
All slain, all dead: "Romeo is banished"!

What does Juliet do when the Nurse wishes harm to Romeo?

---

33. **belong to woe.** Indicate sadness
34. **joy.** Romeo's survival
35. **needly.** Inevitably
36. **rank'd.** Grouped
37. **modern.** Customary
38. **rearward.** Rear guard

words for everyday use

mon • arch (män´ərk) *n.,* ruler. *The <u>monarch</u> ruled her country with a firm hand.*

lam • en • ta • tion (lam´ən tā´shən) *n.,* outward expression of grief. *The <u>lamentation</u> after the massacre moved the journalist, who interviewed some of the grieving crowd members.*

125 There is no end, no limit, measure, bound,
In that word's death, no words can that woe sound.[39]
Where is my father and my mother, nurse?

NURSE. Weeping and wailing over Tybalt's corse.
Will you go to them? I will bring you thither.

130 **JULIET.** Wash they his wounds with tears? Mine shall be spent,
When theirs are dry, for Romeo's banishment.
Take up those cords. Poor ropes, you are beguil'd,[40]
Both you and I, for Romeo is exil'd.
He made you for a highway to my bed,
135 But I, a maid, die maiden-widowed.
Come, cords, come, nurse, I'll to my wedding-bed,
And death, not Romeo, take my maidenhead!

NURSE. Hie to your <u>chamber</u>. I'll find Romeo
To comfort you, I wot[41] well where he is.
140 Hark ye, your Romeo will be here at night.
I'll to him, he is hid at Lawrence' cell.

JULIET. O, find him! Give this ring to my true knight,
And bid him come to take his last farewell.

Exeunt.

Why does the Nurse promise to find Romeo?

SCENE 3: FRIAR LAWRENCE'S CELL

Enter FRIAR LAWRENCE.

FRIAR LAWRENCE. Romeo, come forth, come forth, thou fearful[1] man:
Affliction is enamor'd of thy parts,[2]
And thou art wedded to <u>calamity</u>.

Enter ROMEO.

ROMEO. Father, what news? What is the Prince's doom?[3]
5 What sorrow craves acquaintance at my hand,
That I yet know not?

FRIAR LAWRENCE. Too familiar
Is my dear son with such sour company!
I bring thee tidings of the Prince's doom.

---

39. **sound.** Define; measure
40. **beguil'd.** Deceived
41. **wot.** Know

ACT 3, SCENE 3
1. **fearful.** Frightened
2. **parts.** Traits
3. **doom.** Judgment

---

words for everyday use

cham • ber (chām´bər) *n.,* bedroom. *Melanie's <u>chamber</u> has curtains that match the bedspread.*

ca • lam • i • ty (kə lam´ə tē) *n.,* disaster, misery. *"We must keep this <u>calamity</u> from recurring," stated the mayor after the city bus accident.*

ROMEO. What less than dooms-day[4] is the Prince's doom?

10 **FRIAR LAWRENCE.** A gentler judgment vanish'd[5] from his lips—
Not body's death, but body's banishment.

ROMEO. Ha, banishment? Be merciful, say "death";
For exile hath more terror in his look,
Much more than death. Do not say "banishment"!

What sentence would Romeo choose for himself?

15 **FRIAR LAWRENCE.** Here from Verona art thou banished.
Be patient,[6] for the world is broad and wide.

ROMEO. There is no world without[7] Verona walls,
But purgatory, torture, hell itself.
Hence "banished" is banish'd from the world,
20 And world's exile[8] is death; then "banished"
Is death misterm'd. Calling death "banished,"
Thou cut'st my head off with a golden axe,
And smilest upon the stroke that murders me.

FRIAR LAWRENCE. O deadly sin! O rude unthankfulness!
25 Thy fault our law calls death,[9] but the kind Prince,
Taking thy part, hath rush'd[10] aside the law,
And turn'd that black word "death" to "banishment."
This is dear[11] mercy, and thou seest it not.

What does Friar Lawrence think of the prince's sentence?

ROMEO. 'Tis torture, and not mercy. Heaven is here
30 Where Juliet lives, and every cat and dog
And little mouse, every unworthy thing,
Live here in heaven and may look on her,
But Romeo may not. More validity,[12]
More honorable state, more courtship[13] lives
35 In carrion flies than Romeo; they may seize
On the white wonder of dear Juliet's hand,
And steal immortal blessing from her lips,
Who, even in pure and vestal modesty
Still blush, as thinking their own kisses sin;
40 But Romeo may not, he is banished.
Flies may do this, but I from this must fly;

Why does Romeo think banishment is worse than death?

---

4. **dooms-day.** Death
5. **vanish'd.** Uttered without possibility of recall
6. **Be patient.** Calm yourself
7. **without.** Beyond
8. **world's exile.** Banishment from the world

9. **death.** Capital offense
10. **rush'd.** Pushed
11. **dear.** Unusual
12. **validity.** Honor, worth
13. **courtship.** Courtliness

words for everyday use
car • ri • on (kar´ē ən) *n.*, decaying flesh of a dead body when regarded as food for scavenging animals. *The ravens ate the carrion at the side of the highway.*

They are free men, but I am banished:
And sayest thou yet that exile is not death?
Hadst thou no poison mix'd, no sharp-ground knife,
45 No sudden mean of death, though ne'er so mean,[14]
But "banished" to kill me? "Banished"?
O friar, the damned use that word in hell;
Howling attends it. How hast thou the heart,
Being a divine, a ghostly confessor,
50 A sin-absolver, and my friend profess'd,
To mangle me with that word "banished"?

FRIAR LAWRENCE. Thou fond[15] mad man, hear me a little speak.

ROMEO. O, thou wilt speak again of banishment.

FRIAR LAWRENCE. I'll give thee armor to keep off that word:
55 <u>Adversity</u>'s sweet milk, philosophy,
To comfort thee though thou art banished.

ROMEO. Yet "banished"? Hang up philosophy!
Unless philosophy can make a Juliet,
Displant[16] a town, reverse a prince's doom,
60 It helps not, it prevails not.[17] Talk no more.

FRIAR LAWRENCE. O then I see that madmen have no ears.

ROMEO. How should they when that wise men have no eyes?

FRIAR LAWRENCE. Let me dispute[18] with thee of thy estate.[19]

ROMEO. Thou canst not speak of that thou dost not feel.
65 Wert thou as young as I, Juliet thy love,
An hour but married, Tybalt murdered,
Doting like me, and like me banished,
Then mightst thou speak, then mightst thou tear thy hair,
And fall upon the ground, as I do now,
70 Taking the measure of an unmade grave.

Enter NURSE *within and knock.*

FRIAR LAWRENCE. Arise, one knocks. Good Romeo, hide thyself.

ROMEO. Not I, unless the breath of heart-sick groans
Mist-like infold me from the search of eyes. *Knock.*

---

14. **mean . . . mean.** Means . . . ignoble
15. **fond.** Naïve
16. **Displant.** Relocate

17. **prevails not.** Has no effect
18. **dispute.** Talk
19. **estate.** Situation

words for everyday use

ad • ver • si • ty (ad vʉr´sə tē) *n.*, wretchedness or misfortune. *Mr. Olson bemoaned his <u>adversity</u> after he lost his job.*

FRIAR LAWRENCE.   Hark how they knock!—Who's there?—

75   Romeo, arise,
Thou wilt be taken.—Stay a while![20]—Stand up;   *Loud knock.*
Run to my study.—By and by!—God's will,
What simpleness[21] is this?—I come, I come!   *Knock.*
Who knocks so hard? Whence come you? What's your will?

80   **NURSE.**   [*Within.*] Let me come in, and you shall know my errant.[22]
I come from Lady Juliet.

FRIAR LAWRENCE.   Welcome then.   *Unlocks the door.*

Enter NURSE.

NURSE.   O holy friar, O, tell me, holy friar,
Where's my lady's lord? where's Romeo?

FRIAR LAWRENCE.   There on the ground, with his own tears made drunk.

85   **NURSE.**   O, he is even in my mistress' case,
Just in her case. O woeful sympathy![23]
Piteous predicament! Even so lies she,
Blubb'ring and weeping, weeping and blubb'ring.
Stand up, stand up, stand, and you be a man.
90   For Juliet's sake, for her sake, rise and stand;
Why should you fall into so deep an O?[24]

ROMEO.   Nurse!   *He rises.*

NURSE.   Ah sir, ah sir, death's the end of all.

ROMEO.   Spakest thou of Juliet? How is it with her?
95   Doth not she think me an old[25] murtherer,
Now I have stain'd the childhood of our joy
With blood removed but little from her own?
Where is she? and how doth she? and what says
My conceal'd lady[26] to our cancell'd love?

100   **NURSE.**   O, she says nothing, sir, but weeps and weeps,
And now falls on her bed, and then starts up,
And Tybalt calls, and then on Romeo cries,
And then down falls again.

ROMEO.   As if that name,
Shot from the deadly level[27] of a gun,
105   Did murther her, as that name's cursed hand
Murder'd her kinsman. O, tell me, friar, tell me,
In what vile part of this anatomy
Doth my name lodge? Tell me, that I may sack
The hateful mansion.

> According to the Nurse and Friar Lawrence, how do Romeo and Juliet respond in comparable ways to news of Romeo's banishment?

---

20. **Stay a while.** Wait
21. **simpleness.** Absurdity
22. **errant.** Purpose
23. **sympathy.** Piteous suffering

24. **O.** State of despair
25. **old.** Experienced
26. **conceal'd lady.** Secret wife
27. **level.** Aim

He offers to stab himself, and the NURSE *snatches the dagger away.*

FRIAR LAWRENCE.   Hold thy desperate hand!

What does Romeo attempt to do? Who stops him?

110 Art thou a man? Thy form cries out thou art;
Thy tears are womanish, thy wild acts <u>denote</u>
The unreasonable[28] fury of a beast.
Unseemly woman[29] in a seeming man,
And ill-beseeming beast in seeming both,
115 Thou hast amaz'd me! By my holy order,
I thought thy <u>disposition</u> better temper'd.[30]
Hast thou slain Tybalt? Wilt thou slay thyself,
And slay thy lady that in thy life lives,
By doing damned hate upon thyself?
120 Why railest thou on thy birth? the heaven and earth?[31]
Since birth, and heaven, and earth, all three do meet
In thee at once, which thou at once wouldst lose.
Fie, fie, thou shamest thy shape, thy love, thy wit,[32]
Which[33] like a usurer[34] abound'st in all,

For what does Friar Lawrence scold Romeo?

125 And usest none in that true use indeed
Which should bedeck thy shape, thy love, thy wit.
Thy noble shape is but a form of wax,[35]
Digressing from the valor of a man;
Thy dear love sworn but hollow perjury,
130 Killing that love which thou hast vow'd to cherish;
Thy wit, that ornament to shape and love,
Misshapen[36] in the conduct[37] of them both,
Like powder in a skilless soldier's flask,[38]
Is set afire by thine own ignorance,
135 And thou dismemb'red with thine own defense.
What, rouse thee, man! thy Juliet is alive,
For whose dear sake thou wast but lately dead:
There art thou happy.[39] Tybalt would kill thee,
But thou slewest Tybalt: there art thou happy.
140 The law that threat'ned death becomes thy friend,
And turns it to exile: there art thou happy.
A pack of blessings light upon thy back,

For what should Romeo be grateful?

---

28. **unreasonable.** Irrational
29. **Unseemly woman.** Romeo's behavior is like that of a woman who offends good taste.
30. **temper'd.** Composed; controlled
31. **heaven and earth.** Soul and body
32. **wit.** Mind
33. **Which.** Who

34. **usurer.** One who misuses possessions
35. **form of wax.** Lifeless figure
36. **Misshapen.** Badly trained
37. **conduct.** Use
38. **flask.** Powder horn, container for gunpowder
39. **happy.** Lucky

words for everyday use

de • note (dē nōt´) *vt.*, indicate. *"The symbol <u>denotes</u> repetition of this bar," explained the piano teacher.*

dis • po • si • tion (dis´pə zish´ən) *n.*, one's customary frame of mind. *Sarah's teacher told her parents that she always had a sunny <u>disposition</u>.*

Happiness courts thee in her best array,
But like a mishaved[40] and sullen wench,
145 Thou pouts upon thy fortune and thy love.
Take heed, take heed, for such die miserable.
Go get thee to thy love as was decreed,[41]
<u>Ascend</u> her chamber, hence and comfort her.
But look thou stay not till the watch be set,[42]
150 For then thou canst not pass to Mantua,
Where thou shalt live till we can find a time
To blaze[43] your marriage, reconcile your friends,[44]
Beg pardon of the Prince, and call thee back
With twenty hundred thousand times more joy
155 Than thou went'st forth in lamentation.
Go before, nurse; commend me to thy lady,
And bid her hasten all the house to bed,
Which heavy sorrow makes them apt unto.
Romeo is coming.

160 **NURSE.** O Lord, I could have stay'd here all the night
To hear good counsel. O, what learning is!
My lord, I'll tell my lady you will come.

ROMEO. Do so, and bid my sweet prepare to chide.

What is Friar Lawrence's plan?

NURSE *offers to go in, and turns again.*

NURSE. Here, sir, a ring she bid me give you, sir.
165 Hie you, make haste, for it grows very late.

ROMEO. How well my comfort is reviv'd by this!

Exit NURSE.

FRIAR LAWRENCE. Go hence, good night; and here stands all your state:[45]
Either be gone before the watch be set,
Or by the break of day disguis'd from hence.
170 Sojourn in Mantua. I'll find out your man,
And he shall signify from time to time
Every good hap to you that chances here.
Give me thy hand. 'Tis late; farewell, good night.

ROMEO. But that a joy past joy calls out on me,
175 It were a grief, so brief[46] to part with thee.
Farewell.

Exeunt.

---

40. **mishaved.** Misbehaved
41. **decreed.** Ordered
42. **watch be set.** Guard is posted
43. **blaze.** Announce
44. **friends.** Family
45. **here . . . state.** Your situation is this
46. **brief.** Quickly

words for everyday use

as • cend (ə send´) *vt.,* move upward along; mount; climb; rise. *The tourists <u>ascended</u> the steps that led to the basilica at the top of the hill.*

SCENE 4: CAPULET'S HOUSE

Enter old CAPULET, *his* WIFE, *and* PARIS.

CAPULET. Things have fall'n out, sir, so unluckily
That we have had no time to move our daughter.
Look you, she lov'd her kinsman Tybalt dearly,
And so did I. Well, we were born to die.
5 'Tis very late, she'll not come down to-night.
I promise you, but for your company,
I would have been a-bed an hour ago.

PARIS. These times of woe afford no times to woo.
Madam, good night, commend me to your daughter.

10 **LADY CAPULET.** I will, and know her mind early tomorrow;
To-night she's mewed up to[1] her heaviness.[2]

PARIS *offers to go in, and* CAPULET *calls him again.*

CAPULET. Sir Paris, I will make a desperate tender[3]
Of my child's love. I think she will be rul'd
In all respects by me; nay more, I doubt it not.
15 Wife, go you to her ere you go to bed,
Acquaint her here of my son Paris' love,
And bid her—mark you me?—on We'n'sday next—
But soft, what day is this?

PARIS. Monday, my lord.

CAPULET. Monday! ha, ha![4] Well, We'n'sday is too soon,
20 A'[5] Thursday let it be—a' Thursday, tell her,
She shall be married to this noble earl.
Will you be ready? do you like this haste?
We'll keep no great ado—a friend or two,
For hark you, Tybalt being slain so late,
25 It may be thought we held him carelessly,
Being our kinsman, if we revel much:
Therefore we'll have some half a dozen friends,
And there an end. But what say you to Thursday?

PARIS. My lord, I would that Thursday were tomorrow.

30 **CAPULET.** Well, get you gone, a' Thursday be it then.—
Go you to Juliet ere you go to bed,
Prepare her, wife, against[6] this wedding-day.
Farewell, my lord. Light to my chamber ho!
Afore me,[7] it is so very late that we
35 May call it early by and by. Good night.   *Exeunt.*

> Why does Capulet believe he can offer Paris Juliet's hand in marriage?

ACT 3, SCENE 4
1. **mewed up to.** Shut up with (falconry term)
2. **heaviness.** Sadness
3. **desperate tender.** Daring offer
4. **ha, ha.** Sound he mutters as he thinks
5. **A'.** On
6. **against.** For
7. **Afore me.** I say

Enter ROMEO *and* JULIET *aloft at the window.*

JULIET.   Wilt thou be gone? it is not yet near day.
It was the <u>nightingale</u>, and not the lark,
That pierc'd the fearful hollow of thine ear;
Nightly she sings on yond <u>pomegranate</u> tree.
5   Believe me, love, it was the nightingale.

ROMEO.   It was the lark, the herald of the morn,
No nightingale. Look, love, what envious streaks
Do lace the severing clouds in yonder east.
Night's candles are burnt out, and jocund day
10   Stands tiptoe on the misty mountain tops.
I must be gone and live, or stay and die.

JULIET.   Yond light is not day-light, I know it, I;
It is some meteor that the sun exhal'd[1]
To be to thee this night a torch-bearer
15   And light thee on thy way to Mantua.
Therefore stay yet, thou need'st not to be gone.

ROMEO.   Let me be ta'en, let me be put to death,
I am content, so thou wilt have it so.
I'll say yon grey is not the morning's eye,
20   'Tis but the pale reflex[2] of Cynthia's[3] brow;
Nor that is not the lark whose notes do beat
The vaulty heaven so high above our heads.
I have more care[4] to stay than will to go.
Come, death, and welcome! Juliet wills it so.
25   How is't, my soul? Let's talk, it is not day.

JULIET.   It is, it is! Hie hence, be gone, away!
It is the lark that sings so out of tune,
Straining harsh <u>discords</u> and unpleasing sharps.[5]
Some say the lark makes sweet division;[6]
30   This doth not so, for she divideth us.
Some say the lark and loathed toad change[7] eyes;
O now I would they had chang'd voices too,

ACT 3, SCENE 5
  1. **exhal'd.** Meteors were believed to be vapors from
Earth that were ignited by the sun's heat.
  2. **reflex.** Reflection
  3. **Cynthia's.** The moon's

4. **care.** Wish
5. **sharps.** High-pitched sounds
6. **division.** Melodic variations
7. **change.** Exchange

words for everyday use

night • in • gale (nīt´ən gāl) *n.,* reddish brown songbird noted for the sweet song of the male. *The <u>nightingale</u> ate at Adam's bird feeder.*

pome • gran • ate (päm´gran´it) *n.,* round fruit with a red, leathery rind and many seeds covered with red, juicy, edible flesh. *For dessert the hostess offered <u>pomegranates</u> and other fresh fruit.*

dis • cord (dis´kôrd) *n.,* lack of harmony in tones sounded together. *"Let's try again," said the choir director, pointing out <u>discord</u> in the first verse.*

Since arm from arm[8] that voice doth us affray,[9]
Hunting thee hence with hunt's-up[10] to the day.
35   O now be gone, more light and light it grows.

ROMEO.   More light and light, more dark and dark our woes!

Enter NURSE *hastily.*

NURSE.   Madam!

JULIET.   Nurse?

NURSE.   Your lady mother is coming to your chamber.
40   The day is broke, be wary, look about.   *Exit.*

JULIET.   Then, window, let day in, and let life out.

ROMEO.   Farewell, farewell! One kiss, and I'll descend.   *He goeth down.*

JULIET.   Art thou gone so, love, lord, ay, husband, friend![11]
I must hear from thee every day in the hour,
45   For in a minute there are many days.
O, by this count I shall be much in years[12]
Ere I again behold my Romeo!

ROMEO.   [*From below.*] Farewell!
I will omit no opportunity
50   That may convey my greetings, love, to thee.

JULIET.   O, think'st thou we shall ever meet again?

ROMEO.   I doubt it not, and all these woes shall serve
For sweet discourses in our times to come.

JULIET.   O God, I have an ill-divining[13] soul!
55   Methinks I see thee now, thou art so low,
As one dead in the bottom of a tomb.
Either my eyesight fails, or thou lookest pale.

ROMEO.   And trust me, love, in my eye so do you;
Dry sorrow drinks our blood.[14] Adieu, adieu!   *Exit.*

60   **JULIET.**   O Fortune, Fortune, all men call thee fickle;
If thou art fickle, what dost thou[15] with him
That is renown'd for faith? Be fickle, Fortune:
For then I hope thou wilt not keep him long,
But send him back.

LADY CAPULET.   [*Within.*] Ho, daughter, are you up?

65   **JULIET.**   Who is't that calls? It is my lady mother.
Is she not down[16] so late, or up so early?

---

8. **arm from arm.** From each other's arms
9. **affray.** Startle, scare
10. **hunt's-up.** Song to waken hunters
11. **friend.** Dear one, sweetheart
12. **much in years.** Old

13. **ill-divining.** Sensing evil
14. **Dry . . . blood.** Sorrow was thought to deplete the blood.
15. **what dost thou.** What do you have to do
16. **not down.** Still awake

What unaccustom'd cause procures her hither?

She goeth down from the window.[17]

Enter Mother LADY CAPULET.

LADY CAPULET. Why, how now, Juliet?

JULIET.   Madam, I am not well.

LADY CAPULET. Evermore weeping for your cousin's death?
70   What, wilt thou wash him from his grave with tears?
And if thou couldst, thou couldst not make him live;
Therefore have done. Some grief shows much of love,
But much of grief shows still some want of wit.

JULIET. Yet let me weep for such a feeling[18] loss.

75   **LADY CAPULET.** So shall you feel the loss, but not the friend
Which you weep for.

JULIET.   Feeling so the loss,
I cannot choose but ever weep the friend.

LADY CAPULET. Well, girl, thou weep'st not so much for his death,
As that the villain lives which slaughter'd him.

JULIET. What villain, madam?

80   **LADY CAPULET.**   That same villain Romeo.

JULIET. [*Aside.*] Villain and he be many miles <u>asunder</u>.—
God pardon him! I do with all my heart;
And yet no man like[19] he doth grieve my heart.

LADY CAPULET. That is because the traitor murderer lives.

85   **JULIET.** Ay, madam, from the reach of these my hands.
Would none but I might venge my cousin's death!

LADY CAPULET. We will have vengeance for it, fear thou not.
Then weep no more. I'll send to one in Mantua,
Where that same banish'd runagate[20] doth live,
90   Shall give him such an unaccustom'd dram[21]
That he shall soon keep Tybalt company;
And then I hope thou wilt be satisfied.

JULIET. Indeed I never shall be satisfied
With Romeo, till I behold him—dead—

What does Lady Capulet believe is causing Juliet's sorrow?

What does Lady Capulet plan for Romeo? Why?

---

17. *She . . . window.* Apparently she descends and reenters the main stage, which is no longer the garden but a room in the house.
18. **feeling.** Deep

19. **like.** So much as
20. **runagate.** Renegade
21. **dram.** Unit of weight for apothecaries or druggists; measure of some drug or drink

words for everyday use   **a • sun • der** (ə sun´ dər) *adv.,* apart or separate in direction. *"On this proposal, we are as wide* <u>asunder</u> *as the polar regions,"* *stated the candidate to his opponent.*

95 Is my poor heart, so for a kinsman vex'd.
    Madam, if you could find out but a man
    To bear a poison, I would temper[22] it,
    That Romeo should, upon receipt thereof,
    Soon sleep in quiet. O how my heart <u>abhors</u>
100 To hear him nam'd, and cannot come to him
    To wreak the love I bore my cousin
    Upon his body that[23] hath slaughter'd him!

What does Juliet mean? What does her mother think she means?

LADY CAPULET. Find thou the means, and I'll find such a man.
But now I'll tell thee joyful tidings, girl.

105 **JULIET.** And joy comes well in such a needy time.
What are they, beseech your ladyship?

LADY CAPULET. Well, well, thou hast a careful[24] father, child,
One who, to put thee from thy heaviness,
Hath sorted out a sudden[25] day of joy,
110 That thou expects not, nor I look'd not for.

Why does Juliet's father plan joy for her?

JULIET. Madam, in happy time, what day is that?

LADY CAPULET. Marry, my child, early next Thursday morn,
The gallant, young, and noble gentleman,
The County Paris, at Saint Peter's Church,
115 Shall happily make thee there a joyful bride.

JULIET. Now, by Saint Peter's Church and Peter too,
He shall not make me there a joyful bride.
I wonder at this haste, that I must wed
Ere he that should be husband comes to woo.
120 I pray you tell my lord and father, madam,
I will not marry yet, and when I do, I swear
It shall be Romeo, whom you know I hate,
Rather than Paris. These are news indeed!

How does Juliet respond to the news that she is to marry Paris?

LADY CAPULET. Here comes your father, tell him so yourself;
125 And see how he will take it at your hands.

Enter CAPULET *and* NURSE.

CAPULET. When the sun sets, the earth doth drizzle dew,
But for the sunset of my brother's son
It rains downright.

---

22. **temper.** Prepare
23. **his body that.** Body of the person who
24. **careful.** Caring
25. **sudden.** Fast-approaching

---

words for everyday use ab • hor (ab hôr´) vt., hate; detest. *Nicole <u>abhors</u> doing geometry problems, but she likes algebra equations.*

How now, a conduit,[26] girl? What, still in tears?
Evermore show'ring? In one little body
Thou counterfeits a bark, a sea, a wind:
For still thy eyes, which I may call the sea,
Do ebb and flow with tears; the bark thy body is,
Sailing in this salt flood; the winds, thy sighs,
Who, raging with thy tears, and they with them,
Without a sudden calm,[27] will overset
Thy tempest-tossed body. How now, wife?
Have you delivered to her our decree?

LADY CAPULET.   Ay, sir, but she will none, she gives you thanks.[28]
I would the fool were married to her grave!

CAPULET.   Soft, take me with you, take me with you,[29] wife.
How, will she none? Doth she not give us thanks?
Is she not proud?[30] Doth she not count her blest,
Unworthy as she is, that we have wrought[31]
So worthy a gentleman to be her bride?[32]

JULIET.   Not proud you have, but thankful[33] that you have.
Proud can I never be of what I hate,
But thankful even for hate that is meant love.

CAPULET.   How how, how how, chopp'd logic![34] What is this?
"Proud," and "I thank you," and "I thank you not,"
And yet "not proud," mistress minion[35] you?
Thank me no thankings, nor proud me no prouds,
But fettle[36] your fine joints 'gainst Thursday next,
To go with Paris to Saint Peter's Church,
Or I will drag thee on a hurdle[37] thither.
Out,[38] you green-sickness[39] carrion! Out, you baggage![40]
You tallow-face!

LADY CAPULET.   Fie, fie, what, are you mad?

JULIET.   Good father, I beseech you on my knees,
Hear me with patience but to speak a word.   *She kneels down.*

CAPULET.   Hang thee, young baggage! disobedient wretch!
I tell thee what: get thee to church a' Thursday,
Or never after look me in the face.
Speak not, reply not, do not answer me!
My fingers itch. Wife, we scarce thought us blest

What response does Lady Capulet give to Juliet's refusal to wed Paris?

---

26. **conduit.** Fountain
27. **Without . . . calm.** Unless they stop soon
28. **but . . . thanks.** She declines with thanks.
29. **take . . . you.** Tell me what you mean
30. **proud.** Happy
31. **wrought.** Obtained
32. **bride.** Bridegroom
33. **thankful.** Politely grateful

34. **chopp'd logic.** Misleading but clever argument
35. **minion.** Spoiled child
36. **fettle.** Ready (term usually used for horses)
37. **hurdle.** Sled on which prisoners were taken
38. **Out.** Exclamation of rebuke
39. **green-sickness.** Pale
40. **baggage.** Worthless being

165　That God had lent us but this only child,
　　　But now I see this one is one too much,
　　　And that we have a curse in having her.
　　　Out on her, hilding!

What does Capulet think of Juliet's refusal?

　　　NURSE.　　　　　God in heaven bless her!
　　　You are to blame, my lord, to rate[41] her so.

170　**CAPULET.**　And why, my Lady Wisdom? Hold your tongue,
　　　Good Prudence, smatter[42] with your gossips, go.

　　　NURSE.　I speak no treason.

　　　CAPULET.　　　　　　　O, God-i-goden![43]

　　　NURSE.　May not one speak?

　　　CAPULET.　　　　　　　　Peace, you mumbling fool!
　　　Utter your <u>gravity</u> o'er a gossip's bowl,
　　　For here we need it not.

175　**LADY CAPULET.**　　　You are too hot.

　　　CAPULET.　God's bread, it makes me mad! Day, night, work, play,
　　　Alone, in company, still my care hath been
　　　To have her match'd; and having now provided
　　　A gentleman of noble parentage,
180　Of fair demesnes,[44] youthful and nobly lien'd,[45]
　　　Stuff'd, as they say, with honorable parts,
　　　Proportion'd as one's thought would wish a man,
　　　And then to have a wretched puling[46] fool,
　　　A whining mammet,[47] in her fortune's tender,[48]
185　To answer, "I'll not wed, I cannot love;
　　　I am too young, I pray you pardon me."
　　　But and you will not wed, I'll pardon you.
　　　Graze where you will, you shall not house with me.
　　　Look to't, think on't, I do not use[49] to jest.
190　Thursday is near, lay hand on heart, advise.[50]
　　　And you be mine, I'll give you to my friend;
　　　And you be not, hang, beg, starve, die in the streets,
　　　For, by my soul, I'll ne'er acknowledge thee,
　　　Nor what is mine shall never do thee good.

What threat does Capulet make?

---

41. **rate.** Scold
42. **smatter.** Chatter
43. **God-i-goden.** Exclamation of impatience meaning "for God's sake"
44. **demesnes.** Domain
45. **nobly lien'd.** Of good standing

46. **puling.** Whining
47. **mammet.** Doll
48. **in . . . tender.** When good fortune comes
49. **do not use.** Don't usually
50. **advise.** Think carefully

words for everyday use　grav • i • ty (grav´i tē) *n.,* seriousness or solemnity. *The <u>gravity</u> of the situation alarmed the homeowner, so he called the police.*

195   Trust to't, bethink you, I'll not be forsworn.   *Exit.*

JULIET.   Is there no pity sitting in the clouds,
That sees into the bottom of my grief?
O sweet my mother, cast me not away!
Delay this marriage for a month, a week,
200   Or if you do not, make the bridal bed
In that dim monument where Tybalt lies.

LADY CAPULET.   Talk not to me, for I'll not speak a word.
Do as thou wilt, for I have done with thee.   *Exit.*

JULIET.   O God!—O nurse, how shall this be prevented?
205   My husband is on earth, my faith in heaven;[51]
How shall that faith return again to earth,
Unless that husband send it me from heaven
By leaving earth?[52] Comfort me, counsel me!
Alack, alack, that heaven should practice[53] <u>stratagems</u>
210   Upon so soft a subject as myself!
What say'st thou? Hast thou not a word of joy?
Some comfort, nurse.

NURSE.   Faith, here it is.
Romeo is banished, and all the world to nothing[54]
That he dares ne'er come back to challenge[55] you;
215   Or if he do, it needs must be by stealth.
Then, since the case so stands as now it doth,
I think it best you married with the County.
O he's a lovely gentleman!
Romeo's a dishclout to[56] him. An eagle, madam,
220   Hath not so green, so quick, so fair an eye
As Paris hath. Beshrow[57] my very heart,
I think you are happy in this second match,
For it excels your first; or if it did not,
Your first is dead, or 'twere as good he were
225   As living here[58] and you no use of him.

JULIET.   Speak'st thou from thy heart?

NURSE.   And from my soul too, else beshrew them both.

What does the Nurse advise Juliet to do?

---

51. **my . . . heaven.** I swore my marriage vow before God.
52. **How . . . earth?** How can I remarry unless Romeo dies?
53. **practice.** Invent, contrive
54. **all . . . nothing.** It is a safe bet, the odds are

55. **challenge.** Claim
56. **to.** Compared to
57. **Beshrow.** Beshrew, curse
58. **here.** On earth

words for everyday use

strat • a • gem (strat´ə jəm) n., trick. *The magician's <u>stratagem</u> delighted the children, who had never seen a rabbit pulled out of a hat.*

JULIET. Amen![59]

NURSE. What?

230 **JULIET.** Well, thou hast comforted me marvellous much.
Go in, and tell my lady I am gone,
Having displeas'd my father, to Lawrence' cell,
To make confession and to be absolv'd.

To whom does Juliet turn?

NURSE. Marry, I will, and this is wisely done. *Exit.*

235 **JULIET.** [*She looks after* NURSE.] Ancient damnation![60] O most wicked fiend!
Is it more sin to wish me thus forsworn,
Or to dispraise my lord with that same tongue
Which she hath prais'd him with above compare
So many thousand times? Go, counsellor,
240 Thou and my bosom[61] henceforth shall be twain.[62]
I'll to the friar to know his remedy;
If all else fail, myself have power to die. *Exit.*

---

59. **Amen.** So be it.
60. **Ancient damnation.** Damned old woman

61. **bosom.** Inner thoughts
62. **twain.** Separate

Respond *to the* SELECTION

Which character comes closest to behaving according to your own values—Tybalt, Mercutio, Romeo, or Benvolio? Why?

Investigate, *Inquire,* and Imagine

Recall: GATHERING FACTS

1a. Why does Benvolio want to go inside at the beginning of scene 1? What does he fear?

2a. What name does Tybalt call Romeo? How does Romeo respond? What happens to Mercutio? What is Romeo trying to do when this happens? What happens to Tybalt, and why?

3a. What order does the prince give as a result of the killing of Tybalt? What mistaken impression does Juliet get from the nurse at the beginning of scene 2? What information does Juliet finally get from the nurse?

Interpret: FINDING MEANING

1b. What sort of man is Benvolio? What sort of man is Mercutio? How do they differ in personality?

2b. What do Romeo's actions during the duel reveal about him? What makes Romeo a sympathetic character?

3b. Do you agree with the prince's decision with regard to Romeo? Why, or why not?

Analyze: TAKING THINGS APART

4a. Compare the judgment the Prince imposes on Romeo for the death of Tybalt, to the punishment with which Capulet threatens Juliet if she refuses to marry Paris. What desire or wish motivates the Prince? What motivates Capulet?

Synthesize: BRINGING THINGS TOGETHER

4b. At this point in the story, what might resolve, without further tragedy, the conflict and the complications that have taken place? What would the main characters have to be willing to do? Assess the likelihood of this happening.

Evaluate: MAKING JUDGMENTS

5a. What tragic mistakes have been made and by whom so far in the play? How might the problems Romeo and Juliet now face have been avoided? What is your judgment as to where the blame lies?

Extend: CONNECTING IDEAS

5b. What arguments does Capulet use to suggest that Juliet should obey him? How have generational conflicts changed in five hundred years? How have they stayed the same?

Understanding *Literature*

PLOT AND CRISIS. Review the definitions for **plot** and **crisis** in the Handbook of Literary Terms. In a tragedy, the main character's fortunes improve until the crisis. After the crisis, the main character's fortunes decline, or get worse. What crisis does Romeo face in act 3 of this play? What event occurs that has negative consequences for him? Was Romeo at fault in this crisis? Do you sympathize with his predicament? Why, or why not?

IRONY AND DRAMATIC IRONY. Review the definitions for **irony** and **dramatic irony** in the Handbook of Literary Terms. There are several instances of dramatic irony in act 3. Review the chart you completed on dramatic irony in Literary Tools on page 345. Why do you think Shakespeare used dramatic irony? What feeling might he have wanted to create in the audience? In each case, do you think the character would have acted differently if he or she had known what the audience knows?

Writer's Journal

1. Newspapers as we know them did not exist in Renaissance Italy or in Elizabethan England. For this exercise, however, imagine that a newspaper exists and that you serve as its crime reporter. Write a **news report** about the deaths of Mercutio and Tybalt, and the banishment of Romeo by the prince. You should report the facts and include eyewitness quotes and descriptions of the scene.

2. Imagine that you are Benvolio, Romeo's best friend. Write a **letter** to Juliet, describing what has happened and assuring her that Romeo has behaved honorably.

3. Imagine that you are a theater critic in Elizabethan England. Write a **theater review** of act 3. Provide a brief preview of the action for your readers and describe what they will experience, without giving away the climax.

Integrating the Language Arts

Collaborative Learning & Speaking and Listening

COUNSELING ROMEO. Work with a partner to role-play a counseling session between Friar Lawrence and Romeo on Romeo's plans to marry Juliet. Before the role-play, think about the motivation of Friar Lawrence and of Romeo. What is each most interested in? What points would each want to make? After practicing with your partner, perform your role-play for the class. Then, as a class, discuss whether or not events thus far would have turned out differently if Friar Lawrence had held such a counseling session with Romeo.

Language, Grammar, and Style

PARAPHRASING FRIAR LAWRENCE. Review the Language Arts Survey 5.43, "Paraphrasing, Summarizing, and Quoting." Reread Friar Lawrence's speech in scene 3, lines 110–119 and rewrite it in modern English. Without attempting to rewrite it word for word, try to capture the sense of what Friar Lawrence is saying in terms that modern audiences would find easy to understand.

Study and Research

RESEARCHING ROMEO'S TRAVELS. Locate a map of Italy and find the cities of Verona and Mantua. How far apart are they? Research the typical mode of travel in Renaissance Italy. Estimate the time it would have taken Romeo to travel from Verona to Mantua.

Speaking and Listening & Collaborative Learning

READ ALOUD. Working in pairs read out loud lines 2–60 in act 3, scene 2, Juliet's monologue and the dialogue with her nurse in which she learns of Romeo's death. Take turns reading each part.

Literary TOOLS

PLOT AND CLIMAX. A **plot** is a series of events related to a central conflict, or struggle. The **climax** is the point in the plot where something decisive happens to determine the future course of events and the eventual working out of the conflict. As you read act 4, look for the decisive action—the climax—of the plot.

FORESHADOWING. Foreshadowing is the act of presenting materials that hint at events to occur later in a story. When Juliet first sees Romeo in act 1, she says to her Nurse, "Go ask his name.—If he be married, / My grave is like to be my wedding-bed." This is an example of foreshadowing which hints at the fate of the lovers. As you read act 4, try to find the lines from Capulet that echo or repeat Juliet's line from act 1.

Reader's Journal

If you were Juliet, secretly married to Romeo and being pressured to marry Paris by parents who threaten to disown you, what would you do?

ACT 4
SCENE 1: FRIAR LAWRENCE'S CELL

Enter FRIAR LAWRENCE *and* COUNTY PARIS.

FRIAR LAWRENCE.   On Thursday, sir? The time is very short.

PARIS.   My father Capulet will have it so,
And I am nothing slow to slack his haste.[1]

FRIAR LAWRENCE.   You say you do not know the lady's mind?
5   Uneven is the course, I like it not.

ACT 4, SCENE 1
  1. **I am . . . haste.** I have no desire to cause him to act less hastily.

PARIS.   Immoderately she weeps for Tybalt's death,
And therefore have I little talk'd of love,
For Venus smiles not in a house of tears.
Now, sir, her father counts it dangerous
10   That she do give her sorrow so much sway;
And in his wisdom hastes our marriage,
To stop the <u>inundation</u> of her tears,
Which, too much minded by herself alone,
May be put from her by society.[2]
15   Now do you know the reason of this haste.

FRIAR LAWRENCE.   [*Aside.*] I would[3] I knew not why it should
be slowed.—
Look, sir, here comes the lady toward my cell.

Enter JULIET.

PARIS.   Happily met, my lady and my wife!

20   **JULIET.**   That may be, sir, when I may be a wife.

PARIS.   That may be must be, love, on Thursday next.

JULIET.   What must be shall be.

FRIAR LAWRENCE.   That's a certain text.

PARIS.   Come you to make confession to this father?

JULIET.   To answer that, I should confess to you.

25   **PARIS.**   Do not deny to him that you love me.

JULIET.   I will confess to you that I love him.

PARIS.   So will ye, I am sure, that you love me.

JULIET.   If I do so, it will be of more price,
Being spoke behind your back, than to your face.

30   **PARIS.**   Poor soul, thy face is much abus'd with tears.

JULIET.   The tears have got small victory by that,
For it was bad enough before their spite.

PARIS.   Thou wrong'st it more than tears with that report.

JULIET.   That is no <u>slander</u>, sir, which is a truth,
35   And what I spake, I spake it to my face.[4]

---

2. **too much . . . society.** Paris suggests that Juliet's
sorrow is worse because she is alone and that she would
feel better in the company of others.

3. **would.** Wish
4. **to my face.** About my own face

PARIS.   Thy face is mine, and thou hast sland'red it.

JULIET.   It may be so, for it is not mine own.
Are you at leisure, holy father, now,
Or shall I come to you at evening mass?

40   **FRIAR LAWRENCE.**   My leisure serves me, pensive[5] daughter, now.
My lord, we must entreat the time alone.

PARIS.   God shield[6] I should disturb devotion!
Juliet, on Thursday early will I rouse ye;
Till then adieu, and keep this holy kiss.   *Exit.*

45   **JULIET.**   O, shut the door, and when thou hast done so,
Come weep with me, past hope, past cure, past help!

FRIAR LAWRENCE.   O Juliet, I already know thy grief,
It strains[7] me past the compass[8] of my wits.
I hear thou must, and nothing may prorogue[9] it,
50   On Thursday next be married to this County.

What "pressures" does Friar Lawrence feel?

JULIET.   Tell me not, friar, that thou hearest of this,
Unless thou tell me how I may prevent it.
If in thy wisdom thou canst give no help,
Do thou but call my <u>resolution</u> wise,
55   And with this knife I'll help it presently.[10]
God join'd my heart and Romeo's, thou our hands,
And ere this hand, by thee to Romeo's seal'd,
Shall be the label[11] to another deed,
Or my true heart with treacherous revolt
60   Turn to another, this shall slay them both.
Therefore, out of thy long-experienc'd time,
Give me some present counsel, or, behold,
'Twixt my extremes and me this bloody knife
Shall play the umpeer,[12] arbitrating[13] that
65   Which the commission[14] of thy years and art[15]
Could to no issue of true honor bring.
Be not so long to speak, I long to die,
If what thou speak'st speak not of remedy.

What does Juliet threaten to do if Friar Lawrence has no remedy for her situation?

---

5. **pensive.** Sad and thoughtful
6. **shield.** Forbid
7. **strains.** Forces
8. **compass.** Boundaries or borders
9. **prorogue.** Argue against or prevent
10. **presently.** At this moment

11. **label.** Seal
12. **umpeer.** Umpire
13. **arbitrating.** Deciding
14. **commission.** Authority
15. **art.** Ability

words for everyday use

res • o • lu • tion (rez´ə lü´shən) *n.,* expression of will or intent; determination. *Jamie made a New Year's <u>resolution</u> to lose ten pounds.*

FRIAR LAWRENCE.   Hold, daughter! I do spy a kind of hope,

70 Which craves as desperate an execution
As that is desperate which we would prevent.
If rather than to marry County Paris,
Thou hast the strength of will to slay thyself,
Then is it likely thou wilt undertake
75 A thing like death to chide away this shame,
That cop'st with Death himself to scape from it;[16]
And if thou darest, I'll give thee remedy.

JULIET.   O, bid me leap, rather than marry Paris,
From off the battlements of any tower,
80 Or walk in thievish ways, or bid me lurk
Where serpents are; chain me with roaring bears,
Or hide me nightly in a charnel-house,[17]
O'ercover'd quite with dead men's rattling bones,
With reeky[18] shanks and yellow chapless[19] skulls;
85 Or bid me go into a new-made grave,
And hide me with a dead man in his <u>shroud</u>—
Things that, to hear them told, have made me tremble—
And I will do it without fear or doubt,
To live an unstain'd wife to my sweet love.

90 **FRIAR LAWRENCE.**   Hold then. Go home, be merry, give consent
To marry Paris. We'n'sday is to-morrow;
To-morrow night look that thou lie alone,
Let not the nurse lie with thee in thy chamber.
Take thou this vial, being then in bed,
95 And this distilling liquor drink thou off,
When presently through all thy veins shall run
A cold and drowsy humor;[20] for no pulse
Shall keep his native progress,[21] but surcease;[22]
No warmth, no breath shall testify thou livest;
100 The roses in thy lips and cheeks shall fade
To wanny[23] ashes, thy eyes' windows[24] fall,
Like death when he shuts up the day of life;
Each part, depriv'd of supple government,[25]

> What does Friar Lawrence give Juliet? What will she use it for?

---

16. **That cop'st . . . from it.** You who would have dealings with death in order to escape the death of a marriage to one whom you do not love
17. **charnel-house.** House where corpses are kept
18. **reeky.** Reeking, smelly
19. **chapless.** Jawless

20. **humor.** Fluid
21. **keep . . . progress.** Occur as usual
22. **surcease.** Cease
23. **wanny.** Pale
24. **windows.** Lids
25. **supple goverment.** Control over movements

words for everyday use   shroud (shroud) *n.,* cloth used to wrap a corpse for burial. *The deceased was buried in a black <u>shroud</u>.*

Shall, stiff and stark and cold, appear like death,
105 And in this borrowed likeness of shrunk death
Thou shalt continue two and forty hours,
And then awake as from a pleasant sleep.
Now when the bridegroom in the morning comes
To rouse thee from thy bed, there art thou dead.
110 Then, as the manner of our country is,
In thy best robes, uncovered on the bier,
Thou shall be borne to that same ancient vault
Where all the kindred of the Capulets lie.
In the mean time, against[26] thou shalt awake,
115 Shall Romeo by my letters know our drift,[27]
And hither shall he come, an' he and I
Will watch thy waking, and that very night
Shall Romeo bear thee hence to Mantua.
And this shall free thee from this present shame,
120 If no inconstant toy,[28] nor womanish fear,
Abate thy valor in the acting it.

JULIET. Give me, give me! O, tell not me of fear!

FRIAR LAWRENCE. Hold, get you gone. Be strong and prosperous
In this resolve. I'll send a friar with speed
125 To Mantua, with my letters to thy lord.

JULIET. Love give me strength! and strength shall help afford.
Farewell, dear father! *Exeunt.*

SCENE 2: CAPULET'S HOUSE

Enter FATHER CAPULET, *Mother* LADY CAPULET, NURSE, *and* SERVINGMEN, *two or three.*

CAPULET. So many guests invite as here are writ.

Exit FIRST SERVANT.

Sirrah, go hire me twenty cunning cooks.

2. SERVANT. You shall have none ill, sir, for I'll try if they can lick
their fingers.

5 **CAPULET.** How canst thou try them so?[1]

2. SERVANT. Marry, sir, 'tis an ill cook that cannot lick his own fingers;
therefore he that cannot lick his fingers[2] goes not with me.

---

26. **against.** To prepare for the moment when
27. **drift.** Intentions
28. **inconstant toy.** Change of mind

ACT 4, SCENE 2
  1. **try them so.** By that means tell whether they can cook

2. **lick . . . fingers.** The servant is suggesting that a good cook will be willing to taste his own cooking by licking his fingers.

CAPULET.   Go, be gone.   *Exit* SECOND SERVANT.
We shall be much unfurnish'd[3] for this time.

10   What, is my daughter gone to Friar Lawrence?

NURSE.   Ay forsooth.

CAPULET.   Well, he may chance to do some good on her.
A <u>peevish</u> self-will'd harlotry it is.

Enter JULIET.

NURSE.   See where she comes from shrift with merry look.

15   **CAPULET.**   How now, my headstrong, where have you been gadding?[4]

JULIET.   Where I have learnt me to repent the sin
Of disobedient opposition
To you and your behests, and am enjoin'd
By holy Lawrence to fall <u>prostrate</u> here

20   To beg your pardon. [*She kneels down.*] Pardon, I beseech you!
Henceforward I am ever rul'd by you.

CAPULET.   Send for the County, go tell him of this.
I'll have this knot knit up tomorrow morning.

JULIET.   I met the youthful lord at Lawrence' cell,

25   And gave him what becomed[5] love I might,
Not stepping o'er the bounds of modesty.

CAPULET.   Why, I am glad on't, this is well, stand up.
This is as't should be. Let me see the County;
Ay, marry, go, I say, and fetch him hither.

30   Now, afore God, this reverend holy friar,
All our whole city is much bound to him.

JULIET.   Nurse, will you go with me into my closet[6]
To help me sort such needful ornaments
As you think fit to furnish me tomorrow?

35   **LADY CAPULET.**   No, not till Thursday, there is time enough.

CAPULET.   Go, nurse, go with her, we'll to church tomorrow.
                              Exeunt JULIET *and* NURSE.

LADY CAPULET.   We shall be short in our provision,
'Tis now near night.

CAPULET.   Tush, I will stir about,

---

3. **unfurnish'd.** Unprepared
4. **gadding.** Going in a purposeless manner

5. **becomed.** Fitting
6. **closet.** Room

---

words for everyday use

pee • vish (pēv´ish) *adj.*, hard to please; irritable. *Because her son was <u>peevish</u>, Mrs. Samson made him play alone in his room.*

pros • trate (präs´trāt) *adj.*, lying with the face downward in demonstration of great humility. *Marlene lay <u>prostrate</u> on the floor.*

And all things shall be well, I warrant thee, wife;
40 Go thou to Juliet, help to deck up her.
I'll not to bed tonight; let me alone,
I'll play the huswife[7] for this once. What ho!
They are all forth. Well, I will walk myself
To County Paris, to prepare up him
45 Against to-morrow. My heart is wondrous light,
Since this same wayward girl is so reclaim'd.

Exeunt.

Why does Capulet rejoice?

SCENE 3: CAPULET'S HOUSE

Enter JULIET *and* NURSE.

JULIET.   Ay, those attires are best, but, gentle nurse,
I pray thee leave me to myself tonight,
For I have need of many orisons[1]
To move the heavens to smile upon my state,
5 Which, well thou knowest, is cross and full of sin.

Enter Mother LADY CAPULET.

LADY CAPULET.   What, are you busy, ho? Need you my help?

JULIET.   No, madam, we have cull'd such necessaries
As are behoofeful[2] for our state[3] tomorrow.
So please you, let me now be left alone,
10 And let the nurse this night sit up with you,
For I am sure you have your hands full all,
In this so sudden business.

Why does Juliet send the Nurse away?

LADY CAPULET.   Good night.
Get thee to bed and rest, for thou hast need.

Exeunt LADY CAPULET *and* NURSE.

JULIET.   Farewell! God knows when we shall meet again.
15 I have a faint cold fear thrills through my veins,
That almost freezes up the heat of life.
I'll call them back again to comfort me.
Nurse!—What should she do here?
My dismal scene I needs must act alone.
20 Come, vial.
What if this mixture do not work at all?
Shall I be married then tomorrow morning?
No, no, this shall forbid it. Lie thou there.

Laying down her dagger.

What if it be a poison which the friar
25 Subtilly hath minist'red to have me dead,

---

7. **huswife.** Housewife
ACT 4, SCENE 3
  1. **orisons.** Prayers

2. **behoofeful.** Needed
3. **state.** Ceremony

Lest in this marriage he should be dishonor'd
Because he married me before to Romeo?
I fear it is, and yet methinks it should not,
For he hath still[4] been tried[5] a holy man.
30 How if, when I am laid into the tomb,
I wake before the time that Romeo
Come to redeem me? there's a fearful point!
Shall I not then be stifled in the vault,
To whose foul mouth no healthsome air breathes in,
35 And there die strangled ere my Romeo comes?
Or if I live, is it not very like
The horrible conceit[6] of death and night,
Together with the terror of the place—
As in a vault, an ancient <u>receptacle</u>,
40 Where for this many hundred years the bones
Of all my buried ancestors are pack'd,
Where bloody Tybalt, yet but green in earth,[7]
Lies fest'ring in his shroud, where, as they say,
At some hours in the night spirits resort—
45 Alack, alack, is it not like that I,
So early waking—what with <u>loathsome</u> smells,
And shrikes like mandrakes'[8] torn out of the earth,
That living mortals, hearing them, run mad—
O, if I wake, shall I not be distraught,
50 Environed with all these hideous fears,
And madly play with my forefathers' joints,
And pluck the mangled Tybalt from his shroud,
And in this rage, with some great kinsman's bone,
As with a club, dash out my desp'rate brains?
55 O, look! methinks I see my cousin's ghost
Seeking out Romeo, that did spit his body
Upon a rapier's point. Stay, Tybalt, stay!
Romeo, Romeo, Romeo! Here's drink—I drink to thee.

She falls upon her bed, within the curtains.

According to Juliet, why might Friar Lawrence want to poison her?

What fears does Juliet have about awakening from her sleep in the Capulet burial vault?

---

4. **still.** Always
5. **been tried.** Been shown to be
6. **conceit.** Idea
7. **green in earth.** Newly buried

8. **shrikes like mandrakes'.** Shrieks like those made by mandrakes. The mandrake root, used in magic because of its supposed resemblance to a human being, was believed to shriek when pulled out of the ground.

words for everyday use

re • cep • ta • cle (ri sep´tə kəl) *n.,* anything used to contain or hold something else. *The <u>receptacle</u> held odds and ends for the road trip.*

loath • some (lōth´səm) *adj.,* disgusting; detestable. *Bette put aside her <u>loathsome</u> homework assignment and watched TV.*

Enter lady of the house LADY CAPULET *and* NURSE *with herbs.*

LADY CAPULET.   Hold, take these keys and fetch more spices, nurse.

NURSE.   They call for dates and quinces in the pastry.[1]

Enter old CAPULET.

CAPULET.   Come, stir, stir, stir! the second cock hath crowed,
The curfew-bell hath rung, 'tis three a' clock.
5   Look to the bak'd meats, good Angelica,[2]
Spare not for cost.

NURSE.   Go, you cot-quean,[3] go,
Get you to bed. Faith, you'll be sick tomorrow
For this night's watching.[4]

CAPULET.   No, not a whit. What, I have watch'd ere now
10   All night for lesser cause, and ne'er been sick.

LADY CAPULET.   Ay, you have been a mouse-hunt[5] in your time,
But I will watch you from such watching now.

                Exeunt LADY CAPULET *and* NURSE.

CAPULET.   A jealous hood,[6] a jealous hood!

Enter three or four SERVINGMEN *with spits and logs and baskets.*

Now, fellow, what is there?

15   **1. SERVANT.**   Things for the cook, sir, but I know not what.

CAPULET.   Make haste, make haste. Sirrah, fetch drier logs.

                Exit FIRST SERVANT.

Call Peter, he will show thee where they are.

2. SERVANT.   I have a head, sir, that will find out logs,
And never trouble Peter for the matter.

20   **CAPULET.**   Mass, and well said, a merry whoreson, ha!
Thou shalt be logger-head.[7] Good faith, 'tis day.   *Exit* SECOND SERVANT.
The County will be here with music straight,
For so he said he would. [*Play music within.*] I hear him near.
Nurse! Wife! What ho! What, nurse, I say!

Enter NURSE.

25   Go waken Juliet, go and trim her up,
I'll go and chat with Paris. Hie, make haste,
Make haste, the bridegroom he is come already,
Make haste, I say.   *Exit.*

ACT 4, SCENE 4
  1. **pastry.** Pastry-room
  2. **Angelica.** The nurse
  3. **cot-quean.** Male housekeeper
  4. **watching.** Wakefulness

  5. **mouse-hunt.** Mouse-hunter; one who is up all night, like a cat
  6. **jealous hood.** Jealous person
  7. **logger-head.** Blockhead

NURSE.   Mistress! what, mistress! Juliet!—Fast,[1] I warrant her, she.—
Why, lamb! why, lady! fie, you slug-a-bed!
Why, love, I say! madam! sweet heart! why, bride!
What, not a word? You take your pennyworths[2] now;

5   Sleep for a week, for the next night, I warrant,
The County Paris hath set up his rest
That you shall rest but little. God forgive me!
Marry and amen! How sound is she asleep!
I needs must wake her. Madam, madam, madam!

10   Ay, let the County take you in your bed,
He'll fright you up, i' faith. Will it not be?   *Draws back the curtains.*
What, dress'd, and in your clothes, and down again?
I must needs wake you. Lady, lady, lady!
Alas, alas! Help, help! my lady's dead!

15   O, weraday, that ever I was born!
Some aqua-vitae ho! My lord! my lady!

Enter Mother, LADY CAPULET.

LADY CAPULET.   What noise is here?

NURSE.   O <u>lamentable</u> day!

LADY CAPULET.   What is the matter?

NURSE.   Look, look! O heavy day!

LADY CAPULET.   O me, O me, my child, my only life!

20   Revive, look up, or I will die with thee!
Help, help! Call help.

Enter Father CAPULET.

CAPULET.   For shame, bring Juliet forth, her lord is come.

NURSE.   She's dead, deceas'd, she's dead, alack the day!

LADY CAPULET.   Alack the day, she's dead, she's dead, she's dead!

25   **CAPULET.**   Hah, let me see her. Out alas, she's cold,
Her blood is settled, and her joints are stiff;
Life and these lips have long been separated.
Death lies on her like an untimely frost
Upon the sweetest flower of all the field.

NURSE.   O lamentable day!

30   **LADY CAPULET.**   O woeful time!

> What does the Nurse find?

ACT 4, SCENE 5
1. **Fast.** Fast asleep

2. **pennyworths.** Small amounts (of sleep)

words for everyday use   lam • en • ta • ble (lam ən´tə bəl) *adj.*, grievous; deplorable; distressing. *The argument between Bill and Larry was <u>lamentable</u>, and it upset them both.*

CAPULET. Death, that hath ta'en her hence to make me wail,
Ties up my tongue and will not let me speak.

Enter FRIAR LAWRENCE *and the* COUNTY PARIS *with the* MUSICIANS.

FRIAR LAWRENCE. Come, is the bride ready to go to church?

CAPULET. Ready to go, but never to return.—

35 O son, the night before thy wedding-day
Hath Death lain with thy wife. There she lies,
Flower as she was, deflowered by him.
Death is my son-in-law, Death is my heir,
My daughter he hath wedded. I will die,
40 And leave him all; life, living, all is Death's.

PARIS. Have I thought long to see this morning's face,
And doth it give me such a sight as this?

LADY CAPULET. Accurs'd, unhappy, wretched, hateful day!
Most miserable hour that e'er time saw
45 In lasting labor of his <u>pilgrimage</u>![3]
But one, poor one, one poor and loving child,
But one thing to rejoice and solace in,
And cruel Death hath catch'd[4] it from my sight!

NURSE. O woe! O woeful, woeful, woeful day!
50 Most lamentable day, most woeful day
That ever, ever, I did yet behold!
O day, O day, O day, O hateful day!
Never was seen so black a day as this.
O woeful day, O woeful day!

55 **PARIS.** Beguil'd, divorced, wronged, spited, slain!
Most detestable Death, by thee beguil'd,
By cruel cruel thee quite overthrown!
O love, O life! not life, but love in death!

CAPULET. Despis'd, distressed, hated, martyr'd, kill'd!
60 Uncomfortable time, why cam'st thou now
To murther, murther our solemnity?[5]
O child, O child! my soul, and not my child!
Dead art thou! Alack, my child is dead,
And with my child my joys are buried.

65 **FRIAR LAWRENCE.** Peace ho, for shame! Confusion's cure lives not
In these confusions. Heaven and yourself

---

3. **Most miserable . . . pilgrimage.** The worst hour
since the beginning of time

4. **catch'd.** Stolen, taken

5. **solemnity.** Festivity, ceremony

**words
for
everyday
use**

pil • grim • age (pil´grim ij) *n.,* long journey. *The parishioners made a <u>pilgrimage</u> to Lourdes, France.*

Had part in this fair maid, now heaven hath all,
And all the better is it for the maid.
Your part in her you could not keep from death,
70 But heaven keeps his part in eternal life.
The most you sought was her promotion,
For 'twas your heaven she should be advanc'd,
And weep ye now, seeing she is advanc'd
Above the clouds, as high as heaven itself?
75 O, in this love, you love your child so ill
That you run mad, seeing that she is well.
She's not well married that lives married long,
But she's best married that dies married young.
Dry up your tears, and stick your rosemary[6]
80 On this fair corse, and as the custom is,
And in her best array, bear her to church;
For though fond nature bids us all <u>lament</u>,
Yet nature's tears are reason's merriment.[7]

How does Friar Lawrence attempt to console Capulet?

CAPULET.   All things that we ordained festival,
85 Turn from their office[8] to black funeral:
Our instruments to melancholy bells,
Our wedding cheer to a sad burial feast;
Our solemn hymns to sullen dirges change;
Our bridal flowers serve for a buried corse;[9]
90 And all things change them to the contrary.

What does the planned wedding become?

FRIAR LAWRENCE.   Sir, go you in, and, madam, go with him;
And go, Sir Paris. Every one prepare
To follow this fair corse unto her grave.
The heavens do low'r upon you for some ill;
95 Move them no more by crossing[10] their high will.

They all, but the NURSE *and the* MUSICIANS, *go forth, casting rosemary on her, and shutting the curtains.*

1. MUSICIAN.   Faith, we may put up our pipes and be gone.

NURSE. Honest good fellows, ah, put up, put up,
For well you know this is a pitiful case.   *Exit.*

1. MUSICIAN.   Ay, by my troth, the case may be amended.[11]

Enter PETER.

---

6. **rosemary.** Herb associated with remembrance
7. **nature's . . . merriment.** Human nature weeps at things that reason considers joyful.
8. **office.** Purpose or function

9. **corse.** Corpse, dead body
10. **crossing.** Going against, challenging
11. **amended.** Mended, fixed, repaired

words for everyday use   la • ment (lə ment´) *vi.,* feel deep sorrow. *The townspeople <u>lamented</u> when two of its young men died in battle.*

100 **PETER.** Musicians, O musicians, "Heart's ease," "Heart's ease"![12] O, and you will have me live, play "Heart's ease."

1. MUSICIAN. Why "Heart's ease"?

PETER. O musicians, because my heart itself plays "My heart is full." O, play me some merry dump[13] to comfort me.

105 **1. MUSICIAN.** Not a dump we, 'tis no time to play now.

PETER. You will not then?

1. MUSICIAN. No.

PETER. I will then give it you soundly.

1. MUSICIAN. What will you give us?

110 **PETER.** No money, on my faith, but the gleek;[14] I will give you the minstrel.[15]

1. MUSICIAN. Then will I give you the serving-creature.

PETER. Then will I lay the serving-creature's dagger on your pate.[16] I will carry no crotchets,[17] I'll *re* you, I'll *fa* you.[18] Do you note[19] me?

1. MUSICIAN. And[20] you *re* us and *fa* us, you note us.[21]

115 **2. MUSICIAN.** Pray you put up your dagger, and put out[22] your wit.

PETER. Then have at you with my wit! I will drybeat you with an iron wit, and put up my iron dagger. Answer me like men:
    "When griping griefs the heart doth wound,
    And doleful dumps the mind oppress,
120   Then music with her silver sound"—
why "silver sound"? Why "music with her silver sound"?
What say you, Simon Catling?

1. MUSICIAN. Marry, sir, because silver hath a sweet sound.

PETER. Pretty! What say you, Hugh Rebeck?

125 **2. MUSICIAN.** I say, "silver sound," because musicians sound for silver.

PETER. Pretty too! What say you, James Soundpost?

3. MUSICIAN. Faith, I know not what to say.

PETER. O, I cry you mercy,[23] you are the singer; I will say for you; it is "music with her silver sound," because musicians have no gold for sounding:
130   "Then music with her silver sound
      With speedy help doth lend redress."　　　　　　　*Exit.*

1. MUSICIAN. What a pestilent knave is this same!

2. MUSICIAN. Hang him, Jack! Come, we'll in here, tarry for the mourners, and stay[24] dinner.　　　　　　　*Exeunt.*

---

12. **"Heart's ease."** Title of a popular ballad
13. **dump.** Song
14. **gleek.** Jest, insult
15. **give . . . minstrel.** Call you names
16. **pate.** Head
17. **carry no crotchets.** Pun meaning both "sing no quarternotes" and "endure no gibes"
18. **I'll *re* . . . you.** Pun meaning both "I'll sing the

notes *re* and *fa* to you" and "I'll mess you up and clean you up," from *ray*, "to befoul," and *fay*, "to clean up"
19. **note.** Hear, listen to
20. **And.** If
21. **note us.** Set us to music
22. **put out.** Bring out
23. **cry you mercy.** Beg your pardon
24. **stay.** Wait for

How do you regard Friar Lawrence's plan at this point in the story? Do you think Juliet has done the right thing? Why, or why not?

Investigate, Inquire, and Imagine

Recall: GATHERING FACTS

1a. Whom does Juliet meet when she goes to see Friar Lawrence? What is going to happen on Thursday?

2a. What is Friar Lawrence's new plan? How does it differ from the old one?

3a. What does the Nurse discover when she goes to wake Juliet on her wedding day?

Interpret: FINDING MEANING

1b. How does Juliet feel about the prospect of marrying Paris? How do you know? What does her refusal to marry Paris reveal about her?

2b. Why was it necessary for Friar Lawrence to change his plan?

3b. What consequences have Juliet's actions had for her relationship with her parents? Do her parents share any of the blame for this unfortunate outcome? Why, or why not?

Analyze: TAKING THINGS APART

4a. Compare Juliet's fears about the Friar's plan in act 4, scene 3, lines 24–58, to her feelings in act 4, scene 1, lines 78–89. How have her feelings changed? Also compare Capulet's feelings when he believes Juliet to be dead, in act 4, scene 5, lines 35–40 to the threat he made when Juliet refused to marry Paris in act 3, scene 5, lines 190–195. How have his feelings changed?

Synthesize: BRINGING THINGS TOGETHER

4b. Why have Juliet and Capulet had such changes of heart? What is the common thread between these two cases?

Evaluate: MAKING JUDGMENTS

5a. How would you assess Friar Lawrence's actions at this point in the play? Has he always acted kindly? wisely? Explain.

Extend: CONNECTING IDEAS

5b. Can you predict what the outcome of the play would have been, thus far, if Friar Lawrence had not become involved? Should he have gotten involved? In our culture we refer to bystanders who involve themselves in a problem with good results as "Good Samaritans." We call those who get involved and produce bad results "meddlers" and other, more negative, terms. What do you feel is the proper role of a bystander who becomes aware of a problem in the lives of others? What factors determine whether or not one should get involved?

Understanding *Literature*

PLOT AND CLIMAX. Review the definitions for **plot** and **climax** in the Handbook of Literary Terms. Many people would agree that the climax of this play comes when Juliet drinks the Friar's potion. This is a highly emotional, intense scene. What suspense does the reader feel at the end of the scene? What is the reader wondering about at the end of the act? What character echoes some of the reader's worries about the possible outcome of Friar Lawrence's plan?

FORESHADOWING. Review the definition for **foreshadowing** in Literary Tools on page 373. What lines from Capulet in act 4 echo or repeat Juliet's line from act 1? In what ways has Juliet's statement turned out to be prophetic, an example of foreshadowing?

Writer's Journal

1. Assume the role of Friar Lawrence and write a **personal letter** to Romeo, explaining the plan to free Juliet from marriage to Paris.

2. Imagine that you are the playwright. Brainstorm with a partner about a possible outcome for this play. Then write a **plot summary** of the plot of act 5 as you would write it.

3. Imagine that you are Paris, overcome with grief at the "death" of your fiancée, Juliet. Write a **poem** or a **prose eulogy** about your love for her and your feelings about her death, to be read at her funeral. As an extra challenge, if you elect to write a poem you might want to write it in the form of an Elizabethan sonnet. Review the definition of *sonnet* in the Handbook of Literary Terms.

Integrating the Language Arts

Study and Research & Collaborative Learning

PROBLEM SOLVING AND DECISION MAKING. At the beginning of act 4, Juliet faces the decision of whether to marry Paris and please her parents or honor her marriage to Romeo and follow Friar Lawrence's plan. Review the Language Arts Survey 5.1, "Making Decisions and Solving Problems." Then, working in pairs, brainstorm other possible options for Juliet. How else might she deal with her problem? Finally, complete either a criteria analysis chart or a pro and con chart to arrive at a decision.

Applied English

WRITING A PROCEDURE. Review Friar Lawrence's plan in act 4, scene 1, lines 90–125. Then read the Language Arts Survey 6.4, "Writing a Step-by-Step Procedure." Write a step-by-step procedure for executing Friar Lawrence's plan. Imagine that you are preparing this procedure for a stranger to implement. Make sure that your instructions are clear and in the appropriate order.

Literary
T O O L S

PLOT AND RESOLUTION. A **plot** is a series of events related to a central conflict, or struggle. The **resolution** is the point at which the central conflict is ended, or resolved. As you read, look for the point at which the resolution occurs.

THEME. A **theme** is a central idea in a literary work. As you read the final act of *Romeo and Juliet,* think about what the central ideas are in this play.

TRAGIC FLAW. A **tragic flaw** is a personal weakness that brings about the fall of a character in a tragedy. Reflect back on the play and consider what tragic flaw contributes to the downfall of both Romeo and Juliet.

Reader's
Journal

In what ways, if any, do you believe in fate?

ACT 5
SCENE 1: A STREET IN MANTUA

Enter ROMEO.

ROMEO.   If I may trust the flattering[1] truth of sleep,
My dreams presage some joyful news at hand.
My bosom's lord[2] sits lightly in his throne,[3]
And all this day an unaccustom'd spirit
5   Lifts me above the ground with cheerful thoughts.
I dreamt my lady came and found me dead—
Strange dream, that gives a dead man leave to think!—
And breath'd such life with kisses in my lips
That I reviv'd and was an emperor.
10   Ah me, how sweet is love itself possess'd,
When but love's shadows are so rich in joy!

Enter Romeo's man BALTHASAR, *booted.*

News from Verona! How now, Balthasar?
Dost thou not bring me letters from the friar?
How doth my lady? Is my father well?
15   How doth my Juliet? That I ask again,
For nothing can be ill if she be well.

BALTHASAR.   Then she is well and nothing can be ill:
Her body sleeps in Capel's monument,
And her immortal part with angels lives.
20   I saw her laid low in her kindred's vault,
And presently[4] took post[5] to tell it you.
O, pardon me for bringing these ill news,
Since you did leave it for my office,[6] sir.

ROMEO.   Is it e'en so? Then I defy you, stars!
25   Thou knowest my lodging, get me ink and paper,
And hire post-horses; I will hence tonight.

BALTHASAR.   I do beseech you, sir, have patience.
Your looks are pale and wild, and do import
Some <u>misadventure</u>.

> What was supposed to have reached Romeo before Balthasar's news?

ACT 5, SCENE 1
1. **flattering.** Favorable
2. **My bosom's lord.** Love
3. **his throne.** Romeo's heart
4. **presently.** Immediately
5. **took post.** Traveled by horse
6. **office.** Duty

words for everyday use   **mis • ad • ven • ture** (mis´əd ven´chər) *n.,* unlucky accident; mishap.
Gia got lost in the subway, and her <u>misadventure</u> ended in tears.

ROMEO.   Tush, thou art deceiv'd.

30   Leave me, and do the thing I bid thee do.
Hast thou no letters to me from the friar?

BALTHASAR.   No, my good lord.

ROMEO.   No matter, get thee gone,
And hire those horses; I'll be with thee straight.   *Exit* BALTHASAR.
Well, Juliet, I will lie with thee tonight.

35   Let's see for means.[7] O mischief, thou art swift
To enter in the thoughts of desperate men!
I do remember an apothecary—
And hereabouts 'a dwells—which late I noted
In tatt'red weeds,[8] with overwhelming[9] brows,

40   Culling of simples;[10] meagre were his looks,
Sharp misery had worn him to the bones;
And in his needy shop a tortoise hung,
An alligator stuff'd and other skins
Of ill-shap'd fishes, and about his shelves

45   A beggarly account[11] of empty boxes,
Green earthen pots, bladders, and musty seeds,
Remnants of packthread, and old cakes of roses[12]
Were thinly scattered, to make up a show.
Noting this penury,[13] to myself I said,

50   "An' if[14] a man did need a poison now,
Whose sale is present death[15] in Mantua,
Here lives a caitiff[16] wretch would sell it him."
O, this same thought did but forerun my need,
And this same needy man must sell it me.

55   As I remember, this should be the house.
Being holiday, the beggar's shop is shut.
What ho, apothecary!

Enter APOTHECARY.

APOTHECARY.   Who calls so loud?

ROMEO.   Come hither, man. I see that thou art poor.
Hold, there is forty ducats;[17] let me have

60   A dram of poison, such soon-speeding gear[18]
As will disperse itself through all the veins
That the life-weary taker may fall dead,
And that the trunk may be discharg'd of breath

> What does the apothecary need? What does Romeo need?

---

7. **see for means.** See how
8. **weeds.** Clothes
9. **overwhelming.** Overhanging; large
10. **simples.** Medicines
11. **beggarly account.** Small number
12. **cakes of roses.** Rose petals made into cakes for their scent

13. **penury.** Extreme poverty
14. **An' if.** If
15. **present death.** Capital offense
16. **caitiff.** Cowardly
17. **ducats.** Gold coins
18. **soon-speeding gear.** Fast-acting stuff

As violently as hasty powder fir'd

65   Doth hurry from the fatal cannon's womb.

APOTHECARY.   Such mortal drugs I have, but Mantua's law
Is death to any he[19] that utters[20] them.

ROMEO.   Art thou so bare and full of wretchedness,
And fearest to die? Famine is in thy cheeks,
70   Need and oppression starveth in thy eyes,
Contempt and beggary hangs upon thy back;
The world is not thy friend, nor the world's law,
The world affords no law to make thee rich;
Then be not poor, but break it, and take this.

Why does the apothecary hesitate to sell Romeo poison?

75   **APOTHECARY.**   My poverty, but not my will, consents.

ROMEO.   I pay thy poverty, and not thy will.

APOTHECARY.   Put this in any liquid thing you will
And drink it off, and if you had the strength
Of twenty man, it would dispatch[21] you straight.

80   **ROMEO.**   There is thy gold, worse poison to men's souls,
Doing more murther in this loathsome world,
Than these poor compounds that thou mayest not sell.
I sell thee poison, thou hast sold me none.
Farewell! Buy food, and get thyself in flesh.[22]

Exit APOTHECARY.

85   Come, cordial[23] and not poison, go with me
To Juliet's grave, for there must I use thee.

Exit.

SCENE 2: FRIAR LAWRENCE'S CELL

Enter FRIAR JOHN.

FRIAR JOHN.   Holy Franciscan friar! brother, ho!

Enter FRIAR LAWRENCE.

FRIAR LAWRENCE.   This same should be the voice of Friar John.
Welcome from Mantua! What says Romeo?
Or, if his mind be writ, give me his letter.

5   **FRIAR JOHN.**   Going to find a barefoot brother out,
One of our order, to associate[1] me,
Here in this city visiting the sick,
And finding him, the searchers[2] of the town,

---

19. **any he.** Anyone
20. **utters.** Dispenses
21. **dispatch.** Kill
22. **get . . . flesh.** Become fat (i.e., prosper)

23. **cordial.** Medicine
ACT 5, SCENE 2
  1. **associate.** Accompany
  2. **searchers.** Health officials

Suspecting that we both were in a house
10　Where the infectious pestilence did reign,
Seal'd up the doors and would not let us forth,
So that my speed to Mantua there was stay'd.

Why couldn't Friar John get to Mantua?

FRIAR LAWRENCE.　Who bare my letter then to Romeo?

FRIAR JOHN.　I could not send it—here it is again—
15　Nor get a messenger to bring it thee,
So fearful were they of infection.

What does Friar John return?

FRIAR LAWRENCE.　Unhappy fortune! By my brotherhood,
The letter was not nice[3] but full of charge,[4]
Of dear[5] import, and the neglecting it
20　May do much danger. Friar John, go hence,
Get me an iron crow,[6] and bring it straight
Unto my cell.

FRIAR JOHN.　Brother, I'll go and bring it thee.　　　　*Exit.*

FRIAR LAWRENCE.　Now must I to the monument alone,
25　Within this three hours will fair Juliet wake.
She will beshrew[7] me much that Romeo
Hath had no notice of these accidents;[8]
But I will write again to Mantua,
And keep her at my cell till Romeo come—
30　Poor living corse, clos'd in a dead man's tomb!　　　*Exit.*

SCENE 3: THE CHURCHYARD WHEREIN LIES THE CAPULET FAMILY TOMB

Enter PARIS *and his* PAGE *with flowers and sweet[1] water and a torch.*

PARIS.　Give me thy torch, boy. Hence, and stand aloof.[2]
Yet put it out, for I would not be seen.
Under yond yew trees lay thee all along,[3]
Holding thy ear close to the hollow ground,
5　So shall no foot upon the churchyard tread,
Being[4] loose, unfirm, with digging up of graves,
But thou shalt hear it. Whistle then to me
As signal that thou hearest something approach.
Give me those flowers. Do as I bid thee, go.

10　**PAGE.**　[*Aside.*] I am almost afraid to stand[5] alone
Here in the churchyard, yet I will adventure.[6]

Retires. PARIS *strews the tomb with flowers.*

---

3. **nice.** About small matters
4. **full of charge.** Important
5. **dear.** Extreme, great
6. **crow.** Crowbar
7. **beshrew.** Censure
8. **accidents.** Events

ACT 5, SCENE 3
1. **sweet.** Perfumed
2. **aloof.** Away from here, distant
3. **all along.** Flat against the ground
4. **Being.** Because the ground is
5. **stand.** Stay
6. **adventure.** Try

PARIS.   Sweet flower, with flowers thy bridal bed I strew—
O woe, thy canopy is dust and stones!—
Which with sweet water nightly I will dew,
15   Or wanting that, with tears distill'd by moans.
The obsequies[7] that I for thee will keep
Nightly shall be to strew thy grave and weep.

Whistle Boy.

The boy gives warning, something doth approach.
What cursed foot wanders this way tonight,
20   To cross[8] my obsequies and true love's rite?
What, with a torch? Muffle me, night, a while.   *Retires.*

Enter ROMEO *and* BALTHASAR *with a torch, a mattock, and a crow of iron.*

ROMEO.   Give me that mattock and the wrenching iron.
Hold, take this letter; early in the morning
See thou deliver it to my lord and father.
25   Give me the light. Upon thy life I charge thee,
What e'er thou hearest or seest, stand all aloof,
And do not interrupt me in my course.
Why I descend into this bed of death
Is partly to behold my lady's face,
30   But chiefly to take thence from her dead finger
A precious ring—a ring that I must use
In dear employment—therefore hence be gone.
But if thou, jealous, dost return to pry
In what I farther shall intend to do,
35   By heaven, I will tear thee joint by joint,
And strew this hungry churchyard with thy limbs.
The time and my intents are savage-wild,
More fierce and more inexorable[9] far
Than empty tigers or the roaring sea.

40   **BALTHASAR.**   I will be gone, sir, and not trouble ye.

ROMEO.   So shalt thou show me friendship. Take thou that;
Live and be prosperous, and farewell, good fellow.

BALTHASAR.   [*Aside.*] For all this same, I'll hide me hereabout,
His looks I fear, and his intents I doubt.   *Retires.*

45   **ROMEO.**   Thou detestable maw,[10] thou womb of death,
Gorg'd with the dearest morsel of the earth,
Thus I enforce thy rotten jaws to open,
And in despite I'll cram thee with more food.

ROMEO *begins to open the tomb.*

> What does Romeo order Balthasar to do?

---

7. **obsequies.** Prayers or rites for dead persons
8. **cross.** Interrupt, go against

9. **inexorable.** Not to be persuaded or moved by entreaty
10. **maw.** Mouth

PARIS.   This is that banish'd <u>haughty</u> Montague,
50   That murd'red my love's cousin, with which grief
It is supposed the fair creature died,
And here is come to do some villainous shame
To the dead bodies. I will apprehend him.
Stop thy <u>unhallowed</u> toil, vile Montague!
55   Can vengeance be pursued further than death?
Condemned villain, I do apprehend thee.
Obey and go with me, for thou must die.

ROMEO.   I must indeed, and therefore came I hither.
Good gentle youth, tempt not a desp'rate man.
60   Fly hence and leave me, think upon these gone,
Let them affright thee. I beseech thee, youth,
Put not another sin upon my head,
By urging me to fury: O, be gone!
By heaven, I love thee better than myself,
65   For I come hither arm'd against myself.
Stay not, be gone; live, and hereafter say
A madman's mercy bid thee run away.

PARIS.   I do defy thy conjuration,
And apprehend thee for a felon here.

70   **ROMEO.**   Wilt thou provoke me? Then have at thee, boy!

PAGE.   O Lord, they fight! I will go call the watch.

PARIS.   O, I am slain! [*Falls.*] If thou be merciful,
Open the tomb, lay me with Juliet.

ROMEO.   In faith, I will. Let me peruse this face.
75   Mercutio's kinsman, noble County Paris!
What said my man, when my betossed soul
Did not attend him as we rode? I think
He told me Paris should have married Juliet.
Said he not so? or did I dream it so?
80   Or am I mad, hearing him talk of Juliet,
To think it was so? O, give me thy hand,
One writ with me in sour misfortune's book!
I'll bury thee in a triumphant grave.
A grave? O no, a lanthorn,[11] slaught'red youth;
85   For here lies Juliet, and her beauty makes

> *What does Paris suspect Romeo is doing at Juliet's tomb?*

Steps forth.

They fight.
Exit.

> *What happens to Paris?*

Dies.

---

11. **lanthorn.** Lantern (tower room with glass on all sides)

words for everyday use	
	haugh • ty (hôt´ē) *adj.,* proud; arrogant. *The <u>haughty</u> winning speller indicated by the position of his head that he thought he was better than everyone else.*
	un • hal • lowed (un´hal´ōd) *adj.,* unholy; wicked. *Because of his heinous crime, the murderer was buried in <u>unhallowed</u> ground.*

This vault a feasting presence[12] full of light.
Death, lie thou there, by a dead man interr'd.

Laying PARIS *in the tomb.*

How oft when men are at the point of death
Have they been merry, which their keepers call
90 A lightning before death! O how may I
Call this a lightning? O my love, my wife,
Death, that hath suck'd the honey of thy breath,
Hath had no power yet upon thy beauty:
Thou art not conquer'd, beauty's ensign yet
95 Is crimson in thy lips and in thy cheeks,
And death's pale flag is not advanced[13] there.
Tybalt, liest thou there in thy bloody sheet?
O, what more favor can I do to thee,
Than with that hand that cut thy youth in twain
100 To sunder[14] his that was thine enemy?
Forgive me, cousin! Ah, dear Juliet,
Why art thou yet so fair? Shall I believe
That unsubstantial Death is amorous,
And that the lean abhorred monster keeps
105 Thee here in dark to be his paramour?
For fear of that, I still will stay with thee,
And never from this palace of dim night
Depart again. Here, here will I remain
With worms that are thy chambermaids; O, here
110 Will I set up my everlasting rest,
And shake the yoke of inauspicious stars
From this world-wearied flesh. Eyes, look your last!
Arms, take your last embrace! and, lips, O you
The doors of breath, seal with a righteous kiss
115 A dateless bargain to engrossing death!
Come, bitter conduct,[15] come, unsavory guide!
Thou desperate pilot, now at once run on
The dashing rocks thy sea-sick weary bark!
Here's to my love! [*Drinks.*] O true apothecary!
120 Thy drugs are quick. Thus with a kiss I die. *Dies.*

Enter FRIAR LAWRENCE *with lanthorn, crow, and spade.*

> How does Juliet appear? What does Romeo think?

> What happens to Romeo?

---

12. **feasting presence.** Appear like a place decorated for a feast
13. **advanced.** Raised
14. **sunder.** Cut
15. **conduct.** Guide

---

words for everyday use

par • a • mour (par´ə mür) *n.*, sweetheart. *Maurice bought a box of chocolate candy for his paramour.*

in • aus • pi • cious (in´ô spish´əs) *adj.*, unfavorable; unlucky. *The team thought that Friday the thirteenth was an inauspicious date to hold the regional championship.*

FRIAR LAWRENCE. Saint Francis be my speed! how oft tonight
Have my old feet stumbled at graves! Who's there?

BALTHASAR. Here's one, a friend, and one that knows you well.

FRIAR LAWRENCE. Bliss be upon you! Tell me, good my friend,
125   What torch is yond, that vainly lends his light
To grubs and eyeless skulls? As I <u>discern</u>,
It burneth in the Capels' monument.

BALTHASAR. It doth so, holy sir, and there's my master,
One that you love.

FRIAR LAWRENCE. Who is it?

BALTHASAR.   Romeo.

FRIAR LAWRENCE. How long hath he been there?

130 **BALTHASAR.**   Full half an hour.

FRIAR LAWRENCE. Go with me to the vault.

BALTHASAR.   I dare not, sir.
My master knows not but I am gone hence,
And fearfully did menace me with death
If I did stay to look on his intents.

135 **FRIAR LAWRENCE.** Stay then, I'll go alone. Fear comes upon me.
O, much I fear some ill unthrifty[16] thing.

BALTHASAR. As I did sleep under this yew tree here,
I dreamt my master and another fought,
And that my master slew him.

FRIAR LAWRENCE.   Romeo!
               FRIAR stoops and looks on the blood and weapons.
140 Alack, alack, what blood is this, which stains
The stony entrance of this <u>sepulchre</u>?
What mean these masterless and gory swords
To lie discolor'd by this place of peace?   *Enters the tomb.*
Romeo, O, pale! Who else? What, Paris too?
145 And steep'd in blood? Ah, what an unkind[17] hour
Is guilty of this lamentable chance!
The lady stirs.   JULIET *rises.*

What does Friar Lawrence find?

JULIET. O comfortable friar! where is my lord?
I do remember well where I should be,

---

16. **unthrifty.** Unlucky
17. **unkind.** Unnatural, cruel

words for everyday use

dis • cern (di surn´) vt., recognize; make out clearly. *Without her glasses, Norine could not <u>discern</u> the exit sign.*

sep • ul • chre or sep • ul • cher (sep´əlk ər) n., vault for burial; grave; tomb. *The pop star's fans laid flowers mournfully in front of his <u>sepulchre</u>.*

150 And there I am. Where is my Romeo?   *Noise within.*

FRIAR LAWRENCE.   I hear some noise, lady. Come from that nest
Of death, contagion, and unnatural sleep.
A greater power than we can contradict
Hath thwarted our intents. Come, come away.
155 Thy husband in thy bosom there lies dead;   *What news does Juliet*
And Paris too. Come, I'll dispose of thee   *hear upon awakening?*
Among a sisterhood of holy nuns.
Stay not to question, for the watch is coming.
Come go, good Juliet [*noise again*], I dare no longer stay.   *Exit.*

160 **JULIET.**   Go get thee hence, for I will not away.
What's here? A cup clos'd in my true love's hand?
Poison, I see, hath been his timeless[18] end.
O churl,[19] drunk all, and left no friendly drop
To help me after?[20] I will kiss thy lips,
165 Haply some poison yet doth hang on them,
To make me die with a restorative.[21]   *What does Juliet seek?*
Thy lips are warm.

1. WATCH.   [*Within.*] Lead, boy, which way?

JULIET.   Yea, noise? Then I'll be brief. O happy dagger,
                                                                    Taking Romeo's dagger.
170 This is thy sheath [*stabs herself*]; there rust, and let me die.
                                                                    Falls on Romeo's body and dies.

Enter Paris's BOY *and* WATCH.

PAGE.   This is the place, there where the torch doth burn.

1. WATCH.   The ground is bloody, search about the churchyard.
Go, some of you, whoe'er you find attach.[22]   *Exeunt some.*
Pitiful sight! here lies the County slain,
175 And Juliet bleeding, warm, and newly dead,
Who here hath lain this two days buried.
Go tell the Prince, run to the Capulets,
Raise up the Montagues; some others search.   *Exeunt others.*
We see the ground whereon these woes do lie,
180 But the true ground of all these piteous woes
We cannot without circumstance descry.

Enter some of the WATCH *with Romeo's man* BALTHASAR.

2. WATCH.   Here's Romeo's man, we found him in the churchyard.

1. WATCH.   Hold him in safety till the Prince come hither.

Enter FRIAR LAWRENCE *and another* WATCHMAN.

---

18. **timeless.** Untimely, premature   21. **restorative.** Romeo's kiss will restore Juliet.
19. **churl.** Low person   22. **attach.** Stop, detain
20. **help me after.** Help me to come after or follow you

3. WATCH.   Here is a friar, that trembles, sighs, and weeps.
185   We took this mattock[23] and this spade from him,
As he was coming from this churchyard's side.

1. WATCH.   A great suspicion. Stay the friar too.

Enter the PRINCE *and* ATTENDANTS.

PRINCE.   What misadventure is so early up,
That calls our person from our morning rest?

Enter Capels CAPULET, LADY CAPULET, *and others.*

190   **CAPULET.**   What should it be that is so shrik'd abroad?

LADY CAPULET.   O, the people in the street cry "Romeo,"
Some "Juliet," and some "Paris," and all run
With open outcry toward our monument.

PRINCE.   What fear is this which startles in your ears?

195   **1. WATCH.**   Sovereign, here lies the County Paris slain,
And Romeo dead, and Juliet, dead before,
Warm and new kill'd.

PRINCE.   Search, seek, and know how this foul murder comes.

1. WATCH.   Here is a friar, and slaughter'd Romeo's man,
200   With instruments upon them, fit to open
These dead men's tombs.

CAPULET.   O heavens! O wife, look how our daughter bleeds!
This dagger hath mista'en, for lo his house
Is empty on the back of Montague,
205   And it mis-sheathed in my daughter's bosom!

LADY CAPULET.   O me, this sight of death is as a bell
That warns my old age to a sepulchre.

Enter MONTAGUE *and others.*

PRINCE.   Come, Montague, for thou art early up
To see thy son and heir now early down.

210   **MONTAGUE.**   Alas, my liege,[24] my wife is dead tonight;
Grief of my son's exile hath stopp'd her breath.
What further woe conspires against mine age?

PRINCE.   Look and thou shalt see.

MONTAGUE.   O thou untaught! what manners is in this,
215   To press before thy father to a grave?

PRINCE.   Seal up the mouth of outrage[25] for a while,

What other death does Montague report?

What does Montague see?

---

23. **mattock.** Digging tool
24. **liege.** Lord or master
25. **outrage.** Impassioned grief

Till we can clear these <u>ambiguities</u>,
And know their spring, their head,[26] their true descent,
And then will I be general of[27] your woes,
220 And lead you even to death.[28] Mean time forbear,
And let mischance be slave to patience.
Bring forth the parties of suspicion.[29]

FRIAR LAWRENCE.   I am the greatest, able to do least,
Yet most suspected, as the time and place
225 Doth make against me, of this direful murther;
And here I stand both to impeach and purge
Myself condemned and myself excus'd.

PRINCE.   Then say at once what thou dost know in this.

FRIAR LAWRENCE.   I will be brief, for my short date of breath[30]
230 Is not so long as is a tedious tale.
Romeo, there dead, was husband to that Juliet,
And she, there dead, that Romeo's faithful wife.
I married them, and their stol'n marriage-day
Was Tybalt's dooms-day, whose untimely death
235 Banish'd the new-made bridegroom from this city,
For whom, and not for Tybalt, Juliet pin'd.
You, to remove that siege of grief from her,
Betroth'd and would have married her perforce
To County Paris. Then comes she to me,
240 And with wild looks bid me <u>devise</u> some mean
To rid her from this second marriage,
Or in my cell there would she kill herself.
Then gave I her (so tutor'd by my art)
A sleeping potion, which so took effect
245 As I intended, for it wrought on her
The form of death. Mean time I writ to Romeo,
That he should hither come as[31] this dire night
To help to take her from her borrowed grave,
Being the time the potion's force should cease.
250 But he which bore my letter, Friar John,
Was stayed by accident, and yesternight
Return'd my letter back. Then all alone,

---

26. **their spring, their head.** Their source
27. **be general of.** Learn about
28. **death.** Execution of guilty persons
29. **parties of suspicion.** Suspects
30. **my . . . breath.** Little time left to me in this life
31. **as.** On

---

words for everyday use

am • bi • gu • i • ty (am´bə gyo͞o´ə tē) n., word or statement that is uncertain or unclear. "The <u>ambiguity</u> in your paper makes me wonder which side you're on," wrote the teacher.

de • vise (di vīz´) vt., work out or create; plan. The bandits <u>devised</u> a plan to free their leader from jail.

At the prefixed hour of her waking,
Came I to take her from her kindred's vault,
255 Meaning to keep her closely at my cell,
Till I conveniently could send to Romeo.
But when I came, some minute ere the time
Of her awakening, here untimely lay
The noble Paris and true Romeo dead.
260 She wakes, and I entreated her come forth
And bear this work of heaven with patience.
But then a noise did scare me from the tomb,
And she, too desperate, would not go with me,
But as it seems, did violence on herself.
265 All this I know, and to the marriage
Her nurse is privy; and if aught in this
Miscarried by my fault, let my old life
Be sacrific'd some hour before his time,
Unto the rigor of severest law.

To what penalty does
Friar Lawrence offer to
subject himself?

270 **PRINCE.** We still[32] have known thee for a holy man.
Where's Romeo's man? what can he say to this?

BALTHASAR. I brought my master news of Juliet's death,
And then in post he came from Mantua
To this same place, to this same monument.
275 This letter he early bid me give his father,
And threat'ned me with death, going in the vault,
If I departed not and left him there.

PRINCE. Give me the letter, I will look on it.
Where is the County's page that rais'd the watch?
280 Sirrah, what made[33] your master in this place?

PAGE. He came with flowers to strew his lady's grave,
And bid me stand aloof, and so I did.
Anon comes one with light to ope the tomb,
And by and by my master drew on him,
285 And then I ran away to call the watch.[34]

PRINCE. This letter doth make good the friar's words,
Their course of love, the tidings of her death;
And here he writes that he did buy a poison
Of a poor 'pothecary, and therewithal
290 Came to this vault, to die and lie with Juliet.
Where be these enemies? Capulet! Montague!

32. **still.** Always
33. **made.** Wanted, did
34. **watch.** Watchman

See what a scourge is laid upon your hate,
That heaven finds means to kill your joys with love.
And I for winking at your discords too
295   Have lost a brace[35] of kinsmen. All are punish'd.

CAPULET.   O brother Montague, give me thy hand.
This is my daughter's jointure,[36] for no more
Can I demand.

MONTAGUE.   But I can give thee more,
For I will raise her statue in pure gold,
300   That whiles Verona by that name is known,
There shall no figure at such rate be set
As that of true and faithful Juliet.

CAPULET.   As rich shall Romeo's by his lady's lie,
Poor sacrifices of our enmity!

305   PRINCE.   A glooming[37] peace this morning with it brings,
The sun, for sorrow, will not show his head.
Go hence to have more talk of these sad things;
Some shall be pardon'd, and some punished:
For never was a story of more woe
310   Than this of Juliet and her Romeo.   *Exeunt omnes.*[38]   ■

35. **a brace.** Two
36. **jointure.** Dowry
37. **glooming.** Gloomy
38. ***Exeunt omnes.*** Exit all

How many are punished for the long-running feud, according to the Prince?

What finally happens, after all the deaths?

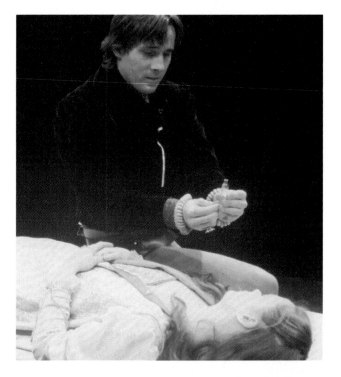

Respond *to the* SELECTION

Who do you feel is to blame for the tragic fate of Romeo and Juliet? Should several people share the blame? Why, or why not?

ROMEO AND JULIET

OVER THE CENTURIES

Romeo and Juliet is probably the best known and best loved of all William Shakespeare's plays. Generations of audiences have been able to relate to the two "star-cross'd" young lovers, whose passion is doomed from the start by the bitter feuding between their families. Since Elizabethan times, the play has been interpreted in many forms, inspiring operas, ballets, musicals, and poetry. It has been translated into nearly every language and has been updated in such modern contexts as gangland New York City, the Israeli-Palestinian conflict in Jerusalem, and war-torn Sarajevo.

The power of the story itself is evident in that it has been told for centuries; in fact, it was not even new to Shakespeare's audience. According to legend, the real story of Romeo and Juliet took place in Verona in 1303, although similar stories were told in Greece dating back to the second century. Shakespeare's source for the play was probably *The Tragicall Historye of Romeus and Juliet,* a long poem written by Englishman Arthur Brooke in 1562. Brooke himself based his poem on an earlier Italian work that had been translated into French.

The timeless story of two lovers found its most treasured and enduring form in the unparalleled poetry of Shakespeare. His version of *Romeo and Juliet* is exceptional for its wit and wordplay, its soaring poetic descriptions, and its frenetic pace. Many lines from *Romeo and Juliet*, like so many others from Shakespeare's body of work, have entered the common lexicon.[1] Everyone knows "a rose by any other name would smell as sweet" and understands the term "Romeo" to mean a lover. The unforgettable balcony scene in act 2 has become an archetype[2] of romantic love.

Shakespeare's plays were meant to be performed, not read. *Romeo and Juliet* in particular, because of its explosive emotion and lack of subtle, introspective brooding, is especially suited for musical interpretations such as those of famous composers like Berlioz and Tchaikovsky. Following are some of the many ways *Romeo and Juliet* has been performed.

- Charles Francois Gounod's **opera** *Romeo and Juliet,* composed in 1867, is the most famous operatic version of Shakespeare's ultimate love story. It continues to be performed in opera houses worldwide.

---

1. **lexicon.** Collection of vocabulary   2. **archetype.** Perfect example

1961 film version of *West Side Story.*

- Leonard Bernstein's 1957 **musical** *West Side Story* moved the setting from Verona to New York City and changed the warring families into rival street gangs. Juliet became "Maria," sister of the leader of the Puerto Rican gang, the Sharks. She falls in love with the leader of the rival Anglo gang, the Jets. The show incorporated modern music and dance. *West Side Story* is also a 1961 movie directed by Robert Wise and starring Natalie Wood as Maria.

- *Romeo and Juliet,* a **ballet** in three acts composed by Serge Prokofiev, had its world premiere in 1965 and starred Margot Fonteyn and Rudolf Nureyev. A 1966 video is available, as well as a 1982 version choreographed by Nureyev.

- The romantic **film** version of *Romeo and Juliet,* directed by Franco Zeffirelli in 1968 and starring teenagers Olivia Hussey as Juliet, and Leonard Whiting as Romeo, is the most popular Shakespearean movie of all time.

Olivia Hussey and Leonard Whiting in the 1967 film *Romeo and Juliet.*

- Director Baz Luhrmann's 1996 **film** *Romeo and Juliet,* starring Leonardo DiCaprio and Claire Danes, changed the scene to fictional Verona Beach, in an otherworldly Los Angeles. The characters and setting are updated to an almost futuristic time, but the language is the original verse of Shakespeare. The movie's lush visuals, modern music, and cutting-edge style have led some to call this "Shakespeare for the MTV generation."

- A new **rock musical** of *Romeo and Juliet,* composed by Jerome Korman and Terrence Mann, and directed by Mann, had its debut onstage in 1999. The musical incorporates modern dance and ballet and puts Shakespeare's verse into contemporary pop/rock for the new millennium. ∎

Claire Danes and Leonardo DiCaprio in the 1996 film *Romeo+Juliet.*

Investigate, Inquire, and Imagine

Recall: GATHERING FACTS

1a. What news does Romeo receive from Balthasar in scene 1?

2a. What does Romeo purchase from the apothecary, or druggist?

3a. To whom did Friar Lawrence give the letter addressed to Romeo? Why wasn't the letter delivered? What did the letter say?

Interpret: FINDING MEANING

1b. What does the scene between Balthasar and Romeo teach us about secondhand reports? Why is it important to verify information for ourselves when we can?

2b. In what way does Romeo act hastily, without considering matters carefully? Is this haste, or impulsiveness, typical or atypical of him? Explain.

3b. How did fate play a role in this?

Analyze: TAKING THINGS APART

4a. At the end of the play, the Prince commands that the vault be sealed "Till we can clear these ambiguities, / And know their spring, their head, their true descent." What are the causes of Romeo and Juliet's tragedy? In what ways are they themselves to blame? In what way are their families to blame? What other factors or forces play a part in causing this tragedy?

Synthesize: BRINGING THINGS TOGETHER

4b. What message does this play teach about feuding and grudges between rival groups? What might the moral of the play be?

Evaluate: MAKING JUDGMENTS

5a. Think back over the play you have read and reflect on the motivation and intentions of the following characters. Imagine that you are each of these characters and write a few sentences for each, explaining your good intentions and the mistake you made because of something you did not know.

- Capulet, in attempting to marry Juliet to Paris
- Paris, in courting Juliet and fighting with Romeo in act 5
- the Nurse, in advising Juliet to marry Paris
- Friar Lawrence, in creating the plan that ultimately leads to the deaths of Romeo and Juliet
- Juliet, in taking the potion and faking her own death
- Romeo, in killing himself

Extend: CONNECTING IDEAS

5b. Describe a time when your own good intentions went awry and you unintentionally caused a bad outcome. What might have averted that bad outcome? What could you have done differently?

Understanding *Literature*

PLOT AND RESOLUTION. Review the definitions for **plot** and **resolution** in the Handbook of Literary Terms. A plot pyramid is a diagram on which to outline the key elements of the plot of a story or play. Copy the pyramid, pictured below, on your own paper. Then identify each of the elements included in it: the central conflict, exposition, inciting incident, complication, crisis, climax, falling action, resolution, and dénouement. What is the central conflict, or struggle, in this play? How is that conflict resolved or ended in act 5? What about this resolution makes this play a tragedy?

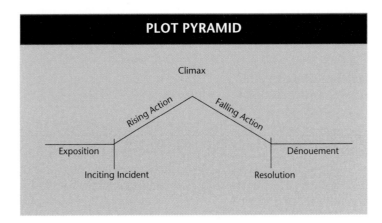

PLOT PYRAMID

Climax

Rising Action

Falling Action

Exposition

Dénouement

Inciting Incident

Resolution

The parts of a plot are as follows:

The **exposition** is the part of a plot that provides background information, often about the characters, setting, or conflict.

The **inciting incident** is the event that introduces the central conflict.

The **rising action**, or **complication**, develops the conflict to a high point of intensity.

The **crisis**, or **turning point**, often the same event as the **climax**, is the point in the plot where something decisive happens to determine the future course of events and the eventual working out of the conflict.

The **falling action** is all the events that follow the climax.

The **resolution** is the point at which the central conflict is ended, or resolved.

The **dénouement** is any material that follows the resolution and that ties up loose ends.

THEME. Review the definition for **theme** in the Handbook of Literary Terms. Working with other students, name at least three central themes of this play. Support your ideas by citing, or noting, particular lines that illustrate these themes.

TRAGIC FLAW. Review the definition for **tragic flaw** in the Handbook of Literary Terms. From what tragic flaw do both Romeo and Juliet suffer? Give examples to support your answer. Why do you think they do so? What does this play teach about the dangers of impulsive young love?

Writer's Journal

1. An *epitaph* is an inscription or verse written to be used on a tomb or written in commemoration of someone who has died. Write an **epitaph** for Romeo, Juliet, Paris, or Lady Montague. You might write your verse in iambic pentameter, in free verse, or in prose.

2. Imagine that you write an **advice column** for a newspaper. You have received the following letter from one of your readers. Answer the letter for your paper. In your answer, refer to *Romeo and Juliet* as an example.

   Dear Mr. Lonelihearts:

   I am fourteen years old. Recently I met a girl whom I like very much. She sits beside me in English class, and we often talk together about our writing and other work. I think that she likes me as much as I like her. However, our families are at odds. My father and her father used to be great friends, but years ago they had a quarrel. To this day they do not speak to one another. Recently my father told me not to have anything to do with "that family." Should I tell him about Marissa, the girl in my class? Is it OK for me to ask Marissa to a dance? What should I do?

   Confused in Columbus

3. Imagine that you are Friar Lawrence and that you wish to deliver a sermon to your church congregation after this tragedy, to help to heal the pain it caused and to make sure such a thing never happens again. What lessons would you want your congregation to learn? Write a brief **sermon** on this subject illustrating the lessons you hope to teach.

Integrating the Language Arts

Language, Grammar, and Style

USING FORMAL ENGLISH. Rewrite the following paragraph in clever, insightful, formal English, eliminating any instances of informal English, jargon, or clichés.

So, the other day I went to the theater to catch this new production of *Romeo and Juliet*. These guys knocked my socks off! Don't be put off by the fact that everyone in the play has a stuck-up way of speaking. At first, I was afraid I'd have trouble understanding what was going on; but once I caught on, I was totally into it. Basically, it goes like this: There's this hunk, Romeo, who digs this babe, Juliet. The problem is, they aren't supposed to fall in love because their families don't get along and no one thinks it's a good idea. But Romeo and Juliet fight against all odds because they know they were made for each other. I don't want to blow the ending, but let me just say you won't believe your eyes! I totally give this one a thumbs up.

Media Literacy & Collaborative Learning

EVALUATING AN ADAPTATION OF *ROMEO AND JULIET*. Read the play *West Side Story* or watch the film and compare it to *Romeo and Juliet*. In a small group, discuss the similarities and differences. Which version is more effective, for you, at conveying the lesson that hatred and feuding cause only grief and heartache? Why?

Language Arts in Action

THE 52nd STREET PROJECT

The 52nd Street Project, also known as The Project, is a nonprofit organization that brings inner-city kids from the Hell's Kitchen neighborhood of New York City together with professional theater artists to create theater. In its nineteen-year history, The Project has produced more than 500 plays involving over 600 children and volunteer theater artists. It has also been recognized nationally for its innovative techniques in drawing young people to the theater arts. Because of the success of The Project, the experience has become available for inner-city kids in nine other locations from Los Angeles, California, to Brooklyn, New York.

The Project first arose out of a need to improve the quality of life for New York City's inner-city kids. Willie Reale, an actor and playwright, responded to this need by creating The Project in 1981. As a company member of the Ensemble Studio Theater (EST), he used his company privileges to reach out to the children of the Hell's Kitchen neighborhood by creating theatrical activities specifically for them. However, the main purpose of this project is not about teaching children to act or to write plays, although they will learn to do both of these activities. The Project is about making children proud of themselves. It is about giving kids between the ages of eight and seventeen the opportunity to prove that they have something valuable, something unique to offer the community.

These goals are achieved through unique mentoring programs that match kids with professional theater artists who volunteer their time to help kids develop their interests and their self-esteem. These mentoring programs are divided into two categories: The Playmaking Program and the Acting Program.

The Playmaking Program is a series of playwriting classes for students. This program is divided into three steps: Playmaking, Replay, and Playback. Playmaking is the first step on The Project ladder. Ten kids enroll in a nine-week playwriting course taught by an artistic director. At the end of the nine weeks, students are taken into the countryside where they are asked to write their own plays for a professional cast of two. The plays are then performed at an Off-Broadway theater in Manhattan.

Replay, the second step in the Playmaking process, is also a nine-week course in playwriting. However, in this step, students are challenged to focus more on plot and character development. They also have the option of adding a third character to their play. The plays are then performed during a day-long picnic in upstate New York.

In Playback, the final step in the Playmaking Program, students write a play during a weekend retreat and an adult partner writes an "answer play." After a rehearsal period, the two partners perform their plays together, side-by-side.

The Acting Program includes progressively challenging activities beginning with One-on-Ones. This is the first level in the Acting Program. A group of ten students are taken to a country retreat during the summer for one week. Each student is then assigned to a playwright who is appointed to write a one-act musical for the student and the playwright to perform together. This activity allows each student the rare opportunity to work with a professional composer, who is also a volunteer.

Jaya Rosado and Michaela Murphy perform their One-on-One in Tyler Hill, Pennsylvania.

The Two-on-Twos activity is designed to give older kids who have graduated from the One-on-Ones activity a new performing challenge. Each student is partnered with another student. The two are matched up with two adults—a playwright and a director. They create a play for the students and perform it in an Off-Broadway theater in Manhattan.

The Teen Project is the final step in the Acting Program. It is for students in their late teens who are well prepared for a major challenge. This activity entails entering a two-year program, focusing on advanced acting of Shakespearean plays. At the end of the program, students are rewarded with a "senior trip." It is during this trip that the Shakespearean play they have worked on for two years is performed. For example, in 1997, a group of nine teens traveled to France and performed *Twelfth Night* in the town of Lorgues. The hard work and dedication required in this activity is rewarded with an experience students will never forget.

For as many programs and activities the 52nd Street Project offers, the organization is very small, with only six full-time staff members. Therefore, The Project is kept alive by the hundreds of people who volunteer because they are the ones who act, direct, write, compose, design, draw, paint, build, drive, usher, issue tickets, tutor, hang lights, and work backstage. The Project welcomes anyone who would like to be a volunteer to submit an application, but requires you to see a performance first. Information on how to become a volunteer and how to access a replication kit of the programs described in the previous paragraphs are listed below.

For more information on volunteering, log on to The Project's "Volunteering and Internships" page at http://www.52project.org/vol_int.html.

To obtain The Replication Kit that includes program and activity manuals and other supporting materials, access http://www.dramatists.com/text/52ndstreet.html.

Guided Writing

> "He was not of an age, but for all time!"
> —Ben Jonson

SCRIPTING A CONTEMPORARY SCENE FOR A PLAY

Shakespeare wrote *The Tragedy of Romeo and Juliet* over 400 years ago, yet the play's themes of love, intrigue, defiance, commitment, generational conflict, and family strife prevail in real life and at the box office. Regardless of how you take on Shakespeare, the experience promises to be an emotional one. As you read, watched, discussed, role-played, wrote about, or acted *Romeo and Juliet*, how did you feel? Delighted? Frustrated? Excited? Amused? Confused? Angered? Saddened? Like those acting, watching, directing, even studying Shakespeare since the days of Elizabeth I, you too may have felt all those emotions and more.

A **scene** is a short section of a literary work that presents action in a single place or at a single time.

WRITING ASSIGNMENT. Create a modern scene with two to four characters based on a theme in *Romeo and Juliet*. Devise a new situation, setting, and character names, but be faithful both to the theme from *Romeo and Juliet* and the basic personalities of the characters. For instance:

Rival groups meet on the street—identify the personalities from the play. Is there a hot-head among them? an agitator? a follow-the-crowd type? Or is there a Romeo—young, impulsive, dynamic—who falls in love with his Juliet—young, bright, strong-willed—at a high school dance? Or a young woman's mother—manipulative, determined, and not unlike her daughter at the same age—who introduces a marriage plan to her strong-willed daughter?

Update the conflict. Determine setting, create dialogue, gather costumes and props, and choreograph action—all modeled after Shakespeare. Whether you're instructed to work alone, with a partner, or in a small group, your teacher will probably want you to take your play from page to stage or scene to screen.

Professional Model

from *The Tragedy of Romeo and Juliet* by William Shakespeare page 322

ROMEO: If I profane with my unworthiest hand
This holy shrine, the gentle sin is this,

My lips, two blushing pilgrims, ready stand
To smooth that rough touch with a tender kiss.

JULIET: Good pilgrim, you do wrong your hand too
much,
Which mannerly devotion shows in this:
For saints have hands that pilgrims' hands do
touch,
And palm to palm is holy palmers' kiss.

ROMEO: Have not saints lips, and holy palmers too?

JULIET: Ay, pilgrim, lips that they must use in pray'r.

ROMEO: O then, dear saint, let lips do what hands do,
They pray—grant thou, lest faith turn to despair.

JULIET: Saints do not move, though grant for prayers'
sake.

ROMEO: Then move not while my prayer's effect I take.

Prewriting

FINDING YOUR VOICE. In this writing, you will be borrowing heavily from Shakespeare: characters, theme, and dramatic form. When you select the language and structure to use, keep in mind the theme you are exploring. In the Professional Model, the scene where Romeo and Juliet meet and fall in love, Shakespeare uses the structure and language playfully, to correspond with the cat-and-mouse stage of early love. Whatever scene you create, make sure your voice is in tune.

WRITING WITH A PLAN. Which theme do you want to explore? Conflict dominates, from "ancient grudge" to "new mutiny." Perhaps you could develop a scene that explains how an "ancient grudge" got started between two feuding families. Was it a corporate takeover? a betrayal of trust? Were the two former business partners? On the other hand, the lingering bitterness and tension between the families may be more compelling. How and where do they continue to fight? How do they attempt to keep their children from interacting? Do males or females control the fight more? How does each generation get involved and nurture the "new mutiny"?

You may be more interested in parent-child relationships that lead to conflict. Think how you would set up a scene for the following: Worried about their absent and morose son, parents ask their son's friend to help them help him. Or a young woman reluctantly considers her parents' choice of a boyfriend, or refuses her father's choice or pretends to accept it. Think about what

EXAMINING THE MODEL. Shakespeare explores the theme of impossible love in his two young characters. Juliet is not yet fourteen, yet she and Romeo fall madly in love at first sight. It's premature and hasty. It's doomed. Yet the two youths are appealingly beautiful. Consider this theme when you look at act I, scene 5. Shakespeare uses the formal structure of the **sonnet**, the poem of love, to frame the exchange between the young people as they meet and fall in love. Usually a sonnet is serious in tone, but Shakespeare uses it for a new effect here. Notice the alternating lines of rhyme. How might this technique suggest the quick-witted back and forth bout of flirtation in which both sides are equally smitten? Where do you notice repetition? What effect does that have? How does Juliet's dissecting of Romeo's "lines" as fast as he can think them up help her display the proper role of a young girl? How do the word choices reflect the mock seriousness of the exchange? What stage directions and gestures would you also include to convey the personalities and feelings of the characters?

Consider who will be your audience. Your teacher may have determined this for you. Whether you are acting live and/or videotaping, your audience will probably be your peers. You want to entertain your audience and at the same time give them something to think about, just as Shakespeare does. Go with something that you trust will be well received, something that will have an emotional impact.

control these parents have or want to have on their children. What obedience or disobedience do the children demonstrate? Maybe you would rather write a scene where characters discover the consequences of defying authority.

Still another conflict or interference in the lives of young people is that of Friar Lawrence and Juliet's Nurse. Think of how you might use the interference of "concerned adults" in the lives of young people. In another time and place, whom might these people be? A school counselor? Neighbor? Family pastor or priest? Longtime daycare provider?

What theme from this "story of more woe" will you explore?

Once you have decided on the situation you are creating, you need to decide which characters will be in the scene. For the main character you'll find the following clustering activity helpful: Put the character's name in a circle in the middle of a sheet of paper. Free associate any ideas about the character that come to you. Among other things, think about what this character wants and needs. Put these in strands that flow out. After you've nearly filled the page, look for interesting connections. Circle that area. Write a lead that grows out of what you have circled. Freewrite for five minutes. In this way you will get to know your main character. You may do this for other characters in your scene as well. Student writer Krista agreed on the theme of unhealthy competition between partners. She did a cluster for her main character, Chris. She did another for George.

Student Model—Graphic Organizer

It is time to get the plot sketched and some dialogue down on paper. You have answered the question of what the character needs. You have determined the situation the character faces.

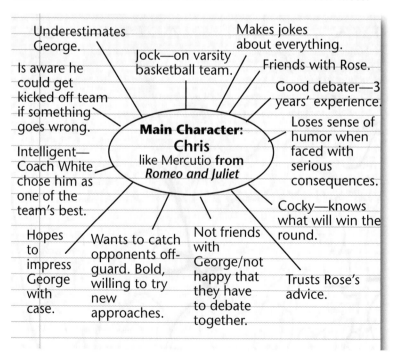

Drafting

Start writing. You don't need to focus on spelling and mechanics at this point. Instead, concentrate on getting your ideas down. Begin with enough exposition to explain to the audience what the situation is, but not so much that you tell the entire scene.

Remember to include **stage directions**. Stage directions are notes included in a play in addition to the dialogue for the purpose of describing how something should be performed on stage. They describe setting, lighting, music, sound effects, entrances and exits, properties, and the movements of characters. Before Chris's opening line, Krista wrote: [scene opens with Chris and Rose standing in the back of the room talking and George seated at one of the tables]. Don't overdo the stage directions, but be sure that your characters do more than just talk to each other.

Continue to write, matching the language, characters, and theme to the scene. Insert stage directions until your scene is complete. Be careful when writing dialogue that it remains suitable for the classroom and true to your characters' voices.

Self- and Peer Evaluation

You don't want others to hear or read your scene before the performance, so for this assignment peer evaluate only in your group. (If you're working by yourself, perhaps you can exchange writing with someone else also working solo.) You probably have already read your work aloud over and over as you've been writing it. Now try reading by parts. Chris reads George's part while George reads Chris's, then they switch. It might be helpful to use toy figures on a piece of paper as you read. See the diagram of the parts of a stage on page 348 to use as a guide. Keep tinkering with the language. Get on your feet and begin to act it out. Add any stage directions that come to mind.

As you evaluate, ask yourself these questions:

- How does the story move forward in this scene, that is, what happens?
- Where does conflict occur in the scene?
- What theme does the scene explore?
- How does the writer use language and structure and tone (voice) to explore the theme?
- Where are examples of vivid verbs? colorful modifiers?
- Where, if anywhere, has the writer used rhyme?
- Where does the voice match the theme? Where, if anywhere, does it sound "off" or discordant?

Reflecting

Writing or rewriting a scene involves a variety of skills: thinking, imagining, planning, writing, staging, working with others. What did you learn about yourself as you progressed through these stages? Which skills were the easiest for you? Which were

Use these tips to help you create your scene:
- Move the story forward.
- Include a beginning, a middle, and an end.
- Create a three-page dialogue scene that will result in three minutes of performance time.

more difficult? How did your appreciation for Shakespeare change as you went through this process? How did your appreciation for language change?

Student Model—Draft

> *Setting: Before the first round of debate Districts. In a [What kind?] [high school] classroom with several desks in the back and center of the room, one small table with two chairs on each side of the room, and a speaking podium at the front.*
>
> *Desk & chairs are shoved together*
>
> *Props: The furniture necessary to create the set; four debate tubs (large, [plastic] square/rectangular tubs filled with files of evidence); papers; pen [What kind?]*
>
> *Characters: Chris [Mercutio], a debater with a sense of humor; George [Tybalt], a debater with a short temper (the two are partners for the competition); Rose, their former teammate; Coach White, their coach. The judge and two negative debaters do not speak, but would be necessary in an [Citizens] actual debate setting. [Benvolio]*
>
> *[The Prince]*
>
> <scene opens with Chris and Rose standing in the back of the room talking and George seated at one of the tables, [sorting] going through his debate tub> [rearranging cards]
>
> *Can you strengthen verbs?*
>
> Chris: I still can't believe Coach White actually put me [partnered] with George for Districts! George is such a loser! [More description?] What was Coach thinking? [Mr. Perfect four-point-oh GPA, over there]
>
> Rose: He was thinking about how you guys are such awesome debaters and how great a team you would make with your

Describe arrangement better

Whom from R&J are these characters based on?

talents. You guys will be great ∧ *impressive*
together. Don't worry about it. *weak word*

Chris: Actually, Rose, I think you're
the awesome debater who should be
partnered with George.

Rose: [chuckling] Well, Chris, I'm
sure I would be the one debating with
George if I hadn't graduated last year.
Besides, I only debated for one season—
you and George have both debated for
three.

Chris: [smug grin] I digress. I suppose
I am the more experienced debater here.
(Even so, would you look over this new
Mozart Education case I wrote? I'm
hoping to surprise a bunch of people
with it because it's something I know
they won't be expecting.)
Can you show his sense of humor?
Rose: [looks over the papers Chris
hands her]

Leave this for next speech. Instead have him pick up on Rose's comment about one season--

Revising and Proofreading

What keeps Shakespeare being read, acted, and filmed is not
the ingeniousness of his plots, but the language that he
employs. As you go back through your scene, attempt to give
the language that extra bit of color and energy that will make
your scene memorable. Make a final copy of the scene.

Publishing and Presenting

Create a playbill to be posted or distributed before the
performance. It should briefly explain the scene and identify the
characters and the actors. Your teacher may wish to collate the
playbills into a booklet for class distribution. Perhaps you and
your classmates could collaborate on illustrations.

   Also finish planning out the performance. Will you need some
music? Do you have the costumes and props together? What
about the backdrop? Costumes, props, and scenery need not be
elaborate. Eyeglasses perched on the end of the actor's nose

Language, Grammar, and Style

Vivid Verbs and Colorful Modifiers

IDENTIFYING VIVID VERBS AND COLORFUL MODIFIERS. Writing can often be improved with the inclusion of vivid action verbs. Without doubt, Shakespeare used action verbs to paint brilliant images. He also added memorable verb modifiers or adverbs, words that expand or explain and add freshness and meaning. See the Language Arts Survey 3.39, "Adding Colorful Language to Sentences," for additional information. Adverbs that end in *–ly* usually explain how something is done: Susie *meticulously* sorted through her grandmother's jewelry. Adverbs not ending in *–ly* give time or degree details: He always arrives *before* you do. Most passages in *Romeo and Juliet* are rich in strong verbs. Find the action verbs and memorable modifiers in the following lines from act 2, scene 2 (page 331):

> Juliet: . . . I should have been more strange, I must confess,
> But that thou overheardst, ere I was ware,
> My true-love passion; therefore pardon me,
> And not impute this yielding to light love,
> Which the dark night hath so discovered.

continued on page 419

---

may be enough for Juliet's father. An artificial plant might suggest a garden while a flashlight could be a torch.

What movements does each actor make? Choreograph all action including entrances and exits, dancing, fighting, and so on. Rehearse lines, timing, sound effects, and action.

Student Model—Revised

The Not-So-Great Debate
by Krista Cady

Setting: Before the first round of debate Districts. In a high school classroom with desks shoved together in the back and center of the room, one small table with two chairs on each side of the room, and a speaking podium at the front.

Props: The furniture necessary to create the set; four debate tubs (large, rectangular plastic tubs filled with files of evidence); papers; pens.

Characters: Chris (Mercutio) a debater with a sense of humor; George (Tybalt), a debater with a short temper (the two are partners for the competition); Rose (Benvolio), their former teammate; Coach White (the Prince), their coach. The judge and two negative debaters (Citizens) do not speak, but would be necessary in an actual debate setting.

[scene opens with Chris and Rose standing in the back of the room talking and George seated at one of the tables, sorting through his debate tub, rearranging cards]

Chris: I still can't believe Coach White actually partnered me with George for Districts! George is such a loser. Mr. Perfect four-point-oh GPA, over there. What was Coach thinking?

Rose: He was thinking about how you guys are such awesome debaters and how great a team you would make with your combined talents. You guys will be impressive together. Don't worry about it.

Chris: Actually, Rose, I think you're the awesome debater who should be teamed with George.

Rose: [chuckling] Well, Chris, I'm sure I would be the one debating with George if I hadn't graduated last year. Besides, I only competed for one season—you and George have both debated for three.

Chris: [smug grin] Hey, one season would be seven years if you were a dog! And you can't tell me that dogs aren't smart—look at Lassie! [scared little kid voice] "Help, Rose! The Debate team has fallen and they can't get up! Go find help, girl!"

Rose: [pretends not to be amused] Very funny, Chris. Even in dog years you're more experienced than I am.

Chris: I digress. I suppose I am the more experienced debater here. Even so, would you look over this new Mozart Education case that I wrote? I'm hoping to shock a bunch of people with it because it's something I know they won't be expecting.

Chris: I guess it's that time, eh? [closes the door and walks to a podium at the front of the room; he looks to the negative team] Negatives ready? [they nod] Judge ready? [s/he nods] Okay. [looks to the papers in his hand] Resolved: That the federal government should establish an education policy to significantly increase academic achievement in secondary schools in the United States. American high school students cannot compete academically with students in many countries around the world. The current methods by which our students are being taught are not enough. As such, we are instituting a program in secondary schools where all students will be required to listen to the music of Mozart throughout the school day. [smiles smugly while back

Romeo: Lady, by yonder blessed moon I vow,
That tips with silver all these fruit-tree tops—

IMPROVING VIVID VERBS AND COLORFUL MODIFIERS. Find two verbs in the student draft that might be improved with the addition of modifiers.

Chris smiles while back at the table, George's face reddens and he growls. The negative team is struck with Chris's case—one drops his pen and stares at Chris, the other puts her face into her hands and shakes her head.

USING VIVID VERBS AND COLORFUL MODIFIERS. Be conscious in your own writing to reduce or eliminate linking verbs in favor of action verbs. Read through your scene to see where you can do this. Also include verb modifiers as appropriate to clarify or add meaning.

at the table, George's face reddens with anger and he growls] They will continue with their current educational programs, but empirically, studies have shown that the addition of Mozart into the classroom will increase their academic achievement. My partner will extend upon these arguments in his speech. Thank you, vote Affirmative. [Chris returns to his seat next to George]

[the negative team is struck dumb by Chris's case—one drops his pen and stares in amazement at Chris, the other puts her face into her hands and shakes head; the judge writes something on the ballot; Rose holds her breath and watches George for his reaction to Chris's new case]

Chris: [whispers] Well, what'd ya think, George?

George: [growls again as he slams his fist down on the table, then stands up] I warned you, Chris. You're on your own. [takes his debate tub and walks out of the room; Rose follows after him; the negative team and judge stare at Chris with wide eyes, waiting for him to decide what to do]

Chris: [shocked] But . . . but . . . oh no. [sits down and talks to himself] Now what am I supposed to do? If I go maverick, we automatically lose and I don't know this argument well enough to do that. I could always forfeit. That may be what I'll have to do. Man, I don't want to, but I don't see what other choice I really have. [he fails to notice as Coach White enters with George and Rose; Chris stands and addresses the judge and negative team] Well, I guess we forfeit. I apologize for wasting your time. Good luck during the rest of the day.

[judge and negatives exit; Rose stands next to the doorway with her arms crossed looking very unhappy; George walks over to the table near where Chris stands; Coach White steps forward]

Coach White: [barely controlling his anger] Chris and George, I honestly cannot express how much you've disappointed me. You both knew how much Districts meant to the team as a whole and your petty, selfish attitudes have cost all of us this entire competition. Frankly, right now, I don't want to see either of you. Effective tomorrow, you are both suspended from this team until further notice. Now, if you'll excuse me, I should be in the Ballot Tabulation Room fulfilling *my* obligation to this team. [turns and exits room]

[Chris and George look down at the floor]

Rose: [uncrosses her arms and shakes her head sadly] That was pretty harsh, guys—I would hate to be in your shoes. You've ruined everyone's chances today. I don't think the team will be quite as easy on you as Coach White was. And you know what? You guys deserve it. [she exits, leaving Chris and George alone]

[scene ends]

UNIT 4 review
Drama

Words for Everyday Use

Check your knowledge of the following vocabulary words from the selections in this unit. Write short sentences using each of these words in context to make the meaning clear. To review the definition or usage of a word, refer back to the page number(s) listed or the Glossary of Words for Everyday Use.

abhor, 370	dexterity, 355	lamentable, 386	purge, 307
adjacent, 327	discern, 399	lamentation, 359	rancor, 336
adversary, 304	discord, 367	lineament, 314	receptacle, 384
adversity, 362	discourse, 328	loathsome, 384	repose, 331
agile, 355	disposition, 364	matron, 356	residence, 334
ambiguity, 402	dissembler, 358	minstrel, 350	resolution, 379
amorous, 356	dote, 336	misadventure, 392	sepulchre or sepulcher,
ascend, 365	drivelling, 339	monarch, 359	399
asunder, 369	eloquence, 357	mutiny, 301	shroud, 380
augment, 305	enmity, 330	nightingale, 367	siege, 308
baleful, 334	flourish, 303	nuptial, 320	singular, 338
bier, 358	forfeit, 304	paramour, 398	slander, 378
bounty, 332	fray, 305	peevish, 382	stratagem, 373
brow, 313	gravity, 372	pernicious, 304	submission, 352
calamity, 360	grievance, 306	pilgrimage, 387	substantial, 332
carrion, 361	haughty, 397	piteous, 357	transgression, 307
chamber, 360	idolatry, 331	plague, 353	unhallowed, 397
chide, 336	impute, 331	pomegranate, 367	valor, 353
confession, 335	inauspicious, 398	posterity, 308	vex, 307
courtier, 317	inconstant, 331	predominant, 334	visage, 316
denote, 364	inundation, 378	procure, 332	
devise, 402	invocation, 327	propagate, 307	
devout, 311	lament, 388	prostrate, 382	

Literary Tools

Define each of the following terms, giving concrete examples of how they are used in the selections in this unit. To review a term, refer to the page number(s) indicated or to the Handbook of Literary Terms.

central conflict, 298	foreshadowing, 377	plot, 298, 326, 349, 377, 392
character, 326	inciting incident, 298	resolution, 392
climax, 377	irony, 349	sonnet, 298
complication, 326	motif, 298	theme, 392
crisis, 349	motivation, 326	tragic flaw, 392
dramatic irony, 349	oxymoron, 298	

Reflecting on your reading

Genre Studies

1. **PLOT.** Identify the elements of plot—exposition, inciting incident, rising action, climax, falling action, resolution, and dénouement—for the play *Romeo and Juliet*.

2. **TRAGEDY.** What characteristics make this play a tragedy? What tragic flaw do Romeo and Juliet have that contributes to their tragic end? Explain, giving examples from the play.

3. **STAGE DIRECTIONS.** Why are stage directions particularly important to *Romeo and Juliet?* What information do they give the actors? Explain, giving examples from the play.

4. **DIALOGUE.** Review the section about dialogue in "Elements of Drama" on page 296. What examples of monologues, soliloquies, and asides can you find in this play?

Thematic Studies

5. **FEUDING.** A central theme of this play is that hatred and violence can breed only tragedy. Cite particular lines in the play that support this theme. How might this message be applied to society today?

6. **LOVE.** Examine the theme of young love in *Romeo and Juliet*. What view is given of love? Consider Romeo's love for Rosaline, and his later passion for Juliet, as well as Juliet's love for Romeo. What causes them to fall in love? What kinds of emotions does love inspire in young people, and what does love lead them to do?

7. **FATE.** A major theme in *Romeo and Juliet* is that humans cannot escape their fortune, or fate. Cite particular lines in the play that support this theme.

8. **PARENTING IN THE RENAISSANCE.** What was a typical relationship like between parents and their daughters in Renaissance times, as portrayed in this play? How were daughters expected to behave toward their parents? Explain, giving examples from the dialogue between Juliet, her mother Lady Capulet, and her father Capulet. Do you think Juliet's parents were too harsh, considering the standards of the day? Why, or why not?

9. **JUSTICE.** Consider the theme of justice in *Romeo and Juliet*. Answer the following questions, quoting lines from the play: With what does the Prince threaten the Montagues and the Capulets if they continue to disturb the peace of Verona with their infighting? How was a man expected to respond to insults, such as thumb-biting, for example, or being called a villain? What was considered just punishment for someone who killed another in a swordfight? Do you think Romeo's banishment was deserved, or was it an unduly harsh or lenient punishment given the standards of justice of the day? Explain.

for your READING LIST

Romeo and Juliet and *West Side Story* by William Shakespeare and Norris Houghton (editor). This book brings you the script of both plays, Shakespeare's great love story, *Romeo and Juliet,* and its modern adaptation, *West Side Story.* One is set in Renaissance Verona, the other in the gang environment of New York's West Side, but both tell the story of young lovers who refuse to allow prejudice and feuding to keep them apart.

Independent Reading Activity

READING GROUP DISCUSSION. In small groups, after having read both *Romeo and Juliet* and *West Side Story*, discuss the similarities between the two plays. How are the characters and plots similar? Which version do you find most appealing and why? Can you think of yet another setting in which you could tell the story of two "star-cross'd lovers"?

Selections for Additional Reading

Romiette and Julio by Sharon M. Draper. This recent book based loosely on *Romeo and Juliet* was written by Sharon M. Draper, an African-American writer of young adult and children's fiction. Romiette Capel, an African-American girl, and Julio Manague, a Hispanic boy, discover that they attend the same high school after falling in love on the Internet, but are harassed by gang members who object to their interracial dating.

Humorous Plays for Teenagers by Christina Hamlett. This collection of short plays will have you laughing in the aisles. "A Rose Is Just a Rose," which brings Shakespeare to modern times in a time machine, would be a fun class production.

The City from Greenwich Village, 1922. John Sloan. National Gallery of Art, Washington, DC.

Nonfiction

" Truth is always exciting.
Speak it, then.
Life is dull without it. "

—*Pearl S. Buck*

ELEMENTS of NONFICTION

Nonfiction is prose writing that deals with real, not imagined, people and experiences. It also explores thoughts and ideas.

Forms of Nonfiction

Histories provide accounts of past events. The textbook you use in history class is a perfect example. Of importance to historians in preparing histories are many types of **public records,** also nonfiction. These include **speeches, sermons, contracts, deeds, constitutions, laws,** and **political tracts**. Examples in this unit include Sojourner Truth's Speech to the Convention of the American Equal Rights Association and Martin Luther King, Jr.'s, "I Have a Dream."

Other types of nonfiction, closely related to histories, are **biographies** and **autobiographies**, which can be thought of as histories of individual people. A biography is the story of a person's life. An autobiography is the story of a person's life, written by that person. Melissa Burdick Harmon's "A Short Life, Intensely Lived: The Adventures of Jack London" (Unit 3) is one example of biography. Examples of autobiographies in this unit include the selection from Maya Angelou's *I Know Why the Caged Bird Sings* and "California Palms" by lê thi diem thúy.

Letters, **diaries**, and **journals**, which are often used by biographers as source material, are also considered nonfiction.

An **essay** is a brief work of prose nonfiction. The original meaning of *essay* was "a trial or attempt," and the word retains some of this original force. An essay need not be a complete or exhaustive treatment of a subject, but rather a tentative exploration of it. A good essay develops a single idea and is characterized by unity and coherence. Examples of essays in this textbook include Aldo Leopold's "Thinking Like a Mountain" and the selection from Rachel Carson's *Silent Spring* (both in this unit). A **personal essay** is a short work of nonfictional prose on a single topic related to the life or interests of the writer. Personal essays are characterized by an intimate and informal style and tone. They are often, but not always, written in the first person. Examples of personal essays in this text include Gish Jen's "An Ethnic Trump" (Unit 7), and Sandra Cisneros's "Straw Into Gold" (Unit 8). **Creative nonfiction** is nonfiction that incorporates some elements of fiction writing, such as imaginative description. One example is the selection "The Gudger House" from James Agee's *Let Us Now Praise Famous Men* (Unit 6).

An **article** is a brief work of nonfiction on a specific topic. The term *article* is typically used for encyclopedia entries and short nonfiction works that appear in newspapers and popular magazines. The term is sometimes used as a synonym of *essay*, though the latter term often connotes a more serious, important, or lasting work. Examples of articles include Linda Wheeler's "'White House' Mystery May Be Solved" (Unit 1), Jerry Adler's "Ghost of Everest" (Unit 6), and Michael Farber's "Where Stars Are Born" (Unit 8).

How-to writing, or writing that explains a procedure or strategy, is also nonfiction. One example of how-to writing is "Research Strategies for the Learning Highway" (Unit 6).

Purposes in Nonfiction

A writer's **purpose,** or *aim,* is what he or she wants to accomplish. All writing, including nonfiction, is generally produced with some overall purpose in mind. The following chart classifies modes, or categories, of prose writing by purpose.

MODE OF WRITING	PURPOSE	EXAMPLE
expository/informative	to inform	news article, research report
imaginative	to entertain, enrich, enlighten, and/or use an artistic medium such as fiction, poetry, or creative nonfiction, to share a perspective	poem, short story, humorous essay
narrative	to share a story about an event, often to make a point	biography, family history
personal/expressive	to reflect	diary entry, personal letter
persuasive/argumentative	to persuade readers or listeners to respond in some way, such as to agree with a position, change a view on an issue, reach an agreement, or perform an action	editorial, petition

Note that a written work can have more than one purpose. For example, a nonfiction work may start with a brief story, or narrative, to introduce the topic or to make a point. It may then incorporate imaginative writing, provide information, express a personal reaction to that information, and strive to persuade the reader to adopt the writer's view. The emerging form known as "creative nonfiction" combines purposes and aims in new ways.

For more information, consult the Language Arts Survey 2.3, "Identifying Your Purpose."

Structure in Nonfiction

A writer may structure, or organize, a piece of writing in different ways in order to communicate more clearly. The following chart describes types of writing that are commonly used in nonfiction, and how these types are typically structured.

TYPE OF WRITING	STRUCTURE OR ORGANIZATIONAL METHOD
Narration	As with the narrative mode, writing with this method tells a story or describes events using time, or chronological order, as a way of organization.
Dialogue	Writing using this method presents words as they are, or were, actually spoken by people. Quotation marks are usually used to set off direct speech.
Description	Writing with this method portrays in words how things look, sound, smell, taste, or feel. Descriptive writing frequently uses spatial order as a way of organization.
Exposition	Writing using this method presents facts or opinions in an organized manner. There are many ways to organize exposition. The following are some of the most common. **Analysis** breaks something into its parts and shows how the parts are related. **Classification** places subjects into categories, or classes, according to their properties or characteristics. **Comparison-contrast** presents similarities as it compares two things and presents differences as it contrasts them. **Process/How-to** writing presents the steps in a process or gives the reader directions on how to do something.

from

I Know Why the Caged Bird Sings

by Maya Angelou

Literary TOOLS

NARRATOR AND POINT OF VIEW. A **narrator** is one who tells a story. In an autobiography—the story of a person's life written by that person—the narrator is usually the author. **Point of view** is the vantage point from which a story is told. Stories are typically written from a *first-person point of view*, in which the narrator uses words such as *I* and *we*, or from a *third-person point of view*, in which the narrator uses words such as *he, she, it,* and *they.* As you read, identify the narrator and the point of view.

SETTING. The **setting** of a literary work is the time and place in which it occurs together with all the details used to create a sense of a particular time and place.

Organizer

As you read, make a cluster chart to list the elements of setting in the story. One example has been done for you.

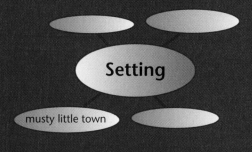

Setting

musty little town

Reader's Journal

Have you ever learned a lesson by watching someone you know? What did you learn?

Reader's resource

The following selection is taken from *I Know Why the Caged Bird Sings* (1970), which tells the story of Maya Angelou's life up to the age of sixteen. The selection tells about Marguerite and her brother Bailey first arriving in, and later returning to, Stamps, Arkansas, where they live with their grandmother and uncle in the Wm. Johnson General Merchandise Store. Angelou continues her life story in the volumes *Gather Together in My Name* (1974), *The Heart of a Woman* (1981), and *All God's Children Need Traveling Shoes* (1986).

In the selection, Angelou's use of concrete words and sensory details creates a portrait of her life in Stamps, Arkansas, that bursts with remembered particulars. Techniques of direct description and portrayal of behavior bring alive the portraits of the inhabitants of Stamps, particularly that of Marguerite's grandmother.

About the AUTHOR

Maya Angelou (1928–) was born Marguerite Johnson in St. Louis, Missouri. Educated in Arkansas and California, Angelou is a poet, playwright, movie and television writer, director, journalist, composer, actor, dancer, and civil rights worker. She has lectured at various American universities and held an administrative position at the University of Ghana. Her collection *Poems*, published in 1986, brings together work from many of her earlier poetry collections. Angelou is most celebrated for her autobiographical work *I Know Why the Caged Bird Sings*. In 1992, Angelou was invited to read her poem "On the Pulse of Morning" at the inauguration of President Clinton.

General Store, Moundville, Alabama, 1936. Walker Evans. Library of Congress.

FROM

I Know Why the Caged Bird Sings   Maya Angelou

FROM CHAPTER 1

When I was three and Bailey four, we had arrived in the <u>musty</u> little town, wearing tags on our wrists which instructed—"To Whom It May Concern"—that we were Marguerite and Bailey Johnson Jr., from Long Beach, California, en route to Stamps, Arkansas, c/o Mrs. Annie Henderson.

Our parents had decided to put an end to their <u>calamitous</u> marriage, and Father shipped us home to his mother. A porter[1] had been

---

1. **porter.** Carrier; in this case, a railroad employee who carries luggage

---

words for everyday use

mus • ty (mus´tē) *adj.*, dull; apathetic. *The <u>musty</u> librarian didn't discuss books with her patrons.*

ca • lam • i • tous (kə lam´ə təs) *adj.*, disastrous. *News of the <u>calamitous</u> living conditions prompted several aid organizations to visit the disaster area.*

charged with our welfare—he got off the train the next day in Arizona—and our tickets were pinned to my brother's inside coat pocket.

Why are Bailey and Marguerite being sent away? To whom are they being sent?

I don't remember much of the trip, but after we reached the segregated southern part of the journey,[2] things must have looked up. Negro passengers, who always traveled with loaded lunch boxes, felt sorry for "the poor little motherless darlings" and <u>plied</u> us with cold fried chicken and potato salad.

Years later I discovered that the United States had been crossed thousands of times by frightened Black children traveling alone to their newly affluent parents in Northern cities, or back to grandmothers in Southern towns when the urban North <u>reneged</u> on its economic promises.

Who else has made a journey similar to that of Marguerite and Bailey, and why?

The town reacted to us as its inhabitants had reacted to all things new before our coming. It regarded us a while without curiosity but with caution, and after we were seen to be harmless (and children) it closed in around us, as a real mother embraces a stranger's child. Warmly, but not too familiarly.

We lived with our grandmother and uncle in the rear of the Store (it was always spoken of with a capital *s*), which she had owned some twenty-five years.

Early in the century, Momma (we soon stopped calling her Grandmother) sold lunches to the sawmen in the lumberyard (east Stamps) and the seedmen at the cotton gin (west Stamps). Her crisp meat pies and cool lemonade, when joined to her miraculous ability to be in two places at the same time, assured her business success. From being a mobile lunch counter,[3]

she set up a stand between the two points of fiscal interest[4] and supplied the workers' needs for a few years. Then she had the Store built in the heart of the Negro area. Over the years it became the lay center[5] of activities in town. On Saturdays, barbers sat their customers in the shade on the porch of the Store, and troubadours[6] on their ceaseless crawlings through the South leaned across its benches and sang their sad songs of The Brazos[7] while they played juice harps and cigar-box guitars.

How did Momma become an entrepreneur?

The formal name of the Store was the Wm. Johnson General Merchandise Store. Customers could find food <u>staples</u>, a good variety of colored thread, mash for hogs, corn for chickens, coal oil for lamps, light bulbs for the wealthy, shoestrings, hair dressing, balloons, and flower seeds. Anything not visible had only to be ordered.

Until we became familiar enough to belong to the Store and it to us, we were locked up in a Fun House of Things where the attendant had gone home for life.

Each year I watched the field across from the Store turn caterpillar green, then gradually frosty white. I knew exactly how long it would be before the big wagons would pull into the front yard and load on the cotton pickers at daybreak to carry them to the remains of slavery's plantations.

---

2. **segregated . . . journey.** Part of the trip took the children through states in which segregation was still practiced. Segregation is enforced separation of people based on race or ethnic origin.

3. **mobile lunch counter.** Lunch stand that could be moved from place to place, for example, in a truck or on a cart

4. **points of . . . interest.** Businesses, here the lumberyard and cotton gin

5. **lay center.** Secular center for all people to gather and talk

6. **troubadours.** Traveling folk singers and storytellers

7. **The Brazos.** River in southeastern and central Texas that flows into the Gulf of Mexico

---

words for everyday use

ply (plī) *vt.*, keep supplying. *Grandmother <u>plies</u> me with cookies when I visit.*

re • nege (ri nig′) *vi.*, back out of an agreement. *If one side <u>reneges</u> on the agreement, the cease-fire will no longer be in effect.*

sta • ple (stā′pəl) *n.*, item of trade, regularly stocked and in constant demand. *Rice is a <u>staple</u> of most Asian diets and is served with almost every meal.*

During the picking season my grandmother would get out of bed at four o'clock (she never used an alarm clock) and creak down to her knees and chant in a sleep-filled voice, "Our Father, thank you for letting me see this New Day. Thank you that you didn't allow the bed I lay on last night to be my cooling board, nor my blanket my winding sheet.[8] Guide my feet this day along the straight and narrow, and help me to put a bridle on my tongue. Bless this house, and everybody in it. Thank you, in the name of your Son, Jesus Christ, Amen."

For what is Momma grateful?

Before she had quite arisen, she called our names and issued orders, and pushed her large feet into homemade slippers and across the bare lye-washed[9] wooden floor to light the coal-oil lamp.

The lamplight in the Store gave a soft make-believe feeling to our world which made me want to whisper and walk about on tiptoe. The odors of onions and oranges and kerosene had been mixing all night and wouldn't be disturbed until the wooden slat was removed from the door and the early morning air forced its way in with the bodies of people who had walked miles to reach the pickup place.

"Sister, I'll have two cans of sardines."

"I'm gonna work so fast today I'm gonna make you look like you standing still."

"Lemme have a hunk uh cheese and some sody crackers."

"Just gimme a coupla them fat peanut paddies." That would be from a picker who was taking his lunch. The greasy brown paper sack was stuck behind the bib of his overalls. He'd use the candy as a snack before the noon sun called the workers to rest.

In those tender mornings the Store was full of laughing, joking, boasting and bragging. One man was going to pick two hundred pounds of cotton, and another three hundred. Even the children were promising to bring home fo' bits and six bits.[10]

The champion picker of the day before was the hero of the dawn. If he prophesied that the cotton in today's field was going to be sparse and stick to the bolls[11] like glue, every listener would grunt a hearty agreement.

The sound of the empty cotton sacks dragging over the floor and the murmurs of waking people were sliced[12] by the cash register as we rang up the five-cent sales.

If the morning sounds and smells were touched with the supernatural, the late afternoon had all the features of the normal Arkansas life. In the dying sunlight the people dragged, rather than their empty cotton sacks.

Brought back to the Store, the pickers would step out of the backs of trucks and fold down, dirt-disappointed, to the ground. No matter how much they had picked, it wasn't enough. Their wages wouldn't even get them out of debt to my grandmother, not to mention the staggering bill that waited on them at the white commissary[13] downtown.

Why are the cotton pickers disappointed in the afternoon?

The sounds of the new morning had been replaced with grumbles about cheating houses, weighted scales, snakes, skimpy cotton and dusty rows. In later years I was to confront the stereotyped picture of gay song-singing cotton pickers

---

8. **cooling board . . . winding sheet.** *Cooling board*—place where a corpse lies while being prepared for burial or cremation; *winding sheet*—sheet in which a corpse is wrapped

9. **lye-washed.** Washed with a harsh, strongly alkaline soap

10. **fo' bits and six bits.** Fifty cents and seventy-five cents

11. **bolls.** Shell-like top parts of the cotton flower that hold the white seed pod, the cotton

12. **sliced.** Interrupted

13. **commissary.** Store

---

with such <u>inordinate</u> rage that I was told even by fellow Blacks that my paranoia was embarrassing. But I had seen the fingers cut by the mean little cotton bolls, and I had witnessed the backs and shoulders and arms and legs resisting any further demands.

Why is the narrator angered by the stereotypes?

Some of the workers would leave their sacks at the Store to be picked up the following morning, but a few had to take them home for repairs. I winced to picture them sewing the coarse material under a coal-oil lamp with fingers stiffening from the day's work. In too few hours they would have to walk back to Sister Henderson's Store, get vittles[14] and load, again, onto the trucks. Then they would face another day of trying to earn enough for the whole year with the heavy knowledge that they were going to end the season as they started it. Without the money or credit necessary to sustain a family for three months. In cotton-picking time the late afternoons revealed the harshness of Black Southern life, which in the early morning had been softened by nature's blessing of grogginess, forgetfulness and the soft lamplight.

FROM CHAPTER 14

The barrenness of Stamps was exactly what I wanted, without will or consciousness. After St. Louis,[15] with its noise and activity, its trucks and buses, and loud family gatherings, I welcomed the <u>obscure</u> lanes and lonely bungalows[16] set back deep in the dirt yards.

The <u>resignation</u> of its inhabitants encouraged me to relax. They showed me a contentment based on the belief that nothing more was coming to them, although a great deal more was due. Their decision to be satisfied with life's <u>inequities</u> was a lesson for me. Entering Stamps, I had the feeling that I was stepping over the border lines of the map and would fall, without fear, right off the end of the world. Nothing more could happen, for in Stamps nothing happened.

What did the narrator learn from the people of Stamps upon her return?

Into this cocoon I crept.

For an <u>indeterminate</u> time, nothing was demanded of me or of Bailey. We were, after all, Mrs. Henderson's California grandchildren, and had been away on a glamorous trip way up North to the fabulous St. Louis. Our father had come the year before driving a big, shiny automobile and speaking the King's English[17] with a big city accent, so all we had to do was lie quiet for months and rake in the profits of our adventures.

Farmers and maids, cooks and handymen, carpenters and all the children in town, made regular pilgrimages to the Store. "Just to see the travelers."

They stood around like cutout cardboard figures and asked, "Well, how is it up North?"

"See any of them big buildings?"

"Ever ride in one of them elevators?"

"Was you scared?"

"Whitefolks any different, like they say?"

Bailey took it upon himself to answer every question, and from a corner of his lively imagination wove a tapestry of entertainment for them that I was sure was as foreign to him as it was to me.

---

14. **vittles.** Food
15. **St. Louis.** The children had been to St. Louis, Missouri, where they had formerly lived, to visit their mother.
16. **bungalows.** One-story houses
17. **the King's English.** English as spoken by the king of England or well-educated people from England; very proper English

---

words for everyday use

in • or • di • nate (in ôr′də nit) *adj.*, lacking moderation. *Because an <u>inordinate</u> number or students had the same incorrect answer, the teacher concluded that many of them had cheated.*

ob • scure (əb skyoor′) *adj.*, inconspicuous; hidden. *The spare key to the front door was kept in an <u>obscure</u> place in the garage.*

res • ig • na • tion (rez′ig nā′shən) *n.*, passive acceptance. *Bill shrugged his shoulders in <u>resignation</u> when he was told he didn't get the job.*

in • eq • ui • ty (in ek′wit ē) *n.*, lack of justice. *Many companies have adopted internal policies to address hiring <u>inequities</u>.*

in • de • ter • mi • nate (in′dē tur′mi nit) *adj.*, uncertain. *The elderly man's exact age is <u>indeterminate</u>, but his family believes he is at least one hundred years old.*

He, as usual, spoke precisely. "They have, in the North, buildings so high that for months, in the winter, you can't see the top floors."

"Tell the truth."

"They've got watermelons twice the size of a cow's head and sweeter than syrup." I distinctly remember his <u>intent</u> face and the fascinated faces of his listeners. "And if you can count the watermelon's seeds, before it's cut open, you can win five zillion dollars and a new car."

Momma, knowing Bailey, warned, "Now Ju, be careful you don't slip up on a not true." (Nice people didn't say "lie.")

"Everybody wears new clothes and have inside toilets. If you fall down in one of them, you get flushed away into the Mississippi River. Some people have iceboxes, only the proper name is Cold Spot or Frigidaire. The snow is so deep you can get buried right outside your door and people won't find you for a year. We made ice cream out of the snow." That was the only fact that I could have supported. During the winter, we had collected a bowl of snow and poured Pet[18] milk over it, and sprinkled it with sugar and called it ice cream.

Momma beamed and Uncle Willie was proud when Bailey <u>regaled</u> the customers with our <u>exploits</u>. We were drawing cards[19] for the Store and objects of the town's adoration. Our journey to magical places alone was a spot of color on the town's drab canvas, and our return made us even more the most enviable of people.

High spots in Stamps were usually negative: droughts, foods, lynchings[20] and deaths.

Bailey played on the country folks' need for diversion. Just after our return he had taken to sarcasm, picked it up as one might pick up a stone, and put it snufflike under his lip. The double entendres,[21] the two-pronged sentences, slid over his tongue to dart rapier-like[22] into anything that happened to be in the way. Our customers, though, generally were so straight thinking and speaking that they were never hurt by his attacks. They didn't comprehend them.

"Bailey Junior sound just like Big Bailey. Got a silver tongue. Just like his daddy."

"I hear tell they don't pick cotton up there. How the people live then?"

Bailey said that the cotton up North was so tall, if ordinary people tried to pick it they'd have to get up on ladders, so the cotton farmers had their cotton picked by machines. ∎

---

18. **Pet.** Brand of evaporated milk
19. **drawing cards.** Performers who attract an audience
20. **lynchings.** Illegal hangings
21. **double entendres.** Double meanings
22. **rapier-like.** Swordlike

---

words for everyday use

in • tent (in tent´) *adj.,* earnest, fixed. *The judge wore an <u>intent</u> expression as she listened to complicated testimony.*

re • gale (ri gāl´) *vt.,* entertain. *During wartime, the U.S.O. <u>regaled</u> soldiers with choreographed shows.*

ex • ploit (eks´ploit) *n.,* daring or bold deed. *The hero's reported <u>exploits</u> turned out to be fictionalized deeds.*

Respond *to the* SELECTION

What kind of a role model is Momma to Marguerite and Bailey?

Investigate, *Inquire,* and imagine

Recall: GATHERING FACTS

1a. What reaction do the people of Stamps show toward the newcomers, Marguerite and Bailey?

2a. Where do the narrator and her brother, Bailey Jr., live in Stamps?

3a. What encourages the narrator to relax upon her return to Stamps from St. Louis?

Interpret: FINDING MEANING

1b. What does the narrator discover years later that suggests she and Bailey were not the only children traveling alone on a train?

2b. What actions on the part of the grandmother show her business talents?

3b. What is probably the reason that the inhabitants of Stamps come to the store "just to see the travelers"?

Analyze: TAKING THINGS APART

4a. Compare and contrast St. Louis and Stamps in the narrator's eyes.

Synthesize: BRINGING THINGS TOGETHER

4b. What do you think motivates Angelou to write about the residents of Stamps? Provide evidence from the text to support your response.

Evaluate: MAKING JUDGMENTS

5a. The narrator, after returning to Stamps, realizes that the townspeople are "satisfied with life's inequities." Evaluate the significance of learning this lesson early in life.

Extend: CONNECTING IDEAS

5b. What are some life lessons that you would like to pass along to a younger brother or sister or to your future offspring?

Understanding *Literature*

NARRATOR AND POINT OF VIEW. Review the definitions for **narrator** and **point of view** in the Handbook of Literary Terms. Who is the narrator? What point of view is used in the story? Find a passage in the selection that reveals the narrator's private, internal thoughts about the cotton pickers.

SETTING. Review the definition for **setting** in the Handbook of Literary Terms and the cluster chart you made for Literary Tools on page 428. What details are used to create the setting of the store in the mornings, before "the wooden slat was removed from the door"? Compare the early morning setting in the store with the late afternoon setting.

Writer's Journal

1. Imagine you are Bailey Jr. visiting St. Louis. Write a **postcard** to a friend back in Stamps describing the sights of the big city. Remember that Bailey exaggerates.

2. Imagine that you are a reporter sent to Stamps to cover the remarkable story of Marguerite's grandmother. Write a brief **article** describing how she started her business, how she starts her day, and how she treats her customers.

3. Imagine that you are the narrator. Write a **journal entry** about the people of Stamps and how you feel about them.

Integrating the Language Arts

Language, Grammar, and Style

THERE SENTENCES. A special kind of inverted sentence is the *there* sentence. Read the Language Arts Survey 3.27, "Working with *There* Sentences."

For each of the sentences below, identify the simple subject(s), verb(s), and complement(s) if any are present.

1. There was a home for Bailey and Maya in Stamps, Arkansas.

2. There wasn't a family raising them; the parents were getting a divorce.

3. Have there ever been more frightened children?

4. Grandmother had a store, and there were many people around.

5. There might have been another way, but Grandmother seemed best.

Collaborative Learning

AUDIO IMPRESSION. The store in the selection is filled with specific sights and sounds unique to that location. Make an audio impression of a familiar place such as a store, home, restaurant, school, or health club. Record definitive sounds such as a cash register, dishwasher, people dining, students talking, or people using exercise equipment. Then, in small groups, play your tape and ask students to identify the location of your audio impression and to write a description of the location.

Media Literacy

BOOK JACKET. Design a book jacket for one of Maya Angelou's books. On the front cover draw a picture suggestive of the content of the book. On the inside cover, write a summary of the book that will make people want to read it. To find out more about Angelou's books, you might want to do research on the Internet; begin by making a search for "Maya Angelou." You might find it useful to read the Language Arts Survey 5.28, "Conducting an Internet Search."

Literary TOOLS

CONFLICT AND INTERNAL CONFLICT. A **conflict** is a struggle between two forces in a literary work. A struggle that takes place within a character is called an **internal conflict.** As you read, determine the internal conflict of the narrator.

METAPHOR AND SIMILE. A **metaphor** is a figure of speech in which one thing is spoken or written about as if it were another. A **simile** is a comparison using like or as. These two figures of speech invite the reader to make a comparison between the two things. The two "things" involved are the writer's actual subject, the *tenor* of the metaphor, and another thing to which the subject is likened, the *vehicle* of the metaphor.

Organizer

As you read, make a chart of the metaphors and similes in the selection. On the left, write the tenor for the figure of speech. On the right, write the vehicle for the figure of speech. One example has been done for you.

Tenor	Vehicle
memories	things dragged from the sea, shaken, and held to the light

Reader's JOURNAL

When have you felt you didn't belong or fit in?

"California Palms"

by lê thi diem thúy

Reader's resource

WORLD HISTORY CONNECTION. In 1975, after America's involvement in the Vietnam War, North Vietnam attacked South Vietnam, and the capital of Saigon fell to the Communists. Not wanting to live under communist rule, hundreds of thousands of South Vietnamese fled their homeland, most in small wooden boats that were not seaworthy. Numerous refugees drowned in the South China Sea or fell prey to pirates, disease, and starvation. Many of these "boat people" who survived emigrated to the United States.

"**California Palms**" is lê thi diem thúy's autobiographical account of her childhood in California, where she fled with her father in 1978. Using colorful description and humorous anecdotes, she describes her attempts to assimilate into American culture as a Vietnamese immigrant.

About the AUTHOR

lê thi diem thúy is a Vietnamese-American poet and performance artist who lives in Massachusetts. Born in South Vietnam in 1972, she left the country by boat in 1978 with her father and eventually settled in Southern California. The rest of her family followed a few years later. lê thi diem thúy wrote about her experiences in the forthcoming memoir, *The Gangster We Are All Looking For.* Her latest book of poetry is titled *Mua He Lua Do: Red Fiery Summer.*

Orange Boats, 1998. Ann Phong. Private Collection.

California PALMS

lê thi diem thúy

Before my mother arrived in the United States from Vietnam, I perceived myself to be an American. Whatever that is. I'd acquired a taste for dill pickles, macaroni and cheese, was an expert at the Hula-Hoop and roller skating backwards. I thought this entitled me to glide along like I imagined everyone else gliding along— merrily—and with no past to speak of. Not only did my mother prompt me to question my taste in American food by reacquainting me with condensed

How does the narrator perceive herself before her mother's arrival in America?

milk, ginger fried fish, lichee nuts, and noodle soup for breakfast, her presence also pointed to an entire history I thought I'd thrown overboard and left for sunken treasure or so much useless luggage adrift in the watery vaults of the Pacific. I thought I had succeeded in making myself light, releasing my longing for Vietnam in order to secure a place in America. Now here was my mother, newly arrived and already dragging memories right out of the sea, shaking them loose on the shore before holding them up to the light and handing them back to me. While my father had <u>instilled</u> in me the belief that we might never go back to Vietnam, my mother came and insisted that we could never leave it.

When my mother arrived in the States in 1980, she had lost three children, survived two wars, was separated from her mother and father, brothers and sisters, and the land of her birth by an entire ocean. My father and I had escaped Vietnam in 1978. During the two years between our departure from Vietnam and my mother's arrival in the United States with my younger sister in 1980, my father and I had sent my mother portraits of ourselves decked out in our best clothes, standing in front of big cars and fancy houses in the wealthy neighborhood of La Jolla, a virtual independent republic of San Diego, California. Through so many smiling images, we led her to believe that the hacienda[1]-style house stretching out behind the two giant California palms was indeed our home in America.

What did the photos lead the narrator's mother to believe?

She arrived to find we had no house. What's more, I claimed she wasn't my real mother. I held on to this belief for months. Even coupling it with the suspicion that this man and woman who assumed the roles of my father and mother were in reality Communist spies, and that the young girl of two or three who was supposedly my sister wasn't really my sister but some child who was cast to be the younger sister just as I had been cast to be the older sister in what appeared to be the portrait of a struggling Vietnamese family newly arrived in America.

My mother was not overly concerned with having been cast as an impostor mother

Where this elaborate drama came from, I do not know except to say that in my worldly travels as an eight-year-old in what were still the Cold War[2] years, I had picked up the common wisdom that the opposite of an American was a Communist. Also, I had a vivid imagination. I was convinced that entire rooms changed once I'd stepped out of them, like a turning stage that twirled one living room away and brought another living room forward, with the same

When did the narrator's mother arrive from Vietnam? When did the narrator and her father escape?

What did the narrator believe was the opposite of an American?

---

1. **hacienda.** Large house in a Spanish style
2. **Cold War.** Ideological conflict between democratic and communist countries after World War II

words for everyday use

in • still (in stil') vt., impart gradually. *My parents <u>instilled</u> a love of learning in me.*

actors in place but in changed costumes and changed characters, which meant that an entirely different drama was about to unfold.

My mother was not overly concerned with having been cast as an <u>impostor</u> mother. After all, she knew she was my mother. She set about correcting my odd Vietnamese—I'd taken to saying things like, "Can I help you shampoo the dishes?"—and acquainting herself with English via songs from television commercials. Her two favorite songs were: "This Bud's for you" and "G.E. We bring good things to life!" Which she pronounced "lie." She often sang these songs—in lieu of[3] the traditional lilting Vietnamese lullaby—to the little girl who, oddly, seemed to like them, especially when my mother thrust a cupped hand in the air, as though toasting the little girl with an invisible twelve-ounce can of Budweiser.

On weekends, she had my father drive us to Thrift village, a warehouse of secondhand clothes and shoes, fat couches and coffee tables, flower-patterned vinyl kitchen chairs, velvet paintings, and tall lamps sporting crushed or otherwise crooked lampshades. It was here that she found a portrait of Jesus with his eyes painted to follow me around the room, so that no matter where I was in our small apartment, whenever I turned to look at him, he, like a <u>demented</u> guard dog my mother had <u>ingeniously</u> convinced to assume the likeness of Jesus, was staring right back at me. It was also here that my father picked out two framed prints, one of the New England countryside alive in the glory of fall <u>foliage</u>, the other of a mother leopard staring into the camera while her baby, protectively curled beside her,

yawned. What, I wondered, did these prints have to do with being a Communist? Yet, it was also at Thrift Village that my mother showed signs of her criminality. She taught my sister and me how to steal.

At Thrift Village, there were no dressing rooms. If you wanted to see whether a shirt fit, you either slipped it on over your shirt or, through some acrobatic feat that consisted in twisting your arms so that the elbow of the right arm almost nestled inside the armpit of the left and vice versa, you were able to loosen your shirt enough so that it became a <u>makeshift</u> tent under which you could try on any number of other shirts. The best thing to do was to hang a long dress over your head and proceed from there, though this did have the effect of making Thrift Village look like a room full of the rear ends of donkeys groping for their more becoming front ends. My mother took advantage of this controlled chaos to pile one article of clothing after another over my sister and me. On top of our own shirts, she had us put on other shirts. Over our own pants, she slipped on more pants, and over those, skirts and dresses. Placing a hat on our heads and a stuffed teddy bear or a toy dinosaur in our arms, my mother pushed my sister and me out the opened doors of Thrift Village with instructions to run and shed the layers of clothes in the back seat of my dad's car. We shed all but our original clothes and ran back to be layered with more. In this way, my sister and I acquired outfits and wardrobes, costumes and new skins.

Though my father was not keen on the <u>phenomenon</u> of my sister and me leaving the thrift

---

3. **in lieu of.** Instead of

store in the guise of two Michelin[4] men and returning as our small-boned, skinny selves, I should have known from the moment my mother arrived in the States that she had the upper hand in determining the direction my family would take. As far as she was concerned, he had failed miserably at keeping things together. Not so much because the hacienda in La Jolla was a fiction but rather because he'd gotten two important details about my identity entirely mixed up.

Back in Vietnam, I'd had an older sister who was called Big Girl, whereas I was called Little Girl. Her given name was thúy and mine was trang. We weren't often called by our given names, which is why, supposedly, my father confused her given name with mine. In the States, I assumed the name thúy and celebrated my birthday on January 15. Neither my father nor I was troubled by this until my mother arrived to set us straight. For one thing, she let us know, my name was trang and my birthday was January 12, not the fifteenth. For a fleeting moment, I entertained the possibility of celebrating my birthday twice in one week, but my mother laughed that one off. Then I thought she'd let me relinquish the name thúy which, pronounced "twee" in English, had caused people to laugh into their hands and make jokes about a certain small cartoon character named Tweety Bird. I didn't necessarily feel that trang, pronounced like a combination of "train" crashing into "tang," was any better, but it was new and, more important, it was supposed to be my name. To this, my mother said no. My older sister, the original thúy, had escaped Vietnam with my mother and younger sister, but she had drowned at the refugee camp in Malaysia.[5] My mother insisted that I keep the name because, due to my father's propitious mistake, it was a part of my older sister that had made it to America. Like a T-shirt stretched to make a tent, I felt my mother's deft logic expanding the familiar one-syllable note of thúy to make room for my dead sister.

The result was, sometimes I felt my name was like an already occupied bed, something I couldn't quite find my place in because someone else was sprawled out and deep in sleep across it. Other times, I felt I had no name or hadn't found my real name yet and was using thúy until then. For a while, I even went by the name of Tina because a friend of mine, an African American girl named Lakeisha, thought thúy was a weird and difficult name to remember. I came to think of names in general and of my name in particular as rough skin, loose approximations of the person underneath.

A name, like any word, can be misspelled, mispronounced, kicked around, and then caressed back to life. Sometimes my mother would say my name in such a way that it didn't seem to be spoken so much as sung and, in its singing, made to linger in the air like a musical note. Through such moments, I came to understand that language is alive as sound, as utterance and invocation. I knew that in one breath she was calling to me and to my older sister, to the past in the present, reaching

> What two details about her life did the narrator's father mix up?

> Why did the narrator's mother make her keep her sister's name?

---

4. **Michelin.** French tire company that is publicized by a chubby white figure
5. **Malaysia.** Country in Southeast Asia

---

words for everyday use

guise (gīz) *n.*, external appearance; manner; fashion. *Jerome appeared at the masked ball in the guise of Napoleon.*
re • lin • quish (ri lin′ kwish) *vt.*, give up. *I relinquished my ticket at the state fair entrance.*
pro • pi • tious (prə pi′ shəs) *adj.*, being of good omen. *The sunny sky was a propitious start to our vacation.*
deft (deft) *adj.*, characterized by facility and skill. *With a few deft strokes of his pen, the artist made a fine caricature of my brother.*
ap • prox • i • ma • tion (ə präk sə mā′ shən) *n.*, quality or state of being close or near. *The light sentence handed down by the jury was only an approximation of justice.*
in • vo • ca • tion (in və kā′ shən) *n.*, prayer of entreaty. *The worship service began with an invocation.*

across the ocean's vastness to touch a particular stretch of beach in front of my grandfather's house.

I remembered the house. The neighbor with the pigeon nest on her roof. A particular rainy Tet[6] evening when I wondered if the firecrackers would light. I remembered a younger brother whom my mother had described as no bigger than a marble when he was first born and an older brother who drowned when I was still in Vietnam but whose death I refused to believe in because my mother had told me, "He fell into a hole in the sea," and I thought that just meant he was hiding under water. I remembered the night my father sat me down in my great-uncle's fishing boat and told me to wait there until he returned. It was the night my mother got into a fight with her father and missed the boat that was taking my father and me away from Vietnam.

My childhood belief that entire rooms disappeared behind me hadn't come out of thin air but out of my own experience of leaving Vietnam. After the days and nights at sea, the months at the refugee camp in Singapore[7], the year and then two with no signs of my mother or other members of my family showing up, as I had imagined they would, my life in Vietnam took on the <u>aura</u> of something remote, like a house I had walked so far away from that when I turned back to look at it, I could barely make out the

To what does the narrator compare leaving her Vietnamese life behind?

house, let alone the toys I'd left in the courtyard or the people sleeping inside. Vietnam became a kind of darkness, a deep silence that would occasionally be interrupted by sudden memories of a rooster crowing or a pigeon cooing. I would see flashes of someone's face, sometimes my older brother's as he turned to see how close I

had come to catching him during a game of chase on the beach. Such memories of Vietnam appeared like intense points of light occasionally capable of piercing through the dark canopy that had come to define my relationship to the past. By the time my mother and sister arrived, I had buried so much of my longing for Vietnam that I could almost believe I had entered the world as a fully formed eight-year-old, emerging from an untraceable black hole.

My mother was the one who alerted me to the simultaneity of worlds. She

How did the narrator's mother speak about Vietnam?

spoke about Vietnam as if it were right around the corner, as alive as where we were, if not more so. While school and mainstream American movies defined Vietnam as a war, from my mother I might have thought there had never been a war, that history hadn't twisted itself around us like a tornado, lifting us up into the heart of it, stomping out our past with a flick of its tail and then depositing us as far from home as possible. She treated the United States like some place we were passing through, made bearable by the belief that no matter how long or how difficult this journey would be, in the end we were still Vietnamese and we would eventually make it back to Vietnam. According to my mother, every <u>ordeal</u> was a test of our strength, meant to build character. Strange, <u>inexplicable</u> things happened. One night, we had boarded a boat in southern Vietnam. One day, we had landed by plane in Southern California. That was fate.

It was fate that had changed my position in the family from the fourth child to the eldest,

---

6. **Tet.** Festival celebrating the lunar New Year in Southeast Asia
7. **Singapore.** Island state south of Malaysia in the South China Sea

---

words for everyday use

au • ra (ôr′ ə) n., distinctive atmosphere. *The island had an <u>aura</u> of mystery and romance.*
or • deal (ôr dēəl′) n., severe trial or experience. *Kathy survived the <u>ordeal</u> of taking all her finals on the same day.*
in • ex • pli • ca • ble (i nik spli′ kə bəl) adj., incapable of being explained, interpreted, or accounted for. *The <u>inexplicable</u> disappearance of the boat owner left the Coast Guard baffled.*

and it was fate which demanded that—even though I was a child—I become the representative head of my family. My mother's conversational English at the time consisted of Yes, No, Maybe, Okay, and Why not?—terms that she used interchangeably to create a cloud of confusion between herself and the listener. My father, who was less <u>verbose</u>, favored nodding solemnly or beginning every explanation with, My name is . . . , I entered with, Excuse me, Pardon me, What time is it?, Where is, We're just looking for, and Thank you. Through the <u>clarity</u> of my pronunciation and the <u>agility</u> of my translation, I was navigating my family through the <u>perils</u> of daily life, from finding milk at the liquor store to locating the correct room to enter at the social services building or the hospital. My mother was impressed with my English. Whenever I spoke, she would gaze into the face of the listening American and observe how my words were smoothing the furrowed brow, unlocking the tight lips, sometimes even <u>eliciting</u> a warm smile. While it might have seemed to my mother that my polite yet directed <u>banter</u> could protect my family from dumbfounded stares and prompt dismissal, I felt that I couldn't truly protect us but was merely delaying our inevitable eviction.

In what way did lê become "the representative head" of her family?

At home, my parents applauded my ability to speak English as well as any American and yet not be an American. In public, I carried myself as the representative of a family most of whose members didn't speak English well but harbored no greater dream than to be Americans. I both hoped and feared that sooner or later I would be found out. The public

What did lê both hope and fear?

would discover that my parents had no desire to become Americans, while my parents would realize that I didn't know how or what it meant to be Vietnamese in America. I could translate sentences from one language to another and back again: tell my mother what my teacher said, ask the sales clerk for what my father wanted. Within our family, I could live life in our small apartment as though it were a distant outpost of Vietnam. Yet every time I turned the television on or stepped out of the house, my parents and Vietnam seemed far away, otherworldly. I had been rowing back and forth, in a relentless manner, between two banks of a wide river. Increasingly, what I wanted was to be a burning boat in the middle of the water, visible to both shores yet <u>indecipherable</u> in my fury.

As early as the age of eight, I had begun to run away. It wasn't long before hunger and darkness brought me back home, but then I would go again, escaping the <u>claustrophobia</u> of my house to run barefoot through the streets.

words for everyday use

ver • bose (vər bōs') *adj.*, given to wordiness. *Randall's <u>verbose</u> style benefited from peer editing.*

clar • i • ty (klar' ə tē) *n.*, quality or state of being clear. *The senator spoke with such <u>clarity</u> that the audience understood the key points of his complicated new proposal.*

agil • i • ty (ə ji' lə tē) *n.*, quality or state of being able to move with quick easy grace. *Mike played football with increasing <u>agility</u>.*

per • il (per' əl) *n.*, exposure to the risk of being injured, destroyed, or lost. *Fire in the flower shop put the businesses on either side of it in <u>peril</u>.*

elic • it (i li' sət) *vt.*, draw forth or bring out. *The Youngs' dinner invitation <u>elicited</u> a quick acceptance from the Quinlans.*

ban • ter (ban' tər) *n.*, good-natured and usually witty and animated speaking. *After the girls won the basketball game, their <u>banter</u> was lively and triumphant.*

in • de • ci • pher • a • ble (in di sī' fər ə bəl) *adj.*, incapable of being decoded or understood. *"I can't read your <u>indecipherable</u> handwriting," complained the social studies teacher to Allison.*

claus • tro • pho • bia (klôs trə fō' bē ə) *n.*, abnormal dread of being in closed or narrow spaces. *Andy was afraid of an attack of <u>claustrophobia</u> when he entered the crowded elevator.*

I'd wander new neighborhoods, look in on other lives, imagine my family stepping out of a station wagon, strolling across the green lawn to unlock the promise of our very own big house. Or, I imagined bringing strangers home to live with us so that they could share the burden of being a witness to my world. I wanted someone to tell me what they saw in my father's <u>stoic</u> silence, my mother's talk about fate, my sister's wide-eyed curiosity, and my own uneasy <u>donning</u> of a dead sister's name. Add to this my father's drinking, my mother's gambling, and their spectacular fights, which left my sister and me hiding in the bathroom until our fear died down. On the flip side of all the <u>tumult</u> was the obvious affection, how with my mother's urging my father could be convinced to sing. He would begin slowly, softly, a hint of a song approaching from far away, and then his voice would rise and he'd clap his hands together. We'd join my father, keeping time, following his voice as it searched all the tones, high and low and back again, moving like a solitary figure leading us through areas of darkness and of light.

> With what does the narrator contrast her parents' fighting?

I think I became a writer in part because I wanted to convey in English the quality of my father's voice as he sang a song in Vietnamese or the peculiar truth of my mother's accented English speaking for General Electric when she declared, "G.E. We bring good things to lie!" Similar to the way my mother has secured my sister's passage to this country by having me bear my sister's name, I have arrived at English through Vietnamese and can't hear one language without feeling the presence of the other.

When I sit down to write, there is a part of me that isn't laying words down so much as dragging my grandfather's fishing boats, sand-and-salt-speckled, clear across the Pacific and right onto the page, and then there is the part of me that continues to stare out from those portraits my father and I used to send to my mother, of our fabled hacienda in La Jolla. I see myself, one of two bodies framed within the space between two enormous California palms, smiling a winning smile. The girl I was then asks the woman I am today, What do you see? Daring me to speak. ∎

> What does the narrator feel when she hears either language—English or Vietnamese?

---

words for everyday use

sto • ic (stō′ ik) *adj.*, firmly restrained response to pain or distress. *Farmer Olson's <u>stoic</u> response to the drought that destroyed his crops did not reflect his internal suffering.*

don • ning (dän′ iŋ) *vt.*, putting on. *Dad's <u>donning</u> of a Santa Claus costume was traditional.*

tu • mult (tü′ məlt) *n.*, violent outburst. *The principal came in to quash the <u>tumult</u> in the classroom.*

Respond *to the* SELECTION

How do you think the narrator would describe herself now?

Investigate, Inquire, and *imagine*

Recall: GATHERING FACTS

1a. What did the narrator believe happened to rooms once she left them?

2a. What names was the narrator called as a child? To what does she compare names?

3a. When the narrator ran away from home as a child to "look in on other lives," what sort of things did she imagine?

Interpret: FINDING MEANING

1b. How might this belief relate to the narrator's experience of leaving Vietnam as a young child?

2b. How does the narrator feel about the name thúy?

3b. What desire influenced the narrator to have these fantasies?

Analyze: TAKING THINGS APART

4a. Identify the role that the narrator played in her family.

Synthesize: BRINGING THINGS TOGETHER

4b. How did this role affect the narrator's identity and her choice of profession?

Evaluate: MAKING JUDGMENTS

5a. Evaluate the degree to which the narrator has been assimilated into American culture. Explain your evaluation with evidence from the story.

Extend: CONNECTING IDEAS

5b. Like the character Mrs. Pan in the story "The Good Deed" by Pearl S. Buck on page 225, lê thi diem thúy had to adjust to life in America. Compare and contrast the two individuals' experiences of assimilation into American culture.

Understanding *Literature*

CONFLICT AND INTERNAL CONFLICT. Review the definitions for **conflict** and **internal conflict** in the Handbook of Literary Terms. With what major internal conflict did the narrator struggle? How did she resolve this internal conflict?

METAPHOR AND SIMILE. Review the definitions for **metaphor** and **simile** in the Handbook of Literary Terms and the chart you made for Literary Tools on page 436. Which metaphor expresses the narrator's feeling of belonging to neither the American nor the Vietnamese culture? Which simile expresses the difficulty the narrator had in assuming her drowned sister's name?

Writer's Journal

1. Imagine you are thúy. Write a **postcard** to your mother, who is still in Vietnam, telling her how Americanized you have become.

2. Imagine you are thúy's mother. Write a **journal entry** about the fears you have for your daughter and the pride you have in her English abilities. What are you afraid your daughter has forgotten? How does she help you in your day-to-day life?

3. Imagine you are the adult thúy who has just sent her autobiography to a publisher for consideration. The publisher has asked you why you titled your story "California Palms." Write the publisher a **letter** explaining what the title means.

Integrating the Language Arts

Language, Grammar, and Style

REDUCING WORDINESS. Good writers use only as many words as needed to convey their thoughts clearly. They correct for wordiness when editing their writing. Read the Language Arts Survey 3.35, "Correcting Wordy Sentences." Then reduce the wordiness in the following sentences.

1. thúy's family found that leaving their home for a country far, far away was really difficult.
2. thúy and her father went to outrageous lengths to give thúy's mother the impression that they lived in a large hacienda-style house in California.
3. thúy felt that her name was like a bed that was used and slept in by someone else.
4. thúy compared her life in Vietnam to a house she had walked so far away from that when she turned back to look at it, she could barely make out the house.
5. The author, who was born in Vietnam, is now American and lives in Massachusetts.

Study and Research & Media Literacy

VIETNAMESE IMMIGRANTS. Research the plight of Vietnamese refugees in the late 1970s after the end of the Vietnam War and the fall of Saigon. These refugees were known as "boat people." What stages did they make in their journey from Vietnam to the United States? What were conditions like in the refugee camps? What difficulties did those who settled in the United States face? What agencies and organizations offered assistance? Prepare a brief oral presentation for the class answering these and other pertinent questions. If you choose to do your research on the Internet, one site you will find useful is The Boat People Connection at http://www.boatpeople.com/stories.

Speaking and Listening

STORYTELLING. In "California Palms," the narrator recounts her adjustments to a new culture. Perhaps you remember what it was like to change schools, move from another city or even from another country. Tell your story to a small group of other students. Where did you feel you belonged at the beginning? How was the new location different from the old one? How did you adjust to the new location? Who helped you to adjust? Where do you feel you belong now? If you can't speak from personal experience, tell the story of a character you know about from a novel, a film, or the TV.

Literary T O O L S

POINT OF VIEW. Point of view is the vantage point from which a story is told. Stories are typically written from a *first-person point of view*, in which the narrator uses words such as *I* and *we*, or from a *third-person point of view*, in which the narrator uses words such as *he, she, it,* and *they*. In this selection, three people speak: Black Elk, Fire Thunder, and Standing Bear. As you read, identify the point of view that each uses.

TONE. Tone is the emotional attitude toward the reader or toward the subject of a literary work. In this selection, the tone is largely dispassionate. In other words, the narrators do not reveal their emotions.

Organizer

As you read, make a cluster chart to reveal examples of the narrators' dispassionate tone in the account of their youth. One example has been done for you.

dispassionate tone

I am a Lakota of the Ogalala band.

Reader's Journal

What dream have you had that made an impression on you?

from

Black Elk Speaks

by Black Elk and John G. Neihardt

Reader's resource

HISTORY CONNECTION. Black Elk was a warrior and medicine man of the Oglala Sioux, a group of Native Americans of the Great Plains. A medicine man is a spiritual advisor as well as a healer. To be a medicine man, one must have a special gift. In this portion of *Black Elk Speaks,* Black Elk tells of his youth, in which he received his first spiritual vision. The vision was a sign that he was indeed gifted and would become a great spiritual leader. The selection also focuses on the difficult time that Black Elk and his people faced as white settlers moved in and claimed ownership of Sioux territory.

About *the* A U T H O R S

John G. Neihardt (1881–1973) was born in Illinois and grew up in Kansas and Nebraska. The close connections he formed with the indigenous populations of these states influenced his work as a poet and fiction writer. He lived among the Oglala Sioux from 1901 to 1907 and became an adopted member of the group. Much of Neihardt's work focused on the time he spent with the Sioux. He worked as a literary critic and a teacher, received several awards and honorary degrees, and was chosen poet laureate of the state of Nebraska.

Black Elk (1863–1950), a Sioux medicine man, chose Neihardt as heir to his spiritual powers, the one who would communicate his message to the outside world.

Last of the Buffalo, 1889. Albert Bierstadt. Corcoran Gallery of Art, Washington, DC.

from Black Elk Speaks

Black Elk and John G. Neihardt

I am a Lakota of the Ogalala[1] band. My father's name was Black Elk, and his father before him bore the name, and the father of his father, so that I am the fourth to bear it. He was a medicine man and so were several of his brothers. Also, he and the great Crazy Horse's father were cousins, having the same grandfather. My mother's name was White Cow Sees; her father was called Refuse-to-go, and her mother, Plenty Eagle Feathers. I can remember my mother's mother and her father. My father's father was killed by the Pawnees when I was too little to know, and his mother, Red Eagle Woman, died soon after.

I was born in the Moon of the Popping Trees (December) on the Little Powder River in the Winter When the Four Crows Were Killed

(1863), and I was three years old when my father's right leg was broken in the Battle of the Hundred Slain.[2] From that wound he limped until the day he died, which was about the time when Big Foot's band was butchered on Wounded Knee[3] (1890). He is buried here in these hills.

I can remember that Winter of the Hundred Slain as a man may remember some bad dream he dreamed when he was little, but I can not tell just how much I heard when I was bigger and how much I understood when I was little. It is like some fearful thing in a fog, for it was a time when everything seemed troubled and afraid.

I had never seen a Wasichu[4] then, and did not know what one looked like; but every one was saying that the Wasichus were coming and that they were going to take our country and rub us all out and that we should all have to die fighting. It was the Wasichus who got rubbed out in that battle, and all the people were talking about it for a long while; but a hundred Wasichus was not much if there were others and others without number where those came from.

What fear did the Oglala Sioux have about the coming of the settlers?

I remember once that I asked my grandfather about this. I said: "When the scouts come back from seeing the prairie full of bison somewhere, the people say the Wasichus are coming; and when strange men are coming to kill us all, they say the Wasichus are coming. What does it mean?" And he said, "That they are many."

When I was older, I learned what the fighting was about that winter and the next summer. Up on the Madison Fork the Wasichus had found much of the yellow metal that they worship and that makes them crazy, and they wanted to have a road up through our country to the place where the yellow metal was; but my people did not want the road. It would scare the bison and make them go away, and also it would let the other Wasichus come in like a river. They told us that they wanted only to use a little land, as much as a wagon would take between the wheels; but our people knew better. And when you look about you now, you can see what it was they wanted.

What word does Black Elk use to describe the Wasichus' attitude toward the "yellow metal"? What does Black Elk think about that attitude? Do you agree with him?

Once we were happy in our own country and we were seldom hungry, for then the two-leggeds and the four-leggeds lived together like relatives, and there was plenty for them and for us. But the Wasichus came, and they have made little islands for us and other little islands for the four-leggeds, and always these islands are becoming smaller, for around them surges the gnawing flood of the Wasichu; and it is dirty with lies and greed.

Who are the "two-leggeds" and the "four-leggeds"? What relationship existed between them before the coming of the Wasichus?

A long time ago my father told me what his father told him, that there was once a Lakota[5] holy man, called Drinks Water, who dreamed what was to be; and this was long before the coming of the Wasichus. He dreamed that the four-leggeds were going back into the earth and that a strange race had woven a spider's web all around the Lakotas. And he said: "When this happens, you shall live in square gray houses, in a barren land, and beside those square gray

---

2. **Battle of the Hundred Slain.** Also called the Fetterman Fight, a Sioux victory in which Captain Fetterman and eighty-one men were slain near Peno Creek in December of 1866

3. **Wounded Knee.** Site in South Dakota of a terrible massacre of Native Americans. This massacre symbolized the defeat of the Sioux and the end of the Indian Wars.

4. **Wasichu.** Term used to describe white settlers

5. **Lakota.** Sioux

words for everyday use

bi • son (bī´sən) n., type of mammal having a shaggy mane, short, curved horns, and a humped back; commonly referred to as the American buffalo. *After being hunted to near extinction, bison where gradually reintroduced to the western United States.*

houses you shall starve." They say he went back to Mother Earth soon after he saw this vision, and it was sorrow that killed him. You can look about you now and see that he meant these dirt-roofed houses we are living in, and that all the rest was true. Sometimes dreams are wiser than waking.

And so when the soldiers came and built themselves a town of logs there on the Piney Fork of the Powder, my people knew they meant to have their road and take our country and maybe kill us all when they were strong enough. Crazy Horse was only about 19 years old then, and Red Cloud was still our great chief. In the Moon of the Changing Season (October) he called together all the scattered bands of the Lakota for a big council on the Powder River, and when we went on the warpath against the soldiers, a horseback could ride through our villages from sunrise until the day was above his head, so far did our camp stretch along the valley of the river; for many of our friends, the Shyela and the Blue Clouds,[6] had come to help us fight.

And it was about when the bitten moon was delayed (last quarter) in the Time of the Popping Trees when the hundred were rubbed out. My friend, Fire Thunder here, who is older than I, was in that fight and he can tell you how it was.

there were more arrows— so many that it was like a cloud of grasshoppers

Fire Thunder Speaks:

I was 16 years old when this happened, and after the big council on the Powder we had moved over to the Tongue River where we were camping at the mouth of Peno Creek. There were many of us there. Red Cloud was over all of us, but the chief of our band was Big Road. We started out on horseback just about sunrise, riding up the creek toward the soldiers' town on the Piney, for we were going to attack it. The sun was about half way up when we stopped at the place where the Wasichus' road came down a steep, narrow ridge and crossed the creek. It was a good place to fight, so we sent some men ahead to coax the soldiers out. While they were gone, we divided into two parts and hid in the gullies on both sides of the ridge and waited. After a long while we heard a shot up over the hill, and we knew the soldiers were coming. So we held the noses of our ponies that they might not whinny at the soldiers' horses. Soon we saw our men coming back, and some of them were walking and leading their horses, so that the soldiers would think they were worn out. Then the men we had sent ahead came running down the road between us, and the soldiers on horseback followed, shooting. When they came to the flat at the bottom of the hill, the fighting began all at once. I had a sorrel horse, and just as I was going to get on him, the soldiers turned around and began to fight their way back up the hill. I

---

6. **Shyela and the Blue Clouds.** Cheyenne and Arapaho, two Native American groups from the Great Plains region

---

words for everyday use

gul • ly (gul´ ē) *n.,* channel or hollow worn by running water. *The log cabin was located at the bottom of a gully.*

sor • rel (sôr´əl) *adj.,* light reddish brown. *Sorrel clay clung to our boots in red clumps.*

had a six-shooter that I had traded for, and also a bow and arrows. When the soldiers started back, I held my sorrel with one hand and began killing them with the six-shooter, for they came close to me. There were many bullets, but there were more arrows—so many that it was like a cloud of grasshoppers all above and around the soldiers; and our people, shooting across, hit each other. The soldiers were falling all the while they were fighting back up the hill, and their horses got loose. Many of our people chased the horses, but I was not after horses; I was after Wasichus. When the soldiers got on top, there were not many of them left and they had no place to hide. They were fighting hard. We were told to crawl up on them, and we did. When we were close, someone yelled: "Let us go! This is a good day to die. Think of the helpless ones at home!" Then we all cried, "Hoka hey!" and rushed at them. I was young then and quick on my feet, and I was one of the first to get in among the soldiers. They got up and fought very hard until not one of them was alive. They had a dog with them, and he started back up the road for the soldiers' town, howling as he ran. He was the only one left. I did not shoot at him because he looked too sweet, but many did shoot, and he died full of arrows. So there was nobody left of the soldiers. Dead men and horses and wounded Indians were scattered all the way up the hill, and their blood was frozen, for a storm had come up and it was very cold and getting colder all the time. We left all the dead lying there, for the ground was solid, and we picked up our wounded and started back; but we lost most of them before we reached our camp at the mouth of the Peno. There was a big blizzard that night; and some of the wounded who did not die on the way, died after we got home.

What was the outcome of the battle?

This was the time when Black Elk's father had his leg broken.

Black Elk Continues:

I am quite sure that I remember the time when my father came home with a broken leg that he got from killing so many Wasichus, and it seems that I can remember all about the battle too, but I think I could not. It must be the fear that I remember most. All this time I was not allowed to play very far away from our tepee, and my mother would say, "If you are not good the Wasichus will get you."

We must have broken camp at the mouth of the Peno soon after the battle, for I can remember my father lying on a pony drag with bison robes all around him, like a baby, and my mother riding the pony. The snow was deep and it was very cold, and I remember sitting in another pony drag beside my father and mother, all wrapped up in fur. We were going away from where the soldiers were, and I do not know where we went, but it was west.

It was a hungry winter, for the deep snow made it hard to find the elk; and also many of the people went snowblind.[7] We wandered a long time, and some of the bands got lost from each other. Then at last we were camping in the woods beside a creek somewhere, and the hunters came back with meat.

What hardships did the Sioux experience that winter?

I think it was this same winter when a medicine man, by the name of Creeping, went around among the people curing snowblinds. He would put snow upon their eyes, and after he had sung a certain sacred song that he had heard in a dream, he would blow on the backs of their heads and they would see again, so I have heard. It was about the dragonfly that he sang, for that was where he got his power, they say.

---

7. **snowblind.** Blinded temporarily by ultraviolet rays reflected from the snow

When it was summer again we were camping on the Rosebud, and I did not feel so much afraid, because the Wasichus seemed farther away and there was peace there in the valley and there was plenty of meat. But all the boys from five or six years up were playing war. The little boys would gather together from the different bands of the tribe and fight each other with mud balls that they threw with willow sticks. And the big boys played the game called Throwing-Them-Off-Their-Horses, which is a battle all but the killing; and sometimes they got hurt. The horsebacks from the different bands would line up and charge upon each other, yelling; and when the ponies came together on the run, they would rear and flounder and scream in a big dust, and the riders would seize each other, wrestling until one side had lost all its men, for those who fell upon the ground were counted dead.

When I was older, I, too, often played this game. We were always naked when we played it, just as warriors are when they go into battle if it is not too cold, because they are swifter without clothes. Once I fell off on my back right in the

art note

Winter Count Calendar. Battiste Good.

Battiste Good (1821–?) of the Sichangu nation in the Dakota territory drew this calendar, which was used to mark the significant events of each year, such as the death of a leader, battles, and seasons of plenty and shortage. The full calendar begins in the year 900, 592 years before the arrival of Columbus, and ends in 1907. This section records the buffalo hunt. How is this different from Albert Bierstadt's depiction of a buffalo hunt on page 447?

Winter Count Calendar [Detail], 1907.
Battiste Good. Library of Congress.

middle of a bed of prickly pears,[8] and it took my mother a long while to pick all the stickers out of me. I was still too little to play war that summer, but I can remember watching the other boys, and I thought that when we all grew up and were big together, maybe we could kill all the Wasichus or drive them far away from our country.

It was in the Moon When the Cherries Turn Black (August) that all the people were talking again about a battle, and our warriors came back with many wounded. It was The Attacking of the Wagons, and it made me afraid again, for we did not win that battle as we did the other one, and there was much mourning for the dead. Fire Thunder was in that fight too, and he can tell you how it was that day.

Fire Thunder Speaks:

It was very bad. There is a wide flat prairie with hills around it, and in the middle of this the Wasichus had put the boxes of their wagons in a circle, so that they could keep their mules there at night. There were not many Wasichus, but they were lying behind the boxes and they shot faster than they ever shot at us before. We thought it was some new medicine of great power that they had, for they shot so fast that it was like tearing a blanket. Afterwards I learned that it was because they had new guns that they loaded from behind, and this was the first time they used these guns. We came on after sunrise. There were many, many of us, and we meant to ride right over them and rub them out. But our ponies were afraid of the ring of fire the guns of the Wasichus made, and

Why did the Wasichus win this battle?

would not go over. Our women were watching us from the hills and we could hear them singing and mourning whenever the shooting stopped. We tried hard, but we could not do it, and there were dead warriors and horses piled all around the boxes and scattered over the plain. Then we left our horses in a gulch and charged on foot, but it was like green grass withering in a fire. So we picked up our wounded and went away. I do not know how many of our people were killed, but there were very many. It was bad.

"Behold, a sacred voice is calling you; All over the sky a sacred voice is calling."

Black Elk Continues:

I do not remember where we camped that winter but it must have been a time of peace and of plenty to eat.

Standing Bear Speaks:

I am four years older than Black Elk, and he and I have been good friends since boyhood. I know it was on the Powder that we camped where there were many cottonwood trees. Ponies like to eat the bark of these trees and it is good for them. That was the winter when High Shirt's mother was killed by a big tree that fell on her tepee. It was a very windy night and there were noises that 'woke me, and then I heard that an old woman had been killed, and it was High Shirt's mother.

Black Elk Continues:

I was four years old then, and I think it must have been the next summer that I first heard the voices. It was a happy summer and nothing was afraid, because in the Moon When the Ponies Shed (May) word came from the Wasichus that

---

8. **prickly pears.** Variety of cactus

there would be peace and that they would not use the road any more and that all the soldiers would go away. The soldiers did go away and their towns were torn down; and in the Moon of Falling Leaves (November), they made a <u>treaty</u> with Red Cloud that said our country would be ours as long as grass should grow and water flow. You can see that it is not the grass and the water that have forgotten.

Why was this a happy summer for the Oglala?

Based on what Black Elk says, what can you conclude about how well the Wasichus honored the treaty that they made?

Maybe it was not this summer when I first heard the voices, but I think it was, because I know it was before I played with bows and arrows or rode a horse, and I was out playing alone when I heard them. It was like somebody calling me, and I thought it was my mother, but there was nobody there. This happened more than once, and always made me afraid, so that I ran home.

It was when I was five years old that my Grandfather made me a bow and some arrows. The grass was young and I was horseback. A thunderstorm was coming from where the sun goes down, and just as I was riding into the woods along a creek, there was a kingbird sitting on a limb. This was not a dream, it happened. And I was going to shoot at the kingbird with the bow my Grandfather made, when the bird spoke and said: "The clouds all over are one-sided." Perhaps it meant that all the clouds were looking at me. And then it said: "Listen! A voice is calling you!" Then I looked up at the clouds, and two men were coming there, headfirst like arrows slanting down; and as they came, they sang a sacred song and the thunder was like drumming. I will sing it for you. The song and the drumming were like this:

Was Black Elk sure that his vision was not a dream? How do you know?

"Behold, a sacred voice is calling you;
All over the sky a sacred voice is calling."

I sat there gazing at them, and they were coming from the place where the giant lives (north). But when they were very close to me, they wheeled about toward where the sun goes down, and suddenly they were geese. Then they were gone, and the rain came with a big wind and a roaring.

I did not tell this vision to any one. I liked to think about it, but was afraid to tell it. ∎

---

words for everyday use
trea • ty (trēt´ē) *n.*, formal agreement between two or more nations, resulting in peace. *The <u>treaty</u> ending World War I was signed at Versailles.*

Respond*to the* SELECTION

After the events described in the selection, what future do you think Black Elk sees for his people?

Investigate, Inquire, and Imagine

Recall: GATHERING FACTS

1a. What did the Oglala believe the Wasichus planned to do? What did the Wasichus wish to build? Why did the Oglala oppose their wishes?

2a. Was the first battle that Black Elk and Fire Thunder described a success for the Oglala? What caused the Oglala to lose the second battle that Black Elk and Fire Thunder described? How did events take a turn for the better in the following spring?

3a. How old was Black Elk when he had his first vision? What appeared to him in the vision?

Interpret: FINDING MEANING

1b. How did the Wasichus change the lives of the Oglala? How did the Oglala in the selection feel about the Wasichus and the things that they seemed to value?

2b. How did real-life events affect the play of the Oglala children? Why did Black Elk say, "You can see that it is not the grass and the water that have forgotten"? How did the Oglala feel about their land?

3b. How did Black Elk feel about his vision?

Analyze: TAKING THINGS APART

4a. Identify specific references to nature that reflect a respect for the natural world in the religion of the Oglala Sioux.

Synthesize: BRINGING THINGS TOGETHER

4b. How might you describe the religion of the Oglala Sioux, based on what you have read in this piece?

Evaluate: MAKING JUDGMENTS

5a. Why did Black Elk's vision have such an impact on him?

Extend: CONNECTING IDEAS

5b. If you were a Wasichu, how would you view the Oglala Sioux based on what is related about them in this selection? Imagine that you are familiar with the actions, beliefs, and culture of the Oglala Sioux.

Understanding Literature

POINT OF VIEW. Review the definition for **point of view** in the Handbook of Literary Terms. Which point of view is used by each of the narrators? How do Black Elk's views differ from those of Fire Thunder and Standing Bear? Do you get a better understanding of the events of the selection because three people tell about them? Why, or why not?

TONE. Review the definition for **tone** in the Handbook of Literary Terms and the cluster chart you made for Literary Tools on page 446. Which citations from your chart would you expect to have a more impassioned tone? In your opinion, why is the tone of the selection dispassionate? How does the tone change when Black Elk speaks of his vision at the end of the selection? What tone does Black Elk use when he discusses the Winter of the Hundred Slain? Where do you find an angry tone?

Writer's Journal

1. Black Elk talks about the seasons in terms of natural events. For example, November is the Moon of Falling Leaves and December is the Moon of the Popping Trees. Create your own **calendar** with titles for each month. The titles need not come from nature, but they should reflect annual events that are important to you.

2. Imagine that you are a mediator negotiating a treaty between the Wasichus and the Oglala Sioux. Write a compromise **document**.

3. Write an **introduction** to a book about the Oglala Sioux based on the information provided in the selection. In the introduction you should include historical events and religious beliefs.

Integrating the Language Arts

Language, Grammar, and Style

PREPOSITIONS AND PREPOSITIONAL PHRASES. Read the Language Arts Survey 3.11, "Prepositions," and 3.30, "Identifying Prepositional Phrases." For each of the sentences below, underline the prepositional phrases.

1. Black Elk was a leader of the Lakota Sioux.
2. His tribe was upset by settlers from Eastern States.
3. These people moved into the lands of the Lakota.
4. After the arrival of the white man, the Lakota lost their land.
5. Land is not property to traditional Native Americans; it is a gift to all creatures.

Study and Research

NATIVE AMERICANS. Select a Native American group that interests you. You might choose from the list below. Then select an aspect of that group's culture to research, such as religion, art, architecture, ceremonies, child rearing, or food gathering. Finally, prepare a report to give to the class. Use visual aids such as maps and pictures from books to make your report vivid and interesting.

Eastern Native Americans: the Penobscot, Algonquin, Iroquois, Ojibway, Delaware
Southeastern Native Americans: the Cherokee, Creek, Chickasaw, Alabama, Choctaw, Apalachee, Seminole Timucua, Catawba
Plains Native Americans: the Blackfoot, Crow, Sioux, Cheyenne, Pawnee, Arapaho, Kiowa, Comanche
Southwestern Native Americans: the Anasazi, Hopi, Navaho, Apache, Zuni, Pima
Northwestern Native Americans: the Coast Salish, Wenatchee

Speaking and Listening & Collaborative Learning

STORYTELLING. This selection relates events important to the Oglala Sioux. Many Native American groups use storytelling to pass history and legends on to future generations. Think about events important to your family history. Select one of them and tell it to a group of classmates.

Literary
T O O L S

AIM. A speaker's or writer's **aim** is his or her purpose, or goal. As you read, determine about what Truth wants to inform her audience and how she wants to persuade them.

DIALECT AND STYLE. A **dialect** is a version of a language spoken by the people of a particular place, time, or social group. A speaker's style or voice is influenced by his or her dialect. **Style** is the manner in which something is said or written.

Organizer

As you read, make a chart to list the examples of dialect found in Truth's speech. On the left, list the examples of dialect. On the right, list how to express the items in standard English. One example has been done for you.

Dialect	Standard English
"I am rejoiced"	I rejoice

Reader's
JOURNAL

For what issues have you spoken up?

Speech to the Convention of the American Equal Rights Association, New York City, 1867

by Sojourner Truth

Reader's
r e s o u r c e

HISTORY CONNECTION. Influenced by Elizabeth Cady Stanton, a leader in the struggle for women's suffrage, Truth lent her unique oratory skills to the women's suffrage movement. Cady Stanton recorded and printed transcripts of some of Truth's speeches in *The History of Women's Suffrage.*

The powerful nature of Sojourner Truth's oratorical style was born in a combination of elements—a personal magnetism, a strong voice, and the courage to speak directly. Speaking English with a Dutch accent, Truth was legendary for her direct platform style. On one particular occasion, Truth challenged Frederick Douglass's stand on the issue of using violence against slavery, exclaiming, "Frederick! Is God dead?"

About *the*
A U T H O R

Sojourner Truth (c.1797–1883) was born to slave parents in Ulster County, New York. Named Isabella, Truth served as a slave in New Paltz, New York, for seventeen years, beginning at the age of thirteen. She escaped to freedom in 1827, initially adopting the name of the Van Wagener family who protected her. One year later, after emancipation became mandatory in New York State, Truth moved to New York City and became involved in social and moral reform. A street-corner preacher, Truth had a wide knowledge of the Bible. In 1843, after adopting the name "Sojourner Truth," she became a wandering orator, launching the speaking tours that made her famous. Illiterate, Truth dictated her life story, barely supporting herself by selling to her audiences the published autobiographical account, *Narrative of Sojourner Truth*, as well as photographs of herself. Truth settled in Battle Creek, Michigan, in the mid-1850s, working and traveling from there for the rest of her life.

Speech to the Convention of the American Equal Rights Association, New York City, 1867

Sojourner Truth

My friends, I am rejoiced that you are glad, but I don't know how you will feel when I get through. I come from another field—the country of the slave. They have got their liberty—so much good luck to have slavery partly destroyed; not entirely. I want it root and branch destroyed. Then we will all be free indeed. I feel that if I have to answer for the deeds done in my body just as much as a man, I have a right to have just as much as a man. There is a great stir about colored men getting their rights, but not a word about the colored women; and if colored men get their rights, and not colored women theirs, you see the colored men will be masters over the women, and it will

> What will happen if African-American men get their rights and African-American women don't? Why should things be stirred up now?

be just as bad as it was before. So I am for keeping the thing going while things are stirring; because if we wait till it is still, it will take a great while to get it going again. White women are a great deal smarter, and know more than colored women, while colored women do not know scarcely anything. They go out washing, which is about as high as a colored woman gets, and their men go about idle, strutting up and down; and when the women come home, they ask for their money and take it all, and then scold because there is no food. I want you to consider on that, chil'n.[1] I call you chil'n; you are somebody's chil'n, and I am old enough to be mother of all that is here. I want women to have their rights. In the courts women have no rights, no voice; nobody speaks for them. I wish woman to have her voice there

---

1. **chil'n.** Dialect word meaning "children"

among the pettifoggers.[2] If it is not a fit place for women, it is unfit for men to be there.

I am above eighty years old; it is about time for me to be going. I have been forty years a slave and forty years free, and would be here forty years more to have equal rights for all. I suppose I am kept here because something remains for me to do; I suppose I am yet to help to break the chain. I have done a great deal of work; as much as a man, but did not get so much pay. I used to work in the field and bind grain, keeping up with the cradler;[3] but men doing no more, got twice as much pay. . . . We do as much, we eat as much, we want as much. I suppose I am about the only colored woman that goes about to speak for the rights of the colored women. I want to keep the thing stirring, now that the ice is cracked. What we want is a little money. You men know that you get as much again as women, when you write, or for what you do. When we get our rights, we shall not have to come to you for money, for then we shall have money enough in our own pockets; and maybe you will ask us for money. But help us now until we get it. It is a good <u>consolation</u> to know that when we have got this battle once fought we shall not be coming to you any more. . . .

Why should men help women in their struggle for rights?

I am glad to see that men are getting their rights, but I want women to get theirs, and while the water is stirring I will step into the pool. Now that there is a great stir about colored men's getting their rights is the time for women to step in and have theirs. I am sometimes told that "Women ain't fit to vote. Why, don't you know that a woman had seven devils in her: and do you suppose a woman is fit to rule the nation?" Seven devils ain't no account; a man had a <u>legion</u> in him. The devils didn't know where to go; and so they asked that they might go into the swine. They thought that was as good a place as they came out from. They didn't ask to go into the sheep—no, into the hog; that was the selfish beast; and man is so selfish that he has got women's rights and his own too, and yet he won't give women their rights. He keeps them all to himself. . . .

How does Truth describe men?

■

---

2. **pettifoggers.** Unethical lawyers
3. **cradler.** Person who cuts grain with a cradle scythe, a cutting instrument with a frame attached so that grain can be laid out as it is cut

---

words for everyday use

con • so • la • tion (kän´sə lā´shən) *n.*, comfort; solace. *After losing the race, Kim sought* <u>consolation</u> *from her best friend.*

le • gion (lē´jən) *n.*, large number; multitude. *In summertime, a* <u>legion</u> *of mosquitoes clouds the lake.*

Respond *to the* SELECTION

Do you think Sojourner Truth would find that men are still selfish in denying women equal rights? Explain.

Investigate, *Inquire,* and Imagine

Recall: GATHERING FACTS

1a. At the beginning of her speech, what prediction does Sojourner Truth make about how the audience will feel when she gets through?

2a. What does Truth want to do "while things are stirring"?

3a. For how many years of her life has Truth been a slave? For how many years has she been free?

➤ Interpret: FINDING MEANING

1b. What concerns Truth about the "great stir about colored men getting their rights"?

2b. What does Truth say will prevent African-American women from being slaves to African-American men?

3b. What is the conclusion Truth draws about why she is still alive?

Analyze: TAKING THINGS APART

4a. Identify how Truth garners respect for her age in her speech. Also identify the strategies Truth uses to be an effective persuasive speaker.

➤ Synthesize: BRINGING THINGS TOGETHER

4b. What kind of a future does Truth envision?

Evaluate: MAKING JUDGMENTS

5a. What experience in Sojourner Truth's working life seems to have had the most impact on her?

➤ Extend: CONNECTING IDEAS

5b. Imagine Sojourner Truth were alive today. For what causes do you think she would speak out?

Understanding *Literature*

AIM. Review the definition for **aim** in the Handbook of Literary Terms. With what observation does Truth inform her audience? What does she want to persuade them to do? Describe the kind of audience to whom you think Truth is speaking.

DIALECT AND STYLE. Review the definitions for **dialect** and **style** in the Handbook of Literary Terms. What effect do you think the use of dialect had on the audience? Truth says, "I wish woman to have her voice there among the pettifoggers." How would the style of that sentence change if she had said, "I wish woman to have her voice there among the lawyers who practice with petty methods"?

Writer's Journal

1. Write a **credo** (statement of belief) for the American Equal Rights Association.

2. Imagine you are a man in the audience who does not believe women should be granted equal rights with men. Write a **rebuttal** of Truth's speech.

3. Imagine that you are a newspaper reporter sent to cover Truth's speech at the Convention of the American Equal Rights Association in New York in 1867. Write a **review** analyzing Truth's main points and her style.

Integrating the Language Arts

Language, Grammar, and Style

DIALECTS OF ENGLISH. Read the Language Arts Survey 3.5, "Dialects of English." In the sentences below identify the example of dialectical language. Then rewrite the sentences, replacing dialectical language with standard English.

1. You are somebody's chil'n.

2. Now there is a great stir about colored men's getting their rights.

3. Some people think that women ain't fit to vote.

4. I am above eighty years old.

5. I did not get so much pay as a man.

Speaking and Listening & Collaborative Learning

DEBATE. Divide into two groups. One group supports equal rights for women. The other group opposes equal rights for women. Hold a debate, making arguments that you think would have been popular in the nineteenth century. For example, it was common to make biblical references to support one's position.

Applied English

PRESS RELEASE. Read the Language Arts Survey 6.9, "Delivering a Press Release." Then write a press release announcing Sojourner Truth's speech at the 1867 Convention of the American Equal Rights Association. Give pertinent biographical information about Truth and tell what her topic is.

"I Have a Dream"
by Martin Luther King, Jr.

Reader's resource

HISTORY CONNECTION. On August 28, 1963, Martin Luther King, Jr., joined other civil rights leaders in the March on Washington in support of civil rights legislation. To an interracial audience of more than two hundred thousand people, he delivered his speech "**I Have a Dream**" at the foot of the Lincoln Memorial. Under the executive leadership of President Lyndon Baines Johnson, the Civil Rights Act was enacted in 1964; it prohibited discrimination for reason of color, race, religion, or national origin in places of public accommodation covered by interstate commerce, such as restaurants, hotels, motels, and theaters. Besides dealing with the desegregation of public schools, the act forbade discrimination in employment. In 1965 the Voting Rights Act was passed to ensure equal voting rights, and the Civil Rights Act of 1968 prohibited housing and real estate discrimination.

King's dynamic and skillful use of rhetoric, or the art of speaking effectively, can be seen in the selection. An emotional and uplifting effect is created through the repetition of words and phrases, the echoes of biblical language, and the description of his vision of a world in which all people would be sisters and brothers.

About the AUTHOR

MARTIN LUTHER KING, JR. (1929–1968) was born in Atlanta, Georgia, the son and grandson of Baptist ministers. Under a special program for gifted students, King entered Morehouse College in Atlanta at the age of fifteen. In his senior year at Morehouse, he decided to enter the ministry. While studying at Crozer Theological Seminary in Chester, Pennsylvania, King was introduced to and strongly influenced by the nonviolent teachings of Henry David Thoreau and Mohandas Gandhi. He received his Ph.D. from Boston University in 1955.

King founded the Southern Christian Leadership Conference, which gave him a platform from which to speak throughout the United States. As a civil rights leader, minister, and orator, King led protests throughout the South, advocating nonviolent civil disobedience to combat racism and bigotry. His writings include *Stride Toward Freedom*, an account of the boycott of the bus system in Birmingham, Alabama, which led to the Supreme Court ruling that segregation of public transportation was unconstitutional. In 1964, the year after his eloquent "I Have a Dream" speech, King was awarded the Nobel Peace Prize. While in Memphis, Tennessee, to show support for striking workers, Martin Luther King, Jr., was assassinated by James Earl Ray.

Literary TOOLS

SIMILE. A **simile** is a comparison using *like* or *as*. As you read, look for similes that King uses about the Emancipation Proclamation.

REPETITION AND STYLE. Repetition is a writer's conscious reuse, of a sound, word, phrase, sentence, or other element. **Style** is the manner in which something is said or written.

Organizer

As you read, make a list on the left of the repeated phrases that King uses in the speech. On the right, explain what ideas are reinforced by the repetition.

Repeated Phrases	Ideas
"one hundred years later"	The idea is reinforced that African Americans are still not free a hundred years after the end of slavery

Reader's Journal

What changes would you like to make in this country?

I Have a Dream

August 28, 1963
Lincoln Memorial, Washington, D.C.

Martin Luther King, Jr.

I'm happy to join with you today in what will go down in history as the greatest demonstration for freedom in the history of our nation.

Fivescore[1] years ago, a great American, in whose symbolic shadow we stand today, signed the Emancipation Proclamation.[2] This momentous decree came as a great beacon light of hope to millions of Negro slaves who had been <u>seared</u> in the flames of withering injustice. It came as a joyous daybreak to end the long night of their captivity.

But one hundred years later, the Negro still is not free; one hundred years later, the life of the Negro is still sadly crippled by the <u>manacles</u> of segregation[3] and the chains of discrimination; one hundred years later, the Negro lives on a lonely island of poverty in the midst of a vast ocean of material prosperity; one hundred years later, the Negro is still <u>languished</u> in the corners of American society and finds himself in exile in his own land. . . .

According to the speech, why was the African American still not free?

Nineteen sixty-three is not an end, but a beginning. And those who hope that the Negro needed to blow off steam and will now be content, will have a rude awakening if the nation returns to business as usual. There will be neither rest nor tranquility in America until the Negro is granted his citizenship rights. The whirlwinds of the revolt will continue to shake the foundations of our nation until the bright day of Justice <u>emerges</u>. . . .

There are those who are asking the devotees of Civil Rights, "When will you be satisfied?" We can never be satisfied as long as the Negro is the victim of the unspeakable horrors of police <u>brutality</u>; we can never be satisfied as long as our bodies, heavy with the fatigue of travel, cannot gain lodging in the motels of the highways and the hotels of the cities; we cannot be satisfied as long as the Negro's basic <u>mobility</u> is from a smaller ghetto[4] to a larger one; we can never be satisfied as long as our children are stripped of their selfhood and robbed of their dignity by signs stating "For Whites Only"; we cannot be satisfied as long as the Negro in Mississippi cannot vote and a

How did King answer the question, "When will you be satisfied?"

---

1. **Fivescore.** One hundred; one score equals twenty
2. **Emancipation Proclamation.** Document signed by Abraham Lincoln in 1863 that legally set free all people held as slaves in the Confederate states

3. **segregation.** Enforced separation of people based on group characteristics
4. **ghetto.** Section of a city in which many members of a minority group live, either by choice or because of economic or social pressure

---

words for everyday use

sear (sir) *vt.*, burn; wither. *The branding iron <u>seared</u> the steer's flesh.*
man • a • cle (man´ə kəl) *n.*, handcuff; shackle; restraint. *On the slave ships, the Africans were kept in <u>manacles</u>.*
lan • guish (lan´gwish) *vi.*, lose vigor or vitality. *Children who don't receive love and affection <u>languish</u>.*
e • merge (ē mʉrj´) *vi.*, become apparent or known; come forth into view. *The faint outlines of my surroundings began to <u>emerge</u> as my eyes adjusted to the dim lighting.*
bru • tal • i • ty (broo tal´ə te) *n.*, cruelty. *Protesters condemned the <u>brutality</u> of the police.*
mo • bil • i • ty (mō´ bil´ə tē) *n.*, ability to move from place to place. *A bicycle increases one's <u>mobility</u>.*

Negro in New York believes he has nothing for which to vote. No! No, we are not satisfied, and we will not be satisfied until "justice rolls down like waters and righteousness like a mighty stream."[5]

I am not unmindful that some of you have come here out of great trials and <u>tribulations</u>. Some of you have come fresh from narrow jail cells. Some of you have come from areas where your quest for freedom left you battered by the storms of persecution and staggered by the winds of police brutality. You have been the veterans of creative suffering. Continue to work with the faith that unearned suffering is <u>redemptive</u>. Go back to Mississippi. Go back to Alabama. Go back to South Carolina. Go back to Georgia. Go back to Louisiana. Go back to the slums and ghettos of our northern cities, knowing that somehow the situation can and will be changed. Let us not <u>wallow</u> in the valley of despair.

I say to you today, my friends, so even though we face the difficulties of today and tomorrow, I still have a dream. It is a dream deeply rooted in the American meaning of its <u>creed</u>, "We hold

5. **"justice rolls down . . . stream."** Biblical reference to Amos 5:24

Martin Luther King, Jr. at the March on Washington, August 28, 1963.

these truths to be self-evident, that all men are created equal."[6] I have a dream that one day on the red hills of Georgia, sons of former slaves and the sons of former slave owners will be able to sit down together at the table of brotherhood. I have a dream that one day even the state of Mississippi, a state sweltering with the heat of injustice, sweltering with the heat of oppression, will be transformed into an oasis of freedom and justice. I have a dream that my four little children will one day live in a nation where they will not be judged by the color of their skin, but the content of their character.

What was the dream King had for his four children?

I have a dream today!

I have a dream that one day down in Alabama—with its vicious racists, with its governor having his lips dripping with the words of interposition and nullification[7]—one day right there in Alabama, little black boys and black girls will be able to join hands with little white boys and white girls as sisters and brothers.

I have a dream today!

I have a dream that one day "every valley shall be <u>exalted</u> and every hill and mountain shall be made low. The rough places will be made plain and the crooked places will be made straight, and the glory of the Lord shall be revealed, and all flesh shall see it together."[8]

This is our hope. This is the faith that I go back to the South with. With this faith we shall be able to transform the jangling <u>discords</u> of our nation into a beautiful symphony of brotherhood. With this faith we will be able to work together, to pray together, to struggle together, to go to jail together, to stand up for freedom together, knowing that we will be free one day. And this will be the day. This will be the day when all of God's children will be able to sing with new meaning, "My country 'tis of thee, sweet land of liberty, of thee I sing. Land where my fathers died, land of the pilgrim's pride, from every mountainside, let freedom ring."[9] And if America is to be a great nation this must become true. . . .

So let freedom ring from the prodigious hilltops of New Hampshire; let freedom ring from the mighty mountains of New York; let freedom ring from the heightening Alleghenies of Pennsylvania; let freedom ring from the snow-capped Rockies of Colorado; let freedom ring from the curvaceous slopes of California. But not only that. Let freedom ring from Stone Mountain of Georgia; let freedom ring from Lookout Mountain of Tennessee; let freedom ring from every hill and molehill of Mississippi. From every mountainside, let freedom ring.

And when this happens and when we allow freedom to ring, when we let it ring from every village and every hamlet, from every state and every city, we will be able to speed up that day when all God's children, black men and white men, Jews and gentiles, Protestants and Catholics, will be able to join hands and sing in the words of the old Negro spiritual: "Free at last. Free at last. Thank God Almighty, we are free at last."

What did King believe would happen if freedom was allowed to ring?

■

---

6. **"We hold these truths to be self-evident, that all men are created equal."** First line of the second paragraph of the Declaration of Independence

7. **interposition and nullification.** Dr. King was talking about the Alabama governor's refusal to obey a federal requirement to allow African-American children to attend public schools. *Interposition* is the disputed theory that a state can reject a federal mandate. *Nullification* refers to the refusal of a state to enforce any federal law.

8. **"every valley shall be . . . see it together."** Biblical reference to Isaiah 40:4–9

9. **"My country 'tis of thee, . . . let freedom ring."** Lines from a well-known American anthem

---

words for everyday use

ex • alt (eg zôlt´) *vt.*, raise in status; elevate by praise. *The head of the relief organization <u>exalted</u> the group for its tireless efforts.*

dis • cord (dis´kôrd) *n.*, conflict. *<u>Discord</u> among siblings is a natural part of family life.*

Martin Luther King, Jr.

Gwendolyn Brooks

A man went forth with gifts.

He was a prose poem.
He was a tragic grace.
He was a warm music.

He tried to heal the vivid volcanoes.
His ashes are
    reading the world.

His Dream still wishes to anoint
    the barricades of faith and of control.

His word still burns the center of the sun,
    above the thousands and the
    hundred thousands.

The word was Justice. It was spoken.

So it shall be spoken.
So it shall be done.

ABOUT THE RELATED READING

Gwendolyn Brooks (1917–2000), poet, novelist, and children's writer, was born in Topeka, Kansas, but lived in the Chicago area for most of her life. Brooks received numerous awards, including a Guggenheim Fellowship, and in 1950 became the first African American to win a Pulitzer Prize. In 1967 Brooks attended the Fisk University Second Black Writers conference, which led to her involvement in the Black Arts movement. In 1985 she was appointed poetry consultant to the Library of Congress and was later selected by the National Endowment for the Humanities as the 1994 Jefferson Lecturer, the highest award in the humanities given by the federal government.

If Martin Luther King, Jr. were to give his speech today, how might it be altered?

Investigate, *Inquire,* and Imagine

Recall: GATHERING FACTS

1a. What does King call the demonstration?

2a. By what is "the life of the Negro" still crippled?

3a. In what kind of nation does King dream that his children will live?

Interpret: FINDING MEANING

1b. "Fivescore years ago, a great American, in whose symbolic shadow we stand today," the opening phrase of King's speech, is a reference to whom and to what? Why is this an appropriate way for King to begin his speech?

2b. What is the reason that "those who hope that the Negro . . . will now be content, will have a rude awakening"?

3b. What will happen "when we allow freedom to ring"?

Analyze: TAKING THINGS APART

4a. Outline the main points King makes in his speech.

Synthesize: BRINGING THINGS TOGETHER

4b. Of what kind of relationship between African-American and white human beings does King dream in his speech? Does that kind of relationship exist today? Explain.

Evaluate: MAKING JUDGMENTS

5a. Evaluate how well King's use of the biblical quote in the eleventh paragraph reinforces his message.

Extend: CONNECTING IDEAS

5b. In the Related Reading, "Martin Luther King, Jr.," what do you think the poet Gwendolyn Brooks meant when she wrote, "His Dream still wishes to anoint / the barricades of faith and of control"?

Understanding *Literature*

SIMILE. Review the definition for **simile** in the Handbook of Literary Terms. What two similes does King use about the Emancipation Proclamation? What two things are being compared in each simile? What do these things have in common? What emotional effect is created in the reader by these two similes?

REPETITION AND STYLE. Review the definitions for **repetition** and **style** in the Handbook of Literary Terms and the chart you made for Literary Tools on page 461. What ideas are reinforced by King's repetitions? What is the effect of these examples of repetition on the style of his speech?

Writer's Journal

1. Imagine that you are a reporter covering the "I Have a Dream" speech in front of the Lincoln Memorial on August 28, 1963. Write a **review** of the speech for your newspaper.
2. Imagine that you are one of the two hundred thousand people in the audience listening to Dr. Martin Luther King, Jr. Write a **journal entry** about the emotional impact the speech has on you.
3. King hoped that segregation would turn into "a beautiful symphony of brotherhood." Write a **letter** to King telling him when you have experienced or witnessed equality and brotherhood between blacks and whites.

Integrating the Language Arts

Speaking and Listening

SPEECH. Write a speech that persuades an audience of your peers to participate in your vision for a better world. For example, you might try to persuade classmates to adopt a child through a relief organization, send money to help refugees, feed homeless people, or help build a home for Habitat for Humanity. Provide background information about the problem you want solved. Also, be sure to give specific tips for how to make your vision come true. For example, if you are advocating the adoption of a poor child in a Third World country, you could tell your audience how to reach the relief organization by phone and how much money the adoption will cost. Before you begin, read the Language Arts Survey 4.15, "Giving a Speech."

Study and Research & Media Literacy

CENTER FOR NONVIOLENT SOCIAL CHANGE. Coretta Scott King, the widow of Dr. Martin Luther King, Jr., founded the Martin Luther King, Jr. Center for Nonviolent Social Change to carry on the nonviolent tradition of her husband. Research the educational and creative programs the Center has been involved with and the research it has conducted. If you want to do part of your research on the Internet, one site you will find useful is the Martin Luther King, Jr. Center for Nonviolent Social Change web page at http://www.nps.gov/malu/documents/kcpage.htm.

Collaborative Learning & Media Literacy

DR. MARTIN LUTHER KING DAY. With several classmates, plan a celebration of Dr. Martin Luther King, Jr. to take place on his birthday or another designated day. You might like to give out a humanitarian award to someone in your community who promotes improved race relations. Other activities could include poetry recitals, dancing, and readings from Dr. King's writings. You might find it useful to see how other communities celebrate Dr. Martin Luther King Day by consulting the Internet.

"Thinking Like a Mountain"

by Aldo Leopold

Literary TOOLS

ANECDOTE. An **anecdote** is a usually short narrative of an interesting, amusing, or biographical incident. As you read, note the anecdote Leopold tells about the wolf in this selection.

PERSONIFICATION. Personification is a figure of speech in which an idea, animal, or thing is described as if it were a person.

Graphic Organizer

Make a chart to list examples of personification in the selection. On the left, write the object of personification. On the right, write the human characteristic(s) given to that object. One example has been done for you.

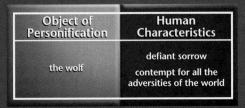

Object of Personification	Human Characteristics
the wolf	defiant sorrow / contempt for all the adversities of the world

Reader's Journal

In what ways have you been respectful toward nature?

Reader's resource

A Sand County Almanac, from which **"Thinking Like a Mountain"** is taken, is a collection of essays about nature and ecology. In its criticism of society's exploitation of nature, *A Sand County Almanac* bears a strong likeness to Thoreau's *Walden*.

In the selection, one of the omnipresent themes in *A Sand County Almanac* emerges—that nature was here first, long before human beings arrived on Earth; therefore, human beings have responsibility to nature and to its ecosystems. Behaving responsibly toward nature begins with the recognition that all things in the natural world are interrelated, a point made clear in Leopold's beautiful, provocative essay.

About the AUTHOR

Aldo Leopold (1887–1948) was born in Burlington, Iowa. After graduating from Yale Forestry School, he became supervisor of Carson National Forest in New Mexico. In 1933, he began teaching at the University of Wisconsin. Two years later, he helped found the Wilderness Society. Throughout his career as a conservationist, Leopold urged a responsible land ethic, confronting issues of economic and industrial expansion and wasteful land use. *A Sand County Almanac*, published the year after Leopold's death, has sold over a million copies.

THINKING LIKE A MOUNTAIN

Aldo Leopold

A deep chesty bawl echoes from rimrock[1] to rimrock, rolls down the mountain, and fades into the far blackness of the night. It is an outburst of wild <u>defiant</u> sorrow, and of contempt for all the <u>adversities</u> of the world.

Every living thing (and perhaps many a dead one as well) pays heed to that call. To the deer it is a reminder of the way of all flesh, to the pine a forecast of midnight scuffles and of blood upon the snow, to the coyote a promise of gleanings[2] to come, to the cowman a threat of red ink at the bank,[3] to the hunter a

What different meanings does the "deep chesty bawl" have?

challenge of fang against bullet. Yet behind these obvious and immediate hopes and fears there lies a deeper meaning, known only to the mountain itself. Only the mountain has lived long enough to listen <u>objectively</u> to the howl of a wolf.

Those unable to <u>decipher</u> the hidden meaning know nevertheless that it is there, for it is felt in all wolf country, and distinguishes that country from all other land. It tingles in the spine of all who hear wolves by night, or who scan their tracks by day. Even without sight or sound of wolf, it is <u>implicit</u> in a hundred small

---

1. **rimrock.** Rock forming on the edge of a cliff
2. **gleanings.** Leftovers; remains

3. **red ink at the bank.** Debt; accountants sometimes use red ink to record debits.

---

words for everyday use

de • fi • ant (dē fī´ənt) *adj.*, openly resisting. *Jeremiah was <u>defiant</u> about going to bed early.*

ad • ver • si • ty (ad vʉr´sə tē) *n.*, state of wretchedness and misfortune. *Gwen lost her job, but even in her <u>adversity</u> she maintained a positive outlook.*

ob • jec • tive • ly (əb jək´tiv lē) *adv.*, without bias or prejudice. *A judge is supposed to consider each case <u>objectively</u>.*

de • ci • pher (dē sī´fər) *vt.*, make out the meaning of. *Language experts are trying to <u>decipher</u> the ancient writing found in the tomb.*

im • plic • it (im plis´it) *adj.*, understood, though not plainly expressed; implied. *<u>Implicit</u> in the invitation to the party was the understanding that I would bring a gift.*

events: the midnight whinny of a pack horse, the rattle of rolling rocks, the bound of a fleeing deer, the way shadows lie under the spruces. Only the ineducable tyro[4] can fail to sense the presence or absence of wolves, or the fact that mountains have a secret opinion about them.

My own <u>conviction</u> on this score dates from the day I saw a wolf die. We were eating lunch on a high rimrock, at the foot of which a turbulent river elbowed its way. We saw what we thought was a doe <u>fording</u> the torrent, her breast awash in white water. When she climbed

What does Leopold personify, or speak of, as though it had human characteristics? What question is Leopold raising in the mind of the reader?

the bank toward us and shook out her tail, we realized our error: it was a wolf. A half-dozen others, evidently grown pups, sprang from the willows and all joined in a welcoming <u>mêlée</u> of wagging tails and playful maulings. What was <u>literally</u> a pile of wolves writhed and tumbled in the center of an open flat at the foot of our rimrock.

In those days we had never heard of passing up a chance to kill a wolf. In a second we were pumping lead into the pack, but with more excitement than accuracy: how to aim a steep downhill shot is always confusing. When our rifles were empty, the old wolf was down, and a

Why did they shoot the wolves?

---

4. **tyro.** Beginner; novice

Mount Moran, Autumn, Grand Teton National Park, Wyoming, 1948. Ansel Adams. Private Collection.

words for everyday use

con • vic • tion (kən vik´shən) n., strong belief. *It is my <u>conviction</u> that these wetlands should be protected.*
ford (fôrd) vt., cross a stream or river by wading. *The pioneers <u>forded</u> the river in summer, when the water level was lower.*
mê • lée (mā´ lā´) n., confused conflict or mixture. *The <u>mêlée</u> of concert-goers jostled for tickets.*
lit • er • al • ly (lit´ər əl ē) adv., actually; in fact. *There are recorded cases of people dying from shock, or being <u>literally</u> "scared to death."*

pup was dragging a leg into impassable slide-rocks.

We reached the old wolf in time to watch a fierce green fire dying in her eyes. I realized then, and have known ever since, that there was something new to me in those eyes—something known only to her and to the mountain. I was young then, and full of trigger-itch; I thought that because fewer wolves meant more deer, that no wolves would mean hunters' paradise. But after seeing the green fire die, I sensed that neither the wolf nor the mountain agreed with such a view.

What idea did the narrator have about killing off all wolves? How did watching the wolf die change this view?

Since then I have lived to see state after state <u>extirpate</u> its wolves. I have watched the face of many a newly wolfless mountain, and seen the south-facing slopes wrinkle with a maze of new deer trails. I have seen every edible bush and seedling browsed, first to anaemic desuetude,[5] and then to death. I have seen every edible tree <u>defoliated</u> to the height of a saddlehorn.[6] Such a mountain looks as if someone had given God a new pruning shears, and forbidden Him all

art note

5. **anaemic desuetude.** Lifeless disuse
6. **saddlehorn.** Handle at the front of a Western-style saddle

other exercise. In the end the starved bones of the hoped-for deer herd, dead of its own too-much, bleach with the bones of the dead sage, or <u>molder</u> under the high-lined junipers.

I now suspect that just as a deer herd lives in mortal fear of its wolves, so does a mountain live in mortal fear of its deer. And perhaps with better cause, for while a buck pulled down by wolves can be replaced in two or three years, a range pulled down by too many deer may fail of replacement in as many decades.

Why does a mountain fear deer?

So also with cows. The cowman who cleans his range of wolves does not realize that he is taking over the wolf's job of trimming the herd to fit the range. He has not learned to think like a mountain. Hence we have dustbowls,[7] and rivers washing the future into the sea.

We all strive for safety, prosperity, comfort, long life, and dullness. The deer strives with his supple legs, the cowman with trap and poison, the statesman with pen, the most of us with machines, votes, and dollars, but it all comes to the same thing: peace in our time. A measure of success in this is all well enough, and perhaps is a <u>requisite</u> to objective thinking, but too much safety seems to yield only danger in the long run. Perhaps this is behind Thoreau's[8] dictum: In wildness is the salvation of the world. Perhaps this is the hidden meaning in the howl of the wolf, long known among mountains, but seldom perceived among men. ∎

What do mountains know that people sometimes do not? What is the hidden meaning in the howl of the wolf?

7. **dustbowls.** Dry, dusty lands from which topsoil has been eroded by wind
8. **Thoreau's.** Henry David Thoreau (1817–1862) was a well-known American naturalist and writer.

words for everyday use

ex • tir • pate (ek´stər pāt´) *vt.*, destroy or remove completely. *White hunters <u>extirpated</u> buffalo from most of North America.*

de • fo • li • ate (dē fō´lē āt´ ed) *vt.*, strip of leaves. *The harmful chemicals can <u>defoliate</u> acres of trees.*

mold • er (mōl´dər) *vi.*, crumble into dust. *Mummified human remains do not <u>molder</u>.*

req • ui • site (rek´wə zit) *n.*, necessity. *It is a <u>requisite</u> that students study math during their freshman and sophomore years.*

What does it mean to think like a mountain?

Investigate, *Inquire,* and Imagine

Recall: GATHERING FACTS

1a. What echoes "from rimrock to rimrock"?

2a. What kind of "opinion" do mountains have about wolves?

3a. What has the narrator seen "state after state" do to wolves?

➤ **Interpret:** FINDING MEANING

1b. To what animal does the "outburst of wild defiant sorrow" belong?

2b. What kind of "small events" distinguish wolf country "from all other land"?

3b. What are the consequences of destroying wolves?

Analyze: TAKING THINGS APART

4a. What kind of relationship between animals and nature is described in the essay? How does that relationship change when humans attempt to tame or destroy the "wildness" of nature?

➤ **Synthesize:** BRINGING THINGS TOGETHER

4b. Does the narrator remain "full of trigger itch"? Explain.

Evaluate: MAKING JUDGMENTS

5a. Are Leopold's attitudes toward preserving a balanced ecosystem still important today?

➤ **Extend:** CONNECTING IDEAS

5b. Today some farmers are growing biologically engineered crops. The pollen from these crops blends with nonbiologically engineered crops. What do you think Aldo Leopold's attitude would be toward this contemporary practice?

Understanding *Literature*

ANECDOTE. Review the definition for **anecdote** in the Handbook of Literary Terms. What anecdote does Leopold tell in the essay? What is Leopold's purpose in telling this anecdote? What lesson did the narrator learn from the experience related in the anecdote?

PERSONIFICATION. Review the definition for **personification** in the Handbook of Literary Terms and the chart you made for Literary Tools on page 468. What human characteristics does the mountain possess? What human characteristics does the wolf possess? How does the use of personification help Leopold to achieve his aim?

Writer's Journal

1. Imagine you are the narrator. Write a **letter to the editor** of an environmental magazine explaining how the death of the wolf changed your convictions about preserving the wolf in mountain life.

2. Write a **contract** between the wolf and the mountain that seeks to preserve them both. What does the wolf promise to do for the mountain? What does the mountain promise to do for the wolf?

3. Write the mountain's **diatribe** against humankind for all the injuries that humans have committed against the mountain. A diatribe is a bitter, abusive criticism or denunciation.

Integrating the Language Arts

Speaking and Listening

TELLING ANECDOTES. With several other students, take turns telling an anecdote about an experience you had in nature. Perhaps you went camping, took a hike, looked at birds, witnessed humankind's disrespect for nature, or saw the interdependence of certain species of animals. Your autobiographical anecdote can be interesting, amusing, or informative. Prepare a nature newsletter made up of the anecdotes from each of the groups in your class.

Study and Research & Media Literacy

WOLVES. Worldwide, the wolf is listed by the International Union for the Conservation of Nature and Natural Resources as a "threatened" species. Estimates from 1995 suggest that there are only 9,200 wolves in the United States, mainly in Alaska and Minnesota. Wolves are being "recovered," or reintroduced, in states such as Montana and Idaho. Research an aspect of wolves such as recovery programs, the social behavior of wolves, or the animals they prey on. Then prepare an oral presentation for the class. Make visual aids to accompany your presentation. If you are interested in doing part of your research on the Internet, you will find it useful to consult the International Wolf Center at http://www.wolf.org.

Collaborative Learning

COMMUNITY PROJECT. With several other students, research recycling in your community. Start by brainstorming a list of questions you want answered about recycling, such as how it is done, what materials can be recycled, what benefits recycling has for the environment, who participates in recycling, and so on. Find out what recycling centers are nearby. You might want to plan a field trip to a local recycling center to get some of your questions answered. Ask your school librarian for suggestions for additional resources. When all the groups have finished their research, hold a class discussion about how your class can become involved in a school or community recycling effort.

Literary TOOLS

AIM AND THESIS. A writer's **aim** is his or her purpose, or goal. A **thesis** is a main idea that is supported in a work of non-fictional prose. As you read, determine Carson's principal aims in writing this selection. Then paraphrase her thesis.

COHERENCE. Coherence is the logical arrangement and progression of ideas in a piece of writing. Writers achieve coherence by presenting their ideas in a logical sequence and by using transitions to show how their ideas are connected to one another.

Organizer

As you read, make a sequence chart to list the development of Carson's ideas.

| The history of the earth is the interaction between living things and their environment. | → | Contamination of air, Earth, rivers, and sea occurs with the use of lethal materials. |

Reader's JOURNAL

If you were given the choice of knowing or not knowing all the facts about environmental pollution and its effects on all forms of life, what choice would you make? Why?

"The Obligation to Endure"
from
Silent Spring
by Rachel Carson

Reader's resource

The danger of environmental pollution, particularly the threat to all life brought about by the widespread use of insecticides, is the theme of this selection. In her careful exploration of the theme, Carson asks why we accept such a dangerous threat to the natural world that supports all life, including human life. She also asks how we expect to endure, to survive as a species, if we do not know the facts about the effects of insecticides. Carson is well known for her precise observations and clear writing style, both of which are evident in this selection from *Silent Spring*.

About the AUTHOR

Rachel Carson (1907–1964) was born in Springdale, Pennsylvania, where, as a child, she developed a deep interest in wildlife. After receiving her M.A. from Johns Hopkins University, Carson did postgraduate work at the Woods Hole Marine Biological Laboratory in Massachusetts. In her long career as a biologist, Carson worked for the U.S. Bureau of Fisheries and the U.S. Fish and Wildlife Service. She won the National Book Award for *The Sea Around Us*, which was published in 1951. Carson's *Silent Spring* (1962), from which this selection is taken, awakened the world to the dangers of environmental pollution. Her other works include *Under the Sea Wind* (1941) and *The Edge of the Sea* (1954).

Environmental Study [Detail], 1999. Julie Delton.

Rachel Carson

The Obligation to Endure

The history of life on earth has been a history of <u>interaction</u> between living things and their surroundings. To a large extent, the physical form and the habits of the earth's vegetation and its animal life have been molded by the environment. Considering the whole span of earthly time, the opposite effect, in which life actually modifies its surroundings, has been relatively slight. Only within the moment of time represented by the present century has one <u>species</u>—man—acquired significant power to alter the nature of his world.

During the past quarter century this power has not only increased to one of disturbing <u>magnitude</u> but it has changed in character. The most alarming of all man's assaults upon the environment is the contamination of air, earth, rivers, and sea with dangerous and even lethal materials. This pollution is for the most part <u>irrecoverable</u>; the chain of evil it initiates not only in the world that must support life but in living tissues is for the most part irreversible. In this now universal contamination of the environment, chemicals are the sinister and little-recognized partners of radiation in changing the very nature of the world—the very nature of its life. Strontium 90, released through nuclear explosions into the air, comes to earth in rain or drifts down as fallout, lodges in soil, enters into the grass or corn or wheat grown there, and in time takes up its abode in the bones of a human being, there to remain until his death. Similarly, chemicals sprayed on croplands or forests or gardens lie long in soil, entering into living organisms, passing from one to another in a chain of poisoning and death. Or they pass mysteriously by underground streams until they emerge and, through the alchemy[1] of air and sunlight, combine into new forms that kill vegetation, sicken cattle, and work unknown harm on those who drink from once pure wells.

> What is the most alarming change humans have made in the environment? Why is this so disturbing?

> Why do poisons have such far-reaching effects?

As Albert Schweitzer[2] has said, "Man can hardly even recognize the devils of his own creation."

It took hundreds of millions of years to produce the life that now inhabits the earth—eons of time in which that developing and evolving and diversifying life reached a state of adjustment and balance with its surroundings. The environment, <u>rigorously</u> shaping and directing the life it supported, contained elements that were hostile as well as supporting. Certain rocks gave out dangerous radiation; even within the light of the sun, from which all life draws its energy, there were short-wave radiations with power to injure. Given time—time not in years but in millennia—life adjusts, and a balance has been reached. For time is the essential ingredient; but in the modern world there is no time.

> How do current changes differ from natural changes of past eons?

The rapidity of change and the speed with which new situations are created follow the <u>impetuous</u> and heedless pace of man rather than the deliberate pace of nature. Radiation is no longer merely the background radiation of rocks, the bombardment of cosmic rays, the ultraviolet of the sun that have existed before there was any life on earth; radiation is now the unnatural creation of man's tampering with the atom. The chemicals to which life is asked to make its adjustment are no longer merely the calcium and silica and copper and all the rest of the minerals washed out of the rocks and carried in rivers to the sea; they are the synthetic creations of man's inventive mind, brewed in his laboratories, and having no counterparts in nature.

---

1. **alchemy.** Scientific method of transmutation, changing a thing into something else

2. **Albert Schweitzer.** (1875–1965) Medical missionary to Africa and noted humanitarian

---

words for everyday use

spe • cies (spē´ shēz) *n.,* population of highly similar organisms that interbreed only among themselves. *Previously unknown <u>species</u> of plant life are still being discovered in the Amazon.*

mag • ni • tude (mag´ nə tood´) *n.,* greatness of importance or influence. *We didn't realize the <u>magnitude</u> of the gang problem until the newspaper article was printed.*

ir • re • cov • er • a • ble (ir´ri kuv´ ər ə bəl) *adj.,* cannot be corrected or remedied. *Financial loss to the district due to crime is considered <u>irrecoverable</u>.*

im • pet • u • ous (im pech´oo əs) *adj.,* moving with great force or violence. *Jake's <u>impetuous</u> temperament got him into a lot of trouble.*

To adjust to these chemicals would require time on the scale that is nature's; it would require not merely the years of a man's life but the life of generations. And even this, were it by some miracle possible, would be futile, for the new chemicals come from our laboratories in an endless stream; almost five hundred annually find their way into actual use in the United States alone. The figure is staggering and its <u>implications</u> are not easily grasped—500 new chemicals to which the bodies of men and animals are required somehow to adapt each year, chemicals totally outside the limits of biologic experience.

Among them are many that are used in man's war against nature. Since the mid-1940's over 200 basic chemicals have been created for use in killing insects, weeds, rodents, and other organisms described in the modern vernacular[3] as "pests"; and they are sold under several thousand different brand names.

These sprays, dusts, and aerosols are now applied almost universally to farms, gardens, forests, and homes—nonselective chemicals[4] that have the power to kill every insect, the "good" and the "bad," to still the song of birds and the leaping of fish in the streams, to coat the leaves with a deadly film, and to linger on in soil—all this though the intended target may be only a few weeds or insects. Can anyone believe it is possible to lay down such a <u>barrage</u> of poisons on the surface of the earth without making it unfit for all life? They should not be called "insecticides," but "biocides."

What is a major problem with most insecticides?

The whole process of spraying seems caught up in an endless spiral. Since DDT was released for civilian use, a process of <u>escalation</u> has been going on in which ever more toxic materials must be found. This has happened because insects, in a triumphant <u>vindication</u> of Darwin's principle of the survival of the fittest, have evolved super races immune to the particular insecticide used, hence a deadlier one has always to be developed—and then a deadlier one than that. It has happened also because, for reasons to be described later, destructive insects often undergo a "flareback," or <u>resurgence</u>, after spraying, in numbers greater than before. Thus the chemical war is never won, and all life is caught in its violent crossfire.

Why is it necessary to create more and more deadly chemicals?

Along with the possibility of the extinction of mankind by nuclear war, the central problem of our age has therefore become the contamination of man's total environment with such substances of incredible potential for harm—substances that accumulate in the tissues of plants and animals and even penetrate the germ cells to shatter or alter the very material of <u>heredity</u> upon which the shape of the future depends.

Besides the possibility of nuclear war, what is the central problem of our age?

Some would-be architects of our future look toward a time when it will be possible to alter the human germ plasm by design. But we may easily be doing so now by <u>inadvertence</u>, for many chemicals, like radiation, bring about gene mutations. It is ironic to think that man might determine his own future by something

---

3. **vernacular.** Common, everyday language

4. **nonselective chemicals.** Substances that contaminate everything they touch

words for everyday use

im • pli • ca • tion (im′pli kā′shən) *n.*, something implied; suggestion. *The implication of the election results is that few people were concerned about the sales tax.*

bar • rage (bə räzh′) *n.*, intense attack. *The sudden barrage of hail dented car hoods.*

es • ca • la • tion (es′kə lā shən) *n.*, step-by-step growth; rapid increase. *The principal is concerned about the recent escalation in vandalism.*

vin • di • ca • tion (vin′də kā′shən) *n.*, justification. *Winning the gold medal was the perfect vindication for the skier, who had been defeated the previous year.*

re • sur • gence (ri sʉrj′əns) *n.*, tendency to rise again. *A resurgence of interest in the culture of the 1970s is evidenced by theme parties and retrospective TV shows.*

in • ad • vert • ence (in′ad vʉrt′ns) *n.*, mistake; oversight. *We found the secluded country inn through inadvertence.*

so seemingly trivial as the choice of an insect spray.

All this has been risked—for what? Future historians may well be amazed by our distorted sense of proportion. How could intelligent beings seek to control a few unwanted species by a method that contaminated the entire environment and brought the threat of disease and death even to their own kind? Yet this is precisely what we have done. We have done it, moreover, for reasons that collapse the moment we examine them. We are told that the enormous and expanding use of pesticides is necessary to maintain farm production. Yet is our real problem not one of *overproduction?* Our farms, despite measures to remove acreages[5] from production and to pay farmers *not* to produce, have yielded such a staggering excess of crops that the American taxpayer in 1962 is paying out more than one billion dollars a year as the total carrying cost of the surplus-food storage program. And is the situation helped when one branch of the Agriculture Department tries to reduce production while another states, as it did in 1958, "It is believed generally that reduction of crop acreages under provisions of the Soil Bank will <u>stimulate</u> interest in use of chemicals to obtain maximum production on the land retained in crops."

All this is not to say there is no insect problem and no need of control. I am saying, rather, that control must be geared to realities, not to mythical situations, and that the methods employed must be such that they do not destroy us along with the insects.

---

5. **acreages.** Large amounts, in acres, of land

The problem whose attempted solution has brought such a train of disaster in its wake is an <u>accompaniment</u> of our modern way of life. Long before the age of man, insects inhabited the earth—a group of extraordinarily varied and adaptable beings. Over the course of time since man's <u>advent</u>, a small percentage of the more than half a million species of insects have come into conflict with human welfare in two principal ways: as competitors for the food supply and as carriers of human disease.

> What two conflicts are there between humans and insects?

Environmental Study, 1999. Julie Delton.

Disease-carrying insects become important where human beings are crowded together, especially under conditions where sanitation is poor, as in time of natural disaster or war or in situations of extreme poverty and deprivation. Then control of some sort becomes necessary. It is a sobering fact, however, as we shall presently see, that the method of massive chemical control has had only limited success, and also threatens to worsen the very conditions it is intended to curb.

Under primitive agricultural conditions the farmer had few insect problems. These arose with the intensification of agriculture—the devotion of immense acreages to a single crop. Such a system set the stage for explosive increases in specific insect populations. Single-crop farming does not take advantage of the principles by which nature works; it is agriculture as an engineer might conceive it to be. Nature has introduced great variety into the landscape, but man has displayed a passion for simplifying it. Thus he undoes the built-in checks and balances[6] by which nature holds the species within bounds. One important natural check is a limit on the amount of suitable habitat for each species. Obviously then, an insect that lives on wheat can build up its population to much higher levels on a farm devoted to wheat than on one in which wheat is intermingled

How did new farming techniques create greater insect problems?

with other crops to which the insect is not adapted.

The same thing happens in other situations. A generation or more ago, the towns of large areas of the United States lined their streets with the noble elm tree. Now the beauty they hopefully created is threatened with complete destruction as disease sweeps through the elms, carried by a beetle that would have only limited chance to build up large populations and to spread from tree to tree if the elms were only occasional trees in a richly diversified planting.

Another factor in the modern insect problem is one that must be viewed against a background of geologic[7] and human history: the spreading of thousands of different kinds of organisms from their native homes to invade new territories. This worldwide migration has been studied and graphically described by the British ecologist Charles Elton in his recent[8] book *The Ecology of Invasions.* During the Cretaceous Period,[9] some hundred million years ago, flooding seas cut many land bridges between continents and living things found themselves confined in what Elton calls "colossal separate nature reserves." There, isolated from others of their kind, they developed many new species. When some of the land masses were joined again, about 15 million years ago, these species began to move out into new territories—a movement that is not only still in progress but is now receiving considerable assistance from man.

---

6. **checks and balances.** Controls and methods of balancing one factor against another
7. **geologic.** Related to the earth, as rocks and minerals
8. **recent.** Carson means recent relative to 1962, the year

Silent Spring was published.
9. **Cretaceous Period.** Geologic period when, most scientists believe, dinosaurs became extinct and small mammals and plants began to develop on Earth

---

words for everyday use

in • ten • si • fi • ca • tion (in ten´ si fi kā´shən) *n.,* increase in magnitude or force. *Marinating the steak will bring about an intensification of flavor.*

con • ceive (kən sēv´) *vt.,* imagine; think. *I can't conceive what caused the package's delay.*

a • dapt (ə dapt´) *vi.,* adjust to fit new circumstances. *The puppy had difficulty adapting to life in the kennel.*

di • ver • si • fied (də vʉr´sə fīd´) *adj.,* varied. *The financial planner talked about the advantages of having a diversified stock portfolio.*

graph • i • cal • ly (graf´ik ə lē) *adv.,* vividly. *As the doctor graphically described the procedure, one of the medical students fainted.*

i • so • lat • ed (ī´sə lāt ed) *adj.,* set apart from others. *The isolated villa was five kilometers away from the nearest village.*

The importation of plants is the primary agent in the modern spread of species, for animals have almost invariably gone along with the plants, quarantine being a comparatively recent and not completely effective <u>innovation</u>. The United States Office of Plant Introduction alone has introduced almost 200,000 species and varieties of plants from all over the world. Nearly half of the 180 or so major insect enemies of plants in the United States are accidental imports from abroad, and most of them have come as hitchhikers on plants.

In new territory, out of reach of the restraining hand of the natural enemies that kept down its numbers in its native land, an invading plant or animal is able to become enormously abundant. Thus it is no accident that our most troublesome insects are introduced species.

> Why can a plant or animal introduced to a new area become troublesome?

These invasions, both the naturally occurring and those dependent on human assistance, are likely to continue indefinitely. Quarantine and massive chemical campaigns are only extremely expensive ways of buying time. We are faced, according to Dr. Elton, "with a life-and-death need not just to find new technological means of <u>suppressing</u> this plant or that animal"; instead we need the basic knowledge of animal populations and their relations to their surroundings that will "promote an even balance and damp down the explosive power of outbreaks and new invasions."

Much of the necessary knowledge is now available but we do not use it. We train ecologists in our universities and even employ them in our governmental agencies but we seldom take their advice. We allow the chemical death rain to fall as though there were no alternative, whereas in fact there are many, and our <u>ingenuity</u> could soon discover many more if given opportunity.

Have we fallen into a mesmerized state[10] that makes us accept as <u>inevitable</u> that which is inferior or <u>detrimental</u>, as though having lost the will or the vision to demand that which is good? Such thinking, in the words of the ecologist Paul Shepard, "idealizes life with only its head out of water, inches above the limits of toleration of the corruption of its own environment. . . . Why should we tolerate a diet of weak poisons, a home in <u>insipid</u> surroundings, a circle of acquaintances who are not quite our enemies, the noise of motors with just enough relief to prevent insanity? Who would want to live in a world which is just not quite fatal?"

Yet such a world is pressed upon us. The crusade to create a chemically sterile, insect-free world seems to have engendered[11] a fanatic <u>zeal</u> on the part of many specialists and most of the so-called control agencies. On every hand there is evidence that those engaged in spraying operations exercise a ruthless power. "The regulatory entomologists . . . function as prosecutor, judge and jury,[12] tax assessor and collector and sheriff to enforce their own orders," said Connecticut entomologist Neely Turner. The

---

10. **mesmerized state.** Hypnotized condition
11. **engendered.** Created

12. **regulatory entomologists . . . jury.** Turner means that the entomologists, experts on insects, who work in government agencies have nobody criticizing the laws they create relating to insects.

---

words for everyday use

in • no • va • tion (in´ə vā´shən) *n.*, something newly introduced. *Students had a hard time getting used to block scheduling, the latest <u>innovation</u> at school.*
sup • press (sə pres´) *vt.*, inhibit; put down by force. *I tried to <u>suppress</u> the urge to laugh in the quiet auditorium.*
in • ge • nu • i • ty (in´jə nōō´ə tē) *n.*, cleverness; originality. *Edison's <u>ingenuity</u> was widely discussed when it became public that he had invented the light bulb.*
in • ev • i • ta • ble (in ev´i tə bəl) *adj.*, that cannot be avoided or evaded. *Because the city is on a major fault line, it is <u>inevitable</u> that it will be hit by an earthquake.*
de • tri • men • tal (de´trə ment´l) *adj.*, harmful. *Smoking is <u>detrimental</u> to one's health.*
in • sip • id (in sip´id) *adj.*, tasteless; dull. *I turned off the <u>insipid</u> TV program and read a good book instead.*
zeal (zēl) *n.*, intense enthusiasm. *The new volunteers demonstrated <u>zeal</u> about serving in the Peace Corps.*

most flagrant[13] abuses go unchecked in both state and federal agencies.

It is not my <u>contention</u> that chemical insecticides must never be used. I do contend that we have put poisonous and biologically potent chemicals indiscriminately into the hands of persons largely or wholly ignorant of their potentials for harm. We have subjected enormous numbers of people to contact with these poisons, without their consent and often without their knowledge. If the Bill of Rights contains no guarantee that a citizen shall be secure against <u>lethal</u> poisons distributed either by private individuals or by public officials, it is surely only because our forefathers, despite their considerable wisdom and <u>foresight</u>, could conceive of no such problem.

I contend, furthermore, that we have allowed these chemicals to be used with little or no advance investigation of their effect on soil, water, wildlife, and man himself. Future generations are unlikely to condone our lack of <u>prudent</u> concern for the <u>integrity</u> of the natural world that supports all life.

There is still very limited awareness of the nature of the threat. This is an era of specialists, each of whom

Why is awareness of this threat so limited?

sees his own problem and is unaware of or intolerant of the larger frame into which it fits. It is also an era dominated by industry, in which the right to make a dollar at whatever cost is seldom challenged. When the public protests, confronted with some obvious evidence of damaging results of pesticide applications, it is fed little tranquilizing pills of half truth. We urgently need an end to these false assurances, to the sugar coating of <u>unpalatable</u> facts. It is the public that is being asked to assume the risks that the insect controllers calculate. The public must decide whether it wishes to continue on the present road, and it can do so only when in full possession of the facts. In the words of Jean Rostand, "The obligation to endure gives us the right to know." ∎

---

13. **flagrant.** Conspicuously offensive

---

words for everyday use

con • ten • tion (kən ten´shən) *n.*, argument. *It is my <u>contention</u> that the Student Council should raise money to send to the refugees.*
le • thal (lē´thəl) *adj.*, capable of causing death. *Mixing medications can sometimes have <u>lethal</u> results.*
fore • sight (fôr´sīt´) *n.*, thoughtful regard for the future. *As no one had the <u>foresight</u> to bring an umbrella, we were drenched by the thunderstorm.*
pru • dent (prōōd´ʹnt) *adj.*, cautious or discreet. *The <u>prudent</u> swimmer wore a life vest.*
in • teg • ri • ty (in teg´rə tē) *n.*, state or condition of wholeness. *The <u>integrity</u> of the sixteenth-century antiques astonished the collector.*
un • pal • at • a • ble (un pal´ə tə bəl) *adj.*, unpleasant. *Too many people turn away from <u>unpalatable</u> scenes of famine in the media.*

Respond *to the* SELECTION

Imagine you are the narrator of the selection, committed to presenting your writing to a group of grade school children. What would you tell them your main message is?

Investigate, *Inquire,* and

Recall: GATHERING FACTS

1a. What "significant power" does humankind have in this century?

2a. What two elements are "changing the very nature of the world"?

3a. What have human beings been trying to destroy since the 1940s with "over 200 basic chemicals"? What does the narrator say that we "urgently need"?

Interpret: FINDING MEANING

1b. What facts emphasize the "disturbing magnitude" of this power?

2b. What evidence supports the prediction that the modern world has "no time" to balance the effects of environmental pollution?

3b. What facts support the statement that a more appropriate name for "insecticides" is "biocides"? What is probably the reason that the public is given "false assurances"?

Analyze: TAKING THINGS APART

4a. What evidence supports the argument that, in our attempt "to control a few unwanted species," we are bringing destruction to ourselves?

Synthesize: BRINGING THINGS TOGETHER

4b. What relationship between preservation and knowledge is described in the selection?

Evaluate: MAKING JUDGMENTS

5a. How effectively can the argument about insecticides be applied to other instances of environmental abuse?

Extend: CONNECTING IDEAS

5b. In what way could Aldo Leopold's "Thinking Like a Mountain" on page 469 provide an argument for Rachel Carson's opening paragraphs from the *Silent Spring* selection?

Understanding *Literature*

AIM AND THESIS. Review the definitions for **aim** and **thesis** in the Handbook of Literary Terms. People may write with the following aims: to inform (expository/informational writing); to entertain, enrich, enlighten, and /or use an artistic medium, such as fiction or poetry, to share a perspective (imaginative writing); to make a point by sharing a story about an event (narrative writing); to reflect (personal/expressive writing); to persuade readers or listeners to respond in some way, such as to agree with a position, change a view on an issue, reach an agreement, or perform an action (persuasive/argumentative writing). What are Carson's aims in writing this selection? What is the thesis of the selection?

COHERENCE. Review the definition for **coherence** in the Handbook of Literary Terms and the chart you created for Literary Tools on page 474. Carson opens with a perspective of life on Earth, establishing a historical context for her ideas and arguments. How is the element of time used to unify and advance the ideas in the selection?

Writer's Journal

1. Imagine that you helped found an organization called The Rachel Carson Environmentalists. Write the **credo** of your organization.

2. Write a **letter** to your senator or state representative explaining why it is important to protect the environment. Use at least one quotation from Rachel Carson.

3. Imagine that you are Rachel Carson, who states, "It is not my contention that chemical insecticides must never be used." Write a **paragraph** explaining when you would use insecticides.

Integrating the Language Arts

Study and Research & Collaborative Learning

THE HISTORY OF DDT. One insecticide that Rachel Carson mentions in the selection from *Silent Spring* is DDT. Working with a group of students, outline what you want to find out about DDT. To get started, you might find it useful to write the words *who, what, where, when, why,* and *how* down the left-hand side of a piece of paper. Next to each word, write questions about the topic that you want to answer or explain. Then divide the questions among your group members and do your research. Finally, make an oral presentation to the class. You might want to use visual aids to make your presentation more interesting.

Media Literacy & Study and Research

WEB PAGE. Design a web page for an Internet site devoted to Rachel Carson. Begin by writing a complete biography. Then create a bibliography of the works she published and a list of books about her. Finally, create a list of other links available on the Internet. If you would like to do part of your research on the Internet, you will find it useful to consult the Pennsylvania Department of Environmental Protection site at http://www.dep.state.pa.us/dep/Rachel_Carson/Rachel_Carson.htm.

Media Literacy

RACHEL CARSON HOMESTEAD. Visit The Rachel Carson Homestead Internet site at http://www.rachelcarson.org. Imagine that you are writing a tour guide for the state of Pennsylvania and want to include the homestead. With a partner, write a tour guide entry about what you can see and do at the Rachel Carson Homestead.

Literary TOOLS

NARRATOR. A **narrator** is one who tells a story. Writers achieve a wide variety of ends by varying the characteristics of the narrator chosen for a particular work. The narrator in this selection is the person being interviewed. As you read, note how the narrator describes himself.

SATIRE. Satire is humorous writing or speech intended to point out errors, falsehoods, foibles, or failings.

Graphic Organizer

As you read, make a chart. On the left, list the satirical elements of the selection. On the right, indicate what is being satirized.

Satire	What is being satirized
Then you spell it with an *I*?	The narrator is satirizing the nature of interviews.

Reader's Journal

Have you ever wanted to make fun of a foolish custom or idea? How could you use humor to expose its foolishness?

"An Encounter with an Interviewer"

by Mark Twain

Reader's resource

Impostors, frauds, and masters of masquerade crowd the cast of characters in Twain's work. Such characters are central to Twain's humor. In fact, Twain once told an audience that it was a humorist's job to expose all shams. In this selection, the narrator assumes a personality other than his own in order to expose the interviewer's foolishness.

In 1894, the same year that he published *The Tragedy of Pudd'nhead Wilson*, the last of his great Mississippi novels, Mark Twain was bankrupt. To pay off his debts, Twain made a worldwide lecture tour. While lecturing, he was interviewed by many journalists. This experience gave him plenty of material to write his satire **"An Encounter with an Interviewer."**

About the AUTHOR

Samuel Langhorne Clemens (1835–1910) was born in Florida, Missouri. In his late twenties, Clemens adopted his pen name, Mark Twain. The phrase *mark twain*, which means "two fathoms deep," was called from Mississippi riverboats when making depth soundings. When Twain was twelve years old, his father died. Twain was apprenticed to a printer, and soon began writing for his brother's newspaper. Then, from 1857 to 1861, he realized his childhood dream of piloting steamboats on the Mississippi River. At the age of thirty-five, Twain began writing about his early experiences of life on the great river. *The Adventures of Tom Sawyer,* published in 1876, was followed by *Life on the Mississippi* and *Adventures of Huckleberry Finn*. These are three books for which Twain will always be remembered. In the 1890s, after Twain suffered a series of financial disasters and the death of his wife and two daughters, the vitality and sly humor of his early work gave way to a dark pessimism. His bitterest works, including *The Mysterious Stranger,* date from this period. Among his numerous other titles are *The Prince and the Pauper, The Tragedy of Pudd'nhead Wilson,* and *A Connecticut Yankee in King Arthur's Court. The Writings of Mark Twain,* published posthumously in 1929, contains thirty-seven volumes.

Mark Twain, 1885.
Joseph Ferdinand Keppler.
Library of Congress.

An Encounter with an Interviewer

Mark Twain

The nervous dapper, "peart"[1] young man took the chair I offered him, and said he was connected with the "Daily Thunderstorm" and added,—

"Hoping it's no harm, I've come to interview you."

"Come to what?"

"*Interview* you."

"Ah! I see. Yes—yes. Um! Yes—yes. I see."

I was not feeling bright that morning. Indeed, my powers seemed a bit under a cloud. However, I went to the bookcase, and when I had been looking six or seven minutes, I found I was obliged to <u>refer</u> to the young man. I said,—

"How do you spell it?"

"Spell what?"

"Interview."

"Oh my goodness! what do you want to spell it for?"

"I don't want to spell it; I want to see what it means."

"Well, this is astonishing, I must say. I can tell you what it means, if you—if you—"

"Oh, all right! That will answer, and much obliged to you, too."

"In, *in,* ter, *ter;* inter—"

"Then you spell it with an *I?*"

Why does the narrator search the bookcase? Why does he turn to the interviewer for help? How does the interviewer react to his question?

---

1. **peart.** Lively; chipper

words for everyday use

re • fer (ri fʉr´) *vi.,* direct attention to. *Refer* to the footnotes for additional information.

"Why, certainly!"

"Oh, that is what took me so long."

"Why, my *dear* sir, what did *you* <u>propose</u> to spell it with?"

"Well, I—I—hardly know. I had the Unabridged,[2] and I was ciphering around the back end, hoping I might tree her among the pictures. But it's a very old edition."

"Why, my friend, they wouldn't have a *picture* of it in even the latest e—My dear sir, I beg your pardon, I mean no harm in the world, but you do not look as—as—intelligent as I had expected you would."

"Oh, don't mention it! It has often been said, and by people who would not flatter and who could have no <u>inducement</u> to flatter, that I am quite remarkable in that way. Yes—yes; they always speak of it with <u>rapture</u>."

"I can easily imagine it. But about this interview. You know it is the custom, now to interview any man who has become <u>notorious</u>."

"Indeed, I had not heard of it before. It must be very interesting. What do you do it with?"

"Ah, well—well—well—this is disheartening. It *ought* to be done with a club in some cases; but <u>customarily</u> it consists in the interviewer asking questions and the interviewed answering them. It is all the rage[3] now. Will you let me ask you certain questions calculated to bring out the <u>salient</u> points of your public and private history?"

> What explanation does the interviewer give of the interviewing process? Do you think he will be successful in this interview? Why, or why not?

"Oh, with pleasure,—with pleasure. I have a very bad memory, but I hope you will not mind that. That is to say, it is an irregular memory,—singularly irregular. Sometimes it goes in a gallop, and then again it will be as much as a fortnight[4] passing a given point. This is a great grief to me."

"Oh, it is no matter, so you will try to do the best you can."

"I will. I will put my whole mind on it."

"Thanks. Are you ready to begin?"

"Ready."

Q.   How old are you?

A.   Nineteen, in June.

Q.   Indeed! I would have taken you to be thirty-five or -six. Where were you born?

A.   In Missouri.

Q.   When did you begin to write?

A.   In 1836.

Q.   Why, how could that be, if you are only nineteen now?

A.   I don't know. It does seem curious, somehow.

> How does the interviewer take all of the narrator's answers?

Q.   It does, indeed. Whom do you consider the most remarkable man you ever met?

A.   Aaron Burr.[5]

Q.   But you never could have met Aaron Burr, if you are only nineteen years—

A.   Now, if you know more about me than I do, what do you ask me for?

Q.   Well, it was only a suggestion—nothing more. How did you happen to meet Burr?

A.   Well, I happened to be at his funeral one day, and he asked me to make less noise and—

Q.   But, good heavens! If you were at his funeral, he must have been dead; and if he was dead, how could he care whether you made a noise or not?

---

2. **Unabridged.** Dictionary that has not been condensed
3. **all the rage.** Craze; fad
4. **fortnight.** Two weeks

5. **Aaron Burr.** (1756–1836) Vice president of the United States from 1801 to 1805

words for everyday use

pro • pose (prō pōz´) *vt.*, intend. *What do you <u>propose</u> to cook for dinner?*

in • duce • ment (in dōōs´mənt) *n.*, motive; incentive. *The promise of attention is an <u>inducement</u> for showing off.*

rap • ture (rap´chər) *n.*, great pleasure. *The music critic expressed her <u>rapture</u> upon hearing the new concerto.*

no • to • ri • ous (nō tôr´ē əs) *adj.*, well known, usually unfavorably. *Wanted posters of the <u>notorious</u> criminal were displayed at the post office.*

cus • tom • ar • i • ly (kus´tə mer´ə lē) *adv.*, according to what is usually done. *<u>Customarily</u>, a Jewish boy is given a bar mitzvah at age thirteen.*

sa • lient (sāl´yənt) *adj.*, prominent. *The <u>salient</u> physical characteristics of the giraffe are its long neck and spotted hide.*

A. I don't know. He was always a particular kind of man that way.

Q. Still, I don't understand it at all! You say he spoke to you, and that he was dead.

A. I didn't say he was dead.

Q. But, wasn't he dead?

A. Well, some said he was, some said he wasn't.

Q. What did you think?

A. Oh, it was none of my business! It wasn't any of my funeral.

> *"Goodness knows! I would give whole worlds to know. This solemn, this awful mystery has cast a gloom over my whole life."*

Q. Did you—However, we can never get this matter straight. Let me ask about something else. What was the date of your birth?

A. Monday, October 31st, 1693.

Q. What! Impossible! That would make you a hundred and eighty years old. How do you account for that?

A. I don't account for it at all.

Q. But you said at first you were only nineteen, and now you make yourself out to be one hundred and eighty. It is an awful <u>discrepancy</u>.

A. Why, have you noticed that? (Shaking hands.) Many a time it has seemed to me like a discrepancy, but somehow I couldn't make up my mind. How quick you notice a thing!

> *What compliment does the narrator give the interviewer? Is he sincere in saying this? Why does he say it?*

Q. Thank you for the compliment, as far as it goes.[6] Had you, or have you, any brothers or sisters?

A. Eh! I—I—I think so—yes—but I don't remember.

Q. Well, this is the most extraordinary statement I ever heard!

A. Why, what makes you think that?

Q. How could I think otherwise? Why, look here! Who is this a picture of on the wall? Isn't that a brother of yours?

A. Oh! yes, yes, yes! Now you remind me of it, that *was* a brother of mine. That's William—*Bill* we called him. Poor old Bill!

Q. Why? Is he dead, then?

A. Ah! well, I suppose so. We never could tell. There was a great mystery about it.

> *Which two people may or may not have been dead? What doesn't the interviewer realize about the narrator and his story?*

Q. That is sad, very sad. He disappeared, then?

A. Well, yes, in a sort of general way. We buried him.

---

6. **as far as it goes.** Limited though it is

words for everyday use

dis • crep • an • cy (di skrep´ən sē) *n.*, inconsistency. *There is a <u>discrepancy</u> between the sales receipts and the amount of money in the cash register.*

Q. *Buried* him. *Buried* him, without knowing whether he was dead or not?

A. Oh, no! Not that. He was dead enough.

Q. Well, I confess that I can't understand this. If you buried him, and you knew he was dead—

A. No! no! We only thought he was.

Q. Oh, I see! He came to life again?

A. I bet he didn't.

Q. Well, I never heard anything like this. *Somebody* was dead. *Somebody* was buried. Now, where was the mystery?

A. Ah! that's just it! That's it exactly. You see, we were twins,—defunct[7] and I,—we got mixed in the bath-tub when we were only two weeks old, and one of us was drowned. But we didn't know which. Some think it was Bill. Some think it was me.

Q. Well, that *is* remarkable. What do *you* think?

A. Goodness knows! I would give whole worlds to know. This solemn, this awful mystery has cast a gloom over my whole life. But I will tell you a secret now, which I never have revealed to any creature before. One of us had a peculiar mark—a large mole on the back of his left hand; that was *me. That child was the one that was drowned!*

---

7. **defunct.** No longer living; dead

Q. Very well, then, I don't see that there is any mystery about it, after all.

A. You don't? Well, I do. Anyway, I don't see how they could ever have been such a <u>blundering</u> lot as to go and bury the wrong child. But, 'sh—don't mention it where the family can hear of it. Heaven knows they have heart-breaking troubles enough without adding this.

Q. Well, I believe I have got material enough for the present, and I am very much obliged to you for the pains you have taken. But I was a good deal interested in that account of Aaron Burr's funeral. Would you mind telling me what particular circumstance it was that made you think Burr was such a remarkable man?

A. Oh! it was a mere trifle! Not one man in fifty would have noticed it at all. When the sermon was over, and the procession all ready to start for the cemetery, and the body all arranged nice in the hearse, he said he wanted to take a last look at the scenery, and so he *got up and rode with the driver—*

Then the young man <u>reverently</u> withdrew. He was very pleasant company, and I was sorry to see him go. ∎

How does the interviewer close the interview? What does he think of the narrator at the end of the interview?

---

words for everyday use	**blun • der • ing** (blun´dər iŋ) *adj.,* clumsy; careless; foolish. *Columbo seemed to be a <u>blundering</u> detective, but he caught the criminal every time.* **rev • er • ent • ly** (rev´ər ənt lē) *adv.,* showing great respect. *Marta spoke <u>reverently</u> of her skilled piano teacher.*

Respond *to the* SELECTION

Imagine you are the interviewer in the selection. How would you summarize your experience of interviewing the narrator?

Investigate, Inquire, and Imagine

Recall: GATHERING FACTS

1a. What information does the narrator provide about the interviewer?

2a. What word does the narrator attempt to look up in the dictionary?

3a. Who does the narrator say is the most remarkable man he ever met?

Interpret: FINDING MEANING

1b. What is probably the reason that the interviewer is "nervous"?

2b. What response on the part of the interviewer reveals his gullibility?

3b. Why does the narrator's response upset the interviewer?

Analyze: TAKING THINGS APART

4a. Analyze the information the narrator gave to the interviewer. Is it possible the interviewer has "got material enough"? Why, or why not?

Synthesize: BRINGING THINGS TOGETHER

4b. What is the narrator trying to do to the interviewer? Is he successful?

Evaluate: MAKING JUDGMENTS

5a. Is the narrator's attitude toward the interviewer understandable? Why, or why not?

Extend: CONNECTING IDEAS

5b. If you were the interviewer, would you have tolerated the narrator's behavior? Why, or why not?

Understanding Literature

NARRATOR. Review the definition for **narrator** in the Handbook of Literary Terms. How does the narrator describe himself at the beginning of the selection? Is this description accurate? If not, why do you think he describes himself this way? How would you describe the narrator?

SATIRE. Review the definition for **satire** in the Handbook of Literary Terms and the chart you made for Literary Tools on page 484. What is being satirized in this selection? What corrective, besides laughter, is implied? How does the writer imply this corrective?

Writer's Journal

1. Imagine that you are the interviewer. Write a **character sketch** of the narrator following your interview.

2. Write a **radio spot** advertising a lecture by Mark Twain in your town.

3. Write a **satirical interview** in which a celebrity makes a fool of a reporter who asks inappropriate questions or questions the celebrity doesn't want to answer.

Integrating the Language Arts

Language, Grammar, and Style

IDENTIFYING COMPLEMENTS. On your own paper, underline the complement in each of the following sentences (if one is present). Then identify the complement as a direct object (DO), indirect object (IO), predicate adjective (PA), predicate noun (PN), or predicate pronoun (PP). To review complements, read the Language Arts Survey 3.19–3.25.

1. The interviewer was young.
2. Twain didn't give good answers to the young reporter.
3. Twain needed spelling instructions.
4. The young reporter was Twain's guest.
5. Was the reporter flustered?

Speaking and Listening & Collaborative Learning

ORAL INTERPRETATION. Select an excerpt from one of Mark Twain's pieces of fiction or some of his humorous quotations to prepare as an oral interpretation. Write an introduction for the material and any needed transitions. Decide how you will interpret your selection. In other words, what tone, facial expressions, and gestures will you employ? Then, imagining you are Mark Twain, present your selection to a classmate. Critique your partner's presentation and give suggestions for improvement.

Collaborative Learning

DRAMATIC ADAPTATION. Write a paragraph that satirizes a social convention or custom, such as shaking hands. Exchange your satirical paragraph with a partner. Collaborate with your partner to adapt each of your paragraphs into a dramatic scene. In your scene, use a particular event or character to show the errors, falsehoods, foibles, or failings of the social convention you satirized in your paragraph. Write a part for you and for your partner in the scene. Rehearse your adaptation and present it to the rest of the class.

Study and Research & Media Literacy

CELEBRITY JOURNALISM. Mark Twain was a celebrity when he made his worldwide lecture tour to pay off his debts. Read several magazines to see how they cover celebrities. Then write an article about Mark Twain in that style. You will need to read more about Mark Twain in order to write an interesting and accurate article. An excellent resource for Mark Twain links on the Internet is The Mining Company at http://marktwain.miningco.com.

Guided Writing

EXPRESSING AN INFORMED OPINION

Persuasive words have power: Sojourner Truth's Speech to the Convention of the American ERA, Martin Luther King, Jr.'s "I Have a Dream" speech, Aldo Leopold's "Thinking Like a Mountain," and Rachel Carson's *Silent Spring*. The powerful ideas these writers express have led to important changes.

You, too, hold powerful tools of persuasion: your awakened heart, your analytical mind, and your writing ability. You can use these tools to make changes in your life and the lives of others.

WRITING ASSIGNMENT. Write an essay in which you express an informed opinion about a topic that interests you.

Professional Model

from *Silent Spring* by Rachel Carson
page 476

During the past quarter century this power has not only increased to one of disturbing magnitude but it has changed in character. The most alarming of all man's assaults upon the environment is the contamination of air, earth, rivers, and sea with dangerous and even lethal materials. This pollution is for the most part irrecoverable. . . . In this now universal contamination of the environment, chemicals are the sinister and little-recognized partners of radiation in changing the very nature of the world—the very nature of its life. Strontium 90, released through nuclear explosions into the air, comes to earth in rain or drifts down as fallout, lodges in soil, enters into the grass or corn or wheat grown there, and in time takes up its abode in the bones of a human being, there to remain until his death. Similarly, chemicals sprayed on croplands or forests or gardens lie long in soil, entering into living organisms, passing from one to another in a chain of poisoning and death. Or they pass mysteriously by underground streams until they emerge and, through the alchemy of air and sunlight, combine into new forms that kill vegetation, sicken cattle, and work unknown harm on those who drink from once pure wells. As Albert Schweitzer has said, "Man can hardly even recognize the devils of his own creation."

EXAMINING THE MODEL. In *Silent Spring*, Rachel Carson sets forth that chemical pollution is bad. She writes, "The most alarming of all man's assaults upon the environment is the contamination of air, earth, rivers, and sea with dangerous and even lethal materials." She goes on to emphasize that the pollution is mostly irrecoverable and irreversible. Most of us would agree with her. However, she doesn't just tell us that it is bad—she gives us examples. Reread the paragraph included here. Find and list the different examples she uses. This essay was written over thirty-five years ago—what additional examples are you familiar with that would update and strengthen the argument? What effect does Carson achieve by ending the paragraph with the quote from Albert Schweitzer?

Prewriting

WRITING WITH A PLAN. Your first step is to choose a topic. You may want to refer to the table in the Language Arts Survey 2.7, "Choosing a Topic." What concerns you? What injustice in the world disturbs you? Where does school, government, or society need to make changes? The following questions will give you some topics to consider:

- Should t-shirts or other clothing with messages be banned?
- Should pagers and cell phones at schools be allowed?
- Should students be academically retained?
- Should dropouts be denied drivers' licenses?
- Should suspension be eliminated?
- Should the government do more to ensure air-traffic safety?
- Should cities have curfews for teens?
- Should the driving age be raised to eighteen?
- Should libraries offer unlimited Internet access?
- Should metal detectors be installed in all schools?

After you have selected a topic, begin by **freewriting** for ten to fifteen minutes. Put down everything you know, feel, or think about this issue. Include points for both sides of the argument. Don't be concerned about organization or writing mechanics yet.

Next, as you read through your freewrite, set up a pro and con chart (see the Language Arts Survey 2.21, "Pro and Con Charts," for more information).

Student writer Rachel decided to examine the issue of separate math and science classes for girls and boys. Her pro and con chart helped her formulate her thesis.

Even though her "pro" list for offering separate classes was slightly longer than her "con" list, Rachel decided that she leaned a little more toward opposing separate classes. To Rachel, having separate classes sent a message that girls couldn't compete with boys academically. She didn't like that thought. Rachel's understanding of both sides of the issue proved invaluable, however, when she drafted the paper.

After you have entered your thesis in your graphic organizer, discuss your topic with several of your classmates. What additional arguments do they offer on this topic? Think about where you need more information or examples. Read about the problem, if necessary. Once you have your arguments and examples, set up a rough or formal outline (see the Language Arts Survey 2.28–2.30, "Outlining," "Rough Outlines," and "Formal Outlines"). Begin with a thesis statement that answers the question and uses the word "should." Plan for at least three arguments to support your stand. Answer any likely objections to your stand.

In persuasive writing the conclusion is crucial. After all, you are trying to persuade your audience to agree with you. The last things you say in your essay will stick with your reader, so it is important to make that concluding paragraph especially strong. This is your call-to-action time. What do you want your

---

IDENTIFYING YOUR AUDIENCE. Consider whom you want to convince in this essay. Whose mind do you need to change to get action on this matter? What adults need to be swayed by your argument? Do you need the support of your peers? Knowing who will read your essay will help you decide what kind of arguments to include. Consider what they already know about the subject, what arguments they've probably heard before, and what objections they may have. In many cases, you will probably decide to appeal to both adults and peers.

audience to do as a result of reading your words? Do you want them to sign a petition? join a group? write a letter? examine their own attitude and consider changing it? Ask your audience to do something.

Student Model—Graphic Organizer

Prewriting

Topic:	Should separate math and/or science be offered for girls and boys?

Pro	Con
• Reduces distraction by opposite sex • Teaching style more aligned to gender learning style • Balances attention and encouragement • Research-based intervention: reduce girls' dropping out of math	• Doesn't parallel real world • Fosters notion that separate is good • Defeatist approach: gender bias

Thesis:	Females should compete with males in math and science classes.

After Self- and Peer Evaluation

Objections to My Stand	My Answers to Those Objections
• What if females do better in classes without males? • What about the idea that females need special attention to do well? • You haven't proven that separated classes is a dated idea.	• Not the way the world works • Need to compete with males • It's a step backward

"Develop interest in life as you see it: in people, things, literature, music— the world is so rich, simply throbbing with rich treasures, beautiful souls and interesting people."
—Henry Miller

FINDING YOUR VOICE. It is important to consider carefully the voice you use in the essay. To convince others of your opinion, you will want to use your most reasonable, sincere voice. Since the adults in your audience will tend to have more power than your peers to make the changes you desire, you must write in a style that connects with adult readers. Of course, you also want to gain the support of your classmates, so you want to appeal to them, too. Don't worry. Your reasonable voice won't offend your peers. Your sincerity and your commitment to your cause will work for you to convince others. While you will not be convincing a jury, you do want to provide support "beyond a reasonable doubt."

Self- and Peer Evaluation

For this essay you want your evaluator to determine specifically if the argument is strong, if the reasoning is sound, and if you have acknowledged the other side of the argument. Complete your graphic organizer to show you what you need to keep and anything you want to add to your final copy.

- What is the single focused point of view the essay presents?
- What are the reasons given for this point of view?
- Which point is the most important? Where is it located in the sequence of points? (Last is often best for most important.)
- What details, examples, and personal observations have been made to support the argument?
- Which point is the weakest logically? Why?
- Where in the essay does the opposing view appear?
- What transitions provide coherence in the essay?
- How does the essay engage the reader in the introduction?
- How does the conclusion invite the reader to act/react?
- How does the conclusion succeed in calling the reader to action?
- What lingering doubts, if any, still exist for the reader?
- What, if anything, links the conclusion to the introduction?

Drafting *Need to Finish*

Write a rough draft of your piece. Do not worry at this point about the details of spelling, grammar, usage, and mechanics. Instead simply concentrate on getting your ideas down on paper. Get your reader's attention in the first paragraph. You can give startling statistics or give a frightening example of the problem. You want to engage the reader's interest or curiosity right away. State your thesis clearly at the end of the first paragraph.

In the body of your essay, include three reasons that support your opinion. Give examples or facts as evidence that your thinking is logical. Discuss concerns or counterarguments your readers may have. Show you have thought through those questions. Consider putting your strongest argument last.

Remember that the purpose for your conclusion is to get the reader to do something. Spell out what you think the reader needs to do.

Use a reasonable and sincere voice. Your audience will be more likely to respect your opinions and respond to your appeals if you are logical and genuine.

Student Model—Draft

~~I read~~ a recent study ~~that~~ found that female students do better in only female classes, especially in math and science. *Transition* Separate classes would reduce the distraction created by the opposite sex, and they would give females more attention and encouragement. The logical conclusion is that high schools should segregate math and science classes by sex. At first glance this may seem to be a logical approach, but in actuality it is a *too informal* pretty lame idea. *flawed* If you would only stop and think a minute, it's obvious girls should compete with males in math and science. *Too much— tone down (sounds insulting)*

Transition

∧ Drive down any street and you will see women construction workers. ~~You can~~ call for assistance from the police or fire departments, and you will as likely have women as men at your door. Go to *Good Examples* the doctor and it may be a woman; look in the phone book for a lawyer and you will find more female than male lawyers. Ask to see the manager or owner of a business, and ~~she~~ *the manager* is as likely to be ∧*either* a woman ~~as~~ *or* a ~~male~~ *man*. ~~All throughout~~ *Across* the employment spectrum women are now doing jobs that (use) *sp* to only be handled by men. How did these women achieve this? ∧*Transition* They did it by learning to compete with men.

A problem with separate classes for males and females is that it supports the dated notion that separate is good. By separating male and female students, schools will send a message that *Put in: civil rights woman's vote* separate is acceptable. Rather than stepping forward, our society will be moving backward.

Good parallel structure if you leave this out. Then you have Drive, Call, Go, Ask to start sentences

Give examples to prove it's dated.

Language, Grammar, and Style
Effective Transitions

IDENTIFYING TRANSITIONS. A **transition** is a word, phrase, sentence, or paragraph used to connect ideas and to show relationships between them. Using transitions, a writer achieves coherence by presenting ideas in a logical sequence. Ways to organize ideas and to incorporate transitions include *chronological order, spatial order, degree order, comparison and contrast order, cause and effect order, classification order,* and *part-by-part order. However, therefore, in addition,* and *in contrast* are common transitions.

continued on page 496

Revising and Proofreading

Use your self- and peer evaluations to decide what changes you want to make in your paper. Note especially where your arguments are clear and where they are weak. Pay attention to how your peers respond to your arguments. If your readers need more convincing, figure out how to strengthen your paper. If you need more information, find it now. If you need to adjust

Look at the examples below from the professional model. Transition words appear in italics.

Similarly, chemicals sprayed on croplands or forests or gardens lie long in soil.

The environment, *rigorously shaping and directing the life it supported*, contained elements that were hostile as well as supporting.

Among them are many that are used in man's war against nature.

Since DDT was released for civilian use, a process of escalation has been going on in which *ever more toxic materials* must be found.

Thus the chemical war is never won.

I contend, *furthermore*, that we have allowed these chemicals to be used with little or no advance investigation of their effects.

FIXING TRANSITIONS. Rachel improved the flow of her essay by adding transitions. The first one is bracketed to show where she inserted it.

A recent study found that female students do better in only female classes, especially in math and science. [Put another way,] separate classes would reduce the distraction created by the opposite sex, and they

your word choice, the argument structure, or the tone of the piece, do that now. See how Rachel revised her paper in the student model on page 496.

Student Model—Revised

Why Classes Separated by Gender
Do Not Work
by Rachel Cobb

A recent study found that female students do better in only female classes, especially in math and science. Put another way, separate classes would reduce the distraction created by the opposite sex, and they would give females more attention and encouragement. While the logical conclusion seems to be that high schools should segregate math and science classes by gender, this idea is actually a very flawed one. In fact, girls should compete with boys in the math and science classroom.

First, the idea of separate classes in math and science for males and females simply doesn't match with what is happening in the real world. For instance, drive down any street and you will see women construction workers. Or call for assistance from the police or fire departments, and you will as likely have women as men at your door. Or go to the doctor and it may be a woman; look in the phone book for a lawyer and you will find more female than male lawyers. Or ask to see the manager or owner of a business, and she is as likely to be a woman as a man. Across the employment spectrum women are now doing jobs that used to be handled only by men. How did these women achieve this? Not by sitting in classrooms with only other women, but by learning to compete with men.

Another problem with separate classes for males and females is that it supports the dated notion that separate is good. For the past 135 years racial minorities have been fighting this stigma. During the 1950s and 1960s there was literally civil war is this country as blacks fought for their constitutional rights. Only in the past generation have blacks enjoyed equal treatment under the law. On the other hand, women have only had the vote since 1920, but Elizabeth Dole was a serious presidential candidate in the 2000 presidential election. By separating male and female students, schools will send a message that separate is acceptable. Consequently, rather than stepping forward, our society will be moving backward.

Furthermore, to accept the attitude that female students cannot compete with males in the "hard classes" is also to accept the attitude that men are better than women. This, of course, is an idea that should have disappeared with the cave men, but unfortunately, there are still some cave men out there. Schools that think they are helping their female students by isolating them from males are really doing them a disservice.

would give females more attention and encouragement.

Insert appropriate transitions into the empty brackets in the next lines of Rachel's essay.

[   ] the idea of separate classes in math and science for males and females [   ] doesn't match with what is happening in the real world. [   ]drive down any street and you will see women construction workers.

[   ] call for assistance from the police or fire departments, and you will as likely have women as men at your door.

USING TRANSITIONS EFFECTIVELY. If your writing lacks coherence, or ideas seem to jump around, then perhaps you need to include more transitions. Examine what you have written, consciously noting inclusion or absence of transitions from sentence to sentence and from paragraph to paragraph. Add transitions wherever necessary.

Another way to convince others of your informed opinion is by delivering your essay as a **persuasive speech.** You can prepare your speech by rehearsing it in pairs or small groups. Look for these elements as you evaluate a speech:

DELIVERY
nonverbal delivery—effective eye contact, facial expressions, gestures, posture, proximity
verbal delivery—appropriate volume, pitch, pace, tone, enunciation
mode of delivery—evidence of comfort, confidence, poise

DESIGN
introduction—gains attention, orients audience to topic, states thesis clearly
organization—clear and simple, appropriate organizational pattern, easy to follow
conclusion—provides closure, summarizes, is memorable

CONTENT
purpose—persuades others to take action or change opinion
supporting materials—uses quality materials
visual aids—relevant to speech, visually appealing, appropriately displayed and explained

For more information, see the Language Arts Survey 4.18, "Guidelines for Giving a Speech," and 6.11, "Displaying Effective Visual Information."

Publishing and Presenting

Write or print a final copy of your informed opinion essay. Read it to your classmates and then send it to a person who could make some changes with this issue. If the person is local, invite him or her to come to your class and discuss the issue with you and your classmates. Other final formats may include an editorial or letter to the editor sent to your local newspaper, an e-mail, or a report. You could also develop your informal opinion essay into a persuasive speech (see the "Delivering Your Essay as a Persuasive Speech" sidebar at left).

Reflecting

When you write an opinion piece, it forces you to think more deeply than you might normally do about a particular issue. How do you feel about the issue you addressed in your paper? Did you learn anything about the topic that helps you understand another viewpoint? How did examining pros and cons benefit you? What discoveries did you make through freewriting? How did peer comments about your topic support or affect your thinking? If your writing was acknowledged by an audience, how did you feel empowered? If your writing was not acknowledged by an audience, what could you try next to have better success?

UNIT 5 review
Nonfiction

Words for Everyday Use

Check your knowledge of the following vocabulary words from the selections in this unit. Write short sentences using these words in context to make the meaning clear. To review the definition or usage of a word, refer back to the page number(s) listed or the Glossary of Words for Everyday Use.

accompaniment, 478
adapt, 479
advent, 478
adversity, 469
agility, 442
approximation, 440
aura, 441
banter, 442
barrage, 477
bison, 448
blundering, 488
brutality, 462
calamitous, 429
clarity, 442
claustrophobia, 442
conceive, 479
consolation, 458
contention, 481
conviction, 470
creed, 463
customarily, 486
decipher, 469
defiant, 469
defoliate, 471
deft, 440
demented, 439
detrimental, 480
discord, 464
discrepancy, 487
diversified, 479

donning, 443
elicit, 442
emerge, 462
escalation, 477
exalt, 464
exploit, 433
extirpate, 471
foliage, 439
ford, 470
foresight, 481
graphically, 479
guise, 440
gully, 449
impetuous, 476
implication, 477
implicit, 469
imposter, 439
inadvertence, 477
indecipherable, 442
indeterminate, 432
inducement, 486
inequity, 432
inevitable, 480
inexplicable, 441
ingeniously, 439
ingenuity, 480
innovation, 480
inordinate, 432
insipid, 480
instill, 438

integrity, 481
intensification, 479
intent, 433
interaction, 475
invocation, 440
irrecoverable, 476
isolated, 479
languish, 462
legion, 458
lethal, 481
literally, 470
magnitude, 476
makeshift, 439
manacle, 462
mêlée, 470
mobility, 462
molder, 471
musty, 429
notorious, 486
objectively, 469
obscure, 432
ordeal, 441
peril, 442
phenomenon, 439
ply, 430
prophesy, 431
propitious, 440
propose, 486
prudent, 481
rapture, 486

redemptive, 463
refer, 485
regale, 433
relinquish, 440
renege, 430
requisite, 471
resignation, 432
resurgence, 477
reverently, 488
salient, 486
sear, 462
sorrel, 449
sparse, 431
species, 476
staple, 430
stereotyped, 431
stimulate, 478
stoic, 443
suppress, 480
treaty, 453
tribulation, 463
tumult, 443
unpalatable, 481
verbose, 442
vindication, 477
wallow, 463
zeal, 480

Literary Tools

Define each of the following terms, giving concrete examples of how they are used in the selections in this unit. To review a term, refer to the page number(s) indicated or the Handbook of Literary Terms.

aim, 456, 474
anecdote, 468
coherence, 474
conflict, 436
dialect, 456
internal conflict, 436

metaphor, 436
narrator, 428, 484
personification, 468
point of view, 428, 446
repetition, 461
satire, 484

setting, 428
simile, 436, 461
style, 456, 461
thesis, 474
tone, 446

Reflecting on your reading

Genre Studies

1. **AUTOBIOGRAPHY.** In *I Know Why the Caged Bird Sings*, Maya Angelou reveals facts about the cotton pickers to create a moving portrait of their suffering. In "California Palms," lê thi diem thúy reveals facts about her mother to create a moving portrait of her trials. What techniques of characterization are used by the authors to create these character portraits? For each autobiography, give an example of each technique used. Review the definition of characterization in the Handbook of Literary Terms.

2. **SPEECHES.** One reason for writing a speech is to persuade people to believe in a certain way or to take certain actions. Which speeches in this unit are persuasive? Of what does each author want to persuade his or her audience?

3. **ESSAY.** A good essay develops a single idea and is characterized by unity. An essay with unity is one in which all the parts help to support the thesis statement, or main idea. Define the thesis statements of "The Obligation to Endure" by Rachel Carson and "Thinking Like a Mountain" by Aldo Leopold. Then give an example of a part of the essay that supports the thesis statement.

Thematic Studies

4. **IDENTITY.** Maya Angelou in *I Know Why the Caged Bird Sings* and lê thi diem thúy in "California Palms" both take up residence in new locations. How is their identity shaped by their new homes? How does their ethnicity inform their identity?

5. **RESPONSIBILITY.** What do Aldo Leopold and Rachel Carson have to say about humankind's responsibility to nature? How are their arguments alike?

6. **HUMAN RIGHTS.** For what human rights do Sojourner Truth and Martin Luther King, Jr. lobby in their speeches? What oppressed people do they represent? How is the content of their speeches similar? How is it different?

7. **JOURNALISM.** What attitudes toward journalism and journalists does Mark Twain adopt in "An Encounter with an Interviewer"? How does Twain use humor to make his points? For whom was the interview a success, Mark Twain or the journalist?

8. **TRIUMPH OF THE SPIRIT.** In his speech, Black Elk recounts defeats of the Oglala Sioux at the hands of white settlers. What personal event in his life marks a triumph of the spirit against this background of defeat? How does this event impact his destiny?

for your READING LIST

High Exposure: An Enduring Passion for Everest and Unforgiving Places
by David Breashears. In the prologue to this book, David Breashears tells
of seeing for the first time a picture of Tenzing Norgay, the Himalayan
sherpa who, along with Sir Edmund Hillary, made the first documented
ascent to the summit of Mt. Everest. He says, "From that moment on, I
equated climbing Everest with man's capacity for hope. Indeed, there's
nothing so exhilarating, so purifying, as standing on its summit more
than 29,00 feet above the sea, surveying the planet below." David
Breashears has spent his life pursuing his passion for mountain climbing
and the exhilaration of challenging himself to do the seemingly impossible. He has reached the
summit of the world's highest peak four times, recording one of those journeys in the IMAX film,
Everest. He won an Emmy for another film, *Red Flag Over Tibet*. This nonfiction account of his
experiences reads like an adventure novel. In it, Breashears describes the thrill of pushing his
body to its limits to achieve a goal, as well as the terrifying tragedy of the 1996 Everest disaster
when, despite the heroic efforts of Breashears's team and others, eight climbers died during one
day. *High Exposure* will take you into a world you will not soon forget.

Independent Reading Activity

BOOK CLUB DISCUSSION. It may be helpful to read Language Arts Survey 1.8, "Guidelines for
Discussing Literature in a Book Club," before beginning to read the book. Decide who will take
on each of the roles outlined there. When everyone has finished reading the book, take some
time individually to prepare for your roles in the discussion.

You may find these questions helpful in your discussion:

- What facts did you learn about mountain climbing from reading this book?
- Why do you think David Breashears is so drawn to mountain climbing?
- Do you feel the same sort of pull toward some challenge? What challenge, and why?
- Why do you think he continues to climb, despite the danger and the many friends who have
  died while climbing?
- Under what circumstances, if any, would you risk your life, and why?
- What lessons has he learned about life from his many experiences climbing?
- What do you think Breashears means when he speaks of the "sense of rebirth that the
  mountain [Mt. Everest] has to offer?
- What do you think was David Breashears's aim in writing this book?
- Would you recommend this book? If so, to whom and why? If not, why not?

Selections for Additional Reading

Zero G: Life and Survival in Space by Peter Bond. A fascinating account of space travel and
exploration with breathtaking photographs.

As Long As the Rivers Flow: The Stories of Nine Native Americans by Paula Gunn Allen and
Patricia Clark Smith. The stories of well-known Native Americans like Jim Thorpe, Will Rogers,
and Louise Erdrich are presented in this collection of dramatic essays.

Pilgrim at Tinker Creek by Annie Dillard. Dillard's personal narrative highlights one year's explorations on foot in the author's own neighborhood, a valley in Virginia's Blue Ridge.

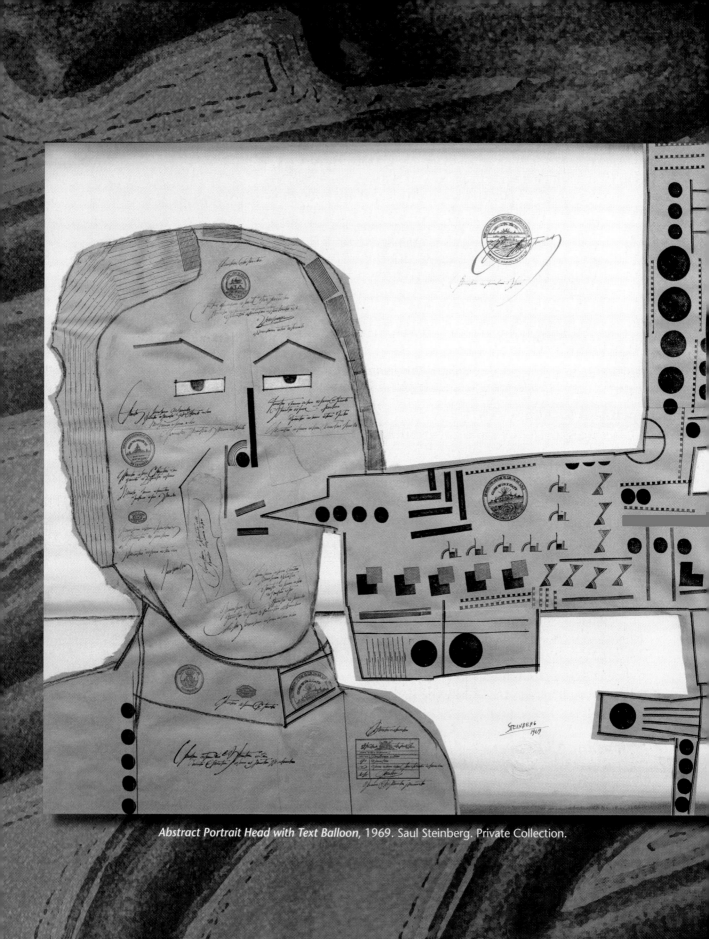

Abstract Portrait Head with Text Balloon, 1969. Saul Steinberg. Private Collection.

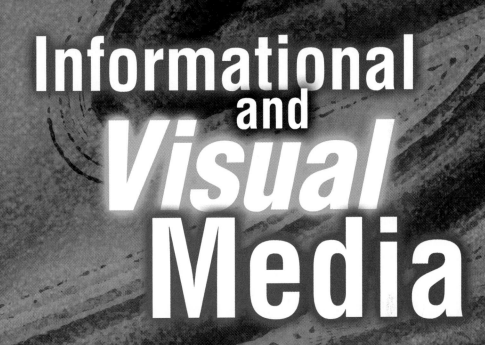

Informational
and
Visual
Media

" The medium is the message. "

—*Marshall McLuhan*

ELEMENTS of INFORMATIONAL AND VISUAL MEDIA

When you are reading for information, you are looking for information that answers a specific immediate question, that helps you learn how to do something, or that will help you make a decision or draw a conclusion about something. One of the most important tasks for you to learn in school is how to access, process, and think about the vast amount of information available to you in online and print reference works, graphic aids, and other visuals.

Informational Media

The term **media**, in most applications, is used as a plural of *medium*, which means a channel or system of communication, information, or entertainment. *Mass media* refers specifically to means of communication, such as newspapers, radio, or television, which are designed to reach the mass of the people. *Journalism* is the gathering, evaluating, and disseminating, through various media, of news and facts of current interest. Originally journalism encompassed only such printed matter as newspapers and periodicals. Today, however, it includes other media used to distribute news, such as radio, television, documentary or newsreel films, the Internet, and computer news services.

Newspapers are publications usually issued on a daily or weekly basis, the main function of which is to report the news. Newspapers also provide commentary on the news, advocate various public policies, furnish special information and advice to readers, and sometimes include features such as comic strips, cartoons, and serialized books. The article "'White House' mystery may be solved" from *The Washington Post* (Unit 1) is an example of a newspaper article.

Periodicals are publications released at regular intervals, such as journals, magazines, or newsletters. Periodicals feature material of special interest to particular audiences. The contents of periodicals can be unrelated to current news stories;—however, when dealing with the news, periodicals tend to do so in the form of commentaries or summaries. Examples of periodical articles include "A Short Life, Intensely Lived: The Adventures of Jack London" (Unit 3), "Where Stars Are Born" and "Spanning the Decades" (Unit 8), and "The "Ghost of Everest" and "For the Future of Florida: Repair the Everglades!" (Unit 6).

Technical writing refers to scientific or process-oriented instructional writing that is of a technical or mechanical nature. Technical writing includes **instruction manuals**, such as computer software manuals, **how-to instructional guides**, and **procedural memos**. In this unit, the step-by-step procedure "Research Strategies for the Learning Highway" is an example of technical writing.

Electronic Media

Electronic media includes online magazines and journals, known as **webzines** or **e-zines, computer news services,** and many **web-based newspapers** that are available on the **Internet.** The **web** is by far the most widely used part of the Internet. Consequently, people often use the terms *net* and *web* interchangeably. There is, however, a difference. Strictly speaking, the Internet is a system of computers, storage devices, and connections, along with the software that allows people to use these connections. The web, in contrast, is the total collection of information available on that portion of the Internet that contains linked HTML documents. In addition to handling web documents, the Internet also provides the physical basis for a number of other computer communications services, allowing people to send e-mail, access archives of files, and participate in discussion groups. The Internet has had a dramatic impact on higher education and business as more universities offer courses and more companies offer goods and services online.

Multimedia is the presentation of information using the combination of text, sound, pictures, animation, and video. Common multimedia computer applications include **games, learning software, presentation software, reference materials,** and **web pages**. Most multimedia applications include links that enable users to switch between media elements and topics. The connectivity provided by these links transforms multimedia from static presentations with pictures and sound into a varied and informative interactive experience.

Visual Media

In today's visually stimulating world, books and news media rely on **visual arts**, such as **fine art, illustrations, photographs,** and other visuals as well as the printed word to convey ideas. Visual arts offer insights into our world in a different way than print does. *Critical viewing* or careful examination of a painting or photograph can help you to comprehend its meaning and be able to compare and contrast the visual image with a literary work or other piece of writing. The Art Notes found throughout this book provide opportunities to critically view the fine art used to illustrate the literature selections.

Ulysses and the Sirens [Detail], 1891. John Waterhouse. National Gallery of Victoria, Melborne, Australia.

ELEMENTS OF INFORMATIONAL MEDIA

NEWS ARTICLES. **News articles** are informational pieces of writing about a particular topic, issue, event, or series of events. News articles can be found in newspapers, magazines, journals, newsletters, and Internet sites such as NewsGroups or Information Services. Broadcast reporters on television and radio verbally present forms of news articles.

EDITORIALS AND COMMENTARIES. An **editorial** is a newspaper or magazine article that gives the opinions of the editors or publishers. A **commentary** is a report of an event usually written by a participant or observer that expresses an opinion.

ESSAYS. An **essay** is a brief work of prose nonfiction that often appears in the media. An essay need not be a complete or exhaustive treatment of a subject, but rather a tentative exploration of it. "Thinking Like a Mountain" by Aldo Leopold (Unit 5) and "It's Not Talent; It's Just Work" by Annie Dillard (Unit 8) are examples of essays.

INTERVIEWS. An **interview** is a meeting usually between a reporter and an individual that consists of a series of questions asked with the intention of getting to know personal details about the person being interviewed or to find out information about a news story or current event. Newspapers and magazines often contain **interviews** with famous celebrities, sports figures, and community leaders.

REVIEWS. A **review,** or *critique,* is a critical evaluation of a work, such as a book, play, movie, or musical performance or recording. For an example, see Roger Ebert's review of the film *Il Postino* (*The Postman*) in Unit 9.

Elements of Electronic Media

ELECTRONIC MAIL. **Electronic mail**, or **e-mail**, is the most widely used communication tool on the Internet. E-mail is used to send written messages between individuals or groups of individuals, often separated geographically by large distances. The proliferation of e-mail is changing the way people communicate as well as the structure of written correspondence. Because of the sometimes almost-immediate response, e-mail tends to be much more informal or conversational in style than previous forms of personal or business correspondence.

WEB PAGES. A **web page** is an electronic "page" on the World Wide Web or Internet that may contain text, pictures, and sometimes animations related to a particular topic. A *website* is a collection of pages grouped together to organize the information offered by the person, company, or group that owns it.

NEWSGROUPS. Another use of e-mail is Usenet, in which discussions on a particular subject are grouped together into **newsgroups**. There are thousands of newsgroups covering an extremely wide range of subjects. Messages to a newsgroup are not posted directly to the user, but are accessible in the form of a list on a local news server. The networking of these servers makes such discussions available worldwide. Associated computer software enables users to choose which messages they want to read, and to reply by posting messages to the newsgroup.

INFORMATION SERVICES. Information services, or *news services,* are providers of electronic news, information, and e-mail services to customers connecting to the service with their computers over modems and telephone lines. Information services may also serve as gateways to other sources of information such as bulletin boards, chat groups, and the Internet.

BULLETIN BOARD SYSTEMS. A **bulletin board system,** or BBS, is an online service that enables users to post and read messages, converse by typing messages (sometimes called a *chat room*), play games with another person online, and copy, or download, programs to their personal computers. Most BBSs are organized around a particular topic. BBSs are usually open to the public and free of cost, but some may require special authorization.

WEBZINES OR E-ZINES. Webzines or **e-zines** are basically periodicals such as magazines or journals that are available online. Some webzines are available only online, while others are the electronic version of a print magazine that is distributed by traditional methods. An online magazine will usually contain all of the features of the print version, but may be more interactive and include more visual effects such as use of color and animation. Some webzines are available free of charge over the Internet, while others may require a subscription fee.

ONLINE NEWSPAPERS. Most major newspapers are now available online and it is possible to read the morning news on your computer screen without a subscription. Online newspapers are usually updated continually and will have the most up-to-date news and weather reports available. They can provide an excellent resource for researching a topic, since often past editions are accessible through an online archive and retrieval system.

ELEMENTS OF VISUAL MEDIA

GRAPHIC AIDS. Graphic aids are **drawings, illustrations, diagrams, charts, graphs, maps, spreadsheets,** and other visual materials that present information. Many people, including scientists, sociologists, economists, business analysts, and school administrators, use graphic aids to present data in understandable ways. Information presented in tables, charts, and graphs can help you find information, see trends, discover facts, and uncover patterns. Learning to interpret graphics and images will help you to more easily understand how things work, what things mean, and how things compare. See the Language Arts Survey 1.15, "Using Graphic Aids," for more information.

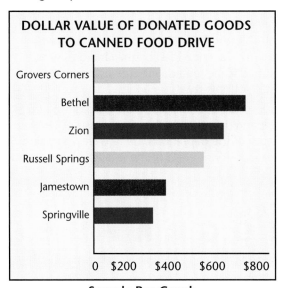

DOLLAR VALUE OF DONATED GOODS TO CANNED FOOD DRIVE

Sample Bar Graph

PHOTOGRAPHS. A photograph is a picture or likeness obtained by *photography*, the art or process of producing exact images on a sensitized surface (as a film) by the action of radiant energy and light. Photography was developed in the early nineteenth century; the word *photography* comes from Greek words and means "drawing with light." Photographs serve as conveyers of news, historical documents, scientific evidence, works of art, and records

of family life. The technology of photography continues to develop rapidly. Electronic technologies have not only changed the way most cameras work, but are changing the fundamental processing of photographs from the traditional developing of film to digital formats that can be stored on disk and downloaded to computers.

DIGITAL PHOTOGRAPHY. Digital photography is a method of making images without the use of conventional photographic film. Instead, a machine called a scanner records visual information and converts it into a code of ones and zeroes that a computer can read. Photographs in digital form can be manipulated by means of various computer programs. Digital photography has become widely used in advertising and graphic design and is quickly replacing conventional photographic technology in areas such as photojournalism.

PHOTOJOURNALISM. Photojournalism is documentary photography that tells a particular story in visual terms. Photojournalists usually work for daily and periodical newspapers, magazines, wire services, and other publications. Photojournalists cover cultural and news events in areas such as politics, war, business, sports, and the arts. They strive to document news events as they happen. The historical photos by Walker Evans in this unit are an example of photojournalism.

VISUAL ARTS. The visual arts include objects that may be two-dimensional or three-dimensional, stationary or moving. Forms of art include painting, sculpture, drawing, printmaking, collage, photography, video, computer-assisted art, and other forms. Art is a two-part process consisting of the creation by the artist and the interpretation by the viewer. It conveys meaning in ways that draw differing interpretations for different viewers. Concepts and uses of art differ greatly throughout the world and throughout history, but every culture has created objects that have no practical function other than to be visually pleasing and to convey ideas or meaning to viewers.

Literary
TOOLS

MOOD. Mood, or *atmosphere*, is the emotion created in the reader by part or all of a literary work. As you read, consider what mood the photographs and the writing convey.

SIMILE AND METAPHOR. A **simile** is a comparison using *like* or *as*. A **metaphor** is a figure of speech in which one thing is spoken or written about as if it were another. Both figures of speech invite the reader to make a comparison between two things. The two "things" involved are the writer's actual subject, the *tenor* of the metaphor, and another thing to which the subject is likened, the *vehicle* of the metaphor.

Organizer

As you read, make a chart like the one below, listing the tenor and the vehicle for the figures of speech in the selection.

TENOR	VEHICLE
the boy's erected head	periscope

Reader's
Journal

Think of a moment in your life that stands out as clear as a photograph in your memory. Describe it as if you were a camera talking about what it sees.

from **Let Us Now Praise Famous Men**

by James Agee and Walker Evans

Reader's
resource

In 1936, Walker Evans and James Agee accepted a commission from *Fortune* magazine to write a series of articles on the condition of white sharecroppers in the rural slums of the South during the Great Depresssion. The two men spent about six weeks in Alabama, mostly with three families. Evans took photographs and Agee took notes. Although their work was rejected by *Fortune*, the material, revised and expanded, was eventually published in 1941 as a book titled **Let Us Now Praise Famous Men**. Breaking with the tradition of photographs illustrating text, Evans displays fifty of his starkly realistic photographs at the beginning of the book. Agee, according to John Hersey, "strove through the sounds and meaning of words to . . . achieve photography" that equaled Evans's images.

HISTORY CONNECTION. Sharecropping was a system of farm tenancy that arose at the end of the Civil War out of the plantation system. Sharecroppers of cotton brought to the farm only their labor. Most other requirements were provided by the landlord, who advanced credit that had to be repaid with interest, keeping sharecroppers in a state of poverty.

The Great Depression was a severe economic crisis during the 1930s that was precipitated by the stock-market crash of 1929. In 1933, during the depth of the depression, there were 16 million unemployed people—about one-third of the available labor force.

About the
PHOTOGRAPHER

Walker Evans (1903–1975) was an important contributor to the development of American documentary photography in the 1930s. Although primarily a photographer of environments rather than people, Evans's social concerns brought him face to face with the Great Depression's victims, whose stoicism in the face of adversity he tried to convey. About his work, Evans said, "The real thing that I'm talking about has purity and a certain severity, rigor, or simplicity, directness, clarity, and it is without artistic pretension in a self-conscious sense of the word." Evans served as an editor for both *Fortune* and *Time* magazines and later became a professor of graphic arts at Yale. His other books include *American Photographs* and *Message from the Interior*.

from *Let Us Now Praise Famous Men*

Documentary Photographs _____ Walker Evans

Who is pictured?

What are the residents of the house doing?

Where is the man looking?

What do you see in this corner of the room?

Let Us Now Praise Famous Men

The Gudger House
James Agee

The house is left alone

Slowly they diminished along the hill path, she, and her daughter, and her three sons, in leisured enfilade beneath the light. The mother first, her daughter next behind, her eldest son, her straggler, whimpering; their bare feet pressed out of the hot earth gentle explosions of gold. She carried her youngest child, his knees locked simian across her, his light hands at her neck, and his erected head, hooded with night, next hers, swiveled mildly upon the world's globe, a periscope. The dog, a convoy, plaited his wanderings round them through the briars. She wore the flowerlike beauty of the sunbonnet in which she is ashamed to appear before us. At length, well up the hill, their talking shrank and became inaudible, and at that point will give safe warning on the hill of their return. Their slanted bodies slowly straightened, one by one, along the brim, and turned into the east, a slow frieze, and sank beneath the brim in order of their height, masts foundered in a horizon; the dog, each of the walking children, at length; at last, the guileless cobra gloatings of the baby, the mother's tall, flared head.

They are gone.

No one is at home, in all this house, in all this land. It is a long while before their return. I shall move as they would trust me not to, and as I could not, were they here. I shall touch nothing but as

Who is alone in the Gudger house?

I would touch the most delicate wounds, the most dedicated objects.

The silence of the brightness of this middle morning is increased upon me moment by moment and upon this house, and upon this house the whole of heaven is drawn into one lens; and this house itself, in each of its objects, it, too, is one lens.

—ᗰᗰ—

In front of the house: The façade

The porch: stands in its short square shade:

The hall: it is in shadow also, save where one wall, fifteen feet back, is slantingly slashed with light:

At the far end of this well of hall, the open earth, lifted a little, bald hard dirt; the faced frontages of the smokehouse and the henhouse, and a segment of the barn: and all of this framed image a little unnaturally brilliant and vital, as all strongly lighted things appear through corridors of darkness:

What buildings are visible besides the house?

And this hall between, as the open valve of a sea creature, steadfastly flushing the free width of ocean through its infinitesimal existence: and on its either side, the square boxes, the square front walls, raised vertical to the earth, and facing us as two squared prows of barge or wooden wings, shadow beneath their lower edge and at their eaves; and the roof:

words for everyday use

en • fil • ade (en′ fə lād) *n.*, interconnected group. *The enfilade of soldiers moved like a serpent through the canyon.*

sim • i • an (si′mē ən) *adj.*, resembling monkeys or apes. *The simian features of the face mask scared the little boy.*

per • i • scope (per′ə skōp) *n.*, tubular optical instrument containing lenses and mirrors by which an observer obtains an otherwise obstructed field of view. *Using its periscope, the submarine found its target.*

frieze (frēz) *n.*, sculptured or richly ornamented band as on a building. *The frieze on the temple showed the goddess Athena.*

in • fin • i • tes • i • mal (in fi nə te′ sə məl) *adj.*, immeasurably or incalculably small. *The infinitesimal size of the organism made it necessary to use a microscope.*

And these walls:

Nailed together of boards on beams, the boards facing the weather, into broad cards of wood inlet with windows stopped with shutters: walls, horizontals, of somewhat narrow weatherboarding; the windows bounded by boards of that same width in a square: the shutters, of wide vertical boards laid edge to edge, not overlapped: each of these boards was once of the living flesh of a pine tree; it was cut next the earth, and was taken between the shrieking of saws into strict ribbons; and now, which was vertical, is horizontal to the earth, and another is clamped against the length of its outward edge and its downward clamps another, and these boards, nailed tightly together upon pine beams, make of their horizontalities a wall: and the sun makes close horizontal parallels along the edges of these weatherboards, of sharp light and shade, the parallels strengthened here in slight straight-line lapse from level, in the subtle knife-edged curve of warping loose in another place: another irregular 'pattern' is made in the endings and piecings-out of boards:

And the roof:

It is of short hand-hewn boards so thick and broad, they are shingles only of a most antique sort: crosswise upon rigid beams, laths[1] have been nailed, not far apart, and upon these laths, in successive rows of dozens and of hundreds, and here again, though regularly, with a certain shuffling of erratism[2] against pure <u>symmetry</u>, these broad thick shingles are laid down over-lapping from the peak to the overhung edge like the plumage of a bird who must meet weather: and not unlike some square and formalized plumage, as of a holy <u>effigy</u>, they seem, and made in <u>profligate</u> plates of a valuable metal; for they have never been stained, nor otherwise

What "stops" the windows?

touched or colored save only by all habits of the sky: nor has any other wood of this house been otherwise ever touched: so that, wherever the weathers of the year have handled it, the wood of the whole of this house shines with the noble gentleness of cherished silver, much as where (yet differently), along the floors, in the pathings of the millions of soft wavelike movements of naked feet, it can be still more melodiously charmed upon its knots, and is as wood long fondled in a tender sea:

Upon these structures, light:

It stands just sufficiently short of vertical that every leaf of shingle, at its edges, and every edge of horizontal plank (blocked, at each center, with squared verticals) is a most black and cutting ink: and every surface struck by light is thus: such an intensity and splendor of silver in the silver light, it seems to burn, and burns and blinds into the eyes almost as snow; yet in none of that burnishment or blazing whereby detail is lost: each texture in the wood, like those of bone, is distinct in the eye as a razor: each nail-head is distinct: each seam and split; and each slight warping; each random knot and knothole: and in each board, as lovely a music as a contour map and unique as a thumbprint, its grain, which was its living strength, and these wild creeks cut stiff across by saws; and moving nearer, the close-laid arcs and shadows even of those tearing wheels: and this, more poor and plain than bone, more naked and noble than sternest

What is the condition of the roof shingles?

What color does the light produce on the exterior of the house?

---

1. **laths.** Thin narrow strips of wood nailed to rafters or studding as a groundwork for slates, tiles, or plaster
2. **erratism.** Variant of erraticism: characterized by lack of consistency, regularity, or uniformity

---

words for everyday use

sym • me • try (si′ mə trē) *n.*, beauty of form arising from balanced proportions. *The <u>symmetry</u> of the driveway derived from an arch of branches formed by two rows of elms.*

ef • fi • gy (e′ fə jē) *n.*, image or representation of a person. *Saint Lucia, in <u>effigy</u>, led the religious procession.*

prof • li • gate (prä′ fli gət) *adj.*, wildly extravagant. *The hostess's <u>profligate</u> expenditures meant caviar and champagne for her guests.*

Doric,[3] more rich and more variant than watered silk, is the fabric and the stature of a house.

It is put together out of the cheapest available pine lumber, and the least of this is used which shall stretch a skin of one thickness alone against the earth and air; and this is all done according to one of the three or four simplest, stingiest, and thus most classical plans contrivable, which are all traditional to that country: and the work is done by half-skilled, half-paid men under no need to do well, who therefore take such vengeance on the world as they may in a cynical and part willful <u>apathy</u>; and this is what comes of it: Most naïve, most massive symmetry and simpleness. Enough lines, enough off-true, that this symmetry is strongly yet most subtly sprained against its centers, into something more powerful than either full symmetry or deliberate breaking and balancing of 'monotonies' can hope to be. A look of being most earnestly hand-made, as a child's drawing, a thing created out of need, love, patience, and strained skill in the innocence of a race. Nowhere one ounce or inch spent with ornament, not one trace of relief or of disguise: a matchless monotony, and in it a matchless variety and this again throughout restrained, held rigid: and of all this, nothing which is not <u>intrinsic</u> between the materials of structure, the earth, and the open heaven. The major lines of structure, each horizontal of each board, and edge of shingle, the strictness yet subtle <u>dishevelment</u> of the shingles, the nail-heads, which are driven according to geometric need, yet are not in perfect order, the grain, differing in each foot of each board and in each

> What is the result of using "half-skilled, half-paid men" to build the house?

board from any other, the many knots in this cheap lumber: all these fluencies and irregularities, all these shadows of pattern upon each piece of wood, all these in <u>rectilinear</u> ribbons caught into one squared, angled, and curled music, compounding a chord of four chambers upon a soul and center of clean air: and upon all these masses and edges and chances and flowerings of grain, the changes of colorings of all weathers, and the slow complexions and marchings of pure light.

Or by another saying:

'In all this house:

'In all of this house not any one inch of lumber being wasted on <u>embellishment</u>, or on trim, or on any form of relief, or even on any doubling of walls: it is, rather, as if a hard thin hide of wood has been stretched to its utmost to cover exactly once, or a little less than once, in all six planes the skeletal beams which, with the inside surface of the weatherboarding, are the inside walls; and no touch, as I have said, of any wash or paint, nor, on the floors, any kind of covering, nor, to three of the rooms, any kind of ceiling, but in all places left bare the plain essences of structure; in result all these almost perfect symmetries have their full strength, and every inch of the structure, and every aspect and placement of the building materials, comes inevitably and purely through into full <u>esthetic</u> existence, the one further conditioner, and discriminator between the functions and properties of indoors and out, being the lights and operations of the sky.' ■

> What is there no trace of in the house?

---

3. **Doric.** Belonging to the simplest Greek architectural style

words for everyday use

ap • a • thy (a′ pə thē) n., lack of interest or concern; indifference. *To counter his students' <u>apathy</u>, Mr. Fields tried a variety of motivational techniques.*

in • trin • sic (in trin′ zik) adj., belonging to the essential nature or constitution of a thing. *The <u>intrinsic</u> value of the diamond was enhanced by its setting.*

di • shev • el • ment (di shev′ əl mənt) n., disorderliness. *The <u>dishevelment</u> of the boys' clothes led their teacher to believe they had been in a fight.*

rec • ti • lin • e • ar (rek tə li′ nē ər) adj., moving in or forming a straight line. *The <u>rectilinear</u> motion of the cardinal led Claire to believe it would fly directly over her.*

em • bel • lish • ment (im be′ lish mənt) n., act or process of making beautiful with ornamentation. *The <u>embellishment</u> of the account of Peter's trip was due to many anecdotes and details.*

es • thet • ic (es thet′ ik) adj., pleasing in appearance. *The <u>esthetic</u> features of the computer pleased Julia.*

Let us now praise famous men, and our fathers that begat us.

The Lord hath wrought great glory by them through his great power from the beginning.

Such as did bear rule in their kingdoms, men renowned for their power, giving counsel by their understanding, and declaring prophecies:

Leaders of the people by their counsels, and by their knowledge of learning meet for the people, wise and eloquent in their instructions:

Such as found out musical tunes, and recited verses in writing:

Rich men furnished with ability, living peaceably in their habitations:

All these were honoured in their generations, and were the glory of their times.

There be of them, that have left a name behind them, that their praises might be reported.

And some there be which have no memorial; who perished, as though they had never been; and are become as though they had never been born; and their children after them.

But these were merciful men, whose righteousness hath not been forgotten.

With their seed shall continually remain a good inheritance, and their children are within the covenant.

Their seed standeth fast, and their children for their sakes. Their seed shall remain for ever, and their glory shall not be blotted out.

Their bodies are buried in peace; but their name liveth for evermore.

—James Agee

Respond *to the* SELECTION

Imagine you are the author. Describe the attitude you take toward the house and the people in it.

About *the* AUTHOR

James Agee (1909–1955) is known for his delicate, moving, and lyrical prose. He worked as a reporter, film critic, and motion picture and television scriptwriter after his collaboration with Walker Evans. His novel *A Death in the Family* (1957), published posthumously and considered his masterpiece, won the Pulitzer Prize. Agee's other books include a volume of poems, *Permit Me Voyage* (1934); another novel, *The Morning Watch* (1951); and several collections of correspondence, reviews, and film scripts. Agee said, "I know I am making the choice most dangerous to an artist in valuing life above art."

Investigate, Inquire, and Imagine

Recall: GATHERING FACTS

1a. What kind of clothes is the family wearing in photograph 1? With what expression is the man in photograph 3 looking into the camera? In what condition is the corner of the room in photograph 4?

2a. How would you describe the construction of the house in photograph 2? In which direction are the exterior wall boards placed?

3a. What isn't the wood wasted on?

Interpret: FINDING MEANING

1b. What do the clothes they wear and the condition of the interior of their house reveal about the family?

2b. How does Agee contrast the wall boards with the pine trees they were made from?

3b. What does this contruction reveal about the residents?

Analyze: TAKING THINGS APART

4a. With what type of eye does the author describe the house?

Synthesize: BRINGING THINGS TOGETHER

4b. How does Agee's writing reinforce Evans's photographic work? What attitude do the two men demonstrate toward their subjects? How are Agee and Evans working in tandem? What do the photographs and the writing invite the viewer/reader to do?

Evaluate: MAKING JUDGMENTS

5a. Which medium, photographs or written description, does a better job of depicting the sharecroppers' lives? Explain your answer.

Extend: CONNECTING IDEAS

5b. Read the poem "Let us now praise famous men" by Agee on page 514. How does the poem reflect the aim of the book?

Understanding Literature

MOOD. Review the definition for **mood** in the Handbook of Literary Terms. What is the mood of the photographs? What is the mood of the selection?

SIMILE AND METAPHOR. Review the definitions for **simile** and **metaphor** in the Handbook of Literary Terms. Which simile highlights the simplicity of the house? Why does Agee compare the roof shingles to a bird's plumage? Does Agee use more similes or more metaphors in the selection? Which of each do you consider to be particularly effective? Why?

Writer's Journal

1. Imagine that you are Walker Evans. Write a **journal entry** explaining why you took each photograph and how each one is representative of the lives of sharecroppers.

2. Imagine that you are the woman in photograph 1 or the man in photograph 3. Write a **letter** to James Agee describing what a typical day is like in your life.

3. Assume that you are the house. Write a **poem** or **short essay** describing what you see when the light descends on your exterior and how the light makes you feel.

Integrating the Language Arts

Language, Grammar, and Style

LINKING VERBS. Read the Language Arts Survey 3.10, "Linking Verbs." On a separate sheet of paper, write out each sentence, underlining the linking verbs.

1. Many people feel fortunate when they see how the sharecroppers lived.
2. Photographs were one means of documenting the lives of the sharecroppers.
3. Does the house in photograph 2 look unfinished to you?
4. Agee was alone in the Gudger house.
5. To the author, the house seemed imbued with "pure light."

Media Literacy

PHOTOGRAPHY CATALOG. Imagine that you are a museum curator in charge of organizing a photography exhibit of Walker Evans's work. Using the Internet, research the subjects he photographed in different periods of his life. Then select ten to twelve representative photographs online. Prepare a catalog for the exhibit, listing the title, year, and a brief description or history for each photograph. A good site to start with is the Farm Administration's web page at http://cti.itc.virginia.edu/~ds8s/walker/farm.html.

Collaborative Learning

MOVIE REVIEW. James Agee wrote the screenplay for the popular 1951 movie *The African Queen*, starring Katharine Hepburn and Humphrey Bogart. View the movie. Then, with a partner, play the roles of television movie critics. Stage a televised movie review in front of the class. One of you should give the movie a "thumbs up" and present reasons why viewers should see the movie; the other should give it a "thumbs down" and present reasons why people should not bother to see it.

"For the Future of Florida: Repair the Everglades!"

by Joette Lorion

Reader's resource

"For the Future of Florida: Repair the Everglades!" is an article from the *Everglades Reporter*, a newsletter published by the organization Friends of the Everglades. You can access the newsletter online at http://www.everglades.org/. Friends of the Everglades was founded in 1969 by Marjory Stoneman Douglas, a pioneer conservationist who formed this grassroots organization to stop a jetport from being built in Big Cypress Swamp, just west of the Everglades. The article describes a plan to restore the Everglades and actions taken by Friends and other organizations to enact the plan.

SCIENCE CONNECTION. The Everglades is a marshy, low-lying tropical area that covers about 5,000 square miles in southern Florida, extending from Lake Okeechobee to Florida Bay. The region is characterized by water, saw grass, hammocks (islandlike masses of vegetation), coastal mangrove forests, and solidly packed black muck (resulting from millions of years of vegetable decay in near-stagnant, warm water). After a century of being ditched, diked, and drained, only half of the Everglades is left. In addition to dying, the Everglades is under assault from pollution. It is the sole source of drinking water for more than five million people in Dade, Monroe, and Palm Beach counties.

About the AUTHOR

Joette Lorion, former president of Friends of the Everglades, is an active environmentalist.

Literary TOOLS

AIM. A writer's **aim** is his or her purpose, or goal. People may write with the following aims: to inform (expository/informational writing); to entertain, enrich, enlighten, and/or use an artistic medium, such as fiction or poetry, to share a perspective (imaginative writing); to tell a story about an event (narrative writing); to reflect (personal/expressive writing); to persuade readers to respond in some way, such as to agree with a position, change a view on an issue, reach an agreement, or perform an action (persuasive/argumentative writing). As you read, try to determine Lorion's main aim in writing the newsletter article.

EXPOSITION. **Exposition** is a type of writing that presents facts or opinions in an organized manner. As you read, identify points that Lorion makes as either facts or opinions.

Organizer

Make a chart. On the left, list several important points that Lorion makes in the newsletter article. On the right, identify each point as a fact or as an opinion. One example has been done for you.

POINTS	FACT OR OPINION
Douglas's words are as true today as when she wrote them.	opinion

Reader's JOURNAL

Select a plant or animal that you appreciate. How does it bring beauty into your life? On what in nature does it depend for survival?

For the Future of Florida:
Repair the Everglades!

Joette Lorion

"If the people will it, if they enforce their will on the water managers of Florida's future, the Everglades can be restored to nature's design."
Marjory Stoneman Douglas.

The Marshall Plan

Marjory Stoneman Douglas recently turned 108 years old, but the above words from her book *The Everglades: River of Grass* are as true today as when she wrote them. Equally true is the headline of this newsletter. This same headline appeared in the *Everglades Reporter* in 1981 when Friends announced a plan to restore the Everglades. The repair plan was developed by ecologist Art Marshall. The message of the "Marshall Plan" was simple: To repair the Everglades Ecosystem, sheetflow[1] must be restored, to the greatest extent possible, from the Kissimmee River down through Lake Okeechobee, south through the central Everglades and into Florida Bay.

What was the message of the "Marshall Plan"?

The purpose of the Plan was to protect and recover a vast array of natural resources which were quickly being degraded—drinking water, freshwater fisheries, marine fisheries and Everglades National Park. Restoration

Which natural resources were quickly being degraded?

of the ecosystem called for, among other things, resolving the pollution problems of Lake Okeechobee and the vast Everglades Agricultural Area, as well as dechannelizing the lower Kissimmee River, which would provide the start of the long sheetflow of water which would pass through Lake Okeechobee and into the Everglades and the Park.

Art Marshall's plan was necessary because the Central and Southern Florida Project, started in 1948, had created an 1800 mile canal and levee system to provide flood control for cities and farms. This ditching, diking, and draining of the Everglades reduced this four million acre wetland by half and resulted in a reduction of nesting wading birds by 94%. The Marshall Plan forms the

By what percentage was the nesting of wading birds reduced because of ditching, diking, and draining of the Everglades?

basis of the plan for restoration being supported by most conservationists today and guides the efforts of Friends of the Everglades.

Marjory spoke of Art Marshall's role in her autobiography *Voice of the River*: "Although my phrase 'River of Grass' first awakened people to the notion of the Everglades as a river, it was Art Marshall who filled in the blanks . . . More than any other person, he stretched our idea of the Everglades and how the system interacts with everything else, which created the most powerful arguments for preserving the water. Self-interest is a more reliable motivation than environmental pity or noblesse oblige,[2] and Marshall accomplished the extraordinary magic

---

1. **sheetflow.** Broad, shallow, relatively unconfined flow of water across sloping terrain (as opposed to controlled, restricted flow as in a channel or river)

2. **noblesse oblige.** Obligation of honorable, generous, and responsible behavior associated with high rank or birth

---

words for everyday use

ar • ray (ə rā') *n.*, large group, number, or quantity of people or things. *An impressive array of scholars sat with heads bent over their books in the library.*

de • grad • ed (di grā' əd) *part.*, reduced in quality or value. *Language purists believe that English is being degraded in much modern advertising.*

e • co • sys • tem (ē' kō sis' təm) *n.*, complex of a community of organisms and its environment functioning as an ecological unit in nature. *The ecosystem along the riverbank was threatened by a new housing development.*

lev • ee (le' vē) *n.*, embankment for preventing flooding. *Levees in Louisiana protect cities and farmland from flooding.*

wet • land (wet' land) *n.*, land or area (as tidal flats or swamps) containing much soil moisture. *Herons build their nests in wetlands.*

con • ser • va • tion • ist (kän sər vā' shə nist) *n.*, person who advocates conservation of natural resources. *Because John Muir was an important American conservationist, Muir Woods National Monument was named for him.*

of taking the Everglades out of the bleeding hearts category forever."

Taking it to the Streets

Art Marshall took it out of the bleeding hearts category and worked with Marjory Stoneman Douglas of Friends of the Everglades and Johnny Jones of the Florida Wildlife Federation to take the plan to the streets. Friends newsletters printed a petition and asked everyone to sign on. They described the environmental and human benefits that would be <u>accrued</u> from the repair of the Everglades system. They told Garden Clubs, Rotary Clubs, political organizations and County Commissions how fixing the Everglades would improve water quality and water quantity, and that restored sheetflow would remove pollutants and restore the health of the system.

Support for Restoration Grows

These Everglades ambassadors were so effective that soon plans to restore the Kissimmee from a canal back to a <u>meandering</u> river began to take form, and today that restoration is underway. By 1992, the movement to restore the Everglades had mushroomed and Congress authorized the Central and South Florida Project

Comprehensive Review Study that directed the Secretary of the Army to study the <u>feasibility</u> of modifying the existing flood control project with particular reference to "modifying the project or its operation for improving the quality of the environment, improving protection of the aquifer,[3] and improving the <u>integrity</u>, capability, and conservation of urban water supplies affected by the project or its operation." In 1996, with public <u>sentiment</u> for restoration still growing, Congress passed the Water Resources and Development Act of 1996 (WRDA). This Act requires the Secretary of the Army to develop a "proposed <u>comprehensive</u> plan for the purpose of restoring, preserving and protecting the South Florida ecosystem." The plan is to provide for the "protection of water quality in, and reduction of fresh water from, the Everglades." It must also include "such features as are necessary to provide for the water-related needs of the region, including flood control, the <u>enhancement</u> of water supplies and other objectives served by the Central and Southern Florida Project." The Army Corps of Engineers must present the Plan to Congress by July 1, 1999.

What mandate was given in the 1996 Water Resources and Development Act (WRDA)?

Currently the Corps is in the process of studying alternative plans to restore the system, now

---

3. **aquifer.** Stratum or zone below the surface of the earth capable of producing water as from a well

---

words for everyday use

ac • crued (ə krüd') *part.*, accumulated after a period of time. *When I learned that interest could be <u>accrued</u>, I lent my sister money.*

me • an • der • ing (mē an' der iŋ) *adj.*, wandering aimlessly or casually without urgent destination. *The <u>meandering</u> tourists found the cobblestone streets and canals of Amsterdam delightful.*

fea • si • bil • i • ty (fē zə bi' lə tē) *n.*, suitability. *The <u>feasibility</u> of the plan to build a large cineplex in the small town was brought into question.*

in • teg • ri • ty (in te' grə tē) *n.*, unimpaired condition; soundness. *The <u>integrity</u> of the ship's hull was compromised when it struck an iceberg.*

sen • ti • ment (sen' tə mənt) *n.*, opinion. *The <u>sentiment</u> of the governor was that a unicameral legislature would be more effective.*

com • pre • hen • sive (căm pri hen' siv) *adj.*, covering completely or broadly; inclusive. *Because the notes he borrowed from Jerry were so <u>comprehensive</u>, Jon felt he wouldn't get behind in biology.*

en • hance • ment (in hant' smənt) *n.*, improvement in value, quality, desirability, or attractiveness. *The <u>enhancement</u> of the ballet costumes was achieved by adding satin waistbands.*

reduced by half and surrounded by cities and farmland. The Restudy plan must consider the Conceptual Plan that was developed by a variety of interests under the Governor's Commission for a <u>Sustainable</u> South Florida. It is a complicated process and the game is currently being played by interest groups and agencies. The environmental groups have scientists studying the alternatives, and Friends serves on the Everglades <u>Coalition's</u> Restudy team. We continue to participate on behalf of the Everglades —calling for the right amount of clean water at the right time and in the right place.

What is the state of the Everglades today?

Marjory's <u>admonition</u> in her 1947 book that the whole thing may depend on our ability to learn to work together is becoming painfully clear. Although restoration of the natural Everglades system is essential to the health of South Florida, it is often difficult for urban, agricultural, and development interests to understand the ecological concept that is critical to a healthy South Florida. The health of South Florida—our people, wildlife, cities, farms, economy and drinking water—depends on a healthy Everglades. ∎

words for everyday use

sus • tain • a • ble (səs stā′ nə bəl) *adj.*, using a resource so that the resource is not depleted or permanently damaged. *<u>Sustainable</u> agriculture is realizable with crop rotation.*

co • a • li • tion (kō ə li′ shən) *n.*, temporary alliance of distinct parties for joint action. *The goal of the <u>coalition</u> is to achieve equal rights for minorities.*

ad • mo • ni • tion (ad mə ni′ shən) *n.*, warning or cautioning. *The teacher's <u>admonition</u> that there would be a quiz unless students started participating led to several hands being raised.*

Do you think Lorion would support a letter-writing campaign to state and federal legislators in support of restoration of the Everglades? Why, or why not?

ABOUT THE RELATED READING

The Related Reading is an excerpt from Marjory Stoneman Douglas's book *The Everglades: River of Grass*, which was published in 1947. The book calls attention to the need for preserving the ecosystem of the Florida Everglades. In addition to being an advocate for the Everglades, Douglas was a journalist, writer of fiction and nonfiction, editor, publisher, and crusader for women's rights and racial justice. In 1993 President Clinton awarded Douglas the Medal of Freedom for her work on behalf of the Everglades. Douglas died in 1998 at the age of 108.

The *Grass*

Marjory Stoneman Douglas

The Everglades begin at Lake Okeechobee.

That is the name later Indians gave the lake, a name

almost as recent as the word "Everglades." It means

"Big Water." Everybody knows it.

Yet few have any idea of those pale, seemingly illimitable waters. Over the shallows, often less than a foot deep but seven hundred fifty or so square miles in actual area, the winds in one gray swift moment can shatter the reflections of sky and cloud whiteness standing still in that shining, polished, shimmering expanse. A boat can push for hours in a day of white sun through the short, crisp lake waves and there will be nothing to be seen anywhere but the brightness where the color of the water and the color of the sky become one. Men out of sight of land can stand in it up to their armpits and slowly "walk in" their long nets to the waiting boats. An everglade kite and his mate, questing in great solitary circles, rising and dipping and rising again on the wind currents, can look down all day long at the water faintly green with floating water lettuce or marked by thin standing lines of reeds, utter their sharp goat cries, and be seen and heard by no one at all.

There are great shallow islands, all brown reeds or shrubby trees thick in the water. There are masses of water weeds and hyacinths and flags rooted so long they seem solid earth, yet there is nothing but lake bottom to stand on. There the egret and the white ibis and the glossy ibis and the little blue herons in their thousands nested and circled and fed.

A long northeast wind, a "norther," can lash all that still surface to dirty vicious gray and white, over which the rain mists shut down like stained rolls of wool, so that from the eastern sand rim under dripping cypresses or the west ridge with its live oaks, no one would guess that all that waste of empty water stretched there but for the long monotonous wash of waves on unseen marshy shores.

Saw grass reaches up both sides of that lake in great enclosing arms, so that it is correct to say that the Everglades are there also. But south, southeast, and southwest, where the lake water slopped and seeped and ran over and under the rock and soil, the greatest mass of the saw grass begins. It stretches as it always has stretched, in one thick enormous curving river of grass, to the very end. This is the Everglades.

It reaches one hundred miles from Lake Okeechobee to the Gulf of Mexico, fifty, sixty, even seventy miles wide. No one has ever fought his way along its full length. Few have ever crossed the northern wilderness of nothing but grass. Down that almost invisible slope the water moves. The grass stands. Where the grass and the water are there is the heart, the current, the meaning of the Everglades.

The grass and the water together make the river as simple as it is unique. There is no other river like it. Yet within that simplicity, enclosed within the river and bordering and intruding on it from each side, there is subtlety and diversity, a crowd of changing forms, of thrusting teeming life. And all that becomes the region of the Everglades.

The truth of the river is the grass. They call it saw grass. Yet in the botanical sense it is not grass at all so much as a fierce, ancient, cutting sedge. It is one of the oldest of the green growing forms in this world.

There are many places in the South where this saw grass, with its sharp central fold and edges set with fine saw teeth like points of glass, this sedge called *Cladium jamaicensis*, exists. But this is the greatest concentration of saw grass in the world. It grows fiercely in the fresh water creeping down below it. When the original saw grass thrust up its spears into the sun, the fierce sun, lord and power and first cause over the Everglades as of all the green world, then the Everglades began. They lie wherever the saw grass extends: 3,500 square miles, hundreds and thousands and millions, of acres, water, and saw grass.

The first saw grass, exactly as it grows today, sprang up and lived in the sweet water and the pouring sunlight, and died in it, and from its own dried and decaying tissues and tough fibers bright with silica sprang up more fiercely again. Year after year it grew and was fed by its own brown rotting, taller and denser in the dark soil of its own death. Year after year after year, hundreds after hundreds of years, not so long as any geologic age but long in botanic time, far longer than anyone can be sure of, the saw grass grew. Four thousand years, they say, it must at least have grown like that, six feet, ten feet, twelve feet, even fifteen in places of deepest water. The edged and folded swords bristled around the delicate straight tube of pith that burst into brown flowering. The brown seed, tight enclosed after the manner of sedges, ripened in dense brownness. The seed was dropped and worked down in the water and its own ropelike mat of roots. All that decay of leaves and seed covers and roots was packed deeper year after year by the elbowing upthrust of its own life. Year after year it laid down new layers of virgin muck under the living water.

There are places now where the depth of the muck is equal to the height of the saw grass. When it is uncovered and brought into the sunlight, its stringy and grainy dullness glitters with the myriad unrotted silica points, like glass dust.

At the edges of the Glades, and toward those southern- and southwesternmost reaches where the great estuary or delta of the Glades river takes another form entirely, the saw grass is shorter and more sparse, and the springy, porous muck deposit under it is shallower and thinner. But where the saw grass grows tallest in the deepest muck, there goes the channel of the Glades.

The water winks and flashes here and there among the sawgrass roots, as the clouds are blown across the sun. To try to make one's way among these impenetrable tufts is to be cut off from all air, to be beaten down by the sun and ripped by the grassy saw-toothed edges as one sinks in mud and water over the roots. The dried yellow stuff holds no weight. There is no earthly way to get through the mud or the standing, keen-edged blades that crowd these interminable miles.

Or in the times of high water in the old days, the flood would rise until the highest tops of that sharp grass were like a thin lawn standing out of water as blue as the sky, rippling and wrinkling, linking the pools and spreading and flowing on its true course southward.

A man standing in the center of it, if he could get there, would be as lost in saw grass, as out of sight of anything but saw grass as a man drowning in the middle of Okeechobee—or the Atlantic Ocean, for that matter—would be out of sight of land.

The water moves. The saw grass, pale green to deep-brown ripeness, stands rigid. It is moved only in sluggish rollings by the vast push of the winds across it. Over its endless acres here and there the shadows of the dazzling clouds quicken and slide, purple-brown, plum-brown, mauve-brown, rust-brown, bronze. The bristling, blossoming tops do not bend easily like standing grain. They do not even in their own growth curve all one way but stand in edged clumps, curving against each other, all the massed curving blades making millions of fine arching lines that at a little distance merge to a huge expanse of brown wires or bristles or, farther beyond, to deep-piled plush. At the horizon they become velvet. The line they make is an edge of velvet against the infinite blue, the blue-and-white, the clear fine primrose yellow,

Marjory Stoneman Douglas in the Florida Everglades.

the burning brass and crimson, the molten silver, the deepening hyacinth sky.

The clear burning light of the sun pours daylong into the saw grass and is lost there, soaked up, never given back. Only the water flashes and glints. The grass yields nothing.

Nothing less than the smashing power of some hurricane can beat it down. Then one can see, from high up in a plane, where the towering weight and velocity of the hurricane was the strongest and where along the edges of its whorl it turned less and less savagely and left the saw grass standing. Even so, the grass is not flattened in a continuous swath but only here and here and over there, as if the storm bounced or lifted and smashed down again in great hammering strokes or enormous cat-licks.

Only one force can conquer it completely and that is fire. Deep in the layers of muck there are layers of ashes, marks of old fires set by lightning or the early Indians. But in the early days the water always came back and there were long slow years in which the saw grass grew and died, laying down again its tough resilient decay.

This is the saw grass, then, which seems to move as the water moved, in a great thick arc south and southwestward from Okeechobee to the Gulf. There at the last imperceptible incline of the land the saw grass goes along the headwaters of many of those wide, slow, mangrove-bordered fresh-water rivers, like a delta or an estuary into which the salt tides flow and draw back and flow again.

The mangrove becomes a solid barrier there, which by its strong, arched, and labyrinthine roots collects the sweepage of the fresh water and the salt and holds back the parent sea. The supple branches, the oily green leaves, set up a barrier against the winds, although the hurricanes prevail easily against them. There the fresh water meets the incoming salt, and is lost.

It may be that the mystery of the Everglades is the saw grass, so simple, so enduring, so hostile. It was the saw grass and the water which divided east coast from west coast and made the central solitudes that held in them the secrets of time, which has moved here so long unmarked.

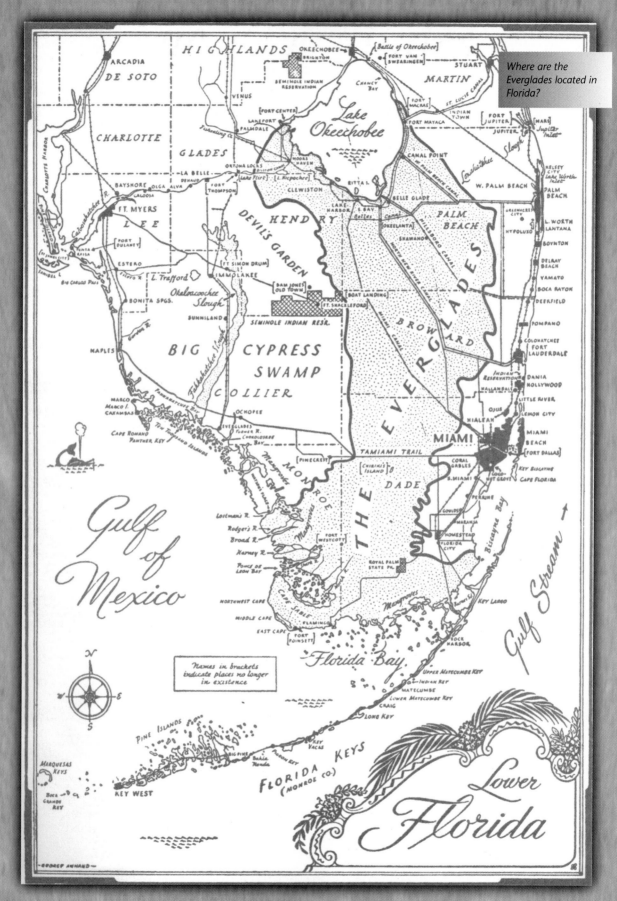

Where are the Everglades located in Florida?

Investigate, Inquire, and Imagine

Recall: GATHERING FACTS

1a. Look at the map on page 526. What main body of water feeds into the Everglades?

2a. According to Marjory Stoneman Douglas, who needs to enforce their will on the water managers of Florida's future? Why?

3a. Who came up with the "Marshall Plan"?

Interpret: FINDING MEANING

1b. What would happen if water from Lake Kissimmee, the Kissimmee River, and Lake Okeechobee were diverted from the Everglades?

2b. What is "nature's design"?

3b. Look up the Marshall Plan in an encyclopedia. Why are quotation marks placed around the Marshall Plan in the selection?

Analyze: TAKING THINGS APART

4a. Identify the different groups that are working together to restore the Everglades.

Synthesize: BRINGING THINGS TOGETHER

4b. *Prescient* means knowing something before it happens. Explain why Marjory Stoneman Douglas's admonition in 1947 was prescient.

Evaluate: MAKING JUDGMENTS

5a. After reading Lorion's article, do you agree or disagree that action should be taken to restore the Everglades? Support your answer.

Extend: CONNECTING IDEAS

5b. Read the Related Reading "The Grass" by Marjory Stoneman Douglas. What characterizes the Everglades, according to Douglas? What descriptions does she give of it? What evidence does she give that the Everglades have changed? How does she write about the Everglades, scientifically or poetically? Explain.

Understanding Literature

AIM. Review the definition for **aim** in the Handbook of Literary Terms. What is Lorion's principal aim in writing this newsletter article? Does she achieve that aim? Explain.

EXPOSITION. Review the definition for **exposition** in the Handbook of Literary Terms and the chart you made for Literary Tools on page 517. How does Lorion organize her newsletter article? What is Lorion's position? Does she support her position with facts or opinions? How does Lorion feel about Marjory Stoneman Douglas? What is the intention of Lorion in making references to Douglas?

Writer's Journal

1. Imagine you are Joette Lorion. Write a **journal entry** explaining why you consider Marjory Stoneman Douglas a personal hero.

2. Imagine you are Marjory Stoneman Douglas. Write a **letter of complaint** to the administrator of the Central and Southern Florida Project expressing your opinion about the changes they are proposing to the Everglades.

3. Write a **summary** of the excerpt from Marjory Stoneman Douglas's book *The Everglades: River of Grass*.

Integrating the Language Arts

Language, Grammar, and Style

COMMAS. Read the Language Arts Survey 3.87, "Commas." Then rewrite the following sentences, inserting commas where they are needed. Some sentences might have more than one comma.

1. Drinking water freshwater fisheries marine fisheries and Everglades National Park were quickly being degraded in the Everglades.

2. The Water Resources and Development Act which was passed in 1996 required the Secretary of the Army to develop a comprehensive plan to restore the Everglades.

3. Douglas was a relentless well-spoken experienced champion of the Everglades.

4. Having written *The Everglades: River of Grass* Douglas founded Friends of the Everglades.

5. She said "The Everglades is a test. If we pass, we get to keep the planet."

Study and Research & Media Literacy

EVERGLADES NATURE GUIDE. Using online and print sources, research plants and animals living in the Everglades. Then select five plants and five animals and make a nature guide that someone visiting the Everglades might find useful. Give the scientific name for each species. Describe where it lives and what it needs to survive. Add illustrations.

Applied English

LETTER-WRITING CAMPAIGN. Write a letter to a congressional representative from your district in support of the restoration of the Everglades. Explain what you feel needs to be done, and why. You might find it helpful to refer to the Language Arts Survey 6.5, "Writing a Business Letter."

"GHOST OF EVEREST"

by Jerry Adler

Reader's resource

This article first appeared in a popular weekly news periodical, *Newsweek,* on May 17, 1999, two weeks after the mountain climber George Mallory's body was found on Mount Everest, and 75 years after he disappeared. Because of the nature of the discovery, the story combines a current news discovery with history. In fact, as the article quotes from another news source, the *Beijing Youth Daily,* "history may be rewritten" because of it. While **"Ghost of Everest"** appeared in *Newsweek*, the news story itself "broke," or first appeared, on the Internet.

GEOGRAPHY CONNECTION. Mount Everest stands in the Himalayan mountain range on the border of Nepal and China (Tibet). It is the highest spot on Earth, reaching 29,029 feet above sea level.

TECHNOLOGY CONNECTION. Mallory communicated by writing handwritten notes and sending Sherpas, Tibetan porters, to carry them to people in the base camps below. Simonson, on the other hand, sent a message by radio to other climbers when the body was discovered. He then wrote a dispatch on his laptop computer from base camp, at 21,300 feet, and posted the news of the discovery of Mallory's body on the Internet that same day.

Graphic Organizer

As you read, use a graphic organizer like the one below to keep track of the facts given in the background information on each of the climbers:

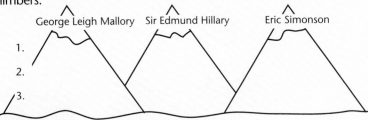

George Leigh Mallory   Sir Edmund Hillary   Eric Simonson

1.

2.

3.

Reader's Journal

How do you feel toward someone who has already succeeded at something you have been working toward?

Literary TOOLS

PERIODICAL AND ARTICLE. A **periodical** is a newspaper, magazine, or newsletter that is published regularly (once a week, for example, as *Newsweek* is). An **article** is a brief work of nonfiction on a specific topic. Encyclopedia entries, newspaper reports, and nonfiction magazine pieces are examples of articles. This selection is an example of a magazine article.

BACKGROUND INFORMATION. **Background information** is information provided in a literary work, often at the beginning, to explain the situation to the reader. A writer may include background information to explain the central conflict, the relationships between the characters, the setting, or any other part of his or her work.

Three famous climbers

- George Leigh Mallory was born in 1886 in England. When he was 38 years old, he and his climbing partner, Andrew Irvine, were the first to attempt to reach the top of Mount Everest. They lost their lives in that attempt on June 8, 1924. It has never been determined whether they made it to the top.
- Sir Edmund Hillary was born in 1919 in New Zealand. He and his Nepalese climbing partner, Tenzing Norgay, became the first people ever to officially reach the peak of Mount Everest, on May 29, 1953. Since the expedition was led and sponsored by Great Britain, Great Britain is the nation that claims to have been the first to reach the peak.
- Eric Simonson, born in 1956 in Washington State, has been a professional guide since 1973, and is one of the most respected expedition organizers in the world. He led the expedition to the peak of Mount Everest to search for Mallory's body.

The last photograph of Mallory, left, and Irvine, right, as they leave for the summit, 1924.

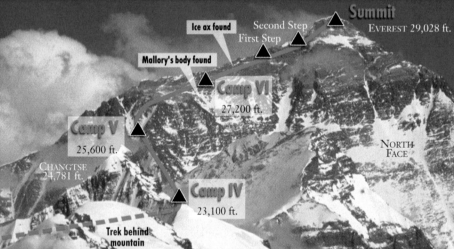

Ice ax found

Second Step
First Step

Mallory's body found

Summit
EVEREST 29,028 ft.

Camp VI
27,200 ft.

Camp V
25,600 ft.

CHANGTSE
24,781 ft.

NORTH
FACE

Camp IV
23,100 ft.

Camp III
(Advanced
base camp)
21,300 ft.

Trek behind
mountain

Camp II
20,000 ft.

Camp I
18,300 ft.

**1999 Mallory & Irvine
Research Expedition Route**

After 75 years, the mountain yields the body of the legendary George Mallory. But the mystery endures: did he reach the top?

Ghost of Everest

Jerry Adler

He must have died near, or even after, sunset, because he had taken off his goggles and stowed them in a pocket. The <u>unnervingly</u> white skin of his back was bare to the sky where the wind had <u>flayed</u> off his clothing, seven layers of cotton and wool. From the evidence, George Mallory, the first man to attempt the <u>summit</u> of Mount Everest, had fallen to his death, landing several hundred feet below the ridge that leads to the peak. The astounding discovery of Mallory's body answers one question about what happened after he and Andrew Irvine disappeared into the clouds one day in June 1924. If it was near dark, he almost certainly fell on his way back down. But that only raises a second question, still unanswered: before turning around, did Mallory reach the summit?

What question is still unanswered?

Among the mountaineers, solving this puzzle would be <u>akin</u> to finding a manuscript of "Othello" in an envelope with Shakespeare's return address. Thus, on the morning of May 1, five American climbers fanned out on a steep and rocky slope at about 27,000 feet. They were part of an eight-member team of some of the world's top mountaineers (and a PBS documentary crew), hoping both to find the remains of Mallory and Irvine and to determine if they had reached the summit before dying—29 years before Sir Edmund Hillary and Tenzing Norgay

---

words for everyday use

un • nerv • ing • ly (ən nər' viŋ lē) *adv.*, deprived of courage and physical strength; cause to become weak and ineffective, especially from fear. *His mother waited <u>unnervingly</u> for the blizzard to hit.*

flayed (flād') *vi.*, strip off the skin or surface of. *His face was <u>flayed</u> by the sharp winds.*

sum • mit (sə' mət) *n.*, highest point, ridge, or level of a mountain; peak. *His goal was to climb to the <u>summit</u> of the mountain.*

a • kin (ə kin') *adj.*, showing the same nature; similar. *Her first roller coaster ride gave her a feeling <u>akin</u> to terror.*

made the first recognized <u>ascent</u>, in 1953. A similar expedition looked for Mallory in 1986, without success. But luck was with the searchers this time. As expedition leader Eric Simonson told Newsweek from base camp "there was very little winter snow, and the temperatures have been moderate by Everest standards," exposing areas usually covered. By Everest standards, "moderate" meant temperatures well below zero with winds of 30 miles an hour or more.

This was on the north, or Tibetan, face of Everest, not Hillary's route up the Southeast Ridge, where five climbers died in the famous 1996 storm. Compared with the southeast approach from Nepal, Simonson said, the north face avoids the dangerous passage under the teetering ice blocks of the Hkumbu Iceface but it requires a little more climbing expertise and involves more time spent above 25,000 feet. Yet Mallory himself was in the opinion of the definitive Everest historian Walt Unsworth, "a <u>competent</u>, rather than great, climber." He was experienced, to be sure, a veteran of two earlier British Everest expeditions, as well as handsome, <u>charismatic</u> and athletic. But he was pushing 38, a married man with three young children and a minor appointment at Cambridge. When the British Alpine Club called him to be second in command of its eight-man team, he almost turned it down. "This is going to be more like war than mountaineering," he told a friend. He and Mallory had seen combat in the war. "I don't expect to come back." Yet he felt the inescapable <u>lure</u> of Everest. He climbed it, he famously told an American reporter,

"because it is there"—a remark that either captured his deeply spiritual approach to mountaineering or (as friends claimed) reflected his <u>exasperation</u> with being asked the same pointless question time after time.

His chosen companion, Irvine, was only 22, a <u>novice</u> climber but exceptionally strong and fit. He was also an expert with the new technologies of bottled oxygen and zippers. Mallory, of the old school, preferred to fasten his anorak with tried-and-true buttons. The

What technology is new to Mallory?

expedition (like most of those today) relied on the indispensable Sherpa porters,[1] but Mallory had no doubt which race made the best mountaineers. When conditions turn bad, he wrote in a <u>dispatch</u> quoted in *The New York Times*, "the splendid fellow who bore his load so proudly has become a veritable child—a child for whom the British officer is at every turn responsible."

On the morning of June 8, the two set out from a camp at 27,000 feet, where they had spent the night alone. Shortly before 1 P.M., another member of their <u>expedition</u>, Noel Odell, spotted from far below two distant figures climbing a rocky ledge. If this was the Second Step, a sheer wall of rock and ice very near the summit, then they almost certainly reached the peak that day. But Odell wasn't certain of what he saw; the climbers may have been at the much lower First Step, with the <u>formidable</u> Second still to come. As Odell watched, the figures disappeared into a cloud. When the

---

1. **Sherpa porters.** Tibetan people skilled in mountain climbing who often accompany climbers as guides

---

words for everyday use

as • cent (ə sent′) n., act of going, traveling, or climbing up. *After the picnic they began their <u>ascent</u> of the mountain.*
com • pe • tent (käm′ pə tənt) adj., possessed of sufficient aptitude, skill, strength, or knowledge. *Before he was hired, he took a test to prove his skills were <u>competent</u>.*
char • is • mat • ic (kar əz ma′ tik) adj., special or magnetic charm or appeal. *The boy's humor made him <u>charismatic</u>.*
lure (loor′) n., temptation. *The <u>lure</u> of the outdoors is recorded in many poems.*
ex • as • per • a • tion (ig zas pə rā′ shən) n., marked irritation or annoyance. *His <u>exasperation</u> over the complicated instructions caused a delay in his work.*
nov • ice (nä′ vəs) adj., beginner; inexperienced person. *He was a <u>novice</u> horseback rider.*
dis • patch (di spach′) n., report, news brief. *They waited for the latest <u>dispatch</u> on the storm.*
ex • pe • di • tion (ek spə di′ shən) n., journey, voyage, or excursion undertaken for a specific purpose. *As an archeologist, he had gone on many such <u>expeditions</u>.*
for • mi • da • ble (for′ mə də bəl) adj,. fearful, dreadful, or intimidating. *The <u>formidable</u> size of the project worried the students.*

weather cleared, hours later, Mallory and Irvine were nowhere to be seen. Nine years later another English expedition recovered an ice ax below the First Step, believed to be Irvine's. But there was no sign of their bodies until 1975, when a Chinese climber spotted what he described as "old English dead" near his expedition's Camp VI. Unfortunately, he kept the news to himself for three years, before confiding in a Japanese climber—and died himself the very next day in an avalanche, taking with him the exact location of the bodies.

What happened to Mallory and Irvine?

Still, that was enough information for Simonson and his team to go on, once they figured out where the Chinese climbers' camp had been. In a posting on the Mountain Zone website (www.mountain-zone.com), an expedition sponsor, climber Conrad Anker described "looking to the west [and then] I saw a patch of white, that was whiter than the rock . . . and also whiter than the snow." "George was lying on his stomach," Simonson reported, "head uphill, arms outstretched, like a frozen statue." Anker put out a coded call on his radio—there were scores of climbers on the mountain, and he didn't want to attract a stampede—and his team-

mates gathered and began carefully digging in the icy gravel.

All along, the climbers had expected to find Irvine, whose ice ax had been recovered nearby. When a tag with Mallory's name turned up, they wondered why Irvine was wearing Mallory's shirt. "Then it hit us," climber Dave Hahn reported on Mountain Zone, ". . . we were in the presence of George Leigh Mallory himself. THE man of the mountain."

How do they know they found Mallory's body?

The body had evidently fallen some distance; a leg was fractured at the boot top, and he was tied to a broken rope—at the other end of which, presumably, had been Irvine. The climbers recovered a few personal objects, including letters, and collected a tissue sample for DNA analysis.[2] Then, with rocks laboriously gathered from the steep slope, they buried Mallory where he lay on his beloved Everest.

What they didn't find, though, was evidence that Mallory had reached the top, such as a notebook or even his camera, which might have contained recoverable images from a summit

Mallory & Irvine Research Expedition, 1999.

"Take one step away and you're not worried about George Mallory's life, you're worried about your own life."

---

2. **DNA analysis.** Deoxyribonucleic acid analysis, a study of cell tissues to determine facts about the body

words for everyday use

spon • sor (spän[t]′ sər) n., one who assumes responsibility for some other person or thing. *Acting as my sponsor, my uncle paid for my study abroad assignment.*

picture snapped 75 years ago. Such a discovery could be politically sensitive, since China claims as a matter of national honor the first recorded ascent of Everest from the north, in 1960. If Mallory did it in 1924, the *Beijing Youth Daily*[3] noted last week, "history may be rewritten."

It may yet be. In 1960 the Second Step was conquered by a climber who found footholds in the rock with his bare feet, sacrificing his toes to frostbite. Modern climbers use a ladder, fixed there in 1975. But sometime this week, Anker hopes to climb the Second Step as Mallory would have done it, without a ladder or ropes, just to see if it can be done. His fellow climbers will search at 27,000 feet again for Irvine. "This expedition," Simonson said, "is not just about going out looking for bodies. We want it to be a celebration of what those guys accomplished 75 years ago in leather boots and tweed jackets." Their achievement, of course, had no <u>practical</u> significance even then. Hillary himself, with a lifetime of honors behind him, said last week he hoped Mallory did make the summit ("but I think it's unlikely"). But who among us, imagining Mallory dying as he hugged the mountain, can help but wonder: at the moment he fell, was he looking down in disappointment—or up at the darkening sky in triumph? ∎

What evidence were they looking for and what would it prove?

What is the purpose of the expedition?

---

3. *Beijing Youth Daily.* Newspaper published in China

---

words for everyday use

prac • ti • cal (prak′ ti kəl) *adj.*, capable of being put to use or account. *Nigel found carrying an umbrella to be <u>practical</u> in London.*

Respond *to the* SELECTION

If you had been a member of Simonson's expedition, what would be the most significant aspects of the discovery of Mallory's body for you?

About *the* AUTHOR

Jerry Adler has been with *Newsweek* magazine since 1979. He has been a senior writer since 1981, and was promoted to senior editor in 1993. He has written articles on a wide variety of topics and has received many awards for his work, especially in the area of science and outer space. Adler received his Bachelor of Arts degree in American history from Yale University.

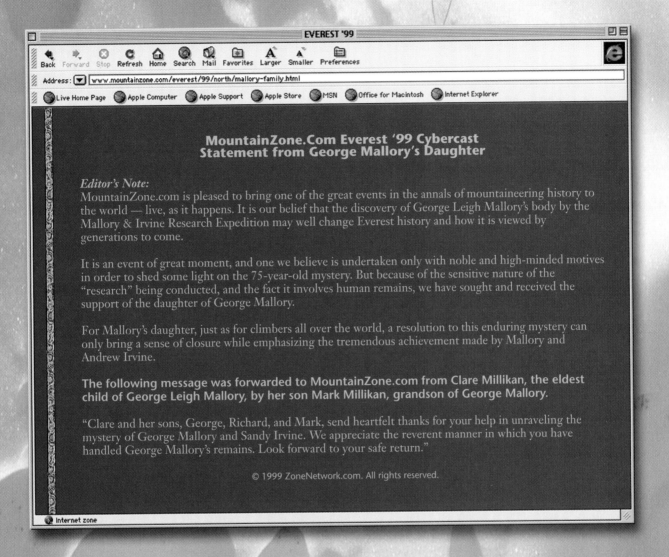

EVEREST '99

Address: www.mountainzone.com/everest/99/north/mallory-family.html

Live Home Page | Apple Computer | Apple Support | Apple Store | MSN | Office for Macintosh | Internet Explorer

MountainZone.Com Everest '99 Cybercast
Statement from George Mallory's Daughter

Editor's Note:
MountainZone.com is pleased to bring one of the great events in the annals of mountaineering history to the world — live, as it happens. It is our belief that the discovery of George Leigh Mallory's body by the Mallory & Irvine Research Expedition may well change Everest history and how it is viewed by generations to come.

It is an event of great moment, and one we believe is undertaken only with noble and high-minded motives in order to shed some light on the 75-year-old mystery. But because of the sensitive nature of the "research" being conducted, and the fact it involves human remains, we have sought and received the support of the daughter of George Mallory.

For Mallory's daughter, just as for climbers all over the world, a resolution to this enduring mystery can only bring a sense of closure while emphasizing the tremendous achievement made by Mallory and Andrew Irvine.

The following message was forwarded to MountainZone.com from Clare Millikan, the eldest child of George Leigh Mallory, by her son Mark Millikan, grandson of George Mallory.

"Clare and her sons, George, Richard, and Mark, send heartfelt thanks for your help in unraveling the mystery of George Mallory and Sandy Irvine. We appreciate the reverent manner in which you have handled George Mallory's remains. Look forward to your safe return."

Internet zone

ABOUT THE RELATED READING

The story of the discovery of George Mallory's body on Mount Everest broke on the Internet at MountainZone.com. Expedition Leader Eric Simonson called in the report on Sunday evening, May 2, from Advanced Base Camp at 21,300 feet on Mount Everest. His report confirmed that the 1999 Mallory and Irvine Research Expedition had found the remains of George Mallory, lost on Mount Everest on June 8, 1924. MountainZone.com posted this cybercast statement including the response from George Mallory's daughter.

Investigate, *Inquire,* and Imagine

Recall: GATHERING FACTS

1a. Identify the nationalities of each of the climbers who led the expeditions mentioned in the article.

2a. What is Mallory famous for saying?

3a. What did the members of Simonson's expedition do with Mallory's body?

→ Interpret: FINDING MEANING

1b. How would you describe the relationship between the climbers? How is mountain climbing also a competition between the nations?

2b. What did he mean by that?

3b. How did the climbers feel toward Mallory?

Analyze: TAKING THINGS APART

4a. What evidence is needed that would prove whether or not Mallory reached the peak?

→ Synthesize: BRINGING THINGS TOGETHER

4b. What would discovering the answer to this question mean? Do you think we will ever know the answer? Explain.

Evaluate: MAKING JUDGMENTS

5a. Simonson called conditions "moderate" by Everest standards. How would you describe the weather conditions?

→ Extend: CONNECTING IDEAS

5b. What hardships would have to be endured to climb Mount Everest?

Understanding *Literature*

PERIODICAL AND ARTICLE. Review the definition of a **periodical** and an **article** in the Literary Tools on page 529. In what other sources might you have read or heard about the information presented in "Ghost of Everest"? What are examples of periodicals other than *Newsweek* that you or your family read regularly?

BACKGROUND INFORMATION. Review the definition of **background information** in the Handbook of Literary Terms. Although the discovery in "Ghost of Everest" is current and newsworthy, it opens a case in history that is seventy-five years old. How does the background information the author provides help the reader understand the significance of the current piece of news?

Writer's Journal

1. Imagine that you are George Mallory on the day of June 8, 1924. Write the last **journal entry** in your climbing log.

2. Assume you are Sir Edmund Hillary. Write a **letter** to a friend describing what it was like to be the first to reach the peak of Mount Everest.

3. Imagine that you are Eric Simonson, leading a contemporary expedition up the mountain. Write a **speech** you would give to your team before setting out.

Integrating the Language Arts

Study and Research & Speaking and Listening

MOUNT EVEREST PRESENTATION. Climbing Mount Everest has been a goal for many mountain climbers. Sir Edmund Hillary was the first to officially reach the top in 1953. Do some research and gather information and dates. Ask questions that will help you explore different topics of the subject Mount Everest. How many climbers have made it to the top since Hillary? How many have attempted to reach the top? How many women have climbed it? Who was the oldest to climb? Who was the youngest? How many people have died? Once you have collected your statistics, organize your information and make a chart of your data. Use the chart to illustrate a presentation of the information to the class.

Collaborative Learning & Media Literacy

DISCUSSING VIDEOS. There have been many movies taken of Mount Everest, including an IMAX production of an expedition. With a group or as a class, view one of these films. Discuss the difference that viewing video footage makes in your understanding of what it would be like to climb Mount Everest and to actually be in the Himalayan mountains. What, for you, are the most stunning and significant visual aspects of Mount Everest? How would you describe the mountain—its weather conditions, its terrain, its physical presence?

Media Literacy & Study and Research

RESEARCHING ON THE INTERNET. The article references the website www.mountainzone.com. Log on to the website. Look at the articles on George Mallory, Mount Everest, and Eric Simonson. As you browse through them, jot down a list of other topics about climbing Mount Everest that you find interesting. Choose one topic and investigate it a bit further on the Internet. From information you find, write an article on a related topic. For example, write about the North face versus the South face, summarize an interview with Simonson, compare the mountain climbing gear Mallory used with gear available today, or investigate the 1996 tragedy in which five people died in a sudden storm on Mount Everest. Be sure to cite the sources you used.

Literary TOOLS

TONE. Tone is the emotional attitude toward the reader or toward the subject implied by a literary work. Examples of the different tones that a work may have include familiar, ironic, playful, sarcastic, and sincere. As you read, notice the tone Berman uses in this article.

ALLITERATION. Alliteration is the repetition of initial consonant sounds, or repeated initial vowel sounds. Find examples of alliteration in this selection.

Graphic Organizer

Fill in the cluster of ovals below with examples of alliteration or humor from the article. What makes the words humorous? Why does a repeated consonant sound funny?

deep pink prominences

Reader's Journal

Think of a time you have seen something magnificent in the sky—a falling star, northern lights, a planet, or a space satellite. How did it feel to see it from Earth?

"Best Sky Sights of the Next Century"

from *The Old Farmer's Almanac*
by Bob Berman

Reader's resource

This article appeared in *The Old Farmer's Almanac,* which is a periodical published once a year in September. An almanac is a publication that provides meteorological and astronomical data arranged according to the days, weeks, and months of a given year. It publishes all kinds of useful information, from gardening and farming tips, to weather predictions, to cooking instructions. It includes sunrise tables, ocean tide tables, and planting charts.

The Old Farmer's Almanac began in 1792 and is North America's oldest continuously published periodical. The founder, Robert B. Thomas, said the *Almanac's* "main endeavour is to be useful, but with a pleasant degree of humour (sic)."

SCIENCE CONNECTION. Astronomy is the science of all bodies in the universe, including stars, planets, comets, and meteors. Astronomers study all aspects of celestial bodies—their origin, evolution, motion, distance, and composition. Babylonians are credited with first recognizing constellations, in as early as 3000 BC. The Greek astronomer Pythagoras first proposed the idea that the earth is round in the sixth century BC.

A **comet** is any small celestial object that orbits the Sun. Comets develop gaseous envelopes and long luminous tails when near the sun. A comet is made up of the nucleus, coma, and tail. The nucleus, or center, is made of ices and soot or carbon dust. It is sometimes compared to a dirty snowball. The coma is the cloud of gas the nucleus gives off as it is melted by the sun. As the solar wind sweeps cometary matter away from the sun, it develops a long tail.

About the AUTHOR

Bob Berman writes a regular column on astronomy for *Discover* magazine. He is director of Storm King Observatory in Cornwall and Overlook Observatory near Woodstock, New York. He produces a weekly radio show called *Skywindow*. He is also the author of two books, *Secrets of the Night Sky* and *Cosmic Adventure: A Renegade Astronomer's Guide to the Universe.* The article Berman wrote for the *Farmer's Almanac* is full of factual information and shows his rich sense of humor.

BEST Sky Sights

OF THE NEXT CENTURY

Bob Berman

The Magnificent Seven Total Solar Eclipses
(Four for Canada)

Totality causes humans and animals alike to moan and babble, as normally invisible deep-pink <u>prominences</u> leap from the Sun's edge like nuclear <u>geysers</u>. Alas, this <u>ineffable</u> experience of totality happens just once every 360 years, on average, from any given site on Earth.

> What is "totality"?

August 21, 2017, will bring the first American totality: the 185-mile-wide shadow will slash the country from coast to coast—west to east—like a calligraphy[1] brushstroke. Another mainland American totality will occur on **April 8, 2024,** followed by the longest eclipse in U.S. history (a six-minute totality) on **August 12, 2045,** that again will cross the country from the Pacific to

> How often does a total solar eclipse happen?

the Atlantic—an inspiration, perhaps, for today's observers to stay healthy.

> What will happen on August 12, 2045?

After a shorter totality over Georgia in **2052,** the continental United States will then receive a rare present: two total solar eclipses within a single year, on **May 11, 2078,** and **May 1, 2079.** Finally, the century will close with a totality for the north-central and mid-Atlantic states in September of **2099.** And that's it—seven opportunities in the next 100 years for stay-at-home Americans to stand fully in the Moon's shadow (we should note, however, that brief totalities occur in northern Alaska in **2033** and **2097**).

> What will happen in 2052?

---

1. **calligraphy.** The art of ornamental, elegant writing.

---

words for everyday use

prom • i • nence (prä' mə nən[t]s) *n.,* object that stands out, or projects beyond a surface or line. *The skyscraper was an unusual <u>prominence</u> in the rural landscape.*

gey • ser (gī' zər) *n.,* spring that throws forth jets of heated water and steam. *Many visitors go to Yellowstone National Park to see its famous <u>geyser</u>, Old Faithful.*

in • ef • fa • ble (i ne' fə bəl) *adj.,* incapable of being expressed in words. *She watched the <u>ineffable</u> beauty of the sunset.*

Halley's comet.

For Canadian eclipse addicts, the **April 8, 2024,** event will also be seen from the Maritime provinces.[2] The next one, on **August 22, 2044,** will actually begin at sunrise on the border with Montana, then will hightail it northward through the western Prairies toward the North Pole. After that, it's a long wait until the eclipse of **May 1, 2079,** visible from the Maritimes, and the totality of **September 14, 2099,** seen in southwestern Canada.

Great Comets

In terms of sheer <u>spectacle</u>, the closest runner-up to solar totality is probably Earth's encounter with a Great Comet. While 1996's Hyakutake and 1997's Hale-Bopp did indeed break a 22-year Great Comet drought, neither was as spec-tacular—that is, bright, with a long tail—as some of the finest historical visitors.

What makes a comet spectacular?

The most-demanding comet-lovers desire a comet with both qualities, like Halley's memorable 1910 visit, or the "Great January comet" of that same extraordinary year. Although most spectacular comets have initially uncharted <u>orbits</u> of thousands of years and therefore visit us with no advance notice, the one trusty short-period comet that *can* be <u>predicted</u> is also the most famous of all—Halley's comet.

Why are we not informed about most comets?

---

2. **Maritime provinces.** Territory bordering on the sea

---

words for everyday use

spec • ta • cle (spek′ ti kəl) *n.,* remarkable or noteworthy site. *He was quite a <u>spectacle</u> in his clown costume.*
or • bit (or′ bət) *n.,* path of a celestial body, artificial satellite, or spacecraft around another body. *He studied the earth's <u>orbit</u> around the sun.*
pre • dict (pri dikt′) *vt.,* declare in advance, to forecast or prophecy. *Amy accurately <u>predicted</u> which dessert Irving would choose from the menu.*

Unfortunately, during Halley's most recent visit, in 1985 and '86, Earth was in nearly the worst possible position, the equivalent of the outfield bleacher seats. But the Earth/Halley geometry will be wonderful for its return in 2061. Then, it should span half the sky. Moreover, it will float in front of the stars of the Big Dipper, making it prominent for observers in the United States and Canada.

Take your vitamins and stick around for the next century's super spectacles, including the longest total solar eclipse in U.S. history (in 2045) or the spectacular return of Halley's Comet in 2061.

Meteor Showers

The finest reliable showers will continue to be summer's Perseids, from **August 11 to 13,** which will slowly creep to **August 12 to 14** as the century advances, and the rich Germinid display on the night of **December 13–14,** which will also migrate ahead one night toward century's end. Anyone can predict which years these will appear at their best by looking up the phases of the Moon for those dates. Meteors are greatly diminished from view by a Moon that falls between the first and last quarter phases.

Of course, for true spectacle, observers will be looking for a meteor "storm," the 50-to-100-shooting-stars-per-second display that happened in **1799, 1833,** and **1966.** Right now, it appears that the on-again, off-again $33\frac{1}{3}$-year periodicity of the Leonids should continue, giving us good opportunities in **2033, 2066,** and **2099.**

Planetary Conjunctions[3]

Truly awesome close encounters require a meeting of at least two of the three planets that can attain dazzling brilliance (Venus, Jupiter, and, rarely, Mars), or the Moon with one or more of these. We'll throw in bright but not brilliant Saturn and Mercury only when a meeting involving them is ultra-close. To qualify, the <u>celestial</u> targets must pass extremely close to each other in the night sky—perhaps even merge into a single, ultra-bright, alien-looking sky object. (Although events involving Venus usually occur in twilight, the sky sightings below remain visible long enough to stand out against a satisfyingly dark backdrop.)

What qualifies as a planetary close encounter?

The following table presents a comprehensive list of the *best* planetary events of the twenty-first century that can be seen during the nightfall-to-10 P.M. period, when most people are willing to venture out.

---

3. **Planetary Conjunctions.** When planets appear very close together in the sky or on a map

---

words for everyday use ce • les • tial (sə les′ chəl) *adj.,* of or relating to the sky: specifically, representing the visible bodies in the sky. *Marvin got a <u>celestial</u> map so he could identify the planets.*

Best Planetary Encounters

Date	Objects	Date	Objects
April 5, 2000	Ma, J	June 21, 2074	V, J
May 10, 2002	V, Ma	June 27, 2074	V, Mn, J
June 30, 2007	V, S	June 28, 2076	Ma, J
December 1, 2008	V, Mn, J	October 31, 2076	Mn, Ma, S
February 20, 2015	V, Mn, Ma	February 27, 2079	V, Ma
June 30–July 1, 2015	V, J	November 7, 2080	Ma, J, S
July 18, 2015	V, Mn, J	November 15, 2080	Ma, J, S
December 20, 2020	J, S	November 17, 2080	Mn, Ma, J, S
March 1, 2023	V, J	December 24, 2080	V, J
December 1–2, 2033	Ma, J	March 6, 2082	V, J
February 23, 2047	V, Ma	April 28, 2085	Mn, Ma, J
March 7, 2047	V, J	June 13, 2085	Me, V, J
May 13, 2066	V, Ma	May 15, 2098	V, Ma
July 1, 2066	V, S	June 29, 2098	V, J
March 14, 2071	V, J		

Me=Mercury   V=Venus   Mn=Moon   Ma=Mars   J=Jupiter   S=Saturn
In all these cases, face west toward the fading evening twilight.

Attach this article to a refrigerator you plan to keep for ten decades. But there's no substitute for keeping your eyes wide open after nightfall—for many of the best celestial spectacles, such as awesome long-period comets, northern lights, and bolides (exploding meteors), arrive with little or no warning, brilliant bombshells in the heavens. ∎

WHEN WILL THE MOON RISE TODAY?

A lunar puzzle involves the timing of moonrise. Folks who enjoy the out-of-doors and the wonders of nature may wish to commit to memory the following gem:

**The new Moon always rises at sunrise
And the first quarter at noon.
The full Moon always rises at
  sunset
And the last quarter at midnight.**

Moonrise occurs about 50 minutes later each day than the day before. The new Moon is invisible because its illuminated side faces completely away from Earth, which occurs when the Moon lines up between Earth and the Sun. One or two days after the date of the new Moon, you can see it in the western sky as a thin crescent setting just after sunset.

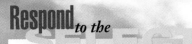

How does the information in the article change how you perceive the sky, and how you perceive time?

Investigate, *Inquire,* and Imagine

Recall: GATHERING FACTS

1a. When will the next sky event take place?

2a. What happened in 1986 that made Halley's comet difficult to view?

3a. What conditions are perfect for viewing a meteor shower?

Interpret: FINDING MEANING

1b. How old will you be on that date?

2b. How will it look when it next appears?

3b. How can conditions be predicted?

Analyze: TAKING THINGS APART

4a. Identify the main celestial events Berman discusses in his article.

Synthesize: BRINGING THINGS TOGETHER

4b. What is their relationship to each other?

Evaluate: MAKING JUDGMENTS

5a. Why does Berman cover events that will be happening over a span of one hundred years?

Extend: CONNECTING IDEAS

5b. Why does he tell us to take our vitamins and stick around, and to hang the article on a refrigerator for ten decades? What sense do you have of your own life span in relation to the life span of, for example, a comet?

Understanding *Literature*

TONE. Review the definition for **tone** in the Handbook of Literary Terms. What is Bob Berman's tone in this article? How would you describe it, and what examples can you find to support your description?

ALLITERATION. Review the definition of **alliteration** in Literary Tools on page 538, and look at the examples of it that you found in this selection. Was the article fun to read? If so, why? What other phrases make a play on words? Jot down a few sentences of your own that contain alliteration.

Writer's Journal

1. Write a **journal entry** describing your reaction to watching the stars "come out" at night. If you have never done it, then do so on the next clear evening and write about the experience.
2. Write a **paragraph** describing the size of the universe; include alliteration in your description.
3. Write a **myth** or **story** about a constellation.

Integrating the Language Arts

Language, Grammar, and Style

GERUNDS AND PARTICIPLES. Read the Language Arts Survey 3.80, "Verbals: Participles, Gerunds, and Infinitives." Then identify the gerunds and present participles in the following sentences.

1. Looking at *The Old Farmer's Almanac* is something farmers have been doing for centuries.
2. In the book you can find practical articles about gardening and farming.
3. A person gazing at the sky on August 21, 2017, will see a solar eclipse.
4. In 2061, night viewers will see a trailing comet.
5. Do you think writing about sky sights of the next century is something Bob Berman enjoys?

Applied English

TIME LINE. Make a time line of all the dates and events listed in this article, both past and future. Use different colors or symbols for each type of event—comets, meteor showers, solar eclipses, and lunar eclipses. Add your own birthdate (using a different color or symbol). What events have happened while you were alive? Add the birthdate of your parents and grandparents and ask them if they recall seeing any of the celestial events on your time line. What events do you hope to be able to see in the future? How old will you be? What events do you think you will not be able to see?

Study and Research

RESEARCHING THE EARTH AND SKY. Log on to the website of *The Old Farmer's Almanac* at http://www.almanac.com and look over some of the various meteorological and astronomical data that is recorded there. Choose a specific topic to research—for example, lunar eclipses, meteors, the planet Mars, high and low tides, or tornadoes. Collect information on this topic from a variety of sources. You may visit http://www.britannica.com or other online encyclopedias. Then write a short informative report. Try to keep your writing in line with the mission of the *Almanac*: make it "useful, but with a pleasant degree of humor."

"Research Strategies for the Learning Highway"

from *The Learning Highway: Smart Students and the Net*

by Trevor Owen and Ron Owston

Reader's resource

"**Research Strategies for the Learning Highway**" is a chapter from *The Learning Highway: Smart Students and the Net*, a book intended to make better students of its readers by providing them information on the latest developments occurring on the Internet. In "Research Strategies for the Learning Highway," Trevor Owen and Ron Owston discuss finding facts, websites, and reading material on the Internet, as well as how to assess the quality of Internet sites. The chapter is an example of *technical writing*, which refers to scientific or process-oriented instructional writing of a technical or mechanical nature.

About *the* AUTHORS

Trevor Owen is the coordinator of Instructional Technology at York University in the Faculty of Education and founder of the Writers in Electronic Residence program. **Ron Owston** is Associate Professor in the Faculty of Education at York University and founding director of the Center for the Study of Computers in Education. Owen and Owston's book *The Learning Highway: Smart Students and the Net* was published in 1998.

Reader's Journal

What are your goals when you use the Internet?

Literary TOOLS

CHRONOLOGICAL ORDER. Chronological order is the arrangement of details in order of their occurrence. It is the primary method of organization used in narrative writing. It is also common in nonfiction writing that describes processes, events, and cause and effect relationships.

EXPOSITION. Exposition is a type of writing that presents facts or opinions in an organized manner. Among the most common ways to organize exposition are the following: *analysis, classification, comparison-contrast,* and *process* or *how-to writing.*

Organizer

As you read, make a cluster chart like the one below, listing the three types of information that the article helps you find.

information provided

how to find facts on the Internet

Research Strategies for the Learning Highway

Trevor Owen and Ron Owston

Four Steps to Finding Facts

Often you'll want to find specific facts, statistics, definitions, and other data. For instance, we might want to know the answer to questions such as:

- How high is Mount Everest?
- What is the GNP of France?
- What countries belong to the British Commonwealth?
- Who wrote the novel *The Sun Also Rises?*

Here are the steps we suggest you take to find answers to questions such as these.

Step 1

Think of the most obvious search words, paying particular attention to key nouns: for example, *height, elevation, Mount Everest* would be good for the first question above. Enter these words into a comprehensive search index, such as Altavista, and connect the keywords with appropriate search operators. For Altavista these might be +*(height or elevation)* + *"Mount Everest."* Then do the search. If you don't find what you want, go to the next step.

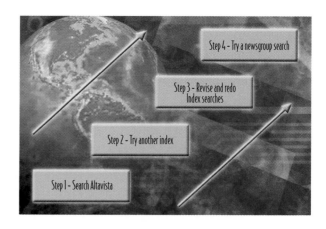

Step 4 - Try a newsgroup search

Step 3 - Revise and redo Index searches

Step 2 - Try another index

Step 1 - Search Altavista

Step 2

Rather than refining your search with Altavista, try

What are the steps for finding specific facts?

one or two Web search indexes because they typically produce remarkably different results with the same search words. You might even try MetaCrawler because it searches all of the major search engines in one step. Go to Step 3 if you still have no luck.

Step 3

Your search skills will now be put to the test because you are going to have to go back and revise your search keywords and operators with the indexes and retry the searches. For example, we might try *(elevation OR height OR high) NEAR "Mount Everest"* in an advanced Altavista search.

Step 4

If you're not successful in Step 3, then you should try searching the newsgroups with DejaNews. Given the vast amount of discussion that takes place in newsgroups, perhaps someone has previously talked about your topic. If you still draw a blank after searching DejaNews, then try posting a message in an appropriate group to see if anyone knows the answer to your question.

Four Steps to Finding Websites

This is a more open-ended kind of search than looking for facts, because if you're trying to locate websites that deal with a certain topic, you may never be satisfied that you've found them all. But more important than finding all the sites on a topic is locating good-quality sites that meet your needs. The steps we outline below will answer some of the following sample questions:

- What websites deal with modern English literature?

- Are there any sites dedicated to tornadoes—how they are formed and what safety precautions you can take if you see one?
- Are there any sites that have tutorials to help me improve my Spanish?
- Where can I go to find information on and see pictures of the Mir space station?

To answer questions like this, we suggest you follow the four steps described below.

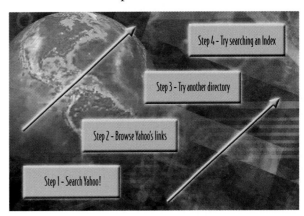

Step 1

Yahoo! is a good starting point. Begin by either browsing your topic or doing a keyword search. For the last example about the Mir space station, browsing the path *Science: Space: Missions* would take you to a list of sites, as would searching on *Mir*. Since Yahoo! is an excellent resource for locating websites you may not need to look any farther, but if you do, try the next step.

Step 2

Follow the path in Yahoo! to a subcategory that takes you closest to your topic and browse some of the links to sites that you find there. There's a good chance that a few of these sites will have links to your topic. But if you don't discover anything relevant, or <u>conversely</u>, if you find too many sites, go to Step 3.

Step 3

Browse another directory. Magellan is a good one to try—pay particular attention to their evaluated sites.

When looking for websites, what should a student do if searching Yahoo! presents no results?

It's possible to browse only sites that are highly rated, for example. You may also want to browse the Top 5% sites at Lycos.

Step 4

Try searching Altavista or any of the other major Web indexes if you still can't find what you want. We suggest using the indexes as a last resort for locating websites, because they often turn up too many links in their results list, especially when you are searching for a relatively broad topic.

Four Steps to Finding Reading Material

These steps will help you find articles, abstracts, essays, book excerpts, research papers, stories, poetry, and other kinds of original reading material. They are designed to help you locate suitable background reading for your courses or special interests, and to find material for assignments or papers. By following these steps, you should be able to answer questions like:

- What has been written recently about the treatment of dyslexia in young children?
- Is there any research that suggests a connection between movie stars smoking on screen and teenage use of tobacco?
- Why was the U.S. involved in the Vietnam War?
- Why do some economists say that high unemployment can be "good" for the economy?

Following are the four steps we suggest you try.

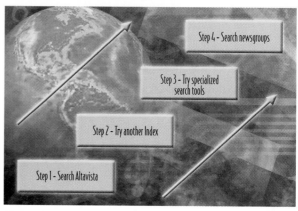

Step 1

Try doing a search on your topic using Altavista. As a first step you may even want to enter a natural language question like any of the above and see how Altavista handles it. If that doesn't work, try entering keywords connected by appropriate operators. At this point don't spend too much time attempting to formulate a "perfect" search.

Step 2

If Altavista doesn't locate what you want after a few tries, search a few other Web indexes or use MetaCrawler. Generally speaking, Yahoo! and the other Web directories are not as useful as the indexes for locating articles about specific topics, but there's no harm in giving them a go too.

Step 3

Try some of the other specialized search tools if you still are not satisfied with what you've found so far. For example, search the catalog of your local library or that of a highly regarded university for your topic. Also try searching Amazon.com. The libraries and bookstores will likely point the way to <u>relevant</u> print materials you might be able to borrow or purchase; they may also suggest authors and keywords you can use for Steps 1 and 2.

---

words for everyday use

rel • e • vant (re′ lə vənt) *adj.,* having significant and demonstrable bearing on the matter at hand. *At the meeting about the prom, Stephen brought up fundraising for new football uniforms, which the chairperson said was not <u>relevant</u>.*

Step 4

Turn to DejaNews and search the newsgroups for your topic, if the first three steps prove unproductive. You won't find actual reading material about your topic there, but you may come across someone who has discussed the topic and has referred to resources on the topic. If a website is mentioned in the body of a newsgroup article, DejaNews turns it into a clickable link that you could pursue with your browser. As a last resort, you could post a newsgroup message for help in an appropriate group.

Why does a person select DejaNews?

Evaluating What You Find

With the traditional publishing of articles, books, magazines, and newspapers there is a built-in editorial process. Publishing houses employ editors to review manuscripts for content and style before they go to press. This process gives the reader some assurance that, at a minimum, someone else has read the material and deemed it worthy of publication. However, as we said earlier, on the Internet anyone can publish anything about any topic he or she wishes and can do so without having it <u>scrutinized</u> by an editor. Therefore, the <u>caveat</u> on the Internet is "Reader Beware!"

Besides looking out for <u>erroneous</u> information and reading critically, there are some other criteria you can use to evaluate what you read on the Internet. Here are some we recommend.

- *Look at the resource's domain name.* Domain names can provide some clues to the credibility of a resource. Generally speaking, we tend to trust documents that have domain names ending in *edu* or *gov*, because those names tell you that the documents come from a U.S. university or government site. If the site is outside the U.S., look for a university or government name as part of the domain name (e.g., *yorku.ca*). Commercial sites (*com*) of well-known, <u>reputable</u> companies are <u>credible</u>, too, but you must watch for <u>biases</u> that may relate to a company's product. For example, would you trust documents at a cigarette manufacturer's site about research linking smoking and cancer? Would these be as objective as a government report? Sites ending in *org* or *net* can be trusted if they are operated by a reputable organization too (e.g., the Public Broadcasting System, whose domain name is <u>http://www.pbs.org</u>), but watch for advocacy and special interest group sites because they may be presenting a specific slant on a topic to further their organization's goals.

- *Look for a document's author.* Never accept or quote from a document that is anonymous. We believe that anyone who publishes a document on the Internet would sign it if they think it's worthwhile. Once you identify the author, try to find out about his or her background. This may be as simple as clicking on a link on the document to the author's home page, or as bothersome as searching for an author's name with a Web index to see what you can unearth.

---

words for everyday use

scru • ti • nized (skrü′ tən īzd) *part.*, closely examined. *The convenience store's videotape was <u>scrutinized</u> in an effort to identify the robber.*

ca • ve • at (ka′ vē ät) *n.*, warning or caution. *The laundromat's <u>caveat</u> was to start your last load of laundry by 9:30 P.M. unless you didn't mind picking it up the next morning.*

er • ro • ne • ous (i rō′ nē əs) *adj.*, containing or characterized by error. *Ron's <u>erroneous</u> assumptions about the weather in England in January led him to pack all the wrong clothes for his trip.*

rep • u • ta • ble (re′ pyə tə bəl) *adj.*, held in esteem. *Because she had a <u>reputable</u> lawyer, Mrs. White Eagle thought she would get a fair settlement.*

cred • i • ble (kre′ də bəl) *adj.*, believable. *Because his student's story sounded <u>credible</u>, Mr. Connell let him hand in his assignment late.*

bi • as (bī′ əs) *n.*, inclination of temperament or outlook. *My grandfather has a <u>bias</u> against foreign-made cars.*

- *Try to determine a document's context if you have doubts about it.* There may be a good reason why a document appears anonymous. For instance, it may be a subdocument of a large publication at a website. Therefore, see if you can find the document's context. Often you need only look higher up the directory in the site's URL.[1] For example, if you find a document with the URL http://www.anyu.edu/faculty/research/report2.html remove report2.html from the URL and enter it into your browser. At that point you may see a menu, with links to documents, that describes what the document is about and who wrote it. Failing that, there may be other clues or links that will help you identify it.

- *Find corroborating documents.* Always look for other documents or sites about the same topic that provide supporting evidence to the point of view or facts presented in a document you want to use for your research. News reporters routinely look for corroborating evidence before running an investigative story. Even though there's no guarantee that if several people say the same thing, it's true, there's a better chance that it is. The search engines that have the option "find more documents like this one" will help you find corroborating information.

What can a person do to evaluate what he or she reads on the Internet?

If you still have doubts about a document's validity, don't hesitate to show it to your teacher or professor. If she welcomes email from students, you may want to use the "mail document" function of your Web browser to send it directly to her.

Finally, make sure to cite the source of material from the Internet that you use in a project or research paper. Your school's or university's policies about academic honesty apply to electronic material as well as printed material. Unless you are told otherwise, use the same reference format you would use for print publications, and add the document's URL and the date you viewed it in parentheses at the end of the reference. ∎

---

1. **URL.** Uniform Resource Locator, or Internet address

---

words for everyday use

cor • rob • o • rat • ing (kə rä′ bə rāt iŋ) *adj.,* supporting with evidence; confirming. *Because of the corroborating witness, the lawyer won the case with the evidence she presented.*

Respond *to the* SELECTION

In what ways can you use the Internet to help you to become a better student?

Investigate, *Inquire,* and Imagine

Recall: GATHERING FACTS

1a. What is step 2 when you are trying to find facts on the Internet?

2a. What is the first step for finding websites?

3a. What is the authors' opinion about anonymous documents on the Internet?

Interpret: FINDING MEANING

1b. Why is this step necessary?

2b. Why do the authors recommend using Yahoo! over other search engines?

3b. Why do the authors say "Reader Beware!" when locating information on the Internet?

Analyze: TAKING THINGS APART

4a. Identify the three research strategies described in the selection.

Synthesize: BRINGING THINGS TOGETHER

4b. Why do the steps for these three research strategies differ?

Evaluate: MAKING JUDGMENTS

5a. Evaluate which Internet site would probably provide more reliable information on Edgar Allan Poe.

http://www.poedecoder.com/PreciselyPoe/

http://raven.ubalt.edu/features/poe

Extend: CONNECTING IDEAS

5b. Write five questions, ranging in difficulty from factual to interpretive, about Edgar Allan Poe for which you would like to know the answer. Then, after each question, write down which research strategy you should follow: 1) finding facts; 2) finding websites; or 3) finding reading material.

Understanding *Literature*

CHRONOLOGICAL ORDER. Review the definition for **chronological order** in the Handbook of Literary Terms. How does the selection use chronological order?

EXPOSITION. Review the definition for **exposition** in the Handbook of Literary Terms and the cluster chart you made in Literary Tools on page 545. Which method of organization do the authors use: analysis, classification, comparison-contrast, or process (how-to) writing?

Writer's Journal

1. Write **directions** for finding factual information on the Internet.
2. Write a **paragraph** summarizing how to evaluate resources on the Internet.
3. Imagine you are one of the authors of *The Learning Highway: Smart Students and the Net.* Write a **letter** to an editor of a publishing company to see if he or she is interested in publishing your book. Identify yourself, state your qualifications and background, and summarize the content of your book.

Integrating the Language Arts

Language, Grammar, and Style

SUBORDINATE CLAUSES. Read the Language Arts Survey 3.72, "Subordinating Conjunctions." Then write out the subordinate clauses in the following sentences.

1. Owen and Owston, who are experts in computer technology, advise using more than one search engine.
2. Keywords that are specific will help you with your online search.
3. Although Yahoo! is the authors' preferred search engine, they admit it may be necessary to try other directories.
4. It is helpful to try specialized search tools such as library catalog indexes, Amazon.com, and newsgroups when looking for reading material.
5. As surfers have discovered, there is a world of information on the Internet.

Media Literacy

CREATING AN INTERNET LOG. Imagine that you are writing a research paper on the contributions of Martin Luther King, Jr. to the Civil Rights movement. Create a research log to track how you find information to use in your paper. Follow the steps outlined in the Language Arts Survey 5.41, "Documenting and Mapping Internet Research." Locate eight sources, evaluating each one according to the guidelines in the Language Arts Survey 5.35, "How to Understand Internet Sites."

Study and Research & Media Literacy

DOCUMENTING SOURCES ON THE INTERNET. Imagine that you have written the research paper on Martin Luther King, Jr. described in the other Media Literacy activity on this page. Select the five most reputable sources on the Internet to use in your paper. Then write a bibliography citing your sources, making sure to add the URL (Uniform Resource Locator, or Internet address) and date for each source. Refer to the Language Arts Survey 5.40, "Making Bibliographies and Bibliography Cards."

Guided Writing

DOCUMENTING A STEP-BY-STEP PROCESS

What fascinates you? Is it sketching a landscape? building incredible biceps? surviving in the wilderness? rebuilding a small engine? writing a poem? interpreting your dreams? What hobby do you have that makes you an expert in a field that may be foreign to the rest of your classmates? Are you a fly fisherperson? a watercolor painter? a rock hound?

Whatever you are interested in doing, this assignment will give you the opportunity to share your interest with others. You will provide information about a task you already know or want to learn how to perform.

WRITING ASSIGNMENT. Write a process paper on how to do something, step by step. Prepare visual documents to illustrate the process. Your writing must be clear, accurate, organized, and, above all, interesting. Make your presentation energetic, sincere, and engaging.

> "You have to know the material as well as you know yourself."
>
> —Virginia Hamilton

Professional Model

from *The Learning Highway: Smart Students and the Net* by Trevor Owen and Ron Owston
page 546

Four Steps to Finding Facts
Often you'll want to find specific facts, statistics, definitions, and other data. For instance, we might want to know the answer to questions such as:
- How high is Mount Everest?
- What is the GNP of France?
- What countries belong to the British Commonwealth?
- Who wrote the novel *The Sun Also Rises?*

Here are the steps we suggest you take to find answers to questions such as these.

Step 1
Think of the most obvious search words, paying particular attention to key nouns: for example, *height, elevation, Mount Everest* would be good for the first question above. Enter

Everyone now wants to be able to use the learning highway not only to find information, but also to assess the value of that information and to evaluate its quality. "Research Strategies for the Learning Highway" appeals to a contemporary audience because of its timeliness and relevance. Also, it is audience-friendly. There is order: finding facts (reprinted in this lesson), finding websites, finding reading material, and evaluating what's found (this appears later in the article). There is parallel structure: four steps to each "find." There is jargon-free information that is easy to understand. Clear visuals illustrate and simplify the text. The learning highway driver, now more comfortable and skilled, puts the car in gear and goes.

these words into a comprehensive search index, such as Altavista, and connect the keywords with appropriate search operators. For Altavista these might be + (*height or elevation*) + "*Mount Everest.*" Then do the search. If you don't find what you want, go to the next step.

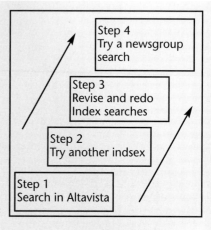

Step 1
Search in Altavista

Step 2
Try another indsex

Step 3
Revise and redo
Index searches

Step 4
Try a newsgroup
search

Step 2
Rather than refining your search with Altavista, try one or two Web search indexes because they typically produce remarkably different results with the same search words. You might even try MetaCrawler because it searches all of the major search engines in one step. Go to Step 3 if you still have no luck.

Step 3
Your search skills will now be put to the test because you are going to have to go back and revise your search keywords and operators with the indexes and retry the searches. For example, we might try (*elevation OR height OR high*) *NEAR* "*Mount Everest*" in an advanced Altavista search.

Step 4
If you're not successful in Step 3, then you should try searching the newsgroups with DejaNews. Given the vast amount of discussion that takes place in newsgroups, perhaps someone has previously talked about your topic.

Prewriting

FINDING YOUR VOICE. This is your chance to teach the class something that you think is either important or fun to know. Consider the voice you will use. **Voice** is the way a writer uses language to reflect his or her unique personality and attitude toward topic, form, and audience. A writer expresses voice through tone, word choice, and sentence structure. The voice you use will depend on your topic and your audience's knowledge of it. Contrast these two statements:

Tarantulas customarily live in deep cylindrical burrows, from which they emerge at dusk and into which they retire at dawn.

Tarantulas live in underground burrows during the day. At night, they creep out.

Which word in the second example suggests a playful voice? Which word in the first example suggests a serious, academic voice? What can you say about the length of the sentences in the two examples? Which would be more interesting to your audience?

IDENTIFYING YOUR AUDIENCE. Have you ever watched a home-improvement show on television? Even if you may not care about how to plan a picnic lunch, there is something hypnotic about such presentations and you can easily watch an entire program; presenters like Martha Stewart know what appeals to and how to hold their audience. Informational commercials, or infomercials, as they sell their products, have a different audience, but the results are the same; it can be difficult to turn the channel.

You will be presenting your step-by-step process to your classmates; therefore, they will be your audience. To hold the attention of your peers, you will need a topic you care deeply about. You will also need visual aids and a well-planned demonstration that will help your audience understand what you are showing them. Even if they may not be interested in your particular topic, your delivery and mode of presentation can still hold their attention.

WRITING WITH A PLAN. You need a compelling topic. What do you know that others should know because it might save a life, make life more enjoyable or interesting, or save people time or money? Topics can include demonstrating the Heimlich maneuver, dancing the salsa, learning to hang glide, or buying a used mountain bike. This is your chance to show your audience something you are passionate about, and, perhaps, pass on that sense of passion.

First you need to separate the process into distinct steps. Next, you will describe each step precisely. Define any terms you use that may not be known to your audience. Aim to be clear. Then place those steps in the proper order. Nothing is more confusing than a misplaced step in a set of directions: "Oh, yes, I forgot to tell you!" just doesn't work.

As you think through each step, consider what will be the best method to give your audience a visual picture: posters, overheads, a slide show, a PowerPoint or Hypercard presentation. Check to see what technologies are available. What if you don't already know how to use the technology? Don't let that stop you. In most cases you can learn what you need to know quite easily. Check around: help is probably waiting to be asked.

Sarah is a promising potter who gets a great deal of joy and satisfaction from her art, and thinks other people would enjoy this hobby. Thus, selecting a topic was easy for her. This is how she set up her graphic organizer:

Using Visuals Effectively

A good presentation skillfully uses visuals. Here are guidelines that will help visuals work well for you.

- Make sure any equipment you need is on hand, plugged in, and working before your presentation begins.
- Keep a visual covered until referring to it.
- Cover a visual when you finish your reference to it.
- Practice using the visuals before the presentation so you can work out any problems.
- Practice in front of a mirror so you can see what your audience will see.
- Face and look at your audience as you refer to your visual.

For more information see the Language Arts Survey, 6.11, "Displaying Effective Visual Information."

"Art is a technique of communication."
—Claes Oldenburg

Baseball

Student Model—Graphic Organizer

Steps and Visuals

Step #1	Materials and clay type	Visual #1	Some of the materials, pictures of materials
Step #2	How to work the potter's wheel	Visual #2	Diagram of potter's wheel
Step #3	Centering the clay	Visual #3	Show hand positions on wheel
Step #4	Making the middle width	Visual #4	Show how to keep it from falling and height apart
Step #5	How to get the pot off the wheel and trimming	Visual #5	Show tool to get it off wheel bisque
Step #6	Glazing-painting or dripping	Visual #6	Show both ways w/ posters and some colors
Step #7	Baking, finishing touches and uses	Visual #7	Show some finished products

Designing a Good Visual

- Keep it simple
- Limit each visual to one idea
- Limit text to six lines, six words to a line
- Make it neat
- Make sure it is correct
- Be sure it adds information and is not just a decoration
- Select lettering thoughtfully
- Make sure it is easy to read
- Use both uppercase and lowercase letters
- Limit the number of typefaces and type sizes
- Select colors carefully (Note: Yellow lettering is not legible; red is difficult to read at a distance.)

Drafting

Depending on your topic, you will need to decide what kind of introduction to use. You might wish to give some history or background: tell the story of how you became interested in your subject. Or let the audience know how this information will benefit them: tell the story of how someone's life was saved or improved with this information. You need to connect with your audience with your first words. Do not begin with the title; begin with your introduction.

As you go through the body of your presentation, giving step-by-step instructions, refer the audience to the visuals. You will also want to include many audience identification words—*you, yours, yourself, we, ours, ourselves*—throughout your script to let your audience know you are talking directly to them.

Conclude with a clincher. It is often a good idea to refer back to your introduction to wrap up your presentation. That will signal your audience that your presentation is ending. You want the last words you speak to leave an impact on the audience. Resist the temptation of adding, "and that's all I have" or "that's it." Those words drain the energy of your impact.

Student Model—Draft

This is your first and only warning: do not even think about doing this if you hate getting messy! Alright, with the [*sp*] useless warning out of the way, we can get started. Most people like getting messy, ~~even if they deny it to their grave.~~ my pottery teacher says everyone has that little inner child. You've probably encountered him or her before, they tell you to have fun without worrying, to eat anything to your heart's content, and to act immature when you know you're an adult and should be mature. Some times we deny them and sometimes we give in. This is one way to give in to you're inner child that says "Get messy!" while giving the excuse that you are being a very mature artist. *Fix to make sense.*

[*Good voice: you engage the audience right away!*]

[*wordy — this doesn't sound right!*]

Making pottery is extremely dirty, ~~the main reason being that~~ [*because*] you're basically playing with dirt and mud. Dirt is the main ingredient for clay, addsome water, and you've got mud. There are other ingredients, of course, so that you can mold and create. Working with clay is good, messy fun, there's also a bonus, pots make great gifts for your mom and grandma. You know how they love when you make something totally original just for them, and if the pot turns out to be a mess, it doesn't matter. A lot of types

[*Better if you just talked about your own experience*]

[*fix comma problem*]

Self- and Peer Evaluation

Once you have finished a draft, let several of your peers read or observe your script and presentation. Are there any key steps either left out or unclear? When we are teaching others something we already know, we sometimes assume the audience also knows. Be careful that you don't assume too much. As you look over your work, ask yourself these questions:

- How does the introduction draw the audience into the subject?
- Where does the writer explain technical terms the audience will need to know?
- Where, if anywhere, in the step-by-step process were you lost?
- What audience identification words are used? (*you, your, we, our, ourselves*)
- Where did the visuals provide information helpful in understanding the subject?
- What errors, if any, did you notice in the visuals?
- What layout techniques did the writer use to create effective visuals? (Consider elements of color, type, spacing, and size.)
- What is the impact of the last sentence in the presentation?

Effective Comma Usage

IDENTIFYING EFFECTIVE COMMA USAGE. Two of the most frequent errors in sentence structure are the sentence run-on and the comma splice.

A **sentence run-on** occurs when the writer doesn't separate sentences with the appropriate conjunction or punctuation.

RUN-ON

First you need to find all the necessary materials then you should clear your work space.

REVISED

First you need to find all the necessary materials, and then you should clear your work space.

A run-on also occurs when you continue connecting sentences together, creating a long, awkward sentence.

RUN-ON

First you need to find all the necessary materials, and then you should clear your work space, and then you will cut all the pieces up, and then you will turn on the oven, and then you will grease the pan.

REVISED

First you should clear your work space. Then you need to find all the necessary materials. At this point, turn the oven on to 400

continued on page 559

---

of art originated from mess-ups. And you can make cool things for your friends, too. I made a gargoyle once for my friend Deenah and she uses it for a bookend. (Somewhere here I need a visual) So, let's get messy. There are five main steps to making something from clay, here they are.

Could you bring in the gargoyle you made?

fix comma splice

Revising and Proofreading

Review your self- and peer evaluations. Revise your writing after considering these comments. Polish the rough edges. Make sure you've considered the audience's level of knowledge and have explained any technical terms. Look over your visuals. Double-check that they are accurate, clear, and necessary. Then practice your presentation aloud in the size voice you will use for your audience. Have you ever had someone try to sell you something that he or she really knew very little about? A salesperson who is reading off a note card, mumbling or looking at the ceiling isn't very convincing. You are a salesperson in this instance, so you want to be sure that you know your subject as well as possible.

Student Model—Revised

Mess Your Way to Success
by Sarah Richards

This is your first and only warning: do not even think about doing this if you hate getting messy! All right, with the useless warning out of the way, we can get started. Most people like getting messy, even if they deny it. Think of mud wrestling. Think of mud pies and dirt fights you had as a kid. This is one way to give in to the voice that says, "Get messy!" while giving the excuse that you are being a very mature artist.

Making pottery is extremely dirty. You're basically playing with dirt and mud. Dirt is the main ingredient for clay. Add some water, and you've got

mud. There are other ingredients, of
course, so that you can mold and
create. Working with clay is good,
messy fun, but there's also a bonus:
pots make great gifts for your
relatives and friends. My grandma loves
it when I make something totally
original just for her, and if the pot
turns out to be a mess, it doesn't
matter. A lot of types of art
originated from mess-ups. And you can
make cool things for your friends, too.
I made this gargoyle for my friend
Deenah. [Show gargoyle to audience.]
She uses it for a bookend.

So let's get messy. There are five
main steps to making your own
masterpiece. Here they are.

Publishing and Presenting

Your final draft is the manuscript for the speech you will deliver
to your classmates. You may wish to deliver the speech to other
interested audiences. Consider who else might be interested in
this information. For instance, if you've done an informative
piece on building a terrarium, what elementary school science
class would be interested in this very subject? If you dealt with
genealogy, perhaps a senior citizens' group would like to hear
your presentation. You can also consider participating in speech
events. Check to see if your school offers a speech team or club.

Reflecting

We have become a world where flash is sometimes more
powerful than substance. Which is more powerful in your
project: flash or substance? Have you ever been influenced by
flash? Remember the toy that made you like a fast-food
hamburger meal? clothes that you wanted because they were
stylish, but went out of fashion in three months? the car you
bought because you liked the color? You need some flash to get
your audience's attention, but you must make sure your
presentations have substance as well as flash. As you reflect on
the step-by-step process you have documented for your
audience, ask yourself these questions:

- What was the substance of my presentation?
- What was its flash?

degrees. While the oven
heats, grease the pan. Then
combine the following dry
ingredients in a mixing
bowl.

A **comma splice** occurs when
you connect two sentences
with a comma instead of a
comma and a conjunction.

COMMA SPLICE

Golfers don't always look
like athletes, golf is
considered the most
difficult sport.

REVISED

Golfers don't always look
like athletes, but golf is
considered the most
difficult sport.

FIXING INCORRECT COMMA USAGE.
Read through the following
paragraph, locate the run-ons
and comma splices, and then
correct them.

After experimenting with the
pedal, turn off the wheel, get the
proper amount of clay for your
piece. If this is your first pot, start
small. A little less than a handful
of clay would be a good amount
to start with. Place it on the
wheel and fill a bucket with water
and put the sponge and any other
tools inside it and then pick up
your clay and slam it down in the
center of the wheel. Slam it down
hard enough so that it sticks to
the wheel, not too hard or else it
will go flying everywhere.

USING COMMAS EFFECTIVELY. Read
back through your own script
and make any corrections that
you think would help the flow
of the presentation. Be sure to
correct any run-ons or comma
splices.

UNIT 6 review
Informational & Visual Media

Words for Everyday Use

Check your knowledge of the following vocabulary words from the selections in this unit. Write short sentences using these words in context to make the meaning clear. To review the definition or usage of a word, refer to the page number(s) listed or the Glossary of Words for Everyday Use.

accrued, 520
admonition, 521
akin, 531
apathy, 513
array, 519
ascent, 532
bias, 549
caveat, 549
celestial, 541
charismatic, 532
coalition, 521
competent, 532
comprehensive, 520
conservationist, 519
conversely, 547
corroborating, 550

credible, 549
degraded, 519
dishevelment, 513
dispatch, 582
ecosystem, 519
effigy, 512
embellishment, 513
enfilade, 511
enhancement, 520
erroneous, 549
esthetic, 513
exasperation, 532
expedition, 532
feasibility, 520
flayed, 531
formidable, 532

frieze, 511
geyser, 539
ineffable, 539
infinitesimal, 511
integrity, 520
intrinsic, 513
levee, 519
lure, 532
meandering, 520
novice, 532
orbit, 540
periscope, 511
practical, 534
predict, 540
profligate, 512
prominence, 539

rectilinear, 513
relevant, 548
reputable, 549
scrutinized, 549
sentiment, 520
simian, 511
spectacle, 540
sponsor, 533
summit, 531
sustainable, 521
symmetry, 512
unnervingly, 531
wetland, 519

Literary Tools

Define the following terms, giving concrete examples of how they are used in the selections in this unit. To review a term, refer to the page number(s) indicated or to the Handbook of Literary Terms.

aim, 517
alliteration, 538
article, 529
background information, 529

chronological order, 545
exposition, 517, 545
metaphor, 508
mood, 508

periodical, 529
simile, 508
tone, 538

Reflecting on your reading

Genre Studies

1. **INFORMATIONAL MEDIA.** Select two examples of informational media from this unit. For example, you might select the newsletter article ("For the Future of Florida: Repair the Everglades!") and the periodical article ("Ghost of Everest"). Describe the intended audience for each and explain how the authors wrote differently from each other in order to reach their intended audience.

2. **VISUAL MEDIA.** Examine the photographs that accompany the excerpt from *Let Us Now Praise Famous Men*. What is the aim, or purpose, of Walker Evans's photojournalism? How do you interpret his photographs? Do you find them visually pleasing or disturbing? Do they persuade you to think in a new way? If so, how?

3. **ESSAYS.** Even though Joette Lorion and Marjory Stoneman Douglas write for the same cause, their approaches to the topic of saving the Everglades are different. Explain Marjory Stoneman Douglas's approach to convincing people to save the Everglades. How does she get the reader's attention? How does she draw the reader into her cause?

Thematic Studies

4. **ENDURANCE.** Which people described in this unit exemplify endurance? What have they endured? What personal qualities do you think enabled them to endure? What do they have to show for their endurance?

5. **EXPLORATION.** How is the exploration described in "Ghost of Everest" different from the exploration described in "Research Strategies for the Learning Highway"? Are they similar in any way?

6. **TECHNOLOGY.** How has the advent of the Internet changed society? What things do many people do differently now that the Internet is an integral part of their lives? What applications for the Internet are predicted for the future?

for your READING LIST

Margaret Bourke-White: Her Pictures Were Her Life by Susan Goldman Rubin. Margaret Bourke-White was a pioneer in photojournalism and helped to define the photo-essay as a form of communication and art. She was one of the chief photographers for *Life* magazine and her style of telling stories with photographs was to become its hallmark. Over the course of her career, she broke many barriers, becoming the first woman photographer for *Fortune* and *Life* magazines, the first woman named war photographer, and the first woman allowed to fly on a bombing mission. She marched into danger countless times to tell the stories she felt were important. This book allows the reader to see much of her most significant work and to understand why, when *Life* magazine published a tribute at her death, the story began, "Her pictures were her life."

Independent Reading Activity

READING MEANING IN PHOTOGRAPHS. Like writers, photographers create their work with a purpose or aim in mind. Some deliberately stage their photographs and some manipulate lighting, shadow, or other elements to create a visual effect and convey a specific idea or emotion. Review the photographs in this book and select the three or four that you find most compelling or interesting. What do you think Margaret Bourke-White's aim was in each of the photographs? What idea, emotion, or information was she trying to convey? How did the choice of subject, lighting, and composition of the photograph help to convey the idea or emotion? How effective are her photographs, in your opinion?

Selections for Additional Reading

The 21st Century is a literary magazine published by The Young Authors Foundation that is written entirely by teens for teens. It is also available online at www.TeenInk.com.

Multi-Media: The Complete Guide published by Dorling Kindersley. This book provides information on topics ranging from CD-ROMs and interactive movies to 3-D games, the Internet, and the World Wide Web.

A Student's Guide to the Internet: Exploring the World Wide Web, Gopherspace, Electronic Mail, and More! by Elizabeth Marshall, describes strategies for gathering information from the Net, using newsgroups, e-mail, and the Web.

Themes in Literature
PART TWO

© Estate of Hughie Lee-Smith/Licensed by VAGA, New York.

The Stranger, c. 1957–1958. Hughie Lee-Smith. National Museum of American Art, Washington, DC.

The
SEARCH
for
SELF

" What we have to be is
what we are. "

—*Thomas Merton*

echoes

➤ If a man does not keep pace with his companions, perhaps it is because he hears a different drummer.

—*Henry David Thoreau*

➤ If you do not tell the truth about yourself you cannot tell it about other people.

—*Virginia Woolf*

➤ To conquer oneself is a greater task than conquering others.

—*Buddha*

➤ She had nothing to fall back on; not maleness, not whiteness, not ladyhood, not anything. And out of the profound desolation of her reality she may well have invented herself.

—*Toni Morrison*

➤ What am I then?
I am at once no one of the races and I am all of them.
I belong to no one of them and I belong to all.
I am, in a strict racial sense, a member of a new race.

—*Jean Toomer*

➤ I want, by understanding myself, to understand others. I want to be all that I am capable of becoming.

—*Katherine Mansfield*

➤ Can one thus resume one's self? Can one know one's self? Is one ever somebody? I don't know anything about it any more. It now seems to me that one changes from day to day and that every few years one becomes a new being.

—*George Sand*

➤ No one remains quite what he was when he recognizes himself.

—*Thomas Mann*

"I'm Nobody! Who are you?"
by Emily Dickinson

Reader's resource

In **"I'm Nobody! Who are you?"** Dickinson subtly criticizes those who clamor for fame. She finds dignity in quietude and a sort of fellowship in the unadvertised, private life. The topics of solitude and privacy are prominent in much of Dickinson's writing.

About the AUTHOR

Amherst College Archives and Special Collections

Emily Dickinson (1830–1886) was born and spent most of her life in Amherst, Massachusetts. She did travel to Boston, Cambridge, and Worcester several times to visit relatives, and to Philadelphia and Washington with her father, who was a member of Congress. When she was seventeen, she attended Mount Holyoke Female Seminary, but left after a year and never returned. As time went on, Dickinson became more and more reclusive and in later life she was seldom seen at all. In her seclusion, Dickinson read widely, exploring the works of such authors as Shakespeare, Milton, Keats, George Eliot, and Elizabeth Barrett Browning. Only eight of Dickinson's poems were published during her life. The rest of her poems were discovered only after her death.

By the time of her death, which occurred in the house of her birth, Dickinson had produced well over one thousand lyrics. These explored a tremendous range of subjects in language remarkable for its wit, inventiveness, and economy of expression. Taken as a whole, her verses, most of them quite brief, present a complex self-portrait, a sort of spiritual autobiography. Her voice is alternately humble and proud, intimate and aloof, ecstatic and sorrowful, but always questioning, reflective, and intensely alive. She was a keen observer of particulars—capable of sudden, breathtaking generalizations that synthesized these particulars into truths.

Literary TOOLS

SIMILE. A **simile** is a comparison using *like* or *as.* As you read "I'm Nobody! Who are you?," look for the simile in the second stanza.

METER. The **meter** of a poem is its rhythmical pattern. As you read, pay attention to the rhythmical pattern of the poem.

Reader's JOURNAL

Do you consider yourself a private, introverted person who needs a lot of time alone? Or are you an extroverted person who is more outgoing and loves to socialize with others? Explain.

The Tea Cup, 1935. André Derain.

I'm Nobody! Who are You?

Emily Dickinson

I'm Nobody! Who are you?
Are you—Nobody—Too?
Then there's a pair of us?
Don't tell! they'd advertise—you know!

How dreary—to be—Somebody!
How public—like a Frog—
To tell one's name—the livelong June—
To an admiring Bog! ■

What does the speaker feel it's like to be "Somebody"?

words for everyday use

bog (bäg) *n.*, wet, spongy ground; small marsh or swamp. *The field guide listed the birds living in the bog.*

Imagine that reporters have found the speaker of "Nobody." How might such a private person feel about being discovered?

Investigate, Inquire, and Imagine

Recall: GATHERING FACTS

1a. Who does the speaker say she is?

2a. What does the speaker not want the reader to do?

→ **Interpret:** FINDING MEANING

1b. How does the speaker feel about her identity?

2b. Why doesn't the speaker want the reader to do this?

Analyze: TAKING THINGS APART

3a. Analyze the speaker's feelings about fame and about people who admire the famous.

→ **Synthesize:** BRINGING THINGS TOGETHER

3b. What seems to be the theme of "I'm Nobody Who are you?"?

Perspective: LOOKING AT OTHER VIEWS →

4a. From what you have learned about her, why do you think Emily Dickinson published so few poems during her life?

Empathy: SEEING FROM INSIDE

4b. If you were Emily Dickinson, how would you react to each of the following?

- a request for a public poetry reading of your poems
- a quiet picnic with a friend
- a newspaper article about your literary contributions and personal life
- a secret you are asked to keep for a friend

Understanding Literature

SIMILE. Review the definition of **simile** in the Handbook of Literary Terms. What simile does Dickinson use in stanza 2? What two things is she comparing? In what way are they similar? What feelings does she express about fame and publicity by using this simile? Think of a contrasting feeling about fame and publicity. What is one simile that would express that idea?

METER. Review the definition for **meter** in the Handbook of Literary Terms. Copy the poem in your notebook and mark its stress pattern. The first line of the poem has been done for you.

‿ / ‿ ‿ ‿ /
I'm Nobody! Who are you?

Writer's Journal

1. Imagine you are a friend of the speaker. Write a **journal entry** describing the speaker's attitude toward fame and publicity, and comparing and contrasting it to your own.

2. Imagine you are the speaker. Write a **greeting card** to celebrate a new friendship with someone who shares your values.

3. Imagine you are the speaker. Write a **letter** to a friend who has publicized your friendship.

Integrating the Language Arts

Language, Grammar, and Style

COMBINING SENTENCES. Read the Language Arts Survey 3.36, "Combining and Expanding Sentences." Then combine each pair of sentences below to create a single sentence.

1. Emily Dickinson lived a private life. She rarely ventured beyond her home and her close circle of family and friends.

2. Dickinson did not seek fame. She had considerable contempt for it.

3. Only eight of her poems were published during her lifetime. They were published anonymously and without her full consent.

4. At her death, which occurred in the house in Amherst, Dickinson had produced well over one thousand poems. She was born in the house where she died.

5. The first volumes of her poetry mangled the work by "correcting" her unconventional punctuation and her purposeful deviations from grammatical propriety. The first volumes of her poetry were published after her death.

Media Literacy

WRITING AN ABSTRACT. Using the Internet, find criticism of Emily Dickinson's poetry that interests you. For example, you might want to explore what critics have to say about the topic of love or nature in her work. Read several articles. One site you will find useful is the Emily Dickinson International Society at the website http://www.cwru.edu/affil/edis/edisindex.html. Then, write an abstract to summarize your favorite article. An abstract is a brief account of the main ideas or arguments presented in a work. A well-made abstract presents those ideas or arguments in the same order as in the original.

Collaborative Learning

COMPILING A POETRY LIST. With a partner, find other poems by Emily Dickinson that deal with the topic of privacy. Make a list of the titles of these poems, circling the titles of the ones you liked best.

Literary TOOLS

METAPHOR. A **metaphor** is a figure of speech in which one thing is spoken or written about as if it were another. As you read, look for the metaphor in stanza 2 of "Mirror."

SPEAKER. The **speaker** is the character who speaks in or narrates a poem—the voice assumed by the writer.

Graphic Organizer

As you read, make a cluster chart to list what you learn about the speaker. One example has been done for you.

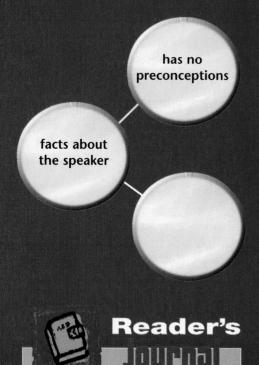

has no preconceptions

facts about the speaker

Reader's Journal

What do you see when you look in the mirror?

"MIRROR"

by Sylvia Plath

Reader's resource

"**Mirror,**" which first appeared in *The New Yorker* in 1963, was published in 1971 in a collection of Plath's poems called *Crossing the Water.* "Mirror" examines the qualities of reflection as the speaker is, in turn, a mirror and a lake.

About the AUTHOR

Born in Boston, **Sylvia Plath** (1932–1963) published poems even as a child and won many academic and literary awards. Her interest in writing continued at Smith College. During her junior year she won a prize for fiction at *Mademoiselle* magazine and spent that summer as a guest editor in the magazine's New York office. After graduating *summa cum laude* from Smith, Plath accepted a Fulbright Scholarship to Cambridge University in England, where she met and married poet Ted Hughes.

The Colossus (1960), the only volume of poetry published during Plath's short life, is well crafted and intensely personal. *Ariel* (1968), considered by many her finest book of verse, was written in the last months of her life. Other volumes include *Crossing the Water* (1971) and *Winter Trees* (1972), both of which reveal an objective detachment from life and a growing fascination with death. Her novel *The Bell Jar* (1963) chronicles the nervous breakdown she suffered while a college student. Most of Plath's work was published posthumously, following her suicide at the age of thirty-one.

art note

Girl before a Mirror, 1932. Pablo Picasso.

A critic noted that the type of mirror in Pablo Picasso's (1881–1973) painting is called a "psyche," meaning "soul." How might that influence your interpretation of the painting?

Sylvia Plath

MIRROR

Girl before a Mirror, 1932. Pablo Picasso.
The Museum of Modern Art, New York.

I am silver and exact. I have no <u>preconceptions</u>.
Whatever I see I swallow immediately
Just as it is, unmisted by love or dislike.
I am not cruel, only truthful—
The eye of a little god, four-cornered.
Most of the time I meditate on the opposite wall.
It is pink, with speckles. I have looked at it so long
I think it is a part of my heart. But it flickers.
Faces and darkness separate us over and over.

Now I am a lake. A woman bends over me,
Searching my reaches for what she really is.
Then she turns to those liars, the candles or the moon.
I see her back, and reflect it faithfully.
She rewards me with tears and an <u>agitation</u> of hands.
I am important to her. She comes and goes.
Each morning it is her face that replaces the darkness.
In me she has drowned a young girl, and in me an old woman
Rises toward her day after day, like a terrible fish. ∎

What does the speaker do?

What is part of the speaker's heart?

Who rises toward the woman by the lake?

What do you think the woman is thinking to herself as she peers at herself in the lake?

Investigate, *Inquire,* and Imagine

Recall: GATHERING FACTS

1a. What adjectives describe the speaker in stanza 1?

2a. What does the speaker in stanza 1 do with whatever it sees? Upon what does the speaker meditate?

3a. Whom has the woman drowned? Who rises toward her "day after day"?

Interpret: FINDING MEANING

1b. What is the speaker in stanza 1?

2b. What is the speaker's attitude toward what it sees? Why might it be ironic that the speaker meditates on such an insignificant thing?

3b. Who are the young girl and the old woman? Why is the old woman "like a terrible fish"?

Analyze: TAKING THINGS APART

4a. What qualities do the mirror and the lake share?

Synthesize: BRINGING THINGS TOGETHER

4b. How does the lake make the woman feel? How can you tell? Why do you think the lake is so important to her?

Evaluate: MAKING JUDGMENTS

5a. Why do you think the speaker calls the moon and candles "liars"?

Extend: CONNECTING IDEAS

5b. Both Narcissus in "The Story of Echo and Narcissus" on page 7 and the woman in "Mirror" bend over the water. How are their perceptions about their reflections different?

Understanding *Literature*

METAPHOR. Review the definition for **metaphor** in the Handbook of Literary Terms. What are the two things being compared in stanza 2? What does being a lake allow the speaker to do?

SPEAKER. Review the definition for **speaker** in the Handbook of Literary Terms and the cluster chart you made in Literary Tools on page 572. What pronoun does the speaker use? What separates the speaker in stanza 1 and in stanza 2? What can be inferred about the speaker from what it says about its reflections?

Writer's Journal

1. Imagine that you are the mirror in your room. Write a **love letter** to one of the objects that you see.

2. The woman by the lake, concerned about aging, writes to your advice column. Write an **advice column** response that reassures her.

3. Write a **dialogue** between the woman and the lake which reflects her image. The lake wants to know why the woman is agitated and crying. The woman tells her story.

Integrating the Language Arts

Language, Grammar, and Style

POSSESSIVE NOUNS. Possessive nouns are hybrids. In the phrase "Mike's paper," *Mike's* looks like a noun because it names *Mike,* but it functions as an adjective because it modifies *paper.* Read more about possessive nouns in the Language Arts Survey 3.90, "Apostrophes." In the following sentences, 1) underline each possessive noun, 2) add appropriate apostrophes, and 3) tell which noun the possessive noun modifies.

1. Sylvia Plaths life was very short.
2. How many poets works were published after they died?
3. What happened to the womans youth in "Mirror"?
4. The poem is told from the mirrors perspective.
5. What is the darknesss replacement?

Vocabulary

SYNONYMS. Read the Language Arts Survey 5.50, "Answering Synonym and Antonym Questions." Then read the underlined words listed below that come from the poem. From the choices listed after each one, choose the one most similar in meaning to the underlined word as it is intended in the poem.

1. <u>exact</u>—fine, precise, correct, punctual
2. <u>preconception</u>—prejudice, idea, birth, construction
3. <u>unmisted</u>—clear, rainy, teary, opaque
4. <u>agitation</u>—disturbance, shaking, commotion, excitement
5. <u>terrible</u>—fearful, awesome, great, difficult

Collaborative Learning

ADAPTING A NOVEL. Read a chapter or two of Sylvia Plath's novel *The Bell Jar.* Then, with a small group, select a scene to dramatize and adapt the novel to the stage.

Use Plath's ideas and words to create a script. You will need to write dialogue and stage directions. Review the Elements of Drama on pages 296–297 for more information.

Media Literacy & Study and Research

RESEARCHING ON THE INTERNET. The novelist Joyce Carol Oates has called Sylvia Plath "our acknowledged Queen of Sorrows, the spokeswoman for our most private, most helpless nightmares. . . ." You may wish to learn more about Plath's tumultuous life and to discover some of her other poetry. Research Sylvia Plath on the Internet and at the library. You may begin by visiting PlathOnline at http://www.plathonline.com. Then select one of Plath's poems to read to the class. Before you present your reading, you may want to review the Language Arts Survey 4.19, "Oral Interpretation."

Literary
T O O L S

IRONY. Irony is a difference between appearance and reality. As you read, decide what makes the poem doubly ironic.

CHARACTERIZATION. Characterization is the use of literary techniques to create a character. Writers use three major techniques to create characters: direct description, portrayal of characters' behavior, and representations of characters' internal states.

Organizer

As you read, make a cluster chart to list all that you know about "you," the character of the poem. One example has been done for you.

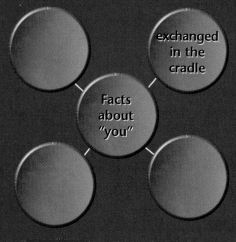

exchanged in the cradle

Facts about "you"

Reader's
JOURNAL

In your journal, write five interesting questions beginning with the words *What if,* for example, *What if I were rich?* Then explain how your life would be different if these conditions were true.

"A Story That Could Be True"
by William Stafford

Reader's
resource

"A Story That Could Be True" was published in William Stafford's collection of poetry *Stories That Could Be True,* which appeared in 1977. The poem invites the reader to consider something that could be true of any of its readers, something that is exotic and wonderful. Like much imaginative literature, the poem begins by posing a "What if" question and ends with an intriguing answer.

About *the*
A U T H O R

William Stafford (1914–1993) was born in Hutchinson, Kansas. After attending the University of Kansas, he began a long-term teaching position at Oregon's Lewis and Clark College. He has also served as consultant in poetry to the Library of Congress. Stafford's poetry explores the difficult choices faced by people all over the world. For example, how can the delicate relationship between nature and humanity be preserved? His simple, poignant verses reflect his reverence for nature and the need to protect it from urban expansion and technological greed.

Stafford often writes deeply personal poems, poems that lay bare private, intimate experiences. His lifelong horror of war led him to register as a conscientious objector during World War II. His personal account of that experience, *Down In My Heart,* was published in 1947. Although he submitted poems to literary journals as a young man, his first collection of poetry, *West of Your City,* was not published until 1960. In 1962, his collection *Traveling Through the Dark* won the National Book Award. Other collections of Stafford's sensitive, moving verse include *The Rescued Year* (1966); *Allegiances* (1970); *Someday, Maybe* (1973); and *Stories That Could Be True* (1977).

A Story That Could Be True

William Stafford

If you were exchanged in the cradle and
your real mother died
without ever telling the story
then no one knows your name,
5   and somewhere in the world
your father is lost and needs you
but you are far away.

He can never find
how true you are, how ready.
10   When the great wind comes
and the robberies of the rain
you stand on the corner shivering.
The people who go by—
you wonder at their calm.

15   They miss the whisper that runs
any day in your mind,
"Who are you really, wanderer?"—
and the answer you have to give
no matter how dark and cold
20   the world around you is:
"Maybe I'm a king."

Why might no one know your name?

What does it mean to be a king?

Investigate, Inquire, *and* Imagine

Recall: GATHERING FACTS

1a. Whom is the speaker addressing in the poem?

2a. What would be true of "your" father?

3a. What do "you" wonder at, and what do other people miss about "you"?

Interpret: FINDING MEANING

1b. What does the phrase "no one knows your name" suggest about how well people know one another's true, inner selves?

2b. What does the speaker of the poem suggest is true about "you"? How would the poem differ if "you" became "he" or "she"?

3b. What characteristics of a king does the speaker suggest "you" possess?

Analyze: TAKING THINGS APART

4a. Identify lines of the poem that show that "you" may not be famous and lines that show that "you" think you may be special.

Synthesize: BRINGING THINGS TOGETHER

4b. Summarize how "you" find the world.

Evaluate: MAKING JUDGMENTS

5a. To what degree has the character of the poem demonstrated kingly qualities?

Extend: CONNECTING IDEAS

5b. What "What if" question have you asked about yourself?

Understanding *Literature*

IRONY. Review the definition for **irony** in the Handbook of Literary Terms. This poem makes the ironic point that even when people feel out of place and different, even when they experience the world as cold and dark, they remain unique: they have unrecognized potentials; in fact, they may be royalty. Note that what is true of the "you" in the poem is also true of all those other people, the ones that go by and cause "you" to "wonder at their calm." Given this observation, what makes the poem doubly ironic?

CHARACTERIZATION. Review the definition for **characterization** in the Handbook of Literary Terms and the cluster chart you made in Literary Tools on page 576. What techniques does the poet employ to describe "you"? Give an example of each.

Writer's Journal

1. The speaker of the poem describes "you" as being "true." Without looking at a dictionary, write a **dictionary entry** for the word *true* as it is used in the poem. Also include the pronunciation, part-of-speech label, and an illustration of usage. To understand these terms, read the Language Arts Survey 1.17, "Using a Dictionary." Finally, write a sentence using the word.

2. As "you," write a **journal entry** saying what the future holds in store. Tell how "your" story will be resolved.

3. In "A Story That Could Be True," William Stafford reminds us that everyone, whether famous or not, has greatness inside. Choose someone you know well but who is not famous, and write a **poem** or **essay** to describe his or her special qualities or achievements.

Integrating the Language Arts

Language, Grammar, and Style

SENTENCE FRAGMENTS. Read the Language Arts Survey 3.33, "Correcting Sentence Fragments." Rewrite the fragments as complete sentences, adding words as needed. If a sentence is not a fragment, write *OK* by its number.

1. Exchanged in the cradle and lost your father.
2. Far away, you stand on the corner shivering in the rain.
3. How dark and cold the world!
4. The people who go by.
5. What you would do if you were king.

Collaborative Learning & Speaking and Listening

A STORY THAT COULD BE TRUE. With several classmates, think of something wildly improbable that could, nonetheless, be true. Some famous examples of "stories that could be true" include the idea that someone was switched at birth, the idea that some famous person from the past didn't really die but is still living an obscure life somewhere on the planet, and the idea that the last hour didn't really happen but was really part of a dream you are having. With your group, brainstorm a list of such "stories that could be true." Choose one of these ideas. Then tell the story in a circle. The first group member introduces the character and the setting. The second group member begins the plot, and so on. You may want to put a time limit on each person's contribution. When you have finished your story, summarize it to the class.

Media Literacy & Study and Research

TRIBUTE TO WILLIAM STAFFORD. Several notable American poets, such as Robert Bly and Kathleen Norris, have written poetic tributes to William Stafford. Read these poems by accessing The Sleep of Grass Internet site at http://www.newsfromnowhere.com/home.html. Then, using the computer, make a booklet of your five favorite poems from the website. Include a short introduction about the poets you selected. To find out information about the poets, use library resources or the Internet.

Literary
T O O L S

FREE VERSE. Free verse is poetry that avoids use of regular rhyme, meter, or division into stanzas. Free verse tends to sound a lot more like ordinary speech than traditional verse does. As you read, note the elements in this poem that show that it resembles speech.

PARADOX. A paradox is a seemingly contradictory statement, idea, or event. Often a writer will express a paradox in order to make a point in an arresting or memorable way. In this poem, Giovanni uses paradox to express what it was like growing up in poverty.

Organizer

As you read, make a cluster chart to list references to poverty during Nikki-Rosa's childhood. One example has been done for you.

poverty

no inside toilet

Reader's
JOURNAL

What would you want a biographer to say about your childhood?

"Nikki-Rosa"
by Nikki Giovanni

Reader's
resource

"Nikki-Rosa" was published in *Black Feeling, Black Talk, Black Judgment* (1970). The title refers to the poet's childhood nickname. In the poem, the speaker discusses good memories of growing up poor.

HISTORY CONNECTION. The late 1950s saw the beginnings in the United States of the Civil Rights movement, which was dedicated to achieving equality for all American citizens, regardless of racial or ethnic background. Slowly, over the next two decades, advances were made in many areas. Laws were passed making discrimination in housing, schooling, and public accommodations illegal. Practices that kept African Americans from being able to vote, such as poll taxes, were banned. Nevertheless, prejudice and economic inequality persisted. In many American cities, persons of African descent lived in poverty, leading many well-intentioned white social and political commentators to write books during that period about the plight of African Americans. However, these books often overlooked strengths in the African-American community, strengths about which Giovanni comments in her poem.

About *the*
A U T H O R

Nikki Giovanni (1943–) is the pen name of Yolande Cornelia Giovanni, a poet, publisher, and educator who gained prominence in the 1960s and 1970s for her poetry and essays on racial issues and the African-American experience. Giovanni was born in Tennessee and grew up in Cincinnati, Ohio. After attending Fisk University, where she received a degree in history, she went on to study at the University of Pennsylvania and at the Columbia School of Fine Arts. She now teaches at Virginia Polytechnic Institute. The recipient of honorary doctorates from many universities, she has written *Gemini* (1971), a collection of essays on literary, autobiographical, and social topics; poetry collections such as *Re: Creation* (1970), *Cotton Candy on a Rainy Day* (1978), and *Those Who Ride the Night Wind* (1983); and two collections of poetry for young people, *Spin a Soft Black Song* (1971) and *Ego Tripping* (1973).

Harriet and Leon, 1941. Allan Rohan Crite. The Boston Athenaeum.

art note

Allan Rohan Crite (1910–) said he portrayed the people of his urban neighborhood as "ordinary human beings going about their business...rather than the exotic sharecropper of the South or the Jazz personality of Harlem, which were popular images being presented." How is that like Nikki Giovanni's poem?

Nikki-Rosa

Nikki Giovanni

childhood remembrances are always a drag
if you're Black
you always remember things like living in Woodlawn[1]
with no inside toilet
5   and if you become famous or something
they never talk about how happy you were to have your mother
all to yourself and
how good the water felt when you got your bath from one of those
big tubs that folk in chicago barbecue in
10   and somehow when you talk about home
it never gets across how much you
understood their feelings
as the whole family attended meetings about Hollydale
and even though you remember
15   your biographers never understand
your father's pain as he sells his stock[2]
and another dream goes
and though you're poor it isn't poverty that
concerns you
20   and though they fought a lot
it isn't your father's drinking that makes any difference
but only that everybody is together and you
and your sister have happy birthdays and very good Christmasses
and I really hope no white person ever has cause to write about me
25   because they never understand Black love is Black wealth and they'll
probably talk about my hard childhood and never understand that
all the while I was quite happy

What positive experiences does the speaker remember from her childhood?

---

1. **Woodlawn.** Neighborhood in Chicago
2. **stock.** Share of ownership in a business that can be bought, sold, or traded

Of what from her childhood is the speaker proud?

Investigate, *Inquire,* and Imagine

Recall: GATHERING FACTS

1a. With what overstatement does this poem begin?

2a. What, according to the speaker, do people not say about the childhoods of famous African Americans?

→ Interpret: FINDING MEANING

1b. Is this overstatement true for the speaker? Why, or why not?

2b. Why does the speaker hope that "no white person ever has cause to write about" her?

Analyze: TAKING THINGS APART

3a. Identify aspects of a darker side to the speaker's childhood.

→ Synthesize: BRINGING THINGS TOGETHER

3b. Summarize what "Black love is Black wealth" means to the speaker.

Perspective: LOOKING AT OTHER VIEWS →

4a. The speaker in this poem reacts to the thought of a biographer recounting her childhood, and she thinks the biographer wouldn't understand what her childhood was all about because she was poor. What could the speaker tell the biographer about her childhood so that he or she would truly understand it?

Empathy: SEEING FROM INSIDE

4b. If you were the speaker and a biographer wrote a misconstrued biography about your childhood, what could you do to set the record straight?

Understanding *Literature*

FREE VERSE. Review the definition for **free verse** in Literary Tools on page 580. What elements in this poem show that it resembles speech?

PARADOX. Review the definition for **paradox** in the Handbook of Literary Terms. What paradox does the speaker of this poem express about poverty? How does the use of paradox make the speaker's point more memorable?

"Hanging Fire"
by Audre Lorde

Literary
T O O L S

REPETITION. **Repetition** is a writer's conscious reuse of a sound, word, phrase, sentence, or other element. As you read, look for the sentence that is repeated throughout the poem.

POINT OF VIEW. **Point of view** is the vantage point from which a story is told. Stories (and poems) are typically written from a first-person point of view, in which the narrator uses words such as *I* and *we,* or from a third-person point of view, in which the narrator uses words such as *he, she, it* and *they.*

Graphic
Organizer

As you read, make a cluster chart listing the speaker's worries and problems from her point of view. One example has been done for you.

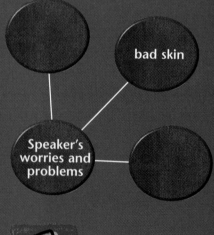

bad skin

Speaker's worries and problems

Reader's
Journal

What worries and problems do you have?

Reader's
resource

"Hanging Fire" was published in Lorde's volume of poetry called *The Black Unicorn* (1978). In "Hanging Fire" a fourteen-year-old girl discusses her problems and worries. The expression *to hang fire* means a delay in the explosion of a gun charge once the primer has been fired or set.

About *the*
AUTHOR

Audre Lorde (1934–1992) was born in Harlem to West Indian parents. She began writing poetry as an adolescent. Lorde has said, "When I couldn't find the poems to express the things I was feeling, that's what started me writing poetry, and that was when I was twelve or thirteen." *Seventeen* magazine published one of her poems when she was still in high school. After graduating from Columbia University and Hunter College, she worked as a librarian and teacher while refining her talents as a writer. "I have come to believe over and over again," said Lorde, "that what is most important to me must be spoken, made verbal and shared, even at the risk of having it bruised or misunderstood." Having come of age during the Civil Rights struggle, Lorde became an activist against oppression on many fronts. In 1991 Lorde was appointed New York's Poet Laureate. She published over a dozen poetry collections and six books of prose. *Collected Poems of Audre Lorde* was published in 1997.

Hanging Fire

Audre Lorde

I am fourteen
and my skin has betrayed me
the boy I cannot live without
still sucks his thumb
in secret
how come my knees are
always so ashy
what if I die
before morning
and momma's in the bedroom
with the door closed.

What problems does the speaker have?

I have to learn how to dance
in time for the next party
my room is too small for me
suppose I die before graduation
they will sing sad melodies
but finally
tell the truth about me
There is nothing I want to do
and too much
that has to be done
and momma's in the bedroom
with the door closed.

What is the speaker afraid of?

Nobody even stops to think
about my side of it
I should have been on Math Team
my marks were better than his
why do I have to be
the one
wearing braces
I have nothing to wear tomorrow
will I live long enough
to grow up
and momma's in the bedroom
with the door closed. ∎

Where is the speaker's mother?

What do you think the speaker would tell her mother if her mother were available?

Investigate, *Inquire,* and Imagine

Recall: GATHERING FACTS

1a. In stanza 2, what problems and worries does the speaker have?

2a. What does the speaker say will happen if she dies before graduation?

Interpret: FINDING MEANING

1b. In what ways is the speaker "hanging fire"—waiting for something to happen?

2b. What is the "truth" about the speaker?

Analyze: TAKING THINGS APART

3a. What evidence can you find that the speaker is troubled?

Synthesize: BRINGING THINGS TOGETHER

3b. Prescribe ways in which the speaker might resolve some of her problems.

Evaluate: MAKING JUDGMENTS

4a. To what degree does the speaker's mother contribute to her problems?

Extend: CONNECTING IDEAS

4b. How do the speaker's problems in "Nikki-Rosa" compare with the speaker's problems in "Hanging Fire"?

Understanding *Literature*

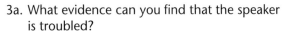

REPETITION. Review the definition for **repetition** in the Handbook of Literary Terms. What sentence is repeated in the poem? What meaning does this repetition suggest to you? What does the repetition of this sentence imply about the speaker's desires? How does this repetition help create the poem's mood?

POINT OF VIEW. Review the definition for **point of view** in the Handbook of Literary Terms and the cluster chart you made for Literary Tools on page 584. What point of view is used in the poem? Who is the *I* in the poem? Why did the poet select the first-person point of view? What might have been lost if the poem had been told in the third-person point of view?

Writer's Journal

1. Imagine you are the mother in "Hanging Fire." Write a **letter** to your daughter explaining why your bedroom door is closed.
2. Write a brief **autobiographical essay** about an event in your childhood. Fill your account with concrete details that will help your readers to feel what it was like to be you as a child undergoing the experience.
3. Write a **poem** modeled on "Hanging Fire" in which you detail the problems of an adolescent. Use the first-person point of view in writing your poem.

Integrating the Language Arts

Language, Grammar, and Style

ACHIEVING PARALLELISM. Read the Language Arts Survey 3.38, "Achieving Parallelism." Then rewrite each of the following sentences to make their parts parallel.

1. As a young girl, Audre Lorde enjoyed reading poetry and to write her own verse.
2. Lorde worked as a librarian and was teaching early in her career.
3. To preserve African-American culture and in celebrating women of color, Lorde founded the Kitchen Table: Women of Color Press.
4. Lorde believed in living honestly and to have compassion for the oppressed.
5. Before her death, Lorde had documented her fourteen-year battle against cancer in "The Cancer Journals" and wrote a series of essays compiled in "A Burst of Light."

Collaborative Learning & Speaking and Listening

AFRICAN-AMERICAN POETRY RECITAL. The 1960s through the 1980s was a period of great creativity and productivity among African-American poets. Active during this period were such outstanding poets as Nikki Giovanni, Audre Lorde, Mari Evans, Gordon Parks, Alice Walker, Gwendolyn Brooks, Robert Hayden, and Imamu Amiri Baraka. Hold a contemporary African-American poetry recital with other students in your class. Research the poets listed here (and any others you might want to include), select poems you wish to present, and write an introduction about each poem and poet. Finally, hold your recital for the class. You may wish to add art, music, or dance to your recital to make it more interesting.

Study and Research

PAIRING GIOVANNI AND LORDE. Read other poems by Nikki Giovanni and Audre Lorde. Then pair Giovanni poems with Lorde poems based on theme, subject, point of view, metaphor, or any other type of classification that you discover. Finally, make a booklet of the paired poems and write an introduction to explain each pairing.

Literary T O O L S

THEME. A **theme** is a central idea in a literary work. A central idea in this story involves the means by which traditional peoples attempt to preserve their ethnic identities against changes introduced from the outside. As you read, think about the story's theme.

SYMBOL. A **symbol** is a thing that stands for or represents both itself and something else. In this story, the dead man is sprinkled with corn meal, pollen, and water. Think about what each symbolizes.

Organizer

As you read, make a chart listing the three items used in the burial ceremony of Teofilo. Indicate the significance of each of the three items to the Pueblo Indians and what you think each item symbolizes in the death rites. One example has been done for you.

Item	Significance to Pueblo Indians	Symbol
corn meal	Food staple	Food/Abundant harvests

Reader's JOURNAL

In what ways have you or your family kept certain traditions or rituals alive that are important to you?

"The Man to Send Rain Clouds"

by Leslie Marmon Silko

Reader's resource

In the Catholic religion, when a person is about to die, a priest is often called to perform a ceremony known as last rites. Last rites include the sprinkling of holy water that has been blessed by a priest. The story **"The Man to Send Rain Clouds"** shows how Pueblo Indians of the southwestern U.S. maintain their own identity by adapting the last rites to fit their own culture's religious beliefs.

WORLD HISTORY CONNECTION. The Spanish were the first Europeans to explore the American Southwest. They brought with them their Catholic religion and established missions, building beautiful churches out of dried mud, or adobe. By 1630, 60,000 Pueblo Indians had been converted to Christianity, and 90 villages had chapels.

SOCIAL STUDIES CONNECTION. Among the native peoples of the Southwest, the Spanish found ancient, established religions that they did not understand. These religions often involved elaborate ceremonies, including ritual dances such as the rain dance, intended to bring rain. Spanish missionaries worked to convert native peoples to the Catholic religion, but many people clung to the older ways, often adding elements of Catholicism to their own rituals and beliefs.

About the AUTHOR

Leslie Marmon Silko (1948–   ), born in New Mexico, grew up on the Laguna Pueblo Reservation. She attended Bureau of Indian Affairs schools, a Catholic high school, and the University of New Mexico (UNM). Silko, who left law school to work on her writing, published her first story in 1969. Since then, she has taught at several colleges, including the University of New Mexico. (Among her honors is a prestigious MacArthur Foundation Fellowship.)

Silko's writings reflect themes from her Native American heritage, including the relationship between humans and nature and the tensions of living within different cultures. Her first novel, *Ceremony* (1977), tells of the feelings of a World War II veteran of mixed parentage who seeks advice from a Native American sage.

The Man to Send RAIN Clouds

Leslie Marmon Silko

They found him under a big cottonwood tree. His Levi jacket and pants were faded light blue so that he had been easy to find. The big cottonwood tree stood apart from a small grove of winterbare cottonwoods which grew in the wide, sandy arroyo.[1] He had been dead for a day or more, and the sheep had wandered and scattered up and down the arroyo. Leon and his brother- in-law, Ken, gathered the sheep and left them in the pen at the sheep camp before they returned to the cottonwood tree. Leon waited under the tree while Ken drove the truck through the deep sand to the edge of the arroyo. He squinted up at the sun and unzipped his jacket— it sure was hot for this time of year. But high and northwest the blue mountains were still in snow. Ken came sliding down the low, crumbling bank about fifty yards down, and he was bringing the red blanket.

Before they wrapped the old man, Leon took a piece of string out of his pocket and tied a small gray feather in the old man's long white hair. Ken gave him the paint. Across the brown wrinkled forehead he drew a streak of white and along the high cheekbones he drew a strip of blue paint. He paused and watched Ken throw pinches of corn meal and pollen into the wind that fluttered the small gray feather. Then Leon painted with yellow under the old man's broad nose, and finally, when he had painted green across the chin, he smiled.

"Send us rain clouds, Grandfather." They laid the bundle in the back of the pickup and covered it with a heavy tarp before they started back to the pueblo.[2]

> What does Leon ask of the dead man?

They turned off the highway onto the sandy pueblo road. Not long after they passed the store and post office they saw Father Paul's car coming toward them. When he recognized their faces he slowed his car and waved for them to stop. The young priest rolled down the car window.

"Did you find old Teofilo?" he asked loudly.

Leon stopped the truck. "Good morning, Father. We were just out to the sheep camp. Everything is O.K. now."

"Thank God for that. Teofilo is a very old man. You really shouldn't allow him to stay at the sheep camp alone."

> What doesn't Leon tell the priest? Why?

"No, he won't do that any more now."

---

1. **arroyo.** Dry gully
2. **pueblo.** Village

"Well, I'm glad you understand. I hope I'll be seeing you at Mass this week—we missed you last Sunday. See if you can get old Teofilo to come with you." The priest smiled and waved at them as they drove away.

Louise and Teresa were waiting. The table was set for lunch, and the coffee was boiling on the black iron stove. Leon looked at Louise and then at Teresa.

"We found him under a cottonwood tree in the big arroyo near sheep camp. I guess he sat down to rest in the shade and never got up again." Leon walked toward the old man's bed. The red plaid shawl had been shaken and spread carefully over the bed, and a new brown flannel shirt and pair of stiff new Levi's were arranged neatly beside the pillow. Louise held the screen door open while Leon and Ken carried in the red blanket. He looked small and <u>shriveled</u>, and after they dressed him in the new shirt and pants he seemed more shrunken.

It was noontime now because the church bells rang the Angelus.[3] They ate the beans with hot bread, and nobody said anything until after Teresa poured the coffee.

Ken stood up and put on his jacket. "I'll see about the gravediggers. Only the top layer of soil is frozen. I think it can be ready before dark."

Leon nodded his head and finished his coffee. After Ken had been gone for a while, the neighbors and clanspeople came quietly to embrace Teofilo's family and to leave food on the table because the gravediggers would come to eat when they were finished.

The sky in the west was full of pale yellow light. Louise stood outside with her hands in the pockets of Leon's green army jacket that was too big for her. The funeral was over, and the old men had taken their candles and medicine bags and were gone. She waited until the body was laid into the pickup before she said anything to Leon. She touched his arm, and he noticed that her hands were still dusty from the corn meal that she had sprinkled around the old man. When she spoke, Leon could not hear her.

"What did you say? I didn't hear you."

"I said that I had been thinking about something."

"About what?"

"About the priest sprinkling holy water for Grandpa. So he won't be thirsty."

Why does Louise want the priest to come sprinkle holy water over the body?

Leon stared at the new moccasins that Teofilo had made for the ceremonial dances in the summer. They were nearly hidden by the red blanket. It was getting colder, and the wind pushed gray dust down the narrow pueblo road. The sun was approaching the long <u>mesa</u> where it disappeared during the winter. Louise stood there shivering and watching his face. Then he zipped up his jacket and opened the truck door. "I'll see if he's there."

Ken stopped the pickup at the church, and Leon got out; and then Ken drove down the hill to the graveyard where people were waiting. Leon knocked at the old carved door with its symbols of the Lamb.[4] While he waited he looked up at the twin bells from the king of Spain[5] with the last sunlight pouring around them in their tower.

The priest opened the door and smiled when he saw who it was. "Come in! What brings you here this evening?"

---

3. **Angelus.** Prayer said at morning, noon, and evening to honor the birth of Jesus Christ
4. **Lamb.** Symbol of Jesus Christ
5. **twin bells. . . king of Spain.** Spain colonized the Americas in the fifteenth and sixteenth centuries; the Spanish monarchy sent priests and financed the building of churches.

---

words for everyday use

shriv • eled (shriv′əld) *adj.,* wrinkled and withered. *A raisin is simply a <u>shriveled</u> grape.*

me • sa (mā′sə) *n.,* high, flat tableland. *The top of the <u>mesa</u> was a perfect place to film the ad for the sports utility vehicle.*

The priest walked toward the kitchen, and Leon stood with his cap in his hand, playing with the earflaps and examining the living room—the brown sofa, the green armchair, and the brass lamp that hung down from the ceiling by links of chain. The priest dragged a chair out of the kitchen and offered it to Leon.

"No thank you, Father. I only came to ask you if you would bring your holy water to the graveyard."

The priest turned away from Leon and looked out the window at the patio full of shadows and the dining-room windows of the nuns' cloister[6] across the patio. The curtains were heavy, and the light from within faintly penetrated; it was impossible to see the nuns inside eating supper. "Why didn't you tell me he was dead? I could have brought the Last Rites[7] anyway."

Leon smiled. "It wasn't necessary, Father."

The priest stared down at his scuffed brown loafers and the worn hem of his cassock. "For a Christian burial it was necessary."

His voice was distant, and Leon thought that his blue eyes looked tired.

"It's O.K. Father, we just want him to have plenty of water."

The priest sank down into the green chair and picked up a glossy missionary magazine. He turned the colored pages full of lepers and pagans[8] without looking at them.

"You know I can't do that, Leon. There should have been the Last Rites and a funeral Mass at the very least."

Why does the priest hesitate?

Leon put on his green cap and pulled the flaps down over his ears. "It's getting late, Father. I've got to go."

When Leon opened the door Father Paul stood up and said, "Wait." He left the room and came back wearing a long brown overcoat. He followed Leon out the door and across the dim churchyard to the adobe steps in front of the church. They both stooped to fit through the low adobe entrance. And when they started down the hill to the graveyard only half of the sun was visible above the mesa.

The priest approached the grave slowly, wondering how they had managed to dig into the frozen ground; and then he remembered that this was New Mexico, and saw the pile of cold loose sand beside the hole. The people stood close to each other with little clouds of steam puffing from their faces. The priest looked at them and saw a pile of jackets, gloves, and scarves in the yellow, dry tumbleweeds that grew in the graveyard. He looked at the red blanket, not sure that Teofilo was so small, wondering if it wasn't some perverse Indian trick—something they did in March to ensure a good harvest—wondering if maybe old Teofilo was actually at sheep camp corraling the sheep for the night. But there he was, facing into a cold dry wind and squinting at the last sunlight, ready to bury a red wool blanket while the faces of his parishioners were in shadow with the last warmth of the sun on their backs.

What does the priest wonder about the situation? What does this show about his position in this community?

His fingers were stiff, and it took him a long time to twist the lid off the holy water. Drops of

---

6. **cloister.** Place of protection and seclusion for people who follow a religious vocation
7. **Last Rites.** Sacrament performed by a Catholic priest or deacon for someone dying
8. **lepers and pagans.** *Lepers*—people afflicted with the disease known as leprosy; *pagan*—a word sometimes used to refer to people who are not Christians.

Sunset Dance—Ceremony to the Evening Sun, 1924. Joseph Henry Sharp.
National Museum of American Art, Washington, DC.

water fell on the red blanket and soaked into dark icy spots. He sprinkled the grave and the water disappeared almost before it touched the dim, cold sand; it reminded him of something—he tried to remember what it was, because he thought if he could remember he might understand this. He sprinkled more water; he shook the container until it was empty, and the water fell through the light from sundown like August rain that fell while the sun was still shining, almost evaporating before it touched the wilted squash flowers.

The wind pulled at the priest's brown Franciscan robe[9] and swirled away the corn meal and pollen that had been sprinkled on the blanket. They lowered the bundle into the ground, and they didn't bother to untie the stiff pieces of new rope that were tied around the ends of the blanket. The sun was gone, and over on the highway the eastbound lane was full of headlights. The priest walked away slowly. Leon watched him climb the hill, and when he had disappeared within the tall, thick walls, Leon turned to look up at the high blue mountains in the deep snow that reflected a faint red light from the west. He felt good because it was finished, and he was happy about the sprinkling

Why does Leon feel happy?

of the holy water; now the old man could send them big thunderclouds for sure. ∎

---

9. **Franciscan robe.** Robe worn by a member of the Franciscan order, the Order of Saint Francis, consisting of a hooded brown full-length tunic tied at the waist with a rope

How should people react to belief systems that differ from their own?

Investigate, Inquire, *and* Imagine

Recall: Gathering Facts → ## Interpret: Finding Meaning

1a. What has happened to the elderly man found by Ken and Leon at the beginning of the story? What word does Leon use to refer to the elderly man? What does Leon put in the man's hair? What does he put on the man's face? What does he ask the man to do?

1b. What purpose might the painting of the elderly man's face serve? Why might the elderly man, according to the beliefs of Ken and Leon, now be in a position to influence the rainfall? What, then, do Ken and Leon probably believe about the afterlife?

2a. What doesn't Leon tell the priest about Teofilo? Why does Leon decide to go to visit the priest?

2b. What does Louise believe that sprinkling holy water on the dead man will do?

3a. What does the priest wish that Leon had told him? What would the priest have done if Leon had told him that?

3b. Why didn't Leon consider informing the priest "necessary"?

Analyze: Taking Things Apart → ## Synthesize: Bringing Things Together

4a. Compare the priest's first reaction to Leon's request to the priest's final decision. Why might he have changed his mind?

4b. What does this response tell you about the priest and about the way cultures come together, clash, and merge?

Evaluate: Making Judgments → ## Extend: Connecting Ideas

5a. How effectively do you think the Pueblo people merge the elements from different cultures and religious traditions? Explain.

5b. Cite examples of how other contemporary cultures or people of various ethnic backgrounds have adapted elements from one culture to another.

Understanding *Literature*

THEME. Review the definition for **theme** in the Handbook of Literary Terms. What does this story tell you about the ways in which traditional peoples attempt to preserve their ethnic identities against changes introduced from the outside? What do you think is the main theme of the selection?

SYMBOL. Review the definition for **symbol** in the Handbook of Literary Terms and the chart you made for Literary Tools on page 588. What function does pollen serve in nature? What significance does corn meal have to the Pueblo people? Why is rain important to them? Why then do Pueblo Indians sprinkle the dead with corn meal and pollen? What do corn meal, pollen, and water symbolize, or represent for them?

Writer's Journal

1. Using some of the clues in the story about his identity, write an **obituary** for Teofilo.
2. Pretend you are writing an encyclopedia article on the Pueblo people and their customs. Based on information from this story, write a **paragraph** on burial customs and belief in an afterlife.
3. Imagine that you are the priest in the story. Write a **letter** to the bishop of your church explaining your decision to sprinkle holy water for an unorthodox purpose.

Integrating the Language Arts

Language, Grammar, and Style

CORRECTING RUN-ONS. Read the Language Arts Survey 3.34, "Correcting Sentence Run-ons." Then revise the sentences below by changing punctuation and capitalization.

1. The Pueblo Indians have the oldest civilization in North America north of Mexico it dates back 700 years.
2. The Spanish named the Pueblo Indians "pueblo" also means "village."
3. In 1680 the Pueblo Indians staged a successful revolt against their Spanish oppressors the Pueblos lost 347 of their number, and the Spanish lost 411.
4. The Pueblos adopted many domestic animals and assorted crafts from the old world chili and many new fruits were introduced.
5. Today men are the weavers women make pottery and build houses.

Study and Research

ANTHROPOLOGICAL REPORT. Choose a ceremony or ritual important in your culture. Possibilities include weddings, birthday parties, bar mitzvahs, high school graduations, first communions, and Christmas celebrations. Write a description of the ceremony to be read by people from a different culture. In describing what takes place, be sure to explain the symbolic significance of the actions, words, and objects used in the ceremony. For example, each candle on a birthday cake symbolizes one year of life. Research some of the historical origins of the ceremony or ritual you select, and include these in your description as well.

Speaking and Listening

INTERVIEW/ORAL REPORT. Interview an individual from a culture or religious background different from your own. Identify some ritual or ceremony that plays an important role in that culture and learn everything you can about it from your interviewee. Then, in an oral report to several of your classmates, present what you have learned. For more information on interviewing, see the Language Arts Survey 4.14, "Conducting an Interview."

Collaborative Learning

WORD ORIGINS. Several of the words in Words for Everyday Use have Spanish origins (*adobe, arroyo, mesa, pueblo*). Can you think of other Spanish words that have been integrated into the English language? Work with a team to list as many as you can, along with their definitions, on a piece of paper. The team with the most English words derived from Spanish wins.

"An *Ethnic* Trump"

by Gish Jen

Reader's resource

"An Ethnic Trump" is a personal essay about Gish Jen's experiences as the mother of a biracial child. Jen is Chinese-American and her husband is of Irish descent. Yet somehow, people think of their son, Luke, as mainly Chinese. Jen ponders what it means to be multiracial in American society, and wonders how important it really is to hold on to one's ethnic heritage.

HISTORY CONNECTION. Many scholars argue that the category of "race" was invented in the seventeenth centrury by Europeans who wished to establish themselves as superior to the Native Americans they conquered and the Africans they enslaved. In the nineteenth and early twentieth century, some people tried to attribute cultural or psychological values to race in order to prove the white race superior. This racism reached a horrifying level in the racial doctrines of Nazi Germany. Today, most people recognize that fixed racial categories are sorely inadequate for describing the variety of individuals living on Earth. Many people prefer to think of themselves simply as belonging to the *human* race.

SOCIOLOGY CONNECTION. Since 1977, United States Census forms have required citizens to check one of the following racial classifications: American Indian or Alaskan native; Asian or Pacific Islander; Black; or White. An additional classification has been added: "Hispanic Origin" or "Not of Hispanic Origin." Today, many people criticize these choices, saying they no longer reflect the racial and ethnic diversity of the United States population. These people would like to see a "multiracial" category on the census forms.

About *the* AUTHOR

Gish Jen (1956–) grew up in Scarsdale, New York, the American-born daughter of immigrant Chinese parents. Her first name is Lillian, but she took the pen name "Gish," a nickname her high school friends called her. Jen writes about the Chinese-American experience in her novels *Typical American* and *Mona in the Promised Land*. However, she hopes her readers will get the message that "ethnicity is a very complicated thing, not a stable, unified thing. Right now many people hold the view that if you're a Chinese American, that is far and away the most important fact about you.... I think that's entirely wrong. I think that all the groups in America have rubbed off on each other, and that no group is pure. There is really no such thing as one who is purely Chinese American or anything else.... To imagine that being just one thing is the be-all-and-end-all truth about yourself is pretty naive."

Literary TOOLS

AIM. A writer's **aim** is his or her purpose, or goal. People may write with one or more of the following aims: to inform, to entertain, to make a point, to reflect, or to persuade. As you read, determine what you think Gish Jen's aim or aims are in writing this selection.

ANECDOTE. An **anecdote** is usually a short narrative of an interesting, amusing, or biographical incident. Although anecdotes are often the basis for short stories, an anecdote differs from a short story in that it lacks a complicated plot and relates a single episode. Anecdotes are sometimes used in nonfiction writing as examples to help support an idea or opinion. In this selection, Gish Jen relates several anecdotes.

Graphic Organizer

Make a chart like the one below to record the anecdotes Gish Jen relates in her essay "An Ethnic Trump." In the right column of the chart, write what you think each anecdote was meant to convey to the reader.

anecdote	meaning

Reader's Journal

How do you define your ethnic heritage?

An *Ethnic* Trump

Gish Jen

That my son, Luke, age four, goes to Chinese-culture school seems <u>inevitable</u> to most people, even though his father is of Irish descent. For certain <u>ethnicities</u> <u>trump</u> others; Chinese, for example, trumps Irish.

What are Luke's two ethnicities? Which one trumps, or overrides, the other?

This has something to do with the relative distance of certain cultures from mainstream American culture, but it also has to do with race. For as we all know, it is not only certain ethnicities that trump others but certain colors: black trumps white, for example, always and forever; a mulatto is not a kind of white person, but a kind of black person.

And so it is, too, that my son is considered a kind of Asian person whose <u>manifest</u> destiny is to embrace Asian things. The Chinese language. Chinese food. Chinese New Year. No one cares whether he speaks Gaelic[1] or wears green on Saint Patrick's Day. For though Luke's skin is fair, and his features mixed, people see his straight black hair and "know" who he is.

But is this how we should define ourselves, by other people's perceptions? My husband, Dave, and I had originally hoped for Luke to grow up embracing his whole complex ethnic heritage. We had hoped to pass on to him values and habits of mind that had actually survived in both of us.

> What had the author and her husband hoped for their son?

Then one day, Luke combed his black hair and said he was turning it yellow. Another day, a fellow mother reported that her son had invited all blond-haired children like himself to his birthday party. And yet another day, Luke was happily scooting around the Cambridge Common playground when a pair of older boys, apparently brothers, blocked his way. "You're Chinese!" they shouted, leaning on the hood of Luke's scooter car. "You are! You're Chinese!" So <u>brazen</u> were these kids that even

> What do the boys on the playground yell at Luke? What is Luke's response?

I told him that he was 100 percent American, . . .

when I, an adult, intervened, they continued to shout. Luke answered, "No, I'm not!"—to no avail; it was not clear if the boys even heard him. Then the boys' mother called to them from some distance away, outside the fence, and though her voice was no louder than Luke's, they left obediently.

Behind them opened a great, rippling quiet, like the wash of a battleship.

Luke and I immediately went over things he could say if anything like that ever happened again. I told him that he was 100 percent American, even though I knew from my own childhood in Yonkers that these words would be met only with <u>derision</u>. It was a sorry chore. Since then, I have not asked him about the incident, hoping he has forgotten about it, and wishing that I could, too. For I wish I could forget the sight of those kids' fingers on the hood of Luke's little car. I wish I could forget their loud attack, but also Luke's soft defense: No, I'm not.

Chinese-culture school. After dozens of phone calls, I was elated to discover the Greater Boston Chinese Cultural Association nearby in West Newton. The school takes children at three, has a wonderful sense of community, and is housed in a center paid for,

---

1. **Gaelic.** The Irish language

---

words for everyday use

man • i • fest (ma' ń fest) adj., obvious. *Megan's path in life was <u>manifest</u> from the very beginning: since she was a toddler, she wanted to be a dancer.*

bra • zen (brā zən) adj., overly bold; disrespectful. *The most <u>brazen</u> of the reporters pursued the movie star relentlessly, sneaking pictures of her in her own backyard.*

de • ri • sion (di ri' zhən) n., scorn. *The French director looked down on American movies and regarded Hollywood productions with <u>derision</u>.*

in part, by great karaoke[2] fund-raising events. (Never mind what the Japanese meant to the Chinese in the old world. In this world, people donate at least two hundred dollars each for a chance at the mike, and the singing goes on all night.) There are even vendors who bring home-style Chinese food to sell after class—stuff you can't get in a restaurant. Dave and I couldn't wait for the second class, and a chance to buy more bao[3] for our freezer.

But in the car on the way to the second class, Luke announced that he didn't want to go to Chinese school anymore. He said that the teacher talked mostly about ducks and bears and that he wasn't interested in ducks and bears. And I knew this was true. I knew that Luke was interested only in whales and ships. And what's more, I knew we wouldn't push him to take swimming lessons if he didn't want to, or music. Chinese school was a wonderful thing, but there was a way in which we were accepting it as somehow nonoptional. Was

that right? Hadn't we always said that we didn't want our son to see himself as more essentially Chinese than Irish?

Yet we didn't want him to deny his Chinese heritage, either. And if there were going to be incidents on the playground, we wanted him to know what Chinese meant. So when Luke said again that he didn't really want to go to Chinese school, I said, "Oh, really?" Later on, we could try to teach him to define himself irrespective of race. For now, though, he was going to Chinese school. I exchanged glances with Dave. And then together, in a most carefully casual manner, we squinted at the road and kept going. ∎

> What do the author and her husband not want Luke to do? What do they want him to know?

---

2. **karaoke.** Device that plays musical accompaniment while the user is recorded singing along with the music (from Japanese *kara*, meaning "empty" + *oke*, short for *okesutura*, meaning "orchestra")

3. **bao.** Chinese name for a type of dried fish

Respond *to the* SELECTION

Do you think Luke's parents made the right decision in insisting that Luke go to Chinese-culture school? What would you have done in their position?

Investigate, *Inquire,* and

Recall: GATHERING FACTS

1a. Which ethnicities "trump" others, according to the author of this selection? Which of Luke's ethnicities trumps the other?

2a. What is Luke's response when some boys at the playground say he is Chinese? How does his mother tell him he should respond?

3a. What does Luke say about Chinese school? How do his parents react?

→ Interpret: FINDING MEANING

1b. Why do people think it inevitable that Luke go to Chinese-culture school? Why don't they expect him to speak Gaelic?

2b. Why do the boys assume Luke is Chinese? Why does Luke respond as he does?

3b. Why do the author and her husband want Luke to continue attending Chinese-culture school?

Analyze: TAKING THINGS APART

4a. According to the author, for what reasons do certain ethnicities trump others? What evidence can you find that Luke is perceived as more ethnically Chinese than Irish?

→ Synthesize: BRINGING THINGS TOGETHER

4b. What do the author and her husband want to pass on to Luke? How have they always wanted him to view his ethnic heritage? In your opinion, should Luke define himself by other people's perceptions?

Perspective: LOOKING AT OTHER VIEWS →

5a. Why do you think Luke's classmate invites only blond children to his party? Why do you think the other children in the park harass Luke? Do you think these children are mean-spirited? Do you think their behavior is different from that of the adults who assume Luke is Chinese? Explain.

Empathy: SEEING FROM INSIDE

5b. If you were Luke, how would you react to being harassed on the playground? How do you think Luke's response affects his mother? Why do you think the author uses the simile of "the wash of a battleship" to describe the quiet after the boys leave the playground?

Understanding *Literature*

AIM. Review the definition for **aim** in the Handbook of Literary Terms. What do you think is Gish Jen's primary aim in writing this essay? Explain. What do you think some of her secondary aims, if any, might be?

ANECDOTE. Review the definition for **anecdote** in the Handbook of Literary Terms. How does each anecdote in "An Ethnic Trump" contribute to the aim or aims of Jen's essay?

Writer's Journal

1. Imagine you are one of Luke's parents. How would you advise him to respond when other kids call him Chinese? Write a **note** to Luke, giving him advice.
2. How do you define yourself? Write a **definition** of yourself that you might provide to a pen pal whom you have never met.
3. Imagine that you are Luke as a teenager. How might you feel about your parents' efforts to educate you about your heritage? Write a **letter** Luke might write to his parents telling them how he feels about having attended Chinese school and about how he sees himself.

Integrating the Language Arts

Critical Thinking & Speaking and Listening

HOLDING A DEBATE. Form groups of four students to research the issue of including racial categories on government forms. On the Internet, use the keywords "mixed race" or "multirace" to find sites or articles that discuss multiracial identity. What are the arguments for and against asking people to define themselves in terms of race or ethnic background? When you have gathered enough information on the topic, meet as a group to discuss what each thinks about the issue. Make sure that each point of view on the issue is brought out and examined.

Study and Research

RESEARCHING AMERICA'S MULTIRACIAL HERITAGE. Conduct research on the presence of multi-racial people in the United States. Your topic could be the Creole people of Louisiana, the Black Seminoles of Florida and the Southwest, or Latinos in the United States. You might also research the controversy surrounding the third president of the United States, Thomas Jefferson, and his relationship with his slave Sally Hemings. Finally, you might also choose a specific well-known person who is multiracial, such as singer Mariah Carey, actress Rae Dawn Chong, golfer Tiger Woods, or musician Lenny Kravitz, and find interviews with the person in which he or she discusses ethnic background and identity. When you have finished your research, prepare an oral report of your findings to be given to the class.

Media Literacy

MAGAZINES AND ONLINE MAGAZINES. Research magazines dealing with interracial issues. Two such magazines are *Interracial Voice* and *Mavin*. Information can be found online at http://www.webcom.com/~intvoice/ and http://www.mavin.net/. What kinds of issues are discussed in these magazines that are not necessarily dealt with by mainstream magazines? What is the aim of these publications?

"Who Am I This Time?"

by Kurt Vonnegut, Jr.

Reader's resource

"Who Am I This Time?" was published in *Welcome to the Monkey House* (1969). In this story, the characters produce *A Streetcar Named Desire,* a play by Tennessee Williams (1911–1983). Made into a movie in 1951, *A Streetcar Named Desire* became a film classic. Brando's cinematic performance as Stanley Kowalski drew rave reviews from critics and audiences alike, and he has been associated with the role ever since. In much the same way Brando *became* Stanley by assuming that character's identity, Vonnegut's Harry becomes Brando in the story.

About *the* AUTHOR

Kurt Vonnegut, Jr. (1922–) has written novels, short stories, plays, television scripts, and essays. Born in Indianapolis, he was educated at Cornell, the Carnegie Institute, and the University of Chicago. His experiences serving in World War II inspired his best-known novel, *Slaughterhouse Five* (1969), about the destruction of Dresden, an event he witnessed firsthand as a prisoner of war in that city. After the war, Vonnegut worked in public relations for the General Electric Company before devoting himself to writing and teaching. By the late 1960s, Vonnegut's novels had made him the most popular writer on college campuses.

In his works Vonnegut protests the horrors of the twentieth century—mass death, dehumanization, pollution of the environment—and supports pacifism. Often labeled science fiction, his novels have fantastic plots, involving time faults, trips to outer space, and apocalyptic destruction. Vonnegut treats his grim themes with wry charm and dark humor. His works of fiction include *Player Piano* (1951), *Mother Night* (1962), *Cat's Cradle* (1963), *Welcome to the Monkey House* (1969), *Breakfast of Champions* (1973), *Galapagos* (1985), and *Hocus Pocus* (1990).

Literary TOOLS

IRONY AND DRAMATIC IRONY. Irony is a difference between appearance and reality. **Dramatic irony** is a type of irony in which something is known by the reader or audience but unknown to the characters. As you read, look for examples of dramatic irony.

ALLUSION. An **allusion** is a rhetorical technique in which reference is made to a person, event, object, or work from history or literature. What literary allusions are presented in this story?

Organizer

As you read, make a chart listing literary allusions in the selection. Include the characters in the play that Helene gives to Harry as a present and the characters Helene says she and Harry interpreted at home after their marriage. On the left write the names of fictitious characters that are mentioned. On the right write what happens to them. One example has been done for you.

Characters	Plot
Helen of Troy	kidnapped by a foreigner

Reader's Journal

When have you pretended to be someone you are not? What was your response to trying on a role?

Who Am I This Time?

Kurt Vonnegut, Jr.

Marlon Brando and Vivien Leigh in *A Streetcar Named Desire,* 1951.

...Harry Nash, the only real actor the club has, had to take the Marlon Brando part in the play.

The North Crawford Mask and Wig Club, an _amateur_ theatrical society I belong to, voted to do Tennessee Williams' *A Streetcar Named Desire* for the spring play. Doris Sawyer, who always directs, said she couldn't direct this time because her mother was so sick. And she said the club ought to develop some other directors anyway, because she couldn't live forever, even though she'd made it safely to seventy-four.

So I got stuck with the directing job, even though the only thing I'd ever directed before was the installation of combination aluminum storm windows and screens I'd sold. That's what I am, a salesman of storm windows and doors, and here and there a bathtub _enclosure_. As far as acting goes, the highest rank I ever held on stage was either butler or policeman, whichever's higher.

What experience does the narrator have with directing plays?

I made a lot of conditions before I took the directing job, and the biggest one was that Harry Nash, the only real actor the club has, had to take the Marlon Brando part in the play. To give you an idea of how _versatile_ Harry is, inside of one year he was Captain Queeg in *The Caine Mutiny Court Martial*, then Abe Lincoln in *Abe Lincoln in Illinois* and then the young architect in *The Moon is Blue.* The year after that, Harry Nash was Henry the Eighth in *Anne of the Thousand Days* and Doc in *Come Back Little Sheba*, and I was after him for Marlon Brando in *A Streetcar Named Desire.* Harry wasn't at the meeting to say whether he'd take the part or not. He never came to meetings. He was too shy. He didn't stay away from meetings because he had something else to do. He wasn't married, didn't go out with women—didn't have any close men friends either. He stayed away from all kinds of gatherings because he never could think of anything to say or do without a script.

Why does Harry Nash stay away from social gatherings?

So I had to go down to Miller's Hardware Store, where Harry was a clerk, the next day and ask him if he'd take the part. I stopped off at the telephone company to complain about a bill I'd gotten for a call to Honolulu, I'd never called Honolulu in my life.

And there was this beautiful girl I'd never seen before behind the counter at the phone company, and she explained that the company had put in an automatic billing machine and that the machine didn't have all the bugs out of it yet. It made mistakes. "Not only did I not call Honolulu," I told her, "I don't think anybody in North Crawford ever has or will."

So she took the charge off the bill, and I asked her if she was from around North Crawford. She said no. She said she just came with the new billing machine to teach local girls how to take care of it. After that, she said, she would go with some other machine to someplace else. "Well," I said, "as long as people have to come along with the machines, I guess we're all right."

---

words for everyday use

am • a • teur (a′ mə tər) *n.*, one who engages in a pursuit, study, science, or sport as a pastime rather than as a profession. *Do you think _amateur_ baseball teams play with as much passion as professionals?*

en • clo • sure (in klō′ zhər) *n.*, structure that encloses or shuts in. *At the back of the house there was a small screened-in _enclosure_.*

ver • sa • tile (vər′ sə təl) *adj.*, embracing a variety of subjects, fields, or skills. *Kim is such a _versatile_ singer that she can sing both the alto and soprano parts.*

"What?" she said.

"When machines start delivering themselves," I said, "I guess that's when the people better start really worrying."

"Oh," she said. She didn't seem very interested in that subject, and I wondered if she was interested in anything. She seemed kind of numb, almost a machine herself, an automatic phone-company politeness machine.

"How long will you be in town here?" I asked her.

"I stay in each town eight weeks, sir," she said. She had pretty blue eyes, but there sure wasn't much hope or curiosity in them. She told me she had been going from town to town like that for two years, always a stranger.

And I got it in my head that she might make a good Stella for the play. Stella was the wife of the Marlon Brando character, the wife of the character I wanted Harry Nash to play. So I told her where and when we were going to hold tryouts, and said the club would be very happy if she'd come.

Why does the narrator invite the woman he just met to tryouts?

She looked surprised, and she warmed up a little. "You know," she said, "that's the first time anybody ever asked me to participate in any community thing."

"Well," I said, "there isn't any other way to get to know a lot of nice people faster than to be in a play with 'em."

She said her name was Helene Shaw. She said she might just surprise me—and herself. She said she just might come.

You would think that North Crawford would be fed up with Harry Nash in plays after all the plays he'd been in. But the fact was that North Crawford probably could have gone on enjoying Harry forever, because he was never Harry on stage. When the maroon curtain went up on the stage in the gymnasium of the Consolidated Junior-Senior High School, Harry, body and

Why does the town like Harry's acting?

...Harry, body and soul, was exactly what the script and the director told him to be.

soul, was exactly what the script and the director told him to be.

Somebody said one time that Harry ought to go to a psychiatrist so he could be something important and colorful in real life, too—so he could get married anyway, and maybe get a better job than just clerking in Miller's Hardware Store for fifty dollars a week. But I don't know what a psychiatrist could have turned up about him that the town didn't already know. The trouble with Harry was he'd been left on the doorstep of the Unitarian Church when he was a baby, and he never did find out who his parents were.

When I told him there in Miller's that I'd been appointed director, that I wanted him in my play, he said what he always said to anybody who asked him to be in a play—and it was kind of sad, if you think about it.

"Who am I this time?" he said.

So I held the tryouts where they're always held—in the meeting room on the second floor of the North Crawford Public Library. Doris Sawyer, the woman who usually directs, came to give me the benefit of all her experience. The two of us sat in state[1] upstairs, while the people who wanted parts waited below. We called them upstairs one by one.

Harry Nash came to the tryouts, even though it was a waste of time. I guess he wanted to get that little bit more acting in.

For Harry's pleasure, and our pleasure, too, we had him read from the scene where he beats

---

1. **sat in state.** Received official visitors, as would a king or queen

up his wife. It was a play in itself, the way Harry did it, and Tennessee Williams hadn't written it all either. Tennessee Williams didn't write the part, for instance, where Harry, who weighs about one hundred forty-five, who's about five feet eight inches tall, added fifty pounds to his weight and four inches to his height by just picking up a playbook.[2] He had a short little double-breasted bellows-back grade-school graduation suit coat on and a dinky little red tie with a horsehead on it. He took off the coat and tie, opened his collar, then turned his back to Doris and me, getting up steam for the part. There was a great big rip in the back of his shirt, and it looked like a fairly new shirt too. He'd ripped it on purpose, so he could be that much more like Marlon Brando, right from the first.

When he faced us again, he was huge and hand-some and conceited and cruel. Doris read the part of Stella, the wife, and Harry bullied that old, old lady into believing that she was a sweet, pregnant girl married to a sexy gorilla who was going to beat her brains out. She had me believing it too. And I read the lines of Blanche, her sister in the play, and darned if Harry didn't scare me into feeling like a drunk and faded Southern belle.

And then, while Doris and I were getting over our emotional experiences, like people coming out from under <u>ether</u>, Harry put down the playbook, put on his coat and tie, and turned into the pale hardware-store clerk again.

"Was—was that all right?" he said, and he seemed pretty sure he wouldn't get the part.

"Well," I said, "for a first reading, that wasn't too bad."

"Is there a chance I'll get the part?" he said. I don't know why he always had to pretend

What aspects of the Brando character did Harry convey?

there was some doubt about his getting a part, but he did.

"I think we can safely say we're leaning pow-erfully in your direction," I told him.

He was very pleased. "Thanks! Thanks a lot!" he said, and he shook my hand.

"Is there a pretty new girl downstairs?" I said, meaning Helene Shaw.

"I didn't notice," said Harry.

It turned out that Helene Shaw *had* come for the tryouts, and Doris and I had our hearts broken. We thought the North Crawford Mask and Wig Club was finally going to put a really good-looking, really young girl on stage, instead of one of the beat-up forty-year-old women we generally have to palm off[3] as girls.

But Helene Shaw couldn't act for sour apples. No matter what we gave her to read, she was the same girl with the same smile for anybody who had a complaint about his phone bill.

Doris tried to coach her some, to make her understand that Stella in the play was a very passionate girl who loved a gorilla because she needed a gorilla. But Helene just read the lines the same way again. I don't think a volcano could have stirred her up enough to say, "Oo."

"Dear," said Doris, "I'm going to ask you a personal question."

"All right," said Helene.

"Have you ever been in love?" said Doris. "The reason I ask," she said, "remembering some old love might help you put more warmth in your acting."

Helene frowned and thought hard. "Well," she said, "I travel a lot, you know. And practi-cally all the men in the different companies I

---

2. **playbook.** script
3. **to palm off.** To deceive by some trickery or fraud

visit are married and I never stay anyplace long enough to know many people who aren't."

"What about school?" said Doris. "What about puppy love and all the other kinds of love in school?"

So Helene thought hard about that, and then she said, "Even in school I was always moving around a lot. My father was a construction worker, following jobs around, so I was always saying hello or good-by to someplace, without anything in between."

"Um," said Doris.

"Would movie stars count?" said Helene. "I don't mean in real life. I never knew any. I just mean up on the screen."

Doris looked at me and rolled her eyes. "I guess that's love of a kind," she said.

And then Helene got a little enthusiastic. "I used to sit through movies over and over again," she said, "and pretend I was married to whoever the man movie star was. They were the only people who came with us. No matter where we moved, movie stars were there."

"Uh huh," said Doris.

For whom has Helene felt love in the past?

"Well, thank you, Miss Shaw," I said. "You go downstairs and wait with the rest. We'll let you know."

So we tried to find another Stella. And there just wasn't one, not one woman in the club with the dew still on her.[4] "All we've got are Blanches," I said, meaning all we had were faded women who could play the part of Blanche, Stella's faded sister. "That's life, I guess—twenty Blanches to one Stella."

"And when you find a Stella," said Doris, "it turns out she doesn't know what love is."

Doris and I decided there was one last thing we could try. We could get Harry Nash to play a scene along with Helene. "He just might make her bubble the least little bit," I said.

"That girl hasn't got a bubble in her," said Doris.

So we called down the stairs for Helene to come back on up, and we told somebody to go

find Harry. Harry never sat with the rest of the people at tryouts—or at rehearsals either. The minute he didn't have a part to play, he'd disappear into some hiding place where he could hear people call him, but where he couldn't be seen. At tryouts in the library he generally hid in the reference room, passing the time looking at flags of different countries in the front of the dictionary.

Helene came back upstairs, and we were very sorry and surprised to see that she'd been crying.

"Oh, dear," said Doris. "Oh, my—now what on earth's the trouble, dear?"

"I was terrible, wasn't I?" said Helene, hanging her head.

Doris said the only thing anybody can say in an amateur theatrical society when somebody cries. She said, "Why, no dear—you were marvelous."

"No, I wasn't," said Helene. "I'm a walking icebox,[5] and I know it."

"Nobody could look at you and say that," said Doris.

"When they get to know me, they can say it," said Helene. "When people get to know me, that's what they *do* say." Her tears got worse. "I don't want to be the way I am," she said. "I just can't help it, living the way I've lived all my life. The only experiences I've had have been in crazy dreams of movie stars. When I meet somebody nice in real life, I feel as though I were in some kind of big bottle, as though I couldn't touch that person, no matter how hard I tried." And Helene pushed on air as though it were a big bottle all around her.

"You ask me if I've ever been in love," she said to Doris. "No—but I want to be. I know what this play's about. I know what Stella's supposed to feel and why she feels it. I—I—I—" she said, and her tears wouldn't let her go on.

"You what, dear?" said Doris gently.

---

4. **with the dew still on her.** Young
5. **icebox.** Refrigerator

"I—" said Helene, and she pushed on the imaginary bottle again. "I just don't know how to begin," she said.

There was heavy clumping on the library stairs. It sounded like a deep-sea diver coming upstairs in his lead shoes. It was Harry Nash, turning himself into Marlon Brando. In he came, practically dragging his knuckles on the floor. And he was so much in character that the sight of a weeping woman made him <u>sneer</u>.

"Harry," I said, "I'd like you to meet Helene Shaw. Helene—this is Harry Nash. If you get the part of Stella, he'll be your husband in the play." Harry didn't offer to shake hands. He put his hands in his pockets, and he hunched over, and he looked her up and down, gave her looks that left her naked. Her tears stopped right then and there.

"I wonder if you two would play the fight scene," I said, "and then the reunion scene right after it."

"Sure," said Harry, his eyes still on her. Those eyes burned up clothes faster than she could put them on. "Sure," he said, "if Stell's game."

"What?" said Helene. She'd turned the color of cranberry juice.

"Stell—Stella," said Harry. "That's you. Stell's my wife."

I handed the two of them playbooks. Harry snatched his from me without a word of thanks. Helene's hands weren't working very well, and I had to kind of mold them around the book.

"I'll want something I can throw," said Harry.

"What?" I said.

"There's one place where I throw a radio out a window," said Harry. "What can I throw?"

So I said an iron paperweight was the radio, and I opened the window wide. Helene Shaw looked scared to death.

"Where you want us to start?" said Harry, and he rolled his shoulders like a prizefighter warming up.

"Start a few lines back from where you throw the radio out the window," I said.

"O.K., O.K.," said Harry, warming up, warming up. He scanned the stage directions. "Let's see," he said, "after I throw the radio, she runs off stage, and I chase her, and I sock her one."

"Right," I said.

"O.K., baby," Harry said to Helene, his eyelids drooping. What was about to happen was wilder than the chariot race in *Ben Hur*. "On your mark," said Harry. "Get ready, baby. Go!"

When the scene was over, Helene Shaw was as hot as a hod carrier,[6] as limp as an eel. She sat down with her mouth open and her head hanging to one side. She wasn't in any bottle any more. There wasn't any bottle to hold her up and keep her safe and clean. The bottle was gone.

"Do I get the part or don't I?" Harry snarled at me.

"You'll do," I said.

"You said a mouthful!" he said. "I'll be going now. . . . See you around, Stella," he said to

> What was about to happen was wilder than the chariot race in Ben Hur.

6. **hod carrier.** Laborer employed in carrying supplies to bricklayers, stone masons, cement finishers, or plasterers

words for everyday use

sneer (snēr) *n.*, smile or laugh accompanied by facial contortions that express scorn or contempt. *Amy delivered her sarcastic retort with a <u>sneer</u>.*

Stage production of *A Streetcar Named Desire,* 1947.

Helene, and he left. He slammed the door behind him.

"Helene?" I said. "Miss Shaw?"

"Me?" she said.

"The part of Stella is yours," I said. "You were great!"

"I was?" she said.

"I had no idea you had that much fire in you, dear," Doris said to her.

"Fire?" said Helene. She didn't know if she was afoot or on horseback.

"Skyrockets! Pinwheels! Roman candles!"[7] said Doris.

"Me," said Helene. And that was all she said. She looked as though she were going to sit in the chair with her mouth open forever.

"Stella," I said.

"Huh?" she said.

"You have my permission to go."

So we started having rehearsals four nights a week on the stage of the Consolidated School. And Harry and Helene set such a pace that everybody in the production was half crazy with excitement and exhaustion before we'd rehearsed four times. Usually a director has to beg people to learn their lines, but I had no such trouble. Harry and Helene were working so well together that everybody else in the cast regarded it as a duty and an honor and a pleasure to support them.

I was certainly lucky—or thought I was. Things were going so well, so hot and heavy, so early in

7. **Roman candles.** Fireworks

the game that I had to say to Harry and Helene after one love scene, "Hold a little something back for the actual performance, would you please? You'll burn yourselves out."

I said that at the fourth or fifth rehearsal, and Lydia Miller, who was playing Blanche, the faded sister, was sitting next to me in the audience. In real life, she's the wife of Verne Miller. Verne owns Miller's Hardware Store. Verne was Harry's boss.

"Lydia," I said to her, "have we got a play or have we got a play?"

"Yes," she said, "you've got a play, all right." She made it sound as though I'd committed some kind of crime, done something just terrible. "You should be very proud of yourself."

"What do you mean by that?" I said.

Before Lydia could answer, Harry yelled at me from the stage, asked if I was through with him, asked if he could go home. I told him he could and, still Marlon Brando, he left, kicking furniture out of his way and slamming doors. Helene was left all alone on the stage, sitting on a couch with the same gaga look she'd had after the tryouts. That girl was drained.

I turned to Lydia again and I said, "Well—until now, I thought I had every reason to be happy and proud. Is there something going on I don't know about?"

"Do you know that girl's in love with Harry?" said Lydia.

"In the play?" I said.

"What play?" said Lydia. "There isn't any play going on now, and look at her up there." She gave a sad cackle. "You aren't directing this play."

"Who is?" I said.

"Mother Nature at her worst," said Lydia. "And think what it's going to do to that girl when she discovers what Harry really is." She corrected herself. "What Harry really isn't," she said.

I didn't do anything about it, because I didn't figure it was any of my business. I heard Lydia

Who does Lydia think is directing the play? What does she think will happen to Helene?

try to do something about it, but she didn't get very far.

"You know," Lydia said to Helene one night, "I once played Ann Rutledge, and Harry was Abraham Lincoln."

Helene clapped her hands. "That must have been heaven!" she said.

"It was, in a way," said Lydia. "Sometimes I'd get so worked up, I'd love Harry the way I'd love Abraham Lincoln. I'd have to come back to earth and remind myself that he wasn't ever going to free the slaves, that he was just a clerk in my husband's hardware store."

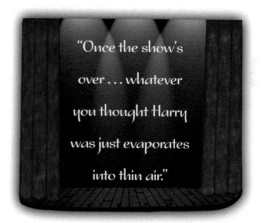

"Once the show's over ... whatever you thought Harry was just evaporates into thin air."

"He's the most marvelous man I ever met," said Helene.

"Of course, one thing you have to get set for, when you're in a play with Harry," said Lydia, "is what happens after the last performance."

"What are you talking about?" said Helene.

"Once the show's over," said Lydia, "whatever you thought Harry was just evaporates into thin air."

"I don't believe it," said Helene.

"I admit it's hard to believe," said Lydia.

Then Helene got a little sore. "Anyway, why tell me about it?" she said. "Even if it is true, what do I care?"

"I—I don't know," said Lydia, backing away. "I—I just thought you might find it interesting."

"Well, I don't," said Helene.

And Lydia slunk away, feeling about as frowzy[8] and unloved as she was supposed to feel in the play. After that nobody said anything more to Helene to warn her about Harry, not even when word got around that she'd told the telephone company that she didn't want to be moved around anymore, that she wanted to stay in North Crawford.

So the time finally came to put on the play. We ran it for three nights—Thursday, Friday, and Saturday—and we murdered those audiences. They believed every word that was said on stage, and when the maroon curtain came

All the Marlon Brando in him was gone... he was everything Harry was famous for being between plays.

down they were ready to go to the nut house along with Blanche, the faded sister.

On Thursday night the other girls at the telephone company sent Helene a dozen red roses. When Helene and Harry were taking a curtain call[9] together, I passed the roses over the footlights to her. She came forward for them, took one rose from the bouquet to give to Harry. But when she turned to give Harry the rose in front of everybody, Harry was gone. The curtain came down on that extra little scene—that girl offering a rose to nothing and nobody.

I went backstage, and I found her still holding that one rose. She'd put the rest of the bouquet aside. There were tears in her eyes. "What did I do wrong?" she said to me. "Did I insult him some way?"

"No," I said. "He always does that after a performance. The minute it's over, he clears out as fast as he can."

"And tomorrow he'll disappear again?"

"Without even taking off his makeup."

"And Saturday?" she said. "He'll stay for the cast party on Saturday, won't he?"

"Harry never goes to parties," I said. "When the curtain comes down on Saturday, that's the last anybody will see of him till he goes to work on Monday."

"How sad," she said.

Helene's performance on Friday night wasn't nearly so good as Thursday's. She seemed to be thinking about other things. She watched Harry take off after curtain call. She didn't say a word.

On Saturday she put on the best performance yet. Ordinarily it was Harry who set the pace. But on Saturday Harry had to work to keep up with Helene.

When the curtain came down on the final curtain call, Harry wanted to get away, but he couldn't. Helene wouldn't let go his hand. The rest of the cast and the stage crew and a lot of well-wishers from the audience were all standing around Harry and Helene, and Harry was trying to get his hand back.

"Well," he said, "I've got to go."

"Where?" she said.

"Oh," he said, "home."

"Won't you please take me to the cast party?" she said.

He got very red. "I'm afraid I'm not much on parties," he said. All the Marlon Brando in him was gone. He was tongue-tied, he was scared, he was shy—he was everything Harry was famous for being between plays.

"All right," she said. "I'll let you go—if you promise me one thing."

---

8. **frowzy.** Slovenly or uncared-for appearance
9. **curtain call.** Appearance by a performer in response to lengthy applause

"What's that?" he said, and I thought he would jump out a window if she let go of him then.

"I want you to promise to stay here until I get you your present," she said.

"Present?" he said, getting even more panicky.

"Promise?" she said.

He promised. It was the only way he could get his hand back. And he stood there miserably while Helene went down to the ladies' dressing room for the present. While he waited, a lot of people congratulated him on being such a fine actor. But congratulations never made him happy. He just wanted to get away.

Helene came back with the present. It turned out to be a little blue book with a big red ribbon for a place marker. It was a copy of *Romeo and Juliet*. Harry was very embarrassed. It was all he could do to say "Thank you."

> What gift does Helene give Harry?

"The marker marks my favorite scene," said Helene.

"Um," said Harry.

"Don't you want to see what my favorite scene is?" she said.

So Harry had to open the book to the red ribbon.

Helene got close to him, and read a line of Juliet's. "'How cam'st thou hither, tell me, and wherefore?'" she read. "'The orchard walls are high and hard to climb, and the place death, considering who thou art, if any of my kinsmen find thee here.'" She pointed to the next line. "Now, look what Romeo says," she said.

"Um," said Harry.

"Read what Romeo says," said Helene.

Harry cleared his throat. He didn't want to read the line, but he had to. "'With love's light wings did I o'erperch these walls,'" he read out loud in his everyday voice. But then a change came over him. "'For stony limits cannot hold love out,'" he read, and he straightened up, and eight years dropped away from him, and he was brave and gay. "'And what love can do, that dares love attempt,'" he read, "'therefore thy kinsmen are no let to me.'"

"'If they do see thee they will murther thee,'" said Helene, and she started him walking toward the wings.

"'Alack!'" said Harry, "'there lies more peril in thine eye than twenty of their swords.'" Helene led him toward the backstage exit. "'Look thou but sweet,'" said Harry, "'and I am proof against their enmity.'"

"'I would not for the world they saw thee here,'" said Helene, and that was the last we heard. The two of them were out the door and gone.

They never did show up at the cast party. One week later they were married.

They seem very happy, although they're kind of strange from time to time, depending on which play they're reading to each other at the time.

I dropped into the phone company office the other day, on account of the billing machine was making dumb mistakes again. I asked her what plays she and Harry'd been reading lately.

"In the past week," she said, "I've been married to Othello, been loved by Faust and been kidnapped by Paris[10]. Wouldn't you say I was the luckiest girl in town?"

> How does Helene feel about her marriage to Harry?

I said I thought so, and I told her most of the women in town thought so too.

"They had their chance," she said.

"Most of 'em couldn't stand the excitement," I said. And I told her I'd been asked to direct another play. I asked if she and Harry would be available for the cast. She gave me a big smile and said, "Who are we this time?" ∎

---

10. **I've been married . . . Paris.** *Othello* is a play by Shakespeare in which the title character strangles his wife, Desdemona. *Faust* is a play by Goethe in which the title character sells his soul to the devil. Paris kidnapped Helen of Troy, considered the most beautiful woman in ancient Greece.

Respond *to the* SELECTION

Do you think that the love that Harry and Helene express for each other will last? Why, or why not?

Investigate, *Inquire,* and Imagine

Recall: GATHERING FACTS →

1a. What does Harry always say when the director proposes a part for him to play?

2a. What image does Vonnegut use to describe Helene's inability to project any emotion in her acting?

3a. What is Helene's reaction to Lydia's telling her that Harry will "evaporate into thin air" after the play is over?

Interpret: FINDING MEANING

1b. Why does the narrator think that Harry's response is sad?

2b. What difficulty does Helene experience because of the moving she did as a child and as an employee for the phone company?

3b. Why does Helene react the way that she does to Lydia's warning?

Analyze: TAKING THINGS APART →

4a. Compare and contrast Harry and Helene before they meet to perform *A Streetcar Named Desire*. In what ways are they similar? different?

Synthesize: BRINGING THINGS TOGETHER

4b. Explain the dynamics of Harry and Helene's marriage.

Evaluate: MAKING JUDGMENTS →

5a. Evaluate Helene's statement that she's "the luckiest girl in town."

Extend: CONNECTING IDEAS

5b. What are some other roles that Harry and Helene could play in order to continue playacting at love?

Understanding *Literature*

IRONY AND DRAMATIC IRONY. Review the definitions for **irony** and **dramatic irony** in the Handbook of Literary Terms. What examples of dramatic irony did you find in the selection?

ALLUSION. Review the definition for **allusion** in the Handbook of Literary Terms and the chart you made for Literary Tools on page 601. Based on the chart you made, what does Vonnegut seem to be saying about Harry and Helene's love affair?

Writer's Journal

1. Imagine you are the narrator-director of this story. Write a **journal entry** speculating on what is happening on stage between Harry and Helene and expressing what concerns you have about their relationship.

2. Imagine you are Harry playing the role of Stanley or Helene playing the part of Stella in *A Streetcar Named Desire*. While staying in character, write a **letter** to your acting partner telling how you feel about her or him.

3. Watch the film version of *A Streetcar Named Desire* starring Marlon Brando. Then, with a partner, write a **character sketch** about Stanley, Stella, or Blanche.

Integrating
the Language Arts

Language, Grammar, and Style

REFLEXIVE AND INTENSIFYING PRONOUNS. Read about reflexive pronouns in the Language Arts Survey 3.58, "Reflexive Pronouns" and about intensifying pronouns in the Language Arts Survey 3.78, "Hybrids." Then, in the sentences below, underline each reflexive or intensifying pronoun, and identify the pronoun as reflexive or intensive.

1. Doris Sawyer couldn't direct the play herself.
2. She herself suggested the narrator direct the play.
3. Harry Nash wasn't himself when he acted.
4. The people in the community enjoyed themselves at the play.
5. Can you yourself act in a play?

Speaking and Listening & Collaborative Learning

CHARACTER CHARADES. With several classmates, come up with a list of characters you know from movies, books, or plays. Write the characters' names on slips of paper and draw slips to choose characters. Take turns imitating the characters while your teammates try to guess each one. If a teammate guesses your imitation within ten seconds of your finished presentation, you earn a point and get another turn. If a teammate does not guess your assumed identity within that time, then the next person in your group gets a turn. At the end of the allotted time, the teammate with the highest points wins.

Media Literacy & Applied English

DRAMA REVIEW. Imagine that it is your job to write reviews of plays. Write a review of the performance of *A Streetcar Named Desire* that is depicted in "Who Am I This Time?" Comment on the performance of the director and the two principal characters. Use your imagination to describe the set.

EXAMINING THE MODEL.
In "An Ethnic Trump," Gish Jen writes about an incident of racism against her four-year-old son. The term "trump" means to override or outrank. Why does her son's Chinese ancestry trump his Irish roots? Look at the lead, the opening statement, for this piece. Notice that Jen manages to catch your interest in the first line. She leads you to wonder why her child would be going to a Chinese culture school, and to consider why most people would think it inevitable that he would be going.

So you know from the start this piece is going to deal with attitudes about race.

continued on page 615

Guided Writing

REFLECTING ON AN AUTOBIOGRAPHICAL INCIDENT

When asked what advice she had for young writers, British novelist Doris Lessing said, "Always the same advice: learn to trust your own judgment, learn inner independence, learn to trust that time will sort the good from the bad—including your own bad." While we tend to remember most clearly those events or experiences in our lives we can label good or bad, those aren't the only experiences we have. Even by age fifteen we've done a lot of living. In fact, American writer Willa Cather declared, "Most of the material a writer works with is acquired before the age of fifteen."

A writer writes about his own experiences, often going back to his or her youth to express an attitude about some belief or idea. Many times an incident happens that at the time doesn't seem significant. Later, however, the writer realizes that this event did have an impact on his or her life, and then writes a narrative to relate that incident to a larger audience. A **narrative** is a shared story about an event, often to make a point.

WRITING ASSIGNMENT. Write an autobiographical narrative about an experience that was meaningful to you.

Professional Model

from "An Ethnic Trump" by Gish Jen
page 596

That my son, Luke, age four, goes to Chinese-culture school seems inevitable to most people, even though his father is of Irish descent. For certain ethnicities trump others; Chinese, for example, trumps Irish.

…And so it is too, that my son is considered a kind of Asian person whose manifest destiny is to embrace Asian things.… For though Luke's skin is fair, and his features mixed, people see his straight black hair and "know" who he is.

…Then one day Luke combed his black hair and said he was turning it yellow. Another day, a fellow mother reported that her son had invited all blond-haired children like himself to his birthday party. And yet another day, Luke was happily scooting around the Cambridge Common playground when a pair of older boys, apparently brothers, blocked his way. "You're Chinese!" they shouted, leaning on the hood of Luke's scooter car. "You are! You're Chinese!" So brazen were these kids that even when I, an adult, intervened, they continued to shout. Luke answered, "No, I'm not!"—to no avail; it was not clear if the boys even heard him. Then the boys' mother called to them from some distance away, outside the fence, and though her voice was no louder than Luke's, they left obediently.

Behind them opened up a great, rippling quiet, like the wash of a battleship.

Luke and I immediately went over things he could say if anything like that ever happened again. I told him he was 100 percent American, even though I knew from my own childhood in Yonkers that these words would be met only with derision. It was a sorry chore.

Now look at how Jen tells about the confrontation between the two older boys and her son. She uses "blocked his way" and "brazen" to describe the actions of the brothers. She says that, "…even when I, an adult, intervened, they continued to shout," to show you how threatening they seemed. You get a clear picture of the situation. Later, in reflection, Jen says, "I wish I could forget the sight of those kids' fingers on the hood of Luke's little car." You know what she feels about the actions of those particular boys. She says that talking about how to meet racism was a "sorry chore" because she, herself, had experienced something similar as a child.

Prewriting

FINDING YOUR VOICE. Because you are writing about an incident that happened to you, your voice should reflect the seriousness of the experience. Convey your thoughts and feelings honestly and clearly in a natural voice. What tone does the voice in "An Ethnic Trump" reflect in the following sentence?

I wish I could forget their loud attack, but also Luke's soft defense: No, I'm not.

IDENTIFYING YOUR AUDIENCE. Who will read your narrative? While a narrative may be entertaining, a good narrative takes the reader beyond entertainment to empathy and understanding. Your classmates may be able to identify with your experience, but so might your 60-year-old grandfather. Consequently, you should write your paper for an audience with a wide age range.

WRITING WITH A PLAN. When you write about an *autobiographical incident*, you will begin by identifying and relating some incident, then responding to what it meant. There are two parts to the writing: the narrative and the reflection. For the narrative, once you have selected the incident, you will want to press the rewind button of your memory. Replay and rewind that tape as much as necessary until you have all the pieces you want to include so that the readers become viewers.

The reflection piece will not be quite so easy, since our VCR of memory has no *reflect* button. However, reflecting is the essential part; it conveys the global or universal significance of a personal experience. Did you have to make a decision that

A narrative often uses chronological order in telling about an incident. **Chronological order** is the arrangement of details in order of their occurrence. The time line you complete as your graphic organizer will help you develop your narrative.

The *reflection* section of your graphic organizer is particularly important to complete. You will draw from it extensively as you draft your narrative.

proved to be a mistake? Did you change your way of thinking or viewing the world? Were you inspired, disappointed, or enlightened? Who besides you was affected? What will be the future implications?

Ariana considered writing about her cross-country season; the year before she had been one of the best on the team, but this year she had dropped down several spots and she had a tough time dealing with it. Another topic was her memory of when she and her parents drove her older sister up to St. Paul to begin college there and her realization that Colleen was truly leaving home. Finally, however, she decided to zoom in on one specific incident she had experienced during her trip to Turkey last summer.

Once she had selected her topic, she used a graphic organizer for her ideas. She listed details of the incident by using headings of *before*, *during*, *after*, and *reflection*.

Student Model—Graphic Organizer

Time Line

Before:	back from sight-seeing
	eating peaches in hotel room
	fell asleep watching Jackie Chan movie

During:	awoke to loud noises from street and became annoyed
	sister yelled my name
	room was shaking, couldn't walk across—earthquake!
	parents said to dress to go out to street
	had to descend in dark, eight flights of stairs

After:	people milled and talked on street; sirens
	disco story eases tension
	dogs barked

Reflection:	panic, fear
	homes and businesses destroyed
	family members missing
	people need shelter and comfort
	different accounts
	in tragedy, people come together

Drafting

For your lead, or introductory paragraph, follow the **2 or 20 rule**: you've got two sentences or twenty seconds to get and keep your reader's attention. You might have some great material later on, but unfortunately, most readers won't be there to find out. A writer must be sure to open with a powerful statement, one that hooks the reader and doesn't let go. Three often-used but effective leads include:

BACKGROUND   "It was a day…"

ACTION   "The screech of the brakes woke me."

DIALOGUE   "The ice will hold us—don't worry. It was five below zero last night."
               "But the sign says, 'Danger: Thin Ice.'"

Once you have a solid lead, you can use your time line from your graphic organizer to draft the narrative.

Pay special attention to see that your *reflection* section, the last item on the graphic organizer, is as complete as you can make it.

> "The events in our lives happen in a sequence in time, but in their significance to ourselves, they find their own order. . . the continuous thread of revelation."
> —Eudora Welty

Student Model—Draft

Ariana Sarar wrote about an incident near the end of her trip in August, 1999, to Turkey, her father's homeland. After you read her draft, revise your work.

> During the night I woke to loud noises from the street. The hotel window had been left open until the air conditioning kicked in, and I could hear shouts from outside. I shoved a pillow over my head to block out the noise and yelled for them to "shut up!" Seconds later, after barely dozing off, I awoke to my sister screaming my name.
>
> "Ariana! Ariana!" she yelled from across the room. She was Standing near the bathroom door holding the frame the room was shaking back and forth. *Was the room holding the door-frame? Reword.*
>
> "What's happening?" I called back. I was utterly confused and couldn't seem to react.

Ariana's new lead---
"Shut up!" I yelled at the loud noises from the street. I shoved a pillow over my head to block out the noise that woke me from my sleep.

Not a bad lead, but you could try leading with dialogue for even more punch.

After living fourteen years in the United States and having my Turkish father as the most diverse part of my life, I had traveled with my family to ~~Turkey~~. It was the end of a three-week *Repeats* trip ~~in Turkey~~ and we had returned to Istanbul from the tourist city of Ayvalik. We had come back from a day of sightseeing and were munching on *juicy* ^ peaches ~~purchased~~ from a grocer across the street from our hotel. It was as typical an evening as it could have been. We had watched a Jackie Chan *Good detail* movie on Turkish television, and soon after I had fallen asleep in the hotel room I shared with my older sister.

Self- and Peer Evaluation

After you finish your draft, complete a self-evaluation of your writing. As time allows, have one or two classmates complete a peer evaluation.

As you evaluate your autobiographical incident or that of a classmate, answer the following questions:

- What incident is clearly identified and narrated? What details might be added or deleted?
- How does the narrative explain why this incident is significant to the writer and why this incident is significant to a larger community?
- What insight or knowledge does the writer gain?
- Is the narrative in a logical order? If not, at what point does the narrative become confusing? What might the reader do to eliminate vagueness or confusion?
- What makes the narrative appealing and meaningful to readers of varying ages? If the narrative seems to be limited to only the writer's classmates, what word choices and details need to be modified to give it wider appeal?
- How does the writer show his/her thoughts and feelings about the incident? What reflection is evident?

- What writing conventions (paragraph structure, sentence structure, grammar, and mechanics) could be improved to make the narrative easier to read?

Revising and Proofreading

Put aside your writing for a day or two, if possible, in order to separate the writing from the revising process. If you begin revising your work too soon, you might still be reading what you think you wrote rather than what you actually wrote. Review your self- and peer evaluations and revise accordingly. Consider content, organization, voice, word choice, and readability of your draft. Think about what you should add, remove, reorganize, or change. Throughout the revision process, stay focused on the two necessary parts: narrative of incident and reflection of incident.

Proofread your revised writing several times. Read your work aloud, listening for meaning and clarity. Check for correct spelling and punctuation. For more information, see the Language Arts Survey 2.45, "A Proofreading Checklist."

Reflecting

Both the writer and the reader have an opportunity to gain insights from an autobiographical incident. Ask yourself what this writing experience has taught you about yourself. Think about what you have learned about other people, communities, or cultures. What is the lasting value of the incident? How has the incident changed or shaped the way you view others, your world, or yourself?

Student Model—Revised

Drawing Together in a Smaller World
by Ariana Sarar

"Shut up!" I yelled at the loud noises from the street. I shoved a pillow over my head to block out the noise that woke me from my sleep. The hotel window had been left open until the air conditioning kicked in, and I could hear shouts from outside. Seconds later, after barely dozing off, I awoke to my sister screaming my name.

"Ariana! Ariana!" she yelled from across the room. She was standing near the bathroom door holding the frame. The room was shaking back and forth.

"What's happening?" I called back. I

Language, Grammar, and Style

Dangling and Misplaced Modifiers

IDENTIFYING PROBLEM MODIFIERS. A **dangling modifier** is a phrase or a clause that, because of its placement in the sentence, describes a word it is not intended to describe or modify. Sometimes the modifier problem occurs because the modifier is too far from the word it should describe. If this is the case, the error is known as a **misplaced modifier**.

While the result of a dangling or misplaced modifier is often comical, comedy is not the intent. Here are examples of both.

DANGLING MODIFIERS
Hearing the wail of an ambulance, the store was emptied. (The store can't hear.)

Wrapped in a lunch bag and hidden under a staircase, the police found the stolen necklace. (What were the police doing wrapped up in a lunch bag?)

Andy's parents started a business in their home in preschool. (It sounds as if Andy's parents started their business at a very young age.)

continued on page 620

MISPLACED MODIFIERS

I watched the sunrise climbing my first 14,000–foot mountain. (It sounds as if the sun can climb mountains.)

The library has several books about dinosaurs in our school. (This sentence makes it sound as if the dinosaurs are in our school.)

I found a coupon for a free case of soda in the newspaper. (The coupon, not the soda, was found in the newspaper.)

FIXING PROBLEM MODIFIERS. To eliminate dangling or misplaced modifiers, add words, change words, and/or reword. Notice these corrections:

Hearing the wail of an ambulance, we cleared a path.

Hearing the wail of an ambulance, drivers pulled over.

The library in our school has several books about dinosaurs.

Fix these sentences that contain dangling or misplaced modifiers.

1. Wrapped in a lunch bag and hidden under a staircase, the police found the stolen necklace.

2. Andy's parents started a business in their home in preschool.

continued on page 621

was utterly confused and couldn't seem to react.

After living fourteen years in the United States and having my Turkish father as the most diverse part of my life, I had traveled with my family to Dad's homeland. It was the end of a three-week trip and we had returned to Istanbul from the tourist city of Ayvalik. We had come back from a day of sightseeing and were munching on juicy peaches from a grocer across the street from our hotel. It was as typical an evening as it could have been. We had watched a Jackie Chan movie on Turkish television, and soon after I had fallen asleep in the hotel room I shared with my older sister.

"Come over here!" my sister ordered. "It's an earthquake!" I didn't know what was happening. I was sleepy and had never experienced an earthquake before. It took awhile for me to understand. I got up and tried to make my way across the room to where she was standing. Walking was much harder than I imagined with the floor shaking beneath me. With a drunken sensation, I stumbled across the room to her and stood clutching her arm until the earthquake subsided. It had to be the longest 45 seconds in my life.

Minutes later my parents rushed into our room and told us to get sweatshirts on and come with them down to the streets. All of the power had gone out and we were in total darkness. From the top floor of our hotel, we had to feel our way down the unlit, winding staircase for eight floors. It was extremely difficult. We were the last ones to come down, but were happy to recognize some other guests in the street outside our hotel.

In the darkness people loitered around, talking quietly to each other. Even though it was summer, the night air was cool, and two young men who worked at the hotel tended to all of us in the street. They brought the Russian women who had fled the hotel in terror pillows and blankets so that they could sleep in a nearby park. My mother, sister, and I sat on the curb and tried to understand the language being spoken. Soon the young men brought us blankets, too. We watched as people poured into the streets. There was an unbelievable tension in the air, and though I never remember being scared, it was obvious others were completely shaken. Groups of women held each other for balance; they were terrified.

As the evening rolled on, the sounds of a city at night were replaced with sirens of ambulances and police cars. Some men stopped to tell their earthquake story to the group who had gathered. They had been in a disco, and the whole place had shaken. It looked like everyone was doing "some new dance move." This got everyone to laugh despite the circumstances. All around dogs barked, and people screamed and shouted. When the aftershocks came, everyone fled into the inner city and parks, trying to stand in open areas to avoid buildings and other structures. In other parts of the city, people had lost everything they had in mere seconds. Family members were missing, and the city was in chaos with homes and businesses caving in. People needed shelter and comfort.

We stayed out in the city's streets all night, listening to the others. In the morning we talked to our taxi drivers. They all had different stories of the earthquake and where they had been when it happened. That night it became evident to me that no matter where you're from, what language you speak, whether you're a vacationer or resident, in tragedy everyone comes together.

In just a couple of days, we were back home. We watched silently as the news reports from Istanbul told of the great loss of life.

3. I watched the sunrise climbing my first 14,000-foot mountain.

4. I found a coupon for a free case of soda in the newspaper.

5. Stored in their lockers, some students keep six months' worth of food.

USING MODIFIERS CORRECTLY. Look over your autobiographical narrative, making certain that all modifying phrases and clauses are placed closely to the words that the modifiers are intended to describe.

Words for Everyday Use

Check your knowledge of the following vocabulary words from the selections in this unit. Write short sentences using each of these words in context to make the meaning clear. To review the definition or usage of a word, refer back to the page number(s) listed or the Glossary of Words for Everyday Use.

adobe, 591
agitation, 573
amateur, 603
bog, 569
brazen, 597
derision, 597
enclosure, 603

ether, 605
ethnicity, 596
inevitable, 596
manifest, 597
mesa, 590
missionary, 591
parishioner, 591

penetrate, 591
perverse, 591
preconception, 573
shriveled, 590
sneer, 607
trump, 596
versatile, 603

Literary Tools

Define each of the following terms, giving concrete examples of how they are used in the selections in this unit. To review a term, refer to the page number(s) indicated or the Handbook of Literary Terms.

aim, 595
allusion, 601
anecdote, 595
characterization, 576
dramatic irony, 601
free verse, 580

irony, 576, 601
metaphor, 572
meter, 567
paradox, 580
point of view, 584
repetition, 584

simile, 567
speaker, 572
symbol, 588
theme, 588

Reflecting on your reading

Genre Studies

1. **NONFICTION.** A *theme* is a central idea in a literary work. What is the theme of "An Ethnic Trump"? How is this theme developed? In other words, what example is the development of the theme dependent upon?

2. **CONFESSIONAL POETRY. Confessional poetry** is verse that describes, sometimes with painful explicitness, the private or personal experiences of the writer. In "Mirror," is the writer's experience directly or indirectly expressed? What do we learn about the writer in this poem?

3. **NARRATIVE POETRY.** "A Story That Could Be True" uses a second-person point of view. How would this **narrative poem** be different if it were told from a first-person or third-person point of view? Who is included in this poem? How involved do you feel in the poem?

Thematic Studies

4. **ETHNICITY.** What role does ethnicity play in "An Ethnic Trump"? How is Gish Jen's son defined by his ethnic background? What is the lesson in his example of ethnic identity in America?

5. **FAMILY LIFE.** The speakers in "Nikki-Rosa" and "Hanging Fire" are influenced by their family life. Are these influences positive or negative? How do you know?

6. **ROLE PLAYING.** What attitude toward role playing do Harry and Helene demonstrate in "Who Am I This Time"? What attitude does the speaker in "I'm Nobody! Who are you?" take toward being someone that one is not?

for your READING LIST

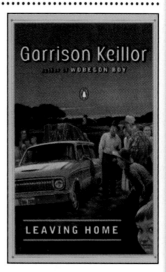

Leaving Home by Garrison Keillor. This collection of stories is about the fictional town of Lake Wobegon, "the town that time forgot, that the decades cannot improve," created by Garrison Keillor in his monologues for the public radio show, *A Prairie Home Companion.* The characters are all simple, small town folk whose church suppers, school projects, and daily routines are the backdrop for Keillor's often touching, always funny, thoughts about life. In these stories, Keillor tells of leaving—leaving home in search of a more exciting life, leaving the scene of a big embarrassment, or simply leaving town for vacation. But these are also stories about home, and the pull it exerts on us even when we leave in search of something else. For the residents of Lake Wobegon, a part of who you are is forever rooted in where you came from.

Independent Reading Activity

INTERVIEW THE AUTHOR. Working with your book circle, imagine that you are the production team for a public television program for teens on books and authors. Garrison Keillor has agreed to be interviewed on your program and to discuss his book, *Leaving Home.* Prepare a list of questions to ask Keillor about his life and his book. You may find the following ideas helpful:
- How is Lake Wobegon similar to and different from your home town?
- How did you "leave home"—how and when did you break away from your parents and your childhood?
- What are your favorite childhood memories?
- Why do you like writing and telling about Lake Wobegon?

Selections for Additional Reading

The Chosen by Chaim Potok. This classic story is about two boys, one a secular Jew and one an Hasidic Jew, the struggles they face over differences and commonalities with each other and with their fathers as each boy comes to an understanding of who he is.

Me, Me, Me, Me, Me: Not a Novel by M. E. Kerr. In this series of vignettes, Kerr, writer of humorous and realistic fiction for young adults, recounts various significant episodes from her childhood and adolescence and describes how they are translated into her novels.

The Acrobats, c.1900s. Fernand Léger. Private Collection.

F.L.

What Is Talent?

> " A genuine talent finds its way. "
>
> —*Goethe*

> Great talent takes time to ripen.
> —*Greek Proverb*

> Talent is like electricity. We don't understand electricity. We use it.
> —*Maya Angelou*

> All of us do not have equal talent, but all of us should have an equal opportunity to develop our talents.
> —*John F. Kennedy*

> Talent is that which is in a man's power; genius is that in whose power a man is.
> —*James Russell Lowell*

> Genius does what it must, and Talent does what it can.
> —*Owen Meredith*

> Everyone has talent; what is rare is the courage to follow the talent to the dark place where it leads.
> —*Erica Jong*

> God has given each normal person a capacity to achieve some end. True, some are endowed with more talent than others, but God has left none of us talentless.
> —*Martin Luther King, Jr.*

> If a man has talent and learns somehow to use the whole of it, he has gloriously succeeded, and won a satisfaction and a triumph that few men ever know.
> —*Thomas Wolfe*

> We can't take any credit for our talents. It's how we use them that counts.
> —*Madeleine L'Engle*

> Talent is something rare and beautiful and precious, and it must not be allowed to go to waste.
> —*George Selden*

> I do not want to die until I have faithfully made the most of my talent and cultivated the seed that was placed in me until the last small twig has grown.
> —*Kathe Kollwitz*

"It's Not Talent; It's Just Work"

by Annie Dillard

Reader's resource

In this essay, author Annie Dillard challenges readers to reconsider the concept of "talent." Dillard's perspective on the topic is unique. Instead of discussing whether talent is the result of forces in nature or in nurture, she focuses on the concept of love and how love motivates a person toward achievement and fulfillment.

About *the* AUTHOR

Annie Dillard (1945–) is a poet and writer of creative nonfiction. In 1975, she won a Pulitzer Prize for *Pilgrim at Tinker Creek*, a detailed account of the four seasons she spent living in the wilderness at Tinker Creek in Virginia. Like American naturalist and writer Henry David Thoreau, Dillard kept a meticulous journal of her observations about nature. She became obsessed with her writing, sometimes spending 15 to 16 hours a day on her journal. Dillard has been praised for her "distinctive passion and intensity" and "intellectual radiance" and has been compared to Thoreau, Ralph Waldo Emerson, and poet Emily Dickinson. Of herself, she says simply, "I am no scientist. I am a wanderer with a background in theology and a penchant for quirky facts."

Annie Dillard has taught writing and poetry at Wesleyan University and also tours the country as a speaker and reader. She is the author of *Tickets for a Prayer Wheel* (1974), a collection of poetry, and has contributed to many magazines and journals. Some of her nonfiction works include *Teaching a Stone to Talk* (1982), a collection of personal essays and narratives; *An American Childhood* (1987, her autobiography); *The Writing Life* (1989), essays on writing; and a novel, *The Living* (1992).

Literary TOOLS

AIM. A writer's **aim** is his or her purpose, or goal. People may write with the following aims:

- to inform (expository/informational writing)
- to entertain, enrich, or enlighten (imaginative writing)
- to tell a story about an event (narrative writing)
- to reflect (personal/expressive writing)
- to persuade (persuasive/argumentative writing)

As you read, think about what aim or aims the author had in writing this essay.

ANALOGY. An **analogy** is a comparison of two things that are alike in some respects. Often an analogy explains or describes something unfamiliar by comparing it to something more familiar. A *simile* is an expressed analogy; a *metaphor* is an implied analogy.

Organizer

As you read this selection, record the examples of analogy Dillard uses in a chart like the one below.

Analogy	Thing described
like they were addressing an armored tank	envious people asking about writing

Reader's Journal

Think of a famous person whom you consider talented, and explain why you think that person has talent.

It's Not Talent; It's Just Work

"You do it for love.

You do it for love and respect for your own life;

you do it for love and respect for the world;

and you do it for love and respect for the task itself."

Annie Dillard

It's hard work, doing something with your life. The very thought of hard work makes me queasy. I'd rather die in peace. Here we are, all equal and alike and none of us much to write home about—and some people choose to make themselves into physicists or thinkers or major-league pitchers, knowing perfectly well that it will be nothing but hard work. But I want to tell you that it's not as bad as it sounds. Doing something does not require discipline; it creates its own discipline—with a little help from caffeine.

> How does the author feel about hard work?

People often ask me if I discipline myself to write, if I work a certain number of hours a day on a schedule. They ask this question with envy in their voices and awe on their faces and a sense of alienation all over them, as if they were addressing an armored tank or a talking giraffe or Niagara Falls. We want to believe that other people are natural wonders; it gets us off the hook.

Now, it happens that when I wrote my first book of prose, I worked an hour or two a day for a while, and then in the last two months, I got excited and worked very hard, for many hours a day. People can lift cars when they want to. People can recite the Koran,[1] too, and run in marathons. These things aren't ways of life; they are merely possibilities for everyone on certain occasions of life. You don't lift cars around the clock or write books every year. But when you do, it's not so hard. It's not superhuman. It's very human. You do it for love. You do it for love and respect for your own life; you do it for love and respect for the world; and you do it for love and respect for the task itself.

> When Dillard wrote her first book of prose, what was her schedule like?

If I had a little baby, it would be hard for me to rise up and feed that little baby in the middle of the night. It would be hard but certainly wouldn't be a discipline. It wouldn't be a regimen I imposed on myself out of masochism, nor would it be the flowering of some extraordinary internal impulse. I would do it, grumbling, for love and because it has to be done.

> What are the two reasons the author would get up in the middle of the night and feed her baby?

Of course it has to be done. And something has to be done with your life too: something specific, something human. But don't wait around to be hit by love. Don't wait for anything. Learn something first. Then, when you are getting to know it, you will get to love it, and that love will direct you in what to do. So many times when I was in college, I used to say of a course like seventeenth-century poetry or European history, "I didn't like it at first, but now I like it." All of life is like that—a sort of dreary course which gradually gets interesting if you work at it.

> What happened to the author while she was in college?

I used to live in perpetual dread that I would one day read all the books that I would ever be interested in and have nothing more to read. I always figured that when that time came I would force myself to learn wildflowers, just to keep awake. I dreaded it, because I was not very interested in wildflowers but thought I should be. But things kept cropping up and one book has led to another and I haven't had to learn wildflowers yet. I don't think there's much danger of coming to the end of the line. The line is endless. I urge you to get in it, to get in line. It's a long line—but it's the only show in town. ■

---

1. **Koran.** Holy book of Islamic faith

words for everyday use

quea • sy (kwē′ ze) *adj.,* nauseated; uneasy. *Riding the ferry made Rochelle seasick and queasy.*

alien • ation (ā lē ə nā′ shən) *n.,* distance or separation because of great differences. *Because Larry was quiet and very different from the others in his class, he often experienced alienation in school.*

prose (prōz) *n.,* broad term used to describe all writing that is not poetry, including fiction and nonfiction. *The novelist writes wonderful prose.*

reg • i • men (re′ jə mən) *n.,* regular course of action, especially strenuous training. *The boxer's daily regimen was to jump rope, lift weights, and spar with a partner.*

mas • och • ism (ma′ sə ki zəm) *n.,* pleasure in suffering. *Mike considered tackle football a form of masochism—he much preferred touch football.*

per • pet • u • al (pər pe′ chə wəl) *adj.,* continuing forever. *Carmen joked that her two-year-old sister was in perpetual motion because she never seemed to run out of energy.*

What things do you love to do? Do you consider yourself talented at these things?

Investigate, *Inquire,* and Imagine

Recall: GATHERING FACTS ➔

1a. According to the author, why do people like to think of talented people as "natural wonders"?

2a. Does the author discipline herself to write? What does she say about discipline? Explain.

3a. What, according the author, "has to be done"? What did she say about some of her courses in college?

Interpret: FINDING MEANING

1b. How does this belief relieve people of responsibility?

2b. According to the author, what enables people to do extraordinary things?

3b. How does a person decide what to do with his or her life?

Analyze: TAKING THINGS APART ➔

4a. In this essay, Dillard presents arguments contradicting some commonly held beliefs about talent and success. Identify these common beliefs.

Synthesize: BRINGING THINGS TOGETHER

4b. What opinions does Dillard present that contradict these beliefs? What does Dillard believe about talent? Does she regard certain people as "superhuman"? Does the author think only a talented few can run marathons or recite the Koran? Explain.

Perspective: LOOKING AT OTHER VIEWS ➔

5a. Knowing the author is a well-known writer and Pulitzer Prize winner, are you surprised by her opinions about talent? Why, or why not? Thomas Alva Edison once said that genius is 1% inspiration and 99% perspiration. Explain whether Dillard would agree with that statement.

Empathy: SEEING FROM INSIDE

5b. How does the author describe some people's attitude toward her as a famous author? Why do you think their attitude bothers her? What do these people believe about Dillard? Why do you think it is important for the author to let people know that writing is hard work?

Understanding *Literature*

AIM. Review the definition for **aim** in the Handbook of Literary Terms. In your opinion, what is the principal aim of this selection? Explain.

ANALOGY. Review the definition for **analogy** in the Handbook of Literary Terms. What do Dillard's uses of analogy add to her essay?

Writer's Journal

1. Imagine that Annie Dillard is coming to visit your class. Write two **questions** you would like to ask her. Explain why you would wish to raise these questions.

2. Imagine you are filling out a **questionnaire** about yourself. One of the sections says, "Describe your interests and talents." Write the answer.

3. Write a **letter** to Annie Dillard explaining why you agree or disagree with her beliefs about talent.

Integrating the Language Arts

Language, Grammar, and Style

SIMPLE TENSES. Read the Language Arts Survey 3.62, "Properties of Verbs: Tense." Then, in the following sentences, underline the verbs and tell which tense they are in.

1. Hard work makes me queasy.
2. Work created its own discipline.
3. I will learn about wildflowers.
4. I worked very hard for several months.
5. We will join; we have no choice.

Collaborative Learning

HOLDING A DISCUSSION. Get into small groups and discuss the essay. Possible questions to discuss include: Do you think there is such a thing as talent? How does the essay make you think about your own future? Does it make you feel inspired, or does it make you worry about the work ahead of you?

Speaking and Listening

CONDUCTING AN INTERVIEW. Find a partner and interview that person. The goal of the interview is to find out what interests and talents that person has. Remember that there are many different types of talent— not just being good at a sport or knowing how to play an instrument. After the interview, switch roles, so the interviewer is now the interviewee.

Study and Research

RESEARCHING ATTITUDES ON TALENT. Gather information about two famous people considered to have great talent. Good sources for such information include autobiographies, magazine articles, or interviews published in magazines or on the Internet. Then, compare the attitudes these two people have toward the importance of discipline and hard work. Also, compare their attitudes about talent. For example, while some stars may downplay their abilities, Muhammad Ali boasted of his talent, referring to himself as "the greatest." Write a comparison-contrast essay discussing both celebrities.

Literary TOOLS

DESCRIPTION AND IMAGE. Description is a type of writing that portrays a character, an object, or a scene. An **image** is language that creates a concrete representation of an object or an experience. Note the images the author uses to describe Geraldine and some of the minor characters in the story.

POETRY. Poetry is imaginative language carefully chosen and arranged to communicate experiences, thoughts, or emotions. It differs from prose in that it compresses more meaning into fewer words and often uses meter, rhyme, rhythm, and techniques such as metaphor and simile. As you read this selection, decide whether Geraldine's poem fits your idea of poetry.

Graphic Organizer

Make a cluster chart. Begin by writing the word *poetry* in the middle of the page and circling it. Then jot down every word and phrase that springs to mind as you think about poetry. For more information on clustering, see the Language Arts Survey 2.13, "Clustering."

Rhythm and Rhyme

POETRY

"Geraldine Moore the Poet"
by Toni Cade Bambara

Reader's resource

In **"Geraldine Moore the Poet"** Bambara writes of an undiscovered talent. Everyone has both strengths and weaknesses. Sometimes a person's strengths go unrecognized, even by that person, for a long time. Sometimes personal hardship hinders a person from discovering his or her strengths, and other times hardship may prove to be the vehicle for unmasking a person's talents.

As you read, also note another message of the story: poetic expression does not depend upon putting every word into standard English or in the use of pretty, flowery images; it depends on expressing emotions or observations in one's own unique voice.

About the AUTHOR

Toni Cade Bambara (1939–1995) grew up in Harlem and Brooklyn, New York, and in Jersey City, New Jersey. After studying theater and English at Queens College and the City College of New York, she worked as a film writer and producer. She also taught college English. During the 1960s and 1970s, Bambara was both politically and culturally active in furthuring the civil rights of African Americans. To Bambara, art and politics were not separate realms. She saw her writing as a vehicle for truth in a "racist, hardheaded, heedless society" and said, "The job of the writer is to make revolution irresistible." Bambara published two story collections, *Gorilla, My Love* (1972), and *The Sea Birds are Still Alive* (1977). She also wrote a novel, *The Salt Eaters* (1980), as well as scripts for television and film.

Reader's Journal

What special abilities do you have? How did you discover them?

Geraldine Moore the Poet

Toni Cade Bambara

Geraldine paused at the corner to pull up her knee socks. The rubber bands she was using to hold them up made her legs itch. She dropped her books on the sidewalk while she gave a good scratch. But when she pulled the socks up again, two fingers poked right through the top of her left one.

"That stupid dog," she <u>muttered</u> to herself, grabbing her books and crossing against traffic. "First he chews up my gym suit and gets me into trouble, and now my socks."

Geraldine shifted her books to the other hand and kept muttering angrily to herself about Mrs. Watson's dog, which she minded two days a week for a dollar. She passed the hot-dog man on the corner and waved. He shrugged as if to say business was very bad.

Must be, she thought to herself. *Three guys before you had to pack up and forget it. Nobody's got hot-dog money around here.*

Geraldine turned down her street, wondering what her sister Anita would have for her lunch. She was glad she didn't have to eat the free lunches in high school any more. She was sick of the funny-looking tomato soup and the dried-out cheese sandwiches and those oranges that were more green than orange.

When Geraldine's mother first took sick and went away, Geraldine had been on her own except when Miss Gladys next door came in on Thursdays and cleaned the apartment and made a meat loaf so Geraldine could have dinner. But in those days Geraldine never quite managed to get breakfast for herself. So she'd sit through social studies class, scraping her feet to cover up the noise of her stomach growling.

Now Anita, Geraldine's older sister, was living at home waiting for her husband to get out of the Army. She usually had something good for lunch—chicken and dumplings if she managed to get up in time, or baked ham from the night before and sweet-potato bread. But even if there was only a hot dog and some baked beans — sometimes just a TV dinner if those soap operas kept Anita glued to the TV set—anything was better than the noisy school lunchroom where <u>monitors</u> kept pushing you into a straight line or rushing you to the tables. Anything was better than that.

Geraldine was almost home when she stopped dead. Right outside her building was a pile of furniture and some boxes. That wasn't anything new.

> What was Geraldine feeling when she saw the items outside her building?

---

words for everyday use

mut • ter (mutʹər) *vt.*, utter words in a low tone. *Joan <u>muttered</u> because she didn't know the answer to the teacher's question.*

mon • i • tor (mänʹi tər) *n.*, person who keeps order. *The hallway <u>monitor</u> looked at my pass and let me go to the art room.*

She had seen people get put out in the street before, but this time the ironing board looked familiar. And she recognized the big, ugly sofa standing on its arm, its underbelly showing the hole where Mrs. Watson's dog had gotten to it.

Miss Gladys was sitting on the stoop, and she looked up and took off her glasses. "Well, Gerry," she said slowly, wiping her glasses on the hem of her dress, "looks like you'll be staying with me for a while." She looked at the men carrying out a big box with an old doll sticking up over the edge. "Anita's upstairs. Go on up and get your lunch."

Mrs. Scott had said to write a poem, and Geraldine had meant to do it at lunch-time....But the men carrying off the furniture had made her forget.

Geraldine stepped past the old woman and almost bumped into the superintendent. He took off his cap to wipe away the sweat.

"Darn shame," he said to no one in particular. "Poor people sure got a hard row to hoe."

"That's the truth," said Miss Gladys, standing up with her hands on her hips to watch the men set things on the sidewalk.

Upstairs, Geraldine went into the apartment and found Anita in the kitchen.

"I dunno, Gerry," Anita said. "I just don't know what we're going to do. But everything's going to be all right soon as Ma gets well." Anita's voice cracked as she set a bowl of soup before Geraldine.

"What's this?" Geraldine said.

"It's tomato soup, Gerry."

Geraldine was about to say something. But when she looked up at her big sister, she saw how Anita's face was getting all twisted as she began to cry.

That afternoon, Mr. Stern, the geometry teacher, started drawing cubes and cylinders on the board. Geraldine sat at her desk adding up a column of figures in her notebook—the rent, the light and gas bills, a new gym suit, some socks. Maybe they would move somewhere else, and she could have her own room. Geraldine turned the squares and triangles into little houses in the country.

What keeps Geraldine from concentrating on her schoolwork?

"For your homework," Mr. Stern was saying with his back to the class, "set up your problems this way." He wrote GIVEN: in large letters, and then gave the formula for the first problem. Then he wrote TO FIND: and listed three items they were to include in their answers.

Geraldine started to raise her hand to ask what all these squares and angles had to do with solving real problems, like the ones she had. *Better not*, she warned herself, and sat on her hands. *Your big mouth got you in trouble last term.*

In hygiene class, Mrs. Potter kept saying that the body was a wonderful machine. Every time Geraldine looked up from her notebook, she would hear the same thing. "Right now your body is manufacturing all the proteins and tissues and energy you will need to get through tomorrow."

And Geraldine kept wondering, *How? How does my body know what it will need, when I don't even know what I'll need to get through tomorrow?*

As she headed down the hall to her next class, Geraldine remembered that she hadn't done the homework for English. Mrs. Scott had said to write a poem, and Geraldine had meant to do it at lunch-time. After all, there was nothing to it—a flower here, a raindrop there, moon, June, rose, nose. But the men carrying off the furniture had made her forget.

---

words for everyday use

for • mu • la (for´myoo lə) *n.*, rule or fact in mathematics. *The alchemist was working on a formula to turn lead into gold.*

hy • giene (hī´jēn) *n.*, health and cleanliness. *In an effort to maintain hygiene in its personnel, the restaurant management posted signs in the bathrooms reminding employees to wash their hands.*

tis • sue (tish´oo) *n.*, group of cells that work together in the body. *Joe's tissue was damaged in a biking accident.*

Endangered Species, 1980. Paul T. Goodnight. National Museum of American Art, Washington, DC.

"And now put away your books," Mrs. Scott was saying as Geraldine tried to scribble a poem quickly. "Today we can give King Arthur's[1] knights a rest. Let's talk about poetry."

Mrs. Scott moved up and down the aisles, talking about her favorite poems and <u>reciting</u> a line now and then. She got very excited whenever she passed a desk and could pick up the homework from a student who had remembered to do the assignment.

"A poem is your own special way of saying what you feel and what you see," Mrs. Scott went on, her lips moist. It was her favorite subject.

"Some poets write about the light that . . . that . . . makes the world sunny," she said, passing Geraldine's desk. "Sometimes an idea takes the form of a picture—an image."

For almost half an hour, Mrs. Scott stood at the front of the room, reading poems and talking about the lives of the great poets. Geraldine drew

How does Mrs. Scott define poetry? What has Geraldine felt and seen lately?

What does Geraldine dream about? What do her dreams tell us about her?

---

1. **King Arthur's.** Belonging to the legendary king of Britain and leader of the knights of the Round Table

words for everyday use

re • cite (rē sīt') *vt.,* repeat words aloud from memory. *At confirmation, each member of the catechism class was asked to <u>recite</u> a favorite Bible verse.*

more houses, and designs for curtains.

"So for those who haven't done their homework, try it now," Mrs. Scott said. "Try expressing what it is like to be . . . to be alive in this . . . this glorious world."

"I can't write a poem, Mrs. Scott, because nothing lovely's been happening in my life."

"Oh, brother," Geraldine muttered to herself as Mrs. Scott moved up and down the aisles again, waving her hands and leaning over the students' shoulders and saying, "That's nice," or "Keep trying." Finally she came to Geraldine's desk and stopped, looking down at her.

"I can't write a poem," Geraldine said flatly, before she even realized she was going to speak at all. She said it very loudly, and the whole class looked up.

"And why not?" Mrs. Scott asked, looking hurt.

"I can't write a poem, Mrs. Scott, because nothing lovely's been happening in my life. I haven't seen a flower since Mother's Day, and the sun don't even shine on my side of the street. No robins come sing on my window sill."

What does Geraldine think poems are usually like?

Geraldine swallowed hard. She thought about saying that her father doesn't even come to visit any more, but changed her mind. "Just the rain comes," she went on, "and the bills come, and the men to move out our furniture. I'm sorry, but I can't write no pretty poem."

Teddy Johnson leaned over and was about to giggle and crack the whole class up, but Mrs. Scott looked so serious that he changed his mind.

"You have just said the most . . . the most poetic thing, Geraldine Moore," said Mrs. Scott. Her hands flew up to touch the silk scarf around her neck. "'Nothing lovely's been happening in my life.'" She repeated it so quietly that everyone had to lean forward to hear.

"Class," Mrs. Scott said very sadly, clearing her throat, "you have just heard the best poem you will ever hear." She went to the board and stood there for a long time staring at the chalk in her hand.

"I'd like you to copy it down," she said. She wrote it just as Geraldine had said it, bad grammar and all.

Nothing lovely's been happening in my life.
I haven't seen a flower since Mother's Day,
And the sun don't even shine on my side
 of the street.
No robins come sing on my window sill.
Just the rain comes, and the bills come,
And the men to move out our furniture.
I'm sorry, but I can't write no pretty poem.

Mrs. Scott stopped writing, but she kept her back to the class for a long time—long after Geraldine had closed her notebook.

And even when the bell rang, and everyone came over to smile at Geraldine or to tap her on the shoulder or to kid her about being the school poet, Geraldine waited for Mrs. Scott to put the chalk down and turn around. Finally Geraldine stacked up her books and started to leave. Then she thought she heard a whimper— the way Mrs. Watson's dog whimpered sometimes—and she saw Mrs. Scott's shoulders shake a little. ∎

words for everyday use

ex • press (ek spres´) vt., put into words. Mr. Blair expressed his displeasure when I entered class after the bell had rung.

With what details in Geraldine's story do you identify?

Investigate, Inquire, and Imagine

Recall: GATHERING FACTS

1a. What is Geraldine worried about at the very beginning of the story?

2a. What does Geraldine see piled up outside her building at lunchtime?

3a. What does Mrs. Scott ask her students to write about?

➤ Interpret: FINDING MEANING

1b. What greater worries does Geraldine have to contend with later in the story?

2b. How does Geraldine feel about what she sees piled up outside her building? How do you know?

3b. What does Mrs. Scott assume about her students' lives when she frames her writing assignment as she does? Why can't Geraldine write a "pretty poem"?

Analyze: TAKING THINGS APART

4a. Analyze Mrs. Scott's initial views and definition of poetry. Do you think her views change? Explain.

➤ Synthesize: BRINGING THINGS TOGETHER

4b. How does Geraldine's poem fit with Mrs. Scott's initial definition?

Evaluate: MAKING JUDGMENTS

5a. What effect do you think Mrs. Scott's reaction to Geraldine's comments will have on Geraldine's future? How will Geraldine's comments affect Mrs. Scott's future definition of poetry?

➤ Extend: CONNECTING IDEAS

5b. Many successful individuals have attributed their success to a mentor or someone who believed in them earlier in their life or career. Why do you think a mentor makes a difference? Do you have a mentor? If so, how has he or she affected your life?

Understanding *Literature*

DESCRIPTION AND IMAGE. Review the definitions for **description** and **image** in the Handbook of Literary Terms. Look back at the opening paragraph of this story. What images are used in the description of Geraldine? To what senses do these images appeal? What do you learn about Geraldine from the opening description?

POETRY. Review the definition for **poetry** in the Handbook of Literary Terms and the cluster chart you made for Literary Tools on page 632. How does Geraldine's poem fit this definition? How well does it fit your own definition of poetry?

Writer's Journal

1. Imagine that Geraldine Moore has grown up to be a famous poet. You are a celebrity reporter for a magazine and have arranged an interview with Ms. Moore. You plan to ask her how she got started as a poet, whether she had any mentors or other writers who influenced her work, how she succeeded despite an impoverished background, etc. Write a list of **interview questions**.

2. Write a **children's story** about a character (human or animal) who discovers that he or she has an unknown talent. Be sure to indicate how this discovery makes the character feel.

3. Pretend that you are Geraldine. Before you go to sleep that evening on Miss Gladys's couch, write a **diary entry** about the events of the day—from your sudden eviction to Mrs. Scott's emotional reaction to your poetic words. Make sure to include your feelings about what has happened to you.

Integrating the Language Arts

Language, Grammar, and Style

REGULAR AND IRREGULAR VERBS. Review the Language Arts Survey 3.41, "Using Irregular Verbs." Select ten verbs from the story—five regular and five irregular. Make a chart like the one below and fill in the four principle forms of each verb: the base form, the present participle, the past, and the past participle.

Base Form	Present Participle	Past	Past Participle
mutter	[is] muttering	muttered	[has] muttered
draw	[is] drawing	drew	[has] drawn

Speaking and Listening & Collaborative Learning

IMPROVISATION. Take a few moments to think about the minor characters in "Geraldine Moore the Poet." Try to imagine what they might be thinking and feeling in their scenes with Geraldine. Then break into small groups of four to six students. Take turns dramatizing some of the scenes below, with one person playing Geraldine and one person playing the other character.

- Anita making lunch and talking to Geraldine about how life has been since their mother became ill
- Geraldine's mother speaking on the phone with Geraldine
- Mrs. Scott telling Geraldine about when she first discovered poetry
- Geraldine speaking to the hot-dog man about business

Media Literacy & Collaborative Learning

SOCIAL SERVICE PROJECT. There are many real people who have experiences like Geraldine's and turn to social services or charity organizations for help. As a class, research in your newspaper articles on local charities. Together select an organization to contact and offer the services of the class. Perhaps you can work on a Habitat for Humanity building project, serve dinner at a soup kitchen, donate toys and books to a homeless shelter, or collect donations of new school supplies and backpacks to give to an organization that outfits children for school.

from *The Man Who Listens to Horses*
by Monty Roberts

Reader's
resource

This selection is an excerpt from the autobiographical book *The Man Who Listens to Horses.* In his autobiography, Monty Roberts tells of his childhood as the son of a horse trainer and of his discovery of an effective, nonviolent method to train horses. Roberts's father used traditional methods to "break" wild horses so that they would take riders. These methods, described in a book written by his father, included roping and tying down horses as well as whipping and hitting them to bring them to submission.

As a child, Roberts spent hours watching wild mustangs in the canyons of Nevada and discovered that the dominant mare in each herd used a special series of body movements to train colts. He used this understanding of how horses communicate with each other to develop a training method based on trust rather than fear. In this excerpt the thirteen-year-old Monty, who has just returned from Nevada, shows his discovery to a friend of his father.

The term *mustang*, which is used to refer to wild horses living in the western plains of the United States, comes from the Spanish word *mesteño*, meaning "stray." Mustangs are descended from horses brought to the New World by Spanish settlers around AD 1500.

About *the*
AUTHOR

Monty Roberts (1935–   ) and his wife, Pat, operate the Flag Is Up Farm in the Santa Ynez Valley near Santa Barbara, California. There they train and race thoroughbred horses using the nonviolent techniques he describes in *The Man Who Listens to Horses.*

Roberts's relationship with his father and the rest of his family has been strained since the publication of this book. His siblings have publicly disputed his description of his father as a harsh and disapproving man who beat his children as well as his horses.

Roberts's father never agreed with his son's method of training horses. Others have, however. The "join-up" method of "starting" horses, as Roberts calls it, is used by Queen Elizabeth II's cavalry. He has been awarded a Lifetime Achievement Award from the American Society for the Prevention for Cruelty to Animals for "making the world a better place for animals."

Literary
TOOLS

PERSONIFICATION. Personification is a figure of speech in which an idea, animal, or thing is described as if it were a person. In this piece, Monty Roberts describes the horse as thinking like a human, in sentences. As you read, notice the instances in which he ascribes thought to the horse.

POINT OF VIEW. Point of view is the vantage point from which a story is told. Stories are typically told from a *first-person point of view,* in which the narrator uses words like *I* and *we,* or from the *third-person point of view,* in which the narrator uses words such as *he, she, it* and *they.* This piece is written from the first-person point of view, as is most autobiography. From this point of view, the author can reveal thoughts and emotions which are unknown to other characters in the action.

Graphic
Organizer

Complete the following graphic organizer, noting the private thoughts and emotions Roberts reveals to the reader.

Private thoughts and emotions — Desire for father's approval

Reader's
Journal

What have you done to prove yourself to someone important in your life?

Cabin Fever, 1976. Susan Rothenberg. Modern Art Museum of Fort Worth.

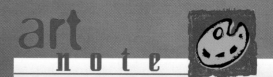

Susan Rothenberg's (1945–) subject matter is almost exclusively the horse, which she portrays in an abstract way. How do you interpret the meaning of the title?

The

Man

Who

Listens

to

Horses

Monty Roberts

Bill was born in 1903. He was a slim six-footer, and always wore round glasses. Were you to see him in a three-piece suit and hear him talk, you might take the straight, stiff man for a banker or an accountant, certainly an educated man. In fact, like his brother, Tom, he had little formal schooling, but there was a remarkable brightness about them both.

Now in his mid-nineties, Bill is still a fine rider and roper but as a young man he was nervous when he competed under pressure in the showring. Bill Dorrance was all about careful calculation. In terms of the psychology of a horse, the study of the horse's mind, he was lightyears ahead of his time. He was the only one who believed in me, and when I was seventeen my father finally forbade me to see him. "Bill Dorrance will destroy you," he predicted one memorable day in Salinas. Bill was a progressive man with new ideas, ideas I shared and understood. When I got back from the desert, I went right to him. He was like a grandfather to me, an armchair philosopher of horsemanship. He was ridiculed for some of the things he said, but I now see how far ahead of his time he really was.

Who was Bill Dorrance?

"You have to cause your horse to be mellow," he once told me, "to be in unison with you, not against you." It was a breathtaking notion for someone of his generation. I owe Bill a great deal. What we shared was a keen awareness of the

What did Bill Dorrance and Monty have in common? What did Bill do for Monty?

possibilities between horses and humans, a sense that we had barely scratched the surface of that ancient connection. "I'm discovering things about horses," he once told me, "and I don't want to die before I pass them on. You're young and talented, and I want to pass them on to you."

I felt I did possess a special <u>affinity</u> with horses. Now that I was beginning to understand their silent language, I could turn a great corner.

What was Monty's ambition?

My ambition was immense: change the way humans relate to horses.

The one hundred mustangs at the competition grounds would be the ideal test of my theory: how to form a natural bond with a wild horse; how to convince the horse you are an ally, not a predator; how to cast myself as the dominant matriarch[1] and speak her language.

I would have to work fast, and with one eye on the whereabouts of my father, because I did not want him to interfere—although, underneath it all, I still sought his acceptance and approval.

As it happened, in the course of starting the mustangs, I discovered something so exciting that I began to believe I could persuade even my tradition-bound father to see things my way. I had identified a <u>phenomenon</u> that I called "join-up." As I

What did Monty call his discovery?

lay in bed at night I could hardly sleep, so convinced was I that I had stumbled on something that truly would change the way we operate with horses.

Surely, I reasoned, my father would see it. He was too experienced a horseman not to. But I knew better than to go to him and show him directly. Instead, I settled on showing Ray Hackworth, hoping that he could prevail upon my father because he had my father's respect.

Whom did Monty want to impress? How does he hope to do it?

Ray Hackworth leased facilities at the competition grounds where we lived. Soft-spoken but also a disciplinarian, he was a noted trainer and a gentleman: I asked him to come and watch what I could do. I told him I had discovered a phenomenon that I could explain only in terms of the horse's own language. I promised him that I could dissolve the natural barrier between horse and man, flight animal and fight animal.

He reminded me that my father had often warned me over the years that my ideas could be dangerous and I should stick to the conventional ways of doing things. But I continued to implore that he come and see for himself what I could do. If I could please Ray, I could surely please my father. . . .

Eventually he agreed.

When we arrived at the round pen, Ray strolled up the ramp on to the viewing deck and leaned against the fence. "OK," he said, tipping his hat to the back of his head. "Let's see it."

I stood in the middle of the pen, together with a three-year-old colt not long past the trauma of the wild horse race. The colt wore no halter,[2] rope, or restraint of any type. The door to the round pen was closed; it was he and I.

From practicing this a hundred times over, I knew what to do. I confidently waited a moment or two to let this unnamed mustang get accustomed to the round pen. He was too nervous to take a single step toward me, although his attention was on me as the main threat currently confronting him. "What I'm

---

1. **matriarch**. Female who dominates or rules a group
2. **halter**. Harness of rope or leather which fits on an animal's head, used to lead the animal

words for everyday use

af • fin • i • ty (ə fin′ ə tē′) *n.*, relationship or attraction between two people or things. *Sam and Rachel had an obvious <u>affinity</u> for one another based on their shared interests.*

phe • nom • e • non (fi nä′ mə nän′) *n.*, observable fact or event; exceptional or unusual person, thing, or occurrence. *When the brilliant northern lights appear in the sky, our family goes outside to see the <u>phenomenon</u>.*

going to do," I said, "is use the same language as the dominant mare in his family group." The silence from the viewing deck told me Ray was not going to ask questions, so I continued. "That language is a silent language, a body language, and the first thing I'm going to ask him is to go away from me, to flee. I'm only doing this because then I will ask him to come back and join up with me."

Whose language does Monty intend to use?

I moved, quite abruptly, toward the colt. I squared my shoulders and fixed my eye on his eye. Straight away, he went into flight, taking off in a canter[3] around the <u>perimeter</u>, staying as close to the wall as he could—and as far from me as possible.

I continued to press him into flight, in the same way that I had observed the matriarch driving away the adolescents in the wild. I remained square on to him, I maintained direct eye contact. For Ray's benefit, I continued to explain what I was doing. "In his own language I'm saying to him, 'Go ahead and <u>flee</u>, but I don't want you to go away a little. I want you to go away a lot. For now, I'll call the shots until we can form a partnership. You see, I speak your language.' "

What message does Monty send to the horse with the first step of the process?

I had a light sash line, and I pitched it at the colt—not to hit him, but to encourage him to flee. Which he did. As he cantered around the pen I used the line and my body posture to keep him in flight; my shoulders were parallel to his long axis. I was facing directly toward his head and, with my body, pressing him away. My eyes were locked on his.

This continued for several minutes. I was watching for the signals—the same signals I had observed in the wild, when the adolescents would ask the dominant mare to be released from their enforced <u>exile</u>. Meanwhile, as a test, I allowed my eyes to drop back to his neck. When I did, he slowed.

I let my eyes drop back farther, to his shoulder . . . and he slowed a bit more; his head started to come off the rail a bit to look over at me. When I let my eyes drop back to his hip, I saw a further reduction in speed, and he began to angle off the wall even more.

What is the meaning of the next signal Monty expects from the horse?

Then I took my eyes back to his eyes, and his speed increased immediately; he moved back toward the wall and was in full flight again. He was reading me. He knew we were dealing with each other in *his* language.

I called to Ray, "I'm waiting for his ear to open onto me, for him to start licking and chewing, and then for him to duck his head and run along holding it a few inches off the ground." It was important that Ray realize I could *predict* what would happen.

What does Monty want Ray to realize?

"Here's the first one, now!" I called. "See?"

The colt's inside ear had opened toward me and stayed fixed in that position. The outside ear was tuned to the surrounding areas, flicking forward and back. The colt was saying, "I don't really know what this is all about, but I'll pay

> The colt was saying, "I don't really know what this is all about, but I'll pay attention to you and we'll see where it goes from here."

---

3. **canter.** Pace of a horse slower than a gallop and faster than a trot

---

words for everyday use	**per • i • met • er** (pə ri′ mə tər) *n.,* border or boundary. *Most people put a fence around the <u>perimeter</u> of their back yards.*
	flee (flē′) *vi.,* run away from. *If I ever see a panther in the woods, I plan to <u>flee</u> immediately.*
	ex • ile (eg′ zīl) *n.,* state of absence from one's country or home. *Like many writers of the Lost Generation, Hemingway spent his <u>exile</u> in Paris.*

attention to you and we'll see where it goes from here."

The colt had made approximately eight revolutions of the round pen before the ear closest to me was adequately locked on. At this point, I pitched the line in front of the colt and stepped a bit to the front of his action, keeping my eyes locked on his to prevent his coming off the wall toward me. Quickly, he reversed field and fled in the opposite direction. In a moment or two, the ear closest to me was locked onto me as before. It was going according to pattern.

Since Ray could not know what to look for down in that pen between the kid and the colt, it was important that I explain my

> What mistake with Ray does Monty fear he may be making?

actions and expectations, but I suddenly sensed this might all be a mistake. A fourteen-year-old explaining things to an older man? It might be seen as arrogant. Still, I hoped, the value of what I was doing would counteract that.

> "I am a herbivore, I am a grazer, and I'm making this eating action with my mouth now because I'm considering whether or not to trust you."

I began to take the pressure off the colt. First, I reduced the number of times I cast the line at him. Then I coiled the line and held it in my hand, slapping my leg with it to encourage him to continue. The colt came back to a trot. By this time he had made twelve revolutions of the round pen.

The next signal came right on time. He started to lick and chew. His tongue actually came through his teeth and outside his mouth, then he pulled his tongue back and chewed with his teeth. There was a ripple effect across the large mandibles.[4]

"There!" I called to Ray. "You see that chewing action with his mouth? That's exactly what I saw them doing out on the range. It means he's ready to discuss this situation. He's gone away and I've pressed him away farther. He's recognized my desire to communicate with him, and now he'd like the chance to renegotiate. This licking and chewing action of the colt is a message to me, it's saying something like, 'I am a herbivore,[5] I am a grazer, and I'm making this eating action with my mouth now because I'm considering whether or not to trust you. Help me out

> What does the colt's licking and chewing mean?

with that decision, can you, please?' "

Then came the final signal I was looking for. As the colt trotted around, he dropped his head so his nose was traveling only an inch or so above ground level.

"And there you go!" I called to Ray. "His head's dropped. I can't tell you the times I've seen this out there in the desert, and it always means the same thing—it means 'Let me back in, I don't want to flee any more.' "

It was time for me—like the dun[6] mare—to turn passive, to let this colt come and join up with me. I allowed my eyes to travel

> What stance will Monty adopt now?

to a point maybe fifteen to twenty feet in front of him. I moved my shoulders around to follow my eyes until they were on a forty-five-degree angle to his long body axis. I was avoiding eye contact and showing him my flanks,[7] as it were.

Immediately, he stopped. He came off the wall and faced me. I maintained my position, my body and my eyeline at forty-five degrees to his. He took a step or two toward me. I waited.

Then he walked right up to me, not stopping until his nose was inches from my shoulder. I could not speak. I wanted to shout to Ray,

---

4. **mandibles.** Jaws
5. **herbivore.** Animal that eats plants, as opposed to meat
6. **dun.** Grayish-brown color
7. **flanks.** Sides

"Look, this is what I mean. How *about* this? Isn't it fantastic?" But I could not afford to break the spell. It was indeed magic: this colt trusted me. No longer a predator, I was his safety zone. The moment of acceptance, or join-up, is what I had discovered, and I felt a shudder of heartfelt emotion. I have felt the same thrill with every one of the 10,000 or more horses I have started this way. I fervently hoped that Ray felt the same way.

What magical thing has happened?

To test the strength of the join-up, I took a slow right turn. The colt followed me into the circle, his nose to my shoulder. Then I took a left turn. He hesitated, and looked to be going the other way.

Immediately I knew to return to a dominant stance, and I began to drive him away. He did not like that, and before he had completed one circuit of the round pen he was flicking his nose out and apologizing, asking to be let back in.

I allowed him back, soothed him and talked to him, and gave him a good stroke between the eyes. It is not essential to use the area between the eyes as the stroking point, but it seems to be more effective to touch the horse here than any other part of the body. There is general <u>consensus</u> that for a horse to let you into a part of his anatomy that he cannot see is the ultimate expression of trust.

Now I had the colt walking comfortably behind me and I knew Ray would be amazed. I imagined him saying to my father, "I tell you, Marvin, that boy of yours had a wild horse walking along behind him like it was his best friend after only twenty-five minutes. He's on to something. Come down and see for yourself."

I called out to Ray, as quietly as possible now that the colt was standing next to me, "Ray, you know, now that he's joined up with me and we're on the same side, it's pretty much of a formality." When I was confident the colt fully trusted me, I brought in another long-line, a saddle, bridle,[8] and a saddle pad, as well as a long stirrup leather—all of which I put on the ground in the middle of the pen. With the click of the gate, the colt's stance changed. He saw something different—a pile of equipment—and became frightened. He had justification for being <u>skeptical</u>, so I waited. I allowed him to choose between me and the equipment. He chose me and calmed down. He stood still while I carefully lifted the saddle pad and the saddle onto his back. He let me fix the girth[9] slowly, smoothly. After taking a step or two away, he steadied and let me continue.

What caused the colt to be fearful again?

Before any rope or lead has been attached to his head, let alone a bridle, he was wearing his first saddle. He was asking me lots of questions, his ears flicking back and forth and his nostrils blowing, but he trusted me.

At this point I stepped away from him and squared up to him, driving him away, not aggressively, but with the confidence I had developed over the last 200 or so horses. He went into flight and began to canter around the perimeter of the round pen. I wanted to familiarize him with the saddle before a rider was on. He bucked hard for several minutes, which I was glad to see because I did not want Ray Hackworth to think this was a <u>fluke</u>. Within a few minutes the colt was cantering steadily around, the bucking over. I saw the same signals—the licking and chewing, the inside ear settling on me, his coming off the

What does Monty do before attempting to ride the colt?

---

8. **bridle.** Harness, bit, and reins used to control a horse
9. **girth.** Strap around a horse's middle, which holds the saddle on snugly

---

words for everyday use

con • sen • sus (kə sen′ səs) *n.,* general or unanimous agreement. *After much debate, the class reached a <u>consensus</u> on where to hold their end-of-year party.*

skep • ti • cal (skep′ ti kəl) *adj.,* uncertain, doubtful. *Lauren told me that Richard Nixon was the only president ever to be impeached, but I was <u>skeptical</u>.*

fluke (flo͞ok′) *n.,* stroke of luck. *Since Marc had never scored in a game before, he considered his three-point basket a total <u>fluke</u>.*

wall to get closer to me. For a minute or two I worked him around the outer limits of the pen, and let him find comfort in carrying the saddle, first one way, then the other. After three or four revolutions in each direction, the colt was telling me he was ready to come back in. I let him join up with me, adjusted his girth, and generally soothed him with my voice. He was doing fine. There was nothing to be frightened about, if he stuck with me. I would look after him and have fun with him, love him like I loved all his brothers and sisters. I took the bridle and lifted it over his ears. The colt accepted the snaffle[10] with no more than a brief lift of his head. I secured the reins under the rear portion of the saddle and took the stirrups down to prepare for long-lining. Then I sent the colt back to work, cantering him around the perimeter, first one way, then the other. He was fully tacked-up,[11] wearing a saddle and a bridle and the long-lines.

How does the colt react to the bit?

I called out, "I want to gain his confidence and make him happy to follow the bit and bridle—as he'll be doing just that for the rest of his working life. I want to make it a happy experience for him."

I turned the colt six or seven times before stopping him and reining back one step. I again adjusted his girth; I brushed the saddle with my hands, rubbed his neck and belly. Then I put my left toe in the stirrup and prepared to lift myself on to his back. I felt the strain in my thigh muscle as I asked the colt if I could put my full weight into the stirrup, testing for his reaction. He took a sideways step to help redistribute the extra weight, but he held firm.

How does the colt react to Monty attempting to ride him?

I lifted myself up. Instead of swinging a leg over, I lay across his back for a while, waiting to see if he was comfortable with this. I hoped I was answering any questions he had with the things I was saying to him. I would find him a good name. We would find him a good home. Perhaps he would enjoy being a ranch horse, or maybe he would go into a Western show, in the pleasure-horse category. He might end up with a kid like me, learning to ride. I let the colt catch sight of me out of both eyes before calmly swinging a leg over and sitting up. I was riding him after only forty minutes.

I sat there <u>jubilant</u> on the back of that horse. An idealistic youth, I was convinced that it was only a matter of weeks before I would enjoy the respect and admiration of my elders and betters all over the county. And especially, my father.

"That was a fluke!" Ray barked out.

He was staring at me, a concerned look on his face. The sound of his voice coincided with the colt's first steps, and I did not try to stop him. As the colt and I walked around together, I heard Ray say, "You're wrong to go against your father. He's worried about you getting hurt—and you could be hurt. These horses are dangerous. I suggest you stop it now."

What is Ray's reaction?

He walked from the viewing deck and disappeared from sight. I rode the colt, feeling crushed at the very moment I should have felt triumphant. The people whose respect and guidance I needed were refusing to give it. I vowed never to mention my ideas to anyone again.   ■

---

10. **snaffle**. Bit; piece of metal which fits in the mouth of a horse, connected to the reins, used to make a horse turn
11. **tacked-up**. Outfitted with the equipment used to ride a horse: harness, bridle, and saddle

words for everyday use

ju • bi • lant (jōō′ bə lənt) *adj.*, filled with joy and triumph. *Sara was <u>jubilant</u> after having won the trophy.*

If you were Monty, would you stop using the new training method? Why, or why not?

Investigate, *Inquire,* and Imagine

Recall: GATHERING FACTS

1a. What special thing did Monty understand about horses?

2a. How did Monty imagine Ray would react to the demonstration of his method?

3a. What was the "ultimate expression of trust" from the horse Monty trained as Ray watched?

→ ### Interpret: FINDING MEANING

1b. Why did this make it possible for him to train them so effectively?

2b. What does he hope his father will think?

3b. What skills and attributes did Monty's achievement call for, in your opinion?

Analyze: TAKING THINGS APART

4a. Explain the training method that Roberts uses to get a horse to "join up."

→ ### Synthesize: BRINGING THINGS TOGETHER

4b. What is it about this method that gains the horse's trust?

Evaluate: MAKING JUDGMENTS

5a. What do you think Monty was trying to prove to his father? After seeing Monty's success, was Ray justified in telling him to stop what he was doing? Why, or why not?

→ ### Extend: CONNECTING IDEAS

5b. Parents often make decisions their children don't like for reasons their children don't understand. What do you think Monty's father might have said about his reasons for disapproving of Monty's work with horses? When is it important to listen to your own instincts, and when is it important to listen to the more experienced people in your life?

Understanding *Literature*

PERSONIFICATION. Review the definition for **personification** in the Handbook of Literary Terms. In this piece, Monty Roberts describes the horse as thinking like a human, in sentences. As you read, notice the instances in which he ascribes thought to the horse. Do you agree with his assumptions about what the horse may be thinking? Why, or why not?

POINT OF VIEW. Review the definition for **point of view** in the Handbook of Literary Terms and the graphic organizer you completed in Literary Tools on page 639. What private thoughts and emotions is Roberts able to reveal in this first-person narration? How does the use of first-person point of view make the piece more effective?

Writer's Journal

1. Imagine that you are Monty. Write a **personal letter** to your father, explaining why this work is important to you.

2. As an adult, Roberts has continued his work with the join-up method and established a center to train horses this way. Imagine that you are his marketing manager. Write a **brochure** advertising his business to train horses.

3. Imagine that you are the horse who has just "joined up" with Roberts in his demonstration for Ray. What would you tell your fellow mustangs about what has just happened? Write an imaginary **dialogue** between this horse and another one about the "join-up" process that has just taken place.

Integrating
the Language Arts

Language, Grammar, and Style

PERFECT TENSES. Read about perfect tenses in the Language Arts Survey 3.62, "Properties of Verbs: Tense." Then, in each of the following sentences, underline each perfect tense verb and tell which tense it is in.

1. Roberts had been around horses as a child.
2. By the end of his career Roberts will have trained hundreds of horses.
3. A successful trainer will have interpreted the language of horses.
4. Roberts had shown Ray Hackworth how to communicate with horses.
5. Today has been a good day for riding.

Study and Research & Speaking and Listening

RESEARCHING ANIMAL TRAINING. Using library and Internet resources, as well as any community resources you may find, research various methods of training animals. You may wish to learn more about the "join-up" method and other methods for training horses, or you may wish to research methods for training dogs or other animals. Learn about at least two methods and compare them. Which is more effective? Why? Share your findings with your class.

Applied English

TECHNICAL WRITING. Review the Language Arts Survey 6.4, "Writing a Step-by-Step Procedure." Then review the story, paying special attention to the steps of the "join-up" method of training a horse to take a saddle and rider. Write a step-by-step technical procedure that could be used as a reference by students in Monty Roberts's school for horse trainers.

"Becoming a Composer"

from *The Music of Light*   by Lindsley Cameron

Reader's
r e s o u r c e

"Becoming a Composer" from the book *The Music of Light: The Extraordinary Story of Hikari and Kenzaburo Oe* (1998), is a nonfiction account of Hikari Oe, the son of famous Japanese author Kenzaburo Oe. Hikari was born with a brain defect which left a large portion of his brain outside his skull. The surgery required to correct this and save his life left him severely damaged, with an Intelligence Quotient (IQ) in the range of 50–75. In addition to this, Hikari was diagnosed with autism. Doctors and acquaintances urged the Oes to allow Hikari to die rather than undertake the demanding responsibilities of raising such a dependent and handicapped child. However, Kenzaburo and his wife, Yukari, decided to devote their lives to raising Hikari to reach his fullest potential and he has far surpassed anyone's expectations. Hikari's name means "light" in Japanese.

Early in his life, Hikari demonstrated an extraordinary interest in, and talent for, music. His parents nurtured this talent, and Hikari is now a world-famous composer. The first CD of his compositions was released to high praise when he was 29. Though Hikari has learned to play simple pieces on the piano, he composes all of his work in his head and writes it down without playing it first.

About *the*
A U T H O R

Lindsley Cameron lived in Japan for eight years and now lives in New York, where she writes about Japanese and Chinese art and culture for *The New York Times* and *The New Yorker*. In addition to *The Music of Light*, she has also published a book of short stories entitled *The Prospect of Detachment* (1991).

Cameron first became aware of Kenzaburo Oe and his work when she read Oe's book *A Personal Matter*. In this book, Oe writes a fictional account of his and his wife's decision not to allow their handicapped son to die, but rather to save his life and raise him. The book held a special power over Cameron because of her own experience as an adopted child. Her adoptive parents adopted a second daughter, but when they found out that she had cerebral palsy they sent her back to the adoption agency, "as though she were a piece of defective merchandise being returned to a department store." Thus, Cameron was drawn to Oe's work and its themes of defective, unwanted, and abandoned children.

Literary
T O O L S

Aim. A writer's **aim** is his or her purpose, or goal. People may write with the following aims: to inform (expository/informational writing); to entertain, enrich, or enlighten (imaginative writing); to tell a story (narrative writing); to reflect (personal/expressive writing); or to persuade (persuasive/argumentative writing). As you read, decide what you think Cameron's main aim was in writing "Becoming a Composer."

Abstract. An **abstract**, précis, or summary is a brief account of the main ideas or arguments presented in a work. Writing an abstract is an excellent way to remember the ideas of an essay or chapter in a textbook. As you read this piece of nonfiction writing, you may find it helpful to jot down notes on the main ideas.

Organizer

Review the Language Arts Survey 2.29, "Rough Outlines." Then, complete the chart below, listing the main ideas and filling in the details the author uses to illustrate these ideas.

Main idea	Supporting details
Hikari loved music as a child	Mother listened to classical music while pregnant with Hikari

Reader's
Journal

When has life presented you with an apparent problem or limitation, that later turned out to be a learning experience, an advantage, or a blessing?

Becoming a Composer

Lindsley Cameron

Hikari has been hearing music all his life. During her pregnancy, his mother listened to lots of Mozart. "They say fetuses begin to hear during their fifth month in the womb," she says, "so maybe he started to like it then." And after he was born, to <u>alleviate</u> her depression, she played recordings of the works of her other favorite classical composers—Chopin and Beethoven, chiefly—over and over. "When he was a toddler, he loved Western classical music. He would listen to it for hours, perfectly absorbed. Whenever we wanted some peace, we'd just put a few symphonies on the record player, and we could be sure Pooh-chan[1] wouldn't bother us at all. At that time, I had no idea how unusual that was. It wasn't until I had my other children that I realized that most normal toddlers won't listen to *any* kind of music for hours in a row—and that Western classical music is something most of them get tired of very fast."

What unusual pastime did Hikari enjoy?

Not Hikari. In a memoir about him, she wrote of how, when he was an infant, she played her favorite Western classical composers again and again until the records wore out. When a wornout record stuck and repeated a passage, Hikari wailed, as he did when a record stopped. She could quiet him only by playing another record. At first, she thought he enjoyed only Western classical music, but by the time he was a toddler she discovered that he liked children's songs and some other music, too. She also discovered that he could remember any tune he had ever heard. Entering a restaurant with his family, if classical music was being played, he could tell them at once what the piece was, even after hearing only a few notes.

What unusual ability did Hikari have?

When he was nine, Yukari began teaching him to read music and to play the piano, reasoning that even if he never got to be very good at it, the attempt might improve his coordination, and even if it didn't, he would probably enjoy it. Every day when he came home from school, all he wanted to do was listen to classical music. Many autistic[2] people limit their activities very narrowly; a tendency to have interests that are both highly restricted and very intense is listed in the diagnostic manual of the

What characteristic is common to both autism and genius?

---

1. **Pooh-chan**. Hikari's nickname, referring to Winnie the Pooh, a character in a children's book
2. **autistic**. Suffering from autism, a mental disorder usually diagnosed in childhood and characterized by withdrawal, inability to interact socially, repetitive behavior, and many different forms of acting out

---

words for everyday use
al • le • vi • ate (ə lē′ vē āt) *vt.*, relieve. *The aspirin <u>alleviated</u> my headache.*

American Psychiatric Association as a symptom of autism. It can also be characteristic of genius, of course, but at this time no one suspected that Hikari's preoccupation would ultimately lead him to <u>transcend</u> the usual limits of his condition.

Hikari's physical handicaps <u>precluded</u> his developing much skill as a pianist. It was hard for him to see the notes and to see and control his fingers on the keys. But he clearly had interest in and <u>aptitude</u> for music. He mastered the contents of Japan's standard introductory piano textbook very quickly. He enjoyed the lessons with his mother, and he had perfect pitch—the ability to correctly identify any note heard instantly and to sing any tone accurately.

> **What unusual ability did Hikari have?**

Inborn absolute pitch is rare. Musicians can be trained to develop relative pitch—that is, the ability to identify notes through recognizing intervals from given memorized pitches—and the earlier they begin musical training, the more likely they are to develop it. There is no definitive figure for the occurrence of inborn perfect pitch in the general population, since the phenomenon has chiefly been studied in musicians, but it is usually estimated as less than 4 percent. It is more common in people with disabilities like Hikari's, and it has recently been linked to a particular gene.

Hikari was extraordinarily sensitive to sounds of all kinds. He had (and to some extent still has) a horror of dogs, apparently because he disliked their barking and growling so. He had an excellent memory for the sounds of spoken language, too. He enjoyed exploiting the comic possibilities of language and was always making puns. And he was—and still is—a talented mimic; he could reproduce the routines of popular television entertainers. And he could remember nearly any piece of music he heard, even music he didn't like particularly. He could even remember that atonal[3] music he detested, if the piece wasn't too long or complicated. What he remembered best, though, was the eighteenth- and nineteenth-century Western classical music he preferred.

> **Which music did Hikari prefer?**

Although such talents made him easy to teach in some ways, Yukari, having three children to take care of, would probably not have been able to instruct him at all if Natsumiko had not proven extraordinarily helpful in taking care of Hikari. Even as a toddler, she understood that her brother needed her help and assumed responsibilities far beyond what might be expected at her age. When her mother went shopping with the children, Natsumiko would take care of the other two. By the time she was six—an age when most children need a parent to escort them when using a public bathroom—she was able to escort Hikari, who couldn't manage such things by himself. (In Japan at that time, most public toilets were unisex.) At home, she often took over the care of her brothers, freeing her mother to get on with her chores. Still, Yukari couldn't manage to give Hikari piano lessons—or even help with practicing—every day, and in any case she had only a beginner's skills herself, having taken lessons for a few years as a child.

Trouble began when Hikari, at age eleven, reached the point of trying to play with both hands simultaneously. He simply couldn't do it, and he stopped making progress. She <u>reprimanded</u> him for not trying hard enough; after all, he had been able to learn everything up to

---

3. **atonal.** Refers to music not organized in one musical key or tonal center

words for everyday use

tran • scend (tran send′) *vt.*, go beyond limits; overcome. *The girl's legs were amputated below the knees, but she transcended her handicap to become a runner.*

pre • clude (pri klüd′) *vt.*, rule out in advance. *Having been born in another country precludes one's chances of becoming President of the United States.*

ap • ti • tude (ap′ tə tüd) *n.*, natural ability or talent; tendency. *Kenji's aptitude for dance was obvious from the time he was a child and would imitate dance moves from television.*

rep • ri • mand (re′ prə mand) *vt.*, scold harshly. *The teacher reprimands anyone who chews gum in the classroom.*

that time, however slowly and laboriously. As his parent, she wanted him to do well and became disappointed and frustrated when he couldn't. And he, of course, wanted to please her and earn her approval, so he, too, became disappointed and frustrated. The lessons weren't fun anymore; in fact, they had become something to be dreaded. Yukari thought it would be a terrible shame if he should come to hate playing the piano, when he seemed to love music more than anything else in the world.

A more knowledgeable teacher was the only solution. The Oes asked around among friends and acquaintances, trying to find someone willing and able to work with a pupil with special needs. Finally, Kumiko Tamura, an amateur classical singer, member of a chorus group, and the wife of a friend of Kenzaburo's, agreed to try, coming to the Oes' house for an hour once every two weeks.

She hadn't been informed in advance about Hikari's disabilities, and once his mother explained his condition, she concluded that she might best begin by teaching him to sing songs with her. She had never worked with a handicapped child before, but she and Hikari got along well from the start. When she found that he could already play the piano a little, she began teaching him to play chords, because his poor physical coordination ruled out the usual fingering exercises.

At first, communication was difficult, and Yukari had to serve as an interpreter at every lesson. But after a couple of months, as they grew used to each other, Ms. Tamura and Hikari were able to talk to each other without her aid, and the lessons became weekly. After the first year, Hikari and his teacher found a way to communicate fluently about musical concepts that were beyond Yukari's level of knowledge, and she couldn't understand what they were saying to each other at all. Ms. Tamura's willingness to accommodate her problematic pupil undoubtedly accelerated their achievements in communicating: in a memoir she wrote a few years ago, Yukari said, "What Hikari likes about his teacher is that she never forces him to practice. Hikari doesn't like to be told what to do and what not to do. He likes to do everything his own way. His teacher knows that and that's why Hikari gets along very well with her."

Among other things, Ms. Tamura taught him to improvise. Sometimes she would play a melody and he would continue it; sometimes the two of them would work out a harmony together. "At such times it often happened that we would come up with a particularly attractive melody or harmony which it seemed a pity to lose, although . . . often . . . Hikari remembered such interesting passages and repeated them later," Ms. Tamura has written in the liner notes for his first CD. This was why she began teaching him how to write down the tunes he made up. He progressed rapidly; soon he could accurately write down anything she played for him. "I was especially eager for him to learn to transcribe music," Yukari remembers. "I had read about how Mozart would write down music as his father played it, and it seemed like the kind of thing Hikari would enjoy a lot."

> What new skill did Ms. Tamura teach Hikari?

> What ability did Hikari share with Mozart?

It wasn't long before he had transcribed music from nearly every record the Oes owned. He enjoyed using his transcribing skills just for fun. He has always loved his maternal grandmother, who lived with the family off and on over the years, always treating him very affectionately.

---

words for everyday use

im • pro • vise (im prə vīz) vt., compose, recite, sing, or play without preparation. *The comedians learned to improvise on stage; they could invent jokes on the spur of the moment.*

trans • cribe (tran skrīb') vt., write down; make a written copy of. *Alan transcribed the interview for us; he typed it out while listening to the recording.*

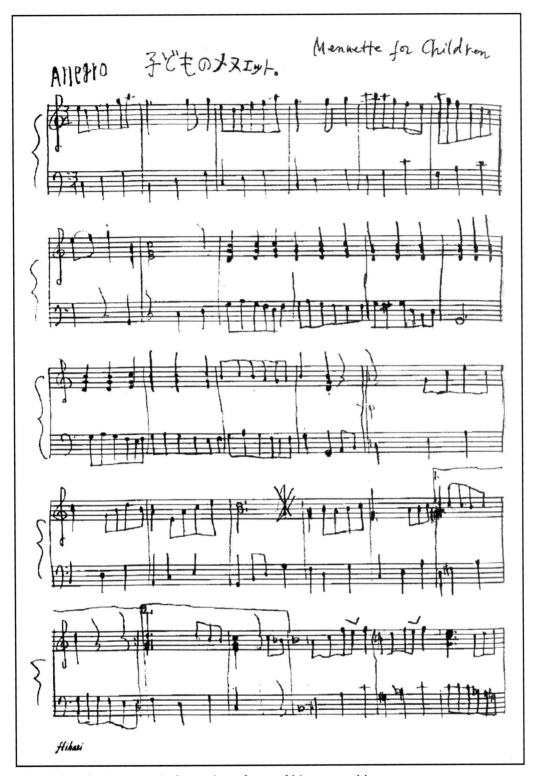

Hikari's handwritten musical notation of one of his compositions.

"Once, when Hikari was still in elementary school, she was hospitalized briefly and we went to visit her. She told him she wanted to find a particular song. She didn't know who wrote it and couldn't remember anything about it but the melody. He took her request very seriously, and wrote the tune down for her on music paper as soon as he got home," Yukari said.

On another occasion, Kenzaburo had been watching a videotape when Hikari was in the room and told him afterward that he had liked the soundtrack, which had been composed by Toru Takemitsu, Japan's best-known composer. His highly original music had made him a celebrity in Japan at an early age, and in 1964, when he was thirty-four, the huge international success of the film *Woman in the Dunes*, with his haunting, otherworldly score, brought him fame all over the world. *November Steps*, a New York Philharmonic commission, a sensation when it was first performed in 1967 and still one of his best-loved pieces, solidified his reputation in the West. Takemitsu, one of Kenzaburo's oldest and closest friends, had been one of the first people he talked to about his son's condition, right after Hikari's birth. And Takemitsu got along in a friendly way with the grown-up Hikari. Kenzaburo especially liked the music for a particular scene in the tape he had been watching, about four minutes long, where a young woman was eating an apple. Hikari promptly transcribed it for him, then played it on the piano as well as he could. Later, Kenzaburo told Takemitsu about it. A journalist who was with them didn't believe that Hikari could have transcribed the music correctly from memory, but Kenzaburo happened to have the notebook Hikari had used and gave it to Takemitsu to check. The composer said it was exactly what he had written, with only a minor error or two.

Hikari had always enjoyed his lessons with Ms. Tamura, but now he could hardly wait for them. When entering a Japanese house, people normally exchange their shoes for slippers at the threshold. Hikari would greet Ms. Tamura at the door carrying not only slippers for her to put on but also an alarm clock set for the time the lesson was to begin; he apparently wanted to make certain that none of the time sacred to music was wasted on pleasantries.

> How did Hikari feel about his piano lessons after working with Ms. Tamura?

He would show her what he had written in his music-manuscript notebook since the last time they met. At first, these were bits and pieces of music he had heard. But soon, by the time he was thirteen, he began writing down fragments he had composed himself, working entirely in his head, without a piano. At first, Ms. Tamura did not know what they were. His favorite compositional method at that time was filling up a manuscript page with broken chords or Alberti basses (a particular left-hand accompaniment of broken triads popular in the classical period), then thinking up a melody to go with them. He wrote mostly in an eighteenth-century idiom, and she thought he must have heard something on the radio that she did not happen to recognize.

> What had Hikari begun to do by the age of thirteen?

His mother thought so, too. "He was always listening to classical music, and he could remember whatever he heard. He knew many more pieces than I did, so I always assumed that he was writing down things I just didn't happen to know." She said in a television interview that

---

words for everyday use

id • i • om (ĭ' dē əm) *n.*, style or form of artistic expression. *The band specialized in the 1940s swing idiom, with a bit of rock and roll mixed in.*

although Hikari would write "This Is My Song" on his music manuscripts, she told Ms. Tamura that he must just be transcribing things he'd heard.

But the day came when his teacher saw four measures she was absolutely certain were his and no one else's. As she put it, in the same television interview, "I yelled out, 'Mrs. Oe, Hikari's composing!' I'm embarrassed to say this, but it reminded me of Annie Sullivan and Helen Keller[4] and the water breakthrough. It was an emotional moment. I couldn't stop crying."

She told a Japanese magazine reporter some details about Hikari's progress: "While having fun with various keys, Hikari began to show very clear likes and dislikes about which keys were good for particular pieces. Hikari remembers everything that he plays on any given day because he has a good memory, and so we started listening practice, too, because he also has a good ear. Listening to the music, he writes it down on a score sheet and afterwards even goes so far as to write in the chords, having thought intently on it for a while. He also does the opposite, writing in the melody while listening to the harmony. He started to write a lot of melodies on notepads the way a small child draws pictures. A lot of these doodled score sheets started to pile up, but after a while I realized that there were pieces that I did not recognize mixed in. They appeared to be Hikari's own compositions. I really could not have been happier at the time! Still, I wondered at first if they might possibly be scores that I didn't know, because he knows everything when it comes to classical music, from symphonic to instrumental pieces." Gradually, though, Ms. Tamura realized that all the works she couldn't

Father and son look together at the liner notes of Hikari's second CD.

identify were entirely Hikari's. And the day came when this was true of everything he wrote in the notebook.

It is not clear when Hikari himself realized that he was composing. He was thirteen when he presented his teacher with the finished score of a short piece by leaving it on the music rack of the piano encircled with a red ribbon tied in a bow; he seemed to know it was something he had made all by himself.

> What was Hikari's first finished composition?

"Birthday Waltz," written for his sister's birthday, was his first finished composition.

And when he graduated from elementary school, he wrote a setting for a poem his father had written called "Graduation." Kenzaburo, as always, took great pride and pleasure in his son's musical development. "Sitting nearby with a book, listening to his piano lessons," he wrote, "I can feel the best, most human things in his character finding lively and fluent expression." ∎

---

4. **Annie Sullivan and Helen Keller**. Helen Keller was a deaf, mute, and blind woman who overcame her handicaps to become a famous author and lecturer. Annie Sullivan was the teacher who taught her to read and speak. The first word that Sullivan got Helen to understand was water.

If you could not speak, what talent or ability would you develop in order to communicate your thoughts and feelings?

Investigate, *Inquire,* and Imagine

Recall: GATHERING FACTS

1a. What tendencies did Hikari have that are typical of autism, as well as of genius? What special talents did Hikari's mother notice in Hikari when he was young?

2a. When did Hikari begin to have trouble with his piano lessons? What did his parents do in response to this?

3a. Who was Kumiko Tamura? What skills did Hikari learn from her? What did Hikari begin to do by the time he was thirteen?

→ Interpret: FINDING MEANING

1b. Why didn't anyone suspect that Hikari was a genius? What made Hikari's talents so special? How might Hikari's autistic tendencies have helped him with his musical progress?

2b. Why did Hikari's mother reprimand him? For what reasons was the experience so frustrating for both Hikari and his mother?

3b. Why did Ms. Tamura think of Annie Sullivan and Helen Keller when she discovered that Hikari was composing music?

Analyze: TAKING THINGS APART

4a. Analyze the development of Hikari's musical ability. The first step in his progression was his early fascination with listening to classical music. What were the other major steps, leading up to his being able to compose his own music?

→ Synthesize: BRINGING THINGS TOGETHER

4b. What expectations did Hikari's mother have of him when she first gave him piano lessons? Based on what Hikari has accomplished, what would Kenzaburo or Yukari Oe tell us about our expectations of the handicapped?

Perspective: LOOKING AT OTHER VIEWS →

5a. What do you think Kenzaburo Oe meant when he said that listening to his son's piano lessons, he "can feel the best, most human things in [Hikari's] character finding lively and fluent expression"?

Empathy: SEEING FROM INSIDE

5b. Kenzaburo Oe says of Hikari, "His existence has...illuminated the dark, deep folds of my consciousness as well as its bright sides." What new consciousness do you think Hikari has brought to his father and others around him? What has he added to their lives?

Understanding *Literature*

AIM. Review the definition of **aim** in the Handbook of Literary Terms. What do you think was Lindsley Cameron's main aim in writing *The Music of Light*? Might she have had more than one aim?

ABSTRACT. Review the definition for **abstract** in the Handbook of Literary Terms. Writing an abstract is an excellent way to remember the ideas of an essay or chapter in a textbook. Write a brief abstract of the selection you have just read. Refer to the graphic organizer you completed in Literary Tools.

Writer's Journal

1. Imagine that you are Hikari's teacher and have just attended the first public performance of one of his compositions. He has just received the applause and praise of hundreds of people. Write a **journal entry** expressing your feelings and thoughts on this occasion.

2. Hikari Oe's music is available on CD and is very popular in Japan and around the world. Imagine that you work for the record company that will distribute his music for the first time in the United States. What would you want to say to potential listeners about the composer and his music? Write the **liner notes** for a CD of Hikari's music.

3. Suppose that Hikari has been nominated for a Grammy Award for one of his compositions. He is too shy to give an acceptance speech, so he has asked his father to prepare and deliver the speech should he win. Imagine that you are Kenzaburo. Write a brief **acceptance speech** to be delivered if Hikari should win the Grammy.

Integrating the Language Arts

Speaking and Listening & Collaborative Learning

CONDUCTING A MOCK INTERVIEW. Work with a partner on this assignment. One of you should imagine that you are a magazine reporter. What questions would you like to ask Kumiko Tamura about Hikari and what it was like to be his teacher? Develop five to six questions, being careful to make sure they are open-ended, requiring more than a *yes* or *no* answer. The other partner should imagine that he or she is Hikari's teacher, Ms. Tamura. Spend some time reviewing the excerpt and considering what it would be like to teach someone like Hikari. Try to stay in character. Role-play an interview, which you may wish to enact for your classmates as well.

Study and Research

RESEARCHING AUTISM. Using library, Internet and other resources, research autism. What sort of disorder is it, how does it affect its victims, and what sort of lives do people with autism lead in this country? How have methods of caring for autistic people changed over the years? Who were some other autistic geniuses or "autistic savants" as they are called? Share your findings with your class.

Media Literacy & Study and Research

APPRECIATING MUSIC. Locate recordings of some of Hikari's music and share them with your class. You may wish to compare his music with that of some of the eighteenth and nineteenth century composers he listened to often, such as his mother's favorites, Beethoven and Chopin.

Literary TOOLS

ESSAY. An **essay** is a brief work of prose nonfiction. The original meaning of essay was "a trial or attempt," and the word retains some of this original force. A good essay develops a single idea and is characterized by unity and coherence. As you read, determine the idea, or focus, of the essay. What details or facts does the author use to support his main points?

ARTICLE. An **article** is a brief work of nonfiction on a specific topic. The term *article* is typically used of encyclopedia entries and short nonfiction works that appear in newspapers and popular magazines. The term is sometimes used as a synonym of *essay*, though the latter term often connotes a more serious, important, or lasting work. As you read "Where Stars Are Born" and the Related Reading, "Spanning the Decades," consider which piece is more serious, important, or lasting.

Graphic Organizer

Make an outline of the essay "Where Stars Are Born." Label the main point or points with Roman numerals and label the supporting details and facts with letters and then numbers as shown below. One example has been done for you.

I. "The Dominican Republic is the real cradle of baseball."
  A. Great players come from that country.
    1. 13 major league players come from San Pedro de Macorís, D.R.
      a)

"Where Stars Are Born"
from *Sports Illustrated*
by Michael Farber

Reader's resource

GEOGRAPHY CONNECTION. The Dominican Republic, where Sammy Sosa was born, is a country in the Caribbean that occupies the eastern two-thirds of the island Hispaniola. The country of Haiti takes up the other, western third of the island. The Dominican Republic's main industries are tourism and sugar production. San Pedro de Macorís, the city where Sammy Sosa was born, is famous for its baseball players.

SPORTS HISTORY CONNECTION. The 1998 baseball season is remembered as the "Summer of 62," the season in which two players, the St. Louis Cardinals' Mark McGwire and the Chicago Cubs' Sammy Sosa, broke Roger Maris's longtime record for most home runs in a single season (1961). Maris's record 61 home runs broke the former record of baseball legend Babe Ruth, who hit 60 home runs in 1927. McGwire went on to set the new home run record of 70, while Sosa ended the '98 season with 66. Although Sosa hit fewer home runs overall, he was overwhelmingly voted Most Valuable Player for the National League that year.

About the AUTHOR

Michael Farber is a senior writer on staff at *Sports Illustrated* magazine. He concentrates mostly on covering baseball, ice hockey, and skiing. After joining the magazine in 1994, he soon established himself as one of *SI's* top writers. Formerly, he was a sports columnist for the *Montreal Gazette*, the *Hackensack* (NJ) *Record*, and Honolulu's *Sun Bulletin*. His efforts have earned him both the National Newspaper Award and the Canadian National Newspaper Award. Born and raised in New Jersey, he graduated from Rutgers University, and now lives in Quebec with his wife and children. His essay "Where Stars Are Born" was published in the October 7, 1998, Special Commemorative Issue of *Sports Illustrated*.

Reader's Journal

Do you have a particular sports star that you admire? If so, what do you admire about that star?

Sammy Sosa hits a home run, 1999.

WHERE Stars ARE BORN

Michael Farber

Sosa's season affirmed for all that the Dominican Republic is the real cradle of the game.

In this summer of statistics, when a nation counted down with more urgency than Casey Kasem,[1] you are asked once again to do the math. From Sammy Sosa's hometown of San Pedro de Macorís (pop. 125,000), there are currently 13 major league baseball players.

For what is Sammy Sosa's hometown noted?

---
1. **Casey Kasem.** Radio deejay who hosts countdowns of popular music hits

A boy plays with a tennis ball and a broken bat in the hurricane-damaged stadium of San Pedro de Macorís.

If, say, New York City produced as many big leaguers per capita, the 30 dugouts would be crammed with 763 men with George Costanza[2] accents. If they played in Peoria[3] the way they do in San Pedro de Macorís, there would be 12 focus-group Americans in the bigs.[4]

In the greatest baseball city on earth they play in the alleys, in the streets, in the sprawling sugarcane fields that line the city's outskirts—with bats made of branches from guava trees, crude gloves crafted from milk cartons, and stuffed socks that stand in for real balls. The fields are often rocky, which has tested not only the occasional protective cup but also the reflexes of the glovemen[5] who have forged San Pedro de Macorís's reputation as a redoubt of shortstops. In the 1980s the city delivered, among others, Tony Fernandez, Julio Franco, Mariano Duncan and Rafael Ramirez to the majors. Frequently overlooked, however, are the boppers,

What gives the short-stops of San Pedro de Macorís such quick reflexes?

2. **George Costanza**. Television sitcom character from New York City
3. **Peoria**. One of the largest cities in Illinois; 1996 pop. 112,306
4. **bigs**. Baseball's big leagues
5. **glovemen**. Slang term for fielders in baseball

words for everyday use

per • cap • i • ta (pər ka′ p´ tə) *adv. or adj.,* per unit of population. *The per capita wage in Rhode Island was high, with each person earning an average of $75,000 a year.*

re • doubt (ri daut′) *n.,* secure retreat or stronghold. *The animal shelter was a redoubt for lost animals.*

men like Rico Carty, George Bell and Pedro Guerrero, all of them Macorisanos. Whereas Sosa spent the summer rewriting the record books, some of us are going to have to spend the winter rewriting the game's mythology.

This was Sosa's glorious role in the home run race: He changed everything. It was supposed to be the summer Ken Griffey Jr. played long-ball cat and mouse with Mark McGwire. Instead, Sosa went on his 20-homer <u>binge</u> in June and established himself as Big Mac's most formidable

challenger. He was the perfect mystery guest, whose humility and joyful, carefree approach to the game leavened[6] the most self-conscious record chase in history. Content to joyride in McGwire's wake, Sosa squeezed every last drop of pleasure from the race and even helped McGwire realize that Chasing Roger should be a kick, not a solemn duty. It was all great fun.

The Summer of 62 will ultimately be recalled as a time when baseball

regained its health. Fans should also remember it as the year of the Dominican Republic, the nation where baseball never took ill. If not for Roger Clemens's remarkable late-season run, Boston Red Sox pitcher Pedro Martinez, of Santo Domingo, would most likely have become the first player to win consecutive Cy Young awards in different leagues. Moises Alou, who also grew up in Santo Domingo, went from Florida to Houston, where he led the Astros to the National League Central title and emerged, along with Sosa, as a leading MVP candidate. And 22-year-old Montreal Expos

outfielder Vladimir Guerrero, from Nizao Bani, quietly morphed into[7] Griffey Jr., putting up numbers that might have challenged for a Triple Crown in another year. Not one of these men, incidentally, is a shortstop.

But it was Sosa who finally made the game a block party that everyone could enjoy. Although baseball has been international for decades and roughly one fifth of today's major leaguers are from Latin America, the Cubs out-fielder is the sport's first true <u>crossover</u> Latin hero, <u>outstripping</u> even his own idol, Roberto Clemente. When Sosa leaped out of the batter's box, skipping two strides as he watched his swats soar toward the bleachers, we skipped along with him. If he didn't shatter any windows along Chicago's Waveland Avenue, he did open plenty of others across the country, letting in some much-needed fresh air. He challenged the assumption that North Americans could never truly embrace Latin players, that they were too "<u>flamboyant</u>" or, in the case of Clemente, too "moody" for gringo tastes. McGwire might have been the first to get to 62, but Sosa's home run quest was richer. It flattered

America's vision of itself as a land of acceptance, as a meritocracy[8] in which color and language and origins don't matter.

In the Summer of 62, National League fences were not the only things Sosa broke down. ∎

---

6. **leaven**. Make lighter by mingling or mixing with some light-ening agent

7. **morphed into**. Became, turned into

8. **meritocracy**. System in which the talented are chosen and moved ahead on the basis of their achievement

---

SPANNING THE DECADES

Puerto Rico honors Sosa, who pays tribute to Clemente

Saturday November 28, 1998

SAN JUAN, PUERTO RICO (AP) — At a ceremony meant to honor him, Sammy Sosa instead made sure Roberto Clemente was not forgotten.

Sosa told Puerto Rican senators who feted him with a special meeting Friday that a photograph he keeps of Clemente inspired him to his 61st and 62nd homers, and later numbers 64 and 65.

"I think I am the reincarnation of Roberto Clemente," Sosa said.

The tribute touched Clemente's widow, Vera. Her husband, a Hall of Famer who is perhaps the greatest player Puerto Rico has produced, died in a 1972 air crash on his way to deliver aid to earthquake victims in Nicaragua.

"He's not just a good baseball player, but a great human being," Vera Clemente said of Sosa in a voice choked with emotion.

Sosa (right) greets Roberto Clemente's son Luis and his widow, Vera, on his trip in Puerto Rico.

Clemente was the National League's Most Valuable Player in 1966. Sosa won the award this year.

"Sammy gave me the opportunity to participate in and enjoy something that I couldn't do when my father was the Most Valuable Player," said Clemente's son, Luis, who was born in 1966.

Sosa, a Dominican, was greeted with cheers and whistles from children dressed in baseball gear and the island's baseball-crazy adults.

"The work that Juan Gonzalez and Sammy Sosa has done is for all Latin Americans, not just for the Dominican Republic," he said. Juan Gonzalez of the Texas Rangers, a Puerto Rican, was voted the American League's Most Valuable Player.

"My career has been very successful....but nobody remembers that Sammy Sosa had to work very hard and cried many tears. This is a very important thing between us Latinos," he said in the Senate.

Later Friday, he visited the Roberto Clemente Sports City in Carolina, just outside San Juan, where the player's family presented him with two paintings of Clemente, one depicting his first hit in the major leagues and the other his last, 3,000th hit.

Sosa attended a gala dinner Friday to raise money for his Miami-based foundation, which has sent relief supplies to his hurricane-ravaged nation. An auction was to be held of memorabilia from Sosa's season, also for the foundation. ∎

Casey at the BAT

Ernest Lawrence Thayer

Baseball Players, 1875. Thomas Eakins.
Rhode Island School of Design, Providence.

The outlook wasn't brilliant for the Mudville nine that day;
The score stood four to two with but one inning more to play.
And then when Cooney died at first, and Barrows did the same,
A sickly silence fell upon the patrons of the game.

5   A straggling few got up to go in deep despair. The rest
Clung to that hope which springs eternal in the human breast;
They thought if only Casey could but get a whack at that—
We'd put up even money now with Casey at the bat.

But Flynn preceded Casey, as did also Jimmy Blake,
10 And the former was a lulu and the latter was a cake;
So upon that stricken multitude grim melancholy sat,
For there seemed to be little chance of Casey's getting to the bat.

But Flynn let drive a single, to the wonderment of all,
And Blake, the much despised, tore the cover off the ball;
15 And when the dust had lifted, and the men saw what had occurred,
There was Jimmy safe at second and Flynn a-hugging third.

Then from five thousand throats and more there rose a lusty yell;
It rumbled through the valley, it rattled in the dell;
It knocked upon the mountain and recoiled upon the flat,
20 For Casey, mighty Casey, was advancing to the bat.

There was ease in Casey's manner as he stepped into his place;
There was pride in Casey's bearing and a smile on Casey's face.

And when, responding to the cheers, he lightly doffed his hat,
No stranger in the crowd could doubt 'twas Casey at the bat.

25 Ten thousand eyes were on him as he rubbed his hands with dirt;
Five thousand tongues applauded when he wiped them on his shirt.
Then while the writhing pitcher ground the ball into his hip,
Defiance gleamed in Casey's eye, a sneer curled Casey's lip.

And now the leather-covered sphere came hurling through the air,
30 And Casey stood a-watching it in haughty grandeur there.
Close by the sturdy batsman the ball unheeded sped—
"That ain't my style," said Casey. "Strike one!" the umpire said.

From the benches, black with people, there went up a muffled roar,
Like the beating of the storm-waves on a stern and distant shore.
35 "Kill him! Kill the umpire!" shouted someone on the stand;
And it's likely they'd have killed him had not Casey raised his hand.

With a smile of Christian charity great Casey's visage shone;
He stilled the rising tumult; he bade the game go on;
He signaled to the pitcher, and once more the spheroid flew;
40 But Casey still ignored it, and the umpire said, "Strike two!"

"Fraud!" cried the maddened thousands, and echo answered "Fraud!"
But one scornful look from Casey and the audience was awed.
They saw his face grow stern and cold, they saw his muscles strain,
And they knew that Casey wouldn't let that ball go by again.

45 The sneer is gone from Casey's lip, his teeth are clenched in hate;
He pounds with cruel violence his bat upon the plate.
And now the pitcher holds the ball, and now he lets it go,
And now the air is shattered by the force of Casey's blow.

Oh, somewhere in this favored land the sun is shining bright;
50 The band is playing somewhere, and somewhere hearts are light,
And somewhere men are laughing, and somewhere children shout;
But there is no joy in Mudville—mighty Casey has struck out. ■

ABOUT THE RELATED READING
Ernest Lawrence Thayer (1863–1940) worked for several years with his college friend William Randolph Hearst, founder of the Hearst chain of newspapers, on the *San Francisco Examiner*. Thayer then left to take over his father's textile business, but he continued to contribute short pieces to the paper. Although Thayer wrote many other works, none achieved the fame of his classic ballad "Casey at the Bat." This poem first appeared in the *San Francisco Examiner* on June 3, 1888. A year later, actor DeWolf Hopper read the poem to a baseball crowd, and the crowd responded with a rousing standing ovation. Thayer's spirited, humorous poem about American's "national pastime" has remained popular for over a hundred years.

If you were Sammy Sosa, what would you do now that you have national fame and respect?

Investigate, Inquire, and Imagine

Recall: GATHERING FACTS

1a. How many major league players are from San Pedro de Macorís? Which major league players from other parts of the Dominican Republic are mentioned in this article?

2a. What are the playing conditions and equipment like for many baseball players in San Pedro de Macorís?

3a. What emotions and attitudes did Sammy Sosa bring to the home run race? What does the author claim Sammy Sosa did for baseball?

Interpret: FINDING MEANING

1b. Why do you think there are so many successful baseball players from the Dominican Republic?

2b. Why do you think the author chose to include this information?

3b. What makes Sammy Sosa such an appealing person? How might the attitudes he brought to the game reflect the feelings about baseball in his hometown?

Analyze: TAKING THINGS APART

4a. Compare and contrast the conditions in which the people of San Pedro de Macorís play baseball with those enjoyed by professional American players. Why do you think Macorisanos continue to play even in such poor conditions? How is their motivation different from that of the pros?

Synthesize: BRINGING THINGS TOGETHER

4b. Predict what would happen if all American players were asked to give up their salaries and expensive playing fields and play in conditions like the Macorisanos do.

Evaluate: MAKING JUDGMENTS

5a. Why was Roberto Clemente such an inspiration to Sammy Sosa? In what ways has his life been similar to Clemente's?

Extend: CONNECTING IDEAS

5b. In the second related reading, Thayer's "Casey at the Bat," the mighty Casey let the team down by striking out in the final inning. Do you think players like Clemente and Sosa might have had similar experiences? How might a failure like this affect a talented athlete?

Understanding *Literature*

ESSAY. Review the definition for **essay** in the Handbook of Literary Terms. Do you think the author of "Where Stars Are Born" did an adequate job in maintaining a single focus, as well as unity and coherence? You may want to look up the definitions of *unity* and *coherence* in the Handbook of Literary Terms. Point out any parts of the essay where you think the author strayed from his main point. Give examples of how you might change the essay to make it clearer and more to the point.

ARTICLE. Review the definition for **article** in the Handbook of Literary Terms. Which of the two articles, "Where Stars Are Born" and the Related Reading, did you think was more serious or had more lasting importance, and why? Is either one of the two articles of lasting interest, or are both only relevant to the time in which they were written? Compare the main points of the two articles. What kinds of articles are they—factual news articles or opinion articles? Explain.

Writer's Journal

1. Write a **fan letter** to Sammy Sosa. Tell him what you admire about him and his life. Think about questions you would ask him if you could talk to him and include these in the letter.

2. Imagine that the people of San Pedro de Macorís have asked you to create a **plaque** for a life-sized bronze statue of Sammy Sosa that will be placed in front of City Hall. Write the message you think should go on this plaque. If you wish, you may draw a design to accompany the words on the plaque.

3. An *anecdote* is a usually short narrative of an interesting, or amusing biographical or autobiographical incident. Write an **anecdote** about a young boy or girl learning to play baseball in San Pedro de Macorís. The story might describe a day on the field and reveal some of the young person's dreams of being a successful ball player.

Integrating *the* Language Arts

Collaborative Learning & Study and Research

RESEARCHING WORLD FIGURES IN BASEBALL. When looking for the next baseball superstar, fans and talent scouts are not limited to the United States. Many people are surprised to hear that Fidel Castro, the Cuban dictator, once tried out as a major league pitcher. Baseball fever has swept Japan, which now has many corporate-sponsored baseball teams. As a group, research a foreign baseball star or team and give a report on them. You may want to present your report as a visual display, as an oral report, or as a media presentation, using video or PowerPoint.

Media Literacy

SPORTSWRITING. What topics are today's sportswriters buzzing about? What does a sportswriter do? What goes into the articles in your sports section of the newspaper and the sports reports you see every day on the news? What different kinds of sportswriters are there? What topics do they cover? When did the first sportswriter get his or her start? Put together a presentation on sportswriters or give a "sports news" presentation to your class on current events in sports.

"Gary Keillor"

by Garrison Keillor

Reader's resource

"Gary Keillor" is a fictional story based on the author's middle-class, Midwestern childhood in the 1950s. In it, Keillor tells of discovering his niche in life as a humorist while participating in a high-school talent show.

CULTURE CONNECTION. The 1950s were a time of peace and prosperity in the United States. After serving in World War II, hundreds of thousands of men and women came home to attend college on the G.I. Bill, which for the first time made college affordable for a broad spectrum of the population. There were plenty of jobs to go around as the economy boomed, subdivisions sprang up in every town, and the baby boom took off. Optimism about the future was high, and it seemed that anything was possible—both for America, and for the average American. Rock and roll music was popular, especially that of superstar Elvis Presley, who skyrocketed to fame in the 1950s and 60s. His hit "All Shook Up" is mentioned in this story by Garrison Keillor.

About the AUTHOR

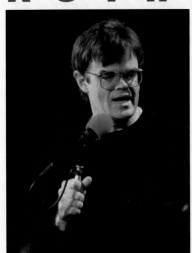

Garrison Keillor (1942–   ) is the host of the very popular public radio show *A Prairie Home Companion*, a variety show loosely based on radio broadcasts of the era before television. The show includes folk and gospel music, comedy sketches, and ad spots for fictitious businesses like Bertha's Kitty Boutique, Ralph's Pretty Good Grocery, and the Chatterbox Café. The best-known portion of the show is "The News from Lake Wobegon," in which Keillor describes with humor and warmth the lives of average people in a fictitious Minnesota town where "all the women are strong, all the men are good looking, and all the children are above average."

Keillor is a native Minnesotan and lives and works in St. Paul. He is the author of eleven books, including *Lake Wobegon Days* (1985), *The Book of Guys* (1993), *The Old Man Who Loved Cheese* (1996), *Wobegon Boy* (1997), and *Lake Wobegon: Summer 1956* (2001).

Literary TOOLS

DESCRIPTION. **Description** is a type of writing that portrays a character, an object, or a scene. Descriptions make use of *sensory details*—words and phrases that describe how things look, sound, smell, taste, or feel. Garrison Keillor describes his classroom and the work he and his classmates were doing there in vivid sensory detail. As you read, make note of these details.

IRONY. **Irony** is a difference between appearance and reality. In "Gary Keillor," the difference between Gary's description of his life, his thoughts, and his dreams and the reality of that life provides an ironic contrast and contributes to much of the humor of this story. As you read, notice the difference between the way Gary sees the situations in which he finds himself and the way we see those situations.

Graphic Organizer

As you read, make a cluster chart, listing examples of ironic humor in the story.

"I was so smart that poor grades didn't bother me in the slightest." — ironic humor

Reader's Journal

When have you been the "star of the show"?

Gary Keillor

Garrison Keillor

When I was sixteen years old, I stood six feet two inches tall and weighed a hundred and forty pounds. I was intense and had the metabolism of a wolverine. I ate two or three lunches a day and three full dinners at night, as my family sat around the kitchen table and observed, and I cleaned off their plates too when they had poor appetites or were finicky. There was no food I disliked except muskmelon, which smelled rotten and loathsome. Everything else I ate. (It was Minnesota so we didn't have seafood, except fish sticks, of course.) I was a remarkable person. I was a junior in high school, Class of 1960. I was smart, so smart that poor grades didn't bother me in the slightest; I considered them no reflection on my intelligence. I read four books a week, and I sometimes walked home from school, all twelve miles, so I could relive favorite chapters out loud, stride along the shoulder of the highway past the potato farms, and say brilliant and outrageous things, and sing in a big throbbing voice great songs like "Til There Was You" and "Love Me Tender."

> Why are grades of no importance to Gary?

I had no wish to sing in front of an audience, songs were a private thing with me. I was an intense person, filled with powerful feelings, and I assumed that I would live alone for the rest of my life, perhaps in a monastery, silent, swishing around in a cassock, my heart broken by a tragic love affair with someone like Natalie Wood,[1] my life dedicated to God.

> What sort of person is Gary? What kind of future does he foresee for himself?

I was a lucky boy. I had learned this two years before on a car trip to Colorado. My Uncle Earl and Aunt Myrna drove there that summer—he had been stationed in Colorado Springs during the war—along with my cousins Gordon and Mel, and I got to go too. I won that trip by dropping over to their house and being extremely nice. I'd say, "Here, let me wash those dishes." I'd say, "Boy, I'm sure in a mood to mow a lawn." And then she'd offer me a glass of nectar and a piece of angel food cake and I'd eat it and say, "Boy, I was looking at *National Geographic* the other night and they had a big article on Colorado. It was so interesting. Just the different rock formations and things. I don't see how people can look at those mountains and not know there's a God." And she'd smile at me, a good boy who mowed lawns and whose faith was pure, and I got to go. Of course my brothers and sisters were fit to be tied. "How come he gets to go? We never get to go. Oh no, we have to stay here all summer and work in the garden while he goes riding out to Colorado." They just didn't get it. Trips to Colorado don't fall in your lap. You've got to go out and earn Colorado.

We took off on the trip, and I was a very good passenger. I sat in the favored front seat between my aunt and uncle, looking at the scenery for hours, no stains on my clothes, my face clean, a good strong bladder, never got carsick, and had a <u>subtle</u> sideways technique for picking my nose—you'd never see it even if you looked straight at me. Far off, the mountains appeared, shining on the horizon for almost a whole day, and then we rose up into them—snowcapped peaks, like the last scene in a western in which justice and romance <u>prevail</u>, and when we reached Denver (*EL. 5280*, the sign said, exactly a mile), we ate dinner at a

> What made Gary a good passenger on the trip to Colorado?

---

1. **Natalie Wood**. An American film actress of the 1950s and 1960s

---

words for everyday use

sub • tle (su'tl) *adj.*, difficult to perceive or identify; crafty. *The catcher's signals to the pitcher were <u>subtle</u> enough that no one else could see.*

pre • vail (pri vāl') *vi.*, triumph or win a victory. *Gail was about to clean her room, but laziness <u>prevailed</u> and she ended up reading a book instead.*

Chinese restaurant and my fortune cookie said: "You are <u>enterprising</u>—take advantage of it." Well, there it was in a nutshell.

The mountains were startling in their whiteness and steepness, the valleys dark in the late afternoon, the peaks glittering in pure sunlight, beautiful stands of light gray-green aspen floating like fog, and my aunt took a picture of me with trees and mountains behind me. Just me, tall and intense. You would never guess I was from Minnesota. I thought, "This is my lucky picture. I'll keep it the rest of my life."

What became Gary's lucky charm?

My family lived in the country, along the Mississippi River between Minneapolis and Tryon, and I attended New Tryon High School, which was bulging under a tidal wave of children from new subdivisions on the other side of the river, places with names like Riverview Estates and Woodlawn and Forest Hills. Our side, South Tryon Township, along the West River Road, was still rural, truck farms, and scattered houses on big rolling tracts, and we West River Roaders were the cream of the school. The editor of the school paper, *The Beacon*, Elaine Eggert, was one of us; so were the stars of the debate team and the speech team, three of the class officers, and the chairperson of the spring talent show, Dede Petersen, who rode on my bus.

Where does Gary's family live?

I had been in love with Dede for two years, in an intense and secret way. She had bouncy blonde hair and wore soft sweaters, plaid skirts, penny loafers and knee socks. One winter day I wrote her a fourteen-page letter (single-spaced) saying that she was my ideal of womanhood, a person of pure taste, excellent judgment, stunning beauty, and natural intelligence, a woman to whom I could pledge myself in a spiritual friendship that would last forever no matter what. If the friendship should turn into physical love, good, and if not, fine. We would be friends for the rest of our lives, our souls communing over vast distances.

I did not, after long thought, give her the letter. I guessed that she might laugh at it and also that her boyfriend Bill Swenson might pound me into the ground. He was an intense person too.

Why didn't Gary give Dede the letter?

One afternoon riding home on the bus, sitting behind her, I heard her complain to her pal Marcy about the miseries of planning the April talent show. Bill Swenson would be in it, lipsynching "All Shook Up," and he was terrific, but there wasn't much other talent around, nothing compared to last year, when all those guys sang "Bali Hai" with the coconuts on their chests, and the skit about school lunch when the kids pretended to vomit and out came green confetti, and of course last year there had been Barbara Lee. Barbara Lee was the most talented person ever to graduate from our school. She danced, she sang, she did the splits, she played the marimba.[2] She was Broadway bound, no doubt about it.

What problem is Dede having with the talent show she is organizing?

I leaned forward and said, "Well, I think we have lots of talent." Oh? like who, for example? she said. I said, "Well, I could do something." *You?* she said. "Or I could get together with some other kids and we could do a skit." *Like what?* she said. I said, "Oh, I don't know. Something

What solution does Gary propose to Dede?

---

2. **marimba**. A musical instrument similar to a xylophone

about the school burning down. It all depends."

"That doesn't sound funny to me," she said. Marcy didn't think it was funny either.

What burned my toast was her saying *"You?"* when I volunteered to be in her talent show. I was only being helpful, I was not claiming to be another Barbara Lee. I had no interest in the stage at all until I heard her incredulity and amusement—*"You?"*—and then I was interested in being interested. A spiritual friendship with Dede was out of the question, if she thought I was the sort of guy you could say *"You?"* to.

What makes Gary angry?

No one in our family sang or performed for entertainment, only for the glory of God and only in groups, never solo. We were Christian people; we did not go in for show. But I was an intense young man. Intensity was my guiding principle. And when I thought about joining that monastery after Natalie Wood rejected me and spending my life in the woodshop making sturdy chairs and tables, I thought that perhaps I ought to get in the talent show at New Tryon High first, get a whiff of show business before I gave my life to God.

Why didn't anyone in Gary's family perform for entertainment?

It was one of those ugly and treacherous springs in the Midwest, when winter refuses to quit, like a big <u>surly</u> drunk who heads for home and then staggers back for another round and a few more songs that everyone has heard before. It was cold and wet, and we sat day after day in dim airless classrooms, the fluorescent lights turned on at midday, the murky sky and bare trees filling the big classroom windows, pools of oil-slicked rain in the parking lot, the grass in front dead, the Stars and Stripes hanging limp and wet like laundry. In plane geometry, I was lost in the wilderness, had been lost since Christmas, and in history, we were slogging through World War I, and in English class, we were memorizing poems. "These are treasures you will carry with you forever," said Miss Rasmussen, a big woman in a blue knit suit. In her wanderings around the classroom as she talked about poetry and metaphor, she often stopped in the aisle and stood looming above me, her voice overhead, her hand resting on my desk, her puffy white hand and red knuckles and short ringless fingers. Her stopping there indicated, I knew, her fondness for me. I was the only student of hers who wrote poems. She had even suggested that I memorize and recite one of my own poems. I declined. Part of the memorization assignment was reciting the poem in front of the class. My poems were far too intense and personal to be said out loud in front of people. I was memorizing Whitman's elegy on the death of Abraham Lincoln, "O Captain! My Captain!" I walked home through the rain one cold day crying out, "O Captain! my Captain! our fearful trip is done, / The ship has weather'd every rack, the prize we sought is won."

Why is Miss Rasmussen fond of Gary?

Why does Gary not want to recite his own poems for his class?

> My poems were far too intense and personal to be said out loud in front of people.

One day a fuel oil truck backed into our driveway and got stuck in the mud and the driver put it into forward gear and got dug in deeper. He gunned it in reverse and gunned it forward

words for everyday use

sur • ly (sər′lē) *adj.*, rude; ill tempered. *Our server was so <u>surly</u> he nearly ruined our evening out.*

and rocked the truck loose and pulled forward and unwound his hose and started filling our fuel oil tank, but meanwhile he had left deep ruts in my mother's garden and the front yard. She was home alone, washing clothes. She heard the grinding and roaring from down in the laundry room and came outdoors to find her garden dug up and the tulips and irises destroyed, and the driver looked at her and said, "You ought to do something about your driveway." Not a word of apology, acted like it was the driveway's fault. My mother was the quietest, politest person ever, she felt that raising your voice indicated a flawed character, but she put her hands on her hips and said, "Mister, if you can't figure out how to drive a truck, then they oughta find you a job you'd be able to handle." And she told him to get out and she would be sending the company a bill for the flower garden. And he did. And she did. And the company sent us a check and an apology from the general manager, a Harold L. Bergstrom.

It was the first time in my memory that my mother had fought back and raised her voice to a stranger, a watershed[3] moment for me. I heard the story from our neighbor, Mr. Couture, and I admired her so much for standing up to the jerk and defending our family's honor. Her principles had always told her to be quiet and polite and turn the other cheek and never make trouble, but there comes a time to let go of principle and do the right thing. To me, this seemed to open the door to show business.

And then, about a week before the talent show, suddenly I was in. The real power behind the show wasn't Dede, it was Miss

Rasmussen, my teacher, the adviser to the talent show, and the day I stood before the class and recited "O Captain! My Captain!" she told Dede to put me in the show. The next day, Miss Rasmussen had me stand up in class and recite it again. It was one of the finest pieces of oral interpretation she had ever seen, she said. She sat in a back corner of the room, her head bowed, her eyes closed, as I stood in front and with dry mouth launched the Captain's ship again, and she did not see the kids smirking and gagging and retching and pulling long invisible skeins of snot from their nostrils and when my Captain died and I got to "O the bleeding drops of red, / Where on the deck my Captain lies, / Fallen cold and dead," they rolled their eyes and clutched at their hearts and died. Then, when she stood up, her eyes moist, and clapped, they all clapped too. "Wasn't that good!" she cried. "You really liked it, didn't you! Oh, I'm glad you did! He's going to recite it in the talent show, too! Won't that be nice!" A couple of boys in front clapped their hands over their mouths and pretended to lose their lunch. They seemed to speak for most of the class.

So I was in the talent show, which I wanted to be, but with an inferior piece of material. I suggested to Miss Rasmussen that "O Captain! My Captain!" might not be right for the talent show audience, that maybe I could find a humorous poem, and she said, "Oh, it'll be just fine," not realizing the gravity of the situation.

How does the class react to Gary's reading of "O Captain! My Captain!"?

> "Never give up on beauty," she said. "Never compromise your standards out of fear that someone may not understand."

---

3. **watershed**. Decisive, critical event which marks the division between two periods or phases of history or of a life

words for everyday use

grav • i • ty (graˈvə tē) n., seriousness. *The passengers of the sinking ship panicked when they realized the gravity of their situation.*

"Never give up on beauty," she said. "Never compromise your standards out of fear that someone may not understand." Teachers were full of useless advice like that.

I tried not to think about "O Captain." I experimented with combing my hair a new way, with the part on the right. I was handsome at certain angles, I thought, and a right-hand part would emphasize a good angle. I stood at the bathroom mirror, a small mirror in my hand, and experimented holding my head cocked back and aimed up and to the right, a pose favored by seniors in their graduation pictures, which looked good from either side, and reciting "O Captain" with my head at that angle. I had good skin except when it flared up, which it did two days before the show, and it took a long time to repair the damage. There were six children in our family and only one bathroom, but I spent fifteen minutes behind a locked door doing surgery and applying alcohol and cold packs and skin-toned cream. The little kids stood banging on the door, pleading to use the toilet. I said, "Well, how bad do you have to go?" I was the one in show business, after all.

What happens two days before the show?

I worked on "O Captain" so that every line was set in my head. I recited it to myself in the mirror ("O Captain! Oh Captain! the fateful day is done, / Your blemishes have disappeared, the skin you sought is won") and for my mother, who said I was holding my head at an unnatural angle, and then, the Friday night before the show, I recited it at a party at Elaine Eggert's house, and there my interpretation of "O Captain! My Captain!" took a sharp turn toward the English stage.

Miss Rasmussen loved a recording of Sir John Gielgud[4] reading "Favourites of English Poetry" and she played it once for our class, a whole hour of it, and from that day, all the boys in the class loved to do English accents. A little lisp, endless dramatic pauses, fruity inflections including shrill birdlike tones of wonder-

ment, and instead of the vowel *o* that delicious English *aaoooww*, a bleating sound not found anywhere in American speech. In the cafeteria, when my friend Ralph Moody came to the table where all of us West River Road rats sat, he stood holding his tray, peering down at us and the welter of milk cartons and comic books and ice cream wrappers and uneaten macaroni-cheese lunches, and after a long pause he cried "Aaaaooooww," with a shudder, a great man forced to sit among savages. So at the party, surrounded by kids from the debate team and the newspaper, the cream of West River Road society, when Elaine had said for the sixth time, "Do the poem you're going to do on Monday," I reached back for Ralph's *Aaooww* and did "O Captain" as Sir John might have done it:

How does Gary change his reading of "O Captain! My Captain!"?

Aoowww Cap-tin, myyyyy Cap-tin,
aower————feeah-fool twip eez done!
Th' sheep has wethah'd————eviddy rack!
th' priiiiiiize we sot————eez won!
But————aaaooooooooowww
th' bleeeeeeeding drrrops————of rrred————
wheahhhh————
on th' deck————
myyyy Captin liiiiiiiies————
fallin————
caaaoooowwwld————
and————————ded!

It was a good party poem. I recited it in the basement, and then everyone upstairs had to come down and hear it, and then Elaine had to call up a friend of hers in the city and I did it on the phone. It got better. "Miss Rasmussen is going to burst a blood vessel," said Elaine. She was a true rebel, despite the editorials she wrote extolling the value of team play and school spirit. I was starting to see some of the

---

4. **Sir John Gielgud.** Classically trained British actor (1904–2000) famed for his elegant bearing and silken voice

virtues in her that I had previously imagined in Dede Petersen.

Bill Swenson had worked for weeks on "All Shook Up," and he looked cool and capable backstage before the curtain went up. His hair was slicked down, he wore heavy eye makeup, and he was dressed in a white suit with gold trim, without a single wrinkle in it. He stood, holding his arms out to the sides, avoiding wrinkling, and practiced moving his lips to "A-wella bless my soul, what'sa wrong with me? I'm itching like a man on a fuzzy tree." Dede knelt, shining his black shoes.

He pretended to be surprised to see me. "What are you doing here? You running the p.a. or what?"

I told him I would be in the show, reciting a poem by Walt Whitman.

"Who? Twitman?" No. Whitman, I said.

"Well, I'm glad I don't have to follow that," he said, with heavy sarcasm. He glanced at my outfit, brown corduroy pants, a green plaid cotton shirt, a charcoal gray sweater vest, and said, "You better change into your stage clothes though."

"These are my stage clothes," I said.

"Oh," he said, his eyebrows raised. "Oh." He smiled. "Well, good luck." He did not know how much luck I had. I had my lucky picture in my pocket, the one of me in the mountains.

> What does Gary bring for good luck?

Dede brushed his forehead with face powder and poofed up his hair. She gave him a light kiss on the lips. "You're going to be great," she said. He smiled. He had no doubt about that. She had put him high on the program, right after "America the Beautiful," a dramatic choral reading from *Antigone*, a solo trumpet rendition of "Nobody Knows the Trouble I've Seen," and a medley of Rodgers and Hammerstein songs performed on the piano by Cheryl Ann Hansen. Then Bill would electrify the crowd with "All Shook Up," and then I would do "O Captain."

> Who is on the program immediately before Gary?

He was Mr. Cool. After Cheryl Ann Hansen's interminable medley, which kids clapped and cheered for only because they knew that her mother had recently died of cancer, Bill grinned at Dede and bounced out on stage and yelled, "Helllllll-ooo baby!" in a Big Bopper[5] voice, and the audience clapped and yelled "Helllllooo baby!" and he yelled, "You knowwwwwwww what I like!" and he was a big hit in the first five seconds. He said it again, "Helllllllllllooo baby!" and the audience yelled back, "Hellllllllllooo baby!" And then Dede carefully set the phonograph needle on the record of "All Shook Up" and Elvis's hoody voice blasted out in the auditorium and Bill started shimmying across the stage and tossing his head like a dustmop. "My friends say I'm acting queer as a bug, I'm in love—huh! I'm all shook up," and on the *huh* he stuck both arms in the air and threw his hip to the left, *huh*, and the audience sang along on the "hmm hmm hmm—oh—yeah yeah"—he was the star of the show right there. Dede ran to look out through a hole in the curtain, leaving me standing by the record player. She was so thrilled, she hopped up and down and squealed.

I could see part of him out there, his white suit hanging loose, the red socks flashing, him pulling out the red satin hanky and tossing it

---

5. **Big Bopper**. J.P. Richardson, rock and roll singer in the 1950s best known for his version of "Chantilly Lace." He died in a plane crash in 1959 along with rock and roll legend Buddy Holly.

---

words for everyday use

ren • di • tion (ren di' shən) n., performance. *The actor won praise for his* rendition *of the Danish prince in Hamlet.*

into the audience, *hmmm hmmm hmmm oh yeah yeah*, and at the end the whole auditorium stood up and screamed. He came off stage bright with sweat, grinning, and went back out and made three deep bows, and threw his hip, *huh*, and came off and Dede wiped his face with a towel and kissed him, and the audience was still screaming and whistling and yelling, "More! More!" and right then Bill made his fateful decision. He went out and did his other number.

It was "Vaya con Dios" by the Conquistadores. Dede put the needle down and the guitars throbbed, and the audience clapped, but Bill hadn't worked as hard on "Vaya con Dios" as on "All Shook Up" and his lips didn't synch very well, but the main problem was that "Vaya con Dios" was "Vaya con Dios," and after "All Shook Up" it seemed like a joke, especially since the Conquistadores were a trio and Bill wasn't. Kids started to laugh, and Bill got mad—perhaps "Vaya con Dios" meant a lot to him personally—and his grim face and his clenched fists made "Vaya con Dios" seem even zanier. Dede ran to the hole in the curtain to see where the hooting and light booing was coming from, and there, standing by the record player, I thought I would help poor Bill out by lightly touching the record with my finger and making the music go flat and sour for a moment.

It was miraculous, the effect this had, like pressing a laugh button. I touched the black vinyl rim and the music warbled, and fifty feet away, people <u>erupted</u> in fits of happiness. I did it again. How wonderful to hear people laugh! and to be able to give them this precious gift of laughter so easily. Then I discovered a speed control that let me slow it down and speed it up. The singers sounded <u>demented</u>, in love one moment, carsick the next. The audience thought this was a stitch. But Bill sort of went to pieces. One prime qualification for a show business career, I would think, is the ability to improvise and go with the audience, but Bill Swenson did not have that ability.

Here he was, rescued from his drippy encore, magically transformed into comedy, and he was too rigid to recognize what a hit he was. His lips stopped moving. He shook his fist at someone in the wings, perhaps me, and yelled a common <u>vulgar</u> expression at someone in the crowd, and wheeled around and walked off.

I didn't care to meet him, so I walked fast right past him onto the stage, and coming out of the bright light into the dark, he didn't see me until I was out of reach. There was still some heavy booing when I arrived at the microphone, and I made a deep English-actor type of bow, with princely flourishes and flutters, and they laughed, and then they were mine all the way. I held on to them for dear life for the next two minutes. I sailed into "O Captain," in my ripest and fruitiest accent, with roundhouse gestures,[6] outflung arms, hand clapped to the forehead————I cried:

> One prime qualification for a show business career, I would think, is the ability to improvise and go with the audience.

What is Bill's encore?

How does Gary "help" Bill?

How does the audience react to Gary's bow?

---

6. **roundhouse gestures**. Wide, sweeping, circular gestures

---

words for everyday use

e • rupt (i rupt′) *vi.*, burst suddenly and violently. *When Mount Vesuvius <u>erupted</u>, it destroyed the city of Pompeii.*

de • men • ted (di men′ təd) *adj.*, insane. *You must be <u>demented</u> if you want to ski down the most dangerous slope.*

vul • gar (vul′ gər) *adj.*, crude and offensive. *When we used <u>vulgar</u> language at home, our mom washed our mouths out with soap.*

AOOWWW CAP-TIN, MYYYYY CAP-TIN,
AOWER———FEEAH-FOOL TWIP EEZ DONE!
TH' SHEEP HAS WETHAH'D———EVIDDY
   RACK!
TH' PRIIIIIIIZE WE SOT———EEZ WON!
BUT———AAAOOOOOOOOWWW
TH' BLEEEEEEEDING DRRROPS———
OF RRRED———
WHEAHH———
ON TH' DECK———
BEEEL SWEN-SON LIIIIIIIES———
FALLIN———
CAAAOOOOWWWLD
———AND———
———DED!

What change does Gary make in the poem?

It wasn't a kind or generous thing to do, but it was successful, especially the "AAAAAOOOOOOOWWWWW" and also the part about Bill Swenson, and at the end there was shouting and whistling and <u>pandemonium</u>, and I left the stage with the audience wanting more, but I had witnessed the perils of success, and did not consider an encore. "Go out and take a bow," said Miss Rasmussen, and out I went, and came back off. Dede and Bill were gone. Dede was not feeling well, said Miss Rasmussen.

I watched the rest of the show standing at the back of the auditorium. The act after me was a girl from the wrong side of the river who did a humorous oral interpretation entitled "Granny on the Phone with Her Minister." The girl had painted big surprise eyebrows and a big red mouth on her so we would know it was comedy, and as the sketch went on, she shrieked to remind us that it was humorous. The joke was that Granny was hard-of-hearing and got the words wrong. Then came an accordionist, a plump young man named David Lee, Barbara's cousin, who was a little overambitious with "Lady of Spain" and should have left out two or three of the variations, and a tap dancer who tapped to a recording of "Nola" and who made the mistake of starting the number all over again after she had made a mistake. I enjoyed watching these dogs, strictly from a professional point of view. And then the choir returned to sing "Climb Every Mountain," and then Miss Rasmussen stood and spoke about the importance of encouraging those with talent and how lucky we should feel to have them in our midst to bring beauty and meaning to our lives. And then the lights came up, and my classmates piled into the aisles and headed for the door and saw me standing in back, modest me, looking off toward the stage. Almost every one of them said how good I was as they trooped past—clapped my shoulder, said, hey, you were great, you should've done more, that was funny—and I stood and patiently endured their attention until the auditorium was empty and then I went home.

At what point does Gary go home?

"You changed the poem a little," Miss Rasmussen said the next day. "Did you forget the line?" "Yes," I said. "Your voice sounded funny," she said. I told her I was nervous. "Oh well," she said, "they seemed to like it anyway."

What does Miss Rasmussen say about Gary's performance?

"Thank you," I said, "thank you very much." ■

---

words for everyday use

pan • de • mon • ium (pan´ də mō´ nē əm) *n.*, wild uproar; chaos. *The <u>pandemonium</u> in the lunchroom reached its height when a food fight broke out.*

How do you think Gary feels about his performance and about himself?

Investigate, *Inquire,* and Imagine

Recall: GATHERING FACTS

1a. Looking at the picture of Gary before the Rocky Mountains, what would you never guess?

2a. What was the watershed moment in Gary's life? What door did it open for him?

3a. What is Bill's "fateful decision"?

Interpret: FINDING MEANING

1b. What do you think Gary would want you to think about him?

2b. Why do you think this moment was crucial to him? How did it mark a change in his life?

3b. What fate does Bill bring on himself through this decision?

Analyze: TAKING THINGS APART

4a. Analyze Gary Keillor's image of himself. What adjectives does he use to describe himself and his thoughts, feelings and ideas? What fantasies does he have about his life?

Synthesize: BRINGING THINGS TOGETHER

4b. In what ways is Gary outstanding and in what ways is he a typical high school kid? What talent does he have that Bill Swenson does not?

Perspective: LOOKING AT OTHER VIEWS

5a. Do you think Gary is justified in slowing down the record on Bill's encore and in using Bill's name to make the audience laugh? Why, or why not?

Empathy: SEEING FROM INSIDE

5b. Why do you think a popular boy like Bill Swenson would make fun of Gary? What is the effect of one group of kids excluding or ridiculing another group? How would you have responded to Bill's unkind comments if you were Gary? How do you think Bill feels after Gary's actions at the talent show?

Understanding *Literature*

DESCRIPTION. Review the definition for **description** in the Handbook of Literary Terms. What is the overall impression you have of Gary's school experience that winter? What descriptive details led you to that impression?

IRONY. Review the definition for **irony** in the Handbook of Literary Terms and the cluster chart you made for Literary Tools on page 667. In "Gary Keillor," the difference between Gary's description of his life, his thoughts, and his dreams, and the reality of that life provides an ironic contrast and contributes to much of the humor of this story. What examples of this sort of irony did you notice as you read?

Writer's Journal

1. Imagine that you are the emcee of the school talent show and must introduce each act. Write a brief **introduction** for both Bill Swenson and Gary Keillor. You will want to give enough of a preview to pique the audience's interest without giving away the surprise of each act.

2. Write a humorous **narrative** like the mother and the truck driver episode that elevates the ordinary to an epiphany (an event that causes a sudden understanding of the nature or meaning of something).

3. Imagine that you are a writer for the school newspaper. Write a **review** of the talent show. You will want to give those who were not there a sense of what they missed as well as give your judgment or opinion of the quality of the performances.

Integrating the Language Arts

Language, Grammar, and Style

USING THE ACTIVE VOICE. Review the Language Arts Survey 3.37, "Making Passive Sentences Active." Determine whether each of the following sentences is written in the passive or the active voice. Rewrite those that are in the passive voice, using the active voice instead.

1. The talent show was enjoyed by all.
2. "All Shook Up" was performed by Bill Swenson before a poetic reading was given by Gary Keillor.
3. Geometry was dreaded by every junior at New Tryon High.
4. Bill Swenson felt embarrassed.
5. Our driveway was ruined by a truck driver.

Speaking and Listening

INTERPRETING POETRY. Locate a copy of Walt Whitman's poem "O Captain! My Captain!" and study it. Poetry comes to life when read aloud. Practice reading this poem the way Gary did in the talent show, for humorous effect. Then develop a different interpretation. You may wish to read it calmly and respectfully or mournfully, or you may take a different emotional approach. How do you think Whitman would have read it? How would Miss Rasmussen have read it? Deliver two different readings for your class. Discuss the different effect that can be achieved with the same words, merely by changing the tone of voice, pacing, and body language.

Study and Research & Media Literacy

RESEARCHING STARS OF THE 1950S. This story refers to many actors, singers, and songs from the 1950s with which you may be unfamiliar. The story will be a richer experience for you, however, if you know something about them. To get the full sense of Gary's experience, locate both recordings of the songs mentioned and films starring the actors cited. You may wish to play the songs and bits of the films for the class to share your findings. If you were updating the story to portray today's high school experience, what actors, singers, and songs would you substitute for those Garrison Keillor remembers? Share these with your class as well.

"Straw Into Gold: The Metamorphosis of the Everyday"
by Sandra Cisneros

Reader's resource

In **"Straw Into Gold: The Metamorphosis of the Everyday,"** Sandra Cisneros gives insights into her own past to show how she has taken advantage of opportunities, despite what some would consider obstacles.

The title of the essay alludes to the fairy tale "Rumpelstiltskin." In this fairy tale, a young woman is told she must spin straw into gold, a task that seems impossible, yet the woman succeeds in her mission.

About *the* AUTHOR

Sandra Cisneros (1954–   ), one of the most powerful Chicana writers in the United States, has won many awards for her work. Her skill blossomed in the late 1970s, when she earned admission to the prestigious University of Iowa Writer's Workshop. At first, she felt like an outsider: "Everyone seemed to have some communal knowledge which I did not have.... My classmates were from the best schools in the country. They had been bred as fine hothouse flowers. I was a yellow weed among the city's cracks." But the recognition that her personal experience, including her childhood in Chicago and her Mexican-American heritage, was unique led Cisneros to find her own literary voice. Cisneros's first book of short stories, *The House on Mango Street* (1983), is based on her childhood in Chicago. Cisneros also incorporates Spanish in her work because she loves the way it "changes the rhythm" of her writing.

Sandra Cisneros's writings include four volumes of poetry, *Bad Boys* (1980), *The Rodrigo Poems* (1985), *My Wicked, Wicked Ways* (1987), and *Loose Woman* (1994); and two volumes of fiction, *The House on Mango Street* (1983) and *Woman Hollering Creek and Other Stories* (1991). She is also the author of a bilingual children's book, *Hairs=Pelitos* (1994).

Reader's Journal

Can you think of a time when you had an opportunity that you passed up, either because you did not recognize it as an opportunity or were fearful of pursuing it? What can you do in the future to recognize opportunities and take advantage of them?

Literary TOOLS

PERSONAL ESSAY. A **personal essay** is a short work of nonfictional prose on a single topic related to the life or interests of the writer. Personal essays are characterized by an intimate and informal style and tone. They are often, but not always, written in the first person. As you read, decide what makes this essay a personal essay.

ANALOGY. An **analogy** is a comparison of two things that are alike in some respects. Often an analogy explains or describes something unfamiliar by comparing it to something more familiar. A *simile* is an expressed analogy; a *metaphor* is an implied analogy. In this essay, Sandra Cisneros uses an event in the fairy tale "Rumpelstiltskin" to create an analogy. As you read, identify the analogy.

Graphic Organizer

In this personal essay, Sandra Cisneros shares details about her life and how they shaped her into becoming a writer. Create a cluster chart showing the people, events, and circumstances that affected Cisneros's writing. Use as many details as you can find. One example has been done for you.

THINGS THAT SHAPED CISNEROS AS A WRITER

poverty

Straw Into Gold

Sandra Cisneros

The Metamorphosis of the Everyday

When I was living in an artists' colony in the south of France, some fellow Latin-Americans who taught at the university in Aix-en-Provence[1] invited me to share a home-cooked meal with them. I had been living abroad almost a year then on an NEA[2] grant, <u>subsisting</u> mainly on French bread and lentils while in France so that my money could last longer. So when the invitation to dinner arrived, I accepted without hesitation. Especially since they had promised Mexican food.

What I didn't realize when they made this invitation was that I was supposed to be involved in preparing this meal. I guess they assumed I knew how to cook Mexican food because I was Mexican. They wanted specifically tortillas, though I'd never made a tortilla in my life.

It's true I had witnessed my mother rolling the little armies of dough into perfect

> *What did the author's hosts want her to make? What did they assume about her?*

circles, but my mother's family is from Guanajuato,[3] *provinciales*,[4] country folk. They only know how to make flour tortillas. My father's family, on the other hand, is *chilango*,[5] from Mexico City. We ate corn tortillas but we didn't make them. Someone was sent to the corner tortilleria to buy some. I'd never seen anybody make corn tortillas. Ever.

Well, somehow my Latino hosts had gotten a hold of a packet of corn flour, and this is what they tossed my way with orders to produce tortillas. *Asi como sea.* Any ol' way, they said and went back to their cooking.

Why did I feel like the woman in the fairy tale who was locked in a room and ordered to spin straw into gold? I had the same sick feeling when I was required to write my critical essay for my MFA[6] exam—the only piece of noncreative writing necessary in order to get my graduate degree. How was I to start? There were rules involved here, unlike writing a poem or story, which I did <u>intuitively</u>. There was a step-by-step process needed and I had better know it. I felt as if making tortillas, or writing

> *What two tasks does the author say seem "impossible"?*

1. **Aixen-Provence** (eks än̩ prō vän̩s'). City in southeastern France
2. **NEA**. National Endowment for the Arts, an organization which funds writers and artists
3. **Guanajuato** (gwä´ nä hwä´ tō). City and state in central Mexico
4. *provinciales* (prō vēn sē ä´ läs). Provincial, or country dwellers
5. *chilango* (chē län' gō). Native of Mexico City
6. **MFA**. Master of Fine Arts

words for everyday use

sub • sist (səb sist') *vi.*, exist; have the necessities of life; nourish oneself. *During a famine, some people are able to <u>subsist</u> on what little grain they can find to eat, but many die.*

in • tu • i • tive • ly (in tōō´ ə tiv lē´) *adv.*, through intuition, which is the ability to know or do something without having to think about it rationally. *Tom seemed to know <u>intuitively</u> that something was going to go wrong; he just had a "feeling."*

Indian Spinning, 1936. Diego Rivera. Phoenix Art Museum, Arizona.

a critical paper for that matter, were tasks so impossible I wanted to break down into tears.

Somehow though, I managed to make those tortillas—crooked and burnt, but edible nonetheless. My hosts were absolutely ignorant when it came to Mexican food; they thought my tortillas were delicious. (I'm glad my mama wasn't there.) Thinking back and looking at the photograph documenting the three of us consuming those lopsided circles I am amazed. Just as I am amazed I could finish my MFA exam (lopsided and crooked, but finished all the same). Didn't think I could do it. But I did.

I've managed to do a lot of things in my life I didn't think I was capable of and which many others didn't think me capable of either. Especially because I am a woman, a Latina, an only daughter in a family of six men. My father would've liked to have seen me married long ago.

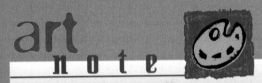

Diego Rivera (1886–1957) is best known for his large, complex murals that illustrated the history of Mexico. Rivera also made more intimate studies of rural people going about everyday tasks, such as this painting. How is this woman like or not like the narrator of this essay?

In our culture, men and women don't leave their father's house except by way of marriage. I crossed my father's threshold with nothing carrying me but my own two feet. A woman whom no one came for and no one chased away.

To make matters worse, I had left before any of my six brothers had ventured away from home. I had broken a terrible <u>taboo</u>. Somehow,

words for everyday use

ta • boo (ta bōō´) *n.*, something forbidden because of social custom or for protection. *The children on the block knew that to cross the street without an adult was an unbreakable <u>taboo</u>.*

looking back at photos of myself as a child, I wonder if I was aware of having begun already my own quiet war.

What "terrible taboo" did the author break?

I like to think that somehow my family, my Mexicanness, my poverty all had something to do with shaping me into a writer. I like to think my parents were preparing me

What factors helped shape Cisneros into a writer?

all along for my life as an artist even though they didn't know it. From my father I inherited a love of wandering. He was born in Mexico City but as a young man he traveled into the U.S. vagabonding. He eventually was drafted and thus became a citizen. Some of the stories he has told about his first months in the U.S. with little or no English surface in my stories in *The House on Mango Street* as well as others I have in mind to write in the future. From him I inherited a sappy heart. (He still cries when he watches the Mexican soaps—especially if they deal with children who have forsaken their parents.)

My mother was born like me—in Chicago but of Mexican descent. It would be her tough, street-wise voice that would haunt all my stories and poems. An amazing woman who loves to draw and read books and can sing an opera. A smart cookie.

When I was a little girl we traveled to Mexico City so much I thought my grandparents' house on La Fortuna, Number 12, was home. It was the only constant in our nomadic ramblings from one Chicago flat to another. The house on Destiny Street, Number 12, in the colonia Tepeyac,[7] would be perhaps the only home I knew, and that nostalgia for a home would be a theme that would obsess me.

My brothers also figured greatly in my art. Especially the oldest two; I grew up in their shadows. Henry, the second oldest and my favorite, appears often in poems I have written and in stories which at times only borrow his nickname, Kiki. He played a major role in my childhood. We were bunkbed mates. We were co-conspirators. We were pals. Until my oldest brother came back from studying in Mexico and left me odd-woman-out for always.

What would my teachers say if they knew I was a writer? Who would've guessed it? I wasn't a very bright student. I didn't much like school because we moved so much and I was always new and funny-looking. In my fifth-grade report card, I have nothing but an avalanche of C's and D's, but I don't remember being that stupid. I was good at art and I read plenty of library books and Kiki laughed at

What was Cisneros like in school?

all my jokes. At home I was fine, but at school I never opened my mouth except when the teacher called on me, the first time I'd speak all day.

When I think how I see myself, it would have to be at age eleven. I know I'm thirty-two on the outside, but inside I'm eleven. I'm the girl in the picture with skinny arms and a crumpled shirt and crooked hair. I didn't like school because all they saw was the outside me. School was lots of rules and sitting with your hands folded and being very afraid all the time. I liked looking out the window and thinking. I liked staring at the girl across the way writing her name over and over again in red ink. I wondered why the boy with the dirty collar in front of me didn't have a mama who took better care of him.

I think my mama and papa did the best they could to keep us warm and clean and never

---

7. **colonia Tepeyac** (cô lō′ nē ä tā pā′ yäc). Neighborhood in Mexico City

words for everyday use

vag • a • bond (va′ gə bänd′) vi., wander or roam about without a fixed home. *During the Depression, some people had to vagabond in search of temporary work and shelter.*

sap • py (sa′pē) adj., overly sentimental or sweet. *My brother thinks that birthday cards with flowers or kittens on them are sappy.*

no • ma • dic (nō ma′dik) adj., roaming from place to place aimlessly. *I tried to give the stray cat a home, but she preferred the nomadic lifestyle.*

no • stal • gia (nä stal′ ja) n., state of sentimental longing, often for something in the past; homesickness. *Whenever Ellen smelled cookies baking, she was overcome with nostalgia for the long-ago days spent in her grandmother's kitchen.*

hungry. We had birthday and graduation parties and things like that, but there was another hunger that had to be fed. There was a hunger I didn't even have a name for. Was this when I began writing?

In 1966 we moved into a house, a real one, our first real home. This meant we didn't have to change schools and be the new kids on the block every couple of years. We could make friends and not be afraid we'd have to say goodbye to them and start all over. My brothers and the flock of boys they brought home would become important characters eventually for my stories—Louie and his cousins, Meme Ortiz and his dog with two names, one in English and one in Spanish.

> What happened in 1966, and what did this mean for Cisneros and her brothers?

My mother flourished in her own home. She took books out of the library and taught herself to garden, producing flowers so envied we had to put a lock on the gate to keep out the midnight flower thieves. My mother is still gardening to this day.

This was the period in my life, that slippery age when you are both child and woman and neither, I was to record in *The House on Mango Street*. I was still shy. I was a girl who couldn't come out of her shell.

How was I to know I would be recording and documenting the women who sat their sadness on an elbow and stared out a window? It would be the city streets of Chicago I would later record, but from a child's eye.

I've done all kinds of things I didn't think I could do since then. I've gone to a <u>prestigious</u> university, studied with famous writers and taken away an MFA degree. I've taught poetry in the schools in Illinois and

> What things has Cisneros done since she was a child that she didn't think she could do?

Texas. I've gotten an NEA grant and run away with it as far as my courage would take me. I've seen the bleached and bitter mountains of the Peloponnesus.[8] I've lived on a Greek island. I've been to Venice[9] twice. In Rapallo, I met Ilona once and forever and took her sad heart with me across the south of France and into Spain.

I've lived in Yugoslavia. I've been to the famous Nice[10] flower market behind the opera house. I've lived in a village in the pre-Alps[11] and witnessed the daily parade of promenaders.[12]

I've moved since Europe to the strange and wonderful country of Texas, land of polaroid-blue skies and big bugs. I met a mayor with my last name. I met famous Chicana and Chicano artists and writers and *políticos.*[13]

Texas is another chapter in my life. It brought with it the Dobie-Piasano Fellowship, a six-month residency on a 265-acre ranch. But most important Texas brought Mexico back to me.

Sitting at my favorite people-watching spot, the snaky Woolworth's counter across the street from the Alamo,[14] I can't think of anything else I'd rather be than a writer. I've traveled and lectured from Cape Cod to San Francisco, to Spain, Yugoslavia, Greece, Mexico, France, Italy, and finally today to Seguin, Texas. Along the way there is straw for the taking. With a little imagination, it can be spun into gold. ∎

> What would she rather be than a writer?

---

8. **Peloponnesus** (pel´ ə pə nē´ səs). Peninsula at the southern tip of Greece

9. **Venice** (ven´ is). A city in Italy on the Mediterranean sea

10. **Nice** (nēs). A port city and summer vacation spot in the south of France

11. **pre-Alps**. The foothills of the Alps, a mountain range in south-central Europe

12. **promenaders**. People strolling in a public place, often a plaza

13. **políticos** (pō lē´ tē cōs). Politicians

14. **Alamo** (al´ ə mō´). Building in San Antonio, Texas, the site of a siege on Texas revolutionaries by Mexican troops in 1836

---

words for everyday use

pres • tig • ious (pre sti´ jəs or pre stē´jəs) *adj.,* highly regarded; honored. *The Nobel Prize is a <u>prestigious</u> award.*

Write about a time you have done something you thought was impossible.

Investigate, Inquire, and Imagine

Recall: GATHERING FACTS

1a. What did the author's friends ask her to prepare for a dinner party? Why was this task difficult for her?

2a. What two traits did Cisneros inherit from her father? What has her mother given her? From whose perspective has she written her stories about Chicago?

3a. For what reasons did the author dislike school?

Interpret: FINDING MEANING

1b. Why did her friends expect her to be able to complete it? Why does she compare the task to the time she had to write a critical essay? What do both tasks have in common?

2b. Why might these traits have helped her as a writer? In what other ways has her family inspired her writing? What period of life do you think has been most influential to her as a writer?

3b. Why do you think the author always felt afraid in school? What does she think about rules? Does she always follow them? Explain.

Analyze: TAKING THINGS APART

4a. What things has the author done that she didn't think she could do? Why did some people, including the author herself, think she was not capable of these things? Outline the obstacles Cisneros faced.

Synthesize: BRINGING THINGS TOGETHER

4b. What things shaped Cisneros into a writer? How has she taken "straw" in her life and spun it into gold?

Perspective: LOOKING AT OTHER VIEWS

5a. Why might the author's former teachers and classmates be surprised to find that Cisneros is a writer? What is Cisneros's "outside me" that people tended to judge her by?

Empathy: SEEING FROM INSIDE

5b. What does Cisneros mean when she says she was "a girl who couldn't come out of her shell"? Have you ever felt the way she did? Explain.

Understanding *Literature*

PERSONAL ESSAY. Review the definition for **personal essay** in the Handbook of Literary Terms. What personal information did you learn about Cisneros from this essay, and how does this information relate to her writing? How might knowing more about an author's life influence the way you read or understand his or her writings?

ANALOGY. Review the definition for **analogy** in the Handbook of Literary Terms. What is the analogy that Cisneros makes about turning straw into gold? What does the analogy refer to the first time she uses it? When she brings the analogy up again at the end, what is she trying to explain to readers?

Writer's Journal

1. Imagine Sandra Cisneros is coming to visit your class. Write five **questions** you'd like to ask her about her life or writing. Indicate why you would like to ask those specific questions.

2. Your own life might contain a multitude of stories waiting to be written. Think of three **story ideas** based on people or events from your life.

3. In the essay, the author describes herself at age eleven. Write a **character sketch** describing what you were like and what you did when you were that age.

Integrating the Language Arts

Language, Grammar, and Style

TRANSITIVE AND INTRANSITIVE VERBS. Read the Language Arts Survey 3.61, "Transitive and Intransitive Verbs." Then underline the verbs in the following sentences and identify them as transitive or intransitive depending on how they are used.

1. Cisneros's friends gave her a cooking task.
2. All Mexican women can make tortillas; at least her friends thought so.
3. Cisneros could write; she couldn't cook anything very well.
5. The hosts didn't know about tortillas.
6. Cisneros read books, but she didn't have domestic skills.

Applied English

FILLING OUT A GRANT APPLICATION. In this essay, Sandra Cisneros mentions getting an NEA grant to support her writing. Imagine you are trying to get grant money to help support your favorite cause. The first essay question on the grant application is "Describe your project or cause." Answer the question in as much detail as possible.

Study and Research

RESEARCHING LATIN AMERICA. Consult a map to determine how many countries are in Latin America. Make a list of the countries. Then choose one country. When was it colonized by Spain or Portugal, and in what year did it gain its independence? What languages are spoken there? Who are some writers native to that country? Prepare a brief report about the country you chose.

Vocabulary

RESEARCHING ETYMOLOGIES. In your dictionary or encyclopedia, find a chart of Indo-European languages. Which languages are descended from Latin, and in what language branch are Latinate languages classified? To which branch does English belong? Look up the following English words in your dictionary and tell what language it is derived from. Not all these words are derived from Indo-European languages.

1. chimpanzee
2. jungle
3. ketchup
4. magic
5. skirt
6. chocolate
7. slogan
8. subsist
9. taboo
10. woman

Guided Writing

Much like a research paper, an **I-Search** project requires you to dig for and into sources, compile and record your findings, and report out in both written and oral form. However, unlike a research paper, an I-Search tends to be less formal, more customized and personal. Your personality will come through.

THE RESEARCH (OR I-SEARCH) PAPER

Want to play the guitar? Acoustic, classical, folk, country, steel, rock? Anybody play whom you know personally? Whose style do you admire: Chet Atkins, Les Paul, Stevie Ray Vaughan, Jimi Hendrix, Eric Clapton? Anyone else? What can great guitarists teach you? Where can you take lessons? How much do lessons cost? Will you need to borrow, rent, or buy a guitar? What other equipment might you need at some point? Want to play in your schools jazz band? Want to start up your own band? Want to write and record your own music? What does a time line for your guitar mastery look like? Want to teach guitar?

The writing you will produce in this lesson is informative: the person posing the questions above wants some answers about a perceived interest or talent. You, too, are invited to ponder your own talents and consider what you might do to develop them. Consider this task as a personal career investigation. Tell the story of where you go, why, and what you find. Don't think of this as a formal research paper, although documentation is required; rather, think of this assignment as an invitation to explore a topic that you have a need to know about *now*. This type of writing is frequently called an **I-Search.**

WRITING ASSIGNMENT. Write an I-Search paper about a talent or potential talent that you would like to develop or learn more about. Include proper documentation for the sources you use to research your topic.

Student Model

excerpted from "Where Do I Want My Talents to Take Me?" I-Search Paper by Neil Rosen

Isaac is twenty-eight now. He always wears a t-shirt, jeans, and a ball cap over his short brown hair, and usually he's chewing gum. He talks fast and nearly every sentence is punctuated with the word "man."

"I was fourteen when I first started playing, man. My dad played guitar when he was young and that is basically what got me started. He had an old Gibson that he could play some Hank Williams on. I didn't care a whole lot for country, man, but Dad taught me some chords and eventually I learned how to play a simple country song. But I was a kid, and I thought country music was for the hicks.

"So I listened to a lot of rock and roll music. I would listen to a song on the radio and then I would try to remember how it went and play it. If I liked the song enough, I would buy the CD, and then play it over and over, each time listening and figuring out the fingering. It was slow learning that way, man, but it made me feel good too when I would finally get a piece down.

"In high school I was in a band called Bad Temper, probably fitting because we were all sort of a bunch of rebels with an attitude. We didn't sound very good, but it was a real kick to play together. A couple times we had gigs at this youth center; playing in front of an audience has got to be the greatest rush there is. It was then that I knew that I wanted to make music for a living. Of course, now I know how tough that is. So I teach and play in a band called Loop. And, you know, man, I get nearly as much satisfaction from teaching punks like you as from the playing." He laughed then.

EXAMINING THE MODEL. Neil does want to play guitar, or at least play better. Since he started lessons less than a year ago, the guitar has become the most important interest in his life, even more important than his snowboard. So he decided he would dig further, seeing what options are available for the guitarist. As part of his search he interviewed his guitar teacher. Notice how Neil tells the story of the interview, giving the information in the words of Isaac. Neil captures his character as well as the information that Isaac provides.

Prewriting

IDENTIFYING YOUR AUDIENCE. For this assignment, your audience is your teacher, of course, but also your classmates. It is human nature to be curious about other people (that's partially why the tabloids at the checkout counter of grocery stores are so popular). Your classmates do want to know who you are, where you are headed, and how you got pointed in that direction. And this should be an important document for *you*. Sometimes you need to write it out before you really realize what you think about it. If you write out your insights, you will be able to better act upon them.

WRITING WITH A PLAN. It's critical in this lesson to map out where your writing is headed. Start by choosing something you want to know more about. Maybe it's something you've been interested in since you were five years old and were asked what you wanted to be when you grew up. Whatever the topic you choose, you **must** be curious about it. Think about it for a few days; always have it somewhere close in mind. The topic needs to be yours, not something that you think your teacher will like, or not something that you already know a lot about, or not something that you think will be easy. How do you picture yourself once you're out of high school, out of college? Under a hard hat running your own construction company? Wearing a uniform and flying a plane? Giving physical therapy to accident

FINDING YOUR VOICE. Voice is the way a writer uses language to reveal his or her personality and attitude toward topic, form, and audience. A writer's tone, word choice, and sentence structure all convey voice. For this assignment you will want to write and share insights and discoveries of particular value to you. So often teachers require that you write in third person only, but this writing is less formal. Write from your mind and heart in first person: "I can spend hours searching for sand dollars along the California coast," or "As I watched the foal emerge, I knew I wanted to become a veterinarian."

CHOOSING YOUR SOURCES. Do not rely on one source; then you are doing a report, not research. One source might not be as informative as you thought it would be, and your final project will be too thin and incomplete. So, if you want to know about the delivery of mail, talk to your mail carrier, but also talk to his supervisor down at the post office, and then you might talk to the supervisor's supervisor, too. Don't worry about getting too much information; it is much easier to cut than to add. As your teacher has instructed, take notes, write source cards, or highlight relevant text. Make sure you know and can account for the origin of anything you plan to use in the paper.

Take care recording information and identifying sources. It's always more difficult to go back to a website, an expert, a book, or a magazine to verify information, so be accurate and complete the first time.

victims? Creating lesson plans for your classroom? However you picture yourself, your topic should focus on what you need to do to get there.

After you have thought about your topic for a few days and are satisfied with it, start by **freewriting** for fifteen minutes. Get down on paper everything you know, everything you want to know about this topic. Perhaps you know little about this topic, but there is something drawing you to it. That's okay! This is a chance for you to dream a little, maybe dream a lot. Common sense is wonderful, but for this assignment, don't let your common sense restrict your dreams. You want to be an astronaut? What will it take? Where can you find out?

INTERVIEWING. This isn't a "go to the encyclopedia" type of paper. You will do some background research, but the substance of your paper, the heart of your search, will be found in people. Ask classmates, friends, and relatives where you might be able to find experts in this field. An expert doesn't have to be someone with degrees or who has written books. Remember Neil and the guitar? He knew he wanted to interview his teacher and included that interview in his paper.

Contact your experts early enough so that you can set up interviews at their convenience. Experts are usually busy people, and they don't like to waste time. But they are also experts because they love what they do, so they will probably be enthusiastic to share their knowledge and love with someone who is genuinely interested in their field. However, you will want to have some basic background information before you approach the expert to avoid asking trite, irrelevant, or yes/no questions. Don't ask a stage actor, for example, if it's difficult to memorize so many lines. Ask instead what tricks she has learned to make the memorization process easier or less painful. Before you interview, check and see what other sources are available: books, film, newspaper or magazine articles, and websites. Be informed as much as you can showing up for the interview.

Once you have arranged an interview, determine how you will record the information. Most people are comfortable if you take written notes; be sure that you ask their permission if you are going to use a cassette recorder. It is important to get the information down quickly and accurately, not only so you don't forget it, but also because you will need to have a **works cited page** at the end of the paper. On this page you will list your sources, in addition to the interviews that you conduct.

Neil filled in the graphic organizer to help him keep track of where he was going as he did his research. He filled in the first two columns as he thought of his topic. He filled in the second two as he found the information.

Student Model—Graphic Organizer

K	W	S	L
*What do you think you **know**?*	*What do you **want to learn**?*	*Where will you **search**?*	*What have you **learned**?*
I know *I like music, especially guitar, had my dad's, got a new one, girlfriend likes it too. Like the guitar shop and gives lessons to make money.*	***I want to know*** *if I could make a living in music.*	***I will search:*** *Interview, books, web site, internet.* *Field, Shelley. Career Opportunities in the Musician. New York: Billboard Books, 1997.* *Penske, Isaac. Personal interview, 3 Feb. 2000.* *www.musicmates. com>4 Feb. 2000.*	***I learned:*** *For every Santana, there are hundreds who can't get a contract.* *Don't have to have a college degree.* *Have to join a union.* *Other jobs for musicians: floorshow band, dance bands (part-time).* *Give lessons.* *Write music.*

Drafting

Tell the story! An I-Search paper is a narrative about your journey of discovery. Consequently, use first person narration. Include the steps you took from the beginning to end. As you tell what you have found out, also tell what is going on in your mind; is your attitude toward the topic changing? How? Why? It might be easier if you divide your paper into four sections, following the graphic organizer:

1. What I **knew**
2. What I **want to learn** (why I'm writing this paper)
3. Where I **searched** for information
4. What I **learned**, or didn't learn

To keep your narrative voice consistent, you will have to take some of the answers that your experts gave you and convert them to keep the flow. *Do not* set up the paper like this:

Question: When did you start playing guitar?
Answer: When I was ten.
Question: What kind of guitar was it?
Answer: Yamaha.

Rather, tell a story:

     Isaac was ten when he first started playing. "I fell in love with Stevie Ray Vaughan's music from the radio, and I listened to it all the time," he said. "All that fall I begged my folks for a guitar, so finally that Christmas, they gave me a

Language, Grammar, and Style

Documenting Sources

IDENTIFYING PROPERLY CITED SOURCES. When writing any research paper, you need to credit the sources you use. Readers may wish to verify your research or read the complete text. Also, citing sources protects you from plagiarism, using sources and failing to credit them. You must identify sources when you directly quote, summarize or paraphrase, or use a fact or statistic unique to a source.

To quote an author's exact words, put the exact words in quotation marks and reference the last name and the page where you found those words.

At times, instead of using a direct quotation, you may paraphrase an author's idea in your essay. When you paraphrase, you're putting someone else's idea into your own words. Even though you are paraphrasing, you must still credit the author by referencing the last name and page where you found the idea. See Language Arts Survey 5.43, "Paraphrasing, Summarizing, and Quoting" for additional information. See also the example below.

    Another problem is that because they have another source of income, part-timers sometimes take less money for gigs, thus lowering the pay scale for all musicians (Levine 7).

continued on page 690

Fixing Citation of Sources.

You need to cite sources correctly. Explain how you would fix the documentation of each source below.

(Field, 241)

(p.191 Field)

(Mike Levine 7)

Using Properly Cited Sources.

Read through your paper again. Be sure you have handled quotations correctly. Check carefully the paraphrased ideas. Is your bibliography page done correctly?

> "I don't have a lot of respect for talent. Talent is genetic. It's what you do with it that counts."
>
> —Martin Ritt

Reflecting

Writing a good I-search paper is one of the more dificult tasks asked of students. What was the most difficult part of the project for you? What do you wish you would have done differently? What did you learn aobut your research and organizational skills? The subject matter? What future reading or research might you be compelled to do? How did your understanding of your goals change or increase?

used Yamaha classic—I think it cost them about 30 bucks. It was the best Christmas present I ever got." Isaac paused here, watched through the window the busy traffic going by, and when he looked back, he had a funny look in his eye. "I still have that guitar, and when my boy is old enough, I'll give it to him," he said in a soft voice.

The conclusion of this paper is important. This is where you determine what you learned or didn't learn about your topic. Perhaps you learned that driving a truck really isn't as appealing as you had thought: long hours away from home and family, driving in all kinds of weather, and lower wages than you would like. But even learning that is worthwhile; it's better to find out the negatives now than when you are thirty-five.

Self- and Peer Evaluation

Exchange papers with a classmate. As you read through each other's papers, consider the following questions:

- What is the thesis of the paper?
- Is the paper organized in a chronological fashion?
- What transitions are used to aid the papers unity?
- What places in the paper need more detail and explanation?
- What places need less detail and explaination?
- Comment on the coherence of the paper. Does the writer ever wander?
- What verbs of being (*is, are, was, were*) can be replaced with strong, active verbs?
- Point out any places where the writer should document information.
- Summarize in a sentence what the writer has learned.

Revising and Proofreading

Review your self- and peer evaluations. Revise your writing after considering these comments. Check the coherence of the paper. Does it progress in a logical manner? If there are any gaps in the narrative, go back and fill in the gaps.

Publishing and Presenting

Your final product should be a paper that you are proud to present to your classmates. When you have done your best, share your work. You may wish to publish the papers as an anthology. Your high school library might wish to shelve a copy, or you might post your papers on your school's website. Perhaps you and your classmates could create a bulletin board complete with portraits and papers.

"Where Do I Want My Talents to Take Me?"
I-Search Paper by Neil Rosen

I started playing guitar about eight months ago when I was still
fifteen. I don't really remember exactly what motivated me to start
playing guitar, but I suppose it was mostly my girlfriend's
influence. She had just gotten an acoustic guitar for Christmas, and
she had even started taking lessons at a local guitar shop. I had
been interested in guitar before that, mainly from seeing
performances of local guitarists that I knew. I play trombone in
the high school band and bass trombone in one of the school jazz
bands. I like playing in jazz band, but I always thought the
guitarists had the coolest parts.

So I started playing with my dad's old classical guitar with the
nylon strings. It had been in my room for ages, gathering dust
underneath my bed, and it was missing a string. He had bought it in
1970, using part of his first paycheck after college to pay for it.
He thought it cost 70 bucks then (Land). It is a Wilson, not
exactly a famous name like Fender or Martin or Gibson.
Unfortunately, it was out of tune so I couldn't do much. Not that I
had the ability anyway.

Eventually I talked my parents into letting me take lessons at
the same guitar shop my girlfriend went to. I paid to restring the
guitar and I started lessons playing that old classical. My lessons
were every week at fifteen dollars a lesson.

That lasted about a month before I realized that I wanted to
play electric, not classical. Todd, the owner of the shop, was
trying to sell some of his low-end guitars in order to make room
for new ones. So, after a couple weeks of trying to remember to do
the chores that my parents think build character (take out the
garbage, pick up the dog poop), I talked them into letting me buy
an electric guitar. I bought a new guitar, choosing a blue one, and
a small Ibanez GT-10 practice amp. I was really excited. I later
realized that it wasn't as cool a guitar as I thought it was.

Eight months later, I still hang out at that guitar shop. It's a
pretty cool place; there are close to a hundred guitars hanging on
the walls, priced anywhere from $89.95 to $3000. The people who
work there are friendly and funny. I'm wondering if being a
professional musician is something I should consider as a career.
It would be a fun place to work, so that's why I decided to
interview my teacher, Isaac Penske.

Before I talked to Isaac, though, I wanted to find out more about
what a career as a musician would cover, so my first stop was the
library.

I admit my first interest was in becoming a recording star. I knew that the big groups like U2 and Metallica could make millions of dollars a year. However, what I hadn't realized was that for every Carlos Santana there are hundreds of groups who can't even get a recording contract (Field 7). I was beginning to realize that owning a guitar did not guarantee success. That was on the down side. On the up side, though, I found out that unlike people in many professions, musicians do not have to have a college degree in order to play professionally. Many of them do, but it's not a requirement. However, professional musicians do need to be able to play very well. In order to get jobs (gigs) I found it is important to join a union (Field 241).

I also found out that there are lots of jobs for musicians, even if they are not recording or making music videos. One of these is as a floorshow band. Such bands perform in nightclubs, hotels, bars, and concert halls, earning anywhere from $250 to $10,000 per engagement (Field 191). Show bands travel a lot, sometimes being on the road for weeks at a time. A step below the show band is the dance band. Dance bands play in schools, bars, club, cafes, hotels, and for private parties (Field 194). Most dance bands play part time, so the members have to have another job to help support themselves. They only make $100 to $1500 per engagement which is maybe enough if one is content to be a part-timer (weekend warrior). However, this also creates problems. Full-time musicians frequently resent these players because they feel that the part-timers take some jobs away from them. Another problem is that because they have another source of income, part-timers sometime take less money for gigs, thus lowering the pay scale for all musicians (Levine 7). Probably the best compromise, if you can't afford to be a full time musician, is to find a job that is related to the music industry like teaching or working in a music store. I was back to Isaac.

Isaac is twenty-eight now. He always wears a t-shirt, jeans, and a ball cap over his short brown hair, and usually he's chewing gum. He talks fast and nearly every sentence is punctuated with the word "man."

"I was fourteen when I first started playing, man. My dad played guitar when he was young and that is basically what got me started. He had an old Gibson that he could play some Hank Williams on. I didn't care a whole lot for country, man, but Dad taught me some chords and eventually I learned how to play a simple country song. But I was a kid, and I thought country music was for the hicks.

"So I listened to a lot of rock and roll music. I would listen to a song on the radio and then I would try to remember how it went and play it. If I liked the song enough, I would buy the CD, and then play it over and over, each time listening and figuring out the fingering. It was slow learning that way, man, but it made me feel good too when I would finally get a piece down.

"In high school I was in a band called Bad Temper, probably fitting because we were all sort of a bunch of rebels with an attitude. We didn't sound very good, but it was a real kick to play together. A couple times we had gigs at this youth center; playing in front of an audience has got to be the greatest rush there is. It was then that I knew that I wanted to make music for a living. Of course, now I know how tough that is. So I teach and play in a band called Loop. And, you know, man, I get nearly as much satisfaction from teaching punks like you as from the playing." He laughed then.

Isaac's inspirations are John Petrucci, Nono Bettencourt, and Paco Delucia. His style of playing is whatever he feels like and he seems to play it all: rock, country, flamenco, and classical. You name it and he can play it. He told me that he plays an average of two hours a day. I only play about half an hour a day. He also plays other instruments such as the bass guitar, piano, drums, and basically any stringed instrument. Since he knows how stringed instruments work, he can play on a basic level.

After talking to Isaac I was beginning to realize how difficult it is to make it in the music industry. He told me about a website that he sometimes looked at to find jobs playing: <www.musicmates.com>. This site lists club schedules, bands seeking musicians, musicians seeking bands, and teachers for hire. I can see there are a lot of guys out there like me who want to make it in music, but the information on the site also is a big reality check.

Some friends and I get together and jam once a week. A couple of months ago I bought a new seven string Ibanez and a much bigger amp. It sounds great! I don't know if we'll keep playing as a group, but now it's fun, and I know that I'll keep playing. And I hope that some day maybe I can write my own music, find some gigs, and give lessons too. I know enough not to count on being a star, but playing music and getting paid for it sounds really good to me.

Bibliography

Field, Shelly. Career Opportunities in the Music Industry. New York: Facts on File, 1995.

Land, Scott. Personal interview, 1 Feb. 2000.

Levine, Mike. How to Be a Working Musician. New York: Billboard Books, 1997.

Music Mates Web Site. Copyright 2000. 4 Feb. 2000. <www.musicmates.com>.

Penske, Isaac. Personal interview, 3 Feb. 2000. <www.musicmates.com> 4 Feb. 2000.

UNIT 8 review
What Is Talent?

Words for Everyday Use

Check your knowledge of the following vocabulary words from the selections in this unit. Write short sentences using each of these words in context to make the meaning clear. To review the definition or usage of a word, refer back to the page number(s) listed or the Glossary of Words for Everyday Use.

affinity, 642	fluke, 645	pandemonium, 676	reprimand, 651
alienation, 629	formula, 634	per capita, 660	sappy, 682
alleviate, 650	gravity, 672	perimeter, 643	skeptical, 645
aptitude, 651	hygiene, 634	perpetual, 629	subsist, 680
binge, 661	idiom, 654	phenomenon, 642	subtle, 669
consensus, 645	improvise, 652	preclude, 651	surly, 671
crossover, 661	intuitively, 680	prestigious, 683	taboo, 681
demented, 675	jubilant, 646	prevail, 669	tissue, 634
enterprising, 670	masochism, 629	prose, 629	transcend, 651
erupt, 675	monitor, 633	queasy, 629	transcribe, 652
exile, 643	mutter, 633	recite, 635	vagabond, 682
express, 636	nomadic, 682	redoubt, 660	vulgar, 675
flamboyamt, 661	nostalgia, 682	regimen, 629	
flee, 643	outstrip, 661	rendition, 674	

Literary Tools

Define each of the following terms, giving concrete examples of how they are used in the selections in this unit. To review a term, refer to the page number(s) indicated or to the Handbook of Literary Terms.

abstract, 649	description, 632, 667	personal essay, 679
aim, 627, 649	essay, 658	personification, 639
analogy, 627, 679	image, 632	poetry, 632
article, 658	irony, 667	point of view, 639

Reflecting on your reading

Genre Studies

1. **PERSONAL ESSAY.** The selections by Annie Dillard and Sandra Cisneros in this unit could both be considered **personal essays**. Why? What personal information do you learn about each author in reading her essay?

2. **SHORT STORY.** Short stories use **description** to make their scenes come alive for the reader. Identify some descriptive details in "Geraldine Moore the Poet" and "Gary Keillor." What overall mood do these details convey?

3. **BIOGRAPHY AND AUTOBIOGRAPHY.** The selection "Becoming a Composer" is a **biography** of Hikari Oe, while the selection from *The Man Who Listens to Horses* is an **autobiography** written by Monty Roberts. From what point of view is each written? What insights do we gain from an

autobiography that we do not from a biography? Which selection do you think might be more objective, and why?

4. **ARTICLE/ESSAY.** Review the definition for *article* in the Handbook of Literary Terms. What makes an **article** different from an **essay**? Considering the article "Where Stars Are Born" as an essay, discuss how the author creates unity and coherence in his essay.

Thematic Studies

5. **BECOMING A WRITER.** Compare the theme of "Geraldine Moore the Poet" with that of "Straw into Gold." Who can become a writer or poet, according to these selections? What does each selection suggest is the best inspiration or subject matter for a writer or poet?

6. **OVERCOMING ADVERSITY.** What adversity does Monty have to overcome in the selection from *The Man Who Listens to Horses*? What adversity does Hikari have to overcome in "Becoming a Composer"? In what ways are their talents remarkable?

7. **UNEXPECTED TALENT.** What talent does Gary Keillor's character discover he has? What talent does Geraldine Moore have? Why are these talents surprising to either the main characters themselves or to other people around them? Explain, using evidence from the story.

8. **TALENT.** What does Annie Dillard's essay suggest is necessary for a person to be talented at something? Does the article "Where Stars Are Born" support this view of talent? Does the essay "Becoming a Composer" support this idea as well?

for your READING LIST

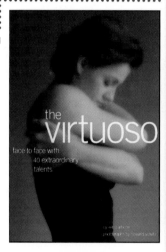

The Virtuoso: Face to Face with 40 Extraordinary Talents by Ken Carbone, photographs by Howard Schatz. This intriguing book pairs spirited profiles of extraordinary people with intimate portraits to reveal what makes truly exceptional people tick. Some, like Muhammad Ali and Mikhail Baryshnikov, are world famous while others are relatively unknown. But all are among the best at what they do, whether it's playing harmonica, drawing maps, or designing typography. Essays by noted figures—Frank Deford on skill, Judith Jamison on mentors, John Russel on genius, and Peter Blake on vision—provide a thoughtful context for exploring the subject of virtuosity.

Independent Reading Activity

INTERVIEW. Interview someone you know who is talented at what he or she does. You may choose to interview a family member, teacher, acquaintance, or anyone you know that is exceptionally good at doing something. Refer to the Language Arts Survey 4.14, "Conducting an Interview" for tips. Write up your interview and compile all of the class interviews into an anthology.

Selections for Additional Reading

Who Says I Can't? by Mary C. Ryan. In this fast-paced, humorous novel, Tessa tries out for student director of the school talent show to exact revenge on a classmate who has insulted her.

What's so Funny about Ninth Grade? by Catherine Clark. After her routine in the school talent show appears to be a failure, Sheila loses her self-confidence as a performer and is afraid to audition for the spring musical.

School's Out, 1936. Allan Rohan Crite. National Museum of American Art, Washington, DC.

Relationships

" A friend may well be reckoned the masterpiece of Nature. "

—*Ralph Waldo Emerson*

➤ If you would be loved, love, and be lovable.
> —*Benjamin Franklin*

➤ Relationships. That's all there really is. There's your relationship with the dust that just blew in your face, or with the person who just kicked you end over end...You have to come to terms, to some kind of equilibrium, with those people around you, those people who care for you, your environment.
> —*Leslie Marmon Silko*

➤ Relationships are like pressures that push you in 36 directions of the compass. But, as in a crowded streetcar, if you learn how to maintain your balance against all the weights, you might arrive at yourself.
> —*Diana Chang*

➤ It no longer bothers me that I may be constantly searching for father figures; by this time, I have found several and dearly enjoyed knowing them all.
> —*Alice Walker*

➤ Happiness is having a large, loving, caring, close-knit family in another city.
> —*George Burns*

➤ To act the part of a true friend requires more conscientious feeling than to fill with credit and complacency any other station or capacity in social life.
> —*Sarah Ellis*

➤ The easiest kind of relationship is with ten thousand people, the hardest is with one.
> —*Joan Baez*

➤ It is the things in common that make relationships enjoyable, but it is the little differences that make them interesting.
> —*Todd Ruthman*

➤ If you're in a relationship and you want to make it work, you have to be a little selfless at times.
> —*Montel Williams*

"Being in Love"

by Marvin Bell

Reader's resource

"**Being in Love**" was originally published in Marvin Bell's third collection of poetry, *Residue of Song*, in 1974, and was reprinted thirteen years later in his collection *New and Selected Poems*. In this poem Bell plays with language as he discusses the problems of being in love.

Bell commented about writing this poem: " 'Being in Love' was a lot of fun to write. The phrase itself is 'loaded.' When you hear those three words, you have a definite feeling about them. I liked playing with the language, using the words again and again so that they stand for more and more. In my poem, the three words 'being in love' are the beginning and the end."

About the AUTHOR

Known as one of America's most prestigious contemporary poets, **Marvin Bell** (1937–) is also an accomplished essayist, critic, editor, and professor. He was born in New York City and grew up on Long Island. Before Bell decided to concentrate on writing poetry, he was a musician, a photographer, and a potter. He now divides his time between Iowa City, Iowa, where he teaches at the University of Iowa, and Port Townsend, Washington. He has published seventeen books of poetry and related writings.

When he was young, Bell thought "that poetry was written in the language of earlier times, expressing flowery sentiments in ways certain to embarrass any red-blooded American boy or girl." But he learned that he was wrong when he realized poetry resembles song lyrics. "Writing poetry is always about being young," says Bell, "because each poem is a fresh beginning, a new world of words to explore, a chance for surprise or a miracle . . . Poetry finds words for what life feels like, and feelings have staying power."

Reader's Journal

Describe a time when your love was not reciprocated.

Literary TOOLS

TONE. **Tone** is the emotional attitude toward the reader or toward the subject implied by a literary work. Examples of the different tones that a work may have include familiar, ironic, playful, sarcastic, serious, and sincere. As you read "Being in Love," determine its tone.

REPETITION. **Repetition** is the writer's conscious reuse of a sound, word, phrase, sentence, or other element. In this poem, Marvin Bell repeats the phrase "being in love" and adds to it in interesting ways.

Organizer

As you read, make a cluster chart like the one below. The center oval should say "being in love." Each connected oval should include an example of the extended phrase. Two examples have been done for you.

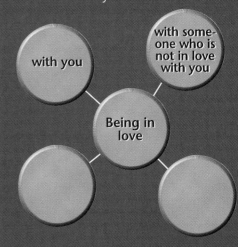

Being in Love

Marvin Bell

with someone who is not in love with
you, you understand my <u>predicament</u>.
Being in love with you, who are not
in love with me, you understand my dilemma.
Being in love with your being in love
with me, which you are not, you understand

the difficulty. Being in love with your
being, you can well imagine how hard it is.
Being in love with your being you,
no matter you are not your being being in
love with me, you can appreciate and pity
being in love with you. Being in love

with someone who is not in love, you know
all about being in love when being in love
is being in love with someone who is not
in love being with you, which is
being in love, which you know only too well,
Love, being in love with being in love. ■

> With whom is the speaker in love?

> What does the speaker expect from the person he or she loves?

words for everyday use	**pre • dic • a • ment** (pri di′ kə mənt) *n.,* complicated, perplexing situation. *Not knowing how to change the baby's diaper, the babysitter found himself in a <u>predicament</u>.*

In the Sky, 1983. Marc Chagall. Marc Chagall Collection, Saint-Paul-de-Vence, France.

art note

Marc Chagall (1887–1985) painted mystical visions of lovers in ecstasy. What about this drawing conveys the mood of the poem?

How would you respond if someone wrote a poem like this about you?

Investigate, *Inquire,* and Imagine

Recall: GATHERING FACTS

1a. What does the speaker believe the person he or she addresses in the poem understands? can appreciate and pity? knows?

2a. How does the speaker define love?

3a. With what phrase does this poem begin and end?

Interpret: FINDING MEANING

1b. Why might the person being addressed in the poem understand, appreciate and pity, and know these things?

2b. What do you think the speaker means by this?

3b. Why might the poet might have chosen to begin and end the poem with the same phrase?

Analyze: TAKING THINGS APART

4a. Identify the ways in which the speaker experiences "being in love." Identify the ways in which the person the speaker addresses in the poem experiences "being in love." Compare and contrast the speaker's definitions for "love" and for "being in love."

Synthesize: BRINGING THINGS TOGETHER

4b. In your own words, summarize the relationship between the speaker and the person the speaker addresses in the poem. Do you think there is more than one way to interpret their relationship, and therefore this poem? Explain.

Perspective: LOOKING AT OTHER VIEWS

5a. Do you think the speaker would continue being in love with the person he or she addresses in the poem if the person addressed were to return the speaker's feelings? Why, or why not?

Empathy: SEEING FROM INSIDE

5b. Imagine that you are the speaker. What might your motivation be for sharing your feelings about being in love with the person with whom you are in love? How do you, as the speaker, feel about love in general?

Understanding *Literature*

TONE. Review the definition for **tone** in the Handbook of Literary Terms. How would you describe the tone of the poem? In what ways does the author establish this tone?

REPETITION. Review the definition for **repetition** in the Handbook of Literary Terms and the cluster chart you made for Literary Tools on page 699. Which phrase is constantly repeated throughout the poem? Where is this phrase turned around and to what effect? What revelations are made with the repetition of "being in love"?

Writer's Journal

1. Imagine you are the speaker. Write a **greeting card** to express your feelings toward the person you love.

2. Imagine you are the person addressed in the poem and the speaker has just expressed his feelings of love for you. Write an informal **note** expressing the type of relationship you wish to have with the speaker.

3. Imagine you are the speaker. Write **song lyrics** to convince the person you love to reconsider the situation and return your love.

Integrating the Language Arts

Language, Grammar, and Style

INTERROGATIVE PRONOUNS. Read the Language Arts Survey 3.57, "Interrogative Pronouns." Then identify each interrogative pronoun below. Remember that to function as an interrogative pronoun, a pronoun must interrogate, or ask a question.

1. What is the most popular subject of poetry?
2. With whom is the speaker in love?
3. Whose heart does he want to win?
4. Which line is the most difficult to understand?
5. What Bell thought when he was young was that poetry used old-fashioned language.

Media Literacy

RESEARCHING ON THE INTERNET. Use the Internet to find another poem about unrequited love. You might do a search for "love poems" or "unrequited love." Then write a short essay comparing and contrasting a poem of your choice with Marvin Bell's "Being in Love." Before you begin writing, review the Language Arts Survey 2.27, "Choosing a Method of Organization." When your essay is complete, ask a classmate to evaluate it. Your peer reviewer might want to review the Language Arts Survey 2.38, "How to Evaluate a Piece of Writing" and 2.39, "How to Deliver Helpful Criticism." After receiving input from your peer reviewer, rewrite your essay.

Collaborative Learning & Media Literacy

BIBLIOGRAPHY. With a classmate, compile an extended bibliography of Marvin Bell's writings, including articles. One of you should do research in your school library. The other should do research on the Internet. Then compare your lists to make sure you have not omitted any works. Finally, incorporate your findings. You might want to review the Language Arts Survey 5.40, "Making Bibliographies and Bibliography Cards."

Literary TOOLS

CHARACTER. A **character** is a person who figures in the action of a literary work. A *static character* is one who does not change during the course of the action. A *dynamic character* is one who does change. As you read, determine whether Luis is a static or dynamic character.

CONFLICT. A **conflict** is a struggle between two forces in a literary work. A struggle that takes place between a character and some outside force is called an *external conflict*. A struggle that takes place within a character is called an *internal conflict*.

Graphic Organizer

As you read, make a chart. On the left list conflicts Luis has in the story. On the right, tell whether the conflict is external or internal.

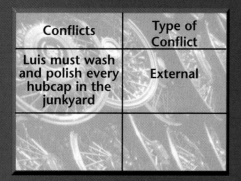

Conflicts	Type of Conflict
Luis must wash and polish every hubcap in the junkyard	External

Reader's Journal

What would you be willing to do to fit into a group?

"Catch the Moon"

by Judith Ortiz Cofer

Reader's resource

"Catch the Moon" appears in Judith Ortiz Cofer's collection of short stories, *An Island Like You* (1996). The Puerto Rican boys and girls depicted in these stories are all struggling in different ways to determine their futures as they advance from adolescence to adulthood. They live in the *barrio*, a Spanish-speaking neighborhood. Luis Cintrón, the protagonist of "Catch the Moon," searches for a way to find meaning in his life after six months in juvenile hall leaves him working off the rest of his time in his father's junk yard.

About *the* AUTHOR

Born in Puerto Rico, **Judith Ortiz Cofer** (1952–) emigrated as a child to the United States with her family who spoke Spanish; therefore, it was "a challenge, not only to learn English, but to master it enough to teach it and—the ultimate goal—to write poetry in it." Ortiz Cofer says that her family is one of the main topics of her poetry: "The place of birth itself becomes a metaphor for the things we all must leave behind; the assimilation of a new culture is the coming into maturity by accepting the terms necessary for survival. My poetry is a study of this process of change, assimilation, and transformation."

Besides poetry, Cofer explored her Puerto Rican heritage in a novel, *The Line of the Sun* (1989). The protagonist, Marisol, learns to balance the American and Puerto Rican aspects of her identity. Living in Paterson, New Jersey, she learns about her Puerto Rican heritage mainly through the stories told by her family. Cofer admits that the obsession called "the island" has always been with her. In her fiction, she recreates the scenes of her youth and transforms them with her imagination. *The Latin Deli* (1993) and *The Year of Our Revolution* (1998) contain both short stories and poems. Her story "Nada" won the O'Henry Short Story Prize. Currently Cofer teaches literature and writing at the University of Georgia in Athens.

Catch the Moon

Judith Ortiz Cofer

Luis Cintrón sits on top of a six-foot pile of hubcaps and watches his father walk away into the steel jungle of his car junkyard. Released into his old man's custody after six months in juvenile hall—for breaking and entering—and he didn't even take anything. He did it on a dare. But the old lady with the million cats was a light sleeper, and good with her aluminum cane. He has a scar on his head to prove it.

Where has Luis spent the last six months? Why?

Now Luis is wondering whether he should have stayed in and done his full time. Jorge Cintrón of Jorge Cintrón & Son, Auto Parts and Salvage, has decided that Luis should wash and pol-ish every hubcap in the yard. The hill he is sit-ting on is only the latest couple of hundred wheel covers that have come in. Luis grunts and stands up on top of his silver mountain. He yells at no one, "Someday, son, all this will be yours," and sweeps his arms like the Pope bless-ing a crowd over the piles of car sandwiches and mounds of metal parts that cover this acre of land outside the city. He is the "Son" of Jorge Cintrón & Son, and so far his father has had more than one reason to wish it was plain Jorge Cintrón on the sign.

Where does Luis work? What task has his father assigned him?

Luis has been getting in trouble since he started high school two years ago, mainly because of the "social group" he organized—a bunch of guys who were into harassing the local authorities. Their thing was taking something to the limit on a dare or, better still, doing something dangerous, like breaking into a house, not to steal, just to prove that they could do it. That was Luis's specialty, coming up with very complicated plans, like military strategies, and

What is Luis's "specialty"?

assigning the "jobs" to guys who wanted to join the Tiburones.

Tiburón means "shark," and Luis had gotten the name from watching an old movie about a Puerto Rican gang called the Sharks[1] with his father. Luis thought it was one of the dumbest films he had ever seen. Everybody sang their lines, and the guys all pointed their toes and leaped in the air when they were supposed to be slaughtering each other. But he liked their name, the Sharks, so he made it Spanish and had it air-painted on his black T-shirt with a killer shark under it, jaws opened wide and dripping with blood. It didn't take long for the other guys in the barrio[2] to ask about it.

Man, had they had a good time. The girls were interested too. Luis outsmarted everybody by calling his organization a social club and registering it at Central High. That meant they were legal, even let out of last-period class on Fridays for their "club" meetings. It was just this year, after a couple of botched jobs, that the teachers had started getting suspicious. The first one to go wrong was when he sent Kenny Matoa to *borrow* some "souvenirs" out of Anita Robles's locker. He got caught. It seems that Matoa had been reading Anita's diary and didn't hear her coming down the hall. Anita was supposed to be in the gym at that time but had copped out with the usual female excuse of cramps. You could hear her screams all the way to Market Street.

How did Luis's group get in trouble?

She told the principal all she knew about the Tiburones, and Luis had to talk fast to convince old Mr. Williams that the club did put on cultur-al activities such as the Save the Animals talent

---

1. **Sharks**. Fictional Puerto Rican gang from the movie *West Side Story*
2. **barrio**. Spanish-speaking neighborhood in the United States

words for everyday use

ha • rass (hə ras′) *vt.*, annoy persistently. *The boy harassed the girl by pulling her ponytail repeatedly.*

show. What Mr. Williams didn't know was that the animal that was being "saved" with the ticket sales was Luis's pet boa, which needed quite a few live mice to stay healthy and happy. They kept E.S. (which stood for "Endangered Species") in Luis's room, but she belonged to the club and it was the members' responsibility to raise the money to feed their mascot. So last year they had sponsored their first annual Save the Animals talent show, and it had been a great success. The Tiburones had come dressed as Latino Elvises and did a grand finale to "All Shook Up" that made the audience go wild. Mr. Williams had smiled when Luis talked, maybe remembering how the math teacher, Mrs. Laguna, had dragged him out in the aisle to rock-and-roll with her. Luis had gotten out of that one, but barely.

His father was a problem too. He objected to the T-shirt logo, calling it disgusting and <u>vulgar</u>. Mr. Cintrón prided himself on his own neat, elegant style of dressing after work, and on his man-

ners and large vocabulary, which he picked up by taking correspondence courses in just about everything. Luis thought that it was just his way of staying busy since Luis's mother had died, almost three years ago, of cancer. He had never gotten over it.

All this was going through Luis's head as he slid down the hill of hubcaps. The tub full of soapy water, the can of polish, and the bag of rags had been neatly placed in front of a <u>makeshift</u> table made from two car seats and a piece of plywood. Luis heard a car drive up and someone honk their horn. His father emerged from inside a new red Mustang that had been totaled. He usually <u>dismantled</u> every small feature by hand before sending the vehicle into the *cementerio*,[3] as he called the lot. Luis watched as the most beautiful girl he had ever seen climbed out of a <u>vintage</u> white Volkswagen Bug. She stood in the sunlight

---

3. *cementerio.* Cemetery (Spanish)

words for everyday use

vul • gar (vəl′gər) *adj.*, lacking in cultivation, perception, or taste. *Emily thought the fake flowers on Jessica's dress were <u>vulgar</u>, or lacking in taste.*

make • shift (māk′ shift) *adj.*, crude and temporary substitute. *A <u>makeshift</u> clinic was set up by the accident site with a table made of plywood and sawhorses.*

dis • man • tle (dis man′ təl) *vt.*, take to pieces. *Jed <u>dismantled</u> the bookcase and placed the disassembled boards in the moving truck.*

vin • tage (vin′ tij) *adj.*, dating from the past. *The <u>vintage</u> ice cream maker was made in the 1930s.*

in her white sundress waiting for his father, while Luis stared. She was like a smooth wood carving. Her skin was <u>mahogany,</u> almost black, and her arms and legs were long and thin, but curved in places so that she did not look bony and hard—more like a ballerina. And her <u>ebony</u> hair was braided close to her head. Luis let his breath out, feeling a little dizzy. He had forgotten to breathe. Both the girl and his father heard him. Mr. Cintrón waved him over.

"Luis, the señorita here has lost a wheel cover. Her car is twenty-five years old, so it will not be an easy match. Come look on this side."

Luis tossed a wrench he'd been holding into a toolbox like he was annoyed, just to make a point about slave labor. Then he followed his father, who knelt on the gravel and began to point out every detail of the hubcap. Luis was hardly listening. He watched the girl take a piece of paper from her handbag.

"Señor Cintrón, I have drawn the hubcap for you, since I will have to leave soon. My home address and telephone number are here, and also my parents' office number." She handed the paper to Mr. Cintrón, who nodded.

"Sí, señorita, very good. This will help my son look for it. Perhaps there is one in that stack there." He pointed to the pile of caps that Luis was supposed to wash and polish. "Yes, I'm almost certain that there is a match there. Of course, I do not know if it's near the top or the bottom. You will give us a few days, yes?"

Luis just stared at his father like he was crazy. But he didn't say anything because the girl was smiling at him with a funny expression on her face. Maybe she thought he had X-ray eyes like Superman, or maybe she was <u>mocking</u> him.

"Please call me Naomi, Señor Cintrón. You know my mother. She is the director of the funeral home. . . ." Mr. Cintrón seemed surprised at first; he prided himself on having a great memory. Then his friendly expression changed to one of sadness as he recalled the day of his wife's burial.

Naomi did not finish her sentence. She reached over and placed her hand on Mr. Cintrón's arm for a moment. Then she said "Adiós" softly, and got in her shiny white car. She waved to them as she left, and her gold bracelets flashing in the sun nearly blinded Luis.

Mr. Cintrón shook his head. "How about that," he said as if to himself. "They are the Dominican owners of Ramirez Funeral Home." And, with a sigh, "She seems like such a nice young woman. Reminds me of your mother when she was her age."

Hearing the funeral parlor's name, Luis remembered too. The day his mother died, he had been in her room at the hospital while his father had gone for coffee. The alarm had gone off on her monitor and nurses had come running in, pushing him outside. After that, all he recalled was the anger that had made him punch a hole in his bedroom wall. And afterward he had refused to talk to anyone at the funeral. Strange, he did see a black girl there who didn't try like the others to talk to him, but actually ignored him as she <u>escorted</u> family members to the viewing room and brought flowers in. Could it be that the skinny girl in a frilly white dress had been Naomi? She didn't

> Why does talking to Naomi sadden Mr. Cintrón? How does Naomi express sympathy for Mr. Cintrón?

---

words for everyday use

ma • hog • a • ny (mə hä′ gə nē) *adj.*, colored deep brown like mahogany wood. *The <u>mahogany</u> cushions matched the wood in the room.*

eb • o • ny (e′ bə nē) *adj.*, black. *The keys on a piano are <u>ebony</u> and ivory.*

mock (mäk) *vt.*, treat with contempt or ridicule. *The boys <u>mocked</u> their new classmate by imitating his gestures and walk.*

es • cort (es′ kärt) *vt.*, accompany as an escort. *The director <u>escorted</u> his leading lady to the premiere.*

act like she had recognized him today, though. Or maybe she thought that he was a jerk.

Luis grabbed the drawing from his father. The old man looked like he wanted to walk down memory lane. But Luis was in no mood to listen to the old stories about his falling in love on a tropical island. The world they'd lived in before he was born wasn't his world. No beaches and palm trees here. Only junk as far as he could see. He climbed back up his hill and studied Naomi's sketch. It had obviously been done very carefully. It was signed "Naomi Ramirez" in the lower right-hand corner. He memorized the telephone number.

Luis washed hubcaps all day until his hands were red and raw, but he did not come across the small silver bowl that would fit the VW. After work he took a few practice Frisbee shots across the yard before showing his father what he had accomplished: rows and rows of shiny rings drying in the sun. His father nodded and showed him the bump on his temple where one of Luis's flying saucers had gotten him.

"Practice makes perfect, you know. Next time you'll probably <u>decapitate</u> me." Luis heard him struggle with the word *decapitate*, which Mr. Cintrón pronounced in syllables. Showing off his big vocabulary again, Luis thought. He looked closely at the bump, though. He felt bad about it.

"They look good, hijo." Mr. Cintrón made a sweeping gesture with his arms over the yard. "You know, all this will have to be classified. My dream is to have all the parts divided by year, make of car, and condition. Maybe now that you are here to help me, this will happen."

"Pop . . ." Luis put his hand on his father's shoulder. They were the same height and build,

What is Mr. Cintrón's plan for the junkyard? What does Luis think of this idea?

about five foot six and muscular. "The judge said six months of free labor for you, not life, okay?" Mr. Cintrón nodded, looking distracted. It was then that Luis suddenly noticed how gray his hair had turned—it used to be shiny black like his own—and that there were deep lines in his face. His father had turned into an old man and he hadn't even noticed.

"Son, you must follow the judge's instructions. Like she said, next time you get in trouble, she's going to treat you like an adult, and I think you know what that means. Hard time, no breaks."

"Yeah, yeah. That's what I'm doing, right? Working my hands to the bone instead of enjoying my summer. But listen, she didn't put me under house arrest, right? I'm going out tonight."

"Home by ten. She did say something about a curfew, Luis." Mr. Cintrón had stopped smiling and was looking upset. It had always been hard for them to talk more than a minute or two before his father got offended at something Luis said, or at his sarcastic tone. He was always doing something wrong.

Why is it difficult for Luis and his father to talk?

Luis threw the rag down on the table and went to sit in his father's ancient Buick, which was in <u>mint</u> condition. They drove home in silence.

After sitting down at the kitchen table with his father to eat a pizza they had picked up on the way home, Luis asked to borrow the car. He didn't get an answer then, just a look that meant "Don't bother me right now."

Before bringing up the subject again, Luis put some ice cubes in a Baggie and handed it to Mr. Cintrón, who had made the little bump on his head worse by rubbing it. It had GUILTY written on it, Luis thought.

"Gracias, hijo." His father placed the bag on the bump and made a face as the ice touched his skin.

words for everyday use	de • cap • i • tate (di ka′ pə tāt) vt., behead. *Marie-Antoinette and Louis XVI were <u>decapitated</u> by the guillotine.* mint (mint) adj., unmarred as if fresh from a mint. *Looking for a silver dollar that did not have any flaws, the coin collector noticed one that was in <u>mint</u> condition.*

They ate in silence for a few minutes more; then Luis decided to ask about the car again.

"I really need some fresh air, Pop. Can I borrow the car for a couple of hours?"

"You don't get enough fresh air at the yard? We're lucky that we don't have to sit in a smelly old factory all day. You know that?"

"Yeah, Pop. We're real lucky." Luis always felt irritated that his father was so grateful to own a junkyard, but he held his anger back and just waited to see if he'd get the keys without having to get in an argument.

> *What irritates Luis?*

"Where are you going?"

"For a ride. Not going anywhere. Just out for a while. Is that okay?"

His father didn't answer, just handed him a set of keys, as shiny as the day they were manufactured. His father polished everything that could be polished: doorknobs, coins, keys, spoons, knives, and forks, like he was King Midas[4] counting his silver and gold. Luis thought his father must be really lonely to polish utensils only he used anymore. They had been picked out by his wife, though, so they were like <u>relics.</u> Nothing she had ever owned could be thrown away. Only now the dishes, forks, and spoons were not used to eat the yellow rice and red beans, the fried chicken, or the mouth-watering sweet plantains[5] that his mother had cooked for them. They were just kept in the cabinets that his father had turned into a museum for her. Mr. Cintrón could cook as well as his wife, but he didn't have the heart to do it anymore. Luis thought that maybe if they ate together once in a while things might get better between them, but he always had something to do around dinnertime and ended up at a hamburger joint.

> *Why doesn't Mr. Cintrón cook anymore?*

Tonight was the first time in months they had sat down at the table together.

Luis took the keys. "Thanks," he said, walking out to take his shower. His father kept looking at him with those sad, patient eyes. "Okay. I'll be back by ten, and keep the ice on that egg," Luis said without looking back.

He had just meant to ride around his old barrio, see if any of the Tiburones were hanging out at El Building, where most of them lived. It wasn't far from the single-family home his father had bought when the business started paying off: a house that his mother lived in for three months before she took up residence at St. Joseph's Hospital. She never came home again. These days Luis wished he still lived in that tiny apartment where there was always something to do, somebody to talk to.

Instead Luis found himself parked in front of the last place his mother had gone to: Ramirez Funeral Home. In the front yard was a huge oak tree that Luis remembered having climbed during the funeral to get away from people. The tree looked different now, not like a skeleton, as it had then, but green with leaves. The branches reached to the second floor of the house, where the family lived.

For a while Luis sat in the car allowing the memories to flood back into his brain. He remembered his mother before the illness changed her. She had not been beautiful, as his father told everyone; she had been a sweet lady, not pretty but not ugly. To him, she had been the person who always told him that she was proud of him and loved him. She did that every night when she came to his bedroom

> *What did Luis's mother always tell him?*

---

4. **King Midas.** Legendary Phrygian king who is given the power of turning everything he touches to gold

5. **plantain.** Banana-like fruit

words for everyday use

rel • ic (re′ lik) *n.,* memento from a past time. *The nineteenth-century communion goblet was a <u>relic</u> that the congregation cherished.*

door to say good-night. As a joke he would sometimes ask her, "Proud of what? I haven't done anything." And she'd always say, "I'm just proud that you are my son." She wasn't perfect or anything. She had bad days when nothing he did could make her smile, especially after she got sick. But he never heard her say anything negative about anyone. She always blamed *el destino*, fate, for what went wrong. He missed her. He missed her so much. Suddenly a flood of tears that had been building up for almost three years started pouring from his eyes. Luis sat in his father's car, with his head on the steering wheel, and cried, "Mami,[6] I miss you."

Why does Luis cry outside the Ramirez Funeral Home?

When he finally looked up, he saw that he was being watched. Sitting at a large window with a pad and a pencil on her lap was Naomi. At first Luis felt angry and embarrassed, but she wasn't laughing at him. Then she told him with her dark eyes that it was okay to come closer. He walked to the window, and she held up the sketch pad on which she had drawn him, not crying like a baby, but sitting on top of a mountain of silver disks, holding one up over his head. He had to smile.

The plate-glass window was locked. It had a security bolt on it. An alarm system, he figured, so nobody would steal the princess. He asked her if he could come in. It was soundproof too. He mouthed the words slowly for her to read his lips. She wrote on the pad, "I can't let you in. My mother is not home tonight." So they looked at each other and talked through the window for a little while. Then Luis got an idea. He signed to her that he'd be back, and drove to the junkyard.

Luis climbed up on his mountain of hubcaps. For hours he sorted the wheel covers by make, size, and condition, stopping only to call his father and tell him where he was and what he was doing. The old man did not ask him for explanations, and Luis was grateful for that. By lamppost light, Luis worked and worked, beginning to understand a little why his father kept busy all the time. Doing something that had a beginning, a middle, and an end did something to your head. It was like the satisfaction Luis got out of planning "adventures" for his Tiburones, but there was another element involved here that had nothing to do with showing off for others. This was a treasure hunt. And he knew what he was looking for.

What does Luis learn while looking for a hubcap for Naomi's car?

Finally, when it seemed that it was a hopeless search, when it was almost midnight and Luis's hands were cut and bruised from his work, he found it. It was the perfect match for Naomi's drawing, the moon-shaped wheel cover for her car, Cinderella's shoe. Luis jumped off the small mound of disks left under him and shouted, "Yes!" He looked around and saw neat stacks of hubcaps that he would wash the next day. He would build a display wall for his father. People would be able to come into the yard and point to whatever they wanted.

Luis washed the VW hubcap and polished it until he could see himself in it. He used it as a mirror as he washed his face and combed his hair. Then he drove to the Ramirez Funeral Home. It was almost pitch-black, since it was a moonless night. As quietly as possible, Luis put some gravel in his pocket and climbed the oak tree to the second floor. He knew he was in front of Naomi's window—he could see her shadow through the curtains. She was at a table, apparently writing or drawing, maybe waiting for him. Luis hung the silver disk carefully on a branch near the window, then threw the gravel at the glass. Naomi ran to the window and drew the curtains aside while Luis held on to the thick branch and waited to give her the first good thing he had given anyone in a long time.

What does the VW hubcap represent to Luis?

■

6. **Mami**. Mom (Spanish)

How do you think Luis's life will change now that he has accepted his mother's death?

Investigate, *Inquire,* and Imagine

Recall: GATHERING FACTS

1a. Why does Luis spend six months in juvenile hall?

2a. Why does Naomi Ramirez come to the junkyard?

3a. What does Luis do when he borrows his father's car?

Interpret: FINDING MEANING

1b. What is the underlying reason for Luis's disruptive behavior? Is he a typical gang member? Explain.

2b. How does Naomi change Luis's attitude?

3b. What does crying for his mother do for Luis? How does his subsequent "treasure hunt" help him understand both his father and himself?

Analyze: TAKING THINGS APART

4a. What behaviors does Luis exhibit to indicate he is a good son?

Synthesize: BRINGING THINGS TOGETHER

4b. Why does Luis want to create a new relationship with his father?

Evaluate: MAKING JUDGMENTS

5a. Is Luis justified in putting down his father because he owns a junkyard?

Extend: CONNECTING IDEAS

5b. Luis thinks that the hubcap he gives Naomi is "the first good thing he had given anyone in a long time." This act represents a turning point in Luis's life. Make predictions about how his life will be different six months later.

Understanding *Literature*

CHARACTER. Review the definitions for **character**, **static character**, and **dynamic character** in the Handbook of Literary Terms. Is Luis a static character or a dynamic character? Explain your answer using evidence from the selection.

CONFLICT. Review the definition for **conflict** in the Handbook of Literary Terms and the chart you made for Literary Tools on page 704. Is this story primarily one of internal or external conflict? Which conflict propels Luis toward transformation?

Writer's Journal

1. Imagine you have been employed by Jorge Cintrón & Son, Auto Parts and Salvage to create a **promotional flyer**. Write text for the flyer intended to encourage shoppers to check out the products at the Cintrón junkyard.
2. Imagine that you are Naomi. Write a **journal entry** telling what you thought of Luis when you first saw him at the junkyard and what you thought of him after he brought the hubcap to your house. Do you plan to see more of Luis? What attracts you to him?
3. Imagine you are Luis's parole officer. Write a **report** summarizing the progress you have observed Luis make since his release from juvenile hall.

Integrating the Language Arts

Language, Grammar, and Style

COORDINATING AND CORRELATIVE CONJUNCTIONS. Read the Language Arts Survey 3.70, "Coordinating Conjunctions," and 3.71, "Correlative Conjunctions." Then, in the following sentences, underline the conjunctions, and identify them as coordinating or correlative conjunctions.

1. Not only did Luis start a gang, but he got caught breaking into a house.
2. Both Luis's father and school officials worried about him.
3. Neither his own house nor the junkyard gave Luis comfort.
4. Luis was planning to see the Tiburones, but he went to see Naomi instead.
5. He could either talk to her or go away.

Applied English

REAL ESTATE ADVERTISEMENT. Imagine that Mr. Cintrón puts Jorge Cintrón & Son, Auto Parts and Salvage on the market after Luis and his father have classified all the auto parts by year, make of car, and condition. Read several commercial real estate ads. Then write a real estate ad for Jorge Cintrón & Son, Auto Parts and Salvage. Be sure to include the size of the company, a summary of its contents, the price it is selling for, and whom to contact.

Speaking and Listening

DIALOGUE. *Dialogue* is conversation involving two or more people or characters. With a partner, present an extemporaneous dialogue between Luis and Naomi after Luis brings Naomi the Volkswagen hubcap.

Critical Thinking

LITERARY TECHNIQUES. At the end of "Catch the Moon," Cofer tells the reader "the moon-shaped wheel cover" for Naomi's car is "Cinderella's shoe." Review the definition for *metaphor* and *allusion* in the Handbook of Literary Terms and determine whether the reference to Cinderella's shoe is metaphor or allusion. Explain your answer. What is the meaning of the comparison? How do you expect the story of Luis and Naomi to end, given this comparison? What is the meaning of the title? Cofer entitles her story "Catch the Moon," but the story ends on a moonless night. How does Luis catch the moon on a night of pitch blackness?

PREREADING

"If You Forget Me"
by Pablo Neruda

Literary TOOLS

SYMBOL. A **symbol** is a thing that stands for or represents both itself and something else. As you read the poem, determine what the flower and the land symbolize.

IMAGE. An **image** is language that creates a concrete representation of an object or an experience.

Graphic Organizer

As you read, make a cluster chart listing the images used in the poem. One example has been done for you.

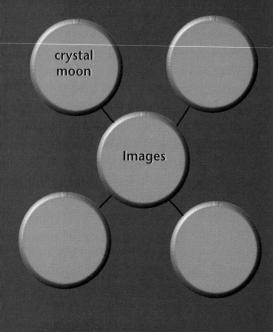

Reader's resource

"If You Forget Me" is a lyric poem, highly musical verse that expresses the emotions of a speaker. *Elegies, odes,* and *sonnets* are examples of important types of lyric poems. In contrast to narrative poetry, which relates events in the form of a story, Pablo Neruda's poem is a melodic and individual expression of the poet's thoughts and feelings. "If You Forget Me" was first published anonymously in one of Neruda's many volumes of love poetry, *Los versos del Capitán (The Captain's Verses).*

MUSIC CONNECTION. The words to "If You Forget Me" were made into lyrics for a song recorded by Madonna that was used in the movie *Il Postino (The Postman)* in 1995.

CULTURE CONNECTION. Although Pablo Neruda was a native of Chile and wrote in Spanish, English speakers consider him one of the most important poets of the late twentieth century.

About the AUTHOR

Pablo Neruda (1904–1973) was a Latin American poet, diplomat, and politician who was awarded the Lenin Peace Prize in 1953 and the Nobel Prize for literature in 1971. Born Neftali Ricardo Reyes Basoalto in Parral, Chile, Neruda became an avid reader as a child and started writing poetry at the age of ten. His father disapproved of his poetry and discouraged him from writing, which is probably why he began to publish under the pseudonym Pablo Neruda, the name he legally adopted in 1946. Upon completing his secondary education in 1920, Neruda moved to Santiago, where he devoted himself to writing poetry. Neruda's first book, *Crepuscalario,* was published in 1923, followed by *Twenty Love Poems and a Song of Despair* in 1924. His other poetry collections include *Canto General* (1949), *Elementary Odes* (1954), and *Isla Negra: A Notebook* (1964).

In addition to writing poetry, Pablo Neruda led an intense political life. From 1927 to 1933 he served as Chilean consul in South Asia—in Burma (now Myanmar), Ceylon (now Sri Lanka), Java (now part of Indonesia), and Singapore. In 1933 and 1934 he represented Chile in Buenos Aires, and from there he went to Spain, where he served through the early part of the Spanish Civil War. His involvement there inspired *Spain in the Heart* (1937). During the rest of his life Neruda traveled extensively and continued writing poetry, gaining an international reputation as one of the twentieth century's noteworthy and most prolific poets.

Reader's Journal

What do your friends or loved ones do to return the love you give them?

If You FORGET Me

Pablo Neruda

I want you to know
one thing.

You know how this is:
if I look
at the crystal moon, at the red branch
of the slow autumn at my window,
if I touch
near the fire
the <u>impalpable</u> ash
or the wrinkled body of the log,
everything carries me to you,
as if everything that exists,
aromas, light, metals,
were little boats
that sail
toward those isles of yours that wait for me.

Well, now,
if little by little you stop loving me
I shall stop loving you little by little.

To whom is the poet speaking?

When will the speaker stop loving the person he is addressing?

words for everyday use

im • pal • pa • ble (im pal′ pə bəl) *adj.,* so finely divided that no grains or grit can be felt. *The powdered sugar was sifted until it was <u>impalpable</u>.*

If suddenly
you forget me
do not look for me,
for I shall already have forgotten you.

If you think it long and mad,
the wind of banners
that passes through my life,
and you decide
to leave me at the shore
of the heart where I have roots,
remember
that on that day,
at that hour,
I shall lift my arms
and my roots will set off
to seek another land.

But
if each day,
each hour,
you feel that you are destined for me
with <u>implacable</u> sweetness,
if each day a flower
climbs up to your lips to seek me,
ah my love, ah my own,
in me all that fire is repeated,
in me nothing is extinguished or forgotten,
my love feeds on your love, beloved,
and as long as you live it will be in your arms
without leaving mine. ■

> Under what circumstances will the speaker's love continue to grow?

---

words for everyday use

im • pla • ca • ble (im pla′ kə bəl) *adj.,* not capable of making concessions. *The renegade sought revenge against his <u>implacable</u> enemy.*

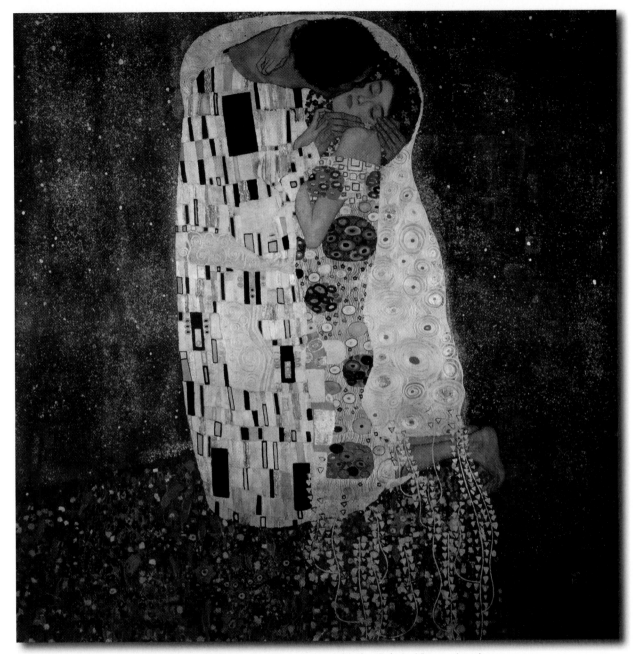

The Kiss, c.1907. Gustav Klimt. Osterreichische Galerie, Vienna, Austria.

art
n o t e

Gustav Klimt (1862–1918) was a major figure in the Art Nouveau movement, which concentrated on the decorative aspects of art: patterns and colors designed primarily to please the eye. How does Klimt use the decorative aspects to also show how these people feel?

ABOUT THE RELATED READING

The movie *Il Postino* was based on Antonio Skarmeta's novel *Burning Patience* and was directed by Michael Radford. The screenplay was written by Anna Pavignano, Michael Radford, Furio Scarpelli, Giacomo Scarpelli, and Massimo Troisi. *Il Postino* received Academy Award nominations for 1995 Best Picture of the Year, Best Director, Best Leading Role Actor, Best Original Score, and Best Screenplay based on Previously Published Media.

Roger Ebert is the movie reviewer for the *Chicago Sun-Times* newspaper and hosted a television movie review show with Gene Siskel until Siskel's death in 1999. Siskel and Ebert coined the review system of giving a movie a "thumbs up" or a "thumbs down" that became the measure of a movie's popular success. Ebert continues to host the television review show and writes movie reviews for the *Chicago Sun-Times.*

Il Postino
(The Postman)

Chicago Sun-Times
Date of publication: 06/23/1995

By Roger Ebert

The first time we see Mario, the hero of "The Postman," we think perhaps he is retarded. He is having a conversation with his father, who seems to be retarded, too, or perhaps just engrossed in his soup. We realize in the next scene or two that Mario is of normal intelligence, but has been raised in a place that provided him with almost nothing to talk about. That is about to change.

Mario (Massimo Troisi) lives on a quiet island where little changes and new ideas arrive slowly, if at all. Then one day the postmaster enlists him to bicycle out to the house of a new arrival. Pablo Neruda (played by Philippe Noiret), the famous poet, has been exiled from his native Chile for political reasons, and has come here to live.

Mario grows fascinated by Neruda, who seems to receive letters mostly from women. He discusses the poet with the village postmaster, a communist who supports Neruda for his political ideas. Neither one of them has much insight into poetry, but Mario agrees to take the job of postman so that he can visit Neruda daily, and maybe find out how to pick up girls.

Their relationship grows slowly. Neruda is a quiet man who lives with a woman, perhaps his wife. Mario sees enough to realize they are deeply in love. Slowly, using every possible conversational opening, the postman forges a friendship. He obtains a book of Neruda's poems, and asks him to sign it. Neruda signs "Regards, Pablo Neruda." Mario is crushed: the book is not even personalized, "To Mario." How can he impress women with it?

As the movie opens, Mario is like the man who came to dinner: He arrives at Neruda's gate, and in a sense never seems to leave. By the end of the film, Mario is more like the mute, inglorious Miltons that Thomas Gray wrote about in his "Elegy Written in a Country Churchyard": We see that Mario, too, might have developed the soul of a poet, had he not been born in such a backwater.

And there is another lesson—Neruda can also learn from the people he has come to live among. Some months after he leaves the village, a newspaper clipping comes into Mario's hands, quoting the poet, who says, "I lived in complete solitude

Massimo Troisi as the postman in "Il Postino."

with the most simple people in the world." Mario's face betrays just the slightest twitch as he learns how "simple" he is.

That twitch is enough to reveal that he is no longer quite so simple.

"The Postman" could have developed its friend-ship between poet and peasant more obviously. The beauty of the film is in its quietness. The director, Michael Radford, is British, born in India. His previous credits ("1984" and "White Mischief") are interesting films, but nothing like this Italian-language production.

The guiding spirit behind the production seems to have been Troisi, an Italian director and actor who co-wrote the screenplay and postponed heart surgery in order to act in the title role. He died the day after the movie was finished. Perhaps it was his illness, or perhaps it was his sense of the material, that caused him to play the role in such a low key. He never seems to push for an effect, never strains, never goes too far. His character

spends the entire film essentially violating Neruda's privacy—but he does it so quietly, you can never quite catch him at it.

I also liked Philippe Noiret, as the poet. He is a French actor, now 65, who has spent decades playing a phlegmatic man of the people. When other people's faces might reflect surprise, his reflects confirmation: He always seems to be nod-ding as if things had turned out as he expected.

Together, they make this good-hearted little film into a quiet meditation on fate, tact, and poetry. If things had been different, Mario might have been the poet, and Neruda the postman, although that is an idea that occurs more easily to Mario. And it is Mario, too, who proves that poet-ry can work to seduce women, although the woman of his dreams, inevitably named Beatrice (Maria Grazia Cucinotta), is initially suspicious. The screenplay is based on a novel, *Burning Patience,* by Antonio Skarmeta, but is the novel based on fact? I don't really want to know. ∎

Respond*to the* SELECTION

If you were the speaker, what signs of reciprocation of your love would you want to have from your beloved?

Investigate, *Inquire,* and Imagine

Recall: GATHERING FACTS **Interpret: FINDING MEANING**

1a. What carries the speaker toward his beloved?

1b. What senses of the speaker are affected by these things?

2a. When should the speaker's lover cease to look for him?

2b. Why does the speaker insist that his lover return his love?

3a. What does the speaker think might make his lover leave him?

3b. What might the "wind of banners" represent?

Analyze: TAKING THINGS APART **Synthesize: BRINGING THINGS TOGETHER**

4a. Identify the images that remind the speaker of the person he is addressing.

4b. What lesson does this poem make about the nature of unrequited love?

Evaluate: MAKING JUDGMENTS **Extend: CONNECTING IDEAS**

5a. Evaluate the value of the lesson expressed in this poem.

5b. Compare the theme of "If You Forget Me" with the theme of Marvin Bell's "Being in Love" on page 700.

Understanding *Literature*

SYMBOL. Review the definition for **symbol** in the Handbook of Literary Terms. What do the flower and the land symbolize?

IMAGE. Review the definition for **image** in the Handbook of Literary Terms and the cluster chart you made for Literary Tools on page 714. What idea does the imagery in the first stanza evoke?

Writer's Journal

1. Imagine you are the speaker five years into the future. Write a **diary entry** that reflects on your relationship during the last five years with the person addressed in the poem. Did the speaker and his or her beloved forget each other and part, or did their love grow? How does the speaker feel about what has happened over this period of time?

2. Imagine you are the person to whom this poem is addressed. Write a **letter** in response to the poem, describing your feelings toward the speaker of the poem.

3. Write a **lyric poem** using images that remind you of someone you love. The poem should directly address the person you are writing about.

Integrating the Language Arts

Language, Grammar, and Style

SUBORDINATING CONJUNCTIONS. Read the Language Arts Survey 3.72, "Subordinating Conjunctions." Then, for each sentence below, identify the subordinating conjunction and the subordinate clause.

1. I preferred Neruda's prose until I read his poetry.
2. If any man could write that well, he deserved to be world famous.
3. Even though Neruda was popular around the world, Chile distrusted his politics.
4. When I heard his poem sung as a popular song, I couldn't believe my ears.
5. If it is with the right person, who wouldn't want the love Neruda describes?

Media Literacy

MOVIE REVIEW. View the movie *Il Postino (The Postman)*. Read the Related Reading movie review by newspaper and television film critic Roger Ebert. Then write a review of the film to be presented on video or posted online. To prepare, you might want to watch movie reviews on television or read reviews on the Internet. Discuss aspects of the film such as setting, characterization, plot, and historical background intelligently. Then tell your audience why they should or should not see this film, and give the movie a rating based on one to four stars. One Internet site you may want to visit to read movie reviews written by high school students and to post your own movie review is The Student Center Network at http://www.teenmovies.studentcenter.org/reviews.php.

Speaking and Listening & Collaborative Learning

ORAL INTERPRETATION. With a classmate, present to the class a love poem by a poet other than Neruda. One of you should introduce the poem and the poet by discussing the poem's subject and theme and presenting biographical information about the poet. The other should orally interpret the poem, deciding what tone, gestures, facial expressions, and body language to use. You may want to review the Language Arts Survey 4.19, "Oral Interpretation."

Literary
T O O L S

AIM. A writer's **aim** is his or her purpose, or goal. People may write with the following aims: to inform (expository/informational writing); to entertain, enrich, enlighten, and/or use an artistic medium, such as fiction or poetry, to share a perspective (imaginative writing); to tell a story about an event (narrative writing); to reflect (personal/expressive writing); to persuade readers or listeners to respond in some way, such as to agree with a position, change a view on an issue, reach an agreement, or perform an action (persuasive/argumentative writing). As you read, determine Saki's principal aim in writing this story.

PLOT AND CONFLICT. A **plot** is a series of events related to a *central conflict,* or struggle. A typical plot involves the introduction of a **conflict,** its development, and its eventual resolution. Sometimes a *catastrophe,* an event marked by the fall of a central character, occurs in a plot.

Graphic
Organizer

As you read, make a plot pyramid like the one in the Elements of Fiction on page 167. Identify the exposition, inciting incident, rising action, climax, falling action, resolution, and catastrophe. One example, for exposition, is "Ulrich von Gradwitz patrols the forest. Family's feud is introduced."

Reader's
Journal

How have you resolved conflict in a relationship or put an end to a grudge?

"The Interlopers"
by Saki

Reader's
r e s o u r c e

"The Interlopers" revolves on a conflict, a struggle between opposing forces. Common types of conflicts in fiction are person versus nature, person versus person, person versus society, person versus self, person versus machine, and person versus the supernatural. "The Interlopers" presents the first kind of conflict, one between the characters Ulrich von Gradwitz and Georg Znaeym. Their conflict over the border between their lands has been burning between their families for three generations. By the end of the story each man realizes that he has more to fear than his neighbor's hatred.

About *the*
A U T H O R

Saki (1870–1916) is the pen name of Hector Hugh Munro. In a series of short stories, he created, the characters Reginald and Clovis, two young men who happily take to task the conventional adult world. His collections of short stories include *Reginald, The Chronicles of Clovis, Beasts and Super Beasts,* and *The Square Egg.* Some of Saki's short stories, such as "Sredni Vashtar" and "The Muse on the Hill," are rather somber. He also wrote two novels, three plays, and one history. At the age of forty-four, Saki volunteered for active duty in World War I and was killed in action. Nearly all of his work is included in *The Complete Works of Saki,* published in 1976.

art
n o t e

The German Romantic painter Caspar-David Friedrich (1774–1840) used landscape as a symbolic language for expressing abstract ideas about life, death and salvation. A fallen tree evokes death while evergreens are symbols of hope and life. The distant mountain peaks rising above the misty clouds suggest the power of faith. The distant light of the moon symbolizes the afterlife.

The Interlopers[1]

Saki

Clearing in the Forest, 1825. Caspar-David Friedrich. Neue Galerie, Linz, Austria.

---

1. **Interlopers.** People who meddle, or intrude, in other people's concerns

In a forest of mixed growth somewhere on the eastern spurs of the Carpathians,[2] a man stood one winter night watching and listening, as though he waited for some beast of the woods to come within the range of his vision, and, later, of his rifle. But the game for whose presence he kept so keen an outlook was none that figured in the sportsman's calendar as lawful and proper for the chase; Ulrich von Gradwitz patrolled the dark forest in quest of a human enemy.

The forest lands of Gradwitz were of wide extent and well stocked with game; the narrow strip of <u>precipitous</u> woodland that lay on its outskirt was not remarkable for the game it harbored or the shooting it afforded, but it was the most jealously guarded of all its owner's territorial possessions. A famous lawsuit, in the days of his grandfather, had wrested it from the illegal possession of a neighboring family of petty landowners;[3] the dispossessed party had never acquiesced in the judgment of the Courts, and a long series of poaching affrays[4] and similar scandals had <u>embittered</u> the relationships between the families for three generations. The neighbor feud had grown into a personal one since Ulrich had come to be head of his family; if there was a man in the world whom he detested and wished ill to it was Georg Znaeym, the inheritor of the quarrel and the tireless game-snatcher and raider of the disputed border-forest. The feud might, perhaps, have died down or been <u>compromised</u> if the personal ill-will of the two men had not stood in the way; as boys they had thirsted for one another's blood, as men each prayed that misfortune might fall on the other, and this wind-scourged winter night Ulrich had banded together his foresters to watch the dark forest, not in quest of four-footed quarry, but to keep a look-out

Ulrich von Gradwitz patrolled the dark forest in quest of a human enemy.

for the prowling thieves whom he suspected of being afoot from across the land boundary. The roebuck,[5] which usually kept in the sheltered hollows during a storm-wind, were running like driven things tonight, and there was movement and unrest among the creatures that were wont to sleep through the dark hours. Assuredly there was a disturbing element in the forest, and Ulrich could guess the quarter from whence it came.

He strayed away by himself from the watchers whom he had placed in ambush on the crest of the hill, and wandered far down the steep slopes amid the wild tangle of undergrowth, peering through the tree-trunks and listening through the whistling and skirling of the wind and the restless beating of the branches for

> With whom has the family of Ulrich von Gradwitz been in dispute? About what?

> Why does Ulrich watch the forest?

---

2. **eastern spurs . . . Carpathians.** Ridges projecting from a mountain chain; the Carpathian Mountains extend from southern Poland to northeastern Romania

3. **petty landowners.** Owners of small pieces of land

4. **poaching affrays.** Attacks for the purpose of stealing game from someone else's property

5. **roebuck.** Male of the roe deer

---

words for everyday use

pre • cip • i • tous (prē sip´ə təs) *adj.*, steep. *The <u>precipitous</u> trail up the steep mountain was difficult even for the most seasoned climbers.*

em • bit • ter (em bit´ər) *vt.*, make resentful. *Lucy didn't let her friend's betrayal <u>embitter</u> her; she was not resentful of her friend.*

com • pro • mise (käm´prə mīz) *vi.*, settle by having both sides make concessions. *Bill wanted a heated dessert and I wanted something cold, so we <u>compromised</u> on a hot fudge sundae.*

sight or sound of the <u>marauders</u>. If only on this wild night, in this dark, lone spot, he might come across Georg Znaeym, man to man, with none to witness—that was the wish that was uppermost in his thoughts. And as he stepped round the trunk of a huge beech he came face to face with the man he sought.

The two enemies stood glaring at one another for a long silent moment. Each had a rifle in his hand, each had hate in his heart and murder uppermost in his mind. The chance had come to give full play to the passions of a lifetime. But a man who has been brought up under the code of a <u>restraining</u> civilization cannot easily nerve himself to shoot down his neighbor in cold blood and without word spoken, except for an offense against his hearth and honor.[6] And before the moment of hesitation had given way to action a deed of Nature's own violence overwhelmed them both. A fierce shriek of the storm had been answered by a splitting crash over their heads, and ere they could leap aside a mass of falling beech tree had thundered down on them. Ulrich von Gradwitz found himself stretched on the ground, one arm numb beneath him and the other held almost as helplessly in a tight tangle of forked branches, while both legs were pinned beneath the fallen mass. His heavy shooting-boots had saved his feet from being crushed to pieces, but if his fractures were not as serious as they might have been, at least it was evident that he could not move from his present position till some one came to release him. The descending twigs had slashed the skin of his face, and he had to wink away some drops of blood from his eyelashes before he could take in a general view of the disaster. At his side, so near that under ordinary cir-

What happens before either man has a chance to speak or shoot?

cumstances he could almost have touched him, lay Georg Znaeym, alive and struggling, but obviously as helplessly <u>pinioned</u> down as himself. All round them lay a thick-strewn wreckage of splintered branches and broken twigs.

Relief at being alive and exasperation at his captive plight brought a strange medley of pious thank-offerings and sharp curses to Ulrich's lips. Georg, who was nearly blinded with the blood which trickled across his eyes, stopped his struggling for a moment to listen, and then gave a short, snarling laugh.

"So you're not killed, as you ought to be, but you're caught, anyway," he cried; "caught fast. Ho, what a jest, Ulrich von Gradwitz snared in his stolen forest. There's real justice for you!"

And he laughed again, mockingly and savagely.

"I'm caught in my own forest-land," retorted Ulrich. "When my men come to release us you will wish, perhaps, that you were in a better <u>plight</u> than caught poaching on a neighbor's land, shame on you."

Georg was silent for a moment; then he answered quietly:

"Are you sure that your men will find much to release? I have men, too, in the forest tonight, close behind me, and *they* will be here first and do the releasing. When they drag me out from under these damned branches it won't need much clumsiness on their part to roll this mass of trunk right over on the top of you. Your men will find you dead under a fallen beech tree. For form's sake I shall send my condolences to your family."

Who do the men believe will save them? What do they believe will happen when they are saved?

"It is a useful hint," said Ulrich fiercely. "My men had orders to follow in ten minutes' time,

6. **hearth and honor.** Home and reputation

seven of which must have gone by already, and when they get me out—I will remember the hint. Only as you will have met your death poaching on my lands I don't think I can decently send any message of condolence to your family."

"Good," snarled Georg, "good. We fight this quarrel out to the death, you and I and our foresters, with no cursed interlopers to come between us. Death and damnation to you, Ulrich von Gradwitz."

"The same to you, Georg Znaeym, forest-thief, game-snatcher."

Both men spoke with the bitterness of possible defeat before them, for each knew that it might be long before his men would seek him out or find him; it was a bare matter of chance which party would arrive first on the scene.

Both had now given up the useless struggle to free themselves from the mass of wood that held them down; Ulrich limited his <u>endeavours</u> to an effort to bring his one partially free arm near enough to his outer coat-pocket to draw out his wine-flask. Even when he had accomplished that operation it was long before he could manage the unscrewing of the stopper or get any of the liquid down his throat. But what a Heaven-sent draught it seemed! It was an open winter, and little snow had fallen as yet, hence the captives suffered less from the cold than might have been the case at that season of the year; nevertheless, the wine was warming and reviving to the wounded man, and he looked across with something like a throb of pity to where his enemy lay, just keeping the groans of pain and weariness from crossing his lips.

"Could you reach this flask if I threw it over to you?" asked Ulrich suddenly; "there is good wine in it, and one may as well be as comfortable as one can. Let us drink, even if tonight one of us dies."

"No, I can scarcely see anything; there is so much blood caked round my eyes," said Georg, "and in any case I don't drink wine with an enemy."

Ulrich was silent for a few minutes, and lay listening to the weary screeching of the wind. An idea was slowly forming and growing in his brain, an idea that gained strength every time that he looked across at the man who was fighting so grimly against pain and exhaustion. In the pain and <u>languor</u> that Ulrich himself was feeling the old fierce hatred seemed to be dying down.

"Neighbor," he said presently, "do as you please if your men come first. It was a fair compact.[7] But as for me, I've changed my mind. If my men are the first to come you shall be the first to be helped, as though you were my guest. We have quarrelled like devils all our lives over this stupid strip of forest, where the trees can't even stand upright in a breath of wind. Lying here tonight, thinking, I've come to think we've been rather fools; there are better things in life than getting the better of a boundary dispute. Neighbor, if you will help me to bury the old quarrel I—I will ask you to be my friend."

Georg Znaeym was silent for so long that Ulrich thought, perhaps, he had fainted with the pain of his injuries. Then he spoke slowly and in jerks.

"How the whole region would stare and gabble[8] if we rode into the market-square together. No one living can remember seeing a Znaeym and a von Gradwitz talking to one another in friendship. And what peace there would be among the forester folk if we ended our feud tonight. And if we choose to make peace among our people there is none other to interfere, no

> *What does Ulrich begin to think as he looks at Georg? What does he decide?*

---

7. **compact.** Agreement
8. **gabble.** Chatter; talk

words for everyday use

en • deav • or or en • deav • our (en devˊər) *n.*, attempt, effort. *Hillary's first <u>endeavor</u> to dock the boat failed; her second attempt succeeded.*

lan • guor (laŋˊgər) *n.*, lack of interest, listlessness. *The speaker's dullness and the stifling room filled us with <u>languor</u>.*

interlopers from outside. . . . You would come and keep the Sylvester night[9] beneath my roof, and I would come and feast on some high day at your castle. . . . I would never fire a shot on your land, save when you invited me as a guest; and you should come and shoot with me down in the marshes where the wildfowl are. In all the countryside there are none that could hinder if we willed to make peace. I never thought to have wanted to do other than hate you all my life, but I think I have changed my mind about things too, this last half-hour. And you offered me your wine-flask. . . . Ulrich von Gradwitz, I will be your friend."

For a space both men were silent, turning over in their minds the wonderful changes that this dramatic <u>reconciliation</u> would bring about. In the cold, gloomy forest, with the wind tearing in fitful gusts through the naked branches and whistling round the tree-trunks, they lay and waited for the help that would now bring release and succor to both parties. And each prayed a private prayer that his men might be the first to arrive, so that he might be the first to show honorable attention to the enemy that had become a friend.

Presently, as the wind dropped for a moment, Ulrich broke silence.

"Let's shout for help," he said; "in this lull our voices may carry a little way."

"They won't carry far through the trees and undergrowth," said Georg, "but we can try. Together, then."

The two raised their voices in a prolonged hunting call.

> **They hear us! They've stopped. Now they see us. They're running down the hill towards us.**

"Together again," said Ulrich a few minutes later, after listening in vain for an answering halloo.

"I heard something that time, I think," said Ulrich.

"I heard nothing but the pestilential[10] wind," said Georg hoarsely.

There was silence again for some minutes, and then Ulrich gave a joyful cry.

"I can see figures coming through the wood. They are following in the way I came down the hillside."

Both men raised their voices in as loud a shout as they could muster.

"They hear us! They've stopped. Now they see us. They're running down the hill towards us," cried Ulrich.

"How many of them are there?" asked Georg.

"I can't see distinctly," said Ulrich; "nine or ten."

"Then they are yours," said Georg; "I had only seven out with me."

"They are making all the speed they can, brave lads," said Ulrich gladly.

"Are they your men?" asked Georg. "Are they your men?" he repeated impatiently as Ulrich did not answer.

"No," said Ulrich with a laugh, the idiotic chattering laugh of a man unstrung with hideous fear.

"Who are they?" asked Georg quickly, straining his eyes to see what the other would gladly not have seen.

"*Wolves.*"

█

> What do the men decide to do?

> Whom do the men think they see in the distance? What do they actually see?

---

9. **Sylvester night.** New Year's Eve, December 31; named after Saint Sylvester
10. **pestilential.** Of or related to a pestilence, regarded as dangerous or harmful

---

words for everyday use

rec • on • cil • i • a • tion (rek´ən sil´ē ā´shən) n., settling of problems or disputes. *Jeff and Hetty put their long grudge aside and reached a <u>reconciliation</u>.*

ABOUT THE RELATED READING

William Blake (1757–1827) was a major poet and one of England's finest visual artists. Nearly all of Blake's poetry focuses on humanity's alternative states of innocence and experience. "A Poison Tree" was published in 1794.

A Poison Tree

William Blake

I was angry with my friend:
I told my wrath, my wrath did end.
I was angry with my foe:
I told it not, my wrath did grow.

And I water'd it in fears,
Night and morning with my tears;
And I sunnéd it with smiles,
And with soft deceitful wiles.

And it grew both day and night,
Till it bore an apple bright;
And my foe beheld it shine,
And he knew that it was mine,

And into my garden stole,
When the night had veil'd the pole:
In the morning glad I see
My foe outstretch'd beneath the tree. ∎

Imagine that you are one of the men, Ulrich or Georg, trapped underneath the beech tree in the forest. Describe your present feelings about all of the years you have spent quarreling with your neighbor.

Investigate, *Inquire,* and Imagine

Recall: GATHERING FACTS

1a. What or whom is Ulrich von Gradwitz pursuing in the forest?

2a. What do the two men do when they meet face to face?

3a. What does Ulrich offer to Georg as a token of friendship?

Interpret: FINDING MEANING

1b. What emotion does Ulrich feel toward Georg Znaeym at the beginning of the story?

2b. What event shows "Nature's own violence" to be stronger than the violence of either man?

3b. What thoughts on the part of both men show that even the villagers would find their reconciliation to be dramatic?

Analyze: TAKING THINGS APART

4a. Identify the changes that take place in Ulrich and Georg while they are trapped together underneath the beech tree.

Synthesize: BRINGING THINGS TOGETHER

4b. Why do you think the changes occur in the two men?

Evaluate: MAKING JUDGMENTS

5a. How strong is the new bond of friendship between Ulrich and Georg? Will it endure if they live?

Extend: CONNECTING IDEAS

5b. Read the poem "A Poison Tree" by William Blake, which also deals with the poisonous nature of feuding. How are the messages of "A Poison Tree" and "The Interlopers" similar? How are the endings different?

Understanding *Literature*

AIM. Review the definition for **aim** in the Handbook of Literary Terms. What do you think is Saki's principal aim in writing the short story "The Interlopers"? Does he accomplish his aim? Explain.

PLOT AND CONFLICT. Review the definitions for **plot**, **conflict**, and **catastrophe**, as well as the plot pyramid you created for Literary Tools on page 722. How is the conflict in the story resolved? Why is the catastrophe that follows the conflict resolution tragic?

Writer's Journal

1. Imagine that Georg has pen and paper while pinned beneath the tree and that he wants to let his men know what has transpired between him and Ulrich. Write a **note** that his men will find so that they will know not to continue the feud.

2. Pretend that Ulrich and Georg are rescued and are able to live out their new vows of friendship. Write a **proclamation** for them to read at a town meeting calling for an end to the feuding by all parties.

3. Write a **conclusion** for the story in which Ulrich and Georg live to prove their friendship for one another.

Integrating the Language Arts

Language, Grammar, and Style

RELATIVE PRONOUNS AND SUBORDINATING CONJUNCTIONS. Read the Language Arts Survey 3.79, "Possessive Nouns and Pronouns," and 3.72, "Subordinating Conjunctions." Then identify the relative pronouns and subordinating conjunctions in the sentences below.

1. If there was a man whose face he didn't want to see, it was Georg Znaeym.
2. He was the person who poached Ulrich's lands.
3. Ulrich could not move from his present position unless someone came to release him.
4. After this ordeal was over, he and Georg would become friends.
5. The wolves that were approaching looked like people.

Collaborative Learning

STORYBOARD. Refer to the plot pyramid you made in Literary Tools on page 722 for this activity. As a class, review the following plot elements in the story: exposition, inciting incident, rising action, climax, falling action, resolution, and catastrophe. Then form seven small groups, assigning one plot element to each group. Within each group, create the appropriate portion of the storyboard, illustrating the key event for that particular plot element. Display in class all eight portions of the storyboard, following the time order used in the story.

Vocabulary

CONTEXT CLUES. Read the Language Arts Survey 1.16, "Using Context Clues to Estimate Word Meaning." Then find the words below in "The Interlopers," and write a definition for each one. Check the definition that you have recorded with the dictionary definition. Finally, write an original sentence that uses each word in context. If a word has more than one definition, use the same definition that it has in the story.

wrest	skirling
acquiesce	ere
wind-scourged	condolences
quarry	succor
wont	muster

from To Kill a Mockingbird
by Harper Lee

Reader's resource

To Kill a Mockingbird addresses the many facets of persecution and intolerance by describing circumstances surrounding the trial of Tom Robinson, an African-American man falsely accused of attacking a white woman. Atticus, father of the six-year-old narrator Scout, acts as Robinson's attorney. Many people in Maycomb, the town in which the novel is set, disapprove of Atticus's actions, but Atticus has the courage to defend a man he knows to be innocent.

The novel also depicts the persecution of the innocent Arthur (Boo) Radley, a mysterious recluse. Rumors about him abound, and he is feared by both children and adults. He is said to peep through windows in the middle of the night, to eat raw squirrels, and to kill flowers with his breath. This selection shows Scout, Jem, and Dill's fascination with Mr. Radley and depicts Scout and Jem's budding friendship with Dill.

The character of Dill is closely based on Lee's childhood friend Truman Capote, who lived with relatives in Monroeville, Lee's home town. Although Lee claims that the novel is not autobiographical, the physical description of Dill matches that of Capote as a boy. Another autobiographical element seems to exist in the description of the activities of Scout and Dill, who enjoyed playing together in a treehouse and acting out scenes from their favorite books and movies, as did Lee and Capote.

About the AUTHOR

Harper Lee (1926–) was born and raised in Monroeville, Alabama. She attended the University of Alabama but left to pursue a writing career before she finished her law degree. While at the university, she wrote for several campus publications, acting on a passion for writing that began when she was seven years old. In the early 1950s she presented two essays and three short stories to a literary agent, who suggested that she expand one of the stories. Acting on this suggestion, Lee produced *To Kill a Mockingbird,* her only novel. When she submitted the manuscript for publication, it was criticized for being merely a string of short stories. After extensive rewriting, the novel was published in 1960. The next year the book won the Pulitzer Prize for fiction, and the following year it was made into a movie starring Gregory Peck.

Literary TOOLS

DESCRIPTION. Description is a type of writing that portrays a character, an object, or a scene. As you read this selection, note how Lee uses *sensory details* to describe the Radley Place. Sensory details are words and phrases that describe how things look, sound, taste, or feel.

NARRATOR. In *To Kill a Mockingbird*, the **narrator**, the person who tells the story, is Scout, a six-year-old girl.

Graphic Organizer

As you read, make a chart to describe how Scout sees people and locations in the world around her. One example has been done for you.

People and Locations in Scout's world	Description
Maycomb	
Atticus	
Calpurnia	
Jem	
Dill	
Mr. Radley	a malevolent phantom

Reader's Journal

Think about an unfamiliar person or place that fascinated you. What about this person or place intrigued you?

From

To Kill a Mockingbird

Harper Lee

Maycomb was an old town,
but it was a tired old town
when I first knew it.

In rainy weather the streets turned to red slop; grass grew on the sidewalks, the courthouse sagged in the square. Somehow, it was hotter then: a black dog suffered on a summer's day; bony mules hitched to Hoover carts flicked flies in the sweltering shade of the live oaks on the square. Men's stiff collars wilted by nine in the morning. Ladies bathed before noon, after their three-o'clock naps, and by nightfall were like soft teacakes with frostings of sweat and sweet talcum.

People moved slowly then. They ambled across the square, shuffled in and out of the stores around it, took their time about everything. A day was twenty-four hours long but seemed longer. There was no hurry, for there was nowhere to go, nothing to buy and no money to buy it with, nothing to see outside the boundaries of Maycomb County. But it was a time of vague optimism for some of the people: Maycomb County had recently been told that it had nothing to fear but fear itself.[1]

We lived on the main residential street in town—Atticus, Jem and I, plus Calpurnia our cook. Jem and I found our father satisfactory: he played with us, read to us, and treated us with courteous <u>detachment</u>.

Calpurnia was something else again. She was all angles and bones; she was nearsighted; she squinted; her hand was wide as a bed slat and twice as hard. She was always ordering me out of the kitchen, asking me why I couldn't behave as well as Jem when she knew he was older, and calling me home when I wasn't ready to come. Our battles were <u>epic</u> and one-sided. Calpurnia always won, mainly because Atticus always took her side. She had been with us ever since Jem

> *What does Calpurnia look like? How does Scout feel about Calpurnia?*

was born, and I had felt her tyrannical presence as long as I could remember.

Our mother died when I was two, so I never felt her absence. She was a Graham from Montgomery; Atticus met her when he was first elected to the state legislature. He was middle-aged then, she was fifteen years his junior. Jem was the product of their first year of marriage; four years later I was born, and two years later our mother died from a sudden heart attack. They said it ran in her family. I did not miss her, but I think Jem did. He remembered her clearly, and sometimes in the middle of a game he would sigh at length, then go off and play by himself behind the car-house. When he was like that, I knew better than to bother him.

> *How did the death of their mother affect Scout and Jem?*

When I was almost six and Jem was nearly ten, our summertime boundaries (within calling distance of Calpurnia) were Mrs. Henry Lafayette Dubose's house two doors to the north of us, and the Radley Place three doors to the south. We were never tempted to break them. The Radley Place was inhabited by an unknown <u>entity</u> the mere description of whom was enough to make us behave for days on end; Mrs. Dubose was plain hell.

> *What do Scout and Jem think about their southern boundary, the Radley Place?*

That was the summer Dill came to us.

Early one morning as we were beginning our day's play in the back yard, Jem and I heard something next door in Miss Rachel Haverford's collard[2] patch. We went to the wire fence to see

---

1. **nothing to fear but fear itself.** Words from a famous radio address by President Franklin D. Roosevelt, intended to reassure people during the Great Depression
2. **collard.** A variety of cabbage

---

words for everyday use

de • tach • ment (dē tach´mənt) n., state of being disinterested. *Do students in your class demonstrate <u>detachment</u>, or are they involved in instruction?*

ep • ic (ep´ik) adj., grand in scale. *The story relates an <u>epic</u> tale of the hero's fantastic adventures.*

en • ti • ty (en´tə tē) n., being. *The <u>entity</u> was able to change shape.*

if there was a puppy—Miss Rachel's rat terrier was expecting—instead we found someone sitting looking at us. Sitting down, he wasn't much higher than the collards. We stared at him until he spoke:

"Hey."

"Hey yourself," said Jem pleasantly.

"I'm Charles Baker Harris," he said. "I can read."

Who is in the collard patch?

"So what?" I said.

"I just thought you'd like to know I can read. You got anything needs readin' I can do it. . . ."

"How old are you," asked Jem, "four-and-a-half?"

"Goin' on seven."

"Shoot no wonder, then," said Jem, jerking his thumb at me. "Scout yonder's been readin' ever since she was born, and she ain't even started to school yet. You look right puny for goin' on seven."

"I'm little but I'm old," he said.

Jem brushed his hair back to get a better look. "Why don't you come over, Charles Baker Harris?" he said. "Lord, what a name."

"'s not any funnier'n yours. Aunt Rachel says your name's Jeremy Atticus Finch."

Jem scowled. "I'm big enough to fit mine," he said. "Your name's longer'n you are. Bet it's a foot longer."

"Folks call me Dill," said Dill, struggling under the fence.

"Do better if you go over it instead of under it," I said. "Where'd you come from?"

Dill was from Meridian, Mississippi, was spending the summer with his aunt, Miss Rachel, and would be spending every summer in Maycomb from now on. His family was from Maycomb County originally, his mother

"Then if he's not dead you've got one, haven't you?"

worked for a photographer in Meridian, had entered his picture in a Beautiful Child contest and won five dollars. She gave the money to Dill, who went to the picture show twenty times on it.

"Don't have any picture shows here, except Jesus ones in the courthouse sometimes," said Jem. "Ever see anything good?"

Dill had seen *Dracula*,[3] a <u>revelation</u> that moved Jem to eye him with the beginning of respect. "Tell it to us," he said.

Dill was a curiosity. He wore blue linen shorts that buttoned to his shirt, his hair was snow white and stuck to his head like duckfluff; he was a year my senior but I towered over him. As he told us the old tale his blue eyes would lighten and darken; his laugh was sudden and happy; he habitually pulled at a cowlick in the center of his forehead.

When Dill reduced Dracula to dust, and Jem said the show sounded better than the book, I asked Dill where his father was: "You ain't said anything about him."

"I haven't got one."

"Is he dead?"

"No . . ."

---

3. *Dracula*. Film based on a novel written by Bram Stoker about an Eastern European count who becomes a vampire

---

words for everyday use

rev • e • la • tion (rev´ə lā´shən) n., striking announcement. *The translation of the Rosetta stone was a <u>revelation</u> to linguists because it gave them the key to Egyptian hieroglyphic.*

"Then if he's not dead you've got one, haven't you?"

Dill blushed and Jem told me to hush, a sure sign that Dill had been studied and found acceptable. Thereafter the summer passed in routine contentment. Routine contentment was: improving our treehouse that rested between giant twin chinaberry trees in the back yard, fussing, running through our list of dramas based on the works of Oliver Optic, Victor Appleton, and Edgar Rice Burroughs.[4] In this matter we were lucky to have Dill. He played the character parts formerly thrust upon me—the ape in *Tarzan*, Mr. Crabtree in *The Rover Boys*, Mr. Damon in *Tom Swift*. Thus we came to know Dill as a pocket Merlin, whose head teemed with eccentric plans, strange longings, and quaint fancies.

> Why does Scout enjoy playing with Dill?

But by the end of August our repertoire was vapid from countless reproductions, and it was then that Dill gave us the idea of making Boo Radley come out.

The Radley Place fascinated Dill. In spite of our warnings and explanations it drew him as the moon draws water, but drew him no nearer than the light-pole on the

> What is Dill's reaction to the Radley Place?

corner, a safe distance from the Radley gate. There he would stand, his arm around the fat pole, staring and wondering.

The Radley Place jutted into a sharp curve beyond our house. Walking south, one faced its porch; the sidewalk turned and ran beside the lot. The house was low, was once white with a deep front porch and green shutters, but had long ago darkened to the color of the slate-gray yard around it. Rainrotted shingles drooped over the eaves of the veranda; oak trees kept the sun away. The remains of a picket drunkenly guarded the front yard—a "swept" yard that was never swept—where johnson grass and rabbit-tobacco grew in abundance.

Inside the house lived a malevolent phantom. People said he existed, but Jem and I had never seen him. People said he went out at night when the moon was down, and peeped in windows.

> What rumors circulated about the "malevolent phantom"?

When people's azaleas froze in a cold snap, it was because he had breathed on them. Any stealthy small crimes committed in Maycomb were his work. ∎

---

4. **Oliver Optic . . . Burroughs.** Writers of adventure stories; for example, Burroughs wrote *Tarzan*

---

words for everyday use

teem (tēm) *vi.*, be full. *The river teemed with salmon making their way upstream to spawn.*

vap • id (vap´id) *adj.*, dull, uninteresting. *Do you find my conversation vapid, or are you just distracted?*

jut (jut) *vi.*, stick out. *The fishing pier juts into the ocean*

ma • lev • o • lent (mə lev´ə lənt) *adj.*, wishing evil or harm to others. *The malevolent witch put a curse on the boy.*

Respond *to the* SELECTION

What would you do to fill your time if you lived in a town like Maycomb?

Investigate, Inquire, and Imagine

Recall: GATHERING FACTS

1a. What kind of town is Maycomb? How does the narrator remember the summers? What were the children's summer boundaries?

2a. How did Dill's mother win money? What did Dill do with the money?

3a. How does Scout define "routine contentment"? What new idea did Dill have?

Interpret: FINDING MEANING

1b. How did the type of town they lived in affect the activities and imaginations of Jem, Scout, and Dill? Why weren't Scout and Jem tempted to break their summer boundaries?

2b. What effect did Dill's knowledge of movies have on Jem and Scout's play?

3b. Why is Dill fascinated by the Radley house?

Analyze: TAKING THINGS APART

4a. Identify the characteristics that differentiate Dill from Jem and Scout.

Synthesize: BRINGING THINGS TOGETHER

4b. Why do you think Dill was the one most interested in getting Boo Radley to come out?

Evaluate: MAKING JUDGMENTS

5a. How effective is the author at using description to portray the look and feel of Maycomb? Explain.

Extend: CONNECTING IDEAS

5b. How does the introduction of Dill create contrast to Jem and Scout's everyday life in Maycomb? What effect does the mention of Boo Radley have on the reader?

Understanding Literature

DESCRIPTION. Review the definition for **description** in the Handbook of Literary Terms. Which sense does Lee appeal to when describing the Radley Place? What sensory details does Lee use? What effect do the sensory details create? Cite specific words and phrases that create this effect.

NARRATOR. Review the definition for **narrator** in the Handbook of Literary Terms and the chart you made for Literary Tools on page 731. Who narrates *To Kill a Mockingbird*? Why do you think Lee chose to have a child tell the story? How might the story differ if it were told by an adult?

Writer's Journal

1. Imagine that you are Atticus and have just viewed one of Jem's, Scout's, and Dill's dramas. Write a **theater review** to share with the children.

2. Imagine that you are Dill. Write an **invitation** to Boo Radley asking him to an activity. Introduce yourself, and explain why you would like to meet Boo.

3. Lee based the character of Dill on her childhood friend Truman Capote. Turn one of your friends into a character for a story. Imagine that you are meeting this friend for the first time. Write a **dialogue** between you and your friend that develops some of your friend's characteristics.

Integrating the Language Arts

Language, Grammar, and Style

PROPER NOUNS AND ADJECTIVES. Read the Language Arts Survey 3.95, "Proper Nouns and Adjectives." Then form a proper noun and a proper adjective for each of the following common nouns.

EXAMPLE: philosopher; Socrates (noun); <u>Socratic</u> method (adjective)

1. state
2. country
3. scientist
4. literary movement
5. writer

Speaking and Listening & Collaborative Learning

ROLE-PLAY. Think about why Jem, Scout, and Dill are so fascinated by Boo Radley and why they want to make him come out. Then, in groups of three, act out the story of Jem, Scout, and Dill, discussing reasons for and reasons against getting Boo to come out. Also discuss certain options that might work to get him to come out. Remember that these characters are ten, six, and seven years old respectively.

Media Literacy

ABSTRACT. Although this novel was published in 1960, its themes of persecution and tolerance continue to be important issues today. Find a newspaper, magazine, or Internet article concerning a recent real-life example of persecution or tolerance. Then write an abstract about the article. An abstract, or summary, is a brief account of the main ideas or arguments presented in an article.

Literary
T O O L S

MOTIVATION. A **motivation** is a force that moves a character to think, feel, or behave in a certain way. As you read, determine what Mrs. Jones's motivation is for helping Roger.

CHARACTERIZATION. Characterization is the use of literary techniques to create a character. Writers use three major techniques to create characters: direct description, portrayal of characters' behavior, and representations of characters' internal states.

Organizer

As you read, make a Venn diagram to list what you know about Mrs. Jones and Roger. One example has been done for you.

Mrs. Jones
strong
forceful

wanted
things in
their youth
they could
not get

Roger
fourteen or
fifteen and
willow-wild

in tennis
shoes and
blue jeans

Reader's

Think about the following situations: a neighbor picks flowers from your garden; your sibling borrows your favorite sweatshirt without asking; a classmate looks at your test answers. How would you respond to each of these situations?

"Thank You, M'am"
by Langston Hughes

Reader's
r e s o u r c e

"Thank You, M'am" tells the story of a boy who tries to steal and is reformed by his victim. These are the only two characters in the story. "Thank You, M'am" was published in 1958 in Hughes's collection of short stories *Something in Common.*

CULTURE CONNECTION. Hughes's stories and poetry portray the joys and miseries of ordinary African Americans. He typically wrote about African Americans living in Harlem, a section of New York City.

About *the*
A U T H O R

Langston Hughes (1902–1967) was born in Joplin, Missouri, and grew up in Lawrence, Kentucky, and Cleveland, Ohio. He came from a family of abolitionists, people who fought for the end of slavery in the United States. Hughes started writing at an early age and published poetry and fiction in his high school magazine. After attending Columbia University for one year, he worked at a series of odd jobs while developing his skills as a writer. He then attended Lincoln University in Pennsylvania and graduated in 1929. By that time, he had published two books of poetry and had become known as a versatile and gifted poet. Hughes became concerned with political issues in the United States and other countries. For twenty years he worked as a columnist for an African-American weekly publication, *The Chicago Defender.* For the column, he wrote the humorous "Semple" stories about Jesse B. Semple, a black urban "Everyman." He also wrote the lyrics for a Broadway musical, *Street Scene.* Hughes eventually settled in Harlem, New York, and produced several volumes of poetry as well as a novel and an autobiography.

Thank You, M'am

Langston Hughes

Minnie, 1930. William H. Johnson. National Museum of American Art, Washington, DC.

She was a large woman with a large purse that had everything in it but hammer and nails. It had a long strap, and she carried it slung across her shoulder. It was about eleven o'clock at night, dark, and she was walking alone, when a boy ran up behind her and tried to snatch her purse.

The strap broke with the single tug the boy gave it from behind. But the boy's weight and the weight of the purse combined caused him to lose his balance. Instead of taking off full blast as he had hoped, the boy fell on his back on the sidewalk and his legs flew up. The large woman simply turned around and kicked him right square in his blue-jeaned sitter. Then she reached down, picked the boy up by his shirt front, and shook him until his teeth rattled.

> What does the boy try to steal? What does his intended victim do to him?

After that the woman said, "Pick up my pocketbook, boy, and give it here."

She still held him tightly. But she bent down enough to permit him to stoop and pick up her purse. Then she said, "Now ain't you ashamed of yourself?"

Firmly gripped by his shirt front, the boy said, "Yes'm."

The woman said, "What did you want to do it for?"

The boy said, "I didn't aim to."

She said, "You a lie!"

By that time two or three people passed, stopped, turned to look, and some stood watching.

"If I turn you loose, will you run?" asked the woman.

"Yes'm," said the boy.

"Then I won't turn you loose," said the woman. She did not release him.

"Lady, I'm sorry," whispered the boy.

"Um-hum! And your face is dirty. I got a great mind to wash your face for you. Ain't you got nobody home to tell you to wash your face?"

"No'm," said the boy.

"Then it will get washed this evening," said the large woman starting up the street, dragging the frightened boy behind her.

He looked as if he were fourteen or fifteen, frail and willow-wild,[1] in tennis shoes and blue jeans.

The woman said, "You ought to be my son. I would teach you right from wrong. Least I can do right now is to wash your face. Are you hungry?"

"No'm," said the being-dragged boy. "I just want you to turn me loose."

"Was I bothering *you* when I turned that corner?" asked the woman.

"No'm."

"But you put yourself in contact with *me*," said the woman. "If you think that that contact is not going to last awhile, you got another thought coming. When I get through with you, sir, you are going to remember Mrs. Luella Bates Washington Jones."

Sweat popped out on the boy's face and he began to struggle. Mrs. Jones stopped, jerked him around in front of her, put a half nelson[2] about his neck, and continued to drag him up the street. When she got to her door, she dragged the boy inside, down a hall, and into a large kitchenette-furnished room[3] at the rear of the house. She switched on the light and left the door open. The boy could hear other roomers laughing and talking in the large house. Some of their doors were open, too, so he knew he and the woman were not alone. The woman still had him by the neck in the middle of her room.

She said, "What is your name?"

"Roger," answered the boy.

"Then, Roger, you go to that sink and wash your face," said the woman, whereupon she turned him loose—at last. Roger looked at the door—

> What does Mrs. Jones tell Roger to do?

looked at the woman—looked at the door—*and went to the sink.*

---

1. **willow-wild.** Thin, graceful, and flexible like a willow tree
2. **half nelson.** Wrestling hold in which one arm is pressed under the opponent's arm and one hand pressed to the back of the neck (as opposed to the full nelson in which both arms are pressed under the opponent's arms and both hands pressed to the back of the neck)
3. **kitchenette-furnished room.** *kitchenette*—very small kitchen typical of urban apartment buildings; *furnished room*—room rented with furniture

Jim, 1930. William H. Johnson. National Museum of American Art, Washington, DC.

"Let the water run until it gets warm," she said. "Here's a clean towel."

"You gonna take me to jail?" asked the boy, bending over the sink.

"Not with that face, I would not take you nowhere," said the woman. "Here I am trying to get home to cook me a bite to eat and you snatch my pocketbook! Maybe you ain't been to your supper either, late as it be. Have you?"

"There's nobody home at my house," said the boy.

"Then we'll eat," said the woman. "I believe you're hungry—or been hungry—to try to snatch my pocketbook!"

"I want a pair of blue suede shoes," said the boy.

art note

William H. Johnson (1901–1970) began his career during the Harlem Renaissance, and for the rest of his life, divided his time between Europe and New York. His style changed dramatically during his career. Compare the style he used for *Jim* and *Minnie* (on the previous page) with that of *Underground Railroad* on page 56. What differences do you see?

"Well, you didn't have to snatch *my* pocketbook to get some suede shoes," said Mrs. Luella Bates Washington Jones. "You could of asked me."

What reason does Roger give for trying to steal money from Mrs. Jones? How does Mrs. Jones respond to this?

"M'am?"

The water dripping from his face, the boy looked at her. There was a long pause. A very long pause. After he had dried his face and not knowing what else to do, dried it again, the boy turned around, wondering what next. The door was open. He could make a dash for it down the hall. He could run, run, run, *run!*

The woman was sitting on the daybed.[4] After a while she said, "I were young once and I wanted things I could not get."

There was another long pause. The boy's mouth opened. Then he frowned, not knowing he frowned.

The woman said, "Um-hum! You thought I was going to say *but*, didn't you? You thought I was going to say, *but I didn't snatch people's pocketbooks.* Well, I wasn't going to say that." Pause. Silence. "I have done things, too, which I would not tell you, son—neither tell God, if He didn't already know. Everybody's got something in common. So you set down while I fix us something to eat. You might run that comb through your hair so you will look presentable."

In another corner of the room behind a screen was a gas plate and an icebox.[5] Mrs. Jones got up and went behind the screen. The woman did not watch the boy to see if he was going to run now, nor did she watch her purse, which she left behind her on the daybed. But the boy took care to sit on the far side of the room, away from the purse, where he thought she could easily see him out of the corner of her eye if she wanted to. He did not trust the woman *not* to trust him.[6] And he did not want to be mistrusted now.

Where did Roger sit as Mrs. Jones prepared the meal? Why?

"Do you need somebody to go to the store," asked the boy, "maybe to get some milk or something?"

"Don't believe I do," said the woman, "unless you just want sweet milk yourself. I was going to make cocoa out of this canned milk I got here."

"That will be fine," said the boy.

She heated some lima beans and ham she had in the icebox, made the cocoa, and set the table. The woman did not ask the boy anything about where he lived, or his folks, or anything else that would embarrass him. Instead, as they ate, she told him about her job in a hotel beauty shop that stayed open late, what the work was like, and how all kinds of women came in and out, blondes, redheads, and Spanish. Then she cut him a half of her ten-cent cake.

"Eat some more, son," she said.

When they were finished eating, she got up and said, "Now here, take this ten dollars and buy yourself some blue suede shoes. And next time, do not make the mistake of latching onto *my* pocketbook *nor nobody else's*—because shoes got by devilish ways will burn your feet. I got to get my rest now. But from here on in, son, I hope you will behave yourself."

What does Mrs. Jones give to Roger? About what does she warn him? What does she wish?

She led him down the hall to the front door and opened it. "Good night! Behave yourself, boy!" she said, looking out into the street as he went down the steps.

The boy wanted to say something other than, "Thank you, m'am," to Mrs. Luella Bates Washington Jones, but although his lips moved, he couldn't even say that as he turned at the foot of the barren stoop and looked up at the large woman in the door. Then she shut the door. ∎

4. **daybed.** Bed that can be a sofa during the day
5. **gas plate and an icebox.** *gas plate*—Small cooking surface fueled by gas; *icebox*—cabinet containing ice for keeping food cold
6. **He did not . . . trust him.** He did not believe that she would mistrust him (but he wasn't sure)

What do you think Roger will do the next time he wants something he cannot afford?

Investigate, *Inquire,* and Imagine

Recall: GATHERING FACTS

1a. What did Roger hope to steal? What happened when he tried to do this? What was his intended victim's first response?

2a. What two things does Mrs. Jones ask Roger about his home life? Where does Mrs. Jones live? What does she tell Roger to do as soon as they arrive at her home?

3a. What did Roger want with Mrs. Jones's money? What does Mrs. Jones tell him he could have done?

Interpret: FINDING MEANING

1b. What does Mrs. Jones's reaction to the attempted robbery say about the kind of person she is?

2b. Why do you think Mrs. Jones wanted to know about Roger's home life?

3b. How does Mrs. Jones try to get Roger to trust her? What personal information does Mrs. Jones share with Roger?

Analyze: TAKING THINGS APART

4a. Why doesn't Mrs. Jones call the police and have Roger arrested? Why does she help him?

Synthesize: BRINGING THINGS TOGETHER

4b. Why do you think Roger goes to the sink instead of the door when he has a chance to run away? What about Mrs. Jones is causing him to stay?

Evaluate: MAKING JUDGMENTS

5a. At the conclusion of the story, Roger is incapable of uttering an expression of thanks to Mrs. Jones. Is this ending realistic? Why, or why not?

Extend: CONNECTING IDEAS

5b. Predict how Roger's encounter with Mrs. Jones will change his life. What life lessons do you think he has learned? What do you think he will do in the future when he wants something he cannot afford?

Understanding *Literature*

MOTIVATION. Review the definition for **motivation** in the Handbook of Literary Tools. What is Mrs. Jones's motivation for helping Roger? What is Roger's motivation for trying to steal Mrs. Jones's purse?

CHARACTERIZATION. Review the definition for **characterization** in the Handbook of Literary Tools and the Venn diagram you made for Literary Tools on page 738. Which techniques of characterization does Hughes employ in his characterization of Mrs. Jones and Roger? Name one example from the story for each of these techniques. What are four things you learned about Mrs. Jones and Roger? What things do they have in common?

Writer's Journal

1. Imagine that Roger goes to the shoe store and buys a pair of blue suede shoes. He even has some money left over, so he decides to buy Mrs. Jones a small gift. Imagine you are Roger and write a **thank-you note**. Explain what the gift is for, tell Mrs. Jones how you like your new shoes, and express what her generosity has meant in your life.

2. Imagine that you are Mrs. Jones who talks to a neighbor in her rooming house the next day about her encounter with Roger. Write the **dialogue** between these two people. Mrs. Jones should give her opinions about Roger and explain why she helped him. The neighbor should make judgments and ask intelligent questions.

3. A rap is an improvised rhymed verse that is chanted or sung, often to a musical accompaniment. Write the words for a **rap song** about learning a lesson.

Integrating the Language Arts

Language, Grammar, and Style

IDENTIFYING MAIN SUBJECTS AND VERBS. Finding the subject and verb of a sentence can be tricky when a sentence contains a subordinate clause. Even though both clauses have a subject and a verb, the subject and verb of the main clause will be the subject and verb of the sentence. Read the Language Arts Survey 3.84, "The Clauses of a Sentence: Simple, Compound, and Complex Sentences." Then rewrite the following sentences, underlining the main subject once and the main verb twice.

1. If I turn you loose, will you run?
2. Sweat popped out on the boy's face after he struggled with Mrs. Jones.
3. As soon as they finished eating, Mrs. Jones gave the boy money for shoes.
4. While Mrs. Jones talked about her past, the boy listened.
5. Although his lips moved, he could say nothing to thank her.

Study and Research & Collaborative Learning

HARLEM RENAISSANCE. Langston Hughes belonged to the Harlem Renaissance, a period of great artistic and literary creativity in the African-American community of Harlem, New York. Working with several classmates, assign a topic to each person, such as the goals of the Harlem Renaissance, the artists and writers involved, and representative works. One classmate might be responsible for creating a time line listing notable events and achievements during this period. Each classmate reports back to the group. One website you will find useful is "Harlem Renaissance" at http://encarta.msn.com/schoolhouse/Harlem/harlem.asp.

Guided *Writing*

EVALUATING COMMUNICATION STYLES

Observing people is critical to effective writing because all writing investigates some aspect of "the human condition" or contemplates life forces in action. Whether you write fiction or nonfiction, essays or poetry, you convey insights about the world around you.

People use both verbal and nonverbal communication to convey meaning and exchange ideas. Have you ever talked to a friend, made everything perfectly clear, and then realized that friend didn't understand you at all? Or, even more disturbing, has a friend, or a parent, given you complete instructions (they thought), while you listened as closely as you could, only to find out later that you missed the message completely?

WRITING ASSIGNMENT. **Observe** the way two people communicate. **Report** what you've observed and heard, and then **analyze** the effectiveness of that communication. This is a great way to understand "the human condition," the people in your own life, and the way you yourself communicate.

Professional Model

from "Thank You, M'am" by Langston Hughes
page 740

She said, "What is your name?"

"Roger," answered the boy.

"Then, Roger, you go to that sink and wash your face," said the woman, whereupon she turned him loose—at last. Roger looked at the door—looked at the woman—looked at the door—*and went to the sink*.

"Let the water run until it gets warm," she said. "Here's a clean towel."

"You gonna take me to jail?" asked the boy, bending over the sink.

"Not with that face, I would not take you nowhere," said the woman. "Here I am trying to get home to cook me a bit to eat and you snatch my pocketbook! Maybe you ain't been to your supper either, late as it be. Have you?"

> "We are given senses to receive our information with. With our own eyes we see, and with our skin we feel."
>
> —Sophy Burnham

The value of communication lies in what is heard. It doesn't much matter what you *meant* to say if the listener did not get it.

Humans communicate with words when they write, words that have both a **denotation** and a **connotation.** You've seen this in that familiar distinction between the literal meaning of "pig = an animal with a curly tail and a flat snout" and the more figurative meaning of "pig = a person who is messy."

But when you are speaking and listening with another communicator, you drape your words in *connotations* passed on in your actions, your expressions, your voice, your *nonverbal* behavior. As much as sixty percent of the meaning of a message may be communicated nonverbally.

EXAMINING THE MODEL.

Langston Hughes, in "Thank you, M'am," describes an intense confrontation between a purse snatcher and his intended victim. Roger is caught by Mrs. Luella Bates Washington Jones, and summarily taken to her rooming house. She intends to teach Roger a lesson, but not by turning him into the police.

Mrs. Luella Bates Washington Jones shows her concern for Roger in the way she talks to him and in the way she treats him. Hughes carefully describes Roger's intentions—running out of her room, escaping—in Roger's nonverbal analysis of the door, the woman, the sink. Hughes does not give us the thoughts going through Roger's mind. He just lets us see him weigh the situation.

Hughes also conveys Mrs. Luella Bates Washington Jones's concern for Roger in the *connotations* behind what she says. In her reply, "Not with that face, I would not take you nowhere," she implies that he's not a criminal, but just a kid with a dirty face, an easily remedied flaw.

Prewriting

FINDING YOUR VOICE. There is no finer skill for a writer than to develop the art of observing and recording what he or she sees and hears. Think of yourself as a reporter preparing a feature article on communication skills. Your voice will be professional, the voice of the research paper. But your notes and observations will come from real conversation and exchange of feelings and ideas. Be accurate in capturing the dialect, the body movements, facial expressions, and the slang you hear.

IDENTIFYING YOUR AUDIENCE. The audience for an informative essay will be other learners, the students in your classroom. You will be informing the audience about what you saw and heard.

You will also be analyzing what you've recorded to persuade your audience that the communication was effective or not effective. When the time comes to persuade, your writing must be targeted to that student audience. Your classmates are going to want to know what you think the message did, or did not, get across. You will have to use your strongest writing skills to convince them of your evaluation.

WRITING WITH A PLAN. Let's examine the steps of this sociological research adventure.

1. **OBSERVING:** Select two people to watch and take copious notes. Because people modify their behavior when they know they are being observed, it's best, therefore, to select people in conversation who are not aware you are observing. This may be hard to do in your own home. If you choose to observe a communication at home, you might want to announce that you have to do this assignment, and that you'll be doing it at some unannounced time so that your sample is not tainted by modified behavior.

    Your simplest opportunities may occur in school, at lunchtime, while you are waiting for the bus, or sitting in a restaurant. It is often easiest to make the detailed notes that observation entails when you are observing strangers. Focus on a short exchange rather than a long, drawn out conversation.

2. **REPORTING THE OBSERVATION:** Your notes should include who said what, and when, but also the nonverbal communication that occurred. The checklist in the graphic organizer will help as you observe and as you complete the write-up.

3. **ANALYZING THE COMMUNICATION:** You will decide what messages have been conveyed by either person, whether a power structure is obvious in the exchange, and perhaps whether each person prefers verbal or nonverbal techniques. To persuade your audience of your opinion, you'll need to be precise and convincing.

    Distinct elements of both verbal and nonverbal

communication can be isolated as you observe an exchange. Use this checklist as a tool as you conduct your observation.

Student Model—Graphic Organizer

	ELEMENT	DEFINITION	EXAMPLES
V E R B A L	Volume	loudness or softness of speech	yelling, booming, hushed
	Melody, Pitch	high tones or bass tones	shrill, nasal, baritone, monotone
	Pace	speed	fast-talking, slow, pauses
	Tone	emotional quality	animated, laconic, solemn
	Enunciation	clearness of speech	slurring, precise pronunciation, mumbling
N O N V E R B A L	Eye contact	focus of the eyes	eyes diverted, eyes directly into eyes, focus on floor, shifting eyes
	Facial expressions	emotions shown on face	frowning, smiling, sneering, head tilting
	Gestures	motions of hands, arms	chopping movements, swinging arms, crossing arms, pointing fingers, twiddling fingers
	Posture	position of the body	turned towards or away from speaker, slumped shoulders, tense body
	Proximity	distance from listener	6" away from listener, several feet apart, arm around shoulder, heads together

> "I think the whole glory of writing lies in the fact that it forces us out of ourselves into the live of others."
>
> —Sherwood Anderson

Drafting

Once you have gathered your data, you are ready to write your first draft of your evaluation. First, write it all out. You will determine the final structure you'd like to use once you've recorded your initial facts and interpretations.

First: Describe the subjects you have observed. Who are they? Where did the observation take place? When? Were you able to observe without being detected?

Second: Describe the nature of the communication—what information was passed on, what decisions were made, what questions were answered?

Language, Grammar, and Style

Formal and Informal English

IDENTIFYING FORMAL AND INFORMAL ENGLISH. In the short story, "Thank you, M'am," the informal nature of the characters' speech is quite pronounced. Mrs. Luella Bates Washington Jones and Roger both use slang and incorrect grammatical structures.

"Now, ain't you ashamed of yourself?"

"Um-hum! And your face is dirty. I got a great mind to wash your face for you. Ain't you got nobody home to tell you to wash your face?"

"You gonna take me to jail?"

"I were young once and I wanted things I could not get."

If Langston Hughes had written these statements in grammatically correct or formal English, he would have (1) failed to reveal the education level of the speakers, and (2) created entirely different people. Can you imagine how you would visualize these two characters had they spoken differently?

"Now, aren't you ashamed of yourself?"

"Thank you for the apology. I notice, however, that your face is

Third: Discuss the verbal communications you heard. What vocabulary or expressions conveyed speaker attitudes or opinions? Record dialogue exchanges to demonstrate the messages conveyed.

Fourth: Discuss the nonverbal implications of the exchange. How did the speakers communicate with their bodies and their faces? Did the nonverbal communication match the verbal? Were there misunderstandings? Were the misunderstandings clarified, and how? Was one person assertive, one nonassertive, and was this conveyed verbally or nonverbally?

Fifth: Analyze the style of communication that each person demonstrated in this exchange. Characterize each speaker's approach to the other, and each speaker's approach to the subject being discussed. Is there an underlying power structure apparent in the exchange? Prove your assertions with your recorded observations. Persuade your reader that your analysis is accurate and backed up by your observations.

Student Model—Draft

Heath Brinker observed a scene in a private home and made the following notes:

Set the scene - How old is daughter? What is going on right before this exchange?
(voice soft, leaning in doorway)
Elise:∧Mom, what's for dinner?

(plunking down in chair)   ⓘtal
Mom:∧I don't know—∨what are you making for dinner?

                          (cocky)
Elise: Nothing∧(walking away). - tone of voice?

(rising voice)   Reword: redundant
Mom:∧Oh yes you are, it's your turn (crescendo-ing voice to loud at the end)   Put stage directions before the speech

Elise: (yelling from bedroom) What about Jake, he hasn't cooked dinner in a while.

Mom: Jake was gone last weekend and he's ̶i̶s̶ still tired (looking straight at Elise through the door)

Elise: So? (pouting expression, crossing her arms)

Mom: So...what!? (standing up and yelling)

consider dropping final g

Elise: So I'm not making dinner tonight! (looking Mom straight in the eye). *[handwritten: g]*

Mom: You are too, young lady (pointing and waving her index finger)

Elise: I'm not! (pouting like a child)

make a contraction

Mom: You are˄too, and <u>that is</u> the end of this discussion. (angry expression)

Elise: I'm not making dinner, so there (running to her bedroom, yelling, slamming the bedroom door shut) *What message? State it*

Mom: Elise! (yelling at the top of her lungs while banging her fists on Elise's bedroom door)

    Analysis: It was obvious that the mom was trying to get her message across but it failed because Jake ended up making dinner. Elise didn't change her tone of voice or make hand gestures very much, but the mother changed her voice a few times while using many hand *in what way?* gestures. That is why I think that the mother uses nonverbal ways to express herself, and Elise uses words, and only a few.

She also uses nonverbal: pouting, crossing her arms, slamming the door
Who had power here?

Self- and Peer Evaluation

Clarity in your description of this exchange is mandatory. Look over your rough draft with these questions in mind:

- Where have you used quotation marks correctly in dialogue?
- Have you fairly described the way words were stated?
- Where have you used ellipses (. . .) to indicate pauses in a statement . . . spots where a speaker hesitates?
- Where are the descriptions of body language vivid enough that the reader can see through your eyes?
- Where have you used figurative language to paint a picture of nonverbal communications?
- What have you concluded about the exchange and the nature of the individuals' relationship?
- What conclusions have you made about the nature of verbal and nonverbal communication in general?
- Where have you used formal, standard English?

dirty. I believe it would be appropriate for me to assist you in washing your face. Haven't you parents at home to instruct you in personal hygiene?"

"Are you planning to take me to the detention center?"

"I was young once, and I did covet material goods that I could not procure."

It just wouldn't have worked!

FIXING FORMAL AND INFORMAL ENGLISH. In Heath's report, you can change some language to make the scene more reflective of informal talk. Add some contractions to make the speech less formal. Look at dropping the final –g for the same effect. Change these sentences to make them less formal:

Original: "What are *you* making for dinner?"

Original: "Jake was gone last weekend and he is still tired."

Original: "You are, too, and that is the end of this discussion."

USING FORMAL AND INFORMAL ENGLISH. Look at your own first draft. Select three statements made by the speakers you observed. Rewrite these so that they more accurately reflect the sound of slang and the cadence of normal speech. Quite often, final consonants are dropped in speech—*goin'* rather than *going*. Another variant in normal speech is the use of

continued on page 750

contractions rather than complete subject-verb constructions—*I've* rather than *I have*—and even more realistically, *I've got* rather than *I have.* Another signal that speech is informal is repetition of phrases—*You know, you know...* or *I wanted to...you know...I wanted to go home then.*

For additional review, see the Language Arts Survey 3.2, "Formal and Informal English." and 3.5, "Dialects of English."

- Where have you accurately conveyed the informal English, e.g. slang, colloquialisms, dialects, of the speakers?
- Where have you covered emotional variations in speech, such as sighs, shrieks, whispers, or coughs?

Revising and Proofreading

Remember that in the Drafting section of this lesson you focused on description and the nature and style of the verbal and nonverbal communication taking place. Use your self- and peer evaluations to make revision decisions. As you look back at your rough draft, be prepared to make major changes when necessary. See the Language Arts Survey 2.45 for a proofreading checklist.

Student Model—Revised

by Heath Brinker

This observation took place in a home where a mother and a daughter were discussing dinner preparations. The daughter has been home from middle school for 2 hours and the mother is just arriving home from work.

Elise (voice soft and gentle, leaning in the doorway): Mom, what's for dinner?

Mom (plunking down in a chair, looking directly at Elise): I don't know. What are *you* making for dinner?

Elise (cocky tone of voice, walking away): Nothin'.

Mom (voice rising from soft at beginning to loud at the end, without any humor in voice): Ooh yes you are! It's your turn.

Elise (yelling from her bedroom across the way, in a honestly questioning voice, but not looking in her mom's direction): What about Jake? He hasn't cooked dinner in a while.

Mom (leaning toward the bedroom, looking directly at Elise): Jake was gone last weekend and he is still tired. Elise (walking back into the kitchen, crossing her arms, pouting voice): So?

Mom (standing up and yelling): So WHAT??

Elise (looking her mother straight in the eyes, stating clearly: So, I'm not makin' dinner tonight.

Mom (pointing at her and waving her index finger, voice speeding up): You are too, young lady.

Elise (pout deepens, arms crossed): I'm not!

Mom (now furious, with the face of someone who has just been kicked): You are too, and THAT'S the end of this discussion.

Elise (yelling as she runs to her bedroom and slams bedroom door shut): I'm NOT making dinner, so there!

Mom (going to bedroom door, yelling at the top of her lungs while banging her fists on Elise's bedroom door): Elise, you get out here right now! You hear me!

Obviously, the mother was trying to get a message across that Elise should make dinner, but it failed because Jake ended up making dinner. Elise resisted the order to make dinner by firm verbal statements and very little emotion. The mother, on the other hand, raised both the volume and the tone of her voice a couple of times, becoming louder and higher pitched with frustration. The mother used many gestures, while the daughter seemed collected and calm until she finally denied the mother, strongly.

The daughter had power over the mother in this exchange because she won in the end. The mother appeared tired and unable to protest, her emotions clearly not affecting the daughter. The daughter did not recognize or sympathize with the mother's stress.

Publishing and Presenting

In professional associations, writers read evaluations such as you have done before a gathering of peers to learn from one another. Share your findings with your class. You have something valuable to say.

Reflecting

Communication matters. Human beings uniquely read, write, speak. Manipulating language is what makes us human, yet we "speak" with our whole selves verbally and nonverbally. What did you learn about communication from your observation? What are you still thinking about? What is your own style of communicating? Do you excel in some elements of communicating, but need work in others? How would you define a good listener?

UNIT **9** *review*
Relationships

Words for Everyday Use

Check your knowledge of the following vocabulary words from the selections in this unit. Write short sentences using each of these words in context to make the meaning clear. To review the definition or usage of a word, refer back to the page number(s) listed or the Glossary of Words for Everyday Use.

compromise, 724	escort, 708	marauder, 725	restraining, 725
decapitate, 709	harass, 706	mint, 709	revelation, 734
detachment, 733	impalpable, 715	mock, 708	teem, 735
dismantle, 707	implacable, 716	pinion, 725	vapid, 735
ebony, 708	jut, 735	plight, 725	vintage, 707
embitter, 724	languor, 726	precipitous, 724	vulgar, 707
endeavor, 726	mahogany, 708	predicament, 700	
entity, 733	makeshift, 707	reconciliation, 727	
epic, 733	malevolent, 735	relic, 710	

Literary Tools

Define each of the following terms, giving concrete examples of how they are used in the selections in this unit. To review a term, refer to the page number(s) indicated or the Handbook of Literary Terms.

aim, 722	description, 731	plot, 722
character, 704	image, 714	repetition, 699
characterization, 738	motivation, 738	symbol, 714
conflict, 704, 722	narrator, 731	tone, 699

Reflecting on your reading

Genre Studies

1. **SHORT STORY.** Select two **short stories** from this unit. Do they rely more on dialogue or description? What does each author accomplish with his or her approach?

2. **LYRIC POETRY.** What makes "If You Forget Me" a **lyric poem** rather than a narrative poem? Review the definition for lyric poem in the Handbook of Literary Terms. What elements of the poem contribute to its musicality? What emotions of the speaker are expressed in the poem?

Thematic Studies

3. **FRIENDSHIP.** In *To Kill a Mockingbird*, Scout and Jem make a new friend, Dill. In "The Interlopers" old enemies Ulrich and Georg become friends. What is friendship? What binds the friends in these stories together?

4. **REFORMATION.** What gets Luis in "Catch the Moon" and Roger in "Thank You, M'am" in trouble? What events lead to their reformation? How have the characters changed? Do you think their reformations are permanent? Why, or why not?

for your READING LIST

A Christmas Memory by Truman Capote. As a young boy, Truman Capote was sent away to live with some distant, elderly cousins in rural Monroeville, Alabama. In this autobiographical account, he tells of the special relationship he shared with one of those cousins, Miss Sook Faulk, a shy and eccentric woman who took the same childish delight in kites and fantasy as seven-year-old Truman. Their Christmas tradition was making fruitcakes for strangers who struck their fancy, like President Franklin Roosevelt and the local knife-grinder. In the loving description of these preparations, Truman Capote shows us how a timid old woman and a lonely child, who both feel misunderstood, find love and a sense of belonging with each other.

Independent Reading Activity

WRITE YOUR OWN MEMOIR. What person in your childhood made you feel special, loved or important? Was this person a family member or a friend? an adult or a child? What memories do you have of that person? What events, conversations, and activities did you share? Freewrite in your journal about this person and your relationship, recalling as much detail as you can. Then select a memory that best portrays the nature of the relationship you shared. Write a brief memoir of the time in your life when this person, and your relationship, was so important to you.

Selections for Additional Reading

Grand Mothers: Poems, Reminiscences, and Short Stories about the Keepers of Our Traditions, edited by Nikki Giovanni. This anthology of stories and poems about grandmothers describes the special nature of the relationships we have with our elders and, through them, with our past.

Iceman by Chris Lynch. Struggling to connect with a family he finds emotionless and unreal, fourteen-year-old Eric takes his frustration out on the ice.

The Friends by Kazumi Yumoto. Three boys puzzle over the meaning of death and life by watching an old man, but they learn more than they bargain for when he begins watching them in return.

The Gulf Stream, 1899. Winslow Homer. Metropolitan Museum of Art, New York.

Courage
and
Perseverance

" All our dreams can come
true, if we have the courage
to pursue them. "

—Walt Disney

echoes

➤ Courage is the first of human qualities because it is the quality which guarantees all others.

—*Winston Churchill*

➤ To be courageous…requires no exceptional qualifications, no magic formula, no special combination of time, place, and circumstances. It is an opportunity that sooner or later is presented to us all.

—*John F. Kennedy*

➤ We must do the things we think we cannot do.

—*Eleanor Roosevelt*

➤ Whatever doesn't kill me, makes me stronger.

—*Friedrich Nietzsche*

➤ Children's talent to endure stems from their ignorance of alternatives.

—*Maya Angelou*

➤ Courage and perseverance have a magical talisman, before which difficulties disappear and obstacles vanish into air.

—*John Quincy Adams*

➤ Courage is fear that has said its prayers.

—*Dorothy Bernard*

➤ Courage is like love; it must have hope to nourish it.

—*Napoleon Bonaparte*

➤ Courage is the power to let go of the familiar.

—*Mary Byrant*

➤ He who loses wealth loses much; he who loses a friend loses more; but he that loses his courage loses all.

—*Miguel de Cervantes*

➤ Until the day of his death, no man can be sure of his courage.

—*Jean Anouilh*

➤ Act boldly and unseen forces will come to your aid.

—*Dorothea Brande*

"Courage"
by Anne Sexton

Reader's resource

The four stanzas of **"Courage"** might be seen to represent four stages in a person's life, beginning with childhood. The poem speaks of the courage one needs to face adversity and painful experiences throughout life. In this poem, Anne Sexton may be revealing some of the pain and despair she herself felt during her long struggle with depression.

About the AUTHOR

Anne Sexton (1928–1974) wrote in an intensely personal, "confessional" style, shining harsh light on the emotional anguish that characterized her life. She shocked readers by dealing with controversial topics that "just weren't talked about" during her day. Sexton is also credited with paving the way for poetry that deals with feminist issues.

Sexton was born in Newton, Massachusetts. She attended Garland Junior College for a year before her marriage in August 1948 to Alfred M. Sexton II. She worked at various times as a fashion model and as a librarian, and had two daughters. She began writing in 1956 after attending a class taught by Robert Lowell at Boston University. Her first book, *To Bedlam and Part Way Back,* published in 1960, described her stay in a mental institution and her recovery from an emotional breakdown. Her second book of poems, *All My Pretty Ones,* appeared in 1962 and continued in uncompromising self-exploration. Sexton won a Pulitzer Prize in 1967 for her collection *Live or Die.* She published five more poetry collections after that. Unfortunately, Sexton struggled with depression all her life and, tragically, committed suicide in October 1974. Two collections of her poetry were published after her death by her daughter Linda.

Reader's Journal

Write about a time when you did something that required courage.

Literary TOOLS

PERSONIFICATION. Personification is a figure of speech in which an idea, animal, or thing is described as if it were a person. As you read this poem, note the use of personification.

METAPHOR AND SIMILE. A **metaphor** is a figure of speech in which one thing is spoken or written about as if it were another. This figure of speech invites the reader to make a comparison between the two things. The two "things" involved are the writer's actual subject, the *tenor* of the metaphor, and another thing to which the subject is likened, the *vehicle* of the metaphor. A **simile** is a comparison using *like* or *as*. A simile is a type of metaphor, and like any other metaphor, can be divided into two parts, the tenor and the vehicle. As you read, note how the author uses metaphor and simile throughout this poem.

Graphic Organizer

Make a chart like the one below to list the metaphors and similes found in the poem "Courage." In the left-hand column, write the tenor of each metaphor or simile, and in the center column, write its vehicle. In the right-hand column, write which type of figurative language each is (whether a metaphor or a simile). One example has been done for you.

Tenor	Vehicle	Type of Language
a child's first step	an earthquake	simile

Courage

Anne Sexton

It is in the small things we see it.
The child's first step,
as awesome as an earthquake.
The first time you rode a bike,
5 <u>wallowing</u> up the sidewalk.
The first spanking when your heart
went on a journey all alone.
When they called you crybaby
or poor or fatty or crazy
10 and made you into an alien,
you drank their acid
and concealed it.

Later,
if you faced the death of bombs and bullets
15 you did not do it with a banner,
you did it with only a hat to
cover your heart.
you did not fondle the weakness inside you
though it was there.
20 Your courage was a small coal
that you kept swallowing.
If your buddy saved you,
and died himself in so doing,
then his courage was not courage,
25 it was love; love as simple as shaving soap.

Later,
if you have endured a great despair,
then you did it alone,
getting a transfusion from the fire,
30 picking the scabs off your heart,
then wringing it out like a sock.

> *What is "as awesome as an earthquake"?*

> *What death might a person face in the course of his or her life?*

art note

The End of the War, c.1931. Horace Pippin.

Horace Pippin (1888–1946) fought in World War I with the legendary 369th Infantry, a segregated African American unit. Despite a wound that paralyzed his right arm, Pippin taught himself to paint. Pippin was courageous in battle and also courageous in pursuing his dream to be an artist.

words for everyday use   wal • low (wä' lō) vi., roll about clumsily; take delight. *The pig <u>wallowed</u> in the cool mud on hot days.*

The End of the War, c.1931. Horace Pippin. Philadelphia Museum of Art.

Next, my kinsman, you powdered your sorrow,
you gave it a back rub
and then you covered it with a blanket
35 and after it had slept a while
it woke to the wings of the roses
and was transformed.

Later,
when you face old age and its natural conclusion
40 your courage will still be shown in the little ways,
each spring will be a sword you'll sharpen,
those you love will live in a fever of love,
and you'll bargain with the calendar
and at the last moment
45 when death opens the back door
you'll put on your carpet slippers
and stride out. ■

What does the speaker say was "powdered" and given a back rub?

With what or whom might a person bargain when near the end of life?

Which of the situations described in the poem do you think would require the most courage? Explain.

Investigate, *Inquire,* and Imagine

Recall: GATHERING FACTS

1a. In what "small things" does the speaker say a child shows courage?

2a. What does the speaker say a courageous person would not fondle when facing the death of bombs and bullets? What would inspire a person to save someone else, risking his or her own death?

3a. In stanza 3, what does the speaker say a person might endure in the course of life? In stanza 4, what things does the speaker say a courageous person might do when facing old age and death?

Interpret: FINDING MEANING

1b. Why might these things require courage?

2b. Under what circumstances might a person face death by "bombs and bullets"? Why do you think the speaker thinks that risking one's life to save another is not courage?

3b. What does the speaker mean by "getting a transfusion from the fire"? What allows a person's sorrow to be "transformed"? What does the speaker mean by "each spring will be a sword you'll sharpen"?

Analyze: TAKING THINGS APART

4a. In this poem, the speaker cites a number of situations that require courage. Classify these situations into different groups. For example, which situations provoke fear of physical harm? Which provoke a different kind of fear? How should a courageous person deal with each of these situations?

Synthesize: BRINGING THINGS TOGETHER

4b. According to this poem, how should a person deal with despair and sorrow? How should one face death? Write the definition of courage you think Anne Sexton would write.

Evaluate: MAKING JUDGMENTS

5a. Do you agree with the speaker that risking one's life to save another is not a courageous act? Explain. Which situation mentioned in the poem do you think would be the most difficult to face?

Extend: CONNECTING IDEAS

5b. Brainstorm a list of things you think require courage. Which of these have you faced?

Understanding *Literature*

PERSONIFICATION. Review the definition for **personification** in the Handbook of Literary Terms. List the examples of personification found in this poem. Then, answer the following questions: What does it mean for a heart to go on a journey all alone? What image comes to mind when you read about "sorrow" being powdered and covered with a blanket? What image comes to mind when you read of "death" opening the back door? How does the use of personification make abstract concepts seem more real or concrete?

METAPHOR AND SIMILE. Review the definitions for **metaphor** and **simile** in the Handbook of Literary Terms. In what sense is a child's first step "as awesome as an earthquake"? Why does the poet use the word "acid" in stanza 1? Why does she use the image of a coal in stanza 2? What do you think the poet means by "the wings of the roses" in stanza 3?

Writer's Journal

1. Recall how you felt when you rode a bicycle for the first time. Who was with you, and what thoughts went through your head? Write a **description** of the experience.

2. Write a **metaphor** or **simile** to describe courage. Hint: your metaphor should begin "Courage is…" and your simile should begin "Courage is like…."

3. In stanza 3 of "Courage," Sexton personifies sorrow. If sorrow was a person, what would it look like? How would it act? Write your own **personification** of sorrow. It need only be a paragraph or so in length.

Integrating the Language Arts

Language, Grammar, and Style
RECOGNIZING CLAUSES AND PHRASES. Read the Language Arts Survey 3.81, "Groups of Words That Function as One Part of Speech," and 3.82, "Phrases." Then identify the underlined parts of the following sentences as clauses (C) or phrases (P).

1. As a toddler, you learned to walk <u>with tiny steps</u>.
2. <u>When you were spanked</u>, your heart went on a journey all alone.
3. You did not fondle the weakness inside you <u>though it was there</u>.
4. When you endured a great despair, you did not talk <u>to anyone</u>.
5. You will show courage <u>when you are dying</u>.

Study and Research
RESEARCHING MILITARY MEDALS. Soldiers who participate in war are given medals of courage such as the Purple Heart. Conduct research to find out how many such honors exist and what they are called. Then, choose one medallion or decoration to write about. What are the criteria that qualify a person for this honor? What does the medallion itself look like? (You may want to include a picture or a drawing of your own.) What is the history of the medal? Present your findings to the class.

Collaborative Learning
COURAGE ROLE-PLAY. In groups of four or five students, brainstorm situations in which courage is required. These situations can be from your everyday life. Then, write a skit in which one or more characters acts courageously. Each student should be given a role in the skit. When you have rehearsed the skit several times, enact it in front of the class.

Literary
T O O L S

HERO. A **hero** is a character whose actions are inspiring and courageous. An epic hero represents the ideals of the culture that creates it. In early literature, a hero is often part divine and has remarkable abilities, such as magical power, superhuman strength, or great courage. A tragic hero is a character of high status who possesses noble qualities but who also has a tragic flaw, or personal weakness. In much contemporary literature, the hero often refers to any main character. Which character is the hero in this story?

DESCRIPTION. Description is a type of writing that portrays a character, an object, or a scene. Descriptions make use of *sensory details*—words and phrases that describe how things look, sound, smell, taste, or feel.

Graphic Organizer

Create a sensory details chart like the one below. As you read, record the sensory details used in "The Leap." You may want to focus on the circus scene and the fire scene in particular. Some examples are given.

SIGHT	sequined costume
SOUND	crackle
SMELL	whiff of smoke
TASTE	
TOUCH	stitches burn fingers

"The Leap" by Louise Erdrich

Reader's
r e s o u r c e

"The Leap" portrays a complex mother/daughter relationship and how it changes over the years. The story reminds us that love never lessens with age and that memories of events often remain as vivid as the day on which they happened. "The Leap" has appeared in various publications: first in *Harper's Magazine,* later in a 1994 anthology, *In Praise of Mothers,* and finally, (in a significantly altered form) in her novel *Tales of Burning Love.*

About *the*
A U T H O R

Louise Erdrich (1954–), is the mother of six children, three of whom were adopted by her late husband, writer Michael Dorris, and three of whom the couple had together. Being a mother has deepened her art, she says. "I find myself emotionally engaged in ways I wouldn't have been otherwise. I wouldn't understand certain things that I'm starting to get now."

Another gift to Erdrich's writing is her unique heritage. Like many of the characters in her books, she is of mixed Native American descent: her mother is French Chippewa (Ojibwa) and her father is German American. While Erdrich was growing up in North Dakota, her parents worked as teachers on a reservation. Today, she is a member of the Turtle Mountain Band of Chippewa. Erdrich has said: "To be of mixed blood is a great gift for a writer. I have one foot on tribal lands and one foot in middle-class life."

Reader's
Journal

Can you think of a time when your parent or guardian protected you or saved you from getting hurt? If someone in your family were in danger, what would you do to help that person?

The Leap

Louise Erdrich

The Acrobat, c.1900s, Marc Chagall. Musee d'Art Moderne de la Ville de Paris.

My mother is the surviving half of a blindfold trapeze act, not a fact I think about much even now that she is sightless, the result of encroaching and stubborn cataracts.[1] She walks slowly through her house here in New Hampshire, lightly touching her way along walls and running her hands over knickknacks, books, the drift of a grown child's belongings and castoffs. She has never upset an object or as much as brushed a magazine onto the floor. She has never lost her balance or bumped into a closet door left carelessly open.

It has occurred to me that the catlike precision of her movements in old age might be the result of her early training, but she shows so little of the drama or flair one might expect from a performer that I tend to forget the Flying Avalons. She has kept no sequined costume, no photographs, no fliers or posters from that part of her youth. I would, in fact, tend to think that all memory of double somersaults and heartstopping catches had left her arms and legs were it not for the fact that sometimes, as I sit sewing in the room of the rebuilt house in which I slept as a child, I hear the crackle, catch a whiff of smoke from the stove downstairs, and suddenly the room goes dark, the stitches burn beneath my fingers, and I am sewing with a needle of hot silver, a thread of fire.

I owe her my existence three times. The first was when she saved herself. In the town square a <u>replica</u> tent pole, cracked and splintered, now stands cast in concrete. It commemorates the disaster that put our town smack on the front page of the Boston and New York tabloids.[2] It is from those old newspapers, now historical records, that I get my information. Not from my mother, Anna of the Flying Avalons, nor

> Who were the Flying Avalons? Where does the narrator get her information about them?

from any of her in-laws, nor certainly from the other half of her particular act, Harold Avalon, her first husband. In one news account it says, "The day was mildly overcast, but nothing in the air or temperature gave any hint of the sudden force with which the deadly <u>gale</u> would strike."

I have lived in the West, where you can see the weather coming for miles, and it is true that out here we are at something of a disadvantage. When extremes of temperature collide, a hot and cold front, winds generate instantaneously behind a hill and crash upon you without warning. That, I think, was the likely situation on that day in June. People probably commented on the pleasant air, grateful that no hot sun beat upon the striped tent that stretched over the entire center green. They bought their tickets and surrendered them in anticipation. They sat. They ate carmelized popcorn and roasted peanuts. There was time, before the storm, for three acts. The White Arabians of Ali-Khazar rose on their hind legs and waltzed. The Mysterious Bernie folded himself into a painted cracker tin,[3] and the Lady of the Mists made herself appear and disappear in surprising places. As the clouds gathered outside, unnoticed, the ringmaster cracked his whip, shouted his introduction, and pointed to the ceiling of the tent, where the Flying Avalons were perched.

They loved to drop gracefully from nowhere, like two sparkling birds,

> What did the trapeze artists do in the final vignette of their act?

and blow kisses as they threw off their plumed helmets and high-collared capes. They laughed and flirted openly as they beat their way up again on the trapeze bars. In the final <u>vignette</u>

---

1. **cataracts.** Clouding of the lenses of the eyes or their membranes that prevents the passage of light
2. **tabloids.** Small newspapers often containing sensationalized material and many photographs
3. **cracker tin.** Cracker box

---

words for everyday use

rep • li • ca (re′ pli kə) *n.*, exact copy. *Many artists make <u>replicas</u> of their work so that more than one copy exists.*
gale (gāl; gāəl) *n.*, strong wind from 32 to 63 miles per hour. *The 45 mile-per-hour <u>gale</u> blew down several trees in our neighborhood.*
vig • nette (vin yet′) *n.*, brief scene. *The opening <u>vignette</u> of the movie was a shot of a couple seated in a park.*

My mother once said that I'd be amazed at how many things a person can do within the act of falling.

That afternoon, as the anticipation increased, as Mr. and Mrs. Avalon tied sparkling strips of cloth onto each other's face and as they puckered their lips in mock kisses, lips destined "never again to meet," as one long breathless article put it, the wind rose, miles off, wrapped itself into a cone, and howled. There came a rumble of electrical energy, drowned out by the sudden roll of drums. One detail not mentioned by the press, perhaps unknown—Anna was pregnant at the time, seven months and hardly showing, her stomach muscles were that strong. It seems incredible that she would work high above the ground when any fall could be so dangerous, but the explanation—I know from watching her go blind—is that my mother lives comfortably in extreme elements. She is one with the constant dark now, just as the air was her home, familiar to her, safe, before the storm that afternoon.

From opposite ends of the tent they waved, blind and smiling, to the crowd below. The ringmaster removed his hat and called for silence, so that the two above could concentrate. They rubbed their hands in chalky powder, then Harry launched himself and swung, once, twice, in huge calibrated[4] beats across space. He hung from his knees and on the third swing stretched wide his arms, held his hands out to receive his pregnant wife as she dove from her shining bar.

It was while the two were in midair, their hands about to meet, that lightning struck the main pole and sizzled down the guy wires,[5] filling the air with a blue radiance that Harry Avalon must certainly have seen through the cloth of his blindfold as the tent buckled and the <u>edifice</u> toppled him forward, the swing continuing and not returning in its sweep, and Harry going down, down into the crowd with his last thought, perhaps, just a prickle of surprise at his empty hands.

My mother once said that I'd be amazed at how many things a person can do within the act of falling. Perhaps, at the time, she was teaching me to dive off a board at the town pool, for I associate the idea with midair somersaults. But I also think she meant that even in that awful doomed second one could think, for she certainly did. When her hands did not meet her husband's, my mother tore her blindfold away. As he swept past her on the wrong side, she could have grasped his ankle, the toe-end of his tights, and gone down clutching him. Instead, she changed direction. Her body twisted toward a heavy wire and she managed to hang on to the braided metal, still hot from the lightning strike. Her palms were burned so terribly that once

of their act, they actually would kiss in midair, pausing, almost hovering as they swooped past one another. On the ground, between bows, Harry Avalon would skip quickly to the front rows and point out the smear of my mother's lipstick, just off the edge of his mouth. They made a romantic pair all right, especially in the blindfold sequence.

> What happened while the Avalons were in midair?

---

4. **calibrated.** Precisely adjusted or measured

5. **guy wires.** Wires attached to the tent pole and used as reinforcement or guides for the performers

words for everyday use

ed • i • fice (e' də fəs) *n.*, building; massive structure. *The marble <u>edifice</u> with the majestic dome is the state capitol building.*

healed they bore no lines, only the blank scar tissue of a quieter future. She was lowered, gently, to the sawdust ring just underneath the dome of the canvas roof, which did not entirely settle but was held up on one end and jabbed through, torn, and still on fire in places from the giant spark, though rain and men's jackets soon put that out.

Three people died, but except for her hands my mother was not seriously harmed until an overeager rescuer broke her arm in extricating her and also, in the process, collapsed a portion of the tent bearing a huge buckle that knocked her unconscious. She was taken to the town hospital, and there she must have hemorrhaged,[6] for they kept her, confined to her bed, a month and a half before her baby was born without life. Harry Avalon had wanted to be buried in the circus cemetery next to the original Avalon, his uncle, so she sent him back with his brothers. The child, however, is buried around the corner, beyond this house and just down the highway. Sometimes I used to walk there just to sit. She was a girl, but I rarely thought of her as a sister or even as a separate person really. I suppose you could call it the egocentrism of a child, of all young children, but I considered her a less finished version of myself.

> *What happened to Anna and her husband as a result of the terrible accident?*

That is the debt we take for granted since none of us asks for life. It is only once we have it that we hang on so dearly.

When the snow falls, throwing shadows among the stones, I can easily pick her out from the road, for it is bigger than the others and in the shape of a lamb at rest, its legs curled beneath. The carved lamb looms larger as the years pass, though it is probably only my eyes, the vision shifting, as what is close to me blurs and distances sharpen. In odd moments, I think it is the edge drawing near, the edge of everything, the unseen horizon we do not really speak of in the eastern woods. And it also seems to me, although this is probably an idle fantasy, that the statue is growing more sharply etched, as if, instead of weathering itself into a porous mass, it is hardening on the hillside with each snowfall, perfecting itself.

It was during her confinement in the hospital that my mother met my father. He was called in to look at the set of her arm, which was complicated. He stayed, sitting at her bedside, for he was something of an armchair traveler and had spent his war quietly, at an air force training grounds, where he became a specialist in arms and legs broken during parachute training exercises. Anna Avalon had been to many of the places he longed to visit—Venice, Rome, Mexico, all through France and Spain. She had no family of her own and was taken in by the Avalons, trained to perform from a very young age. They toured Europe before the war, then based themselves in New York. She was illiterate.

It was in the hospital that she finally learned to read and write, as a way of overcoming the boredom and depression of those weeks, and it was my father who insisted on teaching her. In return for stories of her

> *Who was the narrator's father? What did he teach her mother?*

_____

6. **hemorrhaged.** Suffered internal bleeding

words for everyday use

ex • tri • cate (ek′ strə kāt′) v., free from entanglement or difficulty. *Mike struggled to extricate himself from the ties of the neighborhood gang.*

ego • cen • trism (ē′ gō sen′ tri′ zəm) n., self-centeredness. *Charlotte's egocentrism annoyed her friends, who complained that she only thought of herself.*

por • ous (pōr′ əs) adj., having pores; being permeable to liquids. *Sponges are porous; that is, they soak up water.*

adventures, he graded her first exercises. He bought her her first book, and over her bold letters, which the pale guides of the penmanship pads could not contain, they fell in love.

I wonder if my father calculated the exchange he offered: one form of flight for another. For after that, and for as long as I can remember, my mother has never been without a book. Until now, that is, and it remains the greatest difficulty of her blindness. Since my father's recent death, there is no one to read to her, which is why I returned, in fact, from my failed life where the land is flat. I came home to read to my mother, to read out loud, to read long into the dark if I must, to read all night.

Why did the narrator move back home?

Once my father and mother married, they moved onto the old farm he had inherited but didn't care much for. Though he'd been thinking of moving to a larger city, he settled down and broadened his practice in this valley. It still seems odd to me, when they could have gone anywhere else, that they chose to stay in the town where the disaster had occurred, and which my father in the first place had found so <u>constricting</u>. It was my mother who insisted upon it, after her child did not survive. And then, too, she loved the sagging farmhouse with its scrap of what was left of a vast acreage of woods and hidden hay fields that stretched to the game park.

I owe my existence, the second time then, to the two of them and the hospital that brought them together. That is the debt we take for granted since none of us asks for life. It is only once we have it that we hang on so dearly.

I was seven the year the house caught fire, probably from standing ash. It can <u>rekindle</u>, and my father, forgetful around the house and perpetually exhausted from night hours on call, often emptied what he thought were ashes from cold stoves into wooden or cardboard containers. The fire could have started from a flaming box, or perhaps a buildup of creosote[7] inside the chimney was the <u>culprit</u>. It started right around the stove, and the heart of the house was gutted. The babysitter, fallen asleep in my father's den on the first floor, woke to find the stairway to my upstairs room cut off by flames. She used the phone, then ran outside to stand beneath my window.

When my parents arrived, the two volunteers had drawn water from the fire pond and were spraying the outside of the house, preparing to go inside after me, not knowing at the time that there was only one staircase and that it was lost.

On the other side of the house, the superannuated[8] extension ladder broke in half. Perhaps the clatter of it falling against the walls woke me, for I'd been asleep up to that point.

As soon as I awakened, in the small room that I now use for sewing, I smelled the smoke. I followed things by the letter then, was good at memorizing instructions, and so I did exactly what was taught in the second-grade home fire drill. I got up, I touched the back of my door before opening it. Finding it hot, I left it closed and stuffed my rolled-up rug beneath the crack. I did not hide under my bed or crawl into my closet. I put on my flannel robe, and then I sat down to wait.

What happened to make rescuing the narrator nearly impossible? What did the narrator do when she realized the house was on fire?

Outside, my mother stood below my dark window and saw clearly that there was no rescue. Flames had pierced one side wall, and the glare of the fire lighted the massive limbs and trunk of the vigorous old elm that had probably

---

7. **creosote.** Flammable tar deposited from wood smoke on chimney walls
8. **superannuated.** Very old; ready for retirement

---

words for everyday use

con • stric • ting (kən strik′ tiŋ) adj., limiting; compressing. *Kim's shoes were a size too small and painfully <u>constricting</u>.*

re • kin • dle (ri′ kin′ dəl) v., catch fire again. *The couple's old romance was <u>rekindled</u> when they met again by accident.*

cul • prit (kəl′ prət) n., one guilty of a crime; cause of a problem. *The problem of thefts during basketball practice ended when the coach caught the <u>culprit</u> in the act of breaking into a locker.*

been planted the year the house was built, a hundred years ago at least. No leaf touched the wall, and just one thin branch scraped the roof. From below, it looked as though even a squirrel would have had trouble jumping from the tree onto the house, for the breadth of that small branch was no bigger than my mother's wrist.

Standing there, beside Father, who was preparing to rush back around to the front of the house, my mother asked him to unzip her dress. When he wouldn't be bothered, she made him understand. He couldn't make his hands work, so she finally tore it off and stood there in her pearls and stockings. She directed one of the men to lean the broken half of the extension ladder up against the trunk of the tree. In surprise, he complied. She ascended. She vanished. Then she could be seen among the leafless branches of late November as she made her way up and, along her stomach, inched the length of a bough that curved above the branch that brushed the roof.

Once there, swaying, she stood and balanced. There were plenty of people in the crowd and many who still remember, or think they do, my mother's leap through the ice-dark air toward that thinnest extension, and how she broke the branch falling so that it cracked in

What did Anna do after she climbed up into the tree?

her hands, cracked louder than the flames as she vaulted with it toward the edge of the roof, and how it hurtled down end over end without her, and their eyes went up, again, to see where she had flown.

I didn't see her leap through air, only heard the sudden thump and looked out my window.

She was hanging by the backs of her heels from the new gutter we had put in that year, and she was smiling. I was not surprised to see her, she was so matter-of-fact. She tapped on the window. I remember how she did it, too. It was the friendliest tap, a bit <u>tentative</u>, as if she was afraid she had arrived too early at a friend's house. Then she gestured at the latch, and when I opened the window she told me to raise it wide and prop it up with the stick so it wouldn't crush her fingers. She swung down, caught the ledge, and crawled through the opening. Once she was in my room, I realized she had on only underclothing, a bra of the heavy stitched cotton women used to wear and step-in, lace-trimmed drawers. I remember feeling light-headed, of course, terribly relieved, and then embarrassed for her to be seen by the crowd undressed.

I was still embarrassed as we flew out the window, toward earth, me in her lap, her toes pointed as we skimmed toward the painted target of the fire fighter's net.

How did Anna and her daughter get out of the burning house?

I know that she's right. I knew it even then. As you fall there is time to think. Curled as I was, against her stomach, I was not startled by the cries of the crowd or the <u>looming</u> faces. The wind roared and beat its hot breath at our back, the flames whistled. I slowly wondered what would happen if we missed the circle or bounced out of it. Then I wrapped my hands around my mother's hands. I felt the brush of her lips and heard the beat of her heart in my ears, loud as thunder, long as the roll of drums. ∎

words for everyday use

ten • ta • tive (ten' tə tiv) *adj.*, hesitant; uncertain. *Louise gave the cute boy a <u>tentative</u> smile, uncertain whether he had noticed her.*

loom • ing (lüm' iŋ) *adj.*, appearing exaggeratedly large or distorted. *The eerie shadow of the giant was seen <u>looming</u> over the land.*

Respond *to the* SELECTION

What do you think the daughter learned from her mother?

Her Flying Trapeze

Nikki Giovanni

Some see the world through rose colored glasses

Some can't see the forest for the trees

A stitch in time will always save nine

She rides through the trees with the greatest of ease

Alone on her flying trapeze

Some will tell you the glass is half full

Others see it as mostly empty

An ounce of prevention is one pound of cure

She flies through the sky two tattoos on her thigh

Alone on her flying trapeze

Some ride the Steinway's 88

Some drive an 18 wheeler

Some feel like fools in their gasoline mules

She glides through the breeze with an absolute ease

Alone on her flying trapeze   ■

Investigate, *Inquire,* and Imagine

Recall: GATHERING FACTS

1a. What was Anna Avalon's job when she was young? What is she like today?

2a. The narrator says of her mother, "I owe her my existence three times." What happened each of these three times? What happened to the palms of Anna's hands after the circus accident?

3a. What skill did Anna's second husband teach her? What does the narrator say is her reason for returning home to her mother?

Interpret: FINDING MEANING

1b. What is similar about her act and her present condition? Why do you think she has not kept any mementos of her former life?

2b. How are the first incident and the third one similar? What might Anna's palms symbolize?

3b. How is Anna's new skill similar to the skill she learned in the circus? Why else might the narrator have returned home?

Analyze: TAKING THINGS APART

4a. The narrator says that her mother "lives comfortably in extreme elements." Find evidence to support this statement.

Synthesize: BRINGING THINGS TOGETHER

4b. How does Anna's career as a trapeze artist illustrate the way she leads her life? What do you think she means when she says that it is possible to do many things while one is falling?

Evaluate: MAKING JUDGMENTS

5a. How do you think Anna was able to persevere despite the tragedy in her life? How did Anna show she wanted to move on with her life, despite what had happened as a result of the circus tent accident? How do you think Anna felt when she realized the firefighters could not save her daughter from the fire?

Extend: CONNECTING IDEAS

5b. What do you think it is like to be a trapeze artist? Read the poem "Her Flying Trapeze." Why do you think the poet used the line "Alone on her flying trapeze" to end each stanza? What was she trying to convey?

Understanding *Literature*

HERO. Review the definition for **hero** in the Handbook of Literary Terms. Do you think Anna Avalon fits the definition? Explain, using evidence from the story. Look up the dictionary definition of the word "Avalon." Do you think Erdrich chose the name deliberately? If so, why? Is the woman in "Her Flying Trapeze" a hero? Explain.

DESCRIPTION. Review the definition for **description** in the Handbook of Literary Terms. How do the sensory details used in the circus scene bring the scene alive for the reader? How do the details used in the fire scene contribute to the mood of the scene? Explain, giving examples of sensory details from the two scenes.

Writer's Journal

1. Imagine you are a reporter for a tabloid called *The Inquirer* and witnessed the fire. Write a **tabloid article** describing the scene. Use the most sensational, melodramatic language you can.
2. Imagine you are Anna and you are asked, "What is the secret of true courage?" Write Anna's **definition** of courage.
3. Imagine you are Anna. Anna wants to write a **letter** to give to her daughter when her daughter gets older. She wants to tell her how she felt on the day of the fire. Write that letter.

Integrating the Language Arts

Language, Grammar, and Style

TYPES OF PHRASES. Read the Language Arts Survey 3.82, "Phrases." Then identify the underlined phrases as adjective phrases, adverb phrases, participial phrases, gerund phrases, or infinitive phrases.

1. <u>To fly blindfolded</u> from trapeze to trapeze was normal to the speaker's mother.
2. Sightless, she is still comfortable in rooms <u>with closet doors</u>.
3. The reporter reported <u>to the public</u> that the day of the disaster was mildly overcast.
4. The <u>striking</u> lightning hit the main pole and sizzled down the guy wires.
5. <u>Burying Harry</u> in the circus cemetery was important to his family.

Media Literacy

CONDUCTING AN INTERVIEW. Imagine you are an historian and are interviewing Anna (as an old woman). You plan to videotape the interview and include it in a multimedia presentation of the town's history. Write down questions you will ask Anna. Then work with a partner to role-play the interview.

Collaborative Learning

WRITING A PROMOTION. Imagine you and your group have been asked to promote the circus that is coming to town. Write a radio script, design flyers and signs or think up other ways to promote the event. Present your promotional materials to the class.

Literary
T O O L S

MOOD. Mood, or atmosphere, is the emotion created in the reader by part or all of a literary work. A writer can evoke in the reader an emotional response—such as fear, discomfort, longing, or anticipation—by working carefully with descriptive language and sensory details. The description in the opening paragraph of "The Scarlet Ibis" establishes a haunted, lonely mood. Watch for mood changes as you read the story.

FORESHADOWING. Foreshadowing is the act of presenting materials that hint at events to occur later in the story. Note the foreshadowing of death in the first paragraph of the story as hinted at in the somber descriptions of nature.

Organizer

Create a radiating circle like the one below to explore the use of foreshadowing in "The Scarlet Ibis." Note the many different descriptions and events that foreshadow the end of the story. Then write each example of foreshadowing in a circle radiating out from the center. One example has been done for you.

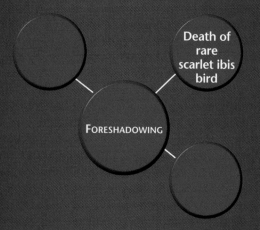

"The Scarlet Ibis" by James Hurst

Reader's
resource

The setting of a literary work is the time and place in which it occurs, together with all the details used to create a sense of a particular time and place. In **"The Scarlet Ibis,"** the setting is particularly important. According to Hurst, it is almost another character. You will notice that Hurst describes colors, weather conditions, plants, and trees in great detail as he creates the world of the story's two main characters. This world is one with which North Carolina-born Hurst is quite familiar. As you read, notice the important role that the setting plays in the story.

About *the*
A U T H O R

James Hurst (1922–) was born and raised on a farm in North Carolina and later attended North Carolina State College. He served in the United States Army during World War II, studied singing at the Juilliard School of Music, and traveled to Rome to further pursue his study of music. For thirty-four years, Hurst worked in the international department of a bank in New York. It was during this period of his life that Hurst wrote and published short stories and a play. "The Scarlet Ibis" was first published in *The Atlantic Monthly* in 1960.

Reader's
Journal

Have you ever had mixed feelings about a family member or a close friend?

The Scarlet Ibis

James Hurst

It was in the clove of seasons,[1] summer was dead but autumn had not yet been born, that the ibis[2] lit in the bleeding tree. The flower garden was stained with rotting brown magnolia petals and ironweeds grew rank amid the purple phlox. The five o'clocks by the chimney still marked time, but the oriole nest in the elm was untenanted and rocked back and forth like

What do the graveyard flowers do?

an empty cradle. The last graveyard flowers were blooming, and their smell drifted across the cotton field and through every room of our house, speaking softly the names of our dead.

It's strange that all this is still so clear to me, now that that summer has long since fled and time has had its way. A grindstone[3] stands where the bleeding tree stood, just outside the kitchen door, and now if an oriole sings in the elm, its song seems to die up in the leaves, a silvery dust. The flower garden is prim, the house a gleaming white, and the pale fence across the yard stands straight and spruce. But sometimes (like right now), as I sit in the cool, green-draped parlor, the grindstone begins to turn, and time with all its changes is ground away—and I remember Doodle.

Doodle was just about the craziest brother a boy ever had. Of course, he wasn't a crazy crazy like old Miss Leedie, who was in love with President Wilson[4] and wrote him a letter every day, but was a nice crazy, like someone you meet in your dreams. He was born when I was six and was, from the outset, a disappointment. He seemed all head, with a tiny body which was red and shriveled like an old man's. Everybody thought he was going to die—everybody except Aunt Nicey, who had delivered him. She said he would live because he was born in a caul and cauls were made from Jesus' nightgown. Daddy had Mr. Heath, the carpenter, build a little mahogany coffin for him. But he didn't die, and when he was three months old Mama and Daddy decided they might as well name him. They named him William Armstrong, which was like

Who is Doodle?

Why does the narrator dislike his brother's name?

tying a big tail on a small kite. Such a name sounds good only on a tombstone.

---

1. **clove of seasons.** Time between seasons
2. **ibis.** Large tropical bird
3. **grindstone.** Revolving stone disk for sharpening or polishing tools
4. **President Wilson.** Thomas Woodrow Wilson (1856–1924), twenty-eighth president of the United States

words for everyday use   caul (kôl) *n.*, membrane enclosing a fetus or a newborn baby. *The caul protects the fetus in the womb.*

I thought myself pretty smart at many things, like holding my breath, running, jumping, or climbing the vines in Old Woman Swamp, and I wanted more than anything else someone to race to Horsehead Landing, someone to box with, and someone to perch with in the top fork of the great pine behind the barn, where across the fields and swamps you could see the sea. I wanted a brother. But Mama, crying, told me that even if William Armstrong lived, he would never do these things with me. He might not, she sobbed, even be "all there." He might, as long as he lived, lie on the rubber sheet in the center of the bed in the front bedroom where the white marquisette curtains billowed out in the afternoon sea breeze, rustling like palmetto fronds.[5]

It was bad enough having an invalid brother, but having one who possibly was not all there was unbearable, so I began to make plans to kill him by smothering him with a pillow. However, one afternoon as I watched him,

> What does the narrator decide to do to his brother? Why? What causes the narrator to change his mind?

my head poked between the iron posts of the foot of the bed, he looked straight at me and grinned. I skipped through the rooms, down the echoing halls, shouting, "Mama, he smiled. He's all there! He's all there!" and he was.

When he was two, if you laid him on his stomach, he began to try to move himself, straining terribly. The doctor said that with his weak heart this strain would probably kill him, but it didn't. Trembling, he'd push himself up, turning first red, then a soft purple, and finally collapse back onto the bed like an old worn-out doll. I can still see Mama watching him, her hand pressed tight across her mouth, her eyes wide and unblinking. But he learned to crawl (it was his third winter), and we brought him out of the front bedroom, putting him on the rug before the fireplace. For the first time he became one of us.

As long as he lay all the time in bed, we called him William Armstrong, even though it was formal and sounded as if we were referring to

Doodle was my brother and he was going to cling to me forever, no matter what I did, so I dragged him across the burning cotton field to share with him the only beauty I knew, Old Woman Swamp.

one of our ancestors, but with his creeping around on the deerskin rug and beginning to talk, something had to be done about his name. It was I who renamed him. When he crawled, he crawled backwards, as if he were in reverse and couldn't change gears. If you called him, he'd turn around as if he were going in the other direction, then he'd back right up to you to be picked up. Crawling backward made him look like a doodlebug, so I began to call him Doodle, and in time even Mama and Daddy thought it was a better name than William Armstrong. Only Aunt Nicey disagreed. She said caul babies should be treated with special respect since they might turn out to be saints. Renaming my

> What does Aunt Nicey believe about the narrator's brother?

brother was perhaps the kindest thing I ever did for him, because nobody expects much from someone called Doodle.

Although Doodle learned to crawl, he showed no signs of walking, but he wasn't idle. He talked so much that we all quit listening to what he said. It was about this time that Daddy built him a go-cart and I had to pull him around. At

---

5. **palmetto fronds.** Fan-shaped leaves of a palm tree

first I just paraded him up and down the piazza,[6] but then he started crying to be taken out into the yard, and it ended up by my having to lug him wherever I went. If I so much as picked up my cap, he'd start crying to go with me and Mama would call from wherever she was, "Take Doodle with you."

He was a burden in many ways. The doctor had said that he mustn't get too excited, too hot, too cold, or too tired and that he must always be treated gently. A long list of don'ts went with him, all of which I ignored once we got out of the house. To discourage his coming with me, I'd run with him across the ends of the cotton rows and careen him around corners on two wheels. Sometimes I accidentally turned him over, but he never told Mama. His skin was very sensitive, and he had to wear a big straw hat whenever he went out. When the going got rough and he had to cling to the sides of the go-cart, the hat slipped all the way down over his ears. He was a sight. Finally, I could see I was licked. Doodle was my brother and he was going to cling to me forever, no matter what I did, so I dragged him across the burning cotton field to share with him the only beauty I knew, Old Woman Swamp. I pulled the go-cart through the saw-tooth fern, down into the green dimness where the palmetto fronds whispered by the stream. I lifted him out and set him down in the soft rubber grass beside a tall pine. His eyes were round with wonder as he gazed about him, and his little hands began to stroke the rubber grass. Then he began to cry.

"For heaven's sake, what's the matter?" I asked, annoyed.

> Why does the narrator find a brother like Doodle to be difficult?

> Why does the narrator stop trying to discourage Doodle's attention?

"It's so pretty," he said. "So pretty, pretty, pretty."

After that day Doodle and I often went down into Old Woman Swamp. I would gather wildflowers, wild violets, honeysuckle, yellow jasmine, snakeflowers, and water lilies, and with wire grass we'd weave them into necklaces and crowns. We'd bedeck ourselves with our handiwork and loll about thus beautified, beyond the touch of the everyday world. Then when the slanted rays of the sun burned orange in the tops of the pines, we'd drop our jewels into the stream and watch them float away toward the sea.

There is within me (and with sadness I have watched it in others) a knot of cruelty borne by the stream of love, much as our blood sometimes bears the seed of our destruction, and at times I was mean to Doodle. One day I took him up to the barn loft and showed him his casket, telling him how we all had believed he would die. It was covered with a film of Paris green[7] sprinkled to kill the rats, and screech owls had built a nest inside it.

> To what does the narrator compare the cruelty that sometimes accompanies love?

Doodle studied the mahogany box for a long time, then said, "It's not mine."

"It is," I said. "And before I'll help you down from the loft, you're going to have to touch it."

> What does the narrator force Doodle to do? What happens when Doodle does it?

"I won't touch it," he said sullenly.

"Then I'll leave you here by yourself," I threatened, and made as if I were going down.

Doodle was frightened of being left. "Don't go leave me, Brother," he cried, and he leaned toward the coffin. His hand, trembling, reached out, and when he touched the casket he screamed. A screech owl flapped out of the box

---

6. **piazza.** Large, covered porch
7. **Paris green.** Green powdered insecticide

The Torn Hat, 1820. Thomas Sully. Boston Museum of Fine Arts.

I hadn't expected such an answer. "So I won't have to haul you around all the time."

"I can't walk, Brother," he said.

"Who says so?" I demanded.

"Mama, the doctor—everybody."

"Oh, you can walk," I said, and I took him by the arms and stood him up. He collapsed onto the grass like a half-empty flour sack. It was as if he had no bones in his little legs.

"Don't hurt me, Brother," he warned.

"Shut up. I'm not going to hurt you. I'm going to teach you to walk." I heaved him up again, and again he collapsed.

This time he did not lift his face up out of the rubber grass. "I just can't do it. Let's make honeysuckle wreaths."

"Oh yes you can, Doodle," I said. "All you got to do is try. Now come on," and I hauled him up once more.

It seemed so hopeless from the beginning that it's a miracle I didn't give up. But all of us must have something or someone to be proud of, and Doodle had become mine. I did not know then that pride is a wonderful, terrible thing, a seed that bears two vines, life and death. Every day that summer we went to the pine beside the stream of Old Woman Swamp, and I put him on his feet at least a hundred times each afternoon. Occasionally I too became discouraged because it didn't seem as if he was trying, and I would say, "Doodle, don't you *want* to learn to walk?"

He'd nod his head, and I'd say, "Well, if you don't keep trying, you'll never learn. Then I'd paint for him a picture of us as old men, white-haired, him with a long white beard and me still pulling him around in the go-cart. This never failed to make him try again.

Finally one day, after many weeks of practicing, he stood alone for a few seconds. When he

into our faces, scaring us and covering us with Paris green. Doodle was paralyzed, so I put him on my shoulder and carried him down the ladder, and even when we were outside in the bright sunshine, he clung to me, crying, "Don't leave me. Don't leave me."

When Doodle was five years old, I was embarrassed at having a brother of that age who couldn't walk, so I set out to teach him. We were down in Old Woman Swamp and it was spring and the sick-sweet smell of bay flowers hung everywhere like a mournful song. "I'm going to teach you to walk, Doodle," I said.

He was sitting comfortably on the soft grass, leaning back against the pine. "Why?" he asked.

fell, I grabbed him in my arms and hugged him, our laughter pealing through the swamp like a ringing bell. Now we knew it could be done. Hope no longer hid in the dark palmetto thicket but perched like a cardinal in the lacy toothbrush tree, brilliantly visible. "Yes, yes," I cried, and he cried it too, and the grass beneath us was soft and the smell of the swamp was sweet.

With success so <u>imminent</u>, we decided not to tell anyone until he could actually walk. Each day, barring rain, we sneaked into Old Woman Swamp, and by cotton-picking time Doodle was ready to show what he could do. He still wasn't able to walk far, but we could wait no longer. Keeping a nice secret is very hard to do, like holding your breath. We chose to reveal all on October eighth, Doodle's sixth birthday, and for weeks ahead we mooned around the house, promising everybody a most spectacular surprise. Aunt Nicey said that, after so much talk, if we produced anything less tremendous than the Resurrection,[8] she was going to be disappointed.

At breakfast on our chosen day, when Mama, Daddy, and Aunt Nicey were in the dining room, I brought Doodle to the door in the go-cart just as usual and had them turn their backs, making them cross their hearts and hope to die if they peeked. I helped Doodle up, and when he was standing alone I let them look. There wasn't a sound as Doodle walked slowly across the room and sat down at his place at the table. Then Mama began to cry and ran over to him, hugging him and kissing him. Daddy hugged him too, so I went to Aunt Nicey, who was thanks praying in the doorway, and began to waltz her around. We danced together quite

> What does the narrator do when Doodle stands on his own? What emotions do the brothers feel when they realize that there is hope for Doodle's success?

well until she came down on my big toe with her brogans,[9] hurting me so badly I thought I was crippled for life.

Doodle told them it was I who had taught him to walk, so everyone wanted to hug me, and I began to cry.

"What are you crying for?" asked Daddy, but I couldn't answer. They did not know that I did it for myself; that pride, whose slave I was, spoke to me louder than all their voices, and that Doodle walked only because I was ashamed of having a crippled brother.

> What reasons does the narrator have for teaching Doodle to walk?

Within a few months Doodle had learned to walk well and his go-cart was put up in the barn loft (it's still there) beside his little mahogany coffin. Now, when we roamed off together, resting often, we never turned back until our destination had been reached, and to help pass the

---

8. **Resurrection.** Jesus' return to life after the Crucifixion
9. **brogans.** Heavy work shoes

But all of us must have something or someone to be proud of, and Doodle had become mine. I did not know then that pride is a wonderful, terrible thing, a seed that bears two vines, life and death.

words for everyday use

im • mi • nent (im´ə nənt) adj., likely to happen. *Park rangers warned that an avalanche was <u>imminent</u> because of the week's heavy snowfall.*

time, we took up lying. From the beginning Doodle was a terrible liar and he got me in the habit. Had anyone stopped to listen to us, we would have been sent off to Dix Hill.[10]

My lies were scary, involved, and usually pointless, but Doodle's were twice as crazy. People in his stories all had wings and flew wherever they wanted to go. His favorite lie was about a boy named Peter who had a pet peacock with a ten-foot tail. Peter wore a golden robe that glittered so brightly that when he walked through the sunflowers they turned away from the sun to face him. When Peter was ready to go to sleep, the peacock spread his magnificent tail, enfolding the boy gently like a closing go-to-sleep flower, burying him in the gloriously <u>iridescent</u>, rustling <u>vortex</u>. Yes, I must admit it. Doodle could beat me lying.

> What can Doodle do more skillfully than his brother? What does this skill reveal about Doodle?

Doodle and I spent lots of time thinking about our future. We decided that when we were grown we'd live in Old Woman Swamp and pick dog-tongue for a living. Beside the stream, he planned, we'd build us a house of whispering leaves and the swamp birds would be our chickens. All day long (when we weren't gathering dog-tongue) we'd swing through the cypresses on the rope vines,

It was too late to turn back, for we had both wandered too far into a net of expectations and had left no crumbs behind.

and if it rained we'd huddle beneath an umbrella tree and play stickfrog. Mama and Daddy could come and live with us if they wanted to. He even came up with the idea that he could marry Mama and I could marry Daddy. Of course, I was old enough to know this wouldn't work out, but the picture he painted was so beautiful and serene that all I could do was whisper Yes, yes.

Once I had succeeded in teaching Doodle to walk, I began to believe in my own <u>infallibility</u> and I prepared a terrific development program for him, unknown to Mama and Daddy, of course. I would teach him to run, to swim, to climb trees, and to fight. He, too, now believed in my infallibility, so we set the deadline for these accomplishments less than a year away, when, it had been decided, Doodle could start to school.

That winter we didn't make much progress, for I was in school and Doodle suffered from one bad cold after another. But when spring came, rich and warm, we raised our sights again. Success lay at the end of summer like a pot of gold, and our campaign got off to a good start. On hot days, Doodle and I went down to Horsehead Landing, and I gave him swimming lessons or showed him how to row a boat. Sometimes we descended into the cool greenness of Old Woman Swamp and climbed the rope vines or boxed scientifically beneath the pine where he had learned to walk. Promise hung about us like the leaves, and wherever we looked, ferns unfurled and birds broke into song.

That summer, the summer of 1918, was blighted. In May and June there was no rain and the crops withered, curled up, then died under the thirsty sun. One morning in July a hurricane came out of the east, tipping over the oaks in the yard and splitting the limbs of the elm trees.

10. **Dix Hill.** The location of Dorothea Dix Hospital, a state institution

---

words for everyday use

ir • i • des • cent (ir´i des´ənt) *adj.*, having shifting changes in color. *The fish's <u>iridescent</u> scales changed from green to blue as it wriggled in the sunlit water.*

vor • tex (vôr´teks´) *n.*, whirlpool or eddy. *Leaves and twigs were sucked into the stream's <u>vortex</u>.*

in • fal • li • bil • i • ty (in fal´ə bil i tē) *n.*, correctness, incapacity for error. *When they become teenagers, most children challenge the idea of their parents' <u>infallibility</u>.*

That afternoon it roared back out of the west, blew the fallen oaks around, snapping their roots and tearing them out of the earth like a hawk at the entrails of a chicken. Cotton bolls were wrenched from the stalks and lay like green walnuts in the valleys between the rows, while the cornfield leaned over uniformly so that the tassels touched the ground. Doodle and I followed Daddy out into the cotton field, where he stood, shoulders sagging, surveying the ruin. When his chin sank down onto his chest, we were frightened, and Doodle slipped his hand into mine. Suddenly Daddy straightened his shoulders, raised a giant knuckly fist, and with a voice that seemed to rumble out of the earth itself began cursing heaven, the weather, hell, and the Republican Party. Doodle and I, prodding each other and giggling, went back to the house, knowing that everything would be all right.

And during that summer, strange names were heard through the house: Château-Thierry, Amiens, Soissons, and in her blessing at the supper table, Mama once said, "And bless the Pearsons, whose boy Joe was lost at Belleau Wood."[11]

So we came to that clove of seasons. School was only a few weeks away, and Doodle was far behind schedule. He could barely clear the ground when climbing up the rope vines and his swimming was certainly not passable. We decided to double our efforts, to make that last drive and reach our pot of gold. I made him swim until he turned blue and row until he couldn't lift an oar. Wherever we went, I purposely walked fast, and although he kept up, his face turned red and his eyes became glazed. Once, he could go no further, so he collapsed on the ground and began to cry.

"Aw, come on, Doodle," I urged. "You can do it. Do you want to be different from everybody else when you start school?"

Is Doodle succeeding in learning the new skills the narrator wishes to teach him?

"Does it make any difference?"

"It certainly does," I said. "Now, come on," and I helped him up.

What does the narrator tell Doodle about being different?

As we slipped through dog days, Doodle began to look feverish, and Mama felt his forehead, asking him if he felt ill. At night he didn't sleep well, and sometimes he had nightmares, crying out until I touched him and said, "Wake up, Doodle. Wake up."

It was Saturday noon, just a few days before school was to start. I should have already admitted defeat, but my pride wouldn't let me. The excitement of our program had now been gone for weeks, but still we kept on with a tired doggedness. It was too late to turn back, for we had both wandered too far into a net of expectations and had left no crumbs behind.

Daddy, Mama, Doodle, and I were seated at the dining-room table having lunch. It was a hot day, with all the windows and doors open in case a breeze should come. In the kitchen Aunt Nicey was humming softly. After a long silence, Daddy spoke. "It's so calm, I wouldn't be surprised if we had a storm this afternoon."

"I haven't heard a rain frog," said Mama, who believed in signs, as she served the bread around the table.

What sound signals a coming storm? Has anyone heard such a sound?

"I did," declared Doodle. "Down in the swamp."

"He didn't," I said contrarily.

"You did, eh?" said Daddy, ignoring my denial.

"I certainly did," Doodle <u>reiterated</u>, scowling at me over the top of his iced-tea glass, and we were quiet again.

Suddenly, from out in the yard, came a strange croaking noise. Doodle stopped eating, with a piece of bread poised ready for his

---

11. **Château-Thierry . . . Belleau Wood.** World War I battlefields in France

mouth, his eyes popped round like two blue buttons. "What's that?" he whispered.

I jumped up, knocking over my chair, and had reached the door when Mama called, "Pick up the chair, sit down again, and say excuse me."

By the time I had done this, Doodle had excused himself and had slipped out into the yard. He was looking up into the bleeding tree. "It's a great big red bird!" he called.

What has produced the croaking sound?

The bird croaked loudly again, and Mama and Daddy came out into the yard. We shaded our eyes with our hands against the hazy glare of the sun and peered up through the still leaves. On the topmost branch a bird the size of a chicken, with scarlet feathers and long legs, was perched precariously. Its wings hung down loosely, and as we watched, a feather dropped away and floated slowly down through the green leaves.

"It's not even frightened of us," Mama said.

"It looks tired," Daddy added. "Or maybe sick."

Doodle's hands were clasped at his throat, and I had never seen him stand still so long. "What is it?" he asked.

Daddy shook his head. "I don't know, maybe it's—"

At that moment the bird began to flutter, but the wings were uncoordinated, and amid much flapping and a spray of flying feathers, it tumbled down, bumping through the limbs of the bleeding tree and landing at our feet with a thud. Its long, graceful neck jerked twice into an S, then straightened out, and the bird was still. A white veil came over the eyes and the long white beak unhinged. Its legs were crossed and its clawlike feet were delicately curved at rest. Even death did not mar its grace, for it lay on the earth like a broken vase of red flowers, and we stood around it, awed by its exotic beauty.

"It's dead," Mama said.

"What is it?" Doodle repeated.

"Go bring me the bird book," said Daddy.

I ran into the house and brought back the bird book. As we watched, Daddy thumbed through its pages. "It's a scarlet ibis," he said, pointing to a picture. "It lives in the tropics—South America to Florida. A storm must have brought it here."

Even death did not mar its grace, for it lay on the earth like a broken vase of red flowers, and we stood around it, awed by its exotic beauty.

Sadly, we all looked back at the bird. A scarlet ibis! How many miles it had traveled to die like this, in *our* yard, beneath the bleeding tree.

How has the bird come to the narrator's yard? What does it do there?

"Let's finish lunch," Mama said, nudging us back toward the dining room.

"I'm not hungry," said Doodle, and he knelt down beside the ibis.

"We've got peach cobbler for dessert," Mama tempted from the doorway.

Doodle remained kneeling. "I'm going to bury him."

"Don't you dare touch him," Mama warned. "There's no telling what disease he might have had."

"All right," said Doodle. "I won't."

Daddy, Mama, and I went back to the dining-room table, but we watched Doodle through the open door. He took out a piece of string from his pocket and, without touching the ibis, looped one end around its neck. Slowly, while singing softly, "Shall We Gather at the River," he carried the bird around to the front yard and dug a hole in the flower garden, next to the petunia

What does Doodle do with the bird?

bed. Now we were watching him through the front window, but he didn't know it. His awkwardness at digging the hole with a shovel whose handle was twice as long as he was made us laugh, and we covered our mouths with our hands so he wouldn't hear.

When Doodle came into the dining room, he found us seriously eating our cobbler. He was pale and lingered just inside the screen door. "Did you get the scarlet ibis buried?" asked Daddy.

Doodle didn't speak but nodded his head.

"Go wash your hands, and then you can have some peach cobbler," said Mama.

"I'm not hungry," he said.

"Dead birds is bad luck," said Aunt Nicey, poking

> What does Aunt Nicey say about the ibis?

her head from the kitchen door. "Specially *red* dead birds!"

As soon as I had finished eating, Doodle and I hurried off to Horsehead Landing. Time was short, and Doodle still had a long way to go if he was going to keep up with the other boys when he started school. The sun, gilded with the yellow cast of autumn, still burned fiercely, but the dark green woods through which we passed were shady and cool. When we reached the landing, Doodle said he was too tired to swim, so we got into a <u>skiff</u> and floated down the creek with the tide. Far off in the marsh a rail was scolding, and over on the beach locusts were singing in the myrtle trees. Doodle did not speak and kept his head turned away, letting one hand trail limply in the water.

After we had drifted a long way, I put the oars in place and made Doodle row back against the tide. Black clouds began to gather in the southwest, and he kept watching them, trying to pull the oars a little faster. When we reached Horsehead Landing, lightning was playing across half the sky and thunder roared out, hiding even the sound of the sea. The sun disappeared and darkness descended, almost like night. Flocks of marsh crows flew by, heading inland to their roosting trees, and two egrets, squawking, arose from the oyster-rock shallows and careened away.

Doodle was both tired and frightened, and when he stepped from the skiff he collapsed onto the mud, sending an armada of fiddler crabs rustling off into the marsh grass. I helped him up, and as he wiped the mud off his trousers, he smiled at me ashamedly. He had failed and we both knew it, so we started back home, racing

> Who has failed? Whose pride has cracked? What has come as Doodle predicted?

the storm. We never spoke (What are the words that can solder cracked pride?), but I knew he was watching me, watching for a sign of mercy. The lightning was near now, and from fear he walked so close behind me he kept stepping on my heels. The faster I walked, the faster he walked, so I began to run. The rain was coming, roaring through the pines, and then like a bursting Roman candle, a gum tree ahead of us was shattered by a bolt of lightning. When the deafening peal of thunder had died, and in the moment before the rain arrived, I heard Doodle, who had fallen behind, cry out, "Brother, Brother, don't leave me! Don't leave me!"

The knowledge that Doodle's and my plans had come to naught was bitter, and that streak of cruelty within me awakened. I ran as fast as I could, leaving him far behind with a wall of rain dividing us. The drops

> What divides the brothers?

stung my face like nettles, and the wind flared the wet glistening leaves of the bordering trees. Soon I could hear his voice no more.

---

words for everyday use skiff (skif) *n.*, small, open boat. *The <u>skiff</u> can hold only two people without capsizing.*

For a long time, it seemed for-ever, I lay there crying sheltering my fallen scarlet ibis from the heresy of rain.

I hadn't run too far before I became tired, and the flood of childish spite <u>evanesced</u> as well. I stopped and waited for Doodle. The sound of rain was everywhere, but the wind had died and it fell straight down in parallel paths like ropes hanging from the sky. As I waited, I peered through the downpour, but no one came. Finally I went back and found him huddled beneath a red nightshade bush beside the road. He was sitting on the ground, his face buried in his arms, which were resting on his drawn-up knees. "Let's go, Doodle," I said.

He didn't answer, so I placed my hand on his forehead and lifted his head. Limply, he fell backwards onto the earth. He had been bleeding from the mouth, and his neck and the front of his shirt were stained a brilliant red.

"Doodle! Doodle!" I cried, shaking him, but there was no answer but the ropy rain. He lay very awkwardly, with his head thrown far back, making his vermilion neck appear unusually long and slim. His little legs, bent sharply at the knees, had never before seemed so fragile, so thin.

Of what does Doodle remind the narrator? Why?

I began to weep, and the tear-blurred vision in red before me looked very familiar. "Doodle!" I screamed above the pounding storm and threw my body to the earth above his. For a long time, it seemed forever, I lay there crying, sheltering my fallen scarlet ibis from the <u>heresy</u> of rain. ■

---

words for everyday use

ev • a • nesce (ev´ən nes´) vi., disappear. *After I had given a few speeches successfully, my fear of public speaking <u>evanesced</u>.*

her • e • sy (her´i sē) n., rejection of a belief that is part of an established set of beliefs. *The Catholic Church accused Martin Luther of <u>heresy</u> because he broke with its teachings.*

Respond *to the* SELECTION

How did you feel about the narrator and Doodle by the last scene of the story?

Investigate, *Inquire,* and Imagine

Recall: GATHERING FACTS

1a. How is the narrator's younger brother different from other children when he is born? What is the baby's original name? How does the narrator come up with the name "Doodle"?

2a. What does the narrator teach Doodle to do? What is the family's reaction to Doodle's accomplishment?

3a. Where are the boys when the storm first hits?

→ Interpret: FINDING MEANING

1b. How do the various family members respond to the new baby? What does the narrator notice about the baby one afternoon, and how does this observation change how the narrator feels toward him? Why does the narrator feel that renaming his brother is the kindest thing he could do for him?

2b. What are the narrator's reasons for taking special interest in his brother and deciding to teach him? What feelings does the narrator display as he spends time with Doodle?

3b. What does the narrator do to his brother for the first time as the two make their way through the rain? How might this action affect the narrator for the rest of his life?

Analyze: TAKING THINGS APART

4a. Identify specific incidents in the story that tell the reader about the relationship between the two brothers.

→ Synthesize: BRINGING THINGS TOGETHER

4b. Based on these examples, how would you describe the narrator's relationship with Doodle?

Perspective: LOOKING AT OTHER VIEWS →

5a. Why do you think Doodle was so much more emotional than the rest of his family over the death of the scarlet ibis?

Empathy: SEEING FROM INSIDE

5b. Describe how you would feel if you were the narrator and had found Doodle dead under the red nightshade bush. How would you tell the rest of your family?

Understanding *Literature*

MOOD. Review the definition for **mood,** or atmosphere, in the Handbook of Literary Terms. How does the author establish mood in the scenes of the story? What bits of dialogue and description make you feel a certain way?

FORESHADOWING. Reread the definition for **foreshadowing** in the Handbook of Literary Terms. Review the chart you completed on foreshadowing for the Graphic Organizer on page 772. What images or events in "The Scarlet Ibis" hint about, or make reference to, Doodle's death at the end of the story? Use the graphic organizer you completed for Literary Tools to help you.

Writer's Journal

1. Write two brief **descriptive paragraphs** that establish setting and mood in a way that is vivid and clear. One paragraph should describe a place with which you are quite familiar. The other paragraph should describe a place to which you have never been but that you can imagine. Try to express the same mood in both pieces.

2. Pretend that you are a close friend of the narrator and he has written to you for help in dealing with the grief and guilt he feels over his brother's death. Write a **letter** of support to him, acknowledging his feelings and show him the facts about his brother's illness to assuage his guilt.

3. Compose a **poem** about Doodle's birth, life, death, personality, or relationship with his brother; include imagery from the story.

Integrating the Language Arts

Language, Grammar, and Style

ADJECTIVE CLAUSES. Read about adjective clauses in the Language Arts Survey 3.83, "Clauses within a Sentence." Then rewrite the following sentences, underlining the adjective clauses.

1. Doodle's brother made him touch the coffin that was built when he was dying.
2. Many thought Doodle, who was slow, would never walk.
3. The family was pleased with the skills that Doodle learned from his brother.
4. Doodle was a lot like the bird who had been blown north in a storm.
5. Doodle was scared by the storm whose wind and rain had just begun.

Study and Research & Speaking and Listening

BIOGRAPHICAL SKETCHES. Think about the expectations people had of Doodle and how he proved them wrong. Many people have had serious illnesses or have been physically challenged in some way, but have surprised and impressed everyone around them by achieving greatness. As a class, brainstorm a list of famous people who fall into this category. Think about different fields—sports, music, art, literature, politics, and science, for example. Working independently or in small groups, research one of these individuals. In a subsequent class discussion, share the information learned about each individual and how each person was able to surpass what was expected of him or her.

Media Literacy

INTERNET RESEARCH. In "The Scarlet Ibis," a hurricane destroys the family's cotton fields and cornfields and was the likely source for the unusual arrival of the tropical scarlet ibis to the family's North Carolina farm. To understand how a storm can wield such fury, use the Internet to research hurricane patterns and create a hurricane map. Concentrate on hurricane patterns along the Atlantic coast. A legend for the map should indicate the times of year when the most hurricanes occur in this region and the locations that are most susceptible to hurricanes.

"Through the Tunnel"

by Doris Lessing

Reader's resource

The passage from childhood to adulthood is the theme of **"Through the Tunnel."** When Jerry first arrives on holiday with his mother, they spend their time together on "the safe beach," but Jerry's thoughts are about "the wild bay." What Jerry experiences about himself in that bay will help him to leave behind the familiar world of childhood and to enter the unfamiliar world of adulthood.

In "Through the Tunnel" Lessing uses the techniques of *symbolism* and *setting* to bring out the theme. A symbol is something that represents both itself and something beyond itself. In this story, emerging from the "tunnel" may be seen as a symbolic second birth into life as an adult. The setting is the time and place in which the story occurs, together with all the details used to create a sense of a particular time and place. The setting and the descriptions of the wild bay where much of the story takes place suggest danger and challenge in contrast to the safe, perhaps boring, beach where the mothers and young children play and rest.

About *the* AUTHOR

Doris Lessing (1919–   ) was born in Kermanshah, Persia (now Iran), and lived for many years in southern Rhodesia (now Zimbabwe), where she was educated. She moved to London in 1949 and one year later published her first novel, *The Grass Is Singing,* which is set in Africa. Throughout her work, Lessing's primary interest is in the subtle and sometimes destructive interactions between women and men. Lessing's experimental novel *The Golden Notebook* has become a classic of feminist literature. She has published numerous novels. Lessing's most highly praised short story collections are *African Stories, The Stories of Doris Lessing,* and *The Habit of Loving,* from which this selection is taken. Her most recent work is the novel *Mara and Dann,* an adventure story. She hopes readers will find it a page-turner.

Reader's Journal

When have you been determined to accomplish a particular feat, such as climbing a rocky hill or swimming a great distance?

Literary TOOLS

CONFLICT. A conflict is a struggle between two forces in a literary work. A struggle that takes place between a character and some outside force is called an *external conflict.* A struggle that takes place within a character is called an *internal conflict.* Are both types of conflict represented in this story?

CHARACTERIZATION. Characterization is the use of literary techniques to create a character. The three major techniques used to create characters are direct description, portrayal of characters' behavior, and representations of characters' internal states. When using the latter, a writer reveals directly the characters' private thoughts and emotions, often by means of what is known as *internal monologue.* Note the use of internal monologue in this story.

Organizer

As you read, make a character chart like the one below and fill in characteristics of Jerry's mother as portrayed by the author. When the chart is complete, note how Lessing has used all three major techniques—direct description, portrayal of the characters' behavior, and representation of the characters' internal states—to develop Jerry's mother.

Direct description: appearance, dress	
Behavior: mannerisms, habits	Worrier
Internal states: private thoughts	

Through the Tunnel

Doris Lessing

The Rocks of Belle-Ile, the Wild Coast, 1886. Claude Monet. Musee d'Orsay, Paris.

4 oing to the shore on the first morning of the vacation, the young English boy stopped at a turning of the path and looked down at a wild and rocky bay, and then over the crowded beach he knew so well from other years. His mother walked on in front of him, carrying a bright striped bag in one hand. Her other arm, swinging loose, was very white in the sun. The boy watched that white, naked arm, and turned his eyes, which had a frown behind them, toward the bay and back again to his mother. When she felt he was not with her, she swung around. "Oh, there you are, Jerry!" she said. She looked impatient, then smiled. "Why, darling, would you rather not come with me? Would you rather—" She frowned, <u>conscientiously</u> worrying over what amusements he might secretly be longing for, which she had been too busy or too careless to imagine. He was very familiar with that anxious, apologetic smile. <u>Contrition</u> sent him running after her. And yet, as he ran, he looked back over his shoulder at the wild bay; and all morning, as he played on the safe beach, he was thinking of it.

Next morning, when it was time for the routine of swimming and sunbathing, his mother said, "Are you tired of the usual beach, Jerry? Would you like to go somewhere else?"

"Oh, no!" he said quickly, smiling at her out of that unfailing impulse of contrition—a sort of <u>chivalry</u>. Yet, walking down the path with her, he blurted out, "I'd like to go and have a look at those rocks down there."

She gave the idea her attention. It was a wild-looking place, and there was no one there; but she said, "Of course, Jerry. When you've had enough, come to the big beach. Or just go straight back to the villa, if you like." She walked away, that bare arm, now slightly reddened from yesterday's sun, swinging. And he almost ran after her again, feeling it unbearable that she should go by herself, but he did not.

She was thinking, Of course he's old enough to be safe without me. Have I been keeping him too close? He mustn't feel he ought to be with me. I must be careful.

> What concern does the boy's mother have? What conflicting goals does she have with regard to her son?

He was an only child, eleven years old. She was a widow. She was determined to be neither possessive nor lacking in devotion. She went worrying off to her beach.

As for Jerry, once he saw that his mother had gained her beach, he began the steep descent to the bay. From where he was, high up among red-brown rocks, it was a scoop of moving bluish green fringed with white. As he went lower, he saw that it spread among small <u>promontories</u> and <u>inlets</u> of rough, sharp rock, and the crisping, lapping surface showed stains of purple and darker blue. Finally, as he ran sliding and scraping down the last few yards, he saw an edge of white surf and the shallow, <u>luminous</u> movement of water over white sand, and, beyond that, a solid, heavy blue.

He ran straight into the water and began swimming. He was a good swimmer. He went out fast over the gleaming sand, over a middle region where rocks lay like discolored monsters under the surface, and then he was in the real

---

words for everyday use

con • sci • en • tious • ly (kän shē en´shəs lē) *adv.,* in a manner governed by doing what one knows is right. *Juan studied <u>conscientiously</u>, always preparing for exams and keeping up with his reading in order to do his best.*

con • tri • tion (kən trish´ən) *n.,* remorse. *Led by a feeling of <u>contrition</u> to make up with June for his surly behavior, Philip bought her a dozen roses.*

chiv • al • ry (shiv´əl rē) *n.,* sense of courage and honor. *Sir Mackleby always behaved with the utmost <u>chivalry</u>, sparing those he conquered in duels and aiding damsels in distress.*

prom • on • to • ry (präm´ən tô rē) *n.,* peak of high land that juts out into a body of water. *Set on a rise of land that juts into the ocean, the inn treats visitors to a spectacular view and the peaceful sound of waves lapping at the base of the <u>promontory</u> far below.*

in • let (in´let) *n.,* narrow strip of water extending into land. *I maneuvered my canoe down one of the many narrow <u>inlets</u> that meandered through the marsh.*

lu • mi • nous (loo´mə nəs) *adj.,* shining; bright. *We stood outside in the darkness, our only light source a <u>luminous</u>, full moon.*

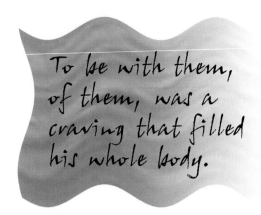

To be with them, of them, was a craving that filled his whole body.

sea—a warm sea where irregular cold currents from the deep water shocked his limbs.

When he was so far out that he could look back not only on the little bay but past the promontory that was between it and the big beach, he floated on the <u>buoyant</u> surface and looked for his mother. There she was, a speck of yellow under an umbrella that looked like a slice of orange peel. He swam back to shore, relieved at being sure she was there, but all at once very lonely.

On the edge of a small cape that marked the side of the bay away from the promontory was a loose scatter of rocks. Above them, some boys were stripping off their clothes. They came running, naked, down to the rocks. The English boy swam toward them, but kept his distance at a stone's throw. They were of that coast; all of them were burned smooth dark brown and speaking a language he did not understand. To be with them, of them, was a craving that filled his whole body. He swam a little closer; they turned and watched him with narrowed, alert dark eyes. Then one smiled and waved. It was enough. In a minute, he had swum in and was on the rocks beside them, smiling with a desperate, nervous <u>supplication</u>. They shouted cheerful greetings

What does the boy want?

at him; and then, as he preserved his nervous, uncomprehending smile, they understood that he was a foreigner strayed from his own beach, and they proceeded to forget him. But he was happy. He was with them.

They began diving again and again from a high point into a well of blue sea between rough, pointed rocks. After they had dived and come up, they swam around, hauled themselves up, and waited their turn to dive again. They were big boys—men, to Jerry. He dived, and they watched him; and when he swam around to take his place, they made way for him. He felt he was accepted and he dived again, carefully, proud of himself.

Soon the biggest of the boys poised himself, shot down into the water, and did not come up. The others stood about, watching. Jerry, after waiting for the sleek brown head to appear, let out a yell of warning; they looked at him idly and turned their eyes back toward the water. After a long time, the boy came up on the other side of a big dark rock, letting the air out of his lungs in a sputtering gasp and a shout of triumph. Immediately the rest of them dived in. One moment, the morning seemed full of chattering boys; the next, the air and the surface of the water were empty. But through the heavy blue, dark shapes could be seen moving and groping.

Jerry dived, shot past the school of underwater swimmers, saw a black wall of rock looming at him, touched it, and bobbed up at once to the surface, where the wall was a low barrier he could see across. There was no one visible; under him, in the water, the dim shapes of the swimmers had disappeared. Then one, and then another of the boys came up on the far side of the barrier of rock, and he understood that they had swum through some gap or hole in it. He plunged down again. He could see nothing through the stinging salt water but the blank rock. When he came up the boys were all on the diving rock, preparing to attempt the feat again. And now, in a panic of failure, he yelled up, in English, "Look at me! Look!" and he began splashing and kicking in the water like a foolish dog.

They looked down gravely, frowning. He knew the frown. At moments of failure, when he clowned to claim his mother's attention, it was with just this grave, embarrassed inspection that she rewarded him. Through his hot shame, feeling the pleading grin on

> What is the boy feeling? Why?

his face like a scar that he could never remove, he looked up at the group of big brown boys on the rock and shouted, *"Bonjour! Merci! Au revoir! Monsieur, monsieur!"*[1] while he hooked his fingers round his ears and waggled them.

Water <u>surged</u> into his mouth; he choked, sank, came up. The rock, lately weighted with boys, seemed to rear up out of the water as their weight was removed. They were flying down past him, now, into the water; the air was full of falling bodies. Then the rock was empty in the hot sunlight. He counted one, two, three. . . .

At fifty, he was terrified. They must all be drowning beneath him, in the watery caves of the rock! At a hundred, he stared around him at the empty hillside, wondering if he should yell for help. He counted faster, faster, to hurry them up, to bring them to the surface quickly, to drown them quickly—anything rather than the terror of counting on and on into the blue emptiness of the morning. And then, at a hundred and

> How long do the boys stay down?

sixty, the water beyond the rock was full of boys blowing like brown whales. They swam back to the shore without a look at him.

He climbed back to the diving rock and sat down, feeling the hot roughness of it under his thighs. The boys were gathering up their bits of clothing and running off along the shore to another promontory. They were leaving to get away from

> Why do the other boys leave? What does Jerry do when they have left?

him. He cried openly, fists in his eyes. There was no one to see him, and he cried himself out.

It seemed to him that a long time had passed, and he swam out to where he could see his mother. Yes, she was still there, a yellow spot under an orange umbrella. He swam back to the big rock, climbed up, and dived into the blue pool among the fanged and angry boulders. Down he went, until he touched the wall of rock again. But the salt was so painful in his eyes that he could not see.

He came to the surface, swam to shore and went back to the villa to wait for his mother. Soon she walked slowly up the path, swinging her striped bag, the flushed, naked arm dangling beside her. "I want some swimming goggles," he panted, defiant and <u>beseeching</u>.

She gave him a patient, inquisitive look as she said casually, "Well, of course, darling."

But now, now, now! He must have them this minute, and no other time. He nagged and pestered until she went with him to a shop. As soon as she had bought the goggles, he grabbed them from her hand as if she were going to claim them for herself, and was off, running down the steep path to the bay.

Jerry swam out to the big barrier rock, adjusted the goggles, and dived. The impact of the water broke the rubber-enclosed vacuum, and

1. **"Bonjour! . . . monsieur!"** French for "Hello! Thank you! Goodbye! Sir, sir!"

---

the goggles came loose. He understood that he must swim down to the base of the rock from the surface of the water. He fixed the goggles tight and firm, filled his lungs, and floated, face down, on the water. Now, he could see. It was as if he had eyes of a different kind—fish eyes that showed everything clear and delicate and wavering in the bright water.

Under him, six or seven feet down, was a floor of perfectly clean, shining white sand, rippled firm and hard by the tides. Two grayish shapes steered there, like long, rounded pieces of wood or slate. They were fish. He saw them nose toward each other, poise motionless, make a dart forward, swerve off, and come around again. It was like a water dance. A few inches above them the water sparkled as if sequins were dropping through it. Fish again—<u>myriads</u> of minute fish, the length of his fingernail, were drifting through the water, and in a moment he could feel the innumerable tiny touches of them against his limbs. It was like swimming in flaked silver. The great rock the big boys had swum through rose sheer out of the white sand—black, tufted lightly with greenish weed. He could see no gap in it. He swam down to its base.

Again and again he rose, took a big chestful of air, and went down. Again and again he groped over the surface of the rock, feeling it, almost hugging it in the desperate need to find the entrance. And then, once, while he was clinging to the black wall, his knees came up and he shot his feet out forward and they met no obstacle. He had found the hole.

He gained the surface, clambered about the stones that littered the barrier rock until he found a big one, and, with this in his arms, let himself down over the side of the rock. He dropped, with the weight, straight to the sandy floor. Clinging tight to the anchor of stone, he lay on his side and looked in under the dark shelf at the place where his feet had gone. He could see the hole. It was an irregular, dark gap; but he could not see deep into it. He let go of his anchor, clung with his hands to the edge of the hole, and tried to push himself in.

He got his head in, found his shoulders jammed, moved them in sidewise, and was inside as far as his waist. He could see nothing ahead. Something soft and clammy touched his mouth; he saw a dark <u>frond</u> moving against the grayish rock, and panic filled him. He thought of octopuses, of clinging weed. He pushed himself out backward and caught a glimpse, as he retreated, of a harmless tentacle of seaweed drifting in the mouth of the tunnel. But it was enough. He reached the sunlight, swam to shore, and lay on the diving rock. He looked down into the blue well of water. He knew he must find his way through that cave, or hole, or tunnel, and out the other side.

> What does the boy feel he must do?

First, he thought, he must learn to control his breathing. He let himself down into the water with another big stone in his arms, so that he could lie effortlessly on the bottom of the sea. He counted. One, two, three. He counted steadily. He could hear the movement of blood in his chest. Fifty-one, fifty-two. . . . His chest was hurting. He let go of the rock and went up into the

> How much longer must the boy stay down in order to go through the tunnel?

air. He saw that the sun was low. He rushed to the villa and found his mother at her supper. She said only "Did you enjoy yourself?" and he said "Yes."

All night the boy dreamed of the water-filled cave in the rock, and as soon as breakfast was over he went to the bay.

---

words for everyday use

myr • i • ad (mir´ē əd) n., indefinitely large number. *In the rainforest there is a <u>myriad</u> of life forms, so many that one can never hope to catalog them all.*

frond (fränd) n., leaflike part of seaweed. *The seaweed grew enormous <u>fronds</u> that served as a supply of food for fish, much as the leaves of trees serve as food for insects.*

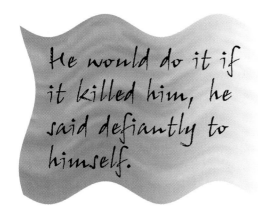

He would do it if it killed him, he said defiantly to himself.

That night, his nose bled badly. For hours he had been under water, learning to hold his breath, and now he felt weak and dizzy. His mother said, "I shouldn't overdo things, darling, if I were you."

That day and the next, Jerry exercised his lungs as if everything, the whole of his life, all that he would become, depended upon it. Again his nose bled at night, and his mother insisted on his coming with her the next day. It was a torment to him to waste a day of his careful self-training, but he stayed with her on that other beach, which now seemed a place for small children, a place where his mother might lie safe in the sun. It was not his beach.

He did not ask for permission, on the following day, to go to his beach. He went, before his mother could consider the complicated rights and wrongs of the matter. A day's rest, he discovered, had improved his count by ten. The big boys had made the passage while he counted a hundred and sixty. He had been counting fast, in his fright. Probably now, if he tried, he could get through the long tunnel, but he was not going to try yet. A curious, most unchildlike persistence, a controlled impatience, made him wait. In the meantime, he lay underwater on the white sand, littered now by

Why does the boy wait? How has he prepared?

stones he had brought down from the upper air, and studied the entrance to the tunnel. He knew every jut and corner of it, as far as it was possible to see. It was as if he already felt its sharpness about his shoulders.

He sat by the clock in the villa, when his mother was not near, and checked his time. He was <u>incredulous</u> and then proud to find he could hold his breath without strain for two minutes. The words "two minutes," authorized by the clock, brought close the adventure that was so necessary to him.

In another four days, his mother said casually one morning, they must go home. On the day before they left, he would do it. He would do it if it killed him, he said defiantly to himself. But two days before they were to leave—a day of triumph when he increased his count by fifteen—his nose bled so badly that he turned dizzy and had to lie limply over the big rock like a bit of seaweed, watching the thick red blood flow on to the rock and trickle slowly down to the sea. He was frightened. Supposing he turned dizzy in the tunnel? Supposing he died there, trapped? Supposing—his head went around, in the hot sun, and he almost gave up. He thought he would return to the house and lie down, and next summer, perhaps, when he had another year's growth in him—*then* he would go through the hole.

But even after he had made the decision, or thought he had, he found himself sitting up on the rock and looking down into the water; and he knew that now, this moment, when his nose had only just stopped bleeding, when his head was still sore and throbbing—this was the moment when he would try. If he did not do it now, he never would. He was trembling with fear that he would not go; and

What two things make the boy tremble?

---

words for everyday use

per • sist • ence (pər sist´əns) *n.,* stubborn continuance; tenacity. *Jim practiced the violin four hours a day despite his busy schedule, and because of his <u>persistence</u> he was accepted to music school.*

in • cred • u • lous (in krej´oo ləs) *adj.,* showing disbelief. *I must have shown that I was <u>incredulous</u> when Alex claimed he could run a marathon, because he put on his running shoes and said, "Just watch me."*

he was trembling with horror at that long, long tunnel under the rock, under the sea. Even in the open sunlight, the barrier rock seemed very wide and very heavy; tons of rock pressed down on where he would go. If he died there, he would lie until one day—perhaps not before next year—those big boys would swim into it and find it blocked.

He put on his goggles, fitted them tight, tested the vacuum. His hands were shaking. Then he chose the biggest stone he could carry and slipped over the edge of the rock until half of him was in the cool, enclosing water and half in the hot sun. He looked up once at the empty sky, filled his lungs once, twice, and then sank fast to the bottom with the stone. He let it go and began to count. He took the edges of the hole in his hands and drew himself into it, wriggling his shoulders in sidewise as he remembered he must, kicking himself along with his feet.

Soon he was clear inside. He was in a small rockbound hole filled with yellowish-gray water. The water was pushing him up against the roof. The roof was sharp and pained his back. He pulled himself along with his hands—fast, fast—and used his legs as levers. His head knocked against something; a sharp pain dizzied him. Fifty, fifty-one, fifty-two. . . . He was without light, and the water seemed to press upon him with the weight of rock.

His head knocked against something; a sharp pain dizzied him.

Seventy-one, seventy-two. . . . There was no strain on his lungs. He felt like an inflated balloon, his lungs were so light and easy, but his head was pulsing.

He was being continually pressed against the sharp roof, which felt slimy as well as sharp. Again he thought of octopuses, and wondered if the tunnel might be filled with weed that could tangle him. He gave himself a panicky, convulsive kick forward, ducked his head, and swam. His feet and hands moved freely, as if in open water. The hole must have widened out. He thought he must be swimming fast, and he was frightened of banging his head if the tunnel narrowed.

A hundred, a hundred and one. . . . The water paled. Victory filled him. His lungs were beginning to hurt. A few more strokes and he would be out. He was counting wildly; he said a hundred and fifteen, and then, a long time later, a hundred and fifteen again. The water was a clear jewel-green all around him. Then he saw, above his head, a crack running up through the rock. Sunlight was falling through it, showing the clean, dark rock of the tunnel, a single mussel shell, and darkness ahead.

How long has the boy been underwater? How does he feel physically and emotionally?

He was at the end of what he could do. He looked up at the crack as if it were filled with air and not water, as if he could put his mouth to it to draw in air. A hundred and fifteen, he heard himself say inside his head—but he had said that long ago. He must go on into the blackness ahead, or he would drown. His head was swelling, his lungs cracking. A hundred and fifteen, a hundred and fifteen pounded through his head, and he feebly clutched at rocks in the dark, pulling himself forward, leaving the brief space of sunlit water behind. He felt he was dying. He was no longer quite conscious. He struggled on in the darkness between lapses into unconsciousness. An immense, swelling pain filled his head, and then the darkness cracked with an explosion of green light. His hands, groping forward, met nothing; and his feet, kicking back, propelled him out into the open sea.

He drifted to the surface, his face turned up to the air. He was gasping like a fish. He felt he would sink now and drown; he could not swim the few feet back to the rock. Then he was clutching it and pulling himself up on to it. He lay face down, gasping. He could see nothing but a red-veined, clotted dark. His eyes must have burst, he thought; they were full of blood. He tore off his goggles and a gout of blood went into the sea. His nose was bleeding, and the blood had filled the goggles.

He scooped up handfuls of water from the cool, salty sea, to splash on his face, and did not know whether it was blood or salt water he tasted. After a time, his heart quieted, his eyes cleared, and he sat up. He could see the local boys diving and playing half a mile away. He did not want them. He wanted nothing but to get back home and lie down.

> *Why does the boy want, at first, to go through the tunnel? What has changed now that he has actually done it?*

In a short while, Jerry swam to shore and climbed slowly up the path to the villa. He flung himself on his bed and slept, waking at the sound of feet on the path outside. His mother was coming back. He rushed to the bathroom, thinking she must not see his face with bloodstains, or tearstains, on it. He came out of the bathroom and met her as she walked into the villa, smiling, her eyes lighting up.

"Have a nice morning?" she asked, laying her hand on his warm brown shoulder.

"Oh, yes, thank you," he said.

"You look a bit pale." And then, sharp and anxious, "How did you bang your head?"

"Oh, just banged it," he told her.

She looked at him closely. He was strained; his eyes were glazed-looking. She was worried. And then she said to herself, Oh, don't fuss! Nothing can happen. He can swim like a fish.

They sat down to lunch together.

"Mummy," he said, "I can stay under water for two minutes—three minutes, at least." It came bursting out of him.

"Can you, darling?" she said. "Well, I shouldn't overdo it. I don't think you ought to swim any more today."

She was ready for a battle of wills, but he gave in at once. It was no longer of the least importance to go to the bay. ∎

> *What is no longer of importance to Jerry?*

Respond *to the* SELECTION

How do you think Jerry's mother would feel if she knew how much danger her son had put himself through?

ABOUT THE RELATED READING ➤

Margaret Atwood grew up in Canada, was educated at the University of Toronto and Harvard, and held various jobs in Canada, the United States, England, and Italy. Atwood published her first poem when she was just nineteen and has won many prizes for her poetry as well as her fiction. A few of her novels include *Edible Woman* (1969), *Lady Oracle* (1976), *Bodily Harm* (1982), and *Cat's Eye* (1988). Many of her stories have been collected in *Dancing Girls and Other Stories* (1978), *Murder in the Dark* (1983), and *Bluebeard's Egg* (1983). The poem "Death of a Young Son by Drowning" was written in 1970 and published by Oxford University Press Canada in *Selected Poems*.

Death of a Young Son by Drowning

Margaret Atwood

He, who navigated with success
the dangerous river of his own birth
once more set forth

on a voyage of discovery
into the land I floated on
but could not touch to claim.

His feet slid on the bank,
the currents took him;
he swirled with ice and trees in the swollen water

and plunged into distant regions,
his head a bathysphere;
through his eyes' thin glass bubbles

he looked out, reckless adventurer
on a landscape stranger than Uranus
we have all been to and some remember.

There was an accident; the air locked,
he was hung in the river like a heart.
They retrieved the swamped body,
cairn of my plans and future charts,
with poles and hooks
from among the nudging logs.

It was spring, the sun kept shining, the new grass
leapt to solidity;
my hands glistened with details.

After the long trip I was tired of waves.
My foot hit rock. The dreamed sails
collapsed, ragged.

I planted him in his country
like a flag.

■

Investigate, *Inquire,* and Imagine

Recall: GATHERING FACTS

1a. What is Jerry's family situation?

2a. What does Jerry do to prepare himself for swimming through the tunnel?

3a. What unexpected problems does Jerry encounter as he swims through the tunnel?

→ Interpret: FINDING MEANING

1b. What worries Jerry's mother when Jerry goes to "his own beach"?

2b. Why doesn't Jerry tell his mother what he is attempting to do?

3b. Why has Jerry no desire to return to the bay and swim again through the tunnel?

Analyze: TAKING THINGS APART

4a. Of what importance is the sea to the setting of the story? Consider the way the bay is described. How does the description of the bay reflect Jerry's feelings after the local boys leave him behind?

→ Synthesize: BRINGING THINGS TOGETHER

4b. Why does Jerry fear swimming through the tunnel? Why does he feel compelled to do it? What does Jerry's journey through the underwater tunnel symbolize?

Evaluate: MAKING JUDGMENTS

5a. Do you think Jerry's mother has prepared him well for his journey to young adulthood? Use evidence from the text to support your response. What other types of challenges might serve as passages from childhood to adulthood?

→ Extend: CONNECTING IDEAS

5b. Compare and contrast Jerry's journey in "Through the Tunnel" to the mother's journey in "Death of a Young Son by Drowning." How does the mother in the poem "follow" her son on his journey through the water?

Understanding *Literature*

CONFLICT. Review the definition for **conflict** in the Literary Tools on page 785. What is the external conflict in this story? What internal conflict does Jerry experience?

CHARACTERIZATION. Review the definition for **characterization** in the Handbook of Literary Terms. Consider the following internal monologue from the story: "She was thinking, Of course he's old enough to be safe without me. Have I been keeping him too close? He mustn't feel he ought to be with me. I must be careful." What is revealed about Jerry's mother in the monologue?

Writer's Journal

1. Write a **narrative paragraph** about an experience you had that challenged you, taught you a lesson, or gave you an opportunity to prove yourself. Begin by writing a sentence that tells what the experience was and what you learned from it. (This will become the topic sentence of your paragraph.)

2. Lessing uses the poetic technique of *alliteration,* the repetition of initial consonant sounds, to heighten her description of the undersea world in paragraph 1, page 790. For example: ". . . the water sparkled as if sequins were dropping through it." Write your own **description** of a scene in nature using alliteration.

3. Imagine that you are Jerry and you write a **letter** to a good friend back home recounting your underwater experience. Tell your friend about how diligently you practiced learning to hold your breath for increasing lengths of time, how you felt and what you were thinking while you were swimming through the tunnel, how it felt to reach the water's surface and the rock, and whether you would do it again.

Integrating the Language Arts

Language, Grammar, and Style

ADVERB CLAUSES. Read about adverb clauses in the Language Arts Survey 3.83, "Clauses within a Sentence." Rewrite the following sentences on a separate sheet of paper, underlining the adverb clauses.

1. Jerry swam through the tunnel like the native boys had been doing.
2. Jerry used a rock after he located the tunnel under water.
3. When he swam through the tunnel, Jerry suffered a nosebleed.
4. If she had known his goal, Jerry's mother would have worried about her son.
5. For Jerry this challenge proved as much as anything could; he was equal to the others.

Study and Research & Media Literacy

RESEARCH REPORT. Many cultures have formal "coming of age" ceremonies to mark a child's emergence into young adulthood. Use the Internet to research such a ceremony and answer the following questions. At what age/time period in a young person's life does the ceremony take place? Are there similar ceremonies for both boys and girls? What happens at the ceremony and what is expected of the child? Where does the ceremony take place? After the ceremony, is the young adult treated differently by family or society members and is he or she expected to behave differently?

Speaking and Listening

CONDUCTING AN INTERVIEW. Talk with a family member or friend about a personal recollection of an experience that marked his or her transition from childhood to young adulthood. Gather details about the time and place as well as the individual's feelings about him or herself and others before, during, and after the transitional experience. Class members can share these stories orally. Do you notice any similarities in the feelings of these individuals?

"miss rosie"
by Lucille Clifton

Reader's resource

The poem "**miss rosie**" is from Lucille Clifton's first poetry collection, *Good Times,* which was published in 1969. A recurring theme throughout the collection—human resilience and survival in the face of life's hardships—can be seen in this poem. The poem creates a strong, clear portrait of Miss Rosie through the use of figurative language, which suggests something more than the literal meanings of the poem's words.

About *the* AUTHOR

Lucille Clifton (1936–   ) was born in DePew, New York. Educated at Howard University and Fredonia State Teachers College, Clifton has taught poetry at many universities. She is currently Distinguished Professor of Humanities at St. Mary's College of Maryland. Expressing pride in her African-American heritage and identity, Clifton has said, "I am a Black woman poet, and I sound like one." In her poems, Clifton often employs African-American language in her examinations of family relationships and life in the urban ghetto. Her nine books of poetry include *Good News About the Earth* (1972), *An Ordinary Woman* (1974), *Two-Headed Woman* (1980), *Good Woman: Poems and a Memoir: 1969–1980* (1987), *Quilting: Poems 1987–1990* (1991), *The Book of Light* (1993), and *The Terrible Stories* (1995). In addition to her collections of poetry, Clifton has written a memoir, *Generations: A Memoir* (1976), and more than sixteen books for children.

Reader's Journal

When have you had to adjust to or recover from a misfortune or difficult change in your life?

Literary TOOLS

SPEAKER. The **speaker** is the character who speaks, or narrates, in a poem—the voice assumed by the writer. The speaker and the writer of a poem are not necessarily the same person. As you read, decide how the speaker feels about Miss Rosie.

SIMILE. A **simile** is a comparison using *like* or *as.* This figure of speech invites the reader to make a comparison between two things. The two "things" involved are the writer's actual subject, the *tenor* of the simile, and another thing to which the subject is likened, the *vehicle* of the simile. As you read, find the two similes used in the poem. See the Handbook of Literary Terms for examples.

Graphic Organizer

Make a chart listing the tenor and vehicle for each simile in the poem.

Tenor	Vehicle

Elderly Lady who lives on Lamont Street, 1942. Gordon Parks. Library of Congress.

miss rosie

Lucille Clifton

When I watch you
wrapped up like garbage
sitting, surrounded by the smell
of too old potato peels
5 or
when I watch you
in your old man's shoes
with the little toe cut out
sitting, waiting for your mind
10 like next week's grocery
I say
when I watch you
you wet brown bag of a woman
who used to be the best looking gal in Georgia
15 used to be called the Georgia Rose
I stand up
through your destruction
I stand up ■

What startling comparison begins this poem? What does that comparison reveal about Miss Rosie?

Why might the toes be cut out of Miss Rosie's shoes?

How has Miss Rosie changed over the years?

art n o t e

Elderly Lady who lives on Lamont Street, 1942. Gordon Parks.

Gordon Parks (1912–) is a renowned photographer in addition to being a poet. Some of his earliest work was with the Farm Services Administration, a government agency that called attention to poverty in America. Do you think the purpose of this photograph is similar to that of Lucille Clifton's poem?

What things have you seen people "stand up" for?

Investigate, *Inquire,* and Imagine

Recall: GATHERING FACTS

1a. What is the speaker doing in the opening line of the poem?

2a. What portrait is presented of Miss Rosie in the first four lines?

3a. What did Miss Rosie "used to be called"?

→ **Interpret: FINDING MEANING**

1b. What can you infer about where the speaker sees Miss Rosie?

2b. What details reinforce the portrait of Miss Rosie?

3b. What does Miss Rosie's former nickname suggest about her appearance when she was young?

Analyze: TAKING THINGS APART

4a. What conditions afflict Miss Rosie?

→ **Synthesize: BRINGING THINGS TOGETHER**

4b. How does Miss Rosie live her life?

Evaluate: MAKING JUDGMENTS

5a. Why might Miss Rosie have such an effect on the speaker?

→ **Extend: CONNECTING IDEAS**

5b. If you were the speaker, what two things could you do for Miss Rosie?

Understanding *Literature*

SPEAKER. Review the definition for **speaker** in the Handbook of Literary Terms. How does the speaker feel about Miss Rosie? What emotions are expressed by the way in which the speaker speaks?

SIMILE. Review the definition for **simile** in Literary Tools on page 797. What is the tenor and vehicle for each of the similes in the poem? What do those things have in common?

Writer's Journal

1. Imagine you are the speaker. Write a **letter** to Miss Rosie offering specific assistance.
2. Imagine you are Miss Rosie. Write a **journal entry** contrasting your present life with your past life when you were known as "the Georgia Rose."
3. Write a **free verse poem** describing something you want to "stand up" for.

Integrating the Language Arts

Language, Grammar, and Style

NOUN CLAUSES. Read about noun subjects and noun clauses in the Language Arts Survey 3.19, "Finding the Complete Subject and Complete Predicate in a Sentence," and 3.83, "Clauses within a Sentence." On a separate sheet of paper, identify the noun subjects and noun clauses in the following sentences.

1. Lucille Clifton pitied whoever had fallen on hard times.
2. The poet knew that Miss Rosie didn't cause her own misfortunes.
3. Whoever wears rags must be very poor.
4. The subject of the poem is wrapped up like garbage.
5. What had happened to Miss Rosie is unknown to the reader.

Collaborative Learning & Study and Research

CELEBRATING NATIONAL POETRY MONTH. National Poetry Month was inaugurated by The Academy of American Poets in April 1996. First, research what events are being held for National Poetry Month throughout the United States this year. If you plan to do your research online, access The Academy of American Poets at http://www.poets.org/ and click on "National Poetry Month." Then plan how your small group can celebrate National Poetry Month at your school. For example, you might want to hold a poetry recital, teach a poetry class at a local elementary school, or pass out booklets of student poems to your classmates.

Applied English

ADVERTISEMENT. Write an advertisement for your student newspaper to entice young people to attend a poetry reading at which Lucille Clifton and the students of your class will read their poems. You may wish to illustrate your ad with sketches, graphics, or photos.

Critical Thinking

BOOK REVIEW. Imagine that your job is to write book reviews for school librarians. Write a review on one of Lucille Clifton's books for children, such as *All Us Come Cross the Water* (1973). What is the book's subject? How can you summarize the book's content? Answer these and other pertinent questions as you write your review.

"The Courage That My Mother Had"
by Edna St. Vincent Millay

Literary
T O O L S

FIGURES OF SPEECH, METAPHOR, AND SIMILE. **Figures of speech** are expressions that have more than a literal meaning. Metaphor and simile are two types of figures of speech. A **metaphor** is a figure of speech in which one thing is spoken or written about as if it were another. A **simile** is a comparison using *like* or *as*. Metaphors and similes invite the reader to make a comparison between two things. The two things involved are the writer's actual subject, the *tenor* of the figure of speech, and another thing to which the subject is likened, the *vehicle* of the figure of speech. As you read, note the figures of speech used in this poem.

RHYME, SIGHT RHYME, AND RHYME SCHEME. **Rhyme** is the repetition of sounds at the ends of words. A **sight rhyme**, or **eye rhyme**, is a pair of words, generally at the ends of lines of verse, that are spelled similarly but pronounced differently, as in *rain* and *again*. A **rhyme scheme** is a pattern of end rhymes, or rhymes at the ends of lines of verse. The rhyme scheme of a poem is designated by letters, with matching letters signifying matching sounds. As you read, note which words rhyme and which rhymes are examples of sight rhyme.

Graphic Organizer

Make a chart like the one below to identify the rhyme scheme of this poem.

line 1	*a*
line 2	*b*
line 3	*c*
line 4	*a*

Reader's
r e s o u r c e

"The Courage That My Mother Had" is a celebration of courage. The poet cherishes her mother's courage and compares her mother's strength to rock from the land on which she lived.

GEOLOGY CONNECTION. Granite is a hard, durable rock that has been used as a building material since ancient times. Gravestones are often made of granite. Granite may be pink, dark gray, or light gray, and is commonly believed to have solidified from molten rock, called magma.

About *the*
AUTHOR

Edna St. Vincent Millay (1892–1950) was born in Rockland, Maine. Her mother raised Millay and her two sisters and encouraged them to be ambitious and independent. Millay was both. She became a noted poet, playwright, feminist, and political activist. At the age of twenty, she won her first major poetry contest. At Vassar College, Millay continued writing poetry and became interested in acting. After graduating in 1917, she lived in Greenwich Village, writing for magazines and acting with the Provincetown Players. From 1921 to 1923 she lived in Europe. In 1923, Millay's poetry collection *The Harp Weaver* won the Pulitzer Prize for poetry, making Millay the first woman to receive that prestigious award. On returning to the United States, she married a Dutch businessman and moved to upstate New York. Her political activism found expression in the many anti-Fascist pieces that she wrote and in her support of Sacco and Vanzetti, two Italian immigrants tried and convicted in Massachusetts for political activities. By the 1930s, Millay's popularity began to decline. She had a nervous breakdown in 1944 and died of a heart attack in 1950.

Reader's
Journal

What quality do you admire in another person that you would like to possess yourself?

The Courage That My Mother Had

Edna St. Vincent Millay

Portrait of Mme Hanka Zborowska, 1917.
Amadeo Modigliani. Galleria Nazionale d'Arte
Moderna, Rome.

The courage that my mother had
Went with her, and is with her still:
Rock from New England <u>quarried</u>;
Now granite in a granite hill.

What did the speaker's mother take with her to the grave?

5   The golden <u>brooch</u> my mother wore
She left behind for me to wear;
I have no thing I treasure more:
Yet, it is something I could spare.

Oh, if instead she'd left to me
10   The thing she took into the grave!—
That courage like a rock, which she
Has no more need of, and I have. ■

What does the speaker wish that her mother had left her?

words for everyday use

quar • ry (kwôr´ē) *vt.,* excavate stone. *The miners <u>quarried</u> the granite by blasting into the hillside.*
brooch (brōch) *n.,* ornamental pin. *Nathalie fastened the <u>brooch</u> on her blazer.*

ABOUT THE RELATED READING

Gordon Parks (1912–   ) is a photographer, poet, and screenwriter. He won an award for a photographic series on a slum in Chicago, which got him a job with the Farm Security Administration (FSA). Parks moved on to work at *Life* magazine for twenty years. After leaving *Life,* Parks wrote novels, poetry, essays, and his autobiography; composed music, including the score and lyrics for a tribute to Martin Luther King Jr.; and directed films. Note the photograph by Gordon Parks on page 798.

In **"The Funeral"** the speaker eulogizes his dead father, not by listing the man's accomplishments or qualities, but rather by using a poetic technique called *hyperbole* (an exaggeration made for effect).

The Funeral

Gordon Parks

After many snows I was home again.
Time had whittled down to mere hills
The great mountains of my childhood.
Raging rivers I once swam trickled now
5   like gentle streams.
And the wide road curving on to China or
Kansas City or perhaps Calcutta,[1]
had withered to a crooked path of dust
Ending abruptly at the county burying ground.
10   Only the giant who was my father
              remained the same.
A hundred strong men strained beneath his coffin
When they bore him to his grave. ■

---

1. **Calcutta.** City in northeast India

Do you agree with the speaker that personal qualities can be more valuable than material possessions? What personal qualities would you like to receive from your parents or from other adults in your life?

Investigate, *Inquire,* and Imagine

Recall: GATHERING FACTS → **Interpret:** FINDING MEANING

1a. What went to the grave with the speaker's mother?

2a. What did the speaker's mother leave for her?

1b. What does the speaker wish that her mother had left her?

2b. How does the speaker feel about her mother's brooch?

Analyze: TAKING THINGS APART → **Synthesize:** BRINGING THINGS TOGETHER

3a. Why might the speaker be in need of her mother's courage right now?

3b. How does the speaker feel about her mother? How can you tell?

Evaluate: MAKING JUDGMENTS → **Extend:** CONNECTING IDEAS

4a. In your opinion, what would be the best way for the speaker to honor the memory of her mother? Explain.

4b. Compare the speaker's view of her mother to the view the speaker of "The Funeral" has of his father. In what way do both speakers honor their parents in their poems? Are their views of their parents realistic, or idealized?

Understanding *Literature*

FIGURES OF SPEECH, METAPHOR, AND SIMILE. Review the difinitions of **figures of speech**, **metaphor**, and **simile** in the Literary Tools on page 802. What metaphor is used in stanza 1? What do the tenor and the vehicle have in common? What simile is used in stanza 3? What is the relationship between these two figures of speech?

RHYME, SIGHT RHYME, AND RHYME SCHEME. Review the definitions of **rhyme**, **sight rhyme**, and **rhyme scheme** in the Handbook of Literary Terms. Which pairs of words rhyme in the poem? Which rhymes are examples of sight rhyme? What is the rhyme scheme of the poem?

Writer's Journal

1. Write a **will**, but instead of giving away your material possessions, give away your character traits to someone who could benefit from them. For example, you might give away your levelheadedness to your impulsive brother.

2. Imagine you are the speaker and you have been asked to say a few words about your mother for an award ceremony in her honor. Write a **short speech** explaining why you admire her courage and giving an example of when she demonstrated that quality.

3. Write a **poem** that highlights an admirable quality in someone you know. You might write a rhyming poem or a free verse poem.

Integrating the Language Arts

Language, Grammar, and Style

REVIEW OF CLAUSES. Review the Language Arts Survey 3.83, "Clauses within a Sentence." Then, on a separate sheet of paper, write out the adjective, adverb, and noun clauses in the following sentences. Identify the type of clause by writing *adjective, adverb,* or *noun* after each clause.

1. The speaker admired the woman who was her mother.
2. The speaker got upset when she learned her mother had died.
3. The brooch that the speaker wore made her think of her mother.
4. When she thought about her mother, it was her courage she remembered most.
5. Whoever reads Millay's poetry is moved by her lyricism.

Media Literacy & Collaborative Learning

STORYTELLING. Read an account of courage in a book, magazine, or newspaper. Then tell the story to a small group of classmates. When you have heard everyone's story, rank the people in order of who was the most courageous to who was the least courageous. Finally, turn in your articles or book exerpts and your group ranking to your teacher.

Media Literacy

POETRY BOOKLET. Explore the thematic exhibits offered by The Academy of American Poets online at http://www.poets.org. Then choose a theme such as courage to create a poetry booklet of your own filled with poems by various poets that reflect that theme. Before each poem, write a short paragraph explaining how the poem explores the theme you selected.

Guided Writing

DEVELOPING A CHARACTER SKETCH

Who are the most interesting people you know? the people who make you laugh? the people who amaze you by doing crazy things? the people you admire? the people who make you think? The writers in this unit have created characters that should live on in our memories, long after we have finished reading each specific piece.

WRITING ASSIGNMENT. Write a fictional character sketch of a character who is a creation of your own imagination. He or she may be a composite (combination) of people you know. Perhaps it's someone from your kindergarten class twenty or thirty years from now or a teacher when he or she was a child. Or perhaps it's someone you see frequently but don't know: a woman walking her Boston terrier you pass every morning on your way to school or the boy who jogs by your house every afternoon regardless of the weather.

Professional Model

> from "Through the Tunnel" by Doris Lessing
> page 787
>
> Going to the shore on the first morning of the vacation, the young English boy stopped at a turning of the path and looked down at a wild and rocky bay, and then over the crowded beach he knew so well from other years. His mother walked on in front of him, carrying a bright striped bag in one hand....When she felt he was not with her, she swung around. "Oh, there you are, Jerry!" she said. She looked impatient, then smiled...He was very familiar with that anxious, apologetic smile. Contrition sent him running after her. And yet, as he ran, he looked back over his shoulder at the wild bay; and all morning, as he played on the safe beach, he was thinking of it.
>
> He was an only child, eleven years old. She was a widow. She was determined to be neither possessive nor lacking in devotion. She went worrying off to her beach.
>
> "I want some swimming goggles," he panted, defiant and beseeching. She gave him a patient, inquisitive look as she said casually, "Well, of course, darling."

EXAMINING THE MODEL. How does the boy's character change in the course of the story? What traits are emphasized at the beginning of the story? In the middle? How do these change by the end of the story? What does Lessing tell you about Jerry's family? Why is this important? Notice how the writer allows you to see Jerry in action. Instead of writing that Jerry was a very impatient child, she shows Jerry demanding goggles. Instead of saying that Jerry was torn between wanting to please his mother and wanting to explore the wild bay, she shows him looking from one to the other. Good writers show instead of tell.

IDENTIFYING YOUR AUDIENCE.
Few of us write without an audience in mind, and this is especially so with imaginative writing. A character comes alive when it talks, walks, interacts, shows emotion. Bring your creation alive in the minds of your classmates so sharply, so vividly, that they will see and think of the character as real.

Prewriting

FINDING YOUR VOICE. In "Through the Tunnel," Lessing's voice reveals how she feels about her subject. Lessing has sympathy for the boy, yet she does not pity him. She lets her characters speak in voices of their own. The voice of the mother reveals her to be a caring, non-prying English woman:

> "Can you, darling?" she said. "Well, you shouldn't overdo it. I don't think you ought to swim any more today."

Jerry's voice is "heard" most often as the narrator describes what he thinks and feels:

> Through his hot shame, feeling the pleading grin on his face like a scar that he could never remove, he looked up at the group of big brown boys on the rock and shouted, *"Bon jour! Merci! Au revoir! Monsieur, monsieur!"* while he hooked his fingers round his ears and waggled them.

WRITING WITH A PLAN. Think about your kindergarten class. Close your eyes and think. Visually, how was the room laid out? What were the different learning centers? Where were the toys? What was your favorite? Where were the animals? What kinds did you have? What board games did you play?

What other games did you enjoy? What games didn't you like? What did your teacher look like? He or she was nice—of course, all kindergarten teachers are nice, but what made him or her special? Did he or she ever get annoyed with anyone? With you? What made her annoyed? Which classmates do you remember? Who was your best friend? Who was the most memorable kid in the class?

Freewrite for ten minutes about your kindergarten class. Put down anything that comes to mind; don't worry about form or structure or coherence. Write about fun times, sad times, smells, tastes, sounds, whatever comes to mind. If you can't remember much, don't worry. You can make up the details as you go along.

Memory is like a muscle in a sense—the more you exercise it, the stronger it gets. From your memories, a fairly clear picture should have emerged of an important time in your life, nine or so years ago.

Of course, characters don't have to be bizarre to be memorable; someone who attempts the impossible—who faces death with courage and dignity, someone who refuses to compromise principles or take the easy way out—these characters are also the people who are remembered in literature.

The best characters in fiction are based loosely on real people, but then the fiction writer does what he or she does best: he or she makes things up. The writer does what we call a *composite* of characters, pulling traits from a variety of people he or she knows and observes and puts these traits together to create a new person.

Roger filled in the following graphic organizer to help him think of and record information about his grandparents.

Student Model—Graphic Organizer

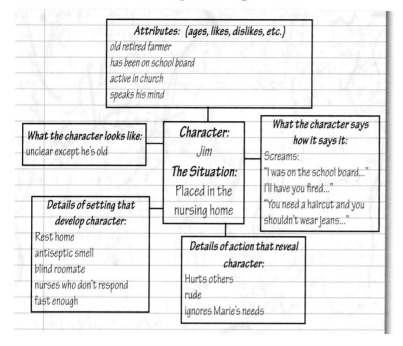

Attributes: (ages, likes, dislikes, etc.)
old retired farmer
has been on school board
active in church
speaks his mind

What the character looks like:
unclear except he's old

Character:
Jim

The Situation:
Placed in the nursing home

What the character says
how it says it:
Screams:
"I was on the school board..."
I'll have you fired..."
"You need a haircut and you shouldn't wear jeans..."

Details of setting that develop character:
Rest home
antiseptic smell
blind roomate
nurses who don't respond fast enough

Details of action that reveal character:
Hurts others
rude
ignores Marie's needs

Begin with some basics: Is the character male or female? How old is he/she? What are his/her favorite foods/movies/books/TV programs? Hobbies? Pet peeves? How does she dress? Where does he live? Who are the character's neighbors, friends, co-workers? How does he/she make a living?

Then go to physical description. What does your character look like? Make a list of his or her physical traits: height, build, hair/eye color, facial features. What makes this person's face distinctive? What is the dominant physical trait?

Next, describe her voice. How does he laugh, cry, snore, whisper? What does he sound like when he is happy, angry, and sad? What expressions does she use?

Put your character is three different hypothetical situations. What would he do if someone asked him for a loan? If she met a famous person? If he realized he was attracted to his best friend's girlfriend? If she lost her job? If he had to report bad news?

Drafting

Put your character into one of your situations. Show what happens. Tell the incident completely, revealing the character's physical appearance and personality. Use sensory details (taste, sight, hearing, touch, and smell): *She gently stroked the dog's injured paw.* Use comparisons: *The air in the room was still like an impending storm.* Use dialogue: *"Will he be released from the hospital today?" my mother asked hopefully. "Well," the doctor drawled, "I don't want to disappoint you but..."*

A **dialect** is a version of a language spoken by the people of a particular place, time, or social group. A writer uses dialect to add realism. A **regional dialect** is spoken by people of a particular place such as Harper Lee's characters from Maycomb, Alabama, in *To Kill a Mockingbird* or Fran Dresher's character in *The Nanny*. A **social dialect**, on the other hand, is spoken by members of a particular social group or class. In *To Kill a Mockingbird,* when Scout and Jem attend church with their housekeeper, Calpurnia, they learn that Calpurnia speaks one way when she's with them and another when she's with "her people." Pay close attention to a standup comedian: a typical mono-logue will reveal dialect, perhaps several if the comedian includes characters in addition to the narrator. Consider how your charcter has both a regional as well as a social dialect.

Language, Grammar, and Style

Writing Dialogue

IDENTIFYING EFFECTIVE DIALOGUE.
When characters speak, they become much more real to the reader. It is important to use that **dialogue** to reveal character. Here are some basic rules for punctuating dialogue:

- Direct quotes must be put in quotation marks.
- Each time you switch speakers, you must start a new paragraph.
- Punctuation for dialogue always goes inside the closing quotation marks.
- When a quotation is followed by a tag line such as "he said" or "she responded," do not end the quotation with a period. Use a comma, exclamation point, or question mark instead. The tag line should not be capitalized.
- Use single quotation marks to denote a quotation within a quotation (when a character quotes someone else).

"I refuse to do your laundry," my mother said, "until you have cleaned your room."

"But I cleaned it just a few days ago," I responded.

"Try a few years ago," she remarked sarcastically.

"But I've been busy."

"Well, 'I've been busy,' too!" she whined. She sounded remarkably like me.

Student Model—Draft

Of course it had been painful leaving Jim in the nursing home, but he couldn't care for himself, and she certainly couldn't. Now he was becoming an angry old man. He had always been outspoken and opinionated, and now that his health was getting so poor, he didn't feel good, ⋀and then he didn't always use good judgment and manners in his conversation.¶"I was on the school

Good quotes! board for ten years!" he screamed one
Describe her day at a ⋀nurse." "You'll come when I
chubby call, by golly or I'll have you fired."
Describe
⟨Another time he told the minister who⟩
Put this ⟨had stopped to visit,⟩¶"You need a *young,*
after haircut!" "And you shouldn't wear *Lutheran*
the quote *new paragraph*

jeans! I'm going to bring that up at
What meeting the next ⋀meeting." "You'll be back
the church board selling shoes, if I have anything to say about it." While her grandchildren and even children found Jim's remarks ~~to and about people~~ somewhat amusing, Marie was just embarrassed by them.

This quote ⋀Jim had also been rude to the kids
really shows and rude to her⋀ I don't know why I
his attitude! have to stay here. Marie can take care of me fine. For crying out loud, I took care of her for 62 years; she can take care of me now." The kids had tried to explain to him that Marie wasn't strong enough to take care of him.
-Explain why. Tell about the care he needs.

Self- and Peer Evaluation

After you have a complete draft, create a subject profile to determine what areas are missing in the sketch. Answer the following questions about your writing and/or exchange drafts with a classmate.

- Who is the subject?
- What is the character's name? If the character doesn't have a name, why is that unimportant or important?
- What is his or her occupation?
- What details of setting or context contribute to character development?
- What are at least 10 details of the character's appearance?
- What does the character reveal through speech or lack of speech?
- What is the character's regional dialect? Social dialect?
- What are at least five details of action that reveal character?
- What role does the narrator play?
- How does the reader feel about the character? Is he or she likable, annoying, amusing?

Revising and Proofreading

Review your self- and peer evaluations. Revise your writing after considering these comments. Fill in the gaps in the profile. Add details and dialogue. Change speech to make it fit the character. Remove inconsistencies or repetitive wording.

Publishing and Presenting

Because your classmates are your audience, you will want to share your finished character sketch. Hold an author party where you and your classmates dress in character, read aloud finished drafts, and partake in refreshments while conversing only in the characters you all have created.

Reflecting

What did you like about this assignment? Who else would you like to share your sketch with? What TV program, movie, book, or comic strip do you see your character fitting into? What actor would you choose to portray him or her? What does the future hold for your character?

See the Student Model—Revised on pages 812–813.

FIXING DIALOGUE. Read the following passage from Roger's draft, punctuating the dialogue correctly.

I was on the school board for ten years! he screamed one day at a nurse. You'll come when I call, by golly or I'll have you fired. Another time he told the minister who had stopped to visit You need a haircut! And you shouldn't wear jeans! I'm going to bring that up at the next meeting. You'll be back selling shoes, if I have anything to say about it.

USING EFFECTIVE DIALOGUE. Remember as you compose your character sketch that strong dialogue adds realism, helps develop character, and makes the narrative livelier. As you write dialogue, be careful to punctuate correctly.

For additional review, see the Language Arts Survey 3.92, "Quotation Marks."

"Dialogue, as much as anything else, reveals the character to the writer and, ultimately, to the reader. I don't have a very clear idea of who the characters are until they start talking."

—Joan Didion

Crazy Quilt

By Roger Jansky

She slowly set herself down on the striped couch and then softly touched her short brown hair. That afternoon she had had her first beauty shop permanent in 12 years; it had been wonderful. Earlier that morning she had walked down for breakfast and seen the announcement that three beauticians would be set up in the commons area. The cost was ten dollars. Without thinking she had put her name on the sign-up list and then sat down for breakfast.

Within two minutes Harold, the old guy from across the hall who always wore a bowtie, was sitting down beside her.

"Care if I join you, Marie?" he asked, but he was already setting his tray down.

"That would be nice," Marie responded. Harold had eaten every meal with her for the last three days. She didn't know where he came from; she had looked around the dining room and hadn't seen him, but then, suddenly, there he was. At first she was somewhat nervous about eating with him. After all, she was still a married woman, but after the first couple times she decided that he was just a friendly man who was probably lonely.

"You should go with us this afternoon dancing," he said. "It's great fun, and I bet you are a jewel of a dancer." Every Tuesday the center's bus took interested people to the Elks lodge for a couple of hours of dancing. Marie smiled.

"That sounds like fun," she said, "but I'm getting my hair done."

Now she breathed deeply, and looked out the large picture window. The view wasn't much: across the lawn of the retirement home was another wing, exactly like the one her two-bedroom apartment was in. Low, one story, red brick, flat roof; very functional, but it wouldn't win any architectural awards. Still, Marie smiled contentedly. It was her first apartment by herself in 62 years, the first time she had been in charge of her own life since she had gotten married back in 1937. It had been a wonderful 62 years: four good children, the beautiful farm, the strong handsome husband, the good friends out in the country, the card parties and the church circle meetings. It had all been wonderful, but now it was time for a new chapter in her life and Marie looked forward to that, too.

Of course it had been painful leaving Jim in the nursing home, but he couldn't care for himself, and she certainly couldn't. Now he was becoming an angry old man. He had always been outspoken and opinionated, and now that his health was getting so poor, he didn't feel good. He didn't always use good judgment and manners in his conversation.

"I was on the school board for ten years!" he screamed one day at a nurse who was slow in coming to his buzzer. "You'll come when I call, by golly, or I'll have you fired."

"You need a haircut! And you shouldn't wear jeans! I'm going to bring that up at the next church board meeting. You'll be back selling shoes, if I have anything to say about it!" he told the young Lutheran minister who had stopped to visit.

While her grandchildren and even children found Jim's remarks somewhat amusing, Marie was just embarrassed by them. Jim had also been rude to the kids and rude to her.

"I don't know why I have to stay here. Marie can take care of me fine. For crying out loud, I took care of her for 62 years; she can take care of me now."

The kids had tried to explain to him that Marie wasn't strong enough to take care of him. With health problems of her own, she couldn't run and get his heart medicine for him; she couldn't get the saltshaker or the butter dish as she had for 62 years, waiting on him like he was a monarch.

Now he shared a room that smelled of antiseptic with an old blind farmer, and she had the apartment all to herself.

She strummed her fingers on the arm of the couch. Tomorrow she would set up her sewing machine, she thought. On the farm there had always been mending of overalls or fixing of work shirts. There had never been time for fun sewing; she had had to take care of the house and cleaning; she had attended to the kids and their school activities. She and the kids had always done the chores in the morning and evening. Jim never had time. He was too busy farming, or he was attending a meeting of the county commissioners, or he was in town having coffee at the pool hall and maybe playing a couple hands of whist.

Later after the kids were grown and Jim had sold the chickens and the milk cows, she had started making quilts, quilting with the church group on winter afternoons. She had loved the piecing together of a quilt, making something new by taking the scraps of material that some women were throwing away. She had never bought material for a quilt. Jim would have thought that was being extravagant. That's what she would do, though, she thought: tomorrow I will start a crazy quilt. She smiled to herself; maybe some bright colors on Jim's bed would make him feel better she thought. She looked out the window then and saw the center's bus returning from the afternoon of dancing. She looked at her watch; it was nearly time for supper.

UNIT 10 *review*
Courage & Perseverance

Words for Everyday Use

Check your knowledge of the following vocabulary words from the selections in this unit. Write short sentences using each of these words in context to make the meaning clear. To review the definition or usage of a word, refer back to the page number(s) listed or the Glossary of Words for Everyday Use.

beseeching, 789	edifice, 765	inlet, 787	rekindle, 767
brooch, 803	egocentrism, 766	iridescent, 778	replica, 764
buoyant, 788	evanesce, 782	looming, 768	skiff, 781
careen, 775	extricate, 766	luminous, 787	sullenly, 775
caul, 773	frond, 790	myriad, 790	supplication, 788
chivalry, 787	gale, 764	persistence, 791	surge, 789
conscientiously, 787	heresy, 782	porous, 766	tentative, 768
constricting, 767	imminent, 777	promontory, 787	vignette, 764
contrition, 787	incredulous, 791	quarry, 803	vortex, 778
culprit, 767	infallibility, 778	reiterate, 779	wallow, 758

Literary Tools

Define each of the following terms, giving concrete examples of how they are used in the selections in this unit. To review a term, refer to the page number(s) indicated or the Handbook of Literary Terms.

characterization, 785	hero, 762	rhyme scheme, 802
conflict, 785	metaphor, 757, 802	sight rhyme, 802
description, 762	mood, 772	simile, 757, 797, 802
figures of speech, 802	personification, 757	speaker, 797
foreshadowing, 772	rhyme, 802	

Reflecting
on your *reading*

Genre Studies

1. **POETRY. Poetry** differs from prose in that it compresses meaning into fewer words, and often uses techniques such as *metaphor* and *simile*. Select one of the poems from this unit. What are the key words that for you seem to convey the most about the meaning of the poem? What are some key metaphors and similes used by the poet? How might the poem be different if it had been written as a short story? For example, what story might the writer have written about Miss Rosie, or about the father in the poem "The Funeral"?

2. **SHORT STORY. A short story** uses characterization to develop its main characters. Review the definition of characterization in the Handbook of Literary Terms. Then explain and give examples of the methods of characterization that were used in one of the following stories: "The Leap" (character of the mother), "The Scarlet Ibis" (character of Doodle or narrator), "Through the Tunnel" (character of Jerry).

Thematic Studies

3. **PERSEVERANCE.** Discuss the theme of perseverance in the selections "The Scarlet Ibis," "Through the Tunnel," and "miss rosie." How do the main characters in each of these works display perseverance? What obstacles must they face? What do they gain, if anything, from their perseverance?

4. **HEROISM.** Discuss the theme of heroism in the selections "Courage," "The Leap," "The Courage that My Mother Had," and "The Funeral." Who are the heroes in these selections? Compare and contrast the definitions of courage in the poem "Courage" and the story "The Leap." According to these two selections, what does it take to be a hero? Explain.

for your READING LIST

Having Our Say: The Delany Sisters' First 100 Years by Sarah L. Delany and A. Elizabeth Delany with Amy Hill Hearth. Two African-American sisters who each lived to be over 100 years old wrote this lively memoir. Their memories span the post-Reconstruction South, the Harlem Renaissance, the Great Depression, World War II, and the Civil Rights movement of the 1960s. Growing up in a time when most women had only one choice, marriage and motherhood, and few African Americans received an advanced education, both Sadie and Bessie went to college and chose a career. Bessie became one of the first African-American women dentists in this country; Sadie became a teacher and was one of the first to integrate the public school system of New York City in the early years of the twentieth century. Their story is a humorous and fascinating personal narrative about two people who faced countless obstacles and refused to allow any barriers to stop them, including Bessie's nearly being lynched. Their wisdom is clear in Sadie's advice: "Life is short, and it's up to you to make it sweet."

Independent Reading Activity

ORAL INTERPRETATION OF LITERATURE. When you read the Delany sisters' book, you can hear their voices speaking. It is as though their words were recorded exactly as they said them, telling the story aloud. Review the Language Arts Survey 4.19, "Oral Interpretation," and prepare an oral presentation of one of the chapters in this book. Before your presentation, read the selection several times aloud to practice pitch, timing and inflection. Do your best to maintain the conversational, informal tone of the book. Your class may enjoy preparing tape-recorded readings of several chapters from the book as a service for those who cannot read for themselves, such as vision-impaired elderly residents of a local nursing home.

Selections for Additional Reading

Ties that Bind, Ties that Break by Lensey Namioka. This novel takes place in turn-of-the-century China, just as revolution is beginning to sweep through the country and change many centuries-old traditions.

The Man from the Other Side by Uri Orlev, translated by Hillel Halkin. Told in the form of a fictional first-person narrative, this is a true story of a fourteen-year-old boy living near the Jewish ghetto in Warsaw during World War II.

Tunda Mawego Bus Service, 1990. Richard Onyango. Private Collection.

Journeys

" The longest journey
of any person
is the journey inward. "

—*Dag Hammerskjold*

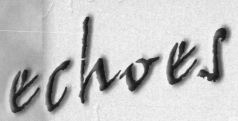
echoes

▶ One approaches the journey's end. But the end is a goal, not a catastrophe.
—*George Sand*

▶ To travel hopefully is a better thing than to arrive.
—*Robert Louis Stevenson*

▶ Everything in life is somewhere else, and you get there in a car.
—*Elwyn Brooks White*

▶ Everywhere is walking distance if you have the time.
—*Stephen Wright*

▶ I soon realized that no journey carries one far unless, as it extends
into the world around us, it goes an equal distance into the world within.
—*Lillian Smith*

▶ There is more to life than increasing its speed.
—*Mohandas Gandhi*

▶ If you let yourself be absorbed completely, if you surrender completely
to the moments as they pass, you live more richly those moments.
—*Anne Morrow Lindbergh*

▶ Do not go where the path may lead; go instead where there is no path
and leave a trail.
—*Ralph Waldo Emerson*

▶ When you come to a fork in the road, take it.
—*Yogi Berra*

▶ Wheresoever you go, go with all your heart.
—*Confucius*

▶ A man travels the world over in search of what he needs and returns home
to find it.
—*George Moore*

▶ Not I, not anyone can travel that journey for you. You must travel it for
yourself.
—*Walt Whitman*

"A JOURNEY"

by Edith Wharton

Reader's resource

"A Journey" was published in 1899 in a volume of stories by Edith Wharton entitled *The Greater Inclination*. One of the author's earliest works, the story takes place on a train as a young wife and her critically ill husband return to New York from a trip to Colorado intended to restore his health. There are parallels in the story to Edith Wharton's own life. At the time the story was written, Wharton and her husband took frequent trips abroad due to his poor health. Also like the young woman in the story, who begins to contemplate a life on her own, Wharton had a troubled marriage and her husband began to show signs of the mental illness that would eventually lead to their divorce.

CULTURE CONNECTION. In the nineteenth and early twentieth centuries, trips to different climates were often prescribed by doctors as remedies for physical and emotional illnesses. During this time period, the status of a woman was tied directly to the social status of her husband. A woman was considered successful if she married well, that is, to a man of high social standing who could provide for her financially.

About *the* AUTHOR

Edith Wharton (1862–1937), American novelist and short story writer, was born into a wealthy and socially prominent old New York City family. Educated privately in New York and Europe, Wharton became an expatriate who resided permanently in France. In 1915 she was awarded the Cross of the Legion of Honor by the French government for her services during World War I.

In her fiction Wharton depicted the suffering of characters caught in the grip of shifting economic forces and restrictive social codes that often encouraged selfish and cruel behavior in the name of respectability. She was also concerned with the subtle interplay of emotions in a society that did not allow the free expression of passion. Her literary reputation was established by *The House of Mirth* (1905). In 1920 she was awarded a Pulitzer Prize for *The Age of Innocence* (1920), which was made into a motion picture starring Daniel Day-Lewis, Michelle Pfeiffer, and Winona Ryder in 1994. Her novella, *Ethan Frome* (1911), one of her most critically acclaimed writings, depicts the tragic fate of three people against the stark background of rural New England. Wharton was also the author of travel books, literary criticism, and poetry.

Literary TOOLS

PSYCHOLOGICAL FICTION. Psychological fiction is fiction that emphasizes the interior, subjective experiences of its characters, and especially such fiction when it deals with emotional or mental disturbance or anguish. As you read "A Journey," determine what upsets the protagonist.

SIMILE AND METAPHOR. A **simile** is a comparison using *like* or *as*. A **metaphor** is a figure of speech in which one thing is spoken or written about as if it were another.

Organizer

As you read, make a chart listing the similes and metaphors in the selection and identifying which they are. One example has been done for you.

Figures of Speech	Type
"Like two faces looking at one another through a sheet of glass they were close together..."	Simile

Reader's Journal

When have you felt that you had to keep something secret, because you feared reactions from those around you?

A Journey

Edith Wharton

As she lay in her berth,[1] staring at the shadows overhead, the rush of the wheels was in her brain, driving her deeper and deeper into circles of wakeful <u>lucidity</u>. The sleeping car had sunk into its night silence. Through the wet windowpane she watched the sudden lights, the long stretches of hurrying blackness. Now and then she turned her head and looked through the opening in the hangings at her husband's curtains across the aisle. . .

With whom is the woman traveling?

She wondered restlessly if he wanted anything and if she could hear him if he called. His voice had grown very weak within the last months and it irritated him when she did not hear. This irritability, this increasing childish petulance[2] seemed to give expression to their <u>imperceptible</u> <u>estrangement</u>. Like two faces looking at one another through a sheet of glass they were close together, almost

What does the woman sense about her relationship with her husband?

---

1. **berth**. Place to sit or sleep on a train
2. **petulance**. Quality or state of unpredictable ill humor

touching, but they could not hear or feel each other: the conductivity between them was broken. She, at least, had this sense of separation, and she fancied sometimes that she saw it reflected in the look with which he supplemented his failing words. Doubtless the fault was hers. She was too impenetrably healthy to be touched by the irrelevancies of disease. Her self-reproachful tenderness was tinged with the sense of his irrationality: she had a vague feeling that there was a purpose in his helpless tyrannies. The suddenness of the change had found her so unprepared. A year ago their pulses had beat to one robust measure; both had the same prodigal confidence in an exhaustless future. Now their energies no longer kept step: hers still bounded ahead of life, preempting unclaimed regions of hope and activity, while his lagged behind, vainly struggling to overtake her.

When they married, she had such arrears of living to make up: her days had been as bare as the white-washed schoolroom where she forced innutritious facts upon reluctant children. His coming had broken in on the slumber of circumstance, widening the present till it became the encloser of remotest chances. But imperceptibly the horizon narrowed. Life had a grudge against her: she was never to be allowed to spread her wings.

What has changed the couple's relationship?

What does the woman resent?

THE SUDDENNESS OF THE CHANGE HAD FOUND HER SO UNPREPARED

At first the doctors had said that six weeks of mild air would set him right, but when he came back this assurance was explained as having of course included a winter in a dry climate. They gave up their pretty house, storing the wedding presents and new furniture, and went to Colorado. She had hated it there from the first. Nobody knew her or cared about her; there was no one to wonder at the good match she had made, or to envy her the new dresses and the visiting cards which were still a surprise to her. And he kept growing worse. She felt herself beset with difficulties too evasive to be fought by so direct a temperament. She still loved him, of course; but he was gradually, undefinably ceasing to be himself. The man she had married had been strong, active, gently masterful: the male whose pleasure it is to clear a way through the material obstructions of life; but now it was she who was the protector, he who must be shielded from importunities and given his drops or his beef juice though the skies were falling. The routine of the sickroom bewildered her; this punctual administering of medicine seemed as idle as some uncomprehended religious mummery.[3]

There were moments, indeed, when warm gushes of pity swept away her instinctive resentment of his condition, when she still found his old self in his eyes as they groped for each other

Why did the couple travel to Colorado?

Who is the strong one in the relationship?

---

3. **mummery.** Pretentious show or ceremony; an act

---

words for everyday use

con • duc • tiv • i • ty (kän dək ti′ və tē) *n.*, quality or power of conducting or transmitting. *The conductivity of the key led to Ben's successful experiment of producing electricity from lightning.*

tyr • an • ny (tir′ ə nē) *n.*, oppressive power. *Dyan felt she lived under the tyranny of the clock and longed for three o'clock and freedom.*

prod • i • gal (prä′ di gəl) *adj.*, recklessly extravagant. *In the biblical parable, the prodigal son squandered his inheritance.*

e • va • sive (i vā′ siv) *adj.*, tending or intended to escape. *Rollo's evasive answers gave Darla no clue as to whether or not he would go to the amusement park.*

im • por • tu • ni • ty (im pər tü′ nə tē) *n.*, quality or state of being troublesomely urgent. *The director resented importunities and directed them to his assistant, who was capable of handling troublesome problems.*

through the dense medium of his weakness. But these moments had grown rare. Sometimes he frightened her: his sunken expressionless face seemed that of a stranger; his voice was weak and hoarse; his thin-lipped smile a mere muscular contraction. Her hand avoided his damp soft skin, which had lost the familiar roughness of health: she caught herself <u>furtively</u> watching him as she might have watched a strange animal. It frightened her to feel that this was the man she loved; there were hours when to tell him what she suffered seemed the one escape from her fears. But in general she judged herself more <u>leniently</u>, reflecting that she had perhaps been too long alone with him, and that she would feel differently when they were at home again, surrounded by her robust and buoyant family. How she had rejoiced when the doctors at last gave their consent to his going home! She knew, of course, what the decision meant; they both knew. It meant that he was to die; but they dressed the truth in hopeful <u>euphemisms</u>, and at times, in the joy of preparation, she really forgot the purpose of their journey, and slipped into an eager allusion to next year's plans.

At last the day of leaving came. She had a dreadful fear that they would never get away; that somehow at the last moment he would fail her; that the doctors held one of their accustomed <u>treacheries</u> in reserve; but nothing happened. They drove to the station, he was installed in a seat with a rug over his knees and a cushion at his back, and she hung out of the window waving unregretful farewells to the acquaintances she had really never liked till then.

The first twenty-four hours had passed off well. He revived a little and it amused him to look out of the window and to observe the humors of the car. The second day he began to grow weary and to chafe under the dispassionate stare of the freckled child with the lump of chewing gum. She had to explain to the child's mother that her husband was too ill to be disturbed: a statement received by that lady with a resentment visibly supported by the maternal sentiment of the whole car. . . .

That night he slept badly and the next morning his temperature frightened her:

> How does the husband's condition change during the journey?

she was sure he was growing worse. The day passed slowly, punctuated by the small irritations of travel. Watching his tired face, she traced in its contractions every rattle and jolt of the train, till her own body vibrated with sympathetic fatigue. She felt the others observing him too, and hovered restlessly between him and the line of interrogative eyes. The freckled child hung about him like a fly; offers of candy and picture books failed to dislodge her: she twisted one leg around the other and watched him <u>imperturbably</u>. The porter, as he passed, lingered with vague proffers of help, probably inspired by <u>philanthropic</u> passengers swelling with the sense that "something ought to be done"; and one nervous man in a skull cap was audibly concerned as to the possible effect on his wife's health.

The hours dragged on in a dreary inoccupation. Towards dusk she sat down beside him and he laid his hand on hers. The touch startled her. He seemed to be calling her from far off. She

> Where are they going now? What does the woman expect to happen there?

looked at him helplessly and his smile went through her like a physical pang.

"Are you very tired?" she asked.

"No, not very."

"We'll be there soon now."

"Yes, very soon."

"This time tomorrow—"

He nodded and they sat silent. When she had put him to bed and crawled into her own berth she tried to cheer herself with the thought that in less than twenty-four hours they would be in New York. Her people would all be at the station to meet her—she pictured their round unanxious faces pressing through the crowd. She only hoped they would not tell him too loudly that he was looking splendidly and would be all right in no time: the subtler sympathies developed by long contact with suffering were making her aware of a certain coarseness of texture in the family <u>sensibilities</u>.

Suddenly she thought she heard him call. She parted the curtains and listened. No, it was only a man snoring at the other end of the car. His snores had a greasy sound, as though they passed through tallow.[4] She lay down and tried to sleep. . . . Had she not heard him move? She started up trembling. . . . The silence frightened her more than any sound. He might not be able to make her hear—he might be calling her now. . . . What made her think of such things? It was merely the familiar tendency of an overtired mind to fasten itself on the most intolerable chance within the range of its <u>forebodings</u> . . . . Putting her head out, she listened: but she could not distinguish his breathing from that of

the other pairs of lungs about her. She longed to get up and look at him, but she knew the impulse was a mere vent for her restlessness, and the fear of disturbing him restrained her. . . . The regular movement of his curtain reassured her, she knew not why; she remembered that he had wished her a cheerful good night; and the sheer inability to endure her fears a moment longer made her put them from her with an effort of her whole sound-tired body. She turned on her side and slept.

She sat up stiffly, staring out at the dawn. The train was rushing through a region of bare hillocks huddled against a lifeless sky. It looked like the first day of creation. The air of the car was close, and she pushed up her window to let in the keen wind. Then she looked at her watch: it was seven o'clock, and soon the people about her would be stirring. She slipped into her clothes, smoothed her <u>disheveled</u> hair and crept to the dressing room. When she had washed her face and adjusted her dress she felt more hopeful. It was always a struggle for her not to be cheerful in the morning. Her cheeks burned deliciously under the coarse towel and the wet hair about her temples broke into strong upward tendrils.[5] Every inch of her was full of life and elasticity. And in ten hours they would be at home!

She stepped to her husband's berth: it was time for him to take his early glass of milk. The window shade was down, and in the dusk of the curtained enclosure she could just see that he lay

THE TRAIN WAS RUSHING THROUGH A REGION OF BARE HILLOCKS HUDDLED AGAINST A LIFELESS SKY

---

4. **tallow.** Hard fat used in making candles
5. **tendril.** Spiral lock of hair

| words for everyday use | **sen • si • bil • i • ty** (sen sə bi lə tē) *n.*, awareness of and responsiveness toward emotions in others. *The teacher took the <u>sensibilities</u> of her kindergarten class into account when she planned her lessons.*
fore • bod • ing (fōr bō′ diŋ) *n.*, omen or presentiment. *Naomi had a <u>foreboding</u> that something bad would happen on her trip.*
di • shev • eled (di shev′ əld) *adj.*, marked by disorder or disarray. *The <u>disheveled</u> apartment was put to order by the cleaning lady.* |

sideways, with his face away from her. She leaned over him and drew up the shade. As she did so she touched one of his hands. It felt cold. . . .

She bent closer, laying her hand on his arm and calling him by name. He did not move. She spoke again more loudly; she grasped his shoulder and gently shook it. He lay motionless. She caught hold of his hand again: it slipped from her limply, like a dead thing. A dead thing?

Her breath caught. She must see his face. She leaned forward, and hurriedly, shrinkingly, with a sickening reluctance of the flesh, laid her hands on his shoulders and turned him over. His head fell back; his face looked small and smooth; he gazed at her with steady eyes.

She remained motionless for a long time, holding him thus; and they looked at each other. Suddenly she shrank back: the longing to scream, to call out, to fly from him, had almost overpowered her. But a strong hand arrested her. Good God! If it were known that he was dead they would be put off the train at the next station.

> What happens to the woman's husband? What does she fear will happen if the train personnel find out?

In a terrifying flash of remembrance there arose before her a scene she had once witnessed in traveling, when a husband and wife, whose child had died in the train, had been thrust out at some chance station. She saw them standing on the platform with the child's body between them; she had never forgotten the dazed look with which they followed the receding train. And this was what would happen to her. Within the next hour she might find herself on the platform of some strange station, alone with her husband's body. . . . Anything but that! It was too horrible—She quivered like a creature at bay.

As she <u>cowered</u> there, she felt the train moving more slowly. It was coming then—they were approaching a station! She saw again the husband and wife standing on the lonely platform; and with a violent gesture she drew down the shade to hide her husband's face.

Feeling dizzy, she sank down on the edge of the berth, keeping away from his outstretched body, and pulling the curtains close, so that he and she were shut into a kind of sepulchral[6] twilight. She tried to think. At all costs she must conceal the fact that he was dead. But how? Her mind refused to act: she could not plan, combine. She could think of no way but to sit there, clutching the curtains, all day long. . . .

She heard the porter making up her bed; people were beginning to move about the car; the dressing-room door was being opened and shut. She tried to rouse herself. At length with a supreme effort she rose to her feet, stepping into the aisle of the car and drawing the curtains tight behind her. She noticed that they still parted slightly with the motion of the car, and finding a pin in her dress she fastened them together. Now she was safe. She looked round and saw the porter. She fancied he was watching her.

"Ain't he awake yet?" he inquired.

"No," she faltered.

"I got his milk all ready when he wants it. You know you told me to have it for him by seven."

She nodded silently and crept into her seat.

At half-past eight the train reached Buffalo. By this time the other passengers were dressed and the berths had been folded back for the day. The porter, moving to and fro under his burden of sheets and pillows, glanced at her as he passed. At length he said: "Ain't he going to get up? You know we're ordered to make up the berths as early as we can."

She turned cold with fear. They were just entering the station. "Oh, not yet," she stammered. "Not till he's had his milk. Won't you get it, please?"

---

6. **sepulchral**. Suggestive of a burial vault or tomb

---

words for everyday use

cow • er (kou′ ər) vi., shrink or crouch from something that frightens. *As the robber approached, the boy <u>cowered</u> under the desk.*

Red Cross Train Passing a Village, 1915. Gino Severini. Guggenheim Museum, New York.

"All right. Soon as we start again."

When the train moved on he reappeared with the milk. She took it from him and sat vaguely looking at it: her brain moved slowly from one idea to another, as though they were stepping-stones set far apart across a whirling flood. At length she became aware that the porter still <u>hovered</u> expectantly.

"Will I give it to him?" he suggested.

"Oh no," she cried, rising. "He—he's asleep yet, I think—"

She waited till the porter had passed on; then she unpinned the curtains and slipped behind them. In the semiobscurity her husband's face stared up at her like a marble mask with agate[7] eyes. The eyes were dreadful. She put out her hand and drew down the lids. Then she remembered the glass of milk in her other hand: what was she to do with it? She thought of raising the

art**note**

Red Cross Train Passing a Village, 1915.
Gino Severini (1883–1966) belonged to a group of artists who called themselves the Futurists. They tried to express motion and speed at the beginning of the modern era. How did Severini try to convey a sense of motion in this painting?

window and throwing it out; but to do so she would have to lean across his body and bring her face close to his. She decided to drink the milk.

What does the woman do with the glass of milk?

She returned to her seat with the empty glass and after a while the porter came back to get it.

"When'll I fold up his bed?" he asked.

---

7. **agate**. Variegated colors blended in clouds or showing mosslike forms

words for everyday use

hov • er (hə′ vər) *vi.*, move to and fro near a place. *Jasmine hated it when her teacher <u>hovered</u> over her desk, looking over her shoulder.*

"Oh, not now—not yet; he's ill—he's very ill. Can't you let him stay as he is? The doctor wants him to lie down as much as possible."

He scratched his head. "Well, if he's *really* sick—"

He took the empty glass and walked away, explaining to the passengers that the party behind the curtains was too sick to get up just yet.

She found herself the center of sympathetic eyes. A motherly woman with an intimate smile sat down beside her.

"I'm really sorry to hear your husband's sick. I've had a remarkable amount of sickness in my family and maybe I could assist you. Can I take a look at him?"

"Oh, no—no please! He mustn't be disturbed." The lady accepted the rebuff indulgently.

"Well, it's just as you say, of course, but you don't look to me as if you'd had much experience in sickness and I'd have been glad to assist you. What do you generally do when your husband's taken this way?"

"I—I let him sleep."

"Too much sleep ain't any too healthful either. Don't you give him any medicine?"

"Y—yes."

"Don't you wake him to take it?"

"Yes."

"When does he take the next dose?"

"Not for—two hours—"

The lady looked disappointed. "Well, if I was you I'd try giving it oftener. That's what I do with my folks."

After that many faces seemed to press upon her. The passengers were on their way to the dining car, and she was conscious that as they passed down the aisle they glanced curiously at the closed curtains. One lantern-jawed man with prominent eyes stood still and tried to shoot his projecting glance through the division between the folds. The freckled child, returning from breakfast, waylaid the passers with a buttery clutch, saying in a loud whisper, "He's sick"; and once the conductor came by, asking for tickets. She shrank into her corner and looked out of the window at the flying trees and houses, meaningless hieroglyphs[8] of an endlessly unrolled papyrus.[9]

Now and then the train stopped, and the newcomers on entering the car stared in turn at the closed curtains. More and more people seemed to pass—their faces began to blend fantastically with the images surging in her brain. . . .

Later in the day a fat man detached himself from the mist of faces. He had a creased stomach and soft pale lips. As he pressed himself into the seat facing her she noticed that he was dressed in black broadcloth, with a soiled white tie.

"Husband's pretty bad this morning, is he?"

"Yes."

"Dear, dear! Now that's terribly distressing, ain't it?" An apostolic smile revealed his gold-filled teeth. "Of course you know there's no sech thing as sickness. Ain't that a lovely thought? Death itself is but a deloosion of our grosser senses. On'y lay yourself open to the influx of the sperrit, submit yourself passively to the action of the divine force, and disease and dissolution will cease to exist for you. If you could indooce your husband to read this little pamphlet—"

The faces about her again grew indistinct. She had a vague recollection of hearing the motherly lady and the parent of the freckled child ardently disputing the relative advantages of trying several medicines at once, or of taking each in turn; the motherly lady maintaining that the competitive

---

8. **hieroglyph.** Character or symbol used in ancient Egyptian writing

9. **papyrus.** Written scroll made of a paper-like substance

---

words for everyday use

re • buff (ri bəf′) *n.,* rejection. *Emily's* rebuff *of his affections led Jeff to wonder whom to like next.*

in • dul • gent • ly (in dəl′ jənt lē) *adv.,* done in a lenient manner. *Mrs. Carpenter listened to her daughters' requests* indulgently, *and then took them shopping for the clothes they wanted.*

ap • os • tol • ic (a pə stä′ lik) *adj.,* relating to the teaching of the New Testament apostles. *The minister commended David for his* apostolic *virtues.*

in • flux (in′ fləks) *n.,* coming in. *The camp was unprepared for the* influx *of refugees.*

dis • so • lu • tion (di sə lü′ shən) *n.,* decay or disintegration. *The army's coup brought about the* dissolution *of the monarchy.*

ar • dent • ly (är′ dənt lē) *adv.,* characterized by passion or zealousness. Ardently, *Joe asked for Melissa's hand in marriage.*

system saved time; the other objecting that you couldn't tell which remedy had effected the cure; their voices went on and on, like bell buoys droning through a fog. . . . The porter came up now and then with questions that she did not understand, but somehow she must have answered since he went away again without repeating them; every two hours the motherly lady reminded her that her husband ought to have his drops; people left the car and others replaced them. . . .

What indicates that the woman is in a confused state of mind?

Her head was spinning and she tried to steady herself by clutching at her thoughts as they swept by, but they slipped away from her like bushes on the side of a sheer <u>precipice</u> down which she seemed to be falling. Suddenly her mind grew clear again and she found herself vividly picturing what would happen when the train reached New York. She shuddered as it occurred to her that he would be quite cold and that someone might perceive he had been dead since morning.

She thought hurriedly. "If they see I am not surprised they will suspect something. They will ask questions, and if I tell them the truth they won't believe me—no one would believe me! It will be terrible"—and she kept repeating to herself—"I must pretend I don't know. I must pretend I don't know. When they open the curtains I must go up to him quite naturally—and then I must scream!" She had an idea that the scream would be very hard to do.

What does the woman plan to do when the train arrives in New York?

Gradually new thoughts crowded upon her, vivid and urgent: she tried to separate and restrain them, but they beset her <u>clamorously</u>, like her school children at the end of a hot day, when she was too tired to silence them. Her head grew confused, and she felt a sick fear of forgetting her part, of betraying herself by some unguarded word or look.

"I must pretend I don't know," she went on murmuring. The words had lost their significance, but she repeated them mechanically, as though they had been a magic formula, until suddenly she heard herself saying: "I can't remember, I can't remember!"

Her voice sounded very loud, and she looked about her in terror; but no one seemed to notice that she had spoken.

As she glanced down the car her eye caught the curtains of her husband's berth, and she began to examine the monotonous arabesques[10] woven through their heavy folds. The pattern was intricate and difficult to trace; she gazed fixedly at the curtains and as she did so the thick stuff grew transparent and through it she saw her husband's face—his dead face. She struggled to <u>avert</u> her look, but her eyes refused to move and her head seemed to be held in a vice. At last, with an effort that left her weak and shaking, she turned away, but it was of no use; close in front of her, small and smooth, was her husband's face. It seemed to be suspended in the air between her and the false braids of the woman who sat in front of her. With an uncontrollable gesture she stretched out her hand to push the face away, and suddenly she felt the touch of his smooth skin. She repressed a cry and half started from her seat. The woman with the false braids looked around, and feeling that she must justify her movement in some way she rose and lifted her traveling bag from the opposite seat. She unlocked the bag and looked into it; but the first object her hand met was a small flask of her husband's, thrust there at the last moment,

What does the woman think she sees through the curtains? Where does it appear again?

_____
10. **arabesque.** Complex design of intertwining floral figures

---

words for everyday use

prec • i • pice (pre′ sə pəs) _n.,_ steep place. _From the cable car they looked down on a steep <u>precipice</u> that looked impossible to climb._
clam • or • ous • ly (kla′ mər əs lē) _adv.,_ noisily insistent. _Merchants <u>clamorously</u> called out the names of the fresh produce and fruit they sold in the market._
a • vert (ə vərt′) _vt.,_ turn away or aside. _Ashamed he had no money to help him, Ken <u>averted</u> his glance from the homeless man begging for money._

in the haste of departure. She locked the bag and closed her eyes . . . his face was there again, hanging between her eyeballs and lids like a waxen mask against a red curtain. . . .

She roused herself with a shiver. Had she fainted or slept? Hours seemed to have <u>elapsed</u>; but it was still broad day, and the people about her were sitting in the same attitudes as before.

A sudden sense of hunger made her aware that she had eaten nothing since morning. The thought of food filled her with disgust, but she dreaded a return of faintness, and remembering that she had some biscuits in her bag she took one out and ate it. The dry crumbs choked her, and she hastily swallowed a little brandy from her husband's flask. The burning sensation in her throat acted as a counterirritant, momentarily relieving the dull ache of her nerves. Then she felt a gently-stealing warmth, as though a soft air fanned her, and the swarming fears relaxed their clutch, receding through the stillness that enclosed her, a stillness soothing as the spacious quietude of a summer day. She slept.

Through her sleep she felt the <u>impetuous</u> rush of the train. It seemed to be life itself that was sweeping her on with headlong <u>inexorable</u> force—sweeping her into darkness and terror, and the awe of unknown days.—Now all at once everything was still—not a sound, not a pulsation. . . . She was dead in her turn, and lay beside him with smooth upstaring face. How quiet it was!— and yet she heard feet coming, the feet of the men who were to carry them away. . . . She could feel too—she felt a sudden prolonged vibration, a series of hard shocks, and then another plunge into darkness, the darkness of death this time—a black whirlwind on which they were both spinning like leaves, in wild uncoiling spirals, with millions and millions of the dead. . . .

She sprang up in terror. Her sleep must have lasted a long time, for the winter day had paled and the lights had been lit. The car was in confusion, and as she regained her self-possession she saw that the passengers were gathering up their wraps and bags. The woman with the false braids had brought from the dressing room a sickly ivy plant in a bottle, and the Christian Scientist was reversing his cuffs. The porter passed down the aisle with his impartial brush. An impersonal figure with a gold-banded cap asked for her husband's ticket. A voice shouted "Baig-gage express!" and she heard the clicking of metal as the passengers handed over their checks.

Presently her window was blocked by an expanse of sooty wall, and the train passed into the Harlem tunnel. The journey was over; in a few minutes she would see her family pushing their joyous way through the <u>throng</u> at the station. Her heart <u>dilated</u>. The worst terror was past. . . .

"We'd better get him up now, hadn't we?" asked the porter, touching her arm.

He had her husband's hat in his hand and was meditatively revolving it under his brush.

She looked at the hat and tried to speak; but suddenly the car grew dark. She flung up her arms, struggling to catch at something and fell face downward, striking her head against the dead man's berth.

What happens to the woman?

■

| words for everyday use | e • lapse (i laps′) *vi.*, slip or glide away. *Four years <u>elapsed</u> before the sailor returned to Cuba.*
im • pet • u • ous (im pech′ wəs) *adj.*, marked by force and violence of movement or action. *The <u>impetuous</u> wind blew the balloon out of sight.*
in • ex • o • ra • ble (i neks′ rə bəl) *adj.*, relentless. *Kyra soon tired of Matt's <u>inexorable</u> demands that never ceased.*
throng (thrän) *n.*, crowd. *The <u>throng</u> in front of the movie theater made it hard for Melanie to find her friend.*
di • late (dī′ lāt) *vt.*, distend, widen, or extend. *The drops <u>dilated</u> Anthony's pupils, but the optometrist assured him they would close again in a couple hours.* |

Respond *to the* SELECTION

What do you think will now happen to the woman in "A Journey"?

The Journey

Mary Oliver

One day you finally knew
what you had to do, and began,
though the voices around you
kept shouting
their bad advice—
though the whole house
began to tremble
and you felt the old tug
at your ankles.
"Mend my life!"
each voice cried.
But you didn't stop.
You knew what you had to do,
though the wind pried
with its stiff fingers
at the very foundations,
though their melancholy
was terrible.
It was already late
enough, and a wild night,
and the road full of fallen
branches and stones.
But little by little,
as you left their voices behind,
the stars began to burn
through the sheets of clouds,
and there was a new voice,
which you slowly
recognized as your own,
that kept you company
as you strode deeper and deeper
into the world,
determined to do
the only thing you could do—
determined to save
the only life you could save. ∎

ABOUT THE RELATED READING

Mary Oliver (1935–) writes poetry that reflects a deep communion with the natural world. As a lonely child she felt her closest friends were poets. From Walt Whitman she learned that "the poem was made not just to exist, but to speak—to be company." To help aspiring poets, she now writes manuals such as *A Poetry Handbook* (1995) that make the techniques of poetry writing accessible. She has been awarded grants from the Guggenheim and the National Endowment for the Arts. In addition, she has won a Pulitzer Prize and a National Book Award for her poetry.

"The Journey" was published in 1996 in Oliver's poetry collection *Dream Work*. The journey described in the poem is both a physical and a spiritual one. It is a physical journey away from negative influences and a spiritual journey that brings one closer to one's true self.

Investigate, Inquire, and Imagine

Recall: Gathering Facts

1a. What was the woman's occupation before she married?

2a. What steps did the doctor prescribe for the woman's husband's health? Did this prescription meet with the woman's approval?

3a. How do the other passengers react when they learn of the woman's husband's illness the day he doesn't rise?

Interpret: Finding Meaning

1b. How did marriage change the woman's view of her life and its potential?

2b. Why do you think the woman felt this way? What did she feel that she had lost?

3b. Does the woman welcome this reaction? Why, or why not?

Analyze: Taking Things Apart

4a. Analyze the woman's conflicted feelings about her husband.

Synthesize: Bringing Things Together

4b. This short story is called "A Journey." What is the woman journeying away from? What is she journeying toward?

Evaluate: Making Judgments

5a. Is the woman a sympathetic character? Do you find her actions and feelings understandable? Why, or why not?

Extend: Connecting Ideas

5b. Compare the Related Reading "The Journey" by Mary Oliver with the Edith Wharton's short story "A Journey." What are the differences and similarities between the kinds of journeys represented? Are these experiences inward or outward journeys? Explain.

Understanding Literature

PSYCHOLOGICAL FICTION. Review the definition for **psychological fiction** in the Handbook of Literary Terms. What upsets the protagonist in "A Journey"? How does her emotional state change? What qualifies the story as psychological fiction?

SIMILE AND METAPHOR. Review the definitions for **simile** and **metaphor** in the Handbook of Literary Terms and the chart you made for Literary Tools on page 819. Does Wharton use more similes or metaphors in "A Journey"? Describing the protagonist and her husband, Wharton writes, "Like two faces looking at one another through a sheet of glass they were close together. . . ." How does this simile describe the changing relationship between the protagonist and her husband? Wharton also compares the "darkness of death" to "a black whirlwind on which they were both spinning like leaves." What does this metaphor reveal about the protagonist's state of mind? What simile is embedded in the metaphor?

Writer's Journal

1. Imagine you are the woman in the story and have just been put off the train by the porter because your husband is dead. Write a **letter** to your family in New York explaining events and describing your regrets.

2. Imagine you are the dying husband. Write a **journal entry** about the changes you have been noticing in your wife since you became ill.

3. Imagine you are a newspaper reporter in New York, who has been assigned to write a story about the arrival of the train from Colorado with a dead body aboard. Think about what information you would get from the passengers, the woman, and the porter, and write a **newspaper article**.

Integrating the Language Arts

Language, Grammar, and Style

COMMAS. Review the Language Arts Survey 3.87, "Commas." Then rewrite the following sentences, inserting commas where they are needed. Some sentences might need more than one comma.

1. The woman was sorry to leave behind her pretty house wedding presents and new furniture.
2. The trip which was ordered by her husband's doctor did not help his condition.
3. Having drunk her husband's milk by his berth the woman returned to her seat.
4. The porter said "Well if he's really sick he can stay in his berth."
5. When the woman awoke she panicked afraid she would be put off the train if her husband's death were discovered.

Media Literacy

APPLYING CRITICISM. Using the Internet, locate critical articles about Edith Wharton's writing. Then apply one criticism to "A Journey." For example, the famous biographer of Wharton, R. W. B. Lewis, pointed out that her writings show "compassion for the wounded or thwarted life that flows through them." Write a paragraph supporting or rejecting the critical comment that you choose.

Study and Research & Media Literacy

WOMEN AT THE TURN OF THE CENTURY. Using your school library and the Internet, research the role of women in America at the turn of the century. What sort of occupations were thought appropriate for women? How long did women live? How many children did the average women have? What legal rights did they have? Then profile an ordinary woman or an extraordinary woman of that time period and explain how she exemplified the time period or challenged it. A woman typical of the time period might be your great-grandmother. Extraordinary women could include Edith Wharton or Susan B. Anthony. When you have completed your research, write a report.

Speaking and Listening & Collaborative Learning

ROLE-PLAY. With a partner, play the roles of the woman in "A Journey" and the coroner who comes to inspect her husband's body on the train when it reaches New York. If you play the role of the coroner, ask questions about the husband's illness and time of death. If you play the role of the woman, answer the coroner's questions the way you think she would based on information given about her in the story.

Literary TOOLS

REPETITION. Repetition is a writer's conscious reuse of a sound, word, phrase, sentence, or other element. As you read the poems "Otherwise" and "The Old Life," determine what is repeated.

DESCRIPTION. Description, is a type of writing that portrays a character, an object, or a scene. Descriptions make use of *sensory details*—words or phrases that describe how things look, sound, touch, taste, or feel.

Organizer

Make a chart to list the examples of sensory details in the poems "Otherwise" and "The Old Life." Then tell what sense the sensory details refer to. One example has been done for you.

Items Described	Sensory Details	Senses
milk	sweet	taste

Reader's Journal

What could have happened today to change your day? How would you describe your morning routine?

"*Otherwise*"
by Jane Kenyon

and

"The Old Life"
by Donald Hall

Reader's resource

Jane Kenyon and Donald Hall were husband and wife and lived together in an old New Hampshire farmhouse that had been Hall's grandparents' home. In 1993, Hall confronted and survived a recurrence of cancer, which spread from his colon to his liver, a threat that made him acutely aware of the fragile nature of life and the importance of treasuring each day. In 1994, Kenyon was diagnosed with leukemia and died just over a year later at the age of 47.

"**Otherwise**" was published prior to Kenyon's illness in a 1993 collection of poems entitled *Constance*. Later, in the final stages of her cancer, she recalled this prophetic poem and made it the centerpiece of her last work, a collection of poems entitled *Otherwise: New and Selected Poems*, which was published posthumously. In one of his own poems, "Last Days," Donald Hall recalls working with her to select poems for the book and to choose hymns for her funeral.

"**The Old Life**" was published in 1995 in a collection entitled *The New Criterion* in which Hall examines the fascination and love he holds for his work. In *Life Work*, a memoir written the year his cancer returned, he describes his excitement as he nears the end of his morning newspaper: "I feel work-excitement building, joy-pressure mounting—until I need resist it no more but sit at the desk and open the folder that holds the day's beginning, its desire and its hope. Then I lose myself. In the best part of the day *absorbedness* occupies me from footsole to skulltop. Hours or minutes or days—who cares?—lapse without signifying."

In both of these poems, the authors explore the journey of a typical day in their lives.

About *the* AUTHORS

Jane Kenyon (1947–1995) was born in Ann Arbor, Michigan, and graduated from the University of Michigan. Prior to her death, she published four collections of poetry: *From Room to Room, The Boat of Quiet Hours, Let Evening Come,* and *Constance.* Kenyon found in the rural New England landscape a subject that allowed her to express her own inner world. She wrote about rural life, the complex currents of human relationships, and her husband's struggle with cancer. Her own lifelong struggle with depression was also a frequent subject of her poetry. Kenyon received a Creative Writing Fellowship from the National Endowment for the Arts and was awarded a Guggenheim Fellowship. In 1995 she was appointed New Hampshire's poet laureate.

Donald Hall (1928–) was born in Hamden, Connecticut, and attended Phillips Exeter and Harvard University. He gave up a long career teaching at the University of Michigan for the quiet life of a full-time poet and writer on Eagle Pond Farm in Wilmot, New Hampshire. Hall, who had spent childhood summers and had written his first poetry there, he described his move to the farm as a "coming home to the place of language." In 1975 he moved to the farm with his second wife, Jane Kenyon, and still lives and writes there. A prolific writer, he has published a number of volumes of poetry and essays as well as children's books, textbooks, and literary criticism. Hall was awarded the National Book Critics Circle Award for his collection *The One Day* and was nominated for the National Book Award for *The Museum of Clear Ideas.* From 1984 to 1989 he was Poet Laureate of New Hampshire.

otherwise

Jane Kenyon

The Breakfast, 1921. Henri Matisse.
Philadelphia Museum of Art.

I got out of bed
on two strong legs.
It might have been
otherwise. I ate
cereal, sweet
milk, ripe, flawless
peach. It might
have been otherwise.
I took the dog uphill
to the birch wood.
All morning I did
the work I love.

What does the speaker say about her work?

At noon I lay down
with my mate. It might
have been otherwise.
We ate dinner together
at a table with silver
candlesticks. It might
have been otherwise.
I slept in a bed
in a room with paintings
on the walls, and
planned another day
just like this day.
But one day, I know,
it will be otherwise. ■

What sort of day does the speaker foresee in the future?

The Old Life

Donald Hall

Snow fell in the night.
At five-fifteen I woke to a bluish
　　mounded softness where
the Honda was. Cat fed and coffee made,
　　I broomed snow off the car
and drove to the Kearsarge Mini-Mart
　　before Amy opened
to yank my Globe[1] out of the bundle.
　　Back, I set my cup of coffee
beside Jane, still half-asleep,
　　murmuring stuporous[2]
thanks in the <u>aquamarine</u> morning.
　　Then I sat in my blue chair
with blueberry bagels and strong
　　black coffee reading news,
the obits, the comics, and the sports.
　　Carrying my cup twenty feet,
I sat myself at the desk
　　for this day's lifelong
<u>engagement</u> with the one task and desire. ■

> When does the speaker get up?

> What does the speaker do after reading his paper and eating bagels?

---

1. **Globe**. *The Boston Globe*, a daily newspaper published in Boston, Massachusetts
2. **stuporous**. Dazed or semi-conscious; not fully alert

---

words for everyday use

aqua • ma • rine (ä kwə mə rēn') *adj.,* pale blue to light greenish blue. *The water of the Mediterranean was <u>aquamarine</u> near the shore.*

en • gage • ment (in gāj' mənt) *n.,* act of being involved. *Brett's <u>engagement</u> in so many extra-curricular activities after school worried his parents.*

How do the speakers of both poems feel about the day they have described? What emotion do the poems generate?

Investigate, *Inquire,* and Imagine

Recall: GATHERING FACTS

1a. In "Otherwise," what does the speaker say about getting out of bed?

2a. In "Otherwise," what does the speaker say will happen "one day"?

3a. In "The Old Life," what does the speaker see when he awakes?

4a. In "The Old Life," why does the speaker sit at his desk?

Interpret: FINDING MEANING

1b. What comment is the speaker making about her health?

2b. What alternate realities do you think the speaker is referring to?

3b. What is the speaker describing?

4b. How can a day's work be "lifelong"? What is the "one task and desire"?

Analyze: TAKING THINGS APART

5a. Compare and contrast the speakers' mornings in "Otherwise" and "The Old Life."

Synthesize: BRINGING THINGS TOGETHER

5b. How do the speakers of both poems interact? Sometimes the speaker of a poem is the poet himself or herself, but sometimes the speaker is a voice assumed by the poet. Which is the case for "Otherwise" and "The Old Life"? How can you tell?

Evaluate: MAKING JUDGMENTS

6a. According to Hall, American poetry after 1950 is "a poetry of experiences more than of ideas. The experience is presented often without comment, and the words of the description must supply the emotion which the experience generates. . . ." Do "Otherwise" and "The Old Life" support this assessment of contemporary poetry?

Extend: CONNECTING IDEAS

6b. What do you think Jane Kenyon and Donald Hall value most in life? What leads you to this conclusion?

Understanding *Literature*

REPETITION. Review the definition for **repetition** in the Handbook of Literary Terms. What is repeated in "Otherwise" and "The Old Life"? What is the effect of this repetition?

DESCRIPTION. Review the definition for **description** in the Handbook of Literary Terms and the chart you made for Literary Tools on page 832. How would the poems be different without the use of sensory details? Which sensory detail in each poem do you find the most striking? Why?

Writer's Journal

1. Write a **paragraph** describing the "otherwise" situations that Kenyon hints at in "Otherwise." Tell how her life might be different in the future.
2. Imagine that you are Donald Hall. Write a **journal entry** describing your frustration or joy with your work in the afternoon.
3. Write a **poem** describing a part of your day or a daily routine. Choose sensory details designed to evoke a particular emotion in your reader.

Integrating the Language Arts

Language, Grammar, and Style

USING VIVID VERBS. Read the Language Arts Survey 3.39, "Adding Colorful Language to Sentences." Then rewrite the following sentences using vivid verbs.

1. Donald made strong coffee.
2. He relaxed in the blue chair.
3. He took the snow off the Honda.
4. Jane said, "Thank you for the coffee."
5. She ate cereal and a peach.

Speaking and Listening

POETRY READING. Imagine that you are Jane Kenyon and you have agreed to give a poetry reading at a bookstore in your area. Select three or four poems that you consider representative of your work and interesting to an audience. Prepare an introduction for each poem. This might be a story about how you came to write the poem, a summary of the poem, or an anecdote intended to pique your audience's interest. Then decide what tone, facial expression, gestures, and body language to use for each poem. Finally, present your poetry reading to the class. Before your presentation, you might want to review the Language Arts Survey 4.19, "Oral Interpretation."

Applied English

FLYER. Imagine that you own a bookstore in New Hampshire and have convinced Donald Hall to read from his poetry for your customers. Having read " The Old Life," you know something of what he values, but you may want to find others of his later works and read them as well. Create a flyer to be sent to your best customers advertising the reading and inviting them to come. You will want to describe it in such a way that your customers will not want to miss it, even if they have never read Hall.

Literary T O O L S

TONE. Tone is the emotional attitude toward the reader or toward the subject implied by a literary work. As you read, try to determine the author's tone toward the subject of the Great Plains.

SIMILE. A **simile** is a comparison using *like* or *as*. This figure of speech invites the reader to make a comparison between two things. The two "things" are the writer's actual subject, the *tenor* of the metaphor, and another thing to which the subject is likened, the *vehicle* of the metaphor.

Graphic Organizer

Make a chart like the one below, listing the tenor and vehicle for the three similes found in the last paragraph of the selection. The first one has been done for you.

Tenor	Vehicle
straight road	laser

Reader's Journal

How would you describe a landscape that you like?

from *GREAT PLAINS*
by Ian Frazier

Reader's resource

This selection is excerpted from Ian Frazier's book *Great Plains* (1989). The Great Plains dazzled and challenged Frazier's imagination when he moved from New York to Montana in 1982. With vivid description, the author describes a long journey across the plains, which he says are "enormous, bountiful, unfenced, empty of buildings, full of names and stories."

GEOGRAPHY CONNECTION. In the United States the Great Plains include parts of North Dakota, South Dakota, Nebraska, Kansas, Oklahoma, Montana, Wyoming, Colorado, New Mexico, and Texas. The Great Plains slope gently eastward from the foothills of the Rocky Mountains at an elevation of 6,000 feet to merge into the prairies at an elevation of 1,500 feet on their eastern side.

HISTORY CONNECTION. At the end of the excerpt, Frazier pays tribute to Crazy Horse, who is revered by the Oglala Sioux as their greatest leader. Crazy Horse successfully battled white encroachment into the Black Hills until he was forced to surrender. Imprisoned because the army feared he was planning a revolt, Crazy Horse was stabbed by a bayonet in 1877 when trying to escape.

About the AUTHOR

Ian Frazier (1951–) was born in Cleveland, Ohio, and earned a B.A. from Harvard in 1973. A staff writer for *The New Yorker*, he has also contributed essays to *The Atlantic Monthly* and other magazines. His books *Dating Your Mom* (1986) and *Nobody Better, Better Than Nobody* (1987) were collections of his pieces from *The New Yorker*. *Great Plains* (1989) grew out of his experiences traveling through that part of the country. Frazier's latest book is *On the Rez* (2000), an account of life on the Pine Ridge Reservation in South Dakota.

Gas, 1940. Edward Hopper. The Museum of Modern Art, New York.

from

Great PLAINS

Ian Frazier

When I went for long drives on the plains, I might be on the road for weeks at a time. I could afford to stay in motels only every third or fourth night, so the others I spent in my van. I slept beneath the mercury lights of highway rest areas where my lone car was visible for six miles in any direction and the inside of the

Where does the author sleep?

men's room looked as if it had been sandblasted with tiny insects, and on the streets of small towns where the lawn sprinklers ran all night, and next to dammed-up waters of the Missouri River where the white top branches of drowned trees rose above the waves. My van had so many pinholes from rust that it created a planetarium effect on the ground when I turned on the interior light. After a day of driving there was usually a lot of dust on the bed, and maybe a stunned grasshopper that had come through the open window.

One night I tried to sleep at a picnic area at the Double Mountain Fork of the Brazos River in Texas, on U.S. Highway 83. Highway 83 runs from Mexico to Canada and is like the Main Street of the Great Plains. Cars went by only occasionally, which somehow made them scarier. The moon was full, and the wind was blowing harder than during the day. I got up and walked around. By moonlight I read a historic marker in the picnic area which said that in 1871 hunters brought more than a million buffalo hides to a trading post near this spot. When I lay down again, the unquiet spirits of a million buffalo were abroad in the windy night. My head kept falling through the pillow. The moon shone, the stars blinked, the trees tossed back and forth, the shadows waited under the picnic kiosks. I got up again and drove until dawn.

In New Mexico I slept well in front of a shuttered vegetable stand on the outskirts of a town. I woke in the morning to blue sky and the sound of small animals playing under my car and scurrying across the roof. On the vegetable stand I saw a sign posted. I went over to see what it said. It said:

> **What does the author call U.S. Highway 83?**

PLAGUE
is passed to man by
WILD RODENTS, Rabbits,
and by their FLEAS
. . . Do not
Pitch tents or lay
Bedrolls on or near
nests or burrows.
Plague is CURABLE
WHEN TREATED IN TIME.

The best places to sleep were truck stops. At two-thirty in the morning a truck-stop parking lot full of trucks is the capital of sleep. The trucks park in close rows, as if for warmth. The drivers sleep with purposeful intent. The big engines idle; together, the trucks snore. Hinged moisture caps on top of the diesel stacks bounce in the exhaust with a pinging noise. I tried to park as close as I could without being presumptuous. Unlike tourists in rest stops, truck drivers seem careful about slamming doors and gunning engines late at night. Sometimes the truck I had gone to sleep next to would quietly leave and another would quietly pull in. One morning when I woke up a semitrailer full of pickup-truck camper tops had been replaced by a stock truck. On the truck's door, in big letters, a poem:

> **What is the "capital of sleep"?**

Buck Hummer
Hog Hauler

In Colorado, Highways 71 and 36 make a big cross on the map when they intersect at the town of Last Chance. Sixty miles to the west, the prairie ends and greater Denver begins, and the uplands are barnacled with houses for a hundred miles along the Rocky Mountain front. Fewer than seventy people live in Last Chance.

words for everyday use

pre • sump • tu • ous (pri zəm(p)′ chə wəs) *adj.,* overstepping bounds of propriety or courtesy; taking liberties. *Anne thought it was* presumptuous *of Lance to assume she would go to the dance with him.*

The wheat fields are eroding, the oil wells are running dry, the only store in town burned down. "However, hope springs eternally in the breasts of our decreasing high school enrollment," a citizen of Last Chance wrote recently. On a night of many thunderstorms, I pulled over to sleep at that intersection. The wind made the streetlight sway, and made its shadows sway inside my van. A full cattle truck came sighing down the road and then squeaked to a stop at the blinking red light. I could hear the animals shifting and bumping inside. They were very likely on their way to one of the largest feedlots[1] in the world, sixty miles north of Denver, where they would stand around with a hundred thousand other cows and eat until they were fat enough to slaughter. The truck sat for a moment. Then the driver revved the engine and found first gear, and the full load of cattle braced themselves for the start. In step, they set their many feet all at once, like a dance revue.

Now, when I have trouble getting to sleep, I sometimes imagine that my bed is on the back of a flatbed pickup truck driving across the Great Plains. I ignore the shouts on the sidewalk and the bass vibrations from the reggae club across the street. The back of this truck has sides but no top. I can see the stars. The air is cool. The truck will go nonstop for nine hours through the night. At first the road is as straight as a laser—State Highway 8, in North Dakota say—where nothing seems to move except the wheels under me and the smell of run-over skunks fading in and out in my nose. Then the road twists to follow a river valley, and cottonwood leaves pass above, and someone has been cutting hay,

What does the author imagine when he has trouble getting to sleep?

and the air is like the inside of a spice cabinet. Then suddenly the wheels rumble on the wooden planks of a one-lane bridge across the River That Scolds at All the Others. Ever since the Great Plains were first called a desert, people have gone a long way toward turning them into one. The Great Plains which I cross in my sleep are bigger than any name people give them. They are enormous, bountiful, unfenced, empty of buildings, full of names and stories. They extend beyond the frame of the photograph. Their hills are hipped, like a woman asleep under a sheet. Their rivers rhyme. Their rows of grain strum past. Their draws[2] hold springwater and wood and game and grass like sugar in the hollow of a hand. They are the place where Crazy Horse will always remain uncaptured. They are the lodge of Crazy Horse. ■

---

1. **feedlot.** Plot of land on which livestock are fattened for market
2. **draw.** Gully shallower than a ravine

Respond *to the* SELECTIONS

If you were Frazier, what would you hope readers would glean from reading "Long Drives on the Plains"?

Investigate, *Inquire,* and Imagine

Recall: GATHERING FACTS → Interpret: FINDING MEANING

1a. In what places did Frazier stay overnight when driving through the Great Plains?

1b. Why does Frazier say he tried to park close to the other trucks in the truck stop without being "presumptuous"?

2a. What did the historic marker in the picnic area say?

2b. Why did Frazier get up and drive until dawn?

3a. What are the uplands like outside of Denver?

3b. Does Frazier prefer the inhabited areas around Denver or the uninhabited plains?

Analyze: TAKING THINGS APART → Synthesize: BRINGING THINGS TOGETHER

4a. Why does Frazier say "[The Great Plains] are the place where Crazy Horse will always remain uncaptured?"

4b. What is the effect of ending the essay with a reference to Crazy Horse?

Perspective: LOOKING AT OTHER VIEWS → Empathy: SEEING FROM INSIDE

5a. If you were Frazier, what would you say you like the most about traveling through the Great Plains?

5b. If you took a trip across the Great Plains, who would you like to interview? Why? What would you ask him or her?

Understanding *Literature*

TONE. Review the definition of **tone** in the Handbook of Literary Terms. How would you describe the tone of the selection? What passages reveal this tone?

SIMILE. Review the definition of **simile** in the Handbook of Literary Terms and the chart you made in Literary Tools on page 838. Which simile describes the flatness of the landscape at the beginning of the imagined journey? Which simile describes the changing face of the landscape as the journey continues? How does Frazier feel about the "springwater and wood and game and grass" on the Great Plains? To what are they compared?

Writer's Journal

1. Imagine you are Frazier. Write a **post card** to a friend describing what you have seen on your journey.

2. Imagine you are Crazy Horse. Write a **letter** to the white settlers expressing what the land means to you and your people.

3. Imagine you are a truck driver passing through your part of the country. Describe what you see in a **travel journal** entry. Try to use at least one simile.

Integrating the Language Arts

Language, Grammar, and Style

VERBALS: PARTICIPLES. Read about participles in the Language Arts Survey 3.80, "Verbals: Participles, Gerunds, and Infinitives. On a separate sheet of paper, identify the participles and the nouns they modify in the following sentences.

1. A posted sign said, "Slow Down!"
2. I was passed by many speeding cars.
3. The author was impressed by the Great Plains' expanding horizons.
4. At night the narrator dreamed of slaughtered buffalo.
5. His truck had many rusted spots.

Collaborative Learning & Study and Research

PLANNING A ROAD TRIP. With a partner, plan a road trip to a part of the United States you would like to know better. Mark your route on a map of the United States. Then read guide books about that area. Finally, pretend you are taking the trip. Write travel journal entries about what you are seeing as you drive. Include descriptions of the land and industry. Write down an interview with a native you have met to reveal what he or she shared about that part of the country. Mention where you stay each night, what foods you eat, and what sites you visit.

Study and Research

RESEARCHING A NATIVE AMERICAN CHIEF. In the closing sentences of his essay, Frazier remarks of the Great Plains, "They are the place where Crazy Horse will always remain uncaptured. They are the lodge of Crazy Horse." Research Crazy Horse or another Native American chief. Then write a biographical sketch about his life, explaining why he was revered by his tribe.

Literary TOOLS

POINT OF VIEW. Point of view is the vantage point from which a story is told. Stories are typically written from a *first-person point of view*, in which the narrator uses words such as *I* and *we*, or from *a third-person point of view*, in which the narrator uses words such as *he, she, it,* and *they*. As you read, determine which point of view Harris selected.

IMAGE. An image is language that creates a concrete representation of an object or an experience.

Graphic Organizer

As you read, make a cluster chart to show the images Harris uses in "Mississippi Solo." One example has been done for you.

Reader's Journal

What journeys would you like to take? Why?

from *Mississippi Solo*
by Eddy L. Harris

Reader's resource

Mississippi Solo is a detailed account of a man's trip down the Mississippi River—from Minnesota to Louisiana—in a borrowed canoe. Friends told Harris that paddling the length of the Mississippi River was foolish and dangerous. Harris, however, felt compelled to make this difficult journey. He states in the opening of his book, "But this dream of mine, still suspended on the breeze and delicate as ever, was just as real as those flimsy summer spider webs hanging in the air, and just as clinging. Once the webs attach themselves to you they are hard to get rid of. And so it was with my desire to ride the river." His friend Robinovich, who is mentioned in the selection you are about to read, played a key role in helping Harris to prepare for his journey and get off to a good start.

HISTORY CONNECTION. The Mississippi River flows southeast from Lake Itasca in Minnesota to the Gulf of Mexico. The river stretches some two thousand three hundred fifty miles and, together with the Missouri River, forms a river system surpassed in length only by the Nile in Africa and the Amazon in South America. The Mississippi River was acquired by the United States through the Louisiana Purchase in 1803 and marked the gateway to the western territories.

About the AUTHOR

Eddy L. Harris, a 1977 graduate of Stanford University, has lived on the East Coast and in Missouri, where he grew up. When he was ten years old his family moved out of the St. Louis ghetto and into the suburbs. He has spent years trying to understand what it means to be a black man and an American. This search has taken him down America's most mythical river in a canoe, a quest that was the basis of his first book, *Mississippi Solo* (1988), and on a long African journey that made him identify with being an American more than ever, *Native Stranger* (1992). For his most recent book, *Still Life in Harlem* (1996), Harris lived for two years in Harlem, which he describes it "the alabaster vessel that holds the Black American heart." Harris has worked as a screenwriter and as a journalist, and has traveled throughout Europe and Central America.

from

Mississippi
Solo

Eddy L. Harris

We were up before the sun. The air was soft and fine, but cold. The morning seemed brittle. When the sun finally rose it looked like it would have taken any excuse at all and gone back to bed. The same for me, so it was quickly tea and soup, break camp and head on down to the lake.

Without much <u>ado</u> we unloosed the canoe from its perch atop the car and set it in the water. I tied an extra paddle to one of the cross struts[1] in the canoe, slipped a line through the stern,[2] and I was ready.

> Right away I
> discover that
> canoeing is an art,
> one which I will
> eventually have
> to learn.

Nothing else needed to be stowed in the canoe because Robinovich had agreed to stay on for the day and meet me periodically along this early portion of the river. Just to make sure I got the hang of it and to put both our minds at ease.

I took a long hug and a kiss, <u>donned</u> my yellow life jacket, and I was away.

The lake invites me with its stillness. Any <u>turbulence</u> might have discouraged me, but the water is so calm and pretty and the morning so quiet and finally beginning to take on some color that I shove off easily and paddle straight out to where the water is deep and cold and scariest. I suddenly have no fear of falling in and if not for the river calling me I could easily stay here and paddle up and down this lake all day.

What is the lake like in the morning? How do the conditions of the lake make Harris feel?

But the river does call. I turn my canoe north and glide toward it.

Right away I discover that canoeing is an art, one which I will eventually have to learn. On the quiet lake my zigzagging poses no problem, but I will need to learn to control this thing or I might find trouble later on. I don't want that.

What does Harris learn on the lake? What does he want to avoid?

I settle in quickly amid the cushioning quiet of this near-wilderness. The lake reflects the dark green trees and the sky striped white and blue. The trail I lay behind me in the water is a soft S-curve of bubbles and swirls. I make so little noise. Only the light swishing of my paddle, the drips of water tapping the lake when I cross the paddle from my left side to my right, a little plop when each time I dig the paddle into the water, and a slight suction sound when I pull it out for the next stroke. And all about me is fine and silent until a handful of ducks skims across the water. Their noise is the flapping of heavy wings and the dragging of duck feet across the lake.

I lengthen my stroking. I'm coming faster and faster across the water now. It's almost effortless,

---

1. **cross struts.** Braces fitted across the framework of a canoe to resist pressure in the direction of its length
2. **stern.** Rear end of a ship or boat

---

words for everyday use

a • do (ə do͞o´) *n.,* fuss; trouble; excitement. *One of Shakespeare's comedies is entitled Much <u>Ado</u> About Nothing.*

don (dän) *vt.,* put on (a garment). *Shane <u>donned</u> a clown suit to entertain the children at the hospital.*

tur • bu • lence (tʉr´byo͞o ləns) *n.,* violent, irregular motion or swirling agitation of water, air, gas, etc. *When the airplane experienced <u>turbulence</u>, drinks and magazines flew off passengers' trays.*

a feeling much like gliding across calm seas in a sail boat. I feel the spirit of this water rising up from the morning's mist and I hear it whispering to me that I have nothing to worry about.

As I carve my path across the water, I see ahead the river falling away as though spilling into a drain. I'm caught in the current. Still paddling, of course; the current isn't *that* strong. It must be a psychological pull that makes me feel I could stop paddling and still not keep from aiming for those rocks and that river.

A father and mother are showing the baby river to their two children. They wave and call to me as I slow to <u>negotiate</u> the rocks that cross the river.

"Where are you headed?"

"New Orleans." I feel like an expert now, an old pro at this. I try to look cool, like I know what I'm doing, but I add, "I hope."

They laugh and wish me luck.

It's a transaction I will undergo a hundred times before I reach the end, each one very much like this one. Some will wish they could go along, others will think I'm a little on the loony side, but each one will encourage me and no one will wish me bad luck or ill. Well, almost no one.

> What reactions will people that Harris meets have to his trip?

When the river finally falls into the gulf, it will have reached a depth of about two hundred feet, but just beyond these big rocks the Mississippi's bottom lies only inches below the surface. My canoe and its 185-pound paddler have a draft[3] of about six inches and when the creek bed rises to its shallowest point, the canoe touches bottom and I'm stuck. Not ten yards

> What happens ten yards from the beginning? What might this suggest about the rest of the trip?

from the beginning and I'm stuck. I hope no one is looking. Is this an <u>omen</u>?

There! I dig my paddle hard into the pebbly bottom and lean against it and just shove until the canoe slides free, dragging bottom at first but finally getting loose and afloat again. This will happen many more times before the river has found a few more inches to <u>accommodate</u> me, but a little strength is all I need. I manage.

Shortly on I come to a little bridge. Lying flat in the canoe I slide under the bridge, scraping bottom again and having to shove my way free while almost lying down. With higher water I could have floated under more easily but my head would have been taken off by the low bridge.

The creek bends left, it bends right. Another footbridge lies across my path and blocks my way. No way can I get under this one, not even if I lie flat and try to slide by again. Easy solution. Get out, set the canoe adrift and let it float under the bridge by itself, then grab it as it comes through the other side. Good idea, but when I get out of the canoe and take the weight of my body with me, the canoe rises in the water and sits too high to squeeze under. The bow[4] of the canoe knocks into the bottom of the bridge. I can stand in the canoe until the front end is under the bridge, climb up onto the bridge myself and then push the canoe through, but the canoe still won't go. It gets stuck in the rafters[5] that support the bridge. I pull it back out and think again.

The bridge is just too low. The <u>embankments</u> are too high to drag the canoe up, but I've no choice. Unless I want to go back and go home.

---

3. **draft.** Depth to which bottom of boat sinks
4. **bow.** Front part of a ship or boat
5. **rafters.** Boards or planks that slope from the ridge of a roof to the eaves and give support to the roof

That remains a possible solution to every difficulty I encounter along the way, but I don't take the consideration seriously here. I'm simply forced to

What is a possible solution to every difficulty of the trip?

get out of the canoe and try to drag this thing up the embankment and across the bridge to the other side.

The canoe is not mine. It's on loan to me from a youth organization in St. Louis, run by a friend of Robinovich's. I hope I don't bend it or break it or put holes in it, but it feels like all of these will happen. In the meantime I'm pulling this boat inch by inch, slipping into the mud and getting my feet wet. At times I go to the back end and lift and shove and finally I get the cursed canoe up and over and back down into the water. No damage to the canoe, only to me and my already weak back.

But soon I'm on my way again along the sparkling waters. I'm in a canyon of trees, two hundred-year-old pines. The river cuts left, it cuts right.

Up ahead another bridge. This time the river has been funneled through what looks like a huge metal sewer pipe and the water builds up there and shoots through to the other side with a rushing noise that sounds like Niagara Falls.[6] I can only go through if I lie down. I do and I'm at the mercy of the river. I hold my breath and go for it. Gathering speed I shoot through the tunnel and out the other side and I feel like I've shot the rapids or done a ride at Disneyland.

How does Harris get by the second bridge? How does this experience make him feel?

For a few minutes I sit in a large, quiet pool at the other end of the tunnel. The river is coming hard and noisily at me. But here it widens and quickly quiets once more and becomes clear and slow again. I move on.

A beaver dam[7] blocks my way. The beavers will create many problems for me before this day is done, and this first dam is the least of them. It stops up the river and a tree has been thrown across half the creek to make getting around it difficult. I wonder if these dams serve a purpose, if beavers really live in them, or if beavers are just great big jokers who like to slow down people in small boats. I'm certainly slowed down. I'm not an expert yet and I struggle to get the canoe going sideways at the right times. Too often I get going backwards. I hit a branch. I'm caught in a snarl of limbs. I get stuck.

What difficulties does Harris face at the beaver dam?

The river here is so gentle. A heron[8] rises up out of nowhere. It squawks: follow me. I do. It drifts downstream to hide, be <u>flushed</u> again, and hide again. It's playing games with me. Eagles in the sky above soar over me and probably laugh at me. Critters scurry through the brush on the banks and never let me see them. The air is crisp and cool but sunny enough and I'm paddling enough to stay warm. Further on I find baby fishes flickering as they dart for cover when I disturb their water. I feel I've got a <u>continuum</u> here, that fish will be with me unlike any other creature all the way to the end and I'll not be so alone. When the river deepens and I encounter the bigger fish <u>loitering</u> in the shade, I know it for certain. But I'm wrong. At the highway bridge just this side of the marsh the river deep-

---

6. **Niagara Falls.** Large waterfall on the Niagara River, divided by an island into two falls, one on the Canadian border and one on the United States border

7. **beaver dam.** Barrier that holds back water built from felled trees by rodents with chisel-like teeth. Beavers build these dams to form pools in which they make dome-shaped island dwellings.

8. **heron.** Any of various wading birds with a long neck, long legs, and a long, tapered bill that live along marshes and riverbanks

words for everyday use

flush (flush) vt., cause to take wing suddenly. *The gunshot <u>flushed</u> the birds from their perches in the trees.*

con • tin • u • um (kən tin′yoō əm) n., unbroken or connected whole. *Eva's classes in art, her visits to art exhibits, and her interviews with local artists form a nice <u>continuum</u> of experience.*

loi • ter • ing (loit′ər iŋ) part., lingering or spending time in an aimless or idle way. *The convenience store discourages teens from <u>loitering</u> in front of the entrance.*

ens considerably and a school of fish lives here, but they are the last fish I see. The river shallows very quickly again and the fish are gone.

I'm totally alone. This is wilderness.

Now the river really <u>meanders</u>. Soft curves become zigzags and I must cover a lot of ground to gain such a short crow-fly[9] distance. I find myself enmeshed in a maze of meanderings and marsh. The trees stand a long way off now but are still all around, and I'm floating in a plain of rice grass. Tall blades of dense pale yellow, the color of ripened wheat, surround me and the river branches infinitely through. I do not know which branch to take.

Advice from an old man in Wallace, Idaho: When you come to a fork in the road, always take the right road.

What decision does Harris have to make? What concerns does he have about this decision?

The route left looks just as good. The right might be the wrong. Maybe they all come out at the same place. Maybe this way is shorter than that. If I only had a helicopter. Or if I had a motor boat and could just plow through the rice fields. Or a pole instead of a paddle.

The sun is behind me and to my left, high in the sky. I'm okay for time, and the branch to the right seems to go the most north. I take it.

Ducks quack up around me, breaking the quiet. A hawk hovers overhead. The rifle shots of deer hunters echo way off in the distance. Other than that I am so totally alone and the day is so serene and noiseless, I can hear the whooshing of the wind through the tall grass. I feel like singing. Even if I take the wrong way and have to double back, I'm doing fine. The weather is fine, I've got my Nature Valley granola bars to eat, and a canteen filled with tasty spring water. As long as I don't get lost in this maze, I'm okay.

These three miles—by park ranger estimation—take forever. Later in the journey I will expect to do three miles in no time, but these three take so long that by the time I reach Wanagan Landing to stop for lunch, I'm actually considering staying here for the night.

Already my legs are stiff, my hands are sore and my back is tense and tired. I pull the canoe up and lie in the grass. I drink from my canteen.

In a moment, Robinovich arrives. She's been out admiring the area on her own, driving dozens of miles in the time it's taken me to make three. And she's laughing at how tired I am.

We get a small fire going and have a simple lunch. I get warm. Robinovich opens up the treats sent along to me by friends. Trail mix, peanuts, cashews, cookies, and a mountain of granola bars, which I never liked before but which by the time this trip ends will be among my favorite snacks.

Never before could I understand why bicycle racers are surrounded by cars carrying extra bikes, food, and drink. I always thought a racer should be out there doing his job, on his own, and if he has a breakdown he just pulls out. I look at Robinovich, my support team—preparing lunch, encouraging me, prodding me with her presence so I'd be too ashamed to quit—and I understand.

What had Harris thought about bicycle racers? What does he learn from his experience on the river?

I'm back on my way and we've agreed to meet twelve miles further on at the campsite called Coffee Pot. The Minnesota Parks and Recreation Department has carved into the wilderness along this first sixty-mile stretch of river a series of landings and campsites. They are beautifully done and clean. Some have fire

---

9. **crow-fly.** In a straight line; direct

words for everyday use

me • an • der (mē an′dər) *vi.*, take a winding course. *Paul* <u>meandered</u> *through the cornfields on his way to the farm.*

rings and pit toilets and water pumps, others picnic tables. Others are primitive. But they all blend in well with the green surroundings and don't intrude much.

Three miles took forever. Twelve more should take four times as long. But no! The next twelve will take much longer. But how can this be? I was rested. The sun was still high. I had just eaten. And the river straightened. On top of that I was gaining experience as a canoeist with every stroke. How could I not make the next twelve miles in a hurry?

I'm feeling really fine. The river deepens and the rice marsh lines only one bank. The other bank is woodsy for now.

> How does Harris feel when he sets off again after lunch?

Too quickly the marsh and the meanderings are back, but only for a short time. Still, the going is not swift. Soon the sun is slipping down beyond the pines. When the sun goes, the cold comes. And now I'm deeper in the woods where the air is naturally fresher and cooler. I put on my gloves and don a sweatshirt with a hood. Robinovich has my warm jacket. I was thinking she would need it more than I. After all, all this paddling so far has kept me warm. In the sun.

I come to a low wooden dam that threatens to force me out of the canoe. But I'm feeling expert. I can ride this. I do, but the riding is tricky and I get wet. The wet makes me colder. The beaver dams take time. Time takes away my light. There is another obstruction and I'm forced out of my canoe to portage around it. More time. More effort. More cold coming fast into the valley. Whose idea *was* this?

> What difficulties face Harris? How have his feelings changed since the beginning of the day?

Rapids. They are loud and swift and the rocks are boulders and I'm scared. I may be expert, but I'm not *that* expert. But what choice have I? I've got to shoot them, and shoot them I do. A long series of rapids after rapids—probably because of the shallow water in autumn—and with each one I gain more and more confidence. After each one I shout with triumph and glee. But with each one I get wetter. And as the darkness descends, each one gets more difficult to see and thus trickier to negotiate.

One time the river spins me into a rock and I nearly fly from my seat. The rock spins me around sideways and soon I'm going swiftly downstream backwards. I can't turn around. The river narrows and the canoe won't fit. I'm stuck.

Another time I'm thrown into the side of the river. Low branches force me into the bank and I can't turn around. The water from the side is too fast and strong for me. I have to get out and push the boat around. My shoes get soaked and my feet get cold and my gloves get wet.

To dry the gloves I lay them on the struts. The next set of rapids tosses up the front end of the canoe. Only a keen sense of balance—no canoeing skill—keeps me from falling into the icy water.

I look. My gloves are gone.

The river has become an adversary. I see deer munching leaves on the shore. They know better than to do what I'm doing and they feel safe from me. How can I get at them even if I want to? They watch me and I feel stupid.

Finally it's dark. Then it's night. I'm freezing right through to the bone and my hands and feet are numb. I'm worried about frostbite. I'm worried about being lost. I'm worried about how to find Robinovich out there in the night. I don't know how far I've come or how far I've got to go. I'm scared. So I sing. I worry

> What worries Harris? What does he do to alleviate his fear?

about running across more rapids, falling in, freezing to death.

That rushing sound, the sound of rapids, terrifies me each time I hear it. The river has begun to meander again and the bank has hidden deep behind the marsh that has popped up again. I can't get out of the river because I can't get out of the canoe. I don't know if I'll find solid ground or if I'll sink to my waist. I'm forced on.

The sound of rapids is the same sound of water falling over those huge beaver dams that threaten my progress. I hate the dams but I fear the rapids even more. The dams I can go around— when I can see them. The ones that completely cross the river I can plow over. The ones that are too thick I can approach and step out on and slide the canoe over. I'm hoping beavers don't bite.

Finally the moon rises and throws down its light. I breathe easier. I can see a bit. But it's still very dark and mostly what I must do is listen. Hearing, smelling: other senses take over when you can't see and right now (despite the moonlight) my eyesight is fairly useless. I rely on a sense I didn't even know I had and it somehow keeps me in the water, upright, away from the marsh and out of too much trouble. I carry on and I sing.

How does Harris compensate for his inability to see in the dark?

I'm wondering how long before the search party comes looking for me. Off in the distant night sky a signal flare[10] shoots a bright arc and falls. Someone, I'm sure, is looking for me. Pretty soon a helicopter will thump through the air overhead and shine down an intense spotlight on the river. A voice in a loud speaker will ask me if I'm all right and will light my path on the water. I'm sure of it.

But no. I'm still all alone and still miserable. My toes are dead numb and my fingers are swollen. They're locked around the paddle and cannot unbend. Frostbite.

Off in the distance, high on a hill, a light. I aim straight for it and tell myself when I get close, I'll get out and hike. It's a good mile straight up a hill, but at least I know there's a house. I can phone from there or get a ride to Coffee Pot. But dogs are howling up there on the hillside. I keep going.

Beaver dams. Each time I step from the canoe to go over them my feet get wetter. I'm just freezing. In my pocket I do have a box of waterproof matches. If I could find a place to pull out I could at least build a fire and dry off and warm up a little.

Up on a rise, not far from the river, a shed. Old and rickety, but made of wood. I can burn that thing if I need to, burn it to the ground for warmth, and yes I need to. My life or the life of this old shack.

But then I smell smoke. Someone else has built a fire. Hunters maybe, or Robinovich. I keep going.

What gives Harris hope?

A big mistake. I find no fire, no hunters, no Robinovich. My spirit is sinking fast. I sing to keep from losing it completely. Between songs I call out to Robinovich. No reply. Just my own voice echoing hollowly back to me from the walls of the night.

I can give up, get out right now and just die. It'll be easier.

What possible action does Harris consider? What does he actually do?

I find every scrap of energy that's in me and push on. I can't see any better now and I don't need too much speed to make me crash into something or send me into the weeds. I pick my way carefully.

And then I see the light from a fire. I smell smoke. I see the lights from a car. I'm yelling my head off but no sound comes back to me. How far away am I?

Finally I arrive. Coffee Pot. The fire, a big smoky blaze, is ours. Robinovich has built it. She's gone, though, when I pull out from the river, gone to search for me. Not knowing where or how to search she quickly returns. The car lights I saw were hers. ■

---

10. **flare.** Bright light used as a distress signal

Do you think that Harris was internally or externally motivated to make his journey down the Mississippi? Explain your answer.

Investigate, *Inquire,* and Imagine

Recall: GATHERING FACTS

1a. At what time of day does Harris begin his journey? What is the first major difficulty he encounters?

2a. Who is assisting Harris?

3a. At what point in the trip does Harris feel "totally alone"? How does he lose his gloves?

Interpret: FINDING MEANING

1b. How does Harris feel on the morning he begins his trip? What clues is the reader given about his state of mind at this time?

2b. How does Robinovich encourage Harris to keep going?

3b. Does Harris feel positive about being alone in the wilderness? In what way do losing his gloves and being tired and hungry affect his spirit?

Analyze: TAKING THINGS APART

4a. Identify the obstacles that Harris encounters on the first day of his trip.

Synthesize: BRINGING THINGS TOGETHER

4b. What does Harris learn about accomplishing goals through his experiences that day?

Perspective: LOOKING AT OTHER VIEWS

5a. Why does Harris keep telling himself that "I can give up, get out right now. . . ."? Why might this statement make him feel temporarily secure?

Empathy: SEEING FROM INSIDE

5b. If you were Harris, how would you summon the strength to reach your goal?

Understanding *Literature*

POINT OF VIEW. Review the definition for **point of view** in the Handbook of Literary Terms. What point of view does Harris use in this selection? What are the advantages of using this point of view? How would the selection be different if it used a different point of view?

IMAGE. Review the definition for **image** in the Handbook of Literary Terms and the cluster chart you made for Literary Tools on page 844. What are some particularly vivid images in this selection?

Writer's Journal

1. Many travelers keep a journal of their travels to remember what happens each day. Imagine that you are Harris. Write a **travel journal entry** in which you summarize the high points and the low points of your first day on the Mississippi.

2. Write a **thank-you note** to Robinovich expressing your gratitude to her for helping you to accomplish your goal on the first day of your trip.

3. Imagine that you work for an organization that organizes canoe trips down the Mississippi. Write a **brochure** intended to stimulate interest in your excursions. Point out the challenges and rewards of making such a trip.

Integrating the Language Arts

Language, Grammar, and Style

VERBALS: GERUNDS. Read about gerunds in the Language Arts Survey 3.80, "Verbals: Participles, Gerunds, and Infinitives." Then identify the gerunds in the following sentences.

1. Traveling down an entire river takes commitment.
2. But paddling in a canoe for the length of a continent seemed foolish to many.
3. The quiet gave the author time for thinking.
4. Toward dark, meeting his support person became very important.
5. As it grew dark, all he could think of was eating and sleeping.

Study and Research & Collaborative Learning

EXPLORING THE MISSISSIPPI. Work with a small group of your classmates to investigate some aspect of the Mississippi River. Each group member should select a different topic. For example, you might research early explorations of the river, major cities along the route, the steamboat era, the history of human use of the Mississippi, how the river was formed and has changed over time, or how Mark Twain treated the river in literature. Then meet as a group to make individual presentations of what you learned. Take notes on the presentations of your classmates. You might want to use visual aids to make your presentation more appealing.

Collaborative Learning & Speaking and Listening

SETTING GOALS. Eddy L. Harris had the goal of traveling down the Mississippi in a canoe. He set steps to reach his goal, such as arranging to borrow a canoe. Decide on a distant goal you want to accomplish. Make a list of what you can do today, this week, this month, and this year to reach your goal. Then, with a small group of classmates, discuss your goal and how you plan to reach it.

Literary T O O L S

CONFLICT. A **conflict** is a struggle between two forces in a literary work. A character may struggle against another character, against the forces of nature, against society or social norms, against fate, or against some element within himself or herself. A struggle that takes place between a character and some outside force is called an *external conflict*. A struggle that takes place within a character is called an *internal conflict*. As you read, identify the conflicts in the story.

CHARACTERIZATION. Characterization is the use of literary techniques to create a character. Writers use three major techniques to create characters: direct description, portrayal of characters' behavior, and representations of characters' internal states.

Organizer

As you read, make a chart to list examples of characterization of Mrs. Crowell and the techniques used by the author. One example has been done for you.

Examples of Characterization	Techniques
Mrs. Crowell sat in the bathtub.	direct description

Reader's Journal

What events in your life do you always want to remember?

"How Did I Get Here?"
by Sybil Carlin

Reader's resource

In **"How Did I Get Here?"** Mrs. Crowell and her daughter Caroline look back on their lives and struggle to discover how they got to where they are now. The story is about the journey of self-discovery. First published in 1973 by *Redbook* and reprinted in their "Famous Fiction" issue in 1977, it was also reprinted internationally in countries such as Australia and the Netherlands.

About *the* AUTHOR

Sybil Carlin (1947–1999), short story and nonfiction writer, graduated from the Pratt Institute. She worked for ten years as an award-winning writer and editor for the Long Island-based *Nassau Herald* newspaper before joining *The Convenience Store News* in 1993. She served on the staff of *CS News* for nearly five years, and as editor-in-chief of the *Journal of Petroleum Marketing* up until the time of her death in 1999. "How Did I Get Here?" was Carlin's first published story in a national magazine and an encouragement, she said, to continue to write. Her nonfiction has appeared in the *New York Times, The Village Voice, T.V. Guide,* and other periodicals.

How Did I Get Here?

Sybil Carlin

Mrs. Crowell sat erect in the bathtub, trying to remember the names of all the stores she had passed every day as she walked the one block from her home to her elementary school, sixty years before.

What is Mrs. Crowell trying to remember?

"Thatcher's Pharmacy on the far corner," she mused aloud, "and there was a cigar store on the corner near the house, but I am having difficulty with the middle. A Chinese hand laundry in there somewhere, and a bakery, but what else? What else?"

She caught herself and continued her <u>recollections</u> in silence. Her daughter might come to visit today. Caroline had her own key, and she would be very upset if she walked in and overheard her mother. Mrs. Crowell had been a bit concerned last week when, sitting by the window with her back to the door, she had suddenly realized that Caroline had entered.

"Mother? Who's here? I heard you talking to someone."

Why is Caroline concerned about her mother?

"No one, Caroline. I was just trying to think of the names of the girls in my high-school class. It helps me recall things if I say them out loud."

"You don't have anyone to talk to here. You must get so lonely. Don't you think you might like to reconsider—"

But Mrs. Crowell had broken in with, "I am not losing my mind. I can take care of myself and I still function perfectly. I don't talk to myself <u>habitually</u>, you know. Just when I'm trying to remember something. It jogs the memory to say things out loud."

"I wasn't suggesting anything, but . . ."

"I know you mean well, all of you. But I'm fine as I am," she had said.

Mrs. Crowell gave Caroline no reason to bring the subject up again until she went to her daughter's for dinner a month later and forgot herself while she helped dry the dishes.

"Mother, you were talking about Calvin, the old dog we had when I was little. I heard you."

"He wasn't always 'old' Calvin. We got him way before you were born, when he was just a pup, and I was trying to remember how he grew up. It seems like one day he was making messes all over the house and the next day he was grown up and trained to wait for his walk. I know I trained him, but I can't remember exactly how I did it or how long it took."

"Why do you want to remember?" Caroline asked softly.

Mrs. Crowell was silent, and then she said, "I have to."

When she went back into the dining room the children were gone and Caroline and Tom were

---

words for everyday use

rec • ol • lec • tion (re kə lek′ shən) *n.*, something remembered. *Dad has a different <u>recollection</u> of the vacation than us kids, who remember it as being a lot of fun.*

ha • bit • u • al • ly (hə bi′ chəw əl ē) *adv.*, done on a regular basis. *Mom <u>habitually</u> cleans the kitchen sink after doing the dishes.*

sitting together, giving each other meaningful looks across the table.

Tom apparently had been elected this time, because he started right up with: "We think it's time you thought seriously about selling the house and coming here to stay with us. Or you could go to a retirement community where there are people your own age to talk over old times with. We're very serious about this."

"I know you both are, and I take you seriously and offer you a serious explanation for my behavior, which I know has worried you. I am

What options does Tom suggest to Mrs. Crowell?

Portrait of Gala, 1935. Salvador Dalí.
The Museum of Modern Art, New York.

art n o t e

Salvador Dalí (1904–1989), known for his bizarre Surrealist paintings, made this subdued double portrait of his wife Gala. She is looking at herself as if in a mirror, but there is no mirror. How might this be a metaphor for the story "How Did I Get Here?"

trying to figure out exactly how I got here."

"Mother!"

"Please let me finish. I was very young once, and I can't seem to remember growing old. The first gray hair, the first wrinkle, the first time I had to stop and get my breath going up to the second floor—I don't remember any of it. I remember the first vacation trip we took with your brother, Caroline, but I don't remember getting into the car or the road we took or arriving at the hotel. I remember the day my son died and parts of the day he was born, but not the night he was conceived or the day I decided to have another child. I remember growing up wanting to be a great artist, and I was talented, too. I don't remember when I gave up the idea of art school exactly, or why."

"Why must you know these things?" Tom asked.

And then she looked at him gently and said, "Because I am leaving here not too long from now, and I am not going to go until I find out how I got here. I stay in the house because it helps me to remember. Do you remember, Caroline, the day you got your college acceptance in the mail? I was carrying an African violet out to the back porch, and I was so excited when you told me that I dropped it right on the dining-room table. It left a scratch that's still there. One day I looked at the scratch and remembered it all, every minute. There are pieces of days like that all over the house."

After Tom had driven Mrs. Crowell home, he and Caroline sat and talked.

"I guess we had to expect this. She was always so alert that it never occurred to us. But at her age we should have been prepared for it and got her over here while she could still think clearly enough to agree."

"I'm worried about her."

"I am too, but I'm not about to carry her bodily over here. She's not that bad off yet. She gets around pretty well."

"I'll talk to her."

"Talk to her."

Caroline talked to her off and on for a year, until the day Mrs. Crowell slipped in the tub and went to the hospital with a broken hip. Pneumonia came, and the nurses assured Tom and Caroline that all old people talked to themselves about the past; when she asked, "How did I get here?" they thought she meant to the hospital.

It was a full year after Mrs. Crowell died that Caroline again thought of the conversation they had had after dinner that night.

She was standing at the stove one sunny morning, cooking breakfast. She thought <u>idly</u> of the time when she and Tom were first married, when the bacon was burned as often as not, and the coffee was either pale or pitch-black and perfect eggs were an occasion. Of the time she had laughed and told Tom that she wasn't cut out for breakfast cooking, being a more intellectual type who definitely was going back for a graduate degree and would never have any messy children.

And now standing here, casually rustling up breakfast for five in ten minutes, with the coffee perfect and the bacon crisp, she could not remember when she had learned to do it or when she had decided not to go back for the degree or what had convinced her to bring three children into the world. And she closed her eyes to keep from crying out the question "How did I get here?" ■

> In the hospital, what does Mrs. Crowell mean when she asks, "How did I get here?" What do Tom and Caroline think she means?

> What can't Caroline remember?

---

words for everyday use

i • dly (īd´ lē) *adv.*, in a slow or inactive manner. *Standing in line at the grocery store, the woman <u>idly</u> flipped through a magazine.*

Late Fragment

Raymond Carver

And did you get what
you wanted from this life, even so?
I did.
And what did you want?
To call myself beloved, to feel myself
beloved on the earth.   ■

ABOUT THE RELATED READING

Raymond Carver (1938–1988) is most well-known for his
spare, unadorned short stories about the wrenching lives of
working-class people. He also published several collections
of poetry, including *Where Water Comes Together with Other
Water* (1985), *In a Marine Light: Selected Poems* (1987), and
A New Path to the Waterfall (1989). Carver is credited as a
major force in the revitalization of the short story in the
twentieth century.

How did you "get here"? What decisions, realizations, and steps toward goals made you who you are today?

Investigate, *Inquire,* and Imagine

Recall: GATHERING FACTS

1a. What sorts of things is Mrs. Crowell trying to remember?

2a. Why do Caroline and Tom think Mrs. Crowell should move in with them or into a retirement community?

3a. What does Caroline do "one sunny morning"?

→ **Interpret:** FINDING MEANING

1b. Why is Mrs. Crowell trying to remember these things?

2b. Why is it important for Mrs. Crowell to remain in her own home?

3b. How is Caroline like her mother?

Analyze: TAKING THINGS APART

4a. Analyze Caroline's growth during the course of the story.

→ **Synthesize:** BRINGING THINGS TOGETHER

4b. What does Caroline's ability to brew a good pot of coffee and make perfect eggs and bacon reveal about her life choices and the process of remembering?

Perspective: LOOKING AT OTHER VIEWS → **Empathy:** SEEING FROM INSIDE

5a. How does Mrs. Crowell react to Tom and Caroline's concern about her behavior?

5b. Read the Related Reading "Late Fragment" by Raymond Carver. Do you think Mrs. Crowell "got what she wanted from this life"? Support your answer with details from the story.

Understanding *Literature*

CONFLICT. Review the definition for **conflict** in the Handbook of Literary Terms. Identify the different conflicts in "How Did I Get Here?" What types of conflicts are they? What do these conflicts reveal about the characters involved in them?

CHARACTERIZATION. Review the definition for **characterization** in the Handbook of Literary Terms and the chart you made for Literary Tools on page 854. What techniques does the author use to create characterization in this story? Give an example of each technique. Which technique does the author use the most? Why?

Writer's Journal

1. Write an **obituary** for Mrs. Crowell based on what is revealed about her in the story. You might find it useful to read several obituaries in the newspaper before you begin. You will need to use your imagination for some of the facts, such as birth and death dates and the name of her husband or other family members.

2. Imagine you are Mrs. Crowell. Write a **letter** to your daughter explaining why you need to remain in your house and why she needn't worry about you.

3. Write a **dialogue** between Caroline and her husband Tom. Caroline explains that she understands now what her mother was going through, and Tom asks pertinent questions and makes appropriate comments.

Integrating the Language Arts

Language, Grammar, and Style

ACTIVE VOICE. Read the Language Arts Survey 3.37, "Making Passive Sentences Active." Then rewrite the sentences below, changing them from the passive voice to the active voice.

1. Mrs. Crowell is struck by forgetfulness.
2. Mrs. Crowell is found speaking to herself by Caroline.
3. For Mrs. Crowell, memories are triggered by things she sees in her house.
4. Options to living alone are provided by Tom.
5. The breakfast is prepared by Caroline.

Speaking and Listening & Collaborative Learning

INTERVIEW. Nostalgia is a sentimental yearning to return to some past period of one's life. Interview a grandparent or an elderly neighbor about a nostalgic event in his or her life. Then interpret this event visually with a painting, drawing, or a collage. Display your art piece representing the event as you tell the person's story to a small group of your classmates.

Study and Research

WRITTEN REPORT. Research an aspect of memory such as short-term memory, long-term memory, amnesia, Alzheimer's disease, forgetting and the theory of disuse, or the theory of interference. Then prepare a written report on what you have learned. Before you begin writing, you might find it useful to review the Language Arts Survey 2.26, "Writing Main Ideas and Supporting Details."

Applied English

BUSINESS LETTER. Imagine that, in her attempts to help her mother, Caroline writes to a nursing home. She explains to the nursing home what has been happening to her mother that gives her concern. In addition, she makes inquiries about the facilities of the nursing home, the cost, and the care provided. Imagine that you are Caroline and write this letter for your mother. Before you begin writing, you might find it useful to review the Language Arts Survey 6.5, "Writing a Business Letter."

Guided Writing

CHRONICLING A JOURNEY

Jenny received another letter from her eighty-eight-year-old great-grandfather who lived several hundred miles away in northern Wisconsin. She could barely decipher the wobbly handwriting.

> Dear Fish Girl,
>
> There's no one to fish with since you left. When will you and Esther come back? I can't see too good to write.
>
> Love,
> Frank

She remembered the first day she had met him. She and her grandma, Esther, had journeyed to his house in the northern woods. Buttoned into a red sweater on a sweltering summer day, he had greeted her by wrapping his bony arms around her like a tall, scrawny bear might have done. Then he wiped his glass eye with a dirty handkerchief and insisted that she and her grandma go fishing with him.

Jenny folded the letter and added it to the stack. They had been corresponding now for three years. Each summer, she had undertaken the journey to see him again, but it had become a journey of the heart. He had taught her to fish, to play canasta, and to navigate country roads in total blackness. Most of all, to her surprise, he had taught her the meaning of friendship.

How about you? What kind of journeys have you undertaken? Have you undertaken an actual journey where you had to overcome physical obstacles? What did you learn about yourself from that experience? Have you undertaken a mental journey where you had to come to grips with new thoughts and ideas? What did you realize from that journey?

WRITING ASSIGNMENT. Chronicle what happened to you on a journey. Instead of writing about your worst camping trip or a field trip to the museum, however, you will write about a journey in which you gained some knowledge or insight about others or yourself. Chronicling your journey will not only put it into perspective for you, it will also allow your readers to experience your journey vicariously. Through their imaginative and sympathetic participation, your readers will be able to understand your experience.

EXAMINING THE MODEL. In this excerpt from *Mississippi Solo,* Eddy Harris chronicles what happens in the first three miles of his solo canoe trip on the Mississippi River. Harris creates a well-written narrative because he uses the first-person point of view, provides lively details, and shares his insights. Readers can experience his journey vicariously: they sympathize with how tired and sore he is after only three miles; they understand his nervousness about his canoeing skills and the journey ahead; they gain new insights about the importance of a support team.

Professional Model

from *Mississippi Solo* by Eddy L. Harris
page 846

Right away, I discover that canoeing is an art, one which I will eventually have to learn. On the quiet lake my zigzagging poses no problems, but I will need to learn to control this thing or I might find trouble later on. I don't want that....

These three miles—by park ranger estimation—take forever. Later in the journey I will expect to do three miles in no time, but these three take so long, that by the time I reach Wanagan Landing to stop for lunch, I'm actually considering staying here for the night.

Already my legs are stiff, my hands are sore and my back is tense and tired. I pull the canoe up and lie in the grass. I drink from my canteen.

In a moment, Robinovitch arrives. She's been out admiring the area on her own, driving dozens of miles in the time it's taken to make three. And she's laughing at how tired I am.

We get a small fire going and have a simple lunch. I get warm. Robinovitch opens up the treats sent along to me by friends. Trail mix, peanuts, cashews, cookies, and a mountain of granola bars, which I never liked before but which by the time this trip ends will be among my favorite snacks.

Never before could I understand why bicycle racers are surrounded by cars carrying extra bikes, food, and drink. I always thought a racer should be out there doing his job, on his own, and if he has a breakdown he just pulls out. I look at Robinovitch, my support team—preparing lunch, encouraging me, prodding me with her presence so I'd be too ashamed to quit—and I understand.

Prewriting

FINDING YOUR VOICE. Harris's voice—his use of words, sentence structures, and style—reveals his personality and his attitude toward the river and the challenges he faces. Harris writes, "Right away I discover that canoeing is an art, one which I will eventually have to learn. On the quiet lake my zigzagging poses no problem, but I will need to learn to control this thing or I might find trouble later on. I don't want that." In this passage, Harris lets readers know about his limited canoeing skills and his desire to improve them. He is aware of the challenges ahead and shows his respect for the river.

As you write your narrative, imagine that you are actually speaking to a close friend. Use the same kind of casual, natural, and informal words that you would say to your friend.

Use a voice that is appropriate to your topic. If you are writing about an encounter with a rattlesnake while hiking in the mountains, your voice will be much different than if you are writing about the journey you took to become a lifeguard.

IDENTIFYING YOUR AUDIENCE. The audience for your narrative will be your peers and teacher. They will want to know about the difficulties you encountered on your journey and how you handled those challenges. They will also want to know what insights you gained on your journey.

WRITING WITH A PLAN. Your first step will be to select a journey to chronicle. It could be an actual trip that involved some conflict or danger: the mountain you climbed or some other wilderness experience you had that changed your life. It could be a trip to a place where you realized that your life is better than you had thought: your volunteering at a soup kitchen or at the Humane Society. It could be a challenge you faced that appeared overwhelming, but wasn't: a campaign to get a skating park in your town. It could be a mental journey in which your faith, beliefs, or value system changed: an experience where you learned something about truth, honor, commitment, and respect.

Create a list of possible journeys you could write about. Join three or four classmates in a small group. Explain why you chose each possibility and get some feedback from your classmates. Then decide which possibility best fits the needs of this assignment.

The next step is to generate your thoughts and feelings about your experience. A good way to begin this process is to make a **cluster chart**. Start with a key word or phrase and write it in the middle of your page. Circle it. What ideas does the key word or phrase jog in your memory? Draw more circles branching out from your center circle, and fill them with ideas related to your key word or phrase. Include sensory details. What smells, sounds, and touch experiences do you recall? Continue to branch out until you have exhausted your memory of the experience. Finally, number the most important words and phrases in your cluster chart in the order that you plan to write about them. For more information about clustering, see the Language Arts Survey 2.13, "Clustering."

Cheryl Mackrory created a cluster chart to generate ideas about her journey from South Africa to New Zealand and finally to the United States. She numbered the ideas in the order she planned to write about them.

> "The beginning of knowledge is the discovery of something we do not understand."
> —Frank Herbert

Student Model—Graphic Organizer

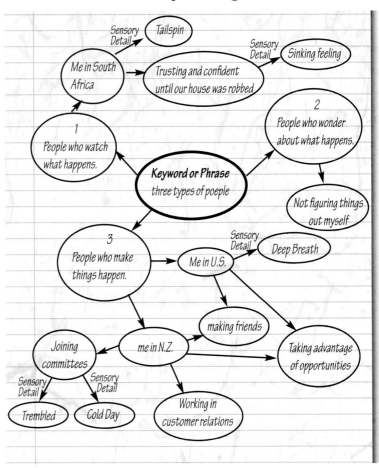

Make a cluster chart on a separate piece of paper. Start with a key word or phrase, then continue with related ideas and sensory details.

Drafting

You do not have to be overly concerned about spelling, grammar, and mechanics as you write your draft. Instead, focus on getting your ideas down in a logical order.

How should you start your draft? You could start at the beginning of your journey and narrate the events in chronological order. You could incorporate the insights you gained at various points of your journey. Eddy Harris used this type of order very effectively in *Mississippi Solo.* He shared his insights as he narrated his journey in chronological order.

You could also start with your insight or accomplishment and then narrate the events that led to that insight or accomplishment. Or, you could start by narrating your story in chronological order and wait until the end to tell what you learned. Experiment with the order that works best for your story.

Notice how detailed Eddy Harris's account of his canoe trip is. Strive to include sensory details. Show what happens, but also include other senses: what smells, sounds, and touch experiences do you recall? Tell enough so the reader can experience this trip as well.

Student Model—Draft

It is said that there are three types of people in this world—those that make things happen, those that watch things happen, and ~~people who~~ wonder *those that (keep parallel)* what happened. I used to be ~~the type of~~ person who just watched things happen. *In South Africa, a* *I was just a watcher* At times I wondered about things that happened, but I never wanted to figure things out for myself. *Then, the world went into a tailspin! Apartheid..* Now, I have become ~~the kind of~~ person that makes *be more specific.* *a* things happen. I have learned to take every opportunity that comes along and learn as much as possible because you have nothing to lose by doing so, only pride. I live each day and by learning from the past, I prepare for tomorrow.

Growing up in South Africa I was quite unaware of the fear that my family lived in. *that haunted both black and white* I was very content with the way we were, thinking that everyone and everything was just fine. That changed in a moment when our house was ~~burgled~~ and *robbed* I had a taste of the real world. I knew *—What does this mean?* that my life could have changed for the *deep and dangerous divisions in the*

Put this sentence last to show a better flow

Tell about the reason for fear

"Wherever we go, whatever we do, self is the sole subject we study and learn."
—Ralph Waldo Emerson, 1833

state what you really feared. *my life could have ended*

<u>worse</u> that night, had the <u>burglar</u> been

armed.   *What does that look like?*

— *looked at my shoes-was shy...*

When we moved to New Zealand, I

became even more timid; I was cautious

and afraid of what people thought of me

because of the problems in South Africa.

Then I realized that if I wanted to make

anything of myself, I had to stop

watching and wondering and start making

What committees?

things happen. I joined committees at

What did you do?

school. I worked part time in a

supermarket. I made friends and I became

in the customer services division,

more confident.   *-helped people make decisions*

Self- and Peer Evaluation

After you finish your first draft, complete a self-evaluation of your writing. You may also want to get one or two peer evaluations if you have time. See the Language Arts Survey 2.37 for more details about self- and peer evaluation.

As you evaluate your narrative or that of a classmate, answer the following questions. Write revision ideas on your draft to use later.

- How would you categorize this journey? Self-discovery? Self knowledge? A changed community or worldview?
- How well does the lead-in engage the reader?
- Does the narrative follow a logical order? What parts of the narrative are not clear?
- Is the first-person point of view used?
- What sensory details enrich the narrative? (Mark with a yellow highlighter.) Where could details be added?
- What thoughts and feelings are revealed? (Mark with a blue highlighter.) Where could details be added?
- What details give the reader a sense of time and place? (Mark with a green highlighter.)
- How would you describe the writer's voice and attitude about this journey?
- What impression is left with the reader?
- How has the reader vicariously experienced the same journey made by the writer?

Cheryl's self-evaluation of her rough draft is shown below. Notice how she began her draft by telling what she learned on her journey.

Revising and Proofreading

As you consider your narrative and your self-evaluation and peer reviews, think about the changes that are suggested. Make decisions about which changes would be of benefit before you begin to revise. Pay particular attention to the highlighted words or passages. If there is little or no highlighting of a certain color, you probably need to develop that part of your narrative.

Proofread your narrative for errors in spelling, grammar, punctuation, capitalization, and other details. Check your sentences for parallel structure.

After reviewing her narrative and considering her self- and peer evaluation notes, Cheryl revised her writing. Note her improvements.

Student Model—Revised

> Live For Tomorrow
> By Cheryl Mackrory
>
> I've heard it said that there are three types of people in this world— those who make things happen, those who watch things happen, and those who wonder what happened. Growing up in South Africa, I was just a watcher. At times I wondered about things, but I never wanted to figure anything out. Then, it was like the world went into a tailspin! Apartheid was over and I had to cope with everything around me changing. I had no control. At first everyone, including me, was insecure. But slowly I learned to take advantage of each opportunity that came along by learning as much as possible from it. Now I'm a person who makes things happen.
>
> I lived in South Africa when I was a young child. I was unaware of the fear that haunted both blacks and whites. I was very content with the way we were. I thought that everyone and everything was just fine. That changed the night our house was robbed. That was my first taste of the deep and dangerous divisions in the real world. It gave me a sick, sinking feeling to think about it. I knew that had the

Language, Grammar, and Style

Achieving Sentence Parallelism

IDENTIFYING SENTENCE PARALLELISM. To make writing clearer and to make it sound better, writers try to keep sentences parallel. A sentence has parallelism when it uses the same grammatical forms to express ideas of equal, or parallel, importance. Use similar grammatical forms to convey a list of items or a series of thoughts. Below are some famous examples from history.

> We cannot dedicate, we cannot consecrate, we cannot hallow this ground.
> —Abraham Lincoln

> Ask not what your country can do for you; ask what you can do for your country.
> —John F. Kennedy

> With this faith we will be able to work together, to pray together, to struggle together, to go to jail together, to stand up for freedom together, knowing that we will be free one day.
> —Martin Luther King, Jr.

continued on page 868

FIXING FAULTY PARALLELISM.

Read the following example. Then read the correction. How does it help the flow of the sentence?

Example

After high school I will be a lawyer, a doctor, or drive a truck.

Correction: After high school I will be a lawyer, a doctor, or a trucker.

Read the following sentences. Correct the errors in parallel structure.

1. The patients all had fever, sore throats, weakness, and their heads ached.
2. Travel lets one learn about other cultures, see distant places, meet people of other nationalities, and one also gets a better understanding of one's own country.
3. The group spent the day picking up cans and refuse in the park, adding gravel to the pathways, and they painted the porch of the shelter.

Read the following sentence from the student model. Correct the errors in parallel structure.

It has been said that there are three types of people in this world—those that make things happen, those that watch things happen, and people who wonder what happened.

USING SENTENCE PARALLELISM.

Read through your narrative.

continued on page 869

intruder been armed with a knife or gun, my life could have ended even as I slept.

When I was older, we moved to New Zealand. I became even more timid. I was afraid of what people thought of me because of the problems in South Africa. I spent a lot of time looking down at my shoes. Then I realized that if I wanted to make anything of myself, I had to stop watching and start making things happen. Though at first it made me tremble, I joined committees at school. I worked part time in the customer service division of a supermarket. There I began to help people make decisions and to appreciate their points of view. I made friends and I became more confident.

Five years after we arrived in New Zealand, my dad was offered a job in the United States. I was so afraid to move that I always kept my hands in my jacket pockets, even on hot days. But then, on a really cold fall day, I took off my jacket and just walked in the cold wind. And I wasn't even cold. I felt great. That day I overcame my fear by realizing that the move was just another change, another opportunity for me to learn. It was sad to leave my friends, but I knew that I had made those friends by being confident and positive. I knew I could make the adjustment and that it would make me stronger.

I have lived in Colorado for six months. I am still learning and growing. It seems like each day I meet another wonderful person. I stay busy by participating in the chess club, the glee club, an after school sports group, and a committee that welcomes new kids to our school. All of this makes me happy and keeps me growing as a person. Sometimes I take a deep breath and remind myself to take it all in. I live each day and by learning from the past rather than fearing the future, I prepare for tomorrow.

Publishing and Presenting

Plan to share your chronicle with your peers. Your teacher may wish to combine the journey chronicles into a classroom anthology. A copy for every member of your class, as well as the library and the principal, would be a good way to share your journey experiences. This anthology is an opportunity for you to shine, both as a writer and as an artist. A cover, page dividers, and your narratives may all require some artwork. A book signing party might be a way to celebrate your writing success and your individual journeys.

Reflecting

In the process of chronicling your journey, you probably gained some insights that you did not have before you started this assignment. What was the most significant insight you learned about yourself or others who were part of your journey? What insights did you gain from your classmates' writing? What do you know about life and the human condition that you did not realize before?

In which sentences did you use parallel structure? How do parallel sentences help your narrative flow better?

Find several sentences that would benefit from parallel structure and make the corrections. Do your changes improve the flow of your narrative?

For more information refer to the Language Arts Survey 3.38, "Achieving Parallelism."

UNIT 11 review
Journeys

Words for Everyday Use

Check your knowledge of the following vocabulary words from the selections in this unit. Write short sentences using each of these words in context to make the meaning clear. To review the definition or usage of a word, refer back to the page number(s) listed or the Glossary of Words for Everyday Use.

accommodate, 847
ado, 846
adversary, 850
apostolic, 826
aquamarine, 835
ardently, 826
avert, 827
clamorously, 827
conductivity, 821
continuum, 848
cower, 824
dilate, 828
disheveled, 823
dissolution, 826

don, 846
elapse, 828
embankment, 847
engagement, 835
estrangement, 820
euphemism, 822
evasive, 821
flush, 848
foreboding, 823
furtively, 822
habitually, 855
hover, 825
idly, 857
imperceptible, 820

imperturbably, 822
impetuous, 828
importunity, 821
indulgently, 826
inexorable, 828
influx, 826
intrude, 850
leniently, 822
loitering, 848
lucidity, 820
meander, 849
negotiate, 847
omen, 847
philanthropic, 822

portage, 850
precipice, 827
presumptuous, 840
prodigal, 821
rebuff, 826
recollection, 855
sensibility, 823
throng, 828
treachery, 822
turbulence, 846
tyranny, 821

Literary Tools

Define each of the following terms, giving concrete examples of how they are used in the selections in this unit. To review a term, refer to the page number(s) indicated or the Handbook of Literary Terms.

characterization, 854
conflict, 854
description, 832
image, 844

metaphor, 819
point of view, 844
psychological fiction, 819
repetition, 832

simile, 819, 838
tone, 838

Reflecting
on your reading

Genre Studies

1. **Short Story.** A **conflict** is a struggle between two forces in a literary work. One side of the central conflict is usually taken by the main character, who may struggle against another character, against the forces of nature, against society or social norms, against fate, or against some element within himself or herself. What is the central conflict in Edith Wharton's story "A Journey"? Is this struggle an external or an internal conflict? Explain.

2. **Nonfiction.** In "Mississippi Solo," what does the narrator expect to learn from making his journey down the Mississippi? Are these goals stated clearly or only implied?

3. **Lyric Poetry. Lyric poetry** is highly musical verse that expresses the emotions of a speaker. Compare and contrast the emotional experiences of the speakers in "Otherwise" by Jane Kenyon and "The Old Life" by Donald Hall.

Thematic Studies

4. **AGING.** What is the central preoccupation of Mrs. Crowell in "How Did I Get Here?" How does this character define herself? Where does Mrs. Crowell want to spend her last days? Why?

5. **ISOLATION.** How does isolation shape the voyages of the woman in "A Journey" and Eddy L. Harris in "Mississippi Solo"? How might the thought processes of each author be different if they were traveling with a companion?

6. **MODES OF TRANSPORTATION.** How are Ian Frazier's and Eddy L. Harris's journeys defined by their mode of transportation? What does traveling by car in "Great Plains" and traveling by canoe in "Mississippi Solo" allow them to see? How would their observations be different if they exchanged modes of transportation?

for your READING LIST

I Heard the Owl Call My Name by Margaret Craven. When the Bishop learns that his young vicar, Mark Brian, has only two or three years to live, he says, "So short a time to learn so much? It leaves me no choice. I shall send him to my hardest parish." Thus begins Mark's journey to live among a primitive, remote Indian tribe. The most basic aspects of life—finding food and keeping shelter—consume much of his time. Working alongside his new parishioners, he comes to appreciate their vanishing way of life and, by sharing their hardships, he gradually earns their trust and friendship. Without modern conveniences and distractions, life is pared down to its essentials, making it "…easier here, where only the fundamentals count, to learn what every man must learn in this world…Enough of the meaning of life to be ready to die."

Independent Reading Activity

BOOK CLUB DISCUSSION. Read the Language Arts Survey 1.7, "Reading with a Book Club or Literature Circle" and 1.8, "Guidelines for Discussing Literature in a Book Club." Then, after reading Margaret Craven's *I Heard the Owl Call My Name,* discuss the following questions in your book club or circle.

- What is it that Mark has learned about life?
- Did the Bishop do Mark a favor by sending him to Kingcome? Why, or why not?
- How would you want to spend the last two years of your life?

Selections for Additional Reading

Leaving Home, stories selected by Hazel Rochman and Darlene Z. McCampbell. This collection of short stories with the theme of taking journeys includes selections by Amy Tan, Tim O'Brien, Sandra Cisneros, Judith Ortiz Cofer, Toni Morrison, and other notable writers.

Running North by Ann Mariah Cook. A husband and wife take a journey across the tundra of Alaska, their young daughter in tow, to run the Yukon Quest, the most demanding dog sled race in the world.

Man at the Crossroads, 1934. Diego Rivera. Palacio de Bellas Artes, Mexico City.

Visions of the Future

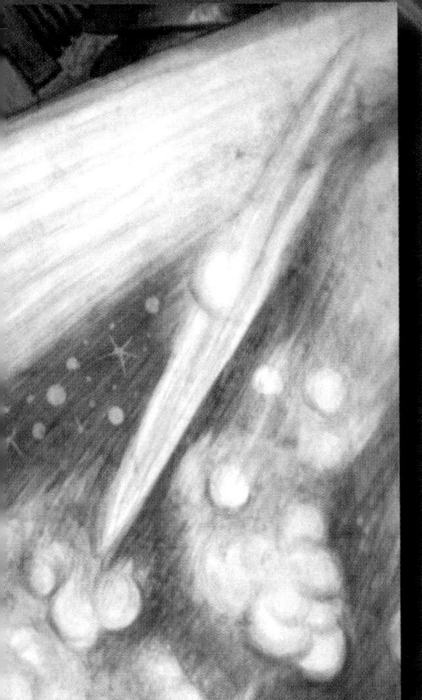

> " When all else is lost,
> the future still remains. "
>
> —*Christian Nestell Bovee*

echoes

▶ I never think of the future. It comes soon enough.

—*Albert Einstein*

▶ The future depends entirely on what each of us does every day.

—*Gloria Steinem*

▶ The future belongs to they who know how to wait.

—*Russian Proverb*

▶ The future is made up of the same stuff as the present.

—*Simone Weil from* On Science, Necessity, and the Love of God

▶ Learn the future by looking at the past.

—*Indian Proverb*

▶ The future belongs to those who believe in the beauty of their dreams.

—*Eleanor Roosevelt*

▶ We should all be concerned about the future because we will have to spend the rest of our lives there.

—*Charles F. Kettering*

▶ Perhaps the best thing about the future is that it only comes one day at a time.

—*Dean Acheson*

▶ No one knows the story of tomorrow's dawn.

—*African Proverb*

▶ We grow in time to trust the future for our answers.

—*Ruth Benedict*

▶ Who controls the present controls the past. Who controls the past controls the future.

—*George Orwell*

"There Will Come Soft Rains"
by Ray Bradbury

Reader's resource

"There Will Come Soft Rains" is written in the science fiction genre—a highly imaginative fiction containing fantastic elements based upon scientific principles, discoveries, or laws. This story is set in the year 2026 in a fully automated house (one in which activities once done by humans are now done by machines). The advanced technology and the futuristic setting make this a science fiction story.

The title of this story is an allusion to a poem by Sara Teasdale that is featured in the story. An *allusion* is a rhetorical technique in which reference is made to a person, event, object, or work from history or literature. Teasdale's poem, like Bradbury's story, deals with the horrific possibility that people might destroy themselves through war. As you read the story and the poem, think about how science fiction writers use stories about the future to warn us about the possible consequences of our present actions.

About the AUTHOR

Born in Illinois, **Ray Bradbury** (1920–) is best known for his science fiction and fantasy stories. Nevertheless, his more than twenty books include novels, children's

books, and collections of short stories, poetry, and plays. His science fiction stories offer social criticism and warnings against the dangers of uncontrolled technological development. For his work in science fiction and fantasy, he has won the World Fantasy Award for lifetime achievement and the Grand Master Award from the Science Fiction Writers of America.

Literary TOOLS

THEME. A **theme** is a central idea in a literary work. As you read the story, think about the theme Ray Bradbury wanted to convey to his readers.

PERSONIFICATION. Personification is a figure of speech in which an idea, animal, or thing is described as if it were a person. In this story the house, by being personified, becomes the main character in the story. Find examples of all the things the house is able to do.

Organizer

As you read the story, make a pro and con chart to discuss the advantages and disadvantages of some of the technological innovations mentioned. Follow the example below.

Task	Pro	Con
Automatic breakfast	Fast, efficient, no one has to get up early to cook or spend time cleaning up.	No choice in menu or time of eating; no joy in cooking/creating

Reader's JOURNAL

Think about the positive and negative aspects of technology in your own life. In what ways are you assisted by it? In what ways can technology sometimes be annoying or dangerous?

There Will Come Soft Rains

Ray Bradbury

In the living room the voice-clock sang, *Tick-tock, seven o'clock, time to get up, time to get up, seven o'clock!* as if it were afraid that nobody would. The morning house lay empty. The clock ticked on, repeating and repeating its sounds into the emptiness. *Seven-nine, breakfast time, seven-nine!*

> To whom is the house speaking? Who is in the house?

In the kitchen the breakfast stove gave a hissing sigh and <u>ejected</u> from its warm interior eight pieces of perfectly browned toast, eight eggs sunnyside up, sixteen slices of bacon, two coffees, and two cool glasses of milk.

"Today is August 4, 2026," said a second voice from the kitchen ceiling, "in the City of Allendale, California." It repeated the date three times for memory's sake. "Today is Mr. Featherstone's birthday. Today is the anniversary of Tilita's marriage. Insurance is payable, as are the water, gas, and light bills."

Somewhere in the walls, relays clicked, memory tapes glided under electric eyes.

Eight-one, tick-tock, eight-one o'clock, off to school, off to work, run, run, eight-one! But no doors slammed, no carpets took the soft <u>tread</u> of rubber heels. It was raining outside. The weather box on the front door sang quietly: "Rain, rain, go away; rubbers, raincoats for today. . . ." And the rain tapped on the empty house, echoing.

> What is the weather like on August 4, 2026? What does the house recommend?

Outside, the garage chimed and lifted its door to reveal the waiting car. After a long wait the door swung down again.

At eight-thirty the eggs were shriveled and the toast was like stone. An aluminum wedge scraped them into the sink, where hot water whirled them down a metal throat that digested and flushed them away to the

> Which conveniences in this passage already exist in today's society?

---

words for everyday use

e • ject (ē jekt´) *vi.*, cast out; emit; discharge. *When his plane lost one of its engines, the pilot <u>ejected</u> from the aircraft and parachuted to safety.*

tread (tred) *n.*, step. *The loud <u>tread</u> of Margaret's footsteps disturbed her sleeping mother.*

distant sea. The dirty dishes were dropped into a hot washer and <u>emerged</u> twinkling dry.

Nine-fifteen, sang the clock, *time to clean.*

Out of warrens[1] in the wall, tiny robot mice darted. The rooms were acrawl with the small cleaning animals, all rubber and metal. They thudded against chairs, whirling their mustached runners, <u>kneading</u> the rug nap, sucking gently at hidden dust. Then, like mysterious invaders, they popped into their burrows. Their pink electric eyes faded. The house was clean.

> What is unusual about the way the house speaks? What is significant about its use of language?

Ten o'clock. The sun came out from behind the rain. The house stood alone in a city of rubble and ashes. This was the one house left standing. At night the ruined city gave off a radioactive[2] glow which could be seen for miles.

> What has happened to the other houses in the city?

Ten-fifteen. The garden sprinklers whirled up in golden founts, filling the soft morning air

---

1. **warrens.** Tunneled homes produced by small mammals such as mice or rabbits
2. **radioactive.** Capable of producing energy in the form of rays (alpha, beta, and gamma) given off by the disintegration of atomic nuclei, as in uranium and plutonium

---

words for everyday use

e • merge (ē mʉrj´) *vi.,* come forth. *From behind the velvet curtain, the actors <u>emerged</u> to take one last bow.*
knead (nēd) *vt.,* press, rub, or squeeze; massage. *To make bread rise properly, you must <u>knead</u> the dough.*

with scatterings of brightness. The water pelted windowpanes, running down the charred west side where the house had been burned evenly free of its white paint. The entire west face of the house was black, save for five places. Here the silhouette in paint of a man mowing a lawn. Here, as in a photograph, a woman bent to pick flowers. Still farther over, their images burned on wood in one <u>titanic</u> instant, a small boy, hands flung into the air; higher up, the image of a thrown ball, and opposite him a girl, hands raised to catch a ball which never came down.

What record is left of the family? How was the record created?

The five spots of paint—the man, the woman, the children, the ball—remained. The rest was a thin charcoaled layer.

The gentle sprinkler rain filled the garden with falling light.

Until this day, how well the house had kept its peace. How carefully it had inquired, "Who goes there? What's the password?" and, getting no answer from lonely foxes and whining cats, it had shut up its windows and drawn shades in a <u>preoccupation</u> with self-protection that bordered on a mechanical <u>paranoia</u>.

It quivered at each sound, the house did. If a sparrow brushed a window, the shade snapped up. The bird, startled, flew off! No, not even a bird must touch the house!

The house was an altar with ten thousand attendants, big, small, servicing, attending, in choirs. But the gods had gone away, and the <u>ritual</u> of the religion continued senselessly, uselessly.

Twelve noon.

A dog whined, shivering, on the front porch.

The front door recognized the dog voice and opened. The dog, once huge and fleshy, but now gone to bone and covered with sores, moved in and through the house, tracking mud. Behind it whirred angry mice, angry at having to pick up mud, angry at inconvenience.

For not a leaf fragment blew under the door but what the wall panels flipped open and the copper scrap rats flashed swiftly out. The offending dust, hair, or paper, seized in miniature steel jaws, was raced back to the burrows. There, down tubes which fed into the cellar, it was dropped into the sighing vent of an incinerator[3] which sat like evil Baal[4] in a dark corner.

The dog ran upstairs, hysterically yelping to each door, at last realizing, as the house realized, that only silence was here.

It sniffed the air and scratched the kitchen door. Behind the door, the stove was making pancakes that filled the house with a rich baked odor and the scent of maple syrup.

The dog frothed at the mouth, lying at the door, sniffing, its eyes turned to fire. It ran wildly in circles, biting at its tail, spun in a frenzy, and died. It lay in the parlor for an hour.

Two o'clock, sang a voice.

Delicately sensing decay at last, the regiments of mice hummed out as softly as blown gray leaves in an electrical wind.

Two-fifteen.

The dog was gone.

What happens to the dog?

In the cellar, the incinerator glowed suddenly and a whirl of sparks leaped up the chimney.

Two thirty-five.

Bridge[5] tables sprouted from patio walls. Playing cards fluttered onto pads in a shower of

---

3. **incinerator.** Furnace designed to burn waste products
4. **Baal.** Pre-Christian god of the Semitic people
5. **Bridge.** Card game involving team strategy

words for everyday use

ti • tan • ic (tī tan´ik) *adj.,* strong; powerful. *Paul Bunyan was a legendary man of <u>titanic</u> size and strength.*

pre • oc • cu • pa • tion (pr ē ăk´yōō pā´shən) *n.,* absorption in thought. *Claudio has a <u>preoccupation</u> with reading fine works of literature; he has an enormous library from which it is impossible to entice him.*

par • a • noi • a (par´ə noi´ə) *n.,* suspiciousness; delusions of persecution. *Mark was subject to bouts of <u>paranoia</u>, during which he would claim that the FBI, the CIA, and other groups were after him.*

rit • u • al (rich´ōō əl) *n.,* religious or ceremonial act. *Many societies perform a <u>ritual</u> to indicate an adolescent's crossing from childhood to adulthood.*

pips.[6] Drinks <u>manifested</u> on an oaken bench with egg-salad sandwiches. Music played.

But the tables were silent and the cards untouched.

At four o'clock the tables folded like great butterflies back through the paneled walls.

Four-thirty.

The nursery walls glowed.

Animals took shape: yellow giraffes, blue lions, pink antelopes, lilac panthers <u>cavorting</u> in crystal substance. The walls were glass. They looked out upon color and fantasy. Hidden films clocked through well-oiled sprockets,[7] and the walls lived. The nursery floor was woven to resemble a crisp, cereal meadow. Over this ran aluminum roaches and iron crickets, and in the hot still air butterflies of delicate red tissue <u>wavered</u> among the sharp aroma of animal spoors![8] There was the sound like a great matted yellow hive of bees within a dark bellows, the lazy bumble of a purring lion. And there was the patter of okapi[9] feet and the murmur of a fresh jungle rain, like other hoofs, falling upon the summer-parched grass. Now the walls <u>dissolved</u> into distances of parched weed, mile on mile, and warm endless sky. The animals drew away into thorn brakes and water holes.

It was the children's hour.

Five o'clock. The bath filled with clear hot water.

Six, seven, eight o'clock. The dinner dishes manipulated like magic tricks, and in the study a *click.* In the metal stand opposite the hearth where a fire now blazed up warmly, a cigar popped out, half an inch of soft gray ash on it, smoking, waiting.

What is ironic about the lifelike images in the nursery?

Nine o'clock. The beds warmed their hidden circuits, for nights were cool here.

Nine-five. A voice spoke from the study ceiling: "Mrs. McClellan, which poem would you like this evening?"

The house was silent.

The voice said at last, "Since you express no preference, I shall select a poem at random." Quiet music rose to back the voice. "Sara Teasdale. As I recall, your favorite . . ."

> There will come soft rains and the
>   smell of the ground,
>
> And swallows circling with their
>   shimmering sound;
>
> And frogs in the pools singing at
>   night,
>
> And wild plum trees in <u>tremulous</u>
>   white;
>
> Robins will wear their feathery fire,
>
> Whistling their whims on a low
>   fence-wire;
>
> And not one will know of the war,
>   not one
>
> Will care at last when it is done.
>
> Not one would mind, neither bird
>   nor tree,
>
> If mankind perished utterly;
>
> And Spring herself, when
>   she woke at dawn
>
> Would scarcely know that
>   we were gone.

What effect has the death of the family had on the house? What effect do you think the end of humankind has had on the world?

---

6. **pips.** Figures on playing cards indicating the suit
7. **clocked through well-oiled sprockets.** Moved regularly through holes lined up in a row, as film in a camera
8. **spoors.** Tracks, trails, or droppings of a hunted animal
9. **okapi.** African animal with zebra-like stripes and a giraffe-like neck

words for everyday use

man • i • fest (man´ə fest) *vi.*, appear. *The ghost <u>manifested</u> itself suddenly; one minute the apparition was there, and the next minute it was gone.*

ca • vort (kə vôrt´) *vi.*, leap about; romp. *It was lovely to see the children <u>cavort</u> about the park, leaping and jumping through their various games.*

wa • ver (wā´vər) *vi.*, swing or sway; flutter. *There is a very slight breeze outside; the leaves of the trees <u>waver</u> ever so gently.*

dis • solve (di zälv´) *vi.*, decompose or disintegrate. *I helped my brother build an enormous snowman, and, for his sake, I was sad to see it <u>dissolve</u> on the first warm, sunny day.*

trem • u • lous (trem´yoŏ ləs) *adj.*, trembling; quivering. *Richard's anxiety about giving a speech was revealed in his <u>tremulous</u> voice.*

The fire burned on the stone hearth, and the cigar fell away into a mound of quiet ash on its tray. The empty chairs faced each other between the silent walls, and the music played.

At ten o'clock the house began to die.

The wind blew. A falling tree bough crashed through the kitchen window. Cleaning solvent,[10] bottled, shattered over the stove. The room was ablaze in an instant!

"Fire!" screamed a voice. The house lights flashed, water pumps shot water from the ceilings. But the solvent spread on the linoleum, licking, eating, under the kitchen door, while the voices took it up in chorus: "Fire, fire, fire!"

The house tried to save itself. Doors sprang tightly shut, but the windows were broken by the heat and the wind blew and sucked upon the fire.

The house gave ground as the fire in ten billion angry sparks moved with flaming ease from room to room and then up the stairs. While scurrying water rats squeaked from the walls, pistoled their water, and ran for more. And the wall sprays let down showers of mechanical rain.

But too late. Somewhere, sighing, a pump shrugged to a stop. The quenching rain ceased. The reserve water supply which had filled baths and washed dishes for many quiet days was gone.

The fire crackled up the stairs. It fed upon Picassos and Matisses[11] in the upper halls, like delicacies, baking off the oily flesh, tenderly crisping the canvases into black shavings.

Now the fire lay in beds, stood in windows, changed the colors of drapes!

And then, <u>reinforcements</u>.

From attic trapdoors, blind robot faces peered down with faucet mouths gushing green chemical.

The fire backed off, as even an elephant must at the sight of a dead snake. Now there were twenty snakes whipping over the floor, killing the fire with a clear cold venom of green froth.

But the fire was clever. It had sent flame outside the house, up through the attic to the pumps there. An explosion! The attic brain which directed the pumps was shattered into bronze shrapnel[12] on the beams.

> What part of the house does the fire attack? What consequence will this attack have for the house?

The fire rushed back into every closet and felt the clothes hung there.

The house shuddered, oak bone on bone, its bared skeleton cringing from the heat, its wire, its nerves <u>revealed</u> as if a surgeon had torn the skin off to let the red veins and capillaries[13] quiver in the scalded air. Help, help; Fire! Run, run! Heat snapped mirrors like the first brittle winter ice. And the voices wailed Fire, fire, run, run, like a tragic nursery rhyme, a dozen voices, high, low, like children dying in a forest, alone, alone. And the voices fading as the wires popped their sheathings like hot chestnuts. One, two, three, four, five voices died.

In the nursery the jungle burned. Blue lions roared, purple giraffes bounded off. The panthers ran in circles, changing color, and ten million animals, running before the fire, vanished off toward a distant steaming river. . . .

Ten more voices died. In the last instant under the fire avalanche, other choruses, <u>oblivious</u>,

---

10. **Cleaning solvent.** Chemical substance that dissolves another substance, such as soil
11. **Picassos and Matisses.** Pieces of art by Spanish artist Pablo Picasso (1881–1973) and French artist Henri Matisse (1869–1964)
12. **shrapnel.** Bits of shattered metal thrown from an explosion
13. **capillaries.** Small blood vessels that carry blood between the arteries (carrying oxygenated blood away from the heart) and the veins (carrying blood depleted of oxygen back to the heart)

---

words for everyday use

re • in • force • ment (rē´in fôrs´mənt) n., additional forces. *We never would have won the battle if we had not cleverly concealed our <u>reinforcements</u>, who brought new life and energy to the battlefield.*

re • veal (ri vēl´) vt., show; expose. *Jamie <u>revealed</u> an artistic side we had never seen when he demonstrated his talent for modern dance.*

ob • liv • i • ous (ə bliv´ ē əs) adj., forgetful or unmindful. *The driver of that blue car must be <u>oblivious</u> to everything around him; he almost hit three parked cars!*

could be heard announcing the time, playing music, cutting the lawn by remote-control mower, or setting an umbrella frantically out and in the slamming and opening front door, a thousand things happening, like a clock shop when each clock strikes the hour insanely before or after the other, a scene of maniac confusion, yet unity; singing, screaming, a few last cleaning mice darting bravely out to carry the horrid ashes away! And one voice, with <u>sublime</u> disregard for the situation, read poetry aloud in the fiery study, until all the film spools burned, until all the wires withered and the circuits cracked.

People have often claimed that at death a person's life "flashes before his or her eyes." In what way is the death of the house similar to the death of a person?

The fire burst the house and let it slam flat down, puffing out skirts of spark and smoke.

In the kitchen, an instant before the rain of fire and timber, the stove could be seen making breakfasts at a psychopathic rate,[14] ten dozen eggs, six loaves of toast, twenty dozen bacon strips, which, eaten by fire, started the stove working again, hysterically hissing!

The crash. The attic smashing into kitchen and parlor. The parlor into cellar, cellar into subcellar. Deep freeze, armchair, film tapes, circuits, beds, and all like skeletons thrown in a cluttered mound deep under.

Smoke and silence. A great quantity of smoke.

Dawn showed faintly in the east. Among the ruins, one wall stood alone. Within the wall, a last voice said, over and over again and again, even as the sun rose to shine upon the heaped rubble and steam:

"Today is August 5, 2026, today is August 5, 2026, today is . . ." ∎

---

14. **psychopathic rate.** Frantic, insanely rapid rate

Respond *to the* SELECTION

Imagine living in an automated house such as this one. What would you like about it? What would you dislike? Might living in an automated house change you in any way? If so, how?

Investigate, Inquire, and Imagine

Recall: GATHERING FACTS

1a. Who is talking in the house on the morning of August 4, 2026? In what ways does the house prepare for people who do not appear?

2a. What happens just after nine o'clock? Which poem does the house select?

3a. What happens at ten o'clock? How does the house react?

Interpret: FINDING MEANING

1b. What is ominous about the house at the beginning of the story?

2b. Why is the action just after nine o'clock somewhat more personal than the others of the day? How does the house choose the poem? Why is it an appropriate poem for the situation?

3b. Describe the scene of the destruction of the house. How is the house left in the end? How does the action of the house in the last line compare to its action in the first line?

Analyze: TAKING THINGS APART

4a. Based on Bradbury's descriptions in the story, how do you think the city and its inhabitants were destroyed?

Synthesize: BRINGING THINGS TOGETHER

4b. Why do you think Bradbury waited until paragraph 10 to explain what had happened to the city? Why do you think he waited to show what had happened to the family?

Evaluate: MAKING JUDGMENTS

5a. What makes the actions of the house senseless? Might it be dangerous to put too much of our lives in the hands of machines? Why, or why not?

Extend: CONNECTING IDEAS

5b. What comment is Bradbury making about the essential stupidity of machines? of mankind? Contrast this with Sara Teasdale's view of nature in her poem "There Will Come Soft Rains."

Understanding Literature

THEME. Review the definition for **theme** in the Handbook of Literary Terms. What do you think the theme of Sara Teasdale's poem is? Why do you think Bradbury chose to use the name of this poem for the title of his story as well as to incorporate the poem into the story? How are the themes of the poem and the story similar?

PERSONIFICATION. Review the definition for **personification** in the Handbook of Literary Terms. What is special about this house that makes it different from other houses? What specific lines, especially in the fire scene, describe the house in human terms? What is ironic about the survival of the house?

Writer's Journal

1. In this story the daily schedule is clear because of the frequent chimings of the house. Write an hourly **schedule** for one day in your life. If desired, write out activities and events in little jingles as the house does to help remind you of things that you have to do.

2. To continue in the personification vein, write a **eulogy** memorializing the dead house, extolling the valued deeds it performed for the family living within its walls. Your eulogy may evoke a solemn, comical, or satirical tone.

3. Write your own short **science fiction story** about technology gone awry.

Integrating the Language Arts

Language, Grammar, and Style

MODIFIERS FOR PARTICIPLES. Review the Language Arts Survey 3.80, "Verbals: Participles, Gerunds, and Infinitives." Then identify the participles and their modifiers in the following sentences.

1. Fast-moving mice cleaned the carpeting.
2. The newly ruined city gave off a radioactive glow.
3. The freshly cooked eggs were unappetizingly shriveled by eight-thirty.
4. The recently emptied house had lost its family.
5. No one heard the gently recited poem the machine had chosen.

Speaking and Listening & Collaborative Learning

INVENTORS' FAIR. Have you ever thought, "There has to be a better way to do this?" Get together in small groups, don your inventor hats, and brainstorm ideas for machines to do your least favorite tasks. Once you have a list of possibilities, vote on the one you think is most workable. Together create a design or model of your machine and write a description of it. Present the idea for your invention to the class.

Study and Research

WRITTEN REPORT. Ray Bradbury is one of the best known writers in the science fiction genre. Research this genre and answer the following questions in a written report: Who were the earliest science fiction writers, and what are some of their most memorable works? Who are some contemporary writers of science fiction? What stories are they famous for? Why has this genre been so popular?

Vocabulary

PREFIXES AND SUFFIXES. Learning new vocabulary can be easier if you learn the meanings of some common prefixes and suffixes. A *prefix* is a letter or group of letters added to the beginning of a word to change its meaning. A *suffix* is a letter or group of letters added to the end of a word. Review the vocabulary in the "Words for Everyday Use" for this selection. Identify all the prefixes and suffixes in the words and look up their meanings in a dictionary. Then relate these definitions to the definitions of the vocabulary words. For example, the suffix *–ous* means "full of" or "having." Thus *tremulous* means "having trembles or tremors."

Literary TOOLS

SIMILE. A **simile** is a comparison using *like* or *as*. A simile can be divided into two parts, the *tenor* (or subject being described) and the *vehicle* (or object being used in the description). Look for similes as you read this poem.

NARRATOR. A **narrator** is one who tells a story. The narrator in a work of fiction may be a central or minor character or simply someone who witnessed or heard about the events being related. Of primary importance is the choice of the narrator's *point of view*. Why do you think Benét chose the type of narrator he did to tell the story in this poem?

Organizer

To give yourself some perspective on how prevalent machines are in your own life, before reading the story create a cluster chart. Try to think of all the machines you use in your own home.

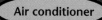

Air conditioner   Washer

Machines Used at Home

Reader's JOURNAL

Do you think humans are too dependent on machinery? Is there a middle ground between accepting conveniences and relinquishing control to machines? Explain your answers.

"NIGHTMARE NUMBER THREE"

by Stephen Vincent Benét

Reader's resource

In **"Nightmare Number Three"** Benét writes on a theme found often in science fiction: technology that is out of control. Benét wrote in the early part of the century, when mechanization was in its infancy. Benét's poem is humorous, but as you read it, consider this: Does overdependence on machines have a dark side?

About the AUTHOR

Stephen Vincent Benét (1898–1943) was born in Bethlehem, Pennsylvania. Because his father was a soldier, the family moved frequently from one army base to the next. Benét's travels and an interest in history greatly affected his writing. He began writing at age fifteen and two years later published his first book of poetry. While a student at Yale, he continued to write poetry. Later Benét received a Guggenheim Fellowship and went to Paris, where he finished a narrative poem about the Civil War, "John Brown's Body" (1928), for which he won a Pulitzer Prize. Later in his career, Benét turned to writing stories and novels. His story "Sobbin Women" (1926) was made into the musical *Seven Brides for Seven Brothers*, and his short story, "The Devil and Daniel Webster" (1937) was made into an opera and a movie. In 1944, Benét was awarded a second Pulitzer Prize posthumously for his epic poem on the westward migration, *Western Star*.

NIGHTMARE NUMBER THREE

Stephen Vincent Benét

We had expected everything but <u>revolt</u>
And I kind of wonder myself when they started thinking—
But there's no dice in that[1] now.

                                I've heard fellows say
5   They must have planned it for years and maybe they did.
Looking back, you can find little incidents here and there,
Like the concrete-mixer in Jersey eating the chap[2]
Or the roto press[3] that printed "Fiddle-dee-dee!"
In a three-color process[4] all over Senator Sloop,

> *What little incidents might have been warnings?*

---

1. **there's no dice in that.** It doesn't matter
2. **chap.** Man
3. **roto press.** Rotogravure press—printing press used in printing color sections of newspapers
4. **three-color process.** Printing method in which the three primary colors— red, yellow, and blue (cyan)—in a picture, or image, are separated. One color is placed on each of three engraved printing plates.

words for everyday use

re • volt (ri vōlt´) n., rebellion; insurrection. *A cruel leader ran that country until several people planned a <u>revolt</u> against his rule.*

10   Just as he was making a speech. The thing about that
Was, how could it walk upstairs? But it *was* upstairs,
Clicking and mumbling in the Senate Chamber.
They had to knock out the wall to take it away
And the wrecking-crew said it grinned.

*What is
inexplicable?*

15   It was only the best
Machines, of course, the <u>superhuman</u> machines,
The ones we'd built to be better than flesh and bone,
But the cars were in it, of course . . .

                              and they hunted us

20   Like rabbits through the cramped streets on that Bloody Monday,
The Madison Avenue buses[5] leading the charge.
The buses were pretty bad—but I'll not forget
The smash of glass when the Duesenberg[6] left the show-room
And pinned three <u>brokers</u> to the Racquet Club steps,

*To what are humans
compared?*

25   Or the long howl of the horns when they saw the men run,
When they saw them looking for holes in the solid ground . . .

I guess they were tired of being ridden in,
And stopped and started by pygmies for silly ends,
Of wrapping cheap cigarettes and bad chocolate bars,
30   Collecting nickels and waving[7] platinum hair,
And letting six million people live in a town.
I guess it was that. I guess they got tired of us
And the whole smell of human hands.

                           But it was a shock

35   To climb sixteen flights of stairs to Art Zuckow's office
(Nobody took the elevators twice)
And find him strangled to death in a nest of telephones,
The octopus-tendrils waving over his head,
And a sort of quiet humming filling the air . . .

*What happened to Art
Zuckow?*

40   Do they eat? . . . There was red . . . But I did not stop to look.
And it's lonely, here on the roof.

                        For a while I thought
That window-cleaner would make it, and keep me company.
But they got him with his own hoist[8] at the sixteenth floor

---

5. **Madison Avenue buses.** Buses that run along one of the main avenues in Manhattan, New York City
6. **Duesenberg.** Elegant automobile produced in the early part of the twentieth century
7. **waving.** Giving a permanent wave to
8. **hoist.** Mechanical pulley attached to a platform and used for lifting heavy objects or people

**words
for
everyday
use**

su • per • hu • man (sōōˈpər hyōōˈmən) *adj.*, having power above that of a normal human being. *That athlete seems
to have superhuman strength.*

bro • ker (brōˈkər) *n.*, person who acts as an agent or intermediary in negotiating contracts, buying, or selling. *The
jewelry broker found someone who would sell my brother a diamond necklace at a good price.*

45   And dragged him in with a squeal.
        You see, they cooperate. Well, we taught them that,
        And it's fair enough, I suppose. You see, we built them.
        We taught them to think for themselves.
        It was bound to come. You can see it was bound to come.

In what way are humans to blame for the revolt?

50   And it won't be so bad, in the country. I hate to think
        Of the reapers, running wild in the Kansas fields,
        And the transport planes[9] like hawks on a chickenyard,
        But the horses might help. We might make a deal with the horses.
        At least you've more chance, out there.

To what are planes compared?

55   And they need us too.
        They're bound to realize that when they once calm down.
        They'll need oil and spare parts and adjustments and tuning up.
        Slaves? Well, in a way, you know, we were slaves before.
        There won't be so much real difference—honest there won't.

What hope do humans have for a future?

60   (I wish I hadn't looked into that beauty-parlor
        And seen what was happening there.
        But those are female machines and a bit high-strung.)
        Oh, we'll settle down. We'll arrange it. We'll compromise.
        It wouldn't make sense to wipe out the whole human race.

65   Why, I bet if I went to my old Plymouth now
        (Of course, you'd have to do it the tactful way)
        And said, "Look here! Who got you the swell French horn?"
        He wouldn't turn me over to those police cars.
        At least I don't *think* he would.

70   Oh, it's going to be jake.[10]
        There won't be so much real difference—honest, there won't—
        And I'd go down in a minute and take my chance—
        I'm a good American and I always liked them—
        Except for one small detail that bothers me

75   And that's the food proposition. Because you see,
        The concrete-mixer may have made a mistake,
        And it looks like just high spirits.
        But, if it's got so they like the flavor . . . well . . .   ■

What worries the speaker?

---

9. **transport planes.** Wide-bodied planes, nearly empty of seating; typically used for carrying freight or soldiers
10. **jake.** Fine (slang)

Respond *to the* SELECTION

Imagine that the machines in your home came to life. What kinds of complaints do you think they would have? Which machine would frighten you the most?

All Watched Over by Machines of Loving Grace

Richard Brautigan

I like to think (and
the sooner the better!)
of a cybernetic[1] meadow
where mammals and computers
5   live together in mutually
programming harmony
like pure water
touching clear sky.

I like to think
10   (right now, please!)
of a cybernetic forest
filled with pines and electronics
where deer stroll peacefully
past computers
15   as if they were flowers
with spinning blossoms.

I like to think
    (it has to be!)
of a cybernetic ecology
20   where we are free of our labors
and joined back to nature,
returned to our mammal
brothers and sisters,
and all watched over
25   by machines of loving grace.

---

1. **cybernetic.** Relating to cybernetics, the comparative study of the control and communication systems of humans and electronics

ABOUT THE RELATED READING

Richard Brautigan (1935–1984) is best known for his first novel, *Trout Fishing in America*, a darkly humorous work that explores the deterioration of both the American landscape and its populace. His novels include *In Watermelon Sugar,* which was mistakenly greeted by young people in the late 1960s as a utopian vision of the future, *A Confederate General from Big Sur,* and *Sombrero Fallout: A Japanese Novel.* Brautigan began his career by writing poetry, and he continued to write poetry throughout his life. His poem "All Watched Over by Machines of Loving Grace" refers to a cybernetic world where people and machines live side by side.

Investigate, *Inquire,* and Imagine

Recall: GATHERING FACTS

1a. What didn't the speaker expect in the beginning of "Nightmare Number Three?"

2a. According to the speaker, what are the possible reasons for the rebellion?

3a. What did humans teach the machines that allowed the revolt to be so successful? What does the speaker think will happen to people?

Interpret: FINDING MEANING

1b. What does hindsight allow the speaker to see about the situation?

2b. What message do you think the poet means to communicate about humans and machines?

3b. How do the machines work together? Do you think that this is something they would have learned from humans? Do you think humans are slaves to machines? Explain your answers.

Analyze: TAKING THINGS APART

4a. Identify what machines are lacking that would make such a rebellion possible.

Synthesize: BRINGING THINGS TOGETHER

4b. Consider how the machine rebellion described in Benét's poem compares to human rebellions.

Evaluate: MAKING JUDGMENTS

5a. Do you think it is unreasonable to think that all of the machines in the world could get fed up or annoyed with humans? Why, or why not?

Extend: CONNECTING IDEAS

5b. The poem "All Watched Over by Machines of Loving Grace" by Richard Brautigan also deals with humans' relationships with technology. How is the message of each poem similar? How are the descriptions of the machines in Benét's rebellion different from Brautigan's vision of the machines in his cybernetic ecology?

Understanding *Literature*

SIMILE. Review the definition for **simile** in the Handbook of Literary Terms. What simile does Benét use to describe how cars acted in the revolt? What is the tenor of this simile? What is the vehicle? How is the image that is created in this simile continued in line 25? What simile does Benét use to describe planes in line 52? What is the tenor? What is the vehicle? To what are people compared in this line? Why might humans be compared to docile, domesticated animals throughout this poem?

NARRATOR. Review the definition for **narrator** in the Handbook of Literary Terms. Is the narrator in this poem *omniscient*, knowing all things, including the internal workings of the minds of the characters in the story? Or is the narrator limited in his or her knowledge? Does the narrator participate in the action of the story or stand outside that action and comment on it? Are the narrator's statements reliable—can they be trusted? Support your answers with evidence from the selection.

Writer's Journal

1. Write three **similes** comparing three of the household machines you noted in your cluster chart to various aspects of nature.

2. Think about what frightens you the most regarding technological advances. Write an **essay** about your own "nightmares" for the future. Include some thoughts on what might prevent these nightmares from coming true.

3. The machines in this poem seem to feel that they are not appreciated for the necessary tasks they do. Choose a machine you use frequently, such as a car, a computer, or a CD player. Write an **ode** to this machine explaining why it is important to you. An ode is a lofty lyric poem on a serious theme.

Integrating the Language Arts

Speaking and Listening & Collaborative Learning

ROLE-PLAY. Imagine a secret meeting of representatives of the various classes of machines. Each person in the class or a small group of students will represent a different group of machines and present their interests. For example, one person or group might represent small kitchen appliances. Maybe they resent being stuck in the house all the time or feel they are not allowed to live up to their potential. How might these concerns differ from those of a car? In your meeting, debate the issues and make a plan for action that will allow all machines to be free.

Study and Research

RESEARCH REPORT. Certain inventions through the years have revolutionized the world—inventions like the wheel, the printing press, the cotton gin, the Model T, the computer. Research one of these or another revolutionary invention and write a report on how it was invented, who invented it, and what kind of impact the invention made on the world.

Applied English

CAREER RESEARCH. Both Stephen Vincent Benét and Richard Brautigan warned their readers of the dangers of technology years before computer technology became as prevalent as it is today. Many people today can't imagine life before computers—consider all the people who earn a living in computer-related careers. Research a few computer careers—programmer, analyst, designer, database administrator, chief information officer, for example—to find out the kind of educational background that is required for each, the types of organizations that hire people for these positions, what the jobs involve, what the job market is for each job, and a typical salary range for each career.

"THE TEST"

by Theodore L. Thomas

Reader's resource

Theodore L. Thomas originally intended for "The Test" to show only what a driver's test of the future might be like. The test was created to judge not only technical driving skills, but moral and emotional fitness as well. The conclusion of the story did not satisfy Thomas, however, and one night before falling asleep he realized the meaning behind the scenes of his story—that human beings never know what is real and what is not real. With this new idea in mind, he was able to write the last two paragraphs of the story.

As we've learned from earlier selections, science fiction is highly imaginative fiction containing fantastic elements based on scientific principles, discoveries, or laws. The genre allows writers to suspend or alter certain elements of reality in order to create fascinating and sometimes instructive alternatives. As you read the story, consider why Thomas altered the world as he did. What might he be trying to say?

About the AUTHOR

Theodore L. Thomas (1920–) has published many stories and articles in anthologies and magazines. After graduating from Massachusetts Institute of Technology, he earned a law degree from Georgetown University. Though employed in fields as diverse as chemical engineering and patent law, Thomas has always found time for his writing.

Literary TOOLS

MOOD. **Mood,** or **atmosphere,** is the emotion created in the reader by part or all of a literary work. Look for mood changes in the story as you read.

THEME. A **theme** is a central idea in a literary work. While reading this story, think about what theme Thomas hoped to convey.

Organizer

This story is fast-paced and has a surprise ending. To help yourself follow the story's events and determine the story's theme, fill out a story map as you read. The chart should include the elements of a short story: setting, mood, conflict, plot, major characters, and theme. Follow the example given below.

SETTING AND MOOD	CONFLICT
Time: Place: Mood:	Internal: External:
MAJOR CHARACTERS	PLOT Inciting incident: Climax: Resolution:
THEME	

Reader's JOURNAL

Have you ever had a dream that seemed so real that when you woke up you were not sure if it had really happened or if it was indeed just a dream? What made the dream seem so real? What convinced you that it was not real?

THE TEST

Theodore L. Thomas

Robert Proctor was a good driver for so young a man. The Turnpike curved gently ahead of him, lightly travelled on this cool morning in May. He felt relaxed and alert. Two hours of driving had not yet produced the twinges of fatigue that appeared first in the muscles in the base of the neck. The sun was bright, but not <u>glaring</u>, and the air smelled fresh and clean. He breathed it deeply, and blew it out noisily. It was a good day for driving.

How does Robert Proctor feel?

He glanced quickly at the slim, grey-haired woman sitting in the front seat with him. Her mouth was curved in a quiet smile. She watched the trees and the fields slip by on her side of the pike. Robert Proctor immediately looked back at the road. He said, "Enjoying it, Mom?"

"Yes, Robert." Her voice was as cool as the morning. "It is very pleasant to sit here. I was thinking of the driving I did for you when you were little. I wonder if you enjoyed it as much as I enjoy this."

He smiled, embarrassed. "Sure I did."

She reached over and patted him gently on the arm, and then turned back to the scenery.

He listened to the smooth purr of the engine. Up ahead he saw a great truck, spouting a geyser of smoke as it sped along the Turnpike. Behind it, not passing it, was a long blue convertible, content to drive in the wake of the truck. Robert Proctor noted the arrangement and filed it in the back of his mind. He was slowly <u>overtaking</u> them, but he would not reach them for another minute or two.

What does Robert notice?

He listened to the purr of the engine, and he was pleased with the sound. He had tuned that engine[1] himself over the objections of the mechanic. The engine idled rough now, but it ran smoothly at high speed. You needed a special feel to do good work on engines, and Robert Proctor knew he had it. No one in the world had a feel like his for the tune of an engine.

How does Robert feel about his ability to work with cars?

It was a good morning for driving, and his mind was filled with good thoughts. He pulled nearly abreast of the blue convertible and began

---

1. **tuned that engine.** Set the timing and replaced the spark plugs, for example, to improve the engine's running condition

---

words for everyday use

glar • ing (gler´iŋ) *adj.*, shining with a strong light. *Al had a headache at the basketball game because of the <u>glaring</u> lights in the gym.*

o • ver • take (ō´vər tāk´) *vt.*, catch up with and go beyond. *Louisa had a slow start, but she will surely <u>overtake</u> the less experienced runners by the end of the race.*

Steering Wheel, 1982. David Hockney.

to pass it. His speed was a few miles per hour above the Turnpike limit, but his car was under perfect control. The blue convertible suddenly swung out from behind the truck. It swung out without warning and struck his car near the right front fender, knocking his car to the shoulder on the left side of the Turnpike lane.

> What happens when Robert starts to pass the convertible?

Robert Proctor was a good driver, too wise to slam on the brakes. He fought the steering wheel to hold the car on a straight path. The left wheels sank into the soft left shoulder, and the car tugged to pull to the left and cross the island and enter the lanes carrying the cars heading in the opposite direction. He held it, then the

art **n o t e**

David Hockney (1937–) is best known as a painter. He had been dissatisfied with photographs because the single image did not hold his interest very long. Hockney claims that his collage of several photographs comes closer to the actual experience of looking: "not all-at-once but rather in discrete, separate glimpses." Do you agree?

HE HEARD NO CRASH WHEN THE TWO CARS COLLIDED HEAD-ON

wheel struck a rock buried in the soft dirt, and the left front tire blew out. The car slewed,[2] and it was then that his mother began to scream.

The car turned sideways and skidded part of the way out into the other lanes. Robert Proctor fought against the steering wheel to straighten the car, but the drag of the blown tire was too much. The scream rang steadily in his ears, and even as he strained at the wheel one part of his mind wondered coolly how a scream could so long be <u>sustained</u> without a breath. An oncoming car struck his radiator from the side and spun him viciously, full into the left-hand lanes.

He was flung into his mother's lap, and she was thrown against the right door. It held. With his left hand he reached for the steering wheel and pulled himself erect against the force of the spin. He turned the wheel to the left, and tried to stop the spin and career out of the lanes of oncoming traffic. His mother was unable to right herself; she lay against the door, her cry rising and falling with the <u>eccentric</u> spin of the car.

The car lost some of its <u>momentum</u>. During one of the spins he twisted the wheel straight, and the car wobblingly stopped spinning and headed down the lane. Before Robert Proctor could turn it off the pike to safety a car loomed ahead of him, bearing down on him. There was a man at the wheel of that other car, sitting rigid, unable to move, eyes wide and staring and filled with fright. Alongside the man was a girl, her head against the back of the seat, soft curls framing a lovely face, her eyes closed in easy sleep. It was not the fear in the man that

reached into Robert Proctor; it was the trusting helplessness in the face of the sleeping girl. The two cars sped closer to each other, and Robert Proctor could not change the direction of his car. The driver of the other car remained frozen at the wheel. At the last moment Robert Proctor sat motionless staring into the face of the <u>onrushing</u>, sleeping girl, his mother's cry still sounding in his ears. He heard no crash when the two cars collided head-on at a high rate of speed. He felt something push into his stomach, and the world began to go grey. Just before he lost consciousness he heard the scream stop, and he knew then that he had been hearing a single, short-lived scream that had only seemed to drag on and on. There came a painless wrench,[3] and then darkness.

Robert Proctor seemed to be at the bottom of a deep black well. There was a spot of faint light in the far distance, and he could hear the rumble of a distant voice. He tried to pull himself toward the light and the sound, but the effort was too great. He lay still and gathered himself and tried again. The light grew brighter and the voice louder. He tried harder, again, and he drew closer. Then he opened his eyes full and looked at the man sitting in front of him.

"You all right, Son?" asked the man. He wore a blue uniform, and his round, beefy face was familiar.

> What catches the attention of Robert and causes him to be immobile?

> What seems to be happening to Robert Proctor? Is he dying? sleeping? Why might this passage be deliberately ambiguous?

---

2. **slewed.** Turned or pivoted around
3. **wrench.** Jolt; sharp, pulling motion

---

words for everyday use

sus • tain (sə stān´) vi., keep up or maintain. *The trumpeter's perfect sound was <u>sustained</u> throughout the long concert.*

ec • cen • tric (ek sen´trik) adj., off-center; departing from a normal pattern. *People often became confused by that <u>eccentric</u> system of roads and highways.*

mo • men • tum (mō men´təm) n., force of an object in motion. *The small child's bowling ball lost its <u>momentum</u> and stopped before it reached the pins.*

on • rush • ing (än´rush´iŋ) adj., dashing forward. *The squirrel started to run into the street, but the <u>onrushing</u> traffic scared it away.*

Robert Proctor <u>tentatively</u> moved his head, and discovered he was seated in a reclining chair, unharmed, and able to move his arms and legs with no trouble. He looked around the room, and he remembered.

The man in the uniform saw the growing intelligence in his eyes and he said, "No harm done, Son. You just took the last part of your driver's test."

Robert Proctor focused his eyes on the man. Though he saw the man clearly, he seemed to see the faint face of the sleeping girl in front of him.

The uniformed man continued to speak. "We put you through an accident under hypnosis—do it to everybody these days before they can get their driver's licenses. Makes better drivers of them, more careful drivers the rest of their lives. Remember it now? Coming in here and all?"

> What does Robert learn about the accident when he wakes up?

Robert Proctor nodded, thinking of the sleeping girl. She never would have awakened; she would have passed right from a sweet, temporary sleep into the dark heavy sleep of death, nothing in between. His mother would have been bad enough; after all, she was pretty old. The sleeping girl was downright waste.

> How does Robert assess the accident damage?

The uniformed man was still speaking. "So you're all set now. You pay me the ten dollar fee, and sign this application, and we'll have your license in the mail in a day or two." He did not look up.

Robert Proctor placed a ten dollar bill on the table in front of him, glanced over the application and signed it. He looked up to find two white-uniformed men, standing one on each side of him, and he frowned in annoyance. He started to speak, but the uniformed man spoke first. "Sorry, Son. You failed. You're sick; you need treatment."

The two men lifted Robert Proctor to his feet, and he said, "Take your hands off me. What is this?"

The uniformed man said, "Nobody should want to drive a car after going through what you just went through. It should take months before you can even think of driving again, but you're ready right now. Killing people doesn't bother you. We don't let your kind run around loose in society any more. But don't you worry now, Son. They'll take good care of you, and they'll fix you up." He nodded to the two men, and they began to march Robert Proctor out.

At the door he spoke, and his voice was so <u>urgent</u> the two men paused. Robert Proctor said, "You can't really mean this. I'm still dreaming, aren't I? This is still part of the test, isn't it?"

> Is Robert still dreaming?

The uniformed man said, *"How do any of us know?"* And they dragged Robert Proctor out the door, knees stiff, feet dragging, his rubber heels sliding along the two grooves worn into the floor. ∎

---

words for everyday use

ten • ta • tive • ly (ten´tə tiv lē) *adv.*, with uncertainty. *I knocked <u>tentatively</u> on the door because I wasn't sure if I was at the right house.*

ur • gent (ʉr´jənt) *adj.*, insistent. *Mario's little brother called to him in an <u>urgent</u> voice, so Mario dropped what he was doing and rushed to the child.*

Respond to the SELECTION

Do you think a virtual reality or hypnosis-type accident experience will ever be required in a driver's license test? Why, or why not?

Auto Wreck

Karl Shapiro

Its quick soft silver bell beating, beating,
And down the dark one ruby flare
Pulsing out red light like an artery,
The ambulance at top speed floating down
5   Past beacons and illuminated clocks
Wings in a heavy curve, dips down,
And brakes speed, entering the crowd.
The doors leap open, emptying light;
Stretchers are laid out, the mangled lifted
10   And stowed into the little hospital.
Then the bell, breaking the hush, tolls once,
And the ambulance with its terrible cargo
Rocking, slightly rocking, moves away,
As the doors, an afterthought, are closed.

15   We are deranged, walking among the cops
Who sweep glass and are large and composed.
One is still making notes under the light.
One with a bucket douches ponds of blood
Into the street and gutter.
20   One hangs lanterns on the wrecks that cling,
Empty husks of locusts, to iron poles.

Our throats were tight as tourniquets,
Our feet were bound with splints, but now,
Like convalescents intimate and gauche,
25   We speak through sickly smiles and warn
With the stubborn saw of common sense,
The grim joke and the banal resolution.
The traffic moves around with care,
But we remain, touching a wound
30   That opens to our richest horror.
Already old, the question Who shall die?
Becomes unspoken Who is innocent?

For death in war is done by hands;
Suicide has cause and stillbirth, logic;
35   And cancer, simple as a flower, blooms.
But this invites the occult mind,
Cancels our physics with a sneer,
And spatters all we knew of dénouement
Across the expedient and wicked stones. ■

White Burning Car III, 1963. Andy Warhol.

ABOUT THE RELATED READING

Karl Shapiro (1913–) received a Pulitzer Prize for his first successful poetry collection, *V-Letter and Other Poems* (1944), written while he was serving in the United States Army in the South Pacific during World War II. His poems were raw expressions of sensations, and he believed in using common, everyday language in poetry. His later poetry, which included *Poems of a Jew* (1957) and *The Bourgeois Poet* (1964), explores his own past. Critical works by Shapiro include his *Essay on Rime* (1945); a verse commentary on modern poetry, *Beyond Criticism* (1953); and *In Defense of Ignorance* (1960). Shapiro has served as editor of the influential literary magazines *Poetry* and *Prairie Schooner* and has taught at many U.S. universities.

Investigate, *Inquire,* and *Imagine*

Recall: GATHERING FACTS

1a. What is Robert Proctor doing when the story begins? Who is with him? What does he notice ahead of him on the road?

2a. What happens as he starts to pass the convertible? What sound does he hear throughout the following ordeal? What holds his attention while he is on the collision course with the other car?

3a. Who appears after Robert completes his application form? Why do they take him away?

Interpret: FINDING MEANING

1b. What kind of mood is Robert in at the beginning of the story? How does he feel about his ability to care for and handle a car?

2b. What is Robert's reaction to the crash? How does he feel when he learns it was not real?

3b. What do the two grooves on the floor indicate? What does the man mean when he says, "How do any of us know?"

Analyze: TAKING THINGS APART

4a. Identify the details that make the crash seem real to you. Are there details that make it seem unreal?

Synthesize: BRINGING THINGS TOGETHER

4b. Do you think Robert had questioned reality before? Do you think he will ever feel that he is in the "real" world again? Support your answers with details from the story.

Evaluate: MAKING JUDGMENTS

5a. What do you think of the driving test that Robert was given? Do you think it is an accurate way to determine if somebody is fit to drive? Do you think the test serves other purposes? What do you think it says about the people who created it?

Extend: CONNECTING IDEAS

5b. In the Related Reading poem "Auto Wreck," Karl Shapiro also writes about an automobile accident. How are the onlookers in his poem different from Robert Proctor in "The Test"? How are they similar to each other?

Understanding *Literature*

MOOD. Review the definition for **mood** in the Handbook of Literary Terms. What mood is created in the beginning of the story? What details help to create this mood? When does the mood change? What new mood is created?

THEME. Review the definition for **theme** in the Handbook of Literary Terms. Do you agree with the uniformed man's suggestion that all of life might be a kind of test? In what ways does life test people every day? In what ways do people pass or fail the tests that life presents to them?

Writer's Journal

1. Pretend that the accident in the story was real, not induced by hypnosis. Prepare a **police/accident report** with information on the whereabouts of the accident, the cars and drivers involved, the cause of the accident, the condition of the drivers and passengers, and any other pertinent information. Fill in gaps in the report with details from your own imagination.

2. As this story progresses, twists in the plot continue to distort what is real and what is not. Add another **plot twist** of your own. Maybe Robert will be taken to the psychiatric ward. Maybe, while there, he'll be hypnotized again. Maybe he'll wake up somewhere else. Try to think of some other possibilities. With what type of "reality" will your story end?

3. Write a **short story** about an everyday activity that takes place in the distant future. Think about how and why this activity might change.

Integrating the Language Arts

Language, Grammar, and Style

REVIEWING VERBALS. Review the Language Arts Survey 3.80, "Verbals: Participles, Gerunds, and Infinitives." Then rewrite the following sentences, underlining the verbals. After each sentence write P for participle, G for gerund, or I for infinitive.

1. Robert Procter was hypnotized for a driving test.
2. His thinking was being examined.
3. To think about the sleeping child troubled Robert.
4. Remembering that child was the worst experience of the test.
5. Two uniformed men prevented him from leaving.

Collaborative Learning

CHOOSE YOUR OWN ENDING. With a group of your classmates, create a choose-your-own-ending book. Use "The Test" as the beginning of your story, and compile the endings that you and your classmates wrote for the plot twist writing assignment. At an appropriate point in the story, insert lines that read something like this: If you think Robert will escape from the men in white, turn to page 4." Put each new ending on a separate page. Add illustrations and put your story together as a book. Some students can work as editors, some as cover designers or illustrators for the interior of the book, and others as word processors. Discuss with your classmates which endings you like the most.

Applied English & Study and Research

EXPLORATION. Examination procedures for a driver's license vary from state to state, as do the qualifications required for driving instructors and testers. Find out what the detailed procedures are for obtaining a driver's license in your state. Also research the qualifications necessary for those who provide driver's education training and those who test new drivers on their skills behind the wheel.

Literary
T O O L S

DRAMATIC IRONY. In **Dramatic irony** something is known by the reader or audience but unknown to the characters. Think about what the reader understands about the ending of this story that the characters do not understand.

SETTING. The **setting** of a literary work is the time and place in which it occurs, together with all the details used to create a sense of a particular time and place. Note the various settings of time and place as you read this story.

Organizer

A time line may be useful in keeping track of the many different time periods discussed in the story. Create a time line for "History Lesson" using actual dates and clues to dates as given in the text. For more information on time lines, read the Language Arts Survey 2.19.

| 2371 | 2372 | 2373 | 2374 |

Reader's
JOURNAL

Do you think that television and movies accurately portray society? In what ways are they accurate? In what ways are they inaccurate?

"HISTORY LESSON"
by Arthur C. Clarke

Reader's
r e s o u r c e

The destruction of the world, exploration of alien civilizations, and the place of humans in the universe—these common themes from science fiction stories are all found in Arthur C. Clarke's amusing and thought-provoking tale **"History Lesson."** Clarke's story makes us question our society: what values it promotes, how powerful it is, and what weaknesses it possesses. It also offers an unusual "history lesson."

About *the*
A U T H O R

Arthur C. Clarke (1917–), who was born in Somerset, England, graduated with honors in physics and mathematics from King's College in London. In the Royal Air Force, he worked with radar. Clarke's fascination with technology led him eventually to write science fiction. Combining his interest in science with a skilled narrative style, he has created numerous entertaining, instructive stories and novels. His science fiction works often focus on exploration and the place of humans in the universe. Clarke is the author of many nonfiction scientific works as well, including one in which he predicted the use of satellites for communication. His fictional works include *Childhood's End* (1953), *The City and The Stars* (1956), *The Nine Billion Names of God* (1967), and *2001: A Space Odyssey* (1968), which was later made into a popular movie.

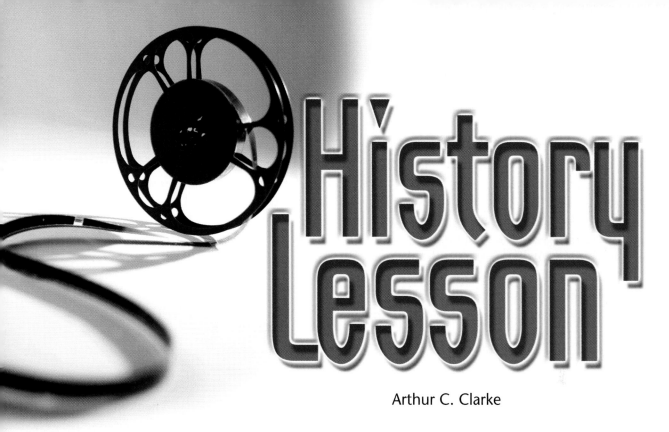

History Lesson

Arthur C. Clarke

No one could remember when the tribe had begun its long journey. The land of great rolling plains that had been its first home was now no more than a half-forgotten dream.

For many years, Shann and his people had been fleeing through a country of low hills and sparkling lakes, and now the mountains lay ahead. This summer they must cross them to the southern lands. There was little time to lose. The white terror that had come down from the Poles, grinding continents to dust and freezing the very air before it, was less than a day's march behind.

Shann wondered if the glaciers could climb the mountains ahead, and within his heart he dared to kindle a little flame of hope. This might prove a barrier against which even the remorseless ice would batter in vain. In the southern lands of which the legends spoke his people might find refuge at last.

It took weeks to discover a pass through which the tribe and the animals could travel. When midsummer came, they had camped in a lonely valley where the air was thin and the stars shone with a brilliance no one had ever seen before.

The summer was waning when Shann took his two sons and went ahead to explore the way. For three days they climbed, and for three nights slept as best they could on the freezing rocks, and on the fourth morning there was nothing ahead but a gentle rise to a cairn of gray stones built by other travelers, centuries ago.

Shann felt himself trembling, and not with cold, as they walked toward the little pyramid of stones. His sons had fallen behind. No one spoke, for too much was at stake. In a little

> Why is Shann leading his people south?

---

words for everyday use

re • morse • less (ri môrs´lis) *adj.*, merciless; cruel. *We asked for an apology, but the remorseless bully just walked away.*
ref • uge (ref´yo͞oj) *n.*, protection; safety. *The homeless people sought refuge from the cold in the city shelter.*
wane (wān´) *vi.*, ebb or fade away. *Roberto ended his speech as the audience's enthusiasm began to wane.*
cairn (kern) *n.*, pile of stones built as a monument or landmark. *The group gathered a few rocks to build a small cairn as a landmark along the nature trail.*

while they would know if all their hopes had been betrayed.

To east and west, the wall of mountains curved away as if embracing the land beneath. Below lay endless miles of undulating[1] plain, with a great river swinging across it in tremendous loops. It was a fertile land, one in which the tribe could raise crops knowing that there would be no need to flee before the harvest came.

Then Shann lifted his eyes to the south, and saw the doom of all his hopes. For there at the edge of the world glimmered that deadly light he had seen so often to the north—the glint of ice below the horizon.

There was no way forward. Through all the years of flight, the glaciers from the south had been advancing to meet them. Soon they would be crushed beneath the moving walls of ice . . . .

Southern glaciers did not reach the mountains until a generation later. In that last summer the sons of Shann

Where do Shann's sons store their treasures? Why might they do this?

carried the sacred treasures of the tribe to the lonely cairn overlooking the plain. The ice that had once gleamed below the horizon was now almost at their feet. By spring it would be splintering against the mountain walls.

No one understood the treasures now. They were from a past too distant for the understanding of any man alive. Their origins were lost in the mists that surrounded the Golden Age,[2] and how they had come at last into the possession of this wandering tribe was a story that now would never be told. For it was the story of a civilization that had passed beyond recall.

Once, all these pitiful relics had been treasured for some good reason, and now they had become sacred though their meaning had long been lost. The print in the old books had faded centuries ago though much of the lettering was still visible—if there had been any to read it. But many generations had passed since anyone had

What do these treasures reveal about Shann's people? Why might this revelation be surprising?

had a use for a set of seven-figure logarithms, an atlas of the world, and the score of Sibelius's[3] Seventh Symphony printed, according to the flyleaf, by H. K. Chu and Sons, at the City of Pekin in the year 2371 AD.

The old books were placed reverently in the little crypt that had been made to receive them. There followed a <u>motley</u> collection of fragments—gold and platinum coins, a broken telephoto lens, a watch, a cold-light lamp, a microphone, the cutter from an electric razor, some midget radio tubes, the <u>flotsam</u> that had been left behind when the great tide of civilization had <u>ebbed</u> forever.

All these treasures were carefully stowed away in their resting place. Then came three more relics, the most sacred of all because the least understood.

The first was a strangely shaped piece of metal, showing the coloration of intense heat. It was, in its way, the most pathetic of all these symbols from the past, for it told of man's greatest achievement and of the future he might have known. The mahogany stand on which it was mounted bore a silver plate with the inscription

Auxiliary Igniter from Starboard Jet Spaceship
"Morning Star"
Earth-Moon, AD 1985

Next followed another miracle of the ancient science—a sphere of transparent plastic with strangely shaped pieces of metal imbedded in it. At its center was a tiny capsule of synthetic radio-element, surrounded by the converting

---

1. **undulating.** Rising and falling
2. **Golden Age.** Period of great prosperity and cultural achievement
3. **Sibelius.** Finnish composer Jean Sibelius (1865–1957)

---

words for everyday use

mot • ley (mät´lē) *adj.*, made of many different elements. *A <u>motley</u> collection of junk—nobody knew exactly what—was in the large kitchen drawer.*

flot • sam (flät´səm) *n.*, odds and ends. *Nothing was floating in the pool of water but dirt, leaves, and other bits of <u>flotsam</u>.*

ebb (eb) *vi.*, recede; decline. *When the tide begins to <u>ebb</u>, we can go for a walk on the beach and look for shells that have been left behind.*

screens that shifted its radiation far down the spectrum. As long as the material remained active, the sphere would be a tiny radio transmitter, broadcasting power in all directions. Only a few of these spheres had ever been made. They had been designed as perpetual beacons to mark the orbits of the asteroids. But man had never reached the asteroids and the beacons had never been used.

Last of all was a flat, circular tin, wide in comparison with its depth. It was heavily sealed, and rattled when shaken. The tribal lore predicted that disaster would follow if it was ever opened, and no one knew that it held one of the great works of art of nearly a thousand years before.

> What is the last sacred object? What do the people know about it? What do they believe?

The work was finished. The two men rolled the stones back into place and slowly began to descend the mountainside. Even to the last, man had given some thought to the future and had tried to preserve something for posterity.

That winter the great waves of ice began their first assault on the mountains, attacking from north and south. The foothills were overwhelmed in the first onslaught, and the glaciers ground them into dust. But the mountains stood firm, and when the summer came the ice retreated for a while.

So, winter after winter, the battle continued, and the roar of the avalanches, the grinding of rock and the explosions of splintering ice filled the air with tumult. No war of man's had been fiercer than this, and even man's battles had not quite engulfed the globe as this had done.

At last the tidal waves of ice began to subside and to creep slowly down the flanks of the mountains they had never quite subdued. The valleys and passes were still firmly in their grip. It was stalemate. The glaciers had met their match, but their defeat was too late to be of any use to man.

So the centuries passed, and presently there happened something that must occur once at least in the history of every world in the universe, no matter how remote and lonely it may be.

The ship from Venus came five thousand years too late, but its crew knew nothing of this. While still many millions of miles away, the telescopes had seen the great shroud of ice that made Earth the most brilliant object in the sky next to the sun itself.

Here and there the dazzling sheet was marred by black specks that revealed the presence of almost buried mountains. That was all. The rolling oceans, the plains and forests, the deserts and lakes—all that had been the world of man was sealed beneath the ice, perhaps forever.

The ship closed in to Earth and established an orbit less than a thousand miles away. For five days it circled the planet, while cameras recorded all that was left to see and a hundred instruments gathered information that would give the Venusian scientists many years of work.

An actual landing was not intended. There seemed little purpose in it. But on the sixth day the picture changed. A panoramic monitor, driven to the limit of its amplification, detected the dying radiation of the five-thousand-year-old beacon. Through all the centuries, it had been sending out its signals with ever-failing strength as its radioactive heart steadily weakened.

> Why might the Venusian scientists not want to land on Earth?

The monitor locked on the beacon frequency. In the control room, a bell clamored for attention. A little later, the Venusian ship broke free from its orbit and slanted down toward Earth, toward a range of mountains that still towered proudly above the ice, and to a cairn of gray stones that the years had scarcely touched. . . .

> Why do the Venusians land on Earth?

The great disk of the sun blazed fiercely in a sky no longer veiled with mist, for the clouds that had once hidden Venus had now completely gone. Whatever force had caused the change in the sun's radiation had doomed one civilization, but had given birth to another. Less than five

> What caused the Ice Age on Earth? What effect did this have on Venus?

thousand years before, the half-savage people of Venus had seen sun and stars for the first time. Just as the science of Earth had begun with astronomy, so had that of Venus, and on the warm, rich world that man had never seen progress had been incredibly rapid.

Perhaps the Venusians had been lucky. They never knew the Dark Age that held man enchained for a thousand years. They missed the long detour into chemistry and mechanics but came at once to the more fundamental laws of radiation physics. In the time that man had taken to progress from the Pyramids to the rocket-propelled spaceship, the Venusians had passed from the discovery of agriculture to anti-gravity itself—the ultimate secret that man had never learned.

The warm ocean that still bore most of the young planet's life rolled its breakers <u>languidly</u> against the sandy shore. So new was this continent that the very sands were coarse and gritty. There had not yet been time enough for the sea to wear them smooth.

The scientists lay half in the water, their beautiful reptilian bodies gleaming in the sunlight. The greatest minds of Venus had gathered on this shore from all the islands of the planet. What they were going to hear they did not know, except that it concerned the Third World and the mysterious race that had peopled it before the coming of the ice.

What sort of beings are the Venusians?

The Historian was standing on the land, for the instruments he wished to use had no love of water. By his side was a large machine which attracted many curious glances from his colleagues. It was clearly concerned with optics, for a lens system projected from it toward a screen of white material a dozen yards away.

The Historian began to speak. Briefly he <u>recapitulated</u> what little had been discovered concerning the Third Planet and its people.

He mentioned the centuries of fruitless research that had failed to interpret a single word of the writings of Earth. The planet had been inhabited by a race of great technical ability. That, at least, was proved by the few pieces of machinery that had been found in the cairn upon the mountain.

"We do not know why so advanced a civilization came to an end," he observed. "Almost certainly, it had sufficient knowledge to survive an Ice Age. There must have been some other factor of which we know nothing. Possibly disease or racial <u>degeneration</u> may have been responsible. It has even been suggested that the tribal conflicts <u>endemic</u> to our own species in prehistoric times may have continued on the Third Planet after the coming of technology.

Did humanity necessarily have to be destroyed by the Ice Age?

"Some philosophers maintain that knowledge of machinery does not necessarily imply a high degree of civilization, and it is theoretically possible to have wars in a society possessing mechanical power, flight, and even radio. Such a conception is alien to our thoughts, but we must admit its possibility. It would certainly account for the downfall of the lost race.

What do the Venusians believe about the effect of technology on war?

"It has always been assumed that we should never know anything of the physical form of the creatures who lived on Planet Three. For centuries our artists have been depicting scenes from the history of the dead world, peopling it with all manner of fantastic beings. Most of these creations have resembled us more or less closely, though it has often been pointed out that because *we* are reptiles it does not follow that all intelligent life must necessarily be reptilian.

What surprises the Venusians about the life forms from Earth? What did they expect other intelligent life forms would be like?

"We now know the answer to one of the most baffling problems of history. At last, after hundreds of years of research, we have discovered the exact form and nature of the ruling life on the Third Planet."

There was a murmur of astonishment from the assembled scientists. Some were so taken aback that they disappeared for a while into the comfort of the ocean, as all Venusians were apt to do in moments of stress. The Historian waited until his colleagues reemerged into the element they so disliked. He himself was quite comfortable, thanks to the tiny sprays that were continually playing over his body. With their help he could live on land for many hours before having to return to the ocean.

The excitement slowly subsided and the lecturer continued:

"One of the most puzzling of the objects found on Planet Three was a flat metal container holding a great length of transparent plastic material, perforated at the edges and wound tightly into a spool. This transparent tape at first seemed quite featureless, but an examination with the new subelectronic microscope has shown that this is not the case. Along the surface of the material, invisible to our eyes but perfectly clear under the correct radiation, are literally thousands of tiny pictures. It is believed that they were imprinted on the material by some chemical means, and have faded with the passage of time.

"These pictures apparently form a record of life as it was on the Third Planet at the height of its civilization They are not independent. Consecutive pictures are almost identical, differing only in the detail of movement. The purpose of such a record is obvious. It is only necessary to project the scenes in rapid succession to give an illusion of continuous movement. We have made a machine to do this, and I have here an exact reproduction of the picture sequence.

"The scenes you are now going to witness take us back many thousands of years, to the great days of our sister planet. They show a complex civilization, many of whose activities we can only dimly understand. Life seems to have been very violent and energetic, and much that you will see is quite baffling.

"It is clear that the Third Planet was inhabited by a number of different species, none of them reptilian. That is a blow to our pride, but the conclusion is inescapable. The dominant type of life appears to have been a two-armed biped. It walked upright and covered its body with some flexible material, possibly for protection against the cold, since even before the Ice Age the planet was at a much lower temperature than our own world. But I will not try your patience any further. You will now see the record of which I have been speaking."

A brilliant light flashed from the projector. There was a gentle whirring, and on the screen appeared hundreds of strange beings moving rather jerkily to and fro. The picture expanded to embrace one of the creatures, and the scientists could see that the Historian's description had been correct.

The creature possessed two eyes, set rather close together, but the other facial adornments were a little obscure. There was a large orifice in the lower portion of the head that was continually opening and closing. Possibly it had something to do with the creature's breathing.

---

words for everyday use

bi • ped (bī´ped´) *n.*, two-footed animal. *It is very difficult to train the average household pet to be a biped; dogs and cats are far more comfortable on all four legs.*

or • i • fice (ôr´ə fis) *n.*, opening; mouth. *There was a small orifice in the rock wall that led to a roomy cave where primitive people once lived, protected from large animals by the narrow opening.*

The scientists watched spellbound as the strange being became involved in a series of fantastic adventures. There was an incredibly violent conflict with another, slightly different creature. It seemed certain that they must both be killed, but when it was all over neither seemed any the worse.

What is surprising about the action in the film?

Then came a furious drive over miles of country in a four-wheeled mechanical device which was capable of extra-ordinary feats of locomotion. The ride ended in a city packed with other vehicles moving in all directions at breathtaking speeds. No one was surprised to see two of the machines meet head on with devastating results.

After that, events became even more complicated. It was now quite obvious that it would take many years of research to analyze and understand all that was happening. It was also clear that the record was a work of art, somewhat stylized, rather than an exact reproduction of life as it actually had been on the Third Planet.

What do the Venusians recognize about the film?

Most of the scientists felt themselves completely dazed when the sequence of pictures came to an end. There was a final flurry of motion, in which the creature that had been the center of interest became involved in some tremendous but <u>incomprehensible</u> catastrophe. The picture contracted to a circle, centered on the creature's head.

The last scene of all was an expanded view of its face, obviously expressing some powerful emotion. But whether it was rage, grief, defiance, resignation or some other feeling could not be guessed. The picture vanished. For a moment some lettering appeared on the screen, then it was all over.

For several minutes there was complete silence, save for the lapping of the waves upon the sand. The scientists were too stunned to speak. The fleeting glimpse of Earth's civilization had had a shattering effect on their minds. Then little groups began to start talking together, first in whispers and then more and more loudly as the implications of what they had seen became clearer. Presently the Historian called for attention and addressed the meeting again.

"We are now planning," he said, "a vast program of research to extract all available knowledge from this record. Thousands of copies are being made for distribution to all workers. You

words for everyday use

in • com • pre • hen • si • ble (in´käm´prē hen´sə bəl) *adj.*, not understandable. *Since the speech was given in Greek, I found it to be <u>incomprehensible</u>.*

will appreciate the problems involved. The psychologists in particular have an immense task confronting them.

"But I do not doubt that we shall succeed. In another generation, who can say what we may not have learned of this wonderful race? Before we leave, let us look again at our remote cousins, whose wisdom may have surpassed our own but of whom so little has survived."

What does the Historian expect to learn?

Once more the final picture flashed on the screen, motionless this time, for the projector had been stopped. With something like awe, the scientists gazed at the still figure from the past, while in turn the little biped stared back at them with its characteristic expression of arrogant bad temper.

For the rest of time it would symbolize the human

What would symbolize the human race?

race. The psychologists of Venus would analyze its actions and watch its every movement until they could reconstruct its mind. Thousands of books would be written about it. Intricate philosophies would be contrived to account for its behavior.

But all this labor, all this research, would be utterly in vain. Perhaps the proud and lonely figure on the screen was smiling <u>sardonically</u> at the scientists who were starting on their age-long <u>fruitless</u> quest.

Its secret would be safe as long as the universe endured, for no one now would ever read the lost language of Earth. Millions of times in the ages to come those last few words would flash across the screen, and none could ever guess their meaning.

A Walt Disney Production. ∎

---

words for everyday use

sar • don • i • cal • ly (sär dän´ i kə lē) *adv.*, sarcastically. *George was irritated because his rival smiled at him <u>sardonically</u>.*

fruit • less (frōōt´lis) *adj.*, unsuccessful. *The Conquistadors considered their journey to be <u>fruitless</u>, as they did not discover the Fountain of Youth as they had hoped.*

Respond *to the* SELECTION

What view of our humanity would you wish other civilizations to understand five thousand years in the future?

Investigate, *Inquire,* and Imagine

Recall: GATHERING FACTS

1a. What do Shann and his tribe fear in the beginning of the story? What hope do they have for survival?

2a. What items do the sons of Shann put into a safe place to save for future generations? Which three items have become the most sacred?

3a. Who finds the preserved items? What secret have they learned that humans never learned?

→ Interpret: FINDING MEANING

1b. What reason is given for the Ice Age? How has this affected the planet Venus?

2b. Why do Shann's people place importance on the items they choose to save? Why have the sacred items become so important?

3b. How does the progression of Venusian knowledge differ from that of humans? How do the accomplishments of humans compare to those of the Venusians?

Analyze: TAKING THINGS APART

4a. What do the Venusians hope to gain by studying the film record? What don't they understand about this record?

→ Synthesize: BRINGING THINGS TOGETHER

4b. What point does this story make about interpreting historical artifacts?

Evaluate: MAKING JUDGMENTS

5a. Reread the passages that describe the cartoon. What misconceptions might the Venusians have about humans based on this film? In what way is it an accurate portrayal of life as we know it on Earth?

→ Extend: CONNECTING IDEAS

5b. Imagine that the Venusians had found some footage from the evening news as well as the cartoon. How would the two films compare?

Understanding *Literature*

DRAMATIC IRONY. Review the definition for **dramatic irony** in the Handbook of Literary Terms. What meaning does the last line of the story have for the reader? What does the reader know at that point about the Venusians' study of human civilization?

SETTING. Review the definition for **setting** in the Handbook of Literary Terms. As you began reading, when did you think the story was set? What details created this effect? What details changed your conception of the setting? What purpose was achieved by using such an ambiguous setting?

Writer's Journal

1. Pretend that you are one of the Venusian scientists who gather for the Historian's revelation. Write a **journal entry** for the day, giving your thoughts about the discoveries and what these mean for your future study.

2. Imagine that you could be any cartoon character in an animated film, television show, or newspaper cartoon. Write a short **essay** about who you would pick and why.

3. Review the list of things that Shann's people left in the cairn. Imagine that the Venusians have set up an exhibit about life on the Third Planet. Write a **museum guide** to this exhibit that includes a short description of each piece with its name, its material, and its possible function. Try to think about these items from a Venusian point of view.

Integrating the Language Arts

Language, Grammar, and Style

SIMPLE SUBJECTS AND VERBS. Review the Language Arts Survey 3.21, "How to Find the Simple Subject and Verb." Then underline the simple subject once and the simple verb twice in each of the following sentences.

1. No one could remember when the tribe had begun its long journey.
2. The tribe had preserved some relics from earlier generations.
3. The Dark Age had held man enchained for a thousand years.
4. The flat metal container holding a great length of transparent plastic material, perforated at the edges and wound tightly into a spool was a mystery.
5. To the Venusians the relic will symbolize the human race.

Media Literacy & Speaking and Listening

INTERNET RESEARCH. Use the Internet to research information about the prehistoric Ice Age and then look up various sites that deal with scientific research on an Ice Age in the future. In a class discussion, compare information with other students.

Collaborative Learning

TIME CAPSULE. Shann and his people preserved items that they thought were important within their history and culture. What items would you include in a time capsule? Think about things that have special significance to you. With your classmates, create a list of items you would choose to save. Collect any of these items that you can; for others that are too large or expensive, use pictures of the items. Make a display of the collection. Perhaps you would like to store this away somewhere to be opened at a much later date.

Study and Research

WRITTEN REPORT. With our own past civilizations, we often depict one specific archaeological or intellectual feat as a symbol of that civilization—for instance the pyramids with the ancient Egyptians. Select a civilization and research one or more of its notable symbols. What do we know of this civilization based on our knowledge of this symbol?

Literary
T O O L S

CARICATURE. In literature, a **caricature** is a piece of writing that exaggerates certain qualities of a character in order to satirize or ridicule that character or type. In "The Feeling of Power," Asimov presents caricatures of types of people. As you read, try to determine which characters are caricatures (or if all of them are).

SATIRE. Satire is humorous writing or speech intended to point out errors, falsehoods, foibles, or failings. It is written for the purpose of reforming human behavior or human institutions. As you read, try to find examples of satire in the story, and then put them in the chart below.

Graphic
Organizer

Create a chart with two columns. One column should be marked "action or dialogue" and the other "what it satirizes." Fill in the chart with the examples of satire you found in the story. One example has been done for you.

Action or Dialogue	what it satirizes
"He smoked Denebian tobacco with the air of one whose patriotism was so notorious, he could be allowed such liberties."	Asimov is making fun of the fact that politicians, who should be good moral and lawful examples, often get away with things unacceptable for the average citizen.

Reader's
Journal

Which do you consider more powerful, a computer or the human brain? Explain your answer.

"THE FEELING OF POWER"
by Isaac Asimov

Reader's
resource

SCIENCE CONNECTION. One of the great abilities of science fiction is its tendency to look ahead at new possibilities for science and technology. Interestingly enough, these predictions often become ideas for cutting edge technology. Cell phones, for instance, are direct imitations of the hand-held "communicators" that the crew of the original "Star Trek" TV series used. **"The Feeling of Power"** gives a different twist to this science fiction tradition. Instead of creating a new science or technology, Asimov shows what might happen if an old science, such as mathematics, is forgotten and then regained.

HISTORY CONNECTION. The war described in "The Feeling of Power" between Earth and Deneb is very similar to the Cold War of the mid- to late 20th century. Rather than a real "war," the Cold War was actually a competition between the U.S. and the Soviet Union to become the world's greatest super power. Isaac Asimov lived through the Cold War, and that experience may color his ideas in this story. In the story, as in the Cold War, both sides are constantly looking for an advantage. During the Cold War the advantage they sought was control of nuclear power, useful as both a source of electricity and of powerful bombs. Mathematics is presented in a similar way in "The Feeling of Power." Although it has many peaceful benefits, the characters of the story view mathematics as a weapon with which to win their war.

About the
A U T H O R

Isaac Asimov (1920–1992) has been called one of the "Big Three" of science fiction, and with good reason. He, along with fellow "Big Three" authors Robert Heinlein and Arthur C. Clarke, ushered in the "Golden Age" of science fiction, when for the first time it was widely accepted by the reading public. Asimov's first lure into the world of storytelling was the collection of science fiction comic books sold in his family's New York City candy store. He desired to tell his own stories and wrote his first book when he was ten. He disliked what he wrote but still decided to share it with a friend. This friend found the story so good that he thought Asimov had copied it from a published book. This encouragement propelled Asimov into becoming one of the great masters of science fiction.

Isaac Asimov

Jehan Shuman was used to dealing with the men in authority on long-embattled Earth. He was only a civilian, but he originated programming patterns that resulted in self-directing war computers of the highest sort. Generals <u>consequently</u> listened to him. Heads of congressional committees, too.

Why do congressmen and generals listen to Jehan Schuman?

There was one of each in the special lounge of New Pentagon. General Weider was space-burnt and had a small mouth puckered almost into a cipher.[1] Congressman Brant was smooth cheeked and clear eyed. He smoked Denebian tobacco with the air of one whose patriotism was so <u>notorious</u>, he could be allowed such liberties.

Shuman, tall, distinguished, and Programmer-first-class, faced them fearlessly.

He said, "This, gentlemen, is Myron Aub."

"The one with the unusual gift that you discovered quite by accident," said Congressman Brant placidly. "Ah." He inspected the little man with the egg-bald head with amiable curiosity.

The little man, in return, twisted the fingers of his hands anxiously. He had never been near such great men before. He was only an aging, low-grade Technician who had long ago failed all tests designed to smoke out the gifted ones among mankind and had settled into the rut of unskilled labor. There was just this hobby of his that the great Programmer had found out about and was now making such a frightening fuss over.

What is Aub's reaction to the powerful men in the room?

---

1. **cipher.** An o-shaped object

words for everyday use

con • se • quent • ly (kän(t)′ sə kwent lē) *adv.*, as a result. *I stole my brother's dessert; <u>consequently</u>, I was punished.*

no • to • ri • ous (nō tōr′ ē əs) *adj.*, widely but unfavorably known. *Jake was <u>notorious</u> for his ability to get out of trouble.*

General Weider said, "I find this atmosphere of mystery childish."

"You won't in a moment," said Shuman. "This is not something we can leak to the first comer.—Aub!" There was something <u>imperative</u> about his manner of biting off that one-syllable name, but then he was a great Programmer speaking to a mere Technician. "Aub! How much is nine times seven?"

Aub hesitated a moment. His pale eyes glimmered with a feeble anxiety. "Sixty-three," he said.

What is Aub's special skill?

Congressman Brant lifted his eyebrows. "Is that right?"

"Check it for yourself, Congressman."

The congressman took out his pocket computer, nudged the milled[2] edges twice, looked at its face as it lay there in the palm of his hand, and put it back. He said, "Is this the gift you brought us here to demonstrate. An illusionist?"[3]

"More than that, sir. Aub has memorized a few operations and with them he computes on paper."

"A paper computer?" said the general. He looked pained.

"No, sir," said Shuman patiently. "Not a paper computer. Simply a sheet of paper. General, would you be so kind as to suggest a number?"

"Seventeen," said the general.

"And you, Congressman?"

"Twenty-three."

"Good! Aub, multiply those numbers and please show the gentlemen your manner of doing it."

"Yes, Programmer," said Aub, ducking his head. He fished a small pad out of one shirt pocket and an artist's hairline stylus[4] out of the other. His forehead corrugated[5] as he made painstaking[6] marks on the paper.

What kind of effort does Aub have to put into multiplying these numbers?

General Weider interrupted him sharply. "Let's see that."

Aub passed him the paper, and Weider said, "Well, it looks like the figure seventeen."

Congressman Brant nodded and said, "So it does, but I suppose anyone can copy figures off a computer. I think I could make a passable seventeen myself, even without practice."

What skill does the congressman (and perhaps the general) seem to lack?

"If you will let Aub continue, gentlemen," said Shuman without heat.

Aub continued, his hand trembling a little. Finally he said in a low voice, "The answer is three hundred and ninety-one."

Congressman Brant took out his computer a second time and flicked it, "By Godfrey, so it is. How did he guess?"

"No guess, Congressman," said Shuman. "He computed that result. He did it on this sheet of paper."

"Humbug," said the general impatiently. "A computer is one thing and marks on paper are another."

"Explain, Aub," said Shuman.

"Yes, Programmer.—Well, gentlemen, I write down seventeen and just underneath it, I write twenty-three. Next, I say to myself: seven times three—"

The congressman interrupted smoothly, "Now, Aub, the problem is seventeen times twenty-three."

"Yes, I know," said the little Technician

---

2. **milled**. Having a raised rim or ridged edge (like some coins)
3. **illusionist**. Someone who tries to convince observers that a false image or object is real
4. **stylus**. An instrument for writing
5. **corrugated**. Settled in wrinkles; furrowed
6. **painstaking**. Requiring diligent, perhaps painful, care and effort

---

words for everyday use

im • per • a • tive (im per′ ə tiv) *adj.*, commanding; absolutely necessary. *It was <u>imperative</u> that we finish the ad campaign before the client arrived or we would be fired.*

earnestly, "but I *start* by saying seven times three because that's the way it works. Now seven times three is twenty-one."

"And how do you know that?" asked the congressman.

"I just remember it. It's always twenty-one on the computer. I've checked it any number of times."

"That doesn't mean it always will be, though, does it?" said the congressman.

Amorous Figures, c.1900s. Giacomo Balla. Private Collection.

What does Aub think he would have to be in order to prove that seven times three is always twenty-one?

"Maybe not," stammered Aub. "I'm not a mathematician. But I always get the right answers, you see."

"Go on."

"Seven times three is twenty-one, so I write down twenty-one. Then one times three is three, so I write down a three under the two of twenty-one."

"Why under the two?" asked Congressman Brant at once.

"Because—" Aub looked helplessly at his superior for support. "It's difficult to explain."

Shuman said, "If you will accept his work for the moment, we can leave the details for the mathematicians."

Brant subsided.

Aub said, "Three plus two makes five, you see, so the twenty-one becomes a fifty-one. Now you let that go for a while and start fresh. You multiply seven and two, that's fourteen, and one and two, that's two. Put them down like this and it adds up to thirty-four. Now if you put the thirty-four under the fifty-one this way and add them, you get three hundred and ninety-one and that's the answer."

There was an instant's silence and then General Weider said, "I don't believe it. He goes through this rigmarole[7] and makes up numbers and multiplies and adds them this way and that, but I don't believe it. It's too complicated to be anything but hornswoggling."[8]

How does the general take Aub's discovery?

"Oh no, sir," said Aub in a sweat. "It only *seems* complicated because you're not used to it. Actually, the rules are quite simple and will work for any numbers."

"Any numbers, eh?" said the general. "Come then." He took out his own computer (a severely styled GI model) and struck it at random. "Make a five seven three eight on the paper. That's five thousand seven hundred and thirty-eight."

"Yes, sir," said Aub, taking a new sheet of paper.

"Now," (more punching of his computer), "seven two three nine. Seven thousand two hundred and thirty-nine."

"Yes, sir."

"And now multiply those two."

---

7. **rigmarole**. Complicated and time-consuming steps in a procedure

8. **hornswoggling**. Trickery

"It will take some time," quavered Aub.

"Take the time," said the general.

"Go ahead, Aub," said Shuman crisply.

Aub set to work, bending low. He took another sheet of paper and another. The general took out his watch finally and stared at it. "Are you through with your magic-making, Technician?"

What does the general call Aub's mathematics?

"I'm almost done, sir.—Here it is, sir. Forty-one million, five hundred and thirty-seven thousand, three hundred and eighty-two." He showed the scrawled figures of the result.

General Weider smiled bitterly. He pushed the multiplication contact on his computer and let the numbers whirl to a halt. And then he stared and said in a surprised squeak, "Great Galaxy, the fella's right."

The President of the Terrestrial Federal had grown <u>haggard</u> in office, and, in private, he allowed a look of settled <u>melancholy</u> to appear on his sensitive features. The Denebian war, after its early start of vast movement and great popularity, had trickled down into a <u>sordid</u> matter of maneuver and countermaneuver, with discontent rising steadily on Earth. Possibly, it was rising on Deneb, too.

And now Congressman Brant, head of the important Committee on Military Appropriations, was cheerfully and smoothly spending his half-hour appointment spouting nonsense.

"Computing without a computer," said the president impatiently, "is a contradiction in terms."

"Computing," said the congressman, "is only a system for handling data. A machine might do it, or the human brain might. Let me give you an example." And, using the new skills he had learned, he worked out sums and products until the president, despite himself, grew interested.

"Does this always work?"

"Every time, Mr. President. It is foolproof."

"Is it hard to learn?"

"It took me a week to get the real hang of it. I think you would do better."

"Well, said the president, considering, "it's an interesting parlor game, but what is the use of it?"

What is the president's reaction to the new knowledge?

"What is the use of a newborn baby, Mr. President? At the moment there is no use, but don't you see that this points the way toward liberation from the machine? Consider, Mr. President"—the congressman rose and his deep voice automatically took on some of the cadences[9] he used in public debate—"that the Denebian war is a war of computer against computer. Their computers forge an impenetrable shield of countermissiles against our missiles, and ours forge one against theirs. If we advance the efficiency of our computers, so do they theirs, and for five years a <u>precarious</u> and profitless balance has existed.

"Now we have in our hands a method for going beyond the computer, leapfrogging it, passing through it. We will combine the mechanics of computation with human thought; we will have the equivalent of intelligent computers; billions of them. I can't predict what the consequences will be in detail, but they will be incalculable. And if Deneb beats us to the punch, they may be unimaginably <u>catastrophic.</u>"

The president said, troubled, "What would you have me do?"

---

9. **cadences**. Rising and falling tone patterns in a speaking voice.

"Put the power of the administration behind the establishment of a secret project on human computation. Call it Project Number, if you like. I can vouch for my committee, but I will need the administration behind me."

"But how far can human computation go?"

"There is no limit. According to Programmer Shuman, who first introduced me to this discovery—"

How powerful does the congressman think the human brain can be?

"I've heard of Shuman, of course."

"Yes. Well, Dr. Shuman tells me that in theory there is nothing the computer can do that the human mind cannot do. The computer merely takes a <u>finite</u> amount of data and performs a finite number of operations upon them. The human mind can duplicate the process."

The president considered that. He said, "If Shuman says this, I am inclined to believe him—in theory. But, in practice, how can anyone know how a computer works?"

Brant laughed <u>genially</u>. "Well, Mr. President, I asked the same question. It seems that at one time computers were designed directly by human beings. Those were simple computers, of course, this being before the time of the rational use of computers to design more advanced computers."

"Yes, yes. Go on."

"Technician Aub apparently had, as his hobby, the reconstruction of some of these ancient devices, and in so doing he studied the details of their workings and found he could imitate them. The multiplication I just performed for you is an imitation of the workings of a computer."

"Amazing!"

The congressman coughed gently. "If I may make another point, Mr. President—the further we can develop this thing, the more we can divert our Federal effort from computer production and computer maintenance. As the human brain takes over, more of our energy can be directed into peacetime pursuits, and the impingement[10] of war on the ordinary man will be less. This will be most advantageous for the party in power, of course."

What benefits would come from human computation?

"Ah," said the president, "I see your point. Well, sit down, Congressman, sit down. I want some time to think about this.—But meanwhile, show me that multiplication trick again. Let's see if I can't catch the point of it."

Programmer Shuman did not try to hurry matters. Loesser was conservative, very conservative, and liked to deal with computers as his father and grandfather had. Still, he controlled the West European computer combine[11], and if he could be persuaded to join Project Number in full enthusiasm, a great deal would be accomplished.

But Loesser was holding back. He said, "I'm not sure I like the idea of relaxing our hold on computers. The human mind is a <u>capricious</u> thing. The computer will give the same answer to the same problem each time. What guarantee have we that the human mind will do the same?"

What concern does Loesser have over the choice of the human brain instead of a computer?

"The human mind, Computer Loesser, only manipulates facts. It doesn't matter whether the

---

10. **impingement**. Effect, often negative
11. **combine**. A group of individuals (computers, in this case) that is unified into a whole.

---

words for everyday use

fi • nite (fī nīt) *adj.*, having definable limits. *There was a <u>finite</u> number of possibilities for the allowance money Charlie had earned.*

ge • ni • al • ly (jē′ nē ə lē) *adv.*, cheerful, friendly, and sympathetic. *The teacher smiled <u>genially</u> to calm her nervous kindergartners.*

ca • pri • cious (kə pri′ shəs) *adj.*, tending to change abruptly; erratic. *My <u>capricious</u> friends were always changing their minds about our weekend plans.*

human mind or a machine does it. They are just tools."

"Yes, yes. I've gone over your <u>ingenious</u> demonstration that the mind can duplicate the computer, but it seems to me a little in the air. I'll grant the theory, but what reason have we for thinking that theory can be converted to practice?"

"I think we have reason, sir. After all, computers have not always existed. The cave men with their triremes,[12] stone axes, and railroads had no computers."

"And possibly they did not compute."

"You know better than that. Even the building of a railroad or a ziggurat[13] called for some computing, and that must have been without computers as we know them."

"Do you suggest they computed in the fashion you demonstrate?"

"Probably not. After all, this method—we call it 'graphitics,' by the way, from the old European word *grapho*, meaning 'to write'—is developed from the computers themselves, so it cannot have antedated[14] them. Still, the cave men must have had *some* method, eh?"

"Lost arts! If you're going to talk about lost arts—"

"No, no. I'm not a lost art enthusiast, though I don't say there may not be some. After all, man was eating grain before hydroponics,[15] and if the primitives ate grain, they must have grown it in soil. What else could they have done?"

"I don't know, but I'll believe in soil-growing when I see someone grow grain in soil. And I'll believe in making fire by rubbing two pieces of flint together when I see that, too."

Why does Shuman think mathematics (graphitics) could not have existed before computers?

Shuman grew placative.[16] "Well, let's stick to graphitics. It's just part of the process of etherealization.[17] Transportation by means of bulky <u>contrivances</u> is giving way to direct mass-transference. Communications devices become less massive and more efficient constantly. For that matter, compare your pocket computer with the massive jobs of a thousand years ago. Why not, then, the last step of doing away with computers altogether? Come, sir, Project Number is a going concern; progress is already <u>headlong</u>. But we want your help. If patriotism doesn't move you, consider the intellectual adventure involved."

What is the next technological advance, according to Shuman? Why is this ironic?

Loesser said <u>skeptically</u>, "What progress? What can you do beyond multiplication? Can you integrate a transcendental[18] function?"

"In time, sir. In time. In the last month I have learned to handle division. I can determine, and correctly, integral quotients and decimal quotients."

"Decimal quotients? To how many places?"

Programmer Shuman tried to keep his tone casual. "Any number!"

Loesser's lower jaw dropped. "Without a computer?"

"Set me a problem."

"Divide twenty-seven by thirteen. Take it to six places."

---

12. **triremes**. Warships of the ancient Greeks, with three decks of oars
13. **ziggurat**. Ancient Assyrian or Babylonian pyramid-shaped structure.
14. **antedated**. Occurred earlier than
15. **hydroponics**. Growing plants without soil, as with a nutrient solution or other material
16. **placative**. Soothing or appeasing; calming
17. **etherealization**. To decrease or eliminate material substance
18. **transcendental**. A function, such as sine, cosine, or tangent, that cannot be separated into a finite number of calculations

---

words for everyday use

in • ge • ni • ous (in jē′ yəs) *adj.*, clever or original. *I had never seen anything like Christine's <u>ingenious</u> science project.*
con • tri • vance (kən trī′ vən(t)s) *n.*, something contrived or constructed, as an invention, plan, etc. *My uncle's house was his own unique <u>contrivance</u>, designed and built in his spare time.*
headlong (hed lôŋ′) *adj.*, moving with uncontrolled speed or force. *Luis's <u>headlong</u> dive allowed him to stop the ball short of the goal.*
skep • ti • cal • ly (skep′ ti kəl) *adv.*, with an attitude of doubt or criticism. *I listened <u>skeptically</u> as my friend explained his wild scheme.*

Five minutes later, Shuman said, "Two point oh seven six nine two three."

Loesser checked it. "Well, now, that's amazing. Multiplication didn't impress me too much because it involved integers after all, and I thought trick manipulation might do it. But decimals—"

"And that is not all. There is a new development that is, so far, top secret and that, strictly speaking, I ought not to mention. Still—we may have made a breakthrough on the square root front."

"Square roots?"

"It involves some tricky points and we haven't licked the bugs yet, but Technician Aub, the man who invented the science and who has an amazing <u>intuition</u> in connection with it, maintains he has the problem almost solved. And he is only a Technician. A man like yourself, a trained and talented mathematician, ought to have no difficulty."

"Square roots," muttered Loesser, attracted.

"Cube roots, too. Are you with us?"

Loesser's hand thrust out suddenly, "Count me in."

General Weider stumped his way back and forth at the head of the room and addressed his listeners after the fashion of a savage teacher facing a group of <u>recalcitrant</u> students. It made no difference to the general that they were the civilian scientists heading Project Number. The general was the overall head, and he so considered himself at every waking moment.

How does the general treat the Project Number scientists?

He said, "Now square roots are all fine. I can't do them myself and I don't understand the methods, but they're fine. Still, the Project will not be sidetracked into what some of you call the <u>fundamentals</u>. You can play with graphics any way you want to after the war is over, but right now we have specific and very practical problems to solve."

In a far corner, Technician Aub listened with painful attention. He was no longer a Technician, of course, having been relieved of his duties and assigned to the Project, with a fine-sounding title and good pay. But, of course, the social distinction[19] remained and the highly placed scientific leaders could never bring themselves to admit him to their ranks on a footing of equality. Nor, to do Aub justice, did he, himself, wish it. He was as uncomfortable with them as they with him.

How is Aub treated by the other scientists?

The general was saying, "Our goal is a simple one, gentlemen; the replacement of the computer. A ship that can navigate space without a computer on board can be constructed in one-fifth the time and at one-tenth the expense of a computer-laden ship. We could build fleets five times, ten times as great as Deneb could if we could but eliminate the computer.

"And I see something even beyond this. It may be fantastic now, a mere dream, but in the future I see the manned missile!"

What is the general's main goal for pursuing graphics?

There was an instant murmur from the audience.

The general drove on. "At the present time, our chief bottleneck[20] is the fact that missiles are limited in intelligence. The computer controlling them can only be so large, and for that reason they can meet the changing nature of anti-missile defenses in an unsatisfactory way. Few missiles, if any, accomplish their goal, and missile warfare is coming to a dead end—for the

---

19. **distinction**. The distinguishing of a difference
20. **bottleneck**. A situation that slows or halts progress

words for everyday use

in • tu • i • tion (in tü wi' shən) *n.*, knowledge of something without conscious reasoning; immediate understanding. *With his natural <u>intuition</u> of physics, Einstein easily grasped difficult ideas such as light-speed travel.*

re • cal • ci • trant (ri kal' sə trənt) *adj.*, obstinately defiant of authority or restraint. *The <u>recalcitrant</u> prisoner refused to leave his cell when summoned by the warden.*

fun • da • men • tal (fən də men' təl) *adj.*, of or forming a foundation or basis. *Reading, writing, and arithmetic were the <u>fundamentals</u> in the one-room schoolhouse.*

enemy, fortunately, as well as for ourselves.

"On the other hand, a missile with a man or two within, controlling flight, by graphitics, would be lighter, more mobile, more intelligent. It would give us a lead that might well mean the margin of victory. Besides which, gentlemen, the exigencies[21] of war compel us to remember one thing. A man is much more dispensable than a computer. Manned missiles could be launched in numbers and under circumstances that no good general would care to undertake as far as computer-directed missiles are concerned—"

How does the general compare manned missiles to computer controlled missiles?

He said much more, but Technician Aub did not wait.

Technician Aub, in the privacy of his quarters, labored long over the note he was leaving behind. It read finally as follows:

"When I began the study of what is now called graphitics, it was no more than a hobby. I saw no more in it than an interesting amusement, an exercise of mind.

"When Project Number began, I thought that others were wiser than I; that graphitics might be put to practical use as a benefit to mankind, to aid in the production of really practical mass-transference devices perhaps. But now I see it is to be used only for death and destruction.

What does Aub think his "invention" is only going to be used for? Is he right?

"I cannot face the responsibility involved in having invented graphitics."

He then deliberately turned the focus of a protein-depolarizer on himself and fell instantly and painlessly dead.

They stood over the grave of the little Technician while tribute was paid to the greatness of his discovery.

Programmer Shuman bowed his head along with the rest of them but remained unmoved. The Technician had done his share and was no longer needed, after all. He might have started graphitics, but now that it had started, it would carry on by itself <u>overwhelmingly</u>, triumphantly, until manned missiles were possible with who knew what else.

Nine times seven, thought Shuman with deep satisfaction, is sixty-three, and I don't need a computer to tell me so. The computer is in my own head.

And it was amazing the feeling of power that gave him. ∎

21. **exigencies**. Immediate demands

---

words for everyday use   o • ver • whelm • ing • ly (ō ver wel′ miŋ lē) *adv.*, overpowering in thought or feeling. *Winning an Olympic medal is an <u>overwhelmingly</u> heady experience.*

Respond *to the* SELECTION

Whose feelings about graphitics do you agree with more, Aub or Shuman? Why?

Investigate, Inquire, and Imagine

Recall: GATHERING FACTS

1a. What is the new science that everyone is so interested in?

2a. How do people initially react to this "new" knowledge?

3a. For what purpose(s) do the characters want to use this knowledge?

Interpret: FINDING MEANING

1b. How is their excitement and interest ironic?

2b. What does this say about their culture and attitudes?

3b. What impression does this give you of the different characters?

Analyze: TAKING THINGS APART

4a. Compare the story's society, with its attitudes on technology and advancement, with today's real human society. What similarities or differences do you notice?

Synthesize: BRINGING THINGS TOGETHER

4b. Classify the similarities of the fictional society and modern society as either good or bad traits. What is Asimov trying to suggest by pointing these out? Is he criticizing or praising our society?

Evaluate: MAKING JUDGMENTS

5a. Do you think Asimov's criticism or praise is justified? Does he create an accurate picture of society, or is he wrong about human nature? Why?

Extend: CONNECTING IDEAS

5b. Does Asimov seem to be suggesting any solutions to societal problems? If so, explain what they are and if you think they would work. If not, then suggest a solution of your own to any problems Asimov raises.

Understanding Literature

CARICATURE. Review the definition of **caricature** in the Handbook of Literary Terms. In "The Feeling of Power," Asimov presents many caricatures of people. Which characters did you see as caricatures? What types of people are they intended to represent, and which of their qualities are exaggerated and satirized? What does Asimov's use of charicatures add to the story's meaning?

SATIRE. Review the definition of **satire** and the chart you made for Literary Tools on page 910. In "The Feeling of Power," Asimov satirizes human nature and dependence on technology through the actions and dialogues of his characters. What examples of satire do you find? What kind of people are they aimed at? Do these examples point to any overall criticisms that Asimov has? What are they?

Writer's Journal

1. Write a **news briefing** on graphitics and Project Number that will be read on the evening news. Include names and some information on people who are important to the project, a summary of how graphitics works, and any other information you think the public should know. Make it complete, but as short as possible, since your story has a limited time slot in this evening's news lineup.

2. Create a quick **survey form** asking people what they think about the new science of graphitics, its effects on society and technology, and its possible uses (such as in manned missiles). You may use true/false or multiple choice questions, short answer questions, a mix of these, or create your own questioning system.

3. Imagine you are a member of an organization that wants to prevent the government from using the new science of graphitics for harmful purposes. Your task is to create a short, persuasive **pamphlet** describing to people what the government wants to use graphitics for and why this is wrong. Use strong, emotional language to influence people to defend your cause.

Integrating the Language Arts

Language, Grammar, and Style

PARTS OF SPEECH. Review the Language Arts Survey 3.7, "Grammar Reference Chart—Parts of Speech Overview." Then identify the part of speech for each underlined word or phrase in the sentences below.

1. Isaac Asimov, <u>a famous science fiction writer</u>, explored science, literature, <u>and</u> other subjects in his <u>writing</u>.
2. <u>His</u> <u>caricatures</u> in "The Feeling of Power" exaggerate <u>character</u> traits.
3. This short story shows Asimov's <u>highly</u> <u>developed</u> sense <u>of</u> humor.
4. This story is especially <u>funny</u> to those of us who had <u>problems</u> learning math.
5. Just <u>imagine</u> a group of scientists without the ability <u>to do</u> simple arithmetic!

Study and Research

REAL WORLD MATH. Research ways math is used in the world today. Is it generally used for good, beneficial things, or is it used mostly in harmful ways? Make a list of harmful and beneficial ways that math is used today. Then, report on whether you found math is in general good or bad, or just a tool that can be used for either. Based on your findings, decide whether math should be banned from use, regulated in its use, or used freely without restriction.

Speaking and Listening & Collaborative Learning

THE GREAT DEBATE. Divide the class into an even number of groups with four or five students in each group. Half of the groups will represent Programmer Shuman and the government, and the other half will represent Technician Aub and others who protest the way graphitics is being used. Each group will research their position and pair up against a group of the opposite opinion. Debates can proceed as follows: Each team gets a three- minute initial argument phase, then each will have seven minutes to argue against the other team's introduction, and finally each will have five minutes for a concluding argument.

"The Monsters Are Due on Maple Street"

by Rod Serling

Reader's resource

A *screenplay* is a drama written for television or film. **"The Monsters Are Due on Maple Street"** is a screenplay for a half-hour television program. Written as an episode for the *Twilight Zone* series, this teleplay is perhaps the best example from the series of Serling's remarkable gift for developing in a few short scenes a believable yet extremely dramatic sequence of events. In typical Serling fashion, these events challenge the characters, causing them to reveal their true selves. As you read the play, you will notice references peculiar to screenwriting, especially notes on camera effects, such as *fading in* (slowly becoming distinct) and *panning* (moving across a field of view).

About *the* AUTHOR

Rod Serling (1924–1975) grew up in the state of New York and became a major screenwriter for both film and television. Early in his career, Serling wrote realistic dramas. However, he soon switched to writing fantasies to avoid censorship. His television series *The Twilight Zone* became one of the most watched series in the history of the medium. Most *Twilight Zone* teleplays combined science fiction or fantasy elements with biting social criticism and satire. Serling received an Academy Award for Best Screenplay for his feature-length realistic drama *Requiem for a Heavyweight*. He also received a number of Emmy Awards. In addition to *The Twilight Zone*, Serling wrote for and directed the television series *Patterns* and *Night Gallery*.

Literary TOOLS

SETTING. The **setting** of a literary work is the time and place in which it occurs, together with all the details used to create a sense of a particular time and place. As you read this screenplay, think about the importance of the setting.

MOTIVATION. A **motivation** is a force that moves a character to think, feel, or behave in a certain way. While reading the screenplay, think about what motivates the people on Maple Street to turn into a mob.

Organizer

Tommy's fear that the aliens likely sent scouts ahead disguised as humans has set off great concern among the neighbors as to which ones of them may actually be aliens. The six different characters listed below are all accused at one time or another. As you read the screenplay, jot down the reason(s) that others feel motivated to accuse these characters.

Character	Reason for Accusation
Les Goodman Steve Brand Charlie Tommy Bob Weaver	
	His house lights flicked off and on.
Don Martin	

Reader's Journal

Have you ever participated in group behavior that you knew to be wrong? What were your motivations for joining in?

The Monsters Are Due on Maple Street

Rod Serling

CHARACTERS

Narrator
Figure One
Figure Two

Residents of Maple Street

Steve Brand
Mrs. Brand
Don Martin
Pete Van Horn
Charlie
Charlie's Wife
Tommy

Sally, Tommy's mother
Les Goodman
Mrs. Goodman
Woman
Man One
Man Two

ACT I

Fade in on a shot of the night sky. The various nebulae[1] and planet bodies stand out in sharp, sparkling relief, and the camera begins a slow pan across the Heavens.

NARRATOR'S VOICE. There is a fifth dimension[2] beyond that which is known to man. It is a dimension as vast as space, and as timeless as infinity. It is the middle ground between light and shadow—between science and superstition. And it lies between the pit of man's fears and the summit of his knowledge. This is the dimension of imagination. It is an area which we call The Twilight Zone.

The camera has begun to pan down until it passes the horizon and is on a sign which reads "Maple Street." Pan down until we are shooting down at an angle toward the street below. It's a tree-lined, quiet residential American street, very typical of the small town. The houses have front porches on which people sit and swing on gliders, conversing across from house to house. Steve Brand polishes his car parked in front of his house. His neighbor, Don Martin, leans against the fender watching him. A Good Humor man rides a bicycle and is just in the process of stopping to sell some ice cream to a couple of kids. Two women gossip on the front lawn. Another man waters his lawn.

NARRATOR'S VOICE. Maple Street, U.S.A., late summer. A tree-lined little world of front porch gliders, hop scotch, the laughter of children, and the bell of an ice cream vendor.

There is a pause and the camera moves over to a shot of the Good Humor man and two small boys who are standing alongside, just buying ice cream.

NARRATOR'S VOICE. At the sound of the roar and the flash of light it will be precisely 6:43 P.M. on Maple Street.

At this moment one of the little boys, Tommy, looks up to listen to a sound of a tremendous screeching roar from overhead. A flash of light plays on both their faces and then it moves down the street past lawns and porches and rooftops and then disappears.

Various people leave their porches and stop what they're doing to stare up at the sky. Steve Brand, the man who's been polishing his car, now stands there <u>transfixed</u>, *staring upwards. He looks at Don Martin, his neighbor from across the street.*

STEVE. What was that? A meteor?

DON. (*Nods*) That's what it looked like. I didn't hear any crash though, did you?

STEVE. (*Shakes his head*) Nope. I didn't hear anything except a roar.

MRS. BRAND. (*From her porch*) Steve? What was that?

STEVE. (*Raising his voice and looking toward porch*) Guess it was a meteor, honey. Came awful close, didn't it?

MRS. BRAND. Too close for my money! Much too close.

The camera pans across the various porches to people who stand there watching and talking in low tones.

NARRATOR'S VOICE. Maple Street. Six-forty-four P.M. on a late September evening. (*A pause*) Maple Street in the last calm and <u>reflective</u> moment . . . before the monsters came!

> What mood is set by the opening of the screenplay?

> How does the Narrator's last line in the opening contrast with the description that preceded it? What makes this line surprising?

---

1. **nebulae.** Groups of stars too far away to be seen distinctly; patches of misty light in the night sky
2. **fifth dimension.** Dimension beyond the three spatial dimensions: length, width, and depth—and also beyond the fourth dimension, which is time

---

words for everyday use

trans • fixed (trans fikst´) *part.*, made motionless. *The raccoon robbing my shed was* <u>transfixed</u> *by the sudden light, his startled eyes glowing through his black mask.*

re • flec • tive (ri flek´ tiv) *adj.*, meditative; thoughtful. *At sunrise he enjoyed a* <u>reflective</u> *pause over black coffee and the newspaper.*

The camera slowly pans across the porches again. We see a man screwing a light bulb on a front porch, then getting down off the stool to flick the switch and finding that nothing happens.

Another man is working on an electric power mower. He plugs in the plug, flicks the switch of the power mower, off and on, with nothing happening.

Through the window of a front porch, we see a woman pushing her finger back and forth on the dial hook. Her voice is indistinct and distant, but intelligible and repetitive.

WOMAN. Operator, operator, something's wrong on the phone, operator!

Mrs. Brand comes out on the porch and calls to Steve.

MRS. BRAND. (*Calling*) Steve, the power's off. I had the soup on the stove and the stove just stopped working.

WOMAN. Same thing over here. I can't get anybody on the phone either. The phone seems to be dead.

We look down on the street as we hear the voices creep up from below, small, mildly disturbed voices highlighting these kinds of phrases:

VOICES. Electricity's off.

Phone won't work.

Can't get a thing on the radio.

My power mower won't move, won't work at all.

Radio's gone dead!

Pete Van Horn, a tall, thin man, is seen standing in front of his house.

VAN HORN. I'll cut through the back yard . . . See if the power's still on on Floral Street. I'll be right back!

He walks past the side of his house and disappears into the back yard.

The camera pans down slowly until we're looking at ten or eleven people standing around the street and overflowing to the curb and sidewalk. In the background is Steve Brand's car.

STEVE. Doesn't make sense. Why should the power go off all of a sudden, and the phone line?

DON. Maybe some sort of an electrical storm or something.

CHARLIE. That don't seem likely. Sky's just as blue as anything. Not a cloud. No lightning. No thunder. No nothing. How could it be a storm?

WOMAN. I can't get a thing on the radio. Not even the portable.

The people again murmur softly in wonderment and question.

CHARLIE. Well, why don't you go downtown and check with the police, though they'll probably think we're crazy or something. A little power failure and right away we get all flustered and everything.

STEVE. It isn't just the power failure, Charlie. If it was, we'd still be able to get a broadcast on the portable.

There's a murmur of reaction to this. Steve looks from face to face and then over to his car.

STEVE. I'll run downtown. We'll get this all straightened out.

He walks over to the car, gets in it, turns the key. Looking through the open car door, we see the crowd watching him from the other side. Steve starts the engine. It turns over sluggishly and then just stops dead. He tries it again and this time he can't get it to turn over. Then, very slowly and reflectively, he turns the key back to "off" and slowly gets out of the car.

The people stare at Steve. He stands for a moment by the car, then walks toward the group.

STEVE. I don't understand it. It was working fine before . . .

DON. Out of gas?

STEVE. (*Shakes his head*) I just had it filled up.

WOMAN. What's it mean?

CHARLIE. It's just as if . . . as if everything had stopped. (*Then he turns toward Steve.*) We'd better walk downtown. (*Another murmur of assent at this.*)

> Why does Van Horn leave?

STEVE. The two of us can go, Charlie. (*He turns to look back at the car.*) It couldn't be the meteor. A meteor couldn't do *this*.

He and Charlie exchange a look, then they start to walk away from the group.

We see Tommy, a serious-faced fourteen-year-old in spectacles who stands a few feet away from the group. He is halfway between them and the two men, who start to walk down the sidewalk.

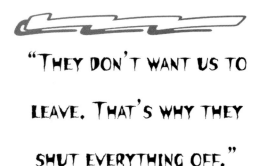

"They don't want us to leave. That's why they shut everything off."

TOMMY. Mr. Brand . . . you better not!

STEVE. Why not?

TOMMY. They don't want you to.

Steve and Charlie exchange a grin, and Steve looks back toward the boy.

STEVE. *Who* doesn't want us to?

TOMMY. (*Jerks his head in the general direction of the distant horizon*) Them!

STEVE. Them?

CHARLIE. Who are them?

TOMMY. (*Very intently*) Whoever was in that thing that came by overhead.

Steve knits his brows for a moment, cocking his head questioningly. His voice is intense.

STEVE. What?

TOMMY. Whoever was in that thing that came over. I don't think they want us to leave here.

Steve leaves Charlie and walks over to the boy. He kneels down in front of him. He forces his voice to remain gentle. He reaches out and holds the boy.

STEVE. What do you mean? What are you talking about?

TOMMY. They don't want us to leave. That's why they shut everything off.

STEVE. What makes you say that? Whatever gave you that idea?

WOMAN. (*From the crowd*) Now isn't that the craziest thing you ever heard?

TOMMY. (*Persistently but a little <u>intimidated</u> by the crowd*) It's always that way, in every story I ever read about a ship landing from outer space.

WOMAN. (*To the boy's mother, Sally, who stands on the fringe of the crowd*) From outer space, yet! Sally, you better get that boy of yours up to bed. He's been reading too many comic books or seeing too many movies or something.

SALLY. Tommy, come over here and stop that kind of talk.

STEVE. Go ahead, Tommy. We'll be right back. And you'll see. That wasn't any ship or anything like it. That was just a . . . a meteor or something. Likely as not—(*He turns to the group, now trying to weight his words with an optimism he obviously doesn't feel but is desperately trying to <u>instill</u> in himself as well as the others.*) No doubt it did have something to do with all this power failure and the rest of it. Meteors can do some crazy things. Like sunspots.[3]

---

3. **sunspots.** Temporarily cooler places on the surface of the sun, which appear as dark spots and are sometimes associated with physical disturbances on earth

---

words for everyday use

in • tim • i • date (in tim´ə dāt´) *vt.*, make timid or afraid. *Larry refused to be <u>intimidated</u> by the gruff manner of his football coach.*

in • still (in stil´) *vt.*, impart gradually. *Long experience with bug-ridden computer software had <u>instilled</u> in Colleen an unshakable distrust of technology.*

DON. (*Picking up the cue*) Sure. That's the kind of thing—like sunspots. They raise Cain with[4] radio reception all over the world. And this thing being so close—why, there's no telling the sort of stuff it can do. (*He wets his lips, smiles nervously.*) Go ahead, Charlie. You and Steve go into town and see if that isn't what's causing it all.

Steve and Charlie again walk away from the group down the sidewalk. The people watch silently.

Tommy stares at them, biting his lips, and finally calling out again.

TOMMY. Mr. Brand!

The two men stop again. Tommy takes a step toward them.

TOMMY. Mr. Brand . . . please don't leave here.

Steve and Charlie stop once again and turn toward the boy. There's a murmur in the crowd, a murmur of irritation and concern as if the boy were bringing up fears that shouldn't be brought up: words which carried with them a strange kind of <u>validity</u> that came without logic but nonetheless registered and had meaning and effect. Again we hear a murmur of reaction from the crowd.

Tommy is partly frightened and partly defiant as well.

TOMMY. You might not even be able to get to town. It was that way in the story. Nobody could leave. Nobody except—

STEVE. Except who?

TOMMY. Except the people they'd sent ahead of them. They looked just like humans. And it wasn't until the ship landed that—

The boy suddenly stops again, conscious of the parents staring at them and of the sudden hush of the crowd.

> Are Steve and Don convinced by their own explanations? Why are they trying so desperately to explain what is going on?

SALLY. (*In a whisper, sensing the antagonism of the crowd*) Tommy, please son . . . honey, don't talk that way—

MAN ONE. That kid shouldn't talk that way . . . and we shouldn't stand here listening to him. Why this is the craziest thing I ever heard of. The kid tells us a comic book plot and here we stand listening—

Steve walks toward the camera, stops by the boy.

STEVE. Go ahead, Tommy. What kind of story was this? What about the people that they sent out ahead?

TOMMY. That was the way they prepared things for the landing. They sent four people. A mother and a father and two kids who looked just like humans . . . but they weren't.

There's another silence as Steve looks toward the crowd and then toward Tommy. He wears a tight grin.

STEVE. Well, I guess what we'd better do then is to run a check on the neighborhood and see which ones of us are really human.

There's laughter at this, but it's a laughter that comes from a desperate attempt to lighten the atmosphere. It's a release kind of laugh. The people look at one another in the middle of their laughter.

> What is unusual about the people's laughter? Why are they laughing in this way?

CHARLIE. There must be somethin' better to do than stand around makin' bum jokes about it. (*Rubs his jaw nervously*) I wonder if Floral Street's got the same deal we got. (*He looks past the houses.*) Where is Pete Van Horn anyway? Didn't he get back yet?

---

4. **raise Cain with.** Create commotion with; biblical reference to Cain, the oldest son of Adam and Eve, who murdered his brother Abel

---

words for everyday use

va • lid • i • ty (və lid´ə tē) *n.*, quality of being firmly grounded on facts. *Although the findings of the doctor's study seemed unbelievable, the <u>validity</u> of his argument was proved later by many scientists.*

Suddenly there's the sound of a car's engine starting to turn over.

We look across the street toward the driveway of Les Goodman's house. He's at the wheel trying to start the car.

SALLY. Can you get it started, Les? (*He gets out of the car, shaking his head.*)

GOODMAN. No dice.

He walks toward the group. He stops suddenly as behind him, _inexplicably_ and with a noise that inserts itself into the silence, the car engine starts up all by itself. Goodman whirls around to stare toward it.

The car idles roughly, smoke coming from the exhaust, the frame shaking gently.

Goodman's eyes go wide, and he runs over to his car. The people stare toward the car.

MAN ONE. He got the car started somehow. He got his car started!

The camera pans along the faces of the people as they stare, somehow caught up by this _revelation_ and somehow, illogically, wildly, frightened.

WOMAN. How come his car just up and started like that?

SALLY. All by itself. He wasn't anywheres near it. It started all by itself.

Don approaches the group, stops a few feet away to look toward Goodman's car and then back toward the group.

DON. And he never did come out to look at that thing that flew overhead. He wasn't even interested. (*He turns to the faces in the group, his face taut and serious.*) Why? Why didn't he come out with the rest of us to look?

CHARLIE. He always was an oddball. Him and his whole family. Real oddball.

DON. What do you say we ask him?

The group suddenly starts toward the house. In this brief fraction of a moment they take the first step toward performing a _metamorphosis_ that changes people from a group into a mob. They begin to head purposefully across the street toward the house at the end. Steve stands in front of them. For a moment their fear almost turns their walk into a wild stampede, but Steve's voice, loud, _incisive_, and commanding, makes them stop.

STEVE. Wait a minute . . . wait a minute! Let's not be a mob!

> About what is Steve worried? What does he want to stop?

The people stop as a group, seem to pause for a moment, and then much more quietly and slowly start to walk across the street. Goodman stands alone facing the people.

GOODMAN. I just don't understand it. I tried to start it and it wouldn't start. You saw me. All of you saw me.

And now, just as suddenly as the engine started, it stops and there's a long silence that is gradually intruded upon by the frightened murmuring of the people.

GOODMAN. I don't understand. I swear . . . I don't understand. What's happening?

DON. Maybe you better tell us. Nothing's working on this street. Nothing. No lights, no power, no radio. (*And then meaningfully*) Nothing except one car—yours!

The people pick this up and now their murmuring becomes a loud chant filling the air with accusations and demands for action. Two of the men pass Don and head toward Goodman, who backs away, backing into his car and now at bay.

words for everyday use

in • ex • pli • ca • bly (in eks´ pli kə blē) *adv.*, without explanation. *The train was _inexplicably_ delayed just a few dozen feet from the station.*

rev • e • la • tion (rev´ə lā´shən) *n.*, something disclosed. *The _revelation_ that his "lost" glasses were perched on top of his head amused the man.*

met • a • mor • pho • sis (met´ə môr´fə sis) *n.*, transformation. *A novel by a German writer named Kafka describes the _metamorphosis_ of a man into an immense cockroach.*

in • ci • sive (in sī´siv) *adj.*, penetrating. *The most _incisive_ wit, political commentary, and general reflections on the state of the world are often heard in a taxicab.*

GOODMAN. Wait a minute now. You keep your distance—all of you. So I've got a car that starts by itself—well, that's a freak thing. I admit it. But does that make me some kind of a criminal or something? I don't know why the car works—it just does!

This stops the crowd momentarily and now Goodman, still backing away, goes toward his front porch. He goes up the steps and then stops to stand facing the mob.

We see a long shot of Steve as he comes through the crowd.

STEVE. (*Quietly*) We're all on a monster kick, Les. Seems that the general impression holds that maybe one family isn't what we

What is Steve's attitude toward the neighbors' growing fear of Goodman?

think they are. Monsters from outer space or something. Different than us. Fifth columnists[5] from the vast beyond. (*He chuckles.*) You know anybody that might fit that description around here on Maple Street?

GOODMAN. What is this, a gag or something? This a practical joke or something?

We see a close-up of the porch light as it suddenly goes out. There's a murmur from the group.

GOODMAN. Now I suppose that's supposed to <u>incriminate</u> me! The light goes on and off. That really does it, doesn't it?

(*He looks around at the faces of the people.*) I just don't understand this—(*He wets his lips, looking*

---

5. **Fifth columnists.** Citizens who help the invading enemies of their nation

---

words for everyday use

in • crim • i • nate (in krim´i nāt) vt., charge with or show evidence of involvement in a crime. *The Fifth Amendment to the Constitution allows people to refuse to <u>incriminate</u> themselves in court.*

from face to face.) Look, you all know me. We've lived here five years. Right in this house. We're no different from any of the rest of you! We're no different at all. Really . . . this whole thing is just . . . just weird—

WOMAN. Well, if that's the case, Les Goodman, explain why—(*She stops suddenly, clamping her mouth shut.*)

GOODMAN. (*Softly*) Explain what?

STEVE. (*Interjecting*) Look, let's forget this—

CHARLIE. (*Overlapping him*) Go ahead, let her talk. What about it? Explain what?

WOMAN. (*A little reluctantly*) Well . . . sometimes I go to bed late at night. A couple of times . . . a couple of times I'd come out on the porch and I'd see Mr. Goodman here in the wee hours of the morning standing out in front of his house . . . looking up at the sky. (*She looks around the circle of faces.*) That's right, looking up at the sky as if . . . as if he were waiting for something. (*A pause*) As if he were looking for something.

There's a murmur of reaction from the crowd again. We cut suddenly to a group shot. As Goodman starts toward them, they back away frightened.

GOODMAN. You know really . . . this is for laughs. You know what I'm guilty of? (*He laughs.*) I'm guilty of insomnia. Now what's the penalty for insomnia? (*At this point the laugh, the humor, leaves his voice.*) Did you hear what I said? I said it was insomnia. (*A pause as he looks around, then shouts.*) I said it was insomnia! You fools. You scared, frightened rabbits, you. You're sick people, do you know that? You're sick people—all of you! And you don't even know what you're starting because let me tell you . . . let me tell you—this thing you're starting—that

> What nightmare is beginning on Maple Street?

should frighten you. As God is my witness . . . you're letting something begin here that's a nightmare!

ACT II

We see a medium shot of the Goodman entry hall at night. On the side table rests an unlit candle. Mrs. Goodman walks into the scene, a glass of milk in hand. She sets the milk down on the table, lights the candle with a match from a box on the table, picks up the glass of milk, and starts out of scene.

Mrs. Goodman comes through her porch door, glass of milk in hand. The entry hall, with table and lit candle, can be seen behind her.

Outside, the camera slowly pans down the sidewalk, taking in little knots of people who stand around talking in low voices. At the end of each conversation they look toward Les Goodman's house. From the various houses we can see candlelight but no electricity, and there's an <u>all-pervading</u> quiet that blankets the whole area, disturbed only by the almost whispered voices of the people as they stand around. The camera pans over to one group where Charlie stands. He stares across at Goodman's house.

We see a long shot of the house. Two men stand across the street in almost sentry-like[6] poses. Then we see a medium shot of a group of people.

SALLY. (*A little timorously*) It just doesn't seem right, though, keeping watch on them. Why . . . he was right when he said he was one of our neighbors. Why, I've known Ethel Goodman ever since they moved in. We've been good friends—

CHARLIE. That don't prove a thing. Any guy who'd spend his time lookin' up at the sky early in the morning—well, there's something wrong with that kind of person. There's something that ain't legitimate. Maybe under normal circum-

---

6. **sentry-like.** Like a military guard

---

words for everyday use

all-per • vad • ing (ôl´ pər vād´ iŋ) *adj.*, prevalent throughout. *The trilling of the frogs in the local ponds created an <u>all-pervading</u> racket on spring nights.*

stances we could let it go by, but these aren't normal circumstances. Why, look at this street! Nothin' but candles. Why, it's like goin' back into the Dark Ages or somethin'!

What makes Charlie's comment ironic? In what way have the people on Maple Street gone "back into the Dark Ages"? Who has led them there?

Steve walks down the steps of his porch, walks down the street over to Les Goodman's house, and then stops at the foot of the steps. Goodman stands there, his wife behind him, very frightened.

GOODMAN. Just stay right where you are, Steve. We don't want any trouble, but this time if anybody sets foot on my porch, that's what they're going to get—trouble!

STEVE. Look, Les—

GOODMAN. I've already explained to you people. I don't sleep very well at night sometimes. I get up and I take a walk and I look up at the sky. I look at the stars!

MRS. GOODMAN. That's exactly what he does. Why this whole thing, it's . . . it's some kind of madness or something.

STEVE. (*Nods grimly*) That's exactly what it is—some kind of madness.

CHARLIE'S VOICE. (*Shrill, from across the street*) You best watch who you're seen with, Steve! Until we get this all straightened out, you ain't exactly above suspicion yourself.

STEVE. (*Whirling around toward him*) Or you, Charlie. Or any of us, it seems. From age eight on up!

WOMAN. What I'd like to know is—what are we gonna do? Just stand around here all night?

CHARLIE. There's nothin' else we can do! (*He turns back looking toward Steve and Goodman again.*) One of 'em'll tip their hand. They got to.

STEVE. (*Raising his voice*) There's something you can do, Charlie. You could go home and keep your mouth shut. You could quit strutting around like a self-appointed hanging judge and just climb into bed and forget it.

CHARLIE. You sound real anxious to have that happen, Steve. I think we better keep our eye on you too!

DON. (*As if he were taking the bit from his teeth, takes a hesitant step to the front*) I think everything might as well come out now. (*He turns toward Steve.*) Your wife's done plenty of talking, Steve, about how odd you are!

CHARLIE. (*Picking this up, his eyes widening*) Go ahead, tell us what she's said.

We see a long shot of Steve as he walks toward them from across the street.

STEVE. Go ahead, what's my wife said? Let's get it all out. Let's pick out every idiosyncrasy of every single man, woman, and child on the street. And then we might as well set up some kind of kangaroo court.[7] How about a firing squad at dawn, Charlie, so we can get rid of all the suspects? Narrow them down. Make it easier for you.

How do Don's comments confirm Steve's fears? What is happening to the neighbors' tolerance for differences, or idiosyncrasies?

DON. There's no need gettin' so upset, Steve. It's just that . . . well . . . Myra's talked about how there's been plenty of nights you spent hours down in your basement workin' on some kind of radio or something. Well, none of us have ever seen that radio—

By this time Steve has reached the group. He stands there defiantly close to them.

---

7. **kangaroo court.** Unauthorized court that disregards regular legal procedure; named because its enforcement of justice occurs rapidly and unpredictably, in leaps and bounds

---

words for everyday use

id • i • o • syn • cra • sy (id´ē ō´siŋ´krə sē) *n.*, any personal peculiarity. *One of the poet's many idiosyncrasies was his habit of twirling his mustache with his fingers while he spoke.*

de • fi • ant • ly (dē fī´ənt lē) *adv.*, openly resisting. *When she was a little girl, Myrtle had defiantly insisted on eating the frosting before the cake.*

CHARLIE. Go ahead, Steve. What kind of "radio set" you workin' on? I never seen it. Neither has anyone else. Who you talk to on that radio set? And who talks to you?

STEVE. I'm surprised at you, Charlie. How come you're so dense all of a sudden? (*A pause*) Who do I talk to? I talk to monsters from outer space. I talk to three-headed green men who fly over here in what look like meteors.

Steve's wife steps down from the porch, bites her lip, calls out.

MRS. BRAND. Steve! Steve, please. (*Then looking around, frightened, she walks toward the group.*) It's just a ham radio set,[8] that's all. I bought him a book on it myself. It's just a ham radio set. A lot of people have them. I can show it to you. It's right down in the basement.

STEVE. (*Whirls around toward her*) Show them nothing! If they want to look inside our house—let them get a search warrant.

CHARLIE. Look, buddy, you can't afford to—

STEVE. (*Interrupting*) Charlie, don't tell me what I can afford! And stop telling me who's dangerous and who isn't and who's safe and who's a menace. (*He turns to the group and shouts.*) And you're with him, too—all of you! You're standing here all set to crucify—all set to find a scapegoat—all desperate to point some kind of a finger at a neighbor! Well now look, friends, the only thing that's gonna happen is that we'll eat each other up alive—

He stops abruptly as Charlie suddenly grabs his arm.

CHARLIE. (*In a hushed voice*) That's not the only thing that can happen to us.

Cut to a long shot looking down the street. A figure has suddenly <u>materialized</u> in the gloom and in the silence we can hear the clickety-clack of slow, measured footsteps on concrete as the figure walks slowly toward them. One of the women lets out a stifled cry. The young mother grabs her boy as do a couple of others.

TOMMY. (*Shouting, frightened*) It's the monster! It's the monster!

Another woman lets out a wail and the people fall back in a group, staring toward the darkness and the approaching figure.

We see a medium group shot of the people as they stand in the shadows watching. Don Martin joins them, carrying a shotgun. He holds it up.

DON. We may need this.

STEVE. A shotgun? (*He pulls it out of Don's hand.*) Good Lord—will anybody think a thought around here? Will you people wise up? What good would a shotgun do against—

Now Charlie pulls the gun from Steve's hand.

CHARLIE. No more talk, Steve. You're going to talk us into a grave! You'd let whatever's out there walk right over us, wouldn't yuh? Well, some of us won't!

He swings the gun around to point it toward the sidewalk.

The dark figure continues to walk toward them.

The group stands there, fearful, apprehensive, mothers clutching children, men standing in front of wives. Charlie slowly raises the gun. As the figure gets closer and closer he suddenly pulls the trigger. The sound of it explodes in the stillness. There is a long angle shot looking down at the figure, who suddenly lets out a small cry, stumbles forward onto his knees and then falls forward on his face. Don, Charlie, and Steve race forward over to him. Steve is there first and turns the man over. Now the crowd gathers around them.

> Again, what is ironic about Charlie's statement? Who actually sends one of his neighbors into a grave?

---

8. **ham radio set.** Amateur radio operator's equipment

---

words for everyday use

ma • te • ri • al • ize (mə tir´ ē əl īz´) *vt.*, appear in physical form. *Joe's impractical plan for acquiring wealth never made so much as a penny <u>materialize</u> in his bank account.*

STEVE. (*Slowly looks up*)   It's Pete Van Horn.

DON. (*In a hushed voice*)   Pete Van Horn! He was just gonna go over to the next block to see if the power was on—

WOMAN.   You killed him, Charlie. You shot him dead!

CHARLIE. (*Looks around at the circle of faces, his eyes frightened, his face <u>contorted</u>*)   But . . . but I didn't know who he was. I certainly didn't know who he was. He comes walkin' out of the darkness—how am I supposed to know who he was? (*He grabs Steve.*) Steve—you know why I shot! How was I supposed to know he wasn't a monster or something? (*He grabs Don now.*) We're all scared of the same thing. I was just tryin' to . . . tryin' to protect my home, that's all! Look, all of you, that's all I was tryin' to do. (*He looks down wildly at the body.*) I didn't know it was somebody we knew! I didn't know—

There's a sudden hush and then an intake of breath. We see a medium shot of the living room window of Charlie's house. The window is not lit, but suddenly the house lights come on behind it.

WOMAN. (*In a very hushed voice*) Charlie . . . Charlie . . . the lights just went on in your house. Why did the lights just go on?

DON.   What about it, Charlie? How come you're the only one with lights now?

GOODMAN.   That's what I'd like to know.

A pause as they all stare toward Charlie.

GOODMAN.   You were so quick to kill, Charlie, and you were so quick to tell us who we had to be careful of. Well, maybe you had to kill. Maybe Peter there was trying to tell us something. Maybe he'd found out something and came back to tell us who there was amongst us we should watch out for—

Charlie backs away from the group, his eyes wide with fright.

CHARLIE.   No . . . no . . . it's nothing of the sort! I don't know why the lights are on. I swear I don't. Somebody's pulling a gag or something.

He bumps against Steve, who grabs him and whirls him around.

"LOOK, LOOK I SWEAR TO YOU . . . IT ISN'T ME . . . BUT I DO KNOW WHO IT IS . . . I SWEAR TO YOU, I DO KNOW WHO IT IS."

STEVE.   A gag? A gag? Charlie, there's a dead man on the sidewalk and you killed him! Does this thing look like a gag to you?

Charlie breaks away and screams as he runs toward his house.

CHARLIE.   No! No! Please!

A man breaks away from the crowd to chase Charlie.

We see a long angle shot looking down as the man tackles Charlie and lands on top of him. The other people start to run toward them. Charlie is up on his feet, breaks away from the other man's grasp, lands a couple of desperate punches that push the man aside. Then he forces his way, fighting, through the crowd to once again break free, jumps up on his front porch. A rock thrown from the group smashes a window along-

side of him, the broken glass flying past him. A couple of pieces cut him. He stands there perspiring, rumpled, blood running down from a cut on the cheek. His wife breaks away from the group to throw herself into his arms. He buries his face against her. We can see the crowd <u>converging</u> on the porch now.

VOICES.   It must have been him.
He's the one.
We got to get Charlie.

Another rock lands on the porch. Now Charlie pushes his wife behind him, facing the group.

CHARLIE.   Look, look I swear to you . . . it isn't me . . . but I do know who it is . . . I swear to you, I do know who it is. I know who the monster is here. I know who it is that doesn't belong. I swear to you I know.

GOODMAN. (*Shouting*)   What are you waiting for?

WOMAN. (*Shouting*)   Come on, Charlie, come on.

MAN ONE. (*Shouting*)   Who is it, Charlie, tell us!

DON. (*Pushing his way to the front of the crowd*) All right, Charlie, let's hear it!

Charlie's eyes dart around wildly.

CHARLIE.   It's . . . it's . . .

MAN ONE. (*Screaming*)   Go ahead, Charlie, tell us.

CHARLIE.   It's . . . it's the kid. It's Tommy. He's the one!

> What are your feelings toward Charlie at this point in the play?

There's a gasp from the crowd as we cut to a shot of Sally holding her son Tommy. The boy at first doesn't understand and then, realizing the eyes are all on him, buries his face against his mother.

SALLY. (*Backs away*)   That's crazy! That's crazy! He's a little boy.

WOMAN.   But he knew! He was the only one who knew! He told us all about it. Well, how did he know? How *could* he have known?

The various people take this up and repeat the question aloud.

VOICES.   How could he know?
Who told him?
Make the kid answer.

DON.   It was Charlie who killed old man Van Horn.

WOMAN.   But it was the kid here who knew what was going to happen all the time. He was the one who knew!

We see a close-up of Steve.

STEVE.   Are you all gone crazy? (*Pause as he looks about*) Stop.

> How would you answer Steve's question?

A fist crashes at Steve's face, staggering him back out of the frame of the picture.

There are several close camera shots suggesting the coming of violence. A hand fires a rifle. A fist clenches. A hand grabs the hammer from Van Horn's body, etc. Meanwhile, we hear the following lines.

DON.   Charlie has to be the one—Where's my rifle—

WOMAN.   Les Goodman's the one. His car started! Let's wreck it.

MRS. GOODMAN.   What about Steve's radio— He's the one that called them—

MR. GOODMAN.   Smash the radio. Get me a hammer. Get me something.

STEVE.   Stop—Stop—

CHARLIE.   Where's that kid—Let's get him.

MAN ONE.   Get Steve—Get Charlie —They're working together.

The crowd starts to converge around the mother, who grabs the child and starts to run with him. The

---

words for everyday use

con • verge (kən vurj´) vi., come together. *The two superhighways <u>converged</u> in a black and grimy wasteland.*

crowd starts to follow, at first walking fast, and then running after him.

We see a full shot of the street as suddenly Charlie's lights go off and the lights in another house go on. They stay on for a moment, then from across the street other lights go on and then off again.

MAN ONE. (*Shouting*) It isn't the kid . . . it's Bob Weaver's house.

WOMAN. It isn't Bob Weaver's house, it's Don Martin's place.

CHARLIE. I tell you it's the kid.

DON. It's Charlie. He's the one.

We move into a series of close-ups of various people as they shout, accuse, scream, <u>interspersing</u> these shots with shots of houses as the lights go on and off, and then slowly in the middle of this nightmarish <u>morass</u> of sight and sound the camera starts to pull away, until once again we've reached the opening shot looking at the Maple Street sign from high above.

The camera continues to move away until we dissolve to a shot looking toward the metal side of a space craft, which sits shrouded in darkness. An open door throws out a beam of light from the illuminated interior. Two figures silhouetted against the bright lights appear. We get only a vague feeling of form, but nothing more explicit than that.

FIGURE ONE. Understand the procedure now? Just stop a few of their machines and radios and telephones and lawn mowers . . . throw them into darkness for a few hours, and then you just sit back and watch the pattern.

FIGURE TWO. And this pattern is always the same?

FIGURE ONE. With few variations. They pick the most dangerous enemy they can find . . . and it's themselves. And all we need do is sit back . . . and watch.

> *Who, according to the aliens, is the most dangerous enemy that people can face? What qualities make this enemy dangerous?*

FIGURE TWO. Then I take it this place . . . this Maple Street . . . is not unique.

FIGURE ONE. (*Shaking his head*) By no means. Their world is full of Maple Streets. And we'll go from one to the other and let them destroy themselves. One to the other . . . one to the other . . . one to the other—

> *What comment is being made by the aliens about human nature?*

Now the camera pans up for a shot of the starry sky and over this we hear the Narrator's voice.

NARRATOR'S VOICE. The tools of conquest do not necessarily come with bombs and explosions and fallout.[9] There are weapons that are simply thoughts, attitudes, prejudices—to be found only in the minds of men. For the record, prejudices can kill and suspicion can destroy and a thoughtless frightened search for a scapegoat has a fallout all its own for the children . . . and the children yet unborn. (*A pause*) And the pity of it is . . . that these things cannot be confined to . . . The Twilight Zone! ■

---

9. **fallout.** Radioactive particles falling to earth; for example, after a nuclear explosion

---

words for everyday use

in • ter • sperse (in´tər spʉrs´) *vt.*, scatter among other things. *Pressed flowers were <u>interspersed</u> among the pages of her grandmother's poetry book.*

mo • rass (mə ras´) *n.*, perplexing state of affairs. *When Godfrey attempted to register his antique car, he found himself caught in a <u>morass</u> of paperwork.*

Respond *to the* SELECTION

Which character or characters in this selection do you admire? What makes this person or these persons different from the rest of the inhabitants of Maple Street?

Investigate, *Inquire,* and Imagine

Recall: GATHERING FACTS

1a. What explanation does the boy Tommy give of the peculiar events occurring on Maple Street? Where did he get his ideas?

2a. Why do the people turn in a mob toward Les Goodman's house? What does Les Goodman do sometimes at night?

3a. Where does Pete Van Horn go at the beginning of the play? What happens to him when he returns?

→ Interpret: FINDING MEANING

1b. What are the neighbors' first reactions to Tommy's story? How do their reactions change and why?

2b. Why do the neighbors consider Les Goodman's nighttime activity odd? What does their reaction to Goodman's nighttime activity reveal about their level of tolerance for differences?

3b. Why does Charlie do what he does to Pete Van Horn? What is the explanation suggested by one of the neighbors?

Analyze: TAKING THINGS APART

4a. How do the people on Maple Street react to what happens to their machines at the beginning of the play? What emotion leads them to react this way?

→ Synthesize: BRINGING THINGS TOGETHER

4b. The play suggests that humans can quickly resort to mob violence because of fears and hatreds. Yet in reality, there are also other motivators of human action that form a powerful force to curtail mob violence. What are some of these motivators?

Evaluate: MAKING JUDGMENTS

5a. Who or what are the real monsters in this screenplay?

→ Extend: CONNECTING IDEAS

5b. In the 1930s and 1940s the countries of Germany and Italy suffered severe economic hardships. Inflation and unemployment led people to look desperately for solutions and for scapegoats. In both countries, extremely brutal dictators came to power. What similarities can you find between these events in Germany and Italy and the events described in this play? What political point might the author be making?

Understanding *Literature*

SETTING. Review the definition of **setting** in the Literary Tools on page 921. Why is it important that this play be set on an ordinary street, one like thousands of others? What details at the beginning of the teleplay contribute to making the setting seem ordinary and wholesome?

MOTIVATION. Review the definition for **motivation** in the Handbook of Literary Terms. What motivates the people on Maple Street to turn into a mob? What small differences between people become magnified in their minds? What is this play saying about how people are capable of reacting toward one another in times of stress or crisis?

Writer's Journal

1. Imagine that you are the captain of the alien spaceship in "The Monsters Are Due on Maple Street." Write an entry for your **ship's log** telling about the experiment that you performed on Maple Street. Explain exactly what you did to bring about the events on Maple Street and why. Also explain the outcome or results of your experiment.

2. Imagine being a police officer who has arrived on the scene at the end of act I. Compose a **speech** that the police officer would deliver to calm the fears and suspicions of the residents of Maple Street.

3. Write a short **essay** on the questions: What are the "monsters" inside us, and what can we do to control them?

Integrating the Language Arts

Media Literacy & Study and Research

WRITTEN REPORT. Mob violence and collective hysteria have plagued American history—consider the Salem witch hunts; the Boston Massacre of 1770, which contributed to tensions before the American Revolution; Civil War anti-draft riots; the communist "witch hunts" led by Senator Joseph McCarthy in the 1950s; and race riots of the 1950s and 60s. Research one of these or a similar event in American or world history. Then research periodicals, newspapers, or Internet sites to find a recent (less than a year old) example of mob violence or collective hysteria in the world. Compare the events. How are the forces that led to the violence or hysteria similar? Write a report giving details of and indicating similarities between the two events.

Collaborative Learning

SCIENCE FICTION FAIR. Organize a science fiction fair. Begin by choosing a common topic in science fiction, such as the dangers of technology, visions of the future, or contacts with extraterrestrial intelligences. Then find science fiction stories, plays, and videotapes that deal with this topic. Working with your teacher and with other classmates, organize an event to present selections from these works. You may wish to do readings from stories, to present skits, and to show parts of films. You may also choose to come dressed as your favorite science fiction characters.

Guided Writing

CREATING A MULTIMEDIA PRESENTATION

What if one day people could inject genes into their bodies that changed the color of their hair or the shape of their eyes? What if astronauts discovered a parallel world in another solar system? What would that world be like? What if the climate of the earth suddenly shifted to steaming tropics? What if all the ice at the North and South Poles melted away? These are the kinds of questions science fiction writers ask when they create future worlds for their stories. In this lesson you have the opportunity to do the same—ask questions, imagine, and then create a future world.

Science fiction is a form of literature that lends itself to bold visions, strong images and intriguing tales. Using media such as computers, videos, artwork, and recordings, you will work in groups to design and produce a multimedia presentation expressing your vision of the future.

WRITING ASSIGNMENT. Your assignment is to work in small groups to script a multimedia presentation that examines a future world.

Student Model

A group of ninth grade students from northern California chose to explore one possible outcome of cloning. The students imagined a future world where cloning was used to create super-people and then came up with this script for their vision.

Multimedia is the presentation of information using the combination of text, sound, pictures, animation, and video. Common multimedia computer applications include *games, learning software, presentation software, reference materials,* and *web pages.* Most multimedia applications include links that enable users to switch between media elements and topics. The connectivity provided by these links transforms multimedia from static presentations with pictures and sound into a varied and informative interactive experience.

Multimedia Presentation
"The Clone Basketball Game"

VISUALS	AUDIO
A girl news anchor sits at a large desk facing the class. Spotlight on her. To the left of girl is a video screen with the words "Six O'clock News."	Music up and out: weird synthesized sounds. Anchor: Good evening. I'm Amy Shaw and thanks for joining us on the 6 o'clock news on this Wednesday, February 16, 2101.

EXAMINING THE MODEL. Science fiction looks at the facts of our current world and then stretches that knowledge to make predictions about the future. What facts are the students' presentation based on and what is their prediction for the future? What issues, moral or otherwise, does their vision touch on? Do you think it is a possible scenario?

The science fiction writer gets us to believe his or her story by including familiar details from our own world to help us experience the future world. You recognize the typical local television news format, the familiar rivalry between schools on the basketball court. What other details do the writers include to convince you their world is realistic? How do the visuals help or hinder the message?

On video: Picture of a basketball team wearing masks of the same face and another team without masks.

Anchor: Headlining the news today: High school students in Redmond, California made history last night. In a stunning first for young athletes, human students were allowed to challenge a clone team from nearby Marino Academy on the basketball court. Stay tuned for this amazing story.

Video fades to black. Spotlight on anchor.

Anchor: Since the first human clones came on the scene twenty years ago, human children have not been allowed to compete with clones in either academics or sports. Last night that all changed. Sara Sequent has the story.

Spotlight on girl reporter at a desk to the right of anchor.

Reporter: Thanks, Amy. So much for the notion that human children cannot compete with handpicked clones. Last night in a demonstration game between clones and human, the human students surprised everyone.

Video: Picture of young man. He is the same face that we saw earlier on all the team members.

Reporter: Marino Academy is an exclusive, private school with a basketball team that has been cloned almost entirely from Sam Waterman, one of the century's finest players. The Marino Comets have never lost a game since the school opened ten years ago. . .

Video: Picture of regular basketball team—all sizes and shapes.

Video: Picture of clone team again—all with identical "Sam" masks and all about the same size and build.

Spotlight on video: Medium Shot, woman coach standing against lockers.

Video: Medium Shot, cut to a human basketball player standing against lockers.

Reporter: On the other hand, the human students from Redmond, California attend public school and represent a mix of sizes and abilities.

Reporter: The clones were given telepathic blockers and told to refrain from astral projection. But these rules didn't appear to cause the Comets any worries. They laughed at their opponents when they came onto the floor. The clones flew into action at the whistle, taking the ball and sinking four baskets in a row with the human students unable to stop them.

Fifteen minutes into the game, human Jaguar, Mike Salens, was tossed off the court for arguing with the referee.

That was the low point for Redmond as Coach Belinda Max and player Rashan Zortex explain.

Coach: We lost our best scorer and we needed to rethink our approach after that.

Player: We were getting beat pretty bad and then we lost Mike. We knew we had to do something different. A bunch of us

"I would rather live in a world where my life is surrounded by mystery than live in a world so small that my mind could comprehend it."
—Harry Emerson Fosdick

noticed that the clone team had habits, like twitching their eyes to the right before they passed and faking with the same shoulder. We picked up on it and I guess we got lucky.

Spotlight back to reporter. Video screen fades to black.

Reporter: Lucky, indeed. In the second half, the Marino Comets stopped laughing. The Jaguars pulled ahead with one solid play after another. Freshman Jaguar, Jacob Case, a 6' 6" shooting guard made 25 points and the Comets couldn't seem to keep up with him. In the end, the Jaguars grabbed the lead to finish their stunning win: Jaguars 85 to the Comets' 70.

Video:
Picture of human Jaguars jumping for joy.

Reporter: Even though this was a demonstration match, it proves that human students are more capable than officials have thought. This historic game may open the future to more matches between the two groups.

Video picture fades away. Spotlight back on anchor and reporter

Anchor: Amazing story, Sara. Who would have thought?

Spotlight fades after anchor's speech.

Reporter: All I've got to say is those clones better watch out.

Prewriting

IDENTIFYING YOUR AUDIENCE. You will present your vision of the future to your classmates, so consider their interests and background when developing your piece.

FINDING YOUR VOICE. Your group will need to discuss and decide what your attitude will be toward your topic. Your voice should fit the attitude and purpose. Graphics, music, color, photographs, and words will be different for a humorous approach than for a serious or scary one. Since this is class presentation, you can, within reason, include references and words that students appreciate and understand.

WRITING WITH A PLAN. Creating a multimedia presentation is an excellent group activity because it requires many different skills. You will need to decide on a concept, write a text, find appropriate media, make a design plan, and create a working presentation. There is plenty for everyone to do and when you work together you will find that ideas flow.

- **Determine what issue you will explore and gather information about your issue.** Discuss as a group what issue you want to explore. The best way to make predictions about the future is to start by finding facts about the current world. Sources for information may include newspapers, television, magazines, the Internet, or organizations. Have one student keep all the information others provide in a notebook. What new technologies point to a different future? Imagine where these advances in science are leading.

- **Brainstorm your predictions of the future based on your research.** For your brainstorm, ask questions beginning with *What if?* to generate ideas. If the issue you want to explore is medical advances in genetic therapy, you might ask, "What if we find a cure for cancer and other lethal diseases? What would the world be like if people lived to be three hundred years of age?" List and analyze your ideas. Which interest the group the most? Which can be best expressed in a multimedia presentation?

- **Brainstorm a scenario and the media you will use to express that scenario.** Do you want to act out a story? Use a news format? Show a future family photo-album? Record a radio show? What media could you use to communicate your concept? Imagine where and how the media might be used.

- **Make a schedule.** Once you have a prediction of the future and a possible scenario, sketch out a brief schedule. Make a calendar that shows each step and when it should be completed. When will the group meet to write the rough draft of the script? When do you need to have a completed script? When do you need to get your equipment, actors, props and locations?

HANDLING DEADLINES. Break each deadline down into tasks and assign who will be responsible for what. This could be as simple as "Jackie will bring in two robot articles from magazines by tomorrow's meeting" or "On Wednesday, Jim will bring in three slides that we will look at for ideas about our made-up world." You may need to change the due dates on your schedule as more information becomes available.

WORKING ON A TEAM. For more information on effective group work, see the Language Arts Survey 6.12, "Working on a Team."

You will also need to research what media are available and when your group can use them. If no one in your group is familiar with the equipment, find someone in or out of school who can teach you. By what date do you need to be ready to shoot or record or create graphics?

The northern California students used the graphic organizer below to generate and organize ideas for their multimedia presentation. Make your own lists of visual and audio ideas that could be used to show your predictions of the future.

Student Model—Graphic Organizer

Visual	Audio
News anchor is live in front of class in spotlight.	News anchor telling the headline.
Video monitor shows photographs of clone team, regular team, action shots of the two teams playing.	Sports reporter tells the story of a basketball game, the clones vs. human kids.
	The human kids win.
Interview on monitor with coach and player.	A commercial break shows how food has changed or maybe how school or clothing has changed.
Commercial for some future product with people eating strange food	

Drafting

Once you know your scenario, you are ready to begin writing the script. Concentrate on writing a clear text that has a vision based on one issue. Include enough details about the future world so that a viewer would be able to describe it easily. Plan on creating a tight piece no more than five to ten minutes long. Print the words of your audio-visual script next to each other in chronological order so that the text is easy to read and follow.

You may decide to use lights, music, recordings, slides, live actors, charts, paintings, or video. There are many options, but keep in mind that too much media can clutter up a presentation and take away from your story. A multimedia presentation with a few media that work flawlessly is a better choice than one that is full of media that doesn't function.

Read your script aloud and time your reading. Make adjustments so that the piece will fit in the time allowed.

Language, Grammar, and Style
Effective Visuals

IDENTIFYING EFFECTIVE VISUAL INFORMATION. Visual information can help your viewer understand and remember your message. Charts, pictures, slides, and art are examples of the kinds of visuals that can enhance your text. Visuals serve many purposes. They can:

- focus and hold audience attention
- make complex ideas easier to understand
- show comparison
- summarize main thoughts
- help the audience grasp facts quickly
- serve as an outline or guide in the presentation

Read over the student model and identify the purpose (or lack of purpose) for each visual.

continued on page 943

Student Model—Draft

VISUALS	AUDIO
A girl news anchor sits at a large desk facing the class. Spotlight on her. To the left of girl is a video screen with the words "Six O'clock News."	Music: weird synthesized sounds.
	Anchor: Good evening. I'm Amy Shaw and thanks for joining us.
	Need to add date
	Wednesday, February 16, 2001

Try to find pictures for each of these headlines

Give more information without telling who won. Use sports writing language like they do in newspapers. ←

Anchor: Headlining the news today: High school students in Redmond, California made history last night. ~~They played a clone team from Marino Academy and won.~~

In a stunning first for young athletes, human students were allowed to challenge a clone team from nearby Marino Academy on the basketball court. Stay tuned for this amazing story.

VISUALS	AUDIO
Video fades to black. Spotlight on anchor.	Anchor: Since the first human clones, *came on the scene twenty years ago* genetically-mixed children have not been allowed to compete with clones in either academics or sports. Last night that changed. Sara Sequent has the story.
Spotlight on girl reporter at a desk to the right of anchor.	Reporter: Thanks, Amy. So much for the notion that human children cannot compete with hand-picked clones. Last night in a demonstration game between clones and human, the human students surprised everyone.

If you think about the purpose of your visuals, it will help you decide when and where to use them. In addition, here are some basic guidelines to help you create and display effective visuals:

- Keep the visuals simple. Avoid too many different fonts, many small pictures, or too many graphics.
- Clearly label visual displays so that your viewer knows what you are showing.
- Make the visual big enough to be easily seen from the back of a classroom.
- Use bullets or numbers to organize visual lists in your presentation.
- Use color with care. It can be distracting or make your graphics or text unreadable.
- Document all sources of graphic information just the way you would information from someone else's text. Give credit on any visual information that is not your own.

FIXING INEFFECTIVE VISUAL INFORMATION. When the students first developed a title page for their newscast, they used the visual below. How would you improve the sign so that viewers could more easily understand it?

The
Six O'Clock
News
WITH AMY SHAW AND SARA SEQUENT
Sponsored by SpeedLearn and ProRobotics Sports.

continued on page 944

USING EFFECTIVE VISUAL INFORMATION. Read over your script and look for visuals that do not follow the guidelines listed above. Does each visual serve a purpose? Are there any visuals that are hard to read or do not fit with the text? Are any of the visuals confusing or misleading? Adjust your script to achieve the best visual impact.

For additional help review the Language Arts Survey 6.11, "Displaying Effective Visual Information."

Video:	Reporter: Marino Academy is an exclusive, private school with a basketball team that has been cloned almost entirely from Sam Waterman, one of the century's finest players. The Marino Comets have never lost a game since the school opened ten years ago.
Picture of team.	
Maybe show the original person, Sam, instead.	

Self- and Peer Evaluation

After you have written your first completed draft, consider the questions below. If time allows, have other students complete a peer evaluation. Make any changes that will help your piece present a tight and effective message.

• What future does the text predict? Summarize the main ideas.
• Is the future world clearly portrayed or are there places where the text could be clearer?
• Which visuals focus or clarify the message of the piece? Which detract from the message?
• Which visuals grab your attention? Where could visuals be stronger?
• Do the visuals and text fit together smoothly into an effective presentation? If not, how could they be better matched?
• How long is the piece? Do you need to shorten or lengthen the text? Where and how could you do that?

Revising and Proofreading

Review your self- and peer evaluations. Revise your text and media elements after considering these comments. After you have completed a final proofreading of your text, test the entire presentation to make sure all elements are functioning.

When the students revised their rough draft, they found several places where they could improve the script by matching the visuals with the text. Do you agree with their changes?

Publishing and Presenting

Practice your presentation and note any difficulties. Make sure that all equipment is in order. Share your completed piece with your class and possibly other classes in the school.

Reflecting

Compare the process of composing an audio-visual script to writing by itself. How is the process different and what advice would you give to someone else just learning how to write a script?

Think about the impact of a multimedia presentation on the viewer. How can it create or influence our perceptions? What is the power of media —including text—to make or distort reality? Where have you seen examples of this?

"All the fun's in how you say a thing."
—Robert Frost

UNIT 12 review
Visions of the Future

Words for Everyday Use

Check your knowledge of the following vocabulary words from the selections in this unit. Write short sentences using each of these words in context to make the meaning clear. To review the definition or usage of a word, refer back to the page number(s) listed or the Glossary of Words for Everyday Use.

all-pervading, 929
biped, 905
broker, 886
cairn, 901
capricious, 915
catastrophic, 914
cavort, 879
consequently, 911
contorted, 932
contrivance, 916
converge, 933
defiantly, 930
degeneration, 904
dissolve, 879
ebb, 902
eccentric, 894
eject, 876
emerge, 877
endemic, 904
finite, 915
flotsam, 902

fruitless, 907
fundamental, 917
genially, 915
glaring, 892
haggard, 914
headlong, 916
idiosyncrasy, 930
imperative, 912
incisive, 927
incomprehensible, 906
incriminate, 928
inexplicably, 927
ingenious, 916
instill, 925
intersperse, 934
intimidate, 925
intuition, 917
knead, 877
languidly, 904
manifest, 879
materialize, 931

melancholy, 914
metamorphosis, 927
momentum, 894
morass, 934
motley, 902
notorious, 911
oblivious, 880
onrushing, 894
orifice, 905
overtake, 892
overwhelmingly, 918
paranoia, 878
precarious, 914
preoccupation, 878
recalcitrant, 917
recapitulate, 904
reflective, 923
refuge, 901
reinforcement, 880
remorseless, 901
reveal, 880

revelation, 927
revolt, 885
ritual, 878
sardonically, 907
skeptically, 916
sordid, 914
sublime, 881
superhuman, 886
sustain, 894
tentatively, 895
titanic, 878
transfixed, 923
tread, 876
tremulous, 879
urgent, 895
validity, 926
wane, 901
waver, 879

Literary Tools

Define each of the following terms, giving concrete examples of how they are used in the selections in this unit. To review a term, refer to the page number(s) indicated or the Handbook of Literary Terms.

caricature, 910
dramatic irony, 900
mood, 891
motivation, 921

narrator, 884
personification, 875
satire, 910
setting, 900, 921

simile, 884
theme, 875, 891

Reflecting
on your reading

Genre Studies

1. SCIENCE FICTION. **Science fiction** is highly imaginative fiction containing fantastic elements based on scientific principles, discoveries, or laws. Find three examples from the selections in this unit that require you, the reader, to suspend or alter certain elements of reality in order for the writer to make his or her point.

2. **SATIRE.** **Satire** is humorous writing intended to point out errors, falsehoods, foibles, or failings. It is written for the purpose of reforming human behavior or its institutions. What selections from this unit could be considered satires? What errors are they trying to point out in humanity and its institutions? What can be done to modify those errors?

3. **SCREENPLAY.** A **screenplay** is a drama written for the television or film. How would "The Monsters Are Due on Maple Street" be different if it were a short story instead of a screenplay? What are the advantages of writing it as a screenplay? What are the disadvantages?

Thematic Studies

4. **TECHNOLOGY.** What messages about technology are conveyed in "There Will Come Soft Rains" and "Nightmare Number Three"? In what ways are the messages negative? In what ways, if any, are the messages positive?

5. **REALITY VS. DISILLUSIONMENT.** In what ways is the theme in "The Test" similar to the theme in "Auto Wreck"? Why do you think both writers chose to write about car accidents to convey this theme?

6. **ESSENCE OF HUMANITY.** What are Arthur C. Clarke in "History Lesson" and Rod Serling in "The Monsters Are Due on Maple Street" saying about humanity? What "weapons" ultimately destroy humanity? How can we be a great civilization and yet be self-destructive?

for your READING LIST

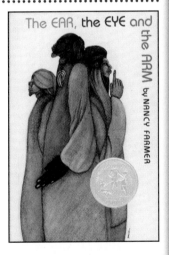

The Ear, the Eye and the Arm by Nancy Farmer. As the oldest son of General Matsika, Tendai knows he is not allowed to leave the grounds of the family home for fear of being kidnapped. But Tendai and his younger brother and sister sneak out of the high-security compound, and promptly disappear. His frantic parents hire a team of mutant detectives to find the children, who maddeningly stay just out of reach. Set in Zimbabwe in the year 2194, this novel creates a vivid picture of a complex futuristic society, while also portraying a young man's struggle to find his own identity and prove his worth to his father and himself.

Independent Reading Activity

PREDICTING THE FUTURE. After reading *The Ear, the Eye and the Arm,* work with a partner or in small groups to list some of the author's predictions of the future. Include inventions, environmental issues, and lifestyle changes. After completing your list, discuss which predictions you think are realistic or useful and which are unrealistic or impractical. Finally, write a list of your own predictions about the future. Select one prediction and plan a way to present it to the rest of the class. Use drawings, models, or other forms of media in your presentation.

Selections for Additional Reading

Tunnel in the Sky by Robert A. Heinlein. Rod Walker and his classmates are sent across the universe for a standard ten-day survival test, but something goes wrong and the students find themselves stranded on an unknown planet.

The Winds of Mars by H. M. Hoover. Annalyn Court, daughter of the president of Mars, had always planned to enter her father's honor guard when she finished her military training, but a revolution changes her plans and reveals dark secrets about her father and the world she has always known.

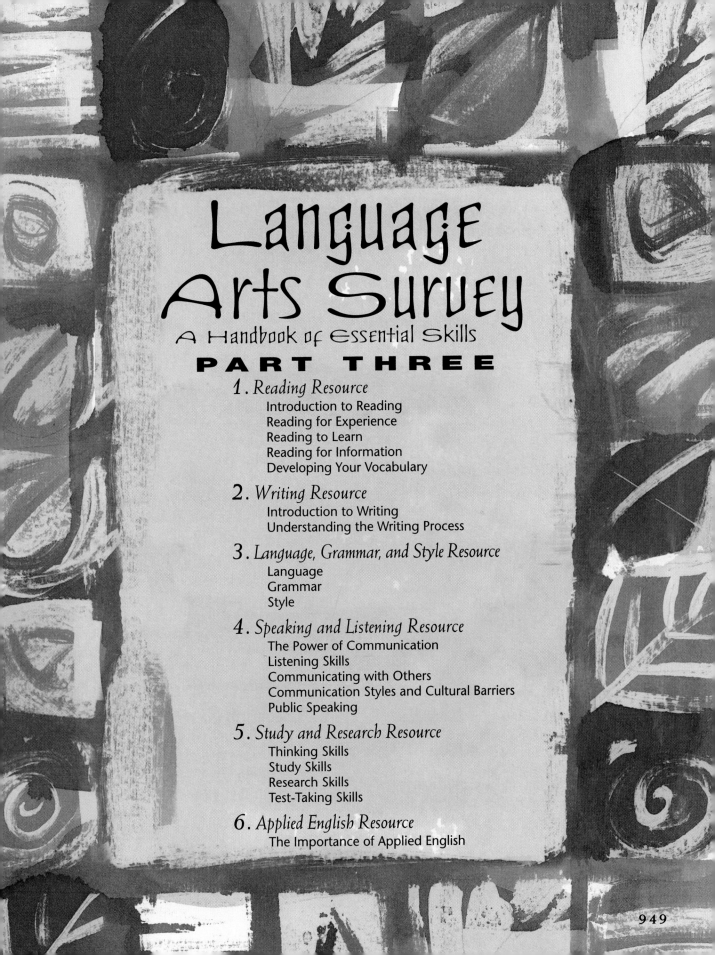

Language Arts Survey

A Handbook of Essential Skills

PART THREE

READING Resource

INTRODUCTION TO READING

1.1 Purposes of Reading

You as a reader read for different purposes. You might **read for experience**—for insights into ideas, other people, and the world around you. You can also **read to learn**. This is the kind of reading done most often in school. When you read to learn, you may read textbooks, newspapers and newsmagazines, and visual "texts" such as art and photographs. The purpose of this type of reading is to gain knowledge. Third, you can **read for information**. When you read in this way, you are looking for specific data in such things as reference materials, tables, databases, and diagrams.

1.2 Reading Independently

Learning to know and value your own response to what you read is one of the rewards of becoming an independent reader. Scanning, skimming, and reading slowly and carefully are three different ways of reading.

SCANNING. When you **scan**, you look through written material quickly to locate particular information. Scanning is useful when you want to find an entry in an index or a definition in a textbook chapter. To scan, simply run your eye down the page, looking for a key word. When you find the key word, slow down and read carefully.

SKIMMING. When you **skim**, you glance through material quickly to get a general idea of what it is about. Skimming is an excellent way to get a quick overview of material. It is useful for previewing a chapter in a textbook, for surveying material to see if it contains information that will be useful to you, and for reviewing material for a test or essay. When skimming, look at titles, headings, and words that appear in boldface or colored type. Also read topic sentences of paragraphs, first and last paragraphs of sections, and any summaries or conclusions. In addition, glance at illustrations, photographs, charts, maps, or other graphics.

SLOW AND CAREFUL READING. When you **read slowly and carefully**, you look at each sentence, taking the time to absorb its meaning before going on. Slow and careful reading is appropriate when reading for pleasure or when studying a textbook chapter for the first time. If you encounter words that you do not understand, try to figure them out from context or look them up in a dictionary. You may want to write such words in a notebook. The act of writing a word will help you to remember it later. When reading for school, take notes using a rough outline form. Writing the material will help you to remember it. For more information, see the Language Arts Survey 5.17, "Taking Notes, Outlining, and Summarizing Information."

READING FOR EXPERIENCE

1.3 Reading Literature: Educating Your Imagination

The most important reason to read literature is to educate your imagination. Reading literature will train you to think and feel in new ways. In the process of reading literary works and thinking about your own and others' responses to them, you will exercise your imagination and grow in ways that might otherwise have been impossible.

1.4 Educating Your Imagination as an Active Reader

Reading literature actively means thinking about what you are reading as you are reading it. Here are some important strategies for reading actively.

ASK QUESTIONS AS YOU READ.

- How does what I am reading make me feel?

- What is the setting of this work? How do things look, sound, taste, feel, or smell?

- Do I identify with any of the characters? What would I do if I were in their place?
- Does what I am reading involve a conflict? If so, what is it? How might it be resolved?
- What main images, ideas, symbols, or themes appear in the work?
- What can be learned from the experiences of these characters?

MAKE PREDICTIONS AS YOU READ. While reading, think often about what will come next. Think about how situations might turn out and what characters might do.

SUMMARIZE PARTS AS YOU READ. Especially when reading longer works, it is a good idea to stop, perhaps at the end of each chapter or section, to summarize on paper what you have read so far. Doing so will help you remember complicated literary works.

1.5 Keeping a Reader's Journal

Keeping a reader's journal will help you get the most out of your experience with literature. A reader's journal can first act as a log in which you record the title and author of the work you are reading. You may want to briefly summarize the work. You can write a journal response to questions such as those in the Reader's Journal and Respond to the Selection features of this textbook. Or you might write your own questions and respond to them.

> Why has the myth about Dædalus and Icarus lasted such a long time? It's probably because people can relate to the idea of wanting to fly higher and higher (in their dreams or goals or whatever), like Icarus did with his new wings. And of course, his father, Dædalus, warned him to be careful, just like most parents would, and Icarus didn't listen. He just took off, "drawn to the vast heaven" as the story goes, and the wings melted and Icarus fell. Well, people still want to fly high, even with the risks. I'm into extreme sports, and I can relate to Icarus.

1.6 Reading Silently versus Reading Out Loud

At times you will find it best to read silently and at other times to read out loud. When reading independently, you will probably make the most progress by reading silently. However, you may find it most helpful to read difficult passages out loud, even if softly. Hearing the words spoken can help make sense of complex passages. Another good time to read out loud is with poetry. By speaking the lines, you will be able to hear the rhythm and rhyme. Plays are also intended to be performed, and as with poetry, they are best appreciated when they are read out loud. This can be particularly helpful when different people take on the roles of different characters.

1.7 Reading with a Book Club or Literature Circle

No two people are exactly alike. Because of this, the experience that you have when reading a particular story, poem, or play will be different from the experience of each of your classmates. That's what makes discussing literature with other students interesting.

In a classroom literature circle, students get together in a small group to exchange insights, interpretations, and questions about literature they have read independently. Students in a literature circle may gather to discuss a selection and work together to understand it. Or they might read different literary works and meet to compare themes, writing styles of different authors, or different selections by the same author. Personal insights recorded in a reading log or journal can be shared when the literature circle meets.

1.8 Guidelines for Discussing Literature in a Book Club

At first, your literature group might need help from your teacher to get started, but soon your group should be able to conduct its own sessions if you follow these guidelines.

BEFORE THE SESSION
- Finish reading the assignment on time.
- Write down ideas in your reader's journal to help yourself get ready for the discussion.

- Mark places in the reading that you don't understand or want to discuss with your group. Also mark passages that you like, disagree with, or find especially worth remembering.
- Make sure you bring the literature to school instead of leaving it home on discussion day.

DURING THE SESSION
- Share your ideas and offer suggestions.
- Speak clearly, loudly, and slowly enough.
- Make eye contact with others.
- Answer questions other people ask.
- Ask questions to help other members clarify or expand on their points.
- Help keep the group on track and focused.
- Encourage others to talk.
- Disagree when you find it necessary without hurting others' feelings.
- Summarize and repeat your ideas when necessary.
- Give reasons for your opinions.
- Listen politely and ask follow-up questions.
- Try to understand and carry out other members' suggestions.

AFTER THE SESSION
- Evaluate your contribution to the group.
- Evaluate the overall success of your group.
- List ways to improve the next time.

READING TO LEARN

When you are reading to learn, you have two main goals: to expand your knowledge on a particular topic and to remember the information later. When you read to learn, you will often work with textbooks, nonfiction library books, newspapers, or journals, newsmagazines, and related art and photographs.

1.9 Reading Textbooks and Nonfiction Books

Textbooks provide a broad overview of a course of study. Textbooks should provide as much material as possible in an objective, factual way. Other nonfiction books provide information about actual people, places, things, events, and ideas. Types of nonfiction books include histories, biographies, autobiographies, and memoirs.

THE PARTS OF A BOOK. When previewing an entire book, you might want to glance at all of its parts. Every book will have some or all of the following parts:

THE PARTS OF A BOOK

Title page	Gives the title, author, and publisher
Copyright page	Gives information regarding the publication of the book and the copyrights protecting it from being copied or sold illegally
Table of contents	Lists the units, chapters, and/or subjects of the book and the page numbers where they are found
Preface, introduction, or foreword	Introduces the book
Text	Contains main part of the book
Afterword or epilogue	Gives conclusion or tells what happened later
Appendix	Gives additional information about subjects covered in the book, often in chart or table form
Glossary	Lists key words used in the book and their definitions
Bibliography	Lists sources used in writing the book or sources for further study
Index	Lists in alphabetical order the subjects mentioned in the book and pages where these subjects are treated

1.10 Reading Newspapers, Journals, and Newsmagazines

Newspapers, journals, and newsmagazines contain an enormous amount of information. Few people have time to read everything that appears in a newspaper each day. Nonetheless, staying aware of the news is important.

To get an overview of a newspaper, journal, or newsmagazine, skim the headlines and leads (the first sentence in a news story that explains the who, what, where, why, and how of the story). Read any news summaries included in the publication. Then read in depth any stories that seem particularly important or interesting. Also take advantage of the features and entertainment sections, which often reflect contemporary culture or the particular flavor of a community.

When reading news stories and editorials, make sure to distinguish between facts and opinions. **Facts** are statements that can be proved by observation or by consulting a reliable and objective source. **Opinions** are predictions or statements of value or belief. When you encounter opinions in the news, try to determine whether they are sound. Sound opinions are supported by facts. For more information, see the Language Arts Survey 5.2, "Distinguishing Fact from Opinion."

1.11 "Reading" Art and Photographs

In today's visually stimulating world, books and news media rely on art, photographs, and other visuals as well as the printed word to convey ideas. Being able to understand and interpret graphic images is important in today's society. Visual arts offer insights into our world in a different way than print does.

Careful examination of a painting can lead you to discover meaning in it and to compare and contrast the painting's meaning with that of a literary work or other piece of writing. The same thing happens with photographs. Learning to interpret other graphics or images—drawings, diagrams, charts, and maps—will help you to understand more easily how things work, what things mean, and how things compare.

1.12 Seeking Knowledge as an Active Reader

Reading to learn requires you to develop and use key skills to acquire knowledge. Reading actively means thinking about what you are reading as you read it. Slow and careful reading—and sometimes rereading—is necessary when reading to understand new and complex material. There are five key skills required for active reading:

- asking questions
- using your prior knowledge to make inferences and predictions about what you are reading
- recognizing what you do not know
- being able to synthesize information or create summaries, and
- knowing when to adapt your reading approach.

ASK QUESTIONS. Questioning allows you to realize what you understand about what you are reading. Before you read, think about your prior knowledge about the subject. When confronted with new information, your mind is doing many things at once. It is trying to figure out what it already knows about the topic and how this information connects to the information already in your brain. During reading, your mind is trying to answer these questions: What is the essential information presented here? How is this new information organized? After reading, you need to examine how your knowledge has grown, and identify the questions you still have about the material.

BEFORE READING

What is this going to be about?
What do I already know about the topic?
What's my purpose for reading this?

DURING READING

What does the author want me to know?
What is the significance of what I am reading?
What do I need to remember from this material?

AFTER READING

What have I learned?
What else do I want to know about this topic?

USE YOUR PRIOR KNOWLEDGE TO MAKE INFERENCES AND PREDICTIONS. While you are reading, you need to use what you already know about the topic to make inferences about what the author is saying. As you read, think about what might come next and try to make predictions about the next section of material.

KNOW WHAT YOU DO NOT KNOW. Recognizing when you do not understand something is as important as knowing that you do understand it. Try to form questions about the material you do not understand. Reread the text. Explain the topic to another student. Teaching someone else forces you to work to understand the material in deeper ways.

SUMMARIZE OR SYNTHESIZE TEXT. Summarizing what you are reading not only helps you identify and understand the main and subordinate points in the text, it is essential for storing and retrieving the information from long-term memory. Write a summary for each major section of the text you read. Create meaningful labels for a list of things or actions.

ADAPT YOUR READING APPROACH. If you become aware that you are not comprehending the material, you need to try another approach. Expert readers alter their reading strategies to compensate for any problems they have. You may need to experiment with different tactics like speeding up, slowing down, rereading, standing up and reading, reading the same material from another book, reading with a dictionary in your lap, or generalizing or visualizing what you are reading.

1.13 Strategies for Reading to Learn: SQ3R

A five-step reading strategy called SQ3R can help you reduce your study time and increase your ability to understand the essential information. The main steps of SQ3R are SURVEY, QUESTION, READ, RECALL, and REVIEW.

SURVEY
- Preview the organization of material.
- Glance at visuals and assess how they contribute to the meaning of the text.
- Skim headings and introductory paragraphs.

- Notice words in italics, boldface, and other terms that stand out.
- Ask yourself: What is the scope of the reading task? What should I learn from this material?

QUESTION
- Turn chapter titles and headings into questions.
- Ask yourself what the text is offering and what the author is saying.
- Ask yourself what you should know about the material and what you already know about it.
- Question graphics and visual materials. Try to translate the information they offer into your own words.
- Use words like *who, what, when, where, why,* and *how* to retrieve information.

READ
- Read and interact with the text.
- Underline or copy in your journal the main points.
- Make note of unusual or interesting ideas.
- Jot down words you need to define.
- Write your reactions to what you read.

RECALL
- Condense the major points of the text by writing recall cues.
- Summarize the material you have read. Reread any sections you don't clearly remember.
- Use graphic organizers to visualize or map out the material.
- Reread the text aloud if you need help recalling.

REVIEW
- After you have finished the chapter or book, go back and reread main headings and compare them to your notes.
- Review your notes, summaries, and definitions. Answer any questions you wrote.
- Ask yourself: What do I now understand? What is still confusing?

READING FOR INFORMATION

1.14 Reading Internet Materials, Reference Works, Graphic Aids, and Other Visuals

When you are reading for information, you are looking for information that answers a specific, immediate question; that helps you learn how to do something; or that will help you make a decision or draw a conclusion about something. One of the most important tasks for you to learn in school is how to access, process, and think about the vast amount of information available to you on the Internet and in online and print reference works, graphic aids, and other visuals.

Skills critical to reading for information include:
- determining your specific purpose for reading or viewing
- determining the creator's or author's purpose
- knowing how to interpret symbols and numeric data, and
- using an appropriate approach for the reading or viewing task.

DETERMINE YOUR SPECIFIC PURPOSE FOR READING OR VIEWING. Know why you are reading and what information you seek. State your purpose for reading as clearly as you can. Are you searching the Internet for a review of the movie you're unsure whether to see? Are you learning to operate a computer program? Are you researching data to determine if city regulations allow pet ferrets?

DETERMINE THE CREATOR'S OR AUTHOR'S PURPOSE. It is important to interpret the creator's or author's viewpoint. Ask yourself what the writer or illustrator wants the reader to think, believe, or do after reading this piece. Ask yourself if the author has bias on the topic that is affecting his or her views. If you are on the Internet, check for the following: Who is sponsoring the site? What hyperlinks are embedded in the site? Can you contact the website? When was the content on the site developed, and how might that affect the information it provides?

DETERMINE HOW THE AUTHOR USES SYMBOLS AND NUMERIC DATA. Work to understand how the creator or author uses symbols, icons, and abbreviated headings on tables. Use any icons as shortcuts for navigating through the text and also for identifying the important from unimportant material.

USE THE SEARCH APPROACH. Although your reading and viewing strategies should vary and relate

directly to your purpose, you may find the SEARCH method helpful when you are reading for information. SEARCH stands for SCAN, EXAMINE, ACT, REVIEW, CONNECT, and HUNT.

SCAN
- Look over the text and determine how the material is structured.
- Look for a table of contents, a glossary, an index, and other helpful sections.
- For an Internet site, look for a site map.

EXAMINE
- Do directions appear in a sequence of steps? Are there diagrams? Do directions reveal exactly what to do, or do you need to experiment a little?
- Is there a pattern in headings or icons?
- Are there any references to other sources of information?
- If you are on the Internet, does the site provide any links?

ACT
- Explore the procedures you are reading and learn by doing.
- If you are seeking data, take notes about the information. Is it exactly what you were looking for, or do you need to keep looking?

REVIEW
- Revisit the steps of a procedure to make sure you have them clear in your head.
- Compare similar resources and read any additional references or links provided.

CONNECT
- Connect the information to what you previously knew about the topic. How did you build on what you knew?
- Connect text with visual aids. How do the visual aids supplement the text? What additional information do they provide?

HUNT
- Look up the meanings of any new words you found.
- Use the help feature on a computer program to find answers to your questions.
- Make a visual diagram of a procedure if it will help you remember it.

1.15 Using Graphic Aids

Graphic aids are pictures, maps, illustrations, charts, graphs, diagrams, spreadsheets, and other visual materials that present information. Many people, including scientists, sociologists, economists, business analysts, and school administrators, use graphic aids to present data in understandable ways. Information presented in tables, charts, and graphs can help you find information, see trends, discover facts, and uncover patterns. Here are some common types of structures for presenting data.

PIE CHARTS. A pie chart is a circle that stands for a whole group or set. The circle is divided into parts to show the divisions of the whole. When you look at a pie chart, you can see the relationships of the parts to one another and to the whole.

BAR GRAPHS. A bar graph compares amounts of something by representing the amounts as bars of different lengths. In the bar graph below, each bar represents the value in dollars of canned goods donated by several communities to a food drive. To read the graph, simply draw in your imagination a line from the edge of the bar to the bottom of the graph. Then read the number. For example, the bar graph below shows that the community of Russell Springs donated $600 worth of goods during the food drive.

MAPS. A map is a representation, usually on a surface such as paper or a sheet of plastic, of a geographic area, showing various significant features of that area.

ARLINGTON HIGH SCHOOL POETRY SURVEY

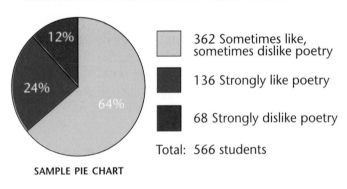

362 Sometimes like, sometimes dislike poetry

136 Strongly like poetry

68 Strongly dislike poetry

Total: 566 students

SAMPLE PIE CHART

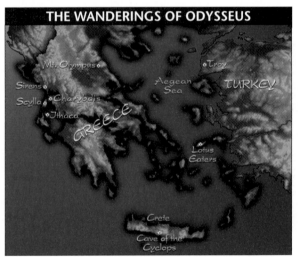

SAMPLE MAP

DOLLAR VALUE OF DONATED GOODS TO CANNED FOOD DRIVE

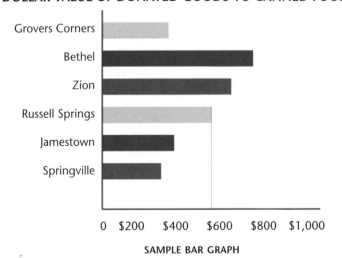

SAMPLE BAR GRAPH

Here are guidelines for working with graphics:

BEFORE READING

- Determine the subject of the graphic by reading the title, headings, and other textual clues.
- Determine how the data are organized, classified, or divided by reading the labels along rows or columns.
- Ask yourself: Why am I reading this document? What do I need to find? Where in this graphic is that information located?

DURING READING

- Survey the data and look for trends by comparing columns and rows, noting changes among information fields, looking for patterns, or navigating map sections.
- Use legends, keys, and other helpful sections in the graphic.
- Ask yourself: How do the data I need compare to other data on the graphic? What do those comparisons mean to me? What in this graphic can I skim or skip?

AFTER READING

- Check footnotes or references for additional information about the data and its sources.
- Ask yourself: Did this graphic answer my questions? If so, what are the answers? If not, where do I go to find the answers?

DEVELOPING YOUR VOCABULARY

1.16 Using Context Clues to Estimate Word Meaning

If you come across an unfamiliar word in your reading and you can't access a dictionary, you can often figure out the meaning of a word by using context clues.

One type of context clue is **restatement**. The author may tell you the meaning of the word you do not know by using different words to express the same idea in another sentence.

EXAMPLES

The dog snarled at Donald malevolently. The dog's vicious behavior warned Donald to stay away.

The restatement provides a context clue that malevolently means "maliciously, with intent to do harm."

Another type of context clue is **apposition**. An apposition is renaming something in different words. Look for a word or phrase that has been placed in the sentence to clarify the word you do not know.

EXAMPLE

Evan's conclusion was based on a fallacy, a false idea about how Maggie felt toward him.

Examples given in a sentence can also be used as context clues.

EXAMPLE

The words *dad*, *radar*, *noon*, and *tenet* are all palindromes; so is the phrase "A man, a plan, a canal, Panama!"

1.17 Using a Dictionary

Dictionary entries provide much more information about words than just their spelling and definitions.

The **pronunciation** is given immediately after the entry word. You can find a complete key to pronunciation symbols in the dictionary's table of contents. In some dictionaries, a simplified key is provided at the bottom of each page.

An abbreviation of the **part of speech** usually follows the pronunciation. This label tells the ways in which a word can be used (see the Language Arts Survey 3.7, "Parts of Speech Overview"). If a word can be used in more than one way, definitions are grouped by part of speech.

An **etymology** is the history of a word. In the first entry, the word *pole* can be traced back through Middle English (ME) and Old English (OE) to the Latin (L) word *palus*, which means "stake." In the second entry, the word *pole* can be traced back through Middle English to the Latin word *polus*, which comes from the Greek word *polos*, meaning "axis of the sphere."

Each **definition** in the entry gives a different meaning of the word. When a word has more than one meaning, the different definitions are numbered. The first definition in an entry is the most common meaning of the word.

Sometimes the entry will include a list of **synonyms**. The entry may also include an **illustration of usage**, which is an example of how the word is used.

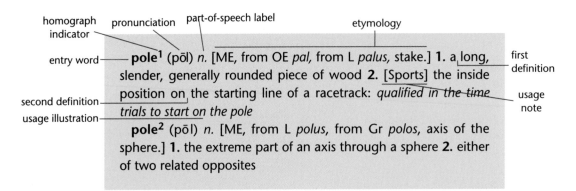

- homograph indicator
- pronunciation
- part-of-speech label
- etymology
- entry word
- first definition
- second definition
- usage note
- usage illustration

pole¹ (pōl) *n.* [ME, from OE *pal,* from L *palus,* stake.] **1.** a long, slender, generally rounded piece of wood **2.** [Sports] the inside position on the starting line of a racetrack: *qualified in the time trials to start on the pole*

pole² (pōl) *n.* [ME, from L *polus,* from Gr *polos,* axis of the sphere.] **1.** the extreme part of an axis through a sphere **2.** either of two related opposites

1.18 Using Glossaries and Footnotes

A **glossary** is an alphabetized list of words and their definitions. Glossaries usually appear at the end of an article, chapter, or book. **Footnotes** appear at the foot, or bottom, of a page. Sometimes they cite a source of information. Other times they define annotated words in order of appearance.

1.19 Learning Base Words, Prefixes, and Suffixes

Many words are formed by adding prefixes or suffixes to base words. (See the Language Arts Survey 3.101, "Using Spelling Rules I.") If you are unfamiliar with a word that is formed with a prefix or a suffix, check to see if you recognize the meaning of the base word and the meaning of its prefix or the suffix.

PREFIX	MEANING	EXAMPLE	MEANING
anti–	"against"	antibacterial	against bacteria
dis–	"not, opposite"	disagreeable	not agreeable
hyper–	"over, excessively"	hyperactive	excessively active
im–, un–	"not"	unusual	not usual
post–	"after"	postseason	after the season
re–	"again"	reprint	print again

SUFFIX	MEANING	EXAMPLE	MEANING
–er, –or	"one who"	narrator	one who narrates
–ful	"full of"	graceful	full of grace
–ish	"like"	childish	like a child
–ity, –ty	"state of, quality"	captivity	state of being captive
–less	"without"	fearless	without fear
–ment	"act of, state of"	achievement	act of achieving

1.20 Learning Synonyms, Antonyms, and Homonyms

A **synonym** is a word that has the same or nearly the same meaning as another word.

EXAMPLES   discover, find, locate, pinpoint

An **antonym** is a word that means the opposite of another word.

EXAMPLES   discover, conceal   give, take   success, defeat

A **homonym** is a word that has the same pronunciation as another word but with a different meaning, origin, and, usually, spelling.

EXAMPLES   bight, bite, byte

1.21 Exploring Word Origins and Word Families

The English language gains new words from many different sources. One source is the names of people and places. Another source of words in the English language is **acronyms**. Acronyms are words formed from the first letter or letters of the major parts of terms.

EXAMPLES

> sonar, from sound navigation ranging; NATO, from North Atlantic Treaty Organization; NASA, from National Aeronautic and Space Administration

Some words in the English language are **borrowed** from other languages.

EXAMPLES **deluxe** (French), **Gesundheit** (German), **kayak** (Eskimo)

Many words are formed by **shortening** longer words.

EXAMPLES

> ad, from advertisement; auto, from automobile; lab, from laboratory; phone, from telephone; stereo, from stereophonic

Brand names are often taken into the English language. People begin to use these words as common nouns, even though most of them are still brand names.

EXAMPLES Scotch tape, Xerox, Rollerblade

HAMBURGER
Originally known as "Hamburg steak," the hamburger takes its name from the city of Hamburg, Germany.

SPOONERISM
A slip of the tongue whereby the beginning sounds of words are switched; named after the Rev. William A. Spooner, who was noted for such slips. For example, after officiating at a wedding, he told the groom, "It is kisstomary to cuss the bride."

1.22 Jargon and Gobbledygook

Jargon is the specialized vocabulary used by members of a profession. It tends to be difficult for people outside the profession to understand. A plumber may speak of a "hubless fitting" or a "street elbow" (kinds of pipe). A computer programmer may talk of "ram cache" (part of computer memory) or a "shell" (a type of operating software for computers).

Jargon is useful to writers who want to describe authentically situations in which jargon would naturally be used. A novel about fighter pilots would probably be full of aviation jargon. A science fiction film might include futuristic jargon about warps in space and energy shields.

Gobbledygook is unclear, wordy jargon used by bureaucrats, government officials, and others. For example, the failure of a program might be called an "incomplete success." A bureaucrat might say, "We are engaged in conducting a study with a view to ascertaining which employees might be assigned to the mobility pool and how we might create revenue enhancement," when he means, "We are planning to cut jobs and increase taxes." Avoid the use of gobbledygook. Effective communication involves using precise language instead of muddy, vague vocabulary.

1.23 Clichés and Euphemisms

A **cliché** is an expression that has been used so often it has been colorless and uninteresting. The use of clichés instantly makes writing dull.

EXAMPLES quick as a wink, pretty as a picture

A **euphemism** is an inoffensive term that substitutes for one considered offensive.

EXAMPLES aerial mishap (for "plane crash")
building engineer (for "janitor")

1.24 Connotation and Denotation

A **connotation** of a word is all the associations it has in addition to its literal meaning. For example, the words *cheap* and *economical* both denote "inexpensive," but *cheap* connotes shoddy and inferior while *economical* connotes a good value for the money. A **denotation** of a word is its dictionary definition. Writers and speakers should be aware of the connotations as well as the denotations of the words they use. Contrast these denotations and connotations:

EXAMPLES

curious: nosy, snoopy, prying, inquisitive, inquiring

WRITING *Resource*

INTRODUCTION TO WRITING

2.1 The Writing Process

We live in an information age in which success in most fields requires well-developed writing skills. The most important action that you can take to shape a successful future for yourself is to learn how to write clearly and effectively. Almost anyone can learn to write well by learning the writing process. The writing process is simply the steps that a person takes to compose a piece of writing.

SEVEN STAGES IN THE PROCESS OF WRITING

PREWRITING · DRAFTING · SELF- AND PEER EVALUATION · REVISING · PROOFREADING · PUBLISHING AND PRESENTING · REFLECTING

STAGE	TASKS
1. **Prewriting**	Plan your writing: choose a topic, audience, purpose, and form; gather ideas; arrange them logically.
2. **Drafting**	Get your ideas down on paper.
3. **Self- and Peer Evaluation**	Evaluate, or judge, the writing piece and suggest ways to improve it. Judging your own writing is called **self-evaluation**. Judging a classmate's writing is called **peer evaluation**.
4. **Revising**	Work to improve the content, organization, and expression of your ideas.
5. **Proofreading**	Check your writing for errors in spelling, grammar, capitalization, and punctuation. Correct these errors, make a final copy of your paper, and proofread it again.
6. **Publishing and Presenting**	Share your work with an audience.
7. **Reflecting**	Think through the writing process to determine what you learned as a writer, what you accomplished, and what you would like to strengthen the next time you write.

While writing moves through these seven stages, it is also is a continuing cycle. You might need to go back to a previous stage before going on to the next step. Returning to a previous stage will strengthen your final work. Note also that the Reflecting stage can be done between any of the other stages. The more you reflect on your writing, the better your writing will become.

UNDERSTANDING THE WRITING PROCESS

2.2 Prewriting

In the **prewriting** stage of the writing process, you make a writing plan. You decide on a purpose, audience, form, and topic. You also begin to discover your voice and gather and organize ideas.

THE PARTS OF A WRITING PLAN

Purpose	A **purpose**, or **aim**, is the goal that you want your writing to accomplish.
Audience	An **audience** is the person or group of people intended to read what you write.
Voice	**Voice** is the quality of a work that tells you that one person wrote it.
Form	A **form** is a kind of writing. For example, you might write a paragraph, an essay, a short story, a poem, or a news article.
Topic	A **topic** is simply something to write about. For example, you might write about a sports hero or about a cultural event in your community.

2.3 IDENTIFYING YOUR PURPOSE. A **purpose**, or **aim**, is the goal that you want your writing to accomplish. For example, you might write to inform, to entertain, to tell a story, to reflect, or to persuade. Your writing might have more than one purpose. For example, a piece of writing might inform about an important event while persuading the audience to respond in a specific way.

MODES AND PURPOSES OF WRITING

MODE	PURPOSE	EXAMPLE
expository/informative writing	to inform	news article, research report
imaginative writing	to entertain, enrich, and enlighten by using a form such as fiction or poetry to share a perspective	poem, short story
narrative writing	to make a point by sharing a story about an event	biography, family history
personal/expressive writing	to reflect	diary entry, personal letter
persuasive/argumentative writing	to persuade readers or listeners to respond in some way, such as to agree with a position, change a view on an issue, reach an agreement, or perform an action	editorial, petition

2.4 IDENTIFYING YOUR AUDIENCE. An **audience** is the person or group of people intended to read what you write. For example, you might write for yourself, for a friend, for a relative, or for your classmates. The best writing usually is intended for a specific audience. Choosing a specific audience beforehand will help you make important decisions about your work. For example, for an audience of young children, you would use simple words and ideas. For an audience of fellow members of a technology club, you would use jargon and other specialized words that they already know. For more information, see the the Language Arts Survey 3.3, "Register, Tone, and Voice."

THINKING ABOUT YOUR AUDIENCE

- What people would be most interested in my topic?
- How much does the audience that I am considering already know about the topic?
- How much background information do I need to provide?
- What words, phrases, or concepts in my writing will my audience not understand? For which ones will I have to provide clear explanations?
- What can I do at the beginning of my writing to capture my audience's interest?

2.5 FINDING YOUR VOICE. Voice is the quality of a work that tells you that one person in particular wrote it. Voice makes a person's writing unique. Beginning with the prewriting stage and continuing through the rest of the writing process, a writer discovers his or her own unique voice. For more information, see the section about voice in the Language Arts Survey 3.3, "Register, Tone, and Voice."

2.6 CHOOSING A FORM. Another important decision that a writer needs to make is what form his or her writing will take. A form is a kind of writing. For example, you might write a paragraph, an essay, a short story, a poem, or a newspaper article. The following chart lists some forms of writing that you might want to consider.

FORMS OF WRITING

Adventure	Directions	Letter	Rap
Advertisement	Dream report	Magazine article	Recipe
Advice column	Editorial	Memorandum	Recommendation
Agenda	Epitaph	Menu	Research report
Apology	Essay	Minutes	Résumé
Appeal	Eulogy	Movie review	Schedule
Autobiography	Experiment	Mystery	Science fiction
Biography	Fable	Myth	Short story
Book review	Family history	Narrative	Slide show
Brochure	Fantasy	Newspaper article	Slogan
Calendar	Greeting card	Obituary	Song lyric
Caption	Headline	Parable	Speech
Cartoon	History	Paraphrase	Sports story
Character sketch	Human interest story	Petition	Statement of belief
Children's story	Instructions	Play	Summary
Comedy	Interview questions	Police/Accident report	Tall tale
Consumer report	Invitation	Poem	Thank-you note
Debate	Itinerary	Poster	Tour guide
Detective story	Joke	Proposal	Want ad
Dialogue	Journal entry	Radio or TV spot	Wish list

2.7 Choosing a Topic. A topic is simply something to write about. For example, you might write about a sports hero or about a cultural event in your community. Here are some ideas that may help you find interesting writing topics:

WAYS TO FIND A WRITING TOPIC	
Check your journal	Search through your journal for ideas that you jotted down in the past. Many professional writers get their ideas from their journals.
Think about your experiences	Think about people, places, or events that affected you strongly. Recall experiences that taught you important lessons or that you felt strongly about.
Look at reference works	Reference works include printed or computerized dictionaries, atlases, almanacs, and encyclopedias.
Browse in a library	Libraries are treasure houses of information and ideas. Simply looking around in the stacks of a library can suggest good ideas for writing.
Use the mass media	Newspapers, magazines, radio, television, and films can suggest good topics for writing. For example, a glance at listings for public television programs might suggest topics related to the arts, to history, or to nature.
Talk to people	Friends, relatives, teachers, and other people you know can be valuable sources for writing.
Do some freewriting	Simply put your pen or pencil down on a piece of paper and write about whatever pops into your mind. Write for two to five minutes without pausing to worry about whether your writing is perfect. Then look back over what you have written to see if you can find any good topics there.
Ask "What if" questions	Ask questions beginning with "What if" to come up with topics for creative writing. For example, you might ask, "What if a kid with a ham radio set received a message from space? Would people believe her?"
Make a cluster chart	Write some general subject such as music or sports in the middle of a piece of paper. Circle this subject. Then, around it, write other ideas that come into your mind as you think about the subject. Circle these and draw lines to connect the outer circles to the inner one.

2.8 Focusing a Topic. Sometimes a topic is too broad to be treated in a short piece of writing. When you have a topic that is too broad, you must **focus**, or limit, the topic.

WAYS TO FOCUS A WRITING TOPIC	
Break the topic into parts	For example, the topic "newspapers" could be broken down into reporting, copyediting, advertising, circulation, and so on.
Ask questions about the topic	Begin your questions with the words *who, what, where, when, why,* and *how.* Then ask what stands out about your topic or what interests you most.
Make a cluster chart or do some freewriting	For information on these techniques, see the Language Arts Survey 2.7, "Choosing a Topic."

GATHERING IDEAS

Once you have made your writing plan by identifying your purpose, form, audience, and topic, the next step in the prewriting stage is to **gather ideas**. There are many ways to gather ideas for writing. This section will introduce you to some of the most useful ones.

2.9 BRAINSTORMING. When you **brainstorm,** you think of as many ideas as you can, as quickly as you can, without stopping to evaluate or criticize the ideas. In brainstorming, anything goes. Sometimes even silly-sounding ideas can lead to productive ones. When you brainstorm in a group, often one person's idea will help another person to build on that concept. It is a good way to come up with creative, new ideas and innovative solutions to problems. Remember that no idea should be rejected in the brainstorming stage. Welcome all ideas with an encouraging response such as, "Great! Any other ideas?" Be sure to get contributions from everyone in your group and to record all ideas so they can be considered and judged later.

2.10 LEARNING FROM PROFESSIONAL MODELS. Professional models are works by published authors. They can be an excellent way to gather your own ideas. For example, one student was impressed by the way Bob Berman wrote about comets in his essay "Best Sky Sights of the Next Century" in Unit 6. He analyzed this informative essay and used it as a model when he wrote his own piece on astronomy for a science fair exhibit. For more examples, see the way Professional Models are used in the Guided Writing lessons at the end of each unit in this textbook.

2.11 KEEPING A JOURNAL. A **journal** is a record of your ideas, dreams, wishes, and experiences. Composition books, spiral notebooks, looseleaf binders, and bound books with blank pages all make excellent journal books. Some people even keep electronic journals on computers.

TYPES OF JOURNALS

A Diary, or Day-to-day Record of Your Life	August 3, 2003. Today I started keeping a journal. My brother Sean saw me writing and asked me what I was doing. When I told him, he said, "Don't go writing about me in that thing!" I guess he thinks he has all kinds of fascinating secrets! In a family as large as ours though, it is pretty difficult to have any privacy. . . .
A Reader Response Journal	There have been times when I have joined in doing something that I knew was wrong, just because my friends were doing it. I always felt guilty afterward and regretted doing it. In "The Monsters Are Due on Maple Street" everyone becomes suspicious of their friends and neighbors out of fear. I think that's what motivates the characters to develop into a mob. It's ironic that the aliens have figured out that humans' most dangerous enemy is themselves, and the attitudes and prejudices they have in their own minds.
A Commonplace Book, or Book of Quotations	"Many a thing is despised that is worth more than is supposed." —Chrétien de Troyes, <u>Arthurian Romances</u> "Who knows why people do what they do?" —Barbara Kingsolver, <u>Animal Dreams</u>
A Writer's Lab, or Collection of Ideas for Writing	What if some new supercomputer fell in love with one of its programmers? That could be a very funny or a very sad story. How would it begin? Let's see. One day Randall Meeks, a programmer for the Department of Defense, goes in to work and sits down at a terminal connected to ERICA, a new top-secret computer whose name means Efficient Risk-Instruction Computational Automaton. He logs onto the computer. A message appears, reading, "Good morning. You are looking quite handsome today." He thinks that one of the other programmers is playing a joke on him—but he's wrong.

CONTINUED

A Learning Log, or Record of What You Have Learned	Science: I read today in my science textbook that at the top of Mt. Everest, the highest point on the planet, there are rocks that were formed when sediment fell to the bottom of an ocean. How could the bottom of an ocean get pushed up to the top of the highest mountain? I'll have to ask in class tomorrow about that. Wow, Earth really is a turbulent thing, constantly changing. I wonder what it will look like millions of years into the future?
A Record of Questions	What causes the sky to glow at sunset? Chandra seems unhappy lately. How could I cheer her up? How does a person get a job as a zookeeper? Do you have to study animal behavior or biology or something like that in college? I think it would be fun to work with animals and to help save endangered species.
A Daily Organizer	Things to do tomorrow: • Go to library for book on Gandhi for social studies report • Go to football practice after school • Call Pete about concert tickets • Turn in overdue math homework

2.12 FREEWRITING. Freewriting is simply taking a pencil and paper and writing whatever comes into your mind. Try to write for several minutes without stopping and without worrying about spelling, grammar, usage, or mechanics. If you get stuck, just repeat the last few words until something new pops into your mind.

I really don't get this freewriting stuff. Just write? About what? Hum. I don't think of myself as a writer. I mean, sure, I can write and all, but . . . OK, I'm stuck . . . OK, I'm stuck. Funny, I was just thinking, what if some character in a short story kept saying that this was just a story that he was stuck in and the other characters thought he was crazy, and maybe he manages to figure out a way to pop in and out of the story that he was in, or maybe he can get into different stories at different times. Weird idea, I know it's like that idea that "maybe this is all just a dream." Dreams are interesting. There's that nursery rhyme, "Life is but a dream." What's that called. Oh, Row, Row, Row Your Boat. We used to sing that on the bus in elementary school.

To gather ideas about a specific topic, you might want to try **focused freewriting**. In a focused freewrite, you still write nonstop for a few minutes, but you stick with one topic and write whatever comes to mind as you think about that topic.

2.13 CLUSTERING. Another good way to tap what you already know is to make a **cluster chart**. To make a cluster chart, draw a circle in the center of your paper. In it write a topic you want to explore. Draw more circles branching out from your center circle, and fill them with subtopics related to your main topic. See the sample cluster chart on page 966.

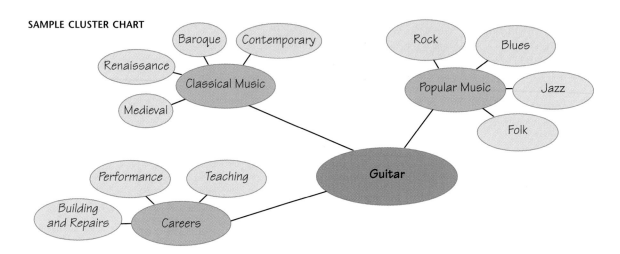

2.14 QUESTIONING: USING THE 5 Ws AND AN H. Using the 5 Ws and an H means asking the **reporting questions** *who, what, where, when, why,* and *how* about your topic. This questioning strategy is especially useful for gathering information about an event or for planning a story.

USING QUESTIONING (TOPIC: COWBOY POETRY)	
Who	Cowboy poets from the United States and other parts of the world
What	The Cowboy Poetry Festival, where cowboy poets gather
Where	Elko, Nevada
When	Held annually the last week in January
Why	So cowboys who love performing their songs, poetry, and stories can share them with others
How	This happens because of the huge interest in cowboy poetry and because of the major help from volunteers; the Western Folklife Center in Elko is a major organizer.

Sample paragraph using this information:

> Cowboy poets from all over the United States and around the world will gather once again this January for the Cowboy Poetry Festival. Hosted annually in Elko, Nevada, by the Western Folklife Center and hundreds of volunteers, the largest cowboy poetry get-together draws huge crowds who love to listen to cowboys share their songs, poetry, and stories.

2.15 IMAGINING: ASKING "WHAT IF" QUESTIONS. If you are doing imaginative or creative writing, ask questions that begin with the words *what if.* "What if" questions can spark your imagination and lead you down unexpected and interesting paths. It can also help you see another side of things and strengthen your own when writing a persuasive piece.

EXAMPLES What if I could run school for a week? What changes would I make?
What if I could go back in time to speak with a historical figure?
What if the greenhouse effect melted the polar icecaps and raised the levels of the oceans around the world? How would people respond?
What if the city council rejects the proposal for a teen center? How will this affect me and the kids I know?

2.16 COMPLETING VENN DIAGRAMS. If you are writing a comparison and contrast essay, one of the best ways to gather ideas is by completing a Venn diagram. A Venn diagram shows two slightly overlapping circles. The outer part of each circle shows what aspects of two things are different from each other. The inner, or shared, part of each circle shows what aspects the two things share.

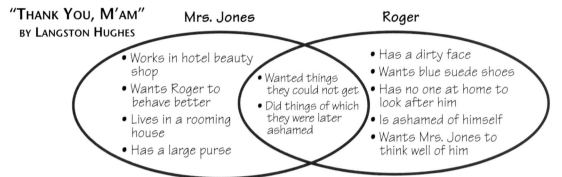

"THANK YOU, M'AM"
BY LANGSTON HUGHES

Mrs. Jones

Roger

- Works in hotel beauty shop
- Wants Roger to behave better
- Lives in a rooming house
- Has a large purse

- Wanted things they could not get
- Did things of which they were later ashamed

- Has a dirty face
- Wants blue suede shoes
- Has no one at home to look after him
- Is ashamed of himself
- Wants Mrs. Jones to think well of him

2.17 ANALYZING. To **analyze** is to break something down into its parts and then think about how the parts are related. Analyzing is a way to sort out information about a topic. An **analysis chart** can help you to list the parts and to describe each one.

ANALYSIS OF "LOCAL SENSIBILITIES" BY WING TEK LUM		
PART	**DESCRIPTION**	**RELATION OF PART TO WHOLE**
Stanza 1	Describes associations with pineapple	Introduces characteristics of Hawaiian industry
Stanza 2	Describes surfer Duke	Introduces a native Hawaiian character
Stanza 3	Describes Portuguese man-of-war	Introduces characteristics of Hawaiian animal life
Stanza 4	Describes what "packages" mean to him	Introduces a colloquial Hawaiian expression
Stanza 5	Describes the Sand Island roundup	Introduces an event from Hawaiian history
Stanza 6	Describes nature of Hawaii	Summarizes what Hawaii means to him

2.18 SENSORY DETAIL CHARTS. Most people have the use of five major **senses**: sight, sound, touch, taste, and smell. The larger the number of these senses you use to observe something, the more you will notice about it. A **sensory detail chart** can help you to collect information about something so that you can describe it thoroughly. To make a sensory detail chart, begin by writing your subject at the top of the page. Make a box with a column for each of the five senses. In the column under each heading, list details about the subject that you learn from that sense.

SENSORY DETAILS OF A MARATHON				
SIGHT	**SOUND**	**TOUCH**	**TASTE**	**SMELL**
hundreds of runners of all ages	starting gun	hot, sore feet from standing so long	hot dogs and lemonade from vendor carts	hot asphalt
news reporters and onlookers	crowds clapping			perspiration
running clothes	running shoes slapping on asphalt	stinging face from sun and wind		

2.19 TIME LINES. A **time line** can be useful when you are planning to write a story or a historical account. It gives you an overview of the sequence of events during a particular time period. To make a time line, draw a line on a piece of paper and divide it into equal parts. Label each part with a date or a time. Then add key events at the right places along the time line.

Landmark Events in the History of the Civil Rights Movement (1950–1975)

1950	1955	1960	1965	1970	1975
	1954 *Brown v. Board of Education*: U.S. Supreme Court bans racial segregation in public schools	**1960** Sit-in at Greensboro, NC, lunch counter	**1965** March for voting rights from Selma to Montgomery, AL; Voting Rights Act passed; Malcolm X assassinated; race riots in Watts section of Los Angeles	**1971** Supreme Court rules that busing of students may be ordered to achieve desegregation	

2.20 STORY MAPS. A **story map** is a chart that shows the various parts of a fable, myth, tall tale, legend, short story, or other fictional work. Most story maps include the following elements:

ELEMENTS OF A STORY MAP	
ELEMENT	**DESCRIPTION**
Setting	The time and place in which the story occurs
Mood	The emotion created in the reader by the story
Conflict	A struggle between two forces in the story
Plot	The series of events taking place in the story
Characters	The people (or sometimes animals) who play roles in the story
Theme	The main idea of the story

2.21 PRO AND CON CHARTS. A **pro and con chart** shows arguments for and against taking a particular position on some issue. To create a pro and con chart, begin by writing a statement, called a **proposition**, at the top of a piece of paper. Under the proposition, make two columns, one labeled *Pro* and the other, *Con*. In the pro column, list arguments in favor of the proposition. In the con column, list arguments against the proposition.

PRO AND CON CHART	
Proposition: All students should take an hour of physical education each day.	
Pro	**Con**
—would keep students in good physical condition	—would take time away from academic studies
—improved health would also improve students' ability to think clearly and work hard	—the same ends might be achieved in less time per day

2.22 INTERVIEWING. In an **interview**, you meet with someone and ask him or her questions. Interviewing experts is an excellent way to gain information about a particular topic. For example, if you are interested in writing about the making of pottery, you might interview an art teacher, a professional potter, or the owner of a ceramics shop. When planning an interview, list the questions you would like to ask, including some about the person's background as well as about your topic. Other questions might occur to you as the interview proceeds. See the Language Arts Survey 4.14, "Conducting an Interview."

2.23 RESEARCHING FOR IDEAS. No matter what your subject, you can probably find information about it by doing research in reference works. **Reference works** include encyclopedias, dictionaries, almanacs, atlases, indexes, Internet sites, and more. For additional information about reference materials and how to find them, see the Language Arts Survey 5.20, "Using Reference Works," and 5.37, "Keeping a Research Journal."

Organizing Ideas

2.24 WRITING PARAGRAPHS. After you have gathered ideas for a piece of writing, the next step is to organize these ideas in a useful and reader-friendly way. The most basic organization of ideas occurs in forming paragraphs. A good paragraph is a carefully organized unit of writing. It develops a sequence in narrative writing or develops a particular topic in informational or persuasive writing.

PARAGRAPHS WITH TOPIC SENTENCES. Many paragraphs include a topic sentence that presents a main idea. The topic sentence can be placed at the beginning, middle or end of the paragraph. Topic sentences usually appear early on in the paragraph and are commonly followed by one or more supporting sentences. Often these supporting sentences begin with transitions that relate them to the other sentences or to the topic sentence. This type of paragraph may end with a clincher sentence, which sums up what has been said in the paragraph.

EXAMPLE

TOPIC SENTENCE	*Romeo and Juliet* is probably the best known and best loved of all William Shakespeare's plays. Generations of audiences have been able to relate to the two "star-cross'd" young lovers, whose passion is doomed from the start by the bitter feuding between their fami-
SUPPORTING SENTENCES	lies. Since Elizabethan times, the play has been interpreted in many forms, inspiring operas, ballets, musicals, and poetry. It has been translated into nearly every language and has been updated in such modern contexts as gangland New York City, the Israeli-
CLINCHER SENTENCE	Palestinian conflict in Jerusalem, and war-torn Sarajevo. The power of the story is evident in that it has been told for centuries.

Insights: Romeo and Juliet over the Centuries, page 405

PARAGRAPHS WITHOUT TOPIC SENTENCES. Most paragraphs do not have topic sentences. In a narrative piece of writing, many paragraphs state a series of events, and no sentence in the paragraph sums up the events. In good narrative writing, the sequence of events appears in chronological order. Descriptive writing may contain paragraphs organized spatially—in the order in which the speaker or narrator sees, hears, feels, smells, and tastes things in a given situation.

EXAMPLE

No one is at home, in all this house, in all this land. It is a long while before their return. I shall move as they would trust me not to, and as I could not, were they here. I shall touch nothing but as I would touch the most delicate wounds, the most delicate objects.

James Agee, from *Let Us Now Praise Famous Men*, page 511

PARAGRAPH UNITY. The ideas in a paragraph should be tightly linked, or "together." They should be ordered and linked in a logical and easily understandable way. You can organize a paragraph in the order of time (chronologically), in the order of importance, or in order to achieve a specific purpose, such as describing or comparing and contrasting. To link the ideas in a paragraph, use connective words and phrases. In informational or persuasive paragraphs, *for example, as a result, finally, therefore,* and *in fact* are common connectives. In narrative and descriptive paragraphs, words like *first, then, suddenly, above, beyond, in the distance,* and *there* are common connectives. In comparison-contrast paragraphs, common phrases include *similarly, on the other hand,* and *in contrast.* In cause and effect paragraphs, linkers include *one cause, another effect, as a result, consequently, finally,* and *therefore.*

2.25 WRITING A THESIS STATEMENT. One way to start organizing your writing, especially if you are writing an informative or persuasive essay, is to identify the main idea of what you want to say. Present this idea in the form of a sentence or two called a thesis statement. A **thesis statement** is simply a sentence that presents the main idea or the position you will take in your essay.

> **THESIS FOR A PERSUASIVE ESSAY**
> The development at Rice Creek Farm should be stopped because it will destroy one of the best natural areas near the city.

> **THESIS FOR AN INFORMATIVE ESSAY**
> Wilma Rudolph was an athlete who succeeded in the elite sport of tennis before the world was willing to recognize her.

2.26 WRITING MAIN IDEAS AND SUPPORTING DETAILS. Once you have a thesis statement, the next step is to select several main ideas to support your thesis statement. Begin by writing your thesis at the top of a piece of paper. Then list the main points that you will use to support your thesis. For each main idea, list several supporting details—statements, facts, examples, quotes, and illustrations that explain or demonstrate your idea.

THESIS: The development at Rice Creek Farm should be stopped because people will be unable to enjoy the area, a considerable amount of wildlife will be harmed, and an important water resource will be lost.

- People will be unable to enjoy the area.
  — Hundreds of people of all ages now bike, run, and swim in the area in the summer and ski in the winter. Last year's recreation survey was completed by 653 people. Eighty-five percent said that they visited Rice Creek Farm at least twice a month.
  — The development of an industrial park would ban people from using the area. It will become a factory site instead of a wooded recreation area. "The industrial park site would be strictly off limits to the public for their own protection," developer Orrin Q. Smedley said in the *Rice Creek Times.*

- A considerable amount of wildlife will be harmed.
  — The wooded area will be completely eliminated, destroying habitat.

CONTINUED

— The species that will be lost will include deer, fox, racoons, skunks, and wild birds, according to the parks board supervisor.

- An important water resource will be lost.
  — The water resource has many uses, including recreational and agricultural.
  — The quality of our city water supply depends on the preservation of this habitat.

2.27 CHOOSING A METHOD OF ORGANIZATION. Writing can be organized in different ways.

METHOD	DESCRIPTION
Chronological Order	Give events in the order in which they happen or should be done; connect events by using transition words such as *first, second, next, then,* and *finally.* Chronological organization would be a good method for relating a narrative, giving a recipe, writing a how-to article on building a bird-feeder, or to describe a process, such as what happens when a volcano erupts.
Spatial Order	Describe parts in order of their location in space, for example, from back to front, left to right, or top to bottom; connect your descriptions with transition words or phrases such as *next to, beside, above, below, beyond,* and *around.* Spatial order would be a useful form for an article describing a kitchen renovation, or a descriptive passage in a science fiction story set in a space station.
Order of Importance	List details from least important to most important or from most important to least important; connect your details with transition phrases such as *more important, less important, most important,* and *least important.* A speech telling voters why they should elect you class president could be organized from the least important reason and build to the most important reason.
Comparison and Contrast Order	Details of two subjects are presented in one of two ways. In the first method, the characteristics of one subject are presented, followed by the characteristics of the second subject. This method would be useful to organize an essay that compares and contrasts two fast-food chains. You could use this method to say why one is superior to another. "BurgerWorld has the most restaurants. They broil their hamburgers, and offer a line of low-fat meals. Ma's Burgers has far fewer restaurants, fries their hamburgers, and offers no low-fat choices." In the second method, both subjects are compared and contrasted with regard to one quality, then with regard to a second quality, and so on. An essay organized according to this method could compare the platforms of two political parties, issue by issue: the environment, the economy, and so on. Ideas are connected by transitional words and phrases that indicate similarities or differences, such as *likewise, similarly, in contrast, a different kind,* and *another difference.*
Cause and Effect Order	One or more causes are presented followed by one or more effects, or one or more effects are presented followed by one or more causes. A public health announcement warning about the dangers of playing with fire would be usefully organized by cause and effect. An essay discussing the outbreak of World War I and the events that led up to it could be organized by effect and causes. Transitional words and phrases that indicate cause and effect include *one cause, another effect, as a result, consequently,* and *therefore.*

CONTINUED

Part by Part Order	Ideas are presented according to no *overall* organizational pattern. However, each idea is connected logically to the one that precedes it and/or to the one that follows it. A letter to a friend might be organized part by part. One paragraph might discuss a party the writer just attended and the next could focus on the writer's feelings about a person he or she met there. After chronological order, this is the most common method for organizing ideas in writing.
	Transitional words or phrases include anything that indicates the relationship or connection between the ideas.

2.28 OUTLINING. An **outline** is an excellent framework for highlighting main ideas and supporting details. Rough and formal outlines are the two main types of outlines writers commonly use.

2.29 ROUGH OUTLINES. To create a **rough outline**, simply list your main ideas in some logical order. Under each main idea, list the supporting details set off by dashes.

What Is Drama?

Definition of Drama
—Tells a story
—Uses actors to play characters
—Uses a stage, properties, lights, costumes, makeup, and special effects

Types of Drama
—Tragedy
  —Definition: A play in which the main character meets a negative fate
  —Examples: <u>Antigone</u>, <u>Romeo and Juliet</u>, <u>Death of a Salesman</u>
—Comedy
  —Definition: A play in which the main character meets a positive fate
  —Examples: <u>A Midsummer Night's Dream</u>, <u>Cyrano de Bergerac</u>, <u>The Odd Couple</u>

2.30 FORMAL OUTLINES. A **formal outline** has headings and subheadings identified by numbers and letters. One type of formal outline is the **topic outline**. Such an outline has entries that are words or phrases rather than complete sentences.

What Is a Myth?

I. Definition of myth
   A. Ancient story involving gods
      1. Multiple gods in mythology
      2. Gods given human characteristics
   B. Often about origins
      1. Reflect prescientific worldview
      2. Gods and humans actively participate
   C. Often about heroes
II. Creation myths
   A. The Greek myth of the origins of the universe
   B. The Greek myth of the origins of human beings
III. Origin myths
   A. Arachne and the origins of spiders
   B. Phaëthon and the origins of deserts
IV. Hero myths
   A. Theseus and the Minotaur
   B. Herakles and the twelve labors

2.31 Drafting

After you have gathered your information and organized it, the next step in writing is to produce a draft. A **draft** is simply an early attempt at writing a paper. When working on a draft, keep in mind that you do not have to get everything just right the first time through. The beauty of a draft is that you can rework it many times until you are satisfied with the final product.

Different writers approach drafting in different ways. Some prefer to work slowly and carefully, perfecting each part as they go. Producing such a **careful draft** can be rewarding because you get to see a finished, polished piece emerging part by part. However, many writers find that perfecting each part as they come to it bogs down the process. These writers prefer to write a discovery draft, getting all their ideas down on paper in rough form and then going back over the paper to work it into shape. When writing a **discovery draft**, you do not focus on spelling, grammar, usage, and mechanics. You can take care of those matters during revision.

2.32 DRAFTING AN INTRODUCTION. The purpose of an introduction is to capture your reader's attention and establish what you want to say. An effective introduction can start with a quotation, a question, an anecdote, an intriguing fact, or a description that hooks the reader to keep reading.

An effective introduction can open with:

A QUOTE	"That's one small step for man, one giant leap for mankind." With these words, Neil Armstrong signaled his success as the first human to set foot on the moon...
A QUESTION	What would it be like if all the birds in the world suddenly stopped their singing?
AN ANECDOTE	When my brother was nineteen, he volunteered in a homeless shelter making sure people had a safe place to spend the night. He told me once that he would never forget the time he met...
A FACT	More than a million new web pages appear each day on the Internet...
A DESCRIPTION	Along the murky bottom of the ocean floor, at the deepest part of the ocean, lies the giant squid, a creature so elusive that few people have ever seen it. For hundreds of years, no one knew it really existed—although tales of sea monsters had long hinted of it.

2.33 DRAFTING BODY PARAGRAPHS. When writing the body of an essay, refer to your outline. Each heading in your outline will become the main idea of one of your paragraphs. To move smoothly from one idea to another, use transitional words or phrases. As you draft, include evidence from documented sources to support the ideas that you present. This evidence can be paraphrased, summarized, or quoted directly. For information on documenting sources, see the Language Arts Survey 5.36, "Documenting Sources," and 5.43, "Paraphrasing, Summarizing, and Quoting."

2.34 DRAFTING A CONCLUSION. In the conclusion, bring together the main ideas you included in the body of your essay and create a sense of closure to the issue you raised in your thesis. There is no single right way to conclude a piece of writing. Possibilities include:

- making a generalization
- restating the thesis and major supporting ideas in different words
- summarizing the points made in the rest of the essay
- drawing a lesson or moral
- calling on the reader to adopt a view or take an action
- expanding on your thesis or main idea by connecting it to the reader's own interests
- linking your thesis to a larger issue or concern

2.35 USING TRANSITIONS EFFECTIVELY. Transitions are words and phrases that help you move smoothly from one idea to the next in your writing. The transition words themselves depend on the method of organization you are using in your paper. For lists of these words and when to use them, see the Language Arts Survey 2.27, "Choosing a Method of Organization."

2.36 WRITING NARRATIVE, DIALOGUE, DESCRIPTION, AND EXPOSITION. Some writing purposes do not require a thesis or a formal outline. They rely on other types of writing to present their ideas effectively. These types include narrative, dialogue, description, and exposition.

TYPE OF WRITING	DESCRIPTION AND ORGANIZATION
Narrative	As with the narrative mode, this method tells a story or presents events using time, or **chronological order**, as a way of organization.
Dialogue	Writing using this method presents words as they were actually spoken by people. Quotation marks are usually used to set off direct speech.
Description	Writing with this method portrays a character, an object, or a scene. Descriptions make use of sensory details—words and phrases that describe how things look, sound, smell, taste, or feel. Descriptive writing frequently uses **spatial order** as a method of organization.
Exposition	Writing using this method presents facts or opinions in an organized manner. There are many ways to organize exposition. Among the most common are the following: **Analysis** breaks something into its parts and shows how the parts are related. **Cause and effect order** identifies and analyzes the causes and effects of something. **Classification order** involves placing subjects into categories, or classes, according to their properties or characteristics. These groups are then presented, one-by-one, in some reasonable order. **Comparison and contrast order** is a method of organization in which details about the similarities and differences between two subjects are presented in one of two ways. In the first method, characteristics of one subject are presented, followed by the characteristics of a second subject. In the second method, both subjects are compared and contrasted with regard to one characteristic, then with regard to a second characteristic, and so on. **Definition** explains a concept or idea and examines its qualities. **Problem/Solution** writing analyzes a problem and proposes possible solutions. It can be objective or persuasive. **Process/How-to** writing presents the steps in a process or gives the reader directions on how to do something.

2.37 Self- and Peer Evaluation

When you evaluate something, you examine it carefully to find its strengths and weaknesses. Evaluating your own writing is called **self-evaluation**. A **peer evaluation** is an evaluation of a piece of writing done by a classmate, or peer.

2.38 HOW TO EVALUATE A PIECE OF WRITING. After producing a rough draft of a piece of writing, the next step is to evaluate that draft to find out what you or the writer you are evaluating should improve.

A good evaluation practice is to read through the piece of writing three times:

- **First, check for content.** If you are evaluating your own writing, make sure that you have said all that you want to say, that you have not left out important details, and that you have not included unimportant or unrelated details. If you are evaluating a peer's writing, make sure the content is clear, that nothing is missing to prevent the work from carrying the reader forward, and that the writer has not included any unrelated details.

- **Second, check for organization.** Make sure that the ideas in the writing are presented in a reasonable order.
- **Third, check the style and language** of the piece. Make sure that the language is appropriately formal or informal, that the tone is appropriate to the message and the audience the piece addresses, and that the writer has defined any key or unfamiliar terms.

As you check the writing piece, make notes about what the writer needs to revise, or change. See the Language Arts Survey 2.42, "A Revision Checklist," for further information on what to look for as you evaluate your or a peer's writing.

2.39 How to Deliver Helpful Criticism

- **Be focused.** Concentrate on content, organization, and style. Do not concentrate at this point on proofreading matters such as spelling and punctuation; they can be fixed later.
- **Be positive.** Let the writer know what he or she has done right. Show how the paper could be improved by making the changes that you are suggesting.
- **Be specific.** Give the writer concrete ideas for improving his or her work. For example, if you think that two ideas seem unconnected, suggest a way in which they might be connected clearly.
- **Be tactful.** Consider the other person's feelings, and use a pleasant tone of voice. Do not criticize the writer. Instead, focus on the writing.

2.40 How to Benefit from Helpful Criticism

- **Tell your evaluator specific concerns.** For example, if you are wondering whether something you have written is clear, ask the evaluator if he or she understands that part of what you have written.
- **Ask questions to clarify comments** that your evaluator makes.
- **Accept your evaluator's comments graciously.** Remember that criticisms can be helpful. They can help you to identify weaknesses and produce a better piece through revision. If, on the other hand, you think that a given suggestion will not truly improve your writing, you do not have to follow it. There are many ways to strengthen writing. By reflecting on reviewer comments and your own self-evaluation, you will be ready to go on to the next step: revision.

2.41 Revising

After identifying weaknesses in a draft through self-evaluation and peer evaluation, the next step is to **revise** the draft. Here are four basic ways to improve meaning and content:

ADDING OR EXPANDING. Sometimes writing can be improved by adding details, examples, or transitions to connect ideas. Often a single added adjective, for example, can make a piece of writing clearer or more vivid.

| UNREVISED | Wind whistled through the park. |
| REVISED | A **bone-chilling** wind whistled through the park. |

At other times, you will find you will need to add details to back up your main idea.

| UNREVISED | Everyone uses the park so its destruction would be a major loss to the community. |
| REVISED | Of the 653 people who responded to the survey, 85 percent said they would consider the destruction of the park a major loss to the community. |

CUTTING OR CONDENSING. Often writing can be improved by cutting unnecessary or unrelated material.

UNREVISED	Watson was firmly determined to find the structure of the DNA molecule.
REVISED	Watson was determined to find the structure of the DNA molecule.

REPLACING. Sometimes weak writing can be made stronger through more concrete, more vivid, or more precise details.

UNREVISED	Several things had been bothering Bill.
REVISED	Several personal problems had been bothering Bill.
UNREVISED	Chandra lived in a house down the street.
REVISED	Chandra lived in a Garrison colonial down Mulberry Street.

MOVING. Often you can improve the organization of your writing by moving part of it so that related ideas appear near one another.

UNREVISED	Mince the garlic in very fine pieces. Then heat a tablespoon of olive oil in a small skillet. Stir it with a wooden spoon and saute just until it starts to brown. Then remove it. Oh—before you put it in the skillet, heat some oil. Use about a tablespoon. Olive oil is best. Use medium-low heat.
REVISED	Mince the garlic in very fine pieces. Heat a tablespoon of olive oil in a small skillet at a medium-low temperature. When the oil is hot, add the garlic. Stir it with a wooden spoon and saute it just until it starts to brown. Then remove the garlic.

When you mark a piece of writing for revision, use the standard proofreading symbols. The symbols for adding, cutting, replacing, and moving are the first four symbols in the Language Arts Survey 2.44, "Using Proofreader's Marks."

2.42 A REVISION CHECKLIST. The following chart lists some questions to ask yourself whenever you are revising your writing. If you cannot answer *yes* to any of these questions, then you need to revise your work. Continue revising until you can answer *yes*.

REVISION CHECKLIST	
Content	• Does the writing achieve its purpose?
	• Are the main ideas clearly stated and supported by details?
Organization	• Are the ideas arranged in a sensible order?
	• Are the ideas connected to one another within paragraphs and between paragraphs?
Style	• Is the language appropriate to the audience and purpose?
	• Is the mood appropriate to the purpose of the writing?

2.43 Proofreading

When you proofread your writing, you read it through to look for errors and mark corrections. When you mark corrections to your writing, use the standard proofreading symbols. With just a little practice you'll find them very easy and convenient.

2.44 USING PROOFREADER'S MARKS. Consult the chart below for standard proofreading marks.

PROOFREADER'S SYMBOLS	
Symbol and Example	**Meaning of Symbol**
The very first time	Delete (cut) this material.
cat cradle	Insert (add) something that is missing.
George	Replace this letter or word.
All the horses king's	Move this word to where the arrow points.
french toast	Capitalize this letter.
the vice-President	Lowercase this letter.
housse	Take out this letter and close up space.
book keeper	Close up space.
gebril	Change the order of these letters.
end. "Watch out," she yelled.	Begin a new paragraph.
Love conquers all	Put a period here.
Welcome friends.	Put a comma here.
Getthe stopwatch	Put a space here.
Dear Madam	Put a colon here.
She walked he rode.	Put a semicolon here.
name brand products	Put a hyphen here.
cats meow	Put an apostrophe here.
cat's cradle stet	Let it stand. (Leave as it is.)

2.45 A PROOFREADING CHECKLIST. After you have revised your draft, make a clean copy of it and proofread it for errors in spelling, grammar, and punctuation. Use the following proofreading checklist.

PROOFREADING CHECKLIST	
Spelling	• Are all words, including names, spelled correctly?
Grammar	• Does each verb agree with its subject?
	• Are verb tenses consistent and correct?
	• Are irregular verbs formed correctly?
	• Are there any sentence fragments or run-ons?
	• Have double negatives been avoided?
	• Have frequently confused words, such as *affect* and *effect*, been used correctly?
Punctuation	• Does every sentence end with an end mark?
	• Are commas used correctly?
	• Do all proper nouns and proper adjectives begin with capital letters?

2.46 PROPER MANUSCRIPT FORM. After proofreading your draft, you will want to prepare your final manuscript. Follow the guidelines given by your teacher or, if your teacher tells you to do so, the guidelines given here. After preparing a final manuscript according to these guidelines, proofread it one last time for errors.

GUIDELINES FOR PREPARING A MANUSCRIPT

- Keyboard your manuscript using a typewriter or word processor, or write it out neatly using blue or black ink.
- Double-space your paper. Leave one blank line between every line of text.
- Use one side of the paper.
- Leave one-inch margins on all sides of the text.
- Indent the first line of each paragraph.
- In the upper right-hand corner of the first page, put your name, class, and date. On every page after the first, include the page number in this heading, as follows:
  Keanna Pérez
  English 7
  October 3, 2001
  p. 2
- Make a cover sheet listing the title of the work, your name, the date, and the class.

2.47 Publishing and Presenting Your Work

In the **publishing and presenting stage**, you share your work with an audience.

2.48 MAINTAINING A WRITING PORTFOLIO. A **writing portfolio** is a collection of your writing. Usually, a portfolio is a file folder with your name on it and your writing in it. Your teacher may ask you to keep a complete portfolio, one that includes all the pieces that you write. Another possibility is that your teacher will ask you to keep a selected portfolio, one that contains only your very best pieces of writing.

When you put a piece of writing in your portfolio, make sure that your name and the date are on it. Attach any notes or earlier versions of the writing that you have.

From time to time, you and your teacher will evaluate, or examine, your portfolio. You will meet in a student-teacher conference and talk about your pieces of writing. Your teacher will help you to find strengths and weaknesses in your writing. He or she also will help you to make plans for improving your writing in the future.

Keeping a writing portfolio can be exciting. In very little time, you can build a collection of your work. Looking over this work, you can take pride in your accomplishments. You can also reflect on how you are growing as a writer.

2.49 SHARING YOUR WORK WITH OTHERS. Some writing is done just for one's self. Journal writing usually falls into that category. Most writing, however, is meant to be shared with others. There are many ways in which to share your work. Here are several ways in which you can publish your writing or present it to others:

- Find a local publication that will accept your work. (A school literary magazine, a school newspaper, or a community newspaper are possibilities.)

- Submit the work to a regional or national publication. Check a reference work such as *Writer's Market* to find information on types of manuscripts accepted, manuscript form, and methods and amounts of payment.

- Enter the work in a contest. Your teacher may be able to tell you about writing contests for students. You can also find out about such contests by looking for announcements in writers' magazines and literary magazines.

- Read your work aloud to classmates, friends, or family members.

- Obtain permission to read your work aloud over the school's public address system.

- Work with other students to prepare a publication—a brochure, online literary magazine, anthology, or newspaper.

- Prepare a poster or bulletin board, perhaps in collaboration with other students, to display your writing.

- Make your own book by typing or word processing the pages and binding them together. Or copy your work into a blank book.

- Hold a reading or performance of student writing as a class or schoolwide project.

- Share your writing with other students in a small writers' group that meets periodically to discuss one or two students' recent work. (Members of the group should receive the work to be discussed beforehand so they can read it and make notes on it.)

- If the work is dramatic in nature, work with other students to present a performance of it, either as straight drama or as readers' theater. If the work is poetry, fiction, or nonfiction, work with others to present it as an oral interpretation.

2.50 Reflecting on Your Writing

In the **reflecting** stage, you think through the writing process to determine what you learned as a writer, what you accomplished, and what skills you would like to strengthen the next time you write. Reflection can be done in a journal, on a self-evaluation form for writing, in small group discussion, or simply in your own thoughts. Here are some questions to ask as you reflect on the writing process and yourself as a writer.

QUESTIONS FOR REFLECTION

- What have I learned in writing about this topic?
- What have I learned in writing for this purpose?
- What have I learned by using this form?
- How do I perceive my audience? What would I like my audience to gain from my writing?
- What kind of voice does my writing have?
- How have I developed as a writer while writing this piece?
- What strengths have I discovered in my work?
- What aspects of my writing do I want to strengthen? What can I do to strengthen them?

LANGUAGE, GRAMMAR, AND STYLE *Resource*

LANGUAGE

3.1 Appropriate Uses of English

Language is a powerful tool for conveying meaning. It is also a complex tool that must be used appropriately if genuine communication is to occur. In deciding how to communicate most effectively, a speaker must make choices concerning use of formal or informal English; what tone to use, the effects of irony, sarcasm, and rudeness; and how dialect affects the communicated message.

3.2 Formal and Informal English

Depending on the situation, you might use either formal English or informal English when you speak or write. Formal English is appropriate for school essays, newspaper and magazine articles, some literary works, oral or written reports, and test answers. Informal English is appropriate when speaking with a friend or writing personal letters or notes; it can also be used in some literary works.

How do you decide whether to use formal or informal English? You will naturally tend to use informal English, so all you need to remember are the situations just described in which formal English may be expected instead. Your audience and purpose help determine whether to use formal or informal English. For example, you would use formal English to discuss a grade with a teacher or to ask for a refund from a store manager. You would use informal English talking with your friends. You might use somewhat formal English in getting to know a new friend, and then relax and use more informal English as the friendship developed.

How do you tell the difference between formal and informal English? Informal English allows grammatical constructions that would not be acceptable in formal English. Many of these constructions are described in the Grammar Handbook (pages 982–1008), where they are labeled "nonstandard." Informal English also uses *colloquialisms* and *slang*.

A **colloquialism** is a word or phrase used in everyday conversation.

> COLLOQUIAL ENGLISH
> **You guys** must be **sick of** doing the same thing day after day.
> He was **totally turned off** by the movie.
>
> FORMAL ENGLISH
> **All of you** must be **weary** of doing the same thing day after day.
> He was completely **displeased** by the movie.

Slang is a form of speech made up of invented words or old words that are given a new meaning.

> SLANG
> You better **chill out** for a while—you're too angry to talk to him now.
>
> FORMAL ENGLISH
> You had better **relax** for a while—you're too angry to talk to him now.

3.3 Register, Tone, and Voice

To understand the concept of register, imagine that all the different kinds of usage in a language—both formal and informal—form one large set. A **register** is a subset of language usage specific to a particular relationship between people. In talking to a friend, for example, you speak in a register that is casual, warm, and open. In speaking to a young child, you speak in a register that is nonthreatening and simple to understand. In speaking to an official such as a police officer or a government clerk, you speak in a register that is polite but forthright—the same register that person should use with you. The words you choose, the grammar you employ to say those words, and your tone of voice will change depending on the register in which you are speaking.

Another way to understand register is to examine its meaning as a musical term. In music, register means the range of notes a singer or instrument is capable of producing. Your speaking and writing, however, are not limited to one range of usage. You can call on any part of a broad scale of usage, ranging from a grunt to a complex and formal declaration of your thought.

One hallmark of people who know how to use the power of language is their ability to choose and use the appropriate register for whatever situation they are in. They do not offend strangers by being too familiar or puzzle their friends by being too formal.

Tone is a writer's or speaker's attitude toward a subject. The tone of a message should reflect the speaker's attitude toward the subject and his or her audience. The speaker shapes the tone of a message by carefully choosing words and phrases. *Diction*, or choice of words, determines much of a speaker's tone. For instance, when writing a letter of complaint, do you want to say, "Your new product is so disgusting that I'll never buy anything you make ever again" or "I am concerned with the danger your new product poses to young children"? The tone you convey will depend greatly upon word choice.

The following examples give two different descriptions of the same scene. In one the scene is described in a tone of fear, and in the other it is described in a tone of awe. If you were telling a story about someone who was afraid of the ocean, you might use the more negative description. If you were writing about someone who enjoyed the ocean, you would probably use the more positive description.

TONE OF FEAR

Menacing black waves rolled in relentlessly, crashing down upon the rocks and threatening to sweep everything in their path out to sea. Mountainous and savage, the waves pounded the shore with a fury that sent a chill of dread through my soul.

TONE OF AWE

Powerful breakers rolled in majestically, splashing against the rocks and sending fountains of spray high into the air. I stood in awe of this force so mighty that nothing could stop it.

Voice is the quality of a work that tells you that one person in particular wrote it—not several, and not just anyone. Voice is one feature that makes a spoken or written work unique. The voice of a work can be difficult to define; it may have to do with the way a writer or speaker views people, events, objects, ideas, the passage of time, even life itself. If this treatment of the subject is consistent throughout, despite variations in tone, register, point of view, and topic, then the writer or speaker has established a voice, a sense of individuality, in the work.

In your own communication, whether in speaking or writing, you should strive to develop your own voice, not to imitate the voices of others. What that voice is, and how it compares to others, are matters no one can decide for you. "To thine own self be true," says Polonius in Shakespeare's *Hamlet*, "and thou canst not then be false to any man." Be true to your own voice, and your experience will speak directly to the experience of others.

3.4 Irony, Sarcasm, and Rudeness

It is easy to mistake the term *rude* to mean anything that is crude, distasteful, or not pleasing to someone. The word *rude* has been adapted and expanded into a general slang term. The standard definition of *rude* means bad-mannered, impolite, or inconsiderate. If someone says something a listener doesn't like, that person is not rude in the original meaning of the word. However, a person who interrupts someone else's conversation, curses, or forgets to say "please," "thank you," or "excuse me" is being selfish and inconsiderate—all characteristics of rude behavior within the original meaning of the word.

Frequently students confuse sarcasm or irony with rudeness. **Verbal irony** is present when someone says or writes the opposite of what he or she means in order to create humor or to make a point. It can be funny or serious. For example, if someone pushes to the front of a line, and someone else says, "What polite behavior," the speaker is expressing verbal irony. **Sarcasm** is a specialized kind of irony; the difference is the speaker's intentions. Sarcastic people say the opposite of what they mean in order to criticize, hurt, or humiliate someone. Sarcasm differs from other forms of irony because it is usually unkind.

Mark Twain uses sarcasm in "An Encounter with an Interviewer" when he asks the interviewer how to spell *interview*:

EXAMPLE

"How do you spell it?"
"Spell what?"
"Interview."
"Oh my goodness! What do you want to spell it for?"
"I don't want to spell it; I want to see what it means."

3.5 Dialects of English

A **dialect** is a version of a language spoken by people of a particular place, time, or group. Dialects are characterized by differences in pronunciation, word choice, grammar, and accent. They are usually based on social differences (upper class, middle class, and lower class) or on regional differences. In the United States, the major regional dialects are northern, southern, midland, and western.

All dialects are equally capable of expressing thought, which is what language is for. Therefore, no dialect is better than any other dialect. The dialect used by the most powerful social class is usually considered the **standard**, and other dialects are considered **nonstandard**. But standard does not mean "correct" or "better than others." Knowledge of the standard dialect is useful because it is widely understood, and because in many situations, speaking or writing in the standard dialect will ensure that people focus on what you say rather than how you say it. They will understand your meaning, without being distracted by your use of an unfamiliar dialect.

Knowing nonstandard dialect is also useful to writers. Consider the way Harper Lee uses dialect to make her writing more authentic.

EXAMPLE

"How old are you," asked Jem, "four-and-a-half?"
"Goin' on seven."
"Shoot no wonder, then," said Jem, jerking his thumb at me. "Scout yonder's been readin' ever since she was born, and she ain't even started to school yet. You look right puny for goin' on seven." from *To Kill a Mockingbird*

Differences in dialect show up especially in the terms speakers use to refer to certain objects in various areas of the country. For example, the generic term for a carbonated beverage is "soda" in Florida and Washington, DC, "pop" in Ohio and Minnesota, "coke" in Georgia and Tennessee, and "tonic" in Boston. Similarly, the grassy strip separating the lanes of an interstate highway is called a "mall" in upstate New York, a "median" in Ohio, a "medial strip" in Pennsylvania, a "meridian" in the upper Midwest, and "neutral ground" in Louisiana.

GRAMMAR

In English the basic unit of meaning is the sentence. In this integrated approach to grammar you will examine sentences to determine what they mean. This should help you to be a better reader and more skillful writer. This approach may be new to you, so here are a series of charts and references to help you as you begin. Do not memorize these charts. The more you use them, the less you will need them. With time, you will develop a feeling for the way language works so you will not need them at all.

3.6 Identifying the Parts of Speech

Each word in a sentence has one of four basic functions: it **names**, **modifies**, **expresses action or state of being**, or **links**.

A fifth "extra" function is to interrupt for effect; words that **interrupt** will be discussed at the end of this section.

English also has words that can work as more than one part of speech. Words that can take on different parts of speech are called **hybrids**. These words will be explained at the end of this section.

Below is an overview of the parts of speech. For a more detailed description of what each part of speech does, see the "Parts of Speech Summary" on page 1071.

3.7 Grammar Reference Chart—Parts of Speech Overview

PARTS OF SPEECH	EXAMPLE(S)
NAMERS (nouns and pronouns) are subjects and objects.	
NOUN. A **noun** names a person, place, thing, or idea.	Adam, journalist, mountain, India, rose, motorcycle, honesty, feeling
PRONOUN. A **pronoun** is used in place of a noun to name a person, place, thing, or idea.	I bought the bricks and used **them** to build a wall. Take Schuyler to the ice cream shop and buy **him** (used in place of Schuyler) a cone.
EXPRESSERS (verbs) name an action or state of being plus the conditions around it.	
VERB. A **verb** expresses action or state of being.	bake, glance, give, build, compose, think, look, feel, am
MODIFIERS (adjectives and adverbs) make other parts of speech more specific.	
ADJECTIVE. An **adjective** modifies, or changes the meaning of, a noun or pronoun.	**gray** skies, **deep** water, **eerie** laughter
ADVERB. An **adverb** modifies, or changes the meaning of, a verb, an adjective, or another adverb.	Leanne gripped the wheel **nervously**. Elliot thought the exam was **extremely** easy. Giovanni peered over the edge of the cliff **very** cautiously.
LINKERS (prepositions and conjunctions) join all the constructions of the English language.	
PREPOSITION. A **preposition** is used to show how a noun or a pronoun is related to other words in the sentence. Common prepositions are *in, after, among, at, behind, beside, off, through, until, upon,* and *with*.	Pablo enjoyed the concert **at** the Wang Center. Theresa squeezed **through** the opening **of** the cave and crawled **into** the narrow passage.
CONJUNCTION. A **conjunction** joins words or groups of words. Common conjunctions are *and, but, for, nor, or, so,* and *yet*.	Wilhelm plays the guitar, **but** Leonard plays drums. Wilhelm **and** Leonard play loudly.
INTERRUPTERS (interjections and other constructions) interrupt a sentence for emphasis.	
INTERJECTION. An **interjection** is a word used to express emotion. Common interjections are *oh, ah, well, say,* and *wow*.	**Hey!** What are you doing in there? **Oh well,** I didn't expect to win the election anyway.
APPOSITIVE. An **appositive** is an interrupter that renames a noun.	My friend **Yang Yardley** did a beautiful project on birds. Mrs. Cokely, **my favorite teacher**, will retire.
NOUN OF DIRECT ADDRESS. **A noun of direct address** says the name of the person or group spoken to and is never the subject of the sentence.	Wait until dark, **Audrey**. **Class**, listen to the instructions. (*Class* is a noun of direct address; the subject of the sentence is *you*; the pronoun *you* is understood.)

CONTINUED

PARTS OF SPEECH	EXAMPLE(S)

HYBRIDS (such as possessive nouns, pronouns, verbals) can act as more than one part of speech.

POSSESSIVE NOUNS AND PRONOUNS. Possessive nouns and **pronouns** are nouns and pronouns that function as adjectives.	Angela read **Scott's** essay. (*Scott's* is a possessive noun modifying *essay*.) Angela read **his** essay. (*His* is a possessive pronoun modifying *essay*.)
VERBALS. Verbals are verb forms such as participles, gerunds, and infinitives that can function as adjectives, nouns, and adverbs.	I love the **swimming** pool. (*Swimming* is a verbal called a participle and acts as an adjective.) **Swimming** is my favorite sport. (*Swimming* is a verbal called a gerund and acts as a noun.) I like **to swim**. (*To swim* is a verbal called an infinitive.)

To understand how a sentence works, here are other groups of words that you should know about.

3.8 Grammar Reference Chart—Helping Verbs

A **helping verb** helps a main verb to express action or state of being.

HELPING VERBS		
be (am, are, is, was, were, being, and been)	have (has, had)	shall
	may	should
can	might	will
could	must	would
do (does, did)		

3.9 Grammar Reference Chart—The Verb *To Be*

Most languages use the verb *to be* more than any other verb because its forms have more uses than any other verb form. It can be the main verb of a sentence, used to express existence. It also can be a helping verb used with action verbs. Here are some forms of *to be*:

THE VERB *TO BE*	
Present: am, is, are **Past:** was, were, has been, had been **Future:** will be, shall be, will have been	**Other expressions and forms that use** *be:* being, can be, could be, could have been, may be, may have been, might be, might have been, must be, must have been, would be, would have been

3.10 Grammar Reference Chart—Linking Verbs

A **linking verb** connects a noun with another noun, a pronoun, or pronoun adjective that describes or defines it. Note that some linking verbs can also be action verbs. For example, <u>I grow</u> tired uses *grow* as a linking verb. <u>I grow</u> flowers uses *grow* as an action verb. Notice how <u>I am a junior</u> and <u>A junior am I</u> mean exactly the same thing. This is because *am* is a linking, not an action verb. Sentences with action verbs cannot be reversed in the same way: *I made a bookshelf* and *A bookshelf* *made me* do not mean the same thing. Here is a list of common linking verbs. *Be* is the most common of all.

LINKING VERBS		
appear	grow	smell
be (am, is, are, was, were, been)	look	sound
become	remain	stay
feel	seem	taste

3.11 Grammar Reference Chart—Prepositions

These are the most commonly used prepositions. Remember, though, that any word on this list may not always be used as a preposition. If it is a preposition, it will always have an object.

PREPOSITIONS				
aboard	at	concerning	off	until
about	before	down	on	up
above	behind	during	over	upon
across	below	except	past	with
after	beside	for	since	within
against	besides	from	through	without
along	between	in	throughout	
amid	beyond	into	to	
among	but	like	under	
around	by	of	underneath	

3.12 What Is Grammar?

The **grammar** of a language refers to two different language areas. First, grammar is the collection of rules and standards that careful speakers use as they write and speak. Second, a **grammar** is any one of several possible descriptions of a language.

Classical grammar has troubled English students because it was originally designed to fit Latin, an inflected language. In Latin every word has an ending or inflection that defines its sentence function, so word order doesn't matter. About the middle of this century, different English grammars began to appear. The most successful of the new grammars were based upon rules of English word order, but frequently the terms used were too confusing to be widely used.

Consequently, the grammar presented here uses elements of both. It demands that students label words and language groups according to what language is doing (which we know by word order). Many terms are familiar because they come from classical grammar, but their meaning may change to fit the grammar of a syntactic language, English.

3.13 English Is a Syntactic Language

Scholars who study language have classified European languages into two major categories: **inflected languages** and **syntactic languages.** The words of **inflected** languages change their forms to tell speakers how the word is used. Word order isn't all that important to meaning. Some inflected languages are Latin and German. English is a **syntactic language**. Word order **(syntax)** determines meaning for **syntactic languages.**

3.14 The Importance of Syntax, or Word Order

EXAMPLE The junior class plans the prom each spring.

In English sentences words are arranged in specific patterns. In the most frequently used sentence, the sentence tells who (The junior class), and then it tells what that *who* does (*plans the prom each spring*). When word order changes, the sentence changes meaning; if the pattern rules are ignored, the sentence may become awkward, or even meaningless.

EXAMPLES
Class the the prom plans each spring junior.
Plans the junior spring the prom class each.
Class the plans each the prom junior spring.

A change in syntax results in a change in meaning; different sentence positions of the same word results in different meanings.

EXAMPLES
Junior prom <u>plans</u> are finished by March.
<u>Plans</u> for our house were completed last fall.
Our family <u>plans</u> a vacation every summer.

In the first two sentences, *plans* names something. In the first sentence it is used to mean arrangements; in the second, it means blueprints. In the third sentence, *plans* is an action. In all sentences the word form is the same, but different positions signal different meanings.

3.15 Inflections in English

English does have some **inflections**, or changes in form, but word order is most important! English verbs, adjectives, and pronouns are inflected. Sometimes we add a suffix (add *–ed* to *work*, *–er* or *–est* to *hard*); other times interior letters or the entire forms change: *drive* becomes *drove*, *my* becomes *mine*, *was* becomes *were*.

EXAMPLES
INFLECTED VERBS
Today I *carry* my lunch. Yesterday I *carried* it, too. (The *y* is replaced by *i*, and the suffix *–ed* is added.)

Today I *have* lots of homework; yesterday I *had* very little. (The entire verb form changes.)

INFLECTED ADJECTIVES
My sister is *wise*; my mother is *wiser*, but my grandmother is the *wisest* woman in the family. (The suffixes *–er* and *–est* are added to indicate higher degrees of quality.)

Kevin's day was *good*; Tua's was *better*, but mine turned out *best*. (The form changes altogether.)

INFLECTED PRONOUNS
Most pronouns change forms: *me, mine; they, them*. A specialized group of pronouns, the reflexive and intensive pronouns, add the suffix *–self* to the singular possessive pronoun forms *my, him, her, it,* and *your,* and add *–selves* to the plural forms *them, your,* and *our.*

3.16 The Sentence: The Basic Building Block of the English Language

Since first grade you have been encouraged to write and speak in sentences because they are the basic units of meaning. English sentences are organized to tell us whom or what a speaker is talking about and information about that whom or what. Classical grammar defines a sentence as "a group of words that expresses a complete thought."

3.17 Functions of Sentences

English speakers use four kinds of sentences to express four different kinds of complete thoughts:

• A **declarative sentence** informs us. First, it tells whom or what a speaker is writing or speaking about, and second, it gives information about that whom or what.

• An **interrogative sentence** asks a question.

• An **imperative sentence** gives orders or makes requests.

• An **exclamatory sentence** expresses strong feeling.

Declarative	I am ready to eat dinner.
Interrogative	Is dinner ready?
Imperative	Give me my food.
Exclamatory	I'm starving to death!

3.18 Subjects and Verbs: The Basic Building Blocks in a Sentence

Good readers and writers analyze meaning by examining the structure of sentences. Finding the parts of a sentence is a basic tool for people who use language well.

3.19 Finding the Complete Subject and Complete Predicate in a Sentence

All simple English sentences can be divided into two parts, the subject and the predicate. In the most common English sentence, the first part of the sentence tells us what it is talking about. This is the **complete subject**. Then it gives us information about the subject; this second part of the sentence is called the **complete predicate**. In the following examples, the complete subject is underlined once and the complete predicate is underlined twice.

> EXAMPLES
>
> One of my brothers fixed his own car.
> Sharyl and Ken will be presenting Friday's history lesson.
> Lala might have been given a wrong classroom number.

NOTE: Every word in every sentence is a part of the complete subject or the complete predicate.

3.20 Finding the Simple Subject and Simple Predicate in a Sentence

Most people need more specific information than that given by the complete subject and the complete predicate. The basic units of meaning are found in the **simple subject** and the **simple predicate** (more frequently called the **verb**). The **simple subject** is the **complete subject** without any of its modifiers. The **verb** is the **complete predicate** without any complements or modifiers.

The **simple subject** is the complete subject without any modifiers or linkers—the extra words.

> EXAMPLES
>
> Little **kids** like pet kittens and puppies.
> Telly's **mother** wants a new car.

The **simple predicate** or **verb** is the complete predicate without any complements, linkers, or modifiers.

> EXAMPLES
>
> Little kids **like** pet kittens and puppies.
> Telly's mother **wants** a new car.

NOTE: Verbs may have more than one word—they may have as many as four! Each of the examples is one verb.

> EXAMPLES
>
> play (one word)
> is playing (two words)
> has been playing (3 words)
> may have been playing (4 words)

3.21 How to Find the Simple Subject and Verb

The following four-step method will help you to find the simple subject and verb.

> EXAMPLE
>
> My older sister might not get a motorcycle for high school graduation.

1. Ask, "What is the action of this sentence?" The action is *get*.
2. Using the Language Arts Survey 3.8, "Helping Verbs," check some of the words around the action word. For the sample sentence, you might want to check *might* and *not*. *Might* is on the list; *not* isn't. Only *might* is a helping verb. The verb of the sentence is *might get*.
3. After finding the verb, ask who (what) did the action? Who *might get? My older sister.*
4. Finally, what words aren't necessary for simplest meaning? *Older sister* makes sense, so omit *my; older* can be left out, too. *Sister* is the simple subject of the sentence.

3.22 Sentence Completers for Action Verbs: Direct and Indirect Objects

A sentence must have a subject and a verb, but sometimes sentences have other parts that complete the meaning. The completers for action verbs are **direct objects** and **indirect objects**.

First, it is important to realize that not all sentences have objects. Here are some examples of sentences without objects. In each of these sentences there is no receiver of the action. The verb expresses the total concept.

> EXAMPLES
>
> Birds fly south.

Work fast.
I have been walking.

DIRECT OBJECTS. A **direct object** receives the action in the sentence. The following sentences do have receivers of the action, or direct objects. In each case, once the verb is found, the direct object answers the question *what?* about the verb.

EXAMPLES

Birds ate grain. (Birds ate what? *grain*)
Work the problems fast. (Work what? *problems*)
I walked the dog. (Walked what? *dog*)

The last step was to get rid of any modifiers. That tells you what the direct object itself is. Also note that a direct object is *never* in a prepositional phrase.

INDIRECT OBJECTS. Sometimes the direct object is received by someone or something. This receiver is called the **indirect object**. A sentence without a direct object cannot have an indirect object.

EXAMPLE   Mike gave me a red pencil.

What is the action (the verb)? *gave*
Who gave? (the subject) *Mike*
What did he give? (the direct object) *pencil*

To find the indirect object, check to see if the direct object had a receiver. Who got the direct object? In this sentence we ask, "Who got the pencil?" The answer is me.

Who received the pencil? (the indirect object) *me*

3.23 Sentence Completers for Linking Verbs: Predicate Nouns, Pronouns, and Adjectives

Unlike action verbs, **linking verbs** do not describe an *action*. They simply join a subject to another word that describes or identifies it. Since no action is being performed, there are no objects or direct objects. Instead, the first noun, or naming word, is assumed to be the subject while the renaming or describing word is called its **complement.**

Because a linking verb has no object or direct object, the order of the sentence can sometimes be reversed without affecting the meaning. For example, *I am a student* and *A student am I* mean

the same thing. *Am* is merely linking the two nouns, no matter what the order. On the other hand, *I made dinner* and *Dinner made me* mean very different things. Because *made* is an action verb, the sentence cannot be reversed. There are three types of sentence completers for linking verbs: predicate nouns, predicate pronouns, and predicate adjectives.

EXAMPLES

PREDICATE NOUN	Tala is my best <u>friend</u>.
PREDICATE PRONOUN	We are the <u>ones</u>!
PREDICATE ADJECTIVES	Tierre felt <u>ill</u>.

3.24 Predicate Nouns and Pronouns as Sentence Completers

Sentences with predicate nouns and pronouns do not use action verbs: they use forms of the verb *to be*. (Forms of *to be* are listed in 3.9, "Grammar Reference Chart—The Verb *To Be*.") To find a **predicate noun** or **predicate pronoun**, ask the same questions asked to find a **direct object**.

EXAMPLE   Mary will have been my friend for six years.

To find the predicate noun, ask, "Mary will have been what?" The answer is *friend*.

EXAMPLE   The most dangerous criminal was he.

To find the predicate pronoun, ask, "The most dangerous criminal was who?" The answer is *he*.

NOTE: Direct and indirect objects include *me, her, him,* and so on. Predicate pronouns include *I, she, he,* and so forth, the same forms as subjects.

3.25 Predicate Adjectives as Sentence Completers

A **predicate adjective** modifies, or describes, the subject of a sentence. Sentences with predicate adjectives may use a variety of linking verbs. Consult 3.10, the "Grammar Reference Chart—Linking Verbs," for a list of linking verbs. Most of these are used just with predicate adjectives, not with predicate nouns or pronouns.

EXAMPLE   Della feels blue today.

To find the predicate adjective, ask, "Della feels what?" The answer is *blue*. *Blue* describes Della.

SUBJECTS AND VERBS: PROBLEM CONSTRUCTIONS

English speakers often rearrange or use different kinds of sentences. Some of these constructions can be challenging!

3.26 Working with Inverted Sentences

A sentence is **inverted** when all or part of the complete predicate comes before the subject. When you ask a question, you automatically invert your sentence. Usually, part of the verb is in front of the subject.

> EXAMPLES
> **DECLARATIVE SENTENCE**
> Sitka did study the math problem.
> **INTERROGATIVE SENTENCE**
> Did Sitka study the math problem?

In both sentences, the verb is *did study*. Part of the verb comes before the subject.

Other sentences may be inverted so that a modifier comes before the subject.

> EXAMPLE   Sitka studied the math problem today.
> Today Sitka studied the math problem.
> *Today* modifies *studied* in both sentences.

Be sure to find all the words in the verb of an inverted sentence.

3.27 Working with *There* Sentences

The word *there* often appears as the first word or as one of the first few words in a sentence. *There* will never be a basic part of the sentence; it is a modifier. To make finding the subject and verb easier, cross out *there* before determining the basic parts of the sentence.

> EXAMPLE
> There will be two standardized tests given this week.

Remove *there*:
> will be two standardized tests given this week

Rearrange words:
> two standardized tests will be given this week

Now the subject and verb are easy to find. The subject is *tests;* the verb is *will be given*.

3.28 Working with Compound Subjects, Verbs, and Sentences

If a sentence has more than one subject, together they are called a **compound subject**.

> EXAMPLE
> Frank and Jesus work at a carwash.

If a sentence has more than one verb, the verbs together are called a **compound verb**.

> EXAMPLE
> Helen cooked dinner, washed dishes, and swept the floor.

Notice that each verb has its own direct object.
Sentences can have both a compound subject and a compound verb.

> EXAMPLE
> Mikka and Juan cut the grass and washed the car.
> Subjects: Mikka, Juan; Verbs: cut, washed.

A **compound sentence** refers to two sentences that are either 1) connected by a semicolon *or* 2) connected with a coordinating conjunction and a comma. Each part of the compound sentence has its own subject and verb.

> EXAMPLES
> Sally wanted a car, but her family wouldn't buy one.
> Sally wanted a car; her family wouldn't buy one.

In both sentences, the subjects are *Sally* and *family;* the verbs are *wanted* and *would buy*. (*Not* is not part of the verb; it only modifies the verb.)

For more information, see the Language Arts Survey 3.36, "Combining and Expanding Sentences."

3.29 Working with Negatives and Contractions

NEGATIVES. Negatives such as *not* and *never* frequently affect verbs. They are adverbs, because they add to the meaning of the verb. The verb tells what an action is, and the negative says that the writer or speaker means the opposite of that.

> EXAMPLES
> I play basketball.
> Negative: I do not play basketball.

Make sure to use only one negative in each sentence. Check your writing to be sure that you have not used a negative word such as *not, nobody, none, nothing, hardly, barely, can't, doesn't, won't, isn't,* or *aren't* with another negative word.

DOUBLE NEGATIVE (NONSTANDARD)

I hardly never eat my lunch at school.
Didn't Joyce never go to Chicago?
It doesn't make no difference!
Why wasn't Jerry hurt no worse when the car was destroyed?

CORRECTED SENTENCES (STANDARD)

I hardly ever eat my lunch at school.
Didn't Joyce ever go to Chicago?
It doesn't make any difference!
Why wasn't Jerry hurt any worse when the car was destroyed?

CONTRACTIONS. Contractions combine two words by shortening and joining them with an apostrophe.

EXAMPLES

isn't, aren't, don't, can't

When you are trying to determine subjects and verbs in a sentence, contractions need to be written out into the two words that they represent. After the contraction is written out, each word should be considered separately. Each of the contractions above contains a negative. Remember that a negative is never part of a verb, but is an adverb.

CONTRACTION	WORDS CONTRACTED	PARTS OF SPEECH
isn't	is not	is (verb or helping verb), not (negative; adverb)
aren't	are not	are (verb), not (negative; adverb)
don't	do not	do (verb), not (negative; adverb)
can't verb),	can not	can (helping not (negative; adverb)

3.30 Identifying Prepositional Phrases

A **prepositional phrase** is a phrase made up of a preposition, the noun or pronoun that is its object, and any words that modify the object. A list of common prepositions can be found in the Language Arts Survey 3.11, "Grammar Reference Chart—Prepositions."

The prepositional phrases have been underlined in the example below:

EXAMPLE

One <u>of my brothers</u> is planning a medical career <u>after college</u>.

NOTE: The simple subject, verb, and complements are *never* in prepositional phrases. If you wish to determine the subject and verb of a sentence, first cross out any prepositional phrases, and you will have fewer words to consider.

3.31 Using Indefinite Pronouns

You seldom have problems with personal pronouns in sentences because they are easy to recognize. When you encounter an **indefinite pronoun** (used to replace a person or a group of people not specifically identified), you might make errors in subject and verb agreement. Subjects and objects are particularly tricky when they are followed by a prepositional phrase, as shown below.

EXAMPLES

<u>Some</u> of the students wrote excellent short stories.
<u>Ten</u> from the senior class were chosen for a legislative workshop.
Mr. James gave <u>several</u> of my friends top grades on their papers.

You might want to cross out prepositional phrases in a sentence before you determine subjects and verbs.

3.32 Avoiding Problems Caused by Understood Subjects and Nouns of Direct Address

Understood subjects are sometimes used in sentences that make requests or give commands. The subject is *you*, but it is not written out, because both the speaker/writer and listener/reader understand who is meant.

Open your books. Give me your attention.
Run outside; the school is burning down!

In each of these the speaker does not have to say the *you* because it is understood.

If you are not sure that the subject is understood, try using *you* in front of the verb.

Nouns of direct address are never a part of the basic sentence. They name the person talked to, and they are always set off from the rest of the sentence using commas. They can appear at any place in a sentence.

<u>Hank,</u> when did you plan to finish your project?
Have you seen the new science lab, <u>Carrie</u>?
I need to know, <u>class</u>, if you had any problems with today's homework.

By paying attention to the comma clues—that is, the way the noun of direct address is set off from the rest of the sentence—you will realize that these nouns are not actually a part of the basic sentence.

WRITER'S WORKSHOP: BUILDING EFFECTIVE SENTENCES

3.33 Correcting Sentence Fragments

A sentence contains a subject and a verb and should express a complete thought. A **sentence fragment** is a phrase or clause that does not express a complete thought but has been punctuated as though it did.

SENTENCE FRAGMENT

So he could explore the clear waters of the lake.

COMPLETE SENTENCE

Teddy bought a new mask and snorkel so he could explore the clear waters of the lake.

SENTENCE FRAGMENT

Looking for the lost little girl.

COMPLETE SENTENCE

The searchers combed the woods looking for the lost little girl.

3.34 Correcting Sentence Run-ons

A **sentence run-on** is made up of two or more sentences that have been run together as if they were one complete thought. You can fix a run-on by dividing it into two separate sentences. Mark the end of each idea with a period, question mark, or exclamation point. Capitalize the first word of each new sentence.

RUN-ON

Jason tried to jump across the swollen stream he slipped in the mud on the other side.

TWO SENTENCES

Jason tried to jump across the swollen stream. He slipped in the mud on the other side.

RUN-ON

Mr. Strauss refused to reconsider his decision, he had made up his mind and didn't want to be bothered with the facts.

TWO SENTENCES

Mr. Strauss refused to reconsider his decision. He had made up his mind and didn't want to be bothered with the facts.

You can also correct a sentence run-on with a semicolon.

RUN-ON

I went to bed early I got up late.

CORRECTED WITH SEMI-COLONS

I went to bed early; I got up late.

A **sentence string** is a sentence run-on formed of several sentences strung together with conjunctions. Edit sentence strings by breaking them into separate sentences and subordinate clauses.

STRINGY

When I decided to audition for the part, I had no idea how to do it so I asked my friend Eileen who has some acting talent what to do and she said to practice in front of a mirror, but I tried that and it didn't help, so I had Eileen come over instead and when I read my lines to her that really helped.

REVISED

When I decided to audition for the part, I had no idea how to do it. I asked my friend Eileen, who has some acting talent, what to do. She said to practice in front of a mirror, but I tried that and it didn't help. I had Eileen come over instead. When I read my lines to her, that really helped.

3.35 Correcting Wordy Sentences

As you write, avoid **wordy sentences**. Use only the words necessary to make your meaning clear to a reader. Edit your sentences so that they are not wordy and complicated. Replace complicated or general words with simple and specific words.

WORDY

Make sure that you are very careful not to forget to lock the door to the house when you leave the house.

CLEAR AND DIRECT

Don't forget to lock the door as you leave.

3.36 Combining and Expanding Sentences

There are many ways to combine and expand sentences to achieve smooth writing and sentence variety.

COMBINING SENTENCES. If you use several short sentences in a paragraph, your writing might sound choppy, and your reader might have trouble understanding how ideas are connected.

Combining sentences is a good way to bring two sentences together that deal with the same main idea. If you combine short sentences, your writing will sound smooth and clear, and your reader will see how ideas are connected to one another.

One way of combining sentences is to take a word or phrase from one sentence and insert it into another sentence. You might need to change the form of the word.

BORING, SHORT SENTENCES

The cowboys walked into the saloon. Their walk was more like a swagger. They were boisterous.

COMBINED SENTENCE

The boisterous cowboys swaggered into the saloon.

Another way of combining sentences is to merge two related sentences into one sentence that states both ideas. Your two sentences can be combined with a comma and a **conjunction** such as *and, or, for, nor, but, so,* or *yet.*

BORING, SHORT SENTENCES

The storm was fierce. The captain brought the ship to safety.

COMBINED SENTENCE

The storm was fierce, but the captain brought the ship to safety.

EXPANDING SENTENCES. You can expand sentences and achieve sentence variety by knowing how to use different types of clauses and sentences. These include independent clauses, compound sentences, complex sentences, and compound-complex sentences.

An **independent clause** expresses a complete thought and can stand by itself as a sentence.

INDEPENDENT CLAUSES

The geese flew away.
The geese flew away at the sound of the plane.

A **compound sentence** is formed by two or more independent clauses joined by a conjunction and a comma, or by a semicolon followed by a transition word such as *however* or *therefore* and a comma.

COMPOUND SENTENCES

The geese flew away at the sound of the plane, and all was quiet.
The geese flew away at the sound of the plane; however, the crows remained.

You can also expand a sentence that has only one independent clause by adding a subordinate clause. You will then have a **complex sentence**—one formed of an independent clause and at least one subordinate clause. In the following examples, the subordinate clauses are underlined.

COMPLEX SENTENCES

<u>After the geese flew away</u>, the crows remained.
The geese flew away, <u>scared by the noise</u>.

If you combine a compound sentence and a complex sentence, you will have a **compound-complex sentence**. This kind of sentence must have two or more independent clauses and at least one subordinate clause. In the following examples, the subordinate clauses are underlined.

COMPOUND-COMPLEX SENTENCES

<u>Although they were accustomed to loud noises</u>, the geese flew away at the sound of the plane; however, the crows remained.

The geese flew away at the sound of the plane; however, the crows remained, <u>greedily eating the corn in the fields</u>.

3.37 Making Passive Sentences Active

A verb is **active** when the subject of the verb performs the action. It is **passive** when the subject of the verb receives the action.

ACTIVE Caroline delivered a powerful speech.
PASSIVE A powerful speech was delivered by Caroline.

Poor writing uses too many passive verbs. Use active verbs unless you have a good reason for using the passive voice. In the examples that follow, note how the active verbs make the writing more natural and interesting.

WITH PASSIVE VERBS

The school was flooded with requests from students for a longer vacation. It was not decided by the school board until later to give them a hearing. The meeting was begun by the student council. The vote was unanimous to extend spring break an extra week. It was considered an unprecedented move favoring all students suffering spring fever.

WITH ACTIVE VERBS

Students flooded the school with requests for a longer vacation. The school board did not decide until later to give them a hearing. The student council began the meeting. Everyone voted to extend spring break an extra week. The unpredecented move favored all students suffering spring fever.

Note that the writer could still combine, expand, and add variety to these sentences. Making such sentences active instead of passive, however, is a good start toward livelier writing.

3.38 Achieving Parallelism

A sentence has **parallelism** when it uses the same grammatical forms to express ideas of equal, or parallel, importance. When you edit your sentences during revision, check to be sure that your parallelism is not faulty.

FAULTY

The teacher told me to think better and having more focus.

PARALLEL

The teacher told me <u>to think</u> better and <u>to have</u> more focus.

FAULTY

Being too late for the bus and to get something to eat, I decided to walk to the mall.

PARALLEL

<u>Being</u> too late for the bus and <u>wanting</u> to get something to eat, I decided to walk to the mall.

FAULTY

I really like playing chess, walking my dog, and vacations in Florida.

PARALLEL

I really like <u>playing</u> chess, <u>walking</u> my dog, and <u>taking</u> vacations in Florida.

3.39 Adding Colorful Language to Sentences

When you write, use words that tell your reader exactly what you mean. Precise and lively language makes your writing more interesting to your reader.

DULL

The <u>people</u> made <u>noise</u>.

COLORFUL

The <u>mob</u> made an <u>uproar</u>.

Specific verbs also help to create a clear picture in a reader's mind. Use verbs that tell the reader exactly what you mean.

DULL

He <u>took</u> the pitcher and <u>drank</u> the cool water.

COLORFUL

He <u>grabbed</u> the pitcher and <u>gulped</u> the cool water.

A **modifier** is a word that modifies—that is, changes or explains—the meaning of another word. Adjectives and adverbs are modifiers. Colorful modifiers can turn dull reading into dynamic reading.

DULL

The <u>cold</u> wind blew <u>hard</u>.

COLORFUL

The <u>frigid</u> wind blew <u>furiously</u>.

EDITING FOR GRAMMAR AND USAGE ERRORS

3.40 Getting Subject and Verb to Agree

A word that describes or stands for *one* person, place, thing, or idea is **singular**. A word that describes or stands for *more than one* person, place, thing, or idea is **plural**.

SINGULAR NOUNS	prize, child, instrument
PLURAL NOUNS	prizes, children, instruments

In a sentence, a verb must be singular if its subject is singular and plural if its subject is plural. **A verb must agree in number with its subject**.

SINGULAR AGREEMENT	<u>Charles</u> <u>needs</u> forty more dollars.
PLURAL AGREEMENT	<u>They</u> <u>need</u> forty more dollars.
SINGULAR AGREEMENT	<u>She</u> <u>exercises</u> every day.
PLURAL AGREEMENT	The <u>girls</u> <u>exercise</u> every day.

The pronouns *I* and *you*, although singular, almost always take the same verb forms as for the plural pronouns *we* and *they*. The only exceptions are the forms *I am* and *I was*.

EXAMPLES

I <u>believe</u> the car industry will continue to rebound.
You <u>sense</u> my uneasiness.

AGREEMENT WITH COMPOUND SUBJECTS. A **compound subject** is formed of two or more nouns or pronouns that are joined by a conjunction and have the same verb. A compound subject joined by the conjunction *and* usually takes a plural verb.

EXAMPLE <u>Salt</u> and <u>acid rain</u> <u>are</u> hard on a car's body.

A compound subject in which the subjects are joined by the conjunction *and* takes a singular verb if the compound subject really names only one person or thing.

EXAMPLE His <u>work and love</u> <u>is</u> writing.

A compound subject formed of two singular subjects joined by the conjunctions *or* or *nor* takes a singular verb.

EXAMPLES

Neither <u>Streep</u> nor <u>Foster</u> <u>is</u> usually guilty of underpreparing.
Either <u>poetry</u> or <u>drama</u> <u>is</u> appropriate for public performance.

A compound subject formed of a singular subject and a plural subject joined by the conjunctions *or* or *nor* takes a verb that agrees in number with the subject nearer the verb.

EXAMPLES

Either <u>Kim</u> or the backup <u>vocalists</u> <u>are</u> responsible for the recording.
Either the backup <u>vocalists</u> or <u>Kim</u> <u>is</u> responsible for the recording.

AGREEMENT WITH INDEFINITE PRONOUNS. These indefinite pronouns are singular and take a singular verb: *anybody, anyone, anything, each, either, everybody, everyone, everything, neither, nobody, no one, nothing, one, somebody, someone,* and *something*.

EXAMPLES

<u>Nobody wants</u> to take the exam on Friday.
<u>Everybody enjoys</u> some kind of music.

These indefinite pronouns are plural and take a plural verb: *both, few, many,* and *several*.

EXAMPLES

<u>Both</u> of these choices <u>are</u> unacceptable.
<u>Several</u> new students <u>are</u> on the honor roll.

The following indefinite pronouns can be singular or plural: *all, any, most, none,* and *some*.

EXAMPLES

<u>All</u> of the cookies <u>were saved</u>. (*All* is plural.)
<u>All</u> of the pie <u>was eaten</u>. (*All* is singular.)

AGREEMENT IN INVERTED SENTENCES. When you invert sentences for emphasis, make sure you maintain agreement in number between subject and verb.

EXAMPLES

For those ghastly performances <u>he takes</u> full credit.
The last straw <u>she took</u>.

AGREEMENT WITH DOESN'T AND DON'T. The contraction *doesn't* (from *does not*) is third-person singular and should be used only with a third-person singular subject (*he, she,* or *it,* for example). The contraction *don't* (from *do not*) should be used with all other subjects.

EXAMPLES

She doesn't want material things.
They don't understand the procedure.
I don't find the subject boring.

OTHER PROBLEMS IN SUBJECT-VERB AGREEMENT. When a sentence begins with *here, there, when,* or *where,* often the subject follows the verb. In editing your writing, use extra care to check that the subject and verb of such sentences agree in number. Remember that the contractions *here's, there's, when's,* and *where's* contain a singular verb *(is)* and should only be used with a singular subject.

EXAMPLES

Here's the team.
There is one more exam being given.
When's the test?
When are the band members joining us?
Where's the rub?

Also check to be sure a verb in a sentence with a predicate nominative agrees in number with the subject and not with the predicate nominative.

EXAMPLES

Essays are the hardest part of school.
The hardest part of school is essays.

A collective noun takes a singular verb when the noun refers to the group as a unit, and it takes a plural verb when it refers to the members of the group as individuals.

AS SINGULAR   The team runs laps every day.
AS PLURAL   The team joke among themselves behind the coach's back.

While editing your work, check for nouns that are plural in form but singular in meaning. They should take singular verbs.

EXAMPLES   cryogenics, slacks, measles

The title of a creative work such as a book or song takes a singular verb, as does a group of words used as a unit.

EXAMPLES

The book *Aphorisms* has been on the bestseller list for two weeks.

Sidney and Austen is the smallest firm in Chicago.

An expression stating an amount is singular and takes a singular verb when the amount is considered as one unit. It is plural and takes a plural verb when the amount is considered as something with many parts.

AS SINGULAR

Three eggs is a high-cholesterol breakfast.

AS PLURAL

Three eggs were found splattered across the windshield.

A fraction or a percentage is singular when it refers to a singular word and plural when it refers to a plural word.

AS SINGULAR

One-fourth of the text was footnotes.

AS PLURAL

One-fourth of all the pages were footnotes.

AS SINGULAR

Over 60 percent of the nation is hopeful about the economy.

AS PLURAL

Over 60 percent of all citizens are hopeful about the economy.

Expressions of measurement, such as area, length, volume, and weight, are usually singular.

EXAMPLE

Two quarts is a lot of milk to drink in one sitting.

3.41 Using Irregular Verbs

To write about something that happened in the past, use past tense verbs (tense means *time* in grammar). For regular verbs, add *–ed* or *–d* to the present form of the verb. For more information, see the Language Arts Survey 3.62, "Properties of Verbs: Tense."

EXAMPLES

The bandit guarded the hideout.
guard (base form) + ed

Carmen gazed at the distant mountains.
gaze (base form) + d

Irregular verbs often have different past tense forms and are formed using a different spelling. The following chart lists some of the most common irregular verbs.

IRREGULAR VERBS	
begin/began	grow/grew
bring/brought	have/had
burst/burst	hurt/hurt
choose/chose	know/knew
come/came	lay/laid
cut/cut	make/made
do/did	ride/rode
draw/drew	run/ran
drink/drank	see/saw
eat/ate	sing/sang
fall/fell	take/took
feel/felt	teach/taught
fly/flew	wear/wore
give/gave	write/ wrote
go/went	

When using irregular verbs in the perfect tense (with *has* or *have*), make sure you do not use the past form instead of the past participle.

NONSTANDARD

I have knew him since I was in middle school.

STANDARD

I have known him since I was in middle school.

Another error to avoid is using the past participle form without a helping verb, or mistaking the past participle for the past.

NONSTANDARD	I flown this plane dozens of times.
STANDARD	I have flown this plane dozens of times.
NONSTANDARD	I done all I could do to convince him.
STANDARD	I did all I could do to convince him.

Finally, do not add *–d* or *–ed* to the past form of an irregular verb.

NONSTANDARD	I ated an apple.
STANDARD	I ate an apple.

3.42 Avoiding Split Infinitives

In the English language, the infinitive is often in the form of two words, *to* and the base word.

EXAMPLES   to catch, to succeed, to entertain

Under traditional rules of grammar, the infinitive should not be "split." In other words, adverbs or other sentence components should not come between *to* and the base word.

NONSTANDARD	Irving begged me to immediately show him the photos.
STANDARD	Irving begged me to show him the photos immediately.

3.43 Using *I* and *Me*

Before you use the words *I* and *me* in a sentence, remember that *I* is always the subject of a verb and *me* is always the object of a verb or of a preposition.

EXAMPLES

I went sailing in Florida.
Amber and I went sailing in Florida.

I is the subject in both of these sentences.

Lester helped me set up for the party.
Lester helped Brianna and me set up for the party.

In both sentences, *me* is the object of the verb *helped*.

If you are not sure which pronoun to use with a compound subject, drop the other part of the subject and use your pronoun separately with the verb.

EXAMPLE

Sam and (I, me) went sledding at the golf course.

After dropping out Sam:
I went sledding at the golf course. OR Me went sledding at the golf course.

Correct: Sam and I went sledding at the golf course.

EXAMPLE

Please apologize for Carol and (I, me).

After dropping out Carol:
Please apologize for me. OR Please apologize for I.

Correct: Please apologize for Carol and me.

3.44 Using *Who* and *Whom*

The pronoun *who* has two different forms. *Who* is used as a subject of a sentence. *Whom* is used as the direct object of a verb or of a preposition.

SUBJECT

<u>Who</u> knows the answer?

Where is the boy <u>who</u> looks after the sheep?

DIRECT OBJECT

<u>Whom</u> did the police arrest?

The plumber <u>whom</u> we called charged a huge fee.

OBJECT OF PREPOSITION

By <u>whom</u> is this painting?

From <u>whom</u> is that gift?

3.45 Getting Pronouns and Antecedents to Agree

Make sure pronouns in your writing agree with their antecedents (the words they refer back to) in number and gender.

Number refers to singular and plural. If the antecedent is singular, the pronoun must also be singular; if the antecedent is plural, the pronoun must also be plural.

Gender is the form a word takes to show whether it is masculine, feminine, or neutral (neither masculine nor feminine). The pronoun must match its antecedent in terms of gender.

INCORRECT NUMBER	Each <u>student</u> must sit in <u>their</u> assigned seat.
CORRECT NUMBER	Each <u>student</u> must sit in <u>his or her</u> assigned seat.
INCORRECT GENDER	<u>Humankind</u> has <u>his</u> own flaws.
CORRECT GENDER	<u>Humankind</u> has <u>its</u> own flaws.

3.46 Avoiding Dangling and Misplaced Modifiers

A **dangling modifier** seems to modify a word it is not intended to modify. If this error occurs when the modifier is too far away from the word it is supposed to modify, it is called a **misplaced modifier**. Edit a dangling or misplaced modifier by rewording the sentence or moving the modifier closer to the phrase it modifies.

DANGLING	Valerie drove to the airport while <u>taking a nap</u>.
WORDS ADDED	Valerie drove to the airport while <u>I was taking a nap</u>.
MISPLACED	Alex walked his dog <u>wearing shorts</u>.
REWORDED	Alex, <u>wearing shorts</u>, walked his dog.

3.47 Recognizing Other Problems with Modifiers

Them is a personal pronoun. *Those* is a demonstrative pronoun, which means it points out a particular person, place, or thing.

NONSTANDARD	Them cars have four-wheel drive.
STANDARD	Those cars have four-wheel drive.

The words *bad* and *badly* often confuse writers. Use *bad* as an adjective, and *badly* as an adverb. The adjective *bad* should follow a linking verb such as *feel, see, smell, sound,* or *taste.*

NONSTANDARD
Reports of the forest fire sounded badly.
STANDARD
Reports of the forest fire sounded bad.
NONSTANDARD
Ricky behaved bad for the babysitter.
STANDARD
Ricky behaved badly for the babysitter.

The words *good* and *well* also tend to confuse writers. *Good* is an adjective used to modify a person, place, thing, or idea, not an action verb. *Well* is an adverb meaning "successfully" or "skillfully" and an adjective meaning "healthy" or "of a satisfactory condition."

NONSTANDARD
Allen swims good.
STANDARD
Allen swims well.
Allen is a good swimmer.
Allen is well now that he is over his cold.

Each modifier has a **positive, comparative,** and **superlative** form of comparison. Most one-syllable modifiers and some two-syllable modifiers form comparative and superlative degrees by adding –*er* and –*est.* Other two-syllable modifiers, and all modifiers of more than two syllables, use *more* and *most* to form these degrees.

	POSITIVE	COMPARATIVE	SUPERLATIVE
ADJECTIVES	hungry	hungrier	hungriest
	daring	more daring	most daring
ADVERBS	late	later	latest
	fully	more fully	most fully

To show a decrease in the quality of any modifier, form the comparative and superlative degrees by using *less* and *least*.

EXAMPLES   dense, less dense, least dense
            skeptically, less skeptically, least skeptically

Some modifiers form comparative and superlative degrees irregularly. Check the dictionary if you are unsure about the comparison of a modifier.

EXAMPLES   good, better, best
            well, better, best
            bad, worse, worst

Use the comparative degree when comparing two things. Use the superlative degree when comparing more than two things.

COMPARATIVE
Santha was the **more easily** intimidated of the two sisters.

SUPERLATIVE
The skin is the **largest** organ of the human body.

3.48 Correcting Common Usage Problems

Watch for these words and learn their correct usage as you edit your own writing.

accept, except. To *accept* is to "welcome something" or to "receive something willingly." To *except* is to "exclude or leave something out." *Except* is also used as a preposition meaning "but."

The Tigers accept our challenge to a rematch.
She excepted Roland from the guest list.
I will eat any vegetable except collard greens.

advice, advise. *Advice* is a noun meaning "guidance or recommendation regarding a decision." To *advise* is to "recommend or inform."

I took your advice about the movie.
I would advise you to avoid that movie.

affect, effect. *Affect* is a verb meaning "have an effect on." *Effect* is a noun meaning "the result of an action."

The short story affected me strangely.
The short story had a strange effect on me.

altogether, all together. *Altogether* is an adverb meaning "thoroughly." Something *done all together* is done as a group or mass.

She was altogether frustrated waiting all day.
We were all together awaiting news of the surgery.

among, between. Use the word *between* when talking about two people or things at a time. Use the word *among* when talking about a group of three or more.

Oscar and Lucas had five dollars between them.
There was disagreement among the team members.

can, may. Use the word *can* to mean "able to do something." Use the word *may* to ask or give permission.

Can you swim across Gull Pond?
May I go swimming? Yes, you may go.

fewer, less. *Fewer* refers to the number of units of something. *Less* refers to bulk quantity.

I have fewer than eight items.
I have less energy when it is very humid.

in, into. The preposition *in* indicates location. The preposition *into* indicates direction from the outside to the inside.

The meeting is being held in the gym.
The students are going into the gym now.

its, it's The word *its* is a possessive pronoun. The word *it's* is a contraction of *it is*.

The turtle dug its nest.
The sun will be up by the time it's over.

lay, lie. *Lay* means to "put" or to "place" and always takes a direct object. *Lie* means to "rest" or to "be in a lying position." *Lie* never takes a direct object. (Note that the past tense of *lie* is *lay*.)

Lay the map on the table.
Gretchen laid the map on the table.
Lie down and keep quiet.
Oliver lay down and kept quiet.

like, as. *Like* is a preposition meaning "similar to." *Like* usually introduces a phrase. *As* should be used as a conjunction. *As* usually introduces a clause that has a subject and a verb.

NONSTANDARD
The sun came out earlier, just like I had hoped.
STANDARD
The sun came out earlier, just as I had hoped.

their, they're, there. These three *homonyms* (words that sound alike but that have different spellings and meanings) sometimes confuse writers. The word *their* is a possessive pronoun. The word *they're* is the contracted form of *they are*. The word *there* refers to a place.

> Marsupials carry their young in a pouch.
> They're complaining about the noise.
> The lamp should go over there.

to, too, two. *To* is a preposition that can mean "in the direction of." *Too* is an adverb that means both "extremely, overly" and "also." *Two* is the spelling for the number 2.

> Take the basket to Granny's house.
> Ivan has too many fish in his tank.
> Sharon is invited, too.
> I have two wishes left.

your, you're. *Your* is a possessive pronoun. *You're* is the contracted form of *you are*.

> Your mittens are in the dryer.
> You're the winner!

PARTS OF SPEECH SUMMARY

As you have seen, the meanings of words depend on their positions in a sentence. As their positions change, both meaning and function change. You have looked at function to determine parts of the sentence.

You can now go one step further. By looking at the relationship of a word to the rest of the words in a sentence, you can determine the parts of speech for individual words. Once again, you will be examining what a word does; then you will label its part of speech.

Remember two important facts: 1) words have four primary functions—they **name**, **express**, **modify**, and **link**. They can also **interrupt**. 2) Groups of words can function as one individual part of speech.

3.49 Namers—Nouns and Pronouns

Namers are **nouns** and **pronouns**, parts of speech that name people, places, ideas, and things or refer to them; you can tell what they are by what they do. Nouns and pronouns are subjects and objects: direct objects, indirect objects, objects of prepositions, and objects of infinitives. Namers:

NAME PEOPLE	Dylan, principal, father, choreographer
NAME PLACES	home, Central Park, Joe's Tacos
NAME IDEAS	love, multiplication, tonality, smell
NAME THINGS	basketball, dance, orbit, trading card

3.50 Specific Kinds of Nouns

There are many kinds of nouns. They include common and proper nouns, concrete and abstract nouns, and collective nouns.

3.51 COMMON NOUNS AND PROPER NOUNS. **Common nouns** are the names given to general objects. **Proper nouns** are names of specific people or things. They are always capitalized.

COMMON NOUNS

> girl, monument, government agency

PROPER NOUNS

> Michelle, Washington Monument, United States Supreme Court

Some proper nouns may have more than one word. *Michelle Adams, Central High School,* and the *United States Department of the Interior* are all names of one person or one place or organization. These multiword names are still considered to be one noun because they name only one person or thing.

3.52 CONCRETE NOUNS AND ABSTRACT NOUNS. A **concrete noun** names anything you can physically taste, touch, smell, see, or hear. An **abstract noun** names something that cannot be physically sensed.

CONCRETE NOUNS	automobile, textbook, lunchbox
ABSTRACT NOUNS	sadness, suffering, mood

3.53 COLLECTIVE NOUNS. **Collective nouns** name groups—family, committee, class. Collectives are interesting nouns because, in their singular forms, they can be either singular or plural, depending upon how the group acts. When the group acts together as one unit to do something, the group is considered singular.

The <u>committee</u> <u>votes</u> on its agenda.

Because the committee acted as one unit (by everyone doing the same one thing at the same time), the noun is singular and takes a singular verb form. The possessive pronoun *its* also reflects that the noun is collective.

When the group acts as individuals instead of as one unit, the group is considered plural.

The <u>committee</u> <u>were</u> giving their reports.

Because individual members gave their reports at different times and functioned as individuals, the group is considered plural. Note how the verb *were giving* and the possessive pronoun *their* reflect this.

3.54 Types of Pronouns

Pronouns replace names (nouns) with reference words. Because we use these references in so many situations, there are four different kinds of pronouns and three hybrids. The four kinds of pronouns are **personal pronouns, indefinite pronouns, interrogative pronouns,** and **reflexive pronouns**.

The three kinds of hybrids are **possessive pronouns, relative pronouns,** and **intensifying pronouns. Possessive pronouns** are hybrids because they take pronoun forms but act as modifiers; **relative pronouns** are hybrids because they are pronoun forms that act as linkers; and **intensifying pronouns** are hybrids because they use the same forms as reflexive pronouns but act as interrupters. The three hybrids are discussed in the hybrids section (see Language Arts Survey 3.78, "Hybrids").

3.55 Personal Pronouns. A **personal pronoun** is a substitute for the name of a person or thing. The personal pronouns are *I, me, we, us, he, she, it, him, her, you, they,* and *them*. Personal pronouns refer to three groups of speakers: first, second, and third person.

FIRST PERSON:	the speaker or speakers talks about themselves: *I, me, we, us*
SECOND PERSON:	the speaker talks about the person talked to: *you*
THIRD PERSON:	the speaker talks about someone or something else: *he, she, it, they*

All personal pronouns require clear **antecedents,** or nouns that come before the pronoun. That means that the person or thing that the pronoun refers to must be obvious.

Have you seen <u>Mary</u>? Yes, I saw <u>her</u> yesterday.
(<u>Mary</u> is the antecedent of <u>her</u>.)

3.56 Indefinite Pronouns. Indefinite pronouns are pronouns used when we may not be sure whom we are talking about. They include *somebody, anybody, few,* and *many*. They also include numbers. Frequently they are used when the reference word is in a prepositional phrase. Below are some indefinite pronouns.

INDEFINITE PRONOUNS

all	few	nothing
another	many	one
any	neither	other
anyone	no one	some
both	nobody	someone
each	none	something
either		

EXAMPLES

A <u>few</u> in our English class are reviewing a new textbook.
We asked for <u>some</u> of the details about the news story.
<u>Nobody</u> knows where the homecoming decorations were stored.
<u>Three</u> of the swimmers qualified for the state meet.

3.57 Interrogative Pronouns. Interrogative pronouns are the question-askers of the pronoun family. *Who, whom, whose, which,* and *what* are the interrogative pronouns.

EXAMPLES

<u>Which</u> of these buses do I take to reach my school?
<u>Whom</u> do I ask for directions?
<u>What</u> do I do now?

Be careful when identifying interrogative pronouns. The same words are used as relative pronouns (discussed in 3.79), but relative pronouns do not ask a question.

3.58 Reflexive Pronouns. Reflexive pronouns refer back to a noun previously used and can be recognized because *–self* and *–selves* have been added to other pronoun forms. Some reflexive pronouns include *myself, herself, yourself, themselves,* and *ourselves.*

EXAMPLES
I talk to <u>myself</u>.
Mike and James helped <u>themselves</u> to more food.

Reflexive pronouns are often parts of the basic sentence or objects of prepositions. (Note that **intensifying pronouns**, discussed in 3.78, "Hybrids," use the same forms, but they are interrupters and are neither a part of a basic sentence nor an object of a preposition.)

3.59 Expressers—Verbs

Verbs are the **expressers** of the English language, and they carry more information than any other single part of speech because they have three major properties: *tense, mood,* and *voice.* They reveal the time something happened or will happen, whether the action is finished or continuing, whether the subject is the actor or receiver of the action, and the manner in which the action occurred. English verbs can be from one to four words long.

EXAMPLES
runs
has run
has been running
may have been running

Note: The same verb may fit into several of the classes below, depending on its uses in different sentences.

3.60 Action Verbs and State of Being Verbs. The verb of any sentence is either an **action verb** or a **state of being verb**, depending on the message the verb expresses in the sentence. **Action verbs** are all of the words that refer to actions and to things you can do.

EXAMPLES   have, get, drive, run, sleep

State of being verbs indicate that something exists. These are all the forms of the verb *to be* that are listed on your Grammar Reference Chart in the Language Arts Survey 3.9, "The Verb *To Be.*"

3.61 Transitive and Intransitive Verbs. Transitive verbs are action verbs that have completers. If a verb has a direct object, it is a transitive verb.

EXAMPLE   Jamie writes short stories.

(*Short stories* is a direct object, so the verb *writes* is transitive.)

Intransitive verbs are action verbs that do not take objects.

EXAMPLE   The sun shines every day in Mexico.

The action *shines* is complete in itself; no extra material is necessary. This makes *shines* an intransitive verb.

3.62 Properties of Verbs: Tense

Verbs carry a concept of time, called **tense**. The simple tenses express simple past, present, and future. The perfect tenses give information about actions that take place over time.

Simple Tenses. Present tense shows that something is happening now. **Past tense** verbs talk about something that happened before now, and **future tense** verbs talk about something that will happen in the future.

SIMPLE TENSES FOR THE VERB *TO STUDY*	
PRESENT TENSE	
I You We They	study. do study.
He/She/It	studies. does study.
PAST	
I You He/She/It We They	studied. did study.

CONTINUED

FUTURE

I
You
He/She/It } will study.
We
They

PERFECT TENSES. The **perfect tenses** express past, present, and future, but they add information about actions that continued over a period of time and were completed in the past or will be completed in the present or future. All perfect tenses use some form of the helping verb *to have* with a past participle.

PERFECT TENSES FOR THE VERB *TO SLEEP*

I
You
We } have slept.
They

He/She/It   has slept.

PRESENT PERFECT

I
You
He/She/It } had slept.
We
They

FUTURE PERFECT

I
You
He/She/It } will have slept.
We
They

PROGRESSIVE VERB FORMS. Each of the simple and perfect tenses has a **progressive** form that shows continuing action. The progressive form is made by using a tense of the helping verb *be* with the present participle (*–ing* form).

PROGRESSIVE TENSES FOR THE VERB *TO WORK*

PRESENT PROGRESSIVE

I   am working.

He/She/It }   is working.

You
We }   are working.
They

PAST PROGRESSIVE

I
He/She/It }   was working.

You
We }   were working.
They

FUTURE PROGRESSIVE

I
You
He/She/It }   will be working.
We
They

PRESENT PERFECT PROGRESSIVE

I
You
We }   have been working.
They

He/She/It }   has been working.

CONTINUED

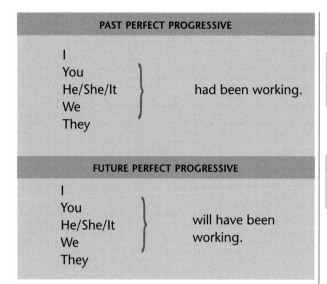

PAST PERFECT PROGRESSIVE

I
You
He/She/It   } had been working.
We
They

FUTURE PERFECT PROGRESSIVE

I
You
He/She/It   } will have been
We   working.
They

3.63 Properties of Verbs: Voice

The **voice** of a verb refers to the relationship between the subject and the action. A verb is in the **active voice** if the subject did the acting. It is in the **passive voice** if someone or something else did the acting and the subject is the receiver of the action.

ACTIVE	Mary gave her sister Rhonda a new skirt.
PASSIVE	Rhonda was given a new skirt for her birthday.

If the sentence is in the active voice, the subject of the sentence, Mary, did the acting—she gave a skirt to Rhonda. The first sentence is in the active voice. In the second sentence, Rhonda did nothing at all. Someone else, not named, did the acting. The second sentence is in the passive voice.

Writing in the active voice strengthens writing; writing in the passive voice usually weakens it. The passive voice can be very effective in many cases, but it should be used seldomly and carefully. For more information, see the Language Arts Survey 3.37, "Making Passive Sentences Active."

3.64 Properties of Verbs: Mood

The **mood** of a verb is the manner in which the verb relates the action. English uses three moods: the **indicative, the declarative**, and the **subjunctive**.

The **indicative mood** (notice how close this word is to *indicate*) is used most frequently. This is the mood used to make a statement or ask a

question. Most declarative and interrogative sentences fall into this mood.

INDICATIVE
Gordon and Caley are my two brothers.
Don't you have two brothers, also?

Imperative sentences are in the **imperative mood**. These make requests or give commands.

IMPERATIVE
Please, hand me the salt.
Run before the flood gets you!

The **subjunctive mood** has few uses in English, and is used much less frequently than it is used in other languages. It is used to express a wish, a possible condition, or a condition contrary to a fact.

SUBJUNCTIVE
If I were you, I would dress more warmly in this weather.
If I had a million dollars, I would buy an airplane and fly around the world.
It is necessary that you be on time.
If they were here, they would win the prize.

Notice the verb form in the first sentence. The only verb that has a unique form in the subjunctive is the verb *to be. Were* is used with all pronouns, not just the singular.

3.65 Modifiers—Adjectives and Adverbs

Adjectives and **adverbs**, two kinds of **modifiers**, add meaning to nouns, adjectives, verbs, and adverbs. To determine whether the word is an adjective or adverb, use the following procedure:

1. Look at the word that is modified.
2. Ask yourself, "Is this modified word a noun or a pronoun?"

If the answer is *yes*, the modifier is an adjective. **Adjectives** modify only nouns and pronouns. If the answer is *no*, the modifier is an **adverb**. **Adverbs** modify verbs, adjectives, and other adverbs.

3.66 ADJECTIVES. **Adjectives** modify nouns or pronouns by making them more specific.

GENERAL REFERENCE	puppy
A LITTLE MORE SPECIFIC	the puppy

MORE SPECIFIC YET	the little puppy
EVEN MORE SPECIFIC	the little, black-spotted puppy
WITH A PREPOSITIONAL PHRASE	the little, black-spotted puppy with the shaggy coat

As each step adds more modifiers (more information), it becomes more possible for the listener or reader to visualize the actual dog.

3.67 ADVERBS. Adverbs are the generalists of the modifier family. They modify anything that is not a namer (noun or pronoun)—verbs, adjectives, and other adverbs. Many times they will specify *where* or *when;* nouns and pronouns specify *who* or *what.*

ADVERBS MODIFY VERBS
Katie came home quickly.

Quickly tells how Katie came home.

ADVERBS MODIFY ADJECTIVES
She wore a really new dress.

New modifies *dress; really* modifies the modifier, *new.* Since *new* is an **adjective**, not a **noun** or **pronoun**, *really* has to be an **adverb**.

ADVERBS MODIFY OTHER ADVERBS
Katie scurried home really fast.

Fast modifies the verb *scurried; really* modifies *fast.* In this sentence, one adverb modifies another.

3.68 Linkers/Joiners

Conjunctions and **prepositions** are the joiners of the English language. These words join everything from individual words to complete sentences to create compound sentences. Because there are many kinds of links that need to be made, there are many kinds of linkers: prepositions, coordinating conjunctions, correlative conjunctions, and subordinating conjunctions.

3.69 PREPOSITIONS. Prepositions are easy to identify because they have objects. If the word does not have an object, then it is another part of speech. See the Language Arts Survey 3.11 for a list of prepositions. If you find one of these words in a sentence, find its object. If it has an object, then the preposition and its object(s)—it may have more than one—form a prepositional phrase.

EXAMPLE I went [to the store] [for a loaf] [of sandwich bread].

In this sentence, three words are on the preposition list: *to, for,* and *of.* Does *to* have an object? Ask, "*to* what?" The answer is *the store. To* has an object, so it is a preposition. *To the store* is a prepositional phrase. After you apply the same test to *for* and *of,* you will find that they are both prepositions and that the sample sentence has three prepositional phrases. These are *to the store, for a loaf,* and *of sandwich bread.*

3.70 COORDINATING CONJUNCTIONS. Coordinating conjunctions join words and groups of words of equal importance. The most common coordinating conjunctions are *and, or, nor, for, but, yet,* and *so.* The word is not important; what is important is that both words or word groups are equally important.

EXAMPLE
Her morning schedule included math and history and music and home room.

Note that joining a series of words using coordinating conjunctions between them is perfectly acceptable grammar. Most writers use commas, however, and save multiple conjunctions for sentences with special emphasis. (Note: All but the last *and* could be replaced by commas.)

When a coordinating conjunction plus a comma joins two or more complete thoughts that could be separate sentences, the resulting structure is called a **compound sentence**.

COMPOUND SENTENCE
I wanted to go to a movie, but nothing sounded very good.

Here a comma plus *but* join two short, complete, independent thoughts. Each of the two parts could be a sentence of its own. Since their ideas are closely related, they can be joined using proper punctuation.

3.71 CORRELATIVE CONJUNCTIONS. Correlative conjunctions travel in pairs that belong together. Some of these pairs are *both...and, neither...nor, either...or,* and *not only...but also.*

EXAMPLES
Both art and graphic design are electives in our school.
Neither Latin nor Greek languages are studied by most high school students.

She wanted to study <u>either</u> architecture <u>or</u> industrial design.
He spoke <u>not only</u> German, <u>but also</u> spoke French and Spanish.

3.72 SUBORDINATING CONJUNCTIONS. Subordinating conjunctions join two phrases or clauses that are not of equal importance. Subordinating conjunctions are used to establish that one idea in a sentence is more important than the other. Subordinating conjunctions include *after, before, if, than, since, unless, when,* and *while;* there are many more. All of the following examples contain subordinating conjunctions.

SUBORDINATING CONJUNCTIONS

We will go on a picnic on Saturday <u>unless</u> it rains.
<u>Whenever</u> the pollen count is high, I start to sneeze and get itchy eyes.
I want to visit my grandmother in Detroit <u>if</u> I can save enough money.
<u>When</u> the deadline arrives, students need to get their projects handed in.

Even though both clauses have subjects and verbs, the parts of the sentence of the most important clause (called the **main clause**) will be the subject and verb of the sentence. The parts of the sentence found in the less important clause (called the **subordinate clause**) can be ignored. These are NOT the main subject and verb of the sentence; they are only the subject and verb of a **dependent clause**.

3.73 Interrupters

Sometimes you will want to interrupt the flow of your sentences and thoughts by adding a word or phrase for emphasis. Most **interrupters** are set off from the rest of the sentences by commas because they are not basic building blocks of meaning. **Interrupters** include **interjections, parenthetical expressions, nouns of direct address**, and **appositives**. Another interrupter, **intensifying pronouns**, is discussed in the Language Arts Survey 3.78, "Hybrids."

Interrupters (with the exception of one-word appositives) are set off from other parts of the sentence using commas. It is important to note that no interrupter is ever a basic part of a sentence.

3.74 INTERJECTIONS. Interjections are parts of speech that express strong feeling or enhance meaning.

EXAMPLES

<u>Yes</u>, I finished my homework.
<u>Good grief</u>, you did what again?
<u>Wow</u>, Sam got a new car for his birthday.

Note that omitting the interjection does not affect the basic meaning of the sentence. Each interjection is set off from the rest of the sentence by commas.

3.75 PARENTHETICAL EXPRESSIONS. Parenthetical expressions are those comments (set off by commas) that explain, comment, or qualify the ideas contained in the sentence. Common parenthetical expressions include *by the way, however, on the other hand, incidentally.*

EXAMPLES

I went right home after school; <u>however</u>, my sister went shopping for school supplies.
Mary misplaced her coat. <u>By the way</u>, have you seen a red raincoat in your closet?

3.76 NOUNS OF DIRECT ADDRESS. A noun of direct address says the name of the person or group spoken to. A noun of direct address is *never* the subject of the sentence. This becomes especially tricky when the subject is understood.

EXAMPLE <u>Class</u>, listen to the instructions.

Class is a noun of direct address; the understood subject is *you.*

3.77 APPOSITIVES. Appositives rename a noun. Like all interrupters, appositives are enclosed or set off from the rest of the sentence by commas. In some cases, word names do not require commas.

EXAMPLES

My friend <u>Yang</u> did a beautiful project on birds. (No punctuation is required.)

Mrs. Cokley, <u>my favorite teacher</u>, will retire this year. (Commas are needed.)

3.78 Hybrids

Hybrids are words usually thought of as one part of speech that occasionally function as another. Each word form should be labeled according to what it does in the sentence. Some common hybrids include **possessive nouns** and **possessive pronouns**, **relative pronouns**, **intensifying pronouns**, and a group of verb forms called **verbals**.

3.79 POSSESSIVE NOUNS AND PRONOUNS. Possessive nouns and **possessive pronouns** are namer forms that work as modifiers. To form a possessive noun, an apostrophe plus an *s* is added to a singular; an apostrophe is added to a plural. Notice how the possessive noun uses a noun form, but with the suffix it becomes a modifier.

EXAMPLE   Linda proofread <u>Marty's</u> assignment.

Marty's modifies *assignment.* Consequently this construction is a hybrid: it looks like a noun, but it functions as an adjective. When listing parts of the sentence, label a possessive noun as an adjective.

   Possessive pronouns act much the same way. Many possessive forms are the same as other pronouns, but a few pronoun forms are uniquely possessive. Some of the unique forms include *mine, your, yours, hers, its, our, their,* and *theirs.* Two other possessive forms, *her* and *him,* are not always possessive.

EXAMPLE   I ate <u>my</u> pizza.

My modifies *pizza. My* looks like a pronoun, but here it works as a modifier by telling whom the pizza belongs to. Because we label parts of speech according to what they are doing in the sentence, this word should be considered a modifier—in this case, an adjective.

   Relative pronouns are pronoun forms that function like **subordinating conjunctions**. The commonly used relative pronouns are *who, whom, whose, which,* and *that.* These words can connect a subordinate clause to the main clause of the sentence. But they also will function as a subject, object, or predicate pronoun—these are exactly the same functions as naming parts of speech.

EXAMPLE

   I want to meet the person <u>who painted that picture</u>.

Who is the **relative pronoun** that connects the subordinate clause (underlined) with the main clause. Also notice that *who* is the subject of the clause; the verb is *painted.*

EXAMPLE

   I want to meet the cousin <u>whom you described</u>.

Whom, the **relative pronoun,** is the connection between the two clauses; it also is the direct object of the verb *described.*

EXAMPLE

   Kate was the one <u>with whom I designed my art sculpture</u>.

In this sentence, *whom* is the object of the preposition *with;* it also connects the two clauses.

3.80 VERBALS: PARTICIPLES, GERUNDS, AND INFINITIVES. Verbals are verb forms that act as namers or modifiers. There are three different forms of verbals. These include participles (that act as modifiers), gerunds (that act like nouns), and infinitives (that can act like nouns, adjectives and adverbs).

   To determine if a verb is used as a verbal, you must be aware of what the word is actually doing in the sentence. Like other verbs, verbals can take objects, modifiers, or both. When a verbal has modifiers and/or objects, the group of words is called a participial phrase, a gerund phrase, or an infinitive phrase. Like all phrases, verbal phrases function as one part of speech.

   Participles are action adjectives. They have two forms: the present participle and the past participle. Both are used the same way.

   The **present participle** uses the *–ing* form.

EXAMPLES   Jana jumped off the <u>diving</u> board.
         My uncle has a <u>hearing</u> aid.
         I love to listen to that <u>marching</u> band.

   The **past participle** uses the *–ed* form.

EXAMPLES   A <u>raided</u> cookie jar is not a pretty sight.
         The <u>forgotten</u> language will never be recovered.
         A <u>watched</u> pot never boils.

   Note that you can find the object of a participle by using the same questioning strategy you use to find the verb of a sentence. The participle and its object form a construction called a **participial phrase**. It acts as one part of speech, an adjective.

The student taking notes got an *A* last semester.

Taking is a participle. If you ask, "taking what?", the answer is *notes*. The object of *taking*, the **participle**, is *notes*. Since *taking notes* modifies *student*, the entire construction (called a participial phrase) is working as an adjective.

Gerunds are verb forms used as namers. When you use any action as a name (running, jumping, writing, singing, playing), you use a gerund.

EXAMPLES

<u>Running</u> was her favorite activity.
(The gerund is the subject of the sentence.)

He liked high <u>jumping</u>.
(The gerund is the direct object.)

She wanted a tutor for <u>writing</u>.
(The gerund is the object of a preposition.)

Like participles, gerunds can take objects. You can find the object of a gerund just as you find the object of a verb.

EXAMPLE

<u>Buying</u> a prom dress took all of Katy's money.

Buying is a **gerund**. If you ask, "Buying what?", the answer is *a prom dress*. After you eliminate the modifiers, you will see that the object of the gerund *buying* is *dress*.

Gerunds can also take modifiers; since the gerund acts as a noun, the modifiers are adjectives.

EXAMPLE Dan began <u>ice skating</u>.

In this case, *ice* modifies *skating*.

EXAMPLE Senna began <u>complaining to her mother</u>.

Note that the prepositional phrase *to her mother* modifies *complaining*. This makes the modifier a prepositional phrase.

In both of the sentences above, the entire **gerund phrase** (the gerund + objects and/or modifiers) acts as one noun. In both these sentences, the phrases are direct objects.

Infinitives are verbals that use the form *to* + the verb. Each of the examples below illustrates a different use of infinitives. Infinitives can be used as nouns or as modifiers (adjectives and adverbs).

EXAMPLES

Her desire <u>to win</u> dominated her entire life. (Adjective)

The entire family gathered <u>to celebrate</u> my grandmother's birthday. (Adverb)

<u>To attend</u> college is my ultimate goal. (Noun)

When I turned sixteen, my parents allowed me <u>to drive</u> my car to school. (Noun)

Like other verbals, infinitives can take modifiers and objects. In the second and third sample sentences, the infinitives have objects. *To celebrate* has an object, *my grandmother's birthday;* the object of *to attend* is *college.* The fourth, *to drive,* has an object, *my car,* and a modifier, *to school.*

Infinitives can get tricky because speakers and writers may leave out *to* when it follows some commonly used verbs. Sometimes the *to* is omitted in infinitives that follow *dare, do, feel, hear, help, let, make, need, see, watch.* These constructions, called **bare infinitives**, are usually direct objects that name an action. The *to* is understood.

EXAMPLES

I heard her (to) play the piano.
Help me (to) carry this table.

Be careful. The *to* is not always left out after these verbs, and no dependable rule seems to exist. Native speakers with good ears will have a sense of this, but others may find it difficult. Fortunately, it is never wrong to include the *to* with an infinitive, although it may sound a little awkward.

3.81 Groups of Words That Function as One Part of Speech

Sometimes groups of words function as one part of speech. These groups fall into two categories: **phrases** and **clauses**. **Clauses** have both subjects and verbs; **phrases** do not.

EXAMPLES

I need <u>to get another spiral notebook</u>. (Phrase)

She will be elected <u>to the Student Council</u>. (Phrase)

I will watch television <u>when I finish my homework</u>. (Clause)

Do you know <u>who will be our next class president</u>?
(Clause)

Most clauses and phrases are named after the functions that they perform.

3.82 PHRASES. Phrases are groups of words that do not contain a subject and verb and that function as one part of speech. The following kinds of phrases are used in the English language:

Adjective phrases are prepositional phrases that modify nouns or pronouns.

Slim wanted a job <u>with good hours</u>.

Adverb phrases are prepositional phrases that modify anything except nouns and pronouns.

I spoke <u>to the two-headed alien</u>.

Participial phrases are verbal phrases that function as adjectives.

Their <u>recently remodeled</u> house is the jewel of the neighborhood.

Gerund phrases are verbal phrases that function as nouns.

<u>Getting good grades</u> is important to many students.

Infinitive phrases are verbal phrases that function as nouns, adjectives, or adverbs.

<u>To see angels</u> is to <u>believe in them</u>.
(Noun)
The ride <u>to go on</u> is the Ferris wheel.
(Adjective)
We are ready <u>to go home</u>. (Adverb)

3.83 CLAUSES WITHIN A SENTENCE. The **clauses** within a sentence are groups of words that 1) contain a subject and verb and that 2) function as one part of speech. The following kinds of clauses are used in the English language:

Adjective clauses are subordinate clauses that function as adjectives; they modify nouns and pronouns.

I admired the girl <u>who won the speech contest</u>.

Adverb clauses are subordinate clauses that function as adverbs, modifiying anything except nouns and pronouns.

My mother got upset <u>when she learned where I was going</u>.

Noun clauses function as subjects and objects.

<u>Whoever gets straight *A*'s in math</u> gets a four-year scholarship from the school's foundation.

3.84 THE CLAUSES OF A SENTENCE: SIMPLE, COMPOUND, AND COMPLEX SENTENCES. The **independent clauses**, or **main clauses**, of a sentence are the parts that contain a subject and verb. Without coordinating and/or subordinating words, they could stand alone. A sentence with only one independent clause is called a **simple sentence**.

Mabel made a broccoli pizza.

A sentence with two or more independent, or main clauses—two ideas of equal importance—is called a **compound sentence**. The independent clauses are usually connected with a comma and a **coordinating conjunction** such as *and, but, for, nor, or,* or *yet.*

Mabel made a broccoli pizza, <u>but</u> I didn't eat it!

A sentence with one independent clause and one or more **dependent**, or **subordinate**, **clauses** (less important clauses) is called a **complex sentence**. The dependent clauses are usually connected to the independent clause with a **subordinating conjunction** such as *after, because, if,* or *when,* or a **relative pronoun** such as *this* or *that*. The dependent clause may begin or end a complex sentence, but when it begins the sentence, a comma must follow it.

After I returned home, I ate a cheese pizza.
I ate a cheese pizza after I returned home.

If a sentence contains both kinds of clauses, it is called a **compound-complex sentence**.

I ate a cheese pizza after I returned home, and Mabel was insulted because I didn't eat the pizza she made.

For more information, see the Language Arts Survey 3.36, "Combining and Expanding Sentences."

3.85 Editing for Punctuation Errors

To avoid punctuation errors, you should know how to use end marks, commas, semicolons, colons, apostrophes, underlining, italics, quotation marks, dashes, and hyphens.

3.86 END MARKS. End marks tell the reader where a sentence ends. An end mark also shows the purpose of the sentence. The three end marks are the period, the question mark, and the exclamation point.

A **declarative sentence** ends with a period.

> **DECLARATIVE**
>
> For many years the Empire State Building was the tallest skyscraper in the world.

An **interrogative sentence** ends with a question mark.

> **INTERROGATIVE**
>
> When did World War I begin?
> How do you spell your name?

An **exclamatory sentence** ends with an exclamation point.

> **EXCLAMATORY**
>
> The view from the top is breathtaking!
> Help! Marvin is choking!

3.87 COMMAS. A comma separates words or groups of words within a sentence. Commas tell the reader to pause at certain spots in the sentence. These pauses help keep the reader from running together certain words and phrases when these phrases should be kept apart for clarity. Following is a list of the most common ways commas should be used.

RULES	EXAMPLES
Use commas to separate **items in a series**. Three or more words make a series.	The primary particles in an atom are protons, neutrons, and electrons. Choices include carrots, green beans, and asparagus.
Use commas when you **combine sentences using and, but, or, nor, yet, so,** or **for**. Place the comma before these words.	Casey was confident that he could hit a home run. He struck out. Casey was confident that he could hit a home run, but he struck out. Joanna will sing in the talent show. Margaret will accompany her. Joanna will sing in the talent show, and Margaret will accompany her.
Use a comma to **set off words or phrases that interrupt sentences**. Use two commas if the word or phrase falls in the middle of the sentence. Use one comma if the word or phrase comes at the beginning or at the end of a sentence.	Emily's twin brothers, Eric and Derrick, look exactly alike. Hercules, a hero of classical mythology, was said to be the strongest man on earth. After the first quarter, the Knicks dominated the game. How did you solve that problem, Jared?

CONTINUED

RULES	EXAMPLES
Use commas to **separate the parts of a date**. Do not use a comma between the month and the day.	The Germans surrendered on May 8, 1945. My appointment is on Wednesday, January 7.
Use commas to **separate items in addresses**. Do not put a comma between the state and the ZIP code.	Francisco was born in Caracas, Venezuela. They live at 210 Newfield Road, DeWitt, New York 13214.

3.88 SEMICOLONS. You have seen how two related sentences can be combined into one using a conjunction such as *and, but, so,* and *or.* Another way to join two related sentences into one is to use a semicolon. The **semicolon** can be used in place of the comma and the conjunction.

A fin was spotted moving through the water, so the bathers scrambled onto the beach.
A fin was spotted moving through the water; the bathers scrambled onto the beach.

Danielle is an exchange student from Paris, and everyone is enjoying getting to know her.
Danielle is an exchange student from Paris; everyone is enjoying getting to know her.

3.89 COLONS. Use a **colon** to introduce a list of items.

Don't forget the following items for the hike: water bottle, food, first-aid kit, extra sweater, and rain gear. Make sure you have all your paperwork in order: passport, visa, and tickets.

You should also use a colon between numbers that tell hours and minutes.

1:07 P.M.   6:00 A.M.   9:54 P.M.

A colon is often used after the greeting in a business letter.

Dear Sirs: Dear Ms. Flanagan:

3.90 APOSTROPHES. An **apostrophe** is used to form the possessive of nouns. To form the possessive of a singular noun, you should add an apostrophe and an *s* to the end of the word.

The sun's diameter is about 864,000 miles. (sun + 's = sun's)

Isaac's room is plastered with posters of the Pacers. (Isaac + 's = Isaac's)

The possessive of a plural noun is formed two different ways. If the plural noun does not end in *s,* you add an apostrophe and an *s* to the end of the word. If the plural noun ends with an *s,* add only an apostrophe.

The women's volleyball team is undefeated. (women + 's = women's)

The Vikings' star quarterback is on the injured list. (Vikings + ' = Vikings')

There are some words that end in *s* and are singular, such as *species* or *Jesus,* that have an irregular possessive form. Form the possessive of these words by adding only an apostrophe.

Moses' staff
Euripedes' tragedies

3.91 UNDERLINING AND ITALICS. Italics are a type of slanted printing used to make a word or phrase stand out. In handwritten documents, or in forms of printing in which italics are not available, underlining is used. You should underline or italicize the titles of books, magazines, works of art, movies, and plays.

BOOKS	*To Kill a Mockingbird, The Learning Highway* or <u>To Kill a Mockingbird, The Learning Highway</u>
MAGAZINES	*Reader's Digest, Sports Illustrated* or <u>Reader's Digest, Sports Illustrated</u>

WORKS OF ART	*The Thinker, The Starry Night* or <u>The Thinker</u>, <u>The Starry Night</u>
MOVIES	*American Beauty, The Matrix* or <u>American Beauty</u>, <u>The Matrix</u>
PLAYS	*The Tragedy of Romeo and Juliet, The Effect of Gamma Rays on Man-in-the-Moon Marigolds* or <u>The Tragedy of Romeo and Juliet</u>, <u>The Effect of Gamma Rays on Man-in-the-Moon Marigolds</u>

3.92 QUOTATION MARKS. When you use a person's exact words in your writing, you are using a **direct quotation**. Enclose the words of a direct quotation in quotation marks.

EXAMPLES

"It looks as if thunderclouds are gathering," Sylvia remarked.
Pietro said, "It's good to be back home."

A direct quotation should always begin with a capital letter. Separate a direct quotation from the rest of the sentence with a comma, question mark, or exclamation point. Do not separate the direct quotation from the rest of the sentence with a period. All punctuation marks that belong to the direct quotation itself should be placed inside the quotation marks.

EXAMPLES

"Your golf game has really improved," Avram remarked.
Victor lamented, "I wish Uncle Don were here."
"Did I turn off the iron?" wondered Mrs. Cameron.
Joy asked, "Have you seen my red blouse?"

Use quotation marks to enclose the titles of short works such as short stories, poems, songs, articles, and parts of books.

SHORT STORIES

"The Monkey's Paw," "To Build a Fire"

POEMS

"Casey at the Bat," "Birches"

SONGS

"John Henry," "If You Forget Me"

ARTICLES, ESSAYS

"Ghost of Everest," "Where Stars are Born"

PARTS OF BOOKS

"The Search for Self"

3.93 HYPHENS AND DASHES. A **hyphen** is used to make a compound word.

EXAMPLES

four-year-old boy, great-grandmother, run-of-the-mill, seventh-grade student, three-time winner

A **dash** is used to show a sudden break or change in thought.

EXAMPLE

Juan surprised his teacher—and himself—by getting an *A* on the science test.

3.94 Editing for Capitalization Errors

To avoid capitalization errors, you should know how to capitalize proper nouns and adjectives; geographical names, directions and historical names; and titles of art and history books.

3.95 PROPER NOUNS AND ADJECTIVES. Using capital letters is called **capitalization**. Always capitalize proper nouns and adjectives. A proper noun names a specific person, place, or thing. A **proper adjective** is an adjective formed from a proper noun.

PROPER NOUNS
Lebanon, Queen Elizabeth, Democrat
PROPER ADJECTIVES
Lebanese, Elizabethan, Democratic

Capitalize the names of people and pets.

PEOPLE AND PETS
Charles A. Lindbergh, Marie Curie, Smoky

There are many different kinds of proper nouns. The chart below should help you to recognize some of them.

PROPER NOUNS	
TITLES USED WITH NAMES	Dr. Stetson, Ms. Dixon, Mr. Meletiadis
MONTHS, DAYS, HOLIDAYS	January, Wednesday, Labor Day
RELIGIONS	Hinduism, Catholicism, Buddhism

CONTINUED

PROPER NOUNS

SACRED BEINGS AND WRITINGS
the Great Spirit, the Bible, the Koran

CITIES, STATES, COUNTRIES
Seattle, Louisiana, Peru

NATIONALITIES
Danish, Brazilian, Greek

STREETS, BRIDGES
Highland Street, Tappan Zee Bridge

BUILDINGS, MONUMENTS
World Trade Center, Washington Monument

CLUBS, ORGANIZATIONS, BUSINESSES
Kiwanis Club, National Audubon Society, Sears Roebuck

3.96 *I* AND FIRST WORDS. Capitalize the first word of every sentence.

EXAMPLES
Did you see that meteor?
The river rose over its banks.

Capitalize the word *I* whenever it appears.

EXAMPLES
Janice and I will buy the present.
Whenever I see horses, I think of Uncle Sherman.

3.97 FAMILY RELATIONSHIPS AND TITLES OF PERSONS. A word for a family relation such as *Mom, Dad,* or *Grandpa* should be capitalized if it is used as the name or part of the name of a particular person. Do not capitalize a word for a family relation if a modifier such as *the, a, my,* or *your* comes before it.

CAPITALIZED
When they were children, Dad, Aunt Polly, and Uncle Richard went down the Grand Canyon on mules.

NOT CAPITALIZED
My grandma has a cousin who lives in Germany.

Capitalize the official title of a person when it is followed by the person's name or when it is used instead of a name in direct address.

President James Polk, Queen Mary, Sir Winston Churchill, Pope Paul
"I am honored to meet you, Ambassador."

Do not capitalize references to occupations.

the electrician, the doctor, the sergeant, the judge, the chef, the editor

3.98 GEOGRAPHICAL NAMES, DIRECTIONS, AND HISTORICAL NAMES. Capitalize the names of specific places, including terms such as *lake, mountain, river,* or *valley* if they are used as part of a name.

BODIES OF WATER	Colorado River, Black Sea
CITIES AND TOWNS	Kansas City, Fayetteville
COUNTIES	Cayuga County, Kosciusko County
COUNTRIES	Switzerland, Indonesia
ISLANDS	Ellis Island, Isle of Wight
MOUNTAINS	Pike's Peak, Mount Rainier
STATES	Montana, South Carolina
STREETS, HIGHWAYS	Erie Boulevard, Route 71

Do not capitalize general names for places.

EXAMPLES
The still lake beautifully reflected the white-capped mountain.
Follow this road for two more miles and you will reach a small town.

Capitalize geographical directions if they are part of a specific name or a commonly recognized region. Do not capitalize words such as east(ern), west(ern), north(ern), and south(ern) if they are used only to indicate direction.

CAPITALIZED
<u>Western</u> Samoa, <u>East</u> Africa, <u>South</u> Bend, <u>Northern</u> Ireland

NOT CAPITALIZED
<u>west</u> of Denver, <u>eastern</u> face of the mountain, <u>south</u> side of the city, <u>northern</u> regions

Capitalize historical events, special events, and recognized periods of time.

HISTORICAL EVENTS
Continental Congress, Boxer Rebellion

HISTORICAL PERIODS
Paleozoic Era, Industrial Age

SPECIAL EVENTS
Empire State Games, Rose Bowl

3.99 TITLES OF ARTWORKS AND LITERARY WORKS.
Apply title capitalization to titles of artworks and literary works. In title capitalization, capitalize the first word, the last word, and all other words except articles (*a, an,* and *the*) and prepositions.

EXAMPLES

Raphael's *The School of Athens*, Matisse's *Joy of Life*, Jackson Pollock's *Autumn Rhythm*, Shakespeare's *The Taming of the Shrew*, Faulkner's *The Sound and the Fury*, Ray Bradbury's "All Summer in a Day"

3.100 Editing for Spelling Errors

You can improve your spelling by following the rules given here, and by memorizing the list of commonly misspelled words.

3.101 USING SPELLING RULES I. Always check your writing for spelling errors, and try to recognize the words that give you more trouble than others. Adding prefixes and suffixes often causes spelling errors. A prefix is a letter or a group of letters added to the beginning of a word to change its meaning. When adding a prefix, do not change the spelling of the word itself.

dis + similar = dissimilar
un + necessary = unnecessary

A **suffix** is a letter or group of letters added to the end of a word to change its meaning. The spelling of most words is not changed when the suffix –*ness* or –*ly* is added.

even + ness = evenness
usual + ly = usually

If you are adding a suffix to a word that ends with *y*, and that *y* follows a vowel, you should usually leave the *y* in place. (**Vowels** are the letters *a, e, i, o,* and *u*.)

employ + ment = employment
stay + ing = staying
destroy + ed = destroyed

If you are adding a suffix to a word that ends with *y*, and that *y* follows a consonant, you should usually change the *y* to *i*. (**Consonants** are all letters that are not vowels.)

silly + est = silliest
sticky + ness = stickiness
cry + ed = cried
cheery + ly = cheerily

If you are adding a suffix that begins with a vowel to a word that ends with a silent *e*, you should usually drop the *e*.

shave + ing = shaving
value + able = valuable
rose + y = rosy
take + ing = taking

If you are adding a suffix that begins with a consonant to a word that ends with a silent *e*, you should usually leave the *e* in place.

tire + less = tireless
sincere + ly = sincerely
fate + ful = fateful
place + ment = placement

3.102 USING SPELLING RULES II. When a word is spelled with the letters *i* and *e* and has the long *e* sound, it is spelled *ie* except after the letter *c*.

thief, relieve, yield, pierce
ceiling, conceive, receipt, deceive

The only word in the English language that ends in –*sede* is *supersede*. Only the following three words end in –*ceed*: *exceed, proceed,* and *succeed*. Every other word that ends with the "seed" sound is spelled –*cede*.

precede, recede, concede, accede

Most noun plurals are formed by simply adding –*s* to the end of the word.

stairs, ducklings, kites, rockets

The plurals of nouns that end in *o, s, x, z, ch,* or *sh* should be formed by adding –*es*.

tomatoes, classes, taxes, topazes, beaches, flashes

An exception to the rule above is that musical terms (and certain other words that end in *o*) are usually pluralized by adding –*s*.

pianos, solos, concertos, sopranos, banjos, radios

Form the plurals of nouns that end in *y* following a vowel by adding –*s*.

EXAMPLES

toy + s = toys
donkey + s = donkeys
Thursday + s = Thursdays
ray + s = rays

Form the plurals of nouns that end in *y* following a consonant by changing the *y* to an *i* and adding –es.

EXAMPLES	pony + s = ponies
	spy + s = spies
	country + s = countries
	story + s = stories

3.103 COMMON SPELLING ERRORS. Some English words are often misspelled. The following box contains a list of 150 commonly misspelled words. If you master this list, you will avoid many errors in your spelling.

COMMONLY MISSPELLED ENGLISH WORDS

absence	biscuit	enormous	liquefy	parallel	siege
abundant	breathe	enthusiastically	magnificent	pastime	significance
academically	business	environment	manageable	peasant	souvenir
accessible	calendar	exhaust	maneuver	permanent	sponsor
accidentally	camouflage	existence	meadow	persistent	succeed
accommodate	catastrophe	fascinating	mediocre	phenomenon	surprise
accurate	cellar	finally	miniature	physician	symbol
acknowledgment	cemetery	forfeit	mischievous	pneumonia	synonymous
acquaintance	changeable	fulfill	misspell	prestige	temperature
adequately	clothes	guidance	mortgage	privilege	tomorrow
adolescent	colossal	guerrilla	mysterious	procedure	transparent
advantageous	column	hindrance	naive	prophesy	twelfth
advisable	committee	hypocrite	necessity	prove	undoubtedly
ancient	conceivable	independent	nickel	receipt	unmistakable
annihilate	conscientious	influential	niece	referred	unnecessary
anonymous	conscious	ingenious	noticeable	rehearsal	vacuum
answer	consistency	institution	nucleus	relieve	vehicle
apparent	deceitful	interference	nuisance	resistance	vengeance
article	descendant	irrelevant	nutritious	resources	villain
attendance	desirable	irresistible	obedience	responsibility	vinegar
bankruptcy	disastrous	judgment	occasionally	rhythm	weird
beautiful	discipline	league	occurrence	schedule	whistle
beggar	efficiency	leisure	orchestra	seize	withhold
beginning	eighth	license	outrageous	separate	yacht
behavior	embarrass	lightning	pageant	sergeant	yield

SPEAKING AND LISTENING *Resource*

THE POWER OF COMMUNICATION

Humans are by nature social creatures. **Communication** is a form of behavior that fulfills the basic human need to connect and interact with other individuals in society. Because democratic government requires the free exchange of ideas, communication is also fundamental to the political way of life in the United States.

4.1 Verbal and Nonverbal Communication

Human beings use both verbal and nonverbal communication to convey meaning and exchange ideas. When a person expresses meaning through words, he or she is using **verbal communication**. When a person expresses meaning without using words, for example by standing up straight or shaking his or her head, he or she is using **nonverbal communication**. When we speak to another person, we usually think that the meaning of what we say comes chiefly from the words we use. However, as much as 60 percent of the meaning of a message may be communicated nonverbally.

ELEMENTS OF VERBAL COMMUNICATION		
ELEMENT	**DESCRIPTION**	**GUIDELINES FOR SPEAKERS**
Volume	loudness or softness	Vary your volume, but make sure that you can be heard.
Melody, Pitch	highness or lowness	Vary your pitch. Avoid speaking in a monotone (at a single pitch).
Pace	speed	Vary the speed of your delivery to suit what you are saying. Excitement, for example, can be communicated by a fast pace, and seriousness can be communicated by slowing down and saying something forcefully.
Tone	emotional quality	Suit your tone to your message, and vary it appropriately as you speak. For example, you might use a light tone for a happy message and a heavier one for a sad message.
Enunciation	clearness with which words are spoken	When speaking before a group, pronounce your words more precisely than you would in ordinary conversation.

ELEMENTS OF NONVERBAL COMMUNICATION

ELEMENT	DESCRIPTION	GUIDELINES FOR SPEAKERS
Eye contact	Looking audience members in the eye	Make eye contact regularly with people in your audience. Try to include all audience members.
Facial expression	Using your face to show your emotions	Use expressions to emphasize your message—raised eyebrows for a question, pursed lips for concentration, eyebrows lowered for anger, and so on.
Gesture	Meaningful motions of the arms and hands	Use gestures to emphasize points. Be careful, however, not to overuse gestures. Too many can be distracting.
Posture	Position of the body	Keep your spine straight and head high, but avoid appearing stiff. Stand with your arms and legs slightly open, except when adopting other postures to express particular emotions.
Proximity	Distance from audience	Keep the right amount of distance between yourself and the audience. You should be a comfortable distance away, but not so far away that the audience cannot hear you.

LISTENING SKILLS

Learning to listen well is essential not only for success in personal life, but also for success in school and, later, on the job. It is estimated that high school and college students spend over half their waking time listening to others, yet most people are rather poor listeners.

4.2 Active versus Passive Listening

Effective listening requires skill and concentration. The mind of a good listener is focused on what a speaker is trying to communicate. In other words, an effective listerner is an active listener. Ineffective listeners view listening as a passive activity, something that simply "happens" without any effort on their part. Passive listening is nothing more than hearing sounds. This type of listening can cause misunderstanding and miscommunication.

Different situations require different listening skills. The following suggestions can help you become a better listener in particular situations.

4.3 Listening to a Lecture or Demonstration

• Think of creative reasons to listen. It can be difficult to pay attention to a lecture or demonstration if you do not think the information being presented is important to you. Try to think of reasons why the information is important by asking yourself: How can I use this information?

• As you listen, show the speaker that you are involved. Remember that in a lecture or demonstration, as in a conversation, the speaker depends on you for positive feedback or response. Try to maintain an attentive posture by sitting up straight, making eye contact, and nodding when you understand.

• Listen for major ideas. Try to identify the speaker's main points and the facts or materials that are offered to support them. Check your understanding of what the speaker is saying by putting it into your own words, in your head, as you listen.

- Take notes as you listen. Note the major ideas and related details. Do not try to write down what the speaker says word for word. Use phrases, symbols, and abbreviations such as *w/* for *with, Amer.* for *American,* and *&* or *+* for *and.* (For more information, see the Language Arts Survey 5.17, "Taking Notes, Outlining, and Summarizing Information.")

- When you do not understand something that the speaker is saying, make a note. Save questions and comments for an appropriate time, usually when the speaker pauses or when he or she invites questions. Then raise your hand before asking your question or making your comment.

- Do not let yourself become distracted. Avoid such things as daydreaming, focusing on the speaker's delivery, or listening to background noise. Giving in to distractions can prevent you from understanding the speaker's message.

4.4 Listening in Conversations

- Do not monopolize the conversation. Give the other person plenty of opportunities to speak.

- When the other person is speaking, pay attention to what he or she is saying. Show through eye contact, body language, and facial expressions that you are interested and attentive.

- Avoid mentally debating the other person while he or she is speaking. This may distract you from truly hearing what the person has to say. Try to withhold judgment until the other person has finished.

- Ask the other person questions. Asking questions is a good way to start a conversation, to keep the conversation going, and to show the other person that you are really listening. The best questions are usually ones that directly relate to what the speaker has been saying.

- When you speak, respond to what the other person has been saying. Relate what you say to what he or she has said.

- Take time to think about what the other speaker has said before responding. Do not be afraid of a lull in the conversation while you think about what has been said and about your response.

- If you find yourself becoming overly emotional during a conversation, stop, take a deep breath, and bring your emotions under control before continuing. If controlling your emotions seems too difficult, consider continuing the conversation at a later time.

4.5 Listening to the Media

- Avoid being a "couch potato." Television, movies, and radio programs can be powerful manipulators. As you watch or listen, think critically about what you are seeing or hearing by evaluating these messages.

- When watching or listening to news programs or commercial advertisements, make sure to distinguish facts from opinions. *Facts* are statements that can be proved by checking a reference work or making observations. *Opinions* are statements of value or statements of policy that express personal beliefs. A statement of value expresses positive or negative attitudes toward a person, object, or idea. For example, "Albert Einstein was a great humanitarian" is a statement of value because it expresses a positive attitude toward Einstein. A statement of policy says what should or should not be done. "Congress should spend more money on education" is a statement of policy because it suggests what Congress should do. When you hear an opinion, ask yourself whether it is supported by the facts. For more information, see the Language Arts Survey 5.2, "Distinguishing Fact from Opinion."

- When watching or listening to an entertainment program, think about the quality of the program. Consider the quality of the acting, directing, and writing. Also consider the production qualities of the program—the lighting, sound effects, staging, camera work, costuming, properties, and music.

- Think about what message or messages are being delivered by the program and whether you agree or disagree with them. Do not assume that just because a program is entertaining, it does not communicate a message.

- Set standards about what you will watch or listen to. Learn to turn off a program or to switch to another program when something does not meet your standards.

- Limit the time that you spend watching or listening to the broadcast media. Remember that there is much more that you might be doing with your life such as reading, learning a new hobby or skill, writing in your journal, exercising, interacting with other people, creating works of art, or simply thinking.

4.6 Adapting Listening Skills to Specific Tasks

Just as different situations require different types of listening, different tasks or goals may also require different listening strategies and skills.

LISTENING FOR COMPREHENSION means listening for information or ideas communicated by other people. For example, you are listening for comprehension when you try to understand directions to a friend's house or your teacher's explanation of how to conduct a classroom debate. When listening for comprehension, your goal is to reach understanding, so it is important to recognize and remember the key information or ideas presented. Concentrate on getting the main points or major ideas of a message rather than all the supporting details. This can prevent you from becoming overwhelmed by the amount of information presented.

You might also use a technique called clarifying and confirming to help you better remember and understand information. The technique involves paraphrasing or repeating back to the speaker in your own words the key information presented to make sure that you have understood correctly. If the situation prevents you from using the technique—for instance, if there is no opportunity for you to respond directly to the speaker—it can still be helpful to rephrase the information in your own words in your head to help you remember and understand it.

LISTENING CRITICALLY means listening to a message in order to comprehend and evaluate it. When listening for comprehension, you usually assume that the information presented is true. Critical listening, on the other hand, includes comprehending and judging the arguments and appeals in a message in order to decide whether to accept or reject them. Critical listening is most useful when you encounter a persuasive message such as a sales pitch, advertisement, campaign speech, or news editorial. When evaluating a persuasive message, you might consider the following: Is the speaker trustworthy and qualified to speak about this subject? Does the speaker present logical arguments supported by solid facts? Does the speaker use unproven assumptions to make a case? Does the speaker use questionable motivational appeals, such as appeals to fear or to prejudice? These questions can help you decide whether or not to be convinced by a persuasive message.

LISTENING TO LEARN VOCABULARY involves a very different kind of listening because the focus is on learning new words and how to use them properly. For instance, if you were to hear a presentation on hip-hop music, the speaker might introduce some of the many slang terms used in this musical style and explain what they mean. Or you might have a conversation with someone who has a more advanced vocabulary and use this as an opportunity to learn new words. The key to listening in order to learn vocabulary is to pay attention to how words are used in context. Sometimes it is possible to figure out what an unfamiliar word means based simply on how the word is used in a sentence. Once you learn a new word, try to use it several times so it becomes more familiar and you become comfortable using it. Also be sure to look up the word in a dictionary to find out whether it has other meanings or connotations of which you are not aware.

LISTENING FOR APPRECIATION means listening purely for enjoyment or entertainment. You might listen appreciatively to a singer, a comedian, a storyteller, an acting company, or a humorous speaker. Appreciation is a very individual matter and there are no rules about how to appreciate something. However, as with all forms of listening, listening for appreciation requires attention and concentration.

COMMUNICATING WITH OTHERS

4.7 Communicating with Another Person

The ordinary human interactions that take place in daily life involve a great deal of interpersonal communication, or communication between two individuals. The following guidelines will help you to communicate more effectively in such daily interactions.

- **Make eye contact** and maintain a relaxed posture.

- **Provide feedback as you listen**. Smile or nod to show understanding and/or agreement. Ask questions or make comments when the speaker pauses for feedback. Try not to interrupt or to finish the speaker's sentences for him or her.

- **Reflect back or rephrase what the speaker has said** to make sure that you understand him or her. For example, suppose that the speaker says, "Crazy Horse never allowed anyone to make a likeness of him or take his photograph." You could reflect back, "So, nobody ever made a likeness of Crazy Horse or took his photograph? That's interesting. Why do you think he felt that way?"

- **Control your emotions**. If you become angry while listening to the speaker, take a deep breath and count to ten. Make sure you haven't misunderstood by rephrasing the statement that angered you. If you can contain your anger, express your objections calmly. If you cannot contain your anger, end your conversation and say that you would like to continue it at another time.

- **Distinguish between facts and opinions**. Facts are statements that can be proven true, whereas opinions are expressions of personal belief that may or may not be true. When presenting factual information in a conversation, it is helpful to explain what the basis for the fact is. When presenting opinions, try to indicate this by introducing these ideas with phrases like "I believe that . . ." or "In my opinion . . ." If you are unsure whether another person is stating a fact or opinion, ask what his or her statement is based on.

4.8 Communicating in a Small Group

Much human activity takes place in small groups. A small group is defined as a group of three to fifteen people, interacting in a face-to-face situation, who have an awareness of a group identity. Everyone is involved in a small group at one point or another in their lives, whether it be a high school clique, an after-school organization, an athletic team, or a family. Although many of the principles of interpersonal communication hold true in small group situations, there are additional factors to consider because of the number of people involved. The following guidelines will help you become a better communicator and participant in small group situations.

- **Respect group norms and culture**. Most groups have norms or rules that govern appropriate behavior for group members. Groups also have their own culture or way of life that may include certain beliefs, rituals, or behaviors. When participating in a small group, be sure to pay attention to and respect the norms and culture of the group.

- **Understand group roles**. Individual members are likely to fulfill particular roles in a group based on what they do best. Constructive roles help the group to achieve its goals. These include the **leader** (directs the work of the group), **secretary** (keeps minutes of group meetings), **gatekeeper** (keeps communication open by encouraging and discouraging participation), and **harmonizer** (helps to resolve conflict or reduce tension between group members). Destructive roles may prevent the group from achieving its goals. These include the **joker** (distracts the group by engaging in horseplay), **dominator** (tries to control the group for his or her own interests), **blocker** (puts down the ideas of others or refuses to cooperate), and **deserter** (withdraws from the group and does not participate). Successful group participants attempt to fulfill positive and constructive roles within the group and encourage others to do so.

- **Take turns participating**. Good group members make contributions to the discussion, but also allow others to participate. If an overly talkative person seems to dominate the discussion, be willing to take on the role of gatekeeper and gently suggest that others be allowed to contribute. For instance, you might say, "I've been interested in what you have to say, Ed. What do other people think about this issue?"

- **Help to foster a positive group climate**. Group climate refers to the degree of warmth or coldness that group members feel toward each other. You have probably been in a group with a cold climate before, where members constantly bicker and argue and never seem to accomplish anything. Positive or warm group climates are characterized by trust, cooperation, and concern for others. Negative or cold group climates are characterized by suspicion, competition, and selfishness. As a good group member, you can help to create a positive and warm climate by being supportive of others ideas, empathizing with others, treating others as equals, and remaining flexible and open to new ideas and information.

- **Establish group goals**. Some groups have a difficult time accomplishing anything because it is not clear what the goals of the group are. Without goals, a group is like a ship that sets sail with no clear destination. Chances are the ship and the group will drift aimlessly until they run aground. You can help your group stay focused by encouraging its members to establish clear goals at the beginning, and referring to these goals whenever the group seems to run aground or lose its way.

4.9 Communicating in a Large Group

Large groups are those that contain more than fifteen people. Generally the larger the size of the group, the less opportunity there is for each individual to participate. However, there are still principles that can help you become a better communicator in large group situations.

- **Share group roles**. In larger groups, it may be difficult to decide who takes what role as many members may have the skills needed for any one role. Sharing roles and responsibilities can allow everyone to contribute to the group.

- **Focus on key relationships**. It may not be possible to get to know everyone in a large group setting. Identify those key individuals in the group that you will most need to interact with in carrying out your assignments or duties, and focus on getting to know them.

- **Emphasize group identity, norms, and goals**. As groups become larger in size, they are likely to become less cohesive. Cohesiveness refers to the level of commitment and attraction members feel to each other and the group. Groups that experience low cohesion are usually not productive or successful. Try to increase cohesion by reinforcing the identity, norms, and goals of the group at every opportunity.

- **Stand up when speaking**. Make sure that everyone in the room can see and hear you. If there is a microphone available, use it. Speak in a normal tone four to six inches from the microphone.

- **Avoid the pressure to conform**. In larger groups, individuals are less comfortable speaking out if they disagree with an idea or decision. This can produce "groupthink," where members give in to the pressure to conform and do not critically evaluate information and/or decisions. If you disagree with an expressed idea or decision, do not hesitate to speak out and share your reservations.

- **Foster responsibility**. In large groups, it is relatively easy for individual members to shirk their duties and avoid responsibility. If something goes wrong, there are usually many people to blame so no one feels individually responsible for the outcomes of the group. Take responsibility yourself, and encourage others in the group to carry out their assigned duties.

4.10 Asking and Answering Questions

There are many situations in which you will find it useful to ask questions of a speaker, or in which you will be asked questions about a presentation. Often a formal speech or presentation will be followed by a question-and-answer period. Keep the following guidelines in mind when asking or answering questions.

ASKING QUESTIONS

- **Wait to be recognized**. In most cases, it is appropriate to raise your hand if you have a question and to wait for the speaker or moderator to call on you.

- **Make questions clear and direct**. The longer your question, the less chance a speaker will understand it. Make your questions short and to the point.

- **Do not debate or argue**. If you disagree with a speaker, the question-and-answer period is not the time to hash out an argument. Ask to speak with the speaker privately after the presentation is over, or agree on a later time and place to meet.

- **Do not take others' time**. Be courteous to other audience members and allow them time to ask questions. If you have a follow-up question, ask the speaker if you may proceed with your follow-up.

- **Do not give a speech**. Sometimes audience members are more interested in expressing their own opinion than in asking the speaker a question. Do not give in to the temptation to present a speech of your own.

ANSWERING QUESTIONS

- **Come prepared** for a question-and-answer period. Although you can never predict the exact questions that people will ask you, you can anticipate many questions that are likely to be asked. Rehearse aloud your answers to the most difficult questions.

- **Be patient**. It may take some time for audience members to formulate questions in response to your speech. Give the audience a moment to do so. Don't run back to your seat the minute your speech is over, or if there is an awkward pause after you invite questions.

- **Be direct and succinct**. Be sure to answer the question directly as it has been asked, and to provide a short but clear answer.

- **Rephrase difficult or ambiguous questions**. If you are not sure what an audience member's question is, repeat the question back to them to clarify. You may also want to repeat the question if not everyone in the audience could hear it.

- **Be courteous**. Sometimes audience members will ask a question you have already answered in your speech. Be tactful in such situations. Briefly repeat the information from your speech in case the audience member did not hear or understand you the first time.

- **Handle difficult audience members gracefully**. Sometimes audience members hog the stage or try to pick a verbal fight with a speaker. In such situations, keep your cool and gently suggest that the audience member talk to you privately after the presentation so you can discuss the issue with him or her more fully.

COMMUNICATION STYLES AND CULTURAL BARRIERS

4.11 Being Considerate of Other Cultures and Communication Styles

Communication styles and behaviors vary greatly between people of different cultures—even those who live and were raised in the same country. There are many possible verbal and nonverbal sources of miscommunication between cultural groups. In some cultures, emotionally intense discussions and insults are expected forms of behavior. In other cultures, such behavior is considered rude. In traditional Asian cultures, a slap on the back is considered insulting and it is not customary to shake hands with people of the opposite sex. In other cultures, a slap on the back expresses friendliness and it is customary to shake hands with anyone you meet for the first time. When listening to someone speak, Native Americans consider a bowed head a sign of respect. In other cultures, lack of eye contact may be seen as a sign of shyness, weakness, or disrespect. In Latino cultures, two speakers in conversation may stand very close and even touch each other. In other cultures, standing close is considered an intrusion on personal space and thought to be rude, and touching is generally acceptable only with close friends or relatives.

These are only a few of the many communication differences that exist among people of different cultures. When interacting with a person from another culture, it is important to remember that such differences may exist and to respect the other individual's cultural practices and behaviors.

4.12 Overcoming Barriers to Effective Multicultural Communication

The following guidelines and suggestions will help you to overcome some common barriers and stumbling blocks to communicating with people of different cultural backgrounds.

- **Treat people as individuals**. Do not assume that everyone is "the same" as you are, or even that people with similar cultural backgrounds are the same. Avoid relying on preconceptions and stereotypes when interacting with someone from another culture. Regardless of what cultural practices, physical characteristics, or behaviors they might share, human beings are individuals and should always be treated as such.

- **Be sensitive to sources of miscommunication**. Remember that both verbal and nonverbal behaviors send messages to others, and that both can lead to miscommunication and misunderstanding. If you think you have done or said something that has offended someone from another culture, ask if this is the case. It may be uncomfortable to do so at first, but you are more likely to overcome your error and become friends if you show respect and sensitivity to the other person.

- **Seek common ground**. One reason people from different cultures may have difficulty communicating is because they focus on differences rather than similarities. A simple way to overcome this problem is to find some common interest, belief, or activity that you share with the other person and that can help to bridge differences.

- **Accept others as they are**. Avoid the temptation to evaluate or judge the behavior, beliefs, feelings, or experiences of others. Instead, learn to accept differences as valid, even if you personally disagree with what someone

else thinks or feels. It is also helpful to remember that the other person is probably doing the best he or she can with whatever resources are available at the time.

- **Avoid provoking language**. Racial, ethnic, or gender slurs have no place in an enlightened society and should never be used. Profanity or swearing is unacceptable, even among close friends, and should be avoided. You-statements ("You are not listening to me," "You should not do that," "You don't know what you're talking about") can feel like an attack, even when they are well intentioned. People often react to you-statements by becoming defensive or hostile. Try to use I-statements instead ("I feel like you aren't listening to me," "I don't think you should do that," "I'm not sure I agree with you").

4.13 Collaborative Learning and Communication

Collaboration is the act of working with one or more other people to achieve a goal. Many common learning situations involve collaboration:

- participating in a small-group discussion
- doing a small-group project
- tutoring another student or being tutored
- doing peer evaluation

GUIDELINES FOR DISCUSSION

- **Listen actively during the discussion**. Maintain eye contact with the speakers. Make notes on what they say. Mentally translate what they say into your own words. Think critically about whether you agree or disagree with each speaker, and why.

- **Be polite**. Wait for your turn to speak. Do not interrupt others. If your discussion has a group leader, ask to be recognized before speaking by raising your hand.

- **Participate in the discussion**. At appropriate times, make your own comments or ask questions of other speakers.

- **Stick to the discussion topic**. Do not introduce unrelated or irrelevant ideas.

- **For a formal discussion, assign roles**. Choose a group leader to guide the discussion and a secretary to record the minutes (the main ideas and proposals made by group members). Also draw up an agenda before the discussion, listing items to be discussed.

GUIDELINES FOR PROJECTS

- **Choose a group leader** to conduct the meetings of your project group.

- **Set a goal** for the group, some specific outcome or set of outcomes that you want to bring about.

- **Make a list of tasks** that need to be performed.

- **Make a schedule** for completing the tasks, including dates and times for completion of each task.

- **Make an assignment sheet**. Assign certain tasks to particular group members. Be fair in distributing the work to be done.

- **Set times for future meetings**. You might want to schedule meetings to evaluate your progress toward your goal as well as meetings to actually carry out specific tasks.

- **Meet to evaluate your overall success** when the project is completed. Also look at the individual contributions of each group member.

GUIDELINES FOR TUTORING

- **Find out what the other student needs to learn**. Help him or her clarify assignments and areas of strength and weakness.

- **Break down your teaching into steps** that can be followed easily. Then help the other student to follow through on each step.

- **Review basic concepts, terms, and processes**. Encourage the other student to explain these to you in his or her own words.

- **Give the other student practice activities or exercises**, and help him or her to complete them.

- **Be patient**. Give the other student time to respond, to make mistakes, and to ask questions.

- **Be encouraging and supportive**. Remember that your job is to help someone else to learn, not to display your own knowledge.

GUIDELINES FOR BEING TUTORED

- **Bring with you all the materials that you need**, such as your textbook, study guides, notes, worksheets, pencils, and paper.

- **Explain as clearly as you can what you need help with**. Prepare questions beforehand.

- **Ask questions about anything that you do not understand**. Remember that no question is silly if it is sincere.

- **Be patient**. Learning takes time.

- **Do not give up if you do not understand immediately**. Practice makes perfect.

- **Be polite** and thank your tutor for his or her help.

GUIDELINES FOR PEER EVALUATION. For more information on peer evaluation, see the Language Arts Survey 2.37, "Self- and Peer Evaluation," 2.39, "How to Deliver Helpful Criticism," and 2.40, "How to Benefit from Helpful Criticism."

4.14 Conducting an Interview

In an interview, you meet with someone and ask him or her questions. Interviewing experts is an excellent way to gain information about a particular topic. For example, if you are interested in writing about the art of making pottery, you might interview an art teacher, a professional potter, or the owner of a ceramics shop.

When planning an interview, you should do some background research on your subject and think carefully about questions you would like to ask. Write out a list of questions, including some about the person's background as well as about your topic. Other questions might occur to you as the interview proceeds, but it is best to be prepared. For guidelines on being a good listener, read the Language Arts Survey 4.2, "Active versus Passive Listening," and 4.4, "Listening in Conversations." Here are some more tips for interviewing:

- **Set up a time for the interview in advance**. Don't just try to work questions into a regular conversation. Set aside time to meet in a quiet place where both you and the person you are interviewing can focus on the interview.

- **Explain the purpose of the interview**. Be sure the person you are interviewing knows what you want to find out and why you need to know it. This will help him or her to answer your questions in a way that is more useful and helpful to you.

- **Ask mostly open-ended questions**. These are questions that allow the person you are interviewing to express a personal point of view. They cannot be answered with a simple "yes" or "no" nor a brief statement of fact. The following are all examples of open-ended questions: "Why did you become a professional potter?" "What is the most challenging thing about owning your own ceramics shop?" "What advice would you give to a beginning potter?" One of the most valuable questions to ask at the end of the interview is, "What would you like to add that I haven't asked about?" This can provide some of the most interesting or vital information of all.

- **If possible, tape-record the interview**. Then you can review the interview at your leisure. Be sure to ask the person you are interviewing whether or not you can tape-record the session. If the person refuses, accept his or her decision.

- **Take notes during the interview**, whether or not you are also tape-recording it. Write down the main points and some key words to help you remember details. Record the person's most important statements word for word.

- **Clarify spelling and get permission for quotes**. Be sure to get the correct spelling of the person's name and to ask permission to quote his or her statements.

- **End the interview on time**. Do not extend the interview beyond the time limits of your appointment. The person you are interviewing has been courteous enough to give you his or her time. Return this courtesy by ending the interview on time, thanking the person for his or her help, and leaving.

- **Write up the results of the interview as soon as possible after you conduct it**. Over time, what seemed like a very clear note may become unclear or confusing. If you are unclear of something important that the person said, contact him or her and ask for clarification.

PUBLIC SPEAKING

4.15 Giving a Speech

The fear of speaking in public, although quite common and quite strong in some people, can be overcome by preparing a speech thoroughly and practicing positive thinking and relaxation. Learning how to give a speech is a valuable skill, one that you most likely will find much opportunity to use in the future.

The nature of a speech, whether formal or informal, is usually determined by the situation or context in which it is presented. **Formal speeches** usually call for a greater degree of preparation, might require special attire such as a suit or dress, and are often presented to larger groups who attend specifically to hear the presentation. A formal speech situation might exist when presenting an assigned speech to classmates, giving a presentation to a community group or organization, or presenting a speech at an awards ceremony. **Informal speech** situations are more casual and might include telling a story among friends, giving a pep talk to your team at halftime, or presenting a toast at the dinner table.

4.16 Types of Speeches

The following are the three main types of speeches:

- **Impromptu speech**. This is a speech given without any advance preparation. For example, if you were surprised by a gift or an award, you might be called upon to give a brief speech that was not written or rehearsed.

- **Memorized speech**. This is a speech that has been written out and memorized word for word. Your teacher may ask you to prepare a memorized speech on a topic you are studying at school.

- **Extemporaneous speech**. This is a speech in which the speaker refers to notes occasionally. Most professional speakers prefer to deliver extemporaneous speeches because they combine the liveliness of an impromptu speech with the careful preparation of a memorized or manuscript speech. While the speaker does not plan what he or she will say word for word, the speaker does create an overall plan for the speech, records important points on cards, and rehearses until she or he is comfortable with the material. You might give an extemporaneous speech at a city council meeting about funding for your school.

4.17 Steps in Preparing an Extemporaneous Speech

1. **Choose a topic for your speech**. Consider the audience, occasion, and your own strengths and weaknesses as a speaker when choosing a topic.

2. **Do prewriting to identify what you know or think about the topic**. As you write, think about different ways to approach the topic.

3. **Do research on the topic**. Use a variety of source materials, including newspapers, magazines, books, interviews, Internet sources, and personal experience.

4. **Determine your specific purpose in speaking about your topic**. What are you trying to accomplish in speaking to your audience? Are you trying to demonstrate something to them? Compare and contrast two things or ideas? Strengthen their commitment to something? Spur them to take action?

5. **Organize your material into three to five main points**. Use a clear, logical, and interesting organizational strategy that is suited to your specific purpose, the audience, and the occasion. Be sure each point flows logically and smoothly from the one that comes before it. Include transitions between main points, and between the introduction, body, and conclusion of the speech.

6. **Create visual aids**. Some material is too difficult to present orally and is best presented visually. Visual aids should be neat, attractive, visible from a distance, and relevant to your speech. For more information, see the Language Arts Survey 6.11, "Displaying Effective Visual Information."

7. **Prepare note cards**. Notecards should be no larger than 4 x 6 inches and should contain as much information as you need to present your speech, but not so much that you are tempted to read from the cards. Write clearly and legibly so you can read your notes at a distance.

8. **Rehearse with your note cards**. Never attempt to speak at length on a subject without practicing what you will say. If possible, practice a few times in front of a live audience. Otherwise, use a mirror or recording device. Rehearse until you feel comfortable with the material and can present the speech with minimal use of notecards. Be sure to rehearse with visual aids if you are using them.

9. **Deliver your speech**.

4.18 Guidelines for Giving a Speech

A speech should always include a beginning, a middle, and an end. The beginning, or introduction, of your speech should spark the audience's interest, present your central idea, and briefly preview your main points. The middle, or body, of your speech should expand upon each of your main points in order to support the central idea. The end, or conclusion, of your speech should be memorable and should give your audience a sense of completion.

TIPS FOR SUCCESSFUL PUBLIC SPEAKING

- **Be sincere and enthusiastic**. Feel what you are speaking about. Apathy is infectious and will quickly spread to your audience.

- **Maintain good but relaxed posture**. Don't slouch or lean. It's fine to move around a bit; it releases normal nervous tension. Keep your hands free to gesture naturally instead of holding on to note cards, props, or the podium so much that you will "tie up" your hands.

- **Speak slowly**. Oral communication is more difficult than written language and visual images for audiences to process and understand. Practice pausing. Don't be afraid of silence. Focus on communicating with the audience. By looking for feedback from the audience, you will be able to pace yourself appropriately.

- **Maintain genuine eye contact**. Treat the audience as individuals, not as a mass of people. Look at individual faces.

- **Speak in a genuine, relaxed, conversational tone**. Don't act or stiffen up. Just be yourself.

- **Communicate**. Focus on conveying your message, not "getting through" the speech. Focus on communicating with the audience, not speaking at or to it.

- **Use strategic pauses**. Pause briefly before proceeding to the next major point, before direct quotations, and to allow important or more complex bits of information to sink in.

- **Remain confident and composed.** Remember that listeners are generally "for you" while you are speaking, and signs of nervousness are usually undetectable. To overcome initial nervousness, take two or three deep breaths as you are stepping up to speak.

4.19 Oral Interpretation

Oral interpretation is the process of presenting a dramatic reading of a literary work or group of works. The presentation should be sufficiently dramatic to convey to the audience a sense of the particular qualities of the work. Here are the steps you need to follow to prepare and present an oral interpretation:

1. **Choose a cutting.** The cutting may be a single piece; a selection from a single piece; or several short, related pieces on a single topic or theme.

2. **Write the introduction and any necessary transitions.** The introduction should mention the name of each piece, the author, and, if appropriate, the translator. It should also present the overall topic or theme of the interpretation. Transitions should introduce and connect the parts of the interpretation.

3. **Rehearse, using appropriate variations in volume, pitch, pace, stress, tone, gestures, facial expressions, and body language.** If your cutting contains different voices (a narrator's voice and characters' voices, for example), distinguish them. Try to make your verbal and nonverbal expression mirror what the piece is saying. However, avoid movement—that's for drama. Practice in front of an audience or mirror or use a video camera or tape recorder.

4. **Present your oral interpretation.** Before actually presenting your interpretation, relax and adopt a confident attitude. If you begin to feel stage fright, try to concentrate on the work you are presenting and the audience, not on yourself.

INTERPRETING POETRY. Here are some additional considerations as you prepare to interpret a poem. The way you prepare your interpretation of a poem will depend on whether the poem you have chosen is a lyric poem, a narrative poem, or a dramatic poem.

- A **lyric poem** has a single speaker who reports his or her own emotions.

- A **narrative poem** tells a story. Usually a narrative poem has lines belonging to narrator, or person who is telling the story. The narrator may or may not take part in the action.

- A **dramatic poem** contains characters who speak. A dramatic poem may be a lyric, in which characters simply report emotions, or a narrative, which tells a story. A dramatic monologue presents a single speaker at a moment of crisis or self-revelation and may be either lyric or narrative.

Before attempting to dramatize any poem, read through the poem carefully several times. Make sure that you understand it well. To check your understanding, try to paraphrase the poem, or restate its ideas, line by line, in your own words.

ANALYZING THE SPEAKER OF A LYRIC POEM. When dramatizing a lyric or dramatic poem, think about the speaker of the poem. Ask yourself:

- Who is the speaker?

- How old is the speaker?

- Is the speaker male or female?

- What is the situation in which the speaker finds himself or herself?

- What does the speaker think about his or her situation?

- What values, opinions, beliefs, wishes, or needs does the speaker have?

- Is the speaker fully aware of the implications of what he or she is saying, or does the reader know more than the speaker?

Try to form a clear image of the speaker in your mind. Think about how such a person might sound, feeling and thinking as he or she does.

ANALYZING THE NARRATOR AND CHARACTERS OF A NARRATIVE OR DRAMATIC POEM. When analyzing a narrative or dramatic poem, ask about the narrator and the characters the same questions that you would ask about the speaker of a lyric poem. How are the narrator and the characters related to one another? In what ways are they different? Is there anything that the narrator understands that one or more of the characters do not?

List the narrator and each of the characters in the poem. After each, list his or her characteristics. Then try to form a clear image of each in your mind. Again, think about how each might sound, feeling and thinking as he or she does. If the poem is narrative, think of how each character reacts to the events in the story that the poem tells.

USING VERBAL AND NONVERBAL COMMUNICATION TO INTERPRET THE POEM. After analyzing the speaker (in a lyric poem) or the narrator and characters (in a narrative or dramatic poem), make a copy of the poem and mark it to show

- the different voices you will use when reading
- the emotions that you will express
- places to increase or decrease your pace
- places to raise or lower your volume
- gestures and facial expressions to use to communicate emotions

MEMORIZING A POEM. To memorize a poem, work line by line. Look at one line. Look away and repeat it. Then check to see that you got it right. Once you get that line right, add a second line. Look away and repeat both lines. Then check them. Continue in this manner until the entire poem is memorized. You may wish to have someone else look at a copy of the poem while you recite it out loud. This second person can prompt you when you forget a line. Memorize the poem thoroughly before you begin working on the qualities of your reading. If you have not thoroughly memorized the lines, you will not be able to concentrate on how you sound.

4.20 Telling a Story

A **story** or **narrative** is a series of events linked together in some meaningful fashion. We use narratives constantly in our daily lives: to make a journal entry, to tell a joke, to report a news story, to recount a historical event, to record a laboratory experiment, and so on. When creating a narrative, consider all of the following elements:

- **Decide on your purpose**. Every story has a point or purpose. It may be simply to entertain or to share a personal experience, but it may have a moral or lesson. Your purpose in telling a story will shape many other parts of the narrative, so it is important to know your purpose before you construct your narrative.

- **Select a focus**. The focus for your narrative will depend largely on your purpose in telling it. For example, if you were telling the story of Abraham Lincoln's life, and your purpose was to show how someone could rise from humble roots to a position of greatness, you would probably choose a broad focus for the story. You might begin with Lincoln's birth in a Kentucky log cabin and end with his eventual rise to the position of president of the United States and his many accomplishments in office. If your purpose was to show that perseverance is an important virtue, you might choose a narrower focus. Your story could ignore Lincoln's early life and instead focus on his long political career and his many defeats on the way to the presidency.

- **Choose your point of view**. The storyteller or narrator determines the point of view from which the story will be told. You can choose to speak in the first person, either as a direct participant in the events or as an observer (real or imagined) who witnessed the events first hand. You can also use the third-person voice to achieve greater objectivity. Once again, your purpose in telling the story may affect your decision about what point of view you choose.

- **Determine sequence of events**. The sequence of events refers to the order in which they are presented. Although it might seem obvious that stories should "begin at the beginning," this is not always the best approach. Some narratives begin with the turning point of the story to create a sense of drama and capture the listener's interest. Others begin at the end of the story and present the events leading up to this point in hindsight. Wherever you choose to begin the story, your narrative should present events in a logical fashion and establish a clear sense of direction for your listeners.

- **Determine duration of events**. Duration refers to how long something lasts. Everyone has experienced an event that seemed to last for hours, when in reality it only took minutes to occur. A good storyteller can likewise manipulate the duration of events in order to affect the way listeners experience them.

- **Select details carefully.** Make them consistent with your focus and make sure they are necessary to your purpose. A well-constructed story should flow smoothly, and should not get bogged down by irrelevant or unnecessary detail. Details can also establish the tone and style of the story and affect how listeners react to the events being described.

- **Choose characters**. All stories include characters, who need to be developed so that they become real for listeners. Try to provide your listeners with vivid, concrete descriptions of the mental and physical qualities of important characters in the story. Remember that listeners need to understand and relate to the characters in order to appreciate their behavior.

- **Create dialogue**. Although it is possible to tell a story in which the characters do not speak directly, conversation and dialogue help to add life to a story. As with detail, dialogue should be used carefully. It is important that dialogue sound authentic, relate to the main action of the story, and advance the narrative. When telling a story, you might choose to enact the characters by creating an individual voice for each one.

4.21 Participating in a Debate

A **debate** is a contest in which two people or groups of people defend opposite sides of a proposition in an attempt to convince a judge or audience to agree with their views. **Propositions** are statements of fact, value, or policy that usually begin with the word *resolved.* The following are examples of typical propositions for debate:

RESOLVED	That lie detector tests are inaccurate. (proposition of fact)
RESOLVED	That imagination is more important than knowledge. (proposition of value
RESOLVED	That Congress should prohibit the sale of handguns to private citizens. (proposition of policy)

The two sides in a debate are usually called the affirmative and the negative. The **affirmative** takes the "pro" side of the debate and argues in favor of the proposition, while the **negative** takes the "con" side and argues against the proposition. Using a single proposition to focus the debate ensures that the two sides argue or clash over a common topic. This allows the participants in the debate to develop their logic and ability to argue their positions persuasively.

Sometimes you may find that you are defending a side of a proposition that you do not personally agree with. For example, you may be asked to defend gun control in class even though you believe that the Second Amendment to the Constitution prohibits regulations on the sale of guns. Although some people may find this distasteful, there is good reason to play the "devil's advocate." First, defending a position you do not believe in will allow you to better understand the position of those who disagree with you. Although you may not change your stance, you may come to appreciate why others see the issue differently. Second, in a society based on the free and open exchange of ideas, debate is a fundamental method for arriving at just and reasonable decisions. Every idea deserves consideration, even if it is ultimately rejected.

Typically, both sides in a debate are allowed an equal amount of time to prepare for the debate and to state their case for or against the proposition. To ensure fairness, the affirmative and negative teams take turns presenting speeches. There are two basic types of speeches: **constructive speeches** in which each side states its case for or against the proposition, and **rebuttal speeches** in which each side refutes or attacks its opponent's arguments, while defending its own case. Sometimes debaters are allowed to cross-examine or ask questions of their opponents during the debate. A typical debate might be organized as follows:

AFFIRMATIVE CONSTRUCTIVE	7 minutes
Cross-Examination by Negative	2 minutes
Negative Constructive	7 minutes
Cross-Examination by Affirmative	2 minutes
Affirmative Rebuttal	3 minutes
Negative Rebuttal	5 minutes
Affirmative Rebuttal	2 minutes

In addition, each side might be granted 4 or 5 minutes of preparation time during the debate to prepare its upcoming speeches. Preparation time may only be used between speeches.

Once the debate is finished, the audience or judge is asked to consider the arguments that have been made and to vote for which side made the more persuasive case. Ideally, judges or audience members will try to be objective and make their decision based not on their personal views of the issue, but rather based on the arguments made by the debaters in the contest.

SUGGESTIONS FOR PARTICIPATING IN A DEBATE

- **Be prepared.** In a debate, it will never be possible to anticipate all the arguments your opponent might make. However, by conducting careful and through research on both sides of the issue, you should be able to prepare for the most likely arguments you will encounter. You can prepare briefs or notes on particular issues in advance of the debate to save yourself preparation time during the debate.

- **Be organized.** Because a debate involves several speeches that concern the same basic arguments or issues, it is important that you remain organized during the debate. When attacking or refuting an opponent's argument, or when advancing or defending your own argument, be sure to follow a logical organizational pattern to avoid confusing the audience or the other team.

- **Take notes** by turning a long sheet of paper sideways. Draw one column for each speaker, taking notes on each speech going down one column, and recording notes about a particular argument or issue across the page as it is discussed in each successive speech.

- **Be audience-centered.** In the argument with your opponent it is easy to forget the goal of the debate: to persuade your audience that your case is correct.

- **Prepare in advance** for the most likely arguments your opponents will raise. Use time sparingly to organize your materials and think of responses to unanticipated arguments. Save time for the end of the debate, during rebuttal speeches, when it will be more valuable.

4.22 Preparing a Multimedia Presentation

Whether you use a simple overhead projector and transparencies or a PowerPoint presentation that involves graphics, video, and sound, multimedia technology can add an important visual element to a presentation. Consider the following guidelines to create a multimedia presentation:

- **Ensure that audio-visual elements enhance understanding.** The multimedia elements should add to the verbal elements, not distract from them. Be sure the content of the presentation is understandable, and that the amount of information—both verbal and visual—will not overwhelm audience members.

- **Make sure the presentation is clearly audible and visible.** Video clips or graphics may appear blurry on a projection screen, or may not be visible to audience members in the back or on the sides of the room. Audio clips may sound muffled or may echo in a larger room or a room with different acoustics. When creating a multimedia presentation, be sure the presentation can be easily heard from all parts of the room.

- **Become familiar with the equipment.** Well before the presentation, be sure you know how to operate the equipment you will need, that you know how to troubleshoot if the equipment malfunctions, and that the equipment you will use during the presentation is the same as that which you practiced with.

- **Be sure the room can accommodate your needs.** Once you know where you will make your presentation, be sure the necessary electrical outlets and extension cords are available, that lights can be dimmed or turned off as needed, that the room can accommodate the equipment you will use, and so forth.

- **Rehearse with the equipment.** Make sure that you can operate the equipment while speaking at the same time. Be sure that the multimedia elements are coordinated with other parts of your presentation. If you will need to turn the lights off in the room, make sure you can operate the equipment in the dark and can still see your note cards.

STUDY AND RESEARCH *Resource*

THINKING SKILLS

Everyone thinks, but not everyone realizes that thinking—like hitting a baseball or playing the piano—is a skill that you can improve by learning and practicing. This section gives you some tips that can greatly improve your ability to make decisions, to solve problems, and to learn and think critically.

5.1 Making Decisions and Solving Problems

MAKING DECISIONS. When you have a decision to make, the best approach is to weigh the alternatives available to you. You can do this by making a **criteria analysis chart**. To make such a chart, list the results that you want to achieve down the left side of the chart. List your choices across the top of the chart. Then assign points from 1 to 5 to each choice, with 1 being the lowest and 5 being the highest. Add up the points for each choice to see which one is best.

CRITERIA ANALYSIS CHART

Purchase of Portable Radio	Brand A	Brand B
1. Low cost	2	3
2. Good warranty	2	1
3. Attractive design	3	1
4. Many features	2	3
Total	9	8

When making a decision, you often must weigh several factors. You can compare your options by making a **pros and cons** chart on paper. First make a list of all your options. For each option list the reasons for choosing it (the pros) and the reasons for not choosing it (the cons). Then compare the lists.

PROS AND CONS

Painting Yearbook Illustration or Drawing It in Pencil		
	Painting	**Drawing in Pencil**
Pros	colorful	easier less expensive
Cons	more expensive more difficult	not colorful

SOLVING PROBLEMS. There are many ways to solve problems. To solve a complex problem, you will probably need to use more than one strategy. Here are two approaches you can try:

- **Trial and error.** Sometimes when you have to solve a problem, you just make a guess and see if it works. In a **trial-and-error approach**, you try one possible solution and if it doesn't work you try another. If you don't know how to solve a particular math problem, you could guess the answer, plug it back into the problem, and then revise your answer as necessary.

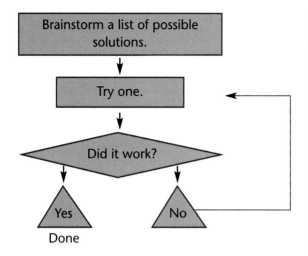

- **Divide and conquer**. Another strategy for problem solving is to divide the problem into parts and then solve each part one at a time in a logical sequence. Here is an example:

PROBLEM
A friend is coming to stay at your house for a few days and you need to prepare a room for him.

SOLUTION
Break down the job into small, manageable goals:

STRATEGY
(1) Move desk and computer from small downstairs room.
(2) Remove storage boxes from closet and put in basement.
(3) Clean the room.
(4) Put cot in room and make bed.

5.2 Distinguishing Fact from Opinion

What is the difference between the following statements?

The language with the greatest number of speakers, over nine hundred million, is Mandarin Chinese.
Mandarin Chinese is the greatest language in the world.

The first statement expresses a **fact**. You can prove this fact by looking in a reference book. The second statement expresses an **opinion**. This statement can be supported but not proved.

A fact is a statement that, at least in principle, could be proved by direct observation. Every statement of fact is either true or false. The following statement is an example of a fact:

Edgar Allan Poe wrote "The Pit and the Pendulum." (This statement can be proved by getting a published copy of the story to see who the author is.)

An opinion is a statement that expresses not a fact about the world, but rather an attitude or desire. Three common types of opinions are value statements, policy statements, and certain types of predictions.

A **value statement** expresses an attitude toward something. Such statements often include judgment words such as the following:

attractive	honest	ugly
awesome	junk	unattractive
beautiful	kind	valuable
cheap	mean	wonderful
dishonest	nice	worthless
excellent	petty	worthwhile
good	treasure	

Ancient Greece produced some <u>beautiful</u> and <u>inspiring</u> myths.
Those violent "action films" are just <u>awful</u>.

A **policy statement** tells not what is, but what someone believes should be. Such statements usually include words such as *should, should not, ought to, ought not to, must,* or *must not*. Examples of policy statements include the following:

The president <u>should be</u> reelected.
You <u>must not</u> play your radio during study hall.

Closely related to policy statements are **requests** and **commands**:

Reelect the president.
Do not play your radio during study hall.

A **prediction** makes a statement about the future. Because the future is unpredictable, most predictions can be considered opinions:

People will live longer in the future.
Tomorrow will be partly cloudy.

EVALUATING FACTS AND OPINIONS. When evaluating a fact, ask yourself whether it can be proved through direct observation or by checking a reliable source such as a reference work or an unbiased expert. An opinion is as good as the facts that support it. The opinion that Mandarin Chinese is the greatest language in the world is supported by such facts as the number of speakers that it has. However, others might argue that English is the greater language because it is spoken more widely around the globe. Of course, no list of facts would conclusively prove or disprove the opinion.

When you write and speak, express opinions sparingly. Usually, you can make a stronger case by substituting related facts for opinions. For example, instead of saying, "This was a wonderful day," you could say something like, "Today the sun was shining, it was 74 degrees outside, and I got an *A* on my math test. That's what made it a great day." When you express an opinion, especially in writing, include facts to back up or support that opinion.

When reading or listening, be critical about the statements that you encounter. Ask yourself, "Is this a fact or an opinion?" If it is a statement of fact, consider whether it can be proved or seems likely. If it is an opinion, consider whether it is supported by facts.

5.3 Avoiding False Arguments and Propaganda

Another very important thinking skill is learning to use good logic. Life is a process of trying to learn what is true and then to live according to what you believe to be true. Not only do you need good facts, but you also need to know how to put those facts together to come up with the right conclusions. Learning how to think clearly will enable you to avoid errors in logic and to arrive at true conclusions. It will also help you to recognize the faulty thinking of others (especially advertisers) who might be trying to persuade you of something. The intentional use of false arguments to persuade others is called **propaganda**. Here are some of the many faulty arguments of which you should be aware.

GLITTERING GENERALITIES AND "SPIN." **Glittering generalities** are statements given to make

something sound more appealing. Such statements can be hard to prove, as they appeal to the emotions.

EXAMPLE
> These trading cards are the best ever in this limited-time collection!

ANALYSIS
> Nothing in this statement tells the listener why the trading cards are the best ever. Adding "limited-time collection" to the statement vaguely implies that the trading cards will be available for only a short while, and that the listener should buy them quickly before they are unavailable.

Spin is a technique used to slant public perception of the news. Public relations firms and advertisers use this technique to create a favorable perception of a product or organization. Unlike more obvious forms of advertising, spin is hard to recognize because it can be invisible. It is important to know how to recognize such manipulative and misleading statements.

EXAMPLE
> The accident was a minor incident because only twenty-five people were injured.

ANALYSIS
> The fact is that twenty-five people were injured. This does not make it a minor incident; someone is merely interpreting the accident as minor.

STEREOTYPES. An overgeneralization about a group of people is known as a **stereotype**. Stereotypes are one of the most dangerous of all overgeneralizations. Remember that the differences among people within a single race or ethnic background are greater than the average differences between races or ethnic groups as a whole. Stereotyping is always based on lack of knowledge or experience. It is the basis of prejudice and is unacceptable in a civilized society.

UNSOUND OPINIONS. A fact is a statement that can be proved. An opinion is a statement that cannot be proved. An opinion is someone's personal idea of what is right and may or may not be true. A sound opinion is one that can be supported by facts. An **unsound opinion** is one that cannot be supported by facts. Always be sure that you make a clear distinction between facts and opinions and that you can back up your opinions with facts.

> FACT
>
> Miss Rivers won this year's award for excellence in teaching.
>
> OPINION
>
> Miss Rivers is the best teacher at Jordan High School.
>
> ANALYSIS
>
> The statement that "Miss Rivers is the best teacher at Jordan High School" is someone's personal feeling about her. However, it is probably a sound opinion because it is backed up by the fact that she received the award for excellence in teaching.

CIRCULAR REASONING. Circular reasoning is the error of trying to support an opinion by restating it in different words. You can avoid circular reasoning by always backing up your opinions with facts.

> EXAMPLE
>
> That adventure book was exciting because it was full of action.
>
> ANALYSIS
>
> The "reason" the speaker gives for saying that the book was exciting is really just another way of saying it was exciting. He or she should mention some specific examples to show what makes the story exciting.

LOADED WORDS. In trying to argue for or against something, people will often use **loaded words**, or words that stir up strong feelings, whether positive or negative. Be careful not to let your feelings interfere with your understanding of the facts.

> EXAMPLE
>
> Representative Philbert is a lazy, good-for-nothing imbecile.
>
> ANALYSIS
>
> This statement, an emotional attack on the representative, uses loaded words that will stir up feelings against him. It is not a reasonable evaluation of his policies or actions in office.

BANDWAGON APPEAL. Bandwagon appeal plays to your desire to be part of the crowd—to be like everyone else and to do what everyone else is doing. Beware of advertisements or arguments that try to get you to think or act like everyone else. Just because "everybody" believes or does something does not make it good or right for you.

> EXAMPLE
>
> Those who want to be cool wear Star jeans.
>
> ANALYSIS
>
> This statement suggests that you aren't really part of the "in" crowd unless you wear this brand of jeans. It does not prove, or even say, anything about the quality of the clothing.

5.4 Classifying

One of the many higher-level thinking skills you can develop is the ability to classify. To **classify** is to put into classes or categories. Items in the same category should share one or more characteristics. For example, whales are classified by their method of eating as baleen or toothed whales. The key step in classifying is choosing categories that fit your purpose. Make sure you clearly define your categories.

5.5 Generalizing

To **generalize** is to make a broad statement based on one or more particular observations. For example, suppose that you observe that several cats like to stare through windows. You might generalize, based on this discovery, that "cats like to stare through windows." Such generalizations are also called **inferences**. People have learned most of what they know about the world by making generalizations based on their experiences.

Generalizing is therefore an extremely important thinking tool. Unfortunately, it is not a perfect one. Generalizations can be proved false by only one exception. Since generalizations can be proved false by a new experience, avoid making generalizations based on too little evidence. Keep an open mind and be willing to revise your ideas about the world.

5.6 Making Inferences, Predictions, and Hypotheses

From careful observation, it is possible to make generalizations, or **inferences**, about the world around us. From there it is possible to **predict** what will happen and to form hypotheses. A **hypothesis** is an educated guess about a cause or an effect. A prediction based on a theory is a hypothesis. A possible explanation for an observed event is also a hypothesis. A hypothesis always needs to be tested against experience. You can test hypotheses the following ways:

- Conduct actual experiments to see if your prediction will occur.
- Examine many relevant examples.
- Conduct a "thought experiment" by asking "What if" questions. (See 2.15, "Imagining: Asking 'What If' Questions.")

Notice that a hypothesis can be disproved by only one exception. However, a hypothesis cannot be proved merely by gathering examples. Theories and hypotheses can change if a discovery shows them to be inadequate.

5.7 Deductive versus Inductive Reasoning

Deduction and induction are two types of logical reasoning. **Deductive reasoning** starts with a generalization to make a statement or statements about something specific. **Inductive reasoning** examines specific facts or instances to make a generalization.

DEDUCTIVE
> All whales live in the sea. (general)
> The beluga whale must live in the sea. (specific)
>
> All students have signed the school policy statement. (general)
> Tom is a student at the school. Therefore, he has signed the policy statement. (specific)

INDUCTIVE
> The blue whale, beluga, and orca live in the sea. (specific)
> Therefore, all whales live in the sea. (general)
>
> More than 100 students have signed the school policy statement. (specific)

> Therefore, all students have signed the policy statement. (general)

Note: With inductive reasoning, only one specific example is needed to prove the generalization false. See the Language Arts Survey 5.5, "Generalizing."

5.8 Estimating and Quantifying

To support an argument, you need to provide facts, and often facts are strengthened by numbers or quantities. If you claim, for instance, that too many people are without health insurance, you should **quantify** your claim by stating how many. The numbers you need may be available in reference works. If not, you might be able to **estimate**, or find the approximate quantity. Sometimes you will have only enough knowledge to estimate a range within which the actual number actually falls. If you need to estimate, always make clear that you are doing so.

QUANTIFYING
> The science fair had 314 registered participants.

ESTIMATING
> The science fair was attended by about 300 students and their parents.

5.9 Analyzing and Synthesizing

When you **analyze** something, you break it down into parts and then think about how the parts are related to each other and to the whole. For example, you might analyze a painting by describing its composition, shapes, lines, colors, and subject. You might analyze a short story by describing its conflict, plot, characters, setting, and theme. You might analyze a movie by describing its acting, directing, writing, settings, and costumes.

When you **synthesize** something, you bring everything that you were considering together into a whole.

5.10 Comparing and Contrasting

Comparing and contrasting are closely related processes. When you **compare** one thing to another, you describe similarities between the two things. When you **contrast** two things, you describe their differences.

To compare and contrast, begin by listing the features of each subject. Then go down both lists and check whether each feature is shared or not. You can also show similarities and differences in a Venn diagram. For more information, see the Language Arts Survey 2.16, "Completing Venn Diagrams," and 2.27, "Choosing a Method of Organization: Comparison and Contrast Order."

5.11 Evaluating

When you **evaluate**, you make a judgment about something. You may be asked to compare two things to determine which is more valuable or effective. Evaluate questions use such words as *evaluate, judge, justify, critique, determine whether, decide the effectiveness of,* and *appraise.*

Determine whether Hawthorne believably portrays Beatrice in "Rappaccini's Daughter," using evidence from the text to support your response.

5.12 Extending

When you **extend** your knowledge, you connect one experience to another. In the study of literature, you extend your knowledge by making connections between two pieces of literature, between the literary work and your own experience, or between a literary work and a cultural or current event. Extend questions use such words as *extend your knowledge, connect, relate,* and *apply.*

In popular culture and throughout history, people have been accused of being poisonous, like Dr. Rappaccini. Name examples of such people and the ways they have influenced the world around them. Then name people who have countered them.

5.13 Perspective, Empathy, and Self-Understanding

When you are asked to use perspective, empathy, and self-understanding to answer a question, you are exercising an important ability to connect the experience of one person or group to your own. Such thinking allows you to see multiple perspectives, generate alternative viewpoints, and understand another person's feelings and

worldview. These questions also allow you to understand your own perspective.

Why do you think Susan B. Anthony was willing to be arrested for her convictions? How would you react if you lost your rights as a citizen? Would you be willing to risk arrest to fight for your rights, as Susan B. Anthony did? Why, or why not?

STUDY SKILLS

5.14 Developing Good Study Habits

Success in a future career depends largely on success in school. No matter what your experience in school so far, you can improve your performance enormously by developing good study habits. Doing so will make learning easier and more enjoyable.

Find a place to work. Homework is best done in a special study area. Follow these guidelines for picking an appropriate place to study:

- Choose a quiet location, away from distractions such as conversation, television, or loud music.

- Choose a place that is well lit and comfortable. Adequate lighting will help you to avoid eyestrain and headaches.

- Choose a study area that is available at regular times. Set aside a specific time each day for study.

- Have all the tools that you will need, such as paper, pencils, textbooks, handouts, and reference works, ready and at hand.

Make a study plan. Many of your assignments will be due on the following day. Others will be long-term projects. At the end of each school day, make a habit of looking over your assignment notebook. Decide what tasks you need to complete for the following day. Break down longer assignments into specific steps that need to be completed by specific times. Record all of these assignments on a calendar or study plan.

5.15 Keeping an Assignment Notebook

Keeping track of assignments in your head can be dangerous because of the possibility of forgetting important details. Instead, write down all your assignments in an assignment notebook. For each assignment, record:

- the name of the subject
- details of the assignment, including what, precisely, you need to do
- the date of the assignment
- the date when the assignment is due

5.16 Understanding the Assignment

Understanding an assignment depends on your ability to follow directions.

FOLLOWING SPOKEN DIRECTIONS. Often teachers give assignments orally. When listening to spoken assignments,

- Listen carefully. Write down the directions as you hear them.
- Notice what steps are involved in the assignment. Also notice the order of these steps.
- Listen for the key word in each step. A key word is one that tells you what to do. Examples are *read, write, organize,* and *memorize.*
- If you do not understand the directions, ask your teacher to explain them.

FOLLOWING WRITTEN DIRECTIONS. Directions for tests usually are written down. Assignment directions also sometimes appear in written form on the board, overhead transparencies, or handouts. When reading written directions,

- Read all the directions completely before you begin the assignment.
- Ask questions to clarify any points not covered in the directions.
- Divide the assignment into steps. Put these steps in a logical order.
- Decide what materials you will need, and assemble them before you begin.
- Reread each step before you actually do it.

5.17 Taking Notes, Outlining, and Summarizing Information

When **taking notes** in class or while conducting your own research, you may find it helpful to use a **rough outline**, or modified outline, form. Write main ideas, capitalizing the first letter of the first word and all proper nouns and proper adjectives. Beneath the main ideas, write related subordinate ideas, preceded by dashes.

Major Cultures in N. Amer., 1492

    —Eastern woodland (incl. Iroquois & Algonquians)
    —Southeastern (incl. Cherokee & Chicasaw)
    —Plains (incl. Dakota, Pawnee, & Kiowa)
    —Southwestern (incl. Navajo, Hopi, & Apache)
    —Great Basin (incl. Ute & Paiute)
    —Plateau (incl. Nez Perce & Yakima)
    —Northwestern (incl. Chinook & Yurok)
    —California (incl. Shasta, Pomo, & Chumash)

Origins

    —Came to Amer. by land bridge across Bering Strait
    — ~ 35,000 bc
    —May have followed herds, mammoths, musk oxen, etc.

To review the material, you might find it helpful to read over your notes and outline, and then to **summarize** what you have learned. Writing a summary of the material is more powerful than thinking through your summary or even saying it out loud. The act of writing reinforces your memory of what you have learned.

RESEARCH SKILLS

Learning is a lifelong process, one that extends far beyond school. Both in school and on your own, it is important to remember that your learning and growth are up to you. One good way to become an independent lifelong learner is to master research skills. Research is the process of gathering ideas and information. One of the best resources for research is the library.

5.18 How Library Materials Are Organized

Each book in a library is assigned a unique number, called a **call number.** The call number is printed on the **spine** (edge) of each book. The numbers serve to classify books as well as to help the library keep track of them.

Libraries commonly use one of two systems for classifying books. Most school and public libraries use the **Dewey Decimal System.** Most college libraries use the **Library of Congress Classification System** (known as the LC system).

5.19 How to Locate Library Materials

If you know the call number of a book or the subject classification number you want, you can usually go to the bookshelves, or stacks, to obtain the book. Use the signs at the ends of the rows to locate the section you need. Then find the

THE LIBRARY OF CONGRESS SYSTEM

Call Letters	Subjects
A	Reference and General Works
B–BJ	Philosophy, Psychology
BK–BX	Religion
C–DF	History
G	Geography, Autobiography, Recreation
H	Social Sciences
J	Political Science
K	Law
L	Education
M	Music
N	Fine Arts
P	Language, Literature
Q	Science, Mathematics
R	Medicine
S	Agriculture
T	Technology
U	Military Science
V	Naval Science
Z	Bibliography, Library Science

THE DEWEY DECIMAL SYSTEM

Call Numbers	Subjects
000–099	Reference and General Works
100–199	Philosophy, Psychology
200–299	Religion
300–399	Social Studies
400–499	Language
500–599	Science, Mathematics
600–699	Technology
700–799	Arts
800–899	Literature
900–999	History, Geography, Biography[1]

1. Biographies (920s) are arranged alphabetically by the name of the person whose life is treated in each biography.

particular shelf that contains call numbers close to yours.

Library collections include many other types of publications besides books, such as magazines, newspapers, audio and video recordings, and government documents. Ask a librarian to tell you where to find the materials you need.

To find the call numbers of books that will help you with your research, use the library's catalog. The catalog lists all the books in the library (or a group of libraries if it is part of a larger system).

COMPUTERIZED CATALOGS. Many libraries today use computerized catalogs. Systems differ from library to library, but most involve using a computer terminal to search through the library's collection. You can usually search by author, title, subject, or key word. If your library has a computerized catalog, you will need to learn how to use your library's particular system. A librarian can help you to master the system. Here is a sample book entry screen from a computerized catalog.

Author	Wallace, David Rains, 1945-
Title	The Quetzal and the Macaw: The story of Costa Rica's National Parks
Publication info.	Sierra Club Books, 1992
No. of pages/size	xvi, 222p. : maps : 24 cm.
ISBN	ISBN 0-87156-585-4
Subjects	National Parks and reserves—Costa Rica—History
	Costa Rica. Servicio de Parques Nacionales—History
	Nature conservation—Costa Rica—History
Dewey call number	333.78

COMPUTERIZED CATALOG SEARCHES

Search By	Example	Hints
Author	gould, stephen j	Type last name first. Type as much of the name as you know.
Title	mismeasure of man	Omit articles such as *a, an,* or *the* at the beginning of titles.
Subject	intelligence tests; ability-testing	Use the list of subjects provided by the library.
Key words	darwin; intelligence; craniology	Use related topics if you can't find anything in your subject.

CARD CATALOGS. Like a computerized catalog, a card catalog contains basic information about each book in the library. In a card catalog the information is typed on paper cards, which are arranged alphabetically in drawers. For each book there is a title card, one author card for each author, and at least one subject card. All of these cards show the book's title, author, and call number, so you can search for a book by title, author, or subject. The following illustration shows a typical title card.

A TITLE CARD

333.78   The Quetzal and the Macaw : the story of Costa Rica's national parks.
Wallace, David Rains, 1945–
The Quetzal and the Macaw : the story of Costa Rica's national parks.—San Francisco: Sierra Club Books, 1992
xvi, 222 p. : maps : 24 cm.
1. National parks and reserves—Costa Rica—History. 2. Costa Rica. Servicio de Parques nacionales—History. 3. Nature conservation—Costa Rica—History. I. Title.
ISBN 0-394-57456-7

When you find the entries for the books you want, write down the call number of each book and then go to the shelves. If you cannot find a particular book you need in the catalog, ask the librarian if your library can request books from another library through an interlibrary loan.

INTERLIBRARY LOANS. Many libraries are part of larger library networks. In these libraries, the computerized catalog covers the collections of several libraries. If you want a book from a different library, you will need to request the book at the library's request desk or by using its computer. Ask your librarian to help you if you have questions. He or she will be able to tell you when the book will be shipped to your library.

5.20 Using Reference Works

Most libraries have an assortment of reference works in which knowledge is collected and organized so that you can find it easily. Usually, reference works cannot be checked out of the library.

5.21 TYPES OF DICTIONARIES. You will find many types of dictionaries in the library reference section. The most common is a dictionary of the English language. Examples include the *American Heritage Dictionary, Webster's New World Dictionary,* and the multi-volume *Oxford English Dictionary.* Other word dictionaries focus on slang, abbreviations and acronyms, English/foreign language translation, and spelling. Biographical, historical, scientific, and world language dictionaries are also some of the works you will find in the reference section.

For more information on using a dictionary to look up specific words in English, see the Language Arts Survey 1.17, "Using a Dictionary."

5.22 USING A THESAURUS. A thesaurus is a reference book that groups synonyms, or words with similar meanings. Suppose that you are writing an essay and have a word that means almost but not quite what you want, or perhaps you find yourself using the same word over and over. A thesaurus can give you fresh and precise words to use. For example, if you look up the word *sing* in a thesaurus, you might find the following synonyms listed:

sing (v.) carol, chant, croon, hum, vocalize, warble, yodel

5.23 USING ALMANACS, YEARBOOKS, AND ATLASES. **Almanacs** and **yearbooks** are published each year. An almanac provides statistics and lists, often related to recent events. In an almanac you can find facts about current events, countries of the world, famous people, sports, entertainment, and many other subjects. An overview of the events of the year can be found in a yearbook.

Some of the more widely used almanacs and yearbooks are *The Guinness Book of World Records;* the *Information Please, Almanac, Atlas, and Yearbook;* the *World Almanac and Book of Facts;* and the *World Book Yearbook of Events.*

An **atlas** is a collection of maps and other geographical information. Some atlases show natural features such as mountains and rivers; others show political features such as countries and cities. If you need to locate a particular feature on a map in an atlas, refer to the gazetteer, an index that lists every item shown on the map.

5.24 Using Biographical References, Encyclopedias, and Periodicals. A **biographical reference** contains information on the lives of famous people. Examples include *Who's Who*, the *Dictionary of American Biography*, and *Contemporary Authors*.

Encyclopedias provide a survey of knowledge. General encyclopedias, such as *World Book*, contain information on many different subjects. Specialized encyclopedias, such as the *LaRousse Encyclopedia of Mythology*, contain information on one particular area of knowledge.

The topics in an encyclopedia are treated in articles, which are usually arranged in alphabetical order. If you look up a topic and do not find it, check the index (usually in the last volume). The index will tell you where in the encyclopedia your topic is covered.

A **periodical** is a publication that comes out regularly, usually once a week, once a month, or four times a year. Magazines and newspapers are periodicals. Because they are published frequently and quickly, periodicals are an excellent source for the latest news and information, but they may not be as accurate as some other sources.

5.25 Using Indexes, Appendices, and Glossaries. An **index** lists in alphabetical order the subjects mentioned in a book or collection of periodicals and pages where these subjects are treated. Indexes help you locate possible sources of information about your topic. An index can be at the back of a book of nonfiction, or it can be a published book itself.

An example of a published index is *The Reader's Guide to Periodic Literature*, a comprehen-sive index to popular magazine and journal articles. Some periodicals, such as the *New York Times* and *National Geographic*, publish their own indexes, listing articles in past issues. Most indexes are published in sequential volumes that are issued yearly or monthly. Indexes are available as bound books, on microfilm, and online on the Internet.

An **appendix** provides additional material, often in chart or table form, at the end of a book or other writing.

A **glossary** lists key words in a book and their definitions.

5.26 Using the Internet

The **Internet** is a vast collection of computer networks that can provide you with a great wealth of information from libraries, government agencies, high schools and universities, nonprofit and educational organizations, museums, user groups, and individuals around the world. The Internet provides a valuable way to do research—if you know how to use it. Here are some guidelines.

5.27 Browsing versus Searching on the Internet. **Browsing** means sifting through Internet sites by means of an Internet browser, or software that connects you to the Internet. **Searching** means conducting focused research by using an Internet search engine. By both browsing and searching, you can gain access to the information you want. Browsing allows you to navigate through different sites, either before or after you have conducted a search. Searching allows you to narrow and expand your research in a focused way to find the particular information you need.

Internet Search Engines

www.alltheweb.com
This enormous engine tracks more than 200 million URLs (Uniform Resource Locators, or Internet addresses).

www.altavista.digital.com
This engine claims to index 30 million Web pages.

www.infoseek.com
This search engine also contains a large database and an associated directory, Infoseek Guide.

www.yahoo.com
This popular search service is maintained by online editors who sift through Internet sites and keep only the valuable ones.

5.28 Conducting an Internet Search

- Access a reliable search engine.

- Browse the search engine's links or do a keyword search.

- Use Boolean search strategies (see the Language Arts Survey 5.29) or other specialized search tools to narrow and expand your search as needed.

- Browse the results of your search.

- Repeat this process using different search engines until you find what you want.

To keep track of your Internet research, see the Language Arts Survey 5.41, "Documenting and Mapping Internet Research."

5.29 USING BOOLEAN SEARCH STRATEGIES. Boolean logic refers to the logical relationship among search terms. It is named for the mathematician George Boole. To conduct a focused search on the Internet, you should know Boolean operators such as AND, OR, NOT, and NEAR. These operators allow you to limit or expand your research. There are several guides to using Boolean search strategies on the Internet. They can be found by searching with the keyword "Boolean."

Boolean Operators

" " Quote marks help limit your search to just the phrase in quotes. "Hitchhiker's Guide to the Galaxy" will find references to that specific book title. Without the quotes, a search engine might list numerous other sites, including those related to hitch-hikers, guide, and galaxy.

AND This operator lets you join two ideas. "Greece" AND "travel" would provide you with travel information to Greece. The two words by themselves would give you listings too general to be helpful.

OR This operator gives you sites that carry information about one or the other of two groups. "Rottweilers OR Huskies" will give you sites that include either one of these dog breeds. "Rottweilers AND Huskies" will list only sites that include both dog breeds.

NOT This command lets you eliminate certain sites. "American food NOT pizza" will find sites on American food but exclude sites related to pizza.

5.30 Evaluating Information and Media Sources

To conduct your research efficiently, you need to evaluate your sources and set priorities among them. Ideally, a source will be:

- **Unbiased.** When an author has a personal stake in what people think about a subject, he or she may withhold or distort information. Investigate the author's background to see if she or he is liable to be biased. Using loaded language and overlooking obvious counterarguments are signs of author bias.

- **Authoritative.** An authoritative source is reliable and trustworthy. An author's reputation, especially among others who conduct research in the same field, is a sign of authority. Likewise, periodicals and publishers acquire reputations for responsible or poor editing and research.

- **Timely.** Information about many subjects changes rapidly. An astronomy text published last year may already be out of date. In other fields—for instance, algebra—older texts may be perfectly adequate. Consult with your teacher and your librarian to decide how current your sources must be.

- **Available.** Borrowing through interlibrary loan, tracing a book that is missing, or recalling a book that has been checked out to another person takes time. Make sure to allow enough time for these materials.

- **Appropriate for your level.** Find sources that present useful information that you can understand. Materials written for "young people" may be too simple to be helpful. Books written for experts may presume knowledge that you do not have. Struggling with a difficult text is often worth the effort, but if you do so, monitor your time and stay on schedule.

5.31 HOW TO READ A NEWSPAPER OR NEWSMAGAZINE. Newspapers and news magazines contain an enormous amount of information. Few people who are not professional politicians or news personnel have the time to read all or most of what appears in a newspaper each day. Nonetheless, reading the news is important. Only by doing that can you take advantage of democratic freedoms and make informed voting decisions.

An excellent way to approach reading a newspaper is as follows: Skim the headlines and leads for world, national, state, and local news stories. Read any news summaries included in your paper. Then read in depth any stories that seem particularly important or interesting. You may also wish to read the feature or entertainment sections of the newspaper, according to your own interests.

When reading news stories and editorials, make sure to distinguish between facts and opinions. Facts are statements that can be proved by observation or by consulting a reliable and objective source. Opinions are predictions or statements of value or policy. When you encounter opinions in a newspaper, try to determine whether these opinions are sound. Sound opinions are ones supported by facts. For more information on distinguishing between facts and opinions, see the Language Arts Survey 5.2, "Distinguishing Fact from Opinion."

5.32 How to Evaluate a Film. We watch movies for a multitude of reasons, but perhaps the most common is that a movie allows us to escape our own realities for a couple of hours. It lets us visit new places, see and try exciting new things, and experience life in someone else's shoes. A great film gives us insight into the lives of others and so expands our understanding and our sympathies. Some films, however, are created solely for the purpose of making money through exploiting sensational elements or gimmicks. Although you cannot control the types of movies Hollywood decides to make, you can control the types of movies you choose to watch. The following guidelines will enable you to become a more discriminating consumer of films.

- **Plan ahead.** Decide in advance which films you would like to see. Don't settle for just any movie that happens to be playing at your local theater or on television.

- **Listen, watch, and read what the critics have to say.** Take what the critics have to say into consideration to help you decide which movies to see. Once you have seen the movie, decide for yourself whether you agree or disagree with a particular critic. Consider what elements of the movie you liked or disliked, and what could have been altered to make it better. If, after a while, you find one particular critic with whom you tend to agree on a regular basis, use his or her opinion to help you choose which movies to see.

- **Be a critic yourself.** Be critical of dialogue and story lines. Many films recycle conventional story lines and dialogue. Many contain sensational scenes that provoke audiences but forfeit quality in story line, dialogue, and content. When you see a film, ask yourself questions such as the following:

  – Does each scene move the story forward?

  – Do the characters' actions fit their motives? Is their dialogue believable?

  – Are the themes raised in the film fully developed?

  – What effects do lighting, camera angle, and musical background produce?

- **Be aware of previews and coming attractions.** These are designed with the help of the production company's marketing and sales departments to motivate you to see their film. Previews can make a film seem more humorous, exciting, and powerful than it really is by showing only the best dialogue and action.

- **Try something new!** Try viewing a film that is much different from the type and genre that you usually see. Keep an open mind; you might just surprise yourself and enjoy it.

- **Never substitute.** Never see a film adaptation of a literary work as a substitute for reading the work itself. While seeing such an adaptation can be a good introduction to a literary work, do not rely on it to capture all the richness of the original.

5.33 How to Evaluate Radio and Television. Television and radio are other communication media. You may not be able to respond directly to the broadcaster, but you can still control the broadcast message. Follow the guidelines below to effectively control television output:

- **Plan your television and radio time.** Rather

than accepting whatever program happens to be on, look at broadcast listings and choose programs that are of interest to you.

- **Be a critic.** Question what you see and hear. What criticisms do you have about a program: its quality, its message, its originality, the depth and reliability of its coverage?

- **Remember that advertisers pay for most broadcast programs.** They also control the content of the programs they sponsor and pay for your attention because they want to sell you something. Listen to and watch these advertisements and programs critically. Read the Language Arts Survey 5.2, "Distinguishing Fact from Opinion," for tips on evaluating information critically.

5.34 HOW TO EVALUATE ADVERTISEMENTS. Advertising messages are everywhere in the media. To sharpen your skills in evaluating them, see the Language Arts Survey 5.2, "Distinguishing Fact from Opinion," and 5.3, "Avoiding False Arguments and Propaganda."

5.35 HOW TO EVALUATE INTERNET SITES. Most published print materials have been checked carefully before publication. But anyone can publish something on the Internet—without having to verify facts or guarantee quality. When you use the Internet for research, be careful to evaluate your sources. Here are some guidelines.

Consider the resource's domain name. Documents that end with .edu and .gov are generally reliable, since they come from educational and governmental organizations. Commercial sites end in .com. They can be reliable, too, but watch for biases that favor the company's product. Sites ending in .org or .net can be trusted if they are from a reliable organization, but watch for special interest group sites that slant or "spin" information to their advantage.

KEY TO INTERNET DOMAINS

.com commercial entitity
.edu educational institution
.firm business entity
.gov government agency or department
.info organizations that provide information
.mil military organization
.net network resource
.org other type of organization, usually nonprofit
.store online stores

Consider the author.
- Is the author's name listed?
- What are this person's credentials?
- What makes him or her qualified to provide this information?
- Does the author provide a way for you to contact him or her?

Evaluate the quality of information.
- How accurate is the information? Does it appear to be reliable and without errors?
- Are there links to other reliable sources? Do the links really work?
- How current is the information? Is the date provided for when the site was authored or revised? Is this the latest information on this topic?
- How clearly does the author provide information?
- How well does the author cover the topic, based on what you know from other sources?
- How does the author support the information—with charts, graphs, a bibliography?

Look for objectivity.
- Is the information given without bias?
- Is the author objective, or does he or she try to influence the way you think?

5.36 Documenting Sources

As you use your research in your writing, you must document your sources of information. Remember to:

- Credit the sources of all ideas and facts that you use.
- Credit original ideas or facts that are expressed in text, tables, charts, and other graphic information.
- Credit all artistic property, including works of literature, song lyrics, and ideas.

5.37 KEEPING A RESEARCH JOURNAL. Just as a writing journal can help you track your thoughts, experiences, and responses to literature, a research journal can help you track your research. A research journal is a notebook, electronic file, or other means to track the information you find as you conduct research. A research journal can include a list of questions you want to research. (Such questions can be an excellent source of writing topics.)

EXAMPLES

How did the Vietnam Veterans Memorial come to be? Why is it one of the most visited memorials in America?

Where can I find more artwork by Faith Ringgold?

Why was Transcendentalism such an important literary movement in America but not in Europe?

5.38 USING YOUR RESEARCH JOURNAL FOR DOCUMENTATION. As you conduct your research, rely on your research journal as a place to take notes on the sources you find and your evaluation of them. Keeping a research journal can be an invaluable way to track your research and to take notes.

5.39 INFORMAL AND FORMAL NOTE-TAKING. **Informal note-taking** is for when you want information for your own use only, and when you will not need to quote or document your sources. You would take informal notes when preparing materials to use in studying, for instance, as you watch a film or listen to a lecture.

Informal note-taking is much like outlining (see 2.29, "Rough Outlines"). Use important ideas as headings, and write relevant details below. You will not be able to copy every word, nor is there any need to. Write phrases instead of sentences.

QUOTATION	"Jerzy Kosinski came to the United States in 1957, and in 1958 he was awarded a Ford Foundation fellowship."
NOTES	Jerzy Kosinski —came to US 1957 —Ford Foundation fellowship 1958

You will also want to record information about the event or performance, including the date, time, place, speaker, and title, as applicable. After you are done taking notes, read them over to ensure that they are legible and meaningful. If you have used idiosyncratic shorthand or abbreviations that you may not later recall, write out your notes more fully.

Formal note-taking is for when you may need to quote or document your sources. When you are keeping formal notes for a project—for instance, for a debate or a research paper—you should use 4" x 6" index cards.

PREPARING NOTE CARDS

1. Identify the source at the top right corner of the card. (Use the source numbers from your bibliography cards.)
2. Identify the subject or topic of the note on the top line of the card. (This will make it easier to organize the cards later.)
3. Use a separate card for each fact or quotation.
4. Write the pertinent source page number or numbers after the note.

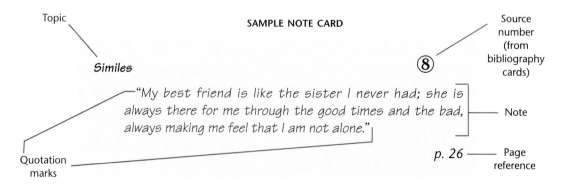

SAMPLE NOTE CARD

Topic

Similes ⑧

Source number (from bibliography cards)

"My best friend is like the sister I never had; she is always there for me through the good times and the bad, always making me feel that I am not alone."

Note

Quotation marks

p. 26 — Page reference

FORMAL NOTE-TAKING

Type of Note	When to Use	What to Watch For
Quotation	When the exact wording of a primary source is important to your topic	Copy spelling, capitalization, punctuation, and numbers exactly as in the source.
	When you are providing a definition	Place quotation marks around all direct quotations.
Paraphrase	When the wording of a secondary source is particularly memorable or insightful	Record, when appropriate, explanatory background information about the speaker or the context of a quotation.
	Most of the time	Focus on your main purpose, and note only points related to your topic.
		Place quotation marks around any quoted words or phrases.
Summary	When the point you are making does not require the detail of a paraphrase	Reread the source after writing your summary to be sure that you have not altered the meaning.

5.40 Making Bibliographies and Bibliography Cards. If you are writing a research paper, your teacher will ask you to include a bibliography to tell where you got your information. A **bibliography** is a list of sources that you used for your writing. A **source** is a book, a magazine, a film, or any other written or audio-visual material that you use to get information. As you work on your paper, you should be writing down on note cards the information for each source that you use. The chart below shows the correct form for different types of bibliography entries.

FORMS FOR BIBLIOGRAPHY ENTRIES

A. A book
Douglass, Frederick. <u>Escape from Slavery: The Boyhood of Frederick Douglass in His Own Words</u>. New York: Alfred A. Knopf, 1994.

B. A magazine article
Reston, James, Jr. "Orion: Where Stars Are Born." <u>National Geographic</u>. December 1995: 90—101.

C. An encyclopedia entry
"Lewis and Clark Expedition." <u>Encyclopedia Americana</u>. Jackson, Donald. 1995 ed.

D. An interview
Campbell, Silas. Personal interview. 6 February 1997.

E. A film
<u>The Big Heat</u>. Dir. Fritz Lang. With Glenn Ford and Gloria Grahame. Writ. Sidney Boehm. Based on the novel of the same title by William P. McGiven. 90 min. Columbia, 1953.

F. The Internet
Durham, Dacia. The Charles A. and Anne Morrow Lindbergh Foundation. 24 Oct. 1995, updated 18 June 1999. <<u>http://www.mtn.org/lindfdtn/</u>>.

For each source used, prepare a **bibliography card** using an index card. Include all of the information in the following chart when preparing your cards.

INFORMATION TO INCLUDE ON A BIBLIOGRAPHY CARD	
Author(s)	Write the complete name(s) of all author(s), editor(s), and translator(s).
Title	Write the complete title. If the piece is contained in a larger work, include the title of the larger work. (For example, write the name of the encyclopedia as well as the name of the article you used.)
Publisher	Write exactly as it appears on the title page.
Place and date of publication	Copy this information from the title page or copyright page of a book. For a magazine, write the date of the issue that you used.
Location and call number	Note where you found the book. If it is in a library collection, write the call number.
Card number	Assign a number to each bibliography card that you prepare. Write that number in the top right corner of the card and circle it. When you take notes from the source, include this number on each note card so that you will be able to identify the source of the note later on.

SAMPLE BIBLIOGRAPHY CARD

②

Van Lawick-Goodall,Jane.
    In the Shadow of Man

      Boston: Houghton, 1971.

    Peabody Institute Library

5.41 DOCUMENTING AND MAPPING INTERNET RESEARCH. Your research journal is an excellent tool for tracking how you find information. It can be especially invaluable for documenting and mapping Internet research. As you browse and search on the Internet, it can be easy to jump from one Internet site to the next and to lose track of how you got from place to place. Especially as you conduct research, it is important to map your path. Here is one way to do so.

- Write a brief statement of the topic of your research.

- Write key words or phrases that will help you search for this information.

- Note the search engines that you will use.

- As you conduct a search, note how many "hits" or Internet sites the search engine has accessed. Determine whether you need to narrow or expand your search. Write down new key words accordingly, and the results of each new search.

- When you find promising sites, write them down.

- Access each promising site. Evaluate its information using the guidelines in The Language Arts Survey 5.35, "How to Understand Internet Sites."

- Once you find information to include in your work, document it carefully. For more information on how to document Internet sites, see the Language Arts Survey 5.40, "Making Bibliographies and Bibliography Cards."

5.42 AVOIDING PLAGIARISM. Plagiarism is taking someone else's words or thoughts and pretending that they are your own. Plagiarism is a very serious problem and has been the downfall of many students and even famous people. Whenever you use someone else's writing to help you with a paper or a speech, you must be careful either to put the ideas in your own words or to use quotation marks. In either case, you must give credit to the person whose ideas you are using.

Giving such credit to others is called documenting your sources.

5.43 PARAPHRASING, SUMMARIZING, AND QUOTING. As you do research, your notes will include paraphrases, summaries, and quotations.

5.44 PARENTHETICAL DOCUMENTATION. Parenthetical documentation is currently the most widely used form of documentation. To use this method to document the source of a quotation or an idea, you place a brief note identifying the source in parentheses immediately after the borrowed material. This type of note is called a **parenthetical citation**, and the act of placing such a note is called **citing a source**.

The first part of a parenthetical citation refers the reader to a source in your List of Works Cited or Works Consulted. For the reader's ease in finding the source in your bibliography, you must cite the work according to how it is listed in the bibliography.

SAMPLE PARENTHETICAL CITATIONS

A. **For works listed by title, use an abbreviated title.**

   Sample bibliographic entry
   "History." _Encyclopedia Britannica: Macropædia_. 1992 ed.

   Sample citation
   Historians go through three stages in textual criticism ("History" 615).

B. **For works listed by author or editor, use the author's or editor's last name.**

   Sample bibliographic entry
   Brown, Dee. _Bury My Heart at Wounded Knee: An Indian History of the American West_. New York: Holt, 1970.

   Sample citation
   "Big Eyes Schurz agreed to the arrest" (Brown 364).

C. **When the listed name or title is stated in the text, cite only the page number.**
   Brown avers that Big Eyes Schurz agreed to it (364).

D. **For works of multiple volumes, use a colon after the volume number.**

   Sample bibliographic entry
   Pepys, Samuel. _The Diary of Samuel Pepys_. Ed. Robert Latham and William Matthews. 10 vols. Berkeley: University of California Press, 1972.

   Sample citation
   On the last day of 1665, Pepys took the occasion of the new year to reflect, but not to celebrate (6: 341-2).

E. **For works quoted in secondary sources, use the abbreviation "qtd. in."**

   Sample citation
   According to R. Bentley, "reason and the facts outweigh a hundred manuscripts" (qtd. in "History" 615).

F. **For classic works that are available in various editions,** give the page number from the edition you are using, followed by a semicolon; then identify the section of the work to help people with other editions find the reference.

5.45 FOOTNOTES AND ENDNOTES. Parenthetical documentation, described in 5.44, is the most common of many accepted systems. Footnoting and endnoting are two other accepted methods.

FOOTNOTES. Instead of putting citations in parentheses within the text, you can place them at the bottom or foot of the page; hence the term **footnote**. In this system, a number or symbol is placed in the text where the parenthetical citation would otherwise be, and a matching number or symbol at the bottom of the page identifies the citation. This textbook, for example, uses numbered footnotes in its literature selections to define obscure words and to provide background information.

ENDNOTES. Many books use endnotes instead of footnotes. Endnotes are like footnotes in that a number or symbol is placed within the text, but the matching citations are compiled at the end of the book, chapter, or article rather than at the foot of the page.

Footnote and endnote entries begin with the author's (or editor's) name in its usual order (first name, then last) and include publication information and a page reference.

SAMPLE FOOTNOTE OR ENDNOTE CITATIONS	
A BOOK WITH ONE AUTHOR	[1]Jean Paul-Sartre, *Being and Nothingness* (New York: The Citadel Press, 1966) 149–151.
A BOOK WITH ONE EDITOR AND NO SINGLE AUTHOR	[2]Shannon Ravenel, ed., *New Stories from the South: The Year's Best, 1992* (Chapel Hill, NC: Algonquin Books, 1992) 305.
A MAGAZINE ARTICLE	[3]Andrew Gore, "Road Test: The Apple Powerbook," *MacUser*, December 1996: 72.

TEST-TAKING SKILLS

5.46 Preparing for Tests

Tests are a common part of school life. These guidelines will help you to prepare for and take a test.

PREPARING FOR A TEST

- **Know exactly what you will be tested on.** If you have questions, ask your teacher.
- **Make a study plan** to allow yourself time to go over the material. Avoid last-minute cramming.
- **Review the subject matter.** Use your notes, your SQ3R strategy, and any study questions given by your teacher.
- **Make lists** of important names, dates, definitions, or events. Ask a friend or family member to quiz you on them.
- **Try to predict questions** that may be on the test. Make sure you can answer them.
- **Get plenty of sleep** the night before the test.

Eat a nutritious breakfast on the morning of the test.

TAKING A TEST

- **Survey the test** to see how long it is and what types of questions are included.
- **Read all directions and questions** carefully. Make sure that you know exactly what to do.
- **Plan your time.** Answer easy questions first. Allow extra time for complicated questions. If a question seems too difficult, skip it and go back to it later. Work quickly, but do not rush.
- **Save time for review.** Once you have finished, look back over the test. Double-check your answers, but do not change answers too often. Your first ideas are often the correct ones.

5.47 Taking Objective Tests

Objective tests require simple right-or-wrong answers. This chart describes the kinds of questions you may see on objective tests.

DESCRIPTION	GUIDELINES
True/False. You are given a statement and asked to tell whether the statement is true or false.	• If any part of a statement is false, then the statement is false. • Words like *all, always, never,* and *everyone* often appear in false statements. • Words like *some, usually, often,* and *most* often appear in true statements. • If you do not know the answer, guess. You have a 50/50 chance of being right.
Matching. You are asked to match items in one column with items in another column.	• Check the directions. See if each item is used only once. Also check to see if some are not used at all. • Read all items before starting. • Match those you know first. • Cross out items as you match them.
Multiple Choice. You are asked to choose the best answer from a group of answers given.	• Read *all* choices first. • Rule out incorrect answers. • Choose the answer that is most complete or accurate. • Pay particular attention to choices such as *none of the above* or *all of the above.*
Short Answer. You are asked to answer the question with a word, a phrase, or a sentence.	• Read the directions to find out if you are required to answer in complete sentences. • Use correct spelling, grammar, punctuation, and capitalization. • If you cannot think of the answer, move on. Something in another question might remind you of the answer.

5.48 Strategies for Taking Standardized Tests

Standardized tests are given to many students in a school district, a state, or a country. You may already have taken a standardized test, such as the Iowa Test of Basic Skills, and you certainly will take more during your school career. Some standardized tests, such as the Scholastic Aptitude Test, or SAT, are used to help determine entrance to colleges and universities. Others must be passed to enter certain vocations or professions. A

standardized test measures overall ability, or achievement over a period of time. Learning how to take standardized tests well can help you to achieve your academic and career goals.

When selecting an answer on a standardized test, remember these points:

• If you do not know the answer, try to rule out some choices and then guess from those remaining.

• If a question seems too difficult, skip it and go back to it later. Be aware, however, that most tests allow you to go back to questions only within a section.

- Always follow the instructions of the test monitor.

5.49 ANALOGY QUESTIONS. Analogy questions ask you to find the relationship between a given pair of words and then to recognize a similar relationship between another pair of words. In an analogy question, the symbols : and :: mean "is to" and "as," respectively. The example below would be "Mare is to horse as . . ." when read aloud. To answer an analogy question, examine all of the answers. If more than one answer seems correct, choose the best one.

To answer an analogy question, think of a sentence that relates the two words. For example, you might think of the sentence "A *mare* is a female *horse*." Then look for another pair of words that would make sense in that sentence: "A *doe* is a female *deer*."

EXAMPLE

> MARE : HORSE ::
> (A) lamb : sheep
> (B) man : woman
> (C) boy : girl
> (D) bee : wasp
> (E) doe : deer

The answer is E.

5.50 SYNONYM AND ANTONYM QUESTIONS. Synonym and **antonym** questions give you a word and ask you to select the word that has the same meaning (for a synonym) or the opposite meaning (for an antonym). You must select the best answer, even if none is exactly correct. For this type of question, you should try all the choices to see which one works best. Always know whether you are looking for a synonym or an antonym, because you will usually find both among the answers.

EXAMPLE

Write the letter of the word that is most nearly the opposite in meaning to the word in capital letters.
1. AMIABLE
  (A) capable
  (B) friendly
  (C) hostile
  (D) lovely

The answer is C.

5.51 SENTENCE COMPLETION QUESTIONS. Sentence completion questions present you with a sentence that has two words missing. You must select the pair of words that best completes the sentence.

EXAMPLE

The expansion of Cedar Hospital was largely_____by the citizens of Minor county, even though it was a major_____for the taxpayers.
  (A)   needed...contribution
  (B)   cheered...burden
  (C)   criticized...expense
  (D)   welcomed...dilemma

The answer is B.

5.52 READING COMPREHENSION QUESTIONS. Reading comprehension questions give you a short piece of writing and then ask you several questions about it. The questions may ask you to figure out something based on information in the passage. Use the following strategies when answering reading comprehension questions:

STEPS IN ANSWERING READING COMPREHENSION QUESTIONS

1. Read all the questions quickly.
2. Read the passage with the questions in mind.
3. Reread the first question carefully.
4. Scan the passage, looking for key words related to the question. When you find a key word, slow down and read carefully.
5. Answer the first question.
6. Repeat this process to answer the rest of the questions.

5.53 Taking Essay Tests

An **essay** is a short piece of writing that expresses the writer's thoughts about a particular subject. To answer an essay question, follow these guidelines.

- **Analyze each question.** Once you understand clearly what you have to do, you will be able to organize and write more effective essays in the time available.

  First, read the *entire* question carefully. Look for key words in the question that tell you what is expected. Underline these words or write them on your own note paper. Then make sure to answer *all* parts of the question.

- **Organize your answer.** Determining how you will spend the time available is an important part of planning an essay. Allow time for planning, writing, and reviewing. Before you begin writing, make a rough outline of the main points you will make. Include main points and key details. Later, if you find yourself running out of time, try at least to state your remaining main points and to add a conclusion.

- **Write a clear introduction.** This will help to keep you on track as you write each paragraph. Your introduction should state the thesis, or main idea, of your essay and should briefly answer the question. In the rest of the essay, you can elaborate on your answer, providing evidence to support it.

- **Review your answer.** Before you turn in your completed essay, take time to review and polish it.

UNDERSTANDING AN ESSAY QUESTION

TYPE OF ESSAY QUESTION	TASKS OF ESSAY
analyze	break into parts and describe the parts and their relationships
compare; compare and contrast	identify and describe similarities and differences
describe; explain	tell the steps in a process; identify causes and effects
define; describe; identify	classify and tell the features of
interpret	tell the meaning and significance of
summarize	retell very briefly, stating only the main points
argue; prove; show	tell and evaluate reasons for believing a statement

QUESTIONS FOR REVIEWING AN ANSWER TO AN ESSAY QUESTION

- Does the essay answer all parts of the question?
- Does the introduction state clearly the main idea of the essay?
- Does the body of the essay provide evidence to support the main idea?
- Does the essay cover all the points in my rough outline?
- Are there any points that could be made more strongly or clearly?
- Is every word in the essay easily readable?
- Is the essay free of errors in grammar, usage, and mechanics?

APPLIED ENGLISH Resource

THE IMPORTANCE OF APPLIED ENGLISH

Applied English is English in the world of work, or practical English. When you apply English skills to real-world situations, you are using your reading, writing, speaking, and listening abilities for practical reasons.

6.1 Filling Out Forms

Entering a new school, going to a new doctor, registering computer software, applying for a job—these are but a few of the thousands of activities that involve filling out forms. The following guidelines will help you to complete a form in a way that will make a good impression.

GUIDELINES FOR COMPLETING FORMS

- Get an extra copy or make a photocopy of the form so that you can complete a practice form.

- Read through the directions and the form itself before completing it.

- Gather the information you will need to complete the form. This information may include former addresses, dates of events, or a social security number.

- Complete the form neatly. Avoid smudges or cross-outs. Use the writing method requested on the form. Most forms request that you either type or use black or blue ink.

- Do not leave any lines blank. Use N.A. for "not applicable" if a request for information does not apply to you. For example, if you have always lived at the same address, you would write N.A. in the blank following "Previous Addresses."

- Proofread your information for errors in punctuation, spelling, or grammar. Make sure all information is correct.

- Submit the form to the appropriate person or address. Use an envelope or folder to keep the form neat and clean.

- Keep a copy of the form for your own records.

6.2 Following Directions

Every day people all over the world face the challenge of doing something they have never done before. Despite their inexperience, many people are able to succeed because they are able to follow directions. At the same time, someone must be able to give them clear, precise directions. Consider these guidelines before you begin following or giving directions.

GUIDELINES FOR FOLLOWING DIRECTIONS

- If the directions are being given in written form, read them carefully before beginning the procedure. If they are being given in spoken form, take notes as you listen. Ask for clarification if something is confusing.

- If written directions include any vocabulary or technical words you do not understand, look them up in a dictionary, or see if the materials include footnotes, a glossary, or an appendix. If an instructor uses words you do not understand, ask him or her to rephrase.

- Take your time and make sure you have performed each step carefully and accurately before proceeding to the next step.

- If you get stuck following directions, retrace your steps or reread the step you are on. If they are available, consult diagrams, maps, or illustrations. You might find it helpful to ask someone else to read the directions and see if he or she arrives at the same conclusion as you do. If the directions include a "help hotline" or other contact information, you may want to use it.

6.3 Giving Directions

GUIDELINES FOR GIVING DIRECTIONS

- Think through the directions completely, from start to finish, before you begin.

- Give each step in the order in which it should be taken.

- Include all necessary steps. Do not assume that your reader or listener already knows any part of the directions unless you are absolutely sure that this is the case.

- Do not include any unnecessary steps.

- Use simple language that can be understood easily.

- Use transition words such as *first*, *second*, *third*, *next*, *then*, and *finally* to connect your ideas.

- When possible, use a parallel or similar sentence structure for each part of the directions.

- When giving directions orally, ask the listener to repeat the directions to you when you have finished. This way you can check to make sure that your directions have been understood.

- If the directions that you are giving are complicated, put them into writing. Number each direction to help you and your reader to keep the steps separate and clear. You may also wish to include a map, diagram, or other illustration to accompany the written directions. For more information, see the Language Arts Survey 6.11, "Displaying Effective Visual Information."

6.4 Writing a Step-by-Step Procedure

A **step-by-step procedure** is a how-to or process piece that uses directions to teach someone something new. Written procedures include textual information and sometimes graphics. Spoken procedures can be given as oral demonstrations. They can include textual and graphic information and other props.

Examples of step-by-step procedures include an oral demonstration of how to saddle a horse; instructions on how to treat a sprained ankle; a video showing how to do the perfect lay-up in basketball; and an interactive Internet site allowing the user to design and send a bouquet of flowers.

To write a step-by-step procedure, review the Language Arts Survey 6.3, "Giving Directions" and 6.11, "Displaying Effective Visual Information."

GUIDELINES FOR WRITING A STEP-BY-STEP PROCEDURE

- If you are showing how to make something, create several different samples to show each step of the procedure. For example, if you are showing how to make a wooden basket, you might want to display the raw materials, the started basket, the basket halfway finished, and then the finished product. You might also want to have a sample showing a variation—a different type of weaving, for example, that the finished product may not have.

- Be prepared. The best way to prevent problems is to anticipate and plan for them. Rehearse an oral demonstration several times. If you are preparing the procedure in written form, go through your directions as if you knew nothing about the process. Anticipate what it would be like to learn this procedure for the first time. See if you can follow your own directions, or have a friend work through the procedure and offer suggestions for improvement.

- Acknowledge mistakes. If you are sharing a procedure "live" as an oral demonstration and you can't talk around or correct a mistake, tell your audience what has gone wrong, and why. If you handle the situation in a calm, direct way, the audience may also learn from your mistake.

- Know your topic well. The better you know it, the better you will be able to teach others.

6.5 Writing a Business Letter

A **business letter** is usually addressed to someone you do not know personally. Therefore, a formal tone is appropriate for such a letter.

Following appropriate form is especially important when writing business letters. If you follow the correct form and avoid errors in spelling, grammar, usage, and mechanics, your letter will sound professional and make a good impression.

Above the salutation, a business letter should contain the name and title of the person to whom you are writing and the name and address of that person's company or organization (see the model on the following page).

One common form for a business letter is the block form. In the block form, each part of the letter begins at the left margin. The parts are separated by line spaces.

Begin the salutation with the word *Dear,* followed by the courtesy or professional title used in the inside address, such as *Ms., Mr.,* or *Dr.,* and a colon. If you are not writing to a specific person, you may use a general salutation such as *Dear Sir or Madam.*

In the body of your letter, use a polite, formal tone and standard English. Make your points clearly, in as few words as possible.

End with a standard closing such as *Sincerely, Yours truly,* or *Respectfully yours.* Capitalize only the first word of the closing. Type your full name below the closing, leaving three or four blank lines for your signature. Sign your name below the closing in blue or black ink (never in red or green). Proofread your letter before you send it. Poor spelling, grammar, or punctuation can ruin an otherwise well-written business letter.

GUIDELINES FOR WRITING A BUSINESS LETTER

- Outline your main points before you begin.
- Word process your letter, if at all possible. Type or print it on clean 8 1/2" x 11" white or off-white paper. Use only one side of the paper.
- Use the block form or another standard business letter form.
- Single space, leaving a blank line between each part, including paragraphs.
- Use a standard salutation and a standard closing.
- Stick to the subject. State your main idea clearly at the beginning of the letter. Keep the letter brief and informative.
- Check your spelling, grammar, usage, and punctuation carefully.

STUDENT MODEL

Jorge loves snorkeling and wants to get a summer job working part time in a dive shop. This is a copy of the letter that he sent to the owner of the shop.

498 Blue Key Rd.
Charleston, SC 02716

May 3, 2001

Mr. Davy Jones, Owner
Deep Sea Divers, Inc.
73 Ocean St.
Charleston, SC 02716

Dear Mr. Jones:

Please consider me for a position as a part-time clerk in your store for the coming summer. I understand that in the summer your business increases considerably and that you might need a conscientious, hard-working clerk. I can offer you considerable knowledge of snorkeling and diving equipment and experience working in a retail shop.

I will be available for work three days per week between June 1 and August 12. I am enclosing a résumé and references. Please contact me if you wish to set up an interview.

Sincerely,

Jorge Alvarez

Jorge Alvarez

6.6 Writing a Memo

In businesses, schools, and other organizations, employees, students, and others often communicate by means of **memoranda**, or **memos.** For example, the director of a school drama club might write a memo to the editor of the student newspaper announcing tryouts for a new play.

Some memos will be more informal than others. If you know the person to whom you are writing well or if the memo has only a social function such as announcing a party, the tone can be fairly informal. Most memos, however, have a fairly formal tone.

A memo begins with a header. Often this header contains the word *memorandum* (the singular form of memoranda) and the following words and abbreviations:

TO:
FR: (from)
DT: (date)
RE: (regarding)
cc: (copy)

STUDENT MODEL

Jack Hart, the president of the drama club at Wheaton High School, wishes to have the upcoming tryouts for his club's production of *Oklahoma!* announced in the school newspaper. He decides to write a memo to the editor of the paper, Lisa Lowry.

MEMORANDUM

TO: Lisa Lowry
FR: Jack Hart
RE: Tryouts for the spring production of *Oklahoma!*
DT: February 12, 2001
cc: Ms. Wise

Please include the following announcement in the upcoming issue of the *Wheaton Crier:* Tryouts for the Wheaton Drama Club's spring production of *Oklahoma!* will be held on Friday, February 26, at 6:00 P.M. in the Wheaton High School Auditorium. Students interested in performing in this musical should come to the auditorium at that time prepared to deliver a monologue less than two minutes long and to sing one song from the musical. Copies of the music and lyrics can be obtained from the sponsor of the Wheaton Drama Club, Ms. Wise. For additional information, please contact Ms. Wise or any member of the Drama Club.

Thank you.

6.7 Writing a Proposal

A **proposal** outlines a project that a person wants to complete. It presents a summary of an idea, the reasons why the idea is important, and an outline of how the project would be carried out. Because the proposal audience is people who can help carry out the proposal, a proposal is both informative and persuasive.

EXAMPLES
- You want funding for an art project that would benefit your community
- Your student council proposes a clothing drive for disaster relief
- You and a group of your friends want to help organize a summer program for teens your age

Proposal: To host a community arts day at the park behind Jordan High School that would allow high school artists to try new art forms and to exhibit their work.

Rationale: The art students at Jordan High School have shown there is a lot of talent here worth sharing. An Arts Day would let everyone interested get involved, and build school and community pride. Art students could lead others through simple art projects, and people could learn new things. At the end, the art could be displayed in an art fair at the community park. Artwork and refreshments could be sold, with all proceeds going to the Jordan High School Art Scholarship.

Schedule/Preparation Outline

Present proposal to School Pride Committee	April 1
Meet with art students to organize event	April 6–15
Contact area businesses for donations	April 6–15
Advertise event and sell tickets	April 16–25
Have practice day to make sure art activities work	April 20
Hold community Arts Day	April 26

BUDGET
Expenses

Posters, mailings, tickets	$30
Art supplies	$200
Refreshments	$75

Note: Expenses will be fewer if we ask area businesses to help sponsor event

Total estimated expenses	$305

Income

Ticket sales (estimated 150 tickets sold @ $3 each)	$450
Refreshment sales	$100
Earnings from art sold at exhibit	$200
Total estimated income	$750
Net proceeds	$445

Note: All proceeds will be donated to the Jordan High School Art Scholarship Fund

GUIDELINES FOR WRITING A PROPOSAL
- Keep the tone positive, courteous, and respectful.
- State your purpose and rationale briefly and clearly.
- Give your audience all necessary information. A proposal with specific details makes it clear what you want approved, and why your audience—often a committee or someone in authority—should approve it.
- Use standard, formal English.
- Format your proposal with headings, lists, and schedules to make your proposed project easy to understand and approve.

6.8 Writing a Résumé

A **résumé** is a summary of a job applicant's career objectives, previous employment experience, and education. Its purpose is to help the applicant obtain the job he or she seeks. A résumé should be accompanied by a cover letter to the employer (see an example in the Language Arts Survey 6.5, "Writing a Business Letter"). Many helpful books and articles are available in libraries and bookstores on writing a résumé. Here are some guidelines.

GUIDELINES FOR WRITING A RÉSUMÉ

- Keep your information brief—to one page if possible. The goal of the resume is to give a potential employer a quick snapshot of your skills and abilities.

- Include all vital contact information—name, address, phone number, and e-mail address, if applicable—at the top of the page.

- Use headings to summarize information regarding job or career objective, education, work experience, skills, extracurricular activities, awards (if applicable), and references. Note that work experience should be listed starting with your most recent job and working backward.

- Key or type your résumé on white or cream-colored paper. Proofread it carefully for any errors; all facts must be accurate as well. Make it as neat as possible.

- You may list references, or simply state that they are available on request.

Pat Mizos
5555 Elm Street
Anytown, NY 20111
(212) 555-5555

Objective:
To gain employment working in a summer camp program for children

Education:
Orchard High School, 2001 graduate

Major area of study: College preparatory, with concentration in science and physical education classes

Grade point average: 3.5 (B+)

Work experience:
Summer 1999   Summer youth counselor, Anytown Parks and Recreation Department

Summer 1998   Dishwasher, the Lobster Shack Anytown, NY

Skills:
Intermediate-level Spanish (three years in high school)
Beginning-level American Sign Language (one semester at Anytown Vocational School)
Certified in CPR

Extracurricular activities:
Swim team, tennis team, youth hotline crisis volunteer

References:
Available on request

6.9 Delivering a Press Release

A **press release** is an informative piece intended for publication in local news media. A press release is usually written to promote an upcoming event or to inform the community of a recent event that promotes, or strengthens, an individual or organization.

EXAMPLES

- a brief notice from the choir director telling the community of the upcoming spring concert
- an informative piece by the district public information officer announcing that your school's art instructor has been named the state Teacher of the Year

GUIDELINES FOR WRITING A PRESS RELEASE

- Know your purpose. What do you want your audience to know from reading your piece?
- Use the 5 *Ws* and an *H—who, what, where, when, why,* and *how*—questioning strategy to convey the important information at the beginning of your story. (For more information, see the Language Arts Survey 2.14, "Questioning: Using the 5 *Ws* and an *H.*")
- Keep the press release brief. Local media are more likely to publish or broadcast your piece if it is short and to the point.
- Include contact information such as your name, phone number, and times you can be reached. Make this information available to the media representative or, if applicable, to the reading public.
- Type your press release using conventional manuscript form. Make sure the text is double-spaced and that you leave margins of at least an inch on all sides of the page.
- At the beginning of the press release, key the day's date and the date the information is to be released. (You can type "For immediate release" or designate the date you would like the press release to be printed in the newspaper.)
- At the end of the press release, key the word "END."

- Check a previous newspaper for deadline information or call the newspaper office to make sure you get your material there on time. Address the press release to the editor.

6.10 Writing a Public Service Announcement

A **public service announcement**, or PSA, is a brief, informative article intended to be helpful to the community. PSAs are written by nonprofit organizations and concerned citizens for print in local newspapers, for broadcast by television and radio stations, and for publication on the Internet.

EXAMPLES

- an article by the American Cancer Society outlining early warning signs of cancer
- an announcement promoting Safety Week
- an informative piece telling coastal residents what to do during a hurricane

GUIDELINES FOR WRITING A PUBLIC SERVICE ANNOUNCEMENT

- Know your purpose. What do you want your audience to know from reading or hearing your piece?
- State your information as objectively as possible.
- As with most informative writing, use the 5 *Ws* and an *H—who, what, where, when, why,* and *how*—questioning strategy to get your important information at the beginning of your story.
- Keep your announcement brief. Local media are more likely to publish or broadcast your piece if it is short and to the point.
- Include contact information in case the media representative has any questions. You might also include contact information in the PSA itself.
- Key or type your PSA in conventional manuscript form. Make sure the text is double-spaced and that you leave margins of at least an inch on all sides of the page.
- At the end of the PSA, key "END" to designate the end of the announcement.
- Be aware of print and broadcast deadlines and make sure your material is sent on time.

6.11 Displaying Effective Visual Information

People frequently learn things best and remember more when information is presented visually. Whenever possible, use charts, tables, pictures, slides, photographs, models, and art to express key points.

PURPOSES OF VISUALS
- focus and hold audience attention
- help the audience grasp facts quickly
- clarify something complicated
- show comparisons
- emphasize key points
- summarize main thoughts
- serve as an outline or guide in a presentation

The quality of your visuals will affect your presentation. Depending on their use, visuals can detract from a presentation or enhance it. Before you use a visual, ask yourself:

- Is it attention-grabbing?
- Is it simple and neat?
- Does it serve a real purpose?
- Can I use it easily?
- Does it fit smoothly into the presentation?

The success of your presentation will depend on how you display visual information. Here are some guidelines.

GUIDELINES FOR DISPLAYING VISUAL INFORMATION
- Keep visual information simple. Do not clutter visual display with multiple lettering or font styles, too many small images, or too much textual or graphic information.
- Design your visual display in a way that the
- Clearly label your visual display. Make it easy for the viewer to know what you are showing. Include a title or caption, labels for different parts, and simple, main points when needed.
- Make the visual visible. Type or graphics that are too small can make the best visual presentation useless. If the display is on a computer screen, make sure you can read it. If the display is for a speech or exhibit, stand back and see if you can see it from the back of the room or wherever your audience members will be. (A general rule is that one-inch letters can be read at 32 feet, two-inch letters at 64 feet, and three-inch letters at 128 feet.)
- Use bullets or numbering to organize your text. For simple presentations, use either one or the other; don't use both.
- Use color carefully. Color can add visual interest, but it can also be distracting or make a graphic or text area illegible.
- Document all sources of graphic information. The ideas in visual information are someone's intellectual property, just like the ideas in text material. Make sure you give proper credit for all work not your own.

For more information on types of visual presentations, see the Language Arts Survey 1.15, "Using Graphic Aids."

6.12 Working on a Team

Working on a team, or doing collaborative learning, is an essential Applied English skill that depends on a strong ability to communicate. This ability can be strengthened with practice.

Individual members of a team or small group are likely to fulfill particular roles or positions based on what they know or do best. Sometimes a group decides before it starts a project who should take on what role. For instance, a group might choose someone to lead it or to act as secretary. At other times, roles emerge as a group progresses. Often, one person fulfills many roles in a group.

Constructive group roles help the group achieve its goals and objectives. These include:

- **leader:** directs the work of the group by assigning tasks or roles to other group members
- **implementer:** carries out or implements group tasks
- **information seeker:** asks for facts, information, or opinions
- **information giver:** offers facts, information, or opinions
- **coordinator:** pulls together ideas, identifies relationships between ideas

- **summarizer:** summarizes group discussions, calls attention to tasks that need to be fulfilled
- **evaluator:** analyzes data, reasoning, conclusions, or decisions of the group
- **energizer:** motivates the group, stimulates greater productivity and discussion
- **administrator:** keeps meetings on track, makes members aware of time and other constraints
- **secretary:** keeps minutes or a record of what occurs at group meetings
- **encourager:** provides understanding, positive reinforcement, and group solidarity
- **harmonizer:** helps to resolve conflict or misunderstandings between group members; encourages compromise
- **gatekeeper:** keeps communication open by encouraging and discouraging participation
- **tension reliever:** uses humor in a productive way to reduce tension and relax group members

Destructive group roles are counterproductive and prevent the group from achieving its goals or objectives.

- **blocker:** puts down others or their ideas; refuses to cooperate
- **aggressor:** picks fights with other members; is too negative and critical
- **recognition seeker:** uses group to boast about personal accomplishments
- **self-confessor:** unloads personal problems on group members, or otherwise uses the group to gain sympathy
- **joker:** uninvolved in group work; creates distractions and engages in "horseplay"

- **dominator:** tries to control group and monopolize its time to advance his or her own interests
- **distractor:** goes off on tangents; offers irrelevant information or ideas
- **deserter:** withdraws from the group; does not participate in group discussions or decision making

TASKS FOR BEING A PRODUCTIVE TEAM MEMBER

AS A PARTICIPANT
- share personal experience
- contribute relevant ideas
- support statements with evidence
- respond to others with respect
- try to understand others' views
- show willingness to change views when appropriate
- show willingness to clarify and defend views
- allow others to speak
- maintain focus on discussion

AS A LEADER
- help the group keep on track
- help ensure that everyone gets a chance to speak
- help the group achieve its goals

AS A RECORD KEEPER
- keep accurate records of the discussion
- make sure all group members have records useful to the project

For more information, see the Language Arts Survey 4.7–4.9, "Communicating with Others," and 4.13, "Collaborative Learning and Communication."

ABRIDGMENT. An **abridgment** is a shortened version of a work. When doing an abridgment, an editor attempts to preserve the most significant elements of the original. See also *abstract* and *paraphrase.*

ABSTRACT. 1. *n.* An **abstract**, *précis,* or *summary* is a brief account of the main ideas or arguments presented in a work. A well-made abstract presents those ideas or arguments in the same order as in the original. Writing an abstract is an excellent way to commit to memory the major ideas of a nonfiction work, such as an essay or a chapter in a textbook. See *paraphrase.* 2. *adj.* An **abstract** word or phrase is one that refers to something that cannot be directly perceived by the senses. *Freedom, love, integrity, honesty,* and *loyalty* are examples of abstract terms. The opposite of *abstract* in this sense is *concrete.* See *concrete.*

ACCENT. See *stress.*

ACRONYM. An **acronym** is a word created from the first, or initial, letters of a series of words. Examples of acronyms include *scuba,* from the words *self-contained underwater breathing apparatus,* and *radar,* from *radio detecting and ranging.*

ACROSTIC. An **acrostic** is a poem organized so that the first or last letters of each line form a word, a phrase, or a regular sequence of letters of the alphabet.

ACT. An **act** is a major division of a drama. The first dramas were not divided into acts, but rather into scenes in which the actors performed and scenes in which the chorus spoke. The dramas of ancient Rome were generally divided into five acts. In modern times, plays are most often divided into three acts, and short plays called "one-acts" are common. There are five acts in Shakespeare's play *The Tragedy of Romeo and Juliet* in Unit 4.

ACTION. The **action** is the sequence of events that actually occur in a literary work, as opposed to those that occur off-scene or that precede or follow the events in the work itself. A common literary technique, inherited from the classical *epic,* is to begin a work *in medias res,* in the middle of the action, and to fill in the background details later through flashbacks. See *flashback.*

ACTOR. An **actor** is one who performs the role of a character in a play. The term is now used both for male and female performers.

ADAGE. See *proverb.*

ADAPTATION. An **adaptation** is a rewriting of a literary work in another form. In modern times, adaptations for film are often made of successful novels, musicals, and plays. Several film adaptations have been made of Shakespeare's *The Tragedy of Romeo and Juliet* in Unit 4.

AFTERWORD. An **afterword** is a statement made at the end of a work, often an analysis, a summary, or a celebration of the preceding work. See *epilogue.*

AIM. A writer's **aim** is his or her purpose, or goal. People may write with the following aims:
- to inform (expository/informational writing)
- to entertain, enrich, enlighten, and/or use an artistic medium, such as fiction or poetry, to share a perspective (imaginative writing)
- to share a story about an event, often to make a point (narrative writing)
- to reflect (personal/expressive writing)
- to persuade readers or listeners to respond in some way, such as to agree with a position, change a view on an issue, reach an agreement, or perform an action (persuasive/argumentative writing)

Here are examples of writing that reflect these five aims:

expository/informational
  news article, research report
imaginative
  poem, short story
narrative
  biography, family history
personal/expressive
  diary entry, personal letter
persuasive/argumentative
  editorial, petition

ALLEGORY. An **allegory** is a work in which each element symbolizes, or represents, something else. Spirituals such as "Go Down, Moses" in

Unit 1 are often allegorical. "Go Down, Moses" is on one level about Moses demanding freedom for the Jews from the Pharaoh in Egypt, but on another level it can be read as being about slaves seeking their freedom in the United States. Yeats's poem "The Song of Wandering Aengus" in Unit 2 is traditionally read as an allegory for a person's aging. In one sense, all literature can be viewed as allegorical in that individual characters, objects, places, and actions can be seen as types representing others of their kind. See *concrete universal* and *extended metaphor.*

ALLITERATION. **Alliteration** is the repetition of initial consonant sounds. Some writers also use the term to describe repeated initial vowel sounds. The following line from Edgar Allan Poe's poem "The Bells," in Unit 2, contains two examples of alliteration:

> **W**hat a **w**orld of **m**erriment their **m**elody foretells!

ALLUSION. An **allusion** is a rhetorical technique in which reference is made to a person, event, object, or work from history or literature. For example, the spiritual "Go Down, Moses" makes an illusion to the biblical story in which Moses demands that the Pharaoh in Egypt free the Jews from bondage. In "Who Am I This Time?" (Unit 7), Kurt Vonnegut, Jr. alludes to many famous plays and characters in Western literature.

AMBIGUITY. An **ambiguity** is a statement that has a double meaning or a meaning that cannot be clearly resolved. In English, the word *cleave* is oddly ambiguous, for it can mean either "to cling together" or "to cut apart." Many literary figures of speech, including *metaphors, similes, personifications,* and *symbols,* are examples of intentional ambiguity, speaking of one thing when another is intended.

ANACHRONISM. An **anachronism** is a reference to something that did not exist at the time being described. Thus, a reference to a computer in a story taking place during the Civil War would be an anachronism because computers had not been invented during the nineteenth century.

ANAGRAM. An **anagram** is a word or a phrase created by rearranging the letters of another word or phrase. The title of Samuel Butler's novel *Erewhon* is an anagram for *nowhere.* See *palindrome.*

ANALOGY. An **analogy** is a comparison of two things that are alike in some respects. Often an analogy explains or describes something unfamiliar by comparing it to something more familiar. A *simile* is an expressed analogy; a *metaphor* is an implied analogy. In "It's Not Talent; It's Just Work" (Unit 8), Annie Dillard makes an analogy between life and a show. See *simile* and *metaphor.*

ANALYSIS. 1. **Analysis** is a thinking strategy in which one divides a subject into parts and then examines the relationships among the parts and between individual parts and the whole. An analysis of a short story, for example, might consist of a division of the work into such parts as the *exposition,* the *rising action,* the *climax,* the *resolution,* and the *dénouement,* along with an examination of the role played by each of these parts in advancing the plot. An analysis of a line of poetry might consist of a careful examination of its rhythm, its figures of speech, its images, and its meaning or meanings. 2. **Analysis** is also a way to organize exposition, a type of nonfiction writing.

ANAPEST. An **anapest** is a poetic foot containing two weakly stressed syllables followed by one strongly stressed syllable, as in the words *unimpressed* and *correlate.* A line of poetry made up of anapests is said to be *anapestic.*

ANECDOTE. An **anecdote** is a usually short narrative of an interesting, amusing, or biographical incident. Although anecdotes are often the basis for short stories, an anecdote differs from a short story in that it lacks a complicated plot and relates a single episode. Anecdotes are sometimes used in nonfiction writing as examples to help support an idea or opinion. In "An Ethnic Trump" (Unit 7), Gish Jen tells several anecdotes about raising her biracial son to underscore the problems that ethnicity raises in American society.

ANTAGONIST. See *character.*

ANTIHERO. An **antihero** is a central character who lacks many of the qualities traditionally associated with heroes. An antihero may be lacking in beauty, courage, grace, intelligence, or moral scruples. Antiheroes are common figures in modern fiction and drama. See *hero.*

APHORISM. An **aphorism** is a short saying or pointed statement. Examples of aphorisms by Benjamin Franklin include "The early bird catches the worm" and "Time is money." An aphorism that gains currency and is passed from generation to generation is called a *proverb* or *adage*. See *proverb*.

APOSTROPHE. An **apostrophe** is a rhetorical device by which a speaker turns from the audience as a whole to address a single person or thing.

APPOSITION. An **apposition** is a grammatical form in which a thing is renamed in a different word, phrase, or clause.

ARCHAIC LANGUAGE. **Archaic language** consists of old or obsolete words or phrases such as *smote* for *hit*.

ARCHETYPE. An **archetype** is an inherited, often unconscious, ancestral memory or motif that recurs throughout history and literature. The notion of the archetype derives from the psychology of Carl Jung, who described archetypes as symbols from humanity's "collective unconscious." The term is often used, more generally, to refer to any element that recurs throughout the literature of the world. Thus the story of the journey, in which someone sets out on a path, experiences adventures, and emerges wiser, may be considered archetypal, for it is found in all cultures and in all times. See *motif*.

ARGUMENT. 1. An **argument** is a summary, in prose, of the plot or meaning of a poem or drama. 2. In nonfiction writing, an **argument** is the case for accepting or rejecting a proposition or course of action.

ARGUMENTATION. **Argumentation** is a type of writing that presents reasons or arguments for accepting a position or for adopting a course of action.

ARGUMENTATIVE WRITING. See *aim*.

ARTICLE. An **article** is a brief work of nonfiction on a specific topic. The term *article* is typically used for encyclopedia entries and short nonfiction works that appear in newspapers and popular magazines. The term is sometimes used as a synonym of *essay*, though the latter term often connotes a more serious, important, or lasting work. "Ghost of Everest" in Unit 6 is an example of a magazine article. See *essay*.

ASIDE. An **aside** is a statement made by a character in a play, intended to be heard by the audience but not by other characters on the stage.

In Shakespeare's *The Tragedy of Romeo and Juliet* in Unit 4, Sampson and Gregory make asides to each other in act 1, scene 1, lines 38–39.

ASSONANCE. **Assonance** is the repetition of vowel sounds in stressed syllables that end with different consonant sounds. An example is the repetition of the long *o* sound in the following line from Edgar Allan Poe's "The Bells" (Unit 2):

From the molten-golden notes

ATMOSPHERE. See *mood*.

AUTOBIOGRAPHY. An **autobiography** is the story of a person's life, written by that person. Some editors and critics distinguish between autobiographies, which focus on personal experiences, and *memoirs*, which focus on public events, though the terms are often used interchangeably. The excerpt from *I Know Why the Caged Bird Sings* by Maya Angelou in Unit 5 is an example of an autobiography.

BACKGROUND INFORMATION. See *flashback*, *plot*, and *setting*.

BALLAD. A **ballad** is a simple narrative poem in four-line stanzas, usually meant to be sung and usually rhyming *abcb*. *Folk ballads*, composed orally and passed by word of mouth from generation to generation, have enjoyed enormous popularity from the Middle Ages to the present. Examples of popular American ballads include "The Ballad of Casey Jones" and "Bonny Barbara Allan." *Literary ballads*, written in imitation of folk ballads, have also been very popular. The folk ballad stanza usually alternates between lines of four and three feet. Common techniques used in ballads include repeated lines, or *refrains*, and *incremental repetition*, the repetition of lines with slight, often cumulative, changes throughout the poem. See *refrain*.

BIBLIOGRAPHY. A **bibliography** is a list of works on a given subject or of works consulted by an author. See *List of Works Cited*.

BIOGRAPHY. A **biography** is the story of a person's life, told by someone other than that person.

BLANK VERSE. **Blank verse** is unrhymed poetry written in iambic pentameter. An *iambic pentameter* line consists of five *feet*, each containing two syllables, the first weakly stressed and the second strongly stressed.

BLEND. A **blend**, or *portmanteau,* is a word created by joining together two previously existing words, such as *smoke* and *fog* for *smog.*

CACOPHONY. **Cacophony** is harsh or unpleasant sound. Writers sometimes intentionally use cacophony for effect.

CÆSURA. A **cæsura** is a major pause in a line of poetry.

CARICATURE. In literature, a **caricature** is a piece of writing that exaggerates certain qualities of a character in order to satirize or ridicule that character or type. See *satire.*

CATALOG. A **catalog** is a list of people or things.

CATASTROPHE. The **catastrophe** is a conclusion of a work, particularly of a tragedy, marked by the fall of the central character. In the catastrophe, the central conflict of the play is ended, or resolved. See *plot.*

CATHARSIS. The ancient Greek philosopher Aristotle described tragedy as bringing about a **catharsis,** or purging, of the emotions of fear and pity. Some critics take Aristotle's words to mean that viewing a tragedy causes the audience to feel emotions of fear and pity, which are then released at the end of the play, leaving the viewer calmer, wiser, and perhaps more thoughtful. The idea that catharsis calms an audience has been contradicted by recent psychological studies that suggest that people tend to imitate enacted feelings and behaviors that they witness. Much of the current debate over violence on television and in movies centers on this question of whether viewing such violence has a cathartic (calming) or an arousing effect on the viewer.

CENSORSHIP. **Censorship** is the act of examining works to see if they meet predetermined standards of political, social, or moral acceptability. Official censorship is aimed at works that will undermine authority or morals and has often in the past resulted in the suppression of works considered dangerous or licentious. Famous American novels that have been targets of censorship include *Adventures of Huckleberry Finn* by Mark Twain and *The Catcher in the Rye* by J. D. Salinger.

CENTRAL CONFLICT. A **central conflict** is the primary struggle dealt with in the plot of a story or drama. See *conflict* and *plot.*

CHARACTER. A **character** is a person (or sometimes an animal) who figures in the action of a literary work. A *protagonist,* or *main character,* is the central figure in a literary work. An *antagonist* is a character who is pitted against a protagonist. *Major characters* are those who play significant roles in a work. *Minor characters* are those who play lesser roles. A *one-dimensional character, flat character,* or *caricature* is one who exhibits a single dominant quality, or *character trait.* In the fable "The Fox and the Crow" (Unit 1), the fox and the crow are one-dimensional characters. A *three-dimensional, full,* or *rounded character* is one who exhibits the complexity of traits associated with actual human beings, like Scout in *To Kill a Mockingbird* (Unit 9). A *static character* is one who does not change during the course of the action. A *dynamic character* is one who does change. A *stock character* is one found again and again in different literary works. An example of a stock character is the mad scientist of nineteenth- and twentieth-century science fiction.

CHARACTERIZATION. **Characterization** is the use of literary techniques to create a character. Writers use three major techniques to create characters: direct description, portrayal of characters' behavior, and representations of characters' internal states. When using direct description, the writer, through a speaker, a narrator, or another character, simply comments on the character, telling the reader about such matters as the character's appearance, habits, dress, background, personality, motivations, and so on. In portrayal of a character's behavior, the writer presents the actions and speech of the character, allowing the reader to draw his or her own conclusions from what the character says or does. When using representations of internal states, the writer reveals directly the character's private thoughts and emotions, often by means of what is known as the *internal monologue.* See *character* and *internal monologue.*

CHORUS. A **chorus** is a person or group of people who speaks directly to the audience to convey the author's viewpoint or to introduce story details.

CHRONOLOGICAL ORDER. **Chronological order** is the arrangement of details in order of their occurrence. It is the primary method of organization used in narrative writing. It is also common in nonfiction writing that describes processes, events, and cause and effect relationships.

CLASSIC. A **classic** is a work of literature that is widely held to be one of the greatest creations within a given literary tradition. The question of what works are to be considered classic is a much-debated one.

CLASSIFICATION ORDER. **Classification order** is a method of organization in which subjects are divided into groups, or classes. These groups are then presented, one-by-one, in some reasonable order. Classification order is commonly used in exposition, or expository writing. See *exposition*, #1.

CLICHÉ. A **cliché** is an overused or unoriginal expression such as *quiet as a mouse* or *couch potato*. Most clichés originate as vivid, colorful expressions but soon lose their interest because of overuse. Careful writers and speakers avoid clichés, which are dull and signify lack of originality.

CLIMAX. The **climax** is the point of highest interest and suspense in a literary work. The term also is sometimes used to describe the *turning point* of the action in a story or play, the point at which the rising action ends and the falling action begins. See *crisis* and *plot*.

CLOSED COUPLET. See *couplet*.

COHERENCE. **Coherence** is the logical arrangement and progression of ideas in a speech or piece of writing. Writers achieve coherence by presenting their ideas in a logical sequence and by using transitions to show how their ideas are connected to one another. See *transition*.

COINED WORDS. **Coined words** are those that are intentionally created, often from the raw materials provided by already existing words and word parts. Examples of recently coined words include *spacewalk* and *e-mail*.

COLLOQUIALISM. **Colloquialism** is the use of informal language. Much modern poetry is characterized by its use of colloquialism. The following passage, which appears in *To Kill a Mockingbird* by Harper Lee (Unit 9), contains colloquialisms.

"How old are you," asked Jem, "four-and-a-half?"

"**Goin'** on seven."

"**Shoot** no wonder, then," said Jem, jerking his thumb at me. "**Scout yonder's been readin'** ever since she was born, and she **ain't** even started to school yet. You look **right puny** for **goin'** on seven."

COMEDY. Originally a literary work with a happy ending, a **comedy** is any lighthearted or humorous work, especially one prepared for the stage or the screen. Comedy is often contrasted with *tragedy*, in which the hero meets an unhappy fate. (It is perhaps only a slight exaggeration to say that comedies end with wedding bells and tragedies with funeral bells.) Comedies typically present less-than-exalted characters who display human limitations, faults, and misunderstandings. The typical progression of the action in a comedy is from initial order to a humorous misunderstanding or confusion and back to order again. Stock elements of comedy include mistaken identities, word play, satire, and exaggerated characters and events. See *tragedy*.

COMIC RELIEF. Writers sometimes insert into a serious work of fiction or drama a humorous scene that is said to provide **comic relief**, because it relieves the seriousness or emotional intensity felt by the audience. Paradoxically, a scene introduced for comic relief can sometimes, because of the contrast it provides, increase the perceived intensity or seriousness of the action around it.

COMPARISON AND CONTRAST ORDER. See *exposition*, #1.

COMPLICATION. The **complication** is the part of a plot in which the conflict is developed or built to its high point of intensity. See *plot*.

CONCRETE. A **concrete** word or phrase is one that names or describes something that can be directly perceived by one or more of the five senses. *Buffalo, geranium, storm,* and *heron* are examples of concrete terms. See *abstract*.

CONCRETE POEM. A **concrete poem**, or *shape poem*, is one printed or written in a shape that suggests its subject matter.

CONCRETE UNIVERSAL. A **concrete universal** is a particular object, person, action, or event that provides an instance or example of a general type.

CONFESSIONAL POETRY. Confessional poetry is verse that describes, sometimes with painful explicitness, the private or personal affairs of the writer. Sylvia Plath's "Mirror" in Unit 7 is an example of confessional poetry.

CONFLICT. A conflict is a struggle between two forces in a literary work. A *plot* involves the introduction, development, and eventual resolution of a conflict. One side of the *central conflict* in a story or drama is usually taken by the *main character*. That character may struggle against another character, against the forces of nature, against society or social norms, against fate, or against some element within himself or herself. In Jack London's short story "To Build a Fire" (Unit 3), the man experiences a man-against-nature conflict. A struggle that takes place between a character and some outside force is called an *external conflict*. A struggle that takes place within a character is called an *internal conflict*. The internal conflict of the narrator in "California Palms" (Unit 5) is whether to be Vietnamese or American. See *central conflict* and *plot*.

CONNOTATION. A connotation is an emotional association or implication attached to an expression. For example, the word *inexpensive* has positive emotional associations, whereas the word *cheap* has negative ones, even though the two words both *denote*, or refer to, low cost. Good writers choose their words carefully in order to express appropriate connotations. See *denotation*.

CONSONANCE. Consonance is a kind of slant rhyme in which the ending consonant sounds of two words match, but the preceding vowel sound does not, as in the words *wind* and *sound*. The following lines from Yeats's poem "The Song of Wandering Aengus" (Unit 2) provide an example:

The silver apples of the moo**n**,
The golden apples of the su**n**.

CONVENTION. A convention is an unrealistic element in a literary work that is accepted by readers or viewers because the element is traditional. One of the conventions of fiction, for example, is that it uses the past tense to describe current or present action. Rhyme schemes and organization into stanzas are among the many commonly employed conventions of poetry.

CONVENTIONAL SYMBOL. See *symbol*.

COUPLET. A couplet is two lines of verse that usually rhyme. These lines from Shakespeare's *Romeo and Juliet* (Unit 4) provide an example:

But passion lends them power, time means, to meet,
Temp'ring extremities with extreme sweet.

A *closed couplet* is a pair of rhyming lines that present a complete statement. A pair of rhyming iambic pentameter lines is also known as a *heroic couplet*.

CRISIS. In the plot of a story or a drama, the **crisis** is that point in the development of the conflict at which a decisive event occurs that causes the main character's situation to become better or worse. See *plot*.

CRITIC. A literary **critic** is a person who evaluates or interprets a work of literature. See *criticism*.

CRITICAL ESSAY. A critical essay is a type of informative or persuasive writing that presents an argument in support of a particular interpretation or evaluation of a work of literature. A well-constructed critical essay presents a clear *thesis*, or main idea, supported by ample evidence from the work or works being considered. See *thesis*.

CRITICISM. Criticism is the act of evaluating or interpreting a work of art or the act of developing general guidelines or principles for such evaluation or interpretation. Over the centuries, many schools, or philosophies, of criticism have been developed. However, most readers and teachers are eclectic critics, drawing consciously or unconsciously upon various schools of critical thought.

DACTYL. A dactyl is a poetic foot made up of a strongly stressed syllable followed by two weakly stressed syllables, as in the word *feverish*. A line of poetry made up of dactyls is said to be *dactylic*.

DEAD METAPHOR. A dead metaphor is one that is so familiar that its original metaphorical meaning is rarely thought of when the expression is used. An example is the word *nightfall*, which describes the coming of darkness as a falling object.

DEFINITION. A definition is an explanation of the meaning of a word or phrase. A dictionary definition typically consists of two parts: the *genus*, or class to which the thing belongs, and the *differentia*, or differences between the thing and other things of its class.

DENOTATION. The **denotation** is the basic meaning or reference of an expression, excluding its emotional associations, or *connotations*. For example, the words *dirt* and *soil* share a single common denotation. However, *dirt* has negative connotations of uncleanliness, whereas *soil* does not. See *connotation*.

DÉNOUEMENT. See *plot*.

DESCRIPTION. **Description** is a type of writing that portrays a character, an object, or a scene. Descriptions make use of *sensory details*—words and phrases that describe how things look, sound, smell, taste, or feel. Effective descriptions contain precise nouns, verbs, adverbs, and adjectives. When Jane Kenyon describes milk with the adjective "sweet" in her poem "Otherwise" (Unit 11), she is appealing to the sense of taste. Descriptions often use *imagery* and *figurative language*.

DIALECT. A **dialect** is a version of a language spoken by the people of a particular place, time, or social group. Writers often use dialect, as in Harper Lee's *To Kill a Mockingbird* (Unit 9), to give their works a realistic flavor. A *regional dialect* is one spoken in a particular place. For example, when John Henry says, "'Tain't nothing but my hammer in the air," he is using a rural southern dialect (Unit 1). A *social dialect* is one spoken by members of a particular social group or class.

DIALOGUE. 1. **Dialogue** is conversation involving two or more people or characters. Plays are made up of dialogue and stage directions. Fictional works are made up of dialogue, narration, and description. 2. **Dialogue** is also used to describe a type of literary composition in which characters debate or discuss an idea.

DIARY. A **diary** is a day-to-day record of a person's activities, experiences, thoughts, and feelings. See *journal*.

DICTION. **Diction**, when applied to writing, refers to word choice. Much of a writer's style is determined by his or her diction, the types of words that he or she chooses. Diction can be formal or informal, simple or complex, contemporary or archaic, ordinary or unusual, foreign or native,

standard or dialectical, coarse or refined, euphemistic or blunt. See *style*.

DIMETER. See *meter*.

DOMINANT IMPRESSION. See *effect*.

DRAMA. A **drama** is a story told through characters played by actors. The script of a drama typically consists of characters' names, dialogue spoken by the characters, and stage directions. Because it is meant to be performed before an audience, drama can be distinguished from other forms of nonperformance-based literary works by the central role played in it by the spectacle—the sensory presentation to the audience, which includes such elements as lighting, costumes, makeup, properties, set pieces, music, sound effects, and the movements and expressions of actors. Another important distinguishing feature of drama is that it is collaborative. The interpretation of the work depends not only upon the author and his or her audience, but also upon the director, the actors, and others involved in mounting a production. Two major types of drama are *comedy* and *tragedy*. See *comedy, dialogue, spectacle, stage directions,* and *tragedy*.

DRAMATIC CONVENTION. A **dramatic convention** is an unreal element in a drama that is accepted as realistic by the audience because it is tradiional. Such conventions include the impersonation of characters by actors, the use of a curtain to open or close an act or a scene, the revelation of a character's thoughts through *asides* and *soliloquies*, and the removal of the so-called *fourth wall* at the front of the stage that allows the audience to see action taking place in an imagined interior. See *convention* and *suspension of disbelief*.

DRAMATIC IRONY. See *irony*.

DRAMATIC MONOLOGUE. A **dramatic monologue** is a poem that presents the speech of a single character in a dramatic situation. The speech is one side of an imagined conversation. See *soliloquy*.

DRAMATIC POEM. A **dramatic poem** is a verse that relies heavily on dramatic elements such as monologue (speech by a single character) or *dialogue* (conversation involving two or more characters). Often dramatic poems are narratives as well. In other words, they often tell stories. Types of dramatic poetry include the *dramatic* *monologue* and the *soliloquy*. See *poetry, lyric poem,* and *narrative poem*.

DRAMATIS PERSONAE. Dramatis personae are the characters in a literary work. The term is most often used for the characters in a drama. See page 300 for a list of the dramatis personae in Shakespeare's *Romeo and Juliet*.

DREAM RECORD. A **dream record** is a diary or journal in which a writer records his or her dreams. See *diary* and *journal*.

DYNAMIC CHARACTER. See *character*.

DYSTOPIA. A **dystopia** is an imaginary, horrible world, the opposite of a *utopia*. Dystopias are common in science fiction. A famous example of a dystopia is the society described in Ray Bradbury's *Fahrenheit 451*. See *utopia*.

EDITORIAL. An **editorial** is a short, persuasive piece that appears in a newspaper, magazine, or other periodical.

EFFECT. The **effect** of a literary work is the general impression or emotional impact that it achieves. Some writers and critics, notably Edgar Allan Poe, have insisted that a successful short story or poem is one in which each detail contributes to the overall effect, or *dominant impression*, produced by the piece.

ELABORATION. Elaboration, or **amplification**, is a writing technique in which a subject is introduced and then expanded upon by means of repetition with slight changes, the addition of details, or similar devices.

ELEGY. An **elegy** is a poem that laments the dead. It is frequently long and formal in tone, but other poems can mourn death or loss as well.

ELIZABETHAN SONNET. See *sonnet*.

EMPHASIS. Emphasis is importance placed on an element in a literary work. Writers achieve emphasis by various means, including *repetition*, *elaboration*, stress, restatement in other words, and placement in a strategic position at the beginning or end of a line or a sentence.

END RHYME. End rhyme is rhyme that occurs at the ends of lines of verse. See *rhyme*.

ENGLISH SONNET. See *sonnet*.

EPIC. An **epic** is a long story, often told in verse, involving heroes and gods. Grand in length and

scope, an epic provides a portrait of an entire culture, of the legends, beliefs, values, laws, arts, and ways of life of a people. Famous epic poems include Homer's *Odyssey* (Unit 2) and *Iliad*, Virgil's *Aeneid*, Dante's *The Divine Comedy*, the anonymous Old English *Beowulf*, and Milton's *Paradise Lost*.

EPIC HERO. See *hero*.

EPIGRAM. An **epigram** is a short, often witty, saying. An example of an epigram is Benjamin Franklin's "Three may keep a secret, if two of them are dead."

EPIGRAPH. An **epigraph** is a quotation or motto used at the beginning of the whole or part of a literary work to help establish the work's theme.

EPILOGUE. An **epilogue** is a concluding section or statement, often one that comments on or draws conclusions from the work as a whole.

EPIPHANY. When applied to literature, the term **epiphany** refers to a moment of sudden insight in which the essence, or nature, of a person, thing, or situation is revealed. The use of the term in this sense was introduced by the Irish author James Joyce.

EPISODE. An **episode** is a complete action within a literary work.

EPISTLE. An **epistle** is a letter, especially one that is highly formal. Letters in verse are sometimes called epistles.

EPITAPH. An **epitaph** is an inscription or verse written to be used on a tomb or written in commemoration of someone who has died. The epitaph on the grave of Benjamin Franklin, written by Franklin himself, reads as follows:

> The body of
> Benjamin Franklin, printer,
> (Like the cover of an old book,
> Its contents worn out,
> And stript of its lettering and gilding)
> Lies here, food for worms!
> Yet the work itself shall not be lost,
> For it will, as he believed, appear once more
> In a new
> And more beautiful edition,
> Corrected and amended
> By its Author!

EPITHET. An **epithet** is a characteristic word or phrase used alongside the name of a person, place, or thing. "Spring, the season of new beginnings," is an example. Sometimes an epithet is so familiar that it can be used in place of a name. In Homer's *Odyssey* (Unit 2), the description of dawn as "rosy-fingered" is an epithet.

EPONYM. An **eponym** is a person or character from whose name a word or title is derived, or a name that has become synonymous with some general characteristic or idea. Narcissus is the eponym of the word *narcissism*, which means extreme preoccupation with one's own appearance and importance.

ESSAY. An **essay** is a brief work of prose nonfiction. The original meaning of essay was "a trial or attempt," and the word retains some of this original force. An essay need not be a complete or exhaustive treatment of a subject but rather a tentative exploration of it. A good essay develops a single idea and is characterized by *coherence* and *unity*. "Where Stars Are Born" by Michael Farber in Unit 8 is an example of an essay. "Straw Into Gold: The Metamorphosis of the Everyday" by Sandra Cisneros, also in Unit 8, is an example of a *personal essay*, or an essay related to the life or interests of the writer. See *coherence* and *unity*.

EUPHEMISM. A **euphemism** is an indirect word or phrase used in place of a direct statement that might be considered too harsh or offensive. The phrase *pass away*, used instead of *die*, and the phrase *waste management*, used in place of *garbage collection*, are euphemisms.

EUPHONY. Euphony is pleasing sound. Writers achieve euphony by various means, including repetitions of vowel and consonant sounds, *rhyme*, and *parallelism*. See *cacophony*.

EXPOSITION. 1. **Exposition** is a type of writing that presents facts or opinions in an organized manner. Among the most common ways to organize exposition are the following: analysis; classification; comparison and contrast; and process or how-to writing. See Types of Nonfiction Writing, page 427, for more information. 2. In a plot, the **exposition** is that part of a narrative that provides background information, often about the characters, setting, or conflict. See *plot*.

EXPOSITORY WRITING. See *aim*.

EXPRESSIVE WRITING. See *aim*.

EXTENDED METAPHOR. An **extended metaphor** is a point-by-point presentation of one thing as though it were another. The description is meant as an implied comparison, inviting the reader to associate the thing being described with something that is quite different from it. Eve Merriam's poem "Metaphor" (Unit 2) is an example of an extended metaphor. In this poem, morning is described as being a blank sheet of paper. Each day's activities, thoughts, and feelings are words on the paper.

EXTERNAL CONFLICT. See *conflict*.

EYE RHYME. See *sight rhyme*.

FABLE. A **fable** is a brief story, often with animal characters, told to express a moral. Famous fables include those of Æsop and Jean de La Fontaine. "The Fox and the Crow," a fable by Æsop, is found in Unit 1.

FAIRY TALE. A **fairy tale** is a story that deals with mischievous spirits and other supernatural occurrences, often in medieval settings. The name is generally applied to stories of the kinds collected by Charles Perrault in France and the Brothers Grimm in Germany or told by Hans Christian Andersen in Denmark. "Cinderella" and "The Little Mermaid" are famous examples. "The White Snake," a fairy tale by Jacob and Wilhelm Grimm, is found in Unit 1.

FALLING ACTION. See *plot*.

FANTASY. A **fantasy** is a literary work that contains highly unrealistic elements. Fantasy is often contrasted with *science fiction*, in which the unreal elements are given a scientific or pseudoscientific basis. Ursula Le Guin's "Gwilan's Harp" (Unit 3) and Stephen Vincent Benét's "Nightmare Number Three" (Unit 12) both contain elements of fantasy. See *Magical Realism* and *science fiction*.

FARCE. A **farce** is a type of comedy that depends heavily on so-called low humor and on improbable, exaggerated, extreme situations or characters.

FICTION. Fiction is prose writing about imagined events or characters. The primary forms of fiction are the *novel* and the *short story*. See *novel* and *short story*.

FIGURATIVE LANGUAGE. Figurative language is writing or speech meant to be understood imaginatively instead of literally. Many writers, especially poets, use figurative language to help readers to see things in new ways. Figurative language includes such literary techniques as *apostrophe, hyperbole, irony, metaphor, metonymy, oxymoron, paradox, personification, simile, synecdoche,* and *understatement.*

FIGURES OF SPEECH. **Figures of speech**, or *tropes,* are expressions that have more than a literal meaning. Hyperbole, metaphor, personification, simile, and understatement are all figures of speech. See *hyperbole, metaphor, personification, simile,* and *understatement.*

FIRST-PERSON POINT OF VIEW. See *point of view.*

FLASHBACK. A **flashback** is a section of a literary work that presents an event or series of events that occurred earlier than the current time in the work. Writers use flashbacks for many purposes, but most notably to provide *background information,* or exposition. In popular melodramatic works, including modern romance fiction and detective stories, flashbacks are often used to end suspense by revealing key elements of the plot such as a character's true identity or the actual perpetrator of a crime. One common technique is to begin a work with a final event and then to tell the rest of the story as a flashback that explains how that event came about. Another common technique is to begin a story *in medias res* (in the middle of the action) and then to use a flashback to fill in the events that occurred before the opening of the story.

FLASH FICTION. See *short short.*

FLAT CHARACTER. See *character.*

FOIL. A **foil** is a character whose attributes, or characteristics, contrast with, and therefore throw into relief, the attributes of another character. In *Romeo and Juliet,* Tybalt's fight-loving character acts as a foil to peace-loving Romeo.

FOLK BALLAD. See *ballad.*

FOLK SONG. A **folk song** is a traditional or composed song typically made up of stanzas, a refrain, and a simple melody. A form of folk literature, folk songs are expressions of commonly shared ideas or feelings and may be narrative or lyric in style. Traditional folk songs are anonymous songs that have been transmitted orally. Examples include the ballad "Bonny Barbara Allan," the sea chantey "Blow the Man Down,"

the children's song "Row, Row, Row Your Boat," the railroad song "Casey Jones," and the cowboy song "The Streets of Laredo." "John Henry" and the spirituals "Steal Away" and "Go Down, Moses" are examples of folk songs found in Unit 1. Contemporary composers of songs in the folk tradition include Bob Dylan, Joan Baez, Pete Seeger, and Joni Mitchell. See *ballad.*

FOLK TALE. A **folk tale** is a brief story passed by word of mouth from generation to generation. Writers often make use of materials from folk tales. Famous collections of folk tales include the German *Märchen,* or fairy tales, collected by the Brothers Grimm; Yeats's collection of Irish stories, *Mythologies*; and Zora Neale Hurston's collection of African-American folk tales and other folklore materials, *Of Mules and Men.* The North African story "Goha and the Pot" in Unit 1 is an example of a folk tale. See *fairy tale, folklore,* and *oral tradition.*

FOLKLORE. **Folklore** is a body of orally transmitted beliefs, customs, rituals, traditions, songs, verses, or stories. *Folk tales, fables, fairy tales, tall tales, nursery rhymes, proverbs, legends, myths, parables, riddles,* charms, spells, and *ballads* are all common kinds of folklore, though each of these can be found, as well, in literary forms made in imitation of works from the oral tradition. See *folk tale, fable, fairy tale, tall tale, nursery rhyme, proverb, myth, parable, riddle,* and *ballad.*

FOOT. In a poem, a **foot** is a unit of rhythm consisting of strongly and weakly stressed syllables. See *meter* and *scansion.* Also see the specific types of feet: *anapest, dactyl, iamb, spondee,* and *trochee.*

FORESHADOWING. **Foreshadowing** is the act of presenting materials that hint at events to occur later in a story. In "The Story of Dædalus and Icarus" (Unit 1), the scene in which Icarus plays with the wax foreshadows his death that occurs when the wax from his wings melts and he plummets to his death.

FOREWORD. See *preface.*

FRAME TALE. A **frame tale** is a story that itself provides a vehicle for the telling of other stories.

FREE VERSE. **Free verse** is poetry that avoids use of regular rhyme, meter, or division into stanzas. Much of the poetry written in the twentieth century is in free verse. Free verse is also referred to as *open verse*. The poems "Local Sensibilities" and "A Simile" (Unit 2), by Wing Tek Lum and N. Scott Momaday, use free verse.

FULL CHARACTER. See *character*.

GENRE. A **genre** (zhän′ rə) is one of the types or categories into which literary works are divided. Some terms used to name literary genres include *autobiography, biography, comedy, drama, epic, essay, lyric, narrative, novel,* pastoral, *poetry, short story,* and *tragedy*. Literary works are sometimes classified into genres based on subject matter. Such a classification might describe *detective stories, mysteries, adventure stories, romances, westerns,* and *science fiction* as different genres of fiction.

HAIKU. A **haiku** is a traditional Japanese three-line poem containing five syllables in the first line, seven in the second, and five again in the third. A haiku presents a picture, or image, in order to arouse in the reader a specific emotional and/or spiritual state.

HALF RHYME. See *slant rhyme*.

HEPTAMETER. See *meter*.

HEPTASTICH. A **heptastich** is a stanza with seven lines. See *stanza*.

HERO. A **hero** is a character whose actions are inspiring and courageous. An epic hero represents the ideals of the culture that creates it. In early literature, a hero is often part divine and has remarkable abilities, such as magical power, superhuman strength, or great courage. Odysseus in the *Odyssey* (Unit 2) is such a hero. A tragic hero is a character of high status who possesses noble qualities but who also has a tragic flaw, or personal weakness. In much contemporary literature, the term *hero* often refers to any main character. Former trapeze artist Anna Avalon is the hero of Louise Erdrich's story "The Leap" (Unit 10). See *antihero* and *tragic flaw*.

HEROIC COUPLET. See *couplet*.

HEROIC EPIC. A **heroic epic** is an epic that has a main purpose of telling the life story of a great hero. The *Odyssey* by Homer (Unit 2) is an example of a heroic epic. See *epic*.

HEXAMETER. See *meter*.

HIGH STYLE. See *style*.

HOW-TO WRITING. See *exposition*, #1.

HYMN. A **hymn** is a song or verse of praise, often religious.

HYPERBOLE. A **hyperbole** (hī pur′ bə lē) is an exaggeration made for rhetorical effect. In "The Devil and Daniel Webster" (Unit 3), Stephen Vincent Benét uses hyperbole when he says that trout leap into Daniel Webster's pockets when he goes fishing.

IAMB. An **iamb** is a poetic foot containing one weakly stressed syllable followed by one strongly stressed syllable, as in the words *afraid* and *release*. A line of poetry made up of iambs is said to be *iambic*.

IAMBIC. See *iamb*.

IMAGE. An **image** is language that creates a concrete representation of an object or an experience. An image is also the vivid mental picture created in the reader's mind by that language. The images in a literary work are referred to, collectively, as the work's *imagery*.

IMAGERY. See *image*.

IMAGINATIVE WRITING. See *aim*.

IN MEDIAS RES. See *action* and *flashback*.

INCITING INCIDENT. See *plot*.

INCREMENTAL REPETITION. See *ballad*.

INFORMATIONAL WRITING. See *aim*.

INTERNAL CONFLICT. See *conflict*.

INTERNAL MONOLOGUE. An **internal monologue** presents the private sensations, thoughts, and emotions of a character. The reader is allowed to overhear what is going on in the character's mind. Which characters' internal states can be revealed in a work of fiction depends on the *point of view* from which the work is told. See *point of view*.

INTRODUCTION. See *preface*.

INVERSION. An **inversion** is a poetic technique in which the normal order of words in an utterance is altered. Robert Frost's famous line "Whose woods these are, I think I know" is an inversion of the usual order of expression: "I think I know whose these woods are."

IRONY. **Irony** is a difference between appearance and reality. Types of irony include the following: *dramatic irony,* in which something is known by the reader or audience but unknown to the characters; *verbal irony*, in which a statement is made that implies its opposite; and *irony of situation*, in which an event occurs that violates the expectations of the characters, the reader, or the audience. Verbal irony occurs in "The Most Dangerous Game" (Unit 3) when General Zaroff states, "We do our best to preserve civilization here." This statement is ironic because his pastime of killing men for sport is the antithesis of civilization. Irony of situation occurs in the same story when Rainsford, a devoted hunter, is forced to become the hunted.

IRONY OF SITUATION. See *irony*.

JOURNAL. A **journal**, like a *diary*, is a day-to-day record of a person's activities, experiences, thoughts, and feelings. In contrast to diary, the word *journal* connotes an outward rather than an inward focus. However, the two terms are often used interchangeably. See *diary*.

LEGEND. A **legend** is a story coming down from the past, often based on real events or characters from older times. Unlike myths, legends are popularly regarded as historical; however, they may contain elements that are fantastic or unverifiable. "The Silver Pool" in Unit 1 is an example of an Irish legend.

LIMITED POINT OF VIEW. See *narrator* and *point of view*.

LIST OF WORKS CITED. A **List of Works Cited** is a type of bibliography that lists works used or referred to by an author. A standard feature of a research paper, the List of Works Cited appears at the end of the paper and is arranged in alphabetical order. See *bibliography*.

LOW STYLE. See *style*.

LYRIC POEM. A **lyric poem** is a highly musical verse that expresses the emotions of a speaker. Lyric poems are often contrasted with narrative poems, which have storytelling as their main purpose. Edgar Allan Poe's "The Bells" (Unit 2) and Emily Dickinson's "I'm Nobody! Who are you?" (Unit 7) are examples of lyric poetry. See *poetry*.

MAGICAL REALISM. **Magical Realism** is a kind of fiction that is for the most part realistic but that contains elements of fantasy. It originated in the works of Latin American writers who wished to communicate non-European worldviews. Magical Realism reflects the fact that Latin

American culture often accepts what Europeans would consider "fantastic occurrences" as part of everyday life. "The Handsomest Drowned Man in the World" by Gabriel García Márquez (Unit 3) is an example of Magical Realism.

MAIN CHARACTER. See *character*.

MAJOR CHARACTER. See *character*.

MEMOIR. A **memoir** is a nonfiction narration that tells a story. A memoir can be autobiographical (about one's life) or biographical (about someone else's life). Memoirs are based on a person's experiences and reactions to historical events. See *autobiography* and *biography*.

METAPHOR. A **metaphor** is a figure of speech in which one thing is spoken or written about as if it were another. This figure of speech invites the reader to make a comparison between the two things. The two "things" involved are the writer's actual subject, the *tenor* of the metaphor, and another thing to which the subject is likened, the *vehicle* of the metaphor. In Unit 2 Eve Merriam uses this metaphor in her poem "Metaphor": "Morning is / a new sheet of paper / for you to write on." The tenor of the metaphor is "Morning," and the vehicle of the metaphor is "new sheet of paper."

Personification and *similes* are types of metaphor. See *dead metaphor*, *mixed metaphor*, *personification*, and *simile*.

METER. The **meter** of a poem is its rhythmical pattern. English verse is generally described as being made up of rhythmical units called feet, as follows:

TYPE OF FOOT	STRESS PATTERN	EXAMPLE
iamb, or iambic foot	⌣ /	insist
trochee, or trochaic foot	/ ⌣	freedom
anapest, or anapestic foot	⌣ ⌣ /	unimpressed
dactyl, or dactylic foot	/ ⌣ ⌣	feverish
spondee, or spondaic foot	/ /	baseball

Some scholars also use the term *pyrrhee*, or *pyrrhic* foot, to describe a foot with two weak stresses. Using this term, the word *unbelievable* might be described as consisting of two feet, an anapest followed by a pyrrhic:

```
 ⌣  ⌣  /  |  ⌣  ⌣
un  be  liev  |  a  ble
```

Terms used to describe the number of feet in a line include the following:

monometer for a one-foot line
dimeter for a two-foot line
trimeter for a three-foot line
tetrameter for a four-foot line
pentameter for a five-foot line
hexameter, or Alexandrine, for a six-foot line
heptameter for a seven-foot line
octameter for an eight-foot line

A seven-foot line of iambic feet is called a *fourteener*.

A complete description of the meter of a line includes both the term for the type of foot that predominates in the line and the term for the number of feet in the line. The most common English meters are iambic tetrameter and iambic pentameter. The following are examples of each:

IAMBIC TETRAMETER:

```
 ⌣  /  ⌣  /  ⌣  /  ⌣  /
O slow | ly, slow | ly rose | she up
```

IAMBIC PENTAMETER:

```
 ⌣  /  ⌣  /  ⌣  /  ⌣  /
The cur | few tolls | the knell | of part |
 ⌣  /
 ing day,
```

METONYMY. Metonymy is the naming of an object associated with a thing in place of the name of the thing itself. Speaking of the *White House* when one means *the administrative* or *executive branch of the United States government* is an example of metonymy.

MIDDLE STYLE. See *style.*

MINOR CHARACTER. See *character.*

MIXED METAPHOR. A **mixed metaphor** is an expression or passage that garbles together two or more metaphors. An example of mixed metaphor would be the sentence "The chariot of the sun screamed across the sky," in which the sun is described, inconsistently, as both a chariot and as something that screams. *metaphor.*

MODE. A **mode** is a form of writing. One common classification system, based on purpose or aim, divides types of writing into five modes: expository/informative, imaginative, narrative, personal/expressive, and persuasive/argumentative. See *aim.*

MONOMETER. See *meter.*

MOOD. Mood, or *atmosphere,* is the emotion created in the reader by part or all of a literary work. The writer can evoke in the reader an emotional response—such as fear, discomfort, longing, or anticipation—by working carefully with descriptive language and sensory details. The author of "The Scarlet Ibis" (Unit 10) establishes a haunted, lonely mood in the story.

MORAL. A **moral** is a practical or moral lesson, usually relating to the principles of right and wrong, to be drawn from a story or other work of literature. The moral of "The Story of Dædalus and Icarus" (Unit 1) is to take the middle course and not live your life in extremes.

MOTIF. A **motif** is any element that recurs in one or more works of literature or art. Examples of common folk tale motifs found in oral traditions throughout the world include grateful animals or the thankful dead, three wishes, the trial or quest, and the magical metamorphosis, or transformation of one thing into another. "Cinderella," "The Ugly Duckling," and the Arthurian "Sword in the Stone" are examples of the transformation motif, in which persons or creatures of humble station are revealed to be exceptional. Much can be revealed about a literary work by studying the motifs within it. In "The White Snake" (Unit 1) a motif is items in sets of three, for example, the three tasks that the hero must complete to win the king's daughter. In *Romeo and Juliet* (Unit 4) the motif of the stars is significant because it underscores the importance of fate in the play.

MOTIVATION. A **motivation** is a force that moves a character to think, feel, or behave in a certain way. Luis, in Judith Ortiz Cofer's short story "Catch the Moon" (Unit 9), is motivated to find the hubcap by his love for Naomi. Roger, in Hughes's short story "Thank You, M'am" (Unit 9), is motivated to steal Mrs. Jones's purse because he wants a pair of blue suede shoes.

MUSE. In ancient Greek and Roman myth, the **Muses**—the nine daughters of Zeus and Mnemosyne, or Memory—were believed to provide the inspiration for the arts and sciences. Calliope was the Muse of epic poetry; Clio, the Muse of history; Erato, the Muse of lyrical poetry; Euterpe, the Muse of music; Melpomene, the Muse of tragedy; Polyhymnia, the Muse of sacred choral poetry; Terpischore, the Muse of choral dance and song; Thalia, the Muse of comedy; and Urania, the Muse of astronomy. The idea of the Muse has often been used by later writers to explain the vagaries and mysteries of literary inspiration. The connection of the Muses with entertainments and the arts survives in our English words *amusing* and *amusement*.

MYTH. A **myth** is a story that explains objects or events in the natural world as resulting from the action of some supernatural force or entity, most often a god. Every early culture around the globe has produced its own myths. "Echo and Narcissus" (Unit 1) is an example of a Greek myth. "The Story of Dædalus and Icarus" (Unit 1) is an example of a Roman myth.

NARRATION. **Narration** is a type of writing that tells a story, or describes events, most often using time, or *chronological order*, as a way of organization. See *chronological order*.

NARRATIVE POEM. A **narrative poem** is a verse that tells a story. "Song" by Gabriela Mistral and "The Creation" by James Weldon Johnson in Unit 2 are examples of narrative poems. See *poetry*.

NARRATIVE WRITING. See *aim*.

NARRATOR. A **narrator** is one who tells a story. In a drama, the narrator may be a character who introduces, concludes, or comments upon the action of the play. However, dramas typically do not have narrators. Works of fiction, on the other hand, always do, unless they consist entirely of dialogue without tag lines, in which case they cease to be fictions and become closet dramas, drama meant to be read but not performed. The narrator in a work of fiction may be a central or minor character or simply someone who witnessed or heard about the events being related. Writers achieve a wide variety of ends by varying the characteristics of the narrator chosen for a particular work. Of primary importance is the choice of the narrator's *point of view*. Will the narrator be omniscient, knowing all things, including the internal workings of the minds of the characters in the story, or will the narrator be limited in his or her knowledge? Will the narrator participate in the action of the story or stand outside that action and comment on it? Will the narrator be reliable or unreliable? That is, will the reader be able to

trust the narrator's statements? These are all questions that a writer must answer when developing a narrator. In Harper Lee's *To Kill a Mockingbird* (Unit 9), the narrator is Scout, a six-year-old girl. See *point of view* and *speaker*.

NEAR RHYME. See *slant rhyme*.

NONFICTION. **Nonfiction** is writing about real events. *Essays, autobiographies, biographies,* and *news articles* are all types of nonfiction. See *prose*.

NONSENSE VERSE. A **nonsense verse** is a kind of light verse that contains elements that are silly, absurd, or meaningless as in this example from "The Owl and the Pussycat" by Edward Lear:

> And there in a wood a Piggy-wig stood,
> With a ring at the end of his nose,
>   His nose
>   His nose,
> With a ring at the end of his nose.

NOVEL. A **novel** is a long work of prose fiction. Often novels have involved plots; many characters, both major and minor; and numerous settings. An excerpt from Harper Lee's novel *To Kill a Mockingbird* is found in Unit 9.

NOVELLA. A **novella** is a short novel.

NURSERY RHYME. A **nursery rhyme** is a children's verse.

OBJECTIVE CORRELATIVE. An **objective correlative** is a group of images that together create a particular emotion in the reader. The term was coined by T. S. Eliot. See *image*.

OCCASIONAL VERSE. An **occasional verse** is one written to celebrate or commemorate some particular event. For example, for President Clinton's first inauguration in 1993, Maya Angelou read a poem she wrote for the occasion, "On the Pulse of Morning."

OCTAMETER. See *meter*.

OCTAVE. An **octave** is an eight-line stanza. A Petrarchan sonnet begins with an octave. See *meter* and *sonnet*.

OFF RHYME. See *slant rhyme*.

OMNISCIENT POINT OF VIEW. See *narrator* and *point of view*.

ONE-ACT. See *act*.

ONE-DIMENSIONAL CHARACTER. See *character*.

ONOMATOPOEIA. Onomatopoeia is the use of words or phrases that sound like the things to which they refer. Examples of onomatopoeia include words such as *buzz, click,* and *pop.* Poets and other writers often make use of onomatopoeia. For example, in Edgar Allan Poe's "The Bells" (Unit 2), sleigh bells make the onomatopoeic sound "tinkle, tinkle, tinkle."

ORAL TRADITION. An **oral tradition** is a work, an idea, or a custom that is passed by word of mouth from generation to generation. Materials transmitted orally may be simplified in the retelling. They also may be sensationalized because of the tendency of retellers to add to or elaborate upon the materials that come down to them. Often, works in an oral tradition contain miraculous or magical elements. Common works found in the oral traditions of peoples around the world include *folk tales, fables, fairy tales, tall tales, nursery rhymes, proverbs, legends, myths, parables, riddles,* charms, spells, and *ballads.* The spirituals "Steal Away" and "Go Down, Moses" in Unit 1 belong to the African-American oral tradition. See *folklore.*

OXYMORON. An **oxymoron** is a statement that contradicts itself. Words like *bittersweet, tragicomedy,* and *pianoforte* (literally, "soft-loud") are oxymorons that develop a complex meaning from two seemingly contradictory elements.

PALINDROME. A **palindrome** is a word, a phrase, or a sentence that reads the same backward as forward. Examples include the word *radar* and the phrase *A man, a plan, a canal—Panama.*

PARABLE. A **parable** is a very brief story told to teach a moral lesson. The most famous parables are those, such as the parable "The Prodigal Son" in Unit 1, told by Jesus in the Bible.

PARADOX. A **paradox** is a seemingly contradictory statement, idea, or event. All forms of *irony* involve paradox. An *oxymoron* is a paradoxical statement. Some paradoxes present unresolvable contradictory ideas. An example of such a paradox is the statement, "This sentence is a lie." If the sentence is true, then it is false; if it is false, then it is true. The paradox in Nikki Giovanni's poem "Nikki-Rosa" (Unit 7) is that she is wealthy (in love) even though she is poor (materialistically). See *irony* and *oxymoron.*

PARALLELISM. Parallelism is a rhetorical technique in which a writer emphasizes the equal value or weight of two or more ideas by expressing them in the same grammatical form. James Weldon Johnson uses parallelism in these lines from "The Creation" (Unit 2):

> Who lit the sun and fixed it in the sky,
> Who flung the stars to the most far corner of
>   the night,
> Who rounded the earth in the middle of his hand.

PARAPHRASE. A **paraphrase** is a rewriting of a passage in different words. A paraphrase is often distinguished from an *abstract* or summary as follows: a summary is shorter than the original, whereas a paraphrase may be as long as or longer than the original. See *abstract.*

PARODY. A **parody** is a literary work that imitates another work for humorous, often satirical, purposes.

PENTAMETER. See *meter.*

PERIODICAL. A **periodical** is a newspaper, magazine, journal, newsletter, or other publication that is produced on a regular basis. *Poetry* magazine has been a leading force in shaping the course of modern American poetry.

PERSONA. A **persona** consists of the qualities of a person or character that are shown through speech or actions.

PERSONAL ESSAY. A **personal essay** is a short work of nonfictional prose on a single topic related to the life or interests of the writer. Personal essays are characterized by an intimate and informal style and tone. They are often, but not always, written in the first person. See *essay.*

PERSONAL SYMBOL. See *symbol.*

PERSONAL WRITING. See *aim.*

PERSONIFICATION. Personification is a figure of speech in which an idea, animal, or thing is described as if it were a person. In her poem "Song" (Unit 2) Gabriela Mistral says "Night grows maternal." Giving night the human characteristic of motherliness is an example of personification. In the *Odyssey* (Unit 2), Homer personifies dawn by giving it hands: "Dawn spread out her finger tips of rose."

PERSUASIVE WRITING. See *aim.*

PLAGIARISM. Plagiarism is the act of using material gathered from another person or work without crediting the source of the material.

PLOT. A **plot** is a series of events related to a central *conflict*, or struggle. A typical plot involves the introduction of a conflict, its development, and its eventual resolution. Terms used to describe elements of plot include the following:

- The **exposition**, or *introduction*, sets the tone or mood, introduces the characters and the setting, and provides necessary background information.
- The **inciting incident** is the event that introduces the central conflict.
- The **rising action**, or *complication*, develops the conflict to a high point of intensity.
- The **climax** is the high point of interest or suspense in the plot.
- The **crisis**, or *turning point*, often the same event as the climax, is the point in the plot where something decisive happens to determine the future course of events and the eventual working out of the conflict.
- The **falling action** is all the events that follow the climax.
- The **resolution** is the point at which the central conflict is ended, or resolved.
- The **dénouement** is any material that follows the resolution and that ties up loose ends.
- The **catastrophe**, in tragedy, is the event that marks the ultimate tragic fall of the central character. Often this event is the character's death.

Plots rarely contain all these elements in precisely this order. Elements of exposition may be introduced at any time in the course of a work. A work may begin with a catastrophe and then use flashback to explain it. The exposition or dénouement or even the resolution may be missing. The inciting incident may occur before the beginning of the action actually described in the work. These are but a few of the many possible variations that plots can exhibit. See *conflict*.

POETIC LICENSE. **Poetic license** is the right, claimed by writers, to change elements of reality to suit the purposes of particular works that they create. Such things do not happen in reality, but they are accepted by readers willing to suspend disbelief in order to have imaginary experiences. See *suspension of disbelief*.

POETRY. **Poetry** is imaginative language carefully chosen and arranged to communicate experiences, thoughts, or emotions. It differs from prose in that it compresses meaning into fewer words, and often uses *meter, rhyme,* and techniques such as *metaphor* and *simile*. Poetry is usually arranged in lines and stanzas as opposed to sentences and paragraphs, and it can be more free in the ordering of words and the use of punctuation. Types of poetry include *narrative, dramatic,* and *lyric*. See *meter, rhyme, narrative poem, dramatic poem,* and *lyric poem*.

POINT OF VIEW. **Point of view** is the vantage point from which a story is told. Stories are typically written from a *first-person point of view*, in which the narrator uses words such as *I* and *we*; from a *second-person point of view*, in which the narrator uses *you*; or from a *third-person point of view*, in which the narrator uses words such as *he, she, it,* and *they*. In stories written from a first-person point of view, the narrator may be a participant or witness of the action. In stories told from a third-person point of view, the narrator generally stands outside the action. In some stories, the narrator's point of view is *limited*. In such stories, the narrator can reveal his or her private, internal thoughts or those of a single character. In other stories, the narrator's point of view is *omniscient*. In such stories the narrator can reveal the private, internal thoughts of any character.

PORTMANTEAU. See *blend*.

PRÉCIS. See *abstract*.

PREFACE. A **preface** is a statement made at the beginning of a literary work, often by way of introduction. The terms *foreword, preface,* and *introduction* are often used interchangeably.

PROCESS WRITING. See *exposition*, #1.

PROLOGUE. A **prologue** is an introduction to a literary work, often one that sets the scene and introduces the conflict or the main characters. In Shakespeare's *Romeo and Juliet* the chorus presents the prologue before act 1.

PROSCENIUM STAGE. See *stage*.

PROSE. **Prose** is the broad term used to describe all writing that is not drama or poetry, including fiction and nonfiction. Types of prose writing include novels, short stories, essays, and news stories. Most biographies, autobiographies, and letters are written in prose. See *fiction*.

PROSE POEM. A **prose poem** is a work of prose, usually a short work, that makes such extensive use of poetic language, such as figures of speech and words that echo their sense, that the line between prose and poetry becomes blurred. Gabriela Mistral's "Song" in Unit 2 is an example of a prose poem.

PROTAGONIST. See *character*.

PROVERB. A **proverb**, or **adage**, is a traditional saying, such as "You can lead a horse to water, but you can't make it drink" or the title of Shakespeare's play *All's Well That Ends Well*.

PSEUDONYM. A **pseudonym** is a name assumed by a writer. For example, Mark Twain was the pseudonym of Samuel Clemens.

PSYCHOLOGICAL FICTION. **Psychological fiction** is fiction that emphasizes the interior, subjective experiences of its characters, and especially such fiction when it deals with emotional or mental disturbance or anguish. Edith Wharton's short story "A Journey" (Unit 11) is an example of psychological fiction.

PUN. A **pun** is a play on words, one that wittily exploits a double meaning. In act 3 of Shakespeare's *Romeo and Juliet*, Mercutio's line, "Ask for me tomorrow, and you shall find me a grave man" is a pun. The word *grave*, in this context, means "having serious thoughts." However, he is also hinting that he might be dead and in a *grave* tomorrow.

PURPOSE. See *aim*.

PYRRHIC. See *meter*.

QUATRAIN. A **quatrain** is a stanza containing four lines.

QUINTAIN. A **quintain**, or **quintet**, is a stanza containing five lines.

QUINTET. See *quintain*.

RAP. **Rap** is improvised, rhymed verse that is chanted or sung, often to a musical accompaniment.

REALISM. **Realism** is the attempt to render in art an accurate portrayal of reality.

REDUNDANCY. **Redundancy** is needless repetition. The phrase *firmly determined* is redundant because the word *determined* already implies firmness.

REFRAIN. A **refrain** is a line or group of lines repeated in a poem or song. Many *ballads* contain refrains.

REGIONAL DIALECT. See *dialect*.

REGIONAL FICTION. **Regional fiction** is writing in which particular settings play an important role. The details used to create a particular regional setting are called *local color*. Many American novels and short stories deal with particular regions of the country (New York City, the western frontier, small towns in the South or Midwest, and so on).

REPETITION. **Repetition** is the writer's conscious reuse of a sound, word, phrase, sentence, or other element.

RESOLUTION. See *plot*.

REVERSAL. A **reversal** is a dramatic change in the direction of events in a drama or narrative, especially a change in the fortunes of the protagonist. See *plot*.

REVIEW. A **review** is a written evaluation of a work of art, a performance, or a literary work, especially one that appears in a periodical or on a broadcast news program. Common subjects of reviews include books, films, art exhibitions, restaurants, and performances of all kinds, from rock concerts to ballets.

RHETORIC. **Rhetoric** is the art of speaking or writing effectively. It involves the study or ways in which speech and writing affect of influence audiences. Rhetoric has also been defined as the art of persuasion.

RHETORICAL QUESTION. A **rhetorical question** is one asked for effect but not meant to be answered because the answer is clear from context.

RHETORICAL TECHNIQUE. A **rhetorical technique** is an extraordinary but literal use of language to achieve a particular effect on an audience. Common rhetorical techniques include *apostrophe*, *catalog*, *parallelism*, *repetition*, and the *rhetorical question*.

RHYME. **Rhyme** is the repetition of sounds at the ends of words. Types of rhyme include *end rhyme* (the use of rhyming words at the ends of lines), *internal rhyme* (the use of rhyming words within lines), *exact rhyme* (in which the rhyming words end with the same sound or sounds), and *slant rhyme* (in which the rhyming sounds are similar but not identical). An example of exact rhyme is the word pair *moon/June*. Examples of slant rhyme are the word pairs *rave/rove* and *rot/rock*. See *poetry, slant rhyme* and *rhyme scheme.*

RHYME SCHEME. A **rhyme scheme** is a pattern of end rhymes, or rhymes at the ends of lines of verse. The rhyme scheme of a poem is designated by letters, with matching letters signifying matching sounds. For example, the rhyme scheme for Yeats's poem "The Song of Wandering Aengus" (Unit 2) is *abcbdefe ababcded abcbdefg.*

RHYTHM. Rhythm is the pattern of beats or stresses in a line of verse or prose. See *meter.*

RIDDLE. A **riddle** is a word game in which something is described in an unusual way and the reader or listener must figure out what that something is. Riddles are common in folklore and myth throughout the world.

RISING ACTION. See *plot.*

ROMANCE. Romance is a term used to refer to four types of literature: 1. medieval stories about the adventures and loves of knights; 2. novels and other fictions involving exotic locales and extraordinary or mysterious events and characters; 3. nonrealistic fictions in general; and 4. in popular, modern usage, love stories of all kinds. Today, the term is quite widely used to refer to love stories, especially popular, sentimental stories.

ROUNDED CHARACTER. See *character.*

RUN-ON LINE. A **run-on line** is a line of verse in which the sense or the grammatical structure does not end with the end of the line but rather is continued on one or more subsequent lines. The following lines from Yeats's "The Song of Wandering Aengus" form a single sentence:

> I went out to the hazel wood,
> Because a fire was in my head,
> And cut and peeled a hazel wand,
> And hooked a berry to a thread;
> And when white moths were on the wing,
> And moth-like stars were flickering out,
> I dropped the berry in a stream
> And caught a little silver trout.

The act of continuing a statement beyond the end of a line is called *enjambment.*

SATIRE. Satire is humorous writing or speech intended to point out errors, falsehoods, foibles, or failings. It is written for the purpose of reform-ing human behavior or human institutions. In "An Encounter with an Interviewer," Mark Twain satirizes reporters and the interview process.

SCANSION. Scansion is the art of analyzing poetry to determine its meter. See *meter.*

SCENE. A **scene** is a short section of a literary work that presents action that occurs in a single place or at a single time. Long divisions of dramas are often divided into scenes.

SCIENCE FICTION. Science fiction is highly imaginative fiction containing fantastic elements based on scientific principles, discoveries, or laws. It is similar to fantasy in that it deals with imaginary worlds but differs from fantasy in having a scientific basis. Often science fiction deals with the future, the distant past, or with worlds other than our own, such as other planets, parallel universes, and worlds under the ground or the sea. The genre allows writers to suspend or alter certain elements of reality in order to create fascinating and sometimes instructive alternatives. Important writers of science fiction include H. G. Wells, Jules Verne, Ray Bradbury, Arthur C. Clarke, Isaac Asimov, Ursula K. Le Guin, Robert Heinlein, and Kurt Vonnegut, Jr. Ray Bradbury's short story "There Will Come Soft Rains" in Unit 12 is an example of science fiction. See *fantasy.*

SENSORY DETAIL. See *description.*

SENTIMENTALITY. Sentimentality is an excessive expression of emotion. Much popular literature of the nineteenth and twentieth centuries is characterized by sentimentality.

SEPTET. A **septet** is a stanza with seven lines.

SESTET. A **sestet** is a stanza with six lines, such as the second part of a Petrarchan sonnet. See *meter* and *sonnet.*

SET. A **set** is a collection of objects on a stage arranged in such a way as to create a scene.

SETTING. The **setting** of a literary work is the time and place in which it occurs, together with all the details used to create a sense of a particular time and place. Writers create setting by various means. In drama, the setting is often revealed by the stage set and the costumes, though it may be revealed through what the characters say about their environs. In fiction, setting is most often revealed by means of description of such elements as landscape, scenery, buildings, furniture, clothing, the weather, and the season. It can also be revealed by how characters talk and behave. In its widest sense, setting includes the general social, political, moral, and psychological conditions in which characters find themselves. The setting of *I Know Why the Caged Bird Sings* (Unit 5) is a small, rural town in Arkansas. Poor, struggling cotton pickers and the narrator's grandmother's store further inform the setting. See *set*.

SHAKESPEAREAN SONNET. See *sonnet*.

SHAPE POEM. See *concrete poem*.

SHORT SHORT. A **short short**, or *flash fiction*, is an extremely brief short story. This recently recognized genre of the short story is currently enjoying considerable popularity among readers of literary magazines and short story collections published in the United States. Short shorts sometimes take the form of anecdotes, or retellings of single incidents. Alternatively, they may attempt to develop an entire plot within the compass of a few paragraphs. Many short shorts are highly poetic and may be considered prose poems. See *anecdote* and *prose poem*.

SHORT STORY. A **short story** is a form of short prose fiction that relates a narrative. Short stories are typically crafted carefully to develop a plot, a conflict, characters, a setting, a mood, and a theme, all within relatively few pages. This form of literature gained popularity in the nineteenth century. See *conflict, character, mood, plot, setting,* and *theme*.

SIGHT RHYME. A **sight rhyme**, or *eye rhyme,* is a pair of words, generally at the ends of lines of verse, that are spelled similarly but pronounced differently. The words *lost* and *ghost* and *give* and *thrive* are examples. The end rhyme between *gone* and *done* in Yeats's poem "The Song of Wandering Aengus" provides an example:

> I will find out where she has **gone,**
> And kiss her lips and take her hands;
> And walk among long dappled grass,
> And pluck till time and times are **done**. . . .

SIMILE. A **simile** is a comparison using *like* or *as*. N. Scott Momaday uses a simile in his poem "A Simile":

> What did we say to each other
> that now we are as the deer. . . .

A simile is a type of *metaphor,* and like any other metaphor, can be divided into two parts, the *tenor* (or subject being described), and the *vehicle* (or object being used in the description). In the simile "your locks are like the snow," the tenor is *locks of hair* and the vehicle is *snow.* They can be compared because they share some quality, in this case, whiteness. See *metaphor*.

SLANG. **Slang** is extremely colloquial speech not suitable for formal occasions and usually associated with a particular group of people. An example of slang current among young people in the United States in the 1920s is "the bee's knees," for something uniquely attractive or wonderful. Among young people in the northeastern United States, the word *wicked* is now sometimes used as a slang term meaning "extremely," as in "That song is wicked good." Writers sometimes use slang in an attempt to render characters and setting vividly.

SLANT RHYME. A **slant rhyme,** or *half rhyme, near rhyme,* or *off rhyme* is the substitution of assonance or consonance for true rhyme. The pairs *world/boiled* and *bear/bore* are examples. See *assonance, consonance,* and *rhyme*.

SOCIAL DIALECT. See *dialect*.

SOLILOQUY. A **soliloquy** is a speech delivered by a lone character that reveals the speaker's thoughts and feelings. In Shakespeare's *Romeo and Juliet*, Juliet's speech, "Farewell! God knows when we shall meet again" (act 4, scene 3), is an example of a soliloquy.

SONNET. A **sonnet** is a fourteen-line poem, usually in iambic pentameter, that follows one of a number of different rhyme schemes. The *English, Elizabethan,* or *Shakespearean* sonnet is divided into four parts: three *quatrains* and a final *couplet.* The rhyme scheme of such a sonnet is *abab cdcd efef gg*. The sonnets that open act 1 and act 2 of Shakespeare's *Romeo and Juliet* (Unit 4) are examples. The *Italian* or *Petrarchan sonnet* is divided into two parts: an *octave* and a *sestet.* The rhyme scheme of the octave is *abbaabba*. The rhyme scheme of the sestet can be *cdecde, cdcdcd,* or *cdedce*.

SOURCE. A **source** is a work from which an author takes his or her materials.

SPEAKER. The **speaker** is the character who speaks in, or narrates, a poem—the voice assumed by the writer. The speaker and the writer of a poem are not necessarily the same person. The speaker in Sylvia Plath's poem "Mirror" (Unit 7) is a mirror and a lake.

SPECTACLE. In drama, the **spectacle** is all the elements that are presented to the senses of the audience, including the lights, setting, costumes, makeup, music, sound effects, and movements of the actors.

SPIRITUAL. A **spiritual** is a folk song of deep religious and emotional character. Spirituals were developed among African Americans in the southern United States during slavery. The words are most often related to biblical passages and frequently reflect patient, profound melancholy, even though the songs seldom refer to slavery itself. Spirituals influenced blues, jazz, and gospel songs. "Steal Away" and "Go Down, Moses" in Unit 1 are examples of spirituals.

SPONDEE. A **spondee** is a poetic foot containing two strongly stressed syllables, as in the words *compound* and *roughhouse*. Such a foot is said to be *spondaic*.

STAGE. A **stage** is any arena on which the action of a drama is performed. In the Middle Ages, stages often consisted of the beds of wagons, which were wheeled from place to place for performances. From the use of such wagons in inn yards, the *thrust stage* developed. This was a platform that extended out into the audience and that was closed at the back. In front of the platform in the first English theaters, such as Shakespeare's Globe Theatre, was an open area, the pit, where common people stood. Around the pit were balconies in imitation of the balconies of inns. The modern *proscenium stage* typically is closed on three sides and open at the front, as though the *fourth wall* had been removed. Sometimes contemporary plays are performed as *theater in the round*, with the audience seated on all sides of the playing area.

STAGE DIRECTIONS. **Stage directions** are notes included in a play, in addition to the dialogue, for the purpose of describing how something should be performed on stage. Stage directions describe setting, lighting, music, sound effects, entrances and exits, properties, and the move-ments of characters. They are usually printed in italics and enclosed in brackets or parentheses.

STANZA. A **stanza** is a group of lines in a poem. The following are some types of stanza:

two-line stanza	*couplet*
three-line stanza	*triplet* or *tercet*
four-line stanza	*quatrain*
five-line stanza	*quintain*
six-line stanza	*sestet*
seven-line stanza	*heptastich*
eight-line stanza	*octave*

STATIC CHARACTER. See *character*.

STEREOTYPE. A **stereotype** is an uncritically accepted, fixed or conventional idea, particularly such an idea held about whole groups of people. A *stereotypical*, or *stock*, character is one who does not deviate from conventional expectations of such a character. Examples of stereotypical characters include the merciless villain, the mad scientist, and the hard-boiled private eye. See *character*.

STOCK CHARACTER. See *character* and *stereotype*.

STORY. A **story,** or **narrative**, is writing or speech that relates a series of events. When these events are causally connected and related to a conflict, they make up a *plot*. See *plot*.

STREAM-OF-CONSCIOUSNESS WRITING. **Stream-of-consciousness writing** is literary work that attempts to render the flow of feelings, thoughts, and impressions within the minds of characters. Modern masters of stream-of-consciousness writing include Virginia Woolf, James Joyce, and William Faulkner.

STRESS. **Stress,** or **accent**, is the level of emphasis given to a syllable. In English metrics, the art of *rhythm* in written and spoken expression, syllables are generally described as being strongly or weakly stressed, in other words, accented or unaccented. A strongly stressed or accented syllable receives a strong emphasis. A weakly stressed or unaccented syllable receives a weak one. In the following line from Yeats's "The Song of Wandering Aengus," the strongly stressed or accented syllables are marked with a slash mark (/).

    /   /   /   /
I went out to the hazel wood,

STYLE. **Style** is the manner in which something is said or written. Traditionally, critics and scholars have referred to three levels of style: high style, for formal occasions or lofty subjects; middle style, for ordinary occasions or subjects; and low style, for extremely informal occasions or subjects. A writer's style depends upon many things, including his or her *diction* (the words that the writer chooses), selection of grammatical structures (simple versus complex sentences, for example), and preference for *abstract* or *concrete* words. Any recurring feature that distinguishes one writer's work from another can be said to be part of that writer's style. See *abstract* and *fiction*.

SUBPLOT. A **subplot** is a subordinate story told in addition to the major story in a work of fiction. Often a subplot mirrors or provides a *foil* for the primary plot. See *plot* and *story*.

SUMMARY. See *abstract*.

SUSPENSE. **Suspense** is a feeling of expectation, anxiousness, or curiosity created by questions raised in the mind of a reader or viewer.

SUSPENSION OF DISBELIEF. **Suspension of disbelief** is the act by which the reader willingly sets aside his or her skepticism in order to participate imaginatively in the work being read. Readers may not believe that animals can talk, but they are willing to suspend that disbelief when reading fairy tales such as "The White Snake" or fables like "The Fox and the Crow" (Unit 1). The willingness to suspend disbelief, to participate imaginatively in a story being read, is the most important attribute, beyond literacy, that a person can bring to the act of reading literature.

SYMBOL. A **symbol** is a thing that stands for or represents both itself and something else. Writers use two types of symbols—conventional, and personal or idiosyncratic. A *conventional symbol* is one with traditional, widely recognized associations. Such symbols include doves for peace; laurel wreaths for heroism or poetic excellence; the color green for jealousy; winter, evening, or night for old age; wind for change or inspiration; the moon for fickleness or inconstancy; roads or paths for the journey through life; woods or darkness for moral or spiritual confusion. A *personal* or *idiosyncratic symbol* is one that assumes its secondary meaning because of the special use to which it is put by a writer. In the parable "The Prodigal Son" (Unit 1), the lost sheep, the lost silver coin, and the prodigal son

all symbolize a lost sinner who returns to God's fold. In Robert Frost's poem "Birches," (Unit 2), swinging on a birch tree toward heaven symbolizes escape from life's demands. In James Hurst's short story "The Scarlet Ibis" (Unit 10), the scarlet ibis becomes a symbol of the uniqueness and fragility of the character Doodle.

SYNAESTHESIA. **Synaesthesia** is a figure of speech that combines in a single expression images related to two or more different senses.

SYNECDOCHE. A **synecdoche** (sin ek' də kē´) is a figure of speech in which the name of part of something is used in place of the name of the whole or vice versa. In the command "All hands on deck!" *hands* is a synecdoche in which a part (hands) is used to refer to a whole (people, sailors). Addressing a representative of the country of France as France would be a synecdoche in which a whole (France) is used to refer to a part (one French person).

SYNTAX. **Syntax** is the pattern of arrangement of words in a statement. Poets often vary the syntax of ordinary speech or experiment with unusual syntactic arrangements. See *inversion*.

TAG LINE. A **tag line** is an expression in a work of fiction that indicates who is speaking and sometimes indicates the manner of speaking. Examples include the familiar *she said* as well as more elaborate expressions such as *Raoul retorted angrily*.

TALL TALE. A **tall tale** is a story, often lighthearted or humorous, that contains highly exaggerated, unrealistic elements. Stories about Paul Bunyan are tall tales.

TENOR. See *metaphor*.

TERCET. See *triplet*.

TETRAMETER. See *meter*.

THEATER (playing area). See *stage*.

THEATER IN THE ROUND. See *stage*.

THEME. A **theme** is a central idea in a literary work. The theme of Emily Dickinson's poem "I'm Nobody! Who are you?" is the value of privacy and solitude. One theme of Ursula Le Guin's story "Gwilan's Harp" (Unit 3) is the ability of the human spirit to rise above grief and loss. The theme of Leslie Marmon Silko's story "The Man to Send Rain Clouds" (Unit 7) is the transforming quality of culture.

THESIS. A **thesis** is a main idea that is supported in a work of nonfictional prose. The thesis of "The Obligation to Endure" by Rachel Carson (Unit 5) is that dangerous insecticides must be controlled now that we know their effect on soil, water, wildlife, and humans.

THIRD-PERSON POINT OF VIEW. See *point of view.*

THREE-DIMENSIONAL CHARACTER. See *character.*

THRUST STAGE. See *stage.*

TONE. **Tone** is the emotional attitude toward the reader or toward the subject implied by a literary work. Examples of the different tones that a work may have include familiar, ironic, playful, sarcastic, serious, and sincere. In the article "Best Sky Sights of the Next Century" (Unit 6), Bob Berman uses a joking, irreverent tone. In the poem "Being in Love" (Unit 9), Marvin Bell employs a playful, hopeful tone.

TRAGEDY. A **tragedy** is a drama (or by extension any work of literature) that tells the story of the fall of a person of high status. It celebrates the courage and dignity of a tragic hero in the face of inevitable doom. Sometimes that doom is made inevitable by a *tragic flaw* in the hero. In the twentieth century, writers have extended the definition of tragedy to cover works that deal with the fall of any sympathetic character, despite his or her status.

TRAGIC FLAW. A **tragic flaw** is a personal weakness that brings about the fall of a character in a tragedy. Both Romeo and Juliet suffer from the tragic flaw of impulsiveness. See *tragedy.*

TRAGIC HERO. See *hero* and *tragedy.*

TRANSITION. A **transition** is a word, phrase, sentence, or paragraph used to connect ideas and to show relationships between them. *However, therefore, in addition,* and *in contrast* are common transitions. Repeated nouns, synonyms, and pronouns can also serve as transitions.

TRANSLATION. Translation is the art of rendering speech or writing into another language.

TRIMETER. See *meter.*

TRIPLET. A **triplet**, or *tercet,* is a stanza of three lines.

TROCHEE. A **trochee** is a poetic foot consisting of a strongly stressed syllable followed by a weakly stressed syllable, as in the word *winter.* A line of poetry made up of trochees is said to be *trochaic.*

TROPE. See *figure of speech.*

TURNING POINT. See *plot.*

UNDERSTATEMENT. An **understatement** is an ironic expression in which something of importance is emphasized by being spoken of as though it were not important, as in "He's sort of dead, I think."

UNITY. A work has **unity** when its various parts all contribute to creating an integrated whole. An essay with unity, for example, is one in which all the parts help to support the thesis statement, or main idea. See *essay.*

UNRELIABLE NARRATOR. An **unreliable narrator** is one whom the reader cannot trust. See *narrator.*

UTOPIA. A **utopia** is an imaginary, idealized world. The term comes from the title of Sir Thomas More's *Utopia,* which described what More believed to be an ideal society. More took the word from the Greek roots meaning "no-place." See *dystopia.*

VEHICLE. See *metaphor.*

VERBAL IRONY. See *irony.*

VERNACULAR. The **vernacular** is the speech of the common people. The term *vernacular* is often used loosely today to refer to dialogue or to writing in general that uses colloquial, dialectical, or slang expressions.

VERS LIBRE. See *free verse.*

VOICE. Voice is the way a writer uses language to reflect his or her unique personality and attitude toward topic, form, and audience. A writer expresses voice through tone, word choice, and sentence structure.

GLOSSARY
Of Words For Everyday Use

PRONUNCIATION KEY

VOWEL SOUNDS

a	hat	i	sit	o͞o (or ü)	blue, stew	ə	extra
ā	play	ī	my	oi (or ȯi)	boy		under
ä	star	ō	go	ou (or aủ)	wow		civil
e	then	ô (or ȯ)	paw, born	u	up		honor
ē	me	o͝o (or ủ)	book, put	ʉ	burn		bogus

CONSONANT SOUNDS

b	but	j	jump	p	pop	th	the
ch	watch	k	brick	r	rod	v	valley
d	do	l	lip	s	see	w	work
f	fudge	m	money	sh	she	y	yell
g	go	n	on	t	sit	z	pleasure
h	hot	ŋ	song, sink	th	with		

a • bashed (ə bashd´) *adj.,* embarrassed; upset.

ab • hor (ab hôr´) *vt.,* hate; detest.

a • broad (ə brôd´) *adv.,* far and wide.

ab • surd (ab sʉrd´) *adj.,* clearly ridiculous.

ac • com • mo • date (ə käm´ə dāt´) *vt.,* have space for.

ac • com • pa • ni • ment (ə kum´pə nə mənt) *n.,* something that goes with something else.

ac • crued (ə krüd´) *part.,* accumulated after a period of time.

a • dapt (ə dapt´) *vi.,* adjust to fit new circumstances.

ad • mo • ni • tion (ad mə ni´ shən) *n.,* warning or cautioning.

a • do (ə do͞o´) *n.,* fuss; trouble; excitement.

a • do • be (ə dō´bē) *n.,* sun-dried brick.

a • dorn • ment (ə dôrn´mənt) *n.,* ornament, decoration.

ad • vent (ad´ vent´) *n.,* coming or arrival.

ad • ver • sar • y (ad´vər ser´ē) *n.,* opponent; enemy.

ad • ver • si • ty (ad vʉr´sə tē) *n.,* state of wretchedness and misfortune.

ag • ile (aj´əl) *adj.,* able to move quickly and easily.

agil • i • ty (ə ji´ lə tē) *n.,* quality or state of being able to move with quick easy grace.

a • gi • ta • tion (a jə tā´ shən) *n.,* movement with an irregular, rapid, or violent action.

a • kin (ə kin´) *adj.,* showing the same nature; similar.

al • cove (al´ kōv´) *n.,* recessed section; nook.

alien • ation (ā lē ə nā´ shən) *n.,* distance or separation because of great differences.

al • le • vi • ate (ə lē´ vē āt) *vt.,* relieve.

all-per • vad • ing (ôl´ pər vād´iŋ) *adj.,* prevalent throughout.

am • a • teur (a´ mə tər; a´ mə chər) *n.,* one who engages in a pursuit, study, science, or sport as a pastime rather than as a profession.

am • bi • gu • i • ty (am´bə gyo͞o´ ə tē) *n.,* word or statement that is uncertain or unclear.

a • mi • a • bly (ā´mē ə blē) *adv.,* pleasantly.

am • o • rous (am´ə res) *adj.,* relating to love.

an • nex (ə neks´) *vt.,* add on or attach.

anx • i • e • ty (aŋ zī´ə tē) *n.,* worry; apprehension.

ap • a • thet • i • cal • ly (ap´ə thet´ə kə lē) *adv.,* without emotion.

ap • a • thy (ap´ə thē) *n.,* indifference; lack of emotion.

ap • os • tol • ic (a pə stä´ lik) *adj.,* relating to the teaching of the New Testament apostles.

ap • per • tain (ap´ər tān´) *vi.,* be a part of.

ap • pre • hen • sion (ap´rē hen´shən) *n.,* anxiety, dread.

ap • prox • i • ma • tion (ə präk sə mā´ shən) *n.,* the quality or state of being close or near.

ap • ti • tude (ap´ tə tüd) *n.,* natural ability or talent; tendency.

aqua • ma • rine (ä kwə mə rēn´) *adj.,* pale blue to light greenish blue.

ar • dent • ly (är´ dənt lē) *adv.,* characterized by passion or zealousness.

ar • dor (är´dər) *n.,* eagerness; passion; enthusiasm.

ar • ray (ə rā´) *n.,* large group, number, or quantity of people or things.

as • cend (ə send´) *vt.,* move upward along; mount; climb; rise.

as • cent (ə sent´) *n.,* act of going, traveling, or climbing up.

as • sail (ə sāl´) *vt.,* attack physically.

a • sun • der (ə sun´ dər) *adv.,* apart or separate in direction.

at • trib • ute (ə trib´yo͞ot) *vt.,* think of as resulting from.

aug • ment (ôg ment´) *vt.,* make greater in size, strength, or quantity.

au • ra (ôr´ə) *n.,* distinctive atmosphere.

av • a • ri • cious (av´ə rish´əs) *adj.,* greedy.

a • venge (ə venj´) *vt.,* get revenge for a wrongdoing.

a • vert (ə vərt´) *vt.,* turn away or aside.

a • vert • ed (ə vᵊrt´ id) *adj.,* turned away.

bale • ful (bāl´fəl) *adj.,* sinister.

balm • y (bäm´ē) *adj.,* soothing; mild; pleasant.

ban • ter (ban´ tər) *n.,* good-natured and usually witty and animated speaking.

bar • ba • rous (bär´ bə rəs) *adj.,* cruel; brutal; uncultured.

bar • rage (bə räzh´) *n.,* intense attack.

bar • ren (ba´rən) *adj.,* empty; not producing crops.

bar • ter (bärt´ər) *vt.,* trade for goods or services.

be • guile (bi gīal´) *vt.,* lead by deception; distract.

be • seech • ing (bē sēch´iŋ) *adj.,* in an earnest manner.

bi • as (bī´ əs) *n.,* inclination of temperament or outlook.

bier (bir) *n.,* coffin and its supporting platform.

binge (binj) *n.,* unrestrained and sometimes excessive indulgence.

bi • ped (bī´ped´) *n.,* two-footed animal.

bi • son (bī´sən) *n.,* type of mammal having a shaggy mane, short, curved horns, and a humped back; commonly referred to as the American buffalo.

blun • der • ing (blun´dər iŋ) *adj.,* clumsy; careless; foolish.

bog (bäg) *n.,* wet, spongy ground; small marsh or swamp.

boun • ti • ful (boun´tə fəl) *adj.,* plentiful; abundant.

boun • ty (boun´tē) *n.,* something given freely; generous gift.

brack • en (brak´ən) *n.,* large, coarse, weedy ferns occurring in meadows and woods.

bra • zen (brā´zən) *adj.,* overly bold; disrespectful.

bro • ker (brō´kər) *n.,* person who acts as an agent or intermediary in negotiating contracts, buying, or selling.

brooch (brōch) *n.,* ornamental pin.

brow (brou) *n.,* forehead.

bru • tal • i • ty (bro͞o tal´ə te) *n.,* cruelty.

buf • fet (bu´ fət) *n.,* blow, esp. by the hand.

buoy • ant (boi´ənt) *adj.,* having power to keep something afloat.

bur • ly (bᵊr´lē) *adj.,* big and strong.

cairn (kern) *n.,* pile of stones built as a monument or landmark.

ca • lam • i • tous (kə lam´ə təs) *adj.,* disastrous.

ca • lam • i • ty (kə lam´ə tē) *n.,* disaster, misery.

ca • pri • cious (kə pri´shəs) *adj.,* tending to change abruptly; erratic.

ca • reen (kə rēn´) *vt.,* lurch from side to side, especially while moving rapidly.

car • mine (kär´ mīn) *adj.,* vivid red.

car • ri • on (kar´ē ən) *n.,* decaying flesh of a dead body when regarded as food for scavenging animals.

ca • ta • stro • phic (ka tə strä´ fik) *adj.,* disastrous, bringing overthrow or ruin.

caul (kôl) *n.,* membrane enclosing a fetus or a newborn baby.

ca • ve • at (ka´ vē ät) *n.,* warning or caution.

ca • vort (kə vôrt´) *vi.,* leap about; romp.

ce • les • tial (sə les´ chəl) *adj.,* of or relating to the sky: specifically, representing the visible bodies in the sky.

chafe (chāf) *vi.,* be impatient or vexed.

cham • ber (chām´bər) *n.,* bedroom.

char • is • mat • ic (kar əz ma´ tik) *adj.,* having a special or magnetic charm or appeal.

chide (chīd) *vt.,* scold.

chiv • al • ry (shiv´əl rē) *n.,* sense of courage and honor.

churl (chᵊrl´) *n.,* rude, vulgar, or unsophisticated person.

civ • il • i • ty (sə vil´ə tē) *n.,* manners; civilized ways.

clam • or (kla´mər) *n.,* loud continuous noice.

clam • or • ous • ly (kla´ mər əs lē) *adv.,* noisily insistent.

clar • i • ty (klar´ ə tē) *n.,* quality or state of being clear.

claus • tro • pho • bia (klôs trə fō´ bē ə) *n.,* abnormal dread of being in closed or narrow spaces.

co • a • li • tion (kō ə li´ shən) *n.,* temporary alliance of distinct parties for joint action.

com • pas • sion (kəm pash´ən) *n.,* sympathy; pity.

com • pel (kəm pel´) *vt.,* force to do something.

com • pen • sa • tion (käm´ pən sā´ shən) *n.,* payment in amends for something.

com • pe • tent (käm´ pə tənt) *adj.,* possessed of sufficient aptitude, skill, strength, or knowledge.

com • pre • hen • sive (cäm pri hen´ siv) *adj.,* covering completely or broadly; inclusive.

com • pro • mise (käm´prə mīz) *vi.,* settle by having both sides make concessions.

con • ceive (kən sēv´) *vt.,* imagine; think.

con • dole (kən dōl´) *vi.,* sympathize.

con • duc • tiv • i • ty (kän dək ti´ və tē) *n.,* quality or power of conducting or transmitting.

con • fer (kən fᵊr´) *vt.,* grant or bestow.

con • fes • sion (kən fesh´ən) *n.,* admission of guilt.

con • fla • gra • tion (kän´flə grā´ shən) *n.,* destructive fire.

con • jec • tur • al (kən jek´chər əl) *adj.,* based on guesses.

con • sci • en • tious • ly (kän shē en´shəs lē) *adv.,* in a manner governed by doing what one knows is right.

con • se • quent • ly (kän(t)´ sə kwent lē) *adv.,* as a result.

con • ser • va • tion • ist (kän sər vā´ shə nist) *n.,* person who advocates conservation of natural resources.

con • so • la • tion (kän´sə lā´shən) *n.,* comfort; solace.

con • sort (kən sôrt´) *vi.,* unite, associate.

con • stric • ting (kən strik´ tiŋ) *adj.,* limiting; compressing.

con • tem • pla • tive • ly (kən tem´plə tiv´lē) *adv.,* in a thoughtful or studious way.

con • ten • tion (kən ten´ shən) *n.,* argument.

con • tin • u • um (kən tin´yo͞o əm) *n.,* unbroken or connected whole.

con • tort • ed (kən tôrt´ əd) *part.,* twisted out of its usual form.

con • tri • tion (kən trish´ən) *n.,* remorse.

con • tri • vance (kən trī´ vən(t)s) *n.,* something contrived or constructed, as an invention, plan, etc.

con • trive (kən trīv´) *vt.,* devise, plan; bring about by strategy or difficulty.

con • verge (kən vᵊrj´) *vi.,* come together.

con • verse • ly (kən vers´ lē) *adv.,* in the opposite manner.

con • vic • tion (kən vik´shən) *n.,* strong belief.

cor • dial (kôr´jəl) *adj.,* friendly.

cor • rob • o • rat • ing (kə rä´ bə rāt iŋ) *adj.,* supporting with evidence; confirming.

cour • ti • er (kôrt´ē ər) *n.,* attendant at a royal court.

cow • er (kou′ ər) *vi.*, shrink or crouch from something that frightens.

cred • i • ble (kre′ də bəl) *adj.*, believable.

cre • du • li • ty (krə dōō′ lə tē) *n.*, tendency to believe too readily.

creed (krēd) *n.*, statement of principle or opinion.

cross • o • ver (kros′ ō vər) *adj.*, breaking into another category.

cull (kul) *vt.*, select from a group; choose.

cul • prit (kəl′ prət) *n.*, one guilty of a crime; cause of a problem.

cur • tail (kər tāl′) *vt.*, make less as if by cutting away a part.

cus • tom • ar • i •ly (kus′tə mer′ə lē) *adv.*, according to what is usually done.

dank (daŋk) *adj.*, disagreeably damp.

dap • pled (dap′əld) *adj.*, spotted.

de • cap • i • tate (di ka′ pə tāt) *vt.*, behead.

de • ci • pher (dē sī′fər) *vt.*, make out the meaning of.

de • cry (dī krī′) *vt.*, express strong disapproval.

de • fi • ant (dē fī′ənt) *adj.*, openly resisting

de • fi • ant • ly (dē fī′ənt lē) *adv.*, openly resisting.

de • fo • li • ate (dē fō′lē āt′ ed) *vt.*, strip of leaves.

deft (deft) *adj.*, characterized by facility and skill.

de • gen • er • a • tion (dē jen′ər ā′shən) *n.*, decline; deterioration.

de • grad • ed (di grā′ əd) *part.*, reduced in quality or value.

de • ment • ed (di men′ təd) *adj.*, mad; insane.

de • note (dē nōt′) *vt.*, indicate.

de • nounce (dē nouns′) *vt.*, condemn strongly as evil or wrong.

de • pre • ci • ate (di prē′shē āt) *vt.*, lower in value.

de • ri • sion (di ri′ zhən) *n.*, scorn.

des • ti • tute (des′tə tōōt) *adj.*, abandoned; forsaken.

de • tach • ment (dē tach′mənt) *n.*, state of being disinterested.

de • tri • men • tal (de′trə ment ′l) *adj.*, harmful.

de • vise (di vīz′) *vt.*, work out or create; plan.

de • vout (di vout′) *adj.*, religious; pious.

dex • ter • i • ty (deks ter′ə tē) *n.*, skill in using one's hands or body.

di • late (dī′ lāt) *vt.*, distend, widen, or extend.

dil • i • gent • ly (dil′ə jənt lē) *adv.*, carefully and steadily.

din (din) *n.*, noise.

dis • cern (dis sʉrn′) *vt.*, recognize; make out clearly.

dis • cord (dis′kôrd) *n.*, conflict; lack of harmony.

dis • course (dis kôrs′) *vi.*, express oneself.

dis • creet (di skrēt′) *adj.*, proper or prudent.

dis • crep • an • cy (di skrep′ən sē) *n.*, inconsistency.

di • shev • eled (di shev′ əld) *adj.*, marked by disorder or disarray.

di • shev • el • ment (di shev′ əl mənt) *n.*, disorderliness.

dis • in • te • grate (di sin′ tə grāt′) *vt.*, break apart.

dis • man • tle (dis man′ təl) *vt.*, take to pieces.

dis • patch (di spach′) *n.*, report, news brief.

dis • po • si • tion (dis′pə zish′ ən) *n.*, one's customary frame of mind.

dis • sem • bler (di sem′blir) *n.*, pretender.

dis • so • lu • tion (di sə lü′ shən) *n.*, decay or disintegration.

dis • solve (di zälv′) *vi.*, decompose or disintegrate.

di • ver • si • fied (də vʉr′sə fīd′) *adj.*, varied.

doc • trine (däk′trin) *n.*, teachings; beliefs.

do • min • ion (də min′yən) *n.*, governed territory.

don (dän) *vt.*, put on (a garment).

don • ning (dän′ iŋ) *n.*, putting on.

dote (dōt) *vi.*, be foolishly or excessively fond.

driv • el • ling (driv′əl iŋ) *part.*, childish.

du • bi • ous • ly (dōō′ bē əs lē) *adv.*, skeptically, doubtfully.

du • pli • ca • tion (dōō′ pli kā′ shən) *n.*, copy, double.

ebb (eb) *vi.*, decline; fall to a lower or worse state.

eb • o • ny (e′ bə nē) *adj.*, black.

ec • cen • tric (ek sen′trik) *adj.*, off-center; departing from a normal pattern.

e • co • sys • tem (ē′ kō sis′ təm) *n.*, complex of a community of organisms and its environment functioning as an ecological unit in nature.

ed • i • fice (e′ də fəs) *n.*, building; massive structure.

ef • fi • gy (e′ fə jē) *n.*, image or representation of a person.

ego • cen • trism (ē′ gō sen′ tri′ zəm) *n.*, self-centeredness.

e • ject (ē jekt′) *vi.*, cast out; emit; discharge.

e • lapse (i laps′) *vi.*, slip or glide away.

elic • it (i li′ sət) *vt.*, draw forth or bring out.

el • o • quence (el′ə kwəns) *n.*, speech or writing that is vivid, forceful, and persuasive.

em • bank • ment (em baŋk′mənt) *n.*, slope of earth; rubble used to keep back water.

em • bel • lish • ment (im be′ lish mənt) *n.*, act or process of making beautiful with ornamentation.

em • bit • ter (em bit′ər) *vt.*, make resentful.

e • merge (ē mʉrj′) *vi.*, become apparent or known; come forth into view.

en • clo • sure (in klō′ zhər) *n.*, structure that encloses or shuts in.

en • deav • or or **en • deav • our** (en dev′ər) *n.*, attempt, effort.

en • dem • ic (en dem′ik) *adj.*, present in.

en • fil • ade (en′ fə lād) *n.*, interconnected group.

en • gage • ment (in gāj′ mənt) *n.*, act of being involved.

en • hance • ment (in hant′ smənt) *n.*, improvement in value, quality, desirability, or attractiveness.

en • ig • ma • tic (e′ nig ma′ tik) *adj.*, mysterious; hard to decipher.

en • mi • ty (en′mə tē) *n.*, hostility; antagonism.

en • ter • pris • ing (en′ tər prī′ziŋ) *adj.*, showing initiative and imagination.

en • thralled (en thrôld′) *adj.*, captivated.

en • ti • ty (en′tə tē) *n.*, being.

en • treat (en trēt′) *vt.*, implore; beg.

ep • ic (ep′ik) *adj.*, grand in scale.

er • ro • ne • ous (i rō′ nē əs) *adj.*, containing or characterized by error.

e • rupt (i rupt′) *vi.*, burst suddenly and violently.

es • ca • la • tion (es′kə lā shən) *n.*, step-by-step growth; rapid increase.

es • carp • ment (e skärp′mənt) *n.*, steep slope.

es • cort (es′ kärt) *vt.*, accompany as an escort.

es • thet • ic (es thet′ ik) *adj.*, pleasing in appearance.

e • ter • nal (ē tʉr′nəl) *adj.*, timeless; everlasting.

ether (ē′ thər) *n.*, liquid used as an anesthetic.

eth • nic • i • ty (eth ni′ sə tē) *n.*, quality such as one's country or tribe of origin, religion, language, or other culturally distinguishing features.

ev • a • nesce (ev′ən nes′) *vi.*, disappear.

e • va • sive (i vā′ siv) *adj.*, tending or intended to escape.

ex • alt (eg zôlt′) *vt.*, raise in status; elevate by praise.

ex • as • per • a • tion (ig zas pə rā′ shən) *n.*, marked irritation or annoyance.

ex • ot • ic (ig zä´tik) *adj.*, not native to the place where found; foreign; exciting or mysterious.

ex • pe • di • tion (ek spə di´ shən) *n.*, journey, voyage, or excursion undertaken for a specific purpose.

ex • ploit (eks´ploit) *n.*, daring or bold deed.

ex • press (ek spres´) *vt.*, put into words.

ex • tir • pate (ek´stər pāt´) *vt.*, destroy or remove completely.

ex • trem • i • ty (ek strem´ə tē) *n.*, greatest degree.

ex • tri • cate (ek´strə kāt´) *vt.*, free from entanglement or difficulty.

fal • ter (fôl´tər) *vi.*, hesitate.

fam • ine (fam´in) *n.*, widespread shortage of food.

fea • si • bil • i • ty (fē zə bi´ lə tē) *n.*, suitability.

fi • nite (fī nīt) *adj.*, having definable limits.

flam • boy • ant (flam boi´ ənt) *adj.*, marked by or given to a strikingly elaborate or colorful display or behavior.

flayed (flād´) *vi.*, strip off the skin or surface of.

flot • sam (flät´səm) *n.*, odds and ends.

flour • ish (flʉr´ish) *vt.*, wave in the air.

flush (flush) *vt.*, cause to take wing suddenly.

fo • liage (fō´ lē ij) *n.*, leaves of one or more plants.

for • ay (fôr´ā) *n.*, sudden invasion or attack; raid.

ford (fôrd) *vt.*, cross a stream or river by wading.

fore • bod • ing (fōr bō´ diŋ) *n.*, omen or presentiment.

fore • sight (fôr´sīt´) *n.*, thoughtful regard for the future.

for • feit (fôr´fit) *n.*, penalty or fine one pays because of a crime or infraction.

forge (fôrj) *vi.*, move forward.

for • mi • da • ble (for´ mə də bəl) *adj.* fearful, dreadful, or intimidating.

for • mu • la (for´myōō lə) *n.*, rule or fact in mathematics.

fray (frā) *n.*, noisy quarrel or fight.

frieze (frēz) *n.*, sculptured or richly ornamented band as on a building.

fri • vol • i • ty (fri väl´ə tē) *n.*, lack of seriousness.

friv • o • lous (friv´ə ləs) *adj.*, not properly serious.

frond (fränd) *n.*, leaflike part of seaweed.

fruit • less (frōōt´lis) *adj.*, unsuccessful.

fume (fyōōm) *n.*, smoke, gas, or vapor.

fun • da • men • tal (fən də men´ təl) *adj.*, of or forming a foundation or basis.

fur • row (fʉr´ō) *n.*, narrow groove.

fur • tive (fʉr´tiv) *adj.*, sneaky; stealthy.

gale (gāl; gāəl) *n.*, strong wind from 32 to 63 miles per hour.

garb (gärb) *n.*, style of clothing.

ge • ni • al • ly (jē´ nē ə lē) *adv.*, cheerful, friendly, and sympathetic.

gey • ser (gī´ zər) *n.*, spring that throws forth jets of heated water and steam.

glar • ing (gler´iŋ) *adj.*, shining too brightly.

graph • i • cal • ly (graf´ik ə lē) *adv.*, vividly.

grav • i • ty (grav´i tē) *n.*, seriousness or solemnity.

griev • ance (grēv´əns) *n.*, complaint or resentment.

guise (gīz) *n.*, external appearance; manner; fashion.

gul • ly (gul´ ē) *n.*, channel or hollow worn by running water.

ha • bit • u • al • ly (hə bi´ chəw əl ē) *adv.*, done on a regular basis.

hag • gard (ha´ gərd) *adj.*, having a wasted, worn look.

hang • dog (haŋ´ dôg´) *adj.*, ashamed and cringing.

ha • rass (hə ras´) *vt.*, annoy persistently.

haugh • ty (hôt´ē) *adj.*, proud; arrogant.

headlong (hed lôŋ´) *adj.*, moving with uncontrolled speed or force.

her • e • sy (her´i sē) *n.*, rejection of a belief that is part of an established set of beliefs.

her • it • age (her´i tij´) *n.*, cultural traditions handed down by ancestors.

home • ly (hōm´lē) *adj.*, simple, plain.

hov • er (hə´ vər) *vi.*, move to and fro near a place.

hy • giene (hī´jēn) *n.*, health and cleanliness.

id • i • om (i´ dē əm) *n.*, style or form of artistic expression.

id • i • o • syn • cra • sy (id ē ō´siŋ´krə sē) *n.*, any personal peculiarity.

i • dly (īd´ lē) *adv.*, in a slow or inactive manner.

i • dol • a • try (ī däl´ə trē) *n.*, excessive devotion or reverence.

il • lu • sion (i lōō´zhən) *n.*, false perception.

im • mi • nent (im´ə nənt) *adj.*, likely to happen.

im • pal • pa • ble (im pal´ pə bəl) *adj.*, so finely divided that no grains or grit can be felt.

im • pas • sioned (im pash´ənd) *adj.*, having a strong feeling.

im • per • a • tive (im per´ə tiv) *adj.*, absolutely necessary.

im • pet • u • ous (im pech´ōō əs) *adj.*, moving with great force or violence.

im • pla • ca • ble (im pla´ kə bəl) *adj.*, not capable of making concessions.

im • pli • ca • tion (im´pli kā´shən) *n.*, something implied; suggestion.

im • plic • it (im plis´it) *adj.*, understood, though not plainly expressed; implied.

im • por • tu • ni • ty (im pər tü´ nə tē) *n.*, quality or state of being troublesomely urgent.

im • pos • tor (im päs´ tər) *n.*, one that assumes false identity for the purpose of deception.

im • pro • vise (im prə vīz) *vt.*, compose, recite, sing, or play without preparation.

im • pu • ta • tion (im pyōō tā´shən) *n.*, charge; claim.

im • pute (im pyōōt´) *vt.*, attribute.

in • ad • vert • ence (in´ad vʉrt ´ns) *n.*, mistake; oversight.

in • au • di • ble (in ôd´ə bəl) *adj.*, that cannot be heard.

in • aus • pi • cious (in´ô spish´əs) *adj.*, unfavorable; unlucky.

in • ci • sive (in sī´siv) *adj.*, penetrating.

in • com • pre • hen • si • ble (in´käm´prē hen´sə bəl) *adj.*, not understandable.

in • con • se • quen • tial (in kän´si kwen´shəl) *adj.*, unimportant.

in • con • stant (in kän´stənt) *adj.*, not remaining firm in mind or purpose.

in • cred • u • lous (in krej´oo ləs) *adj.*, showing disbelief.

in • crim • i • nate (in krim´i nāt´) *vt.*, charge with or show evidence of involvement in a crime.

in • de • ci • pher • a • ble (in di sī´ fəra bəl) *adj.*, incapable of being decoded or understood.

in • de • ter • mi • nate (in´dē tʉr´mi nit) *adj.*, uncertain.

in • dig • nant • ly (in dig´nənt lē) *adv.*, feeling anger as a reaction to ungratefulness.

in • do • lent • ly (in´də lənt lē) *adv.*, idly; lazily.

in • duce • ment (in dōōs´mənt) *n.*, motive; incentive.

in • dul • gent • ly (in dəl´ jənt lē) *adv.*, done in a lenient manner.

in • ef • fa • ble (i ne´ fə bəl) *adj.*, incapable of being expressed in words.

in • eq • ui • ty (in ek´wit ē) *n.*, lack of justice.

in • ev • i • ta • ble (i ne´ və tə bəl) *adj.*, unavoidable.

in • ex • o • ra • ble (i neks' rə bəl) *adj.*, relentless.

in • ex • pli • ca • bly (in eks' pli kə blē) *adv.*, without explanation.

in • fal • li • bil • i • ty (in fal´ə bil i tē) *n.*, correctness, incapacity for error.

in • fin • i • tes • i • mal (in fi nə te' sə məl) *adj.*, immeasurably or incalculably small.

in • flux (in' fləks) *n.*, coming in.

in • ge • ni • ous (in jē' yəs) *adj.*, clever or original.

in • ge • nious • ly (in jēn' yəs lē) *adv.*, done originally, resourcefully, or cleverly

in • ge • nu • i • ty (in´jə nōō´ə tē) *n.*, cleverness; originality.

in • let (in´let) *n.*, narrow strip of water extending into land.

in • no • va • tion (in´ə vā´shən) *n.*, something newly introduced.

in • or • di • nate (in ôr´də nit) *adj.*, lacking moderation.

in • sip • id (in sip´ id) *adj.*, tasteless; dull.

in • still (in stil´) *vt.*, impart gradually.

in • teg • ri • ty (in teg´rə tē) *n.*, state or condition of wholeness.

in • ten • si • fi • ca • tion (in ten´ si fi kā´shən) *n.*, increase in magnitude or force.

in • tent (in tent´) *adj.*, earnest, fixed.

in • ter • ac • tion (in´tər ak´shən) *n.*, reciprocal action or effect.

in • ter • cept (in´tər sept´) *vt.*, seize or stop on the way.

in • ter • sperse (in´tər spʉrs´) *vt.*, scatter among other things.

in • ter • twin • ing (in´tər twīn´iŋ) *adj.*, twisted together.

in • tim • i • date (in tim´ə dāt´) *vt.*, make timid or afraid.

in • trin • sic (in trin' zik) *adj.*, belonging to the essential nature or constitution of a thing.

in • trude (in trōōd´) *vi.*, force upon others without being asked or welcomed.

in • tu • i • tion (in tü wi' shən) *n.*, knowledge of something without conscious reasoning; immediate understanding.

in • tu • i • tive • ly (in tōō' ə tiv lē) *adv.*, through intuition, which is the ability to know or do something without having to think about it rationally.

in • un • da • tion (in´ən dā´shən) *n.*, flood; deluge.

in • vo • ca • tion (in´və kā´shən) *n.*, act of calling on a god for blessing or inspiration.

ir • i • des • cent (ir´i des´ənt) *adj.*, having shifting changes in color.

ir • re • cov • er • a • ble (ir´ri kuv´ ər ə bəl) *adj.*, cannot be corrected or remedied.

i • so • lat • ed (ī´sə lāt ed) *adj.*, set apart from others.

jut (jut) *vi.*, stick out.

keen • ly (kēn´lē) *adv.*, sharply.

kins • man (kinz´mən) *n.*, relative.

knead (nēd) *vt.*, press, rub, or squeeze; massage.

knell (nel) *vi.*, sound ominously or mournfully.

la • bo • ri • ous • ly (lə bôr´ē əs lē) *adv.*, with difficulty.

lab • y • rinth (lab´ər inth´) *n.*, complicated maze

lac • er • at • ed (las´ər āt´əd) *part.*, torn; mangled.

la • ment (lə ment´) *n.*, song of mourning.

la • ment (lə ment´) *vi.*, feel deep sorrow.

lam • en • ta • ble (lam ən´tə bəl) *adj.*, grievous; deplorable; distressing.

lam • en • ta • tion (lam´ən tā´shən) *n.*, outward expression of grief.

lan • guid • ly (laŋ´gwid lē) *adv.*, sluggishly.

lan • guish (lan´gwish) *vi.*, lose vigor or vitality.

lan • guor (laŋ´gər) *n.*, lack of interest, listlessness.

lash (lash) *vt.*, strike hard with great force.

le • ga • cy (le´ge sē) *n.*, gift by will, especially of money or other personal property.

le • gion (lē´jən) *n.*, large number; multitude.

le • thal (lē´ thəl) *adj.*, capable of causing death.

lev • ee (le´ vē) *n.*, embankment for preventing flooding.

li • a • bil • i • ty (lī´ə bil´ə tē) *n.*, state of legal obligation.

lin • e • a • ment (lin´ē ə mənt) *n.*, definite shape, contour, or line, especially of the face.

lit • er • al • ly (lit´ər əl ē) *adv.*, actually; in fact.

loath • some (lōth´sam) *adj.*, disgusting; detestable.

loi • ter • ing (loit´ər iŋ) *part.*, lingering or spending time in an aimless or idle way.

loom • ing (lüm´ iŋ) *adj.*, appearing exaggeratedly large or distorted.

lu • mi • nous (lōō´mə nəs) *adj.*, shining; bright.

lure (lʊr´) *n.*, temptation.

mag • ni • tude (mag´ nə tōōd´) *n.*, greatness of importance or influence.

ma • hog • a • ny (mə hä´ gə nē) *adj.*, colored deep brown like mahogany wood.

make • shift (māk' shift) *adj.*, crude and temporary substitute.

ma • lev • o • lent (mə lev´ə lənt) *adj.*, wishing evil or harm to others.

ma • ligned (mə līnd´) *adj.*, slandered.

mal • treat (mal trēt´) *vt.*, handle in an abusive manner.

man • a • cle (man´ə kəl) *n.*, handcuff; shackle; restraint.

man • i • fest (ma´ ń fest) *adj.*, obvious; appear.

ma • raud • er (mə rôd´ ər) *n.*, one who raids and plunders.

mas • och • ism (ma´ sə ki zəm) *n.*, pleasure in suffering.

mas • tiff (mas´təf) *n.*, any of a breed of large, massive, powerful, smooth-coated dogs.

ma • te • ri • al • ize (mə tir´ē əl īz´) *vt.*, appear in physical form.

ma • tron (mā´trən) *n.*, married woman or widow.

me • an • der (mē an´dər) *vi.*, take a winding course.

me • an • der • ing (mē an´ der iŋ) *adj.*, wandering aimlessly or casually without urgent destination.

mel • an • chol • y (mel´ən käl´ē) *adj.*, sad; gloomy; depressed.

mê • lée (mā´ lā´) *n.*, confused conflict or mixture.

mer • e • tri • cious (mer´ə trish´əs) *adj.*, alluring in a false, showy way.

me • sa (mā´sə) *n.*, high, flat tableland.

met • a • mor • pho • sis (met´ə môr´fə sis) *n.*, transformation.

min • strel (min´strəl) *n.*, medieval entertainer who traveled from place to place.

mint (mint) *adj.*, unmarred as if fresh from a mint.

mis • ad • ven • ture (mis´əd ven´chər) *n.*, unlucky accident; mishap.

mis • sion • ar • y (mish´ ən er´ē) *n.*, person sent to convert others to a religion or to teach religious beliefs.

mo • bil • i • ty (mō´ bil´ə tē) *n.*, ability to move from place to place.

mock (mäk) *vt.*, treat with contempt or ridicule.

mod • u • la • tion (mod ōō lā´shən) *n.*, inflection of tone or pitch of the voice.

mold • er (mōl´dər) *vi.*, crumble into dust.

mo • men • tum (mō men´təm) *n.*, force of an object in motion.

mon • arch (män´ərk) *n.*, ruler.

mon • i • tor (män´ī tər) *n.*, person who keeps order.

mo • rass (mə ras´) *n.*, perplexing state of affairs.

mor • ti • fied (môrt´ə fīd´) *adj.*, shamed, humiliated.

mot • ley (mät´lē) *adj.,* made of many different elements.

mus • ty (mus´tē) *adj.,* dull; apathetic.

mu • ti • ny (myo͞ot´'n ē) *n.,* revolt against constituted authority.

mut • ter (mut´ər) *vt.,* utter words in a low tone.

myr • i • ad (mir´ē əd) *n.,* indefinitely large number.

naught (nôt) *n.,* nothing.

ne • go • ti • ate (ni gō´shē āt´) *vt.,* succeed in crossing, surmounting, moving through.

night • in • gale (nīt´ən gāl) *n.,* reddish brown songbird noted for the sweet song of the male.

nim • ble (nim´bəl) *adj.,* agile.

no • ma • dic (nō ma´dik) *adj.,* roaming from place to place aimlessly.

no • stal • gia (nä stal´ ja) *n.,* state of sentimental longing, often for something in the past; homesickness.

no • to • ri • ous (nō tōr´ ē əs) *adj.,* widely but unfavorably known.

nov • ice (nä´ vəs) *adj.,* beginner; inexperienced person.

nu • cle • us (no͞o´klē əs) *n.,* core; central part.

nup • tial (nup´shəl) *n.,* wedding; marriage (usu. used in plural).

ob • jec • tive • ly (əb jək´tiv lē) *adv.,* without bias or prejudice.

o • bliv • i • ous (ə bli´vē əs) *adj.,* unaware; lacking attention.

ob • scure (əb skyo͞or´) *adj.,* inconspicuous; hidden.

o • men (ō´mən) *n.,* thing or event supposed to foretell a future event.

on • rush • ing (än´rush´iŋ) *adj.,* dashing forward.

op • pres • sive (ə pres´iv) *adj.,* hard to put up with.

or • bit (or´ bət) *n.,* path of a celestial body, artificial satellite, or spacecraft around another body.

or • deal (ôr dēal´) *n.,* severe trial or experience.

or • i • fice (ôr´ə fis) *n.,* opening; mouth.

out • strip (aut strip´) *vt.,* go faster or farther than; get ahead of, leave behind.

o • ver • take (ō´vər tāk´) *vt.,* catch up with and go beyond.

o • ver • whelm • ing • ly (ō ver wel´ miŋ lē) *adv.,* overpowering in thought or feeling.

pall (pôl) *n.,* covering that obscures or cloaks gloomily.

pal • pa • ble (pal´pə bəl) *adj.,* perceptible; noticeable.

pal • pi • tat • ing (pal´pə tāt´iŋ) *part.,* beating rapidly; fluttering.

pan • de • mon • ium (pan´ də mō´ nē əm) *n.,* wild uproar; chaos.

par • a • mour (par´ə mür) *n.,* sweetheart.

par • a • noi • a (par´ə noi´ə) *n.,* suspiciousness; delusions of persecution.

pa • rish • ion • er (pə rish´ə nər) *n.,* member of a church district, or parish.

par • ry (par´ ē) *vt.,* ward off a weapon or a blow.

par • si • mo • ny (pär´sə mō´nē) *n.,* stinginess.

pa • tri • arch (pā´trē ärk) *n.,* male Old Testament leader.

pec • tor • al (pek´tə rəl) *adj.,* located in or on the chest.

pee • vish (pēv´ish) *adj.,* hard to please; irritable.

pen • e • trate (pen´i trāt) *vi.,* pass into.

per • cap • i • ta (pər ka´ p´ tə) *adv. or adj.,* per unit of population.

per • emp • to • ri • ly (pər emp´tə ri lē) *adv.,* commandingly.

per • il (per´ əl) *n.,* exposure to the risk of being injured, destroyed, or lost.

per • i • scope (per´ə skōp) *n.,* tubular optical instrument containing lenses and mirrors by which an observer obtains an otherwise obstructed field of view.

per • ni • cious (pər nish´əs) *adj.,* fatal; deadly.

per • pet • u • al (pər pe´ chə wəl) *adj.,* continuing forever.

per • sist (pər sist´) *vi.,* continue insistently.

per • sist • ence (pər sist´əns) *n.,* stubborn continuance; tenacity.

per • verse (pər vʉrs´) *adj.,* contrary.

phe • nom • e • non (fi nä´ mə nän) *n.,* observable fact or event.

pil • grim • age (pil´grim ij) *n.,* long journey.

pin • ion (pin´ yən) *vt.,* bind.

pit • e • ous (pit´ē əs) *adj.,* arousing or deserving pity or compassion.

plague (plāg) *n.,* anything that afflicts or troubles.

plait (plāt) *vt.,* braid or weave.

plead (plēd) *vi.,* argue a case in a court of law.

plight (plīt) *n.,* dangerous situation.

plum • age (plo͞om´ij) *n.,* bird's feathers.

plume (plo͞om) *vt.,* preen, or clean and arrange one's feathers.

plun • der (plun´dər) *vt.,* steal or take by trickery or by force.

plunge (plunj) *vi.,* move rapidly downward.

ply (plī) *vt.,* keep supplying.

poign • ant (poin´yənt) *adj.,* sharp; painful.

poised (poizd) *part.,* suspended.

pome • gran • ate (päm´gran´it) *n.,* round fruit with a red, leathery rind and many seeds covered with red, juicy, edible flesh.

pon • der • ous (pän´dər es) *adj.,* heavy; bulky; massive.

por • ous (pōr´ əs) *adj.,* having pores; being permeable to liquids.

por • tage (pôr´tij) *vi.,* carry boats or supplies overland from one lake or river to another

pos • ter • i • ty (päs ter´ə tē) *n.,* all succeeding generations.

prac • ti • cal (prak´ ti kəl) *adj.,* capable of being put to use or account.

pre • car • i • ous (pri kar´ ē əs) *adj.,* dependant upon circumstances; uncertain.

prec • i • pice (pre´ sə pəs) *n.,* steep place.

pre • cip • i • tous (prë sip´ə təs) *adj.,* steep.

pre • clude (pri klüd´) *vt.,* rule out in advance.

pre • con • cep • tion (prē kən sep´ shəen) *n.,* an idea formed beforehand.

pre • dic • a • ment (pri di´ kə mənt) *n.,* complicated, perplexing situation.

pre • dict (pri dikt´) *vt.,* declare in advance, forecast or prophecy.

pre • dom • i • nant (prē däm´ə nənt) *adj.,* having dominating influence over others; superior.

pre • dom • i • nate (prē däm´ə nāt´) *vi.,* prevail.

pre • oc • cu • pa • tion (pr ē äk´yo͞o pā´shən) *n.,* absorption in thought.

pres • tig • ious (pre sti´ jəs *or* pre stē´jəs) *adj.,* highly regarded; honored.

pre • sump • tu • ous (prē zump´cho͞o əs) *adj.,* arrogant; overstepping boundaries.

pre • vail (pri vāl´) *vi.,* triumph or win a victory.

pro • cure (prō kyo͞or´) *vt.,* get or bring about by some effort.

prod • i • gal (prä´ di gəl) *adj.,* recklessly extravagant.

pro • di • gious (prō dij´əs) *adj.,* exceptional; of great size or power.

prof • fered (präf´ərd) *part.,* offered courteously.

prof • li • gate (prä´ fli gət) *adj.,* wildly extravagant.

pro • found • ly (prō found´lē) *adv.,* in a deep or intense manner.

prom • i • nence (prä´ mə nən(t)s) *n.,* object that stands out, or projects beyond a surface or line.

prom • on • to • ry (präm´ən tô rē) *n.,* peak of high land that juts out into a body of water.

prop • a • gate (präp´ə gāt) *vt.,* reproduce; multiply.

pro • phe • cy (prä´ fə sē) *n.,* prediction of something to come.

proph • e • sy (präf´ə sī´) *vt.,* predict.

pro • pi • tious (prə pi´ shəs) *adj.,* being of good omen.

pro • pose (prō pōz´) *vt.,* intend.

pro • sa • ic (prō zā´ik) *adj.,* commonplace; dull.

prose (prōz) *n.,* broad term used to describe all writing that is not poetry, including fiction and nonfiction.

pros • trate (präs´trāt) *adj.,* lying with the face downward in demonstration of great humility.

pro • voke (prō vōk´) *vt.,* stir up action or feeling.

pru • dence (prōōd´ns) *n.,* sound judgment.

pru • dent (prōōd´ ´nt) *adj.,* cautious or discreet

purge (pʉrj) *vt.,* cleanse of impurities.

quar • ry (kwôr´ē) *vt.,* excavate stone.

quea • sy (kwē´ ze) *adj.,* nauseated; uneasy.

quiz • zi • cal • ly (kwiz´i kə lē) *adv.,* in a perplexed manner.

ran • cor (raŋ´kər) *n.,* bitter hate or ill will.

rap • ture (rap´chər) *n.,* great pleasure.

re • al • ist (rē´ə list) *n.,* person concerned with real things.

re • buff (ri bəf´) *n.,* rejection.

re • cal • ci • trant (ri kal´ sə trənt) *adj.,* obstinately defiant of authority or restraint.

re • ca • pit • u • late (rē´kə pich´ə lāt´) *vt.,* summarize.

re • ced • ing (ri sēd´iŋ) *part.,* moving away from; becoming more distant.

re • cep • ta • cle (ri sep´tə kəl) *n.,* anything used to contain or hold something else.

re • cite (rē sīt´) *vt.,* repeat words aloud from memory.

rec • ol • lec • tion (re kə lek´ shən) *n.,* something remembered.

re • com • pose (rē´kəm pōz´) *vt.,* restore calmness of mind.

rec • on • cil • i • a • tion (rek´ən sil´ē ā´shən) *n.,* settling of problems or disputes.

rec • ti • lin • e • ar (rek tə li´ nē ər) *adj.,* moving in or forming a straight line.

re • demp • tive (ri demp´tiv) *adj.,* serving to free from the consequences of sin.

re • doubt (ri daut´) *n.,* secure retreat or stronghold.

re • fer (ri fʉr´) *vi.,* direct attention to.

re • flec • tive (ri flek´ tiv) *adj.,* meditative; thoughtful.

ref • uge (ref´yōōj) *n.,* protection; safety.

re • gale (ri gāl´) *vt.,* entertain.

reg • i • men (re´ jə mən) *n.,* regular course of action, especially strenuous training.

re • in • force • ment (rē´in fôrs´mənt) *n.,* additional forces.

re • it • er • ate (rē it´ə rāt´) *vt.,* repeat.

re • kin • dle (ri´ kin´ dəl) *vi.,* catch fire again.

rel • e • vant (re´ lə vənt) *adj.,* having significant and demonstrable bearing on the matter at hand.

rel • ic (re´ lik) *n.,* memento from a past time.

re • lin • quish (ri liŋ´ kwish) *vt.,* give up.

re • luc • tant (ri luk´tənt) *adj.,* unwilling or disinclined.

re • morse • less (ri môrs´lis) *adj.,* merciless; cruel.

ren • di • tion (ren di´ shən) *n.,* performance.

re • ne • gade (re´ni gād) *n.,* someone who rejects lawful behavior or deserts a faith, cause, or allegiance.

re • nege (ri nig´) *vi.,* back out of an agreement.

rep • li • ca (re´ pli kə) *n.,* exact copy.

re • pose (ri pōz´) *n.,* rest; sleep.

re • press (ri pres´) *vt.,* hold back or restrain.

rep • ri • mand (re´ prə mand) *vt.,* scold harshly.

rep • u • ta • ble (re´ pyə tə bəl) *adj.,* held in esteem.

req • ui • site (rek´wə zit) *n.,* necessity.

res • i • dence (rez´i dəns) *n.,* place in which a person or thing resides or lives.

res • ig • na • tion (rez´ig nā´ shən) *n.,* passive acceptance.

res • o • lu • tion (rez´ə lü´shən) *n.,* expression of will or intent; determination.

re • strain • ing (ri strān´ iŋ) *adj.,* controlling or disciplining.

re • sur • gence (ri sʉrj´ əns) *n.,* tendency to rise again.

re • veal (ri vēl´) *vt.,* show; expose.

rev • e • la • tion (rev´ə lā´ shən) *n.,* something disclosed; striking announcement.

re • ver • ber • ate (ri vʉr´ bə rāt´) *vi.,* resound; echo.

re • vere (ri vir´) *vt.,* regard with deep respect and love.

rev • er • ent • ly (rev´ər ənt lē) *adv.,* showing great respect.

re • vile (ri vīl´) *vt.,* subject to verbal abuse.

re • volt (ri vōlt´) *n.,* rebellion; insurrection.

ri • fle (rī´əl) *vt.,* shuffle; move quickly through.

ri • ot • ous (rī´ət əs) *adj.,* without restraint; dissolute.

rit • u • al (rich´ōō əl) *n.,* religious or ceremonial act.

ri • val • ry (rī´vəl rē) *n.,* competition.

roan (rōn) *n.,* solid-colored horse with a sprinkling of white hair.

rogue (rōg) *n.,* wicked or rascally person.

sage (sāj) *adj.,* wise.

sa • lient (sāl´yənt) *adj.,* prominent.

sap • py (sa´pē) *adj.,* overly sentimental or sweet.

sar • don • i • cal • ly (sär dän´i kə lē) *adv.,* sarcastically

scald • ing (skôld´iŋ) *part.,* burning; injuring.

scru • ple (skrōō´ pəl) *n.,* qualm; uneasiness about something one thinks is wrong.

scru • ti • nized (skrü´ tən īzd) *part.,* closely examined.

scru • ti • ny (skrōōt´´n ē) *n.,* careful, searching look.

sear (sir) *vt.,* burn; wither.

se • lect • man (si lek(t)´man) *n.,* elected town official in New England.

sen • si • bil • i • ty (sen sə bi lə tē) *n.,* awareness of and responsiveness toward emotions in others.

sen • ti • ment (sen´ tə mənt) *n.,* opinion.

sep • ul • chre or **sep • ul • cher** (sep´əlk ər) *n.,* vault for burial; grave; tomb.

sheathed (shēthd) *adj.,* encased or covered with something.

shriv • eled (shriv´əld) *adj.,* wrinkled and withered.

shroud (shroud) *n.,* cloth used to wrap a corpse for burial.

siege (sēj) *n.,* persistent attempt to gain control.

sim • i • an (si´mē ən) *adj.,* resembling monkeys or apes.

sin • gu • lar (siŋ´ gyə lər) *adj.,* being the only one of its kind.

skep • ti • cal • ly (skep´ ti kəl) *adv.,* with an attitude of doubt or criticism.

skiff (skif) *n.,* small, open boat.

slan • der (slan´dər) *n.,* false statement damaging another person's character or reputation.

sneer (snēr) *n.,* smile or laugh accompanied by facial contortions that express scorn or contempt.

sor • did (sôr dəd) *adj.,* marked by baseness or grossness; wretched.

sor • rel (sôr´əl) *adj.,* light reddish brown.

sparse (spärs) *adj.,* meager.

spe • cies (spē´ shēz) *n.,* population of highly similar organisms that interbreed only among themselves.

spec • ta • cle (spek' ti kəl) *n.,* remarkable or noteworthy site.

spon • sor (spän(t)' sər) *n.,* one who assumes responsibility for some other person or thing.

spry (sprī) *adj.,* nimble.

sta • ple (stā´pəl) *n.,* item of trade, regularly stocked and in constant demand.

ster • e • o • typed (ster´ē ə tīpt) *adj.,* conventional notion, not allowing for individuality.

stim • u • late (stim´yo͞o lāt) *vt.,* rouse or excite to increase action.

sto • ic (stō' ik) *adj.,* firmly restrained response to pain or distress.

stow (stō) *vt.,* put away, especially aboard a ship.

stra • ta • gem (strā´tə jem) *n.,* trick or scheme used to gain an end.

sub • due (sub do͞o´) *vt.,* overcome; control; reduce.

sub • dued (səb do͞o´d) *part.,* diminished; lessened in intensity.

sub • lime (sə blīm´) *adj.,* outstanding.

sub • mis • sion (sub mish´ən) *n.,* yielding or surrendering.

sub • side (səb sīd´) *vi.,* settle; lessen in intensity.

sub • sist (səb sist´) *vi.,* exist; have the necessities of life; nourish oneself.

sub • stan • tial (səb stan´shəl) *adj.,* real; actual; true.

sub • tle (su'tl) *adj.,* difficult to perceive or identify; crafty.

sul • len • ly (sul´ən lē) *adv.,* gloomily.

sum • mit (sə´ mət) *n.,* highest point, ridge, or level of a mountain; peak.

su • per • hu • man (so͞o´pər hyo͞o´mən) *adj.,* having power above that of a normal human being.

su • per • in • ten • dence (so͞o´pər in tend´ens) *n.,* supervision; management.

sup • pli • ca • tion (sup´lə kā shən) *n.,* humble request.

sup • press (sə pres´) *vt.,* inhibit; put down by force.

surge (sʉrj) *vt.,* have a heavy, swelling motion.

sur • ly (sʉr'lē) *adj.,* rude; ill tempered.

sur • pass (sər pas´) *vt.,* go beyond.

sus • tain (sə stān´) *vi.,* keep up or maintain.

sus • tain • a • ble (səs stā´ nə bəl) *adj.,* using a resource so that the resource is not depleted or permanently damaged.

sym • me • try (si' mə trē) *n.,* beauty of form arising from balanced proportions.

ta • boo (ta bo͞o´) *n.,* something forbidden because of social custom or for protection.

taint (tānt) *vt.,* infect.

tan • gi • ble (tan´jə bəl) *adj.,* having actual form.

tar • ry (tar´ē) *vi.,* delay or be tardy; stay in or at a place.

teem (tēm) *vi.,* be full.

ten • or (ten´ər) *n.,* singer with voice range one octave above and one octave below middle *C*.

ten • ta • tive (ten´ tə tiv) *adj.,* hesitant; uncertain.

ten • ta • tive • ly (ten´tə tiv lē) *adv.,* with uncertainty.

thresh (thresh) *vt.,* thrash; beat or strike; move or stir about violently.

throng (thräŋ´) *n.,* crowd.

tis • sue (tish´o͞o) *n.,* group of cells that work together in the body.

ti • tan • ic (tī tan´ik) *adj.,* of great size, strength, or power.

tor • rent (tôr´ənt) *n.,* swift, violent stream.

tran • scend (tran send) *vt.,* go beyond limits; overcome.

trans • cribe (tran skrīb´) *vt.,* write down; make a written copy of.

trans • gress (trans gres´) *vt.,* break a commandment; sin.

trans • gres • sion (trans gresh´ən) *n.,* offense.

tra • verse (trə vʉrs´) *vi.,* turn; swivel.

tread (tred) *n.,* step.

trea • ty (trēt´ē) *n.,* formal agreement between two or more nations, resulting in peace.

trem • u • lous (trem´yo͞o ləs) *adj.,* trembling; quivering.

trib • u • la • tion (trib´yo͞o lā shən) *n.,* great misery or distress, as from oppression.

trump (trəmp) *vt.,* override or outrank.

tu • mult (tü´ məlt) *n.,* violent outburst.

tur • bu • lence (tʉr´byo͞o ləns) *n.,* violent, irregular motion or swirling agitation of water, air, gas, etc.

tyr • an • ny (tir´ ə nē) *n.,* oppressive power.

un • du • la • tion (un´dyo͞o lā´shən) *n.,* wave; curve.

un • hal • lowed (un´hal´ōd) *adj.,* unholy; wicked.

un • nerv • ing • ly (ən nər´ viŋ lē) *adv.,* deprived of courage and physical strength; cause to become weak and ineffective, especially from fear.

un • pal • at • a • ble (un pal´ə tə bəl) *adj.,* unpleasant.

ur • gent (ʉr´jənt) *adj.,* insistent.

ush • er (ush´ər) *vt.,* escort, conduct.

vag • a • bond (va' gə bänd´) *vi.,* wander or roam about without a fixed home.

va • lid • i • ty (və lid´ə tē) *n.,* quality of being firmly grounded on facts.

val • or (val´ər) *n.,* marked courage or bravery.

vap • id (vap´id) *adj.,* dull, uninteresting.

ver • bose (vər bōs´) *adj.,* given to wordiness.

ver • dant (ver´dənt) *adj.,* green.

ver • sa • tile (vər´ sə təl) *adj.,* embracing a variety of subjects, fields, or skills.

vex (veks) *vt.,* disturb; annoy; irritate.

vig • nette (vin yet') *n.,* brief scene.

vin • di • ca • tion (vin´də kā´shən) *n.,* justification.

vin • tage (vin' tij) *adj.,* dating from the past.

vir • tue (vʉr´ chü) *n.,* beneficial quality or power of a thing.

vis • age (viz´ij) *n.,* face.

vo • lu • mi • nous • ly (və lo͞o´ mə nəs lē) *adv.,* largely; fully.

vor • tex (vôr´teks´) *n.,* whirlpool or eddy.

vul • gar (vul' gər) *adj.,* crude and offensive.

wal • low (wä' lō) *vi.,* take delight; to indulge oneself immoderately.

wane (wān´) *vi.,* ebb or fade away.

wa • ver (w ā´vər) *vi.,* swing or sway; flutter.

wa • ver • ing (wā´ver iŋ) *part.,* swinging or swaying back and forth.

wet • land (wet' land) *n.,* land or area (as tidal flats or swamps) containing much soil moisture.

wrath (rath) *n.,* anger

wry • ly (rī´lē) *adv.,* bitterly or disdainfully ironic.

zeal (zēl) *n.,* intense enthusiasm.

INDEX
Of Titles and Authors

INDEX

Of Skills

WRITING

LANGUAGE, GRAMMAR, AND STYLE

APPLIED ENGLISH

acceptance speech, 657
advertisement, 713, 801
advice column, 32, 36, 281, 325, 409, 575
article, 435
birth announcement, 32
book jacket, 106, 435
book review, 801
brochure, 648, 853
business letter, 241, 860
calendar, 455
career research, 890
choose-your-own-ending book, 899
collaborative learning, 467
contract, 473
costume and set design, 348
credo, 460, 483
directions, 112, 197, 1052–1053
document, 455
Dr. Martin Luther King Day, 467
drama review, 613
editorial, 96, 106
epitaph, 179, 409
eulogy, 391, 883
Everglades nature guide, 528
fan letter, 666
field guide entry, 44
flyer, 837
forms, filling out, 1052
goal setting, 853
goodbye note, 215
grant application, 685
greeting card, 251, 571, 703
interview, 489
invitation, 737
letter, 86, 91, 122, 147, 179, 197, 223, 241, 251, 273,
 325, 376, 391, 445, 467, 483, 516, 528, 537, 552,
 571, 575, 587, 594, 600, 613, 631, 648, 666, 721,
 784, 796, 801, 831, 843, 860
letter of complaint, 528
letter to editor, 473
letter-writing campaign, 528
liner notes, 657
love letter, 91, 575
marriage vows, 347
memo, 1055
movie review, 721
museum guide, 909
news briefing, 920
news report, 44, 376
newspaper article, 215, 223, 831
newspaper editorial, 106
note, 215, 265, 600, 703, 730
obituary, 594, 860
pamphlet, 920

party invitation, 325
personal ad, 241
personal letter, 325, 391, 648
photography catalog, 516
plaque, 666
poetry booklet, 806
police/accident report, 899
post card, 96, 241, 435, 445, 843
press release, 460, 1058
proclamation, 730
promotional materials, 713, 771
proposal, 1055–1056
public service announcement, 1058
questionnaire, 631
radio spot, 489
rap song, 744
real estate advertisement, 713
recycling community project, 473
report, 713
résumé, 102, 265, 1057
review, 721, 737, 801
road trip planning, 843
satirical interview, 489
schedule, 883
science fiction fair, 936
screenplay, 116
ship's log entry, 147, 936
social service project, 638
song lyrics, 273
speech, 537, 657, 806, 936
sports writing, 666
step-by-step procedure, 391, 648
storyboard, 215, 730
survey form, 920
survival guide, 197
tabloid article, 771
team work, 1059–1060
technical writing, 197, 648
television commercial, 32
television interview, 106
thank-you note, 241, 265, 744, 853
theater review, 376, 737
time capsule, 909
time line, 544
tour guide, 96, 483
travel journal, 843, 853
video discussion, 537
video script, 122
visual information, 1059
Web page design, 483
will, 806
wish list, 251, 281
work order, 273

INDEX
Of Internet Sites

At the time of publication, the following were valid, working Internet sites. Due to the changing nature of the Internet, some of these sites may no longer be accessible via the listed address. If an address does not work, try conducting a keyword search by the name of the site, author, or topic. If you find a non-working site, please notify us at educate@emcp.com so that we can update this index.

INDEX

Of Fine Art

ACKNOWLEDGMENTS

ART ACKNOWLEDGMENTS

Cover Hopper: The Museum of Modern Art, New York; **Cover** Van Gogh: Planet Art; **Cover** Hayden: Museum of African American Art, Los Angeles. Gift of Miriam Hayden. Photograph by Armando Solis; **Cover** Bierstadt: Corcoran Gallery of Art. Gift of Albert Bierstadt.; **v** Musées Royaux des Beaux-Arts, Brussels.; **vi** Harris Museum and Art Gallery, Preston, UK./Bridgeman Art Library; **vii** © Ann Phong; **viii** © 2000 Artists Rights Society (ARS), New York / ADAGP, Paris/© Archivo Iconografico, S.A./CORBIS; **ix** © Burstein Collection/CORBIS; **x** © Danny Lehman/CORBIS; **2** © 1952 (renewed 1980) Grandma Moses Properties Co., N.Y., © Geoffrey Clements/CORBIS; **5** © Archivo Iconografico, S.A./CORBIS; **9** © Araldo de Luca/CORBIS; **11** © Archivo Iconograffico, S.A./CORBIS; **12** Musées Royaux des Beaux-Arts, Brussels.; **17** Library of Congress; **18** Bridgeman Art Library; **25** SuperStock; **30** © CORBIS; **33** © Bettmann/CORBIS; **34** The Pennsylvania Academy of Fine Arts, Philadelphia. Joseph E. Temple Fund; **37** Library of Congress; **38** Bridgeman Art Library; **45** Library of Congress; **47** Museum of African American Art, Los Angeles. Gift of Miriam Hayden. Photograph by Armando Solis; **54** Bridgeman Art Library; **56** National Museum of American Art, Washington, DC/Art Resource, NY; **74** Planet Art; **77** © Burstein Collection/CORBIS; **80** Library of Congress; **81** Watercolor over graphite, 77x49.8cm. © The Cleveland Museum of Art, 1999, Gift of Louise Dunn in memory of Henry G. Keller, 1949.544; **87** Yeats: Library of Congress; **87** Celtic Plaque: © Werner Forman/CORBIS; **93** © Catherine Karnow/CORBIS; **100** Photo by Bachrach; **103** Library of Congress; **104** Planet Art; **107** Library of Congress; **109** Digital Stock Corp; **113** © Bettmann/CORBIS; **114** Kactus Foto, Santiago, Chile/SuperStock; **117** Library of Congress; **119** © Aaron Douglas/Howard University Gallery of Art; **124** SEF/Art Resource; **125** National Gallery of Victoria, Melbourne, Australia; **138** Bridgeman Art Library; **141** © Werner Forman/ CORBIS; **162** © 2000 Artists Rights Society (ARS), New York/ADAGP, Paris/National Gallery of Art, Washington, DC.; **165** National Museum of American Art, Washington, DC./Art Resource; **168** Library of Congress; **169** PhotoDisc; **177** Bridgeman Art Library; **180** Library of Congress; **193** © Bettmann/CORBIS; **198** Brandt & Brandt Literary Agents; **207** Bridgeman Art Library; **216** © Colita/CORBIS; **219** The Art Institute of Chicago; **224** Library of Congress; **225** © Catherine Karnow/CORBIS; **230** © Bojan Brecelj/CORBIS; **242** © Roger Ressmeyer/CORBIS; **247** Photo courtesy American Quilts!; **252** Archive Photos; **253** © North Carolina Museum of Art/CORBIS; **256** Library of Congress; **267** PhotoDisc; **268** © Archivo Iconografico, S.A./CORBIS; **274** © Bettmann/CORBIS; **275** Manchester City Art Galleries, England; **294** © National Gallery Collection; By kind permission of the Trustees of the National Gallery, Lond on/CORBIS; **405** © Bettmann/CORBIS; **406** 1967: © Hulton-Deutsch/CORBIS; **406** 1996: 20th Century Fox/Shooting Star; **411** Robert Sean Leonard; **424** © Board of Trustees, National Gallery of Art, Washington, DC. Gift of Helen Farr Sloan; **428** © Bettmann/CORBIS; **429** Library of Congress; **436** Reprinted by permission of le thi diem thuy and the Watkins/Loomis Agency; **437** © Ann Phong. Photo courtesy of the artist.; **446** Ron Nicodemus; **447** Corcoran Gallery of Art. Gift of Albert Bierstadt.; **451** Library of Congress; **457** Library of Congress; **461** Library of Congress; **463** AP/World Wide Photos; **468** Library of Congress; **470** © Ansel Adams Publishing Rights Trust/CORBIS; **474** Library of Congress; **478** © Julie Delton; **485** Library of Congress; **502** © Geoffrey Clements/CORBIS; **508** Library of Congress; **509** All: Walker Evans. Library of Congress; **510** All: Walker Evans. Library of Congress; **514** Library of Congress; **518** © Kevin Fleming /CORBIS; **521** © Kevin Fleming/CORBIS; **525** © Kevin Fleming /CORBIS; **530** Mallory and Irvine: AP/NOVA; **530** Mt. Everest: © Galen Rowell/CORBIS; **533** AP/World Wide Photos; **538** © Dennis di Cicco/CORBIS; **540** © Roger Ressmeyer/CORBIS; **564** © Estate of Hughie Lee-Smith/Licensed by VAGA. National Museum of American Art, Washington, DC/Art Resource, NY; **567** Amherst College Archives and Special Collections. Used by permission of the Trustees of Amherst College; **568** © 2000 Estate of André Derain/Artists Rights Society (ARS), New York/ADAGP, Paris/© Archivo Iconografico, S.A./CORBIS; **573** © 2000 Estate of Pablo Picasso/Artists Rights Society (ARS), New York/The Museum of Modern Art, New York; **576** Photo by Mike Markee. Estate of William Stafford.; **580** Archive Photos; **581** The Boston Athenaeum;

LITERARY ACKNOWLEDGMENTS

Company. Copyright © renewed 1964 by Thomas C. Benét, Stephanie B. Mahin and Rachel Benét Lewis. Reprinted by permission of Brandt & Brandt Literary Agents, Inc. "The Most Dangerous Game" by Richard Connell. Copyright © 1924 by Richard Connell. Copyright © renewed 1952 by Louise Fox Connell. Reprinted by permission of Brandt & Brandt Literary Agents, Inc. "Nightmare Number Three" by Stephen Vincent Benét from *The Selected Works of Stephen Vincent Benét.* Holt, Rinehart and Winston, Inc. Copyright © 1937 by Stephen Vincent Benét. Copyright © renewed 1964 by Thomas C. Benét, Stephanie B. Mahin and Rachel Benét Lewis. Reprinted by permission of Brandt & Brandt Literary Agents, Inc. **Walker Brents.** "Echo and Narcissus" retold by Walker Brents. Copyright 2000 Walker Brents. **Gwendolyn Brooks.** "Martin Luther King, Jr." by Gwendolyn Brooks. Reprinted by permission of the author. **Matthew Carlin.** "How Did I Get Here?" by Sybil Carlin. Reprinted by permission of Matthew Carlin. **Estate of Raymond Carver.** "Late Fragment" from *A New Path to the Waterfall* by Raymond Carver. Copyright © 1989 by the Estate of Raymond Carver. **Jonathan Clowes, Ltd.** "Through the Tunnel" from *The Habit of Loving* by Doris Lessing. Copyright © 1955 by Doris Lessing. Originally appeared in *The New Yorker.* Copyright renewed. Reprinted [in Canada] by kind permission of Jonathan Clowes, Ltd., on behalf of Doris Lessing. **Don Congdon Associates, Inc.** "There Will Come Soft Rains" by Ray Bradbury. Reprinted by permission of Don Congdon Associates, Inc. Copyright © 1950 by the Crowell Collier Publishing Co., renewed 1977 by Ray Bradbury. **The Cowboy Culture Association, Inc.** "Doing Better than My Best!" by Beth Moeller. Reprinted by permission of the author. "The Last Cowboys" by Andrew Huckabee. Reprinted by permission of the author. **Annie Dillard.** "It's Not Talent; It's Just Work" by Annie Dillard from *Seventeen*®, June 1979. Copyright © 1979 by Annie Dillard. Reprinted by permission of the author. **Faber & Faber, Ltd.** "Mirror" from *Crossing the Water* by Sylvia Plath. Copyright © 1963 by Ted Hughes. Originally appeared in *The New Yorker.* Reprinted [in Canada] by permission of Faber & Faber, Ltd. **Farrar, Straus & Giroux, LLC.** From *Great Plains* by Ian Frazier. Copyright © 1989 by Ian Frazier. Reprinted by permission of Farrar, Straus & Giroux, LLC. Excerpt from *Book IX* and excerpt from *Book X* from *The Odyssey of Homer* translated by Robert Fitzgerald. Copyright © 1961, 1963 by Robert Fitzgerald. Copyright renewed 1989 by

Benedict R. C. Fitzgerald, on behalf of the Fitzgerald children. Reprinted by permission of Farrar, Straus and Giroux, LLC. "Thank You, M'am" from *Short Stories* by Langston Hughes. Copyright © 1996 by Ramona Bass and Arnold Rampersad. Reprinted by permission of Hill and Wang, a division of Farrar, Straus and Giroux, LLC. **Floris Books.** "The Silver Pool" from *The Tangle Coated-Horse and Other Tales from the Fionn Saga* by Ella Young. Reprinted by permission of Floris Books, Edinburgh. **Friends of the Everglades.** "For the Future of Florida: Repair the Everglades" from *The Everglades Reporter,* copyright 1997. Reprinted with permission. **Graywolf Press.** "Otherwise" by Jane Kenyon. Copyright 1996 by the Estate of Jane Kenyon. Reprinted from *Otherwise: New & Selected Poems* with the permission of Graywolf Press, Saint Paul, Minnesota. "A Story that Could Be True" by William Stafford. Copyright 1977, 1998 by the Estate of William Stafford. Reprinted from *The Way It Is: New & Selected Poems* with the permission of Graywolf Press, Saint Paul, Minnesota. **Grove/Atlantic, Inc.** "The Journey" from *Dream Work* by Mary Oliver. Copyright © 1986 by Mary Oliver. Used by permission of Grove/Atlantic, Inc. **Harcourt, Inc.** "Everyday Use" from *In Love & Trouble: Stories of Black Women*, copyright © 1973 by Alice Walker, reprinted by permission of Harcourt, Inc. **HarperCollins Publishers, Inc.** "The Good Deed" from *The Good Deed and Other Stories* by Pearl S. Buck. Copyright © 1953, 1962, 1963, 1969. Reprinted by permission of HarperCollins Publishers, Inc. "The Handsomest Drowned Man in the World" from *Leaf Storm and Other Stories* by Gabriel García Márquez. Copyright © 1971 by Gabriel García Márquez. Reprinted by permission of HarperCollins Publishers, Inc. "Her Flying Trapeze" from *Love Poems* by Nikki Giovanni. Copyright © 1968–1997 by Nikki Giovanni. Reprinted by permission of HarperCollins Publishers, Inc. "John Henry" from *Mules and Men* by Zora Neale Hurston. Copyright 1935 by Zora Neale Hurston. Copyright renewed 1963 by John C. Hurston and Joel Hurston. Reprinted by permission of HarperCollins Publishers, Inc. "Mirror" from *Crossing the Water* by Sylvia Plath. Copyright © 1963 by Ted Hughes. Originally appeared in *The New Yorker.* Reprinted [in U.S.] by permission of HarperCollins Publishers, Inc. "Nikki-Rosa" from *Black Feeling, Black Talk, Black Judgement* by Nikki Giovanni. Copyright © 1968, 1970 by Nikki Giovanni. Reprinted by permission of William Morrow and Company, Inc., a division of

HarperCollins Publishers, Inc. "Through the Tunnel" from *The Habit of Loving* by Doris Lessing. Copyright © 1955 by Doris Lessing. Originally appeared in *The New Yorker*. Copyright renewed. Reprinted [in U.S.] by permission of HarperCollins Publishers, Inc. From *To Kill a Mockingbird* by Harper Lee. Copyright © 1960 by Harper Lee. Copyright renewed © 1988 by Harper Lee. Reprinted by permission of HarperCollins Publishers, Inc. **Harvard University Press.** "I'm Nobody! Who are you?" by Emily Dickinson. Reprinted by permission of the publishers and the Trustees of Amherst College from *The Poems of Emily Dickinson,* Ralph W. Franklin, ed., Cambridge, Mass.: The Belknap Press of Harvard University Press, Copyright © 1998 by the President and Fellows of Harvard College. Copyright © 1951, 1955, 1979 by the President and Fellows of Harvard College. **Henry Holt and Company.** "Birches" by Robert Frost from *The Poetry of Robert Frost*, edited by Edward Connery Lathem. Copyright 1944 by Robert Frost. Copyright 1916, © 1969 by Henry Holt and Company, LLC. Reprinted by permission of Henry Holt and Company, LLC. **Houghton Mifflin Company.** "All Watched Over by Machines of Loving Grace" from *The Pill Versus the Springhill Mine Disaster*. Copyright © 1965 by Richard Brautigan. Reprinted by permission of Houghton Mifflin Company. All rights reserved. "Courage" from *The Awful Rowing Toward God* by Anne Sexton. Copyright © 1975 by Loring Conant, Jr., Executor of the Estate of Anne Sexton. Reprinted by permission of Houghton Mifflin Company. All rights reserved. Excerpts from *Let Us Now Praise Famous Men*. Copyright 1939, 1940 by James Agee. Copyright © 1941 by James Agee and Walker Evans. Copyright © renewed 1969 by Mia Fritsch Agee and Walker Evans. Reprinted by permission of Houghton Mifflin Co. All rights reserved. "The Obligation to Endure" from *Silent Spring* by Rachel Carson. Copyright © 1962 by Rachel L. Carson. Copyright © renewed 1990 by Roger Christie. Reprinted by permission of Houghton Mifflin Company. All rights reserved. "The Old Life" from *The Old Life* by Donald Hall. Copyright © 1996 by Donald Hall. Reprinted by permission of Houghton Mifflin Company. All rights reserved. **James Hurst.** "The Scarlet Ibis" by James Hurst from *The Atlantic Monthly,* July 1960. Reprinted by permission of the author. **Indiana University Press.** "The Story of Dædalus and Icarus" by Ovid. From *Metamorphoses,* translated by Rolfe Humphries. Copyright 1955, Indiana University Press. Reprinted by permission of Indiana University Press. **Key Porter Books.** From *The Learning Highway: Smart Students and the Net* by Trevor Owen and Ronald Owston. Copyright © 1998. Reprinted by permission of Key Porter Books. **Virginia Kidd Agency, Inc.** "Gwilan's Harp" by Ursula K. LeGuin, copyright © 1977 by Ursula K. LeGuin; first appeared in *Redbook;* from *The Compass Rose;* reprinted by permission of the author and the author's agents, the Virginia Kidd Agency, Inc. **Ellen Levine Literary Agency, Inc.** "Gary Keillor" from *The Book of Guys* by Garrison Keillor. Reprinted by permission of Garrison Keillor. Copyright © 1993 by Garrison Keillor. **Wing Tek Lum.** "Local Sensibilities" by Wing Tek Lum. Reprinted by permission of the author. **The Lyons Press.** "Mississippi Solo" from *Mississippi Solo: A River Quest* by Eddy L. Harris. Reprinted with the permission of The Lyons Press, New York, NY. *The Magazine of Fantasy and Science Fiction.* "The Test" by Theodore L. Thomas. © 1962 by Mercury Press, Inc. Reprinted from **The Magazine of Fantasy and Science Fiction,** April 1962. © renewed 1990. Reprinted by permission of the author. **N. Scott Momaday.** "A Simile" by N. Scott Momaday from *American Indian Literature: An Anthology.* **Newsweek, Inc.** "Ghost of Everest" by Jerry Adler, from *Newsweek,* May 17, 1999, copyright © 1999 by Newsweek, Inc. All rights reserved. Reprinted by permission. **The New York Times.** "An Ethnic Trump" by Gish Jen. Copyright © 1996 by The New York Times, Co. Used with permission. **W.W. Norton & Company.** "Hanging Fire" from *The Black Unicorn* by Audre Lorde. Copyright © 1978 by Audre Lorde. Reprinted by permission of W.W. Norton & Company, Inc. **Orchard Books.** "Catch the Moon" from *An Island Like You: Stories of the Barrio* by Judith Ortiz Cofer. Copyright © 1995 by Judith Ortiz Cofer. Reprinted by permission of Orchard Books, New York. All rights reserved. **Oxford University Press.** "Thinking Like a Mountain" from *A Sand County Almanac: and Sketches Here and There* by Aldo Leopold. Copyright 1949, 1977 by Oxford University Press, Inc. Used by permission of Oxford University Press, Inc. **Oxford University Press Canada.** "Death of a Young Son by Drowning" from *Selected Poems 1966–1984* by Margaret Atwood. Copyright © Margaret Atwood 1990. Reprinted by permission of Oxford University Press Canada. **Penguin Putnam Inc.** "The Creation" from *God's Trombones* by James Weldon Johnson, copyright 1927 The Viking Press, Inc., renewed © 1955 by Grace Nail Johnson. Used by permission of Viking

Penguin, a division of Penguin Putnam Inc. **Pineapple Press, Inc.** From *The Everglades: River of Grass,* 50th Anniversary Edition, copyright © 1997 by Marjory Stoneman Douglas. Used by permission of Pineapple Press, Inc. **Random House, Inc.** From *I Know Why the Caged Bird Sings* by Maya Angelou. Copyright © 1969 and renewed 1997 by Maya Angelou. Reprinted by permission of Random House, Inc. From *The Man Who Listens to Horses* by Monty Roberts. Copyright © 1996, 1997 by Monty Roberts. Published by The Ballantine Publishing Group, a division of Random House, Inc. "Who Am I This Time?" from *Welcome to the Monkey House* by Kurt Vonnegut, Jr. Copyright © 1961 by Kurt Vonnegut, Jr. Used by permission of Delacourte Press/Seymour Lawrence, a division of Random House, Inc. **Marian Reiner.** "Metaphor" from *A Sky Full of Poems* by Eve Merriam. Copyright © 1964, 1970, 1973 by Eve Merriam. Used by permission of Marian Reiner. **João Guimarães Rosa.** "The Third Bank of the River" from *Modern Brazilian Short Stories,* translated by William L. Grossman. Copyright © 1967 by The Regents of the University of California. **Scovil Chichak Galen Literary Agency, Inc.** "History Lesson" by Arthur C. Clarke. Reprinted by permission of the author and the author's agents, Scovil Chichak Galen Literary Agency, Inc., New York. **Seaver Books.** "The Man to Send Rain Clouds" by Leslie Marmon Silko. Copyright © 1981 by Leslie Marmon Silko. Reprinted from *Storyteller* by Leslie Marmon Silko, published by Seaver Books, New York, New York. **The Rod Serling Trust.** "The Monsters Are Due on Maple Street" by Rod Serling. Reprinted by permission of the Rod Serling Trust. All rights reserved. Copyright © 1960 by Rod Serling. Copyright © 1988 by Carol Serling, Jodi Serling and Ann Serling. **Simon & Schuster.** From *The Music of Light: The Extraordinary Study of Hikari and Kenzaburo Oe* by Lindsley Cameron. Copyright © 1998 Lindsley Cameron. Reprinted with permission of The Free Press, a division of Simon & Schuster, Inc. "The Song of Wandering Aengus" by W. B. Yeats from *The Poems of W. B. Yeats: A New Edition,* edited by Richard J. Finneran. Copyright © 1983 by Anne Yeats. Reprinted by permission of Simon and Schuster, Inc. Reprinted in Canada by permission of AP Watt Ltd. **Sports Illustrated.** "Spanning the Decades: Puerto Rico honors Sosa, who pays tribute to Clemente", copyright © 1998 CNN/Sports Illustrated. A Time Warner Company. All rights reserved. "Where Stars Are Born" by Michael Farber. Reprinted courtesy of *Sports Illustrated,* October 7, 1998. Copyright © 1998, Time Inc. All rights reserved. **Sterling Lord Literistic, Inc.** "The Funeral" from *Whispers of Intimate Things* by Gordon Parks. Copyright 1971 by Gordon Parks. Reprinted by permission of Sterling Lord Literistic, Inc. **University of Nebraska Press.** From *Black Elk Speaks* by John G. Neihardt, reprinted by permission of the University of Nebraska Press. Copyright 1932, 1959, 1972 by John G. Neihardt. Copyright © 1961 by the John G. Neihardt Trust. **University of North Carolina Press.** Lyrics from "John Henry: Tracking Down A Negro Legend", by Guy B. Johnson. Copyright © 1929 by the University of North Carolina Press. Used by permission of the publisher. *The Washington Post.* "White House mystery may be solved" by Linda Wheeler from *The Washington Post, December 8, 1998,* section D. © 1998, *The Washington Post.* Reprinted with permission. **Watkins/Loomis Agency.** "California Palms" by lê thi diem thúy. Reprinted by permission of lê thi diem thúy and the Watkins/Loomis Agency. **Wieser & Wieser, Inc.** "Auto Wreck" by Karl Shapiro. Copyright 1941, 1987 Karl Shapiro. Reprinted by arrangement with Wieser & Wieser, Inc., New York. **Writers House, LLC.** "I Have a Dream", reprinted by arrangement with The Heirs to the Estate of Martin Luther King, Jr., c/o Writers House, Inc. as agent for the proprietor. Copyright 1963 by Martin Luther King, Jr., copyright renewed 1991 by Coretta Scott King. **The Wylie Agency.** "The Leap" from *In Praise of Mothers* by Louise Erdrich. Copyright © 1990 by Louise Erdrich, reprinted with permission of the Wylie Agency, Inc. **Yankee Publishing Inc.** "Best Sky Sights of the Next Century—Guaranteed!" by Bob Berman. From *The Old Farmer's Almanac 2000,* copyright © 2000, Yankee Publishing Inc., Dublin, NH. **ZoneNetwork.com.** "MountainZone.Com Everest '99 Cybercast Statement from George Mallory's Daughter", © 1999 ZoneNetwork.com. All rights reserved.

We have made every effort to trace the ownership of all copyrighted material and to secure permission from copyright holders. In the event of any question arising as to the use of any material, we will be pleased to make the necessary corrections in future printings. Thanks are due to the aforementioned authors, publishers, and agents for permission to use the materials indicated.